FINANCIAL ACCOUNTING

SECOND CANADIAN EDITION

JEFFREY WAYBRIGHT
SPOKANE COMMUNITY COLLEGE

ROBERT KEMP
UNIVERSITY OF VIRGINIA

SHERIF ELBARRAD
MACEWAN UNIVERSITY

PEARSON

Toronto

Vice-President, CMPS: Gary Bennett
Editorial Director: Claudine O'Donnell
Acquisitions Editor: Megan Farrell
Marketing Manager: Claire Varley
Development Team Lead: Suzanne Schaan
Developmental Editor: Toni Chahley
Project Manager: Sarah Gallagher

Editorial Production Service: MPS North America LLC
Compositor: Aptara®, Inc.
Permissions Project Manager: Joanne Tang
Photo Permissions Research: Aptara®, Inc.
Text Permissions Research: Aptara®, Inc.
Cover and Interior Designer: Anthony Leung
Cover Image: Ryan McVay/Allsport Concepts/Getty Images

Credits and acknowledgments for material borrowed from other sources and reproduced, with permission, in this textbook appear on this page or on the appropriate page within text.

Source of financial data from Bombardier Inc.'s 2011 annual report: Bombardier Inc.

Excerpts from CICA Handbook, Part 1 International Financial Reporting Standards, The Canadian Institute of Chartered Accountants. Published by the International Financial Reporting Standards, © 2013.

Original edition published by Pearson Education, Inc., Upper Saddle River, New Jersey, USA. Copyright © 2013, 2010 Pearson Education, Inc. This edition is authorized for sale only in Canada.

If you purchased this book outside the United States or Canada, you should be aware that it has been imported without the approval of the publisher or the author.

10 9 8 7 6 5 4 3 2 1 CKV

Library and Archives Canada Cataloguing in Publication

Waybright, Jeffrey, author
    Financial accounting / Jeffrey Waybright, Spokane Community College, Robert Kemp, University of Virginia, Sherif Elbarrad, MacEwan University. — Second Canadian edition.

Includes indexes.
ISBN 978-0-13-337553-4 (bound)

    1. Accounting—Canada—Textbooks.   I. Kemp, Robert S., author   II. Elbarrad, Sherif, author   III. Title.

HF5636.W38 2015   657'.044   C2014-902629-3

ISBN 978-0-13-337553-4

Dedication

My family—I couldn't have done this without their support
and encouragement.

Jim Kahl—Jim has been a mentor, a colleague, and above all, a tremendous
friend for my entire teaching career.

My students, past, present, and future—without them I would not be doing
that which I love to do, teaching accounting.

Jeffrey Waybright

I dedicate this book to my beloved children: Adam, Meg, and Sarah. I also
dedicate this book to their spouses and children. They give meaning to my
life and are my dream come true.

Robert Kemp

My wife and daughter—I cannot find the words to describe their sacrifice
and encouragement.

To the memory of my parents—My role models in life.

My students—Without their feedback and inspiration, I would not be able
to sharpen my teaching skills.

Sherif Elbarrad

About the Authors

Jeffrey Waybright teaches accounting at Spokane Community College, which is part of a multi-college district in eastern Washington. He has been a full-time, tenured, community college instructor for more than 16 years. In addition to teaching at the community college level, he has taught upper division courses for Linfield College. Jeffrey is a recent co-recipient of the Washington Society of CPA's Outstanding Educator Award.

Jeffrey received his BA in business administration (emphasis in accounting) and MBA from Eastern Washington University. Before becoming a professor, Jeffrey spent eight years as a practicing CPA in Washington State and still holds his licence. During his teaching career, he has taught in many disciplines of accounting, including financial, managerial, computerized, and payroll accounting, as well as in the disciplines of economics, business math, and general business. Jeffrey has developed online courses in accounting, teaches online and traditional courses for financial and managerial accounting, and advises students. Jeffrey is passionate about teaching students the subject of accounting.

Robert S. Kemp, DBA, CPA is the Ramon W. Breeden Sr. Research Professor at the McIntire School of Commerce, University of Virginia. He is a certified public accountant and possesses a baccalaureate, master's, and doctorate in business administration.

Professor Kemp is an accomplished scholar, conducting research and writing in the theory and practice of contemporary business. He currently is conducting research in the funding of pensions, the management of financial institutions, and corporate finance. His scholarly works include 70 completed projects, including monographs, articles, cases, research presentations, and working papers. His work is published in, among other places, *The Financial Review; The Journal of Financial Research; Advances in Accounting, A Research Journal; Benefits Quarterly; The Journal of Mathematics Applied in Business and Industry; The Journal of Accountancy; The Journal of Commercial Bank Lending; The Journal of Bank Accounting and Auditing;* and *The Journal of Business Economics.*

Professor Kemp is likewise an accomplished teacher, to both university students and executives throughout the world. During his 30 years at the University of Virginia, he has taught numerous undergraduate and graduate courses. He has taught classes using lectures, case studies, discussion groups, and distance learning. His consistently high evaluations by students reflect his devotion to the classroom. This high quality is likewise seen in his teaching of business executives. He has worked with and taught for organizations such as Bank of America, the FDIC, Navigant-Tucker Alan, the Siberian Banking Institute, the Barents Group, KPMG, Gerson Lehrman, Wellington Management, the Russian Bankers Association, the Central Asian American Enterprise Fund, the American Institute of Certified Public Accountants, and the Consumer Bankers Association.

Sherif Elbarrad, PhD, CMA is the chair of the Accounting & Finance Department-BCOM program at MacEwan University. He has been involved in teaching accounting at eight universities in Egypt, Germany, Saudi Arabia, and Canada for more than 29 years at both the undergraduate and postgraduate levels. He was the chair of the accounting department at three different universities. Sherif is a Certified Management Accountant (Alberta) and an Associate member of the Montana Society of Certified Public Accountants (USA). He has extensive professional experience in the field of financial and managerial accounting. He has also developed and delivered several workshops in the field of accounting for executive managers in different countries. Sherif has received teaching excellence awards from different universities. He has developed numerous accounting courses at both the undergraduate and postgraduate levels at several universities.

Sherif received both his BCOM (with distinction) and Master of Accounting degrees from Ain-Shams University in Egypt. He received his PhD in Accounting through a joint program between Ain-Shams University in Egypt and the University of Cologne in Germany.

Sherif has numerous publications to his credit. In addition to publishing research articles in reputable peer-reviewed journals, he has authored/co-authored several textbooks for both the undergraduate and postgraduate levels.

Brief Contents

Contents

Preface

Financial Accounting, Second Canadian Edition, in combination with MyAccountingLab, translates the essentials of accounting to students so they understand "why" and "when" financially sound decisions are made in business today. *Financial Accounting* and MyAccountingLab work together to solidify students' understanding of the language of business, leading them to success.

Financial Accounting, Second Canadian Edition, was originally adapted from an innovative text published in the United States. We took on the project of adapting this book for a Canadian audience because we found in the original text a solid foundation on which to build a Canadian financial accounting textbook. The features of the text, such as its focus on decision making, the clarity of its writing style, its innovative pedagogical features and approach to the visuals, and, of course, MyAccountingLab, provided an excellent starting point for the Canadian edition.

Improvements made to the second Canadian edition have been focused on satisfying the differing needs and abilities of students. This edition has been enhanced with new pedagogical features designed to help students approach the material from different perspectives. This new edition also boasts enhanced coverage of the International Financial Reporting Standards (IFRS) and the Accounting Standards for Private Enterprise (ASPE), clearly distinguishing between these two approaches throughout the text.

We have been teaching financial accounting for many years and have prepared this text so that it highlights the relevance of accounting to all students, whether or not they are planning a career in accounting. The text is written in a way that provides students with coverage of the essential financial accounting concepts and in a way that will help them relate these concepts to their everyday lives:

- **Focus on Decision Making**

  Beginning with Chapter 1, an emphasis is placed on the importance of making financially sound business decisions. This emphasis helps students determine how much risk and impact is involved in the types of decisions they may encounter in their future careers. Ethics and ratio coverage are also woven throughout the text to continually support this decision-making focus.

- **Coverage of IFRS and ASPE**

  IFRS and Canadian ASPE are used in Canada for different business sectors—publicly accountable entities and private enterprises. There are many similarities in IFRS and Canadian ASPE; therefore, this textbook focuses its discussion on IFRS. There are specific topics that are treated differently in IFRS and Canadian ASPE, and in these situations, the differences are described and highlighted. Where relevant, we have included a new table at the end of each chapter outlining the differences between IFRS and ASPE as they relate to the topic at hand.

- **Balanced Coverage**

  It is important for students to understand how financial accounting applies in small business scenarios as well as corporate ones. *Financial Accounting*, Second Canadian Edition, provides a straightforward look at the way many different types of organizations use accounting to ensure students are equipped with the knowledge they need.

  Students also need to understand both the "how" and the "why" of accounting. This text offers an appropriate blend of two perspectives—the preparer of accounting information and the user of accounting information—and uses this balanced approach to provide students with a solid grasp of accounting fundamentals and a clear understanding of how accounting information is used to make good business decisions. By demonstrating not only how to create information that communicates the activities of an organization but also why this information is important to a wide variety of users, the reader will see the relevance of financial accounting for anyone in society.

This text would be appropriate for any introductory financial accounting course. The book covers the concepts needed for accounting majors pursuing an accounting designation, but it is also appropriate for non-accounting students due to the interactive and user-friendly approach. The end-of-chapter problems cover a range of levels of difficulty, which, when combined with the Demo Doc problems in each chapter and the unlimited problems available in MyAccountingLab, will enable students who have never been exposed to accounting to work their way up to the more challenging problems, and ensure that those students who excel in the concepts will still be able to work on challenging problems.

This adaptation started with an American text that had many of the necessary elements for a Canadian market. We made a number of important changes to make the text relevant to a Canadian audience. Most importantly, coverage in the Canadian text is based on the IFRS and ASPE. Concepts that were not relevant to Canada, such as LIFO, were replaced with complete coverage of concepts that are relevant. Chapter 1 now incorporates an introduction to the careers in accounting that are available in Canada, both IFRS and ASPE are described and introduced, and terminology changes (for example, from stockholder to shareholder) are implemented. Chapter 4, which details the relationship between ethics and accounting, required significant adaptations to make the material relevant to Canadian students. Canadian accounting scandals and the impact of international accounting scandals on the Canadian accounting system are presented. The perpetual inventory system is illustrated in detail, while the periodic inventory system is presented in the appendix to Chapter 5. The LIFO cost flow assumption is removed from Chapter 6. A new appendix to cover accounting for leases is added to Chapter 8. The concept of par value shares is updated according to Canadian regulations in Chapter 10. The Canadian edition is also full of Canadian examples and stories, which will help to create an interest among students in the Canadian business environment.

ORGANIZATION

The second Canadian edition of *Financial Accounting* takes a cumulative approach to the concepts. Each topic builds on the knowledge of the previous chapters. The placement of a brief look at the financial statements in the first chapter helps to tie each of the following chapters together. The text also incorporates a blend of theory and application. Readers are provided with the tools necessary for understanding the creation of the financial statements through technical details and resources such as the Demo Doc problems and end-of-chapter questions. At the same time, readers are able to see how the concepts are relevant to all users of financial statements through examples, the presentation of various perspectives, and features such as the Focus on Users box.

Financial Accounting, Second Canadian Edition, begins with the introduction of accounting as the language of organizations. This is followed by what a career in accounting might be like, then a brief description of financial statements. This description of the financial statements is used to link the chapters together as each chapter delves deeper into specific elements of the financial statements.

Next, the text demonstrates the accounting equation and works through the accounting cycle, continuously referring back to the accounting equation. Concepts are built one on top of the other in layers that will eventually result in a complete picture of the financial statements, including a wide breadth of knowledge along with significant depth of detail.

Once the fundamentals have been presented, a full chapter is devoted to examining how ethics and accounting merge together. This chapter is filled with real-life examples that will ground the discussion and provide students with an idea of how significant an issue ethics can be.

Chapters 5 through 10 tackle the various groups of accounts (assets, liabilities, shareholders' equity). Each chapter covers the most important concepts for each type of account in enough depth to prepare students for subsequent financial and managerial accounting courses.

The text then returns to the financial statements by demonstrating the creation of the statement of cash flows and its uses, followed by an in-depth look at financial statement analysis in the final chapter. This brings the text full circle from starting with the financial statements, then breaking them down into their various elements, and returning back to the statements in full detail with a view to describing what the financial statements tell us, the users.

NEW TO THE SECOND CANADIAN EDITION

In addition to a thoroughly revised and updated text, the second Canadian edition boasts a number of new features and enhancements.

1. **Conceptual Framework:** The conceptual framework has been enhanced in Chapter 1 and throughout the book.
2. **Coverage of IFRS and ASPE:** Coverage of IFRS and ASPE has been thoroughly updated and enhanced throughout the book. Marginal icons indicate where IFRS and ASPE are mentioned in the main text, and the end of each chapter boasts a table summarizing how IFRS and ASPE approach the key concepts covered in the chapter.
3. **Transaction Analysis:** Transaction analysis has been incorporated in the margins throughout the book, in equation format.
4. **Investment and Lease Appendices:** In response to instructor needs, we have added an appendix at the end of the book dealing with accounting for investments. Chapter 8 contains a new appendix about accounting for leases.
5. **Increased Coverage of Canadian Companies:** Wherever possible, Canadian companies have been used as examples throughout the text.
6. **Student-Friendly Pedagogy:** In addition to the incorporation of transaction analysis, we have also made a number of student-friendly pedagogical enhancements to the book. These include
   a. **Memory Tips:** Found in the margin, these features provide students with helpful tips related to the concept discussed in the main text.
   b. **Still Don't Get It?:** These features assist students with accounting concepts that they tend to struggle with. These marginal icons direct students to MyAccountingLab where they will find an alternate explanation of the concept being discussed in the main text.
   c. **Colour Coding:** To enhance support of visual learners, we have implemented a colour coding strategy across the visuals in the text.

      - **A**ssets: Dark Blue
      - **L**iabilities: Peach
      - **O**wners' Equity: Dark Green
      - **D**ividends: Purple
      - **E**xpenses: Light Green
      - **R**evenues: Red

Changes to Each Chapter

Chapter 1 has been updated to include learning objectives that stress the importance of identifying the needs of different users of accounting information. We have also streamlined and simplified the conceptual framework, adding visuals to represent the different components of the conceptual framework and how they relate to each other.

Chapter 2 boasts new illustrations designed to help students understand how accounts are organized.

Chapter 3 includes new illustrations of the period assumption, as well as several new diagrams that illustrate accrual versus cash basis accounting. We have reclassified the adjusting entries as adjusting expenses and adjusting revenues versus accruals and deferrals, and added an alternate method for adjusting prepaid expenses and unearned revenue. This chapter also includes new adjusting examples.

Chapter 4 includes updates to the petty cash fund appendix with new examples and illustrations for clarity.

Chapter 5 has been updated to focus on the perpetual inventory system. We have moved the periodic inventory system to an appendix for reference. This chapter has been reorganized to divide freight-related activities between purchasing and selling.

Chapter 6 includes a new example of the specific identification method, and a more more in-depth illustration and numerical example of lower of cost or net realizable value (LCNRV). We have also added a numerical example related to damaged goods.

Chapter 7 includes a new section dealing with the need for judgment in recognizing revenue. We have also added an exhibit that illustrates how the direct write-off method violates the matching principle. This chapter also includes a new section, entitled "The Adequacy of the Allowance for Doubtful Accounts," which includes an example that illustrates the case of having a debit AFDA balance at the end of the period.

Chapter 8 has been updated to include a new learning objective on ratio analysis. We have added real-life examples from Canadian companies' financial statements, as well as a CCA explanation with accompanying end-of-chapter questions. We have also added a new appendix on accounting for leases.

Chapter 9 has been enhanced with more real-life examples drawn from the financial statements of Canadian companies. We have also enhanced the coverage of the effective interest method.

Chapter 10 has been enhanced with more real-life examples drawn from the financial statements of Canadian companies.

Chapter 11 includes an introduction to the statement of cash flows using iconic illustrations. We have also added components of the statement of cash flows and an example of loss on sale of assets.

Chapter 12 has been thoroughly updated and includes new illustrations.

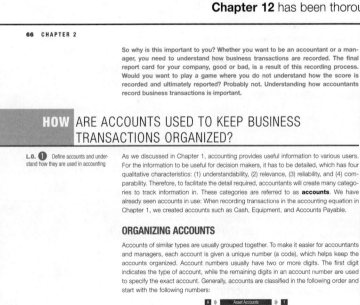

ENHANCEMENTS FOR LEARNING

Presenting Concepts with Clarity and Purpose

The first thing that will distract students is jargon and difficult language, especially when it comes to understanding accounting concepts. Waybright, Kemp, and Elbarrad have crafted a text that is written the way a great teacher would speak in class, with both clarity and purpose. Engaging, easy-to-understand examples are used throughout, facilitating the reader-friendly style of the text.

Question and Answer Format

Some of the most teachable moments happen when a student asks a key question that gets straight to the heart of a topic. This text mirrors that approach by providing key questions in the headers, followed by clear, direct, and detailed explanations.

Seeing It All Together

Waybright, Kemp, and Elbarrad effectively illustrate the connection between accounting equations and big picture concepts by introducing a slight twist on the visuals used in the text. Instead of presenting the details of the journal entries, general ledger, and T-accounts in isolation, *Financial Accounting*, Second Canadian Edition, shows these details within the context of the accounting equation and financial statements. This approach helps students appreciate the steps involved in preparing and interpreting financial statements, which is critical to their understanding of the material and success in the course.

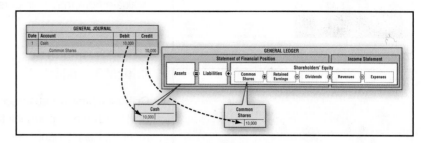

Transaction Analysis

Presented in the margin, transaction analysis has been linked to financial statements throughout the text to illustrate the impact of each transaction on the financial statement, and support the development of a basic understanding of the impact of everyday activities on the business.

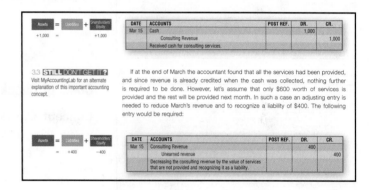

Demo Docs

The **Demo Doc** examples consist of entire problems, worked through step by step, from start to finish, narrated with the kind of comments that instructors would make in class. The Demo Docs are available in most chapters of the text. In addition to the printed Demo Docs, Flash-animated versions are available so that students can watch the problems as they are worked through while listening to the explanations and details. Demo Docs will aid students when they are trying to solve exercises and problems on their own, duplicating the classroom experience outside of class.

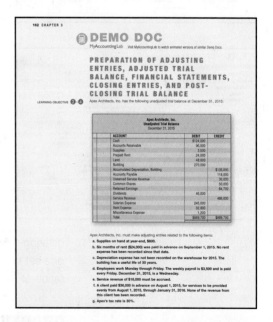

Decision Guidelines

Decision Guidelines summarize the chapter's key terms, concepts, and formulas in the context of business decisions. Found throughout and at the end of each chapter, Decision Guidelines show each decision and how to evaluate it so students can readily see the value in, and for, a business. Overall, these guidelines continue to reinforce how accounting information is used to make decisions in business.

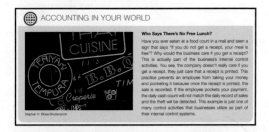

Accounting in Your World

Found in every chapter, the **Accounting in Your World** boxed feature personalizes accounting challenges, issues, and ethical situations for students to evaluate from their own perspective.

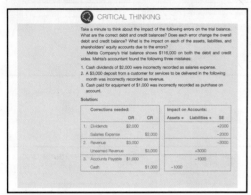

Critical Thinking

Critical Thinking questions appear throughout each chapter, providing students with the opportunity to think about the impact of the accounting treatment on the accounts, the financial statements, as well as on the company's financial objectives and shareholders' objectives. Critical thinking reinforces how accounting information is used to impact decision makers and their respective objectives.

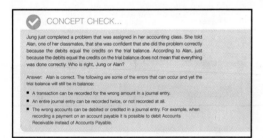

Concept Checks

Concept Checks appear throughout the chapters so that students can review their understanding and interpretation of the material. By showing "what it is" and "why and when it matters" together, these checks allow students a place to pause and interpret what they've just learned.

Focus on Users

The **Focus on Users** feature shows the links between the concepts covered in each chapter and how that accounting information is used by a wide variety of individuals, whether they are inside an organization or outside, accountants or not. The main concepts of each chapter are examined from the viewpoints of various users, such as shareholders and investors, management, competitors, and unions. By demonstrating not only how to create information that communicates the activities of an organization, but also why this information is important to a wide variety of users, the reader will see the relevance of financial accounting for anyone in society. By highlighting these differing viewpoints, the reader also gets a sense of the difficulty in pleasing all users with one set of financial accounting statements and the challenges that arise during the preparation of these statements.

PRACTICE MAKES PERFECT

Accounting Practice

Waybright, Kemp, and Elbarrad understand that the key to students' accounting success is in the practice and work completed in the end-of-chapter problem material. With this in mind, this text presents the material so that students progress from simple calculative exercises, to a mixture of calculative and conceptual exercises, and finally on to more complex, conceptual analysis problems and cases. This progression allows students to build confidence and achieve mastery of the material.

- **Self Check** questions quickly audit the students' understanding of the chapter concepts by presenting them with a series of multiple choice questions.
- **Discussion Questions** help students make the connections between the "how" and the "why" of financial accounting information through a guided series of in-class discussion questions.
- **"A" and "B" sets of Exercises and Problems** provide students and instructors with two sets of exercises and problems in the text. Three sets of alternative exercises and problems are also available in MyAccountingLab to give students more practice opportunities.
- The **Continuing Exercise** highlights the same small business from chapter to chapter, allowing students to apply their understanding of chapter concepts in a business context. As students move through the text, they complete additional steps in this comprehensive exercise. Students are able to see the big picture and learn how the topics build on one another. The Continuing Exercise can be assigned and completed within MyAccountingLab.
- The **Continuing Problem** is a more comprehensive version of the Continuing Exercise, featuring a different small business. Once again, students learn how accounting is a process and the Continuing Problem helps them put it all together.

The questions in the **Know Your Business** section demonstrate how accounting is applicable in real life. Featuring **Financial Analysis**, **Industry Analysis**, and **Small Business Analysis** questions, students learn how to apply the concepts of each chapter to help them understand the significance of financial statement and industry analysis as a means to evaluate the financial health of a company. The financial and industry analysis questions feature one company, Bombardier, allowing students to see how chapter concepts are connected. The financial statements for Bombardier can be found in MyAccountingLab.

STUDENT RESOURCES

MyAccountingLab is a powerful online learning tool that not only provides opportunities for limitless practice, but re-creates the "I get it" moments from the classroom. MyAccountingLab provides a rich suite of learning tools, including:

- Static and algorithmic versions of exercises and problems from the textbook
- An online, interactive Accounting Cycle Tutorial
- Mini-Cases
- Help Me Solve It question-specific interactive coaching
- A dynamic eText with links to media assets
- Accounting videos, animations, and DemoDocs
- "Still Don't Get It?" features that provide alternate explanations to challenging concepts covered in the book

MyAccountingLab

PREMIUM ONLINE COURSEWARE

Pearson's MyAccountingCourse is a premium online course solution that combines fully customizable course lessons and tutorials with the personalized homework and assessment features of MyAccountingLab. Designed to be used in fully online or blended learning environments, MyAccountingCourse can accommodate various term lengths and includes an integrated eText and comprehensive Instructor Resource Guide.

MyAccountingCourse

Features of MyAccountingCourse include:

- A flexible, customizable solution where an instructor may add, delete, and reorganize content. Each topic-based MyAccountingCourse module is built to specific learning outcomes, and MyAccountingCourse includes a comprehensive Instructor Resource Guide complete with course outcomes, lesson objectives, and teaching tips.
- Interactive lesson presentations with a proven learning model, robust content, and relevant video, audio, eText, downloadable MP3 lectures, and other rich media assets.
- Rich MyAccountingLab-based assessment, pre-tests, quizzes, homework, and tests.

COURSESMART FOR STUDENTS

CourseSmart goes beyond traditional expectations—providing instant, online access to the textbooks and course materials you need at a significant savings over the print price. With instant access from any computer and the ability to search your text, you'll find the content you need quickly, no matter where you are. And with online tools like highlighting and note-taking, you can save time and study efficiently. See all the benefits at www.coursesmart.com/students.

PEARSON ETEXT

Pearson eText gives you access to the text whenever and wherever you have access to the Internet. Pearson eText pages look exactly like the printed text, offering powerful new functionality for students and instructors. Users can create notes, highlight text in different colours, create bookmarks, zoom, click hyperlinked words and phrases to view definitions, and view in single-page or two-page view. Pearson eText allows for quick navigation to key parts of the eText using a table of contents and provides full-text search.

LEARNING SOLUTIONS MANAGERS

Pearson's Learning Solutions Managers work with faculty and campus course designers to ensure that Pearson technology products, assessment tools, and online course materials are tailored to meet your specific needs. This highly qualified team is dedicated to helping schools take full advantage of a wide range of educational resources, by assisting in the integration of a variety of instructional materials and media formats. Your local Pearson Education sales representative can provide you with more details on this service program.

INSTRUCTOR'S RESOURCES

Instructor's Teaching Tips Digital eText Resource

Instructors can easily locate useful teaching tips and resources throughout the eText located in MyAccountingLab. Easily identified by an apple icon throughout each chapter, instructors will find Chapter Overviews and Outlines, Assignment Grids, Ten-Minute Quizzes, and other valuable teaching resources, including how to integrate MyAccountingLab into their courses. Collated versions of this resource can also be downloaded from the Instructor Resources page at MyAccountingLab.

The following instructor resources are available to all adopters of this textbook:

- **Instructor's Solutions Manual:** This manual contains thoroughly worked-through solutions to every question, exercise, problem, and case in the text. All solutions were prepared by the authors and technically checked twice by professional accountants.

- **Computerized Test Bank:** Pearson's computerized test banks allow instructors to filter and select questions to create quizzes, tests, or homework. Instructors can revise questions or add their own, and may be able to choose print or online options. These questions are also available in Microsoft Word format.

- **Microsoft PowerPoint Presentations:** PowerPoint presentations offer an outline of the key points for each chapter. The PowerPoint presentations for this edition also include the same useful teaching tips and resources found in the eText. These tips include such helpful resources as illustrative real-life examples, analogies to facilitate learning, examples of problems for in-class use, discussion questions for in-class use, and tips and traps.

- **Image Bank:** The image bank contains digital copies of all of the exhibits and photos in the textbook. Instructors may use these JPEGs to create or enhance their own PowerPoint presentations.

All of these instructor supplements are available for download from a password-protected section of Pearson Canada's online catalogue (www.pearsoncanada.ca/highered). Navigate to your book's catalogue page to view a list of those supplements that are available. See your local sales representative for details and access.

INNOVATIVE SOLUTIONS TEAM

Pearson's Innovative Solutions Team works with faculty and campus course designers to ensure that Pearson technology products, assessment tools, and online course materials are tailored to meet your specific needs. This highly qualified team is dedicated to helping schools take full advantage of a wide range of educational technology by assisting in the integration of a variety of instructional materials and media formats.

PEARSON CUSTOM PUBLISHING

We know that not every instructor follows the exact order of a course text. Some may not even cover all the material in a given volume. Pearson Custom Publishing provides the flexibility to select the chapters you need, presented in the order you want, to tailor fit your text to your course and your students' needs. Contact your Pearson Education Canada Sales and Editorial Representative to learn more.

ACKNOWLEDGMENTS

Financial Accounting has been developed with the help of instructors from across the country who participated in chapter reviews. Their comments and suggestions for the text have been a great help in planning and carrying out the vision of this textbook, and we thank them for their contributions.

For the Second Canadian edition
Ionela Bacain, Humber College
Ron Baker, University of Guelph
Anila Kosta, Concordia University
Carmen Kuczewski, Concordia University
Scott Laing, Dalhousie University
Howard Leaman, University of Guelph-Humber

Fried Pries, University of Guelph
Lianne Smith-Stow, Georgian College
Dragan Stojanovic, University of Toronto
Peggy Wallace, Trent University
Brad Witt, Humber College
Patricia Zima, Mohawk College

For the First Canadian edition
Bharat Aggarwal, Professional Programs, CMA
Mina Ally, Seneca College
Ron Baker, University of Guelph
Maria Belanger, Algonquin College
Stephen L. Bergstrom, SAIT Polytechnic
W. Peter Blake, Sheridan College
Maria Blazkiewicz, Dawson College
Dianne Davis, Nipissing University
Meredith Delaney, Seneca College
Robert G. Ducharme, University of Waterloo
John Harris, Centennial College
David Hoffman, Seneca College of Applied Arts and Technology
Gordon Holyer, Vancouver Island University
Ian Hutchinson, Acadia University
Gerry La Rocca, Vanier College
Howard Leaman, University of Guelph-Humber
Camillo Lento, Lakehead University
Sheila McGillis, Laurentian University
Carol A. Meissner, Georgian College
Ann Clarke-Okah, Carleton University
Clifton Philpott, Kwantlen Polytechnic University
Brad Sacho, Kwantlen Polytechnic University
Barrie Tober, Niagara College
Cindy Trudel, Acadia University
Valerie Warren, Kwantlen Polytechnic University
Brad Witt, Humber ITAL
Patricia Zima, Mohawk College

Thanks to the 2013–2014 Pearson Editorial Advisory Board in Accounting. This group of subject-matter experts helped us develop improved content for our print-based products and online resources:

Chris Deresh, CPA Canada and Douglas College
Fred Pries, University of Guelph
Lianne Smith-Stow, Georgian College
Larry Webster, NAIT
Dr. Eckhard Schuman, University of Toronto
Erica Pimentel, McGill University
Scott Laing, Dalhousie University

Sherif Elbarrad would like to send a sincere thank you to the team at Pearson for their continuous encouragement and support.

Learning objectives are a "roadmap" showing what will be covered and what is especially important in each chapter

LEARNING OBJECTIVES

① Describe the major types of business organizations

② Identify the needs of the different users of accounting information

③ Identify career opportunities in accounting and related fields

④ Explain the key accounting principles and the conceptual framework

⑤ Analyze transactions using the basic accounting equation

⑥ Understand and be able to prepare basic financial statements

CHAPTER OUTLINE

2

Business, Accounting, and You

BUSINESS, ACCOUNTING, AND YOU

You are about to study accounting, so you probably already know a little bit about the subject. But what exactly is accounting? Why is it so important? And why does the study of business typically start with accounting?

Imagine living in a foreign country and not being able to read and speak the native language—that would be difficult. The same thing goes for business: accounting is the language of business, so to understand the world of business you need to understand accounting. It is the process businesspeople use to communicate what they've been doing. To be successful in business, you need to be able to understand, speak, and use the language of business.

In addition, accountants are the scorekeepers of business. Think of the last sporting event you watched or played. Did someone keep score? You bet they did, even if it was an informal hockey match between friends. Can you imagine the end of the game without someone saying who scored, when they scored, and even how they scored? Essentially, accounting lets business managers know if they are winning or losing.

The bottom line is that accounting is at the heart of business. Whether you become an accountant or a business manager, understanding the foundation and process of accounting is critical to your success. At the beginning of each chapter in the section Business, Accounting, and You, we will focus on how accounting keeps track of a business's transactions and helps you, as a manager, make good business decisions.

WHY STUDY ACCOUNTING?

ACCOUNTING TEACHES THE LANGUAGE OF BUSINESS

Many students who enrol in accounting classes often ask the question "Why do I have to take accounting anyway? I am not going to be an accountant." Perhaps the most compelling reason for taking an accounting course, especially if you do not plan on becoming an accountant, is that accounting teaches "the language of business." No matter what your intended area of study, if you want to be successful in business, you need to know how to speak the language of business.

Consider a patient in the hospital. Many health-care professionals, in addition to the doctor, are responsible for ensuring the overall health and welfare of the patient. There are nurses, nursing assistants, x-ray technicians, and others involved in the treatment and care of the patient. Additionally, many pieces of equipment monitor the patient's condition. If the doctor is the only person able to speak "the language of medicine" and read and interpret information provided about the patient's health, the ability of the other health-care professionals to provide quality care to the patient is severely limited. Therefore, all individuals in the health-care profession are required to speak "the language of medicine." They must understand how to speak, read, and interpret information relative to the health of the patients they serve to provide the highest level of care. Similarly, if only the accountants in a business organization are able to speak, read, and interpret financial information regarding the health of the business, the ability of others within the organization to manage the affairs of the business in a manner that ensures the health of the business will be limited. Whether your intended area of study is marketing or management, or even cosmetology or automotive, an understanding of accounting will allow you to monitor and manage the health of the organization for which you work.

ACCOUNTING EMPHASIZES THE IMPORTANCE OF ETHICAL BUSINESS BEHAVIOUR

Boldfaced words are new terms that are explained here and listed in the Accounting Vocabulary at the end of each chapter and defined in the Glossary at the end of the book.

Proper ethical behaviour has taken on renewed importance in the wake of recent accounting scandals, such as Enron, that have occurred in the United States as well as in other countries. **Ethics** refers to the principles of right behaviour that guide decision making. Individuals from top management to front-line workers may be confronted with ethical dilemmas in their jobs. Ethical dilemmas often arise when the actions that most benefit an individual differ from the actions that most benefit the organization or society. Ethical dilemmas are also created when personal beliefs or organizational culture differ from ethical principles.

The study of accounting will help individuals better identify situations that create ethical dilemmas within an organization. More importantly, it helps them discern the proper course of action to take in these situations.

AN UNDERSTANDING OF ACCOUNTING HELPS INDIVIDUALS ENSURE THAT THE BUSINESS IS HEALTHY AND PROFITABLE

Many small business owners and managers within larger businesses are very knowledgeable with regards to many aspects of their position but often fail due to a lack of accounting knowledge. Individuals in these positions often know a lot about the products they sell but are unable to answer questions such as the following:

- What is the true cost of what I am selling?
- Am I being "ripped off" by my employees or my customers?

ACCOUNTING IN YOUR WORLD

Accounting in Your World boxes show you how accounting issues, challenges, and ethical situations affect you in your daily life.

How would you respond to the following situations?

❶ The company CEO asks you to falsify the company's accounting records. He or she says that the company cannot afford to report that it is performing poorly. If it does, some stores will likely have to be closed and people will lose their jobs. The CEO implies that if you are not a "team player" and falsify the records that it will be your fault these people are unemployed.

❷ At the end of the month, your supervisor asks you to create fictitious sales invoices. He or she tells you that your department is just a little bit shy of reaching the sales goal necessary for each member of the department to receive a quarterly bonus. Your supervisor says that you can just delete the fictitious sales at the beginning of the next month and that no one will ever know.

Damato/Shutterstock

❸ A co-worker of yours confides in you that he or she has stolen several MP3 players from the store at which you both work. Your co-worker offers to give you one of the players. He or she says that you both deserve it for all of the long hours you have worked for the company lately.

You may find yourself faced with an ethical dilemma at any time during your career. You only have one chance to make the right decision. In Chapter 4, we take a closer look at ethics and reveal the consequences of other people's poor choices.

- How much does the company need to invest to achieve the growth that has been projected for the upcoming quarter?

An understanding of accounting will allow an individual to answer these and other questions, and monitor the operations that will help the company be profitable.

WHAT IS ACCOUNTING?

Have you noticed how many kids play minor league sports these days, and wondered why so many kids compete in these sports? Some kids play to get into better shape and some kids play just for the fun, but most kids play because they want to win. If you think about it, we live in a very competitive world. This competitiveness makes the job of the scorekeeper very important, because without the scorekeeper, nobody would know which team won the contest. In addition to keeping track of who wins, the scorekeeper in an athletic contest tracks many other statistics, which help the coach and the players judge individual performances. It also allows individuals outside of the team, such as spectators, team owners, journalists, and others, to follow along and keep track of how the team is doing.

The world of business is very much like minor league sports. **Businesses** exist to win, which is usually defined as making money. The scorekeepers in the world of business are the accountants. Their job is to "keep score" to determine if the business has won or lost through a process known as financial accounting. An accountant also tracks other types of information in addition to whether the company made or lost money to help employees and managers judge individual performance. It is the job of the accountant to provide useful information to various users regarding the performance of the organization. The information is used mostly to determine whether or not to invest capital or lend money to a business. Financial accounting produces reports called **financial statements** that show financial information about a business. These reports are "historical" reports that communicate financial information about a business to people or organizations outside the company (such as the investors, creditors, regulators, etc.). The external users of financial statements include those who are not directly involved in the business operations, such as shareholders, potential investors, creditors, suppliers, customers, regulators, government, financial analysts, and the public, while internal users of the financial statements include the CEO, CFO, controller, and managers who run the business. Financial statements

- allow investors and creditors to make investment and credit decisions.

- enable suppliers and customers to determine the financial condition of a business.

- report results, if needed, to regulatory agencies, such as the Ontario Securities Commission (OSC) and the Canada Revenue Agency (CRA).

- allow managers to make operating decisions, and provide feedback for learning and improvement.

Ultimately, the financial statements are the responsibility of the company's managers (the users of the financial statements) rather than the responsibility of the bookkeepers or internal accounting team (the preparers of the statements). This book teaches students the process of **accounting**, or "scorekeeping," for a business organization and the analysis of business performance. This textbook will examine financial accounting with a balanced perspective: It focuses on users of financial information as well as the preparers of financial information. This balanced approach demonstrates that a solid understanding of accounting is needed regardless of whether or not you pursue a career in accounting. Therefore, answering the question "Why is this important?" will be highlighted as well as the question "How do we do this?" Understanding how the processes of accounting work is necessary for understanding what the output tells us. For example, if we want to be an expert racecar driver, understanding the mechanics of automobiles will improve our ability to use the vehicle to maximize its performance. This same concept applies to accounting and businesses. To maximize the performance or understand the performance of an organization, it is important to know how the information on which we are relying was created.

Throughout the book, the "How" will be demonstrated and then followed up with the "Why," or the element of what this information tells us. The Decision Guidelines, Accounting in the Real World, and the Focus on Users boxes, along with other features, are incorporated in this text to assist in demonstrating the relevance of these concepts to all users of financial information.

HOW ARE BUSINESSES ORGANIZED?

TYPES OF BUSINESSES

L.O. ❶ Describe the major types of business organizations

The three types of business are a **service business**, a **merchandising business**, and a **manufacturing business**.

- A service business provides services to its customers. In other words, what it sells is time and knowledge or skills. Common types of service businesses are law firms, accounting firms, physical therapy offices, architecture firms, non-profit organizations (e.g., the Red Cross), etc.

- A merchandise business sells physical goods or products to its customers. Common types of merchandise businesses are automobile dealerships, department stores,

Learning Objectives in the margin signal the beginning of the section that covers the learning objective topic. Look for the Learning Objective when you want to review this topic.

grocery stores, sporting goods stores, etc. A merchandise business may be either a **wholesale business** or a **retail business**. A retailer sells directly to the final customer whereas a wholesaler buys from manufacturers and sells to retailers.

- Manufacturing businesses produce the physical goods that they sell to their customers. Common types of manufacturing businesses are automobile manufacturers, the makers of clothing, soft drink manufacturers, etc.

- A business can also be a blend of different types, or a hybrid. For example, an automobile repair shop provides a service, but also sells parts similar to a retail business.

Bombardier Inc. is a well-known Canadian manufacturer of aerospace and transportation vehicles, but it also provides services, such as repair and maintenance, software development, and technical support.

CHOICE OF BUSINESS ORGANIZATIONS

A business can be organized as a sole proprietorship, partnership, or corporation. But how do you know what type of business organization is best for your business?

- A **sole proprietorship** is a business entity that has one owner. For legal purposes and for tax purposes, the business and the owner are considered the same. The business is not a separate legal entity, and the owner is personally responsible for all of the debts and obligations of the business; in other words, he or she has an unlimited liability. If somebody wants to sue the business, he or she would also have to sue the owner. In addition, all of the income or loss generated by the business is reported on the owner's personal tax return and taxed at individual tax rates.

- A **partnership** is very similar to a sole proprietorship except that it has two or more owners. It should have two or more general partners (who have the right to manage and have unlimited liability—general partnership), or at least one general partner and one or more limited partner(s) (who don't have the right to manage and have limited liability—limited partnership). For legal purposes, the owners (partners) and the business are considered the same. If somebody sues the business, he or she would need to sue one or more of the business owners. For tax purposes, the partners divide all of the income or loss of the partnership among themselves and report it on their personal tax returns. Therefore, it is taxed at individual tax rates just like a sole proprietorship. One advantage of a partnership is flexibility regarding the division of the business income between the partners based on the partnership agreement.

- A **corporation** differs from a sole proprietorship or a partnership because it is a separate legal entity from the owners. This legal separation is very attractive to the business owners because it limits their personal liability to what they have invested in the corporation. The corporation may sue another person or business and it may be sued by another person or business. For tax purposes, the corporation is a separate entity from the owners. Therefore, income tax is imposed on the income of the corporation at corporate tax rates. Any remaining income that is distributed to the owners, or **shareholders**, in the form of dividends is then taxed at the shareholder's individual income tax rates. However, shareholders can claim an enhanced dividend tax credit to reduce the income taxes.

Public versus Private Corporations

A corporation can be publicly held or privately held. A privately held corporation has very few owners and is not traded on a stock exchange. Quite often, corporations start out as privately held organizations and then, through the process of an initial public offering, shares are bought and sold on the stock exchange by shareholders. Once this takes place, the organization becomes a publicly held company.

Due to the different ways a business can be organized, the preparation and presentation of the owners' claims in different business organizations vary. For example, the injection of money or properties from owners in exchange for the ownership of the business is called **owner(s) capital** for sole proprietorships and partnerships, and is called share capital for corporations. The income distributed to owner(s) is called **withdrawals** for sole proprietorships and partnerships, and is called **dividends** for corporations. Corporations are required to prepare a statement to describe the changes in shareholders' equity, including the changes in the number of shares issued and the amount of share capital and earnings.

THE BUSINESS ENTITY CONCEPT

The most basic concept in accounting is that of the business entity. The business entity concept dictates that the financial affairs of a business organization must be kept separate from the personal financial affairs of the business owners. This separation is necessary because if the owners of a business choose to place personal assets into the business, then those assets are now considered to belong to the business and no longer to the owners. For example, if a business owner invests a used car into his or her business, that car should no longer be used by the business owner solely for personal purposes.

Exhibits summarize key ideas in a visual way.

Exhibit 1-1 summarizes the different types of business organizations.

Type of Business	Accounting Status	Legal Status	Tax Status	Benefits	Drawbacks
Sole Proprietorship	Business and owner are considered to be *separate* entities	Business and owner are considered to be one entity	Business income is allocated to the owner and taxed at owner's personal tax rate	• Ease of formation	• Unlimited liability of owner • Difficult to raise capital • Limited life
Partnership	Business and owners are considered to be *separate* entities	Business and owners are considered to be one entity	Business income is allocated to the owners and taxed at owners' personal tax rates	• Ease of formation • Shared investment/ knowledge	• Unlimited liability of owners • Disagreements between partners • Limited life
Corporation	Business and owners are considered to be *separate* entities	Business and owners are considered to be *separate* entities	Business income is taxed at corporate tax rates	• Limited liability of owners • Easier to raise capital • Unlimited life	• More difficult and costly to form • More paperwork • More regulations

Exhibit 1-1 ▲

Although the process of accounting for the different types of business organizations is similar, there are slight variations depending on the type of organization. In this book, we will focus our attention on accounting for corporations.

DECISION GUIDELINES

DECISION	**GUIDELINE**	**ANALYZE**
I am planning to start a new business. What form of business organization should be chosen?	There are many ways to organize a business including the following: a sole proprietorship, partnership, or corporation. Each type of business organization has different advantages and disadvantages.	Know the tax and legal treatments of each type of organization. Weigh the best treatment of taxes and legal liability of each type, and pick the format that is most advantageous for you as an owner.

Decision Guidelines show why accounting principles and concepts are important to business people, not just accountants. They are also an excellent summary of the chapter topics.

WHO ARE THE USERS OF ACCOUNTING INFORMATION?

Information is the main product of accounting. Accounting information is the main resource used by different parties to make business related decisions. There are different users of accounting information, each of which has different information needs to support the decision making process. Those users can be classified into external and internal users since the needs of each class of user is quite different, and accordingly the information provided to each is also different.

 L.O. 2 Identify the needs of the different users of accounting information

EXTERNAL USERS

External users of accounting information are not involved in the day-to-day operations of the business. They include shareholders, investors, banks, government regulatory bodies, such as the Canada Revenue Agency (CRA), etc. **Financial accounting** is a branch of accounting that focuses on serving the needs of external users who need to make sound economic decisions. Those users have limited access to the company's financial information, and hence the information provided to them should be governed by commonly agreed upon principles and assumptions to be understandable and reliable. Accordingly, financial statement preparation is guided by a set of accounting standards, such as the International Financial Reporting Standards (IFRS), Canadian Accounting Standards for Private Enterprises (ASPE), or U.S. Generally Accepted Accounting Principles (US-GAAP) in some cases of companies listed in the United States. Furthermore, the information gathered is past-oriented, meaning that the events reported have already occurred, and the information is gathered from the business entity as a whole. Major tasks involved in financial accounting are financial statement preparation, financial analysis, auditing, etc.

Each of the users requires different information to support their decisions. Investors are looking for information about the profitability and risk of the business so that they can compare different investment opportunities; shareholders are concerned mainly with profitability and profit distributions; banks are looking for information to help in assessing the ability of the business to repay loans and interest; while regulatory bodies, such as the CRA, are concerned with the net income of the business upon which taxes are calculated.

INTERNAL USERS

Internal users are those who are involved in the day-to-day business operations. They include the board of directors, senior managers, heads of departments, etc. They have access to all of the company's financial information, and hence the rules of providing information to these users are more flexible. **Managerial accounting** is a branch of accounting that provides accounting information for internal users to help make business decisions. Major tasks involved in managerial accounting are cost accounting, budgeting, planning and control, performance evaluation, internal auditing, etc. Performing these tasks is not guided by external accounting standards, the information gathered is future-oriented, and it is gathered from the various segments of the business entity.

Each of the users will be looking for information to support his or her decision making process: Boards of directors will be looking at the company's overall profitability, costs, and aggregate figures to help them make strategic decisions; sales managers will be interested in knowing the breakdown of sales figures per product or region; and production managers will be interested in information about the costs of production.

WHAT ARE THE CAREER OPPORTUNITIES IN ACCOUNTING-RELATED FIELDS?

L.O. ❸ Identify career opportunities in accounting and related fields

Careers in accounting and related fields provide rewarding opportunities for professional and personal development and growth, as well as job security and social prestige. There are several broad areas of expertise that accounting professionals build their careers on: financial accounting, managerial accounting, taxation, accounting instructors, and banking and financial services. **Exhibit 1-2** illustrates careers in the field of accounting, the types of tasks typically undertaken, and some examples of common job titles.

We discussed the fields of financial accounting and managerial accounting in the previous section, but with accounting knowledge, accounting professionals can also choose to work in the field of taxation by providing tax planning, tax preparation, and tax audit services to individuals and business taxpayers. Many accountants work in the banking or financial services fields. They help banks and investment companies assess and analyze client risks and credit ratings, and they may work as an investment advisor to help individuals or companies manage and invest their funds.

Exhibit 1-2 ▲

There used to be three professional accounting bodies in Canada: the Certified General Accountants Association of Canada, the Society of Management Accountants of Canada, and the Canadian Institute of Chartered Accountants. Each accounting body was a self-regulated body to grant the qualifying members its respective designation (i.e., CGA, CMA, and CA) and public accounting licence. Professional accounting designations increase the confidence of employers and the general public in accounting professionals who provide accounting-related services. Negotiations are currently taking place to merge the three bodies into one accounting body to be called CPA Canada (Chartered Professional Accountants Canada); the new designation will be the CPA. Many provinces already announced the unification, while others are still underway.

WHAT ACCOUNTING PRINCIPLES AND CONCEPTS GOVERN THE FIELD OF ACCOUNTING?

WHAT ARE THE APPLICABLE ACCOUNTING REPORTING STANDARDS IN CANADA?

L.O. ④ Explain the key accounting principles and the conceptual framework

In sports, there are established rules and principles that dictate how each game is to be played and how the score is to be kept. In accounting, there are reporting standards that guide how business activities should be recognized, measured, and recorded, and how financial information should be reported.

There are several accounting reporting standards in Canada for various types of entities, such as publicly accountable enterprises, private enterprises, not-for-profit organizations, public sector organizations, etc. Canadian publicly accountable enterprises have been required to adopt **International Financial Reporting Standards (IFRS)** since January 1, 2011. Canadian private enterprises, on the other hand, have the option to adopt IFRS or to adopt a new set of "made in Canada" financial reporting standards—the **Accounting Standards for Private Enterprises (ASPE)**—developed by the Accounting Standards Board (AcSB). Some significant differences between IFRS and ASPE lie in the areas of how events that take place are measured and presented, what information needs to be disclosed to people outside of the company, and when certain elements need to be recorded.

The Accounting Standards Board has prepared a five-part *CPA Canada Handbook** for Chartered Professional Accountants Canada that allows different sectors to adopt the appropriate standards to suit their needs. The five parts include:

Part I—International Financial Reporting Standards
Part II—Accounting Standards for Private Enterprises
Part III—Accounting Standards for Not-for-Profit Organizations
Part IV—Accounting Standards for Pension Plans
Part V—A complete set of the existing *CPA Canada Handbook* contents.

Since we will be examining corporations and their financial accounting processes throughout this text, this textbook is based on IFRS and, where applicable, addresses ASPE when they are applicable and relevant. This is due to the fact that publicly accountable enterprises must use IFRS. In addition, some private enterprises may elect to adopt IFRS as a result of having a plan to eventually become public companies or to access capital, funding, and investment opportunities internationally.

INTERNATIONAL FINANCIAL REPORTING STANDARDS

In the 1970s, a set of accounting standards was developed for use primarily by companies located in countries that did not have their own accounting standards. These standards, originally called International Accounting Standards (IAS), evolved into what is currently known as International Financial Reporting Standards, or IFRS. IFRS are created by the International Accounting Standards Board. The members of the International Accounting Standards Board are appointed by the International Accounting Standards Committee. Both the International Accounting Standards Board and the International Accounting Standards Committee have members from many different regions throughout the world. This ensures that the IFRS are the result of input from many different countries throughout the entire world. The goal of the International Accounting Standards Board is to create a set of global, high-quality, enforceable accounting standards. The set of IFRS is referred to as a principles-based system. Instead of creating countless rules that need to be followed, IFRS relies on a **conceptual framework** and a small number of overriding principles coupled with sound decision making and good ethical behaviour.

IFRS have become widespread throughout the world. As a matter of fact, many countries that have their own accounting standards have started to allow the use of IFRS in addition to, or instead of, their own standards. Currently, IFRS are used by more than 100 countries in the world, and a number of economically important countries, such as Japan and the United States, have discussed adopting IFRS.

---

* As of November 1, 2013, the titles of the *CICA Handbook* publications have been changed to the *CPA Canada Handbook*.

THE CONCEPTUAL FRAMEWORK

The conceptual framework is a theoretical foundation that helps accounting standard setters develop consistent and coherent standards, and helps accountants determine the appropriate treatment of events in the absence of specific guidance so that financial information can be properly communicated to the users. The main objective of financial reporting is to provide information that is useful for making economic decisions (e.g., investment and lending). The conceptual framework shows guiding assumptions, principles, and qualities that are considered in the preparation of financial information.

Assumptions

Assumptions are the cornerstone of building financial information. If any of these assumptions change, all of the information that is built on top of these assumptions is affected. The main four assumptions are:

- **Monetary unit assumption:** In accounting, it is assumed that the purchasing power of the dollar is stable. This means that dollars of different time periods are considered to have the same value. This assumption allows accountants to add and subtract dollars of different time periods by their nominal value.

- **Economic entity assumption:** This assumption implies that the organization—the reporting entity—is economically separate from the owners. For example, if you have a business, you would prepare separate accounting records for all the transactions related to the business independent from your own personal transactions to be able to assess the performance of your business. However, for tax and legal purposes, sometimes the owner(s) and the business are considered the same legal entity (refer to Exhibit 1-1).

- **Going concern assumption:** It is assumed that the life of a business is going to continue to operate in the foreseeable future. This assumption is important, because if the business is going to be liquidated, then financial statement elements would be measured differently. For example, assets would be measured at their liquidation value rather than the **historical cost** or fair value because the liquidation value would be more relevant to both creditors and owners in such a situation.

- **Time period assumption:** To be able to assess a business's performance in a timely manner, it is assumed that the operation of a business is divided into a series of time periods. It is *assumed* that business starts at the beginning of a time period and ends its operations at the end of the time period. Accordingly, its performance could be measured during this time period. Such time periods could be a day, a week, a month, a quarter, or a year. Usually, businesses use monthly or quarterly time periods. For tax purposes, annual financial statements must be prepared. Accrual accounting captures the effects of business decisions and other events on the reporting entity's performance and financial position in the periods in which those effects occur.

Accounting Principles

The following accounting principles are the main guidelines that help in preparing the financial statements:

- **Historical cost/fair value:** Basically, all elements of the financial statements are recorded at cost. The historical cost was the basis for measuring the financial statement elements until not so long ago. However, there is another emerging principle—the **fair value** principle—where some financial statement elements in certain situations can be measured at their fair value. This will be discussed in detail in later chapters.

- **Revenue and expense recognition:** The point of time in which revenues or expenses are recognized is crucial because it affects how the performance of a business is measured within a specific period of time. There are several criteria upon which revenues and expenses are recognized, which will be explained throughout this book.

- **Full disclosure principle:** This principle implies that all information that is relevant to a company's financial performance should be included in the financial statements. It could appear either in the body of the financial statements, in the footnotes, or in notes attached to the financial statements.

Constraints

The accounting information is developed and provided in light of two constraints:

- **Cost vs. benefit:** The benefit of the information should exceed its preparation cost. Although the cost of information can be measured accurately, it is always challenging to value the benefits of the information. Therefore, accountants have to use professional judgment to determine if the benefit of providing the information justifies its cost.

- **Materiality: Materiality** refers to the significance or relevance of information to the decision made by financial statement users. If omitting an item would affect the user's decision, this item is considered material. Materiality requires a great amount of judgment.

Qualitative Characteristics

Accounting information should be characterized by certain qualitative characteristics in order to be useful to users of financial statements. Those characteristics are summarized as follows:

- **Relevance:** Information is relevant if it could make a difference in the decision making process. Information would be relevant if users could use it in preparing forecasts, if it confirms users' previous expectations, or if it is provided in an appropriate time for influencing their decisions.

- **Reliability:** Users can rely on financial information if it is complete, verifiable, and free of errors; if it represents faithfully the economic resources available to the reporting entity; and if it is not biased (that is, it is neutral).

- **Comparability and consistency: Comparability** ensures that users will be able to compare the financial information with previous periods and compare it to other companies operating in the same industry. To be comparable, the accounting standards should be consistent. **Consistency** means that the same accounting policies and methods are implemented each accounting period to be able to focus on the real differences. If it is in the best interests of the business to change accounting policies, then it should disclose the effect of such change in the financial statements to make it comparable.

- **Understandability:** When information is understandable, it is usable by users who have a basic knowledge of accounting.

In essence, IFRS provide a general framework and accountants are required to make sound professional judgment calls in various situations. When in doubt, accountants need to refer to the framework and consider whether the financial information to be provided is understandable, comparable, and relevant to users, and whether the financial information can be relied on for users to make economic decisions.

Exhibit 1-3 illustrates the IFRS conceptual framework for financial reporting. IFRS puts the focus on users, as all the preparation and presentation of the financial information is geared toward the users' decision making needs. Accountants need to balance these qualities of information with the above-mentioned assumptions, principles, constraints, and qualitative characteristics in preparing useful financial information for users.

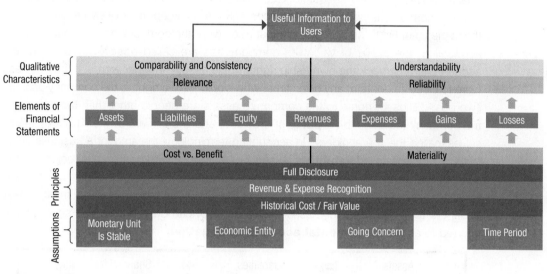

Exhibit 1-3 ▲

Another important aspect of financial statements is that they are prepared on the **accrual basis**, meaning that the business transactions are recognized and recorded when they occur, not when cash is exchanged. When assets (the items that an organization owns or controls, e.g., buildings, equipment, inventory of goods that are sold, etc.) or services are measured and recorded at cost, where cash or cash equivalents were paid to acquire them at the time of their acquisition, this is called historical cost basis measurement. Using the historical cost approach, businesses will keep the historical cost of an asset throughout its useful life because this cost is a reliable measure. This is the most common method of recording the cost of assets. Canadian Accounting Standards for Private Enterprises (ASPE) continues to require the use of the historical cost approach.

ASPE

However, under IFRS, financial statements are prepared on a modified cost basis, with an emphasis on fair value, which is more useful and relevant for users' decision making purposes. Businesses, therefore, may choose one of four recording methods that best reflects their economic activities and reality. These four methods are the historical cost, **current cost, realizable value**, and **present value** approaches. For example, when a business records a purchase of an asset at historical cost, it records the value of the asset as the amount of cash or cash equivalents paid or fair value of the consideration given to purchase it. Using the current cost approach, assets are carried at the amount of cash or cash equivalents that would have to be paid if the same asset were acquired currently; while using the realizable value approach, assets are carried at the amount of cash or cash equivalents that could currently be obtained by selling the asset.

IFRS

The concept of present value will be dealt with in the higher level accounting and finance courses, and we will not discuss this approach in this textbook. We will focus on historical cost with adjustments to current cost or realizable cost in various topics.

HOW IS THE ACCOUNTING EQUATION USED TO RECORD BUSINESS TRANSACTIONS?

L.O. ⑤ Analyze transactions using the basic accounting equation

As we said earlier, one of an accountant's jobs is that of being the scorekeeper for the business. The accountant needs to keep track of information so he or she can tell people how the company is performing. The accountant must keep track of two main things at the same time. First, the accountant must track what the company has that has value. In accounting, the things of value the company has are called **assets**. In addition, the accountant must track the ownership rights to the assets. In other words, if the business were to close its doors at any given time, who would have a right to the company assets? Two possibilities for rights to the company's assets are people other than the owners of the company (called a **third party** or creditors) and the owners of the company themselves (called the shareholders). In accounting terminology, the amount a business owes to third parties is called **liabilities**. Assets not owned by third parties must belong to the shareholders, and the amount of assets owned by the shareholders of the company is called **shareholders' equity**. The amount of assets that a company has must always equal the total rights to those assets. This concept can be expressed as an equation, referred to as the **fundamental accounting equation:**

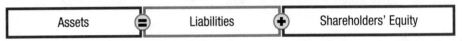

| Assets | = | Liabilities | + | Shareholders' Equity |

Shareholders' equity is also called net assets, the residual interest in the assets of the entity after deducting all its liabilities.

TRANSACTION ANALYSIS

Concept Check questions appear throughout the chapter, giving you the chance to test your mastery of the concepts you just covered before moving on to the next one.

Accountants will record the effects of transactions in this equation. A **transaction** is any event that has a financial impact on the business. If something changes either what the company has or who owns it, it must be recorded in the accounting equation. When the accountant records a transaction that affects the business, he or she will record what

 CONCEPT CHECK...

At the end of its first month of operations, Patel Consulting, Inc. has assets totalling $57,000 and liabilities totalling $25,000. What is the amount of Patel Consulting's total shareholders' equity at the end of the month?

Answer: We can use the fundamental accounting equation to figure out Patel Consulting's total shareholders' equity. First, it helps to restate the equation in a different format by subtracting liabilities from both sides of the equation as follows:

Assets − Liabilities = Shareholders' Equity

Next, insert the amount of Patel Consulting's total assets and the total liabilities into the restated formula.

$57,000 − $25,000 = Shareholders' Equity

Finally, solve the equation to get the total shareholder's equity of $32,000.

$57,000 − $25,000 = $32,000

effect the transaction has on the assets of the business and what effect it has on the ownership of those assets. This process is called transaction analysis.

Throughout this book we will include in the margin a transactional analysis figure to depict the transactions.

SHAREHOLDERS' EQUITY

Before we start looking at how transactions affect the accounting equation, let's take a closer look at the shareholders' equity section of the equation for a corporation. To provide more useful information to various users, the shareholders' equity section of the equation can be broken down into smaller subcategories:

- **Share capital** is used to reflect shareholders' equity that is the result of the owners of the business investing assets or injecting cash into the business. In other words, the assets of the company increased because the shareholders invested those assets into the company. In general, there are two types of share capital: **common shares** and **preferred shares**. The difference between these two types of shares will be discussed in Chapter 10.
- **Retained earnings** is used to reflect shareholders' equity that is the result of the business having earnings that have not been distributed to shareholders but have been retained in the business. As we will see shortly, earnings are created when the business provides goods or services to customers.

An expanded version of the accounting equation would look like this:

(what the business has)   (who owns it)

The retained earnings subcategory can now be further broken down into smaller subcategories to help the accountant provide even better information. These subcategories and what they reflect are as follows:

- **Revenue** is an increase in retained earnings that is the result of the business providing goods and services.
- **Expenses** are used to reflect a decrease in retained earnings that is the result of the business incurring costs related to providing goods and services.
- **Dividends** are used to reflect a decrease in retained earnings that is the result of the owners receiving assets (usually cash) from the business.

An expanded version of the accounting equation would now look like this:

Retained Earnings and, therefore, Shareholders' Equity is increased by adding amounts to Revenues, and is decreased by adding amounts to Expenses and Dividends. These subcategories will make more sense as we see how they are used to record the effects of business transactions. To illustrate, let us analyze the effects of several transactions on the accounting equation for the month of January 2015 for Hooray Consulting, Inc., a new computer consulting business started by Ray Hu.

1. **Issuance of shares.** Ray Hu invests $10,000 to start the business. Hooray Consulting, Inc. sells Ray 1,000 common shares for $10,000 in exchange for his cash investment. The effect of this transaction on the accounting equation is to increase Hooray Consulting's Assets and Shareholders' Equity as follows:

	Assets	=	Liabilities	+	Shareholders' Equity		
					Common Shares	+	Retained Earnings
	Cash	=			**Common Shares**	**+ Revenues − Expenses − Dividends**	
(1)	+$10,000				+$10,000		
Bal	$10,000	=			$10,000		

$10,000
Total Assets

$10,000
Liabilities & Shareholders' Equity

Remember that for each transaction the amount on the left side of the equation must equal the amount on the right side. The amount of assets will be increased by $10,000 because the business now has $10,000 of cash that it did not have before. To keep track of what type of assets the business has, the accountant will create a subcategory under assets for each different type of asset that the business has, so a subcategory for Cash was created. Since the assets have increased, there is now a need to increase the ownership side of the equation. The business does not owe the $10,000 to a creditor so the $10,000 ownership interest must belong to Ray and must be entered in the Shareholders' Equity section of the equation. If we look at the Shareholders' Equity side of the equation, we can see that there are two possible places the $10,000 can be entered to increase Shareholders' Equity: Common Shares and Retained Earnings. Based on the definitions as discussed previously, we see that the $10,000 should be entered in the Common Shares section of Shareholders' Equity because this increase in Shareholders' Equity was the result of Ray investing assets into the business.

2. **Purchase supplies on credit.** Hooray Consulting purchases office supplies, agreeing to pay $350 within 30 days. The effect of this transaction on the accounting equation is to increase Assets and increase Liabilities as follows:

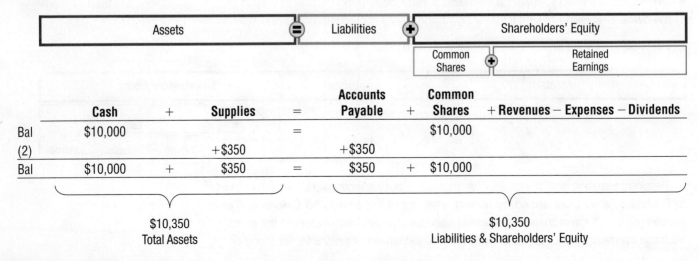

	Assets			=	Liabilities	+	Shareholders' Equity		
							Common Shares	+	Retained Earnings
	Cash	**+**	**Supplies**	**=**	**Accounts Payable**	**+**	**Common Shares**	**+ Revenues − Expenses − Dividends**	
Bal	$10,000			=			$10,000		
(2)			+$350		+$350				
Bal	$10,000	+	$350	=	$350	+	$10,000		

$10,350
Total Assets

$10,350
Liabilities & Shareholders' Equity

The Supplies account is an asset because the supplies that were purchased have not been used yet. Supplies are an example of what we call **prepaid expenses**. A prepaid expense is considered an asset until it has been used up in the business operations. The agreement to pay for them later creates an **accounts payable**, a liability, because the business owes $350 to a creditor.

3. **Purchase equipment for cash.** The business purchases equipment, paying cash of $4,000. The effect of this transaction on the accounting equation is to increase one asset and decrease another asset as follows:

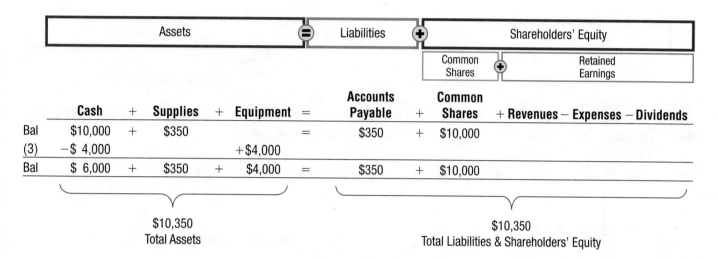

	Cash	+	Supplies	+	Equipment	=	Accounts Payable	+	Common Shares	+ Revenues − Expenses − Dividends
Bal	$10,000	+	$350			=	$350	+	$10,000	
(3)	−$ 4,000				+$4,000					
Bal	$ 6,000	+	$350	+	$4,000	=	$350	+	$10,000	

$10,350
Total Assets

$10,350
Total Liabilities & Shareholders' Equity

The cash purchase of equipment increases one asset, Equipment, and decreases another asset, Cash, by the same amount. After the transaction is completed, Hooray Consulting has total assets of $10,350, liabilities of $350, and shareholders' equity of $10,000. Because there has been no change in the total amount of assets, there should be no change in ownership; therefore, there will be no change in the amount of Shareholders' Equity.

Assets = Liabilities + Shareholders' Equity
−4,000
+4,000

4. **Borrow cash from the bank.** Hooray Consulting borrows $12,000 cash from the bank and signs a two-year note payable to the bank. The effect of this transaction on the accounting equation is to increase Assets and increase Liabilities as follows:

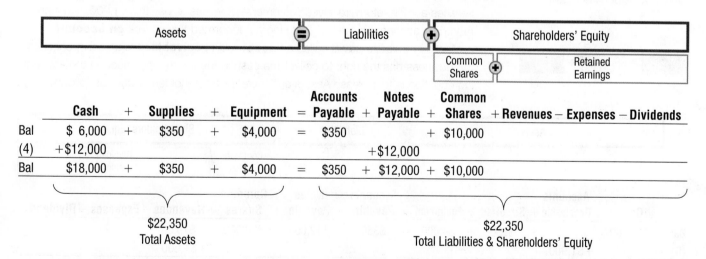

	Cash	+	Supplies	+	Equipment	=	Accounts Payable	+	Notes Payable	+	Common Shares	+ Revenues − Expenses − Dividends
Bal	$ 6,000	+	$350	+	$4,000	=	$350			+	$10,000	
(4)	+$12,000								+$12,000			
Bal	$18,000	+	$350	+	$4,000	=	$350	+	$12,000	+	$10,000	

$22,350
Total Assets

$22,350
Total Liabilities & Shareholders' Equity

A **note payable** is a written promise to pay a specified amount in the future. Often, businesses will borrow money from the bank to purchase assets or to make sure enough cash is available to operate the business. Borrowing cash from the bank increases the asset Cash because the business has $12,000 that it did not have

Assets = Liabilities + Shareholders' Equity
+12,000   +12,000

before. It also increases the liability, Notes Payable, by $12,000 because the business owes $12,000 to the bank. In other words, the bank has an ownership interest for $12,000 of Hooray Consulting's assets. Note that total assets of $22,350 still equal the total liabilities of $12,350 plus the shareholders' equity of $10,000.

5. **Provide services for cash.** Hooray Consulting earns service revenue by providing consulting services for clients. Hooray collects $1,200 cash for services provided. The effect of this transaction on the accounting equation is to increase Assets and increase Shareholders' Equity as follows:

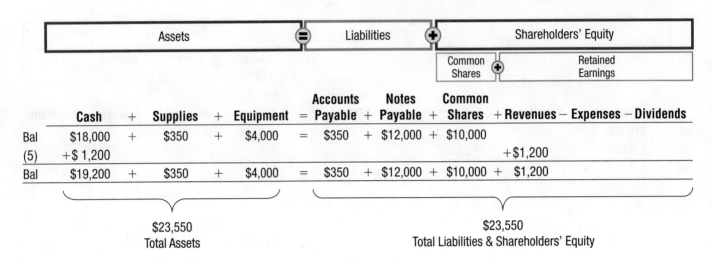

	Cash	+	Supplies	+	Equipment	=	Accounts Payable	+	Notes Payable	+	Common Shares	+	Revenues	−	Expenses	−	Dividends
Bal	$18,000	+	$350	+	$4,000	=	$350	+	$12,000	+	$10,000						
(5)	+$1,200												+$1,200				
Bal	$19,200	+	$350	+	$4,000	=	$350	+	$12,000	+	$10,000	+	$1,200				

$23,550
Total Assets

$23,550
Total Liabilities & Shareholders' Equity

+12,000   +12,000

Providing services increases both Cash and Revenues by $1,200. Cash is increased because the business has $1,200 that it did not have before, and Revenues is increased because Shareholders' Equity must be increased to reflect the fact that Ray, the sole shareholder, has an ownership interest in the increased assets. As was previously discussed, the specific subcategory that is used to increase Retained Earnings (and, therefore, Shareholders' Equity) because of providing goods and services is Revenues.

MEMORY**TIPS**

Revenues increase owners' equity.

+1,900   +1,900

6. **Provide services on credit.** A business can also earn service revenue even if it has not yet received cash for these services. Hooray Consulting performs $1,900 of services and, in return, receives customers' promises to pay this $1,900 within one month. In accounting, we say that Hooray performed this service **on account**. A client's promise to pay is called an **accounts receivable**. It is an asset because the business has the right to collect the cash in the future. The effect on the accounting equation is to increase Assets and increase Shareholders' Equity as follows:

	Cash	+	Accounts Receivable	+	Supplies	+	Equipment	=	Accounts Payable	+	Notes Payable	+	Common Shares	+	Revenues	−	Expenses	−	Dividends
Bal	$19,200			+	$350	+	$4,000	=	$350	+	$12,000	+	$10,000	+	$1,200				
(6)			+$1,900												+$1,900				
Bal	$19,200	+	$1,900	+	$350	+	$4,000	=	$350	+	$12,000	+	$10,000	+	$3,100				

$25,450
Total Assets

$25,450
Total Liabilities & Shareholders' Equity

Notice the Revenue account was increased just as it was in the previous transaction when Hooray Consulting performed services and received cash. The Revenue account was increased to reflect the fact that there has been an increase in the shareholders' ownership interest in the assets of the business.

In Transaction 5, the assets increased because the business received cash, and in Transaction 6, the assets increased because the business received an account receivable.

MEMORY**TIPS**

Any receivable is an asset.

7. **Partial payment of accounts payable.** Hooray Consulting pays $150 to the store where it purchased $350 worth of supplies in Transaction 2. In accounting this is referred to as "paying on account." The effect on the accounting equation is to decrease Assets and decrease Liabilities as follows:

	Cash	+	Accounts Receivable	+	Supplies	+	Equipment	=	Accounts Payable	+	Notes Payable	+	Common Shares	+	Revenues	–	Expenses	–	Dividends
Bal	$19,200	+	$1,900	+	$350	+	$4,000	=	$350	+	$12,000	+	$10,000	+	$3,100				
(7)	–$150								–$150									
Bal	$19,050	+	$1,900	+	$350	+	$4,000	=	$200	+	$12,000	+	$10,000	+	$3,100				

$25,300
Total Assets

$25,300
Total Liabilities & Shareholders' Equity

The payment of cash on account has no effect on Supplies because the payment does not affect the amount of supplies that the business has. Likewise, the payment on account does not affect Expenses because the business is paying off an amount owed, not using those supplies. The Cash account decreases because the business has less cash and the Accounts Payable account decreases because the business owes less to a creditor by paying down a portion of the accounts payable.

8. **Payment of expenses.** During the month, Hooray Consulting paid $1,700 cash for expenses incurred such as wages, building rent, and utilities. Later on we will see that each different type of expense will be shown separately in the accounting equation, but for now we will lump them all together under the heading Expenses. The effect on the accounting equation is to decrease Assets and decrease Shareholders' Equity as follows:

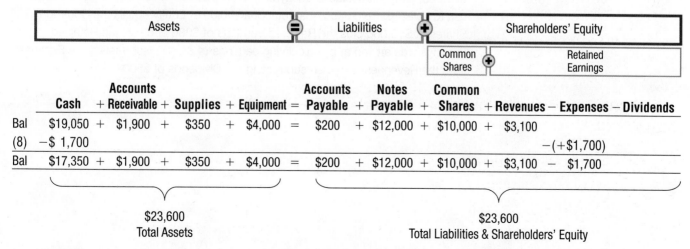

	Cash	+	Accounts Receivable	+	Supplies	+	Equipment	=	Accounts Payable	+	Notes Payable	+	Common Shares	+	Revenues	–	Expenses	–	Dividends
Bal	$19,050	+	$1,900	+	$350	+	$4,000	=	$200	+	$12,000	+	$10,000	+	$3,100				
(8)	–$1,700															–(+$1,700)		
Bal	$17,350	+	$1,900	+	$350	+	$4,000	=	$200	+	$12,000	+	$10,000	+	$3,100	–	$1,700		

$23,600
Total Assets

$23,600
Total Liabilities & Shareholders' Equity

For this transaction, Cash decreases and Expenses increase. Because Expenses are subtracted from Retained Earnings, Retained Earnings (and, therefore, Shareholders' Equity) will decrease. This decrease in Shareholders' Equity reflects that the assets for the business have decreased and, therefore, there has to be less ownership reported. Remember that Expenses are used to decrease Retained Earnings when needed as the result of the business incurring costs related to providing goods and services.

9. **Cash dividends.** Hooray Consulting pays $500 of cash dividends to Ray Hu, the shareholder. The effect on the accounting equation is to decrease Assets and decrease Shareholders' Equity as follows:

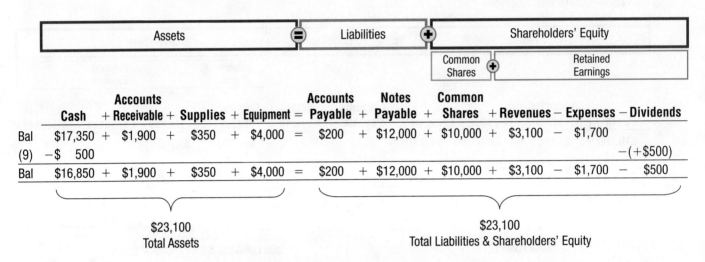

	Cash	+ Accounts Receivable	+ Supplies	+ Equipment	= Accounts Payable	+ Notes Payable	+ Common Shares	+ Revenues	− Expenses	− Dividends
Bal	$17,350	+ $1,900	+ $350	+ $4,000	= $200	+ $12,000	+ $10,000	+ $3,100	− $1,700	
(9)	−$ 500									−(+$500)
Bal	$16,850	+ $1,900	+ $350	+ $4,000	= $200	+ $12,000	+ $10,000	+ $3,100	− $1,700	− $500

$23,100
Total Assets

$23,100
Total Liabilities & Shareholders' Equity

Note that Dividends increased by $500, resulting in a decrease in Shareholders' Equity
(as Dividends decrease Shareholders' Equity).

Assets	=	Liabilities	+	Shareholders' Equity
−500				−500

The payment of dividends causes a decrease in Cash of $500 and an increase in Dividends of $500. Because Dividends are subtracted from Retained Earnings, Retained Earnings (and, therefore, Shareholders' Equity) will decrease. This decrease in Shareholders' Equity reflects that the assets (i.e., Cash) for the business have decreased and, therefore, there has to be less ownership reported. Dividends are different from expenses because the cash is paid directly to the owners rather than being paid for costs that were related to providing goods or services. Once again, we can see that the total assets of $23,100 still equal the total liabilities of $12,200, plus shareholders' equity of $10,900, so the accounting equation continues to balance. Remember that total Shareholders' Equity equals the Common Shares of $10,000 plus the Retained Earnings of $900 and that the Retained Earnings was arrived at by calculating earnings of $1,400 (subtracting the Expenses from the Revenues) and then subtracting the Dividends of $500.

CRITICAL THINKING

Take a minute to think about the impact of the following independent cases on each of the Assets, Liabilities, and Shareholders' Equity accounts. What is the error, if any?

1. A payment of Dividends, $5,000, was recorded as a decrease in Cash and in Expenses.
2. A receipt of $2,500 from a customer who pays her debt was recorded as an increase in Cash and in Service Revenue.
3. A receipt of $12,000 from shareholders in exchange for company's shares was recorded as an increase in Cash and in Liabilities.
4. A purchase of supplies on account for $250 was recorded as an increase in Supplies and in Accounts Payable.

> *Critical Thinking questions appear throughout the chapter, challenging you to think about the real-world implications of accounting issues and challenges raised in the chapter.*

Solution:

1. Recording dividends as an expense will increase the expenses and decrease the company's profitability. Dividends are not expenses; rather they are a distribution of profits, hence equity should decrease. The impact on the accounts after the correction would be:

Assets	Liabilities	Shareholders' Equity
Decrease	No change	Decrease

2. This will overstate service revenue, and since Accounts Receivable should also decrease when collecting payment from a customer, Accounts Receivable will be overstated as well. The impact on the accounts after the correction would be:

Assets	Liabilities	Shareholders' Equity
Increase and decrease equally (increase in Cash and decrease in Accounts Receivable); net effect is no change	No change	No change

3. Investment by shareholders should increase owners' equity. Increasing liabilities will overstate it. The impact on the accounts after the correction would be:

Assets	Liabilities	Shareholders' Equity
Increase	No change	Increase

4. This is correct since the supplies are purchased on account, so both supplies and liabilities would increase. The impact of the transaction would be:

Assets	Liabilities	Shareholders' Equity
Increase	Increase	No change

WHAT DO FINANCIAL STATEMENTS REPORT, AND HOW ARE THEY PREPARED?

L.O. ⑥ Understand and be able to prepare basic financial statements

To present the results of a business's transactions for a period, financial statements need to be prepared. These reports show the entity's financial information to interested stakeholders both inside and outside the organization. Under both IFRS and ASPE, four basic financial statements are prepared by most organizations, but there are some differences that are highlighted as follows:

IFRS	ASPE
Statement of comprehensive income (the income statement is the basis for the statement of comprehensive income; additional details are then added for unrealized gains and losses).	Income statement (includes the income from operations in addition to the gains and losses; however, it does not include unrealized gains and losses).
Statement of changes in equity (the statement of retained earnings is the basis for the statement of changes in equity; additional details are then added for the capital share elements).	Statement of retained earnings (shows the changes in retained earnings during the period).
Statement of financial position or balance sheet (both names are interchangeable and it is fine to use either one).	Balance sheet (shows the assets, liabilities, and owners' equity of a business).
Statement of cash flows (shows the cash generated and used by the business classified into three activities: operating, financing, and investing).	Cash flows statement (the same as IFRS, but the statement title is slightly different).

THE STATEMENT OF COMPREHENSIVE INCOME

A **statement of comprehensive income** is prepared to answer the question, "Is the organization making a **profit**?" Just as a scoreboard shows how many points a team earned and whether the team is winning or losing, a business prepares a statement of comprehensive income to show, for a specific time period, whether the business had **net income** (total revenues were greater than total expenses) or a **net loss** (total revenues are less than total expenses), as well as to show any unrealized gains or losses from holding certain assets, such as investments. Companies can prepare a single statement of comprehensive income or two statements including (1) an income statement ending with net income or net loss, and (2) a statement beginning with the net income or net loss and showing components of other comprehensive income. For the time being, we will focus on the business operations with net income or net loss in an income statement, and in later chapters, we will introduce the statement of comprehensive income. ASPE focuses only on net income and does not consider comprehensive income in the income statement.

ASPE

THE INCOME STATEMENT

To prepare an **income statement**, we set up a form that includes a heading and the body of the statement. The heading of all financial statements should show "who," "what," and "when." The "who" is the name of the business, the "what" is the name of the financial statement, and the "when" is the time *period* covered by the statement. The body of the income statement lists the revenues, then the expenses, and finally the net income or net loss. When revenues are greater than expenses, the business earns net income, or profit. When expenses are greater than revenues, the business has a net loss. Expenses should be listed based on either their nature or their function in the income statement. Since most Canadian companies used to prepare their income statement by function, and companies are permitted to continue with this practice, we will show the income statement classified by function in this textbook.

We can prepare an income statement for Hooray Consulting for the month of January 2015 by referring to the ending balances in the accounting equation that we recently completed.

If we look at **Exhibit 1-4**, we can see what the income statement for Hooray Consulting looks like. In the first month of operations, Hooray Consulting, Inc. earned $3,100 in revenue and had $1,700 in expenses, which resulted in net income of $1,400, ignoring taxes for the time being. This amount can remain part of the shareholders' equity in the business and can be used to "grow" or expand the business, or the business can use all or part of these funds to pay dividends to the shareholders.

 DECISION GUIDELINES

DECISION		**GUIDELINE**		**ANALYZE**
I need to determine if a business is profitable. Which financial statement do I use?	▶	Use the income statement to determine the profitability of a business. The income statement reports the revenues and expenses of a business. Revenues represent what a business earns as a result of providing goods or services. Expenses represent the cost to the business of providing those goods or services.	▶	If revenues exceed expenses, the business is profitable and has earned net income. However, if expenses exceed revenues, the business has incurred a net loss and is not profitable.

THE STATEMENT OF CHANGES IN EQUITY

"How many shares has the corporation issued in exchange for assets, such as cash or equipment?" "How much has the corporation made and kept during the current accounting period?" The **statement of changes in equity** answers these questions by presenting the amount of the share capital, the retained earnings, and the changes to these accounts during a specific time period, such as a month or a year. Increases in common shares are due to issuing more shares, and decreases are due to share buybacks. Likewise, increases in retained earnings come from net income, and decreases result from either a net loss or the payment of dividends.

To prepare the statement of changes in equity, we set up a form that includes a heading and body similar to what we did for the income statement. The heading includes the name of the business, the name of the financial statement, and the time period covered by the statement. The body of the statement lists the beginning of each account that belongs to shareholders' equity; for example, common shares and retained earnings balances, any new shares issued, net income earned or net loss incurred, any dividends paid, and the ending balance of Common Shares and Retained Earnings. Using the information from the income statement that we just prepared and the dividend information from our accounting equation, we can prepare the portion of the changes in the retained earnings account in the statement of changes in equity.

Exhibit 1-4 shows what Hooray Consulting's statement of changes in equity looks like. Because this is the first month that Hooray Consulting has been in business, there is a zero balance in beginning common shares and retained earnings. During the first month of operations, Hooray Consulting, Inc. issued $10,000 of common shares to Ray Hu and paid dividends of $500, which, when combined with the $1,400 of net income for January, leaves

---

Hooray Consulting, Inc.
Income Statement
Month Ended January 31, 2015

Revenue		$3,100
Expenses		(1,700)
Net Income		$1,400

Hooray Consulting, Inc.
Statement of Changes in Equity
Month Ended January 31, 2015

IFRS

	Common Shares		Retained Earnings	Total
	Number of Shares	$		
Balance, January 1, 2015	—	$ 0	$ 0	$ 0
Issued Common Shares	1,000	$10,000		10,000
Net Income			$1,400	1,400
Dividends			(500)	(500)
Balance, January 31, 2015	1,000	$10,000	$ 900	$10,900

Hooray Consulting, Inc.
Statement of Financial Position
As of January 31, 2015

ASSETS		LIABILITIES	
Cash	$16,850	Accounts Payable	$ 200
Accounts Receivable	1,900	Note Payable	12,000
Supplies	350	Total Liabilities	12,200
Equipment	4,000		
		SHAREHOLDERS' EQUITY	
		Common Shares	10,000
		Retained Earnings	900
		Total Shareholders' Equity	10,900
		Total Liabilities &	
Total Assets	$23,100	Shareholders' Equity	$23,100

Exhibit 1-4 ▲

Notice the dollar signs on the first and last amounts and the double underline under the last amount, Net Income, presented on the statement. It is common practice to place a dollar sign on the first number and the last number in each column on a financial statement and to foot (double underline) the final amount.

an ending retained earnings balance at January 31 of $900. We can see that of the $1,400 that Hooray Consulting earned during January, $900 was retained in the business.

Under Canadian Accounting Standards for Private Enterprises, a business is not required to prepare a statement of changes in equity. Instead, a business is required to prepare a statement of retained earnings, which is one of the components in the statement of changes in equity. The statement of retained earnings shows the changes in the retained earnings account. **Exhibit 1-5** shows what Hooray Consulting's statement of retained earnings looks like.

ASPE

Hooray Consulting, Inc. Statement of Retained Earnings Month Ended January 31, 2015	
Retained Earnings, January 1, 2015	$ 0
Add: Net Income for the month	1,400
Subtotal	1,400
Less: Dividends	500
Retained Earnings, January 31, 2015	$ 900

Exhibit 1-5 ▲

 DECISION GUIDELINES

DECISION

I want to know if a company was profitable, and if it was, what it did with the profits. Which financial statement do I use?

GUIDELINE

Use the statement of changes in equity to find out. The retained earnings account in the statement of changes in equity shows whether the net income of a business was paid out as dividends or retained in the business.

ANALYZE

If a business is planning on growth, it will often issue low or no dividends to shareholders. This way, it retains the income in the business.

THE STATEMENT OF FINANCIAL POSITION (OR THE BALANCE SHEET)

"What assets does the company have, and who has ownership rights to those assets?" The **statement of financial position**, also known as the **balance sheet**, answers this question by listing all of an entity's assets, liabilities, and shareholders' equity as of a specific date, usually the end of a month or a year. Since the balance of each account may change from one day to the next, the amount of each account in the statement of financial position shows the balance on a specific date, not for a period of time. Basically, the statement of financial position shows the accounting equation for a business and reflects the fact that assets equal liabilities plus shareholders' equity.

 IFRS ASPE

Using the information from the statement of changes in equity that we just prepared and information from our accounting equation, we can prepare a statement of financial position for Hooray Consulting. Exhibit 1-4 shows what Hooray Consulting's statement of financial position will look like. Notice that total assets equal the combined total of liabilities and shareholders' equity. When a statement of financial position is presented in side-by-side format so that assets are listed on the left-hand side and liabilities and shareholders' equity are the right-hand side, it is said to be in *account format*. It may be more convenient to list assets, then liabilities, and shareholders' equity vertically in a computer spreadsheet. This vertical format is called *report format*. Companies can use either title of the financial statement—either "Statement of Financial Position" if they are adopting IFRS or "Balance Sheet" if they are adopting ASPE.

 DECISION GUIDELINES

DECISION

I want to know who would get its assets if a business were to close its doors. Which financial statement would I use?

GUIDELINE

Use the statement of financial position to determine who has claims to the company's assets.

ANALYZE

The liabilities of a business reflect the claims of creditors to the assets of the business. Once those claims are settled, the remaining assets (called "net assets") belong to the shareholders (the owners) of the business. This amount is reflected by the shareholders' equity on the statement of financial position.

THE STATEMENT OF CASH FLOWS

"Where did the business get the money it needed to operate, and where did it spend its money?" The **statement of cash flows** answers this question by showing stakeholders all of the sources and all of the uses of cash by a business for a specified period of time. Businesses can get cash and use cash through three business activities: operating activities, investing activities, and financing activities. The statement of cash flows is a complex statement to prepare; therefore, we will postpone the coverage of the statement of cash flows until Chapter 11.

However, to get a sense of what it looks like, **Exhibit 1-6** shows a statement of cash flows for Hooray Consulting. Note that only cash transactions are included. Also note that the cash balance at the end of the period matches the cash balance presented on the statement of financial position in Exhibit 1-4.

Hooray Consulting, Inc.
Statement of Cash Flows
Month Ended January 2015

Cash Flows from Operating Activities		
Cash collections from clients	$ 1,200	
Cash payment to suppliers	(150)	
Cash payment to cover expenses	(1,700)	
Net Cash Flows from Operating Activities		($ 650)
Cash Flows from Investing Activities		
Purchase of equipment	($4,000)	
Net Cash Flows from Investing Activities		(4,000)
Cash Flows from Financing Activities		
Issuing of shares	$10,000	
Borrowing from bank	12,000	
Paying dividends	(500)	
Net Cash Flows from Financing Activities		21,500
Net Cash Flows from All Activities		$ 16,850
Cash Balance at the beginning of period		0
Cash Balance at the end of period		$16,850

Exhibit 1-6 ▲

 DECISION GUIDELINES

DECISION	**GUIDELINE**	**ANALYZE**
I want to know where a business gets its cash and where it is spent. Which financial statement would I use?	Use the statement of cash flows to see all of the sources and uses of cash for a business.	You can see whether a company's operations generated cash for the business and how much cash the business invested in the purchase of assets, such as buildings and equipment. If a company's operations generated insufficient funds to finance its investments in assets, you can determine how the business financed these acquisitions.

RELATIONSHIPS AMONG THE FINANCIAL STATEMENTS

The financial statements are prepared in the following order:

1. Income statement and statement of comprehensive income
2. Statement of changes in equity

3. Statement of financial position

4. Statement of cash flows

The reason for this order is that the net income figure from the income statement is needed to prepare the comprehensive income statement and then the retained earnings in the statement of changes in equity. Likewise, the ending share capital and retained earnings balances from the statement of changes in equity are needed to prepare the statement of financial position (refer to Exhibit 1-4). Finally, information from both the statement of comprehensive income and the statement of financial position is needed to prepare the statement of cash flows.

FOCUS ON USERS

The Focus on Users box found at the end of each chapter shows you who the users of the financial statements are, and why the concepts discussed in the chapter are important to them. This box demonstrates the relevance of accounting concepts to everyone, regardless of their career choices.

These boxes will be presented in each chapter to demonstrate the relevance of accounting concepts to everyone, regardless of their career choices. Each Focus on Users box features concepts covered in each chapter and discusses why they might be important to the users of financial statements. Some of the users of financial statements include:

1. Bookkeepers—as the preparers of financial statements, the bookkeepers will be interested in seeing the completed output, preparing internal audits to check their own work, and preparing the work for the next set of financial statements.

2. Managers—the managers of organizations need to be able to evaluate the performance of the organization, make recommendations for improvement, and plan for the future. All of these elements will require financial statements, which are indications of the past performance of the organization.

3. Shareholders and Potential Investors—this group of individuals (or other organizations) will be looking to evaluate the performance of the organization to determine if it is a sound investment, if it is providing them with an appropriate return on their investment (are they getting something out of being an investor), and if the company is showing signs that may indicate that it is time to sell, or perhaps time to invest even further. This is a section that many people will be able to relate to in their lifetime as they invest their own personal funds for their retirement or for "playing" on the stock market.

4. Creditors—individuals and institutions that loan funds to organizations will want to examine the financial statements of an organization to determine whether they are an appropriate risk to lend to and if they have the ability to repay their debt.

5. Competitors—individuals and other organizations that compete with a company can examine the financial statements of competitors to compare the performance of each company and assess the strengths and weaknesses.

6. Government and Regulatory Bodies—governments and regulatory organizations will examine financial statements to determine the amount of taxes to be paid, or to ensure that specific regulations are being followed.

7. Unions—employee unions will be interested in the financial statements of the organization to assess whether or not the employees are receiving appropriate levels of pay and benefits, etc.

This list of users of financial statements is not exhaustive and could also include people such as financial advisors, venture capitalists, journalists, customers, suppliers, etc.

The Focus on Users Box at the end of each chapter will discuss the perspectives of a variety of users and how the concepts of the chapter relate to them. Not all users of financial statements are included in the discussion, but some will be highlighted. It is important to recognize that the organization creates one set of financial statements that needs to satisfy all of these external users. For the organization, this can create a problem as there may be conflicting images that the organization wants to portray. For example, an organization would want the financial statements to show as profitable an image as possible when communicating with creditors to obtain loans; however, the organization, to minimize taxes to the government, would need to show a minimal amount of profit. It is impossible to both minimize and maximize profit at the same time; therefore, the organization needs to make decisions regarding the reporting of activities that will balance the needs of all users. As you read through this text and come across areas where there are a variety of ways to report the same activity, try to keep in mind the variety of users of the financial statements and how the decisions that are made will influence the message that is conveyed to them.

FOCUS ON USERS

Concept	User	Why Is This Important to This User?
Guidelines (IFRS, Accounting Standards for Private Enterprises, etc.)	Bookkeepers Managers Shareholders & Potential Investors Creditors Competitors Government & Regulatory Bodies Unions	All users of financial statements need to understand what guidelines were used to know what types of decisions have been made in the creation of the statements. Managers, in particular, will need to pay close attention to the decision of which set of guidelines should be used to facilitate the most effective communication with the users of financial statements.
Conceptual Framework	Bookkeepers Managers Shareholders & Potential Investors Creditors Competitors Government & Regulatory Bodies Unions	All users of financial statements are at the core of the conceptual framework. The users need to be aware of the balance between the qualitative characteristics of accounting and the constraints on what is feasible to include in the presentation of the financial statements.
Financial Statements	Managers	Managers need to be able to organize, plan, control, and evaluate the performance of individuals, departments, and the organization as a whole. The financial statements assist the managers in all of these functions. The income statement or statement of comprehensive income will demonstrate whether or not the organization has been profitable, in what areas, and how revenues and expenses have changed from one period to the next. The statement of financial position will highlight what is owned, what the organization owes to third parties, and the rights to ownership held by shareholders. This statement will assist managers in understanding whether they can take on more debt or perhaps raise funds through bringing on more shareholders.

Concept	User	Why Is This Important to This User?
Financial Statements (*cont.*)	**Shareholders & Potential Investors**	Shareholders and potential investors are looking to ensure that their investment is in a good position to provide returns on their investment. Dividends are the way that the profits of the organization are distributed to the owners, so shareholders and potential investors will specifically examine the statement of changes in equity to evaluate the changes in the areas that are most important to them.
	Creditors	Creditors will be examining the financial statements for the organization's ability to repay debts. The statement of cash flows will show where the cash comes from and how it is used, which will demonstrate if the organization has the capacity to repay debt. The income statement will demonstrate if the organization is profitable and how much of the profits are taken up with interest (the cost of borrowing). The statement of financial position can be used to highlight what the company owns that may be able to be used as collateral for a loan, and how much cash is actually held by the organization.
	Competitors	Competitors may examine financial statements to assess the strengths and weaknesses of an organization. This could provide the competitor with areas on which to capitalize.

DEMO DOC 📄

Demo Docs walk you through an extensive, challenging review problem that pulls together the chapter concepts. The worked solution provides a full solution so you can check progress and provides some reminders and hints for how to find the solution.

MyAccountingLab   Visit MyAccountingLab to watch animated versions of similar Demo Docs.

These references to MyAccountingLab are reminders that you can review animated versions of the Demo Docs on MyAccountingLab.

TRANSACTION ANALYSIS USING THE ACCOUNTING EQUATION/FINANCIAL STATEMENT PREPARATION

On June 1, 2015, Raj Chopra started a webpage design business named MyWeb, Inc. The business is organized as a corporation. During June 2015, MyWeb, Inc. engaged in the following transactions:

LEARNING OBJECTIVE 5–6

a. Raj invested $25,000 in exchange for 5,000 shares to start the business.

b. The business paid $7,500 cash to acquire computer equipment.

c. Supplies costing $350 were purchased on account.

d. Performed design services and received $1,100 cash.

e. Performed $1,800 of design services for a customer. The customer agreed to pay next week.

f. Paid $200 cash toward the supplies purchased in Transaction c.

g. Paid $600 for employee salaries for the month.

h. Paid $500 of dividends to Raj, the only shareholder.

i. Collected $1,000 from the customer in Transaction e.

REQUIREMENTS:

① **Enter these transactions in the expanded accounting equation of MyWeb, Inc.**

② **Prepare the income statement, statement of changes in equity, and statement of financial position of MyWeb, Inc. after recording the transactions.**

DEMO DOC SOLUTIONS

REQUIREMENT ①

Enter these transactions in the expanded accounting equation of MyWeb, Inc.

Part 1	Part 2	Demo Doc Complete

a. Raj invested $25,000 in exchange for 5,000 shares to start the business.

Raj is using his own money, but he is paying it *to the business*. Because the business is involved, it is a recordable transaction. From the business's perspective, this transaction will increase Cash (an asset) by $25,000 and increase Common Shares (shareholders' equity) by $25,000.

The effect of this transaction on the accounting equation is as follows:

	Cash	+ Accounts Receivable	+ Supplies	+ Equipment =	Accounts Payable	+ Common Shares	+ Service Revenue	− Salaries Expense	− Dividends
a)	+$25,000					+$25,000			
Bal	$25,000			=		$25,000			

To record this transaction in the equation, we add $25,000 to Cash and add $25,000 to Common Shares. Before we move on, we bring down the account balances and check to see that the left side of the equation equals the right side. It is important to remember that the equation must balance after each transaction is recorded.

b. The business paid $7,500 cash to acquire computer equipment.

Equipment (an asset) is increased by $7,500, while Cash (an asset) is decreased by $7,500.

The effect of this transaction on the accounting equation is as follows:

	Cash	+ Accounts Receivable	+ Supplies	+ Equipment =	Accounts Payable	+ Common Shares	+ Service Revenue	− Salaries Expense	− Dividends
Bal	$25,000			=		$25,000			
b)	−$ 7,500			+$7,500					
Bal	$17,500	+		$7,500 =		$25,000			

Notice that transactions do not have to affect both sides of the equation, but for any transaction there has to be at least two accounts affected, and that is why we call it double entry accounting. However, the accounting equation *must always balance*.

c. Supplies costing $350 were purchased on account.

Supplies is an asset that is increased by $350. However, the supplies were not paid for in cash, but instead *on account*. This transaction involves accounts *pay*able (because it will have to be *paid* later). Because we now have *more* money that has to be paid later, it is an increase in Accounts Payable (a liability) of $350.

The effect of this transaction on the accounting equation is as follows:

		Assets			=	Liabilities	+		Shareholders' Equity			
								Common Shares +		Retained Earnings		
	Cash	+ Accounts Receivable +	Supplies +	Equipment =		Accounts Payable +		Common Shares +	Service Revenue −	Salaries Expense −	Dividends
Bal	$17,500			+ $7,500 =				$25,000			
c)			+$350			+$350					
Bal	$17,500	+	$350 +	$7,500 =		$350 +		$25,000			

Remember that the supplies will be recorded as an asset until the time that they are used by the business (we will learn how to adjust for supplies used in a later chapter). The obligation to pay the $350 will remain in Accounts Payable until it is paid.

d. Performed design services and received $1,100 cash.

When the business designs webpages, it is doing work for customers. Doing work for customers (or performing services) is the way that the business makes money. By performing these services, the business is earning service revenues. This means that Service Revenue increases (which increases retained earnings) by $1,100. Because the customer paid in cash, this transaction also results in an increase in Cash (an asset) of $1,100.

The effect of this transaction on the accounting equation is as follows:

		Assets			=	Liabilities	+		Shareholders' Equity			
								Common Shares +		Retained Earnings		
	Cash	+ Accounts Receivable +	Supplies +	Equipment =		Accounts Payable +		Common Shares +	Service Revenue −	Salaries Expense −	Dividends
Bal	$17,500		+ $350 +	$7,500 =		$350 +		$25,000			
d)	+$ 1,100								+$1,100		
Bal	$18,600		+ $350 +	$7,500 =		$350 +		$25,000 +	$1,100		

e. Performed $1,800 of design services for a customer. The customer agreed to pay next week.

Again, the business is performing services for customers, which means that it is earning service revenues. This transaction results in an increase in Service Revenue (retained earnings) of $1,800.

This transaction is similar to Transaction d, except that the business is not receiving the cash immediately. Should we wait to record the revenue until the cash is received? Now, refer to the underlying assumptions and the conceptual framework. Accrual basis accounting specifies that businesses should record transactions based on when they occur, not when cash is exchanged. Therefore, the answer is no, because MyWeb, Inc. should recognize the revenue when the service is performed, regardless of whether or not it has received the cash.

However, this time the client did not pay in cash but instead agreed to pay later, which is the same as charging the services *on account*. The business will *receive* this money in the future (when the customer eventually pays), so it is called an accounts *receivable*. Accounts Receivable (an asset) is increased by $1,800. Accounts Receivable represents amounts owed to the business and decreases when a customer pays.

The effect of this transaction on the accounting equation is as follows:

	Cash	+	Accounts Receivable	+	Supplies	+	Equipment	=	Accounts Payable	+	Common Shares	+	Service Revenue	−	Salaries Expense	−	Dividends
Bal	$18,600			+	$350	+	$7,500	=	$350	+	$25,000		$1,100				
e)			+$1,800										+$1,800				
Bal	$18,600	+	$1,800	+	$350	+	$7,500	=	$350	+	$25,000	+	$2,900				

Assets = Liabilities + Shareholders' Equity
+1,800 = +1,800

f. Paid $200 cash toward the supplies purchased in Transaction c.

Think of Accounts Payable (a liability) as a list of companies to which the business owes money. In other words, it is a list of companies to which the business will *pay* money. In this particular problem, the business owes money to the company from which it purchased supplies on account in Transaction c. When the business *pays* the money in full, it can cross this company off of the list. Right now, the business is paying only *part* of the money owed.

This transaction results in a decrease to Accounts Payable (a liability) of $200 and a decrease to Cash (an asset) of $200. Because the business is only paying part of the money it owes to the supply store, the balance to Accounts Payable is still $150 ($350−$200).

You should note that this transaction does not affect Supplies because we are not buying more supplies. We are simply paying off a liability, not acquiring more assets or incurring a new expense.

Assets = Liabilities + Shareholders' Equity
−200 = −200

The effect of this transaction on the accounting equation is as follows:

	Cash	+	Accounts Receivable	+	Supplies	+	Equipment	=	Accounts Payable	+	Common Shares	+	Service Revenue	−	Salaries Expense	−	Dividends
Bal	$18,600	+	$1,800	+	$350	+	$7,500	=	$350	+	$25,000	+	$2,900				
f)	−$ 200								−$200								
Bal	$18,400	+	$1,800	+	$350	+	$7,500	=	$150	+	$25,000	+	$2,900				

g. Paid $600 for employee salaries for the month.

The work the employees have given to the business has *already been used*. By the end of June, MyWeb's employees have worked for the entire month. Therefore, the *benefit* of the employees' work has *already been received*, which means that it is a salaries *expense*. Salaries Expense increases by $600, which is a decrease to retained earnings. Remember, expenses *decrease* retained earnings.

The salaries were paid in cash, so Cash (an asset) also decreases by $600.

Assets = Liabilities + Shareholders' Equity
−600 = −600

The effect of this transaction on the accounting equation is as follows:

	Cash	+	Accounts Receivable	+	Supplies	+	Equipment	=	Accounts Payable	+	Common Shares	+	Service Revenue	−	Salaries Expense	−	Dividends
Bal	$18,400	+	$1,800	+	$350	+	$7,500	=	$150	+	$25,000	+	$2,900				
g)	−$ 600														−(+$600)		
Bal	$17,800	+	$1,800	+	$350	+	$7,500	=	$150	+	$25,000	+	$2,900	−	$600		

h. Paid $500 of dividends to Raj, the only shareholder.

A decrease to Cash (an asset) is recorded because the business paid Raj $500. This transaction also results in a $500 increase to the Dividend account, which results in a decrease of $500 to Retained Earnings. You should note that *the dividend is not an expense* because the cash is not used by the business. A dividend is a distribution of the profit of a business in that the business pays part of its profit to the shareholder for his or her investment in the business.

The effect of this transaction on the accounting equation is as follows:

Assets				=	Liabilities	+	Shareholders' Equity					
									Common Shares +		Retained Earnings	
		Accounts				Accounts		Common		Service	Salaries	
	Cash	+ Receivable +	Supplies	+ Equipment =		Payable	+	Shares	+	Revenue –	Expense	– Dividends
Bal	$17,800 +	$1,800 +	$350	+ $7,500 =		$150	+	$25,000 +		$2,900 –	$600	
h)	–$ 500											–(+$500)
Bal	$17,300 +	$1,800 +	$350	+ $7,500 =		$150	+	$25,000 +		$2,900 –	$600	– $500

i. Collected $1,000 from the customer in Transaction e.

Think of Accounts Receivable (an asset) as a list of people/companies from which the business will *receive* money at some point in the future. Later, when the business collects (receives) the cash in full from any particular customer, it can cross that customer off the list.

In Transaction e, MyWeb, Inc. performed services for a client who did not pay at that time. Now MyWeb, Inc. is receiving *part* of the money owed ($1,000). Because cash is received, this is an increase to Cash (an asset) of $1,000. This collection also decreases Accounts Receivable (an asset) by $1,000 because the customer no longer owes this amount to MyWeb, Inc.

The effect of this transaction on the accounting equation is as follows:

Assets				=	Liabilities	+	Shareholders' Equity					
									Common Shares +		Retained Earnings	
		Accounts				Accounts		Common		Service	Salaries	
	Cash	+ Receivable +	Supplies	+ Equipment =		Payable	+	Shares	+	Revenue –	Expense	– Dividends
Bal	$17,300 +	$1,800 +	$350	+ $7,500 =		$150	+	$25,000 +		$2,900 –	$600	– $500
i)	+$ 1,000	–$1,000										
Bal	$18,300 +	$ 800 +	$350	+ $7,500 =		$150	+	$25,000 +		$2,900 –	$600	– $500

REQUIREMENT ②

Prepare the income statement, statement of changes in equity, and statement of financial position of MyWeb, Inc. after recording the transactions.

Part 1	Part 2	Demo Doc Complete

Income Statement

The income statement is the first statement that should be prepared because the other financial statements rely upon the net income number calculated on the income statement.

The income statement reports the profitability of the business. To prepare an income statement, begin with the proper heading. A proper heading includes the name of the company (MyWeb, Inc.), the name of the statement (Income Statement), and the time period covered (Month Ended June 30, 2015). Notice that we are reporting income for a period of time, rather than a single date.

The income statement lists all revenues and expenses. It uses the following formula to calculate net income (ignoring taxes for this case):

$$\text{Revenues} - \text{Expenses} = \text{Net Income or Net Loss}$$

First, you should list revenues. Secondly, list the expenses. After you have listed and totalled the revenues and expenses, you subtract the total expenses from total revenues to determine net income or net loss. If you have a positive number, then you report net income. A negative number indicates that expenses exceeded revenues, and you will report a net loss.

In the case of MyWeb, Inc., Transactions d and e increased Service Revenue (by $1,100 and $1,800, respectively). These transactions mean that total service revenue for the month was $2,900 ($1,100 + 1,800).

The only expenses incurred were in Transaction g, which resulted in a salaries expense of $600. The income statement for MyWeb, Inc. is presented next:

MyWeb, Inc. Income Statement Month Ended June 30, 2015	
Revenue	$2,900
Expenses	(600)
Net Income	$2,300

You will use the $2,300 net income on the statement of changes in equity.

Statement of Changes in Equity

The statement of changes in equity shows the changes in common shares and retained earnings for a period of time. To prepare a statement of changes in equity, begin with the proper heading. A proper heading includes the name of the company (MyWeb, Inc.), the name of the statement (Statement of Changes in Equity), and the time period covered (Month Ended June 30, 2015). As with the income statement, we are reporting changes for a period of time, rather than a single date.

Net income is used on the statement of changes in equity to calculate the new balance in the Retained Earnings account. This calculation uses the following formula:

$$\begin{aligned} &\text{Beginning Retained Earnings} \\ &+ \text{Net Income or} - \text{Net Loss} \\ &\underline{- \text{Dividends}} \\ &= \text{Ending Retained Earnings} \end{aligned}$$

You will begin the body of the statement by reporting each account that belongs to the shareholders' equity—common shares and the retained earnings—at the beginning of the period (June 1). List each account on the top of the statement and show the date on the left column. Then, list the events that caused the change in each account; for example, net income increases the retained earnings, net loss and dividends decrease the retained earnings. You should notice that the amount of net income comes directly from the income statement.

In this case, because the company is new, the beginning balances of common shares and retained earnings are both zero. New shares worth $25,000 are issued and added to the zero balance in common shares, and the net income of $2,300 is added to the zero balance in retained earnings for a subtotal of $2,300. The $500 of dividends is subtracted from the $2,300 subtotal to arrive at the ending balance in retained earnings of $1,800. MyWeb's statement of changes in equity would appear as follows:

	Common Shares			
	Number of Shares	$	Retained Earnings	Total
Balance, June 1, 2015	—	$ 0	$ 0	$ 0
Issued Common Shares	5,000	$25,000		25,000
Net Income			$2,300	2,300
Dividends			(500)	(500)
Balance, June 30, 2015	5,000	$25,000	$1,800	$26,800

MyWeb, Inc.
Statement of Changes in Shareholders' Equity
Month Ended June 30, 2015

You will use the $25,000 and $1,800 ending balance in common shares and retained earnings on the statement of financial position.

Statement of Financial Position

The statement of financial position reports the financial position of the business. To prepare a statement of financial position, begin with the proper heading. A proper heading includes the name of the company (MyWeb, Inc.), the name of the statement (Statement of Financial Position), and the date (June 30, 2015). Unlike the income statement and statement of changes in equity, we are reporting the financial position of the company for a *specific date*, rather than a period of time.

The statement of financial position is just a listing of all assets, liabilities, and equity, with the equality of the accounting equation verified at the bottom.

To prepare the body of the statement, begin by listing assets. Next, list the liabilities and shareholders' equity. Notice that the statement of financial position is organized in the same order as the accounting equation. You should also note that the amount of common shares and retained earnings come from the ending common shares and retained earnings on your statement of changes in equity. You should then total both sides to make sure that they are equal. If they are not equal, you need to look for an error.

The figures for assets and liabilities come directly from the accounting equation. In this case, assets include the total cash balance of $18,300, accounts receivable of $800, supplies worth $350, and the equipment's value of $7,500, for a total of $26,950 in assets. Liabilities total $150: the balance in the Accounts Payable account. The $25,000 common shares balance is added to the ending retained earnings of $1,800 (from the statement of changes in equity) to give us total shareholders' equity of $26,800. The shareholders' equity is then added to the liabilities to get total liabilities and shareholders' equity of $26,950. The $26,950 of total assets equals the $26,950 of total liabilities plus shareholders' equity, which confirms the accounting equation:

Assets = Liabilities + Shareholders' Equity

MyWeb, Inc. Statement of Financial Position As of June 30, 2015			
ASSETS		**LIABILITIES**	
Cash	$18,300	Accounts Payable	$ 150
Accounts Receivable	800		
Supplies	350		
Equipment	7,500		
		SHAREHOLDERS' EQUITY	
		Common Shares	25,000
		Retained Earnings	1,800
		Total Shareholders' Equity	$26,800
		Total Liabilities &	
Total Assets	$26,950	Shareholders' Equity	$26,950

DEMO DOC COMPLETE

Part 1	Part 2	Demo Doc Complete

 ## DECISION GUIDELINES

Accounting and the Business Environment

Suppose you open a business. Here are some questions you should consider:

DECISION	GUIDELINE	ANALYZE
I am planning to start a new business. What form of business organization is the best?	There are many ways to organize a business including the following: a sole proprietorship, partnership, or corporation. Each type of business organization has different advantages and disadvantages.	Know the tax and legal treatments of each type of organization. Weigh the best treatment of taxes and legal liability of each type and pick the format that is most advantageous for you as an owner.
I need to determine if a business is profitable. Which financial statement do I use?	Use the income statement to determine the profitability of a business. The income statement reports the revenues and expenses of a business. Revenues represent what a business earns as a result of providing goods or services. Expenses represent the cost to the business of providing those goods or services.	If revenues exceed expenses, the business is profitable and has earned net income. However, if expenses exceed revenue, the business has incurred a net loss and is not profitable.
I want to know if a company was profitable, and if it was, what it did with the profits. Which financial statement do I use?	Use the statement of changes in equity to find out. The statement of changes in equity shows whether the net income of a business was paid out as dividends or retained in the business.	If a business is planning on growth, it will often issue low or no dividends to shareholders. This way, it retains the income in the business.

DECISION

I want to know who would get its assets if a business were to close its doors. Which financial statement would I use?

I want to know where a business gets its cash and where it is spent. Which financial statement would I use?

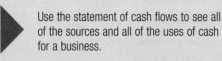

GUIDELINE

Use the statement of financial position to determine who has claims to the company's assets.

Use the statement of cash flows to see all of the sources and all of the uses of cash for a business.

ANALYZE

The liabilities of a business reflect the claims of third parties to the assets of the business. Once those claims are settled, the remaining assets belong to the shareholders (the owners) of the business. This amount is reflected by the shareholders' equity on the statement of financial position.

You can see whether a company's operations generated cash for the business and how much cash the business invested in the purchase of assets, such as buildings and equipment. If a company's operations generated insufficient funds to finance its investments in assets, you can determine how the business financed these acquisitions.

POINT OF COMPARISON	IFRS	ASPE
When to use?	To be used for all publicly traded corporations in Canada as of January 2011.	Privately held corporations, partnerships, or sole proprietorships can choose to adopt either IFRS or ASPE.
Asset Measurement	Allows historical cost, current cost, realizable value, and present value approaches.	Requires historical cost approach.
Financial Statements	Statement of financial position (which shows the assets, liabilities, and owners' equity of a business) is the most commonly used term rather than "balance sheet."	Balance sheet is the most commonly used term rather than "statement of financial position."
	Income statement in addition to statement of comprehensive income, which includes "other comprehensive income." Other comprehensive income includes unrealized gains and losses.	Income statement includes income from operations in addition to other gains and losses.
	Requires the preparation of a statement of changes in equity, which includes changes in shareholders' equity in addition to retained earnings.	Requires the preparation of a statement of retained earnings, which focuses on changes in retained earnings only.
	Cash flows are represented by the statement of cash flows (the most commonly used term) and is prepared by either the direct or indirect method (see Chapter 11).	Cash flows are represented by the cash flow statement (the most commonly used term) and is prepared also by either the direct or indirect method.

ACCOUNTING VOCABULARY

Accounting Vocabulary lists all the new boldfaced terms that were explained in the chapter along with their definitions. Page references help you to review the terms.

THE LANGUAGE OF BUSINESS

Accounts payable (p. 19)

Accounts receivable (p. 20)

Accounting (p. 6)

Accounting Standards for Private Enterprises (ASPE) (p. 12)

Accrual basis accounting (p. 15)

Assets (p. 16)

Balance sheet (p. 27)

Businesses (p. 5)

Common shares (p. 17)

Comparability (p. 14)

Conceptual framework (p. 12)

Consistency (p. 14)

Corporation (p. 7)

Cost vs. benefit (p. 14)

Current cost (p. 15)

Dividends (p. 8)

Economic entity assumption (p. 13)

Ethics (p. 4)

Expenses (p. 17)

Fair value (p. 13)

Financial accounting (p. 9)

Financial statements (p. 6)

Full disclosure principle (p. 14)

Fundamental accounting equation (p. 16)

Going-concern assumption (p. 13)

Historical cost (p. 13)

Income statement (p. 24)

International Financial Reporting Standards (IFRS) (p. 12)

Liabilities (p. 16)

Managerial accounting (p. 10)

Manufacturing business (p. 6)

Materiality (p. 14)

Merchandising business (p. 6)

Monetary unit assumption (p. 13)

Net income (p. 24)

Net loss (p. 24)

Note payable (p. 19)

On account (p. 20)

Owner(s) capital (p. 8)

Partnership (p. 7)

Preferred shares (p. 17)

Prepaid expenses (p. 19)

Present value (p. 15)

Profit (p. 24)

Realizable value (p. 15)

Relevance (p. 14)

Reliability (p. 14)

Retail business (p. 7)

Retained earnings (p. 17)

Revenue (p. 17)

Service business (p. 6)

Share capital (p. 17)

Shareholder (p. 7)

Shareholders' equity (p. 16)

Sole proprietorship (p. 7)

Statement of cash flows (p. 28)

Statement of changes in equity (p. 25)

Statement of comprehensive income (p. 24)

Statement of financial position (p. 27)

Third party (p. 16)

Time period assumption (p. 13)

Transaction (p. 16)

Understandability (p. 14)

Wholesale business (p. 7)

Withdrawals (p. 8)

ACCOUNTING PRACTICE

DISCUSSION QUESTIONS

1. The text states that accounting is the "language of business." What does this mean? Why is it important to know the language?

2. Would you describe accounting as being primarily a technical discipline or primarily an ethical discipline? Why?

3. What are the streams of accounting career opportunities available for accounting professionals? What tasks do financial accountants do? What tasks do management accountants do?

4. What are some reasons why accounting has adopted "historical" financial statements as the model? What are some disadvantages associated with presenting "historical" financial statements?

5. What are some of the uses of financial statements?

6. What is the primary way in which corporations differ from proprietorships and partnerships? What are some of the factors that might affect a person's decision about the form of organization that would be best in a given situation?

7. What is the fundamental accounting equation? Define each of the components of this equation.

8. How is the accounting equation affected by each of the following transactions?
   a. Owners contribute cash to start the business.
   b. The company borrows money from the bank.
   c. The company provides services for a client who promises to pay later.
   d. The company collects from the customer in option c.

9. In what order would the financial statements be prepared? Why?

10. Which financial statement would be most useful to answer each of the following questions?
    a. Does the corporation have enough resources to pay its short-term debts?
    b. What is the corporation's policy toward "growing the company" versus distributing its wealth to owners?
    c. Did the corporation pay its operating costs with resources generated from operations, money borrowed from banks, or money generated from selling off its buildings and equipment?
    d. Did the corporation make a profit last year?

SELF CHECK

1. Which type of business organization is owned by its shareholders?
   a. Proprietorship
   b. Partnership
   c. Corporation
   d. All of the above are owned by shareholders.

2. International Financial Reporting Standards (IFRS) are created by the
   a. Ontario Securities Commission
   b. Canadian Revenue Agency
   c. Accounting Standards Board
   d. International Accounting Standards Board

Test your understanding with these multiple choice questions. The answers are given at the end of each chapter.

MyAccountingLab

The exercises and problems in this chapter can be found on MyAccountingLab. You can practise them as often as you want, and they feature step-by-step guided solutions to help you find the right answer.

This reference to MyAccountingLab reminds you that all of the Exercises and Problems in this chapter can also be found on MyAccountingLab.

3. Which accounting concept or principle specifically states that we should record transactions at amounts that can be verified?

   a. Entity concept
   b. Reliability
   c. Relevance
   d. Going-concern concept

4. Greenlawn is a famous lawn mowing company. At the end of a recent year, Greenlawn's total assets added up to $62,200, and shareholders' equity was $48,700. How much did Greenlawn owe creditors?

   a. $110,900
   b. $62,200
   c. $13,500
   d. $48,700

5. Assume that Greenlawn provided services to customers for $3,500 cash. How would this transaction affect Greenlawn's accounting equation?

   a. Increase both assets and shareholders' equity by $3,500
   b. Increase both assets and liabilities by $3,500
   c. Increase both liabilities and shareholders' equity by $3,500
   d. It will not affect the accounting equation because the effects cancel out.

6. Assume that Greenlawn purchased supplies for $2,200 on account. Which parts of the accounting equation does a purchase on account affect?

   a. Assets and owners' equity
   b. Only the assets side is affected.
   c. Liabilities and owners' equity
   d. Assets and liabilities

7. Assume that Greenlawn paid expenses totalling $3,800. How does this transaction affect Greenlawn's accounting equation?

   a. Increases assets and decreases liabilities
   b. Increases both assets and shareholders' equity
   c. Decreases both assets and shareholders' equity
   d. Decreases assets and increases liabilities

8. Consider the overall effects of transactions in questions 5, 6, and 7 on Greenlawn. What is Greenlawn's net income or net loss?

   a. Net income of $3,500
   b. Net loss of $2,500
   c. Net loss of $300
   d. It cannot be determined from the data given.

9. The statement of financial position reports

   a. financial position on a specific date.
   b. results of operations on a specific date.
   c. financial position for a specific period.
   d. results of operations for a specific period.

10. The income statement reports

   a. financial position on a specific date.
   b. results of operations on a specific date.
   c. financial position for a specific period.
   d. results of operations for a specific period.

Answers are given after Written Communication on p. 63.

SHORT EXERCISES

S1-1. Accounting principles and conceptual framework (*Learning Objective 4*)
5–10 min.

The Learning Objectives covered appear beside each Exercise and Problem.

Place the corresponding letter of the definition next to the term.

a. An organization that stands as a separate economic unit must not have its financial affairs confused with that of other entities.

b. Data must be verifiable.

c. Standards developed by IASB.

d. Acquired assets and services should be recorded at their actual cost.

_____ **1.** Historical cost principle

_____ **2.** Entity concept

_____ **3.** International Financial Reporting Standards

_____ **4.** Reliability

S1-2. Accounting principles and conceptual framework (*Learning Objective 4*)
5–10 min.

Jill Riggins owns and operates Jill's Java coffee shop. She proposes to account for the shop's revenue when she receives cash. Which accounting concept or principle does Jill violate?

a. Accrual basis accounting

b. Entity concept

c. Going-concern concept

d. Comparability

S1-3. Types of accounting (*Learning Objective 3*) 5–10 min.

Place the corresponding letter next to the appropriate term.

_____ **1.** Cost accounting

_____ **2.** Accounts receivable and accounts payable management

_____ **3.** Auditing

_____ **4.** Budget and planning

_____ **5.** Investment and financial planning

_____ **6.** Financial statement preparation

_____ **7.** Tax planning

a. Financial Accounting

b. Managerial Accounting

c. Taxation

d. Banking and Financial Services

S1-4. Conceptual framework and qualitative financial information (*Learning Objective 4*) 5–10 min.

Place the corresponding letter next to the appropriate term.

_____ 1. Financial information should provide predictable value for decision making.

_____ 2. The value of financial information obtained should outweigh the cost of obtaining it.

_____ 3. Financial statements are prepared using the same accounting standards consistently from year to year.

_____ 4. Financial information is included in the financial statement for completeness, as a lack of information will likely impact the decision making.

_____ 5. Financial information should verifiable, neutral, and complete.

a. Comparability

b. Cost–Benefit

c. Reliability

d. Materiality

e. Relevance

S1-5. Accounting terminology (*Learning Objective 1 & 5*) 10–15 min.

Place the corresponding letter of the definition next to the term.

_____ 1. Liabilities

_____ 2. Assets

_____ 3. Corporation

_____ 4. Dividends

_____ 5. Sole proprietorship

_____ 6. Partnership

_____ 7. Transaction

a. Any event that affects financial position.

b. Organization form with a single owner.

c. Organization form with two or more owners.

d. Organization form that can have an indefinite life.

e. Debts owed to outsiders.

f. Economic resources of the business.

g. Payment of cash or other assets to the owners of a corporation.

S1-6. Basic accounting equation (*Learning Objective 5*) 5–10 min

Determine the missing amounts in the following accounting equations.

	Assets	=	Liabilities	+	Shareholders' Equity
a.	$75,000	=	$32,000	+	?
b.	?	=	$43,000	+	$37,000
c.	$92,000	=	?	+	$60,000

S1-7. Basic accounting equation (*Learning Objective 5*) 5–10 min

Ming An owns Ming's Lawncare Service. The business has cash of $3,000 and equipment that costs $12,000. Debts of the business include accounts payable of $6,000 and a $5,000 note payable. Determine the amount of shareholders' equity Ming has in the business. Write the accounting equation for Ming's Lawncare Service.

S1-8. Basic accounting equation (*Learning Objective 5*) 5–10 min.

Apex Financial Services, Inc. has cash of $2,000, supplies costing $800, and shareholders' equity of $1,300. Determine the liabilities of the business. Write the accounting equation for Apex Financial Services, Inc.

S1-9. Basic accounting equation (*Learning Objective 5*) 5–10 min.

Syed Foods, Inc. started as a business when Mr. Syed purchased $8,000 of shares in the business. Before starting operations, Syed Foods, Inc. borrowed $5,000

cash by signing a note payable to First National Bank. Account for these two transactions in the accounting equation.

S1-10. Entering transactions in the accounting equation (*Learning Objective 5*) 5–10 min.

T & T Towing Service, Inc. earns service revenue by towing vehicles for CAA. T & T
Towing Service's main expenses are the salaries paid to its employees. Account for
the following transactions in the expanded accounting equation:

a. T & T Towing Service, Inc. earned $14,000 of service revenue on account.

b. T & T Towing Service, Inc. paid $8,000 in salaries expense.

S1-11. Basic accounting equation (*Learning Objective 5*) 5–10 min.

Match each of the following items with its location in the accounting equation. Use the
most detailed category appropriate:

a. Assets

b. Liabilities

c. Shareholders' Equity

d. Revenues

e. Expenses

_____ **1.** Utilities Expense

_____ **2.** Accounts Receivable

_____ **3.** Common Shares

_____ **4.** Office Supplies

_____ **5.** Lease Expense, Computer

_____ **6.** Salaries Expense

_____ **7.** Cash

_____ **8.** Rent Expense, Office

_____ **9.** Service Revenue

_____ **10.** Accounts Payable

_____ **11.** Land

S1-12. Basic financial statements (*Learning Objective 5*) 5–10 min.

Label each of the items listed with the abbreviation of the financial statement on
which it appears. Items may appear on more than one statement.

- Income Statement (IS)
- Statement of Changes in Equity (SCE)
- Statement of Financial Position (SFP)

_____ **1.** Accounts Receivable

_____ **2.** Notes Payable

_____ **3.** Advertising Expense

_____ **4.** Service Revenue

_____ **5.** Retained Earnings

_____ **6.** Office Supplies

_____ **7.** Common Shares

_____ **8.** Cash

_____ **9.** Salaries Expense

_____ **10.** Dividends

S1-13. Entering transactions in the accounting equation
(*Learning Objective* 5) 5–10 min.

As a manager of a department store, you must deal with a variety of business transactions. Place the letter of each of the following transactions next to the effect it has on the accounting equation.

   a. Paid cash to the shareholders as a distribution of earnings.

   b. Purchased land for building site in cash.

   c. Paid cash on an account payable.

   d. Sold shares to shareholders.

   e. Received cash from the bank in exchange for a note payable.

   _____ **1.** Increase an asset and increase shareholders' equity.

   _____ **2.** Increase an asset and increase a liability.

   _____ **3.** Increase one asset and decrease another asset.

   _____ **4.** Decrease an asset and decrease shareholders' equity.

   _____ **5.** Decrease an asset and decrease a liability.

S1-14. Transaction analysis (*Learning Objective* 5) 5–10 min.

PWC Motorsports, Inc., a corporation, sells and services personal watercraft. The business experienced the following events. State whether each event (a) increased, (b) decreased, or (c) had no effect on the total assets of the business, and identify the asset(s) involved in each transaction.

   1. PWC Motorsports, Inc. sold additional shares to shareholders.

   2. Purchased land as a building site for cash.

   3. Paid cash on accounts payable.

   4. Purchased machinery and equipment; signed a promissory note in payment.

   5. Performed service for a customer on account.

   6. Paid cash to the shareholders as a distribution of earnings.

   7. Received cash from a customer on accounts receivable.

   8. Sold land for a price equal to the cost of the land; received cash.

   9. Borrowed money from the bank.

S1-15. Transaction analysis (*Learning Objective* 5) 5–10 min.

Presented here are nine transactions and the analysis used to account for them. Evaluate each of the suggested accounting treatments and indicate whether it is true or false.

   1. Received cash of $38,000 from the shareholders, who bought shares in the business.
   Answer: Increase asset, increase shareholders' equity. _____ True _____ False

   2. Paid $450 cash to purchase supplies.
   Answer: Increase asset, increase shareholders' equity. _____ True _____ False

   3. Earned service revenue on account, $500.
   Answer: Increase asset, increase retained earnings. _____ True _____ False

   4. Purchased office furniture on account at a cost of $850.
   Answer: Increase asset, increase liability. _____ True _____ False

   5. Received cash on account, $1,400.
   Answer: Increase asset, decrease asset. _____ True _____ False

   6. Paid cash on account, $675.
   Answer: Increase asset, increase liability. _____ True _____ False

   7. Sold land for $38,000, which was the cost of the land.
   Answer: Increase asset, decrease asset. _____ True _____ False

8. Serviced automobiles and received cash of $680.

  Answer: Increase asset, increase revenue. _____ True _____ False

9. Paid monthly office rent of $1,200.

  Answer: Decrease asset, increase shareholders' equity. _____ True _____ False

S1-16. Transaction analysis and calculating net income (*Learning Objective 5 & 6*)
5–10 min.

The analysis of Nelson's Painting Service's first seven transactions follows. The business only sold shares once and paid no dividends.

	Assets			=	Liabilities		+	Shareholders' Equity	
	Cash	+ Accounts Receivable	+ Equipment =		Accounts Payable	+ Notes Payable	+	Common Shares	+ Retained Earnings
1.	+ $40,000		=					+ $40,000	
2.	– 1,200		+ $ 1,200 =						
3.			+ 25,000 =			+ $25,000			
4.		+ $400	=						+ 400
5.	– 750		=						– 750
6.	+ 1,800		=						+ 1,800
7.	+ 200	– 200	=						

1. Label each of the transactions in the preceding analysis with the corresponding letter of the description that best fits it:

  a. Earned revenue for painting services provided, but customer will pay later.

  b. Customers paid cash for painting services completed earlier in the month.

  c. Received cash for revenue earned by providing painting services.

  d. Paid cash for expenses incurred to operate the business.

  e. Paid cash to purchase painting equipment.

  f. Sold shares to start the painting service business.

  g. Borrowed money from the bank to purchase painting equipment.

2. If these transactions fully describe the operations of Nelson's Painting Service, Inc. during the month, what was the amount of its net income or net loss?

EXERCISES (GROUP A)

E1-1A Basic accounting equation (*Learning Objective 5*) 10–15 min.

Determine the missing amounts in the following accounting equations.

	Assets	=	Liabilities	+	Shareholders' Equity
Fresh Produce, Corp.	?	=	$51,600	+	$12,200
Hudson Gift and Cards, Inc.	$ 97,000	=	?	+	$35,000
Nice Cuts, Inc.	$115,700	=	$95,900	+	?

E1-2A. Basic accounting equation (*Learning Objective 5*) 10–15 min.

Styles Salon had $87,000 of total assets and $52,000 of total shareholders' equity at December 31, 2015. At December 31, 2016, Styles Salon had assets totalling $153,000 and shareholders' equity totalling $81,000.

After analyzing the data, answer the following questions:

1. What was the amount of the increase or decrease in liabilities?

2. Identify a possible reason for the change in liabilities during the year.

Quick solution:

$37,000 increase.

Quick Solutions appear in the margin when applicable to help you make sure you are "on track"

E1-3A. Basic accounting equation (*Learning Objective 5*) 10–15 min.

Anthony's Consulting, Inc. started business in 2015 with total assets of $32,000 and total liabilities of $14,000. At the end of 2015, Anthony's total assets were $42,000 and total liabilities were $18,500.

After analyzing the data, answer the following questions:

1. What was the amount of the increase or decrease in shareholders' equity?

2. Identify two possible reasons for the change in shareholders' equity during the year.

E1-4A. Using the accounting equation to determine net income (*Learning Objective 5 & 6*) 15–20 min.

The balance sheet data for Quick Care, Inc. at August 31, 2015, and September 30, 2015, follow:

	Aug 31, 2015	Sep 30, 2015
Total Assets..	$130,000	$165,000
Total Liabilities	87,000	131,000
Common Shares	15,000	15,000
Total Shareholders' Equity............................	?	?

Requirement

1. The following are three *independent* assumptions about the business during September. For each assumption, compute the amount of net income or net loss during September 2015. Find the solution by preparing the statement of changes in equity. First, use the amounts of total assets, total liabilities, and common shares given previously and the accounting equation to determine the beginning and ending retained earnings amounts. Then, plug those and the other amounts given in each assumption into the statement of changes in equity to determine the net income or net loss.

   a. The business paid no dividends.

   b. The business paid $8,000 of dividends.

   c. The business paid $14,000 of dividends.

E1-5A. Transaction analysis (*Learning Objective 5*) 15–20 min.

Suzuka Ito opened a massage practice titled Suzuka Ito Health, Inc. During March, the first month of operations, the business experienced the following events:

Mar 2	Ito bought $65,000 of stock in the business by opening a bank account in the name of Suzuka Ito Health, Inc.
6	The business paid $55,000 cash for land with the intention of building an office building on the land.
11	The business purchased supplies for $1,000 on account.
15	The business officially opened for business.
17	The business treated patients and earned service revenue of $7,000, receiving cash.
19	The business paid office rent, $1,800.
22	The business sold supplies to another massage therapist for the cost of those supplies, $250.
30	The business paid $500 on account related to the March 11 purchase.

Requirement

1. Analyze the effects of these events on the accounting equation of the massage practice of Suzuka Ito Health, Inc. Use headings for Cash, Clinic Supplies, Land, Accounts Payable, Common Shares, Service Revenue, and Rent Expense.

E1-6A. Types of business organizations and balance sheet preparation (Learning Objective 1 & 5) 10–15 min.

The following are the balances of the assets, liabilities, and equity of Hair Today Salon at July 31, 2015:

Cash	$3,500	Office Equipment	$6,300
Retained Earnings	2,200	Common Shares	3,000
Accounts Payable	2,500	Note Payable	4,000
Accounts Receivable	1,200	Supplies	700

Requirements

1. What type of business organization is Hair Today Salon?
2. Prepare the statement of financial position of the business at July 31, 2015.
3. What does the balance sheet report?

E1-7A. Transaction analysis and statement of changes in equity (Learning Objective 6) 10–15 min.

Yuan Spa Inc.'s statement of changes in equity shows the following information:

	Common Shares	Retained Earnings	Total
Balance, Jan. 1, 2015	$12,000	?	$18,000
Issued Common Shares	?		?
Net Income (Loss)		?	?
Dividends		$(3,000)	?
Balance, Dec. 31, 2015	$20,000	?	$42,000

Requirement

1. Calculate the missing amounts.
2. If Yuan Spa's revenue was $45,000, what were the expenses for the year?

E1-8A. Types of accounts and income statement preparation (Learning Objective 5 & 6) 15–20 min.

Selected accounts of Armstrong Consulting, Inc., a financial services business, have the following balances at December 31, 2015, the end of its first year of operations. During the year, Lori Armstrong, the only shareholder, bought $20,000 of shares in the business.

Office Furniture	$ 28,000	Rent Expense	$36,000
Utilities Expense	12,600	Cash	5,400
Accounts Payable	3,800	Office Supplies	800
Note Payable	21,500	Salaries Expense	43,000
Service Revenue	141,500	Salaries Payable	2,000
Accounts Receivable	9,500	Property Tax Expense	2,300
Supplies Expense	4,200	Equipment	22,000

Requirements

1. Identify each as an asset, liability, revenue, or expense.
2. Prepare the income statement of Armstrong Consulting, Inc. for the year ended December 31, 2015. What is the result of operations for 2015?
3. Assuming the balance in Retained Earnings on December 31, 2015, was $18,400, what was the amount of the Dividends during the year? Answer by preparing a statement of retained earnings to solve for the dividends. Recall that the business has just completed its first year and has no beginning balance for retained earnings.

E1-9A. Using the accounting equation to determine net income (*Learning Objective 5 & 6***) 15–20 min.**

Presented here is information for Telco, Inc. for the year ended December 31, 2015.

Telco, Inc.	
Beginning:	
Assets	$ 66,000
Liabilities	15,000
Ending:	
Assets	$ 94,000
Liabilities	28,000
Shareholders' Equity:	
Sale of Shares	$ 7,000
Payment of Dividends	20,000

Requirements

1. What is the beginning shareholders' equity of Telco, Inc.?

2. What is the ending shareholders' equity of Telco, Inc.?

3. What is the net income or net loss for the year?

EXERCISES (GROUP B)

E1-1B. Basic accounting equation (*Learning Objective 5***) 10–15 min.**

Determine the missing amounts in the following accounting equations.

	Assets	=	Liabilities	+	Shareholders' Equity
Corner Grocery, Corp.	?	=	$45,000	+	$27,900
Sampson Hardware, Inc.	$104,000	=	?	+	$44,000
Perfect Cleaners, Inc.	$108,800	=	$92,600	+	?

E1-2B. Basic accounting equation (*Learning Objective 5***) 10–15 min.**

Great Wall Chinese Cuisine had $93,000 of total assets and $31,000 of total shareholders' equity at May 31, 2015. At May 31, 2016, Great Wall Chinese Cuisine had assets totalling $147,000 and shareholders' equity totalling $87,000.

After analyzing the data, answer the following questions:

1. What was the amount of the increase or decrease in liabilities?

2. Identify a possible reason for the change in liabilities during the year.

E1-3B. Basic accounting equation (*Learning Objective 5***) 10–15 min.**

Kablossom started business in 2015 with total assets of $35,000 and total liabilities of $32,000. At the end of 2015, Kablossom's total assets were $65,000, and total liabilities were $20,000.

After analyzing the data, answer the following questions:

1. What was the amount of the increase or decrease in shareholders' equity?

2. Identify two possible reasons for the change in shareholders' equity during the year.

E1-4B. Using the accounting equation to determine net income (*Learning Objective 5 & 6*) 15–20 min.

The statement of financial position data for Bob's Electronics, Corp. at October 31, 2015, and November 30, 2015, follow:

	Oct 31, 2015	Nov 30, 2015
Total Assets...	$140,000	$175,000
Total Liabilities	75,000	117,000
Common Shares	45,000	45,000
Total Shareholders' Equity....................................	?	?

Requirement

1. The following are three *independent* assumptions about the business during November. For each assumption, compute the amount of net income or net loss during November 2015. Find the solution by preparing the statement of changes in equity. First, use the amounts of total assets, total liabilities, and common shares given previously and the accounting equation to determine the beginning and ending retained earnings amounts. Then plug those and the other amounts given in each assumption into the statement of changes in equity to determine the net income or net loss.

   a. The business paid no dividends.

   b. The business paid $17,000 of dividends.

   c. The business paid $25,000 of dividends.

E1-5B. Transaction analysis (*Learning Objective 5*) 15–20 min.

Shuo Lin opened a yoga centre titled Shuo Lin Yoga, Inc. During January, the first month of operations, the business experienced the following events:

Jan 2	Shuo Lin bought $80,000 of shares in the business by opening a bank account in the name of Shuo Lin Yoga, Inc.
6	The business paid $30,000 cash for land with the intention of building an office building on the land.
11	The business purchased supplies for $600 on account.
15	The business officially opened for business.
17	The business earned revenue of $13,000, receiving cash.
19	The business paid office rent, $1,100.
22	The business sold supplies to another yoga studio for the cost of those supplies, $400.
30	The business paid $150 on account related to the January 11 purchase.

Requirement

1. Analyze the effects of these events on the accounting equation of the yoga centre of Shuo Lin Yoga, Inc. Use headings for Cash, Supplies, Land, Accounts Payable, Common Shares, Service Revenue, and Rent Expense.

E1-6B. Types of business organizations and statement of financial position preparation (*Learning Objective 1 & 6*) 10–15 min.

The following are the balances of the assets, liabilities, and equity of Kite Runner, Inc. at August 31, 2015:

Cash......................................	$24,000	Office Equipment...............................	$4,100
Retained Earnings..................	18,400	Common Shares................................	5,000
Accounts Payable...................	5,000	Note Payable.....................................	1,000
Accounts Receivable..............	600	Supplies..	700

Requirements

1. What type of business organization is Kite Runner, Inc.?

2. Prepare the statement of financial position of the business at August 31, 2015.

3. What is the information provided by the statement of financial position?

E1-7B. Transaction analysis and statement of changes in equity (*Learning Objective 6*) 10–15 min.

Omar Fitness Inc.'s statement of changes in equity shows the following information:

	Common Shares	Retained Earnings	Total
Balance, Jan. 1, 2015	?	$28,000	?
Issued Common Shares	$24,000		$24,000
Net Income		?	?
Dividends		$(5,000)	$(5,000)
Balance, Dec. 31, 2015	$34,000	?	$48,000

Requirements

1. Calculate the missing amounts.

2. If Omar Fitness Inc.'s revenue was $26,000, what were the expenses for the year?

E1-8B. Types of accounts and income statement preparation (*Learning Objective 5 & 6*) 15–20 min.

Selected accounts of Albright Consulting, Inc., a financial services business, have the following balances at January 31, 2015, the end of its first year of operations. During the year, Lilly Albright, the only shareholder, bought $49,700 of shares in the business.

Office Furniture......................	$ 20,000	Rent Expense...........................	$36,000
Utilities Expense....................	13,500	Cash...	15,600
Accounts Payable..................	9,500	Office Supplies........................	1,400
Notes Payable.......................	21,500	Salaries Expense.....................	43,000
Service Revenue....................	155,000	Salaries Payable......................	1,000
Accounts Receivable..............	10,500	Property Tax Expense..............	3,000
Supplies Expense..................	3,700	Equipment...............................	40,000

Requirements

1. Identify each as an asset, liability, revenue, or expense.

2. Prepare the income statement of Albright Consulting, Inc. for the year ended January 31, 2015. What is the result of operations for 2015?

3. Assuming the balance in Retained Earnings on January 31, 2015, was $5,800, what was the amount of the dividends during the year? Answer by preparing a statement of changes in retained earnings to solve for the dividends. Recall that the business has just completed its first year and has no beginning balance for retained earnings.

E1-9B. Using the accounting equation to determine net income (*Learning Objective 5 & 6*)
15–20 min.

Presented here is information for Edo, Inc. for the year ended August 31, 2015.

Edo, Inc.

Beginning:	
Assets	$ 99,000
Liabilities	15,000
Ending:	
Assets	$164,000
Liabilities	70,000
Shareholders' Equity:	
Sale of Shares	$ 17,000
Payment of Dividends.	55,000

Requirements

1. What is the beginning shareholders' equity of Edo, Inc.?

2. What is the ending shareholders' equity of Edo, Inc.?

3. What is the net income or net loss for the year?

EXERCISES (ALTERNATES 1, 2, AND 3)

These alternative exercise sets are available for your practice benefit on
MyAccountingLab.

PROBLEMS (GROUP A)

P1-1A. Transaction analysis and the calculation of net income (*Learning Objective 5 & 6*)
20–25 min.

Dan Oliver worked as an accountant at a local accounting firm for five years after
graduating from university. Recently, he opened his own accounting practice, which
he operates as a corporation. The name of the new entity is Oliver and Associates,
Inc. Dan experienced the following events during the first month of operations. Some
of the events were personal and did not affect the accounting practice. Others were
business transactions and should be accounted for by the business.

Jun 3	Received $30,000 cash proceeds from refinancing his house.
5	$60,000 of shares in the business were sold to Dan Oliver. The cash proceeds were deposited in a new business bank account titled Oliver and Associates, Inc.
7	Paid $450 cash for office supplies for the new accounting practice.
9	Purchased $3,800 of office furniture for the accounting practice and agreed to pay the vendor within three months.
10	Dan sold 500 shares of General Motors stock, which he had owned for several years, receiving $48,000 cash. The cash from the sale of shares was deposited in his personal bank account.
14	A representative of a large company telephoned Dan and told him of the company's intention to hire Oliver and Associates, Inc. as its accountants.
20	Finished accounting work for a client and sent the client a bill for $3,800. The client is expected to pay within two weeks.
27	Paid office rent, $1,600.
30	Paid $1,000 of dividends to Oliver and Associates, Inc. shareholders.

Requirements

1. Enter each transaction in the expanded accounting equation of Oliver and Associates, Inc. as needed, calculating new balances after each transaction.

2. Determine the following items on June 30:

   a. Total assets

   b. Total liabilities

   c. Total shareholders' equity

   d. Net income or net loss for June

P1-2A. Income statement and statement of financial position transactions; prepare the income statement and statement of financial position (*Learning Objective 5 & 6*) 25–30 min.

Donna Au started an interior design company called Interiors by Donna, Inc. on September 1, 2015. The following amounts summarize the financial position of her business on September 14, 2015, after the first two weeks of operations:

Assets				=	Liabilities	+	Shareholders' Equity			
							Common Shares +		Retained Earnings	

Cash	+ Accounts Receivable +	Supplies +	Equipment =	Accounts Payable +	Common Shares +	Service Revenue –	Salaries Expense –	Dividends
$1,540 +	$3,680 +		+ $24,000 =	$5,100 +	$21,000 +	$5,100 –	$1,980	

During the remainder of September, the following events occurred:

a. Au received $10,000 as a gift and used it to buy 5,000 shares in the business.

b. Paid off the beginning balance of Accounts Payable.

c. Performed services for a client and received cash of $2,500.

d. Collected cash from a customer on account, $850.

e. Purchased supplies on account, $600.

f. Consulted on the interior design of a major office building and billed the client for services performed, $5,000.

g. Sold an additional 1,000 shares for $2,500 in the business.

h. Paid salaries of $2,400.

i. Sold supplies at cost to another interior designer for $110 cash.

j. Paid dividends of $1,500 to Au.

Requirements

1. Enter the remaining transactions for the month of September into the expanded accounting equation, calculating new balances after each transaction.

2. Prepare the income statement of Interiors by Donna, Inc. for the month ended September 30, 2015.

3. Prepare the statement of changes in equity of Interiors by Donna, Inc. for the month ended September 30, 2015.

4. Prepare the statement of financial position of Interiors by Donna, Inc. at September 30, 2015.

P1-3A. Prepare the income statement, statement of changes in equity, and statement of financial position (*Learning Objective 6*) 20–25 min.

Gear Heads, Inc. restores antique automobiles. The common shares and retained earnings balances of the corporation were $20,000 and $32,000 respectively at December 31, 2014. During 2015, the corporation paid $40,000 in dividends to its shareholders. At December 31, 2015, the business's accounting records show these balances:

Accounts Receivable..............	$ 5,000	Cash..	$ 7,000
Note Payable.........................	25,000	Accounts Payable....................	2,000
Retained Earnings..................	?	Advertising Expense................	3,000
Salaries Expense....................	14,000	Service Revenue......................	72,000
Equipment..............................	78,000	Common Shares......................	20,000
Insurance Expense.................	4,000		

Requirement

1. Prepare the following financial statements for Gear Heads, Inc.:

   a. Income statement for the year ended December 31, 2015.

   b. Statement of changes in equity for the year ended December 31, 2015.

   c. Statement of financial position at December 31, 2015.

Quick solution:

a. Net income = $51,000

b. Ending Retained earnings = $43,000

c. Total assets = $90,000

P1-4A. Prepare the income statement and statement of financial position; identify certain financial information (*Learning Objective 6*) 25–30 min.

Presented here are the amounts of Assets, Liabilities, Shareholders' Equity, Revenues, and Expenses of The Better Body, Inc. at December 31, 2015. The items are listed in alphabetical order.

Accounts Payable..................	$ 15,000	Interest Expense....................	$ 9,000
Accounts Receivable.............	14,000	Land.......................................	40,000
Advertising Expense..............	13,000	Note Payable..........................	65,000
Building.................................	130,000	Property Tax Expense.............	3,000
Cash......................................	16,000	Rent Expense.........................	24,000
Common Shares....................	40,000	Salaries Expense....................	71,000
Dividends..............................	36,000	Salaries Payable.....................	2,000
Equipment.............................	45,000	Service Revenue.....................	185,000
Insurance Expense................	1,000	Supplies.................................	2,000

The common shares and retained earnings balances of the business were $40,000 and $97,000 respectively at December 31, 2014.

Requirements

1. Identify each amount shown as an asset, liability, or shareholders' equity.

2. Prepare the company's income statement and statement of changes in equity for the year ended December 31, 2015.

3. Prepare the company's statement of financial position at December 31, 2015.

4. Answer these questions about the company:

   a. What was the profit or loss for the year?

   b. What was the increase or decrease of retained earnings for the year?

   c. What is the amount of economic resources on December 31, 2015?

   d. What is the amount owed on December 31, 2015?

P1-5A. Error analysis and preparation of statement of financial position (*Learning Objective 6*) 20–25 min.

The IT manager of Aztec Realty, Inc. prepared the statement of financial position of the company while the accountant was ill. The statement of financial position contains numerous errors. In particular, the IT manager knew that the statement of financial position should balance, so she plugged in the retained earnings amount to achieve this balance. The retained earnings amount, however, is not correct. All other amounts are accurate, but some are out of place.

ASSETS		LIABILITIES	
Aztec Realty, Inc.			
Statement of Financial Position			
Month Ended June 30, 2015			
Cash	$ 9,000	Accounts Payable	$ 200
Rent Expense	1,000	Utilities Expense	900
Supplies Expense	350	Accounts Receivable	1,400
Salaries Payable	1,750	Notes Payable	5,700
Equipment	7,500		
		SHAREHOLDERS' EQUITY	
		Common Shares	8,000
		Supplies	800
		Retained Earnings	2,600
		Total Shareholders' Equity	11,400
		Total Liabilities &	
Total Assets	$19,600	Shareholders' Equity	$19,600

Requirement

1. Prepare a new, corrected statement of financial position for Aztec Realty, Inc.

PROBLEMS (GROUP B)

P1-1B. Transaction analysis and the calculation of net income (*Learning Objective 5 & 6*) 20–25 min.

Don Griffin worked as an accountant at a local accounting firm for five years after graduating from university. Recently, he opened his own accounting practice, which he operates as a corporation. The name of the new entity is Griffin and Associates, Inc. Don experienced the following events during the first month of operations. Some of the events were personal and did not affect the accounting practice. Others were business transactions and should be accounted for by the business.

Apr 3	Received $20,000 cash proceeds from refinancing his house.
5	$90,000 of shares in the business were sold to Don Griffin. The cash proceeds were deposited in a new business bank account titled Griffin and Associates, Inc.
7	Paid $600 cash for office supplies for the new accounting practice.
9	Purchased $4,000 of office furniture for the accounting practice and agreed to pay the vendor within three months.
10	Don sold 1,200 Mercedes shares, which he had owned for several years, receiving $22,000 cash. The cash from the sale of shares was deposited in his personal bank account.
14	A representative of a large company telephoned Don and told him of the company's intention to hire Griffin and Associates, Inc. as its accountants.
20	Finished accounting work for a client and sent the client a bill for $3,900. The client is expected to pay within two weeks.
27	Paid office rent, $1,200.
30	Paid $500 of dividends to Griffin and Associates, Inc. shareholders.

Requirements

1. Enter each transaction in the expanded accounting equation of Griffin and Associates, Inc. as needed, calculating new balances after each transaction.

2. Determine the following items:

   a. Total assets

   b. Total liabilities

   c. Total shareholders' equity

   d. Net income or net loss for April

P1-2B. Income statement and statement of financial position transactions; prepare the income statement and statement of financial position (*Learning Objective 5 & 6*) 25–30 min.

Daiyi Gong started a renovation company called Reno by Daiyi, Inc. on November 1, 2015. The following amounts summarize the financial position of her business on November 14, 2015, after the first two weeks of operations:

Assets				=	Liabilities	+	Shareholders' Equity				
							Common Shares	+		Retained Earnings	
Cash	+ Accounts Receivable +	Supplies	+ Equipment =		Accounts Payable	+	Common Shares	+	Service Revenue	– Salaries Expense	– Dividends
$1,750	+ $3,210 +		+ $24,000 =		$5,400	+	$18,020	+	$6,900	– $1,360	

During the remainder of November, the following events occurred:

a. Gong received $6,900 as a gift and used it to buy 3,000 shares in the business.

b. Paid off the beginning balance of Accounts Payable.

c. Performed services for a client and received cash of $1,500.

d. Collected cash from a customer on account, $850.

e. Purchased supplies on account, $400.

f. Consulted on the renovation of a major office building and billed the client for services performed, $9,000.

g. Sold an additional 2,200 shares for $5,500 in the business.

h. Paid salaries of $2,550.

i. Sold supplies at cost to a renovation company for $250 cash.

j. Paid dividends of $1,200 to Gong.

Requirements

1. Enter the remaining transactions for the month of November into the expanded accounting equation, calculating new balances after each transaction.

2. Prepare the income statement of Reno by Daiyi, Inc. for the month ended November 30, 2015.

3. Prepare the statement of retained earnings of Reno by Daiyi, Inc. for the month ended November 30, 2015.

4. Prepare the statement of financial position for Reno by Daiyi, Inc. at November 30, 2015.

P1-3B. Prepare the income statement, statement of changes in equity, and statement of financial position (*Learning Objective 6*) 20–25 min.

Barrett, Inc. restores antique automobiles. The common shares and retained earnings balances of the corporation were $32,000 and $28,500 respectively at

December 31, 2014. During 2015, the corporation paid $35,000 in dividends to its shareholders. At December 31, 2015, the business's accounting records show these balances:

Accounts Receivable...............	$ 5,000	Cash..	$10,000
Note Payable...........................	16,000	Accounts Payable....................	2,000
Retained Earnings...................	?	Advertising Expense................	3,500
Salaries Expense.....................	16,000	Service Revenue......................	70,000
Equipment...............................	70,000	Common Shares......................	32,000
Insurance Expense..................	9,000		

Requirement

1. Prepare the following financial statements for Barrett, Inc.:

   a. Income statement for the year ended December 31, 2015.

   b. Statement of changes in equity for the year ended December 31, 2015.

   c. Statement of financial position at December 31, 2015.

P1-4B. **Prepare the income statement and statement of financial position; identify certain financial information (*Learning Objective 6*) 25–30 min.**

Presented here are the amounts of Assets, Liabilities, Shareholders' Equity, Revenues, and Expenses of Camp Out, Inc. at October 31, 2015. The items are listed in alphabetical order.

Accounts Payable...................	$ 13,000	Interest Expense....................	$ 7,000
Accounts Receivable..............	21,000	Land.......................................	36,000
Advertising Expense..............	17,000	Note Payable.........................	64,000
Building.................................	150,000	Property Tax Expense............	2,500
Cash......................................	17,000	Rent Expense.........................	22,000
Common Shares....................	75,000	Salaries Expense...................	71,000
Dividends..............................	33,000	Salaries Payable....................	1,900
Equipment.............................	50,000	Service Revenue....................	195,000
Insurance Expense................	1,000	Supplies.................................	1,100

The common shares and retained earnings balance of the business were $75,000 and $79,700 respectively at October 31, 2014.

Requirements

1. Identify each amount shown as an asset, liability, or shareholders' equity.

2. Prepare the company's income statement and statement of changes in equity for the year ended October 31, 2015.

3. Prepare the company's statement of financial position at October 31, 2015.

4. Answer these questions about the company:

   a. What was the profit or loss for the year?

   b. What was the increase or decrease of retained earnings for the year?

   c. What is the amount of economic resources on October 31, 2015?

   d. What is the amount owed on October 31, 2015?

P1-5B. **Error analysis and preparation of statement of financial position (*Learning Objective 6*) 20–25 min.**

The IT manager of Right Away Realty, Inc. prepared the statement of financial position of the company while the accountant was ill. The statement of financial position contains numerous errors. In particular, the IT manager knew that the statement of financial position should balance, so she plugged in the retained earnings amount to achieve this balance. The retained earnings amount, however, is not correct. All other amounts are accurate, but some are out of place.

ASSETS		LIABILITIES	
Right Away Realty, Inc. **Statement of Financial Position** Month Ended September 30, 2015			
Cash	$14,000	Accounts Payable	$ 300
Rent Expense	1,600	Utilities Expense	700
Supplies Expense	100	Accounts Receivable	2,200
Salaries Payable	1,950	Notes Payable	7,000
Equipment	8,300		
		SHAREHOLDERS' EQUITY	
		Common Shares	12,000
		Supplies	600
		Retained Earnings	3,150
		Total Shareholders' Equity	15,750
		Total Liabilities &	
Total Assets	$25,950	Shareholders' Equity	$25,950

Requirement

1. Prepare a new, corrected statement of financial position for Right Away Realty, Inc.

PROBLEMS (ALTERNATES 1, 2, AND 3)

These alternative problem sets are available for your practice benefit on MyAccountingLab.

CONTINUING EXERCISE

This exercise is the first exercise in a sequence that begins an accounting cycle. The cycle is continued in Chapter 2 and completed in Chapter 3.

Graham's Yard Care, Inc. began operations and completed the following transactions during June:

Jun 1	Received $1,000 and issued 100 common shares. Deposited this amount in bank account titled Graham's Yard Care, Inc.
3	Purchased on account a mower, $1,000, and weed whacker, $400. The equipment is expected to remain in service for four years.
5	Purchased $20 of gas. Wrote cheque #1 from the new bank account.
6	Performed lawn services for client on account, $200.
8	Purchased $50 of fertilizer from the lawn store. Wrote cheque #2 from the new bank account.
17	Completed landscaping job for client; received cash $500.
30	Received $50 on account from June 6 sale.

Requirement

1. Analyze the effects of Graham's Yard Care, Inc.'s transactions on the accounting equation. Include these headings: Cash, Accounts Receivable, Lawn Supplies, Equipment, Accounts Payable, Common Shares, Retained Earnings, Dividends, Service Revenue, and Fuel Expense.

CONTINUING PROBLEM

This problem is the first problem in a sequence that begins an accounting cycle. The cycle is continued in Chapter 2 and completed in Chapter 3.

Mike Han recently left his job at a local pool company to open his own pool and spa maintenance business. Mike Han took all of the money he and his wife had in their personal savings account and used it to open Aqua Elite, Inc. on May 1, 2015. Presented next are the transactions for the first month of operations for Aqua Elite, Inc.:

May 1	Mike invested $15,000 cash and a used truck worth $13,500 in the business in exchange for 2,000 company shares.
3	Paid $4,700 cash to purchase office equipment.
7	Purchased $860 of supplies on account.
12	Performed services for cash customers and received $850.
15	Paid salaries of $675 to the office receptionist.
16	Sold the company truck for $13,500.
18	Signed a note payable for $31,000 to purchase a new truck.
21	Performed $3,200 of services on account for a local hotel chain.
27	Paid $500 of the amount owed from the purchase of supplies on May 7.
30	Received $2,000 on account from credit customers.
31	Received the utility bill for the month of May, $480. The bill is not due until June 15.
31	Paid $1,000 dividends to the shareholder, Mike Han.

Requirements

1. Enter the transactions for Aqua Elite, Inc. for the month of May into the expanded accounting equation. Calculate the ending balances at the end of May.

2. Prepare the income statement for Aqua Elite, Inc. for the first month of operations.

3. Prepare the statement of changes in equity for Aqua Elite, Inc. for the first month of operations.

4. Prepare the statement of financial position for Aqua Elite, Inc. for the first month of operations.

5. Did Mike make a wise decision leaving his job to start Aqua Elite, Inc.?

APPLY YOUR KNOWLEDGE

ETHICS IN ACTION

Case 1. Wen Bai and her husband Jung were the owners of WJ Enterprises, Inc. They applied for a small business loan, and the bank requested the most recent business financial statements. When Wen compiled the statement of financial position, she noticed that the business assets and related owner's equity were small. Accordingly, she told Jung that they should contribute some of their personal assets to the business so that the assets and equity would appear much larger and thus the bank would more likely agree to the business loan. Jung agreed that the statement of financial position would appear stronger with more assets and equity but his concern was with the income statement. The sales for the latest period were low, which resulted in a slight net loss because expenses were slightly higher than revenues. Jung reasoned that contributing assets would show a stronger statement of financial position but felt something had to be done to also improve the income statement. He then told Wen that their business could "sell" back some of the assets they had contributed and report higher sales on the income statement, which would result in net income rather than the actual net loss. Wen did not feel comfortable buying back assets from their business just to increase reported sales.

Discuss any ethical concerns you may have with Wen's proposal. Discuss any ethical concerns you may have with Jung's proposal. Do you think it is ethical for a business to "dress up" its financial statements when applying for a loan?

Case 2. Eagle Ridge, Inc. was in the final phase of completing a land development project it started earlier in the year. Eagle Ridge, Inc. had acquired 100 acres of raw land for $250,000 and then spent an additional $1,650,000 in land development costs to create a new subdivision with 200 residential lots. With a total cost of $1,900,000 and 200 lots, each lot had a cost of $9,500; however, the lots were listed for sale at $32,000 per lot. Eagle Ridge, Inc. was applying for a business loan and needed to provide current financial statements to the bank. Jill Hamilton, the company president, wanted to include the total current value of the lots, $6,400,000 (200 lots × $32,000 per lot), rather than the total cost currently listed on the statement of financial position, $1,900,000. Dave Jamison, the company accountant, told Jill that the lots were inventory and the cost principle required that they be included on the statement of financial position at the $1,900,000 rather than the fair market value. Furthermore, even though the lots were listed for sale at $32,000 each, there was no guarantee that they would actually all sell at this value, and according to the objectivity principle, the more reliable cost figure should be used for this reason, too.

Is the accountant right about recording the lots using historical cost? What alternative approaches could be used to measure the cost of assets? Should the statement of financial position for Eagle Ridge, Inc. list the lots at their total cost of $1,900,000 or their total selling price of $6,400,000? If Eagle Ridge, Inc. records the realizable value of the assets, where should this unrealized gain be reported?

KNOW YOUR BUSINESS

FINANCIAL ANALYSIS

Purpose: To help familiarize you with the financial reporting of a real company to further your understanding of the chapter material you are learning.

Each chapter will have a financial statement case that will focus on material contained in that chapter. You will be asked questions, and you will then refer to MyAccountingLab where you will find the Bombardier Annual Report, Year Ended December 31, 2012. Bombardier Inc. is a Canadian company that operates in the aerospace and rail transportation industries. In aerospace, the company designs and manufactures aircraft and provides support services to the business and commercial sectors. In rail transportation, Bombardier manufactures and sells rail cars in addition to systems and support services. Use the annual report to answer these questions. As you progress through each chapter, you will gain a real understanding of actual corporate financial reporting in addition to the basic accounting concepts you are learning within each textbook chapter. This added learning experience will further reinforce your understanding of accounting.

Note that Bombardier reports in U.S. dollars, so all of your answers may be given in U.S. dollars. There is no need to convert these to Canadian dollars.

Requirements

1. Look at all the financial statements starting on page 132 of the annual report, and see whether you can identify the statement of financial position, income statement, statement of comprehensive income, and statement of cash flows. (Note that the term *consolidated* simply means combined.)

2. What was the total amount of assets Bombardier reported as of December 31, 2012? Did the total assets increase or decrease from December 31, 2011?

3. What was the total amount of revenues Bombardier reported for the year ended December 31, 2012? Did the revenues increase or decrease from the previous years presented?

4. What was the total cash flow provided from operating activities reported for Bombardier? Did this increase or decrease from December 31, 2011?

INDUSTRY ANALYSIS

Purpose: To help you understand and compare the performance of two companies in the same industry.

Go to the Bombardier Inc. annual report located in MyAccountingLab and find the Consolidated Balance Sheets on page 132. Now access the December 31, 2012, annual report for The Boeing Company. To do this from the internet, go to their webpage for the Investor Relations at www.boeing.com/companyoffices/financial/quarterly.htm and under annual reports go to the 2012 Annual Report. (Hint: you can search using a key term such as "Full-Year Results 2012," which will make finding this report much easier). Their Consolidated Balance Sheet is located on page 51.

Bombardier Inc. and The Boeing Company are in similar industries; that is, the design and manufacturing of aircraft for the commercial sector. However, Boeing also designs and manufactures aircraft for the defence sector, and Bombardier designs and manufactures rail cars. To gauge a company's performance, it is often helpful to compare a company's financial data against other companies in its industry.

Requirement

1. Look at the data from the Consolidated Balance Sheets for each of the companies. Which company's shareholders have a higher percentage claim to their company's assets? To find out, divide the total shareholders' equity for each company by its total liabilities and shareholders' equity.

SMALL BUSINESS ANALYSIS

Purpose: To help you understand the importance of cash flows in the operation of a small business.

You have just received your year-end financial statements from your accountant and you notice one very disturbing item. The net income from your income statement shows $40,000! Your very first thought is "Where is it?" Then you look at your cash balance and see that it decreased $10,000 from last year to this year. You're thinking there has to be something wrong here. So you call up your accountant and ask for a meeting to discuss this obvious error. After all, how can you possibly have a positive net income and have your cash balance *decrease*?

At the meeting, the accountant lays out the financial statements in front of you and begins to explain how this would have happened. The following is a condensed income statement, statement of changes in equity, and statement of financial position.

BCS Consultants, Inc. Income Statement For Year Ended December 31, 2015	
Revenue	$150,000
Expenses	(110,000)
Net Income	$ 40,000

BCS Consultants, Inc.
Statement of Changes in Equity
For Year Ended December 31, 2015

	Common Shares		Retained Earnings	Total
	Number of Shares	$		
Balance, December 31, 2014	—	$ 0	$ 91,000	$ 91,000
Issued Common Shares	2,000	$20,000		20,000
Net Income			40,000	40,000
Dividends			(13,000)	(13,000)
Balance, December 31, 2015	2,000	$20,000	$118,000	$138,000

BCS Consultants, Inc.
Statement of Financial Position
As of December 31, 2016 & 2015

		2016	2015
Assets:			
Cash		$ 30,000	$ 40,000
Equipment		158,000	146,000
Total Assets		$188,000	$186,000
Liabilities:			
Notes Payable—Bank		$ 50,000	$ 75,000
Shareholders' Equity:			
Common Shares		20,000	20,000
Retained Earnings		118,000	91,000
Total Shareholders' Equity		$138,000	$111,000
Total Liabilities and Shareholders' Equity		$188,000	$186,000

Requirement

1. By looking at the three financial statements, can you anticipate what the accountant is going to tell you about why the cash decreased even though you had net income for the year? What changed from 2015 to 2016? And are transactions that affect the income statement the only transactions that affect your cash balance?

WRITTEN COMMUNICATION

You just got an email from a potential new client who contacted you from your website. This client has indicated to you that he or she is planning to start a new business. The client would like to find out from you what different types of business organizations are available. And also, he or she is wondering exactly what role an accountant would have in the running of the client's business.

Requirement

1. Prepare an email back to this potential client addressing his or her questions about the different types of business organizations and why he or she needs to have an accountant involved in the business.

Self Check Answers
1. c 2. d 3. b 4. c 5. a 6. d 7. c 8. c 9. a 10. d

Check how well you answered the Self Check questions.

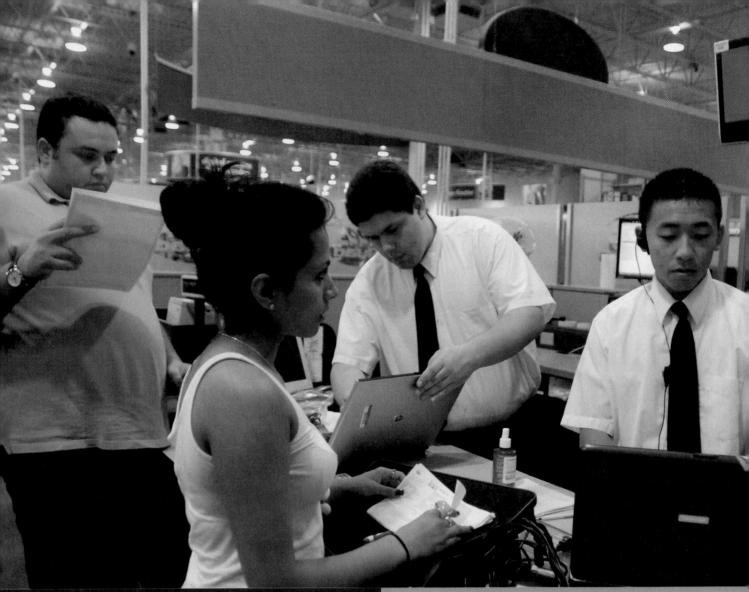

LEARNING OBJECTIVES

① Define accounts and understand how they are used in accounting

② Explain debits, credits, and the double-entry system of accounting

③ Demonstrate the use of the general journal and the general ledger to record business transactions

④ Use a trial balance to prepare financial statements

CHAPTER OUTLINE

CHAPTER 2

Analyzing and Recording Business Transactions

BUSINESS, ACCOUNTING, AND YOU

Walk into your local Best Buy and stand near the Geek Squad counter and observe. What do you see? Most likely, you will see people standing in line, each one with a computer problem that needs to be fixed. There will be Geek Squad employees listening to the customers' problems, offering solutions, and estimating repair bills. Also, you will see customers picking up their newly repaired computers and paying for the repairs with cash, cheques, or credit cards. These are all business transactions that are occurring simultaneously—you are witnessing business in action.

Now, think about it. How does the Geek Squad keep up with the cause and effect of all those transactions? How does a business keep track of all its assets, liabilities, revenue, costs, and other activities? There must be a "scorekeeper" or systematic process that recognizes, measures, records, and reports these business transactions in an understandable, reliable, and relevant manner. That's the role of accounting in business.

To ensure accounting information is understandable, reliable, and relevant, accountants have rules. IFRS and ASPE, as noted in Chapter 1, set the rules for recognizing and measuring business transactions; this part of the process will be explored throughout the book. However, the rules for recording and reporting business transactions are based on a set of proven techniques that have evolved over time. The result is a set of standard, universally accepted procedures that work. The key to using these techniques and procedures is understanding *accounts* and *double-entry accounting*.

▲ Peter Hvizdak/The Image Works

So why is this important to you? Whether you want to be an accountant or a manager, you need to understand how business transactions are recorded. The final report card for your company, good or bad, is a result of this recording process. Would you want to play a game where you do not understand how the score is recorded and ultimately reported? Probably not. Understanding how accountants record business transactions is important.

HOW ARE ACCOUNTS USED TO KEEP BUSINESS TRANSACTIONS ORGANIZED?

L.O. 1 Define accounts and understand how they are used in accounting

As we discussed in Chapter 1, accounting provides useful information to various users. For the information to be useful for decision makers, it has to be detailed, which has four qualitative characteristics: (1) understandability, (2) relevance, (3) reliability, and (4) comparability. Therefore, to facilitate the detail required, accountants will create many categories to track information in. These categories are referred to as **accounts**. We have already seen accounts in use: When recording transactions in the accounting equation in Chapter 1, we created accounts such as Cash, Equipment, and Accounts Payable.

ORGANIZING ACCOUNTS

Accounts of similar types are usually grouped together. To make it easier for accountants and managers, each account is given a unique number (a code), which helps keep the accounts organized. Account numbers usually have two or more digits. The first digit indicates the type of account, while the remaining digits in an account number are used to specify the exact account. Generally, accounts are classified in the following order and start with the following numbers:

Accounts that start with 6, 7, 8, or 9 are used by some businesses to record special types of accounts, such as other revenues and expenses.

To illustrate, a Cash account may be coded 1120 and an Account Payable may be coded 2163:

A gap in numbers is usually left between the different accounts to allow for additional accounts to be added later. A listing of all of the accounts is referred to as a **chart of accounts**. The accounts are typically listed in the chart of accounts in the order that they appear in the accounting equation. Therefore, assets would be listed first, followed by the liabilities, and then the shareholders' equity accounts. **Exhibit 2-1** shows a simple form of a chart of accounts (actual businesses would have a much more detailed chart of accounts). Typical types of accounts for many businesses are discussed in the sections that follow.

Super Trader ⊠ Chart of Accounts			
ACCT #	Account Title	ACCT #	Account Title
1100	Cash	4100	Sales Revenue
1200	Accounts Receivable	4200	Other Revenues
1300	Inventory		
1500	Notes Receivable	5100	Cost of Goods Sold
1600	Prepaid Expenses	5200	Salaries Expense
1700	Land	5300	Supplies Expense
1800	Buildings	5400	Rent Expense
1890	Acc. Depreciation Buildings	5500	Depreciation Expense
1900	Equipment		
1990	Acc. Depreciation Equip.	6100	Advertising Expense
		6200	Insurance Expense
2100	Accounts Payable		
2200	Wages Payable	7100	Interest Expense
2300	Interest Payable	7200	Income Tax Expense
2400	Unearned Revenue		
2500	Notes Payable		
3100	Common Shares		
3200	Retained Earnings		
3300	Dividends		

Exhibit 2-1 ▲

ASSETS

As described in Chapter 1, assets are things of value the company has. They are economic resources or properties owned or controlled by a business that will generate future benefits. Most businesses use the following asset accounts:

- **Cash.** Cash typically includes the business's bank account balance, paper currency, coins, and cheques.
- **Accounts Receivable.** A business may sell goods or services in exchange for a promise of a future cash receipt. Such sales are said to be made on credit or on account. The Accounts Receivable account reflects the amounts that customers owe the business for goods or services that have already been provided. In other words, it shows how much money the company can expect to *receive* from customers in the future.
- **Inventory.** A business may purchase merchandise for resale or purchase raw materials to produce goods as a part of business operation.
- **Notes Receivable.** A business may sell goods or services or loan money and receive a promissory note. A note receivable is a written promise that the customer or borrower will pay a fixed amount of money by a certain date. Notes Receivable reflects the amount of the **promissory notes** that the business expects to collect in cash at a later date. Interest fees are associated with Notes Receivable; however, they are calculated and recorded separately and at a different time.
- **Prepaid Expenses.** A business often pays certain expenses, such as rent and insurance, in advance. A prepaid expense is an asset because the prepayment provides a future benefit for the business. A separate asset account is used for each prepaid expense. Prepaid Rent and Prepaid Insurance are examples of prepaid expense accounts.
- **Land.** The Land account is used to track the cost of land a business owns and uses in its operations.

- **Buildings.** The cost of a business's buildings, offices, warehouses, etc., is recorded in the Buildings account.
- **Equipment, Furniture, and Fixtures.** A business typically has a separate asset account for each type of equipment. Examples include Computer Equipment, Office Equipment, Store Equipment, and Furniture and Fixtures.

Depending on the nature and timing of the use of assets, assets can be grouped or *classified* into different categories to help users understand the company's financial position. Assets can be grouped into two classifications: current assets and long-term assets. **Current assets** are the ones that are expected to be converted to cash, sold, or consumed either within a year or within the **operating cycle**, whichever is longer. For example, cash, accounts receivable, inventory, and prepaid expenses are current assets. **Long-term assets** are those that the business will hold for more than one year or longer than the operating cycle, and depending on the nature of the assets, they may be grouped into (1) long-term investments, (2) property, plant, and equipment, and (3) intangible assets (assets such as patents and copyrights—things that are typically not physical items but still have future value for the business). Long-term assets are also sometimes referred to as non-current assets, fixed assets, or capital assets.

LIABILITIES

As defined in Chapter 1, liabilities are amounts owed to third parties. A business's liabilities can be summarized in categories such as the following:

- **Accounts Payable.** A business may purchase goods or services in exchange for a promise of future payment. Such purchases are said to be made on credit or on account. The Accounts Payable account reflects how much cash the business must pay to suppliers for goods or services that have already been received.
- **Unearned Revenue. Unearned revenue** is created when customers pay in advance or make a deposit for goods or services to be delivered in the future. At the point when cash is received, the company has an obligation to fulfill and has not earned the revenue. The rules for when revenues are earned will be discussed in Chapter 7, but it is important to note that when revenue is earned and when the cash is received do not necessarily have to happen at the same time.
- **Notes Payable.** Notes Payable represents amounts the business must pay because it signed promissory notes to borrow money or to purchase goods or services on credit.
- **Accrued Liabilities.** An accrued liability is a liability for an expense that has been incurred but has not yet been paid. An incurred expense means that a resource has been used. For example, a company will use electricity for a month but the invoice for this will not be received until the following month. Since the electricity has been used, it has been incurred. The same is true for salaries of employees. Employees will work throughout a certain time frame and as they work, the salaries payable accrues until the employees are paid for their work. Taxes Payable, Interest Payable, and Wages Payable are also examples of accrued liability accounts.

Depending on the timing of the debt or obligation repayment, liabilities can also be grouped or *classified* into two different categories. **Current liabilities** are the ones that are expected to be paid or obligations fulfilled within the current operating cycle (usually a year). For example, accounts payable, accrued liabilities, and short-term bank loans are current liabilities. **Long-term liabilities** (also known as non-current liabilities) are those expected to be paid after more than one year or at a point in time longer than the operating cycle, such as a mortgage payable. Long-term liabilities will be discussed further in later chapters.

SHAREHOLDERS' EQUITY

As we saw in Chapter 1, the owners' claim to the assets of the business is called shareholders' equity. We have already discussed the different types of shareholders' equity accounts and what they're used for, but they are listed here again for review.

- **Share Capital.** The Share Capital account represents the investment of assets, usually cash, the shareholders have invested into a business in exchange for the company's shares. A business may issue different classes of shares, for example, preferred shares and/or common shares.

- **Retained Earnings.** The Retained Earnings account tracks the cumulative earnings of the business since it began, less any dividends given to shareholders.

- **Revenues.** Increases in retained earnings (and, therefore, shareholders' equity) created by selling goods or services to customers are called revenues. Review the conceptual framework related to accrual-basis accounting discussed in Chapter 1. This account represents amounts *earned* by the company even if the company has not yet received payment for the goods and services provided. A business may have several revenue accounts depending on how many ways it earns its revenue.

- **Expenses.** Expenses are decreases in retained earnings (and, therefore, shareholders' equity) from using resources to deliver goods and services to customers. Again, based on accrual accounting, expenses are incurred when resources or services are consumed, not when they are paid. A business needs a separate account for each type of expense, such as Insurance Expense, Rent Expense, Wages Expense, and Utilities Expense. Businesses often have numerous expense accounts because many different types of costs are associated with providing goods and services to customers.

- **Dividends.** This account reflects the amount of earnings that have been distributed to the shareholders. Dividends decrease retained earnings (and, therefore, shareholders' equity).

WHAT ARE DEBITS, CREDITS, AND T-ACCOUNTS?

In Chapter 1, we learned that every time we entered a transaction in the accounting equation, it affected at least two accounts. In accounting, the requirement that every transaction impact at least two accounts is called **double-entry accounting**. To simplify the process of accounting, each account is broken down into two sides. This can be visualized as a large T. For each account, one side of the T will represent an increase to the account, while the other side represents a decrease. Whether it is the left side of the T or the right side that increases the account depends on the type of account and on which side of the accounting equation it can be found. Some accounts will increase on the left side and some will increase on the right side. In accounting terms, the left side of an account is referred to as the **debit** side. The right side of an account is referred to as the **credit** side. An example of a **T-account** is as follows:

L.O. 2 Explain debits, credits, and the double-entry system of accounting

Account Title	
Debit = left side Dr.	Credit = right side Cr.

Although T-accounts are not an official accounting tool, some accounting professors and accounting practitioners use them to help visualize and analyze accounts. When first learning accounting, it can be very confusing to understand why some accounts are increased with debits (on the left side) while other accounts are increased with credits (on the right side).

To explain how it works, let's look at the main categories in the accounting equation:

Expenses and dividends decrease shareholders' equity and are on the right side of the equation. To give them a positive sign we will move them to the other side of the equation:

Accordingly, the equation will look like this, and it is still balanced.

When trying to learn which accounts are increased with debits and which accounts are increased with credits, you may create your own memory tool, but it can be helpful to re-visualize the above illustration and to think of the acronym ADE and the acronym LCR. In the acronym ADE, the A stands for Assets, the D for Dividends, and the E for Expenses. These accounts are increased on the debit side (think of the DE in ADE). In the acronym LCR, the L stands for Liabilities, the C stands for Common Shares, and the R stands for both Revenues and Retained Earnings. These accounts are increased on the credit side (think of the CR in LCR). The rules of using T-accounts to record an increase or decrease of each type of account are shown below.

NORMAL BALANCE

The increase side is called the **normal balance** of the account, meaning that normally the account balance should be either 0 or positive on that side. The normal balance of an account is on the same side that we record increases in the account:

- Assets increase on the debit side, so the normal balance of an asset is on the debit side.
- Dividends increase on the debit side, so the normal balance of the Dividends account is on the debit side.
- Expenses increase on the debit side, so the normal balance of an expense is on the debit side.
- Liabilities increase on the credit side, so the normal balance of a liability is on the credit side.

⊕ ACCOUNTING IN YOUR WORLD

Jung recently purchased a train ticket online from Via Rail and used her debit card to pay for it. When she checked her bank account activity online, the bank "debited" her account when it took money out of her account to pay for the purchase. Jung read in the textbook that a debit would increase her cash account. Now Jung is really confused.

Shoosmith Railway Collection/Alamy

Many students feel this way when first introduced to debits and credits. It is really just a matter of perspective. You see, your bank account is an asset to you because it represents cash that is yours. However, your account is a liability to the bank because it represents money that the bank owes you. So, when the bank removes money from your account, it will debit the account to lower the liability because it no longer owes you the money. This is why it is called a *debit* card. You would actually need to credit your cash account, an asset, to show a decrease to your cash. Because you view your account as an asset and the bank views it as a liability, what you do (debit or credit) to the account to increase or decrease it will be exactly opposite of what the bank does.

You	Your Account	Bank
Christopher Nuzzaco/Getty Images	Feng Yu/Fotolia	James Steidl/Fotolia

- Common Shares increase on the credit side, so the normal balance of this account is on the credit side.
- Retained Earnings and Shareholders' Equity increase on the credit side, so the normal balance of these accounts is on the credit side.
- Revenues increase on the credit side, so the normal balance of a revenue is on the credit side.

Exhibit 2-2 shows the normal balance of the major accounts categories.

Exhibit 2-2 ▲

HOW ARE THE GENERAL JOURNAL AND GENERAL LEDGER USED TO KEEP TRACK OF BUSINESS TRANSACTIONS?

L.O. ③ Demonstrate the use of the general journal and the general ledger to record business transactions

Although it would be possible to enter transactions directly into the T-accounts, if we were to try to do this for a real company, it would become very cumbersome and inefficient. Accountants need to enter transactions efficiently and in a timely manner. To do this, the **general journal** was created. The general journal is a chronological, or date order, record of the transactions of a business. The general journal can be compared to an individual person's diary. Like an individual person's diary, the general journal is a place to **record** events that have affected the business. Recording a transaction in the general journal is referred to as **journalizing** the transaction.

To properly record, or journalize, transactions in the general journal, it is helpful to complete a six-step process. Steps 1 through 5 analyze the transaction for the journal entry and step 6 reflects the journalizing of the transaction and the posting from the journal into the accounts that will be introduced later.

TRANSACTION ANALYSIS AND RECORDING

Before recording any transaction, you should go through a five-step process. The five-step process is as follows:

Step 1 Ask what accounts are involved (e.g., Cash, Accounts Payable, Salaries Expense, etc.). If you have difficulty identifying the accounts, try to find the nouns, such as computer, equipment, or salary; otherwise, try to find the verbs, such as paid (cash) or borrowed (from a bank loan or note payable).

Step 2 For each account involved, what type of account is it? Is it an asset, liability, or one of the shareholders' equity accounts? (e.g., Cash is an asset.)

Step 3 What is the normal balance of the account? For example, Cash is an asset account with a debit normal balance. Common Shares is a Shareholders' Equity account with a credit normal balance.

Step 4 What is the direction of change? Did the balance of the account increase or decrease because of the transaction?

Step 5 Should the account be debited or credited? The rule is an account increases on the side of its normal balance and decreases on the opposite side. For example, Cash is an asset account and has a debit normal balance, so when it increases it will increase on the side of its normal balance, which is debit; if an asset decreases, the opposite side of its normal balance is affected, which is credit. While Common Shares is an equity account that has a normal balance on the credit side, when it increases it does so on the side of its normal balance, which is the credit side; if Common Shares decreases it will do so on the opposite side of its normal balance, which is the debit side.

The five-step analysis looks like the following in chart form:

Step 6 Record the entry and post to the accounts in the general ledger.

To record a journal entry in the journal:

1. Record the date.
2. Analyze the transaction, determine the accounts affected, and decide whether they are going to be debited or credited (as shown above).

3. Record the debit entry (or entries) by entering the account title and then entering the amount in the debit column.

4. Record the credit entry (or entries) on the next line by indenting the account title and then entering the amount in the credit column.

5. Write an explanation describing the entry.

Exhibit 2-3, Panel A, describes a transaction: how it is analyzed, how the accounts involved are determined, and how to apply the debit and credit rules. Panel B shows how this transaction is entered in the journal. The page number of the journal appears in its upper right corner.

Because the information in the general journal is organized by date and not by account, the information that it provides is not very useful. For example, if you want to find out how much cash you have at the end of the month, you may not be able to find it from the general

MEMORY TIPS

Remember: If assets, liabilities, and shareholders' equity (including revenue, expenses, and dividends) are not affected in an economic event, it is not a transaction.

PANEL A—Illustrative Transaction:

DATE	TRANSACTION
Jan 1, 2015	Hooray Consulting, Inc., sold $10,000 of shares to Ray Hu, who was investing in the business.

PANEL B—Journal:

Exhibit 2-3 ▲

journal, unless you add all the debits (increases) and then subtract the credits (decreases) in the Cash account. In order to be more useful, information must be organized by account. Therefore, the **general ledger** was created. The general ledger is a grouping of all the accounts of a business with their balances in the order of the statement of financial position. It shows the amount of assets, liabilities, and the shareholders' equity accounts on a given date. Once transactions have been entered in the general journal, the information is then transferred to the general ledger. The process of transferring information from the general journal to the general ledger is called **posting**, which simply means copying the amounts from the journal to the ledger. Debits in the journal are posted as debits in the ledger, and credits in the journal are posted as credits in the ledger. In essence, all the increases and decreases of every account are now grouped or *posted* into each individual account, and then, we can easily figure out the balance of each account. Exhibit 2-3, Panel C, demonstrates how an entry is posted from the journal to the ledger.

The posting process demonstrated in Exhibit 2-3 includes four steps. The four steps required to post the first part of the journal entry are as follows:

Arrow ❶ Copy the transaction date from the journal to the Cash account in the ledger.

Arrow ❷ Copy the journal page number from the journal to the **posting reference** column in the Cash account in the ledger. "J.1" refers to Journal page 1. Since there may be more than one type of journal, sometimes GJ1 (for General Journal page 1) or another acronym is used to be as clear as possible about where to find the entry. This provides a reference that links the entry in the ledger back to the journal.

Arrow ❸ Copy the dollar amount of the debit, $10,000, from the journal as a debit into the Cash account in the ledger.

Arrow ❹ Copy the account number, 1010, from the Cash account in the ledger back to the posting reference column in the journal. This step indicates that the $10,000 debit to Cash was posted to the Cash account in the ledger.

The journal entry is posted to Cash first because this is the first account listed in the entry. Once posting to Cash is complete, repeat the process to post the entry to Common Shares. The account format that is utilized in Exhibit 2-3 is called a four-column account. The first pair of debit and credit columns contains the individual transaction amounts that have been posted from journal entries, such as the $10,000 debit. The second pair of debit and credit columns is used to show the cumulative effect on the account's balance after each entry. Posting used to be performed on a periodic basis, such as daily or weekly. However, most modern computerized accounting systems post transactions immediately after they have been entered.

APPLYING ANALYSIS AND RECORDING TRANSACTIONS

Check out how the transactions for the first month of operations for Hooray Consulting, Inc. are analyzed and recorded. *For illustration purposes, journal entries are shown being posted to T-accounts within the accounting equation. In actual practice, the journal entries would be posted to four-column accounts in the general ledger.*

1. **Sale of shares.** The business sold Ray Hu 1,000 common shares for $10,000.

   Analysis of Transaction (1)

   Step 1 What accounts are involved? The business received cash in exchange for shares, so the accounts involved are Cash and Common Shares.

   Step 2 What type of account is it? Cash is an asset. Common Shares is an account within shareholders' equity.

Step 3 What is the normal balance of each account? Cash is an asset and its normal balance is "debit." Common Shares is equity and its normal balance is "credit."

Step 4 Does the account balance increase or decrease? Because cash was received, Cash is increased. Common Shares also increases because there have been more shares issued.

Step 5 Do you debit or credit the account in the journal entry? According to the rules of debits and credits, an increase in Cash would be a debit (as its normal balance) and an increase in Common Shares would be a credit (as its normal balance).

The first five steps can be summarized as follows:

Step 6 Journalize and post the transactions as follows:

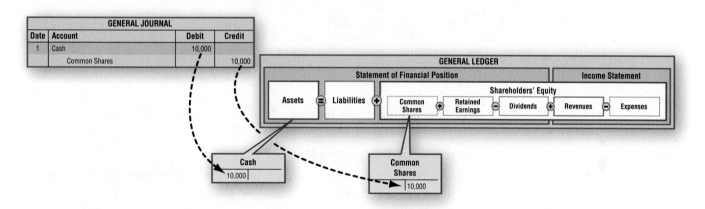

   Notice that the name of the account being credited is indented in the journal. This format is a standard way to differentiate the accounts that are credited from the accounts that are debited. Also, note again that every transaction affects at least two accounts and that the total amount added to the debit side equals the total amount added to the credit side. This demonstrates double-entry accounting, which keeps the accounting equation in balance.

2. **Purchase supplies on credit.** Hooray Consulting purchases office supplies, agreeing to pay $350 within 30 days.

Analysis of Transaction (2)

Step 1 The business received supplies in exchange for a promise to pay cash to the supplier next month. The accounts involved in the transaction are Supplies and Accounts Payable.

Step 2 Supplies is an asset; Accounts Payable is a liability.

Step 3 The asset has a debit normal balance. The liability has a credit normal balance.

Step 4 The asset Supplies increases. The liability Accounts Payable increases because the business owes more than it did before this transaction.

Step 5 An increase in Supplies would be a debit (its normal balance) and an increase in Accounts Payable would be a credit (its normal balance) as illustrated below.

Step 6 Journalize and post the transaction as follows:

3. **Purchase equipment for cash.** The business purchases equipment, paying cash of $4,000.

Analysis of Transaction (3)

Step 1 The business received equipment in exchange for cash paid to the equipment manufacturing company. The accounts involved in the transaction are Equipment and Cash.

Step 2 Equipment and Cash are both assets.

Step 3 The asset Equipment has a debit balance. The asset Cash also has a debit balance.

Step 4 The asset Equipment increases. The asset Cash decreases because a cheque was written to pay for the equipment.

Step 5 An increase in Equipment would be a debit (its normal balance) and a decrease in Cash would be a credit (opposite to its normal balance) as illustrated below.

Step 6 Journalize and post the transaction as follows:

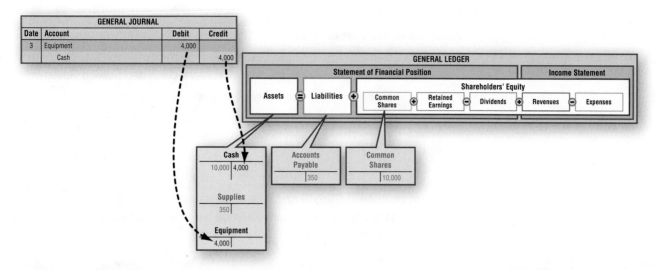

4. Borrow cash from the bank. Hooray Consulting borrows $12,000 cash from the bank and signs a two-year note payable to the bank.

Analysis of Transaction (4)

Step 1 Hooray Consulting received cash from the bank in exchange for a signed note agreeing to pay the cash back in two years. The accounts involved in the transaction are Cash and Notes Payable.

Step 2 Cash is an asset; Notes Payable is a liability.

Step 3 The asset Cash has a debit normal balance; Notes Payable has a credit normal balance.

Step 4 The asset Cash increases. The liability Notes Payable also increases because it represents an obligation owed to the bank.

Step 5 An increase in cash would be a debit (its normal balance) and an increase in Notes Payable would be a credit (its normal balance) as illustrated below.

Step 6 Journalize and post the transaction as follows:

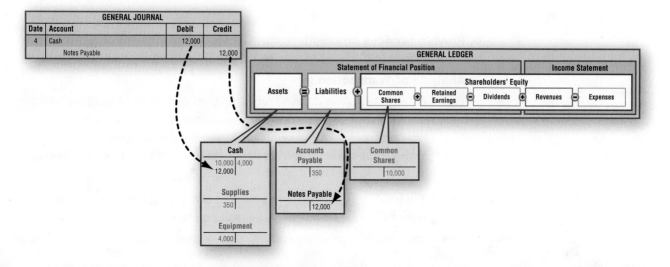

5. Provide services for cash. Hooray collects $1,200 of cash for services provided.

Analysis of Transaction (5)

Step 1 The business received cash in exchange for computer consulting services. The accounts involved in the transaction are Cash and Service Revenue.

Step 2 Cash is an asset; Service Revenue is a revenue.

Step 3 The asset Cash has a debit normal balance; the revenue Service Revenue has a credit normal balance.

Step 4 The asset Cash increases. The revenue Service Revenue also increases because the business has earned revenue by providing services.

Step 5 An increase in Cash would be a debit (its normal balance) and an increase in Service Revenue would be a credit (its normal balance) as illustrated below.

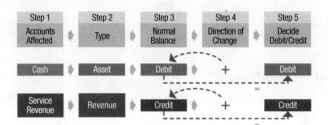

Step 6 Journalize and post the transaction as follows:

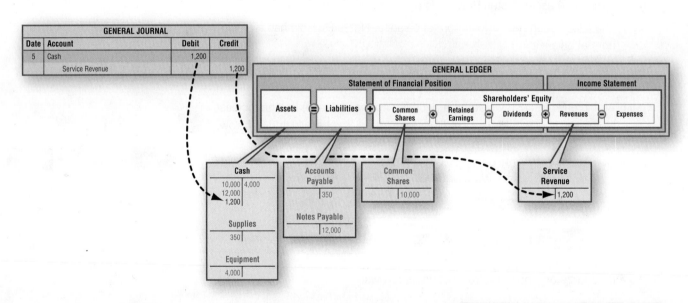

6. Provide services on credit. Hooray Consulting performs $1,900 of services to clients who have promised to pay the business next month.

Analysis of Transaction (6)

Step 1 Hooray Consulting received promises from customers to send cash next month in exchange for consulting services provided. Again, the business earned this money, although it has not received it yet. The accounts involved in the transaction are Accounts Receivable and Service Revenue.

Step 2 Accounts Receivable is an asset; Service Revenue is a revenue.

Step 3 The asset Accounts Receivable has a normal debit balance, while the revenue Service Revenue has a credit normal balance.

Step 4 The asset Accounts Receivable and the revenue Service Revenue both increase.

Step 5 An increase in Accounts Receivable would be a debit (its normal balance) and an increase in Service Revenue would be a credit (its normal balance) as illustrated below.

Step 6 Journalize and post the transaction as follows:

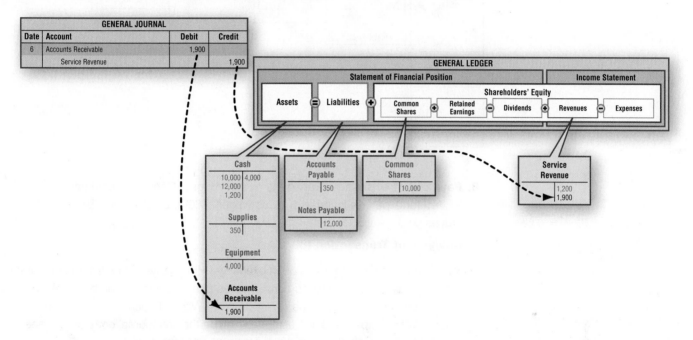

7. **Partial payment of accounts payable.** Hooray Consulting pays $150 to the store where it purchased $350 worth of supplies in Transaction (2).

Analysis of Transaction (7)

Step 1 Hooray Consulting paid $150 of the $350 that it owed to a supplier. The accounts involved in the transaction are Accounts Payable and Cash.

Step 2 Accounts Payable is a liability; Cash is an asset.

Step 3 The liability Accounts Payable has a normal credit balance, while the asset Cash has a normal debit balance.

Step 4 The liability Accounts Payable decreases because Hooray Consulting now owes less in total. The asset Cash also decreases.

Step 5 A decrease in Accounts Payable would be a debit (opposite to its normal balance) and a decrease in Cash would be a credit (opposite to its normal balance) as illustrated below.

Step 6 Journalize and post the transaction as follows:

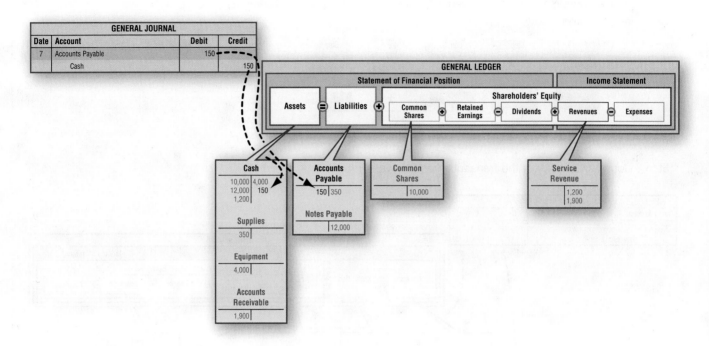

8. **Payment of expenses.** During the month, Hooray Consulting paid cash of $1,700 for expenses incurred such as wages ($600), building rent ($900), and utilities ($200).

Analysis of Transaction (8)

Step 1 The business paid $1,700 in exchange for employee services, the use of the building, and for utilities consumed as part of operating the business. The accounts involved in the transaction are Wages Expense, Rent Expense, Utilities Expense, and Cash. (This will be the first journal entry we will see that has more than two accounts involved in the entry.)

Step 2 Wages Expense, Rent Expense, and Utilities Expense are expenses; Cash is an asset.

Step 3 The expense accounts and the Cash account all have normal debit balances.

Step 4 The expense accounts increase (more resources have been used, so the total expenses increase). The asset Cash decreases.

Step 5 An increase in the expense accounts, Wages, Rent, and Utilities, would be a debit (their normal balance) and a decrease in Cash would be a credit (opposite to its normal balance) as illustrated below.

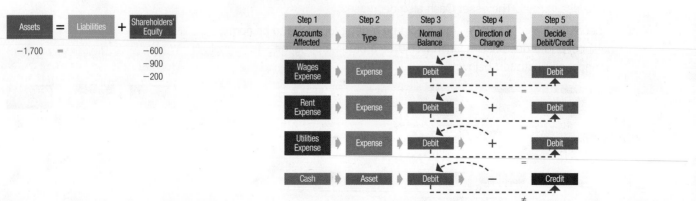

Step 6 Journalize and post the transaction as follows:

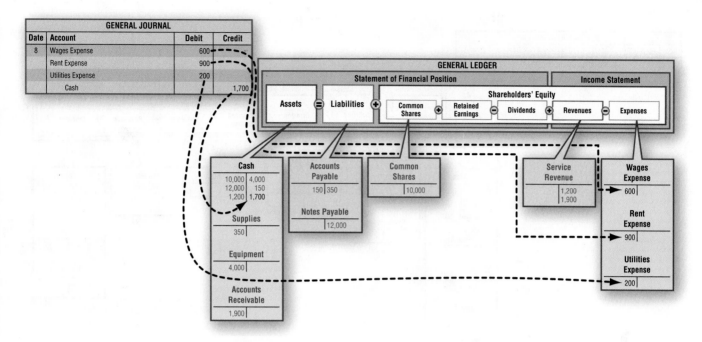

As we can see by this entry, it is possible to have more than two accounts utilized in an entry. This is referred to as a **compound journal entry**. Note that the total amount of debits must still equal the total amount of credits.

9. **Cash dividends.** Hooray Consulting pays $500 of cash dividends to Ray Hu, the only shareholder.

Analysis of Transaction (9)

Step 1 The shareholder received cash dividends because the business has distributed some of the accumulated earnings of the business to the owners. The business reduced the shareholders' equity interest because of dividends paid to the shareholder. The accounts involved in the transaction are Dividends and Cash.

Step 2 Dividends is an account within shareholders' equity, but it reduces shareholders' equity by reducing retained earnings. So it could be regarded as a contra-equity account (contra accounts will be discussed in later chapters; see Chapter 3 in particular). Cash is an asset.

Step 3 The Dividends account is a contra-equity account and has a normal debit balance; the asset Cash has a normal debit balance.

Step 4 The Dividends account increases because the amount of money distributed to the shareholder increased. The asset Cash decreases.

Step 5 An increase in Dividends would be a debit (its normal balance) and a decrease in Cash would be a credit (opposite to its normal balance) as illustrated below.

Step 6 Journalize and post the transaction as follows:

DECISION GUIDELINES

DECISION	GUIDELINE	ANALYZE
How do I know if an event should be entered into a company's accounting records?	Examine the effect of the event on the company's accounting equation.	If the event increases or decreases the assets, liabilities, or shareholders' equity of the business, it represents a transaction that should be recorded in the company's accounting records. If the event doesn't impact the assets, liabilities, or shareholders' equity of the company, then a recordable transaction has not occurred.

CRITICAL THINKING

Take a minute to think about the impact of the following independent cases on each of the assets, liabilities, and shareholders' equity accounts. Should each of the events be entered into a company's accounting records?

1. Ordered a computer system costing $12,000, which will be delivered by the vendor early next month.
2. Received a deposit of $2,000 from a customer for a service to be provided next month.
3. Signed a contract of $5,000 with a customer for a service to be provided next month.
4. Received a shipment of supplies costing $500. The payment will be made by the end of the month.

Solution:

			Shareholders'	
	Assets	**Liabilities**	**Equity**	**Entry in Accounting Record**
1.	No	No	No	No Entry—the item was ordered but not paid for, so cash is not affected and the item has not been used yet, so no expense has been incurred. In other words, there is no effect on the financial position of the company.
2.	+ 2,000	+ 2,000	No	Yes: Cash (Dr); Unearned Revenue (Cr)
3.	No	No	No	No Entry—the contract was signed, but no cash was received and the business has not earned the revenues yet because it has not actually done the work.
4.	+ 500	+ 500	No	Yes: Supplies (Dr); Accounts Payable (Cr)

Impact on Accounts

BALANCING THE T-ACCOUNTS

After the transactions are recorded and posted to the T-accounts, you will calculate each account's **balance**. The balance is the difference between the account's total debits and its total credits. Every account has a balance shown as "Bal" in the following T-account:

	Cash		**1010**
(1) Bal	0	(3)	300
(2)	1,000		
(4) Bal	700		

1. The beginning balance for the current accounting period is the ending balance brought forward from the previous period. In this example, the business is new, so its beginning balance is $0.

2. If, for example, the business receives $1,000 from the sale of shares during the first accounting period, this transaction will show up as a debit to the Cash account.

3. If the company then pays $300 cash for supplies purchased, the amount will be entered on the credit side of the account.

4. Because the company just started, this account had a beginning debit balance of $0. Add increases of $1,000 that appear on the debit side, and subtract decreases of $300 that appear on the credit side. The resulting ending balance of Cash is $700.

A horizontal line separates the transaction amounts from the account balance at the end of an accounting period. The "Bal 700" under the horizontal line shows that the balance in Cash at the end of the accounting period was $700. In the next accounting period, this balance will be the new beginning balance and will change as the business receives more cash and pays out more cash.

If an account's total debits are more than its total credits, then that account has a debit balance. If an account's total credits are more than its total debits, then that account has a credit balance. The ending balance of any T-account can be found in the same way that we just did for the Cash account.

The ending balances for Hooray Consulting would be as follows:

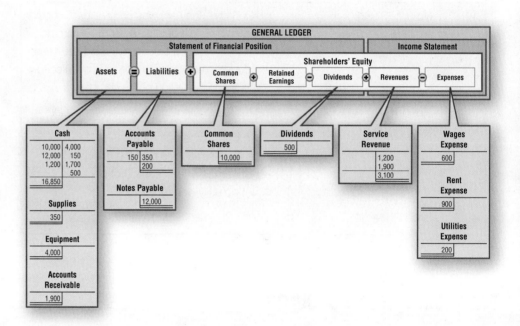

HOW IS A TRIAL BALANCE PREPARED, AND WHAT IS IT USED FOR?

L.O. ④ Use a trial balance to prepare financial statements

Once transactions have been recorded in the journal and posted to accounts in the ledger, a **trial balance** is prepared. A trial balance is a list of all the accounts of a business and their balances at a specific point in time. The trial balance is not an official financial statement, rather it is an internal document whose main purpose is to ensure that the total debits are equal to the total credits. The first step in preparing a trial balance is to complete the heading. Similar to the financial statements that were prepared in Chapter 1, the heading should show the company name, the statement name, and the date of the statement. Next, the account number and name of each account are entered into the first two columns of the trial balance in the order that the account appears in the general ledger. Then, two columns are created labelled "debit" and "credit" and the balance of each account is entered into the correct column. Finally, the debit and credit columns are totalled.

As was done when preparing the financial statements in Chapter 1, the first and last amount in each column has a dollar sign placed before it and the last amounts in both columns are double underlined. A trial balance can be prepared at any time, but is most commonly done at the end of the **accounting period**. An accounting period is usually defined as a month, a quarter, or a year. **Exhibit 2-4** shows the trial balance for Hooray Consulting, Inc. after all transactions have been journalized and posted for January 2015. Note that the trial balance is prepared at a point in time (as the balances of the accounts change each minute), so the day upon which the trial balance is prepared must be stated.

Hooray Consulting, Inc.
Trial Balance
January 31, 2015

ACCT #	ACCOUNT	DEBIT	CREDIT
1010	Cash	$16,850	
1020	Accounts Receivable	1,900	
1030	Supplies	350	
1040	Equipment	4,000	
2010	Accounts Payable		$ 200
2050	Notes Payable		12,000
3010	Common Shares		10,000
3030	Retained Earnings		0
3040	Dividends	500	
4010	Service Revenues		3,100
5010	Wages Expense	900	
5020	Rent Expense	600	
5030	Utilities Expense	200	
	Total	$25,300	$25,300

Exhibit 2-4 ▲

MEMORY **TIPS**
Order of Accounts on a Trial Balance

ALORE

ASSETS

LIABILITIES

OWNER'S EQUITY/
SHAREHOLDER'S
EQUITY

REVENUES

EXPENSES

CONCEPT CHECK...

Jung just completed a problem that was assigned in her accounting class. She told Alan, one of her classmates, that she was confident that she did the problem correctly because the debits equal the credits on the trial balance. According to Alan, just because the debits equal the credits on the trial balance does not mean that everything was done correctly. Who is right, Jung or Alan?

Answer: Alan is correct. The following are some of the errors that can occur and yet the trial balance will still be in balance:

- A transaction can be recorded for the wrong amount in a journal entry.

- An entire journal entry can be recorded twice, or not recorded at all.

- The wrong accounts can be debited or credited in a journal entry. For example, when recording a payment on an account payable it is possible to debit Accounts Receivable instead of Accounts Payable.

CORRECTING ERRORS

If an error has occurred, the steps required to correct it depend on the type of error that was made. If a journal entry has been made to the wrong accounts or for the wrong amount, it is easiest to reverse, or undo, the incorrect entry. A new entry should then be prepared that contains the correct accounts or amount. To correct an entry that has been made twice, one of the entries should be reversed. If an entry was erroneously omitted, it simply needs to be entered.

If the trial balance does not balance, you will need to check all entries and postings to find the errors and correct them. Otherwise, the financial statements are not accurate. Three frequent errors are (1) transposition error, where two digits are reversed or transposed,

(2) adding or dropping a zero (0), and (3) entering the amount in the wrong column (for example, the debit column instead of the credit column). If you make only one of the errors, then there are a couple of things that you can do to help you identify the error. First, take the difference between the total debits and credits. Second, divide the difference by 9. If the number can be divided evenly, then there is a possibility of a transposition error or an adding/dropping zero error.

| Transposition Error: | 530 − 350 = 180 | 180 ÷ 9 = 20 |
| Adding/Dropping "0" Error: | 5,000 − 500 = 4,500 | 4,500 ÷ 9 = 500 |

If this does not help you identify the error, then once again take the difference between the total debits and credits. Instead of dividing the difference by 9, divide the difference by 2. Check for this number in the debit column and credit column to ensure the number is entered in the proper column. For example, if Utilities Expense of $200 were incorrectly entered in the credit column, then the total debit balance would be $25,100, and the total credit balance would be $25,500.

| $25,500 − $25,100 = $400 | $400 ÷ 2 = $200 |

CRITICAL THINKING

Take a minute to think about the impact of the following errors on the trial balance. What are the correct debit and credit balances? Does each error change the overall debit and credit balance? What is the impact on each of the assets, liabilities, and shareholders' equity accounts due to the errors?

Mehta Company's trial balance shows $116,000 on both the debit and credit sides. Mehta's accountant found the following three mistakes:

1. Cash dividends of $2,000 were incorrectly recorded as salaries expense.
2. A $3,000 deposit from a customer for services to be delivered in the following month was incorrectly recorded as revenue.
3. Cash paid for equipment of $1,000 was incorrectly recorded as purchase on account.

Solution:

Corrections needed:	DR	CR		Impact on Accounts: Assets =	Liabilities +	SE
1. Dividends	$2,000					+2000
Salaries Expense		$2,000				−2000
2. Revenue	$3,000					−3000
Unearned Revenue		$3,000			+3000	
3. Accounts Payable	$1,000				−1000	
Cash		$1,000		−1000		

Only the third error will affect the total debits and credits, as both sides of the equation decrease by an equal amount. Let's assume that the trial balance (before the corrections are made) appeared as follows in the box below on the left. If we now make the corrections to the balances of the accounts, we will see that the totals of the debits and the credits in the box on the right change by only $1,000.

	DR	CR
Cash	$12,000	
A/P		$6,000
Unearned Revenue		7,000
Revenue		12,000
Salaries Expense	9,000	
Dividends	4,000	
Total	$25,000	$25,000

	DR	CR
Cash	$11,000	
A/P		$5,000
Unearned Revenue		10,000
Revenue		9,000
Salaries Expense	7,000	
Dividends	6,000	
Total	$24,000	$24,000

DECISION GUIDELINES

DECISION	GUIDELINE	ANALYZE
As the manager of a department, I am responsible for the budget for the department and for evaluating how well the department has performed. When looking at the financial statements for my department, some of the numbers do not feel right and I'm wondering if something was perhaps recorded incorrectly (for example, perhaps someone else's expenses were recorded in my department's records by mistake). I need to check the detail of these accounts that do not seem right. Where can I find more detail?	Review the trial balance or the general ledger.	The trial balance is a summary of all of a company's accounts with their respective balances on a given day. The general ledger provides the detail of all of the transactions that have impacted an account along with a running balance of the account. Having quick access to the account balances often allows managers and owners to make better decisions.

PREPARATION OF FINANCIAL STATEMENTS

After completing the trial balance, you can use it to prepare the financial statements because it shows all of the accounts with their balances. First, set up the financial statements as we did in Chapter 1, starting with the titles to the financial statements. Now, using the account balances from the trial balance, insert the account names and their balances into the financial statements, starting with the income statement, then the statement of changes in equity, and finishing with the statement of financial position. Make sure the statement of financial position is in balance! That is, total assets equal total liabilities plus shareholders' equity.

Exhibit 2-5 shows the income statement, statement of changes in equity, and statement of financial position for Hooray Consulting, Inc. at January 31, 2015. You can see once again how the information flows from one statement to another.

Hooray Consulting, Inc.
Income Statement
Month Ended January 31, 2015

Revenue:		
Service Revenues		$3,100
Expenses:		
Wages Expense	$900	
Rent Expense	600	
Utilities Expense	200	
Total Expenses		1,700
Net Income		$1,400

Hooray Consulting, Inc.
Statement of Changes in Equity
Month Ended January 31, 2015

	Common Shares		Retained Earnings	Total
	Number of Shares	$		
Balance, January 1, 2015	—	$ 0	$ 0	$ 0
Issued Common Shares	1,000	$10,000		10,000
Net Income			$1,400	1,400
Dividends			(500)	(500)
Balance, January 31, 2015	1,000	$10,000	$ 900	$10,900

Hooray Consulting, Inc.
Statement of Financial Position
As of January 31, 2015

ASSETS		LIABILITIES	
Cash	$16,850	Accounts Payable	$ 200
Accounts Receivable	1,900	Note Payable	12,000
Supplies	350	Total Liabilities	12,200
Equipment	4,000		
		SHAREHOLDERS' EQUITY	
		Common Shares	10,000
		Retained Earnings	900
		Total Shareholders' Equity	10,900
		Total Liabilities &	
Total Assets	$23,100	Shareholders' Equity	$23,100

Exhibit 2-5 ▲

These statements look the same as they did in Chapter 1, except now on the income statement we see detailed information for revenues and expenses. Also, notice that the income statement now has two columns. Many students assume, erroneously, that these columns represent debits and credits as they did on the trial balance. Debits and credits are used to *record* increases and decreases of accounts due to the business transaction. Financial statements are used to *report* the balance of each account. On financial statements, the company reports its performance for the period and its financial position at the end of the period. Columns are used to make the statement more organized and easier to read; they are not used to signify debits and credits.

 DECISION GUIDELINES

DECISION

I am considering changing the companies that I'm invested in for my pension. Where do I find feedback on the performance of the companies in order to decide where best to invest my funds?

GUIDELINE

A company's financial statements will provide feedback regarding the performance of the company.

ANALYZE

The income statement reflects how profitable a business has been for a specified period of time. The statement of changes in equity shows the amount of the share capital, the retained earnings, including the earnings that have been distributed to the shareholders, and the changes to these accounts during the time period. The statement of financial position shows the assets that a business owns, the liabilities it owes, and owners' claims on the business on a given date. In other words, it shows what assets the business has and who has rights to those assets.

The process of analyzing transactions, entering them into the journal, posting them to the ledger, preparing a trial balance, and preparing financial statements is only a part of what is called the accounting cycle. This accounting cycle is completed by a business for every accounting period, and then it is repeated for the next accounting period, and the next, and the next, and so on. Shown next is a visual representation of the accounting cycle:

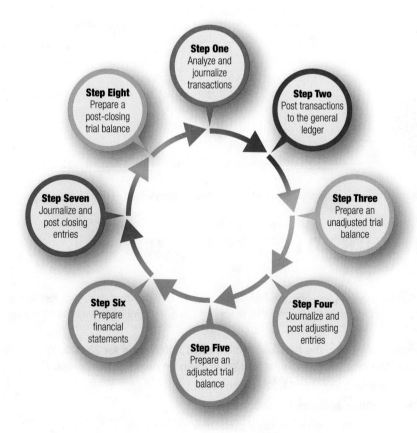

In the next chapter, you will learn the remaining steps in the accounting cycle, which includes preparing, adjusting, and closing entries.

FOCUS ON USERS

Concept	User	Why Is This Important to This User?
Recording and Posting Transactions	**Bookkeepers**	Bookkeepers need to understand the process of accounting to be able to complete their jobs. The analysis of transactions is an important element of what they do. Even in a computerized environment it is important to understand the process because if something goes wrong technically, you need to be able to continue, fix the problem, and understand any hidden issues.
Trial Balance	**Managers**	Managers need to understand the process of accounting particularly for internal auditing and control purposes. For example, management needs to be able to verify the accuracy of what is recorded to be able to have confidence in what the financial statements are presenting.
	Government and Regulatory Bodies	Regulators are interested in the ways in which transactions are recorded and the impact of the choices made in recording transactions on the financial statements to make any necessary changes to regulations and guidelines.
	Bookkeepers	A bookkeeper will use the trial balance as a tool to double-check that the transactions in the general journal have been recorded properly. A balanced trial balance does not guarantee that the transactions are error-free, but it does provide a check-point where the accounting department can assess the transactions prior to creating the financial statements.

DEMO DOC

MyAccountingLab   Visit MyAccountingLab to watch animated versions of similar Demo Docs.

DEBIT/CREDIT TRANSACTION ANALYSIS

LEARNING OBJECTIVE

On June 1, 2015, Jean Dion opened PaintPro, Inc., a company that provides residential and commercial painting services. During the month of June, the business incurred the following transactions:

    a. To begin operations, the business sold Jean 1,000 shares for $8,000. The business received the cash from the sale and gave Jean an ownership interest.

    b. Purchased equipment for $4,800 on account.

    c. Purchased office supplies for $500 cash.

    d. Performed $1,600 of services for a customer on account.

    e. Paid $2,000 cash toward the equipment purchased on account in Transaction b.

f. Received $2,300 in cash for services provided to a new customer.

g. Paid $350 cash to repair equipment.

h. Paid $1,150 cash in salaries expense.

i. Received $700 cash from customers on account.

j. Paid $1,000 of dividends to its only shareholder, Jean Dion.

REQUIREMENTS

① Create blank T-accounts for the following accounts: Cash, 1010; Accounts Receivable, 1020; Supplies, 1030; Equipment, 1040; Accounts Payable, 2010; Common Shares, 3010; Dividends, 3020; Service Revenue, 4010; Salaries Expense, 5010; and Repairs Expense, 5020.

② Journalize the transactions and show how they are posted in T-accounts.

③ Total all the T-accounts to determine their balances at the end of the month.

DEMO DOC SOLUTIONS
REQUIREMENT ①

Create blank T-accounts for the following accounts:

Cash, 1010; Accounts Receivable, 1020; Supplies, 1030; Equipment, 1040; Accounts Payable, 2010; Common Shares, 3010; Dividends, 3020; Service Revenue, 4010; Salaries Expense, 5010; and Repairs Expense, 5020.

Part 1	Part 2	Part 3	Demo Doc Complete

Opening a T-account simply means drawing a blank account (the T) and putting the account title (and the account number, if used) on top. To help find the accounts later, they are usually organized into assets, liabilities, shareholders' equity, revenue, and expenses (in that order). Note that the account numbers also follow this order.

Draw empty T-accounts for every account listed in the question.

REQUIREMENT ②

Journalize the transactions and show how they are posted in T-accounts.

| Part 1 | **Part 2** | Part 3 | Demo Doc Complete |

a. To begin operations, the business sold Jean 1,000 shares for $8,000. The business received the cash from the sale and gave Jean an ownership interest.

Remember the transaction analysis steps listed earlier in the chapter. First, we must determine which accounts are affected.

The business received $8,000 cash when it sold Jean 1,000 shares. In exchange, Jean received an equity interest in the business. So, the accounts involved are Cash and Common Shares.

The next step is to determine what type of accounts they are. Cash is an asset, while Common Shares is part of shareholders' equity.

The next step is to determine the normal balance of the account. Then, we need to determine whether these accounts increased or decreased. From *the business's* point of view, Cash (an asset) increased. Common Shares (equity) also increased.

Now we must determine whether these accounts should be debited or credited. According to the rules of debits and credits, an increase in assets is a debit, while an increase in common shares (equity) is a credit.

So, Cash (an asset) increases, which is a debit. Common Shares (equity) also increases, which is a credit.

The journal entry would be as follows:

DATE	ACCOUNTS	POST REF.	DR.	CR.
a.	Cash		8,000	
	Common Shares			8,000
	Sold shares			

Note that the total dollar amounts of debits will equal the total dollar amounts of credits. Remember to use the transaction letters for references. This will help when we post this entry to the T-accounts.

Posting to the T-accounts is the last step in transaction analysis.

To post the transaction to the T-accounts, simply transfer the amount of each debit to its correct account as a debit (left side) entry, and transfer the amount of each credit to its correct account as a credit (right side) entry.

For this transaction, a debit of $8,000 to Cash means that we enter $8,000 on the left side of the Cash T-account. A credit of $8,000 to Common Shares means that we enter $8,000 on the right side of the Common Shares T-account:

Cash	1010		Common Shares	3010
(a) 8,000				(a) 8,000

b. Purchased equipment for $4,800 on account.

Because it is a new transaction, we perform the transaction analysis steps again.

The business received equipment in exchange for a promise to pay for the cost ($4,800) at a future date. So the accounts involved in the transaction are Equipment and Accounts Payable.

Equipment is an asset, and Accounts Payable is a liability. Equipment (an asset) increased. Accounts Payable (a liability) also increased.

According to the debit and credit rules, an increase in assets is a debit, while an increase in liabilities is a credit.

So, Equipment (an asset) increases, which is a debit. Accounts Payable (a liability) also increases, which is a credit.

The journal entry would be as follows:

DATE	ACCOUNTS	POST REF.	DR.	CR.
b.	Equipment		4,800	
	Accounts Payable			4,800
	Purchased equipment on account.			

We enter $4,800 on the debit (left) side of the Equipment T-account and $4,800 on the credit (right) side of the Accounts Payable T-account.

Equipment 1040	Accounts Payable 2010
(b) 4,800	(b) 4,800

c. Purchased office supplies for $500 cash.

The business purchased supplies in exchange for cash ($500). The accounts involved in the transaction are Supplies and Cash.

Supplies and Cash are both assets. Supplies (an asset) increased. Cash (an asset) decreased.

An increase in assets is a debit, while a decrease in assets is a credit.

So, Supplies (an asset) increases, which is a debit. Cash (an asset) decreases, which is a credit.

The journal entry would be as follows:

DATE	ACCOUNTS	POST REF.	DR.	CR.
c.	Supplies		500	
	Cash			500
	Purchased supplies for cash.			

We enter $500 on the debit (left) side of the Supplies T-account and $500 on the credit (right) side of the Cash T-account.

Cash		1010
(a)	8,000	(c)	500

Supplies		1030
(c)	500	

d. Performed $1,600 of services for a customer on account.

The business received promises from customers to send cash ($1,600) next month in exchange for painting services rendered. So the accounts involved in the transaction are Accounts Receivable and Service Revenue.

Accounts Receivable is an asset and Service Revenue is a revenue. Accounts Receivable (an asset) increased. Service Revenue (revenue) also increased.

An increase in assets is a debit, while an increase in a revenue is a credit.

So, Accounts Receivable (an asset) increases, which is a debit. Service Revenue (revenue) increases, which is a credit.

The journal entry is as follows:

DATE	ACCOUNTS	POST REF.	DR.	CR.
d.	Accounts Receivable		1,600	
	Service Revenue			1,600
	Performed services on account.			

We enter $1,600 on the debit (left) side of the Accounts Receivable T-account and $1,600 on the credit (right) side of the Service Revenue T-account.

Accounts Receivable 1020		
(d)	1,600	

Service Revenue		4010
	(d)	1,600

e. Paid $2,000 cash toward the equipment purchased on account in Transaction b.

The business paid *some* of the money that was owed on the purchase of equipment in Transaction b. The accounts involved in the transaction are Accounts Payable and Cash.

Accounts Payable is a liability, and Cash is an asset. Accounts Payable (a liability) decreased. Cash (an asset) also decreased.

Remember, the Accounts Payable account is the total amount owed to creditors to which the business will have to make payments in the future (a liability). When the business makes these payments to the creditors, the amount of this account decreases, because the business now owes less (in this case, it reduces from $4,800—in Transaction b—to $2,800).

A decrease in liabilities is a debit, while a decrease in assets is a credit.

So, Accounts Payable (a liability) decreases, which is a debit. Cash (an asset) decreases, which is a credit.

The journal entry is as follows:

DATE	ACCOUNTS	POST REF.	DR.	CR.
e.	Accounts Payable		2,000	
	Cash			2,000
	Made a partial payment on account.			

We enter $2,000 on the debit (left) side of the Accounts Payable T-account and $2,000 on the credit (right) side of the Cash T-account.

Cash		1010
(a)	8,000	(c)	500
		(e)	2,000

Accounts Payable		2010
(e)	2,000	(b)	4,800

f. Received $2,300 in cash for services provided to a new customer.

The business received cash ($2,300) in exchange for painting services rendered to a client. The accounts involved in the transaction are Cash and Service Revenue.

Cash is an asset, and Service Revenue is a revenue. Cash (an asset) increased. Service Revenue (revenue) also increased.

An increase in assets is a debit, while an increase in a revenue is a credit.

So, Cash (an asset) increases, which is a debit. Service Revenue (revenue) increases, which is a credit.

The journal entry is as follows:

DATE	ACCOUNTS	POST REF.	DR.	CR.
f.	Cash		2,300	
	Service Revenue			2,300
	Received cash for services performed.			

We enter $2,300 on the debit (left) side of the Cash T-account and $2,300 on the credit (right) side of the Service Revenue T-account.

Cash		**1010**		**Service Revenue**		**4010**
(a)	8,000	(c) 500			(d)	1,600
(f)	2,300	(e) 2,000			(f)	2,300

Notice how we keep adding onto the T-accounts. The values from previous transactions are already in place.

g. Paid $350 cash to repair equipment.

The business paid $350 cash to repair equipment. Because the benefit of the repairs has already been used, the repairs are recorded as Repairs Expense. Because the repairs were paid in cash, the Cash account is also involved.

Repairs Expense is an expense and Cash is an asset. Repairs Expense (an expense) increased. Cash (an asset) decreased.

An increase in expenses is a debit, while a decrease in an asset is a credit.

So, Repairs Expense (an expense) increases, which is a debit. Cash (an asset) decreases, which is a credit.

The journal entry is as follows:

DATE	ACCOUNTS	POST REF.	DR.	CR.
g.	Repairs Expense		350	
	Cash			350
	Paid cash for repairs.			

We enter $350 on the debit (left) side of the Repairs Expense T-account and $350 on the credit (right) side of the Cash T-account.

Cash		**1010**		**Repairs Expense**		**5020**
(a)	8,000	(c) 500		(g)	350	
(f)	2,300	(e) 2,000				
		(g) 350				

h. Paid $1,150 cash in salaries expense.

The business paid employees $1,150 in cash. Because the benefit of the employee's work has already been used, the salary is recorded as Salaries Expense. Because the salary was paid in cash, the Cash account is also involved.

Salaries Expense is an expense, and Cash is an asset. Salaries Expense (an expense) increased. Cash (an asset) decreased.

An increase in expenses is a debit, while a decrease in an asset is a credit.

So, Salaries Expense (an expense) increases, which is a debit. Cash (an asset) decreases, which is a credit.

The journal entry is as follows:

DATE	ACCOUNTS	POST REF.	DR.	CR.
h.	Salaries Expense		1,150	
	Cash			1,150
	Paid salary with cash.			

We enter $1,150 on the debit (left) side of the Salaries Expense T-account and $1,150 on the credit (right) side of the Cash T-account.

Cash			1010
(a)	8,000	(c)	500
(f)	2,300	(e)	2,000
		(g)	350
		(h)	1,150

Salaries Expense		5010
(h)	1,150	

i. Received $700 cash from customers on account.

The business received payments ($700) from customers for services previously provided in Transaction d. The accounts involved in this transaction are Cash and Accounts Receivable.

Cash and Accounts Receivable are both assets. Cash (an asset) increased. Accounts Receivable (an asset) decreased.

Remember, accounts receivable is the total amount due from customers from which the business will receive money. When the business receives these payments from its customers, the amount of this account decreases, because the business now has less to receive in the future (in this case, it reduces from $1,600—in Transaction d—to $900).

An increase in assets is a debit, while a decrease in assets is a credit.

So Cash (an asset) increases, which is a debit. Accounts Receivable (an asset) decreases, which is a credit.

The journal entry is as follows:

DATE	ACCOUNTS	POST REF.	DR.	CR.
i.	Cash		700	
	Accounts Receivable			700
	Collected cash from customers on account.			

We enter $700 on the debit (left) side of the Cash T-account and $700 on the credit (right) side of the Accounts Receivable account.

Cash		**1010**			**Accounts Receivable**	**1020**
(a)	8,000	(c)	500	(d)	1,600	(i) 700
(f)	2,300	(e)	2,000			
(i)	700	(g)	350			
		(h)	1,150			

j. Paid $1,000 of dividends to its only shareholder, Jean Dion.

The business distributed $1,000 of earnings to Jean by paying him dividends. The business paid cash to Jean, whose ownership interest (equity) decreased. The accounts involved in the transaction are Dividends and Cash.

Dividends is a contra-shareholders' equity account, and Cash is an asset. Dividends increased and Cash (an asset) decreased.

An increase in dividends is a debit, while a decrease in an asset is a credit.

The journal entry is as follows:

DATE	ACCOUNTS	POST REF.	DR.	CR.
j.	Dividends		1,000	
	Cash			1,000
	Paid dividends.			

We enter $1,000 on the debit (left) side of the Dividends T-account and $1,000 on the credit (right) side of the Cash account.

Cash		**1010**			**Dividends**	**3020**
(a)	8,000	(c)	500	(j)	1,000	
(f)	2,300	(e)	2,000			
(i)	700	(g)	350			
		(h)	1,150			
		(j)	1,000			

Now we will summarize the journal entries for the month.

DATE	ACCOUNTS	POST REF.	DR.	CR.
a.	Cash	1010	8,000	
	Common Shares	3010		8,000
	Sold 1,000 shares.			
b.	Equipment	1040	4,800	
	Accounts Payable	2010		4,800
	Purchased equipment on account.			
c.	Supplies	1030	500	
	Cash	1010		500
	Purchased supplies for cash.			
d.	Accounts Receivable	1020	1,600	
	Service Revenue	4010		1,600
	Performed services on account.			
e.	Accounts Payable	2010	2,000	
	Cash	1010		2,000
	Made a partial payment on account.			
f.	Cash	1010	2,300	
	Service Revenue	4010		2,300
	Received cash for services performed.			
g.	Repairs Expense	5020	350	
	Cash	1010		350
	Paid cash for repairs.			
h.	Salaries Expense	5010	1,150	
	Cash	1010		1,150
	Paid salary with cash.			
i.	Cash	1010	700	
	Accounts Receivable	1020		700
	Collected cash from customers on account.			
j.	Dividends	3020	1,000	
	Cash	1010		1,000
	Paid dividends.			

Notice how the posting reference field now contains the account number that indicates that the entries have been posted to the general ledger (or in this case, the T-accounts).

REQUIREMENT ③

Total all the T-accounts to determine their balances at the end of the month.

Part 1	Part 2	**Part 3**	Demo Doc Complete

To compute the balance in a T-account (total the T-account), add up the numbers on the debit/left side of the account and (separately) the credit/right side of the account. Subtract the smaller number from the bigger number and put the difference on the side of the bigger number. This procedure gives the balance in the T-account (the net total of both sides combined). For example, for the Cash account, the numbers on the left side total $8,000 + $2,300 + $700 = $11,000. The credit/right side = $500 + $2,000 + $350 + $1,150 + $1,000 = $5,000.

The difference is $11,000 − $5,000 = $6,000. We put the $6,000 on the debit side because it is the side of the bigger number of $11,000.

Another way to think of adding up (totalling) T-accounts is the following:

Beginning Balance in T-account
+ Increases to T-account
− Decreases to T-account
= Ending Balance in T-account

The T-accounts should look like the following after posting all transactions and totalling each account:

DEMO DOC COMPLETE

| Part 1 | Part 2 | Part 3 | Demo Doc Complete |

 DECISION GUIDELINES

Recording Business Transactions

Here are some decisions that you would make as you record and summarize transactions in your business:

DECISION

How do I know if an event should be entered into a company's accounting records?

GUIDELINE

Examine the effect of the event on the company's accounting equation.

ANALYZE

If the event increases or decreases the assets, liabilities, or shareholders' equity of the business, it represents a transaction that should be recorded in the company's accounting records. If the event doesn't impact the assets, liabilities, or shareholders' equity of the company, then a recordable transaction has not occurred.

DECISION		GUIDELINE		ANALYZE

DECISION

As the manager of a department, I am responsible for the budget for the department and for evaluating how well the department has performed. When looking at the financial statements for my department, some of the numbers do not feel right and I'm wondering if something was perhaps recorded incorrectly (for example, perhaps someone else's expenses were recorded in my department's records by mistake). I need to check the detail of these accounts that do not seem right. Where can I find more detail?

I am considering changing the companies that I'm invested in for my pension. Where do I find feedback on the performance of the companies in order to decide where best to invest my funds?

GUIDELINE

Review the trial balance or the general ledger.

A company's financial statements will provide feedback regarding performance of the company.

ANALYZE

The trial balance is a summary of all of a company's accounts with their respective balances on a given day. The general ledger provides the detail of all of the transactions that have impacted an account along with a running balance of the account. Having quick access to the account balances often allows managers and owners to make better decisions.

The income statement reflects how profitable a business has been for a specified period of time. The statement of changes in equity shows the amount of the share capital, the retained earnings, including the earnings that have been distributed to the shareholders, and the changes to these accounts during the time period. And, the statement of financial position shows the assets that a business owns, the liabilities it owes and the owners' claims in the business on a given date. In other words, it shows what assets the business has and who has rights to those assets.

ACCOUNTING VOCABULARY

THE LANGUAGE OF BUSINESS

Account (p. 66)

Accounting cycle (p. 66)

Accounting period (p. 84)

Balance (p. 83)

Chart of accounts (p. 66)

Compound journal entry (p. 81)

Credit (p. 69)

Current assets (p. 68)

Current liabilities (p. 68)

Debit (p. 69)

Double-entry accounting (p. 69)

General journal (p. 72)

General ledger (p. 74)

Journalize (p. 72)

Long-term asset (p. 68)

Long-term liability (p. 68)

Normal balance (p. 70)

Operating cycle (p. 68)

Posting (p. 74)

Posting reference (p. 74)

Promissory note (p. 67)

Record (p. 72)

T-account (p. 69)

Trial balance (p. 84)

Unearned revenue (p. 68)

ACCOUNTING PRACTICE

DISCUSSION QUESTIONS

1. The order in which assets were listed and described in the text is the order in which you will see them listed on the statement of financial position. What is the organizing principle behind the order in which assets are listed?

2. What type of transaction would result in the recording of a prepaid asset? What do you think will happen to that prepaid asset eventually?

3. How is revenue related to retained earnings?

4. Distinguish between an event and a transaction. Are all transactions events? Are all events transactions? Why or why not? What are the implications of your answers with respect to journal entries?

5. What is a "normal balance"? What are normal balances for the following accounts?
   a. Accounts Receivable
   b. Prepaid Expenses
   c. Notes Payable
   d. Retained Earnings
   e. Salaries Expense

6. You learned in this chapter that cash is increased with a debit. When you deposit your paycheque in your account, however, the teller might say that he or she is going to credit your account. Why?

7. What would be the implications of a credit balance in the cash account?

8. Distinguish between journalizing and posting.

9. True or false: If the trial balance is in balance, the financial statements will be accurate. Why or why not?

10. When it comes time to prepare the financial statements, from where do the financial statement numbers come?

SELF CHECK

MyAccountingLab

The exercises and problems in this chapter can be found on MyAccountingLab. You can practise them as often as you want, and they feature step-by-step guided solutions to help you find the right answer.

1. Which sequence of actions correctly summarizes the accounting process?
   a. Prepare a trial balance, journalize transactions, post to the accounts
   b. Post to the accounts, journalize transactions, prepare a trial balance
   c. Journalize transactions, post to the accounts, prepare a trial balance
   d. Journalize transactions, prepare a trial balance, post to the accounts

2. The left side of an account is used to record
   a. debits.
   b. credits.
   c. debits or credits, depending on the type of account.
   d. increases.

3. Suppose Sunshine Florists, Inc. has cash of $40,000, receivables of $30,000, and furniture and fixtures totalling $170,000. Sunshine Florists, Inc. owes $60,000 on account and has a $120,000 note payable. How much is the shareholders' equity?
   a. $240,000
   b. $120,000
   c. $180,000
   d. $60,000

4. Lori's Catering, Inc. purchased $400 of supplies on account. The journal entry to record this transaction is denoted by which of the following?

DATE	ACCOUNTS	POST REF.	DR.	CR.
a.	Inventory		400	
	Accounts Payable			400
b.	Accounts Payable		400	
	Supplies			400
c.	Supplies		400	
	Accounts Payable			400
d.	Supplies		400	
	Accounts Receivable			400

5. Posting an $800 purchase of supplies on account appears as which of the following?

a.

Supplies	Accounts Receivable
800	800

c.

Supplies	Accounts Payable
800	800

b.

Supplies	Accounts Payable
800	800

d.

Cash	Supplies
800	800

6. Which journal entry records obtaining a bank loan of $15,000?

DATE	ACCOUNTS	POST REF.	DR.	CR.
a.	Notes Payable		15,000	
	Accounts Receivable			15,000
b.	Notes Payable		15,000	
	Cash			15,000
c.	Cash		15,000	
	Notes Payable			15,000
d.	Cash		15,000	
	Accounts Payable			15,000

7. S & S Janitorial, Inc. paid $600 for supplies and purchased additional supplies on account for $800. S & S Janitorial, Inc. also paid $300 of the accounts payable. Assuming no supplies have been used yet, what is the balance in the Supplies account?

a. $800
b. $1,100
c. $1,400
d. $1,700

8. The Blue Ox Restaurant recorded a cash collection on account by debiting Cash and crediting Accounts Payable. What will the trial balance show for this error?

    a. Too much for liabilities
    b. Too much for assets
    c. The trial balance will not balance
    d. Both a and b

9. TingTing Wu, an interior designer, has a corporation, TTW Design, Inc., that began the year with total assets of $110,000 and total liabilities of $80,000. During the year, TTW Design, Inc. earned revenue of $90,000 and paid expenses of $40,000. TTW Design, Inc. also sold an additional $10,000 of shares and paid $20,000 in dividends. How much is the shareholders' equity in TTW Design, Inc. at year-end?

    a. $70,000
    b. $110,000
    c. $130,000
    d. $160,000

10. The entry to record the payment of $1,200 rent expense would be which of the following?

DATE	ACCOUNTS	POST REF.	DR.	CR.
a.	Rent Expense		1,200	
	Accounts Payable			1,200
b.	Cash		1,200	
	Rent Expense			1,200
c.	Rent Expense		1,200	
	Cash			1,200
d.	Accounts Payable		1,200	
	Rent Expense			1,200

Answers are given after Written Communication.

SHORT EXERCISES

S2-1. Accounting terms (*Learning Objective 1*) 5–10 min.

Match the accounting terms at the left with the corresponding definitions at the right.

_____ 1. Account   a. Any economic event that has a financial impact on the business

_____ 2. Assets   b. The detailed record of the changes in a particular asset, liability, or shareholders' equity

_____ 3. Shareholders' Equity   c. Economic resources that provide a future benefit for a business

_____ 4. Expenses   d. Debts or obligations of a business

_____ 5. Liabilities   e. Shareholders' claim to the assets of a corporation

_____ 6. Revenues   f. Increases in shareholders' equity from selling goods or services to customers

_____ 7. Transactions   g. Decreases in shareholders' equity from using resources to sell goods or services

S2-2. Account types (*Learning Objective 1*) 5–10 min.

For each of the following accounts, place the corresponding letter(s) of its account type in the space provided. Use the most detailed account type appropriate.

(A) Asset (L) Liability (SE) Shareholders' Equity (R) Revenue (E) Expense

_SE_   Dividends

____ 1. Accounts Payable

____ 2. Cash

____ 3. Service Revenue

____ 4. Prepaid Rent

____ 5. Rent Expense

____ 6. Common Shares

S2-3. Accounting cycle steps (*Learning Objectives 2, 3, & 4*) 5–10 min.

The following list names the activities involved in the accounting process of recording and summarizing business transactions. Place the number corresponding with the order the activity occurs next to the activity, starting with 1.

_1_ Transaction occurs.

____ Prepare the financial statements.

____ Prepare the trial balance.

____ Post the transactions from the journal to the ledger.

____ Record the transactions in the journal.

S2-4. Account types (*Learning Objective 1*) 5–10 min.

For each of the following accounts, indicate the account type by labelling it as an asset (A), liability (L), shareholders' equity (SE), revenue (R), or expense (E). Also give the digit each account number would begin with in the chart of accounts. Use the most detailed account type appropriate.

_A,1_ Land

____ 1. Service Revenue

____ 2. Dividends

____ 3. Accounts Receivable

____ 4. Salaries Expense

____ 5. Notes Payable

____ 6. Common Shares

____ 7. Rent Expense

S2-5. Accounting terminology (*Learning Objectives 2, 3, & 4*) 5–10 min.

Demonstrate your knowledge of accounting terminology by filling in the blanks to review some key definitions.

Dillon Baker is describing the accounting process for a friend who is a psychology major. Dillon states, "The basic summary device in accounting is the _____. The left side of an account is called the _____ side, and the right side is called the _____ side. We record transactions first in a _____. Then we post, or copy, the data to the _____. It is helpful to list all the accounts with their balances on a _____ _____."

S2-6. Effects of debits and credits on accounts (*Learning Objective 2*) 5–10 min.

For each of the following accounts, indicate if the account's normal balance is a debit balance (DR) or a credit balance (CR).

DR   Cash

____ 1. Rent Expense

____ 2. Accounts Payable

____ 3. Service Revenue

____ 4. Office Furniture

____ 5. Common Shares

____ 6. Land

____ 7. Dividends

S2-7. Balancing accounts and normal balances (*Learning Objective 2*) 5–10 min.

Calculate each account balance.

	Supplies	1030				Note Payable	2030	
3/8	400	3/27	600		3/20	2,000	3/5	10,000
3/17	500				3/31	4,000		

S2-8. Types of accounts and effects of debits and credits (*Learning Objective 2*) 5–10 min.

Complete the following table. For each account listed, identify the type of account, how the account is increased (debit or credit), and how the account is decreased (debit or credit). Use the most detailed account type appropriate.

Account	Type	Normal Balance	↑	↓
Office Equipment	Asset	Dr.	Dr.	Cr.
Dividends				
Service Revenue				
Accounts Payable				
Rent Expense				
Cash				

S2-9. Recreating journal entries from T-account postings (*Learning Objective 2*) 15–20 min.

IPW, Inc. began operations on January 1, 2015. The seven transactions recorded during January by the company accountant are shown in the following T-accounts:

	Cash	1010				Equipment	1040				Dividends	3020	
(1)	15,000	(2)	3,000		(2)	3,000				(7)	1,000		
		(5)	250		Bal	3,000				Bal	1,000		
		(6)	2,300										
		(7)	1,000										
Bal	8,450												

	Accounts Payable	2010				Service Revenue	4010	
(5)	250	(3)	600				(4)	4,500
		Bal	350				Bal	4,500

	Accounts Receivable	1020
(4)	4,500	
Bal	4,500	

	Common Shares	3010
	(1)	15,000
	Bal	15,000

	Operating Expenses	5010–5040
(6)	2,300	
Bal	2,300	

	Supplies	1030
(3)	600	
Bal	600	

Complete the following table. For each transaction shown, determine the accounts affected, the type of account, whether the account increases or decreases, and whether it would be recorded in the journal on the debit or credit side.

Transaction	Accounts Affected	Type	Normal Balance	↑↓	Dr. or Cr.
(1)	Cash	Asset	Dr.	Increase	Dr.
	Common Shares	Shareholders' Equity	Cr.	Increase	Cr.

S2-10. Journalizing transactions (*Learning Objective 3*) 10–15 min.

Shohei Oda opened a DJ service in Vancouver, British Columbia as a corporation. The following transactions took place in June:

Jun 1	Sold $20,000 of shares to Shohei to start the business.
5	Purchased party supplies on account, $4,600.
7	Paid monthly office rent of $2,400.
10	Provided $4,000 of DJ services to customers. Received cash of $1,700 for these services and sent bills to clients for the remainder.

Using the steps outlined in the five-step transaction analysis, record the transactions in the journal.

S2-11. Journalizing transactions (*Learning Objective 3*) 10–15 min.

After operating for a month, Shohei Oda's DJ services completed the following transactions during July:

Jul 3	The business borrowed $40,000 from the bank, signing a note payable.
9	Performed DJ service for clients on account, $1,600.
16	Received cash on account from clients, $400.
22	Received a utility bill, $475, which will be paid during August.
31	Paid the monthly salary to its employee, $2,600.
31	Paid interest expense of $110 on the bank loan.

Using the steps outlined in the five-step transaction analysis, record the transactions in the journal.

S2-12. Prepare a trial balance (*Learning Objective 4*) 10–15 min.

The accounting records for Amazing Sounds, Corp. contain the following amounts on April 30, 2015. The accounts appear in no particular order.

Service Revenue	$87,000	Utilities Expense	$19,000
Prepaid Rent	500	Note Payable	10,000
Accounts Payable	1,000	Cash	16,400
Equipment	19,000	Rent Expense	40,000
Dividends	21,000	Common Shares	17,900

Prepare the trial balance for Amazing Sounds at April 30, 2015. List the accounts in proper order.

S2-13. Preparation of financial statements from a trial balance (*Learning Objective 4*) 5–10 min.

To the left of each account listed on the trial balance, indicate the financial statement that will include the account: income statement (IS), statement of changes in equity (SCE), or statement of financial position (SFP).

		ACCOUNT	DEBIT	CREDIT
		Wirt's Dirt, Inc. **Trial Balance** December 31, 2015		
		Cash	$13,900	
		Accounts Receivable	2,100	
		Supplies	400	
		Equipment	5,200	
		Accounts Payable		$ 1,900
		Notes Payable		11,000
		Common Shares		8,000
		Dividends	500	
		Service Revenues		3,300
		Wages Expense	1,300	
		Rent Expense	600	
		Utilities Expense	200	
		Total	$24,200	$24,200

S2-14. Accounting terminology (*Learning Objectives 1, 2, & 3*) 5–10 min.

Accounting has its own vocabulary and basic relationships. Match the accounting terms at the left with the corresponding phrase at the right.

_____ 1. Posting

_____ 2. Normal balance

_____ 3. Payable

_____ 4. Journal

_____ 5. Receivable

_____ 6. Chart of accounts

_____ 7. Debit

_____ 8. Trial balance

_____ 9. Credit

a. Chronological record of transactions

b. An asset

c. Left side of an account

d. Side of an account where increases are recorded

e. Copying data from the journal to the ledger

f. List of all accounts with their balances

g. A liability

h. List of all of the accounts of a business

i. Right side of an account

S2-15. Types of accounts and effects of debits and credits (*Learning Objective 2*) 10–15 min.

Fill in the chart using the first line as an example. The account that is listed on the right column has specific features that you are to list in the chart. For example, Accounts Payable is a liability (account classification), it is increased by a credit (second column), decreased by a debit (third column), has a normal balance as a credit, and it is found on the statement of financial position (financial statement).

Account Classification	Increase	Decrease	Normal Balance	Normal Financial	Statement Account
Liability	Credit	Debit	Credit	SFP	Accounts Payable
_____	_____	_____	_____	_____	Accounts Receivable
_____	_____	_____	_____	_____	Dividends
_____	_____	_____	_____	_____	Building
_____	_____	_____	_____	_____	Consulting Revenue
_____	_____	_____	_____	_____	Inventory
_____	_____	_____	_____	_____	Licence
_____	_____	_____	_____	_____	Preferred Shares
_____	_____	_____	_____	_____	Salaries Expense
_____	_____	_____	_____	_____	Unearned Revenue
_____	_____	_____	_____	_____	Prepaid Rent

EXERCISES (GROUP A)

E2-1A. Journalizing transactions (*Learning Objectives 2 & 3*) 10–15 min.

The following are six transactions for Gonzalez Engineering, Inc. during the month of July.

Jul	1	Paid advertising expense, $275.
	3	Performed service for customers and received cash, $3,000.
	5	Purchased supplies on account, $450.
	9	Received cash of $1,200 from credit customers on account.
	12	Paid $900 on accounts payable.
	17	Performed service for customers on account, $2,800.

Requirement

1. Complete the following table. For each transaction shown, determine the accounts affected, the type of account, whether the account increases or decreases, and whether it would be recorded in the journal on the debit or credit side.

Transaction	Accounts Affected	Account Type	↑↓	Dr. or Cr.
(1)	Advertising Expense	Shareholders' Equity	↑	Dr.
	Cash	Asset	↓	Cr.

E2-2A. Journalizing transactions (*Learning Objective 3*) 15–20 min.

Using the steps outlined for transaction analysis, record the following transactions in the general journal for Alread Plumbing, Inc. Explanations are not required.

Feb	1	Paid interest expense, $300.
	5	Purchased office furniture on account, $2,200.
	10	Performed service on account for a customer, $1,700.
	12	Borrowed $4,500 cash, signing a note payable.
	19	Sold for $85,000 land that had cost the company $85,000.
	21	Purchased building for $290,000; signed a note payable.
	27	Paid $1,500 on account.

E2-3A. Journalizing transactions (*Learning Objective 3*) 15–20 min.

Williams & Associates, Inc. completed the following transactions during October 2015, its first month of operations:

Oct	1	Sold 2,000 shares for $50,000 to Kirsten Williams to start the business.
	3	Purchased supplies on account, $300.
	5	Paid cash for a building to use for storage, $42,000.
	6	Performed service for customers and received cash, $1,600.
	11	Paid on accounts payable, $200.
	18	Performed service for customers on account, $2,400.
	24	Received cash from a customer on account, $800.
	31	Paid the following expenses: salary, $500; and rent, $1,200.

Requirement

1. Using the steps outlined in the five-step transaction analysis, journalize the transactions of Williams & Associates, Inc. List transactions by date. Use the following accounts: Cash, Accounts Receivable, Supplies, Building, Accounts Payable, Common Shares, Service Revenue, Salaries Expense, and Rent Expense.

E2-4A. Balance accounts and prepare trial balance (*Learning Objectives 3 & 4*) 10–15 min.

The transactions for Little Tykes Daycare, Inc. for the month of January 2015 are posted in the following T-accounts.

Cash			1010
Jan 1	25,000	Jan 4	6,800
6	3,000	9	100
23	1,200	29	700
Bal			

Accounts Receivable			1020
Jan 17	1,600	Jan 23	1,200
Bal			

Supplies			1030
Jan 2	200		
Bal			

Equipment			1040
Jan 4	6,800		
Bal			

Accounts Payable			2010
Jan 9	100	Jan 2	200
		Bal	

Common Shares			3010
		Jan 1	25,000
		Bal	

Service Revenue			4010
		Jan 6	3,000
		17	1,600
		Bal	

Salaries Expense			5010
Jan 29	700		
Bal			

Quick solution:

1. Cash balance = $21,600;
2. Trial balance totals = $29,700

Requirements

1. Calculate account balances.

2. Prepare the trial balance for Little Tykes Daycare, Inc. at January 31, 2015.

E2-5A. Record transactions and prepare a trial balance (*Learning Objectives 3 & 4*) 15–20 min.

Baldwin Realty, Inc. had the following transactions for the month of May 2015.

May	2	Paid Rent Expense, $600.
	4	Performed service for a customer and received cash, $1,000.
	8	Purchased supplies on account, $400.
	11	Received cash from credit customers on account, $1,200.
	15	Sold an additional $5,000 of common shares.
	19	Paid $500 on account.
	27	Performed service for customers on account, $1,600.
	31	Made a payment on the Notes Payable, $3,000.

The following T-accounts have been set up for Baldwin Realty, Inc. with their beginning balances as of May 1, 2015.

Cash	1010
May 1 3,000	

Accounts Payable	2010
	May 1 800

Accounts Receivable	1020
May 1 1,800	

Notes Payable	2030
	May 1 10,000

Supplies	1030
May 1 300	

Common Shares	3010
	May 1 30,000

Office Furniture	1050
May 1 1,200	

Service Revenue	4010
	May 1 2,100

Building	1060
May 1 36,000	

Rent Expense	5050
May 1 600	

Requirements

1. Journalize the transactions for the month of May.
2. Post the journal entries to the appropriate T-accounts. Identify all items by date.
3. Calculate the balance of each account at May 31, 2015.
4. Prove that the total of all the debit balances equals the total of all of the credit balances by preparing a trial balance.

E2-6A. Journalize transactions, prepare a trial balance and statement of financial position (*Learning Objectives 3 & 4*) 20–25 min.

The transactions for Crazy Curlz, Inc. for the month of June 2015 have been posted to the accounts as follows:

Cash			
(1) 16,000	(4) 8,000		
	(5) 5,000		
	(6) 300		

Supplies	
(2) 800	

Equipment	
(4) 8,000	

Building	
(3) 60,000	

Accounts Payable	
(6) 300	(2) 800

Notes Payable	
(5) 5,000	(3) 60,000

Common Shares	
	(1) 16,000

Requirements

1. Prepare the journal entries that served as the sources for the six transactions.
2. Calculate the balance in each account.
3. Prepare the trial balance for Crazy Curlz, Inc. at June 30, 2015.
4. Prepare a statement of financial position for Crazy Curlz, Inc. as of June 30, 2015.

E2-7A. Explaining the effects of transactions on accounts using T-accounts and inferring the missing amount (Learning Objectives 2 & 3) 10–15 min.

The following transactions occurred during April 2015 in Sion, Inc.'s operations:

1. Salaries Expense for the month of April was $4,600. Sion made a monthly payment to employees on the fifteenth of the month.

2. Sales on account were $8,270.

3. The Cash, Accounts Receivable, and Salaries Payable beginning and ending balances were:

Cash		Accounts Receivable		Salaries Payable	
8,650	(2)	3,780	(4)	(2)	4,200
(4)		(3)			(1)
(5)		4,350			3,600

Requirements

1. What was the amount paid for salaries in April?

2. What was the amount received from customers in April?

3. What do (1) and (3) represent?

4. What was the Cash ending balance?

E2-8A. Journalizing, posting, trial balance, income statement, and statement of financial position (Learning Objectives 3 & 4) 25–30 min.

McDonald Consulting, Inc. completed the following transactions during December 2015, its first month of operations:

Dec	2	Sold $10,000 of shares to Dan McDonald to start the consulting practice.
	3	Paid monthly office rent, $800.
	6	Paid cash for a new computer, $1,600.
	8	Purchased office furniture on account, $2,100.
	11	Purchased supplies on account, $200.
	19	Performed consulting service for a client on account, $900.
	20	Paid utility expenses, $300.
	28	Performed service for a client and received cash for the full amount of $1,100.

Requirements

1. Open, or set up, T-accounts in the ledger: Cash; Accounts Receivable; Supplies; Equipment; Furniture; Accounts Payable; Common Shares; Service Revenue; Rent Expense; Utilities Expense.

2. Record transactions in the journal. Explanations are not required.

3. Post the transactions to the T-accounts, identify all items by date. Calculate the balance in each account.

4. Prepare a trial balance at December 31, 2015.

5. Prepare the income statement, statement of changes in equity, and statement of financial position.

E2-9A. Error correction (*Learning Objective 4*) 20–25 min.

Julie Palmer has trouble keeping her debits and credits equal. During a recent month, Julie made the following errors:

a. Julie recorded a $750 payment of rent by debiting Rent Expense for $75 and crediting Cash for $75.

b. In recording a $250 payment on account, Julie debited Accounts Receivable and credited Cash.

c. Julie recorded the receipt of cash for service revenue by debiting Cash for $130 instead of the correct amount of $310. Julie also credited Service Revenue for $130, the incorrect amount.

d. Julie recorded a $120 purchase of supplies on account by debiting Accounts Payable and crediting Supplies.

e. In preparing the trial balance, Julie omitted a $15,000 note payable.

Requirements

1. For each of these errors, state whether Julie's mistake would cause the total debits and total credits on the trial balance to be unequal.

2. Identify each account with an incorrect balance, and indicate the amount and direction of the error.

Use the following format:

Effect on Trial Balance	Account(s) Misstated
Total debits = Total credits	Cash $675 too high Rent Expense $675 too low

E2-10A. Error correction (*Learning Objective 4*) 20–25 min.

Kwik Klean, Inc.'s trial balance shows $96,000 on both debit and credit sides. Kwik Klean's accountant found the following mistakes:

1. Purchase of supplies $2,000 on account was incorrectly recorded as supplies expense.

2. A $560 deposit from a customer for services to be delivered in the following month was incorrectly recorded as $650.

3. Cash paid for salaries expense of $2,500 was incorrectly recorded as salaries payable.

4. Borrowed $10,000 from one of the shareholders that was incorrectly recorded as common shares.

5. Paid $3,500 for salaries expense was incorrectly recorded as dividends.

Requirements

1. What are the correct debit and credit balances?

2. Does each error change the overall debit and credit balance?

3. What is the impact on each of the Assets, Liabilities, and Shareholders' Equity accounts due to these errors?

EXERCISES (GROUP B)

E2-1B. Journalizing transactions (*Learning Objectives 2 & 3*) 10–15 min.

The following are six journal entries Keene Engineering, Inc. made during the month of April.

Apr 1	Paid advertising expense, $275.
3	Paid $4,000 cash to purchase a new piece of equipment.
5	Issued shares in exchange for $7,000 cash.
9	Borrowed $5,000 on a note payable from the bank.
12	Paid monthly telephone bill, $325.
17	Purchased supplies for $175, paid cash.

Requirement

1. For each transaction shown, determine the accounts affected, the type of account, whether the account increases or decreases, and whether it would be recorded in the journal on the debit or credit side. The first transaction has been analyzed for you.

Transaction	Accounts Affected	Type	Increase/Decrease	Dr. or Cr.
(1)	Advertising Expense	Shareholders' Equity	Increase	Dr.
	Cash	Asset	Decrease	Cr.

E2-2B. Journalizing transactions (*Learning Objective 3*) 15–20 min.

Using the steps outlined for transaction analysis, record the following transactions in the general journal for Laverden Plumbing, Inc. Explanations are not required.

May 1	Paid interest expense, $500.
5	Purchased office furniture on account, $2,500.
10	Performed service on account for a customer, $2,700.
12	Borrowed $4,500 cash, signing a note payable.
19	Sold for $50,000 land that had cost the company $50,000.
21	Purchased building for $800,000; signed a note payable.
27	Paid $700 on account.

E2-3B. Journalizing transactions (*Learning Objective 3*) 15–20 min.

Welch & Associates, Inc. completed the following transactions during September 2015, its first month of operations:

Sep 1	Sold $40,000 of shares to Katie Welch to start the business.
3	Purchased supplies on account, $200.
5	Paid cash for a building to use for storage, $32,000.
6	Performed service for customers and received cash, $3,000.
11	Paid on accounts payable, $100.
18	Performed service for customers on account, $2,900.
24	Received cash from a customer on account, $1,500.
30	Paid the following expenses: salary, $650; and rent, $1,100.

Requirement

1. Using the steps outlined in the five-step transaction analysis, journalize the transactions of Welch & Associates, Inc. List transactions by date.

E2-4B. Balancing accounts and preparing a trial balance (*Learning Objectives 3 & 4*)
10–15 min.

The transactions for Learning Fun Daycare, Inc. for the month of May 2015 are posted in the following T-accounts.

Cash			1010
May 1	45,000	May 4	12,700
6	7,500	9	200
23	900	29	1,100
Bal			

Accounts Receivable			1020
May 17	3,600	May 23	900
Bal			

Supplies			1030
May 2	700		
Bal			

Equipment			1040
May 4	12,700		
Bal			

Accounts Payable			2010
May 9	200	May 2	700
		Bal	

Common Shares			3010
		May 1	45,000
		Bal	

Service Revenue			4010
		May 6	7,500
		17	3,600
		Bal	

Salaries Expense			5010
May 29	1,100		
Bal			

Requirements

1. Calculate account balances.
2. Prepare the trial balance for Learning Fun Daycare, Inc. at May 31, 2015.

E2-5B. Record transactions and prepare a trial balance (*Learning Objectives 3 & 4*)
15–20 min.

Spadina Realty, Inc. had the following transactions for the month of June 2015.

Jun 2	Paid rent expense, $900.
4	Performed service for a customer and received cash, $1,500.
8	Purchased supplies on account, $900.
11	Received cash from credit customers on account, $1,100.
15	Sold an additional $15,000 of common shares.
19	Paid $600 on account.
27	Performed service for customers on account, $3,000.
30	Made a payment on the Notes Payable, $3,500.

The following T-accounts have been set up for Spadina Realty, Inc. with their beginning balances as of June 1, 2015.

Cash		1010
Jun 1	9,000	

Accounts Receivable		1020
Jun 1	1,800	

Supplies		1030
Jun 1	600	

Office Furniture		1050
Jun 1	1,900	

Building		1060
Jun 1	36,000	

Accounts Payable		2010
	Jun 1	2,600

Notes Payable		2030
	Jun 1	10,000

Common Shares		3010
	Jun 1	34,500

Service Revenue		4010
	Jun 1	3,700

Rent Expense		5050
Jun 1	1,500	

Requirements

1. Journalize the transactions for the month of June.
2. Post the journal entries to the appropriate T-accounts. Identify all items by date.
3. Calculate the balance of each account at June 30, 2015.
4. Prove that the total of all the debit balances equals the total of all of the credit balances by preparing a trial balance.

E2-6B. Journalize transactions, prepare a trial balance and statement of financial position (*Learning Objectives 3 & 4*) 20–25 min.

The transactions for Dancing Antz, Inc. for the month of September 2015 have been posted to the accounts as follows:

Cash			
(1)	28,000	(4)	2,000
		(5)	6,000
		(6)	150

Supplies	
(2)	600

Equipment	
(4)	2,000

Building	
(3)	80,000

Accounts Payable			
(6)	150	(2)	600

Notes Payable			
(5)	6,000	(3)	80,000

Common Shares		
	(1)	28,000

Requirements

1. Prepare the journal entries that served as the sources for the six transactions.
2. Calculate the balance in each account.
3. Prepare the trial balance for Dancing Antz, Inc. at September 30, 2015.
4. Prepare a statement of financial position for Dancing Antz, Inc. as of September 30, 2015.

E2-7B. Explaining the effects of transactions on accounts using T-accounts and inferring the missing amount (*Learning Objective 3*) 10–15 min.

The following transactions occurred during May 2015 of Lion, Inc.'s operations:

1. Sales on account were $5,700.

2. Interest Expense for the month of May was $1,600. Lion made a monthly interest payment on the twentieth of the month.

3. The Cash, Accounts Receivable, and Interest Payable beginning and ending balances were:

Cash			Accounts Receivable			Interest Payable		
4,850	(2)		2,480	(4)		(2)	2,200	
(4)			(3)				(1)	
(5)			1,730				1,400	

Requirements

1. What was the amount paid for interest in May?

2. What was the amount received from customers in May?

3. What do (1) and (3) represent?

4. What was the Cash ending balance?

E2-8B. Journalizing, posting, trial balance, income statement, and statement of financial position (*Learning Objectives 3 & 4*) 25–30 min.

Meo Consulting, Inc. completed the following transactions during February 2015, its first month of operations:

Feb 2	Sold 6,500 shares for $65,000 to DaPing Meo to start the consulting practice.
3	Paid monthly office rent, $800.
6	Paid cash for a new computer, $1,900.
8	Purchased office furniture on account, $2,500.
11	Purchased supplies on account, $500.
19	Performed consulting service for a client on account, $2,700.
20	Paid utility expenses, $450.
28	Performed service for a client and received cash for the full amount of $2,000.

Requirements

1. Record transactions in the journal. Explanations are not required.

2. Create the necessary T-accounts and post the transactions to the T-accounts. Identify all items by date. Calculate the balance in each account.

3. Prepare a trial balance at February 28, 2015.

4. Prepare the income statement, statement of changes in equity, and statement of financial position.

E2-9B. Error correction (*Learning Objective 4*) 20–25 min.

Chester Hinkson has trouble keeping his debits and credits equal. During a recent month, Chester made the following errors:

a. Chester recorded an $850 payment of rent by debiting Rent Expense for $85 and crediting Cash for $85.

b. In recording a $600 payment on account, Chester debited Accounts Receivable and credited Cash.

c. Chester recorded the receipt of cash for service revenue by debiting Cash for $280 instead of the correct amount of $820. Chester also credited Service Revenue for the $280, the incorrect amount.

d. Chester posted a $350 purchase of supplies on account by debiting Accounts Payable and crediting Supplies.

e. In preparing the trial balance, Chester omitted a $50,000 note payable.

Requirements

1. For each of these errors, state whether Chester's mistake would cause the total debits and total credits on the trial balance to be unequal.

2. Identify each account with an incorrect balance, and indicate the amount and direction of the error.

E2-10B. Error correction (*Learning Objective 4*) 20–25 min.

Top Cut, Inc.'s trial balance shows $42,000 on both debit and credit sides. Top Cut's accountant found the following mistakes:

1. Purchase of Equipment $2,000 on account was incorrectly recorded as cash payment.

2. A payment of $1,200 to a supplier on account was incorrectly recorded as $2,100.

3. Cash paid for dividends of $1,500 was incorrectly recorded as salaries expense.

4. Issued 2,000 shares for $6,000 to shareholders, which was incorrectly recorded as Revenue.

5. Paid $750 for an insurance policy that was incorrectly recorded as insurance expense.

Requirements

1. What are the correct debit and credit balances?

2. Does each error change the overall debit and credit balance?

3. What is the impact on each of the Assets, Liabilities, and Shareholders' Equity accounts due to the errors?

EXERCISES (ALTERNATES 1, 2, AND 3)

These alternative exercise sets are available for your practice benefit on **MyAccountingLab**.

PROBLEMS (GROUP A)

P2-1A. Journalizing transactions (*Learning Objective 3*) 15–20 min.

Allison Marshall practices law under the business title Allison Marshall, Lawyer, Inc. During April, her law practice engaged in the following transactions:

Apr	1	Sold $40,000 of common shares to Marshall to start the business.
	3	Paid $600 for the purchase of office supplies.
	8	Paid $28,000 cash to purchase land for an office site.
	12	Purchased office equipment on account, $1,800.
	17	Borrowed $5,000 from the bank. Marshall signed a note payable to the bank in the name of the business.
	26	Paid $2,600 on account.

30	Revenues earned during the month included $15,000 cash and $27,000 on account.
30	Paid employees' salaries, $2,900; office rent, $1,400; and utilities, $700.
30	Paid $9,000 of dividends to shareholder, Marshall.

Marshall's business uses the following accounts: Cash, Accounts Receivable, Supplies, Land, Office Equipment, Accounts Payable, Notes Payable, Common Shares, Dividends, Service Revenue, Salaries Expense, Rent Expense, and Utilities Expense.

Requirement

1. Journalize each transaction. Omit explanations.

P2-2A. Journalizing transactions (*Learning Objective 3*) 15–20 min.

Advantage Advertising, Inc. engaged in the following business transactions during November of 2015:

Nov 1	Borrowed $200,000 from First National Bank. The company president signed a note payable to the bank in the name of Advantage Advertising, Inc.
3	Paid $145,000 cash to purchase an office building.
6	Provided services to customers on account, $14,700.
9	Purchased $1,600 of office supplies on account.
13	Provided services to cash customers, $8,100.
15	Paid $6,000 of dividends to company shareholders.
17	Received payment on account from credit customers, $6,600.
18	Paid property tax expense on office building, $1,600.
22	Paid employee salaries, $2,800.
26	Paid cash to purchase supplies, $700.
30	Paid $2,000 on account.

Advantage Advertising, Inc. uses the following accounts: Cash, Accounts Receivable, Supplies, Building, Accounts Payable, Notes Payable, Common Shares, Dividends, Sales Revenue, Salaries Expense, and Property Tax Expense.

Requirement

1. Journalize each transaction. Omit explanations.

P2-3A. Journalizing, posting, and trial balance preparation (*Learning Objectives 3 & 4*) 20–25 min.

Fang Sun opened a financial services firm on March 1, 2015. During the month of March, the business completed the following transactions:

Mar 1	The business sold $40,000 shares to open the firm, Sun & Associates, Inc.
3	Purchased supplies, $400, and furniture, $2,100, on account.
5	Performed financial service for a client and received cash, $1,700.
8	Paid cash to acquire land for a future office site, $18,000.
11	Prepared tax returns for a client on account, $500.
14	Paid assistant's salary, $1,100.
16	Paid for the furniture purchased March 3 on account.
19	Received $800 cash for accounting services performed.
23	Billed a client for $1,300 of accounting services.
28	Received $300 from client on account.
31	Paid assistant's salary, $900.
31	Paid rent expense, $1,200.
31	Paid $1,800 of dividends.

Requirements

1. Open, or set up, the following T-accounts: Cash, Accounts Receivable, Supplies, Furniture, Land, Accounts Payable, Common Shares, Dividends, Service Revenue, Salaries Expense, and Rent Expense.

2. Journalize transactions. Explanations are not required.

3. Post the transactions to the T-accounts, using transaction dates as posting references.

4. Calculate the balance in each account.

5. Prepare the trial balance for Sun & Associates, Inc. at the end of March.

P2-4A. Journalizing, posting, and trial balance preparation (*Learning Objectives 3 & 4*) 25–30 min.

The trial balance for TDR Systems, Inc. at July 15, 2015, follows:

	TDR Systems, Inc. Trial Balance July 15, 2015		
ACCT #	**ACCOUNT**	**DEBIT**	**CREDIT**
110	Cash	$ 3,500	
112	Accounts Receivable	7,700	
115	Supplies	700	
140	Equipment	13,200	
210	Accounts Payable		$ 4,500
311	Common Shares		20,000
315	Dividends	2,600	
411	Service Revenues		6,700
511	Salaries Expense	2,200	
515	Rent Expense	1,300	
	Total	$31,200	$31,200

During the remainder of July, TDR Systems, Inc. completed the following transactions:

Jul 16	Collected $2,500 cash from a client on account.
18	Performed services on account, $1,900.
21	Received $1,700 cash for services performed.
23	Purchased supplies on account, $600.
25	Paid $1,400 in dividends.
27	Paid $3,200 on account.
29	Received $2,900 cash for services performed.
30	Paid rent, $1,200.
30	Paid employees' salaries, $2,500.

Quick solution:

2. Cash balance = $2,300;

3. Trial balance totals = $35,100

Requirements

1. Journalize the transactions that occurred July 16 to July 30.

2. Open the ledger accounts listed in the trial balance together with their beginning balances at July 15. Use the four-column account format illustrated in the chapter. Enter "Bal" for the previous balance in the Item column. Post the transactions to the ledger using dates, account numbers, and posting references. Calculate the new account balances.

3. Prepare the trial balance for TDR Systems, Inc. at the end of July.

P2-5A. Prepare a trial balance, income statement, statement of changes in equity, and statement of financial position (*Learning Objective 4*) 20–25 min.

The accounts of Cascade Consulting, Inc. follow with their normal balances at December 31, 2015. The accounts are listed in no particular order.

Account	Balance
Common Shares	$ 65,000
Insurance Expense	1,700
Accounts Payable	3,700
Service Revenue	83,000
Land	24,000
Supplies Expense	2,800
Cash	8,300
Salaries Expense	51,000
Building	110,000
Rent Expense	12,800
Dividends	13,500
Utilities Expense	6,400
Retained Earnings	9,700
Accounts Receivable	6,500
Notes Payable	76,000
Supplies	400

Requirements

1. Prepare the company's trial balance at December 31, 2015, listing accounts in the proper order. List the largest expense first, the second-largest expense next, and so on.

2. Prepare the financial statements: income statement, statement of changes in equity, and statement of financial position. The retained earnings balance of $9,700 is the beginning balance for the year; it has not been updated for the current year's income or loss.

3. Was it a profitable year for Cascade Consulting, Inc.? Why or why not?

P2-6A. Error correction (*Learning Objective 4*) 15–20 min.

The following errors occurred in the accounting records of Pacific Outfitters, Inc.:

a. The company accountant recorded the receipt of cash for service revenue by debiting Cash for $890 instead of the correct amount of $980. Service Revenue was also credited for $890, the incorrect amount.

b. A $270 purchase of supplies on account was recorded by debiting Accounts Payable and crediting Supplies.

c. The company accountant recorded a $1,200 payment of rent by debiting rent expense for $12,000 and crediting Cash for $12,000.

d. In recording an $850 payment on account, Accounts Receivable was debited and Cash was credited.

Requirements

1. Prepare the necessary journal entries to correct each of these errors.

2. For each of the errors, determine if the error would cause net income to be overstated, understated, or unchanged.

P2-7A. Explaining the effects of transactions on accounts using T-accounts, inferring the missing amount, and preparing a trial balance (*Learning Objectives 3 & 4*) 20–25 min.

The following transactions occurred during March 2015 from KopyKat, Inc.'s operations:

Cash	
5,000	2,500
(1)	900
4,100	

Accounts Payable	
900	2,400
	(4)
	2,700

Revenue	
	(2)

Accounts Receivable	
2,400	
(2)	5,000
2,300	

Unearned Revenue	
	(1)

Utilities Expense	
(4)	

Equipment	
3,200	
(3)	
?	

Note Payable	
2,500	3,200
	(3)
	4,700

Requirements

1. For each T-account, calculate the missing amount.
2. Explain transactions (1) to (4), which resulted in the entries in the T-accounts.
3. Prepare the trial balance for KopyKat, Inc. at the end of March.

P2-8A. Journalizing, trial balance, income statement, statement of changes in equity preparation (*Learning Objectives 3 & 4*) 30–40 min.

Gleaner Advertising, Inc.'s trial balance on September 30, 2015, shows the following:

	Gleaner Advertising, Inc. Trial Balance September 30, 2015		
ACCT #	**ACCOUNT TITLE**	**DEBIT**	**CREDIT**
1010	Cash	$ 8,600	
1020	Accounts Receivable	4,200	
1030	Prepaid Insurance	1,200	
1040	Prepaid Rent		
1400	Equipment	42,000	
2010	Accounts Payable		$ 5,000
2020	Unearned Advertising Revenue		3,000
2100	Long-term Note Payable		32,000
3010	Preferred Shares		
3015	Common Shares (5,000 shares)		10,000
3030	Retained Earnings		6,000
3040	Dividends		
4010	Advertising Revenue		
5010	Advertising Expense		
5020	Salaries Expense		
5030	Rent Expense		
	Total	$56,000	$56,000

Gleaner completed the following transactions in October:

Oct	2	Paid three months rent for $1,200/month.
	3	Signed a contract for $1,800/month for four months with a local radio station for radio ads.
	10	Sold 2,000 common shares for $5,000 and 3,000 preferred shares for $9,000.
	14	Paid half of the accounts payable owed to suppliers.
	20	Received $6,500 cash for advertising project from a client. The project will start in November.
	30	The advertising revenue for October was $9,300, of which two-thirds was on account.
	31	Received an invoice for $1,800 from the local radio station for the radio ads for October. The payment is due on November 7.
	31	Paid $4,300 for employee salaries.
	31	Paid $2,400 dividends to shareholders.

Requirements

1. Set up T-accounts with the beginning balances for each account.

2. Journalize the above transactions and post to the appropriate T-accounts.

3. Prepare the trial balance on October 31, 2015.

4. Prepare the income statement and the statement of changes in equity for the month of October.

PROBLEMS (GROUP B)

P2-1B. Journalizing transactions (*Learning Objective 3*) 15–20 min.

Avery Alton practices law under the business title Avery Alton, Lawyer, Inc. During September, her law practice engaged in the following transactions:

Sep	1	Sold $50,000 of common shares to Alton to start the business.
	3	Paid $300 for the purchase of office supplies.
	8	Paid $32,000 cash to purchase land for an office site.
	12	Purchased office equipment on account, $3,000.
	17	Borrowed $45,000 from the bank. Alton signed a note payable to the bank in the name of the business.
	26	Paid $2,500 on account.
	30	Service Revenues earned during the month included $9,000 cash and $11,000 on account.
	30	Paid employees' salaries, $2,650; office rent, $1,200; and utilities, $600.
	30	Paid $2,500 of dividends to shareholder, Alton.

Alton's business uses the following accounts: Cash, Accounts Receivable, Supplies, Land, Office Equipment, Accounts Payable, Notes Payable, Common Shares, Dividends, Service Revenue, Salaries Expense, Rent Expense, and Utilities Expense.

Requirement

1. Journalize each transaction. Omit explanations.

P2-2B. Journalizing transactions (*Learning Objective 3*) 15–20 min.

Tip Top Advertising, Inc. engaged in the following business transactions during July of 2015:

Jul	1	Borrowed $190,000 from Oakville Bank. The company president signed a note payable to the bank in the name of Tip Top Advertising, Inc.
	3	Paid $110,000 cash to purchase an office building.
	6	Provided services to customers on account, $18,400.
	9	Purchased $1,200 of office supplies on account.
	13	Provided services to cash customers, $8,500.
	15	Paid $3,000 of dividends to company shareholders.
	17	Received payment on account from credit customers, $2,900.
	18	Paid property tax expense on office building, $1,400.
	22	Paid employee salaries, $3,150.
	26	Paid cash to purchase supplies, $500.
	31	Paid $2,200 on account.

Tip Top Advertising, Inc. uses the following accounts: Cash, Accounts Receivable, Supplies, Building, Accounts Payable, Notes Payable, Common Shares, Dividends, Sales Revenue, Salaries Expense, and Property Tax Expense.

Requirement

1. Journalize each transaction. Omit explanations.

P2-3B. Journalizing, posting, and trial balance preparation (*Learning Objectives 3 & 4*) 20–25 min.

Teddy Sargent opened an accounting firm on May 1, 2015. During the month of May the business completed the following transactions:

May	1	The business sold $80,000 of shares to open the firm, Sargent & Associates, Inc.
	3	Purchased supplies, $500, and furniture, $1,200, on account.
	5	Performed accounting service for a client and received cash, $2,700.
	8	Paid cash to acquire land for a future office site, $22,000.
	11	Prepared tax returns for a client on account, $2,500.
	14	Paid assistant's salary, $1,200.
	16	Paid for the furniture purchased May 3 on account.
	19	Received $700 cash for accounting services performed.
	23	Billed a client for $1,300 of accounting services.
	28	Received $400 from client on account.
	31	Paid assistant's salary, $1,200.
	31	Paid rent expense, $1,700.
	31	Paid $1,200 of dividends.

Requirements

1. Open, or set up, the following T-accounts: Cash, Accounts Receivable, Supplies, Furniture, Land, Accounts Payable, Common Shares, Dividends, Service Revenue, Salaries Expense, and Rent Expense.
2. Journalize transactions. Explanations are not required.
3. Post the transactions to the T-accounts, using transaction dates as posting references.
4. Calculate the balance in each account.
5. Prepare the trial balance for Sargent & Associates, Inc. at the end of May.

**P2-4B. Journalizing, posting, and trial balance preparation (*Learning Objectives 3 & 4*)
25–30 min.**

The trial balance for BFF Systems, Inc. at March 15, 2015, follows:

BFF Systems, Inc.
Trial Balance
March 15, 2015

ACCT #	ACCOUNT	DEBIT	CREDIT
1010	Cash	$ 4,400	
1020	Accounts Receivable	8,900	
1030	Supplies	100	
1040	Equipment	16,000	
2010	Accounts Payable		$ 4,100
3010	Common Shares		23,900
3020	Dividends	2,800	
4010	Service Revenue		7,700
5010	Salaries Expense	2,200	
5050	Rent Expense	1,300	
	Total	$35,700	$35,700

During the remainder of March, BFF Systems, Inc. completed the following transactions:

Mar 16	Collected $1,700 cash from a client on account.
18	Performed services on account, $1,900.
21	Received $1,500 cash for services performed.
23	Purchased supplies on account, $700.
25	Paid $1,300 in dividends.
27	Paid $3,300 on account.
29	Received $2,500 cash for services performed.
30	Paid rent, $1,600.
30	Paid employees' salaries, $2,600.

Requirements

1. Journalize the transactions that occurred March 16 to March 30 in the journal.

2. Open the ledger accounts listed in the trial balance together with their beginning balances at March 15, 2015. Use the four-column account format illustrated in the chapter. Enter "Bal." for the previous balance in the Item column. Post the transactions to the ledger, using dates, account numbers, and posting references. Calculate the new account balances.

3. Prepare the trial balance for BFF Systems, Inc. at the end of March.

P2-5B. Prepare a trial balance, income statement, statement of changes in equity, and statement of financial position (*Learning Objective 4*) 20–25 min.

The accounts of Highland Consulting, Inc. follow with their normal balances at August 31, 2015. The accounts are listed in no particular order.

Account	Balance
Common Shares	$107,700
Insurance Expense	1,300
Accounts Payable	4,000
Service Revenue	86,500
Land	89,000
Supplies Expense	3,100
Cash	9,200
Salaries Expense	56,000
Building	91,000
Rent Expense	8,700
Dividends	10,000
Utilities Expense	5,400
Retained Earnings	13,600
Accounts Receivable	5,500
Notes Payable	68,000
Supplies	600

Requirements

1. Prepare the company's trial balance at August 31, 2015, listing accounts in the proper order. For the expenses, list the largest expense first, the second-largest expense next, and so on.

2. Prepare the financial statements: income statement, statement of changes in equity, and statement of financial position. The retained earnings balance of $13,600 is the beginning balance for the year; it has not been updated for the current year's net income or loss.

3. Was it a profitable year for Highland Consulting, Inc.? Why or why not?

P2-6B. Error correction (*Learning Objective 4*) 15–20 min.

The following errors occurred in the accounting records of Over Side, Inc.:

a. The company accountant recorded the receipt of cash for service revenue by debiting Cash for $1,140 instead of the correct amount of $1,410. Service revenue was also credited for $1,140, the incorrect amount.

b. A $150 purchase of supplies on account was recorded by debiting Accounts Payable and crediting Supplies.

c. The company accountant recorded an $800 payment of rent by debiting Rent Expense for $8,000 and crediting Cash for $8,000.

d. In recording an $815 payment on account, Accounts Receivable was debited and Cash was credited.

Requirements

1. Prepare the necessary journal entries to correct each of these errors.

2. For each of the errors, determine if the error would cause net income to be overstated, understated, or unchanged.

P2-7B. Explaining the effects of transactions on accounts using T-accounts, inferring the missing amount, and preparing a trial balance (*Learning Objectives 3 & 4*) 20–25 min.

The following transactions occurred during July 2015 from Dragon Boat, Inc.'s operations:

Cash	
2,000	2,500
5,900	800
	(4)
1,600	

Accounts Payable	
800	1,300
	(2)
	2,100

Revenue	
	(1)

Accounts Receivable	
2,400	
(1)	5,900
2,300	

Salaries Payable	
2,500	4,400
	(3)
	6,100

Salaries Expense	
(3)	

Supplies	
1,300	
(2)	
2,900	

Dividends	
(4)	

Requirements

1. For each T-account, calculate the missing amount.
2. Explain transactions (1) to (4), which resulted in the entries in the T-accounts.
3. Prepare the trial balance for Dragon Boat, Inc. at the end of July.

P2-8B. Journalizing, trial balance, income statement, statement of changes in equity preparation (*Learning Objectives 3 & 4*) 30–40 min.

Smile Maids, Inc.'s trial balance on February 28, 2015, shows the following:

Smile Maids, Inc.
Trial Balance
February 28, 2015

ACCT #	ACCOUNT TITLE	DEBIT	CREDIT
1010	Cash	$ 7,200	
1020	Accounts Receivable	3,800	
1030	Cleaning Supplies	500	
1040	Prepaid Rent		
1400	Truck	52,000	
2010	Accounts Payable		$ 6,600
2020	Unearned Cleaning Revenue		4,400
2100	Long-term Note Payable		34,000
3010	Preferred Shares		
3015	Common Shares (4,000 shares)		12,000
3030	Retained Earnings		6,500
3040	Dividends		
4010	Cleaning Revenue		
5010	Cleaning Supplies Expense		
5020	Salaries Expense		
5030	Rent Expense		
	Total	$63,500	$63,500

Smile Maids, Inc. completed the following transactions in March:

Mar 2	Signed a contract worth $1,200/month for a year to provide cleaning service to an office building.
3	Paid one third of amount owing to the suppliers.
4	Paid four months rent in advance, $1,500 per month.
10	Sold 2,000 common shares for $6,800, and 2,500 preferred shares for $10,000.
14	Ordered cleaning supplies, $3,400.
20	Received $4,800 cash from a client for cleaning services starting in April for 3 months.
25	Received cleaning supplies ordered on the fourteenth; half of the supplies were used. The invoice will be paid on April 7.
30	The cleaning revenue for March was $8,400, of which one quarter was on account.
31	Paid $3,600 for employee salaries.
31	Paid $1,800 dividends to shareholders.

Requirements

1. Set up T-accounts with the beginning balances for each account.

2. Journalize the above transactions and post to the appropriate T-accounts.

3. Prepare the trial balance on March 31, 2015.

4. Prepare the income statement and the statement of changes in equity for the month of March.

PROBLEMS (ALTERNATES 1, 2, AND 3)

These alternative problem sets are available for your practice benefit on **MyAccountingLab**.

CONTINUING EXERCISE

This exercise continues with the business of Graham's Yard Care, Inc. begun in the Continuing Exercise in Chapter 1. Here you will account for Graham's Yard Care, Inc.'s transactions in the general journal. Graham's Yard Care, Inc. completed the following transactions during June:

Jun 1	Received $1,000 and issued 100 common shares. Deposited this amount in bank account titled Graham's Yard Care, Inc.
3	Purchased on account a mower, $1,000, and weed whacker, $400. The equipment is expected to remain in service for four years.
5	Purchased $20 of gas. Wrote cheque #1 from the new bank account.
6	Performed lawn services for client on account, $200.
8	Purchased $50 of fertilizer from the lawn store. Wrote cheque #2 from the new bank account.
17	Completed landscaping job for client, received cash $500.
30	Received $50 on account from June 6 sale.

Requirements

1. Open T-accounts in the ledger: Cash, Accounts Receivable, Lawn Supplies, Equipment, Accounts Payable, Common Shares, Retained Earnings, Service Revenue, and Fuel Expense.

2. Journalize the transactions. Explanations are not required.

3. Post to the T-accounts. Key all items by date and denote an account balance as "Bal." Formal posting references are not required.

4. Prepare a trial balance at June 30, 2015.

CONTINUING PROBLEM

This problem continues with the business of Aqua Elite, Inc. begun in the Continuing Problem in Chapter 1. Here you will account for Aqua Elite, Inc.'s transactions using formal accounting practices. The trial balance for Aqua Elite, Inc. as of May 31, 2015, is presented below.

Aqua Elite, Inc.
Trial Balance
May 31, 2015

ACCOUNT	DEBIT	CREDIT
Cash	$24,475	
Accounts Receivable	1,200	
Supplies	860	
Equipment	4,700	
Vehicles	31,000	
Accounts Payable		$ 840
Notes Payable		31,000
Common Shares		28,500
Dividends	1,000	
Service Revenues		4,050
Salaries Expense	675	
Utilities Expense	480	
Total	$64,390	$64,390

During June the following transactions occurred:

Jun 1	Paid receptionist's salary, $675.
2	Paid cash to acquire land for a future office site, $15,000.
3	Moved into a new location for the business and paid the first month's rent, $1,800.
4	Performed service for a customer and received cash, $1,700.
5	Received $500 on account.
8	Purchased $750 of supplies on account.
11	Billed customers for services performed, $3,800.
13	Sold an additional $10,000 of common shares to Mike Hanson.
16	Paid receptionist's salary, $675.
17	Received $1,350 cash for services performed.
18	Received $1,500 from customers on account.
19	Paid $325 to be listed in the Yellow Pages telephone directory.
21	Paid $1,000 on account.
22	Purchased office furniture on account, $3,300.
24	Paid miscellaneous expenses, $275.
26	Billed customers for services provided, $1,100.
28	Received $300 from customers on account.
30	Paid utility bill, $745.
30	Paid receptionist's salary, $675.
30	Paid $1,800 of dividends.

Requirements

1. Journalize the transactions that occurred in June. Omit explanations.
2. Open the ledger accounts listed in the trial balance together with their beginning balances at May 31. Use the four-column account format illustrated in the chapter. Enter "Bal" for the previous balance in the Item column. Post the transactions to the ledger creating new ledger accounts as necessary, omitting posting references. Calculate the new account balances.
3. Prepare the trial balance for Aqua Elite, Inc. at the end of June.

APPLY YOUR KNOWLEDGE

ETHICS IN ACTION

Case 1. Jamie Hanson was recording the daily transactions of Alpine Physical Therapy, Inc. into the accounting records so she could prepare financial statements and apply for a bank loan. Some of the business expenses were higher than she had expected, and Jamie was worried about the effect of these expenses on net income. Jamie was recording a $5,000 payment for legal fees incurred by the business by debiting Legal Expense and crediting Cash to properly record the journal entry. She then thought that, rather than debiting the expense account for the $5,000 payment, she could debit the Dividends account, which also had a normal debit balance. Jamie knew that debits had to equal credits so debiting the Dividends account instead of the Legal Expense account would not affect the trial balance. Further, the net income would be $5,000 higher because now no legal expense would be recorded. She thought that either way the retained earnings would be lower, and besides, it really didn't matter how the $5,000 payment was shown as long as she showed it somewhere.

Should Jamie debit the Dividends account rather than the Legal Expense account? Do you agree with her thought that it really doesn't matter how the $5,000 payment is shown as long as it is shown somewhere? Considering that Jamie owns all of Alpine Physical Therapy, Inc.'s common shares, does she have any ethical responsibilities to properly record each business transaction?

Case 2. Jim Peterson is the accountant for ProCare Lawnservice, Inc. During the month, numerous payments were made for wages and, therefore, he was properly debiting the Wage Expense account and crediting Cash. Jim became concerned that if he kept debiting the Wage Expense account it would end up with a balance much higher than any of the other expense accounts. Accordingly, he began debiting other expense accounts for some of the wage payments and thus "spread the expenses around" to other expense accounts. When he was done posting all the journal entries to the ledger accounts, he printed a trial balance. He saw that the Wage Expense debit balance was $38,000 and the total of all the other expense accounts was $24,000. Had he properly posted all the wage expense transactions, Wage Expense would have totalled $52,000 and the other expense accounts would have totalled $10,000. Jim reasoned that his actions provided for "more balanced" expense account totals and, regardless of his postings, the total expenses were still $62,000, so the overall net income would be the same.

Were Jim's actions justified? Do they cause any ethical concerns? If you were the owner of ProCare Lawnservice, Inc. would you have a problem with what Jim did?

KNOW YOUR BUSINESS

FINANCIAL ANALYSIS

Purpose: To help familiarize you with the financial reporting of companies to further your understanding of the chapter material you are learning.

Although we do not have access to the journals used by Bombardier Inc., we can still understand various business transactions that Bombardier Inc. had as seen on the financial statements in its annual report. Refer to Bombardier's income statements (Consolidated Earnings), and Bombardier's balance sheet in MyAccountingLab. Assume Bombardier completed the following transactions during January 2012:

Jan 3	Purchased $485,000 of equipment for cash.
7	Paid cash for $45,000 of employee wages.
10	Purchased materials to be used directly in the manufacturing of aircraft inventory of $500,000 on account.
15	Made $642,000 of sales on account.
29	Paid $167,500 on account from the January 10 purchase.

Requirements

1. Prepare journal entries to record the transactions listed. Use the account titles found in the Bombardier Inc. financial statements: Cash and Cash Equivalents; Receivables; PP&E (Plant, Property and Equipment); Accounts Payable and Accrued Liabilities; and Revenues.

2. Look at the financial statements and locate the accounts that you included in your journal entries. Note that the balances Bombardier Inc. reported include millions of dollars in transactions for the year. Imagine how much activity and how many transactions Bombardier has every day!

INDUSTRY ANALYSIS

Purpose: To help you understand and compare the performance of two companies in the same industry.

Go to the Bombardier Inc. annual report located in MyAccountingLab. Now access the 2012 Annual Report for The Boeing Company. To do this from the internet, go to their webpage for Investor Relations at http://www.boeing.com/companyoffices/financial/quarterly.htm and under Annual Reports, download the annual report for the year ended December 31, 2012.

Requirements

Answer these questions about the two companies:

1. In terms of total revenue, which is the larger company? Which financial statement did you look at to find that information?

2. In terms of total assets, which is the larger company? Which financial statement did you look at to find that information?

3. Which company has more total debt? Which financial statement did you look at to find that information?

4. Which company has the higher gross profit percentage? Don't know that one? On the Consolidated Statements of Income, calculate the Gross Profit by taking Total Revenues minus Total Cost of Sales for Bombardier. For Boeing,

Gross Profit is represented by the Income from Operating Investments. Determine the gross profit percentage by taking Gross Profit divided by Total Revenues. What does it mean to have a higher gross profit percentage? What might affect this percentage for these two companies?

5. Who paid more cash dividends to its shareholders in the past year? Which financial statement did you look at to find that information?

6. Based on this preliminary information, which company's shares would you prefer to own? Why?

SMALL BUSINESS ANALYSIS

Purpose: To help you understand the importance of cash flows in the operation of a small business.

You're sitting in your CA office late on a Friday afternoon when you get an email from a friend. You know that she has been working on setting up a new accounting system in her office for a new business that she just started. You figured that this would eventually generate some communication between the two of you because you know that she has relatively limited accounting knowledge. Here's her email to you.

"Jerry, I'm pretty frustrated right now! As you know, I've been installing this new accounting system here in the office and I've run into a problem. I don't understand this cash account. I have purchased some items on my debit card and I've purchased some items on my credit card. So logically, when I purchased the items on my debit card, I debited the cash account. But when I used my credit card, it made sense to credit my cash account. And to make things even worse, my cash account ends up with a credit balance, and I'm pretty sure that's not right. This is too confusing and it's Friday afternoon; I'm going home!"

The following journal entries were attached to your friend's email.

DATE	ACCOUNTS	POST REF.	DR.	CR.
May 5	Cash		400	
	Supplies			400
	Purchased supplies using debit card.			

DATE	ACCOUNTS	POST REF.	DR.	CR.
May 6	Utilities Expense		250	
	Cash			250
	Paid utilities bill using credit card.			

Requirement

1. Since cash is the lifeblood of any business, having a correct balance in the cash account is of utmost importance. Correctly entering cash transactions is equally as important. Suggest to your friend the corrections that need to be made to the journal entries she made.

WRITTEN COMMUNICATION

Consider the situation that was presented in the Small Business Analysis. Your friend had two concerns that she asked you about. The first one is that she was concerned that her cash balance was showing as a credit balance instead of a debit balance. And even after the corrections were made, the cash balance was still a credit. The second concern she had was how to record transactions when she uses her debit card as opposed to transactions when she uses her credit card.

Write a short memo or letter to your friend addressing these two situations and what you would consider to be the proper accounting treatment for each of the two. More specifically, if the cash account was showing as a credit balance, how would that have happened? Is it possible for that to happen? And regarding the use of the debit card versus the credit card, from the information contained in the chapter, explain the difference between the two types of cards and how each transaction should be recorded from an accounting point of view.

Self Check Answers
1. c 2. a 3. d 4. c 5. b 6. c 7. c 8. d 9. a 10. c

LEARNING OBJECTIVES

1. Understand the time period assumption and differentiate between revenue and expense recognition under both accrual and cash basis accounting

2. Understand the four types of adjustments and prepare adjusting entries

3. Prepare financial statements from an adjusted trial balance

4. Prepare closing entries and a post-closing trial balance

5. Prepare a worksheet

CHAPTER OUTLINE

HOW Does a Company Accurately Report Its Income? p. 136

WHAT Is the Role of Adjusting Entries, and When Are They Prepared? p. 140

HOW Are Financial Statements Prepared from an Adjusted Trial Balance? p. 152

HOW Does a Company Prepare for a New Accounting Period? p. 155

CHAPTER 3

Adjusting and Closing Entries

BUSINESS, ACCOUNTING, AND YOU

It's year end and closing time at Best Buy. Everyone has worked hard. Millions of transactions have occurred and been recorded by the accountants, and it's time to wrap up the year and tabulate the score for Best Buy. How does Best Buy conclude a year's activities and prepare for a new year? There has to be an end for a new beginning.

Think of a sporting event, where there must be an end to the game. At the end of the game the scorekeeper must make sure the score properly reflects what happened. Accountants are the scorekeepers of the business, and they have things to do at the end of a period of time. They may need to go back and make sure they have recognized, measured, and reported all the business's transactions properly; given IFRS or ASPE rules, they may need to adjust the scorecard to better reflect what happened. They then need to summarize the transactions and prepare the final reports.

Whether you are an accountant or a manager who uses accounting information, you need to understand the process used by accountants to adjust and conclude (close) a business's financial records. Why? Because they affect the reports used to manage the business—they affect the final score used to judge a business's success.

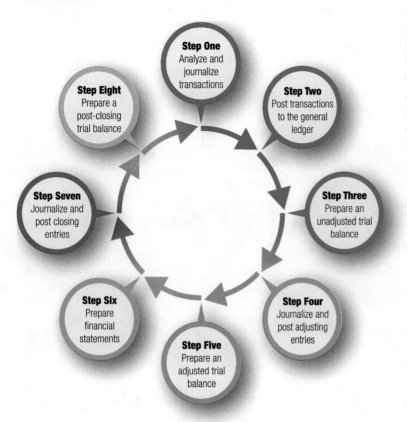

In Chapter 2, we learned about journalizing and posting transactions for a business as well as how to prepare a trial balance and financial statements. These were steps one, two, three, and six of the accounting cycle, as you can see in the visual representation. Here in Chapter 3, we will learn how to prepare steps four to eight.

HOW DOES A COMPANY ACCURATELY REPORT ITS INCOME?

THE TIME PERIOD ASSUMPTION

L.O. ❶ Understand the time period assumption and differentiate between revenue and expense recognition under both accrual and cash basis accounting

We briefly discussed the time period assumption in Chapter 1, but now we are going to see the implications it has for revenue and expense recognition. A business usually continues for many years. Owners, managers, and other stakeholders, however, would like to know the business's financial performance (mainly net income) more frequently and in shorter periods of time. Income is directly related to a period of time—whenever you mention an income figure it should be associated with a period of time. A company cannot declare that it generated a certain amount of income without mentioning the period in which this income was generated. Accountants must make a clear cut between each period of time to be able to measure net income during such period. This period is known as the **accounting period**. The accounting period artificially divides the life of a business into smaller periods. The accounting period could cover any period of time, such as a week, month, quarter, or year. Accounting financial statements that cover periods that are less than a year are usually referred to as **interim financial statements**. Annual financial statements usually cover a **fiscal year**, which is a set of 12 successive months, and hence, could differ from or comply with a calendar year. So, if the company starts its fiscal year in January and ends it at the end of December, then the fiscal year complies with the calendar year. Other companies might have an accounting period different from the calendar year, for example starting at the beginning of July and ending at the end of June, but this is still a 12-month period. Usually, the fiscal year-end date is the low point in business activity for the year.

WHEN TO RECOGNIZE REVENUES AND EXPENSES

The **revenue recognition principle** states that revenues should be recognized, or recorded, when they are *earned* regardless of when cash is received. Revenue is earned when the business fulfills its obligation towards its client in a certain business transaction. Obligations are fulfilled in most transactions by delivering goods or providing services.

Expenses are recognized or recorded when incurred. Expenses are incurred when assets are used up in generating revenues. Hence, expenses are related to revenues, and they are recognized in the same period in which the related revenues are generated. Expenses are matched with the related revenues, which is called the **matching principle**.

CASH VERSUS ACCRUAL ACCOUNTING

It is possible for a business to record revenues and expenses only when cash is received or paid, respectively. This is referred to **cash-basis accounting**. In many instances, when a company uses cash-basis accounting its financial statements usually do not present an accurate picture of how the company is performing. This is because a business may provide goods and services to customers "on account." In this case, the business has earned revenue prior to receiving cash from the customer. A business may also purchase goods and services from suppliers on account. In this case, expenses are incurred before cash is paid, so the flow of cash does not resemble the real activity. When revenues are earned before cash is received, or expenses are incurred before cash is paid, it is called an **accrual**. We have already seen accruals in Chapter 1 and Chapter 2 when we recorded transactions in Accounts Receivable and Accounts Payable. In such cases, revenues and expenses are recorded when the services or goods are delivered or when the expense is incurred regardless of when the cash changes hands. This is referred to as *accrual-basis accounting*. So under accrual-basis accounting there are three possible scenarios of completing a business transaction: either cash is exchanged before, at the same time as, or after services are provided or goods are delivered. Let us focus on services for now.

Exhibit 3-1 illustrates the first scenario, where cash is exchanged prior to the service being provided or goods delivered.

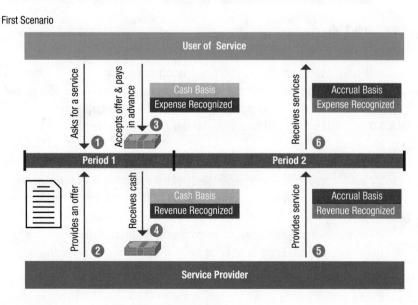

First Scenario

Exhibit 3-1 ▲

According to *cash-basis* accounting, revenues and expenses are recognized at *the time of cash transfer* regardless of when the services are provided (in Exhibit 3-1, expense is recognized for the user of service in step 3, and revenue is recognized for the service provided in step 4; in other words, recognition occurs in Period 1), while the *accrual basis* recognizes expenses and revenues based on *the timing of providing the service* regardless of the timing of transferring the cash (in Exhibit 3-1, expense is recognized for the user of service in step 5, and revenue is recognized for the service provided in step 6; in other words, in Period 2). In this case, from a service provider perspective, cash is received before revenue is earned, and therefore revenue is deferred (**unearned revenue**) until the service is provided. From a user of service perspective, payment might be paid for services prior to receiving those services from the supplier. In this case, cash is paid before an expense is incurred, and therefore the expense is deferred (prepaid) until it is consumed. When cash is received for services prior to the recognition of revenue, or cash is paid for services prior to the recognition of the expense, it is called a **deferral** (deferred revenues or deferred expenses, respectively).

Exhibit 3-2 illustrates the second scenario of completing a business transaction, where cash is exchanged at the time of providing the service.

Second Scenario

Exhibit 3-2 ▲

Both cash and accrual-basis accounting recognize revenues and expenses at the same point of time (Period 2) when cash is exchanged at the time of providing the service. In such a case there would be no difference between the two bases.

Exhibit 3-3 illustrates the third scenario, where cash is exchanged after providing the service or delivering the goods.

Since the service is provided before the cash is exchanged, accrual-basis accounting would recognize the revenues and expenses before the cash basis would. Referring to Exhibit 3-3, the service provider recognized revenue in step 4 when the service is delivered before receiving the cash in step 6 (Period 3) if *accrual-basis* accounting is implemented. However, revenue will only be recognized in step 6 (Period 3) if *cash-basis* accounting is implemented. From a user of service perspective under the *accrual basis*,

Third Scenario

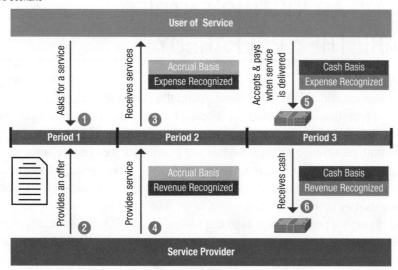

Exhibit 3-3 ▲

the expense will incur on step 3 (Period 2) when the service is used. However, under the *cash basis* the expense will only be recognized when the cash is paid in step 5 (Period 3).

Most businesses apply accrual-basis accounting because it reflects the business's performance more accurately than the cash basis since it recognizes revenues and expenses when services are provided or goods are delivered. Because the timing of transferring cash would differ from the timing of providing services or delivering goods, the cash basis would not reflect actual performance and hence it is not accurate in measuring business performance. In Exhibit 3-3, for example, all the efforts have been made in Period 2; however, the cash basis only recognized revenue in Period 3. For this reason, various accounting standards, such as IFRS and ASPE, require the use of accrual accounting. Accruals and deferrals can be summarized as follows:

3.1 **STILL** DON'T GET IT**?**
Visit MyAccountingLab for an alternate explanation of this important accounting concept.

	Now	Later
Accrued Revenue	Revenue is recognized	Cash is received
Accrued Expense	Expense is recognized	Cash is paid
Deferred (Unearned) Revenue	Cash is received	Revenue is recognized
Deferred (Prepaid) Expense	Cash is paid	Expense is recognized

As we saw in Chapter 2, a business records transactions throughout the accounting period as the transactions occur. At the end of the period, the accountant prepares a trial balance and uses it to prepare financial statements. However, before most businesses can prepare accurate, up-to-date financial statements, the accountant will have to prepare **adjusting entries**.

WHAT IS THE ROLE OF ADJUSTING ENTRIES, AND WHEN ARE THEY PREPARED?

L.O. ② Understand the four types of adjustments and prepare adjusting entries

Adjusting entries are journal entries that are needed at the end of the period to ensure that all revenues and expenses incurred during the period are recognized.

Adjustments may be needed for *accruals* when revenues have been earned or expenses incurred before cash is exchanged. Since cash has not been exchanged, it is possible that the revenue or expense has not been recorded. Hence, an adjusting entry is needed to record the revenue or expense. On the other hand, a *deferral* is created when cash is exchanged before the related revenue or expense is recognized. Adjustments may be needed for deferrals when revenues have been earned or expenses incurred during the period. Since cash has been exchanged in advance, it is possible that the revenue or expense has not been updated after being earned. **Exhibit 3-4** summarizes the required adjustments for both revenues and expenses under accrual accounting.

Exhibit 3-4 ▲

At the end of the accounting period, accountants prepare a trial balance from the account information contained in the general ledger. This trial balance lists most of the revenues and expenses of the business, but these amounts are incomplete because the adjusting entries have not yet been prepared. Therefore, this trial balance is called an **unadjusted trial balance** (step three in the accounting cycle). Remember Hooray Consulting, Inc. from Chapter 2? **Exhibit 3-5** shows the unadjusted trial balance for Hooray Consulting at the end of its first quarter of operations at March 31, 2015.

Remember from Chapter 2 that transactions are recorded in the journal and posted to accounts in the general ledger. This process is still performed when adjusting the accounts. In this chapter, we will show how to record adjusting entries and how to post them to accounts. However, instead of using the real ledger account form, we will post adjustments to T-accounts. We use this method because it is easier to see how these entries affect the specific accounts as well as the accounting equation.

ADJUSTING ENTRIES FOR EXPENSES

Expenses need adjustments if there are accrued expenses that haven't been recorded or prepaid expenses that have been used up during the period.

Hooray Consulting, Inc.
(Unadjusted) Trial Balance
March 31, 2015

ACCOUNT TITLE	BALANCE	
	DEBIT	CREDIT
Cash	$26,300	
Accounts Receivable	8,100	
Supplies	900	
Prepaid Rent	3,000	
Equipment	12,600	
Accounts Payable		$13,100
Unearned Service Revenue		450
Note Payable		5,000
Common Shares		20,000
Retained Earnings		10,150
Dividends	3,200	
Service Revenue		7,000
Salaries Expense	1,200	
Utilities Expense	400	
Total	$55,700	$55,700

Exhibit 3-5 ▲

Adjusting Accrued Expenses

If an expense is accrued and not recorded, this will result in net income being inflated since expenses would be understated. To adjust that, the accrued expense must be debited and a liability must be credited. Let's look at some examples.

Salaries Payable: Suppose Hooray Consulting pays its employee a monthly salary of $600. Hooray pays the employee on the 15th of each month for the past month's work. So, on March 15, when salaries are paid, salaries expense is debited and cash is credited. On March 31, the following adjustment must be made to record the salaries expense for March:

This is referred to as accruing the expense. **Accrued expenses**, such as the accrual for salaries expense, are expenses that the business has incurred but not paid.

Interest Payable: Businesses pay interest on loans. Interest is payable at a specific point in time, but interest accumulates during the period. At the end of the period, interest that has accumulated and not been paid should be recognized as an expense and a liability should be recorded.

Suppose Hooray Consulting, Inc. had obtained a loan for $5,000 on March 1 and signed a six-month note payable bearing interest of 6%. Interest accrues during the month, and the interest due is calculated as follows:

$$\text{Principal amount} \times \text{Interest rate} \times \text{period of time}$$
$$\$5,000 \times 6\% \times 1/12 = \$25$$

On March 31, the following adjustment must be made to record the interest expense for the month of March:

Income Tax Payable: Suppose Hooray Consulting, Inc. had calculated its taxes to be $1,058. Taxes are regarded as an expense because they decrease shareholders' equity. However, Hooray will not make the income tax payment to CRA (Canada Revenue Agency) on March 31. Therefore, Hooray needs to recognize a liability to CRA. On March 31, the following adjustment must be made to record the tax expense for the month of March:

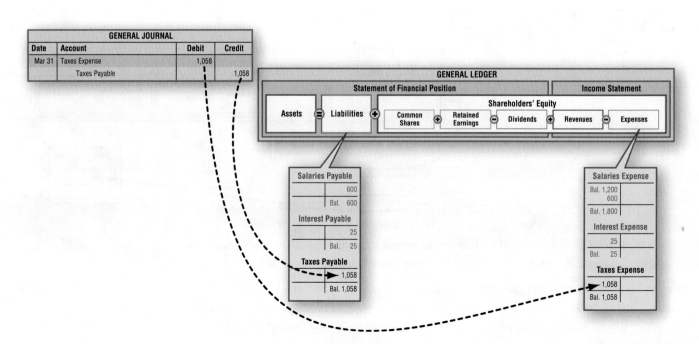

Adjusting Prepaid Expenses

When an expense is paid in advance, such as prepaid rent or prepaid insurance, an asset account is created and it is debited by the appropriate amount. Prepaid expenses, also called **deferred expenses**, represent items that are paid for before they are used; as time passes, these assets are used up. Accordingly, at the end of the period an adjusting entry is needed to reduce the asset account by crediting it and to increase the expense account by debiting it. Let's have a closer look at some types of prepaid expenses.

MEMORY TIPS

Prepaid expenses are assets.

Prepaid Rent: Suppose Hooray Consulting, Inc. moves to a new office and prepays three months' office rent on March 1, 2015. If the lease specifies a monthly rental of $1,000, the amount of cash paid is $3,000 ($1,000 × 3 months). The entry to record the payment is as follows:

DATE	ACCOUNTS	POST REF.	DR.	CR.
Mar 1	Prepaid Rent		3,000	
	Cash			3,000
	Paid three months' rent in advance.			

After posting, Prepaid Rent has a $3,000 debit balance. During March, Hooray Consulting has used the rented space for one month; therefore, the balance in Prepaid Rent is reduced by $1,000 (one month's rent). The required adjusting entry is as follows:

Assets = Liabilities + Shareholders' Equity

3,000
–3,000

The Building Rent Expense account is increased with a debit, which reduces Retained Earnings and, therefore, Shareholders' Equity. The asset account Prepaid Rent is decreased with a credit for the same amount. After posting, Prepaid Rent and Building Rent Expense show the correct ending balances.

Assets = Liabilities + Shareholders' Equity

–1,000   –1,000

If Hooray Consulting, Inc. had prepaid insurance, the same analysis would also apply to this asset account. The difference in the adjusting entry would be in the account titles, which would be Prepaid Insurance instead of Prepaid Rent and Insurance Expense instead of Building Rent Expense. The amount of the entry would also be different.

Supplies: Supplies receive the same treatment as prepaid expenses. On March 5, Hooray Consulting pays $900 for office supplies. The asset accounts Supplies and Cash are both affected—supplies increase by $900 while Cash decreases by $900, as shown here:

DATE	ACCOUNTS	POST REF.	DR.	CR.
Mar 5	Supplies		900	
	Cash			900
	Purchased office supplies.			

During March, Hooray Consulting uses some of these supplies to conduct business. Therefore, Hooray Consulting's March 31 statement of financial position should *not* report supplies of $900. To figure out the amount of supplies used, Hooray Consulting counts the supplies on hand at the end of March, which are still an asset to the business. Assume that Hooray Consulting has supplies costing $600 at March 31. The supplies purchased ($900) minus the supplies on hand at the end of March ($600) equals the value of the supplies used during the month ($300). The amount of supplies used during the month will become the Supplies Expense. The March 31 adjusting entry updates the Supplies account and records Supplies Expense for the month:

After the entry is posted to the general ledger, the correct account balances for Supplies and Supplies Expense are reflected.

Depreciation of Long-Term Assets: **Long-term assets** are assets that last for more than one year or one operating cycle, whichever is longer. Examples include land, buildings, equipment, and furniture. All of these assets (except land) are used up over time. As a long-term asset is used up, part of the asset's cost becomes an expense, just as supplies become supplies expense when they are used up. Expensing a long-term asset's cost over its useful life is called **depreciation**. No depreciation is recorded for land because it is never really used up.

We account for long-term assets in the same way as prepaid expenses and supplies because they are all assets. The major difference is the length of time it takes for the asset to be used up. Prepaid expenses and supplies are typically used within a year, while most long-term assets remain functional for several years. Suppose that on March 1 Hooray Consulting purchases equipment on account for $12,600 and records this journal entry:

DATE	ACCOUNTS	POST REF.	DR.	CR.
Mar 1	Equipment		12,600	
	Accounts Payable			12,600
	Purchased equipment on account.			

After posting the entry, the Equipment account has a $12,600 balance. It is difficult to measure the amount of a long-term asset that has been used up over time, so the amount must be estimated. Several methods can be used to estimate the amount of depreciation. The most common method, which Hooray Consulting, Inc. uses, is called the **straight-line depreciation** method. Hooray Consulting believes the equipment will be useful for three years and will be worthless and have no **salvage (or residual) value** at the end of its life. Depreciation of this equipment is calculated using the straight-line method as follows:

Assets	=	Liabilities	+	Shareholders' Equity
+12,600	=	+12,600		

$$\text{Depreciation Expense per Year} = \frac{\text{Cost of Asset} - \text{Salvage Value of Asset}}{\text{Useful Life of Asset}} = \frac{\$12,600}{3} = \$4,200$$

Because Hooray Consulting purchased the equipment in the month of March, the accountant needs to calculate one month's depreciation expense. To do so, divide the yearly depreciation by twelve ($4,200/12 months = $350).

The Accumulated Depreciation Account: The depreciation expense for March is recorded by debiting the account Depreciation Expense. However, instead of crediting the asset account (as with supplies and prepaid expenses) to reduce it, an account called **Accumulated Depreciation**—Equipment will be credited. This is because the asset itself does not vanish, as in the case of supplies.

The journal entry to record depreciation expense for the month of March is as follows:

Assets	=	Liabilities	+	Shareholders' Equity
−350				−350

Accumulated Depreciation—Equipment is a contra-asset account. A **contra-account** has three main characteristics:

- It is linked to another account and will always appear with this account in the financial statements.
- The normal balance is always opposite of the account it is linked to.
- The balance is subtracted from the balance of the account it is linked to in order to find the **net value** of the two accounts.

Because it is linked to Equipment (an asset account), Accumulated Depreciation—Equipment will appear on the statement of financial position. Being an asset, the Equipment account has a debit balance, so the Accumulated Depreciation—Equipment account will have a credit balance because it is a contra-asset account. Since it's a contra-account, the balance of Accumulated Depreciation—Equipment is subtracted from Equipment. The net amount of a long-term asset is called its **book value**, or **carrying value**, and is calculated as follows:

Book Value of a Long-Term Asset		
Cost	Equipment...	$12,600
− Accumulated Depreciation	Less: Accumulated Depreciation, Equipment.........	350
= Book (or Carrying) Value	Book Value...	$12,250

Accumulated Depreciation—Equipment increases over the life of the asset as the asset is used up, which reduces the book value of the equipment. By keeping the cost of the equipment separate from its accumulated depreciation, financial statement users can look at the Equipment account to see how much the asset originally cost and also look at the Accumulated Depreciation—Equipment account to see how much of the original cost has been used up. A business usually keeps an Accumulated Depreciation account for each type of depreciable long-term asset. If Hooray Consulting, Inc. had both buildings and equipment, it would use two Accumulated Depreciation accounts: Accumulated Depreciation—Buildings and Accumulated Depreciation—Equipment. Depreciation will be covered in more depth in Chapter 8.

An Alternate Way to Record Prepaid Expenses

Some accountants would find it more practical to record some prepaid expenses as expenses when they are first paid. If the prepaid expense is consumed totally during the period, then the accountant doesn't need to do any adjustments. However, if it is not totally consumed, an adjusting entry is required. To illustrate, assume that a company bought supplies on March 1 for $500 in cash. The accountant would record the total amount as an expense as follows:

DATE	ACCOUNTS	POST REF.	DR.	CR.
Mar 1	Supplies Expense		500	
	Cash			500
	Purchase of supplies to be used during the period.			

On March 31, a physical count is taken and if the supplies are used up, then nothing further is required to be done. However, let's assume that $200 worth of supplies are left. In such a case, an adjusting entry is required to recognize the existence of supplies as an asset and to decrease the expense which is now overstated by $200. The following entry is required:

DATE	ACCOUNTS	POST REF.	DR.	CR.
Mar 31	Supplies		200	
	Supplies Expense			200
	Adjusting the supplies expense and recognizing the supplies on hand.			

The previous entry increased the assets (in the form of supplies) by the amount of supplies on hand, and decreased the expense Supplies Expense (hence increasing shareholder's equity) since the Supplies Expense account was previously debited by $500, while it should be debited by $300 only. The following T-account shows the balance of the Supplies Expense account after the adjustments are done:

Supplies Expense			
Mar 1	$500	Mar 31 Adj.	$200
Mar 31 Bal.	$300		

Assets = Liabilities + Shareholders' Equity

+200 =   +200

3.2 **STILL** DON'T GET IT**?**
Visit MyAccountingLab for an alternate explanation of this important accounting concept.

 CONCEPT CHECK...

Jim Oda is the accountant for Crazy Critters, Inc., a local veterinary clinic. After Jim finished preparing the financial statements for the year, he realized that he had failed to make an adjusting entry to record $1,800 of depreciation expense for the year. What effect does this error have on Crazy Critter's financial statements?

Answer: To determine the effect of omitting an adjusting entry, we must examine what the adjusting entry should have been. The adjusting entry Jim should have recorded is as follows:

DATE	ACCOUNTS	POST REF.	DR.	CR.
	Depreciation Expense		1,800	
	Accumulated Depreciation			1,800

As we can see from the journal entry, Depreciation Expense should have been debited (increased), which would have increased total expenses for the year. An increase in total expenses causes a decrease in net income. So the omission of the adjusting entry for depreciation expense causes net income, and therefore retained earnings, to be overstated. We also see that the Accumulated Depreciation account should have been credited (increased), which would cause total assets to decrease because Accumulated Depreciation is a contra-asset account. So the omission of the adjusting entry for depreciation expense also causes the total assets to be overstated.

Assets = Liabilities + Shareholders' Equity

−1,800 =   −1,800

ADJUSTING ENTRIES FOR REVENUES

Revenues need adjustments if there are accrued revenues that haven't yet been recorded or if there are unearned revenues that have either partially or totally been earned during the period. Let's have a closer look at some types of accrued revenues.

L.O. **2**   Understand the four types of adjustments and prepare adjusting entries

Accounts Receivable

Businesses sometimes earn revenue by providing goods or services before they receive cash. Assume that a local car dealership hires Hooray Consulting, Inc. on March 15 as a computer consultant. Hooray Consulting, Inc. agrees to a monthly fee of $500, which the car dealership pays on the 15th of each month beginning on April 15. During March, Hooray earns half a month's fee, $250 ($500 × 1/2 month), for consulting work performed March 15 through March 31. On March 31, Hooray makes the following adjusting entry to reflect the accrual of the revenue earned during March (the beginning balance of each account is found on the unadjusted trial balance presented in Exhibit 3-5):

Without the adjustment, Hooray Consulting's financial statements are inaccurate because they would understate both Accounts Receivable and Service Revenue.

Adjusting Deferred (Unearned) Revenues

Unearned Revenue is a liability.

It is possible for a business to collect cash from customers prior to providing goods or services. Receiving cash from a customer before earning it creates a liability called unearned revenue, or **deferred revenue**. It is classified as a liability because the company owes a product or service to the customer. Even though the account has the word "revenue" in its title, it is not a revenue account because the amounts in the account represent what has *not* yet been earned.

Suppose a local real estate agency hires Hooray Consulting to provide consulting services, agreeing to pay $450 monthly, beginning immediately. Hooray Consulting collects the first amount from the real estate agency on March 21. Hooray Consulting records the cash receipt and a liability as follows:

DATE	ACCOUNTS	POST REF.	DR.	CR.
Mar 21	Cash		450	
	Unearned Service Revenue			450
	Collected revenue in advance.			

The liability account Unearned Service Revenue now shows that Hooray Consulting owes $450 of services because of its obligation to provide consulting services to the real estate agency.

During the last 10 days of March, Hooray Consulting earned one-third of the $450, or $150 ($450 × 1/3). Therefore, Hooray Consulting makes the following adjustment to record earning $150 of the revenue:

Service Revenue increases by $150, and Unearned Service Revenue decreases by $150. Now both accounts are up to date at March 31.

An Alternate Method for Adjusting Unearned Revenues

Some accountants will find it more practical to record all the cash collected in advance to provide service or to deliver goods as revenue. Then at the end of the period, if the service is not provided or the goods are not delivered, an adjusting entry is recorded; otherwise, nothing is required. To illustrate, assume that a customer paid a consulting company $1,000 on March 15 to provide consulting services. The accountant using such a method would record the entry as follows when the cash is received:

DATE	ACCOUNTS	POST REF.	DR.	CR.
Mar 15	Cash		1,000	
	Consulting Revenue			1,000
	Received cash for consulting services.			

3.3 STILL DON'T GET IT?

Visit MyAccountingLab for an alternate explanation of this important accounting concept.

If at the end of March the accountant found that all the services had been provided, and since revenue is already credited when the cash was collected, nothing further is required to be done. However, let's assume that only $600 worth of services is provided and the rest will be provided next month. In such a case an adjusting entry is needed to reduce March's revenue and to recognize a liability of $400. The following entry would be required:

DATE	ACCOUNTS	POST REF.	DR.	CR.
Mar 15	Consulting Revenue		400	
	Unearned revenue			400
	Decreasing the consulting revenue by the value of services that are not provided and recognizing it as a liability.			

ACCOUNTING IN YOUR WORLD

StreetStock/Alamy

To better understand the difference between a prepaid expense and an unearned revenue, consider this example:

At the start of this semester in school, you paid your school the tuition that was due for the upcoming term. Your tuition will ultimately be an expense to you. However, before the term began, the amount you paid was not yet an expense to you because the school had not yet provided any classes. In other words, you had not yet received anything for your payment. Instead, the amount you paid represented an asset known as a prepaid expense. It was an asset because the school owes you either the classes or your money back.

Once classes started, you began to incur an expense. Technically, the amount of your asset, prepaid expense, would have decreased and the amount of your expenses would have increased every day. By the end of the semester, none of the tuition you paid would be considered to be a prepaid expense. Instead, it becomes an expense.

Now, let's look at the same example from the perspective of your school. When your school received the tuition payment from you, it did not have the right to record it as a revenue because it had not provided you with any classes. Instead, the school would record your tuition as a liability called unearned revenue. Unearned revenue represents a liability to the school because the school owes you either the classes or your money back.

Once classes started, your school began to earn revenue. The amount of its unearned revenue would have decreased and the amount of its revenue would have increased. By the end of the semester, the entire amount of tuition you paid would be considered to be revenue to your school. As you can see, one entity's prepaid expense is another entity's unearned revenue and vice versa.

DECISION GUIDELINES

DECISION	GUIDELINE	ANALYZE
I'm a new manager for a company, and I noticed that cash is collected in advance before the service is rendered. However, it is recorded as Service Revenue, assuming that service is going to be provided during the period. Can I trust the income figure?	To produce accurate income measurement, the revenue and expense recognition principle should be followed.	The income figure cannot be trusted without making the necessary adjustments. The revenue recognition principle requires that revenues be recorded only when they are earned regardless of when cash is received. The expense recognition principle requires that expenses are recorded only when they incur regardless of when the cash is paid. When the revenue and expense recognition principle is followed it is referred to as *accrual accounting*. The resulting income figure would then reflect the real performance.

 # CRITICAL THINKING

Take a minute to think about the impact of the errors in the following independent cases on each of the assets, liabilities, and shareholders' equity accounts, based on each of the scenarios. What are the entries required to make the account balance correct? Who might have found these errors?

- Depreciation of $1,000 on a delivery truck was debited as Depreciation Expense $1,000, and credited as Delivery Truck $1,000.
- An annual insurance premium of $1,200 was originally recorded in the Insurance Expense account. Four months of insurance premium have expired. No adjusting entry was made at the year end.
- A receipt of $6,000 from a customer for a three-month service contract was originally recorded in the Service Revenue account. One month of service has been provided. No adjusting entry was made at the year end.

Solution:

	Impact on Accounts					
	Assets	Liabilities	Shareholders' Equity	Required Entries to Correct Account Balances	Debit	Credit
1.	No	No	No	(a) Delivery Truck	1,000	
	There is no impact on the Assets account since the error involved recording the increase in the Accumulated Depreciation account as a reduction in the Delivery Truck account instead. The net effect on the total assets is the same.			Depreciation Expense		1,000
				(b) Depreciation Expense	1,000	
				Accumulated Depreciation, Delivery Truck		1,000
2.	Understated	No	Understated	(a) Prepaid Insurance	1,200	
	The Shareholders' Equity account is understated because the expenses are recorded too high, which reduced Retained Earnings and in turn reduces Shareholders' Equity.			Insurance Expense		1,200
				(b) Insurance Expense	400	
				Prepaid Insurance		400
3.	No	Understated	Overstated	(a) Service Revenue	6,000	
	Liabilities are understated because the Unearned Revenue account should have been increased, but wasn't.			Unearned Revenue		6,000
				(b) Unearned Revenue	2,000	
				Service Revenue		2,000

The first error may have been noticed by the manager responsible for the fleet of delivery trucks. The manager would notice that the recorded value of the trucks decreased for no reason. The second error would be spotted by the manager responsible for organizing the insurance. In a comparison from the previous year and the current year, there would be a noticeable increase in the insurance costs for the current year. The last error would be noticed by an internal auditor. The list of jobs that are not complete yet would not balance with the Unearned Revenue account since this job was not set up as a liability.

HOW ARE FINANCIAL STATEMENTS PREPARED FROM AN ADJUSTED TRIAL BALANCE?

THE ADJUSTED TRIAL BALANCE

L.O. 3 Prepare financial statements from an adjusted trial balance

Earlier in the chapter, the unadjusted trial balance in Exhibit 3-5 on page 141 showed the account balances for Hooray Consulting, Inc. before the adjustments had been made. After adjustment, Hooray Consulting's accounts would appear as presented in **Exhibit 3-6.**

Exhibit 3-6 ▲

Prior to preparing the financial statements, an **adjusted trial balance** is prepared to make sure total debits still equal total credits after adjusting entries have been recorded and posted. The adjusted trial balance for Hooray Consulting is presented in **Exhibit 3-7.**

ACCT #	ACCOUNT	DEBIT	CREDIT
	Hooray Consulting, Inc.		
	Adjusted Trial Balance		
	March 31, 2015		
1010	Cash	$26,300	
1020	Accounts Receivable	8,350	
1030	Supplies	600	
1035	Prepaid Rent	2,000	
1040	Equipment	12,600	
1041	Accumulated Depreciation, Equipment		$ 350
2010	Accounts Payable		13,100
2020	Salaries Payable		600
2025	Interest Payable		25
2040	Unearned Service Revenue		300
2050	Taxes Payable		1,058
2080	Notes Payable		5,000
3010	Common Shares		20,000
3030	Retained Earnings		10,150
3040	Dividends	3,200	
4010	Service Revenue		7,400
5010	Salaries Expense	1,800	
5015	Building Rent Expense	1,000	
5030	Utilities Expense	400	
5040	Depreciation Expense, Equipment	350	
5050	Supplies Expense	300	
5060	Interest Expense	25	
5070	Tax Expense	1,058	
	Total	$57,983	$57,983

Exhibit 3-7 ▲

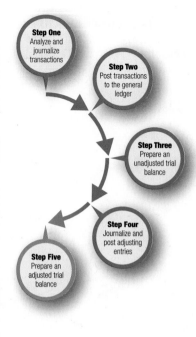

PREPARING THE FINANCIAL STATEMENTS

The March financial statements of Hooray Consulting, Inc. are prepared from the adjusted trial balance in Exhibit 3-7. The financial statements should be prepared in the same order that we used in previous chapters:

1. The income statement (**Exhibit 3-8**) reports the revenues and the expenses to determine net income or net loss for a period of time. Assume Hooray Consulting, Inc. pays 30% income tax on its profit.

2. The statement of retained earnings (**Exhibit 3-9**, a component of the statement of changes in equity) shows the changes in retained earnings during the period and computes the ending balance of retained earnings. Notice that the Retained Earnings balance of $10,150 on the adjusted trial balance does *not* represent the ending Retained Earnings balance because the account has not yet been updated for the current period's earnings or dividends.

3. The classified statement of financial position (**Exhibit 3-10**) reports the assets, liabilities, and shareholders' equity to see the financial position of the business at a specific point in time. There are two classes of assets: (a) current assets, which are assets that will be used or converted to cash within one year or one operating cycle, and (b) long-term assets, which will be kept for more than one year or one operating cycle.

3.4 **STILL** DON'T GET IT?
Visit MyAccountingLab for an alternate explanation of this important accounting concept.

Hooray Consulting, Inc.
Income Statement
Month Ended March 31, 2015

Revenue:		
Service Revenue		$7,400
Expenses:		
Salaries Expense	$1,800	
Building Rent Expense	1,000	
Utilities Expense	400	
Depreciation Expense—Equipment	350	
Supplies Expense	300	
Interest Expense	25	
Total Operating Expenses		3,875
Operating Income		3,525
Income Tax (30%)*		1,058
Net Income		$2,467

*During the preparation of the income statement, income taxes need to be recorded. At 30% of the income before taxes, the income tax expense becomes $3,525 × 30% = $1,058

Exhibit 3-8 ▲

Hooray Consulting, Inc.
Statement of Retained Earnings
Month Ended March 31, 2015

Retained Earnings, March 1, 2015	$10,150	
Add: Net Income	2,467	
Subtotal		12,617
Less: Dividends		3,200
Retained Earnings, March 31, 2015		$9,417

Exhibit 3-9 ▲

Hooray Consulting, Inc.
Statement of Financial Position
March 31, 2015

ASSETS			LIABILITIES		
Current Assets			Current Liabilities		
Cash	$26,300		Accounts Payable	$13,100	
Accounts Receivable	8,350		Salaries Payable	600	
Supplies	600		Unearned Service Revenue	300	
Prepaid Rent	2,000		Interest Payable	25	
Total Current Assets		$37,250	Income Tax Payable	1,058	
			Total Liabilities		$15,083
			Long Term Liabilities		
			Notes Payable	5,000	
			Total Long Term Liabilities		5,000
Equipment	$12,600		**SHAREHOLDERS' EQUITY**		
Less: Accumulated			Common Shares	$20,000	
			Retained Earnings	9,417	
Depreciation—Equipment	350	12,250	Total Shareholders' Equity		29,417
			Total Liabilities &		
Total Assets		$49,500	Shareholders' Equity		$49,500

Exhibit 3-10 ▲

As we first discussed in Chapter 1, all financial statements include these elements:

- Heading
  1. Name of the entity, such as Hooray Consulting, Inc.
  2. Title of the statement: income statement, statement of retained earnings, statement of financial position
  3. Date or period covered by the statement: Month ended March 31, 2015, or March 31, 2015
- Body of the statement

HOW DOES A COMPANY PREPARE FOR A NEW ACCOUNTING PERIOD?

COMPLETING THE ACCOUNTING CYCLE

We have now seen steps one through six in the accounting cycle completed for Hooray Consulting. The entire accounting cycle can be completed by finishing steps seven and eight. Step seven of the accounting cycle is the journalizing and posting of the closing entries, and step eight is the preparation of a post-closing trial balance.

In order to complete the accounting cycle, **closing entries** must be journalized and posted. Earlier in the chapter, we processed the transactions for Hooray Consulting and prepared the financial statements for the month of March. If we continue recording information in the revenue, expense, and dividend accounts, we will lose track of what activity happened in March compared to what happens in April, making it impossible to prepare accurate financial statements for the month of April.

In order to not confuse the transactions from the two different months, the revenue, expense, and dividend accounts must be reset back to zero before we start recording transactions for April. It is similar to resetting the scoreboard at the end of a game before you start a new game. Since we must keep the accounting equation in balance, we cannot just erase the balances in the revenue, expense, and dividend accounts. To keep the accounting equation in balance and still be able to zero out these accounts, we will use closing entries. Closing entries are utilized to accomplish two things:

- The revenue, expense, and dividend account balances from the current accounting period are set back to zero so that accounting for the next period can begin.
- The revenue, expense, and dividend account balances from the current accounting period are transferred into Retained Earnings so that the accounting equation stays in balance. Transferring the revenue and expense account balances into retained earnings actually transfers the net income, or net loss, for the current period into Retained Earnings. Transferring the dividend account balance into Retained Earnings decreases Retained Earnings by the amount of dividends for the period.

The revenue, expense, and dividend accounts are known as **temporary accounts**. They are called temporary because they are used temporarily to record activity for a specific period, the accounting period, and then they are closed into Retained Earnings. It is easy to remember the temporary accounts if you think of the color RED. The R in RED stands for revenues, the E stands for expenses, and the D stands for dividends. The RED accounts are closed at the end of each accounting period.

L.O. ④ Prepare closing entries and a post-closing trial balance

Step One — Analyze and journalize transactions
Step Two — Post transactions to the general ledger
Step Three — Prepare an unadjusted trial balance
Step Four — Journalize and post adjusting entries
Step Five — Prepare an adjusted trial balance
Step Six — Prepare financial statements
Step Seven — Journalize and post closing entries
Step Eight — Prepare a post-closing trial balance

MEMORY **TIPS**

R EVENUE

E XPENSES

D IVIDENDS

RED
Accounts are closed at the end of the period.

Before closing the accounts, the accounting equation for a corporation would be as follows:

After closing the accounts, the accounting equation would be as follows:

The accounts that remain in the accounting equation after closing are called **permanent accounts**. Assets, liabilities, common shares, and retained earnings are *not* closed at the end of the period because they are not used to measure activity for a specific period. Consider Cash, Accounts Receivable, Accounts Payable, and Common Shares. These accounts do not represent business activity for a single period, so they are not closed at the end of the period. Their balances carry over to the next period. For example, the Cash balance at March 31, 2015, becomes the beginning balance on April 1, 2015.

THE THREE CLOSING ENTRIES: REVENUES, EXPENSES, AND DIVIDENDS

To journalize closing entries, complete the following steps:

Step 1 Close the revenue accounts and move their balances into the Retained Earnings account. To close revenues, debit each revenue account for the amount of its credit balance. Transfer the revenue balances to Retained Earnings by crediting the Retained Earnings account for the total amount of the revenues. This closing entry transfers total revenues to the credit side of Retained Earnings.

Step 2 Close the expense accounts and move their balances into the Retained Earnings account. To close expenses, credit each expense account for the amount of its debit balance. Transfer the expense balances to Retained Earnings by debiting the Retained Earnings account for the total amount of the expenses. This closing entry transfers total expenses to the debit side of Retained Earnings.

Step 3 Close the Dividends account and move its balance into the Retained Earnings account. To close the Dividends account, credit it for the amount of its debit balance and debit the Retained Earnings account. This entry transfers the dividends to the debit side of Retained Earnings.

Remember that net income is equal to revenues minus expenses. So, closing the revenues and expenses into retained earnings, Steps 1 and 2, has the effect of adding net income for the period to, or deducting a net loss for the period from, retained earnings. Once the Dividends account has been subtracted from retained earnings, Step 3, the balance in the retained earnings account should match ending retained earnings on the statement of retained earnings.

The process for making closing entries is the same as it is for making any entry: record the entries in the journal and post them to the proper accounts in the ledger.

Now, let's apply this process to Hooray Consulting, Inc. for the month of March:

Step 1

$-7,400$
$+7,400$

Step 2

Step 3

−3,200
+3,200

At this point, the Retained Earnings account balance reflects all the net income earned, net loss incurred, and dividends paid during the life of Hooray Consulting, Inc. to date. After the closing entries, Retained Earnings ends with a balance of $9,417. This balance should, and does, match the balance on the statement of retained earnings and the statement of financial position presented in Exhibits 3-9 and 3-10 on page 154.

POST-CLOSING TRIAL BALANCE

The accounting cycle ends with the preparation of a **post-closing trial balance**, as seen in **Exhibit 3-11**. This trial balance lists the accounts and their adjusted balances after

	Hooray Consulting, Inc. Post-Closing Trial Balance March 31, 2015		
ACCT #	**ACCOUNT**	**DEBIT**	**CREDIT**
1010	Cash	$26,300	
1020	Accounts Receivable	8,350	
1030	Supplies	600	
1035	Prepaid Rent	2,000	
1040	Equipment	12,600	
1041	Accumulated Depreciation, Equipment		$ 350
2010	Accounts Payable		13,100
2020	Salaries Payable		600
2025	Interest Payable		25
2040	Unearned Service Revenue		300
2050	Taxes Payable		1,058
2080	Notes Payable		5,000
3010	Common Shares		20,000
3020	Retained Earnings		9,417
	Total	$49,850	$49,850

Exhibit 3-11 ▲

DECISION GUIDELINES

DECISION	GUIDELINE	ANALYZE
As the bookkeeper for a company, how do I ensure that my accounting records are ready to start a new period?	Prepare *closing entries* for the *temporary accounts*: • Revenues • Expenses • Dividends	The *temporary accounts* have balances that relate only to one accounting period and need to be reset to $0 before accounting for the next period can begin. To reset the temporary accounts, closing entries are made that close the account balances into Retained Earnings. This ensures that the net income for the following period can be tracked accurately. Assets, Liabilities, Common Shares, and Retained Earnings do not get closed. These accounts are referred to as *permanent accounts*. Their balances are carried forward into the next period. After temporary accounts have been closed, a post-closing trial balance is prepared to ensure that all of the temporary accounts were properly closed.

closing. Only assets, liabilities, and shareholders' equity appear on the post-closing trial balance. No temporary accounts—revenues, expenses, or dividends—are included because they have been closed. The accounts in the ledger are now up to date and ready for the next period's transactions.

SUMMARY OF THE ADJUSTING AND CLOSING PROCESS

Businesses record adjusting entries at the *end* of the accounting period to accomplish two purposes:

1. Report net income or net loss accurately on the income statement.

2. Reflect the correct account balances on the statement of financial position.

Each adjusting entry will always affect one income statement account, a revenue or an expense, and one statement of financial position account, an asset or a liability. *Cash is never included in a period-end adjusting entry because cash should always be recorded accurately at the time it is received or paid.*

Deferrals and accruals can be summarized as follows:

- A *deferred revenue or expense* is paid first, and recorded as a revenue or expense later as the revenue is earned or the expense is incurred.

- An *accrued revenue or expense* is recorded as a revenue or expense first as the revenue is earned or the expense is incurred, and paid later.

Exhibit 3-12 summarizes the accrual and deferral adjustments.

Businesses record closing entries at the *end* of the accounting period to accomplish two purposes:

1. Zero out the revenue, expense, and dividend accounts.

2. Transfer the balance of the revenue, expense, and dividend accounts into Retained Earnings.

Closing entries are the end-of-period journal entries that get the temporary accounts—revenues, expenses, and dividends—ready for the next accounting period by zeroing them out. Closing entries also transfer the balances from the temporary accounts into the Retained Earnings account. The post-closing trial balance is the final step in the accounting cycle. The post-closing trial balance is prepared to ensure that debits still equal credits before a new accounting period is started.

Adjusting Entries

Deferrals: Cash transaction comes first.

	First	Dr.	Cr.	Later	Dr.	Cr.
Prepaid Expenses, Depreciable Assets	*Pay cash and record an asset:* Prepaid Rent	XXX		*Record an expense and decrease the asset:* Rent Expense	XXX	
	Cash		XXX	Prepaid Rent		XXX
Unearned Revenues	*Receive cash and record a liability:* Cash	XXX		*Record a revenue and decrease the liability:* Unearned Service Revenue	XXX	
	Unearned Service Revenue		XXX	Service Revenue		XXX

Accruals: Cash transaction comes later.

	First	Dr.	Cr.	Later	Dr.	Cr.
Accrued Expenses	*Accrue an expense and the related liability:* Salaries Expense	XXX		*Pay cash and decrease the liability:* Salaries Payable	XXX	
	Salaries Payable		XXX	Cash		XXX
Accrued Revenues	*Accrue a revenue and the related asset:* Accounts Receivable	XXX		*Receive cash and decrease the asset:* Cash	XXX	
	Service Revenue		XXX	Accounts Receivable		XXX

Exhibit 3-12 ▲

FOCUS ON USERS

Concept	User	Why Is This Important to This User?
Adjusting Entries	**Creditors, Shareholders, and Potential Investors**	Creditors, shareholders, and potential investors are interested in the effect of adjusting entries because the adjusting entries highlight the difference between the timing of when cash is paid or received and when the revenues or expenses are recorded. This may have an impact on the ability of a company to pay its debts. It also has an impact on income measurement.
	Managers	Managers need to understand the adjusting entries because adjusting entries are quite often based on estimations. For example, an adjusting entry to change unearned revenue to revenue may be based on an estimate of how much of the work has been completed for the job that has been prepaid by the customer. What this means is that the adjusting entry is subjective and those in charge of making the estimations may be able to exaggerate situations for their own reasons. For example, a sales manager who receives a bonus based on the amount of revenues recorded would be interested in estimating as high an amount of revenues as possible to maximize his or her bonus.
Depreciation	**Shareholders and Potential Investors**	Shareholders watch the statement of financial position for the value of assets, the accumulated depreciation, and the net book value of long-term assets. Since the accumulated depreciation is an indication of the usage of the assets, the smaller the value of the net book assets, the more likely it is that the organization will need to invest in additional long-term assets.

One optional step that accountants may choose to include is to prepare adjusting entries and closing entries using a worksheet. A worksheet can be easily set up in a spreadsheet program, such as Excel. One of the benefits of preparing a worksheet is that it provides a bird's-eye view of the accounting process and adjusting and closing transactions. **Exhibit 3-13** shows a worksheet for Hooray Consulting, Inc. There are five sets of double columns of debit and credit: the first set of columns shows the unadjusted trial balance, the next set shows the six adjusting entries that updated the account balances, the third set is the adjusted trial balance, the fourth set shows the three closing entries that are required to zero out the temporary accounts, and the last set shows the post-closing trial balance. The only change occurring in the permanent accounts from the adjusted trial balance to the post-closing trial balance is in the Retained Earnings account. The net income and dividends have been closed to the Retained Earnings account, and therefore, the new balance of the Retained Earnings account reflects these changes.

L.O. ⑤ Prepare a worksheet

Hooray Consulting, Inc.
Worksheet
For the Month Ended March 31, 2015

ACCT #	ACCOUNT	Unadjusted Trial Balance DR.	Unadjusted Trial Balance CR.	Adjustments DR.	Adjustments CR.	Adjusted Trial Balance DR.	Adjusted Trial Balance CR.	Closing Entries DR.	Closing Entries CR.	Post-Closing Trial Balance DR.	Post-Closing Trial Balance CR.
1010	Cash	$26,300				$26,300				$26,300	
1020	Accounts Receivable	8,100		① 250		$ 8,350				8,350	
1030	Supplies	900			⑤ 300	$ 600				600	
1035	Prepaid Rent	3,000			④ 1,000	$ 2,000				2,000	
1040	Equipment	12,600				$12,600				12,600	
1041	Accumulated Depreciation, Equipment				⑥ 350		350				$ 350
2010	Accounts Payable		$13,100				13,100				13,100
2020	Salaries Payable				② 600		600				600
2025	Interest Payable				⑧ 25		25				25
2020	Unearned Service Revenue		450	③ 150			300				300
2030	Income Tax Payable				⑦ 1,058		1,058				1,058
2080	Notes Payable		5000				5,000				5,000
3010	Common Shares		20,000				20,000				20,000
3030	Retained Earnings		10,150				10,150	②③ 8,133	① 7,400		9,417
3040	Dividends	3,200				$ 3,200			③ 3,200		
4010	Service Revenue		7,000		①③ 400		7,400	① 7,400			
5010	Salaries Expense	1,200		② 600		$ 1,800			② 1,800		
5015	Building Rent Expense			④ 1,000		$ 1,000			② 1,000		
5030	Utilities Expense	400				$ 400			② 400		
5040	Depreciation Expense, Equipment			⑥ 350		$ 350			② 350		
5050	Supplies Expense			⑤ 300		$ 300			② 300		
5060	Interest Expense			⑧ 25		$ 25			② 25		
5070	Income Tax Expense			⑦ 1,058		$ 1,058			② 1,058		
	Total	$55,700	$55,700	$3,733	$3,733	$57,983	$57,983	$15,533	$15,533	$49,850	$49,850

Exhibit 3-13 ▲

DEMO DOC

MyAccountingLab   Visit MyAccountingLab to watch animated versions of similar Demo Docs.

PREPARATION OF ADJUSTING ENTRIES, ADJUSTED TRIAL BALANCE, FINANCIAL STATEMENTS, CLOSING ENTRIES, AND POST-CLOSING TRIAL BALANCE

LEARNING OBJECTIVE

Apex Architects, Inc. has the following unadjusted trial balance at December 31, 2015:

		ACCOUNT	DEBIT	CREDIT
		Apex Architects, Inc. **Unadjusted Trial Balance** December 31, 2015		
		Cash	$124,000	
		Accounts Receivable	96,000	
		Supplies	3,500	
		Prepaid Rent	24,000	
		Land	48,000	
		Building	270,000	
		Accumulated Depreciation, Building		$135,000
		Accounts Payable		118,000
		Unearned Service Revenue		36,000
		Common Shares		50,000
		Retained Earnings		64,700
		Dividends	46,000	
		Service Revenue		486,000
		Salaries Expense	245,000	
		Rent Expense	32,000	
		Miscellaneous Expense	1,200	
		Total	$889,700	$889,700

Apex Architects, Inc. must make adjusting entries related to the following items:

a. **Supplies on hand at year-end, $800.**

b. **Six months of rent ($24,000) was paid in advance on September 1, 2015. No rent expense has been recorded since that date.**

c. **Depreciation expense has not been recorded on the warehouse for 2015. The building has a useful life of 30 years.**

d. **Employees work Monday through Friday. The weekly payroll is $3,500 and is paid every Friday. December 31, 2015, is a Wednesday.**

e. **Service revenue of $18,000 must be accrued.**

f. **A client paid $36,000 in advance on August 1, 2015, for services to be provided evenly from August 1, 2015, through January 31, 2016. None of the revenue from this client has been recorded.**

g. **Apex's tax rate is 30%.**

REQUIREMENTS:

① Open the ledger T-accounts with their unadjusted balances.

② Journalize Apex Architects' adjusting entries at December 31, 2015, and post the entries to the T-accounts.

③ Total all the T-accounts in the ledger.

④ Prepare an adjusted trial balance.

⑤ Prepare the income statement, the statement of retained earnings, and the statement of financial position. Draw arrows linking the three financial statements.

⑥ Journalize and post Apex Architects' closing entries.

⑦ Prepare a post-closing trial balance.

DEMO DOC SOLUTION

REQUIREMENT ①

Open the ledger T-accounts with their unadjusted balances.

| Part 1 | Part 2 | Part 3 | Part 4 | Part 5 | Part 6 | Part 7 | Demo Doc Complete |

Remember from Chapter 2 that opening a T-account means drawing a blank account that looks like a capital T and putting the account title across the top. To help find the accounts later, they are usually organized into assets, liabilities, shareholders' equity, revenue, and expenses (in that order). If the account has a beginning balance, it *must* be put in on the correct side.

Remember that debits are always on the left side of the T-account and credits are always on the right side. This rule is true for *every* account.

The correct side to enter each account's beginning balance is the side of *increase* in the account. We expect all accounts to have a *positive* balance, or more increases than decreases.

For assets, an increase is a debit, so we would expect all assets to have a debit balance. For liabilities and shareholders' equity, an increase is a credit, so we would expect all of these accounts to have a credit balance. By the same reasoning, we expect revenues to have a credit balance and expenses and dividends to have a debit balance.

The unadjusted balances to be posted into the T-accounts are simply the amounts from the unadjusted trial balance.

REQUIREMENT ②

Journalize Apex Architects' adjusting entries at December 31, 2015, and post the entries to the T-accounts.

Part 1	**Part 2**	Part 3	Part 4	Part 5	Part 6	Part 7	Demo Doc Complete

a. Supplies on hand at year-end, $800.

On December 31, 2015, the unadjusted balance in supplies was $3,500. However, a count shows that only $800 of supplies actually remains on hand. The supplies that are no longer there have been used. When assets/benefits are used, an expense is created.

Apex Architects, Inc. will need to make an adjusting journal entry to reflect the correct amount of supplies on the statement of financial position. The amount to be shown on the statement is the actual amount of supplies on hand of $800. However, right now the Supplies account shows $3,500 (as we can see from the trial balance). This $3,500 is the "cost of asset available."

Cost of asset available	−	Cost of asset on hand at the end of the period	=	Cost of asset used (expense) during the period
$3,500	−	$800	=	$2,700

The supplies have decreased because they have been used up. The $2,700 of supplies expense must be recorded to show the value of supplies that were used.

Assets = Liabilities + Shareholders' Equity

−2,700   −2,700

DATE	ACCOUNTS	POST REF.	DR.	CR.
Dec 31	Supplies Expense		2,700	
	Supplies			2,700
	Record supply expense.			

After posting, Supplies and Supplies Expense reflect correct ending balances:

EXPENSES

Supplies Expense		
(a)	2,700	
Bal	2,700	

ASSETS

Supplies			
Bal	3,500	(a)	2,700
Bal	800		

b. Six months of rent ($24,000) was paid in advance on September 1, 2015 for renting a warehouse. No rent expense has been recorded since that date.

When something is prepaid, it is a *future* benefit (an asset) because the business is now entitled to receive goods or services. Once those goods or services are received (in this case, once Apex Architects, Inc. has occupied the warehouse being rented), they become a *past* benefit, and therefore an expense.

Apex Architects, Inc. prepaid $24,000 for six months of rent on September 1, which means that Apex Architects, Inc. pays $24,000/6 = $4,000 a month for rent. At December 31, prepaid rent is adjusted for the amount of the asset that has been used up. Because Apex Architects, Inc. occupied the warehouse being rented for four months, we know that four months of the prepayment has been used. The amount of rent used is as follows:

$$4 \times \$4,000 = \$16,000$$

The amount of prepaid rent that will appear on the statement of financial position is the amount of prepaid rent that has not been used. In this case, two months' worth of prepaid rent has not been used, $2 \times \$4,000 = \$8,000$. However, right now the Prepaid Rent account shows $24,000 (as we can see from the trial balance). This $24,000 is the "total asset to account for."

$$\text{Total asset to account for} - \frac{\text{Asset remaining}}{\text{at end of period}} = \frac{\text{Cost of asset used (expense)}}{\text{during the period}}$$

$$\$24,000 \quad - \quad \$8,000 \quad = \quad \$16,000$$

Because the $16,000 of prepaid rent is a *past* benefit, an expense is recorded. Rent Expense must be increased (a debit) and Prepaid Rent (an asset) must be decreased (a credit).

DATE	ACCOUNTS	POST REF.	DR.	CR.
Dec 31	Rent Expense		16,000	
	Prepaid Rent			16,000
	Record rent expense.			

Assets = Liabilities + Shareholders' Equity
−16,000   −16,000

ASSETS

Prepaid Rent

Bal	24,000	(b)	16,000
Bal	8,000		

EXPENSES

Rent Expense

Bal	32,000		
(b)	16,000		
Bal	48,000		

c. Depreciation expense has not been recorded on the building for 2015. The building has a useful life of 30 years.

Depreciation expense per year is calculated as follows:

$$\text{Depreciation Expense per Year} = \frac{(\text{Cost of Asset} - \text{Salvage Value of Asset})}{\text{Useful Life of Asset}}$$

The cost principle compels us to keep the original cost of a plant asset in that asset account. Because the Building account has a balance of $270,000, we know that this is the original cost of the building. No salvage value is mentioned in the question, so we assume it is $0. We are told in the question that the building's useful life is 30 years.

$$\text{Depreciation Expense per Year} = \frac{(\$270,000 - \$0)}{30 \text{ Years}}$$

$$= \$9,000 \text{ per Year}$$

We will record depreciation of $9,000 in the adjusting journal entry.

The journal entry to record depreciation expense is *always* the same. It is only the *number* (dollar amount) in the entry that changes. It always involves an increase to Depreciation Expense (a debit) and an increase to the contra-asset account of Accumulated Depreciation (a credit).

DATE	ACCOUNTS	POST REF.	DR.	CR.
Dec 31	Depreciation Expense		9,000	
	Accumulated Depreciation, Building			9,000
	Record depreciation expense.			

Assets = Liabilities + Shareholders' Equity
−9,000   −9,000

ASSETS			EXPENSES
ASSET		**CONTRA-ASSET**	

Building		
Bal	270,000	
Bal	270,000	

Accumulated Depreciation, Building		
	Bal	135,000
	(c)	9,000
	Bal	144,000

Depreciation Expense, Building		
(c)	9,000	
Bal	9,000	

The book value of the building is its original cost (the amount in the Building T-account) minus the accumulated depreciation on the building:

Book Value of Plant Assets	
Building..	$ 270,000
Less: Accumulated Depreciation, Building.................	(144,000)
Book Value of the Building.......................................	$ 126,000

d. Employees work Monday through Friday. The weekly payroll is $3,500 and is paid every Friday. December 31, 2015, is a Wednesday.

Salary is an accrued expense. That is, it is a liability that incurs from an *expense* that hasn't been paid yet. Most employers pay their employees *after* the work has been done, which means that the work is a *past* benefit. This is salaries expense, and it grows each pay period until payday.

Apex Architects' employees are paid $3,500 for five days of work (Monday through Friday), which means they earn $3,500/5 = $700 per day. By the end of the day on Wednesday, December 31, the employees have worked for three days and have not been paid. Therefore, Apex Architects, Inc. owes employees $700 × 3 = $2,100 of salary at December 31.

If the salaries have not been paid, then they are pay*able* (or in other words, they are *owed*). They must be recorded in a payable account. We might be tempted to use Accounts Payable, but this account is usually reserved for *bills* received. Employees do not typically send their employers a bill. They simply expect to be paid and Apex Architects, Inc. knows that the salaries are owed. For this reason, we put this amount into another payable account. In this case, Salaries Payable is most appropriate.

Salary is not owed until work is performed, and we know that Apex Architects' employees have already worked for three days. We therefore need to record an expense (in this case, Salaries Expense) for the past benefit Apex Architects, Inc. received from its employees.

We record an increase to Salaries Expense (a debit) and an increase to the liability Salaries Payable (a credit) of $2,100.

Assets	=	Liabilities	+	Shareholders' Equity
+2,100				−2,100

DATE	ACCOUNTS	POST REF.	DR.	CR.
Dec 31	Salaries Expense		2,100	
	Salaries Payable			2,100
	Accrue salaries expense.			

EXPENSES		LIABILITIES	

Salaries Expense		
Bal	245,000	
(d)	2,100	
Bal	247,100	

Salaries Payable		
	(d)	2,100
	Bal	2,100

e. Service revenue of $18,000 must be accrued.

Accrued revenue is another way of saying "receivable" (or receipt in the future). If *accrued* revenue is recorded, it means that an account or note receivable is also recorded. Customers have received goods or services from the business, but the business has not yet received the cash. The business is entitled to these receivables because the revenue has been earned.

Service Revenue must be increased by $18,000 (a credit) and the Accounts Receivable asset must be increased by $18,000 (a debit).

DATE	ACCOUNTS	POST REF.	DR.	CR.
Dec 31	Accounts Receivable		18,000	
	Service Revenue			18,000
	Accrue service revenue.			

Assets	=	Liabilities	+	Shareholders' Equity
+18,000				+18,000

ASSETS

Accounts Receivable

Bal	96,000	
(e)	18,000	
Bal	114,000	

REVENUES

Service Revenue

	Bal	486,000
	(e)	18,000
	Bal	504,000

f. A client paid $36,000 in advance on August 1, 2015, for services to be provided evenly from August 1, 2015, through January 31, 2016. None of the revenue from this client has been recorded.

Apex Architects, Inc. received cash in advance for work not yet performed for the client. By accepting the cash, Apex Architects, Inc. also accepted the obligation to perform that work (or provide a refund if it did not). In accounting, an obligation is a liability. We call this liability "unearned revenue" because it *will* be revenue (after the work is performed) but it is not revenue *yet*.

The $36,000 paid in advance is still in the Unearned Service Revenue account. However, some of the revenue has been earned as of December 31. Five months of the earnings period have passed (August 1 through December 31), so five months' worth of the revenue has been earned.

The entire revenue earnings period is six months (August 1 through January 31), so the revenue earned per month is $36,000/6 = $6,000. The five months of revenue earned total:

$$5 \times \$6,000 = \$30,000$$

The amount of unearned revenue that will appear on the statement of financial position is the amount of unearned revenue that remains at the end of the period. In this case, one month of unearned revenue remains: $1 \times \$6,000 = \$6,000$. However, right now the Unearned Service Revenue account shows a balance of $36,000 (as we can see from the trial balance). This $36,000 is the "total to account for."

Total unearned revenue to account for	−	Unearned revenue remaining at the end of period	=	Revenue earned during the period
$36,000	−	$6,000	=	$30,000

So Unearned Service Revenue, a liability, must be decreased by $30,000 (a debit). Because the revenue is now earned, it can be recorded as normal service revenue. Therefore, Service Revenue also increases by $30,000 (a credit).

DATE	ACCOUNTS	POST REF.	DR.	CR.
Dec 31	Unearned Service Revenue		30,000	
	Service Revenue			30,000
	Record unearned service revenue that has been earned.			

Essentially, the $30,000 has been shifted from "unearned" to "earned" revenue.

LIABILITIES

Unearned Service Revenue

(f)	30,000	Bal	36,000
		Bal	6,000

REVENUES

Service Revenue

	Bal	486,000
	(e)	18,000
	(f)	30,000
	Bal	534,000

Now we will summarize all of the adjusting journal entries:

DATE	ACCOUNTS	POST REF.	DR.	CR.
Dec 31	Supplies Expense		2,700	
	Supplies			2,700
	Record supply expense.			
Dec 31	Rent Expense		16,000	
	Prepaid Rent			16,000
	Record rent expense.			
Dec 31	Depreciation Expense, Building		9,000	
	Accumulated Depreciation, Building			9,000
	Record depreciation expense.			
Dec 31	Salaries Expense		2,100	
	Salaries Payable			2,100
	Accrue salaries expense.			
Dec 31	Accounts Receivable		18,000	
	Service Revenue			18,000
	Accrue service revenue.			
Dec 31	Unearned Service Revenue		30,000	
	Service Revenue			30,000
	Record unearned service revenue that has been earned.			

REQUIREMENT ③

Total all the T-accounts in the ledger.

Part 1   Part 2   **Part 3**   Part 4   Part 5   Part 6   Part 7   Demo Doc Complete

After posting all of these entries and totalling all of the T-accounts, we have the following:

REQUIREMENT ④

Prepare an adjusted trial balance.

Part 1   Part 2   Part 3   **Part 4**   Part 5   Part 6   Part 7   Demo Doc Complete

		ACCOUNT	DEBIT	CREDIT
		Apex Architects, Inc. **Adjusted Trial Balance** December 31, 2015		
		Cash	$124,000	
		Accounts Receivable	114,000	
		Supplies	800	
		Prepaid Rent	8,000	
		Land	48,000	
		Building	270,000	
		Accumulated Depreciation, Building		$144,000
		Accounts Payable		118,000
		Salaries Payable		2,100
		Unearned Service Revenue		6,000
		Common Shares		50,000
		Retained Earnings		64,700
		Dividends	46,000	
		Service Revenue		534,000
		Salaries Expense	247,100	
		Rent Expense	48,000	
		Depreciation Expense, Building	9,000	
		Supplies Expense	2,700	
		Miscellaneous Expense	1,200	
		Total	$918,800	$918,800

REQUIREMENT ⑤

Prepare the income statement, the statement of retained earnings, and the statement of financial position. Draw arrows linking the three financial statements.

| Part 1 | Part 2 | Part 3 | Part 4 | **Part 5** | Part 6 | Part 7 | Demo Doc Complete |

Apex Architects, Inc.
Income Statement
Year Ended December 31, 2015

Revenue:			
Service Revenue			$534,000
Expenses:			
Salaries Expense		$247,100	
Rent Expense		48,000	
Depreciation Expense, Building		9,000	
Supplies Expense		2,700	
Miscellaneous Expense		1,200	
Total Operating Expenses			308,000
Operating Income			226,000
Income Tax (30%)			67,800
Net Income			$158,200

Apex Architects, Inc.
Statement of Retained Earnings
Year Ended December 31, 2015

Retained Earnings, January 1, 2015	$ 64,700
Add: Net Income	158,200
Subtotal	222,900
Less: Dividends	46,000
Retained Earnings, December 31, 2015	$176,900

Apex Architects, Inc.
Statement of Financial Position
December 31, 2015

ASSETS			LIABILITIES	
Current Assets			Accounts Payable	$118,000
Cash	$124,000		Salaries Payable	2,100
Accounts Receivable	114,000		Unearned Service Revenue	6,000
Supplies	800		Income Tax Payable	67,800
Prepaid Rent	8,000		Total Liabilities	$193,900
Total Current Assets		$246,800		
			SHAREHOLDERS' EQUITY	
Land		48,000	Common Shares	$ 50,000
Equipment	$270,000		Retained Earnings	176,900
Less: Accumulated			Total Shareholders'	
Depreciation	144,000	$126,000	Equity	$226,900
			Total Liabilities &	
Total Assets		$420,800	Shareholders' Equity	$420,800

The balance of the Income Tax Payable will be added to the liabilities in the statement of financial position, and the balance of the Income Tax Expense will be included within the expenses on the income statement.

g. Apex's tax rate is 30%.

Once the income statement is prepared, Apex knows the amount of tax expense incurred, which will need to be paid to the government shortly after the year-end. The income tax expense, $67,800, is calculated based on the income before taxes. Apex Architects, Inc. will need to make one additional adjusting entry to reflect the income tax incurred but not yet paid on December 31.

DATE	ACCOUNTS	POST REF.	DR.	CR.
Dec 31	Income Tax Expense		67,800	
	Income Tax Payable			67,800

Assets = Liabilities + Shareholders' Equity

+67,800   −67,800

After posting, Income Tax Payable and Income Tax Expense reflect correct ending balances:

LIABILITIES			EXPENSES		
Income Tax Payable			**Income Tax Expense**		
	(g)	67,800	(g)	67,800	
	Bal	67,800	Bal	67,800	

REQUIREMENT ⑥

Journalize and post Apex Architects' closing entries.

Part 1	Part 2	Part 3	Part 4	Part 5	**Part 6**	Part 7	Demo Doc Complete

We prepare closing entries for two reasons. First, we need to clear out the temporary accounts (the revenue, expense, and dividends accounts) to a zero balance. They need to begin the next period empty so that the next period's income statement can begin fresh. Second, we need to update the Retained Earnings account.

The first step in the closing process is to close the revenue accounts. Apex Architects, Inc. only has one revenue account, Service Revenue. Because the Service Revenue account has a credit balance we will need to debit it to bring its balance to zero. The credit side of the entry is to Retained Earnings. The effect of this entry is to move the revenues into the Retained Earnings account.

DATE	ACCOUNTS	POST REF.	DR.	CR.
Dec 31	Service Revenue		534,000	
	Retained Earnings			534,000
	Close revenue accounts.			

Assets = Liabilities + Shareholders' Equity

−534,000
+534,000

Service Revenue				**Retained Earnings**		
		Bal	486,000		Bal	64,700
		(e)	18,000		Clo	534,000
		(f)	30,000			
Clo	534,000	Bal	534,000			
		Bal	-0-			

The next step in the closing process is to close the expenses into the Retained Earnings account.

Each of the expenses has a *debit* balance. To bring the accounts to zero, we must *credit* them. The debit side of the entry will go to the Retained Earnings account:

Assets	=	Liabilities	+	Shareholders' Equity
				−375,800
				+247,100
				+ 48,000
				+ 9,000
				+ 2,700
				+ 1,200
				+ 67,800

DATE	ACCOUNTS	POST REF.	DR.	CR.
Dec 31	Retained Earnings		375,800	
	Salaries Expense			247,100
	Rent Expense			48,000
	Depreciation Expense, Building			9,000
	Supplies Expense			2,700
	Miscellaneous Expense			1,200
	Income Tax Expense			67,800
	Close expense accounts.			

Salaries Expense

Bal	245,000		
(d)	2,100		
Bal	247,100	Clo	247,100
Bal	0		

Rent Expense

Bal	32,000		
(b)	16,000		
Bal	48,000	Clo	48,000
Bal	0		

Depreciation Expense, Building

(c)	9,000		
Bal	9,000	Clo	9,000
Bal	0		

Supplies Expense

(a)	2,700		
Bal	2,700	Clo	2,700
Bal	0		

Miscellaneous Expense

Bal	1,200	Clo	1,200
Bal	0		

Retained Earnings

Clo	308,000	Bal	64,700
		Clo	534,000

Income Tax Expense

(g)	67,800		
Bal	67,800	Clo	67,800
Bal	0		

The final step in the closing process is to close the Dividends account to the Retained Earnings account, which moves the amount from Dividends to Retained Earnings. The Dividends account has a debit balance of $46,000, so to bring that to zero, we *credit* the Dividends account for $46,000. The balancing debit goes to the Retained Earnings account:

Assets	=	Liabilities	+	Shareholders' Equity
				−46,000
				+46,000

DATE	ACCOUNTS	POST REF.	DR.	CR.
Dec 31	Retained Earnings		46,000	
	Dividends			46,000
	Close Dividends account.			

Dividends

Bal	46,000	Clo	46,000
Bal	0		

Retained Earnings

Clo	375,800	Bal	64,700
Clo	46,000	Clo	534,000
		Bal	176,900

Notice that all temporary accounts (that is, the revenue, the expense, and the dividends accounts) now return to a zero balance and are ready to begin the next year.

REQUIREMENT ⑦

Prepare a post-closing trial balance.

| Part 1 | Part 2 | Part 3 | Part 4 | Part 5 | Part 6 | **Part 7** | Demo Doc Complete |

	Apex Architects, Inc. Post-Closing Trial Balance December 31, 2015		
	ACCOUNT	**DEBIT**	**CREDIT**
	Cash	$124,000	
	Accounts Receivable	114,000	
	Supplies	800	
	Prepaid Rent	8,000	
	Land	48,000	
	Building	270,000	
	Accumulated Depreciation, Building		$144,000
	Accounts Payable		118,000
	Salaries Payable		2,100
	Unearned Service Revenue		6,000
	Income Tax Payable		67,800
	Common Shares		50,000
	Retained Earnings		176,900
	Total	$564,800	$564,800

Notice that the post-closing trial balance only contains permanent accounts. This is because all of the temporary accounts have been closed and have zero balances.

DEMO DOC COMPLETE

| Part 1 | Part 2 | Part 3 | Part 4 | Part 5 | Part 6 | Part 7 | **Demo Doc Complete** |

DECISION GUIDELINES

Completing the Accounting Cycle

In completing the accounting cycle for your business, you might encounter the following decisions:

DECISION

As the bookkeeper for a company, how do I ensure that my accounting records are ready to start a new period?

GUIDELINE

Prepare *closing entries* for the *temporary accounts*:

- Revenues
- Expenses
- Dividends

ANALYZE

The *temporary accounts* have balances that relate only to one accounting period and need to be reset to $0 before accounting for the next period can begin. To reset the temporary accounts, closing entries are made that close the account balances into Retained Earnings. This ensures that the net income for the following period can be tracked accurately.

Assets, Liabilities, Common Shares, and Retained Earnings do not get closed. These accounts are referred to as *permanent accounts*. Their balances are carried forward into the next period.

After temporary accounts have been closed, a post-closing trial balance is prepared to ensure that all of the temporary accounts were properly closed.

ACCOUNTING VOCABULARY

THE LANGUAGE OF BUSINESS

Accounting period (p. 136)

Accruals (p. 137)

Accrued expenses (p. 141)

Accumulated Depreciation (p. 145)

Adjusted trial balance (p. 152)

Adjusting entries (p. 139)

Book value (p. 146)

Carrying value (p. 146)

Cash-basis accounting (p. 137)

Closing entries (p. 155)

Contra-account (p. 146)

Deferrals (p. 138)

Deferred expenses (p. 143)

Deferred revenue (p. 148)

Depreciation (p. 144)

Fiscal year (p. 136)

Interim financial statements (p. 136)

Long-term assets (p. 144)

Matching principle (p. 137)

Net value (p. 146)

Permanent accounts (p. 156)

Post-closing trial balance (p. 158)

Revenue recognition principle (p. 137)

Salvage (residual) value (p. 145)

Straight-line depreciation (p. 145)

Temporary accounts (p. 155)

Unadjusted trial balance (p. 140)

Unearned revenue (p. 138)

ACCOUNTING PRACTICE

1. If XYZ Consulting performs a consulting service in June and bills the customer on June 28 and receives payment from the customer on July 19, on what date would revenue be recorded if

   a. XYZ uses the cash basis of accounting?

   b. XYZ uses the accrual basis of accounting?

2. Why does the time period in which revenue is recognized matter?

3. What is a deferral? Under which basis of accounting, cash or accrual, would deferrals come into play? Under what circumstances would a company record a deferral?

4. Why do companies prepare adjusting entries?

5. What are some similarities and differences between assets and expenses?

6. What type of account (asset, liability, revenue, or expense) would Joe's Towing debit when it pays (credits) cash for each of the following transactions?

   a. Pays $100 to fill tow truck with gas

   b. Pays $1,000 to have a gas company deliver gas for its on-site refueling station to be used next month.

   Did you choose the same type of account or different ones? Why?

7. Describe the type of transaction that gives rise to a deferred revenue journal entry during the year. Why might deferred revenues require adjustment?

8. What kind of account is Accumulated Depreciation? How is it reported on the financial statements?

9. What are the objectives of the closing process? Which kind of accounts get closed? What is the only account that is affected by the closing process but not closed?

1. The revenue recognition principle says

   a. record revenue only after you have earned it.

   b. record revenue only when you receive cash.

   c. match revenues and expenses to compute net income.

   d. divide time into equal periods to measure net income or net loss properly.

2. Adjusting the accounts is the process of

   a. recording transactions as they occur during the period.

   b. updating the accounts at the end of the period.

   c. zeroing out account balances to prepare for the next period.

   d. subtracting expenses from revenues to measure net income.

3. Which of the following terms describe the types of adjusting entries?

   a. Deferrals and depreciation

   b. Expenses and revenues

   c. Deferrals and accruals

   d. Prepaid expenses and prepaid revenues

4. Assume that the weekly payroll of IDT, Inc. is $3,500. December 31, the end of the year, falls on Tuesday, but the company won't pay employees for the full week until its usual payday, Friday. What adjusting entry will IDT, Inc. make on Tuesday, December 31?

MyAccountingLab

The exercises and problems in this chapter can be found on MyAccountingLab. You can practise them as often as you want, and they feature step-by-step guided solutions to help you find the right answer.

DATE	ACCOUNTS	POST REF.	DR.	CR.
a.	Salaries Expense		1,400	
	Accumulated Salaries			1,400
b.	Salaries Expense		1,400	
	Cash			1,400
c.	Salaries Payable		1,400	
	Salaries Expense			1,400
d.	Salaries Expense		1,400	
	Salaries Payable			1,400

5. Unearned Revenue is always

  a. a liability.
  b. revenue.
  c. an asset.
  d. shareholders' equity.

6. The adjusted trial balance shows

  a. amounts that may be out of balance.
  b. revenues and expenses only.
  c. assets, liabilities, and common shares only.
  d. amounts that are ready for the financial statements.

7. Which of the following accounts is not closed?

  a. Salaries Expense
  b. Service Revenue
  c. Accumulated Depreciation, Equipment
  d. Dividends

8. What do closing entries accomplish?

  a. Transfer revenues, expenses, and dividends to retained earnings
  b. Zero out the revenues, expenses, and dividends to prepare them for the next period
  c. Bring the Retained Earnings account to its correct ending balance
  d. All of the above

9. Which of the following is not a closing entry?

DATE	ACCOUNTS	POST REF.	DR.	CR.
a.	Retained Earnings		300	
	Building Rent Expense			300
b.	Salaries Payable		700	
	Retained Earnings			700
c.	Service Revenue		1,100	
	Retained Earnings			1,100
d.	Retained Earnings		600	
	Dividends			600

10. Which correctly represents the flow of information from one financial statement to another?

a. Income statement to the statement of retained earnings

b. Statement of retained earnings to the statement of financial position

c. Both a and b are correct

d. None of the above is correct

Answers are given after Written Communication.

SHORT EXERCISES

S3-1. Accounting principles (*Learning Objective 1*) 5–10 min.

Match the accounting term with the corresponding definition.

____ 1. Accrual basis accounting	a. Any consecutive 12-month period.
____ 2. Revenue recognition principle	b. Records the impact of a business event as it occurs regardless of whether the transaction affected cash.
____ 3. Fiscal period	c. Records revenue when it is earned.

S3-2. Accounting terminology (*Learning Objectives 2 & 3*) 5–10 min.

Match the accounting term with the corresponding definition.

____ 1. Accumulated depreciation	a. An account whose normal balance is opposite that of its companion account.
____ 2. Adjusted trial balance	b. Entry made to assign revenues to the period in which they are earned and expenses to the period incurred.
____ 3. Adjusting entry	c. A list of accounts with their adjusted balances.
____ 4. Book value	d. The cumulative sum of all depreciation recorded for an asset.
____ 5. Contra-account	e. The allocation of a long-term asset's cost to expense over its useful life.
____ 6. Depreciation	f. The asset's cost less its accumulated depreciation.
____ 7. Long-term asset	g. Long-lived asset used to operate the business.

S3-3. Types of adjusting entries (*Learning Objective 2*) 5–10 min.

The trial balance of Sampson & Associates includes the following statement of financial position accounts. For each account, identify the type of adjusting entry that is typically made for the account (deferred expense, deferred revenue, accrued expense, or accrued revenue), and give the related income statement account used in that adjustment. Example: Prepaid Insurance: deferred expense.

a. Interest Payable

b. Unearned Service Revenue

c. Accounts Receivable

d. Supplies

e. Accumulated Depreciation

S3-4. Adjusting journal entry—prepaid rent (*Learning Objective 2*) 5–10 min.

Alpine Ski Shop's Prepaid Rent balance is $4,500 on June 1. This prepaid rent represents six months' rent. Journalize and post the adjusting entry on June 30 to record one month's rent. Compute the balances of the two accounts involved.

S3-5. Adjusting journal entry—supplies (*Learning Objective 2*) 5–10 min.

Alpine Ski Shop's Office Supplies balance on September 1 is $1,200 and the balance in Office Supplies Expense is $0. On September 30, there is $500 of supplies on hand. Journalize and post the adjusting entry on September 30 for the supplies used. Compute the balances of the two accounts involved.

S3-6. Adjusting journal entry—interest expense (*Learning Objective 2*) 5–10 min.

To purchase equipment and supplies, ProPaint, Inc. borrowed $30,000 on August 1 by signing a note payable to First Nations Bank. Interest expense for ProPaint, Inc. is $200 per month. Journalize an adjusting entry to accrue interest expense at December 31, assuming no other adjusting entries have been made for the year. Use T-accounts to post to the two accounts affected by the adjustment.

S3-7. Adjusting journal entry—magazine subscriptions (*Learning Objective 2*) 5–10 min.

Wild Wonders, an outdoor magazine, collected $2,400 on April 1 for one-year subscriptions from subscribers in advance. Journalize and use T-accounts to post the adjusting entry on December 31 to record the revenue that *Wild Wonders* has earned, assuming no other adjusting entries have been made for the year. Compute the balances of the two accounts involved.

S3-8. Adjusting journal entry—salaries, accrued revenue, interest expense (*Learning Objective 2*) 5–10 min.

Journalize the following adjusting entries at December 31:

1. Services provided but not recorded, $1,500.
2. Salaries earned by employees but not recorded, $2,300.
3. Accrued interest on a note payable, $375.

S3-9. Adjusting journal entry—accrued service revenue (*Learning Objective 2*) 5–10 min.

Suppose you work summers mowing yards. Most of your customers pay you immediately after their lawn is mowed, but a few customers ask you to bill them at the end of the month. It is now September 30 and you have collected $1,200 from cash-paying customers. Your remaining customers owe you $150. How much service revenue would you record for the month of September according to accrual basis accounting?

S3-10. Closing entries (*Learning Objective 4*) 5–10 min.

From the following list of accounts from the adjusted trial balance, identify each as an asset, liability, shareholders' equity, revenue, or expense. Use the most detailed account type appropriate. Also state whether each account is a permanent or temporary account and if it is an account that gets closed at the end of the accounting period. Following the accounts is a sample of the format to use.

1. Depreciation Expense
2. Sales Revenue
3. Building
4. Cash
5. Unearned Service Revenue
6. Prepaid Rent
7. Dividends

Account	Type of Account	Permanent/Temporary	Closed
Supplies	Asset	Permanent	No

S3-11. Financial statements and closing entries (*Learning Objectives 3 & 4*) 10–15 min.

The following selected accounts and balances appear on the adjusted trial balance for Ray Service, Inc. on December 31, 2015:

Service Revenue	$1,200
Building Rent Expense	200
Salaries Expense	300
Dividends	500
Common Shares	4,000
Retained Earnings	3,500

1. What is the net income or net loss?
2. What is the change in Retained Earnings?
3. Journalize the closing entries required.

S3-12. Adjusting and closing entries (*Learning Objectives 2 & 4*) 5–10 min.

For the following series of journal entries, indicate whether each is an adjusting entry (ADJ) or a closing entry (CL).

TYPE OF ENTRY (ADJ OR CL)	ACCOUNTS	POST REF.	DR.	CR.
	Salaries Expense		400	
	Salaries Payable			400
	Service Revenue		900	
	Retained Earnings			900
	Retained Earnings		1,500	
	Dividends			1,500
	Unearned Revenue		800	
	Service Revenue			800

S3-13. Preparing a post-closing trial balance (*Learning Objective 4*) 5–10 min.

After closing its accounts at October 31, 2015, Simmons Realty, Inc. had the following account balances:

Notes Payable	$2,000	Cash	$1,850
Prepaid Rent	975	Service Revenue	0
Accounts Receivable	2,450	Retained Earnings	1,075
Prepaid Insurance	1,300	Common Shares	5,000
Accounts Payable	300	Salaries Expense	0
Equipment	1,800		

Prepare Simmons Realty's post-closing trial balance at October 31, 2015. List accounts in proper order.

E3-1A. Adjusting journal entries—unearned revenue and accrued revenue (*Learning Objective 2*) 10–15 min.

Suppose you started up your own tree trimming business. A customer paid you $175 in advance to trim his or her tree while he or she was on vacation. You trimmed trees for other customers but they have not paid you the due fees of $340 yet. A new customer pays you $150 cash for tree trimming. Answer the following questions about the correct way to account for your revenue under accrual basis accounting:

1. Name the accounts used to record these events.

2. Prepare the journal entries to record the three transactions.

E3-2A. Adjusting journal entry—prepaid insurance (*Learning Objective 2*) 5–10 min.

Calculate the missing amounts for each of the following Prepaid Insurance situations. For situation A, journalize the adjusting entry. Consider each situation separately.

	Situation			
	A	B	C	D
Beginning Prepaid Insurance	$ 300	$ 600	$?	$ 400
Payments for Prepaid Insurance during the year..........	1,200	?	1,300	?
Total amount to account for	?	?	2,000	1,900
Ending Prepaid Insurance.......................................	400	500	?	?
Insurance Expense...	$?	$1,000	$1,200	$ 800

E3-3A. Common adjusting journal entries (*Learning Objective 2*) 10–15 min.

Journalize the adjusting entries for the following adjustments at December 31, the end of the accounting period, omitting explanations.

a. Employee salaries owed for Monday through Thursday of a five-day workweek equals $6,000.

b. Unearned service revenue now earned, $750.

c. Depreciation, $1,800.

d. Prepaid rent expired, $450.

e. Interest revenue accrued, $875.

E3-4A. Error analysis (*Learning Objective 2*) 10–15 min.

The adjusting entries for the following adjustments were omitted at year-end:

a. Prepaid insurance expired, $2,400.

b. Depreciation, $1,800.

c. Employee salaries owed for Monday through Wednesday of a five-day workweek, $2,700.

d. Supplies used during the year, $700.

e. Unearned service revenue now earned, $3,500.

Requirement

1. Compute the amount that net income for the year is overstated or understated by for each omitted entry. Use the following format to help analyze the transactions.

Transaction	Overstated/Understated	Amount
Sample a., b., etc.	Overstated	$5,000

E3-5A. Common adjusting journal entries (*Learning Objective 2*) 15–20 min.

Journalize the adjusting entry needed at October 31, the fiscal year-end, for each of the following independent situations (put the transaction letter in the date column to identify each transaction). No other adjusting entries have been made for the year.

a. On September 1, we collected $4,800 rent in advance. We debited Cash and credited Unearned Rent Revenue. The tenant was paying six months' rent in advance.

b. The business holds a $30,000 note receivable. Interest revenue of $650 has been earned on the note but not yet received.

c. Salaries expense is $1,700 per day, Monday through Friday, and the business pays employees each Friday. This year, October 31 falls on a Thursday.

d. The unadjusted balance of the Supplies account is $2,200. Supplies on hand total $700.

e. Equipment was purchased last year at a cost of $18,000. The equipment's useful life is four years.

f. On June 1, when we prepaid $1,500 for a one-year insurance policy, we debited Prepaid Insurance and credited Cash.

E3-6A. Common adjusting journal entries (*Learning Objective 2*) 15–20 min.

The accounting records of Vacations Unlimited include the following unadjusted balances at June 30: Accounts Receivable, $1,500; Supplies, $800; Salaries Payable, $0; Unearned Service Revenue, $900; Service Revenue, $3,900; Salaries Expense, $1,700; and Supplies Expense, $0. The following data pertain to the June 30 adjusting entries:

a. Service revenue accrued, $1,200.

b. Unearned service revenue that has been earned, $500.

c. Supplies on hand, $150.

d. Salary owed to employees, $1,100.

Requirement

1. Record the adjustments, then post them to T-accounts, labelling each adjustment by letter. Calculate each account's adjusted balance.

E3-7A. Income statement preparation (*Learning Objective 3*) 15–20 min.

The accountant for Henderson Roofing, Inc. posted adjusting entries (a) through (e) to the accounts at December 31, 2015. Selected statement of financial position accounts and all the revenues and expenses of the entity follow in T-account form.

Accounts Receivable	
21,000	
(e) 1,500	

Supplies	
2,800	(a) 1,200

Accumulated Depreciation, Equipment	
	5,600
	(b) 1,400

Accumulated Depreciation, Building	
	28,000
	(c) 2,000

Salaries Payable	
	(d) 2,900

Service Revenue	
	97,000
	(e) 1,500

Salaries Expense	
14,000	
(d) 2,900	

Supplies Expense	
(a) 1,200	

Depreciation Expense, Equipment	
(b) 1,400	

Depreciation Expense, Building	
(c) 2,000	

Requirements

1. Calculate balances in the accounts and use the appropriate accounts to prepare the income statement of Henderson Roofing, Inc. for the year ended December 31, 2015. List expenses in order from largest to smallest.

2. Were the 2015 operations successful? Give the reason for your answer.

E3-8A. Statement of retained earnings preparation (*Learning Objective 3*) 10–15 min.

Sigma Security, Inc. began the year with $15,000 of common shares and $32,000 of retained earnings. On May 5, investors bought $12,000 of additional shares in the business. On August 22, the business purchased land valued at $65,000. The income statement for the year ended December 31, 2015, reported a net loss of $11,000. During this fiscal year, the business paid $800 each month for dividends.

Requirements

1. Prepare Sigma Security's statement of retained earnings for the year ended December 31, 2015.

2. Did the retained earnings of the business increase or decrease during the year? What caused this change?

E3-9A. Recreating adjusting journal entries (*Learning Objective 2*) 10–15 min.

The adjusted trial balances of PDQ, Inc. at December 31, 2015 and December 31, 2016 include these amounts:

	2015	2016
Supplies	$ 2,800	$ 1,700
Salaries Payable	2,800	3,700
Unearned Service Revenue	18,000	16,300

Analysis of the accounts at December 31, 2016 reveals these transactions for 2016:

Purchase of supplies	$ 8,700
Cash payments for salaries	52,300
Cash receipts in advance for services revenue	106,400

Requirement

1. Compute the amount of supplies expense, salaries expense, and service revenue PDQ, Inc. will report for the year ended December 31, 2016. Solve by making T-accounts and posting the information to solve for the unknown amounts.

E3-10A. Financial statement preparation (*Learning Objective 3*) 15–20 min.

The adjusted trial balance for Country Cookin Catering, Inc. is presented next. Prepare the income statement, statement of retained earnings, and statement of financial position for Country Cookin Catering, Inc. for the month ended March 31, 2015.

Country Cookin Catering, Inc.
Adjusted Trial Balance
March 31, 2015

ACCOUNT	DEBIT	CREDIT
Cash	$ 4,000	
Accounts Receivable	8,000	
Supplies	1,300	
Equipment	22,500	
Accumulated Depreciation, Equipment		$ 8,800
Accounts Payable		2,100
Salaries Payable		600
Unearned Service Revenue		1,400
Common Shares		5,000
Retained Earnings		5,800
Dividends	800	
Service Revenues		18,600
Salaries Expense	3,600	
Rent Expense	1,200	
Depreciation Expense, Equipment	600	
Supplies Expense	300	
Total	$42,300	$42,300

E3-11A. Prepare closing entries (*Learning Objective 4*) 10–15 min.

Requirements

1. Using the following selected accounts of A to Z Electrical, Inc. at April 30, 2015, prepare the entity's closing entries:

Common Shares	$ 18,000	Accounts Receivable	$ 9,000
Service Revenue	127,000	Retained Earnings	6,500
Unearned Revenues	1,800	Salaries Payable	800
Salaries Expense	18,500	Depreciation Expense	8,200
Accumulated Depreciation	32,600	Building Rent Expense	5,100
Supplies Expense	1,700	Dividends	18,000
Interest Revenue	800	Supplies	1,800
Interest Expense	2,300		

2. What is A to Z Electrical's ending retained earnings balance at April 30, 2015?

E3-12A. Statement of retained earnings preparation (*Learning Objective 3*) 10–15 min.

From the following accounts of Kurlz Salon, Inc., prepare the business's statement of retained earnings for the year ended December 31, 2015:

Retained Earnings			
Clo	95,000	Jan 1	188,000
Clo	76,000	Clo	234,000
		Bal	251,000

Dividends			
Mar 31	18,000		
Jun 30	14,000		
Sep 30	23,000		
Dec 31	21,000		
Bal	76,000	Clo	76,000

E3-13A. Prepare a post-closing trial balance (*Learning Objective 4*) 10–15 min.

The following post-closing trial balance was prepared for Cunningham Photography, Inc. Prepare a corrected post-closing trial balance. Assume all accounts have normal balances and the amounts are correct.

ACCOUNT	DEBIT	CREDIT
Cunningham Photography, Inc.		
Post-Closing Trial Balance		
December 31, 2015		
Cash	$ 9,450	
Accounts Receivable	33,100	
Supplies		$ 1,900
Equipment		68,000
Accumulated Depreciation, Equipment	19,700	
Accounts Payable	11,450	
Salaries Payable		2,500
Unearned Service Revenue	5,600	
Common Shares		30,000
Retained Earnings	43,200	
Total	$122,500	$102,400

E3-14A. Prepare closing entries (*Learning Objective 4*) 10–15 min.

The following is the adjusted trial balance of Qwik Care Clinic, Inc. for December 31, 2015.

Requirement

1. Journalize the closing entries at December 31.

ACCOUNT	DEBIT	CREDIT
Qwik Care Clinic, Inc.		
Adjusted Trial Balance		
December 31, 2015		
Cash	$ 7,400	
Accounts Receivable	8,700	
Supplies	200	
Furniture	4,800	
Accumulated Depreciation, Furniture		$ 1,200
Equipment	32,000	
Accumulated Depreciation, Equipment		8,800
Accounts Payable		1,300
Salaries Payable		3,500
Unearned Service Revenue		3,100
Common Shares		10,000
Retained Earnings		18,500
Dividends	14,000	
Service Revenues		73,000
Salaries Expense	31,000	
Rent Expense	18,600	
Depreciation Expense, Equipment	1,600	
Depreciation Expense, Furniture	400	
Supplies Expense	700	
Total	$119,400	$119,400

E3-15A. Common adjusting journal entries and financial statement reporting (*Learning Objectives 2 & 3*) 15–20 min.

Chen Financial Services (CFS) is making adjusting entries for the year ended June 30, 2015. The accounting clerk gathered the following information:

a. Paid one-year insurance premium of $2,400 on December 1, 2014, for coverage beginning on January 1, 2015.

b. Office Supplies account showed a balance of $480 and $270 on June 30, 2014 and 2015, respectively. During the year, CFS purchased $860 of office supplies.

c. Received $3,600 from a customer who paid for a three-month financial service contract starting on June 1. Financial Services Revenue account was credited on June 1.

d. An employee borrowed $12,000 by signing a one-year, 5% interest-bearing note from CFS on April 1, 2015. The note specified that interest was payable on the 5th of each month starting May 2015.

e. Signed a contract on June 1 with a local advertising company for $1,500 monthly advertising fee. The advertising service started immediately after signing the contract, and the payment was to be made on the 2nd of each month, starting July 2015.

Requirements

1. Prepare the adjusting entry for each item (a) to (e).

2. What amount should be reported for revenue and expense accounts, from (a) to (e) on the income statement, for the year ended June 30, 2015?

3. What amount should be reported for each asset and liability account in the statement of financial position?

E3-16A. Analyzing the effects of errors on accounts and adjusting entries (*Learning Objective 2*) 10–15 min.

Patel Instruments, Inc. made the following errors in the year-end account adjustments on December 31:

a. Did not record $1,200 salary owed to employees for four days of work.

b. Did not adjust $1,600 of revenue earned from the Unearned Revenue account for the second half of December.

c. Recorded a full year of depreciation, based on an equipment cost of $26,000 and salvage value of $2,000, with a useful life of four years. The equipment was purchased on October 1.

d. Did not adjust $600 of unused office supplies that was originally recorded in the Office Supplies Expense account.

Requirements

1. What is the impact that each item has had on net income, and on the asset, liability, and shareholders' equity accounts? Show understatements by "U," overstatements by "O," and no effect by "NE," and identify their amounts.

2. Based on each item (a) to (d) described above, prepare the appropriate adjusting entry for each item to reflect the correct account balance.

E3-17A. Identify the type of adjustment and adjusting entries (*Learning Objectives 1 & 2*) 10–15 min.

Techco Computer Services had the following transactions during the year. Its year-end is on September 30.

a. One-year insurance premium $1,800 was purchased on April 30. Coverage began on May 1.

b. The monthly payroll was $4,200, and the payment to employees was on the 1st of the following month.

c. A server was purchased on February 1 for $16,000. Techco estimated that the server could last five years, with a salvage value of $1,000 at the end of the fifth year.

d. Computer maintenance service was performed for a client on September 28 for $2,600. The invoice was sent on October 5, after the year-end date.

e. The Unearned Service Revenue account showed a balance of $5,200, which represents a four-month service contract. Three-quarters of the service was performed by the end of September.

Requirements

1. Identify each of the above transactions as accrued revenue, accrued expense, deferred revenue, or deferred expense.

2. Record the adjusting entry for each transaction.

E3-18A. Adjusting entries and inferring transactions (*Learning Objectives 2 & 3*) 10–15 min.

Park Management Ltd's selected account balances are presented below.

Account Title	November 30	December 31
Rent Receivable	$8,200	$5,600
Prepaid Insurance	1,300	900
Unearned Rent Revenue	3,800	2,500
Salaries Payable	3,000	5,000

Additional information regarding transactions that occurred in December:

a. Collection from rent receivable was $12,500.

b. Additional insurance purchased was $600.

c. Cash paid in advance from customers was $1,600.

d. Salary paid to employees was $4,000.

Requirements

1. Record the transactions that occurred during December.

2. Record the adjusting entries on December 31.

3. What amount should be reported for revenue and expense accounts on the income statement for the month ended December 31?

EXERCISES (GROUP B)

E3-1B. Adjusting journal entries—unearned revenue and accrued revenue (*Learning Objective 2*) 10–15 min.

Suppose you started up your own landscaping business. A customer paid you $120 in advance to mow his or her lawn while he or she was on vacation. You performed landscaping services for a local business but the business hasn't paid you the $425 fee yet. A customer pays you $110 cash for landscaping services. Answer the following questions about the correct way to account for your revenue under accrual-basis accounting:

1. Name the accounts used to record these events.

2. Prepare the journal entries to record the three transactions.

E3-2B. Adjusting journal entry—prepaid advertising (*Learning Objective 2*) 5–10 min.

Calculate the missing amounts for each of the Prepaid Insurance situations.
For situation A, journalize the adjusting entry. Consider each situation separately.

	Situation			
	A	B	C	D
Beginning Prepaid Insurance	$ 800	$1,100	?	$ 300
Payments for Prepaid Insurance during the year..........	1,500	?	1,600	?
Total amount to account for.....................................	?	?	3,200	2,700
Ending Prepaid Insurance	700	1,200	?	?
Insurance Expense...	$?	$ 500	$2,600	$1,400

E3-3B. Common adjusting journal entries (*Learning Objective 2*) 10–15 min.

Journalize the adjusting entries at May 31, the end of the accounting period. Omit explanations.

   a. Employee salaries owed for Monday through Thursday of a five-day workweek equals $7,500.

   b. Unearned service revenue now earned, $1,250.

   c. Depreciation, $1,900.

   d. Prepaid rent expired, $550.

   e. Interest revenue accrued, $980.

E3-4B. Error analysis (*Learning Objective 2*) 10–15 min.

The adjusting entries for the following adjustments were omitted at year-end:

   a. Prepaid rent expired, $2,500.

   b. Depreciation, $1,000.

   c. Employee salaries owed for Monday through Wednesday of a five-day workweek, $3,100.

   d. Supplies used during the year, $800.

   e. Unearned service revenue now earned, $4,500.

Requirement

   1. Compute the amount that net income for the year is overstated or understated for each omitted entry. Use the following format to help analyze the transactions.

Transaction	Overstated/Understated	Amount
Sample a., b., etc.	Overstated	$5,000

E3-5B. Common adjusting journal entries (*Learning Objective 2*) 15–20 min.

Journalize the adjusting entry needed at August 31, the fiscal year-end, for each of the following independent situations. No other adjusting entries have been made for the year.

   a. On July 1, we collected $3,000 rent in advance. We debited Cash and credited Unearned Rent Revenue. The tenant was paying six months' rent in advance.

   b. The business holds a $35,000 note receivable. Interest revenue of $520 has been earned on the note but not yet received.

   c. Salaries expense is $2,900 per day, Monday through Friday, and the business pays employees each Friday. This year, August 31 falls on a Tuesday.

   d. The unadjusted balance of the Supplies account is $1,400. Supplies on hand total $200.

e. Equipment was purchased last year at a cost of $8,000. The equipment's useful life is 10 years.

f. On April 1, when we prepaid $1,560 for a one-year insurance policy, we debited Prepaid Insurance and credited Cash.

E3-6B. Common adjusting journal entries (*Learning Objective 2*) 15–20 min.

The accounting records of Weddings Unlimited include the following unadjusted balances at April 30: Accounts Receivable, $1,900; Supplies, $1,100; Salaries Payable, $0; Unearned Service Revenue, $1,300; Service Revenue, $5,300; Salaries Expense, $3,100; and Supplies Expense, $0. The following data pertains to April 30 adjusting entries:

a. Service revenue accrued, $2,200.

b. Unearned service revenue that has been earned, $300.

c. Supplies on hand, $150.

d. Salary owed to employees, $700.

Requirement

1. Record the adjustments, then post them to T-accounts, labelling each adjustment by letter. Calculate each account's adjusted balance.

E3-7B. Income statement preparation (*Learning Objective 3*) 15–20 min.

The accountant for Metal Main, Inc. posted adjusting entries (a) through (e) to the accounts at August 31, 2015. Selected statement of financial position accounts and all the revenues and expenses of the entity follow in T-account form.

Accounts Receivable		Supplies		Accumulated Depreciation, Equipment		Accumulated Depreciation, Building	
19,200		2,200	(a) 1,600		4,200		46,000
(e) 2,250					(b) 1,400		(c) 1,000

Salaries Payable				Service Revenue	
	(d) 2,500				6,400
					(e) 2,250

Salaries Expense		Supplies Expense		Depreciation Expense, Equipment		Depreciation Expense, Building	
13,500		(a) 1,600		(b) 1,400		(c) 1,000	
(d) 2,500							

Requirements

1. Calculate balances in the accounts and use the appropriate accounts to prepare the income statement of Metal Main, Inc. for the year ended August 31, 2015. List expenses in order from largest to smallest.

2. Were the 2015 operations successful? Give the reason for your answer.

E3-8B. Statement of retained earnings preparation (*Learning Objective 3*) 10–15 min.

Zeta Safety, Inc. began the year with $15,000 of common shares and $34,000 of retained earnings. On August 5, investors bought $19,000 of additional shares in the business. On October 22, the business purchased land valued at $45,000. The income statement for the year ended December 31, 2015, reported a net loss of $5,000. During this fiscal year, the business paid $550 each month for dividends.

Requirements

1. Prepare Zeta Safety's statement of retained earnings for the year ended December 31, 2015.

2. Did the retained earnings of the business increase or decrease during the year? What caused this change?

E3-9B. Recreating adjusting journal entries (*Learning Objective 2*) 10–15 min.

The adjusted trial balances of CAS, Inc. at March 31, 2015, and March 31, 2016, include these amounts:

	2015	2016
Supplies...	$ 1,700	$ 1,200
Salaries Payable..	4,000	4,500
Unearned Service Revenue	17,000	15,100

Analysis of the accounts at March 31, 2016, reveals these transactions for 2016:

Purchases of supplies..	$ 9,000
Cash payments for salaries..	55,500
Cash receipts in advance for service revenue...	58,000

Requirement

1. Compute the amount of supplies expense, salaries expense, and service revenue CAS, Inc. will report for the year ended March 31, 2016. Solve by making T-accounts and posting the information to solve for the unknown amounts.

E3-10B. Financial statement preparation (*Learning Objective 3*) 15–20 min.

The adjusted trial balance for Spruce Up Catering, Inc. is presented next. Prepare the income statement, statement of retained earnings, and statement of financial position for Spruce Up Catering, Inc. for the month ended January 31, 2015.

Spruce Up Catering, Inc. Adjusted Trial Balance January 31, 2015		
ACCOUNT	**DEBIT**	**CREDIT**
Cash	$ 6,500	
Accounts Receivable	6,000	
Supplies	400	
Equipment	26,600	
Accumulated Depreciation, Equipment		$ 6,800
Accounts Payable		2,300
Salaries Payable		1,100
Unearned Service Revenue		1,900
Common Shares		5,200
Retained Earnings		11,100
Dividends	1,100	
Service Revenue		20,100
Salaries Expense	3,800	
Rent Expense	1,700	
Depreciation Expense, Equipment	1,500	
Supplies Expense	900	
Total	$48,500	$48,500

E3-11B. Prepare closing entries (*Learning Objective 4*) 10–15 min.

Requirements

1. Using the following selected accounts of Juba Electrical, Inc. at September 30, 2015, prepare the entity's closing entries:

Common Shares	$17,000	Accounts Receivable	$14,000
Service Revenue	49,000	Retained Earnings	7,900
Unearned Revenues	2,500	Salaries Payable	700
Salaries Expense	21,900	Depreciation Expense	5,000
Accumulated Depreciation	32,600	Building Rent Expense	5,600
Supplies Expense	2,300	Dividends	14,000
Interest Revenue	300	Supplies	2,300
Interest Expense	2,400		

2. What is Juba Electrical's ending retained earnings balance at September 30, 2015?

E3-12B. Statement of retained earnings preparation (*Learning Objective 3*) 10–15 min.

From the following accounts of Resch Restore, Inc. prepare the business's statement of retained earnings for the year ended January 31, 2015:

Retained Earnings					Dividends		
Clo	110,000	Feb 1	77,000	Apr 30	17,000		
Clo	82,000	Clo	299,000	Jul 31	14,000		
		Bal	184,000	Oct 31	24,000		
				Jan 31	27,000		
				Bal	82,000	Clo	82,000

E3-13B. Prepare a post-closing trial balance (*Learning Objective 4*) 10–15 min.

The following post-closing trial balance was prepared for Fonzarelli Photo, Inc. Prepare a corrected post-closing trial balance. Assume all accounts have normal balances and the amounts are correct.

Fonzarelli Photo, Inc. Post-Closing Trial Balance March 31, 2015		
ACCOUNT	**DEBIT**	**CREDIT**
Cash	$10,250	
Accounts Receivable	25,000	
Supplies		$ 600
Equipment		17,000
Accumulated Depreciation, Equip.	5,000	
Accounts Payable	8,800	
Salaries Payable		5,200
Unearned Service Revenue	2,200	
Common Shares		20,000
Retained Earnings	11,650	
Total	$62,900	$42,800

E3-14B. Prepare closing entries (*Learning Objective 4*) 10–15 min.

The following is the adjusted trial balance of Happy Health, Inc. for August 31, 2015.

Happy Health, Inc. Adjusted Trial Balance August 31, 2015		
ACCOUNT	DEBIT	CREDIT
Cash	$ 9,000	
Accounts Receivable	11,000	
Supplies	170	
Furniture	5,200	
Accumulated Depreciation, Furniture		$ 1,800
Equipment	39,000	
Accumulated Depreciation, Equipment		4,500
Accounts Payable		1,200
Salaries Payable		3,500
Unearned Service Revenue		2,200
Common Shares		18,000
Retained Earnings		7,970
Dividends	14,000	
Service Revenue		77,000
Salaries Expense	27,000	
Rent Expense	6,000	
Depreciation Expense, Equipment	1,500	
Depreciation Expense, Furniture	1,300	
Supplies Expense	2,000	
Total	$116,170	$116,170

Requirement

1. Journalize the closing entries at August 31.

E3-15B. Common adjusting journal entries and financial statement reporting (*Learning Objectives 2 & 3*) 15–20 min.

Fung Cleaning Services (FCS) is making adjusting entries for the year ended September 30, 2015. The accounting clerk gathered the following information:

a. Paid one-year insurance premium of $1,800 on January 21, 2015, for coverage beginning on February 1, 2015.

b. Cleaning Supplies account showed a balance of $520 and $430 on September 30, 2014 and 2015, respectively. During the year, FCS purchased $780 of cleaning supplies.

c. Received $3,600 from a restaurant customer who paid for a six-month cleaning service contract starting on July 1. Cleaning Services Revenue account was credited on July 1.

d. An employee borrowed $9,000 by signing a one-year, 4% interest-bearing note from FCS on September 1. The note specified that interest was payable on the 5th of each month, starting October 2015.

e. Signed a contract on July 1 with a local advertising company for $1,750 monthly advertising fee. The advertising service started immediately after signing the contract, and the payment was to be made on the 2nd of each month, starting August 2015.

Requirements

1. Prepare the adjusting entry for each item (a) to (e).

2. What amount should be reported for revenue and expense accounts, from (a) to (e) on the income statement, for the year ended September 30, 2015?

3. What amount should be reported for each asset and liability account on the statement of financial position? (You can assume that interest payments have been received on time and payments for advertising have been made on time.)

E3-16B. Analyzing the effects of errors on accounts and adjusting entries (*Learning Objective 2*) 10–15 min.

Rupinder Delivery Services made the following errors in the year-end account adjustments on June 30:

a. Did not record $1,800 gasoline charges on the credit card for the week of June 26.

b. Did not adjust $900 of delivery services provided to a client for the second half of June. The invoice for the service was sent out on July 3.

c. Recorded a full year of depreciation, based on a delivery truck cost of $27,000 and salvage value of $2,000, with a useful life of five years. The delivery truck was purchased on April 1.

d. Did not adjust for unexpired insurance. A one-year insurance premium of $2,400 was paid on February 1 and the coverage started immediately. The transaction was recorded in the Insurance Expense account.

Requirements

1. What is the impact that each item has had on net income, and asset, liability, and shareholders' equity accounts? Show understatements by "U," overstatements by "O," and no effect by "NE," and identify their amounts.

2. Based on each item described above, prepare the appropriate adjusting entry to reflect the correct account balance.

E3-17B. Identify the type of adjustment and adjusting entries (*Learning Objectives 1 & 2*) 10–15 min.

BT Spa had the following transactions during the year. Its year-end is on June 30.

a. The Unearned Revenue account showed a balance of $800, which represented four gift certificates of $200 each sold in June. Three gift certificates had been redeemed in June.

b. The Prepaid Rent account showed a balance of $6,000, which represented six months' rent paid on April 1.

c. An exercise machine was purchased on March 1 for $7,500. BT estimated that the machine could last eight years, with a salvage value of $300 at the end of the eighth year.

d. Five employees each earned $100/day. Salary for the last seven days of June would be paid on July 2.

e. A fitness service was performed for a business client on June 30 for $350. The invoice was sent on July 5, after the year-end date.

Requirements

1. Identify each of the above transactions as accrued revenue, accrued expense, deferred revenue, or deferred expense.

2. Record the adjusting entry for each transaction.

**E3-18B. Adjusting entries and inferring transactions (*Learning Objectives 2 & 3*)
10–15 min.**

Giuseppe Landscaping Ltd's selected account balances are presented below.

Account Title	May 31	June 30
Accounts Receivable	$4,200	$6,300
Landscaping Supplies	1,200	1,400
Unearned Revenue	2,100	2,400
Salaries Payable	4,000	3,500

Additional information regarding transactions that occurred in June:

a. Collection from accounts receivable was $7,500.

b. Additional landscaping supplies purchased were $1,000.

c. Cash paid in advance from customers was $1,800.

d. Salary paid to employee that was owing from the previous month was $4,000.

Requirements

1. Record the transactions that occurred during June.

2. Record the adjusting entries on June 30.

3. What amount should be reported for revenue and expense accounts on the income statement for the month ended June 30?

EXERCISES (ALTERNATES 1, 2, AND 3)

These alternative exercise sets are available for your practice benefit on
MyAccountingLab.

PROBLEMS (GROUP A)

P3-1A. Common adjusting journal entries (*Learning Objective 2*) 15–20 min.

Journalize the adjusting entry needed at December 31, the end of the current accounting year, for each of the following independent cases affecting Canyon Riders, Inc. No other adjusting entries have been made for the year.

a. Prior to making the adjusting entry on December 31, the balance in Prepaid Insurance is $3,600. Canyon Riders, Inc. pays liability insurance each year on August 1.

b. Canyon Riders, Inc. pays employees each Friday. The amount of the weekly payroll is $16,500 for a five-day workweek. December 31, the fiscal year-end, is a Tuesday.

c. Canyon Riders, Inc. received notes receivable from some customers for services provided. For the current year, accrued interest amounts to $300 and will be collected next year.

d. The beginning balance of Supplies was $900. During the year, $4,500 of supplies were purchased. At December 31, the supplies on hand total $1,800.

e. During the year, Canyon Riders, Inc. received $17,200 in advance for services to be provided at a later date. As of December 31, Canyon Riders, Inc. earned $5,100 of the total fees received in advance during the current year.

f. Depreciation for the current year includes Vehicles, $2,990, and Equipment, $1,300.

P3-2A. Recreating adjusting journal entries from trial balances (*Learning Objective 2*) 15–20 min.

Assume the unadjusted and adjusted trial balances for Kristy's Consulting, Inc. at June 30, 2015, show the following data:

Kristy's Consulting, Inc.
Trial Balance
June 30, 2015

ACCOUNT	UNADJUSTED TRIAL BALANCE DR.	UNADJUSTED TRIAL BALANCE CR.	ADJUSTED TRIAL BALANCE DR.	ADJUSTED TRIAL BALANCE CR.
Cash	$ 6,200		$ 6,200	
Accounts Receivable	5,800		5,800	
Supplies	1,400		300	
Prepaid Rent	2,800		2,100	
Equipment	18,000		18,000	
Accumulated Depreciation, Equipment		$ 7,500		$ 7,750
Accounts Payable		1,800		1,800
Salaries Payable				1,250
Interest Payable				150
Unearned Service Revenue		2,600		900
Notes Payable		7,000		7,000
Common Shares		5,000		5,000
Retained Earnings		4,900		4,900
Dividends	13,600		13,600	
Service Revenues		47,400		49,100
Salaries Expense	23,400		24,650	
Rent Expense	3,500		4,200	
Depreciation Expense, Equipment	1,250		1,500	
Interest Expense	250		400	
Supplies Expense			1,100	
Total	$76,200	$76,200	$77,850	$77,850

Requirement

1. Journalize the adjusting entries that account for the differences between the two trial balances.

P3-3A. Prepare adjusting journal entries and an adjusted trial balance
(*Learning Objectives 2 & 3*) 25–30 min.

The trial balance of Alpha Advertising, Inc. at November 30, 2015, and the data
needed for the month-end adjustments follow:

		Alpha Advertising, Inc. Trial Balance November 30, 2015		
		ACCOUNT	DEBIT	CREDIT
		Cash	$ 22,800	
		Accounts Receivable	39,400	
		Prepaid Insurance	2,700	
		Supplies	900	
		Equipment	83,800	
		Accumulated Depreciation, Equipment		$ 64,300
		Accounts Payable		1,900
		Salaries Payable		
		Unearned Service Revenue		2,200
		Common Shares		50,000
		Retained Earnings		29,300
		Dividends	3,600	
		Service Revenues		8,400
		Salaries Expense	2,900	
		Insurance Expense		
		Depreciation Expense, Equipment		
		Utilities Expense		
		Supplies Expense		
		Total	$156,100	$156,100

a. Insurance coverage still remaining at November 30, $300.

b. Supplies used during the month, $250.

c. Depreciation for the month, $1,200.

d. Accrued utilities expense at November 30, $300. (Use Accounts Payable as
the liability account needed.)

e. Accrued salaries at November 30, $450.

f. Service revenue still unearned at November 30, $800.

Requirements

1. Open T-accounts for the accounts listed in the trial balance and insert their
November 30 unadjusted balances.

2. Journalize the adjusting entries and post them to the T-accounts. Reference the
posted amounts by letters (a) through (f). Calculate the adjusted balance in each
account.

3. Prepare the adjusted trial balance.

4. How will the company use the adjusted trial balance?

P3-4A. Effects of adjusting journal entries on income statement accounts
(*Learning Objectives 2 & 3*) 20–25 min.

Helgeson Enterprises, Corp. completed the following selected transactions and prepared these adjusting entries during January:

Jan 1	Prepaid insurance for January through March, $750.
3	Performed service on account, $1,800.
6	Purchased office furniture on account, $350.
8	Paid property tax expense, $600.
12	Purchased office equipment for cash, $1,400.
18	Performed services and received cash, $4,700.
23	Collected $900 on account.
26	Paid the account payable from the January 6 transaction.
30	Paid salaries expense, $2,400.
31	Recorded an adjusting entry for January insurance expense related to the January 1 transaction.
31	Recorded an adjusting entry for unearned revenue now earned, $400.

Requirements

1. State whether the transaction would increase revenues, decrease revenues, increase expenses, decrease expenses, or have no effect on revenues or expenses. If revenues or expenses are affected, give the amount of the impact on revenues or expenses for January. Use the following format for your answer.

Revenues and Expenses for January		
Date	**Impact on Revenues or Expenses**	**$ Effect on Revenues or Expenses**
Jan XX	Increase Revenues	$500

2. Compute January net income or net loss under the accrual basis of accounting.

3. State why the accrual basis of accounting results in an accurate measurement of income.

P3-5A. Prepare financial statements (*Learning Objective 3*) 20–25 min.

The adjusted trial balance of Lighthouse Realty, Inc. at December 31, 2015, follows:

ACCOUNT	DEBIT	CREDIT
Cash	$ 6,300	
Accounts Receivable	11,600	
Prepaid Rent	1,200	
Supplies	900	
Equipment	48,000	
Accumulated Depreciation, Equipment		$ 12,000
Accounts Payable		5,400
Unearned Service Revenue		2,100
Interest Payable		750
Salaries Payable		1,800
Notes Payable		12,000
Common Shares		20,000
Retained Earnings		8,200
Dividends	14,000	
Service Revenue		97,000
Interest Revenue		650
Salaries Expense	51,000	
Rent Expense	18,000	
Depreciation Expense, Equipment	4,200	
Utilities Expense	2,700	
Interest Expense	1,300	
Supplies Expense	700	
Total	$159,900	$159,900

Lighthouse Realty, Inc.
Adjusted Trial Balance
December 31, 2015

Requirements

1. Prepare Lighthouse Realty's 2015 income statement, statement of retained earnings, and year-end statement of financial position. List expenses in decreasing order on the income statement.

2. **a.** Which financial statement reports Lighthouse Realty's results of operations? Were operations successful during 2015? Cite specifics from the financial statements to support your evaluation.

   b. Which statement reports the company's financial position?

P3-6A. Prepare closing entries and a post-closing trial balance (*Learning Objective 4*) 20–25 min.

The June 30, 2015, adjusted trial balance of Energized Espresso, Inc. is shown next.

		ACCOUNT	DEBIT	CREDIT
		Energized Espresso, Inc.		
		Adjusted Trial Balance		
		June 30, 2015		
		Cash	$ 4,900	
		Accounts Receivable	9,600	
		Prepaid Rent	1,800	
		Supplies	600	
		Equipment	26,000	
		Accumulated Depreciation, Equipment		$ 4,200
		Accounts Payable		2,400
		Unearned Service Revenue		1,100
		Salaries Payable		1,800
		Notes Payable		3,000
		Common Shares		10,000
		Retained Earnings		11,950
		Dividends	2,000	
		Service Revenue		43,000
		Interest Revenue		400
		Salaries Expense	24,500	
		Rent Expense	6,000	
		Depreciation Expense, Equipment	1,200	
		Utilities Expense	700	
		Supplies Expense	550	
		Total	$77,850	$77,850

Quick solution:

2. Retained Earnings = $20,400

3. Trial balance totals = $42,900

Requirements

1. Prepare the June closing entries for Energized Espresso, Inc.

2. Calculate the ending balance in retained earnings.

3. Prepare a post-closing trial balance.

P3-7A. Effects of errors on assets, liabilities, shareholders' equity, and net income (*Learning Objectives 2 & 3*) 15–20 min.

The following errors were made in the accounting records of Garceau Corp. in 2015 and were not discovered until 2016.

a. The journal entry to record a receipt of $3,170 for Consulting Revenue was incorrectly recorded as $7,310.

b. A $2,400 credit to Accumulated Amortization, Automobile account was incorrectly credited to Automobile account.

c. A payment of $2,800 for dividends was incorrectly debited to Salaries Expense account.

d. Salaries expense for 2015 of $1,650 was not recorded. It was recorded as Salaries Expense in 2016 when it was paid.

e. A $1,850 credit to Unearned Revenue was posted to Accounts Receivable.

Requirements

For each of the independent errors in parts (a) through (e), identify the net effect on assets, liabilities, shareholders' equity, and net income for 2015 and 2016. Show

understatements by "U," overstatements by "O," and no effect by "NE," and identify
their amounts.

	Assets		Liabilities		Shareholders' Equity		Net Income	
	2015	2016	2015	2016	2015	2016	2015	2016
a								
b								
c								
d								
e								

P3-8A. Adjusting entries using a worksheet (*Learning Objectives 1, 2, 3 & 5*)
35–40 min.

Klean Laundry Services (KLS) has been providing commercial laundry services to restaurants and hotels for several years. KLS's year-end is on June 30. The unadjusted
trial balance on June 30, 2015, was as follows:

Klean Laundry Services
Worksheet
For Month Ended June 30, 2015

ACCT #	ACCOUNT	UNADJUSTED TRIAL BALANCE DR.	CR.	ADJUSTMENTS DR.	CR.	ADJUSTED TRIAL BALANCE DR.	CR.
1010	Cash	$ 5,100					
1020	Accounts Receivable	9,300					
1030	Laundry Supplies	8,600					
1035	Prepaid Insurance	3,600					
1040	Laundry Machines	50,000					
1041	Accumulated Depreciation, Laundry Machines		$ 15,000				
2010	Accounts Payable		3,700				
2015	Salaries Payable						
2020	Unearned Laundry Revenue		2,100				
2025	Interest Payable						
2030	Income Tax Payable						
2100	Note Payable – 3 years		21,000				
3010	Common Shares		10,000				
3030	Retained Earnings		18,500				
3040	Dividends	4,500					
4010	Laundry Revenue		98,000				
5010	Salaries Expense	62,000					
5015	Insurance Expense	9,000					
5030	Utilities Expense	8,400					
5040	Depreciation Expense, Laundry Machines						
5050	Laundry Supplies Expense	7,800					
5060	Interest Expense						
5070	Income Tax Expense						
	Total	$168,300	$168,300				

Additional information about several transactions that occurred during the year:

a. Laundry services provided to hotels amounted to $7,500 in June. The client would pay on July 5.

b. A physical count of laundry supplies showed that there was $3,200 of cleaning supplies on hand on June 30. The balance of Laundry Supplies Expense, $7,800 on June 30, represents laundry supplies purchased during the year.

c. The balance of Prepaid Insurance represents one-year insurance premium paid on February 1.

d. Laundry machines were estimated to last for eight years, with a salvage value of $2,000 at the end of the eigth year. No adjustment was made for this fiscal year.

e. Four workers each earned $60/day. Six days of wages were earned by employees, but not paid by June 30.

f. Seventy percent of the unearned revenue was earned in June.

g. On March 1, KLS borrowed $21,000 from the RBC bank by signing a three-year note with a 5% interest rate. KLS was required to make annual interest payments at the end of each year.

h. The utilities expense for June was estimated at $1,200. The utility bill usually arrived during the first week of the following month.

i. KLS's income tax rate was 30%.

Requirements

1. Indicate the type of adjustments for each transaction.
2. Prepare the adjusting entry and enter the amount for each transaction in the worksheet.
3. Prepare the adjusted trial balance in the worksheet.
4. What is the age of the laundry machines?
5. Prepare the income statement, statement of retained earnings, and statement of financial position.
6. Record the adjusting entry for the income tax.

P3-9A. Closing entries using a worksheet (*Learning Objectives 4 & 5*) 10–15 min.

Refer to P3-8A.

Requirement

Using the adjusted trial balance from P3-8A, prepare the closing entries for 2015 and the post-closing trial balance in the worksheet.

PROBLEMS (GROUP B)

P3-1B. Common adjusting journal entries (*Learning Objective 2*) 15–20 min.

Journalize the adjusting entries needed at December 31, the end of the current accounting year, for each of the following independent cases affecting Mountain Mania, Inc. No other adjusting entries have been made for the year.

a. Prior to making the adjusting entry on December 31, the balance in Prepaid Insurance is $1,200. Mountain Mania, Inc. pays liability insurance each year on April 30.

b. Mountain Mania, Inc. pays employees each Friday. The amount of the weekly payroll is $12,500 for a five-day workweek. December 31, the fiscal year-end, is a Monday.

c. Mountain Mania, Inc. received notes receivable from some customers for services provided. For the current year, accrued interest amounts to $640 and will be collected next year.

d. The beginning balance of Supplies was $1,025. During the year, $4,300 of supplies were purchased. At December 31, the supplies on hand total $2,500.

e. During the year, Mountain Mania, Inc. received $17,200 in advance for services to be provided at a later date. As of December 31, Mountain Mania, Inc. earned $4,700 of the total fees received in advance during the current year.

f. Depreciation for the current year includes Vehicles, $2,550, and Equipment, $1,300.

P3-2B. Recreating adjusting journal entries from trial balances (*Learning Objective 2*) 15–20 min.

Assume the unadjusted and adjusted trial balances for Milky Way Theatre, Inc. at November 30, 2015, show the following data:

<table>
<tr><td colspan="5">**Milky Way Theatre, Inc.**
Trial Balance
November 30, 2015</td></tr>
<tr><td></td><td colspan="2">UNADJUSTED
TRIAL BALANCE</td><td colspan="2">ADJUSTED
TRIAL BALANCE</td></tr>
<tr><td>**ACCOUNT**</td><td>**DR.**</td><td>**CR.**</td><td>**DR.**</td><td>**CR.**</td></tr>
<tr><td>Cash</td><td>$ 9,200</td><td></td><td>$ 9,200</td><td></td></tr>
<tr><td>Accounts Receivable</td><td>6,200</td><td></td><td>6,200</td><td></td></tr>
<tr><td>Supplies</td><td>2,200</td><td></td><td>800</td><td></td></tr>
<tr><td>Prepaid Rent</td><td>3,600</td><td></td><td>2,700</td><td></td></tr>
<tr><td>Equipment</td><td>26,000</td><td></td><td>26,000</td><td></td></tr>
<tr><td>Accumulated Depreciation, Equipment</td><td></td><td>$ 4,700</td><td></td><td>$ 6,200</td></tr>
<tr><td>Accounts Payable</td><td></td><td>2,600</td><td></td><td>2,600</td></tr>
<tr><td>Salaries Payable</td><td></td><td></td><td></td><td>1,250</td></tr>
<tr><td>Interest Payable</td><td></td><td></td><td></td><td>290</td></tr>
<tr><td>Unearned Service Revenue</td><td></td><td>3,000</td><td></td><td>2,100</td></tr>
<tr><td>Notes Payable</td><td></td><td>7,000</td><td></td><td>7,000</td></tr>
<tr><td>Common Shares</td><td></td><td>15,000</td><td></td><td>15,000</td></tr>
<tr><td>Retained Earnings</td><td></td><td>2,900</td><td></td><td>2,900</td></tr>
<tr><td>Dividends</td><td>12,000</td><td></td><td>12,000</td><td></td></tr>
<tr><td>Service Revenue</td><td></td><td>53,400</td><td></td><td>54,300</td></tr>
<tr><td>Salaries Expense</td><td>23,600</td><td></td><td>24,850</td><td></td></tr>
<tr><td>Rent Expense</td><td>4,800</td><td></td><td>5,700</td><td></td></tr>
<tr><td>Depreciation Expense, Equipment</td><td>750</td><td></td><td>2,250</td><td></td></tr>
<tr><td>Interest Expense</td><td>250</td><td></td><td>540</td><td></td></tr>
<tr><td>Supplies Expense</td><td></td><td></td><td>1,400</td><td></td></tr>
<tr><td>Total</td><td>$88,600</td><td>$88,600</td><td>$91,640</td><td>$91,640</td></tr>
</table>

Requirement

1. Journalize the adjusting entries that account for the differences between the two trial balances.

P3-3B. Prepare adjusting journal entries and an adjusted trial balance
(*Learning Objectives 2 & 3*) 25–30 min.

The trial balance of Nina's Novelty, Inc. at September 30, 2015, and the data needed for the month-end adjustments follow:

	Nina's Novelty, Inc. Trial Balance September 30, 2015		
	ACCOUNT	**DEBIT**	**CREDIT**
	Cash	$ 25,000	
	Accounts Receivable	17,400	
	Prepaid Insurance	2,400	
	Supplies	1,200	
	Equipment	59,000	
	Accumulated Depreciation, Equipment		$ 50,000
	Accounts Payable		2,000
	Salaries Payable		
	Unearned Service Revenue		2,400
	Common Shares		25,000
	Retained Earnings		22,800
	Dividends	9,700	
	Service Revenue		16,200
	Salaries Expense	3,700	
	Insurance Expense		
	Depreciation Expense		
	Utilities Expense		
	Supplies Expense		
	Total	$118,400	$118,400

a. Insurance coverage still remaining at September 30, $800.

b. Supplies used during the month, $900.

c. Depreciation for the month, $2,200.

d. Accrued utilities expense at September 30, $1,000. (Use Accounts Payable as the liability account needed.)

e. Accrued salaries at September 30, $800.

f. Service revenue still unearned at September 30, $1,600.

Requirements

1. Journalize the adjusting entries.
2. Open T-accounts for the accounts listed in the trial balance and insert their September 30 unadjusted balances. Post the adjusting entries to the T-accounts. Reference the posted amounts by letters (a) through (f). Calculate the adjusted balance in each account.
3. Prepare the adjusted trial balance.
4. How will the company use the adjusted trial balance?

P3-4B. **Effects of adjusting journal entries on income statement accounts**
(*Learning Objectives 2 & 3*) **20–25 min.**

Moore, Corp. completed the following selected transactions and prepared these adjusting entries during May:

May 1	Prepaid insurance for May through July, $2,700.
3	Performed service on account, $2,500.
6	Purchased office furniture on account, $900.
8	Paid property tax expense, $500.
12	Purchased office equipment for cash, $1,500.
18	Performed services and received cash, $3,500.
23	Collected $800 on account.
26	Paid the account payable from the May 6 transaction.
30	Paid salaries expense, $1,300.
31	Recorded an adjusting entry for May insurance expense related to the May 1 transaction.
31	Recorded an adjusting entry for unearned revenue now earned, $1,100.

Requirements

1. State whether the transaction would increase revenues, decrease revenues, increase expenses, decrease expenses, or have no effect on revenues or expenses. If revenues or expenses are affected, give the amount of the impact on revenues or expenses for May. Use the following format for your answer.

Revenues and Expenses for May		
Date	**Impact on Revenues or Expenses**	**$ Effect on Revenues or Expenses**
May XX	Increase Revenues	$XXX

2. Compute May net income or net loss under the accrual basis of accounting.

3. State why the accrual basis of accounting results in an accurate measurement of income.

P3-5B. Prepare financial statements (*Learning Objective 3*) 20–25 min.

The adjusted trial balance for Destination Realty, Inc. at October 31, 2015, follows:

		ACCOUNT	DEBIT	CREDIT
		Destination Realty, Inc.		
		Adjusted Trial Balance		
		October 31, 2015		
		Cash	$ 6,500	
		Accounts Receivable	12,100	
		Prepaid Rent	2,500	
		Supplies	500	
		Equipment	42,500	
		Accumulated Depreciation, Equipment		$ 11,300
		Accounts Payable		4,300
		Unearned Service Revenue		2,800
		Interest Payable		720
		Salaries Payable		9,000
		Notes Payable		8,000
		Common Shares		3,960
		Retained Earnings		9,700
		Dividends	5,000	
		Service Revenue		85,000
		Interest Revenue		420
		Salaries Expense	40,000	
		Rent Expense	20,000	
		Depreciation Expense, Equipment	2,500	
		Utilities Expense	1,800	
		Interest Expense	1,100	
		Supplies Expense	700	
		Total	$135,200	$135,200

Requirements

1. Prepare Destination Realty's income statement, statement of retained earnings, and year-end statement of financial position. List expenses in decreasing order on the income statement.

2. **a.** Which financial statement reports Destination Realty's results of operations? Were operations successful during 2015? Cite specifics from the financial statements to support your evaluation.

   b. Which statement reports the company's financial position?

P3-6B. Prepare closing entries and a post-closing trial balance (*Learning Objective 4*) 20–25 min.

The September 30, 2015, adjusted trial balance of Java Jolt, Inc. is shown next.

Java Jolt, Inc.
Adjusted Trial Balance
September 30, 2015

ACCOUNT	DEBIT	CREDIT
Cash	$ 5,800	
Accounts Receivable	7,000	
Prepaid Rent	2,300	
Supplies	300	
Equipment	30,000	
Accumulated Depreciation, Equipment		$ 3,800
Accounts Payable		3,000
Unearned Service Revenue		1,900
Salaries Payable		1,400
Notes Payable		10,000
Common Shares		3,100
Retained Earnings		11,200
Dividends	4,000	
Service Revenue		41,000
Interest Revenue		1,000
Salaries Expense	18,500	
Rent Expense	5,400	
Depreciation Expense, Equipment	1,700	
Utilities Expense	800	
Supplies Expense	600	
Total	$76,400	$76,400

Requirements

1. Prepare the September closing entries for Java Jolt, Inc.
2. Calculate the ending balance in retained earnings.
3. Prepare a post-closing trial balance.

P3-7B. Effects of errors on assets, liabilities, shareholders' equity, and net income
(*Learning Objectives 2 & 3*) 15–20 min.

The following errors were made in the accounting records of Gagnon Corp. in 2015 and were not discovered until 2016.

  a. Management revenue of $3,750 earned in 2015 was not recorded until it was collected in 2016.

  b. One year of Amortization Expense, $4,200, was recorded instead of three-quarters of the amount.

  c. A deposit of $4,000 for Management Service to be delivered in 2016 was recorded as Management Revenue in 2015.

  d. One-year insurance premium of $3,300 for 2016 was recorded as Insurance Expense for 2015 when it was paid.

  e. Half of the unearned revenue of $4,500 was earned in 2015, but was not recorded.

Requirements

1. For each of the independent errors in parts (a) through (e), identify the net effect on assets, liabilities, shareholders' equity, and net income for 2015 and 2016. Show understatements by "U," overstatements by "O," and no effect by "NE," and identify their amounts.

	Assets		Liabilities		Shareholders' Equity		Net Income	
	2015	2016	2015	2016	2015	2016	2015	2016
a								
b								
c								
d								
e								

P3-8B. Adjusting entries using a worksheet (*Learning Objectives 1, 2, 3 & 5*)
35–40 min.

Muse Daycare Centre (MDC) has been providing daycare services to its local community for several years. MDC's year-end is on December 31. The unadjusted trial balance on December 31, 2015 was as follows:

Muse Daycare Centre
Worksheet
For Year Ended December 31, 2015

ACCT #	ACCOUNT	UNADJUSTED TRIAL BALANCE DR.	UNADJUSTED TRIAL BALANCE CR.	ADJUSTMENTS DR.	ADJUSTMENTS CR.	ADJUSTED TRIAL BALANCE DR.	ADJUSTED TRIAL BALANCE CR.
1010	Cash	$ 6,200					
1020	Accounts Receivable	2,700					
1030	Art Supplies	3,200					
1035	Prepaid Rent	3,600					
1040	Playground Equipment	43,000					
1041	Accumulated Depreciation, Playground Equipment		$ 7,800				
2010	Accounts Payable		2,450				
2015	Salaries Payable						
2020	Unearned Daycare Revenue		2,100				
2030	Income Tax Payable						
3010	Common Shares		25,000				
3030	Retained Earnings		10,500				
3040	Dividends	5,000					
4010	Daycare Revenue		95,000				
5010	Salaries Expense	60,000					
5015	Rent Expense	9,000					
5030	Utilities Expense	5,350					
5040	Depreciation Expense, Playground Equipment						
5050	Art Supplies Expense	4,800					
5060	Income Tax Expense						
	Total	$142,850	$142,850				

Additional information about several transactions that occurred during the year:

a. Several parents did not pay the fee for the last week of daycare. These parents would pay $1,400 (which included $700 owed in December) in the first week of January.

b. A physical count of art supplies showed that there was $1,500 of art supplies on hand on December 31. The balance of Art Supplies Expense, $4,800 on December 31, represents art supplies purchased during the year.

c. The balance of Prepaid Rent represents the four months of rent paid on November 1.

d. Playground Equipment was estimated to last for 10 years, with a salvage value of $4,000 at the end of the tenth year. No adjustment was made in 2015.

e. Three daycare workers each earned $80/day. Seven days of wages were earned by employees, but not paid on December 31.

f. Half of the unearned revenue was earned in December.

g. The utilities expense for December was estimated at $480. The utility bill usually arrived during the first week of the following month.

h. MDC's income tax rate was 30%.

Requirements

1. Indicate the type of adjustments for each transaction.

2. Prepare the adjusting entry and enter the amount for each transaction in the worksheet.

3. Prepared the adjusted trial balance in the worksheet.

4. What is the age of the playground equipment?

5. Prepare the income statement, statement of retained earnings, and classified statement of financial position.

6. Record the adjusting entry for the income tax.

P3-9B. Closing entries using a worksheet (*Learning Objectives 4 & 5*) 10–15 min.

Refer to P3-8B.

Requirements

Using the adjusted trial balance from P3-8B, prepare the closing entries for 2015 and the post-closing trial balance in the worksheet.

PROBLEMS (ALTERNATES 1, 2, AND 3)

These alternative problem sets are available for your practice benefit on **MyAccountingLab**.

CONTINUING EXERCISE

This exercise continues the accounting process for Graham's Yard Care, Inc. from the Continuing Exercise in Chapter 2. Refer to the T-accounts and the trial balance that you prepared for Graham's Yard Care, Inc. at June 30, 2015.

Requirements

1. Open these additional T-accounts: Accumulated Depreciation, Equipment; Depreciation Expense, Equipment; Supplies Expense.

2. A physical count shows $20 of lawn supplies on hand at June 30, 2015. Depreciation on equipment for the month totals $30. Journalize any required adjusting journal entries and post to the T-accounts, identifying all items by date.

3. Prepare the adjusted trial balance.

4. Journalize and post the closing entries at June 30.

5. Prepare a post-closing trial balance.

This problem continues the accounting process for Aqua Elite, Inc. from the Continuing Problem in Chapter 2. The trial balance for Aqua Elite, Inc. at June 30, 2015, should look like this:

		ACCOUNT	DEBIT	CREDIT
		Aqua Elite, Inc. Trial Balance June 30, 2015		
		Cash	$16,855	
		Accounts Receivable	3,800	
		Supplies	1,610	
		Land	15,000	
		Furniture	3,300	
		Equipment	4,700	
		Vehicles	31,000	
		Accounts Payable		$ 3,890
		Notes Payable		31,000
		Common Shares		38,500
		Dividends	2,800	
		Service Revenue		12,000
		Salaries Expense	2,700	
		Rent Expense	1,800	
		Utilities Expense	1,225	
		Advertising Expense	325	
		Miscellaneous Expense	275	
		Total	$85,390	$85,390

During July, the following transactions occurred:

Jul 1	Paid three months' rent, $5,400.
4	Performed service for a customer and received cash, $2,100.
9	Received $3,600 from customers for services to be performed later.
12	Purchased $750 of supplies on account.
15	Billed customers for services performed, $2,800.
16	Paid receptionist's salary, $675.
22	Received $3,100 on account.
25	Paid $2,800 on account.
28	Received $1,200 cash for services performed.
30	Paid $600 of dividends.

Requirements

1. Journalize the transactions that occurred in July. Omit explanations.

2. Using the four-column accounts from the Continuing Problem in Chapter 2, post the transactions to the ledger creating new ledger accounts as necessary; omit posting references. Calculate the new account balances.

3. Prepare the unadjusted trial balance for Aqua Elite, Inc. at the end of July.

4. Journalize and post the adjusting entries for July based on the following adjustment information.

   a. Record the expired rent.

   b. Supplies on hand, $350.

   c. Depreciation: $400 equipment, $210 furniture, $650 vehicles.

   d. Services performed but unbilled, $1,900.

   e. Accrued salaries, $675.

   f. Unearned service revenue earned as of July 31, $800.

5. Prepare an adjusted trial balance for Aqua Elite, Inc. at the end of July.

6. Prepare the income statement, statement of retained earnings, and statement of financial position for the three-month period May through July, 2015.

7. Prepare and post closing entries.

8. Prepare a post-closing trial balance for the end of the period.

APPLY YOUR KNOWLEDGE

ETHICS IN ACTION

Case 1. Jennifer Baxter was preparing the adjusting journal entries for Jennifer's Java, a business that uses the accrual basis of accounting, to prepare the adjusted trial balance and financial statements. She knew that $750 of salaries related to the current accounting period had accrued but wouldn't be paid until the next period. Jennifer thought that simply not including the adjustment for these salaries would mean that salaries expense would be lower, and reported net income would be higher than it would have been if she had made the adjustment. Further, she knew that the Salaries Payable account would be zero, so the liabilities reported on the statement of financial position would be less, and her business would look even better. Besides, she reasoned that these salaries would be reported eventually, so it was merely a matter of showing them in one period instead of another. Dismissing the reporting as just a timing issue, she ignored the adjustment for the additional salaries expense.

Is Jennifer acting unethically by failing to record the adjustment for accrued salaries? Does it matter that, shortly into the new accounting period, the salaries will ultimately be paid? Is it really simply a matter of timing? What are the potential problems of failing to include all the adjusting journal entries?

Case 2. Jim Anderson and his banker were reviewing the quarterly income statements for his consulting business, Anderson and Associates, Inc. The banker was impressed with the growth of sales revenue and net income for the second quarter this year as compared to the second quarter of last year. Jim knew it had been a good quarter, but didn't think it had been spectacular. Suddenly, Jim realized that he failed to close out the revenue and expense accounts for the prior quarter, which ended in March. Because those temporary accounts were not closed out, their balances were included in the second quarter amounts for the current year. Jim then realized that the banker had the financial statements but not the general ledger or any trial balances. Thus, the banker would not be able to see that the accounting cycle was not properly closed and that this failure was creating a misstated income statement for the second quarter of the current year. The banker then commented that the business appeared to be performing so well that he would approve a line of credit for the business. Jim decided to not say anything because he did not want to lose the line of credit. Besides, he thought, it really did not matter that the income statement was misstated because his business would be sure to repay any amounts borrowed.

Should Jim have informed the banker of the mistake made and should he have redone the second quarter's income statement? Was Jim's failure to close the prior quarter's revenue and expense accounts unethical? Does the fact that the business will repay the loan matter?

KNOW YOUR BUSINESS

FINANCIAL ANALYSIS

Purpose: To help familiarize you with the financial reporting of a real company to further your understanding of the chapter material you are learning.

This case will help you to better understand the effect of adjusting journal entries on the financial statements. We do not have access to the journals and ledgers used by Bombardier Inc., but we can see some of the adjusted accounts on the company's financial statements. Refer to the Bombardier Inc. income statements, "Consolidated Statements of Income," and the Bombardier Inc. statements of financial position in MyAccountingLab. Also, Note 19 titled "Property, Plant and Equipment" on page 168 of the Bombardier Annual Report uses the term amortization instead of depreciation. You can consider these two terms to mean the same thing at this point.

Requirements

1. Open T-accounts for the following accounts and their balances as of December 31, 2012, prior to closing. (All amounts in millions of US$.)

PP&E...	$4,330
Trade and other payables...	$3,361
Advances and progress billings in excess of related long-term contract Inventories....	$1,232
Accumulated amortization and impairment...................................	$2,146

2. Using the following information for Bombardier Inc.'s 2012 operations, make the appropriate year-end journal entries.

   a. Payment of Accrued Liabilities of $1,021.

   b. Amortization expense, $156.

   c. Accrued Accounts Payable and Accrued Liabilities, $1,213.

   d. Additional Advances and progress billings in excess of related long-term contract costs, $783.

3. Post the journal entries to the T-accounts you set up. Check the updated ending balances in each account against the balances reported by Bombardier Inc. as of January 31, 2012. You can determine the net PP&E by subtracting the Amortization from PP&E balance.

INDUSTRY ANALYSIS

Purpose: To help you understand and compare the performance of two companies in the same industry.

Go to the Bombardier Annual Report located in MyAccountingLab. Now access the Annual Report for The Boeing Company. To do this from the internet, go to the company's web page for Investor Relations at http://www.boeing.com/companyoffices/financial/quarterly.htm and download the annual report for the year ended December 31, 2012.

Requirement

1. Identify three accounts for each company that indicate that both Bombardier and Boeing use the accrual basis of accounting. Why do you think using the accrual basis of accounting would be more helpful for analysis purposes than the cash basis for these two companies?

SMALL BUSINESS ANALYSIS

Purpose: To help you understand the importance of cash flows in the operation of a small business.

It's the end of the month and cash flow has been a little slow, as it usually is during this time of the accounting period. It just seems to be a little slower this month. You know that Wednesday the 31st is payday, which always requires a large cash outlay. However, you also know that your bank is looking for a set of financial statements as of the end of the month because the loan on your building is coming up for renewal soon. In some of the previous meetings with your bankers, you know that they were always concerned with the cash balance, so you want to have your cash balance as high as possible.

You come up with a tentative plan to not only preserve some of your cash balance at the end of the month, but you believe it will also help your bottom line, your net income. That's the other thing that the bankers are always concerned about. You don't want to make any mistakes with your financial statements at this crucial point, so you decide to contact your accountant to run the idea by her. The conversation goes something like this:

"Good morning, Linda. This is Jerry from BCS Consultants, Inc. Our financial statements have to look really good this month because the bank is going to be scrutinizing them pretty closely for our pending loan renewal. I know that the two things they concentrate on are the cash balance and the net income. So, I've got a plan to help in both of those areas. I'm going to hold off paying my employees until after the first of the month. Plus, last month, I made a big insurance payment to cover me for the next six months, so I won't need to show any insurance expense this month. Both of those will help my net income because I won't be showing those expenses on my income statement. Plus, by not writing the paycheques until the first of the month, I'll be helping to show a higher cash balance. It's really only one day, but the bank won't know that my cash balance should be lower. These certainly sound like some good ideas that would help with my situation, but just in case, I wanted to check with you to see what you thought. Any comments?"

The first words out of the accountant's mouth are "Jerry, you know that your financial statements are prepared using the accrual basis of accounting."

Requirement

1. Complete the thought process of the accountant concerning Jerry's plan. What does she mean by the accrual basis of accounting? What effect will that have on the net income? Is Jerry correct in his assessment of the big insurance payment he made last month covering the next six months? What effect will that have on the net income? And in regard to the last item, what about Jerry's plan to keep the cash balance as high as possible and his statement "the bank won't know that my cash balance should be lower"?

WRITTEN COMMUNICATION

You received a letter from a disgruntled client concerning this year's tax return that you just completed for his or her company. The client's business is in the second year of operations, and you remembered that it seemed to be much more profitable this year than during the first year of operations. You also recall that this particular client's year-end work was assigned to a relatively new staff accountant, which might be part of the problem. The gist of the letter is that last year's taxable net income was about $25,000, and according to the company's calculations, the net income from this year should have been about $50,000. And so the client is wondering why the company is showing taxable net income of $75,000 on this year's return and paying income tax on that amount. You retrieve the file to review it and immediately see the problem. The staff accountant failed to make the closing entries at the end of the first year of operations!

Requirement

1. Prepare a letter to this client explaining the situation and, most importantly, explaining the importance of doing closing entries at the end of each and every year. Also, suggest a solution to this problem for the client, knowing that just explaining the accounting issue might not be enough to retain this client in the future.

Self Check Answers
1. a 2. b 3. c 4. d 5. a 6. d 7. c 8. d 9. b 10. c

COMPREHENSIVE PROBLEM

JOURNALIZING, POSTING, ADJUSTING, PREPARING FINANCIAL STATEMENTS, AND CLOSING

Waters Landscaping, Inc. completed the following transactions during its first month of operations for January 2015:

a. Gary Waters invested $7,500 cash and a truck valued at $15,000 to start Waters Landscaping, Inc. The business issued common shares in exchange for these assets.

b. Purchased $300 of supplies on account.

c. Paid $1,200 for a six-month insurance policy.

d. Performed landscape services for a customer and received $800 cash.

e. Completed a $4,500 landscaping job on account.

f. Paid employee salary, $600.

g. Received $1,100 cash for performing landscaping services.

h. Collected $1,500 in advance for landscaping service to be performed later.

i. Collected $2,500 cash from a customer on account.

j. Purchased fuel for the truck, paying $80 with a company credit card. Credit Accounts Payable.

k. Performed landscaping services on account, $1,600.

l. Paid the current month's office rent, $750.

m. Paid $50 on account.

n. Paid cash dividends of $500.

Requirements

1. Record each transaction in the general journal. Use the letter corresponding to each transaction as the transaction date. Explanations are not required.

2. Post the transactions that you recorded in Requirement 1 in the following T-accounts.

Cash	Salaries Payable	Service Revenue
Accounts Receivable	Unearned Service Revenue	Salaries Expense
Supplies	Common Shares	Depreciation Expense
Prepaid Insurance	Retained Earnings	Insurance Expense
Truck	Dividends	Fuel Expense
Accumulated Depreciation		Rent Expense
Accounts Payable		Supplies Expense

3. Prepare an unadjusted trial balance as of January 31, 2015.

4. Journalize and post the adjusting journal entries based on the following information:

   a. Accrued salaries expense, $600.

   b. Depreciation expense, $375.

   c. Record the expiration of one month's insurance.

   d. Supplies on hand, $75.

   e. Earned 1/3 of the Unearned Service Revenue during January.

   f. Waters Landscaping's income tax rate is 30%.

5. Prepare an adjusted trial balance as of January 31, 2015. Use the adjusted trial balance to prepare Waters Landscaping's income statement, statement of retained earnings, and statement of financial position for January. On the income statement list expenses in decreasing order by amount—that is, the largest expense first, the smallest expense last.

6. Journalize and post the closing entries.

7. Prepare a post-closing trial balance at January 31, 2015.

LEARNING OBJECTIVES

1. Understand the role of ethics in business and accounting

2. Define fraud and describe the different types of fraud in business

3. Identify the three elements of the fraud triangle

4. Define *internal control* and describe the objectives of an internal control system

5. Identify the elements of a good internal control system

6. Describe the major requirements of the Sarbanes-Oxley Act and how they impacted Canadian provincial regulations

7. Discuss internal controls for cash and prepare a bank reconciliation

8. Report cash on the statement of financial position

9. (Appendix 4A) Account for the petty cash fund

CHAPTER OUTLINE

214

4

Ethics, Internal Control, and Cash

Think of your favourite sports team. How do they play the game? How do they keep score to see who won and who lost the game? What happens if someone cheats? It takes rules, but it also takes someone to make, monitor, and enforce the rules of the game.

Business also has rules. In the game of business, businesses compete to win at creating value. However, a business cannot just do anything it wants. For instance, it's illegal for a business to knowingly make or sell a product that hurts a customer, a business must provide a safe place for employees to work, and a business cannot falsely advertise what a product can or cannot do. Businesses compete, but they operate using rules designed to create fairness for all stakeholders.

Businesses also have rules about financial information. A business cannot provide shareholders and lenders with false information—this is called *fraud* and it is against the law. But what is false information? The answer is that it depends on the rules.

So who sets the rules for businesses regarding financial information? How does a business create a system to ensure the rules are fairly applied? Who makes sure a business is following the rules? What happens if a business does not follow the rules?

In the early part of the 1990s, the management of a company called Phar-Mor committed an accounting **fraud** that amounted to somewhere between $350 and $500 million. Unfortunately, this pales in comparison to some of the more recent scandals that have affected North American businesses. The recent fraudulent activities of companies such as Enron, Livent, Nortel, and Hollinger International have resulted in losses of hundreds of millions of dollars, but that is only a portion of the impact of the activities of a small group of people. Exhibit 4-1 outlines these recent scandals.

Company and Year Detected	Type of Company	Who Perpetrated Fraud?	Nature of Fraud	Fallout
Enron 2001	Enron was an American company that was formed in 1985 from the merger of two gas and pipeline companies. By 1999, the company was enjoying many successes, including being highly ranked on the Fortune 500 and having its stock price at $90 per share. In October 2001, the company reported its first ever quarterly loss. By November the company's stock was below $1 per share and in December, the company filed for bankruptcy.	The Chairman of the Board, Ken Lay, the Chief Executive Officer, Jeffrey Skilling, the Chief Financial Officer, Andrew Fastow, as well as others under their direction.	Complex relationships with offshore partnerships along with questionable accounting practices were used to overstate revenues, understate expenses, and hide the true amount of Enron's liabilities.	Enron filed for bankruptcy. Lay, Skilling, Fastow, and other top executives were convicted of fraud and/or other related charges. Numerous individuals were also convicted of insider trading. Enron's auditor, Arthur Andersen, was convicted of obstruction of justice for shredding documents related to the audit. Arthur Andersen dissolved its U.S. operations despite the conviction being overturned by the U.S. Supreme Court. Around 5,600 Enron employees lost their jobs with the company's collapse.
Conrad Black and Hollinger International 2003	Conrad Black started buying newspaper companies while he was in his twenties and by 1985 Hollinger Inc. was formed through an amalgamation of three companies. In 2003, Black was called to testify in front of the U.S. Securities and Exchange Commission. Early in 2004, Hollinger International removed Black as chairman and announced a lawsuit against Black and another executive for $200 million, based on alleged financial irregularities. A criminal investigation began in March 2005 and Black was charged with racketeering, money laundering, fraud, and obstruction of justice. By the end of 2007 Conrad Black was sentenced to 6.5 years in jail for obstruction of justice and mail fraud.	Conrad Black, David Radler (former executive), and two other executives of Hollinger International.	Diversion of funds from Hollinger International to reduce assets, understatement of income to evade paying taxes, violations of securities laws, and obstruction of justice through the removal of 12 boxes of unknown content assumed to be evidence from Black's Toronto offices.	David Radler pleaded guilty to mail fraud for a reduced sentence and testified against Conrad Black. Conrad Black was sentenced to 6.5 years in jail. In October 2010, Black won an appeal and two fraud convictions were thrown out. The remaining convictions were not overturned.

Exhibit 4-1 ▲

Company and Year Detected	Type of Company	Who Perpetrated Fraud?	Nature of Fraud	Fallout
Livent 1998	Garth Drabinsky and Myron Gottlieb founded Cineplex Odeon in 1979. Drabinsky and Gottlieb were forced by the shareholders to resign from Cineplex Odeon after accounting irregularities were discovered in 1989. In the negotiations to leave the company, Drabinsky and Gottlieb acquired the Pantages Theatre in Toronto and by 1993, Livent, a live theatrical production company, was formed. By 1998 the productions performed in their theatres had earned twenty Tony Awards. In the summer of 1998, shareholders discovered significant financial irregularities and trading in the company's stock was suspended and lawsuits were filed against the company and its officers. In 1998 Livent was under investigation by a number of agencies including the RCMP, the Ontario Securities Commission, the American Securities Exchange Commission, the U.S. Department of Justice, and others.	Maria Messina, CA (CFO of Livent and former audit manager and partner at Deloitte & Touche)	Kickback schemes where suppliers would overcharge Livent for services and then the extra payments would be given directly to Gottlieb and Drabinsky to the amount of $7 million. Accounting manipulations (such as just eliminating expenses from the records) to hide losses and achieve targeted goals.	Messina pleaded guilty to a federal indictment. Livent filed for bankruptcy citing debts of $334 million and the remaining assets were bought by SFX Entertainment. Both Gottlieb and Drabinsky were found guilty of fraud and forgery. Drabinsky was sentenced to seven years while Gottlieb was sentenced to six years.
Nortel 2004	Nortel began in 1895 as Northern Electric and Manufacturing and supplied telecommunications equipment and services globally. The company grew to an organization valued at over $300 billion and in January 2009 dropped to a low of about $200 million. In 2004, the company delayed publishing financial statements for 2003 and fired a number of executives including the CEO and CFO.	CEO Frank Dunn, CFO, controller, at least four more executives, and at least seven additional people from the finance department.	Overstating earnings so much that the earnings for 2003 needed to be restated at less than 50% of the original reported amount.	More than 60,000 jobs were lost. In March 2007, Dunn and three former executives were charged with civil fraud from making "material misstatements" by the Securities and Exchange Commission (U.S.) and the Ontario Securities Commission. In 2008, the RCMP charged Dunn and two former executives with fraud. The first quarter financial results for 2011 showed revenues of $20 million, which was drastically reduced from previous quarters due to "the sale of substantially all of its businesses" (www.nortel.com).

Exhibit 4-1 ▲ (cont.)

These and other scandals rocked the business community and eroded investor confidence. Innocent people lost their jobs, and the stock market suffered when stock prices dropped. Therefore, it is no surprise that these scandals ushered in a new era in the field of accounting and business in general—the need for higher ethical standards and improved internal controls.

WHY IS ETHICS IMPORTANT IN BUSINESS AND ACCOUNTING?

L.O. ① Understand the role of ethics in business and accounting

Some accounting professionals contend that the accounting rules (for example, IFRS or ASPE) may have contributed to the recent accounting scandals. How could that be, you might wonder? Well, accounting rules do not always have many specific rules but instead consist of a small number of overriding principles. Accountants were expected to exercise their professional judgment to ensure that proper accounting treatment was being applied to adhere to these overriding principles. Over time, accounting rules and guidelines have evolved into a system with numerous rules that have been adopted to address very specific accounting situations. With this evolution of the rules, some feel, has come an attitude that "if the rules don't prohibit a specific accounting treatment, then it must be acceptable and, therefore, I am not acting unethically if I utilize this accounting treatment." This attitude may encourage some individuals to search for unique ways of accounting for certain transactions that, although not specifically prohibited, most likely would have been considered to violate the original overriding accounting principles. It is impossible to write enough rules to cover every situation. To promote ethical behaviour, the accounting profession may need to return to a system with a small number of overriding principles and the expectation that sound judgment be applied to ensure that the principles are followed.

Whether or not the current system of accounting rules contributed to the recent accounting scandals is a topic for debate. What is certain is that most, if not all, of these scandals were the result of poor ethical behaviour on the part of one or more individuals. In Chapter 1, ethics was defined as principles of right behaviour that guide decision making. Scandals, such as those that have occurred in the last decade, do not result from decision making based on proper ethical behaviour. Proper ethical behaviour is more than just following the rules or doing what is legal; it is characterized by honesty, fairness, and integrity. Proper ethical behaviour can be summarized by the "golden rule," which says to treat others the same way that you would want to be treated in the same situation. For organizations to earn and keep the public's trust, they must practise good ethical behaviour at every level within the organization. Some of the steps that many organizations utilize to accomplish this include, but are not limited to, the following:

- Develop a written **code of ethics**. A code of ethics defines standards of behaviour all members of an organization are expected to follow.
- Communicate the code of ethics to all members of the organization. A good idea is to distribute the code of ethics in written format to all employees at least annually. Then, have employees acknowledge in writing that they have received, read, and understood what is expected of them.
- Ensure top management within the organization models good ethical behaviour at all times because ethics is better "caught than taught." As any parent can tell you, expecting your children to "do as I say, not as I do" does not work very well.
- Establish a method that allows for ethics violations to be reported anonymously. A person who reports unethical behaviour, a **whistleblower**, must be able to make a report without fear of punishment or retaliation.
- Enforce the ethics code. Ethics violations should always be addressed in a timely fashion. This helps ensure that the ethics code is taken seriously.

The three Canadian accounting regulatory bodies, CA, CGA, and CMA, have their own codes of ethics to guide their members' conduct and ethical standards. Some code of ethics principles include responsibility to society, trust and duties, due care and professional judgment, deceptive information, and responsibilities to the profession. Currently the three Canadian accounting regulatory bodies are in the process of merging into one accounting regulatory body: Chartered Professional Accountants (CPA)-Canada. As mergers are completed, codes of ethics are developed on a province by province basis.

WHAT IS FRAUD AND WHO COMMITS IT?

The scandalous activities referred to previously involve the commission of fraud by company management. So what exactly is fraud? Although there are many definitions of fraud, in its broadest sense fraud can be defined as the use of deception or trickery for personal gain. In North America, fraud is one of the fastest growing crimes. It accounts for more losses than robbery. In the business world, fraud is committed either by a business organization or against a business organization.

L.O. **2** Define fraud and describe the different types of fraud in business

MANAGEMENT FRAUD

An organization's top management is usually responsible for fraud that is committed by a business organization. This **management fraud** typically involves fraudulent financial reporting. Fraudulent financial reporting most often makes a company's earnings look better than they are. The goal of overstating earnings is to help increase a company's stock price or to ensure larger year-end bonuses for upper management. Fraudulent financial reporting is achieved when management does activites to falsify the real financial position of the company, such as:

- Overstates revenues by
  1. overstating receivables related to revenue that has not yet been earned
  2. understating unearned revenue (recording revenue when cash is received even though goods or services have not yet been provided)
- Understates expenses by
  1. overstating the value of assets such as inventory, equipment, and buildings, or recording assets that do not exist
  2. understating amounts owed to suppliers, employees, or creditors

EMPLOYEE EMBEZZLEMENT

The primary form of fraud committed against a business organization is **employee embezzlement**. Employee embezzlement usually involves the misappropriation of business assets by an employee. Employees can

- steal cash, inventory, tools, supplies, or other assets from the employer.
- establish fake companies and have the employer pay these phony companies for goods or services that are never delivered, then intercept and fraudulently cash the cheques.
- engage in **disbursement schemes**. Employee embezzlement involving disbursement schemes takes place when an employee tricks a company into giving up cash for an invalid reason. Examples of disbursement schemes include the following:
  1. Cheque tampering: The employee writes a fraudulent cheque and makes the cheque payable to him- or herself. Alternatively, the employee obtains a cheque intended for an outside party, endorses the cheque, and then cashes it.

2. **Cash register schemes:** The employee gives a false refund for returned merchandise by filling out a refund form and putting it in the cash register. The employee then pockets the cash. Another related scheme happens when the employee accepts cash from a customer for a purchase but does not record the transaction in the cash register. The employee then keeps the cash for personal use.

3. **Expense schemes:** The employee overbills the company for travel or other business-related expenses, such as lunches, hotels, air travel, parking fees, and cab fares.

Another form of employee embezzlement occurs when an employee takes **bribes** or **kickbacks** from

- suppliers in exchange for the employee turning a blind eye to a supplier charging the employer higher purchase prices.
- suppliers in exchange for the employee turning a blind eye to delivery of inferior goods.
- suppliers in exchange for the employee authorizing payments to the supplier for goods not delivered to the employer.
- customers in exchange for granting the customer a lower sales price.
- customers in exchange for giving the customer goods or services for which the employer is never paid.

 DECISION GUIDELINES

DECISION

As the credit manager for a bank, do I need to be concerned about fraud?

GUIDELINE

Fraud is deceit or trickery causing financial harm. It may be perpetrated by management or by employees.

ANALYZE

Management fraud typically involves fraudulent financial reporting. Fraudulent financial reporting occurs when financial information is manipulated so that the business looks more profitable than it really is. Managers may record revenues prematurely or fictitiously, or understate expenses.

Employee embezzlement usually involves the misappropriation of assets. Employee embezzlement can include stealing cash or other assets; taking kickbacks from suppliers or customers; or using cheque tampering, cash register schemes, or expense schemes that result in improper payment from the employer.

Both management fraud and employee embezzlement can cause financial ruin for a company as well as result in criminal prosecution for the perpetrators. Therefore, as a credit manager for a bank, you will need to understand fraud and the signs of fraud to protect the bank from companies that engage in fraud, such as by borrowing funds and then going out of business without repaying the debt.

WHAT FACTORS ARE USUALLY PRESENT WHEN FRAUD IS COMMITTED?

L.O. 3 Identify the three elements of the fraud triangle

Anyone who has done much camping knows that it takes three things to build a fire: fuel, oxygen, and ignition. For fraud to occur, three factors must also exist: perceived pressure, rationalization, and perceived opportunity. **Exhibit 4-2** on the following page presents the **fraud triangle**, which shows the connection of the three factors necessary to commit fraud.

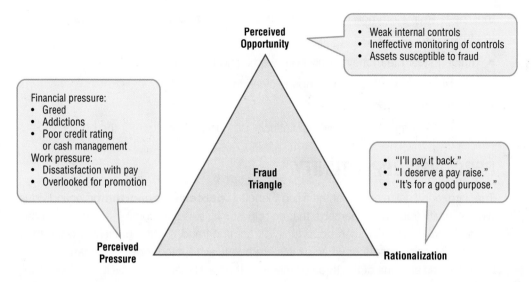

Exhibit 4-2 ▲

Let's take a closer look at the three elements of the fraud triangle.

PERCEIVED PRESSURE

Numerous reasons exist that could cause an individual to feel pressured to commit fraud. However, the most likely sources of **perceived pressure** are usually financial pressure or work-related pressure. Financial pressure can be caused by, but is not limited to, the following:

- Unexpected financial needs, such as perceived family needs

- A drug or alcohol habit

- Living beyond one's means

- A gambling addiction

- Unanticipated financial losses

- Excessive bills or personal debt

   Work-related pressure also has several possible causes. An employee might feel dissatisfied with his or her job because of a sense of being underpaid or underappreciated. An employee might have recently been overlooked for a promotion. Either of these things can motivate an employee to "get even" with the company by committing fraud. Also, if a company is performing poorly, it is possible for people within management to feel they are personally responsible and to feel that they are at risk of being terminated. The perceived pressure caused by this feeling of personal responsibility can lead them to commit management fraud by falsifying the financial statements.

RATIONALIZATION

The next element of the fraud triangle that must be present for fraud to occur is **rationalization**. Rationalization is simply finding good reasons for doing things that we really know are wrong. Rationalization is human nature and very few people, if any, do not rationalize their behaviour at some time or another. For example, you may have rationalized going out to a movie with your friends last night when you knew that you really needed to study for an important quiz. Employees who commit fraud attempt to justify their actions and convince themselves that fraud is not wrong by rationalizing their behaviour. Common rationalizations used by individuals involved in fraud include the following:

- "I didn't steal the money; I only borrowed it and I will pay it back."
- "I deserve a pay raise. The company owes this to me."
- "It won't hurt anyone."
- "Once the company gets over its financial difficulties, I will correct the books."

PERCEIVED OPPORTUNITY

The third, and final, element of the fraud triangle is **perceived opportunity**. An individual who commits fraud must perceive that an opportunity exists to commit the fraud, conceal it, and avoid punishment. An opportunity to commit fraud is often perceived when there is easy access to assets or when assets are poorly accounted for by an organization.

Removing any one of the three elements of the fraud triangle makes it much less likely that fraud will occur. Consider the following examples:

- No perceived pressure: An employee may see an opportunity to steal a company computer. He or she may even be able to justify taking the computer by telling him- or herself that the computer is an older one the company no longer uses. However, if he or she can afford to purchase a new computer, the employee will have a low incentive to steal.

- No rationalization: An employee may desperately need cash to pay overdue bills and may see a way to steal money without detection. However, the employee's moral beliefs may make it impossible for him or her to justify taking the money.

- No perceived opportunity: An employee may feel pressured to steal money to cover a personal debt. He or she may rationalize the theft by convincing him- or herself that he or she will repay the company next month. However, if it is not possible for the employee to steal money without detection, it is unlikely that he or she will commit fraud. This situation arises because the employee sees no opportunity to engage in fraudulent activity without discovery.

Of the three elements of the fraud triangle, a business can have the most influence over the element of perceived opportunity. A business generally has limited control over perceived pressure felt by an employee or an employee's ability to rationalize unethical behaviour. The most effective way for a business to prevent fraud is to reduce, or eliminate, the perceived opportunity for an employee to misappropriate company assets or for a manager to falsify financial information. Perceived opportunity can be reduced through a good system of **internal control**.

 DECISION GUIDELINES

DECISION	GUIDELINE	ANALYZE
As the owner of my own company, I have some cash to invest in deterring fraudulent activities by my employees. How should I spend my money?	When all three "legs," or elements, of the fraud triangle are present, fraud is more likely to occur. These elements are as follows: • Perceived pressure • Rationalization • Perceived opportunity	If you remove one of the legs from a three-legged stool, the stool will fall down. In a similar manner, if you can remove one of the elements of the fraud triangle, it is much less likely that fraud will occur. Perceived pressure and rationalization are influenced more by a perpetrator of fraud and are, therefore, very hard to remove. However, it is possible to control the element of perceived opportunity and, therefore, reduce the risk of fraud occurring.

WHAT IS AN INTERNAL CONTROL SYSTEM?

Internal control is a comprehensive system that helps an organization do the following:

- Safeguard assets
- Operate efficiently and effectively
- Ensure proper reporting of financial information
- Ensure compliance with applicable laws and regulations

An organization's management is responsible for the design and implementation of the internal control system. Internal control systems vary from one company to another. Usually, large companies have better developed, more complex internal control systems than small companies. Despite being less formal and less structured, the internal control systems of small companies can still be effective.

L.O. 4 Define *internal control* and describe the objectives of an internal control system

L.O. 5 Identify the elements of a good internal control system

ELEMENTS OF AN INTERNAL CONTROL SYSTEM

There are five key elements that affect an organization's internal control system. The complexity of, and the effectiveness of, the internal control system depends upon these elements. These elements are as follows:

- Control environment
- Risk assessment
- Control activities
- Information and communication
- Monitoring

Control Environment

The **control environment** is the foundation for all other components of internal control. The control environment reflects management and staff attitudes regarding internal control and sets the tone for the entire organization. Control environment factors include the following:

- Leadership philosophy and operating style (an effective control environment cannot exist if management has a "do as I say, not as I do" attitude)
- The competency of the employees within an organization
- The integrity and ethical values of the company personnel
- The organizational structure of the company, namely the delegation of authority and responsibility

Risk Assessment

Risk is a fact of life. Every day, a company will face a variety of risks from both internal and external sources. **Risk assessment** is an ongoing process that identifies and analyzes risks and takes steps to reduce them. For example, a fast food restaurant that hires predominately younger workers would be at a higher risk of violating child labour laws. Also, a company that has a large amount of cash on hand will have a higher risk of having cash stolen from it.

Control Activities

There are two elements related to **control activities**: policies establishing what should be done and the procedures that should be followed to implement the policies. The types of control activities used by an organization vary from company to company. Control activities occur at all levels and in all functions throughout the entire organization. Generally, the controls chosen for an organization are based on its control environment, its assessment of risk, the size and structure of the organization, and the nature of its operations. Examples of common control activities include the following:

■ Employment of competent personnel: Employees must be competent and trustworthy. They should have written job descriptions and be properly trained and adequately supervised.

■ Separation of duties: Responsibility for more than one of the following functions should not be given to any one employee:

 1. Authorizing transactions

 2. Maintaining custody of assets

 3. Keeping accounting records

 Assigning an individual responsibility for more than one of these duties creates an opportunity for fraud. For example, if an employee has access to cash or other assets and he or she can record transactions, that employee can steal from the company and falsify financial information to hide the theft.

Authorizing a transaction

These functions must be segregated.

Recording in the books

Custody of Assets

■ Mandatory vacations: Employees should be required to take annual vacations. If an employee knows that another person will be performing his or her duties during the vacation, there is less perceived opportunity to commit fraud. The vacationing employee will be concerned that any improper activities will be detected.

■ Restricted access: Limit the number of employees who have access to company assets, such as cash, inventory, and supplies. For instance, use cash registers, vaults, and locked storage units to control access to assets. Also, access to computerized accounting records should be restricted to authorized personnel through the use of passwords. Allowing too many people access to assets and records creates opportunity for fraud to occur. It also makes it more difficult to find the perpetrator should fraud occur.

- Security measures: Proper security measures should be implemented to deter theft. These measures can include the use of security cameras and alarm systems. Cash registers that print a receipt should also be utilized with a requirement that all customers receive a receipt.

- Proper authorization: Requiring proper authorization for certain activities, for example, requiring proper authorization for all sales returns, can help prevent improper refunds from being issued.

- Maintenance of adequate documents and records: A trail of business documents and records, called an **audit trail**, should be maintained. The audit trail provides evidence of, and the details supporting, business transactions. Documents should be pre-numbered so gaps in the numbered sequence draw attention. Creating an effective audit trail lowers the chance that inappropriate activity will go unnoticed.

 ## ACCOUNTING IN YOUR WORLD

Stephen H. Blose/Shutterstock

Who Says There's No Free Lunch?

Have you ever eaten at a food court in a mall and seen a sign that says "If you do not get a receipt, your meal is free"? Why would the business care if you get a receipt? This is actually part of the business's internal control activities. You see, the company doesn't really care if you get a receipt, they just care that a receipt is printed. This practice prevents an employee from taking your money and pocketing it because once the receipt is printed, the sale is recorded. If the employee pockets your payment, the daily cash count will not match the daily record of sales and the theft will be detected. This example is just one of many control activities that businesses utilize as part of their internal control systems.

Information and Communication

To maximize the effectiveness of an internal control system, information about the control environment, the risk assessment, and the control activities must be communicated at all levels of the organization. This information should be communicated up, down, and across the organizational structure of the company. It is also critical that management communicates to all personnel that internal control must be taken seriously.

Monitoring

The internal control system must be continually monitored to locate weaknesses in the system. Monitoring can be accomplished through ongoing activities or through separate evaluations. Ongoing monitoring activities include regular management and supervisory activities. It also includes the assessment of the performance of the internal control system by employees as they perform their required duties. The need for separate evaluations depends on the effectiveness of the ongoing monitoring procedures.

INTERNAL CONTROL LIMITATIONS

A good internal control system reduces the risk of undetected errors and irregularities. However, an internal control system cannot provide absolute assurance that no errors will occur. It also does not guarantee that fraud will be prevented or detected. The effectiveness of an internal control system is limited because of the following:

- Employees can become tired, careless, or distracted and make mistakes. They may also use poor judgment or misunderstand policies and procedures.

- Controls can be poorly designed.

- Staff size limitations may hinder efforts to properly segregate duties.

- Two or more people can work together to circumvent controls. This is known as **collusion**.

- Management can override controls.

- The cost of implementing some internal controls may exceed the benefits of these controls.

    Some examples of these limitations are as follows:

- An employee may forget to check authorization for the extension of credit to a customer when the phone rings in the middle of the transaction.

- A disgruntled employee may convince another employee to help steal from the company.

- Management may override controls and direct the accounting staff to record revenue for services that have not yet been performed.

- In small businesses, the cost of employing enough people for separation of duties may exceed the benefits of the segregation.

 CONCEPT CHECK...

Goodguys Tire Company is a small retail tire outlet located in Aurora, Ontario. Bill Han, the president of Goodguys Tire Company, has assigned the bookkeeper the responsibility of processing all cash receipts as well as all cash disbursements. The bookkeeper also prepares the daily cash deposits and takes them to the bank. Bill knows that he has not achieved a very good separation of duties, but the limited number of employees (due to the size of the company) did not allow it. Is there anything Bill can do in light of the fact that there is not a good separation of duties to help prevent fraud from occurring?

Answer: Yes, although there is no substitute for proper separation of duties, some of the steps Bill could take to help detect/deter fraud include, but are not limited to, the following:

- Ensure that someone other than the bookkeeper receives the unopened bank statement and prepares a bank reconciliation on a monthly basis.

- Require that all adjustments to customer accounts be authorized by someone other than the bookkeeper. A periodic review of the customer account detail should also be performed by someone other than the bookkeeper. Any unauthorized adjustments to the accounts should be noted and investigated.

- Require that someone other than the bookkeeper authorize all cash disbursements. The cash disbursement detail should also be reviewed for unusual disbursements periodically by someone other than the bookkeeper.

DECISION GUIDELINES

DECISION	GUIDELINE	ANALYZE
As the owner of my own small business, I know I need to incorporate internal controls, but I don't know where to start. What do I need to consider to make an effective internal control system?	A good system of internal control must achieve the following objectives: • Safeguard assets • Operate efficiently and effectively • Ensure proper reporting of financial information • Ensure compliance with applicable laws and regulations	The internal control system consists of all of the policies and procedures that a business has in place to achieve these objectives. One of the most important things that can be done to help prevent fraud is to ensure that there is adequate separation of duties within the organization. However, no matter how good a system of internal controls is, there are still limitations. For example, two or more employees can work together (collude) to commit fraud even though there is adequate separation of duties.

WHO IS RESPONSIBLE FOR INTERNAL CONTROL?

Audits confirm, or validate, the accounting records and reports of a business. Auditors examine the company's financial statements and the accounting system that produces them. Audits may be internal or external. Employees conduct **internal audits** of a business. These employees, or internal auditors, verify that company personnel are following policies and procedures, and that operations are running efficiently. Internal auditors also determine whether the company is following applicable legal requirements.

Public accountants are the auditors who are licensed to perform **external audits** of an organization's financial statements. Public accountants are independent of the organization. The provincial securities commissions require that all companies that sell shares and bonds to the general public be audited by independent public accountants. This audit includes an assessment of the company's financial statements to determine whether they are fairly presented in accordance with the appropriate guidelines, whether the company uses IFRS or ASPE, as well as an examination of the company's internal control system. **Exhibit 4-3** illustrates a typical organizational chart.

L.O. 6 Describe the major requirements of the Sarbanes-Oxley Act and how they impacted Canadian provincial regulations

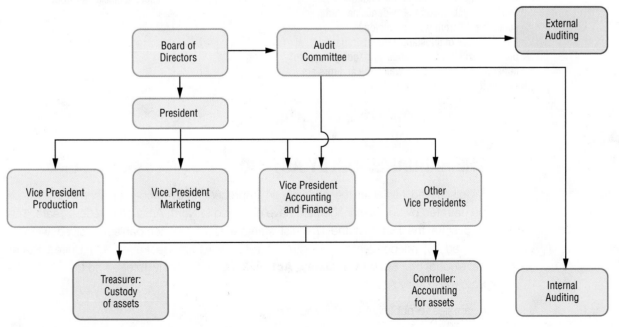

Exhibit 4-3 ▲

AUDIT OPINIONS

The outcome of an external audit is the issuance of an opinion by the independent public accountant. **Exhibit 4-4** describes the four different types of audit opinions.

Type of Opinion	Reason Supporting the Opinion	Impact as a Result of the Opinion
Unqualified (also called a "clean" opinion)	An unqualified opinion means that, in the auditors' opinion, the financial statements are fairly presented. In addition, they are free of material misstatements, and have been prepared in accordance with the appropriate accounting guidelines, unless otherwise noted.	This is the best type of opinion. It gives the financial statement users assurance that the financial statements can be relied upon.
Qualified (also called an "except for" opinion)	A qualified opinion is issued when one of the following occurs: • The auditors have taken exception to an accounting application or treatment the company being audited used • The auditors were unable to gather the information they felt was necessary to issue an unqualified opinion • The auditors were unable to determine the outcome of an uncertainty, which could have an effect on the financial statements	A qualified opinion includes a separate paragraph outlining the reason for the qualification. A qualified opinion is used to help financial statement users make more informed decisions about the company. It allows the auditor to bring to the attention of the users circumstances or situations that may affect the user's reliance on the financial statements.
Adverse	By issuing an adverse opinion, the auditors are stating that in their opinion one of the following situations exists: • The financial statements are not fairly presented in accordance with appropriate accounting guidelines • There are material misstatements in the financial statements	An adverse opinion will be accompanied by a paragraph explaining the reason for the negative opinion. An adverse opinion is very detrimental to a company as it basically informs users that the financial statements should not be relied upon.
Disclaimer	A disclaimer indicates that the auditors are unable to express an opinion based on their audit. A disclaimer of opinion may be issued because of the following: • A lack of independence on the auditors' part • The inability to obtain the evidence needed to support a different type of opinion • The existence of substantial doubts regarding the business's ability to continue as a "going concern" • Material uncertainties for which the auditors are unable to determine the outcome	Since the auditors are unable, or unwilling, to express an opinion on the financial statements, investors will give considerable thought before investing in a company that has been issued a disclaimer of opinion.

Exhibit 4-4 ▲

THE SARBANES-OXLEY ACT

As discussed earlier in the chapter, an unprecedented number of accounting frauds perpetrated by upper management have occurred in North America in recent years. This is despite the fact that the financial statements of the companies involved were all audited by independent auditors. As a response to these frauds, the United States developed the **Sarbanes-Oxley Act** in 2002, commonly referred to as SOX. The Sarbanes-Oxley Act

■ applies to publicly traded companies.

■ established the Public Company Accounting Oversight Board (PCAOB). The PCAOB is a private sector, nonprofit corporation that oversees the auditors of public companies.

The PCAOB protects the interests of investors by helping ensure fair, independent audit reports.

- requires that external auditors report to an audit committee, rather than to an organization's management. Prior to Sarbanes-Oxley, the external auditors often reported to a company's upper management.
- requires that a company's Chief Executive Officer (CEO) and Chief Financial Officer (CFO) certify all annual, or quarterly, reports filed by an organization. By signing the reports, the executives certify the following:

1. They have reviewed the report.
2. The report does not contain any materially untrue statements.
3. The financial statements and related information contained in the report fairly present the financial condition and the results of operations in all material respects of the organization.
4. The signing officers are responsible for internal controls and have evaluated these internal controls within the previous 90 days and have reported on their findings.
5. They have disclosed

   a. a list of all deficiencies in the internal controls and information on any fraud that involves employees who are involved with internal activities.

   b. any significant changes in internal controls or related factors that could have a negative impact on the internal controls.

While SOX has been costly to implement for many companies (as it requires additional internal audit requirements and documentation), it has had a definite impact on improving internal controls in corporate America. SOX has also had an impact on Canadian regulations. Canadian regulators were able to learn from the implementation of the Sarbanes-Oxley Act in America as the Canadian regulations began to be implemented in 2005. The Canadian system is substantially different from the American system in that each province in Canada has its own securities commission. The Canadian Securities Administrators (CSA) is an umbrella organization that makes recommendations for each of the provincial bodies. The CSA, in combination with the Ontario Securities Commission, drafted recommendations based on the Sarbanes-Oxley Act that incorporated CEO/CFO certification of annual reports, new rules for more independence of the audit committee, the implementation and testing of new internal controls, and the formation of a new accounting supervisory body, the Canadian Public Accountability Board. The recommendations are not mandatory for each province, but most recommendations have been adopted by each province. In addition to these recommendations for corporate reporting, the Ontario government implemented tougher penalties for public companies that do not adhere to the regulations, and the federal government made changes to the Criminal Code to toughen the rules against insider trading, to protect from threatening against whistleblowing, and to increase the penalties for public market-related offences.

WHAT INTERNAL CONTROL PROCEDURES SHOULD BE USED FOR CASH?

L.O. 7 Discuss internal controls for cash and prepare a bank reconciliation

Regardless of whether sales are cash sales, credit/debit card sales, or sales on account, ultimately a business will collect cash from the transaction. Cash is one of the most vulnerable assets a business has. Cash is easy to conceal and has no identifying marks that link it to its owner, making it relatively easy to steal. Transactions that affect the Cash account also impact other accounts, so misstatements of cash can result in misstatements of other items. As a result, it is important to have good internal controls over cash.

INTERNAL CONTROLS OVER CASH RECEIPTS

Companies typically receive cash over the counter and through the mail. Good internal control dictates that all cash receipts be deposited in the bank quickly. Each source of cash needs its own security measures.

Over the Counter Cash Receipts

The cash register provides control over the cash receipts for a retail business. Consider a Shoppers Drug Mart store. Shoppers Drug Mart issues a receipt for each transaction to ensure that every sale is recorded; a customer cannot receive a receipt unless the register records the transaction. When the sales associate enters a transaction in the register, the machine records it and the cash drawer opens to receive cash. At the end of the day, the cash in the drawer is reconciled against the machine's record of cash sales to ensure the proper amount of cash is on hand. The machine's record of sales is then used as the source for the journal entry to record sales.

At the end of the day, or several times daily if the company is making a lot of sales, cash should be deposited in the bank. Any cash not in a cash register should be kept in a locked location within the business, such as a safe, until it can be deposited in the bank. These measures, coupled with oversight by management, help discourage theft.

Cash Receipts by Mail

Many companies receive payments by mail, especially if they sell products or services on credit. **Exhibit 4-5** shows how companies can control cash received by mail. Generally, an employee who has no other involvement in the sales or collection process, often a mailroom employee, opens all incoming mail and prepares a control listing of amounts received. At this time a **remittance advice** is prepared if one did not accompany the payment. The mailroom then sends all customer cheques to the treasurer, who oversees having the money deposited in the bank. The remittance advices, often cheque stubs, go to the Accounting Department and serve as a basis for making journal entries to Cash and the customer accounts receivable. As a final step, the controller compares the bank deposit amount from the treasurer with the debit to Cash from the Accounting Department.

The payments received according to the mailroom should match the debit to Cash and should equal the amount deposited in the bank. This procedure ensures that cash receipts are safe in the bank and the company accounting records are up to date.

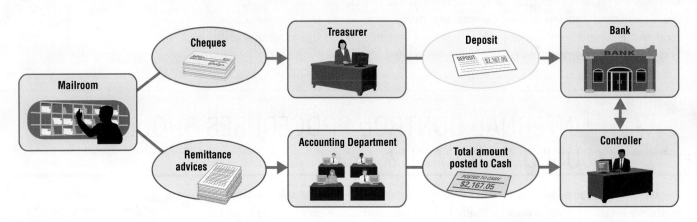

Exhibit 4-5 ▲

INTERNAL CONTROL OVER CASH PAYMENTS

A good separation of duties between operations and cash payments provides internal control over those payments. Also, making payments by cheque is another important control for several reasons:

- The cheque provides a written record of the payment.
- An authorized official studies the evidence supporting the payment.
- The official approves the payment by signing the cheque.

Purchase and Payment Process

To illustrate the internal control over cash payments by cheque in a company large enough to separate duties, suppose Joe's Sporting Goods buys snowboard inventory from Burton Snowboards. This purchase and payment process will generally follow steps similar to those shown in **Exhibit 4-6**:

1. Joe's Sporting Goods sends a **purchase order** to Burton Snowboards, its supplier. By preparing this document, Joe's is placing an order to buy snowboards.
2. Burton Snowboards ships the goods and sends an invoice back to Joe's.
3. Joe's receives the snowboards and prepares a **receiving report** as evidence that it received the goods.
4. After matching the information on these documents, Joe's sends a cheque to Burton Snowboards to pay for the goods together with a remittance advice.

For good internal control, the **purchasing agent**, the individual who places the order, should neither receive the goods nor approve the payment. Otherwise, the purchasing agent could buy goods and have them shipped to his or her home. Or he or she could receive kickbacks from suppliers by having the supplier bill his or her employer too much, approving the payment and splitting the excess with the supplier. The **controller**, as the person responsible for the accounting function, should not sign the cheques for similar reasons; he or she could sign a cheque payable to him- or herself and then manipulate the accounting records to hide this improper payment.

Before signing the cheque, the **treasurer**, who usually assumes responsibility for the custody of cash, should examine each set of documents, including the purchase order,

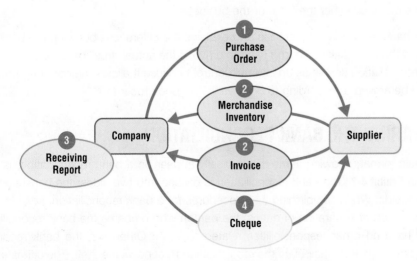

Exhibit 4-6 ▲

receiving report, purchase invoice, and cheque, to prove that they agree. This helps the company ensure that

1. the goods it received were the goods it ordered, as proved by the purchase order and receiving report.
2. it is paying only for the goods ordered and received, as proved by the purchase order, receiving report, invoice, and cheque.

The payment should be issued using pre-numbered cheques. After payment, the cheque signer should deface the set of documents. This can be accomplished by punching a hole through the payment packet or stamping the documents "PAID." This hole or stamp confirms the bill has been paid and prevents the documents from being used to generate a second payment.

Streamlined Payment Procedures

For many companies, the purchase and payment process is made more efficient through the use of **electronic data interchange (EDI)**. EDI is a streamlined process that bypasses people and documents altogether. For example, in electronic data interchange, Walmart's computers communicate directly with the computers of suppliers such as Proctor & Gamble and Hershey Foods. When Walmart's inventory of Hershey chocolate candy reaches a low level, the computer sends a purchase order to Hershey. Hershey ships the candy and invoices Walmart electronically. Then an **electronic funds transfer (EFT)** sends Walmart's payment to Hershey via electronic communication.

THE BANK RECONCILIATION

Preparing a **bank reconciliation** is an important internal control that should be performed regularly. On a monthly basis a company will receive a **bank statement** from its bank that shows the **bank balance**, the cash balance in the company's account according to the bank. This balance usually does not agree with the **book balance**, the cash balance according to the company's records. Differences between the bank balance and the book balance arise because of

- differences, called timing differences, between the time when the bank records a transaction and when the business records it.
- errors made by either the bank or the business.

The bank reconciliation identifies and explains the differences between the bank balance and the book balance and is used to arrive at the actual "true" balance of cash. The bank reconciliation serves as an internal control because it allows the correct amount of cash to be arrived at according to both bank and book records.

PREPARING THE BANK RECONCILIATION

The basic format, showing items that typically appear on a bank reconciliation, is illustrated in **Exhibit 4-7**. The bank reconciliation is divided into two sides: the bank side and the book side. When establishing the procedures for a bank reconciliation, keep in mind our discussion of separation of duties: the person who prepares the bank reconciliation should have no other responsibilities related to cash. Otherwise, the bank reconciler could steal cash and manipulate the reconciliation to conceal the theft. The ultimate goal of the bank reconciliation is to ensure that after the adjustments, the bank balance will equal the book balance.

Exhibit 4-7 ▲

Bank Side of the Reconciliation

When preparing a bank reconciliation, the following items are included on the bank side of the reconciliation:

1. **Deposits in transit** are deposits that the business has recorded but the bank has not. This could happen if the deposit is deposited after banking hours on the date of printing the bank statement. Deposits in transit are added to the bank balance, because by the next day the bank will recognize the deposit.

2. **Outstanding cheques** are cheques that the business has recorded but the bank has not yet paid. This could happen if the beneficiary didn't submit the cheque to the bank for withdrawal. Outstanding cheques are subtracted from the bank balance because sooner or later this cheque is going to be withdrawn from the bank.

3. Bank errors include the bank recording a deposit or a cheque for the wrong amount. The bank may also record a deposit or cheque that belongs in another bank customer's account. The bank must correct the errors that it has made. Adjust the bank balance for the amount of the error, adding or subtracting as necessary depending on the nature of the error.

Book Side of the Reconciliation

When preparing a bank reconciliation, the following items are included on the book side of the reconciliation:

1. **Bank collections** are cash collections made by the bank on behalf of the business. Many businesses have their customers pay their bank directly. One way customers make payment is through a **lock-box system** in which they send their payments to a business's post office box. The bank then collects payments from the box and

deposits them in the business's account, thus reducing the chance of theft. Another example is a bank collection of a depositor's note receivable. Because the bank statement is often the first communication that cash was received, the business has not yet recorded the receipt. These collections are added to the book balance.

2. Electronic fund transfers (EFT) occur when the bank receives or pays cash on the depositor's behalf electronically. Because the bank statement is often the first communication of the transactions, the book balance may need to be adjusted accordingly for the cash receipt or cash payment.

3. Interest revenue may be earned on an account depending on the balance in that account. Interest revenue is added to the book balance as it has not been previously recorded.

4. **Nonsufficient funds (NSF) cheques** represent customer cheques that the business has previously deposited that have turned out to be worthless. In other words, there were not sufficient funds in the customers' bank accounts to pay the cheques. These amounts are subtracted from the book balance to reverse the deposit amount made earlier.

5. Service charges represent bank fees for processing transactions, printing cheques, etc. These amounts are subtracted from the book balance because they have not been recorded yet.

6. Book errors include mistakes made by the account holder in recording cash transactions. For example, an error might involve recording a cheque in the accounting records for a different amount than what the cheque was written for. Another mistake might be failing to record a deposit that was made. The book balance is adjusted for the amount of the error, adding or subtracting as necessary depending on the nature of the error.

ACCOUNTING IN YOUR WORLD

Juice Images/Alamy

I don't need a cheque register; I use online banking.

Jean-Paul got a job his senior year in high school and opened a bank account to keep the money he earns. Jean-Paul deposits his paycheques into the account and then uses a debit card to make purchases. Jean-Paul's dad encouraged him to keep track of his finances using a cheque register and to reconcile his account balance each month when his bank statement arrived. Instead, Jean-Paul decided to just check his account activity every few days online to see that the deductions from his account agree with what he remembers purchasing. A few days after going out for pizza with a couple of friends, Jean-Paul was looking at his account activity online. Jean-Paul happened to have his receipt from the pizza parlor in his wallet, which was unusual as he normally throws them away, and decided to check it against his account activity. The receipt from the pizza parlor showed that the cost of the pizza was $18.53 and that Jean-Paul had added a $2 tip bringing the total amount to $20.53. However, the amount deducted from Jean-Paul's account was $22.53. It appears that the amount of the tip was, accidentally or purposefully, added into the total amount charged twice. Jean-Paul feels lucky that he caught this mistake but wonders how many mistakes like this have occurred in the past that he didn't catch. Now Jean-Paul understands why it is important to maintain a cheque register and to reconcile the account activity each month when he gets his bank statement.

Bank Reconciliation Illustrated

The January bank statement of Acrofab, Inc. is presented in **Exhibit 4-8**. The summary at the top shows the beginning balance, total deposits, total withdrawals, service charges, and the resulting ending balance. Details of the transactions for the month appear on the statement following this summary. The statement shows that the January 31 bank balance of Acrofab, Inc. is $5,875.

INWNB
INLAND NORTHWEST NATIONAL BANK.

Acrofab, Inc.
161 Bay St
Toronto, Ontario M5J 2S4

CHEQUING ACCOUNT 136-213733

CHEQUING ACCOUNT SUMMARY AS OF 1/31/2015

BEGINNING BALANCE	TOTAL DEPOSITS	TOTAL WITHDRAWALS	SERVICE CHARGES	ENDING BALANCE
6,500	4,362	4,972	15	5,875

DEPOSITS	DATE	AMOUNT
Deposits	4-Jan	1,000
Deposits	4-Jan	112
Deposits	8-Jan	200
EFT-Rent	17-Jan	905
Bank collection	26-Jan	2,115
Interest	31-Jan	30

CHARGES	DATE	AMOUNT
Service charges	31-Jan	15

CHEQUES

Number	Amount
956	100
732	3,000
733	160
734	100
735	100
736	1,100

DAILY BALANCE

Date	Balance	Date	Balance
31-Dec	6,500	20-Jan	4,845
4-Jan	7,560	26-Jan	6,960
6-Jan	7,360	31-Jan	5,875
8-Jan	7,560		
10-Jan	7,460		
17-Jan	5,205		

OTHER CHARGES	DATE	AMOUNT
NSF	4-Jan	52
EFT-Insurance	20-Jan	360

MONTHLY SUMMARY

Withdrawals: 8	Minimum Balance: 4,845	Average Balance: 6,085

Exhibit 4-8 ▲

Acrofab's Cash account has a balance of $3,147, as shown in **Exhibit 4-9**. Notice that the cash payments appear as one deduction, or credit, to the Cash account in the general ledger to make the process more efficient because businesses often write and record many cheques at once.

General Ledger:							
Cash							Account No. 1010
			POST			BALANCE	
DATE	ITEM		REF.	DEBIT	CREDIT	DEBIT	CREDIT
2015							
Jan 1	Balance					6,500	
2			J. 30	1,112		7,612	
7			J. 30	200		7,812	
31			J. 32		6,265*	1,547	
31			J. 32	1,600		3,147	

Cash Payments: *Supporting Detail for Jan 31 Credit to Cash			
CHEQUE NO.	AMOUNT	CHEQUE NO.	AMOUNT
732	$3,000	738	$ 320
733	610	739	85
734	100	740	205
735	100	741	460
736	1,100		
737	285	Total	$6,265

Exhibit 4-9 ▲

4.1 **STILL** DON'T GET IT?
Visit MyAccountingLab for an alternate explanation of this important accounting concept.

MEMORY **TIPS**

Only book-side adjustments are journalized.

MEMORY **TIPS**

Outstanding cheques and deposits in transit do not require journal entries on the company's books.

The bank reconciliation in **Exhibit 4-10** identifies and explains the differences between the balance according to the bank statement and the balance according to Acrofab's records, thus determining the correct Cash balance at the end of January. Exhibit 4-10, Panel A, lists the reconciling items, and Panel B shows the completed reconciliation.

Journalizing Transactions from the Reconciliation

Once the bank reconciliation has been prepared, the true balance of cash is known. However, the Cash account in the general ledger still reflects the original book balance if we do not update the book records. Therefore, journal entries must be made and posted to the general ledger so that it reflects the updated cash balance. All items on the book side of the bank reconciliation require journal entries, whereas none of the items on the bank side require journal entries since those are all things that the company has already recorded.

The journal entries listed here bring the Cash account up to date as a result of completing the reconciliation. The letters of the entries correspond to the letters of the reconciling items listed in Exhibit 4-10, Panel A. Entry (i), the entry for the NSF cheque, needs explanation. When L. Ross's cheque was first deposited, Inland Northwest National Bank added $52 to Acrofab's account. When L. Ross's cheque was returned to Inland Northwest National Bank due to insufficient funds, the bank deducted $52 from Acrofab's account. Because the funds are still receivable from Ross, Accounts Receivable—L. Ross is debited to reestablish the amount due from Ross.

PANEL A—Reconciling Items

a. Deposit in transit: $1,600
b. Bank error: The bank mistakenly deducted $100 for a cheque written by another company. Add $100 to bank balance because this balance will be $100 higher once the bank fixes its error.
c. Outstanding cheques:

Cheque No.	Amount
737	$285
738	320
739	85
740	205
741	460

d. EFT receipt of rent revenue: $905
e. Bank collection of a note receivable: $2,115, which includes interest revenue of $115
f. Interest revenue earned on bank balance: $30
g. Book error: Cheque no. 733 for $160 paid to Brown Company on account was recorded as $610; add $450 to the book balance.
h. Bank service charge: $15
i. NSF cheque from L. Ross: $52
j. EFT payment of insurance expense: $360

PANEL B—Completed Reconciliation

Acrofab, Inc.
Bank Reconciliation
January 31, 2015

BANK		BOOKS	
Bal, Jan 31	$5,875	Bal, Jan 31	$3,147
Add:		Add:	
a. Deposit of January 31 in transit	1,600	d. EFT receipt of rent revenue	905
b. Correction of bank error	100	e. Bank collection of note receivable,	
	7,575	$2,000 plus interest revenue of $115	2,115
		f. Interest revenue earned on bank balance	30
Less:		g. Correction of book error—overstated	
c. Outstanding cheques		our cheque no. 733 ($610 – $160)	450
No. 737	(285)		6,647
No. 738	(320)	Less:	
No. 739	(85)	h. Service charge	(15)
No. 740	(205)	i. NSF cheque	(52)
No. 741	(460)	j. EFT payment of insurance expense	(360)
Adjusted bank balance	$6,220	Adjusted book balance	$6,220

These amounts must agree, or the reconciliation is not complete.

Here is a summary of how to treat the reconciling items encountered most often:

Bank Balance—Always:
- *Add* deposits in transit.
- *Subtract* outstanding cheques.
- *Add* or *subtract* corrections of bank errors.

Book Balance—Always:
- *Add* bank collections, interest revenue, and EFT receipts.
- *Subtract* NSF cheques, the cost of printed cheques, service charges, and EFT payments.
- *Add* or *subtract* corrections of book errors.

Exhibit 4-10 ▲

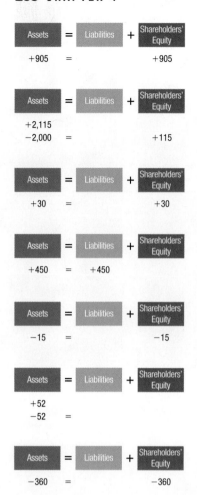

DATE	ACCOUNTS	POST REF.	DR.	CR.
d.	Cash		905	
	Rent Revenue			905
	Record receipt of monthly rent.			
e.	Cash		2,115	
	Notes Receivable			2,000
	Interest Revenue			115
	Record note receivable and interest collected by bank.			
f.	Cash		30	
	Interest Revenue			30
	Record interest earned on bank balance.			
g.	Cash		450	
	Accounts Payable—Brown, Co.			450
	Correct recording of cheque no. 733			
h.	Bank Charges Expense		15	
	Cash			15
	Record bank service charge.			
i.	Accounts Receivable—L. Ross		52	
	Cash			52
	Record NSF cheque returned by bank.			
j.	Insurance Expense		360	
	Cash			360
	Record payment of monthly insurance premium.			

ONLINE BANKING

Online banking allows businesses to pay bills and view account activity electronically. The company doesn't have to wait until the end of the month to get a bank statement. The account history is like a bank statement since it lists all transactions including deposits, cheques, EFT receipts and payments, ATM withdrawals, and interest earned on the bank balance. Because of this, it can be used instead of a bank statement to reconcile the bank account at any time.

 DECISION GUIDELINES

DECISION	**GUIDELINE**	**ANALYZE**
As a manager of a business, I would like to complete some renovations for my retail space. I do not want a loan for this, so I am limited by the amount of cash I have available. But the amount of cash on the bank statement is different from the cash in my general ledger Cash account. Which amount is the amount that I can spend?	Neither. The correct cash balance can only be obtained by preparing a bank reconciliation.	The bank reconciliation identifies differences that arise from the following: • *Timing differences* resulting from items that have been recorded by the business but not yet by the bank or vice versa • *Errors* that have been made by the business or by the bank Once the bank reconciliation has been completed, journal entries are made to adjust the business's Cash account balance to the balance according to the bank reconciliation. This is the correct cash balance.

CRITICAL THINKING

Take a minute to think about the impact of the following cases on each of the assets, liabilities, and shareholders' equity accounts, if the adjusting entries were not recorded in the books. Please indicate understatements "U," overstatements "O," or no effect "NE," identify their amounts, and record the correct entries that should have been made.

1. A cheque for $450 issued to pay for utilities expense was mistakenly recorded in the books as $540.
2. A cheque for $380 deposited in the bank was shown as $330 on the bank statement.
3. An NSF cheque for $260 paid by a customer was returned with the bank statement.
4. An EFT receipt for $150 from a credit customer was not recorded in the book.

Solutions:

	Impact on Accounts			
	Assets	Liabilities	Shareholders' Equity	Correct Entry
1.	U $90	No	U $90	Cash (Dr) .... 90 Utilities Expense (Cr) 90
2.	NE	NE	NE	No Entry
3.	NE	NE	NE	Accounts Receivable (Dr) .... 260 Cash (Cr) 260
4.	NE	NE	NE	Cash (Dr) .... 150 Accounts Receivable (Cr) 150

HOW IS CASH REPORTED ON THE STATEMENT OF FINANCIAL POSITION?

L.O. **8** Report cash on the statement of financial position

Remember from our discussion of the statement of financial position in Chapter 2 that Cash is the first asset listed because it's the most liquid. Businesses often have several bank accounts, but they customarily combine all cash amounts into a single total. On the statement of financial position, this total may be called Cash, or it may be called **Cash and Cash Equivalents**.

Cash on the statement of financial position includes coin, currency, cheques on hand, **petty cash** (discussed in Appendix 4A), chequing accounts, money orders, and traveller's cheques. In short, cash consists of anything that a bank will take as a deposit.

Cash equivalents include very liquid, very safe short-term investments. They include time deposits, money market funds, certificates of deposit, and Treasury bills and Treasury notes. Although Treasury bills and Treasury notes and other cash equivalents can have maturity dates, they are considered cash equivalents if they mature within

90 days of the statement of financial position date. These items are liquid because they can readily be converted into cash, and are safe because they have little risk of losing their value. Cash equivalents so closely resemble cash that they are included with cash on the statement of financial position.

FOCUS ON USERS

Concept	User	Why Is This Important to This User?
Ethical Behaviour	**Bookkeepers**	A bookkeeper will need to have a strong sense of the code of ethics for an organization and how to report unethical behaviour. The bookkeeper may be the first person to notice irregularities since the bookkeeper is typically quite knowledgeable about the accounts of the organization.
	Shareholders and Potential Investors	Shareholders are the people with the ability to set the ethical standard for the company and to ensure that the top executives fulfill their roles in managing the organization while adhering to the ethical code.
Audit Opinions	**Bookkeepers** **Managers** **Shareholders and Potential Investors** **Creditors** **Competitors** **Government & Regulatory Bodies** **Unions**	All users should pay close attention to the audit opinions in the annual report. The audit opinion will identify any concerns regarding the creation and reporting of the financial statements. There are no guarantees that there are no errors or misstatements because the auditors cannot possibly check every transaction, but there is reasonable assurance that the financial statements represent the actual actions of the organization. It is important to remember that ultimately it is management's responsibility to ensure that the financial statements are accurate and fairly represent the accounts of the organization.

ACCOUNTING VOCABULARY

THE LANGUAGE OF BUSINESS

Audit (p. 227)
Audit trail (p. 225)
Bank balance (p. 232)
Bank collection (p. 233)
Bank reconciliation (p. 232)
Bank statement (p. 232)
Book balance (p. 232)
Bribe (p. 220)
Cash (p. 239)
Cash and Cash Equivalents (p. 239)
Cash equivalents (p. 239)

Cash register scheme (p. 220)
Cheque tampering (p. 219)
Code of ethics (p. 218)
Collusion (p. 226)
Control activities (p. 223)
Control environment (p. 223)
Controller (p. 231)
Deposits in transit (p. 233)
Disbursement scheme (p. 219)
Electronic data interchange (EDI) (p. 232)
Electronic funds transfer (EFT) (p. 232)

Employee embezzlement (p. 219)

Expense scheme (p. 220)

External audit (p. 227)

Fraud (p. 216)

Fraud triangle (p. 220)

Internal audit (p. 227)

Internal control (p. 222)

Kickback (p. 220)

Lock-box system (p. 233)

Management fraud (p. 219)

Nonsufficient funds (NSF) cheque (p. 234)

Outstanding cheques (p. 233)

Perceived opportunity (p. 222)

Perceived pressure (p. 221)

Petty cash (p. 239)

Public accountant (p. 227)

Purchase order (p. 231)

Purchasing agent (p. 231)

Rationalization (p. 221)

Receiving report (p. 231)

Remittance advice (p. 230)

Risk assessment (p. 223)

Sarbanes-Oxley Act (SOX) (p. 228)

Treasurer (p. 231)

Whistleblower (p. 218)

ACCOUNTING PRACTICE

DISCUSSION QUESTIONS

1. Can ethics be taught in the college or university classroom? Why or why not?

2. Is there a distinction between personal and professional ethics? What are the implications for the study of ethics in the college or university classroom?

3. What is management fraud? What is employee fraud? Give some examples of each.

4. What are the three components of the fraud triangle? How can they be helpful in fighting fraud in an organization?

5. Do you think the risk factors for management fraud are the same as the risk factors for employee fraud? Why or why not?

6. What is the control environment? Discuss how the control environment had a strong influence over a situation with which you are personally familiar (e.g., a place where you work, your family, your living group in college or university, a classroom, etc.).

7. What part of the fraud triangle is most closely associated with the control activities component of internal control? That is, if control activities are improved, which corner of the fraud triangle is most affected? Why?

8. What are the implications of the fact that every internal control structure has inherent limitations? That is, how does the knowledge that no internal control structure is perfect help management run the organization more effectively?

9. What effect does the Sarbanes-Oxley Act have on the role and influence of the CEO in the corporation?

10. What duties should be segregated in the purchasing process? Why? That is, what could go wrong if two or more of those duties are not segregated?

11. After preparing a bank reconciliation, which reconciling items will require journal entries? Why?

SELF CHECK

MyAccountingLab

The exercises and problems in this chapter can be found on MyAccountingLab. You can practise them as often as you want, and they feature step-by-step guided solutions to help you find the right answer.

1. On what element of the fraud triangle do most organizations usually focus their fraud prevention efforts?

   a. Perceived pressure
   b. Perceived opportunity
   c. Rationalization
   d. All three are targeted

2. Internal control is

   a. the act of stealing a business's assets.
   b. the preparation of fraudulent financial statements.
   c. the process that helps a business achieve its objectives, such as operating efficiently and effectively.
   d. the reconciliation of the bank's cash balance to the book's cash balance.

3. Which of the following is *not* an element of an internal control system?

   a. Auditing
   b. The control environment
   c. Monitoring
   d. Information and communication

4. Separation of duties refers to separating all of these functions *except* which of the following?

   a. Authorizing transactions
   b. Keeping accounting records
   c. Hiring personnel
   d. Maintaining custody of assets

5. Darice Goodrich receives cash from customers as part of her job duties. Her other duty is to post the receipts to customer accounts receivable. Based on these duties, her company has (a) weak

   a. ethics.
   b. fraud triangle.
   c. separation of duties.
   d. disbursement schemes.

6. The document that identifies and explains all differences between the company's record of cash and the bank's record of that cash is the

   a. bank reconciliation.
   b. bank collection.
   c. bank statement.
   d. electronic fund transfer.

7. Which item(s) appears as a reconciling item(s) to the book balance in a bank reconciliation?

   a. Outstanding cheques
   b. Deposits in transit
   c. Both a and b
   d. None of the above

8. Which item(s) appears as a reconciling item(s) to the bank balance in a bank reconciliation?

   a. Outstanding cheques
   b. Deposits in transit
   c. Both a and b
   d. None of the above

9. On its books, Nobu Company's Cash account shows an ending balance of $770. The bank statement for the current period shows a $20 service charge and an NSF cheque for $100. A $250 deposit is in transit, and outstanding cheques total $400. What is Nobu's adjusted book balance for Cash?

   a. $530   b. $650   c. $680   d. $1,050

10. After performing a bank reconciliation, journal entries are required for

    a. all items on the bank side of the reconciliation.

    b. all items on the book side of the reconciliation.

    c. all items on the reconciliation.

    d. no items from the reconciliation because the Cash account needs no adjustment.

Answers are given after Written Communication.

SHORT EXERCISES

S4-1. Internal controls (*Learning Objective 2*) 5–10 min.

Indicate by letters the type of fraud committed:

Cheque tampering (CT)

Cash register scheme (CR)

Expense scheme (E)

Bribe (B)

Fraudulent financial reporting (F)

Here is an example:

  _CT_ Employee writes a fraudulent cheque making it payable to herself.

  _____ At the end of the year, the chief financial officer for Electra International recorded $100,000 in sales that had not been made.

  _____ Carrie is a cashier at a local restaurant. Once a day, she leaves the cash register open and does not record the sale in the cash register when she takes the customer's cash.

  _____ Harry's major customer in Iowa asked Harry to take 20% off of the sales price on the next shipment of jeans to his stores. In return, the customer will give him part of the money saved from the reduced sales price. Harry agrees to lower the price.

  _____ Frank Farmer, owner of Farmer Real Estate, asked the accountant to ignore any depreciation that should be recorded on assets owned.

  _____ Judson submits a cash reimbursement request form for a cab ride he never took.

S4-2. Fraud triangle (*Learning Objective 3*) 5–10 min.

Identify each of the following as an example of a perceived pressure (P), perceived opportunity (O), or rationalization (R) in the fraud triangle:

  _____ 1. Job dissatisfaction

  _____ 2. Greed

  _____ 3. "It's for a good purpose."

  _____ 4. Weak internal control

  _____ 5. Gambling addiction

S4-3. Internal controls (*Learning Objective 4*) 5–10 min.

Internal controls are designed to safeguard assets, encourage employees to follow company policies, promote operational efficiency, and ensure accurate records.

Which objective is most important? Which must the internal controls accomplish for the business to survive? Give your reason.

S4-4. Internal controls (*Learning Objective 5*) 5–10 min.

Indicate by letters which of the following control activities match with the following descriptions:

Separation of duties (SD)

Restricted access (RA)

Proper authorization (PA)

Adequate documents and records (ADR)

_____ 1. Prenumbered invoices

_____ 2. Locking inventory in a warehouse

_____ 3. Manager approval of sales returns

_____ 4. Password protection of accounting software

_____ 5. Not allowing the accounts payable clerk to sign cheques

S4-5. Internal controls (*Learning Objective 5*) 10–15 min.

Explain in your own words why separation of duties is often described as the cornerstone of internal control for safeguarding assets. Describe what can happen if the same person has custody of an asset and also accounts for the asset.

S4-6. Fraud triangle (*Learning Objective 3*) 5–10 min.

Look at each of the following employees of Agetro's Restaurant. Which of the elements of the fraud triangle apply?

Perceived pressure (P)

Perceived opportunity (O)

Rationalization (R)

_____ 1. As the waiter puts $100 in tips in his pocket, he thinks, "Nobody will get hurt" (tips money is divided among waiters at the end of the day).

_____ 2. Tina uses the stolen money to pay for her mother's high medical bills.

_____ 3. Hector knows he will be fired if he doesn't record some fictitious sales.

_____ 4. Roxanne, the night shift manager, knows that upper management does not monitor internal control.

_____ 5. Leo, a waiter, drove to work in a BMW and bragged about his recent vacation to the French Riviera.

_____ 6. Victoria, a cashier for the past five years, was caught stealing cash. When questioned about the theft, she said that she had not received a promotion and deserved more pay.

S4-7. Internal controls (*Learning Objectives 4 & 5*) 5–10 min.

Identify each of the following as an internal control objective (O), an internal control activity (A), or a limitation of internal control (L).

_____ 1. Separation of duties

_____ 2. Collusion

_____ 3. Proper authorization

_____ 4. Reports financial information properly

_____ 5. Mandatory vacations

_____ 6. Management override

_____ 7. Complies with laws and regulations

_____ 8. Adequate documents and records

_____ 9. Poor design

_____ 10. Operates efficiently and effectively

S4-8. Internal controls (*Learning Objective 5*) 5–10 min.

Hazel's Video Store maintains the following policies/procedures with regard to internal control. Indicate by letter which of the following control activities applies to each of the following policies/procedures:

_____ 1. Every day, all cheques written are recorded in the accounting records, using the information on the cheque stubs.

_____ 2. All stores utilize electronic theft detection systems.

_____ 3. Purchases of new DVDs must be approved by the store manager.

_____ 4. Daily sales are recorded in the accounting records by someone other than the sales associates.

_____ 5. The company maintains passwords that limit access to its computerized accounting records.

a. Proper authorization

b. Adequate documents and records

c. Restricted access

d. Security measures

e. Separation of duties

S4-9. Internal controls (*Learning Objective 5*) 5–10 min.

The following situations suggest a strength or a weakness in internal control. Identify each as a strength or weakness, and give the reason for your answer.

a. All employees must take at least five consecutive days off each year.

b. The accounting department orders merchandise and approves invoices for payment.

c. Cash received over the counter is controlled by the sales clerk, who rings up the sale and places the cash in the register. The daily sales are recorded in the accounting records by the accounting department.

d. The officer who signs the cheques need not examine the payment packet because he is confident the amounts are correct.

S4-10. Internal controls (*Learning Objective 5*) 5–10 min.

Identify the missing internal control in the following situations. Select from these activities:

- Proper authorization
- Separation of duties
- Adequate documents and records

a. While reviewing the records of Discount Pharmacy, you find that the same employee orders merchandise and approves invoices for payment.

b. Business is slow at Fun City Amusement Park on Tuesday, Wednesday, and Thursday nights. To reduce expenses, the owner decides not to use a ticket taker on those nights. The ticket seller is told to keep the tickets as a record of the number sold.

c. When business is brisk, a company does not give customers a written receipt unless they ask for it.

d. Jim has worked for Peter's hardware for over 10 years. Due to his length of employment, he has been allowed to grant sales returns at his discretion.

e. At a grocery store, the manager decides to reduce paperwork. She eliminates the requirement that the receiving department prepare a receiving report.

S4-11. Fraud and internal controls (*Learning Objectives 2, 4, & 5*) 15–20 min.

Each of the following situations has an internal control weakness.

a. Betty Grable has been your trusted employee for 30 years. She performs all cash-handling and accounting duties. Betty Grable just purchased a new Lexus and a new home in an expensive suburb. As owner of the company you wonder how she can afford these luxuries because you pay her only $35,000 a year and she has no sources of outside income.

b. Sanchez Hardwoods, a private company, falsified sales and inventory figures to get an important loan. The loan went through, but Sanchez Hardwoods later went bankrupt and couldn't repay the bank.

c. The office supply company where Champ's Sporting Goods purchases its business forms recently notified Champ's Sporting Goods that its documents were no longer going to be prenumbered. Alex Champ, the owner, replied that he never uses the receipt numbers anyway.

d. Discount stores such as Giant Tiger make most of their sales in cash, with the remainder in credit card sales. To reduce expenses, one store manager allows the cashiers to record sales in the accounting records.

Identify the missing internal control in each situation. Answers should include audit, documentation, and separation of duties. Identify the possible problem caused by each control weakness. Answers should include theft and unreliable financial statements. Propose a solution to each internal control problem.

S4-12. Sarbanes-Oxley Act (*Learning Objective 6*) 20–25 min.

What are the main provisions of the Sarbanes-Oxley Act? Be specific.

S4-13. Bank reconciliation adjustments (*Learning Objective 7*) 5–10 min.

For each of the following, indicate whether the item is an adjustment to the bank balance or the book balance:

_____ 1. Bank service charge

_____ 2. Deposit in transit

_____ 3. Bank collection of amount due from customer

_____ 4. Interest revenue on bank balance

_____ 5. Outstanding cheque

S4-14. Bank reconciliation adjustments (*Learning Objective 7*) 10–15 min.

Classify each of the following items as one of the following:

Addition to the book balance (+ Book)
Subtraction from the book balance (− Book)
Addition to the bank balance (+ Bank)
Subtraction from the bank balance (− Bank)

_____ 1. Outstanding cheques

_____ 2. Deposits in transit

_____ 3. NSF cheque

_____ 4. Bank collection of our note receivable

_____ 5. Interest earned on bank balance

_____ 6. Bank service charge

_____ 7. Book error: We credited Cash for $200. The correct amount of the cheque was $2,000.

_____ 8. Bank error: The bank decreased our account for a cheque written by another customer.

S4-15. Prepare a bank reconciliation (*Learning Objective 7*) 5–10 min.

The T-account for cash and the bank statement of Mee Auto Services for the month of March 2015 follows:

Cash			
Mar 1	3,200	Cheque #704	540
Mar 10 deposit	750	Cheque #705	210
Mar 31 deposit	200	Cheque #706	900
Pre-adjusted			
Bal @ Mar 31	2,500		

Bank Statement:

Bal, Mar 1			$3,200
Deposits:			
Deposits		$750	
Bank collection		710	
Interest		10	1,470
Cheques:	No.	Amount	
	704	540	
	705	210	(750)
Other Charges:			
Service charge		$ 20	(20)
Bal, Mar 31			$3,900

Prepare Mee Auto Services' bank reconciliation at March 31.

S4-16. Prepare bank reconciliation journal entries (*Learning Objective 7*) 5–10 min.

Make the necessary journal entries arising from Dee Zee Motor's bank reconciliation presented next. Date each entry March 31 and include an explanation with each entry.

Dee Zee Motors Bank Reconciliation March			
BANK		**BOOKS**	
Bal, Mar 31	$ 500	Bal, Mar 31	$ 740
Add:		Add:	
Deposit in transit	300	Interest revenue	10
	800		750
		Less:	
Less:		Service charge	(20)
Outstanding cheques	(250)	NSF cheques	(180)
Adjusted bank balance	$ 550	Adjusted book balance	$ 550

S4-17. Statement of financial position presentation of cash (*Learning Objective 8*) 5–10 min.

Prepare the current assets section of the statement of financial position as of December 31, 2015, for Lipton, Inc. using the following information:

Accounts Receivable	$63,000
Petty Cash	500
Cash in Bank Accounts	22,000
Inventory	55,500

S4-18. Bank reconciliation adjustments (*Learning Objective 7*) 10–15 min.

Assess each of the following items and indicate the proper treatment of each case as one of the following:

Addition to the book balance (+ Book)

Subtraction from the book balance (− Book)

Addition to the bank balance (+ Bank)

Subtraction from the bank balance (− Bank)

_____ 1. A cheque for $680 received from a customer was recorded as $860 in the books.

_____ 2. A deposit for $580 was shown in the bank statement as $530.

_____ 3. A cheque for $1,250 issued to pay a supplier was not cleared from the bank.

_____ 4. An NSF cheque for $720 was returned with the bank statement.

_____ 5. An EFT receipt for $50 from a purchase rebate.

EXERCISES (GROUP A)

E4-1A. Bank reconciliation adjustments (*Learning Objective 7*) 10–15 min.

Calculate the answers for the missing data:

BANK		BOOKS	
Bal, Jan 31	$1,030	Bal, Jan 31	(c)
Add:		Add:	
Deposit in transit	660	Bank collection	505
	(a)	Interest revenue	25
			(d)
Less:		Less:	
Outstanding cheques	(b)	Service charge	(70)
Adjusted bank balance	$1,290	Adjusted book balance	$1,290

E4-2A. Prepare a bank reconciliation and journal entries (*Learning Objective 7*) 20–25 min.

Dirk Cole's chequebook lists the following:

Date	Cheque No.	Item	Amount	Deposit	Balance
9/ 1					$1,425
5	922	Mesilla Kitchen	$ 22		1,403
10		Dividends received		$ 115	1,518
14	923	Best Products	25		1,493
15	924	Fina (payment on account)	60		1,433
19	925	Cash	200		1,233
27	926	Staples	175		1,058
29	927	Hobart Properties	1,000		58
30		Paycheque		4,095	4,153

Dirk Cole's September bank statement shows the following:

Bal, Sep 1				$1,425
Deposits:				115
Cheques:	No.	Amount		
	922	$ 22		
	923	25		
	924	70*		
	925	200		(317)
Other Charges:				
Printed cheques			$20	
Service charge			15	(35)
Bal, Sep 30				$1,188

*This amount is correct for cheque no. 924.

Requirements

1. Prepare Dirk Cole's bank reconciliation on September 30. How much cash does Dirk Cole actually have on September 30?

2. Prepare all necessary journal entries for Dirk Cole to update the Cash account as a result of the bank reconciliation.

E4-3A. Prepare a bank reconciliation (*Learning Objective 7*) 20–25 min.

Information from Goddard Picture Frames' Cash account as well as the January bank statement are presented next.

Cash			
Jan 1	1,400	Cheque #210	30
Jan 30	2,700	Cheque #211	400
		Cheque #212	110
		Cheque #213	325
		Cheque #214	200
Pre-adjusted			
Bal @ Jan 31	3,035		

Bank Statement:				
Bal, Jan 1				$1,400
Deposits:				
EFT—rent				500
Cheques:	No.	Amount		
	210	300		
	211	400		
	212	110		(810)
Other Charges:				
Service charge			$ 15	
Cheque printing			10	
NSF cheque #201			65	(90)
Bal, Jan 31				$1,000

Cheque #210 was written for $300 to pay salaries.

Requirements

1. Prepare the bank reconciliation on January 31.

2. Prepare all necessary journal entries for Goddard Picture Frames to update the Cash account as a result of the bank reconciliation.

Quick solution:

1. Adjusted cash balance = $3,175

E4-4A. Bank reconciliation adjustments (*Learning Objective 7*) 15–20 min.

MiThai's new accounting clerk could not get the bank reconciliation balanced. She needs your help and has provided you with her bank reconciliation and all the information she used to prepare the bank reconciliation:

Bank	7,610	Book	8,620
Deposit	2,100	Cheque No. 125 (outstanding)	1,680
EFT – Collection	1,200		
Subtotal	10,910	Subtotal	10,300
Subtract		Subtract	
Interest charges	24	NSF cheque	1,735
Bank service charges	16	NSF fee	15
Total	40	Total	1,750
Reconciled bank balance	10,870	Reconciled book balance	8,550

Additional Information:

a. The July 31 bank statement showed a cash balance of $7,610, EFT collection of $1,200, interest charges of $24, bank service charges of $16, NSF cheque of $1,735, and NSF fee of $15.

b. The book ledger showed a cash balance of $8,620. In addition, the book records showed that both cheque #125 for the amount of $1,680 and a deposit of $2,100 were not included in the bank statement.

Requirement

1. Prepare MiThai's bank reconciliation on July 31. What is the reconciled book balance?

E4-5A. Bank reconciliation adjustments (*Learning Objective 7*) 20–25 min.

The following information is for Jae Kim, Ltd. in June:

a. Cash balance on June 30 in the ledger was $12,450, and cash balance on June 30's bank statement was $14,860.

b. Deposit in transit for the amount of $1,500 from May 31 was recorded in the bank statement on June 1. Deposit in transit for the amount of $1,800 from June 30 was not recorded in the June bank statement.

c. Cheque #103 for the amount of $1,720 was outstanding on May 31, 2015 and was still outstanding on June 30, 2015.

d. Cheque #125 for the amount of $680 was outstanding on June 30.

e. EFT collection of $1,200 from a tenant for his rent payment was shown on June 2 in the bank statement.

f. NSF cheque for the amount of $760 and an NSF fee of $20 were included in the bank statement.

g. Interest and bank service charges for June were $15 and $35 respectively.

h. A cheque for cash sales for the amount of $1,600 was mistakenly recorded as $160 in the books.

Requirements

1. Prepare Jae Kim's bank reconciliation on June 30, 2015. What is the reconciled book balance?

2. Record the entries to update the Cash account balance. Include an explanation for each entry.

3. If the entries were not recorded in (2), what is the impact on each of the assets, liabilities, and shareholders' equity accounts?

EXERCISES (GROUP B)

E4-1B. Bank reconciliation adjustments (*Learning Objective 7*) 10–15 min.

Calculate the answers for the missing data:

BANK			BOOKS	
Bal, Dec 31	$1,060		Bal, Dec 31	(c)
Add:			Add:	
Deposit in transit	680		Bank collection	425
	(a)		Interest revenue	35
				(d)
Less:			Less:	
Outstanding cheques	(b)		Service charge	(45)
Adjusted bank balance	$1,340		Adjusted book balance	$1,340

E4-2B. Prepare a bank reconciliation and journal entries (*Learning Objective 7*) 20–25 min.

Dan Cryer's chequebook lists the following:

Date	Cheque No.	Item	Amount	Deposit	Balance
10/ 1					$1,435
5	922	Rivertown Kitchen	$ 40		1,395
10		Dividends received		$ 125	1,520
14	923	Everyday Products	37		1,483
15	924	Fauna (payment on account)	63		1,420
19	925	Cash	200		1,220
27	926	Office Supply	117		1,103
28	927	North East Properties	984		119
31		Paycheque		5,285	5,404

Dan Cryer's October bank statement shows the following:

Bal, Oct 1				$1,435
Deposits:				125
Cheques:	No.	Amount		
	922	$ 40		
	923	37		
	924	163*		
	925	200		(440)
Other Charges:				
Printed cheques			$25	
Service charge			10	(35)
Bal, Oct 31				$1,085

*This amount is correct for cheque no. 924.

Requirements

1. Prepare Dan Cryer's bank reconciliation on October 31. How much cash does Dan Cryer actually have on October 31?

2. Prepare all necessary journal entries for Dan Cryer to update the Cash account as a result of the bank reconciliation.

E4-3B. Prepare a bank reconciliation (*Learning Objective 7*) 20–25 min.

Information from Sheppard Picture Frames' cash account as well as the November bank statement are presented next.

Cash			
Nov 1	2,100	Cheque #210	60
Nov 30	2,000	Cheque #211	400
		Cheque #212	137
		Cheque #213	310
		Cheque #214	180
Pre-adjusted			
Bal @ Nov 30	3,013		

Bank Statement:			
Bal, Nov 1			$ 2,100
Deposits:			
EFT—rent			750
Cheques:	No.	Amount	
	210	600	
	211	400	
	212	137	(1,137)
Other Charges:			
Service charge		$ 30	
Cheque printing		16	
NSF cheque #201		80	(126)
Bal, Nov 30			$ 1,587

Cheque #210 was written for $600 to pay salaries.

Requirements

1. Prepare the bank reconciliation on November 30.

2. Prepare all necessary journal entries for Sheppard Picture Frames to update the Cash account as a result of the bank reconciliation.

E4-4B. Bank reconciliation adjustments (*Learning Objective 7*) 15–20 min.

Patel Ltd.'s new accounting clerk could not get the bank reconciliation balanced. He needs your help and provided you with his bank reconciliation and all the information he used to prepare the bank reconciliation:

Bank	6,750	Book	7,520
Deposit	1,650	Cheque No. 578 (outstanding)	1,320
EFT – Collection	1,040		
Subtotal	9,440	Subtotal	8,840
Subtract		Subtract	
NSF cheque	1,400	Interest charges	25
NSF fee	20	Bank service charges	35
Total	1,420	Total	60
Reconciled bank balance	8,020	Reconciled book balance	8,780

Additional Information:

a. The May 31 bank statement showed a cash balance of $6,750, EFT collection of $1,040, interest charges of $25, bank service charges of $35, an NSF cheque of $1,400, and an NSF fee of $20.

b. The book ledger showed a cash balance of $7,520. In addition, the book records showed that both cheque #578 for the amount of $1,320 and a deposit of $1,650 were not included in the bank statement.

Requirement

1. Prepare Patel Ltd.'s bank reconciliation on May 31. What is the reconciled book balance?

E4-5B. Bank reconciliation adjustments (*Learning Objective 7*) 20–25 min.

The following information is for Yamada, Ltd. In April:

1. Cash balance on April 30 in the ledger was $8,645, and cash balance on April 30's bank statement was $10,750.

2. Deposit in transit for the amount of $1,180 from February 28 was recorded in the bank statement on March 1. Deposit in transit for the amount of $720 from April 30 was not recorded in the April bank statement.

3. Cheque #683 for the amount of $1,400 was outstanding on March 31 and was still outstanding on April 30.

4. Cheque #705 for the amount of $1,020 was outstanding on April 30.

5. EFT collection of $620 from a tenant for his rent payment was shown on April 2 in the bank statement.

6. A cheque for cash sales for the amount of $630 was mistakenly recorded as $360 in the book.

7. An NSF cheque for the amount of $425 together with an NSF fee of $15 were included in the bank statement.

8. Interest and bank service charges for April were $30 and $15 respectively.

Requirements

1. Prepare Yamada's bank reconciliation on April 30. What is the reconciled book balance?

2. Record the entries to update the Cash account balance. Include an explanation for each entry.

3. If the entries were not recorded in (2), what is the impact on each of the assets, liabilities, and shareholders' equity accounts?

EXERCISES (ALTERNATES 1, 2, AND 3)

These alternative exercise sets are available for your practice benefit on **MyAccountingLab**.

PROBLEMS (GROUP A)

P4-1A. Prepare a bank reconciliation (*Learning Objective 7*) 20–25 min.

The May cash records of Nielson, Inc. follow:

Cash Receipts (CR)		Cash Payments (CP)	
Date	Cash Debit	Cheque No.	Cash Credit
May 4	$2,716	1416	$ 8
9	544	1417	775
14	896	1418	88
17	367	1419	126
31	2,037	1420	970
		1421	200
		1422	2,267

Nielson's Cash account shows the balance of $6,171 on May 31. On May 31, Nielson, Inc. received the following bank statement:

Bank Statement for May			
Beginning Balance			$ 4,045
Deposits and other additions			
May 1		$ 625 EFT	
5		2,716	
10		544	
15		896	
18		367	
31		1,000 BC	6,148
Cheques and other deductions			
May 8		$ 441 NSF	
15	(Cheque #1416)	8	
19		340 EFT	
22	(Cheque #1417)	775	
29	(Cheque #1418)	88	
31	(Cheque #1419)	216	
31		25 SC	(1,893)
Ending Balance			$ 8,300

Explanations: BC—bank collection; EFT—electronic funds transfer; NSF—nonsufficient funds cheque; SC—service charge.

Additional data for the bank reconciliation:

a. The EFT deposit was a receipt of rent revenue. The EFT debit was payment of insurance expense.

b. The NSF cheque was received from a customer.

c. The $1,000 bank collection was for a note receivable.

d. The correct amount of cheque #1419 is $216. Nielson, Inc. mistakenly recorded the cheque for $126.

Requirement

1. Prepare Nielson's bank reconciliation at May 31.

P4-2A. Prepare a bank reconciliation (*Learning Objective 7*) 20–25 min.

The October bank statement of Blake's Hamburger just arrived from First National Bank.

October Bank Statement:				
Bal, Oct 1				$12,769
Deposits:				
EFT—rent			$900	
EFT—deposit			200	
Interest			16	1,116
Cheques:	No.	Amount		
	807	600		
	808	400		
	1668	410		(1,410)
Other Charges:				
Service charge			$ 7	
NSF cheque #998			67	
NSF cheque #201			192	(266)
Bal, Oct 31				$12,209

To prepare the bank reconciliation, you gather the following additional data:

a. The following cheques are outstanding at October 31:

Cheque No.	Amount
800	$402
802	74
806	36
809	161
810	229
811	48

b. On October 31, Blake's Hamburger's treasurer deposited $381, but this deposit does not appear on the bank statement.

c. The bank statement includes a $410 deduction for cheque #1668 written by Danson Freight rather than Blake's Hamburger. Blake's Hamburger notified the bank of this bank error.

d. Blake's Hamburger's Cash account shows a balance of $11,200 on October 31.

Requirements

1. Prepare the bank reconciliation for October 31.
2. Record the entries called for by the reconciliation. Include an explanation for each entry in the memo line of the journal.

P4-3A. Prepare a bank reconciliation (*Learning Objective 7*) 25–30 min.

The following is Oishi Sushi's bank statement:

Date	Description	Debit	Credit	Balance
May 31				12,650
Jun 1	Deposit		4,250	16,900
3	Cheque #144	780		16,120
4	Cheque #162	2,705		13,415
7	Deposit		3,480	16,895
10	Cheque #183	625		16,270
12	Cheque #184	1,680		14,590
15	EFT - Salaries	3,600		10,990
16	Deposit		1,720	12,710
16	Cheque #185	840		11,870
18	Cheque #188	550		11,320
20	NSF Cheque - Fundy Bay FishMart	620		10,700
20	NSF Fee	15		10,685
24	EFT - Collection Dalhousie Inc.		1,425	12,110
27	Cheque #190	630		11,480
30	Deposit		2,430	13,910
30	EFT - Salaries	3,600		10,310
30	Bank Service Charges	35		10,275
30	Interest Charges	25		10,250

Oishi Sushi's ledger shows the following transactions in the Cash account in June:

Date	Description	Debit	Credit	Balance
May 31				12,650
Jun 1	Deposit	3,480		16,130
Jun 8	Cheque #183		625	15,505
Jun 9	Cheque #184		1,680	13,825
Jun 10	Cheque #185		840	12,985
Jun 12	Cheque #186		1,360	11,625
Jun 12	Cheque #187		950	10,675
Jun 16	Deposit	1,720		12,395
Jun 16	Cheque #188		550	11,845
Jun 20	Cheque #189		365	11,480
Jun 22	Cheque #190		680	10,800
Jun 28	Deposit	2,340		13,140
Jun 30	Deposit	4,520		17,660

Additional information:

a. Deposit of $4,250 on May 31 was deposited in the bank on June 1.

b. Cheque #178 for $140 and cheque #180 for $625 were issued in May, and they were not cashed in June.

c. Oishi Sushi made an error in recording cheque #190 and the June 28 deposit. Cheque #190 was for an advertisement, and the deposit was a collection from ABC Corp.

Requirements

1. Prepare Oishi Sushi's bank reconciliation at June 30.

2. Record the entries to update the Cash account balance. Include an explanation for each entry.

3. If the entries were not recorded in (2), what is the impact on each of the assets, liabilities, and shareholders' equity accounts?

P4-4A. Prepare a bank reconciliation (*Learning Objective 7*) 20–25 min.

Dion Ltd.'s ledger showed a cash balance of $12,134 on December 31, 2015. In preparing the bank reconciliation, the following information was determined:

a. EFT collection by bank from a credit customer was $5,620.

b. A deposit of $2,600 was correctly recorded in the books, but it was shown as $26.00 on the bank statement.

c. Cheque #205 issued by Dion Ltd. in the amount of $550, for the payment of the bank loan $500 and 10% of interest, had been incorrectly recorded in the books as $55 ($50 allocated for the loan and $5 for the interest expense).

d. Cheque #221 issued by Dion Ltd. in the amount of $2,460, for the purchase of a computer, had been incorrectly paid by the bank as $246.

e. A cheque for $521 paid by a customer for his purchase was incorrectly recorded in the books as $125.

f. An NSF cheque for $2,850 was returned with the bank statement, with a bank charge of $15 for this transaction.

g. Cheque #201 issued by Dion Ltd. in the amount of $1,250 was not included in the bank statement.

h. The bank statement showed interest charges and bank service charges were $52 and $28 respectively.

Requirements

1. Prepare Dion's bank reconciliation at December 31, 2015.

2. What was the reconciled book balance? What was the bank statement balance before reconciliation?

3. Record the entries to update the Cash account balance. Include an explanation for each entry.

4. If the entries were not recorded in (3), what is the impact on each of the assets, liabilities, and shareholders' equity accounts?

PROBLEMS (GROUP B)

P4-1B. Prepare a bank reconciliation (*Learning Objective 7*) 20–25 min.

The November cash records of Stenback, Inc. follow:

Cash Receipts (CR)		Cash Payments (CP)	
Date	Cash Debit	Cheque No.	Cash Credit
Nov 4	$2,725	1416	$ 9
9	530	1417	750
14	880	1418	93
17	353	1419	124
31	2,040	1420	960
		1421	210
		1422	2,250

Stenback's Cash account shows the balance of $6,172 on November 30. On November 30, Stenback received the following bank statement:

Bank Statement for November		
Beginning Balance		$ 4,040
Deposits and other additions:		
Nov 1	$ 635 EFT	
5	2,725	
10	530	
15	880	
18	353	
31	1,800 BC	6,923
Cheques and other deductions:		
Nov 8	$ 452 NSF	
15 (Cheque no. 1416)	9	
19	350 EFT	
22 (Cheque no. 1417)	750	
29 (Cheque no. 1418)	93	
31 (Cheque no. 1419)	214	
31	45 SC	(1,913)
Ending Balance		$ 9,050

Explanations: BC—bank collection; EFT—electronic funds transfer; NSF—nonsufficient funds cheque; SC—service charge.

Additional data for the bank reconciliation:

a. The EFT deposit was a receipt of rent revenue. The EFT debit was payment of insurance expense.

b. The NSF cheque was received from a customer.

c. The $1,800 bank collection was for a note receivable.

d. The correct amount of cheque #1419 is $214. Stenback, Inc. mistakenly recorded the cheque for $124.

Requirement

1. Prepare Stenback's bank reconciliation on November 30.

P4-2B. Prepare a bank reconciliation (*Learning Objective 7*) 20–25 min.

The December 31 bank statement of Billy's Hamburger just arrived from Safety Bank.

Bank Statement for December			
Bal, Dec 1			$13,384
Deposits:			
EFT—rent		$700	
EFT—deposit		400	
Interest		12	1,112
Cheques:	No.	Amount	
	807	$600	
	808	200	
	1668	410	(1,210)
Other Charges:			
Service charge		$ 19	
NSF cheque #998		60	
NSF cheque #201		205	(284)
Bal, Dec 31			$13,002

To prepare the bank reconciliation, you gather the following additional data:

a. The following cheques are outstanding on December 31:

Cheque No.	Amount
800	$415
802	75
806	34
809	123
810	228
811	39

b. On December 31, Billy's Hamburger's treasurer deposited $330, but this deposit does not appear on the bank statement.

c. The bank statement includes a $410 deduction for a cheque written by Jenny's Jump Ropes rather than Billy's Hamburger. Billy's Hamburger notified the bank of this bank error.

d. Billy's Cash account shows a balance of $12,000 on December 31.

Requirements

1. Prepare the bank reconciliation for December 31.
2. Record the journal entries called for by the reconciliation. Include an explanation for each entry.

P4-3B. Prepare a bank reconciliation (*Learning Objective 7*) 25–30 min.

The following is the MaMa Pizza's bank statement on August 31, 2015:

Date	Description	Debit	Credit	Balance
July 31				14,220
August 1	Deposit		2,560	16,780
3	Cheque #264	860		15,920
4	Cheque #283	180		15,740
7	Deposit		3,165	18,905
10	Cheque #303	865		18,040
12	Cheque #304	1,460		16,580
15	EFT - Salaries	2,400		14,180
16	Deposit		1,580	15,760
16	Cheque #305	1,250		14,510
18	Cheque #308	2,120		12,390
20	NSF cheque -Toni Ltd.	1,680		10,710
20	NSF Fee	15		10,695
24	EFT - Collection Roma Inc.		3,080	13,775
27	Cheque #310	830		12,945
28	Deposit		2,160	15,105
30	EFT - Salaries	2,400		12,705
30	Bank service charges	60		12,645
30	Interest charges	105		12,540

MaMa Pizza's ledger shows the following transactions in the Cash account in June:

Date	Description	Debit	Credit	Balance
July 31				14,220
August 1	Deposit	3,165		17,385
8	Cheque #303		865	16,520
9	Cheque #304		1,460	15,060
10	Cheque #305		1,250	13,810
12	Cheque #306		970	12,840
12	Cheque #307		655	12,185
16	Deposit	1,580		13,765
16	Cheque #308		212	13,553
20	Cheque #309		1,040	12,513
22	Cheque #310		830	11,683
28	Deposit	1,260		12,943
30	Deposit	5,250		18,193

Additional information:

a. Deposit of $2,560 on August 31 was deposited in the bank on September 1.

b. Cheque #278 for $260 and cheque #298 for $1,260 were issued in July, and they were not cashed in August.

c. MaMa Pizza made an error in recording cheque #308 and the August 28 deposit. Cheque #308 was for delivery car rental fees, and the deposit was a collection from a catering event.

Requirements

1. Prepare MaMa Pizza's bank reconciliation at August 31.

2. Record the entries to update the Cash account balance. Include an explanation for each entry.

3. If the entries were not recorded in (2), what is the impact on each of the assets, liabilities, and shareholders' equity accounts?

P4-4B. Prepare a bank reconciliation (*Learning Objective 7*) 20–25 min.

Vihn Ltd.'s ledger showed a cash balance of $22,977 on March 31. In preparing the bank reconciliation, the following information was determined:

a. EFT collection by bank from a credit customer was $3,280.

b. A deposit of $1,800 was correctly recorded in the books, but it was shown as $18.00 on the bank statement.

c. Cheque #725 issued by Vihn Ltd. in the amount of $880, for the payment of the bank loan $800 and 10% of interest, had been incorrectly recorded in the books as $88 ($80 allocated for the loan and $8 for the interest expense).

d. Cheque #741 issued by Vihn Ltd. in the amount of $2,580, for the purchase of a computer, had been incorrectly paid by the bank as $258.

e. A cheque of $425 paid by a customer for his purchase was incorrectly recorded in the books as $245.

f. An NSF cheque for $1,370 was returned with the bank statement, with a bank charge of $18 for this transaction.

g. Cheque #701 issued by Vihn Ltd. in the amount of $1,680 was not included in the bank statement.

h. The bank statement showed interest charges and bank service charges were $26 and $54 respectively.

Requirements

1. Prepare Vihn's bank reconciliation at March 31.

2. What was the reconciled book balance? What was the bank statement balance before reconciliation?

3. Record the entries to update the Cash account balance. Include an explanation for each entry.

4. If the entries were not recorded in (3), what is the impact on each of the assets, liabilities, and shareholders' equity accounts?

PROBLEMS (ALTERNATES 1, 2, AND 3)

These alternative problem sets are available for your practice benefit on **MyAccountingLab**.

APPLY YOUR KNOWLEDGE

ETHICS IN ACTION

Case 1.   Jake needed a summer job and was lucky enough to land a job as a ticket collector at a local amusement park. On his first day, he was assigned to work alongside Tim, who had worked at the park for the past two summers. Tim explained to Jake that tickets are purchased from the box office outside the gate, and that park-goers present their tickets at the gate when they are ready to enter. Each ticket has a stub that is torn off and given back to the park-goer so they can leave and return the same day.

Jake decided this was not going to be a bad summer job considering that one of the "perks" of working at the park was that on his days off he could enter the park free. However, he had remembered from reading the employee handbook that only employees were admitted free. Any friends or family accompanying the employee must pay full price. Tim showed Jake the gate that employees used on their days off. He said, "just swipe your employee ID card through the card reader on the outside of the gate and you are in the park."

Soon after Jake started working at the park, he began to notice that many of the employees would hold the employee gate open while their friends and family entered without purchasing a ticket. One day Jake asked Tim about what he had saw. Tim replied, "Oh, nobody around here follows that policy. Last week I even saw the park superintendent come in with his entire family without paying."

A few weeks later on one of his days off, Jake was hanging out with his friends when one of them said, "Hey Jake, since you are working at the amusement park, can't you get us all in free today?" Jake thought about how much more fun it would be to go to the park with his friends and he began to reason "Why should I follow the rules if no one else does, not even the park superintendent? Anyway, it's not like I would really be stealing anything."

Requirement

1. What are the ethical considerations in this case?

Case 2.   Marybeth Jones is the controller at Patterson Supply Company, a publicly traded distributor of floral supplies. It is the end of the third quarter and Marybeth is working under a deadline to get the quarterly financial statements prepared before the board of directors meeting at 2 P.M. The board of directors approves the quarterly financial statements before they are sent to the provincial securities commission.

Unfortunately, Marybeth has a bit of a problem. The debit and credit columns of the general ledger trial balance do not balance. She is certain that this is a simple mistake that someone made in recording a journal entry, but she just doesn't have time to look for the mistake. To make the deadline, Marybeth decides to force the trial balance into balance by adding the $200,000 that she is out-of-balance to the Inventory account. Since inventory is the company's largest asset, Marybeth justified her actions by thinking that this wouldn't make a difference to anyone looking at the financial statements. She wished she had more time to look for the mistake, but the clock is ticking away.

Requirement

1. Is there any evidence of unethical behaviour in this case? Explain your answer.

Case 3.   Rex Banner is the manager of a Stop Mart convenience store. He has been employed by the company for 12 years, the last 9 years of which was as a store manager. Rex applied for a promotion to regional manager, which oversees all 30 locations, but was once again denied promotion. Had he been promoted, the regional manager salary would have given Rex $14,000 more per year.

Rex was upset and decided that if the company would not give him the additional compensation he deserved then he would give himself a raise at the expense of the company.

He knew that whenever he hired a new employee, the required paperwork sent to the corporate headquarters was simply filed without being reviewed. Thus, Rex completed all the company employment forms for a fictitious new employee he named "Sam Jones." He figured that, when the company was notified by Service Canada that the Social Insurance Number for "Sam Jones" was fraudulent, Rex would simply report that the employee had just quit and that Rex had no way to contact him. Rex's scheme involved the following actions:

- He put "Sam" on the schedule.
- Every week, he submitted a signed time card for "Sam" along with all the other legitimate employee time cards.
- Every two weeks when Rex received the employee paycheques, he pulled "Sam's" paycheque and hid it in his briefcase.
- He then cashed the paycheque for "Sam" and enjoyed the extra money.

Requirement

1. While Rex's actions are clearly unethical, were they justified, given that he was again denied a promotion and therefore undercompensated? Will Rex be caught? Does the company bear some responsibility too? If the company required direct deposit of its employee paycheques, could this type of fraud be prevented? Can you recommend any other procedures the company could adopt that would help to prevent Rex's fraud?

Case 4. RAS, Inc. is a supplier of residence alarm systems to building contractors. Sam Jennings, the company's new CEO, is out to make a name for himself and makes it known to his management team that he plans for the company to meet, if not exceed, its sales target each quarter.

Sam begins to realize that the company is falling short of its goal and he quickly calls a management meeting to announce his new plan. He says he has arranged sweet deals with several of the company's largest customers. RAS will pay the contractors a 1% fee to buy a large quantity of alarm systems just before the end of each quarter, with the understanding that RAS will buy the alarm systems back shortly after the beginning of the next quarter. Sam uses the term "buy" loosely since there is no plan for an exchange of cash. RAS will record the sales transaction by debiting Accounts Receivable and crediting Sales Revenue. When the alarm systems are bought back, RAS will debit Inventory and credit Accounts Receivable, which, of course, will have no impact on the income statement.

Lisa Barlow, the company's accountant, tells Sam that there is a problem with his plan. She explains that under International Financial Reporting Standards (IFRS), RAS has not earned revenue until inventory is delivered to customers. Sam quickly responds that he has everything under control. He explains to Lisa that the contractors have agreed to accept automatic shipments of the alarm systems and carry them in the company's inventory as of quarter-end. Sam says this is a "win-win" situation for everyone.

The plan did exactly what Sam hoped it would do. The company reported sales that consistently exceeded expectations. These inflated sales figures helped to boost the company's stock price to an all-time high. Sam considered himself a true winner. His compensation package included a lucrative stock bonus plan tied to the company's sales growth. As a result of the company's reported sales revenue, Sam received shares in the company that he was able to sell for thousands of dollars at the inflated stock price.

Requirements

1. Is there any evidence of unethical behaviour in this case? Explain your answer.
2. Other than Sam and the contractors, who could be harmed by Sam's plan?

Case 5. Mary Rel was hired as the new store manager for the Bargain Bin. The store used four cash registers, and 10 cashiers worked various shifts in the store. Store operations include the following procedures:

- At the start of each shift, a cashier counts the beginning cash balance in the drawer, which is supposed to be $550.
- At the end of each shift, the cashier then does the following:
  1. Counts the ending cash balance in the drawer and adds to it any amounts dropped in the safe.
  2. Completes the shift cash form that reconciles the cash received to the total register sales tape.
  3. Reports any difference between the cash on hand and the cash that should be on hand based on receipts.

As a manager, Mary was responsible for preparing the cash drawers for each shift. She decided to test the honesty of the cashiers so she added an additional $50 to the beginning balance of one cash drawer. Mary planned to look at the shift cash form to see whether the cashier reported the extra $50 that was part of the beginning balance or just reported the $550 expected balance, taking the $50 for personal use.

Mary also tested her assistant manager. She gave him the bank deposit bag containing $5,246.24, but included a deposit ticket that was exactly $100 less, listing $5,146.24 as the deposit amount. Mary wanted to see whether the assistant manager would report the extra $100 in the deposit bag.

Mary planned to never let her employees or even her assistant manager know that she had tested them; instead she would just say that she made a simple mistake in counting the cash if they questioned her.

Requirement

1. Should Mary distrust her employees? Is it ethical for a manager to test employees without their knowledge? Should Mary ever inform the employees that they had been tested? Was it unethical for Mary to test an assistant manager?

Case 6. Assume that you were recently hired as a staff accountant for Environmental Solutions, Inc. You report to Karen, the director of financial reporting, who in turn reports to the CFO. One of your first assignments is to prepare the adjusting entries for the end of the second quarter and to draft the income statement. Karen instructs you to let her know as soon as you have the estimated earnings for the quarter. She says she will need to review the adjusting entries and earnings calculation with the CFO.

After reviewing your work with the CFO, Karen tells you to change the entry that you recorded for depreciation expense on the company's fleet of trucks from $229,000 to $184,000. At first you thought that you must have made some mistake in calculating the amount of depreciation, so you re-check your calculations. Surprisingly, you come up with the same amount again. So tactfully you ask Karen for an explanation for the change. She tells you that depreciation is only an estimate and that the CFO will change his mind about estimates based on earnings.

Requirements

1. What is the effect of the change in the amount of the depreciation expense on the company's second-quarter earnings?
2. What is the ethical dilemma that you face?
3. What are the alternatives that you might consider, and what are the potential consequences of each alternative?
4. What are some of the common pitfalls used to rationalize unethical behaviour?

Case 7. Marvin Silverstein, a trusted employee of Progressive Supply Company, found himself in a difficult financial situation. His son's college tuition had to be paid in full by the end of the month. The family had experienced some unexpected expenses and the money was just not there to pay the tuition. Marvin knew his son could not register for classes until the tuition was paid, and classes filled quickly, so this could cause his son not to get the classes that he needed to graduate on time.

Marvin considered himself a "true company man" who never missed work and was always willing to work until the job was finished. Although he had been with the company for 10 years and was entitled to two weeks vacation per year, Marvin never found time to take vacation. Because of his loyalty to the company over the years, he knew that his boss would probably loan him the money that he needed for his son's tuition, but he just couldn't bring himself to ask his boss for a loan. As Marvin thought about the situation, he realized how simple it would be for him to "borrow" some money from the company to help him through these rough times and pay it back before anyone noticed.

Marvin was responsible for all of the bookkeeping functions, plus opening the mail, counting the cash in the registers at the end of the day, and making the daily bank deposit. With these combined duties, Marvin found it fairly simple to give himself a "loan." He removed $2,500 in cash from the cash register and replaced it with a $2,500 cheque from the incoming mail that day. The cheque was from a customer who was paying his or her account in full. Marvin made a journal entry crediting *Accounts Receivable* to clear the customer's account, but rather than debiting Cash, he debited Inventory. Marvin knew that inventory was not counted and reconciled until year-end. This would give Marvin plenty of time to get the "loan" repaid before anyone noticed.

Requirements

1. What are the ethical considerations in this case?

2. Discuss the primary internal control weakness in this case that could have contributed to Marvin's actions.

Case 8. You are the controller for CrystalClean Services, a company that provides janitorial services to large commercial customers. The company has been very successful during its first two years of operations, but to expand its customer base the company is in need of additional capital to be used for equipment purchases. The two brothers who started the business, Chuck and Josh Wisher, invested their life savings in the business, so they have contacted a local bank about securing a loan for $150,000.

The bank has asked for a set of financial statements, and Chuck, being the businessperson that he is, knows that the bank is going to be looking for a growth in earnings each year. Although the company's earnings have increased, Chuck would like the past year to look better than it does now.

Chuck stops by your office late in the afternoon on December 31 to find out when the financial statements will be ready. You explain that you still have to close out the end of the year, but should have them ready by the end of the week. Chuck tells you that he is aware of a major contract that Josh is working on that will be signed on January 2, and asks you to delay the closing process a couple of days so the new contract can be included in this year's operating results. You attempt to explain to Chuck that you cannot do that, but you can tell that he is not listening to you. Chuck interrupts by saying, "I don't know why you accountants get so worked up over a couple of days. Let me just say that *it would be in your best interest* to include this contract in the current year's operating results." Chuck left your office in a hurry and you heard him mutter under his breath as he turned the corner, "That accountant—who does he think he is trying to tell me how to run my business?"

Requirements

1. What are the accounting issues related to Chuck's request?

2. What is the ethical issue involved in this case?

3. What would be the appropriate course of action for you to take?

KNOW YOUR BUSINESS

FINANCIAL ANALYSIS

Purpose: To help familiarize you with the financial reporting of a real company to further your understanding of the chapter material you are learning.

The Bombardier Annual Report (2012) in MyAccountingLab contains much more information than what is reported in the financial statements and related notes. In this case, you will explore other information presented in the annual report to determine the responsibilities of both management and the independent auditors for the annual report content. In addition, you will investigate the respective roles of both management and the auditors in the company's internal control system.

Refer to the Bombardier Annual Report in MyAccountingLab. You will need to find and then read the following reports:

- Management's Responsibility for Financial Reporting
- Independent Auditors' Report to the Shareholders of Bombardier Inc.

Requirements

1. Who is responsible for the information in the consolidated financial statements and the annual report? How are these responsibilities fulfilled?

2. Who were the independent auditors? Under what standards did they conduct their audit? What was their opinion of the audited financial statements? Who do the auditors primarily interact with and report to?

3. Who is responsible for establishing and maintaining adequate internal control over financial reporting? Is the effectiveness of the internal controls ever reviewed? Do you think that internal control procedures are necessary? Why?

INDUSTRY ANALYSIS

Purpose: To help you understand and compare the performance of two companies in the same industry.

Find the Bombardier Annual Report located in MyAccountingLab and look for information regarding their internal control systems. Now access the 2012 annual report for The Boeing Company. To do this from the internet, go to their webpage for the Investor Relations at http://www.boeing.com/companyoffices/financial/quarterly.htm and, under annual reports, go to the 2012 Annual Report. You'll find a section (Item 9A) where they discuss the company's Controls and Procedures.

Requirement

1. Compare the two annual reports as they relate to their disclosure of internal control procedures and the system of internal control. (These are found on page 122 of the Bombardier report in the "Controls and Procedures" section, and on page 111 of The Boeing Company report under "Item 9A. Controls and Procedures.")

SMALL BUSINESS ANALYSIS

Purpose: To help you understand the importance of cash flows in the operation of a small business.

You're having a tough time figuring out why your actual cash is always coming up less than the amount that the general ledger says should be there. You would hate to think that any of your employees would be stealing from you, because they have all been with you since you opened the business five years ago. But maybe it's time to do a little investigative work. After all, cash is the lifeblood of the business, and if it's being misappropriated, you need to find out fast!

You start to think back over some of the observations you've made recently and some of the conversations you've overheard, and one startling conclusion is staring you in the face. Joe's been a good employee, but lately he's been bragging about his wild weekends and some of the gambling casinos he's been going to. Joe never used to be like that. You overheard one of his fellow employees ask him where he's getting all this money, and he said that his wife just got a really good raise at her job and they're celebrating. Then just last week, Joe drove to work in a new sports car and again you overheard him tell someone about the great deal his brother-in-law got for him on this car.

Joe is in charge of billing and collecting. Since your office is so small, you always felt like these two jobs could be done more efficiently by the same person. You also remember that Joe's uncle is one of your vendors and there was that situation last year where you discovered a double billing to his uncle's company. When you brought it to Joe's attention, he immediately admitted his error and took care of it.

Requirement

1. Respond to the following: You are wondering whether or not you should call Joe into your office and have a talk with him, or just observe a little bit more to see if you can discover any irregularities in Joe's area.

WRITTEN COMMUNICATION

You've been asked by your boss to write a brief description of what the control activities should be as part of the development of a strong internal control system in your office. You know that the office is small in terms of personnel, which does create some control problems. So your boss has also asked you to make some recommendations on ways to strengthen any weaknesses that you discover in the internal control system.

Self Check Answers
1. b 2. c 3. a 4. c 5. c 6. a 7. d 8. c 9. b 10. b

Appendix 4A

WHAT IS A PETTY CASH FUND?

A business may choose to keep a petty cash fund, which is a fund containing a small amount of cash used to pay for minor expenditures, such as the purchase of postage stamps or a shipment of a small package. Cash is easy to steal and the thief is often able to do so without leaving evidence. For this reason, petty cash funds need controls such as the following:

- Designate a custodian for the petty cash fund. This assigns responsibility for the fund.
- Establish the fund by keeping a specific, fixed amount of cash on hand so that any missing amount can be easily identified.
- Keep the fund in a safe, locked location and only allow the custodian to have access to the fund.
- Support all payments from the fund with a written record documenting the purpose and amount of the payment.

L.O. ⑨ (Appendix 4A) Account for the petty cash fund

Setting Up the Petty Cash Fund

Businesses establish a petty cash fund by writing a cheque for the designated amount, usually between $200 and $500, depending on the size and the needs of the business. They typically make the cheque payable to Petty Cash, cash the cheque, and place the money in the fund. Every business may have its own form for documenting petty cash payments, but the form is usually signed by the recipient of the petty cash and the custodian to verify the transaction. *The cash in the fund plus the total of the payment forms should always equal the fund balance at all times*.

Suppose that Inland Equipment established a petty cash fund of $200 on June 1. The journal entry to record the creation of the fund is as follows:

DATE	ACCOUNTS	POST REF.	DR.	CR.
Jun 1	Petty Cash		200	
	Cash			200
	Establish the petty cash fund.			

Assets = Liabilities + Shareholders' Equity
+200
−200 =

Now assume that on June 21 Suzanne Kimmel, the fund custodian, approved a cash payment from the petty cash fund to Jim Dirks to reimburse Jim for $25 of envelopes he purchased for the business. Suzanne prepared a record of the disbursement, much like the petty cash ticket in **Exhibit 4A-1**, and both she and Jim signed it. Suzanne kept the form in the fund as a replacement for the cash taken.

```
                    PETTY CASH TICKET
Date  Jun 21

Amount  $25

For  Envelopes

Debit  Office Supplies

Received by  Jim Dirks          Fund Custodian  SK
```

Exhibit 4A-1 ▲

Replenishing the Petty Cash Fund

Payments deplete the petty cash fund, so periodically it must be replenished. The custodian will pay expenses in cash and collect tickets and invoices. When the cash in the fund is about to end or at the end of the period, the custodian will ask for a cheque to replenish it. **Exhibit 4A-2** illustrates the process of paying the expenses by the custodian.

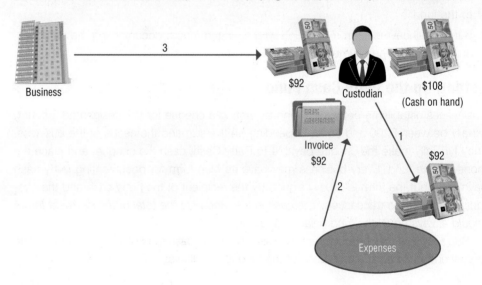

Exhibit 4A-2 ▲

The custodian will count the cash on hand and add up the total of the invoices, which should equal the original amount. If not, then the fund is either cash short or over, as will be explained below.

Let's assume that on July 31 the petty cash fund of Inland Equipment holds the following:

- $108 cash on hand
- $92 in petty cash tickets: office supplies, $53; delivery expense, $29; transportation expenses $10

Notice that when the $108 of cash on hand is added to the $92 of petty cash tickets, the total comes to $200, which is the original amount of the fund's balance.

To replenish the petty cash fund and make the cash on hand equal to $200 again, the company writes a cheque, payable to Petty Cash, for the $92 ($200 – $108) difference between the cash on hand and the fund balance. The fund custodian cashes this cheque and puts $92 back in the fund. Now the fund holds $200 cash as required.

Exhibit 4A-3 illustrates the required journal entry and how to check the replenished amount:

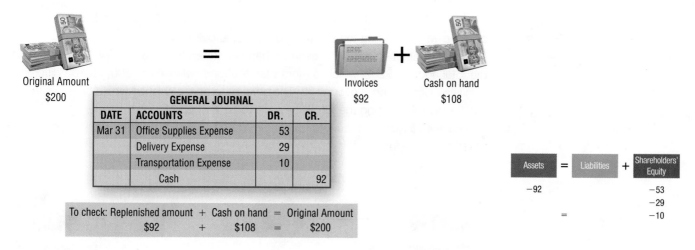

GENERAL JOURNAL			
DATE	ACCOUNTS	DR.	CR.
Mar 31	Office Supplies Expense	53	
	Delivery Expense	29	
	Transportation Expense	10	
	Cash		92

To check: Replenished amount + Cash on hand = Original Amount
$92 + $108 = $200

Assets	=	Liabilities	+	Shareholders' Equity
−92				−53
				−29
	=			−10

Exhibit 4A-3 ▲

Note that the cash paid to the custodian is always the difference between the original balance of the fund and the cash on hand at the time of the replenishment.

The accounts debited in the entry represent the expense accounts associated with what the petty cash funds were used to purchase. Notice that the journal entry included a credit to Cash, not Petty Cash. This is because the money to replenish the petty cash fund was taken from the Cash account. The Petty Cash account is only affected when

- the petty cash fund is established.
- the petty cash fund balance is increased or decreased.

Now let's assume that on July 31 the cash fund of Inland Equipment holds only $106 cash on hand while incurring the same expenses as above.

Notice that when the $106 cash on hand is added to the $92 of petty cash tickets, the total adds to $198, which is less than the fund balance of $200. The $2 difference signifies that $2 was misplaced from the fund. The amount to be replenished would be equal to $94 ($200 – $106), covering the shortage in cash and bringing the fund's balance to $200 again.

Exhibit 4A-4 illustrates how to determine the shortage in cash and the required journal entry to replenish the fund:

MEMORY TIPS

Replenished amount + Cash on hand = Petty cash original amount

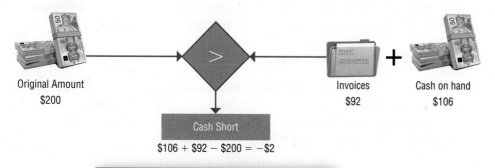

Original Amount
$200

Invoices
$92

Cash on hand
$106

Cash Short

$106 + $92 − $200 = −$2

GENERAL JOURNAL			
DATE	ACCOUNTS	DR.	CR.
Jul 31	Office Supplies Expense	53	
	Delivery Expense	29	
	Transportation Expense	10	
	Cash Short	2	
	Cash		94

To check: Replenished amount + Cash on hand = Original Amount
$94 + $106 = $200

Assets	=	Liabilities	+	Shareholders' Equity
−94				−53
				−29
				−10
	=			−2

Exhibit 4A-4 ▲

Now let's assume that on July 31 the cash fund of Inland Equipment holds $110 cash on hand while incurring the same expenses as above.

Notice that when the $110 cash on hand is added to the $92 of petty cash tickets, the total adds to $202, which is more than the fund balance of $200. The $2 difference signifies that the fund is over by $2. The amount to be replenished would be equal to $90 ($200 − $110), bringing the fund's balance to $200 again.

Exhibit 4A-5 illustrates how to determine the cash over and the required journal entry to replenish the fund.

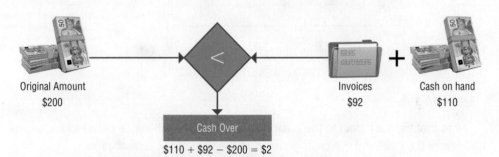

Original Amount
$200

Invoices
$92

Cash on hand
$110

Cash Over
$110 + $92 − $200 = $2

Assets	=	Liabilities	+	Shareholders' Equity
−90				−53
				−29
				−10
	=			+2

GENERAL JOURNAL			
DATE	ACCOUNTS	DR.	CR.
Jul 31	Office Supplies Expense	53	
	Delivery Expense	29	
	Transportation Expense	10	
	Cash Over		2
	Cash		90

To check: Replenished amount + Cash on hand = Original Amount
$90 + $110 = $200

Exhibit 4A-5 ▲

Note that some companies would use one account, Cash Over and Short, instead of having two separate accounts as illustrated above. In such a case, this account would be debited when cash is short and credited when cash is over. The balance of the account would show the net of the cash over and short.

Changing the Petty Cash Fund

Assume that Inland Equipment wants to increase the size of its fund from $200 to $300 on August 1. The business writes a $100 cheque payable to Petty Cash, and the custodian cashes it and places the money in the fund. In this case, the journal entry to record this $100 increase will look like the following:

Assets	=	Liabilities	+	Shareholders' Equity
+100				
−100	=			

DATE	ACCOUNTS	POST REF.	DR.	CR.
Aug 1	Petty Cash		100	
	Cash			100
	Increase petty cash fund balance.			

Petty Cash	
Bal.	200
Aug 1	100
New Bal.	300

ACCOUNTING PRACTICE

S4A-1. Petty cash transactions (*Learning Objective 9*) 5–10 min.

Record the following petty cash transactions of Handy Dan in the journal; explanations are not required.

Nov 1	Established a petty cash fund with a $100 balance.
30	The petty cash fund had $33 in cash and $67 in petty cash tickets that were issued to pay for postage. Replenished the fund with cash.

S4A-2. Petty cash transactions (*Learning Objective 9*) 5–10 min.

Record the following petty cash transactions of Xeno, Corp. in the journal; explanations are not required.

Jun 1	Established a petty cash fund with a $200 balance.
30	The petty cash fund had $22 in cash and $174 in petty cash tickets that were issued to pay for office supplies ($104) and entertainment expense ($70). Replenished the fund.
30	Increased the petty cash fund balance to $300.

E4A-1A. Petty cash transactions (*Learning Objective 9*) 10–15 min.

Jamie's Music School created a $200 petty cash fund on March 1. During the month, the fund custodian authorized and signed petty cash tickets as follows:

Petty Cash			
Ticket No.	Item	Account Debited	Amount
1	Delivery of programs to customers	Delivery Expense	$20
2	Mail package	Postage Expense	40
3	Newsletter	Supplies Expense	44
4	Key to closet	Miscellaneous Expense	16
5	Blank DVDs	Supplies Expense	30

Requirements

1. Record the journal entry to create the petty cash fund.
2. Assuming that the cash in the fund totals $45 on March 31, make the journal entry to replenish the petty cash fund.

E4A-2A. Petty cash transactions (*Learning Objective 9*) 10–15 min.

Hazelnut maintains a petty cash fund of $150. On November 30, the fund holds $7 cash, and petty cash tickets for office supplies, $90, and delivery expense, $50.

Requirements

1. Make the journal entry to replenish the petty cash fund.
2. Hazelnut decided to increase the petty cash fund by $100. Prepare the journal entry.

EXERCISES (GROUP B)

E4A-1B. Petty cash transactions (*Learning Objective 9*) 10–15 min.

Christine's Music School created a $220 petty cash fund on October 1. During the month, the fund custodian authorized and signed petty cash tickets as follows:

Petty Cash			
Ticket No.	Item	Account Debited	Amount
1	Delivery of programs to customers	Delivery Expense	$15
2	Mail package	Postage Expense	50
3	Newsletter	Supplies Expense	43
4	Key to closet	Miscellaneous Expense	19
5	Blank DVDs	Supplies Expense	10

Requirements

1. Record the journal entry to create the petty cash fund.

2. Assuming that the cash in the fund totals $55 on October 31, make the journal entry to replenish the petty cash fund.

E4A-2B. Petty cash transactions (*Learning Objective 9*) 10–15 min.

Maple maintains a petty cash fund of $250. On April 30, the fund holds $19 cash, petty cash tickets for office supplies, $185, and delivery expense, $40.

Requirements

1. Make the journal entry to replenish the petty cash fund.

2. Maple decided to increase the petty cash fund by $120. Prepare the journal entry.

EXERCISES (ALTERNATES 1, 2, AND 3)

These alternative exercise sets are available for your practice benefit on **MyAccountingLab**.

PROBLEMS (GROUP A)

P4A-1A. Petty cash transactions (*Learning Objective 9*) 10–15 min.

On July 1, Chi Kong creates a petty cash fund with a balance of $300. During July, Elise Sautter, the fund custodian, signs the following petty cash tickets:

Petty Cash Ticket Number	Item	Amount
101	Office supplies	$86
102	Cab fare for executive	25
103	Delivery of package across town	17
104	Dinner money for president and a potential customer	90

On July 31, prior to replenishment, the fund contains these tickets plus cash of $62. The accounts affected by petty cash payments are Office Supplies Expense, Travel Expense, Delivery Expense, and Entertainment Expense.

Requirements

1. Record the journal entry to create the petty cash fund.

2. Record the journal entry to replenish the petty cash fund on July 31. Do you have any concerns regarding the Over/Short account?

3. Make the August 1 entry to increase the fund balance to $350. Include an explanation, and briefly describe what the custodian does when the balance is increased.

PROBLEMS (GROUP B)

P4A-1B. Petty cash transactions (*Learning Objectives 9*) 10–15 min.

On March 1, Fab Kong creates a petty cash fund with a balance of $300. During March, Elise Sautter, the fund custodian, signs the following petty cash tickets:

Petty Cash Ticket Number	Item	Amount
101	Office supplies	$86
102	Cab fare for executive	27
103	Delivery of package across town	10
104	Dinner money for president and a potential customer	110

On March 31, prior to replenishment, the fund contains these tickets plus cash of $37. The accounts affected by petty cash payments are Office Supplies Expense, Travel Expense, Delivery Expense, and Entertainment Expense.

Requirements

1. Record the journal entry to create the petty cash fund.

2. Record the journal entry to replenish the petty cash fund on March 31. Do you have any concerns over the Over/Short account?

3. Make the entry on April 1 to increase the fund balance to $375. Include an explanation, and briefly describe what the custodian does when the balance is increased.

PROBLEMS (ALTERNATES 1, 2, AND 3)

These alternative problem sets are available for your practice benefit on **MyAccountingLab**.

LEARNING OBJECTIVES

1. Describe the relationship among wholesalers, retailers, and customers

2. Define periodic and perpetual inventory systems

3. Journalize transactions for the purchase of inventory and related purchasing costs using a perpetual inventory system

4. Journalize transactions for the sale of inventory and related selling costs using a perpetual inventory system

5. Prepare a multi-step income statement and a classified statement of financial position

6. Compute the gross profit percentage and the current ratio

7. (Appendix 5A) Explain how a business accounts for transactions using the periodic inventory system

CHAPTER OUTLINE

WHAT Is the Relationship among Wholesalers, Retailers, and Customers? p. 276

HOW Do Periodic and Perpetual Inventory Systems Differ? p. 276

HOW Do You Account for the Purchase of Inventory and the Related Purchasing Costs Using a Perpetual Inventory System? p. 278

HOW Do You Account for the Sale of Inventory and the Related Selling Expenses Using a Perpetual Inventory System? p. 285

HOW Do You Prepare a Merchandiser's Financial Statements? p. 292

FOCUS On Decision Making: Ratios p. 296

HOW Do You Account for Merchandising Transactions Using a Periodic Inventory System? p. 326

274

CHAPTER 5

Accounting for a Merchandising Business

BUSINESS, ACCOUNTING, AND YOU

What do you see when you walk into your local Best Buy and look around? You see employees, products, and customers. You might see employees unloading products, called inventory, from trucks of suppliers, or placing the products on display shelves, or demonstrating products and helping customers make informed decisions. You see customers taking products from the shelves, going to checkout stations, and purchasing products. In other words, you see thousands of business transactions.

So how does a business like Best Buy account for the operations of its business? How does Best Buy recognize, measure, record, and report the purchase and sale of inventory? How does Best Buy account for employee wages, advertising, and other operating expenses such as utilities? How does Best Buy account for customers buying inventory and giving Best Buy, in exchange, cash or promises to pay cash? How does Best Buy account for the merchandising of products? Business is about operating and earning net income, which starts with buying and selling products. As an accountant or manager, you need to understand how products flow from suppliers to customers. You need to understand how accountants keep score and determine whether the sale of a product results in net income or net loss.

WHAT IS THE RELATIONSHIP AMONG WHOLESALERS, RETAILERS, AND CUSTOMERS?

L.O. ❶ Describe the relationship among wholesalers, retailers, and customers

Throughout the previous chapters you have learned how to account for a service business. In this chapter, you will learn about the special accounting methods for a merchandising business. A merchandising business buys and sells products, called **merchandise inventory**, instead of services. Inventory is a very important asset to a merchandising business because it reflects the value and amount of goods the business has available to sell to its customers. Throughout the remainder of the book, we will refer to merchandise inventory simply as **inventory**.

A merchandising business can be either a **wholesaler** or a **retailer**. Wholesalers generally purchase large lots of products from manufacturers and resell them to retailers. Retailers buy goods from wholesalers and resell them to the final consumers, the general public. It is also possible for a retailer to purchase products directly from a manufacturer.

Exhibit 5-1 shows the relationship among manufacturers, wholesalers, retailers, and customers.

Exhibit 5-1 ▲

The discount chain Giant Tiger and the internet merchandiser Amazon.ca are familiar examples of retailers. In this chapter, a fictitious merchandiser named Cosmic Cellular, Inc. is used to illustrate merchandising operations. Cosmic Cellular is a mall retailer that sells cell phones and accessories. We will learn how Cosmic Cellular records entries related to purchases from its suppliers. In addition, we will learn the entries Cosmic uses to record sales of merchandise to its customers. We will also learn how the type of inventory tracking system chosen by Cosmic will impact the journal entries that it must make.

HOW DO PERIODIC AND PERPETUAL INVENTORY SYSTEMS DIFFER?

L.O. ❷ Define periodic and perpetual inventory systems

Merchandisers use one of two inventory tracking systems:

- The **periodic inventory system** is a system of accounting for inventory that does *not* keep a continuous, running record of inventory as it is bought and sold. Instead, the business physically counts the goods in inventory at the end of the accounting period. It then multiplies the quantity of each item by its cost to get the total value of the ending inventory. Once the ending inventory has been determined, a business will calculate the cost of the inventory it has sold during the period.

Exhibit 5-2 shows the components of inventory activities and the calculation of cost of goods sold using these components.

Historically, businesses that sold large quantities of relatively inexpensive goods used the periodic inventory system because it was too costly and time consuming to track the inventory items that were sold. Currently, thanks to innovations in inventory tracking technology, most businesses utilize a perpetual inventory system.

■ The **perpetual inventory system** is a system of accounting for inventory that keeps a running record of inventory as it is bought and sold. Every time the business engages in a transaction involving inventory, the balance in the inventory account is immediately updated. By doing this, the inventory balance is *perpetually* up-to-date. However, the business must still physically count inventory at least once a year to see whether any goods have been lost, improperly recorded, damaged, or stolen. Just because the accounting records indicate that a certain amount of inventory exists, it doesn't mean that this amount is actually on hand. If the actual inventory count is different than the perpetual records indicate, the perpetual records are adjusted to reflect the physical count. The general ledger is also updated by debiting or crediting the inventory account as needed. The offsetting debit or credit is to the Cost of Goods Sold account. Technology makes it easier for almost any business to use the perpetual system. Usually, a cash register used in a perpetual system is connected to a barcode scanner. When an inventory item is scanned, not only is the sale recorded, but the inventory records are simultaneously updated.

In the next sections, the perpetual inventory system will be presented in detail as it is the mostly widely used system, while the periodic inventory system will be presented in this chapter's appendix.

Beginning Inventory
+ Purchases
―――――――――――――
= Cost of Goods Available for Sale
― Ending Inventory
―――――――――――――
= Cost of Goods Sold

Exhibit 5-2 ▲

 DECISION GUIDELINES

DECISION	**GUIDELINE**	**ANALYZE**
Which inventory system should my business use?	This decision depends on whether or not you plan on utilizing a computer system to help with inventory management. It also depends on the variety and number of goods your business sells.	The *perpetual system* shows the current, correct amounts of inventory on hand and the cost of goods sold at all times.
		The *periodic system* requires that a physical count of the inventory be taken to know the correct balances of inventory and cost of goods sold.
		Before computers, only businesses that sold smaller quantities of higher cost items, like a car dealership, could use the perpetual method. Today, thanks to computers and other technology, most companies utilize the perpetual method even if they sell a high quantity of low cost items.

HOW DO YOU ACCOUNT FOR THE PURCHASE OF INVENTORY AND THE RELATED PURCHASING COSTS USING A PERPETUAL INVENTORY SYSTEM?

L.O. ③ Journalize transactions for the purchase of inventory and related purchasing costs using a perpetual inventory system

Throughout the year, merchandisers engage in a number of inventory transactions with suppliers including cash purchases, credit purchases, **purchase returns and allowances**, and **purchase discounts**. Depending on the inventory system the merchandiser uses, the recording of the purchase of inventory and the sale of inventory are accounted for differently. The perpetual inventory system requires updating the inventory account balance, so when inventory is purchased, we need to increase inventory, and when inventory is sold, we also need to decrease inventory. Let's examine how Cosmic Cellular accounts for these types of transactions.

CASH AND CREDIT PURCHASES

Cosmic Cellular purchases 300 cell phone cases (model XZ413) from Accessories Unlimited on account at a cost of $25 each. Therefore, the total value of Cosmic's purchase is $7,500 (300 cases × $25). Cosmic Cellular receives the goods on February 1 and records this purchase as follows:

+7,500 = +7,500

DATE	ACCOUNTS	DR.	CR.
Feb 1	Inventory—XZ413	7,500	
	Accounts Payable—Accessories Unlimited		7,500
	Record purchase of inventory on account.		

Using the perpetual inventory system, purchase of inventory on account increases both Cosmic Cellular's assets and liabilities. The Inventory account reflects the cost of goods purchased for resale; the balance increases every time inventory is purchased. Inventory is an asset until it is sold because, as discussed in Chapter 1, assets represent things of value that the business owns.

Notice that besides Inventory in the previous entry, the specific inventory item is mentioned. This is simply because the perpetual system needs to track changes for each single inventory item, so it uses a **subsidiary ledger**. To be more specific, it uses an **inventory subsidiary ledger** for each item. An inventory subsidiary ledger maintains a separate account for each inventory item, where changes in the balance of that item are recorded in both quantity and value. Any change in the balance of any item is recorded in the respective inventory subsidiary ledger in addition to the inventory controlling account or general ledger account. If entries are correctly recorded in the subsidiary ledger, the total cost of the inventory in the subsidiary ledger should be equal to the total cost appearing in the inventory controlling account. This way, a merchandiser can keep track of the balance of each single inventory item. A detailed illustration of how to use inventory subsidiary ledgers is presented in Chapter 6. The same thing applies for the suppliers. The supplier's name is used because the amount owed to each individual supplier will be posted to a subsidiary ledger in addition to the Accounts Payable account in the general ledger. This way, a merchandiser can keep track of the amount of accounts payable owed to each individual supplier.

Some suppliers may require cash to be paid at the time of shipment. If Accessories Unlimited required cash payment for the 300 cell phone cases at the time of sale, Cosmic Cellular would record the cash purchase as follows:

DATE	ACCOUNTS	DR.	CR.
Feb 1	Inventory—XZ413	7,500	
	Cash		7,500
	Record purchase of inventory for cash.		

Assets = Liabilities + Shareholders' Equity

+7,500 =
−7,500

PURCHASE RETURNS AND ALLOWANCES

Occasionally, merchandisers buy goods that are not satisfactory. In these cases, most suppliers allow the goods to be returned. Or, they may allow the merchandiser to keep the unsuitable goods and receive a deduction, or allowance, from the amount they owe for the merchandise. Both purchase returns and allowances decrease the merchandiser's cost of the inventory.

Suppose Cosmic Cellular buys 20 hands-free headsets for $20 each from Mega Mobile, and these headsets become damaged in shipment. If Cosmic returns the merchandise to Mega Mobile, it will issue a **debit memorandum**. A debit memorandum is a document that supports the return of goods to the supplier, as illustrated in **Exhibit 5-3**.

COSMIC CELLULAR

1471 Front St.
Toronto, Ontario

DEBIT MEMORANDUM #47

To: Mega Mobile   Date: April 5, 2015
    21 Dundas Street
    Hamilton, Ontario

We debit your account balance for the following:

20 T180 Headsets @ $20 each   **$400**

Exhibit 5-3 ▲

A debit memorandum gets its name from the fact that the issuer's Accounts Payable account will be debited as a result of the return of the goods. Upon issuing the debit memorandum, Cosmic will *debit*, or reduce, its Accounts Payable balance for the value of the merchandise returned. Cosmic will also reduce the Inventory account by the amount of the return because it no longer has this inventory. Cosmic records the purchase return as follows:

DATE	ACCOUNTS	DR.	CR.
Apr 5	Accounts Payable—Mega Mobile	400	
	Inventory—T180		400
	Record inventory returned to manufacturer.		

Assets = Liabilities + Shareholders' Equity

−400 = −400

PURCHASE DISCOUNTS

Exhibit 5-4 illustrates Accessories Unlimited's invoice for Cosmic's $7,500 purchase of inventory. A **sales invoice** is a bill that documents the sale of goods to a business customer. The invoice includes **credit terms**, or the payment terms, for customers who buy on account. A customer may pay cash when it receives the goods or it may pay within a period of time following the receipt of those goods. Merchandisers use credit terms on sales to communicate to the customer when payment is due. Often, merchandisers will use the term **n/30**, which means that the sales price for the goods must be paid within 30 days after the date of the invoice. If the amount is due at the end of the month, the invoice will include the phrase **n/eom** or just **eom**.

All businesses want to have enough cash to pay their bills on time. Therefore, suppliers often offer merchandisers purchase discounts for early payment to improve their cash inflow.

Accessories UNLIMITED

Accessories Unlimited
P.O. Box 873
Windsor, Ont.

	Invoice	
	Date	Number
	2/1/15	644

Shipped to: Cosmic Cellular
1471 Front St.
Toronto, Ontario

Terms: 3/15, n/30

Quantity	Item	Unit Price	Total
300 each	Cell phone cases	$ 25	$ 7,500

	Subtotal	$ 7,500
	Shipping Charge	–
	Tax	–
	Total	$ 7,500

Exhibit 5-4 ▲

By rewarding the merchandiser for paying amounts before the due date, these companies get cash sooner. The time period in which the merchandiser may pay and receive the discount is called the **discount period**. If the merchandiser takes advantage of this offer and pays early, then these discounts represent a reduction in the cost of the merchandise purchased.

Review Accessories Unlimited's invoice in Exhibit 5-4. Accessories Unlimited's credit terms of "3/15, n/30" mean that Cosmic Cellular may deduct 3% of the total amount due to Accessories Unlimited if it pays within 15 days of the invoice date. Otherwise, the full amount is due in 30 days. In this case, the discount period covers 15 days. However, if Accessories Unlimited listed terms of "n/30" instead of "3/15, n/30," it would mean that it was not offering a discount at all, and payment is due 30 days after the invoice date.

MEMORY**TIPS**

Terms of Payment

3/15, n/30

Amount
of Discount
(in percent)

Discount
Period
(usually in days)

Credit Limit
Period
(full amount should
be paid)

If Cosmic Cellular pays within the discount period, it will pay $7,275, or 97% of the purchase invoice amount of $7,500:

Invoice Total	$7,500 (100% of invoice amount)
− Purchase Discount	(225) (3% of invoice amount, or .03 × $7,500)
= Cash Paid	$7,275 (97% of invoice amount, or .97 × $7,500)

Cosmic records its payment on February 13, which is within the discount period, as shown:

DATE	ACCOUNTS	DR.	CR.
Feb 13	Accounts Payable—Accessories Unlimited	7,500	
	Cash		7,275
	Inventory—XZ413		225
	Record payment of inventory purchases within the discount period.		

In the perpetual inventory system, the discount is credited to the Inventory account. This is because the discount decreases the cost of the cell phone cases that Cosmic Cellular bought from Accessories Unlimited. Note that the full invoice amount of the payable, $7,500, should be debited, rather than the net amount of $7,275; otherwise, the Accounts Payable—Accessories Unlimited account will show an outstanding amount of $225.

If Cosmic Cellular pays this invoice after the discount period, it pays the full amount of $7,500. In this case, it records the payment as follows:

DATE	ACCOUNTS	DR.	CR.
Feb 13	Accounts Payable—Accessories Unlimited	7,500	
	Cash		7500
	Record payment of inventory purchases after the discount period.		

It is important to note that discounts are not granted on any portion of a purchase that is returned to the supplier. For example, if Cosmic Cellular returned four damaged cell phone cases at $25 each to Accessories Unlimited on February 3, the balance owed to Accessories Unlimited on February 13 before the payment was made would be $7,400. Cosmic records the purchase returns on February 3 and payment on February 13, which is within the discount period, as shown:

DATE	ACCOUNTS	DR.	CR.
Feb 3	Accounts Payable—Accessories Unlimited	100	
	Inventory		100
	Record inventory returned to manufacturer.		
Feb 13	Accounts Payable—Accessories Unlimited	7,400	
	Cash		7,178
	Inventory		222*
	Record payment of inventory purchases within the discount period.		

*7,400 × .03 = 222

Many companies take advantage of this discount, if they have cash or have access to cash to pay the invoice within 15 days.

COSTS RELATED TO THE RECEIPT OF GOODS FROM SUPPLIERS

In addition to purchases transactions, a merchandiser also accounts for shipping costs. Merchandisers often pay costs related to receiving goods from suppliers.

When merchandisers order items, they often pay the cost of shipping the items to their place of business. These shipping costs are referred to as **freight charges**. Buyers and sellers specify who pays shipping costs by agreeing to shipping terms. In addition to dictating who is responsible for paying shipping costs, shipping terms also specify the point at which ownership of the goods, or **title**, transfers from seller to buyer. Shipping terms may be **free on board (FOB) shipping point** or **free on board (FOB) destination**.

- Under free on board (FOB) shipping point, ownership transfers from the seller to the buyer at the point where the goods are shipped. Also, this term means that the buyer pays the shipping charges to have the merchandise delivered to their place of business. The buyer adds the shipping costs to inventory by debiting Inventory because these amounts increase the cost of the goods purchased.

- Free on board (FOB) destination denotes the opposite arrangement. Ownership transfers from the seller to the buyer when the goods reach their destination. This term means that the seller must pay to ship goods to that point. The seller records the shipping costs with a debit to Delivery Expense.

MEMORY TIPS

Ownership transfers at the point listed after FOB.

Exhibit 5-5 summarizes FOB terms.

Exhibit 5-5 ▲

 ACCOUNTING IN YOUR WORLD

Dmitrimaruta/Fotolia

Have you ever purchased something online or from a catalogue and thought you received a really great deal until you received the bill and realized that the company charged you a significant amount for "shipping and handling"? The reason that you were required to pay these shipping charges is because the merchandise was sold with shipping terms of "FOB shipping point." Next time, you should purchase items from a company that offers "FOB destination" shipping terms.

Now let's see how Cosmic Cellular records shipping costs when it purchases goods. When it buys products under FOB shipping point, Cosmic either pays the shipping company directly or reimburses the seller for the freight charges if they have been prepaid by the seller. When Cosmic buys products under FOB destination, the supplier pays the freight charges.

FOB Shipping Point: Pay the Shipping Company

Suppose Cosmic Cellular incurs shipping costs related to the purchase of merchandise (FOB shipping point) from Accessories Unlimited. Cosmic pays $60 to the carrier for the February 1 shipment. Cosmic Cellular's entry to record payment of the shipping charge is as follows:

DATE	ACCOUNTS	DR.	CR.
Feb 1	Inventory—AV707	60	
	Cash		60
	Record payment of shipping bill for the February 1 purchase.		

Note that the shipping cost is debited to the Inventory account, as the cost of the inventory is increased.

FOB Shipping Point: Repay the Seller for Prepaid Shipping Costs

Under FOB shipping point, the seller sometimes prepays the shipping costs as a convenience to the buyer. These costs are added to the invoice for the merchandise.

Let's see how Cosmic records the following purchase transactions. On July 15, Cosmic buys $1,000 of goods on account from CellTel, Inc. The terms of the purchase are 2/10, n/30, FOB shipping point. CellTel prepaid $80 of shipping costs and added the charges to the invoice for an invoice total of $1,080. Cosmic then returns $100 of these goods for credit on July 20. On July 25, Cosmic makes payment in full for the purchase. First, Cosmic records the purchase of goods:

DATE	ACCOUNTS	DR.	CR.
Jul 15	Inventory—AV707	1,080	
	Accounts Payable—CellTel, Inc.		1,080
	Record purchase of inventory on account.		

Next, Cosmic records the return of inventory, as follows:

DATE	ACCOUNTS	DR.	CR.
Jul 20	Accounts Payable—CellTel, Inc.	100	
	Inventory—AV707		100
	Record inventory returned to the manufacturer.		

Finally, Cosmic records the payment for the purchase by calculating the purchase discount and the balance due. Cosmic pays on July 25, which is within the 10-day discount period, so it receives a discount of $18: 2% of the $1,000 original cost of the goods minus $100 of returned goods, or 0.02 × $900. Although shipping costs increase the invoice amount of the merchandise purchased, they are not included in the calculation of any purchase discount. The purchase discount is computed only on the amount due to the supplier for the goods purchased. The calculation of the payment amount is as follows:

Purchase Amount:	$1,000	
− Purchase Return	(100)	
Amount of Purchase	900	→ Discount is applied on this amount
− Purchase Discount	(18)	→ 900 × 2%
Net Amount of Purchase	882	
+ Shipping	80	→ Note that discount does not apply on shipping
Cash Paid	962	

The journal entry to record the cash payment is as follows:

Assets = Liabilities + Shareholders' Equity

−18 = −980
−962

DATE	ACCOUNTS	DR.	CR.
Jul 25	Accounts Payable—CellTel, Inc.	980	
	($1,000 + $80 − $100)		
	Inventory—AV707 [($1,000 − $100) × 0.02]		18
	Cash ($1,000 + $80 − $100 − $18)		962
	Record payment of inventory purchases within the discount period.		

FOB Destination

Under FOB destination, the seller pays to ship the goods to the destination requested by the customer. If Cosmic Cellular purchased goods under these terms, it has no shipping costs to record because the supplier pays the freight. **Exhibit 5-6** summarizes the purchases-related journal entries using the perpetual inventory system.

ACCOUNTS	DR.	CR.
Inventory—XYZ	xx	
Accounts Payable		xx
Record purchase of inventory on account.		
Accounts Payable	xx	
Inventory—XYZ		xx
Record inventory returned to manufacturer.		
Inventory—XYZ	xx	
Cash		xx
Record payment for transportation.		
Accounts Payable	xx	
Inventory—XYZ		xx
Cash		xx
Record payment of inventory purchases within the discount period.		

Exhibit 5-6 ▲

Note that in a perpetual inventory system, the Inventory account is used to record purchases, purchase returns and allowances, purchase discounts, and transportation-in because each single inventory item is tracked.

PERIOD-END COST OF GOODS SOLD AND INVENTORY ADJUSTMENTS

The Cost of Goods Sold and Inventory accounts are used to account for all the purchases, purchase returns, sales, and sales returns; therefore, the Cost of Goods Sold and Inventory should be up to date, and there should be no need for period-end adjustments. Calculation of Cost of Goods Sold would be required when a periodic inventory system is used.

HOW DO YOU ACCOUNT FOR THE SALE OF INVENTORY AND THE RELATED SELLING EXPENSES USING A PERPETUAL INVENTORY SYSTEM?

Merchandisers engage in several different types of business transactions with customers:

- Cash sales: Goods are sold for cash.
- Credit sales: Goods are sold on account.
- Sales returns and allowances: Damaged goods are returned by a customer for a refund. However, sometimes the customer keeps the damaged goods and accepts an allowance (price reduction) on the goods.
- Sales discounts: Suppliers grant customers a reduction in the amount owed as an incentive for paying within a discount period.

Let's examine how Cosmic Cellular accounts for these types of transactions.

L.O. 4 Journalize transactions for the sale of inventory and related selling costs using a perpetual inventory system

CASH SALES

Merchandisers, such as Cosmic Cellular, often receive cash at the time they sell merchandise. The journal entry to record a cash sale increases the asset Cash and increases the revenue account, **Sales Revenue**. Sales Revenue is the account used by merchandisers to track the value of merchandise sold to customers at the price that the merchandiser charges those customers.

Using the perpetual inventory system, Cosmic Cellular not only needs to account for the sales, but also to reduce the Inventory balance for the value of the merchandise sold. By doing this, the Inventory account is updated so that it always, or perpetually, reflects the current balance. The value of the merchandise sold is accounted for in the **Cost of Goods Sold (COGS)** account. This income statement account reflects the cost of merchandise sold during the period. The Cost of Goods Sold is deducted from Sales Revenue as a step in determining the amount of net income or loss for the period. So when merchandise is sold, two successive entries are required: one to recognize revenue and the other to reflect the decrease in inventory and increase in COGS.

Assume that on June 9, Cosmic Cellular sells $3,000 of merchandise to customers for cash. The goods that Cosmic sold its customers cost Cosmic $1,900. The journal entry to record the sale is as follows:

MEMORY **TIPS**

Remember that in a *perpetual* system any selling transaction requires two sets of entries: one to record the sale using the *selling price*, and the other to record the COGS and the reduction of inventory at *cost*.

DATE	ACCOUNTS	DR.	CR.
Jun 9	Cash	3,000	
	Sales Revenue		3,000
	Cost of Goods Sold	1,900	
	Inventory—XZ413		1,900
	Record sale of inventory for cash.		

Some merchandisers allow customers to use credit cards and debit cards rather than currency. These transactions are treated as cash sales because the merchandiser receives cash from the credit/debit card company within a short period of time. The credit/debit card company then collects the amount due from the customer. The merchandiser, however, usually must pay a service charge to the credit/debit card company in exchange for its processing of the transactions. Accounting for debit and credit card sales is discussed in Chapter 7 in more detail.

CREDIT SALES

Many merchandisers establish charge accounts for their customers. Assume that Cosmic Cellular sold on account a cell phone and accessories to Jim Kahl on June 11 for $500. The goods cost Cosmic $290. The entry to record this transaction is similar to accounting for a cash sale except Accounts Receivable is debited instead of Cash. Cosmic records this sale on account as follows:

DATE	ACCOUNTS	DR.	CR.
Jun 11	Accounts Receivable—Jim Kahl	500	
	Sales Revenue		500
	Cost of Goods Sold	290	
	Inventory—XZ413		290
	Record sale of inventory on account, invoice no. 322.		

When Jim sends Cosmic his payment for this merchandise, Cosmic records the cash receipt on account as follows:

DATE	ACCOUNTS	DR.	CR.
Jun 19	Cash	500	
	Accounts Receivable—Jim Kahl		500
	Record payment received on invoice no. 322.		

Notice that the name of the customer is listed in the journal entry following Accounts Receivable. This is similar to what is done for Accounts Payable. A separate account is kept in an accounts receivable subsidiary ledger for each charge customer. Each entry affecting accounts receivable is posted to the customer's account in the subsidiary ledger as well as to the Accounts Receivable account in the general ledger. After all entries are posted, the total of the account balances in the accounts receivable subsidiary ledger will equal the Accounts Receivable account balance in the general ledger. This way, the merchandiser can keep track of the amount of accounts receivable owed by each individual customer.

SALES RETURNS AND ALLOWANCES

Merchandisers may allow customers to return unwanted merchandise or they may let customers keep the goods and request an allowance. A business tracks these returns so that it can analyze and manage the causes behind the returns and measure the related costs to the business. To track returns accurately, the amount of returns is recorded in a contra-account called **Sales Returns and Allowances**. Remember from Chapter 3 that a contra-account is an account with a balance opposite of the account to which it is linked. Sales Returns and Allowances is linked to Sales Revenue, which has a credit balance. Therefore, Sales Returns and Allowances will have a debit balance. As we will see later, Sales Returns and Allowances appears on the income statement and is deducted from Sales Revenue to arrive at Net Sales.

Exhibit 5-7 illustrates a **credit memorandum**, a document that acknowledges the return of goods from a customer. The credit memo gets its name from the effect that it has on the balance of the customer's account. Because the credit memo decreases the amount due from the customer, the merchandiser *credits* the accounts receivable balance for that customer. The merchandiser sends a credit memorandum to the customer as notification that an adjustment has been made to the amount the customer owes the merchandiser.

COSMIC CELLULAR

1471 Front St.
Toronto, Ontario

CREDIT MEMORANDUM #14

To: Jill Harris
28 St. George St.
Calgary, Alberta

Date: August 15, 2015

We credit your account balance for the following:

3 car chargers @ $25 each	**$75**

Exhibit 5-7 ▲

Sales Returns

When a customer returns goods, the merchandiser will

- decrease net sales revenue by increasing Sales Returns and Allowances, and decrease the customer's Accounts Receivable account balance for the sales price of those goods.
- decrease Cost of Goods Sold and increase Inventory for the cost of the returned goods to update its level.

Let's see how Cosmic records the return illustrated in the credit memo in Exhibit 5-7. The credit memo reflects the return of three car chargers, originally purchased for $75, by Jill Harris, a customer. The returned car chargers cost Cosmic $30. Cosmic Cellular records the sales return as follows:

DATE	ACCOUNTS	DR.	CR.
Aug 15	Sales Returns and Allowances	75	
	Accounts Receivable—Jill Harris		75
	Inventory	30	
	Costs of Goods Sold		30
	Record receipt of returned goods, credit memo no. 14.		

Notice that Accounts Receivable decreases because the customer no longer owes Cosmic for the returned goods. Cosmic also updates its inventory because its perpetual inventory system needs to reflect the increase to Inventory because of the return of the goods. Cosmic also decreases the Cost of Goods Sold because the goods are no longer sold.

Sales Allowances

Rather than return goods to the merchandiser, some customers may be willing to keep unwanted goods and accept an allowance. Assume Cosmic Cellular grants credit customer Bill Logan a $100 sales allowance for damaged goods. Cosmic records the sales allowance as follows:

−100 = −100

DATE	ACCOUNTS	DR.	CR.
Aug 15	Sales Returns and Allowances	100	
	Accounts Receivable—Bill Logan		100
	Record sales allowance for damaged goods, credit memo no. 15.		

Notice that the journal entry for a sales allowance does not affect Inventory or Cost of Goods Sold because the customer did not return any goods to the merchandiser.

SALES DISCOUNTS

Do you recall the discount that Cosmic Cellular received from Accessories Unlimited for early payment? It is possible for Cosmic to offer discounts to its credit customers for early payment. Let's assume that Cosmic sells merchandise to Kelly Harding for $450. The sale is made on account with credit terms of 2/15, n/30. If Kelly chooses to pay the invoice within the 15-day discount period, she will get a 2%, or $9, discount on her $450 purchase ($450 × 0.02). Kelly will pay $441, or 98% of the invoice amount of $450. This discount represents a reduction in the value of sales to Cosmic.

Businesses track the amount of these sales discounts so they can measure the impact on their sales revenue. To do so, businesses record these discounts in a contra-account called **Sales Discounts**. Because Sales Discounts is linked to Sales Revenue, it will normally have a debit balance. The Sales Discounts account tracks decreases in sales revenue that result from a discount to customers. Similar to the treatment of Sales Returns and Allowances, Sales Discounts appears on the income statement and is deducted from Sales Revenue to arrive at net sales. Because the Sales Returns and Allowances and the Sales Discount accounts have debit balances, they will be closed along with the expense accounts at the end of the period.

 CONCEPT CHECK...

If a customer returned $2,500 of merchandise and the transaction was recorded by debiting Sales and crediting Accounts Receivable, instead of debiting Sales Returns and Allowances and crediting Accounts Receivable, would the net income on the income statement be incorrect?

Answer: No. Let's assume that the company has $20,000 of total sales at the time the return is made and that this is the first time merchandise is returned during the period. If the transaction is recorded by debiting Sales, the Sales balance will be reduced to $17,500. Because there have been no other sales returns, the balance in the Sales Returns and Allowances will be zero. Therefore, the amount of net sales will be $17,500. If, instead of debiting Sales, the Sales Returns and Allowances account is debited, the Sales account will have a balance of $20,000 and the Sales Returns and Allowances account will have a balance of $2,500. Therefore, the amount of net sales will still be $17,500 ($20,000 − $2,500). If the amount of net sales is $17,500 regardless of which way the transaction is recorded, the net income will be the same. The reason for using the Sales Returns and Allowances account is simply to keep track of the amount of merchandise returned during the period. Managers often use this information to determine if there are quality issues with their products.

Assume that Cosmic receives payment of $441 from Kelly on February 13 within the discount period. The journal entry to record the receipt of cash and the sales discount is as follows:

DATE	ACCOUNTS	DR.	CR.
Feb 13	Cash	441	
	Sales Discounts	9	
	Accounts Receivable—Kelly Harding		450

Assets = Liabilities + Shareholders' Equity

+441 = −9
−450

If Kelly fails to pay within the 15-day discount period, she will have to pay the full invoice price of $450. If Cosmic receives payment from Kelly on February 24, it records the payment as follows:

DATE	ACCOUNTS	DR.	CR.
Feb 24	Cash	450	
	Accounts Receivable—Kelly Harding		450

Assets = Liabilities + Shareholders' Equity

+450 =
−450

Notice that there is no entry for inventory because this is a receipt of payment from the customer.

COSTS RELATED TO DELIVERING GOODS TO CUSTOMERS

In addition to selling activities, a merchandiser sometimes also has to account for shipping costs and other selling expenses. Merchandisers often pay costs related to

- shipping goods to customers
- advertising and other selling costs

The cost of shipping goods to customers is recorded in an expense account titled Delivery Expense. This cost occurs when the seller agrees to shipping terms of FOB destination. Delivery Expense is an expense on the income statement and, as an expense account, normally has a debit balance.

Let's see how the sale of goods and payment of shipping costs affect Cosmic Cellular in different situations. Rob Macklin, a frequent customer at Cosmic Cellular, has an account with the store. Rob buys a Bluetooth headset as a Christmas gift for his sister who lives in Vancouver. Cosmic purchases the headset for $45 and sells it to Rob for $100. Shipping costs to Vancouver total $15.

FOB Destination

Let's assume that Cosmic advertises that shipping costs are free with any purchase of $100 or more. Assume Rob buys the headset on November 30 and charges it to his account. He asks Cosmic to ship it to Vancouver. Cosmic records the sale and payment of shipping costs as follows:

DATE	ACCOUNTS	DR.	CR.
Nov 30	Accounts Receivable—Rob Macklin	100	
	Sales Revenue		100
	Cost of Goods Sold	45	
	Inventory—BTHS-414		45
	Record sale of inventory on account.		

DATE	ACCOUNTS	DR.	CR.
Nov 30	Delivery Expense	15	
	Cash		15
	Record shipping on sale.		

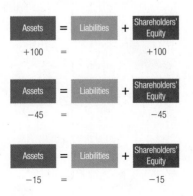

Assets = Liabilities + Shareholders' Equity

+100 = +100

Assets = Liabilities + Shareholders' Equity

−45 = −45

Assets = Liabilities + Shareholders' Equity

−15 = −15

In this case, income from the sale is $40 ($100 − $45 − $15).

FOB Shipping Point

Now, let's assume that Cosmic does not offer free shipping. Because Cosmic sold the goods FOB shipping point, Rob pays for the shipping costs. Rob purchases the headset on November 30 and takes it home to wrap and send with another gift. Cosmic would record the sale as follows:

DATE	ACCOUNTS	DR.	CR.
Nov 30	Accounts Receivable—Rob Macklin	100	
	Sales Revenue		100
	Cost of Goods Sold	45	
	Inventory—BTHS-414		45
	Record sale of inventory on account.		

In this situation, income from the sale would be $55 ($100 − $45).

FOB Shipping Point: Seller Agrees to Prepay the Shipping Costs

Now assume that Rob buys the headset on November 30 and asks Cosmic to ship it to Vancouver for him. Again, because the goods are sold FOB shipping point, Rob is responsible for the shipping charges. In this case, Cosmic pays for shipping the goods and adds the cost to Rob's invoice. Cosmic records the sale, including the payment of shipping costs, as follows:

DATE	ACCOUNTS	DR.	CR.
Nov 30	Accounts Receivable—Rob Macklin	100	
	Sales Revenue		100
	Cost of Goods Sold	45	
	Inventory—BTHS-414		45
	Record sale of inventory on account.		

DATE	ACCOUNTS	DR.	CR.
Nov 30	Accounts Receivable—Rob Macklin	15	
	Cash		15
	Record prepayment of shipping costs.		

Income from the sale is again $55 ($100 − $45). The $15 Cosmic paid to ship the headset to Vancouver is not an expense as it will be reimbursed by Rob. A comparison reveals that the income from the sale under FOB shipping point remains the same whether or not Cosmic prepays the shipping charges:

	FOB Destination	FOB Shipping Point	FOB Shipping Point, Seller Prepays
Sales Revenue	$100	$100	$100
− Cost of Goods Sold.........	(45)	(45)	(45)
− Delivery Expense	(15)	—	—
= Income from Sale	$ 40	$ 55	$ 55

OTHER SELLING COSTS

Selling expenses represent the costs associated with advertising and selling inventory. Examples of selling expenses usually found on a merchandiser's income statement include the following:

- Sales salaries, wages, and commissions
- Advertising and promotion
- Depreciation for the use of stores, parking lots, counters, displays, shelves, vehicles of salespeople, and storage space (such as warehouses and refrigerators)
- Delivery of merchandise to customers

As we will see in the next section, selling expenses are a deduction when arriving at the net income of a merchandiser.

 ## CRITICAL THINKING

Take a minute to think about the impact of the following independent cases on each of the assets, liabilities, and shareholders' equity accounts, based on each of the scenarios. Examine the impact of the cost of the inventory only.

1. Using the perpetual inventory method, the sale of inventory for $8,500 (with a cost of $6,200) on account was recorded, but the cost of inventory was not recorded.

2. Using the perpetual inventory method, the purchase of inventory with a term FOB shipping point, the shipping cost of $500 on account was recorded in the Shipping Expense account.

3. Using the perpetual inventory method, purchase returns of $250 were not recorded.

Solutions:

Impact on Accounts			
Assets	Liabilities	Shareholders' Equity	Entry in Accounting Record
1. + 6,200	No	+ 6,200	Assets and Shareholders' Equity would be overstated because the change in inventory was not recorded. The correct entry should include: Cost of Goods Sold (Dr); Inventory (Cr) in the amount of $6,200.
2. − 500	No	− 500	Assets and Shareholders' Equity would be understated because the cost of the shipping should have been included in the Inventory account rather than in a Shipping Expense account. To correct the entry, the buyer should record the adjusting entry: Inventory (Dr); Shipping Expense (Cr).
3. + 250	+ 250		Assets and liabilities would be overstated because the returns should have reduced the Inventory account and the respective accounts payable account. To correct the entry, the buyer should record the adjusting entry: Accounts Payable (Dr); Inventory (Cr).

HOW DO YOU PREPARE A MERCHANDISER'S FINANCIAL STATEMENTS?

THE INCOME STATEMENT

L.O. 5 Prepare a multi-step income statement and a classified statement of financial position

In earlier chapters, you learned how to complete the financial statements for a service business. Many service businesses use a **single-step income statement**. The single-step income statement groups all revenues together and all expenses together. Then, the total expenses are subtracted from total revenues in a single step without calculating any subtotals. The advantage of the single-step format is that it clearly distinguishes revenues from expenses. Although Cosmic Cellular is a merchandiser, **Exhibit 5-8** illustrates its income statement for the year ended December 31, 2015, prepared using the single-step format.

	Cosmic Cellular, Inc.		
	Income Statement		
	Year Ended December 31, 2015		
Revenues:			
Net Sales Revenue			$167,900
Expenses:			
Cost of Goods Sold		$90,300	
Selling Expenses		1,200	
General and Administrative Expenses		19,650	
Interest Expense		1,100	
Total Expenses			112,250
Net Income			$ 55,650

Exhibit 5-8 ▲

Most merchandisers use a **multi-step income statement**. The multi-step income statement is prepared in steps. Important subtotals are computed as part of the calculation of net income or net loss. Investors prefer this format because it provides step-by-step information about the profitability of the business. This format makes it more useful for managers within the business as well as investors outside of the business. The multi-step income statement for most merchandisers will contain most, but not necessarily all, of the following items:

- **Net Sales Revenue** is presented first, and is calculated by subtracting both Sales Returns and Allowances and Sales Discounts from Sales Revenue. Keep in mind that a company may not offer its customers any sales discounts. Also, even if sales discounts are offered, customers may not take advantage of them. Therefore, it is possible that no sales discounts will appear on a company's income statement.

- The cost of the merchandise that is sold appears next as Cost of Goods Sold. Remember, cost of goods sold is already known since this is recorded with the sales transactions.

- **Gross profit**, also called **gross margin**, is a subtotal computed next. The gross profit equals Net Sales Revenue minus Cost of Goods Sold. This figure is usually important for many companies because it shows the profitability of the company before being distorted by other expenses.

- **Operating expenses** (sometimes referred to as "period expenses") are the expenses, other than cost of goods sold, of operating the business. Operating expenses are listed after gross profit. Many companies report operating expenses in two categories:

  1. Selling expenses include sales salaries, commissions, advertising, promotion, depreciation for items used in sales, and delivery costs to customers.

  2. **General and administrative expenses** include office expenses, such as the salaries of the company president and office employees, depreciation of items used in administration, rent, utilities, and property taxes on the office building.

- On the multi-step income statement, gross profit minus operating expenses equals **operating income**, or **income from operations**. Operating income measures the results of the entity's primary, ongoing business activities.

- The last section of a multi-step income statement is **other revenues and expenses**. This category reports revenues and expenses that fall outside of a business's main operations. Examples include interest revenue, interest expense, dividend revenue, and gains and losses on the sale of long-term assets. Because not every business has revenues and expenses outside its business operations, not all income statements will include this section.

- The last line of the multi-step income statement is net income or net loss. To calculate this total, add other revenues and subtract other expenses from operating income. The final results of operations, net income or net loss, is a company's *bottom line,* a commonly used business term.

  Exhibit 5-9 illustrates the relationship between the different components of a multi-step income statement.

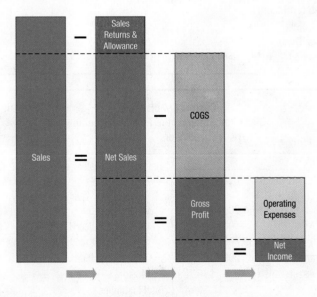

Exhibit 5-9 ▲

Cosmic Cellular's multi-step income statement for the year ended December 31, 2015, appears in **Exhibit 5-10** along with the statement of retained earnings and the statement of financial position.

After you review Cosmic Cellular's multi-step income statement in Exhibit 5-10, look again at its single-step version in Exhibit 5-8. Notice that in both formats net income is exactly the same. The format of the income statement does not change the net income or net loss of a business. It simply changes how the calculation of net income or net loss is presented.

Cosmic Cellular, Inc.
Income Statement
Year Ended December 31, 2015

Sales Revenue		$171,300	
Less: Sales Returns and Allowances		3,400	
Net Sales Revenue			$167,900
Cost of Goods Sold			90,300
Gross Profit			77,600
Operating Expenses:			
Selling Expenses:			
Advertising	$ 1,000		
Delivery Expense	200	1,200	
General and Administrative Expenses:			
Wage Expense	10,200		
Rent Expense	7,300		
Insurance Expense	1,000		
Depreciation Expense, Office Equipment	600		
Supplies Expense	550	19,650	20,850
Operating Income			56,750
Other Revenues and (Expenses):			
Interest Expense			(1,100)
Net Income			$ 55,650

Cosmic Cellular, Inc.
Statement of Retained Earnings
Year Ended December 31, 2015

Retained Earnings, December 31, 2014	$ 20,900
Add: Net Income	55,650
Subtotal	76,550
Less: Dividends	55,900
Retained Earnings, December 31, 2015	$ 20,650

Cosmic Cellular, Inc.
Classified Statement of Financial Position
December 31, 2015

ASSETS			LIABILITIES		
Current Assets:			Current Liabilities:		
Cash	$ 3,150		Accounts Payable	$30,000	
Accounts Receivable	4,600		Wages Payable	400	
Supplies	100		Unearned Sales Revenue	700	
Inventory	39,700		Total Current Liabilities		$31,100
Prepaid Insurance	200		Long-Term Liabilities		
Total Current Assets		$47,750	Mortgage Payable		10,000
Long-Term Assets:			Total Liabilities		41,100
Office Equipment	32,000				
Less: Accumulated			**SHAREHOLDERS'**		
Depreciation, Office			**EQUITY**		
Equipment	3,000	29,000	Common Shares	15,000	
			Retained Earnings	20,650	
			Total Equity		35,650
			Total Liabilities &		
Total Assets		$76,750	Shareholders' Equity		$76,750

Exhibit 5-10 ▲

DECISION GUIDELINES

DECISION	**GUIDELINE**	**ANALYZE**
My manager wants me to analyze our company's income statement to report on its profitability. Which format of income statement should I use?	The choice of the format for the statement depends on who the intended users of the financial statements are and what the purpose is for using the income statement.	The *single-step format* shows the calculation of net income or net loss by subtracting all expenses from all revenues in a single step. The single-step format typically shows summary information and is intended for users who do not need much detail. This format would not be a good format for creditors or investors to use, but it would be great to use in a press release or newspaper article. In this case, it will not be helpful in assessing the company's profitability since all revenues from all sources and all expenses are grouped together.

The *multi-step format* shows the calculation of net income or net loss in a series of steps with subtotals for *gross profit* and *operating income*. This format shows detailed information and is best suited for creditors and investors and those wanting to assess the company's profitability. |

THE STATEMENT OF RETAINED EARNINGS

A merchandiser's statement of retained earnings, which is one component of the statement of changes in equity, looks exactly like that of a service business. Cosmic's statement of retained earnings is presented in Exhibit 5-10.

THE CLASSIFIED STATEMENT OF FINANCIAL POSITION

To provide more useful information, merchandisers, as well as most service businesses, usually prepare a **classified statement of financial position**. A classified statement of financial position lists assets in classes in the order of their **liquidity**. Liquidity refers to how close an asset is to becoming cash or being used up. Similar to the assets, the liabilities are listed in classes based on how soon the obligation will be paid or fulfilled. By listing the assets and liabilities in these classes, financial statement users can better analyze the business's ability to pay its bills on time.

Assets

The most liquid assets are presented on a classified statement of financial position in a class called current assets. Current assets are assets that will be converted to cash, sold, or used up during the next 12 months or within a business's normal operating cycle if longer than one year.

For most businesses, the operating cycle is a few months; hence, current assets usually include Cash, Accounts Receivable, short-term Notes Receivable, and any other prepaid expense or asset that will be consumed (such as supplies) or transferred into cash (such as inventory) within a year. If the business is a merchandiser, then the major difference between its statement of financial position and that of a service business is that it also shows Inventory as a current asset.

All assets other than current assets are reported in a class called long-term assets. One category of long-term assets is called **property, plant, and equipment**. Land, buildings, furniture, fixtures, and equipment are examples of these assets.

IFRS

Long-term assets are also referred to as non-current assets.

Liabilities

The debts or obligations of a business that must be paid for or fulfilled within one year (or within the entity's operating cycle if the cycle is longer than a year) are reported in a class called current liabilities. Accounts Payable, Notes Payable due within one year, Salaries Payable, Interest Payable, and Unearned Revenue are current liabilities.

Obligations that extend beyond one year or one operating cycle (whichever is longer) are reported as **long-term liabilities**. Often, a business owner signs a contract to repay a note or mortgage over several years. The portion of the note or mortgage that must be paid within one year is classified as a current liability. However, the remaining balance is a long-term liability.

IFRS

Long-term liabilities are also referred to as non-current liabilities.

The statement of financial position for Cosmic Cellular is presented in Exhibit 5-10 and is presented in **account form**. The account form lists the assets on the left and the liabilities and shareholders' equity on the right, just as these accounts appear in the accounting equation. It is also acceptable to present the statement of financial position in **report form**, which lists the assets at the top and the liabilities and shareholders' equity on the bottom.

FOCUS ON DECISION MAKING: RATIOS

THE GROSS PROFIT PERCENTAGE

L.O. 6 Compute the gross profit percentage and the current ratio

Gross profit, also called gross margin, is a key tool in evaluating merchandising operations. Remember that gross profit is net sales revenue minus the cost of goods sold. Thus, gross profit is the amount left over from sales after deducting the cost of the merchandise sold. Merchandisers strive to maximize gross profit to help maximize net income. The **gross profit percentage**, also called the **gross margin percentage**, shows how well a merchandising business meets this goal. The gross profit percentage measures the relationship between gross profit and sales.

The gross profit percentage is one of the most carefully watched measures of profitability by investors and business managers. This information is used to compare changes in gross profit from year to year for the business. Also, it is used to compare the company to other businesses in the same industry. For most businesses, the gross profit percentage changes little from year to year. To investors, a significant change in the gross profit percentage signals a significant change in the business's operations meriting further investigation.

To compute the gross profit percentage, divide gross profit by net sales revenue. Based on information provided from the income statement in Exhibit 5-10, the gross profit percentage for Cosmic Cellular is 46.2%, calculated as follows:

$$\text{Gross Profit Percentage} = \frac{\text{Gross Profit}}{\text{Net Sales Revenue}} = \frac{\$77,600}{\$167,900} = 0.462 = 46.2\%$$

A 46.2% gross margin percentage means that each dollar of net sales generates 46.2 cents of gross profit. Every time Cosmic Cellular sells $1 of merchandise, it produces 46.2 cents of gross profit that hopefully covers operating expenses and generates net income.

THE CURRENT RATIO

The **current ratio** is one of the most widely used tools by investors, creditors, and suppliers. They use the current ratio to evaluate a company's ability to pay its obligations as they come due. The granting of credit is often based upon a company having a strong current ratio. The current ratio measures a company's ability to pay its current liabilities by comparing those liabilities to its current assets. The formula for calculating the current ratio is as follows:

$$\text{Current Ratio} = \frac{\text{Current Assets}}{\text{Current Liabilities}}$$

A high current ratio is desired because that means a company has plenty of current assets to pay its current liabilities. An increasing current ratio over time indicates improvement in a company's ability to pay current debts. A general benchmark is that a strong current ratio is 1.50. This indicates that the company has $1.50 in current assets for every $1.00 in current liabilities. A company with a current ratio of 1.50 would probably have little trouble paying its current liabilities. A current ratio below 1.00 is considered low.

However, an extremely high current ratio would give an indication that a company is not efficiently managing its assets. The high ratio could indicate that a company is keeping its assets idle in current assets rather than investing them in more productive cash-generating assets. Also, it is worth mentioning that the current ratio is different from one industry to another, and hence it is beneficial to benchmark a company's current ratio against other companies in the same industry.

Based on information provided from Cosmic's statement of financial position in Exhibit 5-10, the current ratio for Cosmic Cellular is 1.54, calculated as follows:

$$\text{Current Ratio} = \frac{\text{Current Assets}}{\text{Current Liabilities}} = \frac{\$47,750}{\$31,100} = 1.54$$

It appears that Cosmic Cellular should have no trouble paying its obligations as they come due. Cosmic Cellular could also compare its current ratio to its industry average current ratio.

 DECISION GUIDELINES

DECISION	**GUIDELINE**	**ANALYZE**
As a supplier, I am looking at a new customer's financial statements to determine whether or not to grant credit for the customer to make purchases. What can I use to evaluate the company's performance for this decision?	Key ratios are often used as a quick way to measure a business's performance.	The *gross profit percentage* helps analyze the profitability of a merchandiser. The gross profit percentage provides a measurement of how much of each sales dollar remains after covering the cost of the goods sold. The *current ratio* can be used to determine a business's ability to pay its obligations as they come due. A current ratio that is above 1.5 is generally considered to be good. However, if a current ratio gets too high it can be an indicator that the business has too much tied up in current assets and, therefore, is not utilizing its assets as effectively as it could be.

FOCUS ON USERS

Concept	User	Why Is This Important to This User?
Perpetual and Periodic Inventory	**Managers**	Management needs to know whether the inventory amounts that are showing in the general ledger are reliable for decision making. If the company uses a perpetual system, then the inventory account is continually updated and will only be missing any details for inventory that has disappeared but not been sold (stolen, damaged, etc.). If the company uses a periodic system, then a visual inspection or manual count of the inventory would be needed to know the amount in inventory.
Free on Board (FOB) Destination/ Shipping Point	**Managers**	It is important for management to understand what is included in the ending inventory amounts so that management can plan for inventory purchases in the next month. For any purchases that have been sold and are in the process of being delivered, the FOB details need to be known to understand if these items are included in the ending inventory account. If the items were sold FOB destination, then the ending inventory amounts will still include these items even though they have been sold.
	Creditors	Similar to managers, creditors need to understand the composition of the ending inventory, but creditors would want to know this information because the inventory may be used as collateral for loans.
Multi-Step Income Statement	**Shareholders and Potential Investors**	Shareholders and potential investors will closely examine a multi-step income statement for details on gross profit. Gross profit shows how much the company has to contribute to expenses after the cost of the inventory sold is deducted. The gross profit percentage would be compared to other companies in the same industry, which can help determine the strategy of the company as either a high-volume low-price strategy (such as a dollar store or discount retailer) or as a low-volume high-price strategy (such as a high-quality brand retailer).
	Creditors	Creditors would be interested in the operating income amount on a multi-step income statement as this gives an indication of how effectively the company operates its normal operations. For example, a pizza company that also has a warehouse that it rents to other companies would show how much it has earned in income from just making and selling pizzas in the operating income.

POINT OF COMPARISON	IFRS	ASPE
Assets Classification	Assets classified as long-lived assets are called "non-current assets," and assets that are consumed or transferred into cash within a year or an operating cycle (whichever is longer) are called "current assets."	Assets that are consumed or transferred into cash within a year or an operating cycle (whichever is longer) are called "current assets," and long-lived assets are called "long-term assets."
Liabilities Classification	Obligations that are going to exceed one year or operating cycle are called "non-current liabilities"; otherwise they are classified as "current liabilities."	Obligations that are going to be paid within one year or operating cycle are called "current liabilities"; otherwise they are classified as "long-term liabilities."
Statement of Financial Position: Presentation of Assets	Non-current assets sometimes are presented first, followed by current assets.	Usually, current assets are presented first, followed by long-term assets.
Statement of Financial Position: Presentation of Liabilities	Non-current liabilities sometimes are presented first, followed by current liabilities.	Usually, current liabilities are presented first, followed by long-term liabilities.
Income Statement	An income statement and a statement of comprehensive income are prepared. Alternatively, a single statement of comprehensive income incorporating the income statement could be prepared.	Only an income statement is prepared. A statement of comprehensive income is not required.

DEMO DOC 📄

MyAccountingLab   Visit MyAccountingLab to watch animated versions of these Demo Docs.

TRANSACTION ANALYSIS FOR A MERCHANDISER USING THE PERPETUAL INVENTORY SYSTEM

Spokane Paper Products, Inc. had the following transactions in March 2015:

LEARNING OBJECTIVES ③—④

Mar	1	Purchased $1,500 of inventory on account. Terms were 2/10, n/30, FOB destination.
	2	Sold inventory for cash, $800 (cost, $550).
	7	Returned $400 of the inventory purchased on March 1 because it was defective.
	9	Paid supplier for goods purchased on March 1.
	11	Purchased inventory for $1,800 on account. Terms were 3/15, n/30, FOB shipping point.
	14	Paid freight bill on merchandise purchased on March 11, $125.
	18	Sold inventory for $2,200 (cost, $1,500) on account. Terms were 2/10, n/30, FOB shipping point.
	24	Paid supplier for goods purchased on March 11.
	26	The customer from the March 18 sale returned $750 ($500 cost) of goods.
	28	Received cash in full settlement of its account from the customer who purchased inventory on March 18.

REQUIREMENT:

① **Journalize these transactions by using the perpetual inventory system. Omit explanations.**

DEMO DOC SOLUTION
REQUIREMENT ①

Journalize these transactions. Omit explanations.

Part 1	Demo Doc Complete

Mar 1   Purchased $1,500 of inventory on account. Terms were 2/10, n/30, FOB destination.

The purchase of inventory causes the Inventory account to increase by $1,500. The Inventory account is an asset and is, therefore, increased with a debit. Because the purchase was made on account, Accounts Payable is increased (credited) by $1,500. The credit terms are not relevant until the *payment* is made to the supplier. The freight terms indicate that the supplier is responsible for paying the freight charges.

DATE	ACCOUNTS	POST REF.	DR.	CR.
Mar 1	Inventory		1,500	
	Accounts Payable			1,500

Assets	=	Liabilities	+	Shareholders' Equity
+1,500		+1,500		

Mar 2   Sold inventory for cash, $800 (cost, $550).

Under the perpetual inventory method, the entry required to account for a sale requires two parts. The first part of the entry is required to record the recognition of revenue. Because the sale was a cash sale, the Cash account is increased (debited) by $800. When merchandise is sold (and delivered) to a customer, the company earns sales revenue. By selling merchandise, Spokane Paper Products, Inc. has earned sales revenue of $800. Therefore, Sales Revenue is increased (credited) by $800.

The second part of the entry is required to record the cost of the goods sold. The Cost of Goods Sold account is increased (debited) for $550 (Spokane Paper Products' cost of the merchandise). Remember, Cost of Goods Sold is an *expense*. Because goods from inventory were given to the customer, the Inventory account is decreased (credited) by $550.

DATE	ACCOUNTS	POST REF.	DR.	CR.
Mar 2	Cash		800	
	Sales Revenue			800
	Cost of Goods Sold		550	
	Inventory			550

Mar 7   Returned $400 of the inventory purchased on March 1 because it was defective.

Because Spokane Paper Products, Inc. has not yet paid for the purchase, the return of the merchandise will result in a $400 decrease (debit) to Accounts Payable. Also, because the goods were returned to the supplier, the Inventory account will be decreased (credited) by $400.

DATE	ACCOUNTS	POST REF.	DR.	CR.
Mar 7	Accounts Payable		400	
	Inventory			400

Mar 9   Paid supplier for goods purchased on March 1.

Because the original purchase was made on account, we need to consider the credit terms, which were 2/10, n/30. Because Spokane Paper Products, Inc. is paying within the 10-day discount period, it is entitled to take a 2% discount. However, the discount does not apply to the $400 of goods that Spokane Paper Products, Inc. has returned. It only applies to the net account payable that Spokane Paper Products, Inc. owes after the return.

Original purchase price of goods	$1,500
Less amount of goods returned	$ 400
Net account payable.................................	$1,100

The discount, and the amount of cash paid, is calculated as follows:

Net account payable.................	$1,100
Less 2% discount	$ 22 (2% × $1,100)
Total cash paid	$1,078

Accounts Payable is decreased (debited) by the remaining amount due of $1,100. The Cash account will be decreased (credited) by the $1,078 of cash paid. The $22 difference is the discount and is treated as a reduction to the Inventory account because it represents a reduction in the cost of the inventory. So, Inventory is decreased (credited) by the $22 amount of the discount.

DATE	ACCOUNTS	POST REF.	DR.	CR.
Mar 9	Accounts Payable		1,100	
	Cash			1,078
	Inventory			22

Mar 11 Purchased inventory for $1,800 on account. Terms were 3/15, n/30, FOB shipping point.

The purchase of inventory causes the Inventory account to increase (debit) by $1,800. Because the purchase was made on account, Accounts Payable is increased by $1,800 with a credit. The credit terms are not relevant until the *payment* is made to the supplier. The freight terms indicate that Spokane Paper Products, Inc. is responsible for paying the freight charges.

DATE	ACCOUNTS	POST REF.	DR.	CR.
Mar 11	Inventory		1,800	
	Accounts Payable			1,800

−1,800   −1,800

Mar 14 Paid freight bill on merchandise purchased on March 11, $125.

The shipping terms of FOB shipping point means that Spokane Paper Products, Inc. is responsible for paying the freight charges. Because the freight charges represent an increase in the cost of the inventory to Spokane Paper Products, the Inventory account will be increased (debited) by $125. Cash will be decreased (credited) by $125.

DATE	ACCOUNTS	POST REF.	DR.	CR.
Mar 14	Inventory		125	
	Cash			125

+125
−125

Mar 18 Sold inventory for $2,200 (cost, $1,500) on account. Terms were 2/10, n/30, FOB shipping point.

Remember, under the perpetual inventory method, the entry required to account for a sale requires two parts. The first part of the entry is required to record the recognition of revenue. Because the sale was on account, the Accounts Receivable account is increased (debited) by $2,200. Sales revenue is increased (credited) by $2,200. The second part of the entry is required to record the cost of the goods sold. The Cost of Goods Sold account is increased (debited) for $1,500 and Inventory is decreased (credited) by $1,500.

DATE	ACCOUNTS	POST REF.	DR.	CR.
Mar 18	Accounts Receivable		2,200	
	Sales Revenue			2,200
	Cost of Goods Sold		1,500	
	Inventory			1,500

+2,200   +2,200

−1,500   −1,500

Mar 24 Paid supplier for goods purchased on March 11.

Because the original purchase was made on account, we need to consider the credit terms, which were 3/15, n/30. Because Spokane Paper Products, Inc. is paying within the 15-day discount period, it is entitled to take a 3% discount. There were no returns related to this purchase so the discount, and the amount of cash paid, is calculated as follows:

Net account payable	$ 1,800
Less 3% discount (3% × $1,800)	$ (54)
Total cash paid	$ 1,746

Accounts Payable is decreased (debited) by the amount due of $1,800. The Cash account will be decreased (credited) by the $1,746 of cash paid. The $54 difference is the discount and is treated as a reduction to the Inventory account because it represents a reduction in the cost of the inventory. So, Inventory is decreased (credited) by the $54 amount of the discount.

DATE	ACCOUNTS	POST REF.	DR.	CR.
Mar 24	Accounts Payable		1,800	
	Cash			1,746
	Inventory			54

Mar 26 The customer from the March 18 sale returned $750 ($500 cost) of goods.

Just as the sale of goods under the perpetual inventory method requires a two-part entry, so does the return of goods from a customer. The first part of the entry "undoes" the sale and is recorded by increasing (debiting) the contra-account Sales Returns and Allowances by $750. The customer has not yet paid the account, so the return of the goods will result in a decrease (credit) to Accounts Receivable for $750. The second part of the entry will record the physical return of the goods. The Inventory account is increased (debited) by $500, the value of the goods returned and put back for resale. Because the goods were returned and were put back for resale, they are no longer "sold," so the Cost of Goods Sold account is decreased (credited) by $500.

DATE	ACCOUNTS	POST REF.	DR.	CR.
Mar 26	Sales Returns and Allowances		750	
	Accounts Receivable			750
	Inventory		500	
	Cost of Goods Sold			500

Mar 28 Received cash in full settlement of its account from the customer who purchased inventory on March 18.

Because the original purchase was made on account, we need to consider the credit terms, which were 2/10, n/30. Because the customer is paying within the 10-day discount period, he or she is entitled to take a 2% discount. However, the discount does not apply to the $750 of goods that the customer returned. It only applies to the net account receivable that the customer still owes to Spokane Paper Products, Inc. after the return.

Original sales price of goods	$ 2,200
Less amount of goods returned	$ (750)
Net account receivable..............................	$ 1,450

The discount, and the amount of cash Spokane Paper Products, Inc. receives, is calculated as follows:

Net account receivable..............................	$ 1,450
Less 2% discount (2% × $1,450)...............	$ (29)
Total cash received....................................	$ 1,421

The Cash account will be increased (debited) by the $1,421 of cash received. The amount of the discount, $29, is recorded as an increase (debit) to the contra-account, Sales Discounts. Accounts Receivable is decreased (credited) by the net account receivable of $1,450.

DATE	ACCOUNTS	POST REF.	DR.	CR.
Mar 28	Cash		1,421	
	Sales Discounts		29	
	Accounts Receivable			1,450

DEMO DOC COMPLETE

Part 1	Demo Doc Complete

DECISION GUIDELINES

Accounting for a Merchandising Business

As a merchandiser, you might be faced with decisions such as the following:

DECISION	GUIDELINE	ANALYZE

Which inventory system should my business use?

This decision depends on whether or not you plan on utilizing a computer system to help with inventory management. It also depends on the variety and number of goods your business sells.

The *perpetual system* shows the current, correct amounts of inventory on hand and the cost of goods sold at all times.

The *periodic system* requires that a physical count of the inventory be taken to know the correct balances of inventory and cost of goods sold.

Before computers, only businesses that sold smaller quantities of higher cost items could use the perpetual method. Today, thanks to computers and other technology, most companies utilize the perpetual method even if they sell a high quantity of low-cost items.

My manager wants me to analyze our company's income statement to report on its profitability. Which format of income statement should I use?

The choice of the format for the statement depends on the intended users of the financial statements and what the purpose is for using the income statement.

The *single-step format* shows the calculation of net income or net loss by subtracting all expenses from all revenues in a single step. The single-step format typically shows summary information and is intended for users who do not need much detail. This format would not be a good format for creditors or investors to use but it would be great to use in a press release or newspaper article. In this case, it will not be helpful in assessing the company's profitability since all revenues from all sources and all expenses are grouped together.

The *multi-step format* shows the calculation of net income or net loss in a series of steps with subtotals for *gross profit* and *operating income*. This format shows detailed information and is best suited for creditors and investors and those wanting to assess the company's profitability.

As a supplier, I am looking at a new customer's financial statements to determine whether or not to grant credit for the customer to make purchases. What can I use to evaluate the company's performance for this decision?

Key ratios are often used as a quick way to measure a business's performance.

The *gross profit percentage* helps analyze the profitability of a merchandiser. The gross profit percentage provides a measurement of how much of each sales dollar remains after covering the cost of the inventory.

The *current ratio* can be used to determine a business's ability to pay its obligations as they come due. A current ratio that is above 1.5 is generally considered to be good.

However, if a current ratio gets too high it can be an indicator that the business has too much tied up in current assets and, therefore, is not utilizing its assets as effectively as it could be.

ACCOUNTING VOCABULARY

THE LANGUAGE OF BUSINESS

Account form (p. 296)

Classified statement of financial position (p. 295)

Cost of Goods Sold (COGS) (p. 285)

Credit memorandum (p. 286)

Credit terms (p. 280)

Current ratio (p. 297)

Debit memorandum (p. 279)

Discount period (p. 280)

Eom (p. 280)

Free on board (FOB) destination (p. 282)

ACCOUNTING PRACTICE

DISCUSSION QUESTIONS

1. What accounts will appear on the financial statements of a merchandiser that will not appear on those of a service-oriented company?

2. What are some reasons why a merchandiser might prefer to use a perpetual inventory system over a periodic inventory system?

3. Why do businesses use subsidiary ledgers?

4. What do the terms 2/10, n/30 mean? If you were advising a company who bought goods under these terms, what would you advise it to do with respect to payment? Why?

5. What are the accounts involved in recording the sale of merchandise on credit?

6. What kind of account is Sales Returns and Allowances? Where would it appear on the financial statements?

7. What is a debit memorandum? What is a credit memorandum? Give an example of the types of transactions for which each would be used.

8. What does the term "free on board" mean? Why is this an important term to understand if you are involved in making decisions about the purchasing of inventory or the setting of prices for your products?

9. What is the difference between a single-step and multi-step income statement? For what type of business is a multi-step income statement most appropriate?

10. What situation might explain why a company's gross profit percentage went down from 60% to 40% from one year to the next?

SELF CHECK

1. Which account does a merchandiser use that a service company does not use?

   a. Cost of Goods Sold
   b. Inventory
   c. Sales Revenue
   d. All of the above

2. The two main inventory accounting systems are the

   a. perpetual and periodic.
   b. purchase and sale.
   c. returns and allowances.
   d. cash and accrual.

3. Which of the following journal entries for the purchase of $900 of inventory on account, using the perpetual inventory system, is correct?

DATE	ACCOUNTS	POST REF.	DR.	CR.
a.	Cost of Goods Sold		900	
	Accounts Payable			900
b.	Inventory		900	
	Accounts Payable			900
c.	Accounts Payable		900	
	Inventory			900
d.	Inventory		900	
	Cash			900

4. Roy Photography Supply, Inc. purchased inventory for $2,400 and also paid $85 freight to have the inventory delivered. Roy Photography Supply, Inc. returned $100 of the goods to the seller and later took a 2.5% purchase discount. What is the final cost of the inventory that Roy Photography Supply, Inc. kept? (Round your answer up to the next whole number.)

   a. $2,423
   b. $2,325
   c. $2,425
   d. $2,328

5. Suppose Bonzai Boards, Inc. had sales of $180,000 and sales returns of $22,000. Cost of goods sold was $110,000. How much gross profit did Bonzai Boards, Inc. report?

   a. $48,000
   b. $70,000
   c. $92,000
   d. $158,000

6. Suppose Apex Electrical Supply's Inventory account showed a balance of $43,000. A physical count showed $41,800 of goods on hand. It was discovered that the accountant didn't complete the entry of a sales transaction. To adjust the Inventory account, Apex Electrical Supply, Inc. would make which of the following entries:

MyAccountingLab

The exercises and problems in this chapter can be found on MyAccountingLab. You can practise them as often as you want, and they feature step-by-step guided solutions to help you find the right answer.

DATE	ACCOUNTS	POST REF.	DR.	CR.
a.	Cost of Goods Sold		1,200	
	Inventory			1,200
b.	Accounts Payable		1,200	
	Inventory			1,200
c.	Inventory		1,200	
	Cost of Goods Sold			1,200
d.	Inventory		1,200	
	Accounts Payable			1,200

7. If Bonzai Boards, Inc. returned $3,600 of snowboards to a supplier it would record the transaction as which of the following?

DATE	ACCOUNTS	POST REF.	DR.	CR.
a.	Cost of Goods Sold		3,600	
	Inventory			3,600
b.	Accounts Payable		3,600	
	Sales Returns and Allowances			3,600
c.	Inventory		3,600	
	Accounts Payable			3,600
d.	Accounts Payable		3,600	
	Inventory			3,600

8. An asset is classified as current if it
   a. was purchased within the last six months.
   b. will become cash, be sold, or be used up within 12 months.
   c. was purchased with cash.
   d. will last longer than one year.

9. The income statement format that shows important subtotals is referred to as
   a. a classified income statement.
   b. a single-step income statement.
   c. a multi-step income statement.
   d. a subtotalled income statement.

10. Suppose Bonzai Boards, Inc. had sales of $210,000 and sales returns of $18,000. Cost of goods sold was $125,000. What was Bonzai Boards' gross profit percentage (rounded) for this period?
   a. 35%
   b. 54%
   c. 40%
   d. 32%

Answers are given after Written Communication.

SHORT EXERCISES

Questions also cover the periodic inventory system, which is included in Appendix 5A.

S5-1. Inventory methods (*Learning Objective 2*) 5–10 min.

The following characteristics are related to either periodic inventory or perpetual inventory systems.

a. A physical count of goods on hand at year end is required.

b. Inventory records are continuously updated.

c. Purchases of inventory are recorded in an asset account at the time of purchase.

d. Bar code scanners are often utilized when using this inventory system.

e. It is necessary to calculate the cost of goods sold at the end of the year with this inventory system.

Identify each characteristic as one of the following:

a. Periodic inventory

b. Perpetual inventory

c. Both periodic and perpetual inventory

d. Neither periodic nor perpetual inventory

S5-2. Adjusting inventory due to error (*Learning Objective 2*) 5–10 min.

Charleston's Furniture uses the perpetual inventory method. At the end of the year, Charleston's Furniture's Inventory account had a ledger balance of $87,000. A physical inventory count revealed that the actual inventory on hand totaled $85,300. By investigating the matter it was discovered that the difference resulted from an accounting error. The accountant recorded one of the sales transactions and missed the entry to update the inventory.

Journalize the transaction necessary to adjust the Inventory account at the end of the year.

S5-3. Journalizing inventory purchases (*Learning Objectives 3 & 7*) 5–10 min.

Suppose Sports-R-Us purchases $40,000 of sportswear on account from Pacific Trail on March 1, 2015. Credit terms are 2/10, net 30. Sports-R-Us pays Pacific Trail on March 8, 2015.

1. Journalize the transactions for Sports-R-Us on March 1, 2015, and March 8, 2015, using (1) the perpetual system and (2) the periodic inventory system.

2. What was the final cost of this inventory for Sports-R-Us?

S5-4. Inventory purchases and returns (*Learning Objective 3*) 5–10 min.

Sonny's Spas, Inc. purchased $8,000 worth of inventory from the Pool Warehouse on account, terms of 2/10, n/30. Some of the goods were damaged in shipment, so Sonny's Spas, Inc. returns $1,100 of the merchandise to the Pool Warehouse.

How much must Sonny's Spas, Inc. pay the Pool Warehouse

1. after the discount period?
2. within the discount period?

S5-5. Journalizing inventory purchases and returns (*Learning Objectives 3 & 7*) 5–10 min.

Sonny's Spas, Inc. purchased $8,000 worth of inventory from the Pool Warehouse on account, terms of 2/10, n/30. Some of the goods were damaged in shipment, so Sonny's Spas, Inc. returns $1,100 of the merchandise to the Pool Warehouse.

Journalize the following transactions, using (1) the perpetual system and (2) the periodic inventory system, for Sonny's Spas, Inc. Explanations are not required.

a. Purchase of the goods

b. Return of the damaged goods

c. Payment for the goods within the discount period

S5-6. Journalizing inventory purchases and freight charges (*Learning Objectives 3 & 7*) 5–10 min.

Journalize the following transactions, using (1) the perpetual system and (2) the periodic inventory system, for the Jazz Man music store.

a. Purchased $8,700 of merchandise on account, terms 2/10, n/30, FOB shipping point.

b. Paid $175 to the freight company for the delivery of the merchandise purchased.

c. Paid for the inventory purchased in (a) within the discount period.

S5-7. Journalizing sales transactions (*Learning Objective 4*) 5–10 min.

Journalize the following transactions for the Pool Warehouse. Explanations are not required.

a. The Pool Warehouse sold $55,000 of merchandise to Sonny's Spas, Inc. on account, terms 2/15, n/30. The merchandise cost the Pool Warehouse $30,250.

b. Received payment for the goods from Sonny's Spas, Inc. within the discount period.

S5-8. Journalizing sales and return transactions (*Learning Objectives 4 & 7*) 5–10 min.

Suppose Peter's Hardware sells merchandise on account, terms 2/10, n/45, for $750 (cost of the inventory is $460) on May 17, 2015. Peter's Hardware later received $200 of goods (cost, $140) as sales returns on May 21, 2015. The customer paid the balance due on May 26, 2015.

Journalize the May 2015 transactions, using (1) the perpetual system and (2) the periodic inventory system, for Peter's Hardware.

S5-9. Calculate income statement items (*Learning Objective 5*) 5–10 min.

Suppose Peter's Hardware sells merchandise on account, terms 2/10, n/45, for $750 (cost of the inventory is $460) on May 17, 2015. Peter's Hardware later received $200 of goods (cost, $140) as sales returns on May 21, 2015. The customer paid the balance due on May 26, 2015.

1. Calculate net sales revenue for May 2015.
2. Calculate gross profit for May 2015.

S5-10. Calculate classified statement of financial position amounts (*Learning Objective 5*) 5–10 min.

Selected account balances for Jill's Java at the end of the month are listed below in random order:

Accounts Payable	$19,500
Unearned Revenue	2,000
Equipment	33,000
Inventory	37,000
Accounts Receivable	6,000
Wages Payable	1,500
Note Payable, Long-Term	28,000
Accumulated Depreciation, Equipment	4,500
Common Shares	25,000
Supplies	3,400
Building	87,000
Cash	5,200
Accumulated Depreciation, Building	24,000
Prepaid Rent	6,200
Retained Earnings	15,000

Identify or compute the following amounts for Jill's Java:

a. Total current assets
b. Total current liabilities
c. Book value of plant assets
d. Total long-term liabilities

S5-11. Prepare a multi-step income statement (*Learning Objective 5*) 10–15 min.

The accounting records for ADR, Inc. reflected the following amounts at the end of August 31, 2015.

Cash..	$3,500	Cost of Goods Sold..................	$19,500
Total Operating Expenses...........	3,700	Equipment, Net........................	6,100
Accounts Payable.......................	4,500	Accrued Liabilities...................	1,900
Total Shareholders' Equity.........	5,200	Net Sales Revenue...................	28,000
Long-Term Notes Payable..........	2,300	Accounts Receivable................	2,900
Inventory....................................	1,700	Prepaid Rent............................	800
Wages Payable...........................	1,100		

Prepare ADR's multi-step income statement for the fiscal year ended August 31, 2015.

S5-12. Prepare a classified statement of financial position (*Learning Objective 5*) 10–15 min.

The accounting records for ADR, Inc. reflected the following amounts at the end of August 2015:

Cash..	$3,500	Cost of Goods Sold..................	$19,500
Total Operating Expenses...........	3,700	Equipment, Net........................	6,100
Accounts Payable.......................	4,500	Accrued Liabilities...................	1,900
Total Shareholders' Equity.........	5,200	Net Sales Revenue...................	28,000
Long-Term Notes Payable..........	2,300	Accounts Receivable................	2,900
Inventory....................................	1,700	Prepaid Rent............................	800
Wages Payable...........................	1,100		

Prepare the ADR, Inc. classified statement of financial position at August 31, 2015. Use the report format.

S5-13. Calculate gross profit and current ratio (*Learning Objective 6*) 10–15 min.

The accounting records for ADR, Inc. reflected the following amounts at the end of August, 2015:

Cash..	$3,500	Cost of Goods Sold..................	$19,500
Total Operating Expenses...........	3,700	Equipment, Net........................	6,100
Accounts Payable.......................	4,500	Accrued Liabilities...................	1,900
Total Shareholders' Equity.........	5,200	Net Sales Revenue...................	28,000
Long-Term Notes Payable..........	2,300	Accounts Receivable................	2,900
Inventory....................................	1,700	Prepaid Rent............................	800
Wages Payable...........................	1,100		

Calculate the gross profit percentage and current ratio for 2015.

EXERCISES (GROUP A)

E5-1A. Journalizing inventory purchases, returns, and freight transactions (*Learning Objectives 3 & 7*) 10–15 min.

On June 15, 2015, Bailey's Department Store purchased $4,300 of inventory on account from one of its suppliers. The terms were 3/15, n/45, FOB shipping point. On June 18 Bailey's Department Store paid freight charges of $350 related to the delivery of the goods purchased on June 15. Upon receiving the goods, Bailey's Department Store checked the order and found $900 of unsuitable merchandise, which was returned to the supplier on June 20. Then, on June 28, Bailey's Department Store paid the invoice.

Requirement

1. Journalize all necessary transactions for Bailey's Department Store, using (1) the perpetual inventory system, and (2) the periodic inventory system. Omit explanations.

E5-2A. Journalizing inventory purchases, returns, and freight transactions (*Learning Objectives 3 & 7*) 10–15 min.

Journalize the following transactions for Amazing Audio, Inc. that occurred during the month of March, using (1) the perpetual inventory system, and (2) the periodic inventory system. Omit explanations.

Mar 3	Purchased $4,600 of merchandise on account, terms 2/10, n/30, FOB shipping point. The supplier prepaid freight charges of $250 and added the amount to the invoice.
6	Returned damaged goods to the supplier and received a credit memorandum in the amount of $600.
12	Paid for the goods purchased on March 3.

E5-3A. Journalizing inventory sales, returns, and freight transactions (*Learning Objectives 4 & 7*) 10–15 min.

On September 14, 2015, C & T Machinery, Inc. sold $2,300 of inventory (cost is $1,350) on account to one of its customers. The terms were 1/10, n/30, FOB destination. On September 16, C & T Machinery, Inc. paid freight charges of $75 related to the delivery of the goods sold on September 14. On September 20, $900 of damaged goods (cost is $540) were returned by the customer. On September 23, C & T Machinery, Inc. received payment in full from the customer.

Requirement

1. Journalize all necessary transactions for C & T Machinery, Inc. using (1) the perpetual inventory system, and (2) the periodic inventory system. Omit explanations.

E5-4A. Journalizing inventory sales, returns, and freight transactions (*Learning Objectives 4 & 7*) 10–15 min.

Journalize the following transactions for Amazing Audio, Inc. that occurred during the month of November using (1) the perpetual inventory system and (2) the periodic inventory system. Omit explanations. Amazing Audio's cost of inventory is 65% of the sales price.

Nov 3	Sold $1,600 of merchandise on account, terms 2/15, n/45, FOB shipping point. Amazing Audio, Inc. prepaid $85 of shipping costs and added the amount to the customer's invoice.
7	Issued a credit memo to the customer acknowledging the return of $300 of damaged goods.
16	Received payment in full from the customer for the November 3 invoice.

E5-5A. Journalizing inventory purchases, sales, returns, and freight transactions (*Learning Objectives 3, 4, & 7*) 15–20 min.

The following transactions occurred during April 2015 for Angelo's Garden Centre, Inc.:

Apr 3	Purchased $3,500 of goods on account, terms 2/10, n/30, FOB shipping point.
6	Returned $400 of defective merchandise purchased on April 3.
8	Paid freight charges of $110 for delivery of goods purchased on April 3.
11	Sold $4,300 of inventory to a customer on account, terms 3/15, n/45, FOB shipping point. The cost of the goods was $2,100.
12	Paid amount owed on the April 3 purchase.
18	Granted a $300 sales allowance on the April 11 sale because the goods were the wrong colour.
25	Received payment in full from customer for the April 11 sale.

Requirement

1. Journalize all necessary transactions for Angelo's Garden Centre, Inc. using (1) the perpetual inventory system, and (2) the periodic inventory system. Omit explanations.

E5-6A. Calculate multi-step income statement items (*Learning Objective 5*)
10–15 min.

Consider the following incomplete table of a merchandiser's profit data:

Sales	Sales Discounts	Net Sales	Cost of Goods Sold	Gross Profit
$ (a)	$2,500	$ (b)	$68,300	$32,100
64,000	1,700	(c)	44,600	(d)
102,000	(e)	93,500	(f)	28,600
(g)	2,100	86,300	57,700	(h)

Requirement

1. Complete the table by computing the missing amounts.

E5-7A. Prepare a single-step income statement (*Learning Objective 5*) 10–15 min.

The account balances for Atlantis Aquatics, Inc. for the year ended December 31, 2015, are presented next in random order:

Cash...............................	$ 3,700	Cost of Goods Sold.................	$136,400
Equipment...........................	13,700	Accumulated Depreciation,	
Accounts Payable.................	4,500	Equipment...........................	6,100
Common Shares...................	35,000	Unearned Revenues...............	1,900
Long-Term Notes Payable......	10,000	Sales Revenue........................	243,500
General Expenses.................	18,200	Accounts Receivable...............	3,200
Wages Payable.....................	1,100	Accumulated Depreciation,	
Supplies.............................	900	Building.............................	18,500
Building.............................	125,000	Mortgage Payable	
Sales Returns and		(Long-Term)......................	37,000
Allowances.......................	4,800	Dividends.............................	34,000
Prepaid Rent........................	800	Sales Discounts.....................	2,200
Retained Earnings.................	13,800	Selling Expenses....................	26,800
Inventory.............................	1,700		

Requirements

1. Prepare Atlantis Aquatics' *single-step* income statement.

2. Would you recommend the use of the single-step income statement format by a merchandiser? Why?

Quick solution:
1. Net Income = $55,100.

E5-8A. Prepare a multi-step income statement; calculate gross profit percentage (*Learning Objectives 5 & 6*) 15–20 min.

Use the data for Atlantis Aquatics, Inc. from E5-7A.

Requirements

1. Prepare Atlantis Aquatics' *multi-step* income statement.

2. Calculate the gross profit percentage.

3. The gross profit percentage for 2014 was 38.7%. Did the gross profit percentage improve or deteriorate during 2015?

E5-9A. Prepare a classified statement of financial position; calculate current ratio (*Learning Objectives 5 & 6*) 15–20 min.

Use the data for Atlantis Aquatics, Inc. from E5-7A.

Requirements

1. Prepare Atlantis Aquatics' classified statement of financial position. Use the account format. The balance shown for retained earnings represents the balance prior to closing the temporary accounts for the year.

2. Calculate the current ratio.

3. The current ratio for 2014 was 1.25. Did the current ratio improve or deteriorate during 2015?

E5-10A. Calculate gross profit percentage and current ratio (*Learning Objective 6*) 10–15 min.

Apex, Inc. had sales revenue of $47 million, sales returns and allowances of $2 million, and sales discounts of $0.5 million in 2015. Cost of goods sold was $24 million, and net income was $7 million for the year. At December 31, the company had total assets of $36 million, of which total current assets amounted to $15 million. Apex's current liabilities were $9 million and its long-term liabilities were $4 million.

Requirement

1. Compute Apex's gross profit percentage and current ratio for 2015.

EXERCISES (GROUP B)

E5-1B. Journalizing inventory purchases, returns, and freight transactions (*Learning Objectives 3 & 7*) 10–15 min.

On November 15, 2015, Chandler's Department Store purchased $5,100 of inventory on account from one of its suppliers. The terms were 3/15, n/45, FOB shipping point. On November 18 Chandler's Department Store paid freight charges of $175 related to the delivery of the goods purchased on November 15. Upon receiving the goods, Chandler's Department Store checked the order and found $600 of unsuitable merchandise, which was returned to the supplier on November 20. Then, on November 28, Chandler's Department Store paid the invoice.

Requirement

1. Journalize all necessary transactions for Chandler's Department Store, using (1) the perpetual inventory system, and (2) the periodic inventory system. Omit explanations.

E5-2B. Journalizing inventory purchases, returns, and freight transactions (*Learning Objectives 3 & 7*) 10–15 min.

Journalize the following transactions for Antique Furniture, Inc. that occurred during the month of January. Omit explanations, and use (1) the perpetual inventory system and (2) the periodic inventory system.

Jan	3	Purchased $5,700 of merchandise on account, terms 1/10, n/30, FOB shipping point. The supplier prepaid freight charges of $225 and added the amount to the invoice.
	6	Returned damaged goods to the supplier and received a credit memorandum in the amount of $500.
	12	Paid for the goods purchased on January 3.

E5-3B. Journalizing inventory sales, returns, and freight transactions (*Learning Objectives 4 & 7*) 10–15 min.

On November 14, 2015, Amazing Sound, Inc. sold $3,100 of inventory (cost is $1,330) on account to one of its customers. The terms were 3/10, n/30, FOB destination. On November 16, Amazing Sound, Inc. paid freight charges of $65 related to the delivery of the goods sold on November 14. On November 20, $800 of damaged goods (cost is $420) were returned by the customer. On November 23, Amazing Sound, Inc. received payment in full from the customer.

Requirement

1. Journalize all necessary transactions for Amazing Sound, Inc. using (1) the perpetual inventory system and (2) the periodic inventory system. Omit explanations.

E5-4B. Journalizing inventory sales, returns, and freight transactions (*Learning Objectives 4 & 7*) 10–15 min.

Journalize the following transactions for Antique Furniture, Inc. that occurred during the month of April using (1) the perpetual inventory system and (2) the periodic inventory system. Antique Furniture's cost of inventory is 70% of the sales price.

Apr 3	Sold $2,100 of merchandise on account, terms 1/15, n/45, FOB shipping point. Antique Furniture, Inc. prepaid $50 of shipping costs and added the amount to the customer's invoice.
7	Issued a credit memo to the customer acknowledging the return of $200 of damaged goods.
16	Received payment in full from the customer for the April 3 invoice.

E5-5B. Journalizing inventory purchases, sales, returns, and freight transactions (*Learning Objectives 3, 4, & 7*) 15–20 min.

The following transactions occurred during April 2015 for Sandy Salon Products, Inc.:

Apr 3	Purchased $3,400 of goods on account, terms 1/15, n/30, FOB shipping point.
6	Returned $500 of defective merchandise purchased on April 3.
8	Paid freight charges of $130 for delivery of goods purchased on April 3.
11	Sold $2,800 of inventory to a customer on account, terms 3/15, n/45, FOB shipping point. The cost of the goods was $1,600.
12	Paid amount owed on the April 3 purchase.
18	Granted a $200 sales allowance on the April 11 sale because the goods were the wrong colour.
25	Received payment in full from customer for the April 11 sale.

Requirement

1. Journalize all necessary transactions for Sandy Salon Products, Inc. using (1) the perpetual inventory system, and (2) the periodic inventory system. Omit explanations.

E5-6B. Calculate multi-step income statement items (*Learning Objective 5*) 10–15 min.

Consider the following incomplete table of a merchandiser's profit data:

Sales	Sales Discounts	Net Sales	Cost of Goods Sold	Gross Profit
$ (a)	$1,700	$ (b)	$67,500	$37,700
89,600	2,900	(c)	55,700	(d)
103,000	(e)	94,300	(f)	31,500
(g)	1,400	88,000	51,900	(h)

Requirement

1. Complete the table by computing the missing amounts.

E5-7B. Prepare a single-step income statement (*Learning Objective 5*) 10–15 min.

The account balances for Great Gadget, Inc. for the year ended December 31, 2015, are presented next in random order:

Cash	$ 9,300	Cost of Goods Sold	$135,000
Equipment	39,800	Accumulated Depreciation,	
Accounts Payable	6,300	Equipment	13,700
Common Shares	25,000	Unearned Revenues	1,900
Long-Term Notes Payable	35,000	Sales Revenue	257,000
General Expenses	18,200	Accounts Receivable	4,500
Wages Payable	1,300	Accumulated Depreciation,	
Supplies	3,300	Building	25,900
Building	130,000	Mortgage Payable	
Sales Returns and		(Long-Term)	43,500
Allowances	2,900	Dividends	41,000
Prepaid Rent	2,600	Sales Discounts	1,500
Retained Earnings	25,700	Selling Expenses	43,500
Inventory	3,700		

Requirements

1. Prepare Great Gadget's *single-step* income statement.

2. Would you recommend the use of the single-step income statement format by a merchandiser? Why?

E5-8B. Prepare a multi-step income statement; calculate gross profit percentage (*Learning Objectives 5 & 6*) 15–20 min.

Use the data for Great Gadget, Inc. from E5-7B.

Requirements

1. Prepare Great Gadget's *multi-step* income statement.

2. Calculate the gross profit percentage.

3. The gross profit percentage for 2014 was 52.3%. Did the gross profit percentage improve or deteriorate during 2015?

E5-9B. Prepare a classified statement of financial position; calculate current ratio (*Learning Objectives 5 & 6*) 15–20 min.

Use the data for Great Gadget, Inc. from E5-7B.

Requirements

1. Prepare Great Gadget's classified statement of financial position. Use the account format. The balance shown for retained earnings represents the balance prior to closing the temporary accounts for the year.

2. Calculate the current ratio.

3. The current ratio for 2014 was 3.62. Did the current ratio improve or deteriorate during 2015?

E5-10B. Calculate gross profit percentage and current ratio (*Learning Objective 6*) 10–15 min.

Sunny Day Sunlamps, Inc. had sales revenue of $53 million, sales returns and allowances of $2 million, and sales discounts of $0.3 million in 2015. Cost of goods sold was $23 million, and net income was $12 million for the year. At December 31, the company had total assets of $33 million, of which total current assets amounted to $13 million. Sunny Day Sunlamps' current liabilities were $7 million and its long-term liabilities were $4 million.

Requirement

1. Compute Sunny Day Sunlamps' gross profit percentage and current ratio for 2015.

EXERCISES (ALTERNATES 1, 2, AND 3)

These alternative exercise sets are available for your practice benefit on
MyAccountingLab.

PROBLEMS (GROUP A)

P5-1A. Journalizing inventory purchases, returns, and freight transactions (*Learning Objective 3 & 7*) 15–20 min.

The following purchase-related transactions for Axiom, Inc. occurred during the month of February.

Feb 3	Purchased $5,400 of merchandise, paid cash.
9	Purchased $650 of supplies on account from Supplies Unlimited, terms n/30, FOB destination.
16	Purchased $6,800 of merchandise on account from A to Z, Inc., terms 2/15, n/30, FOB shipping point.
22	Received a credit memo in the amount of $1,200 from A to Z, Inc. for damaged goods from the February 16 purchase that were returned.
28	Paid for the supplies purchased on February 9.
28	Paid A to Z, Inc. in full for the February 16 purchase.

Requirement

1. Journalize all necessary transactions for Axiom, Inc. using (1) the perpetual inventory system, and (2) the periodic inventory system. Omit explanations.

P5-2A. Journalizing inventory sales, returns, and freight transactions (*Learning Objectives 4 & 7*) 15–20 min.

The following sales-related transactions for Brunswick Hardware, Inc. occurred during the month of April.

Apr 3	Sold $4,200 (cost $2,000) of merchandise on account to P. William. Terms, 2/15, n/45, FOB destination.
4	Paid $120 to ship the goods sold on April 3 to P. William.
10	Sold $2,100 (cost $900) of merchandise to cash customers.
17	Received payment in full from P. William for the April 3 sale.
22	Sold $4,700 (cost $2,800) of merchandise on account to S. Fraser. Terms, 2/10, n/30, FOB shipping point.
26	Granted S. Fraser a $700 allowance on the April 22 sale due to minor defects in the goods shipped.
30	Received payment in full from S. Fraser for the April 22 sale.

Requirement

1. Journalize the transactions for Brunswick Hardware, Inc. using (a) the perpetual inventory system, and (b) the periodic inventory system. Omit explanations.

P5-3A. Journalizing inventory purchases, sales, returns, and freight transactions (*Learning Objectives 3, 4, & 7*) 20–25 min.

The following transactions occurred between Kinzer Furniture and M & L Furniture Warehouse during May of the current year:

May 4	Kinzer Furniture purchased $5,800 of merchandise from M & L Furniture Warehouse on account, terms 2/15, n/30, FOB shipping point. The goods cost M & L Furniture Warehouse $3,300.
7	Kinzer Furniture paid a $125 freight bill for delivery of the goods purchased on May 4.
10	Kinzer Furniture returned $1,400 of the merchandise purchased on May 4. The goods cost M & L Furniture Warehouse $800.
18	Kinzer Furniture paid $2,000 of the May 4 invoice less the discount.
31	Kinzer Furniture paid the remaining amount owed on the May 4 invoice.

Requirements

1. Journalize all necessary transactions for Kinzer Furniture, using
   a. The perpetual inventory system
   b. The periodic inventory system
2. Journalize these transactions on the books of M & L Furniture Warehouse, using
   a. The perpetual inventory system
   b. The periodic inventory system

Omit explanations.

P5-4A. Journalizing inventory purchases, sales, returns, and freight transactions; calculate gross profit (*Learning Objectives 3, 4, & 7*) 25–30 min.

The following transactions for Liberty Tire, Co. occurred during October:

Oct 4	Purchased $5,900 of merchandise on account from Firerock Tire, terms 2/15, n/45, FOB shipping point. Firerock Tire prepaid the $300 shipping cost and added the amount to the invoice.
7	Purchased $350 of supplies on account from Office Maxx, terms 2/10, n/30, FOB destination.
9	Sold $975 (cost, $500) of merchandise on account to L. Simpson, terms 3/15, n/45, FOB destination.
11	Paid $75 freight charges to deliver goods to L. Simpson.
13	Returned $1,400 of the merchandise purchased on October 4 and received a credit.
15	Sold $650 (cost, $350) of merchandise to cash customers.
16	Paid for the supplies purchased on October 7.
18	Paid Firerock Tire the amount due from the October 4 purchase in full.
20	L. Simpson returned $175 (cost, $100) of merchandise from the October 9 sale.
22	Purchased $2,100 of inventory. Paid cash.
23	Received payment in full from L. Simpson for the October 9 sale.

Quick solution:
2. Gross Profit for the month of October = $651.75.

Requirements

1. Journalize the transactions on the books of Liberty Tire, Co. using
   a. the perpetual inventory system.
   b. the periodic inventory system.
2. What was Liberty Tire's gross profit for the month of October?

P5-5A. Prepare a multi-step income statement; calculate gross profit percentage (*Learning Objectives 5 & 6*) 20–25 min.

The adjusted trial balance for Sparky's Electrical Supply, Inc. as of November 30, 2015, is presented next:

Sparky's Electrical Supply, Inc.
Trial Balance
November 30, 2015

ACCOUNT	DEBIT	CREDIT
Cash	$ 15,000	
Accounts Receivable	37,300	
Inventory	18,500	
Supplies	900	
Equipment	68,000	
Accumulated Depreciation, Equipment		$ 8,000
Accounts Payable		12,900
Unearned Sales Revenue		5,300
Note Payable, Long-Term		15,000
Common Shares		10,000
Retained Earnings		73,300
Dividends	22,000	
Sales Revenue		193,200
Sales Returns and Allowances	8,700	
Sales Discounts	2,600	
Cost of Goods Sold	103,400	
Selling Expense	25,200	
General Expense	16,100	
Total	$317,700	$317,700

Requirements

1. Prepare the multi-step income statement for November for Sparky's Electrical Supply, Inc.
2. Calculate the gross profit percentage for November for Sparky's Electrical Supply, Inc.
3. What does Sparky's Electrical Supply, Inc.'s gross profit percentage mean?

P5-6A. Prepare a multi-step income statement, a statement of retained earnings, and a classified statement of financial position (*Learning Objective 5*) 25–30 min.

The account balances for the year ended December 31, 2015, for Williams Industries are listed next:

Sales Revenue	$322,800	Cost of Goods Sold	$158,400
Equipment	104,000	Accumulated Depreciation,	
Accounts Payable	16,500	Equipment	26,400
Sales Discounts	2,200	Unearned Sales Revenue	2,500
Advertising Expense	12,600	Prepaid Rent	1,200
Interest Expense	1,700	Office Salaries Expense	52,000
Wages Payable	1,600	Accumulated Depreciation,	
Accounts Receivable	6,900	Building	40,500
Building	140,000	Rent Expense	5,800
Sales Returns and		Dividends	14,000
Allowances	6,700	Cash	7,800
Common Shares	35,000	Retained Earnings	87,600
Utilities Expense	10,300	Delivery Expense	1,300
Inventory	16,400	Insurance Expense	5,700
Commission Expense	22,300	Mortgage Payable	
Supplies	600	(Long-Term)	37,000

Requirements

1. Prepare Williams' Industries' *multi-step* income statement.

2. Prepare Williams' Industries' statement of retained earnings.

3. Prepare Williams' Industries' classified statement of financial position in *report form*.

P5-7A. Calculate gross profit percentage and current ratio (*Learning Objective 6*) 20–25 min.

Using the data from P5-6A above:

Requirements

1. Calculate the gross profit percentage for Williams Industries for the year.

2. The gross profit percentage for 2014 was 51.3%. Did the gross profit percentage improve or deteriorate during 2015?

3. Calculate the current ratio for Williams Industries.

4. The current ratio for 2014 was 1.47. Did the current ratio improve or deteriorate during 2015?

PROBLEMS (GROUP B)

P5-1B. Journalizing inventory purchases, returns, and freight transactions (*Learning Objectives 3 & 7*) 15–20 min.

The following purchase-related transactions for Lavery, Inc. occurred during the month of September.

Sep 3	Purchased $5,100 of merchandise, paid cash.
9	Purchased $800 of supplies on account from Chandler Unlimited, terms n/30, FOB destination.
16	Purchased $4,300 of merchandise on account from Garden Supplies, Inc., terms 3/15, n/30, FOB shipping point.
22	Received a credit memo in the amount of $1,100 from Garden Supplies, Inc. for damaged goods from the September 16 purchase that were returned.
30	Paid for the supplies purchased on September 9.
30	Paid Garden Supplies, Inc. in full for the September 16 purchase.

Requirement

1. Journalize all necessary transactions for Lavery, Inc. using (1) the perpetual inventory system, and (2) the periodic inventory system. Omit explanations.

P5-2B. Journalizing inventory sales, returns, and freight transactions (*Learning Objectives 4 & 7*) 15–20 min.

The following sales-related transactions for Budget Decor, Inc., occurred during the month of April:

Apr 3	Sold $3,200 (cost $1,400) of merchandise on account to B. Levin. Terms, 1/15, n/45, FOB destination.
4	Paid $85 to ship the goods sold on April 3 to B. Levin.
10	Sold $2,300 (cost $1,025) of merchandise to cash customers.
17	Received payment in full from B. Levin for the April 3 sale.
22	Sold $4,800 (cost $2,800) of merchandise on account to A. Klecans. Terms, 2/10, n/30, FOB shipping point.
26	Granted A. Klecans a $900 allowance on the April 22 sale due to minor defects in the goods shipped.
30	Received payment in full from A. Klecans for the April 22 sale.

Requirement

1. Journalize all necessary transactions for Budget Decor, Inc. using (a) the perpetual inventory system, and (b) the periodic inventory system. Omit explanations.

P5-3B. Journalizing inventory purchases, sales, returns, and freight transactions (*Learning Objectives 3, 4, & 7*) 20–25 min.

The following transactions occurred between Retro Furniture and E & S Furniture Warehouse during October of the current year:

Oct 4	Retro Furniture purchased $8,000 of merchandise from E & S Furniture Warehouse on account, terms 1/15, n/30. FOB shipping point. The goods cost E & S Furniture Warehouse $2,900.
7	Retro Furniture paid a $200 freight bill for delivery of the goods purchased on October 4.
10	Retro Furniture returned $1,000 of the merchandise purchased on October 4. The goods cost E & S Furniture Warehouse $450.
18	Retro Furniture paid $2,000 of the October 4 invoice less the discount.
31	Retro Furniture paid the remaining amount owed on the October 4 invoice.

Requirements

1. Journalize all necessary transactions for Retro Furniture, using

    a. The perpetual inventory system

    b. The periodic inventory system

2. Journalize these transactions on the books of E & S Furniture Warehouse, using

    a. The perpetual inventory system

    b. The periodic inventory system

P5-4B. Journalizing inventory purchases, sales, returns, and freight transactions; calculate gross profit (*Learning Objectives 3, 4, 5, & 7*) 25–30 min.

The following transactions for Best Deal Tire, Co. occurred during May:

May 4	Purchased $5,400 of merchandise on account from Bargain Tire, terms 3/15, n/45, FOB shipping point. Bargain Tire prepaid the $125 shipping cost and added the amount to the invoice.
7	Purchased $400 of supplies on account from Office Maxx, terms 3/10, n/30, FOB destination.
9	Sold $975 (cost, $250) of merchandise on account to W. Furmick, terms 3/15, n/45, FOB destination.
11	Paid $25 freight charges to deliver goods to W. Furmick.
13	Returned $600 of the merchandise purchased on May 4 and received a credit.
15	Sold $900 (cost, $350) of merchandise to cash customers.
16	Paid for the supplies purchased on May 7.
18	Paid Bargain Tire the amount due from the May 4 purchase in full.
20	W. Furmick returned $175 (cost, $100) of merchandise from the May 9 sale.
22	Purchased $3,900 of inventory. Paid cash.
23	Received payment in full from W. Furmick for the May 9 sale.

Requirements

1. Journalize the transactions on the books of Best Deal Tire, Co. using (1) the perpetual inventory system, and (2) the periodic inventory system.

2. What was Best Deal Tire's gross profit for the month of May?

P5-5B. Prepare a multi-step income statement; calculate gross profit percentage (*Learning Objectives 5 & 6*) 20–25 min.

The adjusted trial balance for CED Electric, Inc. as of June 30, 2015, is presented next:

CED Electric, Inc.
Trial Balance
June 30, 2015

ACCOUNT	DEBIT	CREDIT
Cash	$ 13,600	
Accounts Receivable	32,600	
Inventory	19,600	
Supplies	2,600	
Equipment	69,000	
Accumulated Depreciation, Equipment		$ 13,700
Accounts Payable		5,100
Unearned Sales Revenue		2,800
Note Payable, Long-Term		40,000
Common Shares		25,000
Retained Earnings		68,200
Dividends	48,000	
Sales Revenue		197,500
Sales Returns and Allowances	4,800	
Sales Discount	3,100	
Cost of Goods Sold	101,400	
Selling Expense	37,000	
General Expense	20,600	
Total	$352,300	$352,300

Requirements

1. Prepare the multi-step income statement for June for CED Electric, Inc.
2. Calculate the gross profit percentage for June for CED Electric, Inc.
3. What does CED Electric Inc.'s gross profit percentage mean?

P5-6B. Prepare a multi-step income statement, a statement of retained earnings, and a classified statement of financial position (*Learning Objective 5*) 25–30 min.

The accounts for the year ended March 31, 2015, for Clark Industries, Inc. are listed next:

Sales Revenue..........................	$275,100	Cost of Goods Sold................	$119,000
Equipment...............................	27,000	Accumulated Depreciation,	
Accounts Payable....................	16,500	Equipment..........................	13,000
Sales Discounts	2,500	Unearned Sales Revenue	2,500
Advertising Expense...............	11,500	Prepaid Rent	5,000
Interest Expense	700	Office Salaries Expense..........	54,000
Wages Payable........................	1,000	Accumulated Depreciation,	
Accounts Receivable..............	8,800	Building..............................	52,500
Building..................................	190,000	Rent Expense	5,200
Sales Returns and		Dividends..............................	12,000
Allowances........................	4,900	Cash......................................	22,500
Common Shares	35,000	Retained Earnings..................	112,800
Utilities Expense.....................	14,000	Delivery Expense....................	1,200
Inventory................................	29,000	Insurance Expense.................	10,200
Commission Expense.............	31,700	Mortgage Payable	
Supplies.................................	1,200	(Long-Term)	42,000

Requirements

1. Prepare Clark Industries' *multi-step* income statement.
2. Prepare Clark Industries' statement of retained earnings.
3. Prepare Clark Industries' classified statement of financial position in *report form*.

P5-7B. Calculate gross profit percentage and current ratio (*Learning Objective 6*)
20–25 min.

Using the data from P5-6B above:

Requirements

1. Calculate the gross profit percentage for Clark Industries for the year.
2. The gross profit percentage for 2014 was 39.1%. Did the gross profit percentage improve or deteriorate during 2015?
3. Calculate the current ratio for Clark Industries.
4. The current ratio for 2014 was 2.33. Did the current ratio improve or deteriorate during 2015?

PROBLEMS (ALTERNATES 1, 2, AND 3)

These alternative problem sets are available for your practice benefit on **MyAccountingLab**.

CONTINUING EXERCISE

Let's continue our accounting for Graham's Yard Care, Inc. from Chapter 3. Starting in July, Graham's Yard Care, Inc. has begun selling plants that it purchases from a wholesaler. During July, Graham's Yard Care, Inc. completed the following transactions:

Jul	2	Completed lawn service and received cash of $500.
	5	Purchased 100 plants on account for inventory, $250, plus freight in of $10.
	15	Sold 40 plants on account, $400 (cost $104).
	17	Consulted with a client on landscaping design for a fee of $150 on account.
	20	Purchased 100 plants on account for inventory, $300.
	21	Paid on account, $100.
	25	Sold 100 plants for cash, $700 (cost $276).
	31	Recorded the following adjusting entries: Accrued salaries for the month of July equal $225 Depreciation on equipment $30 Physical count of plant inventory, 50 plants (cost $150)

Refer to the T-accounts for Graham's Yard Care, Inc. from the Continuing Exercise in Chapter 3.

Requirements

1. Journalize and post the July transactions using the perpetual inventory system. Omit explanations. Compute each account balance, and denote the balance as *Bal*. Open additional accounts as necessary.
2. Prepare the July income statement of Graham's Yard Care, Inc. using the single-step format.

CONTINUING PROBLEM

In this problem, we continue the accounting for Aqua Elite, Inc. from Chapter 3. On August 1, Aqua Elite, Inc. expanded its business and began selling and installing swimming pools and spas. The post-closing trial balance for Aqua Elite, Inc. as of July 31, 2015, is presented next.

Aqua Elite, Inc. Trial Balance July 31, 2015		
ACCOUNT	DEBIT	CREDIT
Cash	$17,380	
Accounts Receivable	5,400	
Supplies	350	
Prepaid Rent	3,600	
Land	15,000	
Furniture	3,300	
Accumulated Depreciation, Furniture		$ 210
Equipment	4,700	
Accumulated Depreciation, Equipment		400
Vehicles	31,000	
Accumulated Depreciation, Vehicles		650
Accounts Payable		1,840
Salaries Payable		675
Unearned Service Revenue		2,800
Notes Payable		31,000
Common Shares		38,500
Retained Earnings		4,655
Total	$80,730	$80,730

The following transactions occurred during the month of August:

Aug 2	Paid the receptionist's salary, which was accrued on July 31.
3	Purchased $20,600 of merchandise on account from the Spa Superstore, terms 3/15, n/45, FOB shipping point.
5	Purchased $750 of supplies. Paid cash.
6	Paid freight charges of $475 related to the August 3 purchase.
8	Sold a spa for $5,800 (cost, $3,600) on account to R. Tanaka, terms 2/15, n/30, FOB shipping point.
10	Purchased office furniture for $1,200. Paid cash.
11	Paid advertising expense, $625.
12	Returned a defective spa, which was purchased on August 3. Received a $3,400 credit from the Spa Superstore.
13	Sold a spa for $6,750 (cost, $3,360) to a cash customer.
15	Granted R. Tanaka a $300 allowance because of imperfections she detected upon receiving her spa.
16	Paid receptionist's salary, $675.
17	Paid the Spa Superstore the amount due from the August 3 purchase in full.
19	Purchased $12,100 of inventory on account from Pool Universe, terms 2/10, n/30, FOB destination.
21	Sold an above-ground pool for $13,700 (cost, $8,500) on account to B. Wagoner, terms 2/10, n/30, FOB destination.
22	Received payment in full from R. Tanaka for the August 8 sale.
24	Paid freight charges of $560 to have the pool sold to B. Wagoner on August 21 delivered.

25	Purchased equipment on account from Betterbuy, Inc. for $2,600, terms n/30, FOB destination.
27	Received payment in full from B. Wagoner for the August 21 sale.
28	Paid in full the invoice from the August 19 purchase from Pool Universe.
30	Paid monthly utilities, $850.
31	Paid sales commissions of $1,300 to the sales staff.

Requirements

1. Journalize the transactions that occurred in August, using the perpetual inventory system.

2. Using the four-column accounts from the continuing problem in Chapter 3, post the transactions to the ledger creating new ledger accounts as necessary; omit posting references. Calculate the new account balances.

3. Prepare the unadjusted trial balance for Aqua Elite, Inc. at the end of August.

4. Journalize and post the adjusting entries for August based on the following adjustment information.

   a. Record the expired rent, $1800.

   b. Supplies on hand, $445.

   c. Depreciation: $575 equipment, $380 furniture, $650 vehicles.

   d. A physical count of inventory revealed $13,387 of inventory on hand.

5. Prepare an adjusted trial balance for Aqua Elite, Inc. at the end of August.

6. Prepare the multi-step income statement, statement of retained earnings, and classified statement of financial position for the month of August.

7. Prepare and post closing entries.

8. Prepare a post-closing trial balance for the end of the period.

APPLY YOUR KNOWLEDGE

ETHICS IN ACTION

Case 1. Tim Jackson works as a salesperson at Conway, Inc. In addition to a base monthly salary, Tim receives a commission that is based on the amount of sales that he makes during the month. Tim was hoping to have enough money for a down payment on a new car but sales have been low due to a downturn in the economy. Tim was aware that Conway, Inc. granted credit terms of 2/10, n/30 to its credit customers. In addition, Tim knew that Conway, Inc. had a "no questions asked" return policy. Based on this knowledge, Tim had an idea. Tim contacted a regular customer and convinced the customer to make a substantial purchase of merchandise so that he could earn the commission on the sale. Tim explained to the customer that they would not have to pay for the goods for thirty days and that they could return part, or all, of the goods prior to paying for them. However, Tim asked the customer not to return any of the goods until the following month to ensure that he would earn the full commission.

Requirements

1. Do you feel Tim acted unethically? Why or why not?

2. How can Conway, Inc. deter actions like Tim's?

Case 2. Tina Adams owns and operates the Cottage Café. Tina has requested a credit application from UMT, Inc., a major food supplier that she hopes to begin purchasing inventory from. UMT, Inc. has requested that Tina submit a full set of financial statements for the Cottage Café with the credit application. Tina is concerned because the most recent statement of financial position for the Cottage Café reflects a current ratio of 1.24. Tina has heard that most creditors like to see a current ratio that is 1.5 or higher. To increase the Cottage Café's current ratio, Tina has convinced her parents to loan the business $25,000 on an 18-month long-term note payable. Tina's parents are apprehensive about having their money "tied up" for over a year. Tina reassured them that even though the note is an 18-month note, the Cottage Café can, and probably will, repay the $25,000 sooner.

Requirements

1. Discuss the ethical issues related to the loan from Tina's parents.
2. Why do you think creditors like to see current ratios of 1.5 or higher?

KNOW YOUR BUSINESS

FINANCIAL ANALYSIS

Purpose: To help familiarize you with the financial reporting of a real company to further your understanding of the chapter material you are learning.

This case uses both the income statement (statement of operations) and the statement of financial position of Bombardier Inc. in MyAccountingLab.

Requirements

1. What income statement format does Bombardier Inc. use? How can you tell?
2. Calculate the gross profit ratio for Bombardier Inc. for 2012 and 2011. Has the gross profit rate improved or deteriorated? (Hints on how this is calculated were provided in Chapter 2 questions.)
3. Does Bombardier Inc. report a classified statement of financial position? How can you tell? Why do you think Bombardier reports the statement of financial position in this manner?

INDUSTRY ANALYSIS

Purpose: To help you understand and compare the performance of two companies in the same industry.

Find the Bombardier Annual Report located in MyAccountingLab and go to the financial statements. Now access the 2012 annual report for The Boeing Company. To do this from the internet, go to their webpage for the Investor Relations at http://www.boeing.com/companyoffices/financial/quarterly.htm and, under Financial Information, go to the 4th Quarter & Full-Year Results 2012.

Requirements

1. Calculate the current ratio for Boeing for 2012 and 2011. Has the current ratio improved or deteriorated?
2. Which of these companies is also involved in providing customer financing? How did you determine this? Which accounts on the consolidated statements of financial position indicate this?

SMALL BUSINESS ANALYSIS

Purpose: To help you understand the importance of cash flows in the operation of a small business.

The end of the year is approaching. You're going to meet with your CPA next week to do some end-of-the-year tax planning, so in preparation for that meeting you look at your last month's income statement. You know that you've had a pretty good year, which means that you're going to have to pay some income taxes. But you know if you can get your taxable income down, you won't have to pay as much in income taxes.

You remember that one of your suppliers was offering a pretty good discount if you purchased from the company in bulk. The only problem is you have to pay for the purchases at the time of purchase. Knowing that you want to decrease your taxable income, you call up the supplier and place a large order and write the supplier a cheque.

At your meeting with the CPA, you tell of the large inventory purchase for cash that you just made and how much income tax that will save you on this year's income tax return. The CPA has a rather troubled look on his face; that look usually means you've made some kind of an error. So you pose this question to him:

"Steve, you got that look on your face right after I told you about the big inventory purchase that I made. Even though I used up a lot of my available cash, the reason I did it was to save money on my tax return. A big purchase like that has to knock down my taxable income pretty good, huh? And besides, I got these products for a really good price, which means I'll make more profit when I sell them. So why do you have that look? Did I mess up?"

Requirement

1. If you were the CPA, how would you respond to this client? Is the large inventory purchase going to have any effect on his income statement? What about the fact that he paid for this large purchase in cash? Was that a good idea to use a large portion of available cash for a purchase like this? Keeping in mind that inventory can have a significant amount of carrying cost (storage, personnel, opportunity cost of the money, etc.) would you tell your client that this was a good thing that he did, or not?

WRITTEN COMMUNICATION

You just got a letter from one of your good customers complaining about the shipment of your product that he or she just received. Football season is approaching and the customer had ordered a large shipment of regulation size footballs. Instead, he or she received youth size footballs for half of the order. The customer is asking you what can be done about this mistake. Knowing that this client is located halfway across the country, it's not feasible to just have him or her drop by your facility and trade the footballs.

The customer also had a question about a line item on his or her invoice under shipping terms. It said FOB Destination and the customer noticed that he or she was charged freight, which the customer normally doesn't have to pay. The customer wants to know if that is correct.

Requirement

1. Write a letter to your customer explaining how you intend to handle this purchase return or this purchase allowance (you choose which one you're going to do). Explain the accounting forms that will need to be prepared to document this transaction. Also address the customer's concern about the shipping terms.

Self Check Answers
1. d 2. a 3. b 4. d 5. a 6. a 7. d 8. b 9. c 10. a

Appendix 5A

HOW DO YOU ACCOUNT FOR MERCHANDISING TRANSACTIONS USING A PERIODIC INVENTORY SYSTEM?

L.O. 7 Explain how a business accounts for transactions using the periodic inventory system

As mentioned earlier in this chapter, a periodic inventory system of accounting for inventory does not keep a continuous, running record of inventory as it is bought and sold. Instead, the business physically counts the goods in inventory at the end of the accounting period. It then multiplies the quantity of each item by its cost to get the total value of the ending inventory. Once the ending inventory has been determined, a business will calculate the cost of the inventory it has sold during the period.

Accordingly a business implementing a periodic inventory system would not use an Inventory account; rather, it would use a Purchases account. Such a system would not provide the balance of inventory at any point in time except when a physical count is done. Since the periodic inventory does not require constant updating of the inventory level, we use separate accounts for recording purchases, purchase returns and allowances, transportation-in, and purchase discounts. To illustrate, let's use the same example that is used in the chapter and apply a periodic inventory system.

Cosmic Cellular purchases 300 cell phone cases from Accessories Unlimited on account at a cost of $25 each. Therefore, the total value of Cosmic's purchase is $7,500 (300 cases × $25). Cosmic Cellular receives the goods on February 1 and records this purchase as follows:

DATE	ACCOUNTS	DR.	CR.
Feb 1	Purchases	7,500	
	Accounts Payable—Accessories Unlimited		7,500
	Record purchase of inventory on account.		

Using the periodic inventory system, a purchase of inventory does not increase assets, as the Inventory account is not updated. Instead, the Purchases account, which is one of the cost of goods sold accounts, is increased. This amount will be used to calculate the overall cost of goods sold for the period. The periodic system does not track changes for each single item, and hence, an inventory subsidiary ledger is not needed. If Cosmic Cellular paid cash instead for the merchandise, Accounts Payable will be substituted with Cash in the previous entry.

Purchase Returns and Allowances

Suppose Cosmic Cellular buys 20 hands-free headsets for $20 each from Mega Mobile, and these headsets become damaged in shipment. If Cosmic returns the merchandise to Mega Mobile the following entry is required:

DATE	ACCOUNTS	DR.	CR.
Apr 5	Accounts Payable—Mega Mobile	400	
	Purchase Returns and Allowances		400
	Record inventory returned to manufacturer.		

The invoice from Accessories Unlimited shows credit terms of 3/15, n/30. If Cosmic Cellular pays within the discount period, it will pay $7,275, or 97% of the purchase invoice amount of $7,500. Cosmic records its payment on February 13, which is within the discount period, as shown:

DATE	ACCOUNTS	DR.	CR.
Feb 13	Accounts Payable—Accessories Unlimited	7,500	
	Cash		7,275
	Purchase Discount		225
	Record payment of inventory purchases within the discount period.		

Assets	=	Liabilities	+	Shareholders' Equity
−7,275		−7,500		+225

Using the periodic inventory system, the discount taken is credited directly to the Purchase Discount account, a contra-purchases account.

If Cosmic Cellular pays this invoice after the discount period, it pays the full amount of $7,500. In this case, it records the payment as follows:

DATE	ACCOUNTS	DR.	CR.
Feb 13	Accounts Payable—Accessories Unlimited	7,500	
	Cash		7,500
	Record payment of inventory purchases after the discount period.		

Assets	=	Liabilities	+	Shareholders' Equity
−7,500		−7,500		

Costs Related to the Receipt of Goods from Suppliers

Suppose Cosmic Cellular incurs shipping costs related to the purchase of merchandise (FOB shipping point) from Accessories Unlimited. Cosmic pays $60 to the carrier for the February 1 shipment. Cosmic Cellular's entry to record payment of the shipping charge is as follows:

DATE	ACCOUNTS	DR.	CR.
Feb 1	Transportation-In	60	
	Cash		60
	Record payment of shipping bill for the February 1 purchase.		

Assets	=	Liabilities	+	Shareholders' Equity
−60				−60

Notice that the shipping cost is recorded in the Transportation-in account, which is one of the cost of goods sold accounts.

Let's see how Cosmic records the following purchase transactions. On July 15, Cosmic buys $1,000 of goods on account from CellTel, Inc. The terms of the purchase are 2/10, n/30, FOB shipping point. CellTel prepaid $80 of shipping costs and added the charges to the invoice for an invoice total of $1,080. Cosmic then returns $100 of these goods for credit on July 20. On July 25, Cosmic makes payment in full for the purchase. First, Cosmic records the purchase of goods:

DATE	ACCOUNTS	DR.	CR.
Jul 15	Purchases	1,080	
	Accounts Payable—CellTel, Inc.		1,080
	Record purchase of inventory on account.		

Assets	=	Liabilities	+	Shareholders' Equity
		+1,080		−1,080

Next, Cosmic records the return of inventory, as follows:

DATE	ACCOUNTS	DR.	CR.
Jul 20	Accounts Payable—CellTel, Inc.	100	
	Purchase Returns and Allowances		100
	Record inventory returned to the manufacturer.		

Finally, it records the payment for the purchase by calculating the purchase discount and the balance due. Cosmic pays on July 25, which is within the 10-day discount period, so it receives a discount of $18: 2% of the $1,000 original cost of the goods minus $100 of returned goods, or 0.02 × $900.

DATE	ACCOUNTS	DR.	CR.
Jul 25	Accounts Payable—CellTel, Inc.	980	
	($1,000 + $80 − $100)		
	Purchase Discounts [($1,000 − $100) × 0.02]		18
	Cash ($1,000 + $80 − $100 − $18)		962
	Record payment of inventory purchases within the discount period.		

Exhibit 5A-1 summarizes the purchases-related journal entries using the periodic inventory system.

PERIODIC INVENTORY SYSTEM	DR.	CR.
Purchases	xxx	
Accounts Payable		xxx
Record purchase of inventory on account.		
Accounts Payable	xxx	
Purchase Returns and Allowances		xxx
Record inventory returned to manufacturer.		
Transportation-in	xxx	
Cash		xxx
Record payment for transportation		
Accounts Payable	xxx	
Purchase Discounts		xxx
Cash		xxx
Record payment of inventory purchases within the discount period.		

Exhibit 5A-1 ▲

Period-End Cost of Goods Sold and Inventory Adjustments

At the end of the period, companies need to know the amount of cost of goods sold to be able to calculate their profitability during the period. Calculations of cost of goods sold will differ according to the inventory system being implemented. Let's assume that Cosmic Cellular's ledger shows the account balances on December 31, 2015, that are illustrated in **Exhibit 5A-2**. The year-end inventory physical count shows the inventory is $28,000.

Inventory		Purchases		Purchases Returns and Allowances	
Beg. 35,800		80,500			7,500

Purchases Discount		Transportation-in	
	2,500	12,000	

Exhibit 5A-2 ▲

The cost of goods sold is calculated as follows:

Beginning Inventory		$ 35,800
+ Purchases	80,500	
− Purchases Returns and Allowances	(7,500)	
− Purchases Discounts	(2,500)	
+ Tranportation-in	12,000	
= Total Cost of Goods Purchased		82,500
Goods Available for Sale		$ 118,300
− Ending Inventory		(28,000)
= Cost of Goods Sold		$ 90,300

The Cost of Goods Sold and Inventory accounts have not been updated for the entire accounting period. Hence, we need to calculate the cost of goods sold and update the Inventory account balance.

Two period-end adjusting entries are required to close the beginning inventory and all purchase-related accounts to the Cost of Goods Sold account and to update the inventory balance. Once these two entries are recorded, both the Cost of Goods Sold account ($90,300) and Inventory account ($28,000) are updated.

DATE	ACCOUNTS	DR.	CR.
Dec 31	Cost of Goods Sold	128,300	
	Inventory		35,800
	Purchases		80,500
	Transportation-in		12,000
	To close beginning Inventory, Purchases, and Transportation-in to the Cost of Goods Sold account		
Dec 31	Inventory	28,000	
	Purchase Returns and Allowances	7,500	
	Purchase Discounts	2,500	
	Cost of Goods Sold		38,000
	To update ending Inventory, close Purchase Returns and Allowance and Purchase Discount accounts to the Cost of Goods Sold account		

Accounting for the Sale of Inventory

Using the periodic system, Cosmic Cellular only needs to record the sales as they are made, since the reduction of inventory is not updated.

Assume that on June 9, Cosmic Cellular sells $3,000 of merchandise to customers for cash. The goods that Cosmic sold its customers cost Cosmic $1,900. The journal entry to record the sale is as follows:

DATE	ACCOUNTS	DR.	CR.
Jun 9	Cash	3,000	
	Sales Revenue		3,000
	Record sale of inventory for cash.		

Notice that no entry is required to reduce the Inventory and increase the Cost of Goods Sold accounts as was the case under the perpetual system. This is because inventory is not tracked under the periodic system. If the sale was made on account, Accounts Receivable would be debited instead of Cash.

Sales Returns

The credit memo reflects the return of three car chargers, originally purchased for $75, by Jill Harris, a customer. The returned car chargers cost Cosmic $30. Cosmic Cellular records the sales return as follows:

DATE	ACCOUNTS	DR.	CR.
Aug 15	Sales Returns and Allowances	75	
	Accounts Receivable—Jill Harris		75
	Record receipt of returned goods, credit memo no. 14.		

MEMORY TIPS

In a periodic inventory system, COGS is calculated at the end of the period after taking a physical count.

Again, notice that there is no entry to update the Inventory or the Cost of Goods Sold accounts like there was under the perpetual system.

Sales Allowances

Assume that Cosmic Cellular grants credit customer Bill Logan a $100 sales allowance for damaged goods. Cosmic records the sales allowance as follows:

DATE	ACCOUNTS	DR.	CR.
Aug 15	Sales Returns and Allowances	100	
	Accounts Receivable—Bill Logan		100
	Record sales allowance for damaged goods, credit memo no. 15.		

This is the same entry that is made under the perpetual system, since no inventory is being returned to the store.

Cost Related to Delivering Goods to Customers

FOB Destination

Let's assume that Cosmic advertises that shipping costs are free with any purchase of $100 or more. Assume that customer Rob Macklin buys a headset on November 30 and charges it to his account. He asks Cosmic to ship it to Vancouver for him. Cosmic records the sale and payment of shipping costs as follows:

DATE	ACCOUNTS	DR.	CR.
Nov 30	Accounts Receivable—Rob Macklin	100	
	Sales Revenue		100
	Record sale of inventory on account.		

DATE	ACCOUNTS	DR.	CR.
Nov 30	Delivery Expense	15	
	Cash		15
	Record shipping on sale.		

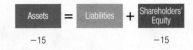

As in other transactions under the periodic system, no entries are made to the Inventory or Cost of Goods accounts.

FOB Shipping Point

Now, let's assume that Cosmic does not offer free shipping. Because Cosmic sold the goods FOB shipping point, Rob pays for the shipping costs. Cosmic would record the sale as follows:

DATE	ACCOUNTS	DR.	CR.
Nov 30	Accounts Receivable—Rob Macklin	100	
	Sales Revenue		100
	Record sale of inventory on account.		

Exhibit 5A-3 summarizes the sales-related journal entries using a periodic inventory system.

ACCOUNTS	DR.	CR.
Accounts Receivable	XXX	
Sales		XXX
To record the sales of inventory.		
Sales Returns and Allowances	XXX	
Accounts Receivable		XXX
Record receipt of returned goods.		
Cash	XXX	
Sales Discounts	XXX	
Accounts Receivable		XXX
Record payment received.		

Exhibit 5A-3 ▲

LEARNING OBJECTIVES

① Describe the three different inventory costing methods

② Compute inventory costs using specific-identification; first-in, first-out (FIFO); and average cost methods and journalize inventory transactions

③ Compare the effects of the different costing methods on the financial statements

④ Value inventory using the lower of cost or net realizable value rule

⑤ Illustrate the reporting of inventory in the financial statements

⑥ Determine the effect of inventory errors on the financial statements

⑦ Use the gross profit method to estimate ending inventory

⑧ Compute the inventory turnover rate

⑨ (Appendix 6A) Compute inventory costs using different methods under a periodic inventory system

CHAPTER 6

Inventory

BUSINESS, ACCOUNTING, AND YOU

Walk down the aisles of a Best Buy store and look at all the products. There are television sets, computers, cameras, computer games, movies, cell phones, MP3 players, and much more—there are literally thousands of items of inventory! Now blink your eyes. What happened? The inventory changed. Customers are constantly buying and removing inventory from Best Buy, and employees are constantly restocking inventory with new items.

Inventory is at the heart of operating a merchandise business. Businesses like Best Buy purchase inventory and plan that customers will buy it at a price above what it cost the business. If this occurs, the business earns net income if they can cover operating expenses. If this does not occur, the business incurs a net loss. Inventory is important and at the centre of creating a return by taking risks.

Now ask yourself: How does Best Buy keep up with its inventory? Who counts the inventory? How does Best Buy figure out the cost of the items sold? How does Best Buy determine the cost of the items that it owns and plans to sell in the future? These concerns are complicated when prices constantly change. Best Buy must have a method to account for the quantity and cost of the thousands of items it buys, owns, and sells. Business is about earning net income, which is simply revenues less costs. How a business accounts for the cost of the items it buys and sells is important. As an accountant or manager, you need to understand how merchandising businesses recognize, measure, record, and report the cost of inventory. It's all about the scorecard of business and figuring out whether the merchandise business is winning or losing; that is, if the business is making a profit or loss.

WHAT INVENTORY COSTING METHODS ARE ALLOWED?

L.O. ❶ Describe the three different inventory costing methods

IFRS
ASPE

As discussed in Chapter 5, merchandise inventory represents the goods that a merchandiser has available to sell to its customers. A manufacturer also has goods it holds for sale to its customers. These goods are called **finished goods** inventory. In addition, a manufacturer maintains two other types of inventory: **raw materials** inventory, which it uses to produce the goods it sells, and **work in process** inventory, which represents partially completed goods. In other words, work in process inventory represents goods that are in the process of becoming finished goods. A more detailed discussion of the inventory accounts of a manufacturer will be left to a managerial or cost accounting course. In this chapter, we focus on managing and accounting for inventory in merchandise businesses. Inventory represents a key asset for a merchandiser and is probably the business's largest current asset.

Recall from Chapter 5 that most companies utilize a perpetual inventory system. Under a perpetual system, the cost of goods purchased is added to the Inventory account in the general ledger when goods are purchased. When the goods are sold, the cost of the goods is removed from the Inventory account and added to the Cost of Goods Sold account. Most merchandisers purchase large quantities of identical items. Due to inflation and other market forces, the cost the merchandiser pays for the items often differs from one purchase to the next. This raises an important accounting dilemma: If the goods are identical, but have different costs, how does the business know which costs to remove from the Inventory account and transfer to Cost of Goods Sold at the time merchandise is sold?

According to IFRS and ASPE, a business can assign costs using one of three different inventory costing methods. The three costing methods allowed by IFRS and ASPE are as follows:

1. **Specific-identification** method—Assumes that the cost assigned to an inventory item when it is sold is the actual cost paid for that specific item. Therefore, the cost of goods sold represents the actual cost of the items that were sold. Also, the ending inventory represents the actual cost of the goods remaining in inventory. Under specific-identification, the cost flow of the goods through the accounting records will *exactly* match the physical flow of the goods through the business. Jewellery stores would use the specific-identification method.

2. **First-in, first-out (FIFO)** method—Assumes that the earliest inventory costs are assigned to items as they are sold. The cost of goods sold represents the oldest costs incurred to purchase inventory items. The ending inventory represents the most recent costs incurred to purchase inventory items. Walmart values its inventory using FIFO.

3. **Average cost** method—Assumes that an average cost per item of the entire inventory purchased is assigned to items as they are sold. Two types of average cost can be used, depending on whether the company utilizes a perpetual inventory system (moving average cost) or a periodic inventory system (weighted average cost). Both the cost of goods sold and the ending inventory represent an average of the cost incurred to purchase inventory items. Under the average cost method, the cost of goods sold does not match the physical flow of goods, but the method smooths the cost fluctuations. Nestle uses the weighted average cost method to account for most of its inventories.

ACCOUNTING IN YOUR WORLD

Jill was at the grocery store the other day picking up a container of milk when she started thinking about FIFO, which she had been learning about in her accounting class. It did not make sense to her that any customer would want the company to use FIFO. After all, she reasoned, if the grocery store used FIFO, it would be selling milk that it purchased a while ago and would leave fresh milk on the shelves. Jill wonders how she can be sure that the container of milk she took off the shelf is fresh and not one that has been on the shelf for weeks, or even months.

Jill is confusing the flow of costs through the accounting records with the physical flow of inventory through a store. Accountants are *assuming* that the first bags of milk the company receives are also the first bags of milk that the company sells, even though that may not be what is actually happening on the shelves. The flow of costs through the accounting records can match, or be exactly opposite of, the physical flow of goods through a store. Jill can rest assured that even if the store uses FIFO, her milk is fresh.

Does this taste funny to you?

COST FLOW VERSUS PHYSICAL FLOW OF INVENTORY

The inventory costing method (FIFO, weighted average, etc.) is an assumption about the flow of costs through a merchandiser's accounting records rather than about the physical flow of the goods through the business. The physical flow of the goods through the business will depend on how the goods are stocked and in what order customers, or employees, remove the goods from the shelves when they are sold. The flow of the *costs* through the accounting records will depend upon which inventory costing method the business chooses.

Imagine that every inventory item that is purchased has a yellow sticky note attached to it with the price that was paid for the item written on the sticky note. Next, assume that when the business receives a shipment of inventory items, the sticky notes reflecting the cost of the items are removed from each item and given to the accounting department. The accounting department will keep track of the sticky notes for each separate purchase in what is referred to as an **inventory layer**. The quantity purchased of each item along with the purchase price is tracked as an inventory layer for every separate purchase.

The physical inventory will most likely be managed in a manner that causes the oldest inventory to be sold first, followed by more recent purchases, and so on. The physical flow of the inventory is maintained in this manner to prevent inventory items from spoiling if they are perishable, or to prevent having items that look outdated should the manufacturer choose to change the packaging of the items. The accounting department calculates the cost flow of the inventory without any consideration of the actual physical flow of the merchandise (unless the specific-identification inventory method is used). The accounting department only needs to know *how many* units were sold, not *which* units were sold. The accounting department then applies the cost flow method to the inventory layers that it has recorded. In other words, the inventory costs are assigned based on the layers of sticky notes. **Exhibit 6-1** demonstrates the difference between cost flow and physical flow.

6.1 **STILL** DON'T GET IT?
Visit MyAccountingLab for an alternate explanation of this important accounting concept.

Exhibit 6-1 ▲

 DECISION GUIDELINES

DECISION

The cost of my products will determine the price that I can sell them for as well as impact other decisions. How do I determine the cost of the inventory I sell?

GUIDELINE

The physical flow of the inventory and the cost flow of the inventory can be different. The cost assigned to the units sold may be based on one of the following three methods:

• Specific-identification
• First-in, first-out (FIFO)
• Average cost

ANALYZE

Specific-identification: Inventory items are specifically labelled or identified and the actual cost of each item sold is assigned to cost of goods sold.

First-in, first-out (FIFO): The first inventory costs incurred are the first costs to be assigned to cost of goods sold.

Average cost: After each purchase of inventory, a new weighted-average cost per unit is computed and assigned to cost of goods sold.

HOW ARE THE THREE INVENTORY COSTING METHODS APPLIED?

INVENTORY COST FLOWS

L.O. ❷ Compute inventory costs using specific-identification; first-in, first-out (FIFO); and average cost methods and journalize inventory transactions

Recollect from Chapter 5 that, in a perpetual inventory system, purchases of goods for resale increase the balance of the Inventory account, while sales of goods to customers decrease the account. The Inventory account also reflects purchase discounts, purchase returns and allowances, and shipping costs related to the purchase of goods:

Inventory			
Bal	XX		
Purchases	XX	Purchase Discounts	XX
Shipping	XX	Purchase Returns and Allowances	XX
		Sales	XX
Bal	XX		

The cost of the inventory flows through the Inventory account as items are purchased and sold. The cost of the units on hand in inventory at the beginning of the period is added to the net cost of units purchased for the period to determine the **cost of goods available for sale**. The objective of tracking the inventory cost is to allocate the cost of the goods available for sale between the following:

- Units sold, which is recorded as Cost of Goods Sold and is subtracted from net sales revenue on the income statement to arrive at gross profit.

- Units on hand, or unsold, which is reflected as ending inventory, a current asset on the statement of financial position.

Let's follow the September inventory activity for ski parkas sold by Northwest Outfitters, Inc. assuming the following:

Sep 1	One parka costing $40 is on hand, unsold from the previous month.
5	Purchased six parkas for $45 each.
15	Sold four parkas for $80 each.
26	Purchased seven parkas for $50 each.
30	Sold eight parkas for $80 each.
30	Two parkas are on hand, unsold.

During September, Northwest Outfitters had 14 parkas available for sale: 1 unit on hand in beginning inventory plus 13 units purchased during the month. Northwest Outfitters' goods available for sale would be calculated as follows:

Beginning Inventory	1 @ $40	= $ 40
+ Purchases	6 @ $45 = $270	
	7 @ $50 = 350	620
= Goods Available for Sale	14	$660

Of the 14 parkas available for sale, Northwest sold 12 parkas and still had 2 parkas on hand in ending inventory at the end of the month. What would be the cost of the goods sold for the month and the ending inventory balance for that month? The answer depends on which inventory costing method Northwest Outfitters elects to use. **Exhibit 6-2** illustrates the objective of calculating inventory costs for Northwest Outfitters.

As we shall see, the various inventory costing methods produce different values for ending inventory and cost of goods sold.

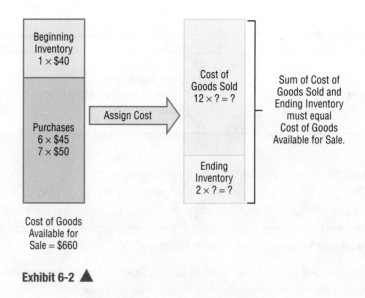

Exhibit 6-2 ▲

SPECIFIC-IDENTIFICATION METHOD

The specific-identification method is also called the **specific-unit cost** method. This method values inventory according to the specific cost of each item of inventory. This method is used predominately by businesses that sell unique items with very different costs. Some examples are businesses that sell automobiles, houses, and artwork. For instance, an automobile dealer may have two vehicles on its car lot, a "basic" model that costs $22,000 and a "fully-equipped" model that costs $29,000. Accordingly, the sales price of the basic model would be less than the sales price for the fully equipped model. It would not make sense for the dealer to assign the cost of the fully equipped model to the basic model when the basic model is sold. This would cause gross profit to be inaccurately stated because the higher cost of the fully equipped model would be subtracted from the lower selling price of the basic model. The dealer would want to specifically identify which model it sold and assign the actual cost of that model to the cost of goods sold. To utilize the specific-identification method, each inventory item must be able to be distinguished from other items with some identifying mark such as a serial number.

This method is not widely used because it requires a lot of effort to track the specific items. In addition, management could easily manipulate the results by using such a method because the cost of goods sold would be determined by the specific item sold, which can be controlled by management. To illustrate, let's assume that a company that trades in laptops uses this method to calculate its cost of goods sold. At the beginning of the period the company had one laptop on hand that cost $1,000. It bought three laptops during the month of the same exact model at $1,100; $900; and $850 respectively. If the company sold one laptop for $1,200, what would the gross profit be? The answer would be that it depends on which laptop is sold. **Exhibit 6-3** illustrates the different alternatives.

Clearly, the profitability of the company depends on which laptop is chosen to be sold. If management wants to increase its profitability, it would choose the last laptop purchased (because it cost the company the least). In such a case the profitability would be $350 ($1,200 − $850). If management chose another laptop, such as the one purchased first during the period, the profitability would be only $100 ($1,200 − $1,100).

Now let's see how to compute inventory amounts using the FIFO and average cost methods for Northwest Outfitters, which are the more popular methods.

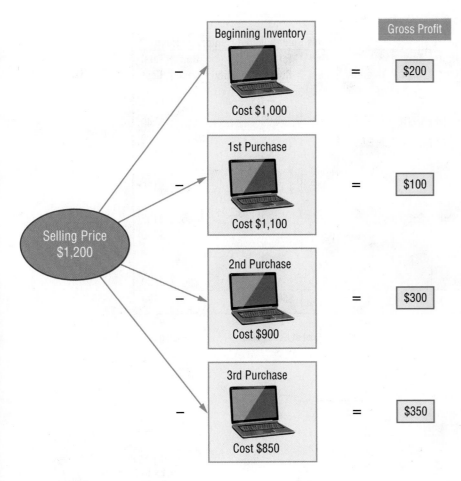

Exhibit 6-3 ▲

FIRST-IN, FIRST-OUT (FIFO) METHOD IN A PERPETUAL INVENTORY SYSTEM

Assume that Northwest Outfitters uses the FIFO method to account for its inventory. Under FIFO, the first inventory costs incurred by Northwest each period are the first costs to be assigned to cost of goods sold. *Simply put, FIFO assumes that the first inventory items Northwest purchased are the first inventory items it sold.* To efficiently track inventory costs, an **inventory subsidiary ledger** is often utilized. The inventory subsidiary ledger maintains the detail supporting the quantity of, and costs assigned to, the inventory items as they are purchased and sold. It also maintains a running balance of the inventory on hand. When preparing the inventory subsidiary ledger, it is critical that the inventory "layers" are kept in the proper order. An inventory layer consists of the quantity of inventory and its purchase cost. **Exhibit 6-4** illustrates the FIFO inventory subsidiary ledger for Northwest Outfitters, while **Exhibit 6-5** illustrates the flow of costs using FIFO.

Northwest began September with one parka that cost $40. After the September 5 purchase, the inventory on hand consists of seven units: one at $40 plus six at $45. Accordingly, the inventory is now composed of two layers: the first layer is composed of one unit for $40 and the second layer is composed of six units for $45 each. Altogether this represents seven units for $310 ($270 + $40). On September 15, Northwest sold four units. Under FIFO, the first layer is assumed to be sold first, then the remaining units are assumed to be sold from the second layer. Since the first layer is composed of only one unit, it will be sold first and the other three units (to complete the four units sold) are

Parkas										
	Purchases			**Cost of Goods Sold**			**Inventory on Hand**			
Date	**Quantity**	**Unit Cost**	**Total Cost**	**Quantity**	**Unit Cost**	**Total Cost**	**Quantity**	**Unit Cost**	**Total Cost**	
Sep 1							1	$40	$ 40	
5	6	$45	$270				1	$40	$ 40	Inventory composed of two layers
							6	$45	$270	
15				1	$40	$ 40				
				3	$45	$135	3	$45	$135	
26	7	$50	$350				3	$45	$135	Inventory composed of one layer
							7	$50	$350	
30				3	$45	$135				
				5	$50	$250	2	$50	$100	
30	**13**		**$620**	**12**		**$560**	**2**		**$100**	

Notice that the first layer which is composed of "1" unit is sold first then "3" units are sold from the second layer leaving "3" units on hand.

Notice that the first layer which is composed of "3" units are sold first then "5" units are sold from the second layer leaving "2" units on hand.

Cost of Goods Sold

Ending Inventory

Exhibit 6-4 ▲

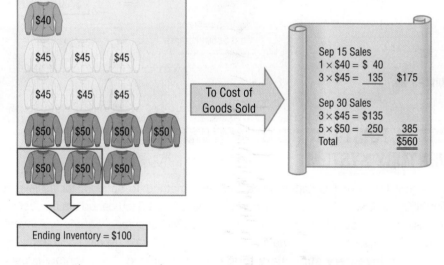

Exhibit 6-5 ▲

taken from the second layer. That leaves three units in inventory on hand, and those units cost $45 each. Each time a purchase is made at a different price, a new layer is formed. The units sold are withdrawn from the first layer at the top and then from the lower layers. The remainder of the inventory subsidiary ledger is completed in the same manner.

The FIFO monthly summary on September 30 is as follows:

- Cost of Goods Sold: 12 units that cost a total of $560

- Ending Inventory: 2 units that cost a total of $100

Look for these amounts in the last row of the inventory subsidiary ledger in Exhibit 6-4 as well as in Exhibit 6-5. If Northwest uses the FIFO method, it will use these amounts for the cost of goods sold and inventory in its financial statements. Notice that the sum of the cost of goods sold plus ending inventory equals the cost of goods available for sale, $660 ($560 + $100).

MOVING AVERAGE COST METHOD IN A PERPETUAL INVENTORY SYSTEM

Suppose Northwest Outfitters uses the average cost method to account for its inventory of parkas. *With this method, the business computes a new, weighted-average cost per unit after each purchase* based on the number of items purchased at each price. Ending inventory and cost of goods sold are then based on the average cost per unit. **Exhibit 6-6** shows an inventory subsidiary ledger for the average cost method. We round average unit cost to the nearest cent and total cost to the nearest dollar.

Parkas									
	Purchases			Cost of Goods Sold			Inventory on Hand		
Date	Quantity	Unit Cost	Total Cost	Quantity	Unit Cost	Total Cost	Quantity	Unit Cost	Total Cost
Sep 1							1	$40.00	$ 40
5	6	$45	$270				7	$44.29	$310
15				4	$44.29	$177	3	$44.29	$133
26	7	$50	$350				10	$48.30	$483
30				8	$48.30	$386	2	$48.30	$ 97
30	13		$620	12		$563	2		$ 97

Cost of Goods Sold   Ending Inventory

$310/7 = $44.29

Exhibit 6-6 ▲

In a perpetual inventory system, the average unit cost on September 5 is based on the cost of the unit on hand at the beginning of September plus the cost of the six units purchased on September 5 as follows:

		Number of Units	Unit Cost	Total Cost
Sep 1	Beginning Inventory	1	$40	$ 40
5	Purchase	6	$45	$270
Total		7		$310

Total Cost of Inventory on Hand ÷	Number of Units on Hand =	Average Cost per Unit
$310	7 Units	$44.29

The four items sold on September 15 are assigned a cost of $44.29 per unit and the remaining three units are carried forward at a cost of $44.29 each. Northwest then computes a new average cost after the September 26 purchase in the same manner.

The average cost monthly summary on September 30 is as follows:

- Cost of Goods Sold: 12 units that cost a total of $563
- Ending Inventory: 2 units that cost a total of $97 ($48.30 times 2 units, then rounded to the nearest dollar)

Once again, these amounts can be seen in the last row of the inventory subsidiary ledger presented in Exhibit 6-6. If Northwest uses the average cost method, it will use these amounts to prepare its financial statements. Yet again, the sum of the cost of goods sold and ending inventory equals the cost of goods available for sale, $660 ($563 + $97).

JOURNALIZING INVENTORY TRANSACTIONS

The journal entries to record the inventory transactions for Northwest Outfitters for the month of September are presented below. **Exhibit 6-7** shows the journal entries using the perpetual inventory system. Assume the following information:

- All purchases and sales in September were made on account.
- The sales price of a parka charged to a customer was $80.

Notice that the journal entries to record the purchases of inventory on account are the same, regardless of the costing method chosen. *The differences occur in the second part of the sales entries that removes the cost of the parkas sold from the Inventory account and transfers it to Cost of Goods Sold.*

			FIFO		Moving Average	
DATE	ACCOUNTS		DR.	CR.	DR.	CR.
Sep 05	Inventory		270		270	
	Accounts Payable			270		270
	Purchase inventory on account (6 parkas @ $45 each)					
15	Accounts Receivable		320		320	
	Sales Revenue			320		320
	Cost of Goods Sold		175		177	
	Inventory			175		177
26	Inventory		350		350	
	Accounts Payable			350		350
	Purchase inventory on account (7 parkas @ $50 each)					
30	Accounts Receivable		640		640	
	Sales Revenue			640		640
	Cost of Goods Sold		385		386	
	Inventory			385		386

Assets = Liabilities + Shareholders' Equity
+270 = +270

Assets = Liabilities + Shareholders' Equity
+320 = +320

Assets = Liabilities + Shareholders' Equity
FIFO   −175 = −175
Average −177 = −177

Assets = Liabilities + Shareholders' Equity
+350 = +350

Assets = Liabilities + Shareholders' Equity
+640 = +640

Assets = Liabilities + Shareholders' Equity
FIFO   −385 = −385
Average −386 = −386

Exhibit 6-7 ▲

WHAT EFFECT DO THE DIFFERENT COSTING METHODS HAVE ON NET INCOME?

L.O. ③ Compare the effects of the different costing methods on the financial statements

The choice of inventory costing method often has an effect on the amount of net income a company reports on its income statement.

Exhibit 6-8 compares the FIFO and average cost methods of costing inventory assuming that, over time, inventory costs are *increasing*. As you can see, different methods have different benefits. FIFO is the most popular inventory costing method.

Inventory Costing Method	Description	Benefit
First-In, First-Out (FIFO)	Cost of goods sold has older, lower costs. Ending inventory has the newer, higher costs (in the case of increasing prices).	Most closely matches actual flow of goods in most cases. Maximizes net income (in the case of increasing prices).
Average Cost	Averages costs in ending inventory and cost of goods sold.	A "middle-ground solution" for reporting net income and inventory.

Exhibit 6-8 ▲

Exhibit 6-9 summarizes the effect that rising and declining inventory cost have on the ending inventory, cost of goods sold, gross profit, and net income. In comparing FIFO to weighted average cost, when the cost of inventory is rising, using the FIFO method will show higher ending inventory cost than the weighted average method, which will result in higher gross income and net income. The reverse is true when the cost of inventory is declining.

Cost of inventory is rising   Cost of inventory is declining

	Rising Cost of Inventory		Declining Cost of Inventory	
	FIFO	**MA**	**FIFO**	**MA**
Cost of Goods Sold	lower	higher	higher	lower
Ending Inventory	higher	lower	lower	higher
Gross Profit	higher	lower	lower	higher
Net Income	higher	lower	lower	higher

Exhibit 6-9 ▲

Exhibit 6-10 summarizes the results of the two inventory methods as used for Northwest Outfitters. It shows sales revenue, cost of goods sold, and gross profit for FIFO and average cost. Net income is the highest under FIFO when inventory costs are rising.

	Perpetual FIFO	Perpetual Moving Average
Sales Revenue	$960.00	$960.00
Cost of Goods Sold	$560.00	$563.00
Gross Profit	$400.00	$397.00

Exhibit 6-10 ▲

Based upon the previous information, it appears that a business could "manage its income" by switching back and forth between costing methods depending upon the circumstances. This is not the case due to the **consistency** principle mandated by IFRS and ASPE. The consistency principle states that businesses should use the same accounting methods and *procedures* from period to period. The consistency principle does not mean that a company can never change its accounting methods, for instance changing from the average cost to FIFO inventory valuation method, but that it can only do so if it can justify the change. A good reason to switch costing methods would be that the new method will make the financial statements more reliable and will give a better presentation of the financial position of the company. Or it could be required to comply with other companies working in the same industry. Change could also be mandatory, such as if the company is using the LIFO (last-in, first-out) method and is going to adopt IFRS, which does not accept LIFO. In this case the company has to change to another approved IFRS method, such as FIFO or weighted average. Also, any changes in accounting methods must be disclosed to the financial statement users.

Suppose you are analyzing a company's net income pattern over a two-year period and costs are rising. If the company switched from average cost to FIFO during that time, its net income likely increased significantly. The problem is that much, if not all, of the increase in income could be the result of the change in inventory method. If you were unaware of the change, you might believe that the company's income increased because of improved operations. Therefore, companies must report any changes in the accounting methods they use and they generally must retrospectively apply the impact of the change as an adjustment to beginning retained earnings, unless it is impractical to do so. Consistency helps investors compare a company's financial statements from one period to the next and make better decisions.

 DECISION GUIDELINES

DECISION		**GUIDELINE**		**ANALYZE**
As a shareholder, I need to evaluate how well management has done in achieving goals for net income in order to award executive bonuses. How do inventory costing methods impact this decision?		The combination of increasing or decreasing costs with inventory costing methods will create opportunities for affecting net income.		When costs are rising • FIFO reports the highest ending inventory value and lowest cost of goods sold and, therefore, the highest net income. • average cost method reports an average cost for the value of ending inventory and cost of goods sold. Average cost can be used to stabilize fluctuations in net income if inventory costs are continually fluctuating. This means that an unethical manager could simply change inventory costing methods and manipulate the net income. Evaluations for executives need to examine not only the results, but the methods that are chosen to achieve the results.

HOW DOES A COMPANY APPLY THE LOWER OF COST OR NET REALIZABLE VALUE RULE?

L.O. ④ Value inventory using the lower of cost or net realizable value rule

Inventory is initially recorded at cost to comply with the cost principle. However, merchandisers are often faced with a situation where the cost of replacing an inventory item is lower than what was originally paid for the item. To take a conservative approach when these situations arise, businesses will often apply the **lower of cost or net realizable value (LCNRV) rule**. Net realizable value (NRV) is the estimated selling price less the estimated costs to complete the sale. The LCNRV rule requires businesses to report inventory in the financial statements at whichever is lower, the amount originally paid or the net realizable value, of each inventory item. The comparison of cost and net realizable value should be done on an item-by-item basis. If the net realizable value of inventory is less than its historical cost, a company writes down the inventory value by decreasing inventory and increasing cost of goods sold. In this way, net income is decreased in the period in which the decrease in the market value of the inventory occurred. However, if the circumstances change, and net realizable value has increased, then inventory that has been written down can be reversed up to cost. Consider the example of a jewellery store, where the price of gold (its inventory) could be fluctuating.

Let's look at the process of valuing inventory according to the lower of cost or net realizable value rule for the inventory in **Exhibit 6-11**.

- Prepare a table listing each inventory item, its quantity, unit cost, and net realizable value.

- Calculate the total cost and total net realizable value for each item. Inventory Item 122A, for example, has a total cost of $2,000 (40 units × $50 cost per unit) and a total net realizable value of $2,080 (40 units × $52 market value per unit).

- Place the lower of the cost or net realizable value for each item in the "LCNRV" (lower of cost or net realizable value) column. Item 122A would have a value of $2,000.

- Add the amounts in each column to obtain the total cost, total net realizable value, and total lower of cost or net realizable value amounts.

- Adjust the inventory balance to reflect the lower of cost or net realizable value amount. The total cost is $14,800 and the total LCNRV amount is $14,425, so a journal entry is made to reduce the inventory amount by the difference of $375 ($14,800 – $14,425).

The application of LCNRV is actually more complex than what is demonstrated in Exhibit 6-11; however, more in-depth coverage will be left to a more advanced accounting course. Application of the LCNRV rule is a continuation of the process of valuing inventory. Businesses using LCNRV will record inventory transactions, assigning a cost to each inventory item sold using the specific-identification, FIFO, or average cost method. Then, at the end of the accounting period, they will apply the LCNRV rule to the ending inventory. In this way, businesses report more prudent values for inventory and net income.

Most businesses will report inventory on the statement of financial position at the lower of cost or net realizable value; however, others will use the concept of materiality to decide whether inventory needs to be written down to its current replacement cost. The materiality concept states that a company must perform strictly proper accounting *only* for items that have a material effect on the company's financial statements. An item is considered to have a material effect when it would cause someone to change a decision; stated differently, a material amount is one large enough to make a difference to a

					Total	
Inventory Item	Inventory Quantity	Unit Cost	Unit Net Realizable Value	Cost	Net Realizable Value	LCNRV
122A	40	$ 50	$ 52	$ 2,000	$ 2,080	$ 2,000
1587L	75	$ 80	$ 75	6,000	5,625	5,625
394CZ	68	$100	$101	6,800	6,868	6,800
				$14,800	$14,573	$14,425

Exhibit 6-11 ▲

6.2 **STILL** DON'T GET IT?
Visit MyAccountingLab for an alternate explanation of this important accounting concept.

user of the financial statements. For example, if the lower of cost or net realizable value comparison in Exhibit 6-11 resulted in a difference between total cost and total LCNRV of $3, the company would have been appropriate in ignoring any adjustment to inventory for the $3. Hence, the materiality concept frees accountants from having to report every account in strict accordance with IFRS or ASPE, yet still report items properly.

HOW IS INVENTORY REPORTED ON THE STATEMENT OF FINANCIAL POSITION?

L.O. ⑤ Illustrate the reporting of inventory in the financial statements

Inventory is reported as a current asset and is often listed after receivables on the statement of financial postition. In addition to showing the inventory amount, a business must disclose the costing method used to value inventory (specific-identification, FIFO, or average cost) and whether the inventory is valued using LCNRV. This disclosure helps a business adhere to the **full-disclosure** principle. The full-disclosure principle requires that a company's financial statements report enough information for outsiders to make knowledgeable decisions about the company. To provide this information, accountants typically include a set of **notes** that accompany the financial statements. Note disclosures help ensure that companies report relevant, reliable, and comparable financial information. A common note related to inventory would look like this:

> NOTE 2: Statement of Significant Accounting Policies:
> *Inventory*. Inventory is carried at the *lower of cost or net realizable value*. Cost is determined using the first-in, first-out method.

Suppose a banker is comparing two companies, one using average cost and the other FIFO. When prices are rising, the company using the FIFO inventory costing method reports higher net income, but only because it uses FIFO. Without knowledge of the accounting methods the companies are using, the banker could lend money to the wrong business, or lend the wrong amount of money to each.

INVENTORY SHRINKAGE

The perpetual inventory method keeps a continuous record of the inventory on hand at all times. However, the actual amount of inventory on hand may differ from the amount on hand according to the accounting records due to errors in recording inventory-related transactions or due to **inventory shrinkage**. Inventory shrinkage represents a loss of inventory. Inventory shrinkage is most often the result of employee theft, customer theft, and the damage, spillage, or spoilage of inventory items.

A physical inventory count is used to determine the amount of inventory actually on hand at the end of the accounting period. A number of commonly used procedures help ensure the accuracy of the count. It usually occurs when the store is closed. Individuals assigned to the count can use maps of inventory locations, pre-numbered count sheets, and ink pens, and may count in pairs. The count may also involve prewritten inventory instructions and tags to identify merchandise to be counted, and is typically supervised. To save time and increase objectivity for the count, an outside inventory-taking firm may be used to take counts instead of, or in addition to, employees. If the entity has its financial statements audited, a representative of the audit firm will usually be present at the count to take test counts and determine whether inventory instructions are being adequately followed. This allows the auditor to evaluate whether inventory and cost of goods sold are fairly presented in the statements.

The inventory value derived from the physical inventory count is used as the inventory account balance on the statement of financial position. The accounting records are adjusted for any difference between the inventory value determined by the count and the value according to the perpetual records. The Inventory account is debited or credited as necessary with a corresponding credit or debit to the Cost of Goods Sold account.

To illustrate, assume that Cosmic Cellular discovered that one of the inventory items, AV707, which costs $100, is totally damaged. The following adjusting entry would be required:

DATE	ACCOUNTS	DR.	CR.
Jul 31	Cost of Goods Sold	100	
	Inventory—AV707		100
	Recording a damaged inventory item.		

Assets	=	Liabilities	+	Shareholders' Equity
−100	=			−100

Notice that Cost of Goods Sold increases (hence increasing expenses and decreasing company profitability) and Inventory is decreased to recognize the damaged unit and comply with the physical count.

HOW DO INVENTORY ERRORS AFFECT THE FINANCIAL STATEMENTS?

A correct count of the inventory items on hand is necessary to ensure the accurate reporting of the inventory's value. However, errors in the inventory count can and do occur such as the following:

L.O. 6 Determine the effect of inventory errors on the financial statements

- Improperly counting inventory
- Double counting inventory; for example, counting it in one location and then moving it to another location where it is counted again
- Not counting one section of the storeroom or excluding incoming goods shipped FOB shipping point
- Failure to recognize obsolete or damaged goods, resulting in failure to write down their value accordingly

What is the impact of a counting error? Remember that the Inventory account balance is adjusted to reflect the value arrived at by the physical count. A wrong count will result in making a journal entry that causes both the Inventory balance and the Cost of Goods Sold to be incorrect.

To demonstrate, let's look at the income statements for a company for two consecutive years. To keep the example simple, we will assume that the company has a $20,000 balance in both beginning inventory and ending inventory for the first year. We will also assume that it has a $20,000 balance in ending inventory in the second year (remember that the beginning balance in the inventory account in year 2 is the ending inventory balance from year 1). We will also assume that the company made purchases of $75,000 and that it had sales of $160,000 and operating expenses of $40,000 in both years. In other words, the activity for both years is exactly the same. **Exhibit 6-12**, Panel A, illustrates the income statements for both years assuming that inventory was properly counted.

Now, let's assume that the ending inventory was incorrectly valued at $25,000 (instead of the correct amount of $20,000) due to an error in the physical count. Exhibit 6-12, Panel B, illustrates the income statements for both years assuming that ending inventory was overstated by $5,000.

Panel A—Ending Inventory correctly stated	Year 1		Year 2	
Sales Revenue		$160,000		$160,000
Cost of Goods Sold:				
Beginning Inventory	$20,000	➤$ 20,000		
Purchases	75,000	75,000		
Cost of Goods Available for Sale	95,000	95,000		
Ending Inventory	20,000	20,000		
Cost of Goods Sold		75,000		75,000
Gross Profit		85,000		85,000
Operating Expenses		40,000		40,000
Net Income		$45,000		$45,000

Panel B—Ending Inventory overstated by $5,000				
Sales Revenue		$160,000		$160,000
Cost of Goods Sold:				
Beginning Inventory	$20,000	➤$ 25,000		
Purchases	75,000	75,000		
Cost of Goods Available for Sale	95,000	100,000		
Ending Inventory	25,000	20,000		
Cost of Goods Sold		70,000		80,000
Gross Profit		90,000		80,000
Operating Expenses		40,000		40,000
Net Income		$ 50,000		$ 40,000

Exhibit 6-12 ▲

A comparison of the statements in Panel A and Panel B of Exhibit 6-12 reveals the following for year 1:

- Cost of goods sold is understated by $5,000.
- Gross profit is overstated by $5,000.
- Net income is overstated by $5,000.
- Retained earnings will be overstated because net income is closed into retained earnings.

Recall from Chapter 3 that Inventory, as an asset, is a permanent account that carries its balance over to the next period. So, one period's ending inventory becomes the next period's beginning inventory. Thus, the error in ending inventory in year 1 carries over as an error in the beginning inventory in year 2. A comparison of the statements in Panel A and Panel B of Exhibit 6-12 reveals the following for year 2:

- Cost of goods available for sale is overstated by $5,000.
- Cost of goods sold is overstated by $5,000.
- Gross profit is understated by $5,000.
- Net income is understated by $5,000.
- Retained earnings will now be correctly stated because the understatement in net income in year 2 will offset the overstatement from year 1 when the net income from year 2 is closed into retained earnings.

As you can see, the error cancels out after two periods. The total net income, $90,000, from Panel B for the two periods combined when there is an error is the same as it is in Panel A for the two periods when there are no errors. The effects of inventory errors are summarized in **Exhibit 6-13**.

	Year 1		Year 2	
	COGS	**Income**	**COGS**	**Income**
Ending inventory overstated in first year, correct in second year	understated	overstated	overstated	understated
Ending inventory understated in first year, correct in second year	overstated	understated	understated	overstated

Exhibit 6-13 ▲

We can use the following mathematical equation of the calculation of the cost of goods sold to explain the understatement or overstatement of the items in the income statement and the statement of financial position:

DECISION GUIDELINES

DECISION	**GUIDELINE**	**ANALYZE**

I just realized that the company that I hired to count my inventory missed a section that I forgot to tell them about. I'll make sure they count it correctly next time, so should I bother to inform the CEO about this error?	In addition to causing an overstatement or understatement of Inventory on the statement of financial position, a misstatement of ending inventory will cause an error on the income statement, and will affect other financial statements, too. You must inform the CEO about this error.	If ending inventory is overstated, then
		• Cost of goods sold is understated.
		• Gross profit is overstated.
		• Net income is overstated.
		If ending inventory is understated, then
		• Cost of goods sold is overstated.
		• Gross profit is understated.
		• Net income is understated.
		Because ending inventory for one period becomes beginning inventory for the next period, the cost of goods sold, gross profit, and net income of the next period are also misstated.

IS IT POSSIBLE TO ESTIMATE THE VALUE OF INVENTORY IF THE INVENTORY IS ACCIDENTALLY DESTROYED?

Often a business must estimate the value of its inventory. Suppose the company suffers a fire loss. To collect insurance, it must estimate the cost of the inventory destroyed; that is, it must estimate the ending inventory.

L.O. ⑦ Use the gross profit method to estimate ending inventory

The **gross profit method** estimates inventory by using the format for the cost of goods sold:

> Beginning Inventory
> + Purchases (Net of Discounts and Returns and
>   Allowances, plus Shipping Costs)
> = Cost of Goods Available for Sale
> − Ending Inventory
> = Cost of Goods Sold

Rearranging ending inventory and cost of goods sold helps to estimate ending inventory. Let's look at an example. We can estimate ending inventory through the following steps and amounts, as shown in **Exhibits 6-14** and **6-15**:

Step 1	Beginning Inventory		$ 14,000
	+ Purchases (net)		66,000
	= Cost of Goods Available for Sale		80,000
Step 2	Estimated Cost of Goods Sold:		
	Net Sales Revenue	$100,000	
	− Estimated Gross Profit of 40% ($100,000 × 40%)	(40,000)	
	= Estimated Cost of Goods Sold		(60,000)
Step 3	Estimated Ending Inventory		$ 20,000

Exhibit 6-14 ▲

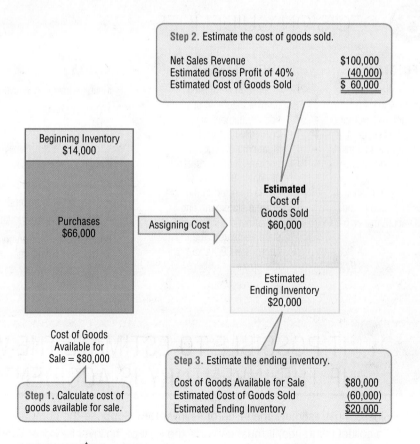

Exhibit 6-15 ▲

Step 1 Calculate the cost of goods available for sale. Add the beginning balance of inventory and the net cost of purchases for the accounting period ($14,000 + $66,000 = $80,000).

Step 2 Estimate the cost of goods sold. Do you remember calculating the gross profit percentage in Chapter 5? The historical gross profit percentage of a business can be used to estimate the current period's gross profit. Calculate the estimated gross profit by multiplying the net sales revenue by the historical gross profit percentage ($100,000 × 40% = $40,000). Subtract the estimated gross profit from the net sales revenue to get the estimated cost of goods sold ($100,000 – $40,000 = $60,000).

Step 3 Estimate the ending inventory. Subtract estimated cost of goods sold from the cost of goods available for sale ($80,000 – $60,000 = $20,000).

FOCUS ON DECISION MAKING: RATIOS

THE RATE OF INVENTORY TURNOVER

Inventory is the most important asset for a merchandising business because it is often the largest current asset and the focus of a company's operations. Owners and managers strive to sell inventory quickly because inventory generates no profit until it is sold. The faster a business produces sales, the higher the sales revenue available to create income will be. **Inventory turnover**, the ratio of cost of goods sold to average inventory, measures the number of times a company sells, or *turns over*, its average level of inventory during a period. To demonstrate the inventory turnover we will use the financial statements for Cosmic Cellular from Exhibit 5-10 in Chapter 5. Cosmic Cellular's rate of inventory turnover is calculated as follows:

L.O. 8 Compute the inventory turnover rate

$$\text{Inventory Turnover} = \frac{\text{Cost of Goods Sold}}{\text{Average Inventory}} = \frac{\text{Cost of Goods Sold}}{(\text{Beginning Inventory} + \text{Ending Inventory})/2}$$

$$= \frac{\$90,300}{(\$40,000^* + \$39,700^{**})/2} = 2.27 \text{ Times Per Year}$$

*The $40,000 beginning inventory balance is the ending inventory balance for the prior period and is not shown in Exhibit 5-10.
**The $39,700 is the ending inventory balance for the current period as shown on the statement of financial position in Exhibit 5-10.

Cosmic's inventory turnover rate shows that it is selling its merchandise inventory a little more than two times a year. Converting the inventory turnover rate into an amount that tells you how long the inventory is usually on hand before it is sold can help you understand how efficiently the inventory is being used. To do the conversion, you simply take 365 and divide by the inventory turnover rate as follows:

$$365 \div 2.27 = 160.8 \text{ days}$$

This means that, on average, the inventory is held for almost 161 days before it is sold. For a product that is not perishable, having the inventory around for that long may be fine; however, the product might also go out of style or become obsolete if it is held onto for too long. For a product that is perishable, such as fresh fruit, it is obvious that having it on hand for 160 days would not be good. Analysis of the type of product is important for a full understanding of the days in inventory calculation.

Inventory turnover is usually computed for an annual period, so the cost of goods sold figure is the amount for the entire year. Average inventory is computed by adding the beginning inventory balance to the ending inventory balance, and dividing the total by two. Remember that statement of financial position accounts, such as Inventory, carry their balances from one period to the next, so the ending inventory for one year becomes the beginning inventory for the next year. A high turnover rate is desirable because it indicates that the inventory is turning over, or being sold, fast; an increase in the turnover rate usually means increasing profits will result from increasing sales.

Regardless of the turnover rate, merchandisers need to keep sufficient levels of inventory on hand to meet sales demand. However, they also need to avoid purchasing too much inventory because more money will be needed to pay for the inventory and to store it until the goods are sold. These actions will increase interest expense if the funds needed are borrowed, and warehouse rent expense, if warehouse storage space is rented.

 DECISION GUIDELINES

DECISION	GUIDELINE	ANALYZE
As a creditor, I have used a company's inventory as collateral towards its loan with my bank. How do I assess the company's management of its inventory?	Use the inventory turnover ratios: $$\text{Inventory Turnover} = \frac{\text{Cost of Goods Sold}}{\text{Average Inventory}}$$ $$\text{Days in Inventory} = \frac{365}{\text{Inventory Turnover}}$$	The inventory turnover ratios can indicate that a business is poorly managing its inventory. For example, a turnover ratio that is low compared to the industry average or a turnover ratio that has declined from the prior year may indicate that the business has damaged or obsolete inventory. It is sometimes more clear to use the days in inventory calculation to determine how well the inventory is managed.

FOCUS ON USERS

Concept	User	Why Is This Important to This User?
Inventory Costing Method	Bookkeepers Managers Shareholders Creditors Competitors Government and Regulatory Bodies Unions	All users need to understand the inventory costing methods used and any changes in the costing methods since this can have a drastic impact on the COGS, net income, and ending inventory amounts that are reported by a company.
	Creditors	Creditors would need to carefully consider the inventory costing methods for decisions regarding the value of the inventory for collateral purposes and the quality of the net income for representing a company's ability to generate sufficient income to support a loan.
	Shareholders	Shareholders need to be sure to understand the inventory amounts reported and how they impact net income (and therefore retained earnings and shareholders' equity).
	Government and Regulatory Bodies	Since income can be manipulated by changes in inventory, government regulators and accounting regulators want to ensure that consistency is applied so that each year's financial statements are based on the same assumptions and cost flow methods. This will make comparison from one year to the next easier and help alleviate the chance of cost flow methods being changed simply to serve a specific purpose for the company (such as showing high income to attract investors).
	Unions	Unions are interested in the ways in which companies report their earnings because union negotiations will revolve around what the company can afford to do with salaries and other benefits to the employees. If changing the cost flow method can alter the net income and the COGS (and therefore the expenses) of the company, the union will want to make sure that the impact of the cost flow assumption is understood for their own purposes of negotiating for the best support of the employees.

DEMO DOC

INVENTORY COSTING

Mackay Specialty Products, Inc., which uses the perpetual inventory method, had the following inventory information for the month of June, 2015:

LEARNING OBJECTIVE ②

Jun 1	Beginning inventory was 200 units costing $9.00 per unit.
3	Purchased 125 units at $9.25 per unit.
7	Sold 180 units.
13	Purchased 100 units at $9.40 per unit.
18	Sold 115 units.
25	Sold 65 units.

REQUIREMENTS:

① Without resorting to calculations, determine which costing method, FIFO or average cost, will result in the highest reported income for Mackay Specialty Products, Inc.

② Calculate the cost of goods sold and the value of ending inventory for Mackay Specialty Products, Inc. for the month of June 2015 under the following costing methods:

a. FIFO

b. Average cost

DEMO DOC SOLUTIONS

REQUIREMENT ①

Without resorting to calculations, determine which costing method, FIFO or average cost, will result in the highest reported income for Mackay Specialty Products, Inc.

Part 1	Part 2	Demo Doc Complete

To determine whether the FIFO or average cost costing method would result in the highest income, we must first look to see if the cost of inventory is increasing or decreasing. A review of the data indicates that the cost of inventory has steadily increased from $9.00 to $9.40 per unit during the month. To have the highest income possible, we must choose the inventory costing method that results in the lowest cost of goods sold. The FIFO costing method assumes that the earliest inventory costs become part of cost of goods sold, which leaves the most recent costs in ending inventory. The average cost smooths out the cost. Because the inventory costs for Mackay Specialty Products, Inc. have steadily increased, the earliest inventory costs are lower than the most recent purchases. Therefore, choosing the FIFO costing method will result in the highest income for Mackay Specialty Products, Inc. as it will result in the lowest cost of goods sold.

REQUIREMENT ②

Calculate the cost of goods sold and the value of ending inventory for Mackay Specialty Products, Inc. for the month of June 2015 under the following costing methods:

Part 1	Part 2	Demo Doc Complete

a. FIFO

An easy way to determine the cost of goods sold and the value of ending inventory is to prepare an inventory subsidiary ledger. The first entry necessary in the ledger records the beginning inventory of 200 units at $9.00 each for a total of $1,800.00. This information is entered in the inventory on hand columns of the ledger as follows:

Date	Purchases Quantity	Purchases Unit Cost	Purchases Total Cost	Cost of Goods Sold Quantity	Cost of Goods Sold Unit Cost	Cost of Goods Sold Total Cost	Inventory on Hand Quantity	Inventory on Hand Unit Cost	Inventory on Hand Total Cost
Jun 1							200	$9.00	$1,800.00

Next, we enter the June 3 purchase of 125 units costing $9.25 each for a total of $1,156.25 in the purchases columns of the ledger.

Date	Purchases Quantity	Purchases Unit Cost	Purchases Total Cost	Cost of Goods Sold Quantity	Cost of Goods Sold Unit Cost	Cost of Goods Sold Total Cost	Inventory on Hand Quantity	Inventory on Hand Unit Cost	Inventory on Hand Total Cost
Jun 1							200	$9.00	$1,800.00
Jun 3	125	$9.25	$1,156.25						

The inventory on hand columns are completed by carrying down the original layer of inventory (200 units at $9.00) and then adding the new layer (125 units at $9.25).

Date	Purchases Quantity	Purchases Unit Cost	Purchases Total Cost	Cost of Goods Sold Quantity	Cost of Goods Sold Unit Cost	Cost of Goods Sold Total Cost	Inventory on Hand Quantity	Inventory on Hand Unit Cost	Inventory on Hand Total Cost
Jun 1							200	$9.00	$1,800.00
Jun 3	125	$9.25	$1,156.25				200	$9.00	$1,800.00
							125	$9.25	$1,156.25

Next, we will enter the June 7 sale transaction. Under FIFO, costs are assigned to cost of goods sold based on the *oldest* units on hand (the *first* units in). The oldest units we have are the units in beginning inventory (200 units at $9.00 each). The 180 units sold are, therefore, assigned a cost of $9.00 each for a total of $1,620.00. This information is entered into the cost of goods sold columns of the ledger.

Date	Purchases Quantity	Purchases Unit Cost	Purchases Total Cost	Cost of Goods Sold Quantity	Cost of Goods Sold Unit Cost	Cost of Goods Sold Total Cost	Inventory on Hand Quantity	Inventory on Hand Unit Cost	Inventory on Hand Total Cost
Jun 1							200	$9.00	$1,800.00
Jun 3	125	$9.25	$1,156.25				200	$9.00	$1,800.00
							125	$9.25	$1,156.25
Jun 7				180	$9.00	$1,620.00			

The inventory on hand columns are completed next. Of the original 200 units in beginning inventory, only 20 (200 − 180) are left. We also still have the 125 units purchased on June 3 for $9.25 each.

Date	Purchases Quantity	Purchases Unit Cost	Purchases Total Cost	Cost of Goods Sold Quantity	Cost of Goods Sold Unit Cost	Cost of Goods Sold Total Cost	Inventory on Hand Quantity	Inventory on Hand Unit Cost	Inventory on Hand Total Cost
Jun 1							200	$9.00	$1,800.00
Jun 3	125	$9.25	$1,156.25				200	$9.00	$1,800.00
							125	$9.25	$1,156.25
Jun 7				180	$9.00	$1,620.00	20	$9.00	$ 180.00
							125	$9.25	$1,156.25

The June 13 purchase of 100 units at $9.40 each is entered into the purchases columns of the ledger.

Date	Purchases Quantity	Purchases Unit Cost	Purchases Total Cost	Cost of Goods Sold Quantity	Cost of Goods Sold Unit Cost	Cost of Goods Sold Total Cost	Inventory on Hand Quantity	Inventory on Hand Unit Cost	Inventory on Hand Total Cost
Jun 1							200	$9.00	$1,800.00
Jun 3	125	$9.25	$1,156.25				200	$9.00	$1,800.00
							125	$9.25	$1,156.25
Jun 7				180	$9.00	$1,620.00	20	$9.00	$ 180.00
							125	$9.25	$1,156.25
Jun 13	100	$9.40	$ 940.00						

The inventory on hand columns are now completed by carrying down the layers of inventory from June 7 and adding a layer consisting of the 100 units purchased on June 13.

Date	Purchases Quantity	Purchases Unit Cost	Purchases Total Cost	Cost of Goods Sold Quantity	Cost of Goods Sold Unit Cost	Cost of Goods Sold Total Cost	Inventory on Hand Quantity	Inventory on Hand Unit Cost	Inventory on Hand Total Cost
Jun 1							200	$9.00	$1,800.00
Jun 3	125	$9.25	$1,156.25				200	$9.00	$1,800.00
							125	$9.25	$1,156.25
Jun 7				180	$9.00	$1,620.00	20	$9.00	$ 180.00
							125	$9.25	$1,156.25
Jun 13	100	$9.40	$ 940.00				20	$9.00	$ 180.00
							125	$9.25	$1,156.25
							100	$9.40	$ 940.00

On June 18, 115 units are sold. Remember that under FIFO we must assign the oldest cost to cost of goods sold first. The oldest cost of inventory on hand is the 20 units at $9.00 each. Because we sold more than 20 units, we must look to the next inventory layer for the cost to assign to the remaining 95 units (115 – 20). These 95 units are assigned a cost of $9.25 each. The sale is entered into the cost of goods sold columns of the ledger as follows:

Date	Purchases Quantity	Purchases Unit Cost	Purchases Total Cost	Cost of Goods Sold Quantity	Cost of Goods Sold Unit Cost	Cost of Goods Sold Total Cost	Inventory on Hand Quantity	Inventory on Hand Unit Cost	Inventory on Hand Total Cost
Jun 1							200	$9.00	$1,800.00
Jun 3	125	$9.25	$1,156.25				200	$9.00	$1,800.00
							125	$9.25	$1,156.25
Jun 7				180	$9.00	$1,620.00	20	$9.00	$ 180.00
							125	$9.25	$1,156.25
Jun 13	100	$9.40	$ 940.00				20	$9.00	$ 180.00
							125	$9.25	$1,156.25
							100	$9.40	$ 940.00
Jun 18				20	$9.00	$ 180.00			
				95	$9.25	$ 878.75			

After this sale, all of the beginning inventory items are assumed to be sold as well as 95 of the units costing $9.25. Therefore, the remaining inventory is made up of 30 units (125 – 95) at $9.25 and 100 units at $9.40. These amounts are entered into the inventory on hand columns of the ledger.

Date	Purchases			Cost of Goods Sold			Inventory on Hand		
	Quantity	Unit Cost	Total Cost	Quantity	Unit Cost	Total Cost	Quantity	Unit Cost	Total Cost
Jun 1							200	$9.00	$1,800.00
Jun 3	125	$9.25	$1,156.25				200	$9.00	$1,800.00
							125	$9.25	$1,156.25
Jun 7				180	$9.00	$1,620.00	20	$9.00	$ 180.00
							125	$9.25	$1,156.25
Jun 13	100	$9.40	$ 940.00				20	$9.00	$ 180.00
							125	$9.25	$1,156.25
							100	$9.40	$ 940.00
Jun 18				20	$9.00	$ 180.00	30	$9.25	$ 277.50
				95	$9.25	$ 878.75	100	$9.40	$ 940.00

In the last transaction on June 25, 65 units were sold. Of these 65 units, 30 are assumed to cost $9.25 and the remaining 35 (65 – 30) are assumed to cost $9.40.

Date	Purchases			Cost of Goods Sold			Inventory on Hand		
	Quantity	Unit Cost	Total Cost	Quantity	Unit Cost	Total Cost	Quantity	Unit Cost	Total Cost
Jun 1							200	$9.00	$1,800.00
Jun 3	125	$9.25	$1,156.25				200	$9.00	$1,800.00
							125	$9.25	$1,156.25
Jun 7				180	$9.00	$1,620.00	20	$9.00	$ 180.00
							125	$9.25	$1,156.25
Jun 13	100	$9.40	$ 940.00				20	$9.00	$ 180.00
							125	$9.25	$1,156.25
							100	$9.40	$ 940.00
Jun 18				20	$9.00	$ 180.00	30	$9.25	$ 277.50
				95	$9.25	$ 878.75	100	$9.40	$ 940.00
Jun 25				30	$9.25	$ 277.50			
				35	$9.40	$ 329.00			

After this sale, all units costing $9.25 are assumed to be sold as well as 35 of the units costing $9.40. Therefore, the remaining inventory is made up of 65 units (100 – 35) at $9.40. These amounts are entered into the inventory on hand columns of the ledger.

Date	Purchases Quantity	Purchases Unit Cost	Purchases Total Cost	Cost of Goods Sold Quantity	Cost of Goods Sold Unit Cost	Cost of Goods Sold Total Cost	Inventory on Hand Quantity	Inventory on Hand Unit Cost	Inventory on Hand Total Cost
Jun 1							200	$9.00	$1,800.00
Jun 3	125	$9.25	$1,156.25				200	$9.00	$1,800.00
							125	$9.25	$1,156.25
Jun 7				180	$9.00	$1,620.00	20	$9.00	$ 180.00
							125	$9.25	$1,156.25
Jun 13	100	$9.40	$ 940.00				20	$9.00	$ 180.00
							125	$9.25	$1,156.25
							100	$9.40	$ 940.00
Jun 18				20	$9.00	$ 180.00	30	$9.25	$ 277.50
				95	$9.25	$ 878.75	100	$9.40	$ 940.00
Jun 25				30	$9.25	$ 277.50			
				35	$9.40	$ 329.00	65	$9.40	$ 611.00

The inventory subsidiary ledger is completed by calculating the total quantity and total cost for the purchases, cost of goods sold, and inventory on hand columns and entering the results in the last row. Notice that the amounts in the inventory on hand columns only reflect the amounts that existed after the last transaction.

Date	Purchases Quantity	Purchases Unit Cost	Purchases Total Cost	Cost of Goods Sold Quantity	Cost of Goods Sold Unit Cost	Cost of Goods Sold Total Cost	Inventory on Hand Quantity	Inventory on Hand Unit Cost	Inventory on Hand Total Cost
Jun 1							200	$9.00	$1,800.00
Jun 3	125	$9.25	$1,156.25				200	$9.00	$1,800.00
							125	$9.25	$1,156.25
Jun 7				180	$9.00	$1,620.00	20	$9.00	$ 180.00
							125	$9.25	$1,156.25
Jun 13	100	$9.40	$ 940.00				20	$9.00	$ 180.00
							125	$9.25	$1,156.25
							100	$9.40	$ 940.00
Jun 18				20	$9.00	$ 180.00	30	$9.25	$ 277.50
				95	$9.25	$ 878.75	100	$9.40	$ 940.00
Jun 25				30	$9.25	$ 277.50			
				35	$9.40	$ 329.00	65	$9.40	$ 611.00
Jun 30	225		$2,096.25	360		$3,285.25	65		$ 611.00

We can double-check our calculations using the following formula:

Cost of Goods Sold = (Beginning Inventory + Purchases − Ending Inventory)

Using this formula, the cost of goods sold is $3,285.25 ($1,800.00 + $2,096.25 − $611.00). This agrees with the cost of goods sold total on the inventory subsidiary ledger so our calculations are correct.

b. Average cost

We will now complete an inventory subsidiary ledger using average cost. As we did for the FIFO inventory subsidiary ledgers, the first entry is to record the beginning inventory of 200 units costing $9.00 each.

Date	Purchases			Cost of Goods Sold			Inventory on Hand		
	Quantity	Unit Cost	Total Cost	Quantity	Unit Cost	Total Cost	Quantity	Unit Cost	Total Cost
Jun 1							200	$9.00	$1,800.00

The entry for the first purchase of 125 units on June 3 is the same as for the FIFO inventory subsidiary ledgers.

Date	Purchases			Cost of Goods Sold			Inventory on Hand		
	Quantity	Unit Cost	Total Cost	Quantity	Unit Cost	Total Cost	Quantity	Unit Cost	Total Cost
Jun 1							200	$9.00	$1,800.00
Jun 3	125	$9.25	$1,156.25						

Once a purchase is made, the average cost per unit must be calculated. The average cost per unit is calculated by dividing the total cost of inventory on hand by the total quantity of inventory on hand. The total cost of inventory equals $2,956.25 ($1,800.00 beginning inventory + $1,156.25 purchased on June 3). The total quantity of inventory on hand equals the 200 units in beginning inventory plus the 125 units purchased for a total of 325 units. The average cost per unit is calculated as follows:

$$\frac{\$2,956.25}{325} = \$9.10^* \text{ per unit}$$

*Rounded

This transaction leaves 325 units (200 + 125) in inventory at $9.10 each. This information is now entered in the inventory on hand columns of the ledger.

Date	Purchases			Cost of Goods Sold			Inventory on Hand		
	Quantity	Unit Cost	Total Cost	Quantity	Unit Cost	Total Cost	Quantity	Unit Cost	Total Cost
Jun 1							200	$9.00	$1,800.00
Jun 3	125	$9.25	$1,156.25				325	$9.10	$2,957.50

On June 7, 180 units are sold. The units in inventory have an average cost of $9.10 each, so the units sold are assigned a cost of $9.10 for a total of $1,638.00. This information is entered into the cost of goods sold columns of the ledger.

Date	Purchases			Cost of Goods Sold			Inventory on Hand		
	Quantity	Unit Cost	Total Cost	Quantity	Unit Cost	Total Cost	Quantity	Unit Cost	Total Cost
Jun 1							200	$9.00	$1,800.00
Jun 3	125	$9.25	$1,156.25				325	$9.10	2,957.50
Jun 7				180	$9.10	$1,638.00			

The inventory on hand consists of 145 units (325 − 180) at $9.10 each. This information is entered into the inventory on hand columns of the inventory subsidiary ledger.

Date	Purchases Quantity	Unit Cost	Total Cost	Cost of Goods Sold Quantity	Unit Cost	Total Cost	Inventory on Hand Quantity	Unit Cost	Total Cost
Jun 1							200	$9.00	$1,800.00
Jun 3	125	$9.25	$1,156.25				325	$9.10	$2,957.50
Jun 7				180	$9.10	$1,638.00	145	$9.10	$1,319.50

The June 13 purchase of 100 units at $9.40 each is now entered into the purchases columns of the inventory subsidiary ledger.

Date	Purchases Quantity	Unit Cost	Total Cost	Cost of Goods Sold Quantity	Unit Cost	Total Cost	Inventory on Hand Quantity	Unit Cost	Total Cost
Jun 1							200	$9.00	$1,800.00
Jun 3	125	$9.25	$1,156.25				325	$9.10	$2,957.50
Jun 7				180	$9.10	$1,638.00	145	$9.10	$1,319.50
Jun 13	100	$9.40	$ 940.00						

Because another purchase has been made, the average cost per unit must be recalculated. The total cost of inventory equals $2,259.50 ($1,319.50 June 7 remaining inventory + $940.00 purchased on June 13). The total quantity of inventory on hand equals the 145 units remaining in inventory on June 7 plus the 100 units purchased for a total of 245 units. The average cost per unit is calculated as follows:

$$\frac{\$2,259.50}{245} = \$9.22^* \text{ per unit}$$

*Rounded

The inventory on hand consists of 245 units at $9.22 each. This information is entered into the inventory on hand columns of the inventory subsidiary ledger.

Date	Purchases Quantity	Unit Cost	Total Cost	Cost of Goods Sold Quantity	Unit Cost	Total Cost	Inventory on Hand Quantity	Unit Cost	Total Cost
Jun 1							200	$9.00	$1,800.00
Jun 3	125	$9.25	$1,156.25				325	$9.10	$2,957.50
Jun 7				180	$9.10	$1,638.00	145	$9.10	$1,319.50
Jun 13	100	$9.40	$ 940.00				245	$9.22	$2,258.90

On June 18, 115 units are sold. The units in inventory have an average cost of $9.22 each, so the units sold are assigned a cost of $9.22 for a total of $1,060.30. This information is entered into the cost of goods sold columns of the ledger.

Date	Purchases Quantity	Unit Cost	Total Cost	Cost of Goods Sold Quantity	Unit Cost	Total Cost	Inventory on Hand Quantity	Unit Cost	Total Cost
Jun 1							200	$9.00	$1,800.00
Jun 3	125	$9.25	$1,156.25				325	$9.10	$2,957.50
Jun 7				180	$9.10	$1,638.00	145	$9.10	$1,319.50
Jun 13	100	$9.40	$ 940.00				245	$9.22	$2,258.90
Jun 18				115	$9.22	$1,060.30			

This transaction leaves 130 units (245 – 115) in inventory at $9.22 each. This information is now entered in the inventory on hand columns of the ledger.

Date	Purchases			Cost of Goods Sold			Inventory on Hand		
	Quantity	Unit Cost	Total Cost	Quantity	Unit Cost	Total Cost	Quantity	Unit Cost	Total Cost
Jun 1							200	$9.00	$1,800.00
Jun 3	125	$9.25	$1,156.25				325	$9.10	$2,957.50
Jun 7				180	$9.10	$1,638.00	145	$9.10	$1,319.50
Jun 13	100	$9.40	$ 940.00				245	$9.22	$2,258.90
Jun 18				115	$9.22	$1,060.30	130	$9.22	$1,198.60

The last transaction on June 25 was for the sale of 65 units. Because there have been no purchases since the last transaction, there is no need to recalculate the average cost per unit. So the cost assigned to the 65 units will be $9.22 each. This information is entered into the cost of goods sold columns of the ledger.

Date	Purchases			Cost of Goods Sold			Inventory on Hand		
	Quantity	Unit Cost	Total Cost	Quantity	Unit Cost	Total Cost	Quantity	Unit Cost	Total Cost
Jun 1							200	$9.00	$1,800.00
Jun 3	125	$9.25	$1,156.25				325	$9.10	$2,957.50
Jun 7				180	$9.10	$1,638.00	145	$9.10	$1,319.50
Jun 13	100	$9.40	$ 940.00				245	$9.22	$2,258.90
Jun 18				115	$9.22	$1,060.30	130	$9.22	$1,198.60
Jun 25				65	$9.22	$ 599.30			

This transaction leaves 65 units (130 – 65) in inventory at $9.22 each. This information is now entered in the inventory on hand columns of the ledger.

Date	Purchases			Cost of Goods Sold			Inventory on Hand		
	Quantity	Unit Cost	Total Cost	Quantity	Unit Cost	Total Cost	Quantity	Unit Cost	Total Cost
Jun 1							200	$9.00	$1,800.00
Jun 3	125	$9.25	$1,156.25				325	$9.10	$2,957.50
Jun 7				180	$9.10	$1,638.00	145	$9.10	$1,319.50
Jun 13	100	$9.40	$ 940.00				245	$9.22	$2,258.90
Jun 18				115	$9.22	$1,060.30	130	$9.22	$1,198.60
Jun 25				65	$9.22	$ 599.30	65	$9.22	$ 599.30

As we did with FIFO, the inventory subsidiary ledger is completed by calculating the total quantity and total cost for the purchases, cost of goods sold, and inventory on hand columns and entering the results in the last row. Notice that the amounts in the inventory on hand columns only reflect the amounts that existed after the last transaction.

Date	Purchases			Cost of Goods Sold			Inventory on Hand		
	Quantity	Unit Cost	Total Cost	Quantity	Unit Cost	Total Cost	Quantity	Unit Cost	Total Cost
Jun 1							200	$9.00	$1,800.00
Jun 3	125	$9.25	$1,156.25				325	$9.10	$2,957.50
Jun 7				180	$9.10	$1,638.00	145	$9.10	$1,319.50
Jun 13	100	$9.40	$ 940.00				245	$9.22	$2,258.90
Jun 18				115	$9.22	$1,060.30	130	$9.22	$1,198.60
Jun 25				65	$9.22	$ 599.30	65	$9.22	$ 599.30
Jun 30	225		$2,096.25	360		$3,297.60	65		$ 599.30

Once again, we can double-check our calculations by calculating the cost of goods sold using the same formula that we used in steps a and b. Using this formula, the cost of goods sold is $3,296.95 ($1,800.00 + $2,096.25 − $599.30). The difference ($0.65) between this amount and the cost of goods sold found on our inventory subsidiary ledger ($3,297.60) is due to rounding when calculating the average unit costs and is immaterial.

DEMO DOC COMPLETE

Part 1	Part 2	Demo Doc Complete

DECISION GUIDELINES

Inventories

If you own or work for a merchandiser, here are some decisions related to inventory that you may encounter.

DECISION	GUIDELINE	ANALYZE
The cost of my products will determine the price that I can sell them for as well as impact other decisions. How do I determine the cost of the inventory I sell?	The physical flow of the inventory and the cost flow of the inventory can be different. The cost assigned to the units sold may be based on one of the following three methods: • Specific-identification • First-in, first-out (FIFO) • Average cost	*Specific-identification:* Inventory items are specifically labelled or identified and the actual cost of each item sold is assigned to cost of goods sold. *First-in, first-out (FIFO):* The first inventory costs incurred are the first costs to be assigned to cost of goods sold. *Average cost:* With the perpetual system, a new moving average cost per unit is computed after each purchase and assigned to cost of goods sold. With the periodic system, a new weighted-average cost per unit is calculated at the end of each period.
As a shareholder, I need to evaluate how well management has done in achieving goals for net income to award executive bonuses. How do inventory costing methods impact this decision?	The combination of increasing or decreasing costs with inventory costing methods will create opportunities for affecting net income.	When costs are rising • FIFO reports the highest ending inventory value and lowest cost of goods sold and, therefore, the highest net income. • average cost reports an average cost for the value of ending inventory and cost of goods sold. Average cost can be used to stabilize fluctuations in net income if inventory costs are continually fluctuating. This means that an unethical manager could simply change inventory costing methods to manipulate the net income. Evaluations for executives need to examine not only the results, but the methods that are chosen to achieve the results.

I just realized that the company that I hired to count my inventory missed a section that I forgot to tell them about. I'll make sure they count it correctly next time, so should I bother to inform the CEO about this error?	In addition to causing an understatement of Inventory on the statement of financial position, a misstatement of ending inventory will cause an error on the income statement. You must inform the CEO about this error.	If ending inventory is overstated, then
		• Cost of goods sold is understated.
		• Gross profit is overstated.
		• Net income is overstated.
		
		If ending inventory is understated, then
		• Cost of goods sold is overstated.
		• Gross profit is understated.
		• Net income is understated.
		
		Because ending inventory for one period becomes beginning inventory for the next period, the cost of goods sold, gross profit, and net income of the next period are also misstated.

As a creditor, I have used a company's inventory as collateral towards its loan with my bank. How do I assess the company's management of its inventory?	Use the inventory turnover ratios: $$\text{Inventory Turnover} = \frac{\text{Cost of Goods Sold}}{\text{Average Inventory}}$$ $$\text{Days in Inventory} = \frac{365}{\text{Inventory Turnover}}$$	The inventory turnover ratio can be an indicator that a business is poorly managing its inventory. For example, a turnover ratio that is low compared to the industry average or a turnover ratio that has declined from the prior year may indicate that the business has damaged or obsolete inventory. It is sometimes more clear to use the Days in Inventory calculation to determine how well the inventory is managed.

POINT OF COMPARISON	IFRS	ASPE
There are no significant differences.		

ACCOUNTING VOCABULARY

THE LANGUAGE OF BUSINESS

Average cost (p. 334)

Consistency (p. 343)

Cost of goods available for sale (p. 337)

Finished goods (p. 334)

First-in, first-out (FIFO) (p. 334)

Full disclosure (p. 346)

Gross profit method (p. 350)

Inventory layer (p. 335)

Inventory shrinkage (p. 346)

Inventory subsidiary ledger (p. 339)

Inventory turnover (p. 351)

Lower of cost or net realizable value (LCNRV) rule (p. 344)

Moving average cost (p. 392)

Notes (p. 346)

Raw materials (p. 334)

Specific-identification (p. 334)

Specific-unit cost (p. 338)

Weighted average cost (p. 392)

Work in process (p. 334)

ACCOUNTING PRACTICE

DISCUSSION QUESTIONS

1. The introduction to this chapter suggests that the chapter will explore the answers to some questions about inventory. Did you get the answers to those questions? Specifically,

   a. why does inventory need to be counted?

   b. what would happen if the count was done incorrectly?

   c. what does the term FIFO have to do with inventory?

2. How are the financial statements of a manufacturer different from those of a merchandiser with respect to inventory?

3. What is a cost-flow assumption? Why is a cost-flow assumption necessary in accounting for inventory?

4. If a company had two units that cost $1 each in its beginning inventory and purchased two more units for $2 each, what would be the cost of goods sold associated with a sale of three units under each of the following assumptions?

   a. FIFO

   b. Average cost

5. If a company had two units that cost $1 each in its beginning inventory and purchased two more units for $2 each, what would be the gross profit reported on the income statement under each of the following assumptions if three units were sold for $3 each?

   a. FIFO

   b. Average cost

6. In a period of rising prices, which cost-flow assumption would produce the highest net income? Why?

7. Let's say that two companies, identical in every way except that one used FIFO and one used average cost, went into a bank on the same day to get a loan to deal with the rising cost of acquiring inventory. Despite the fact that they both engaged in the same transactions at the same dollar values, one company reported higher net income and higher total assets on the financial statements. Which one was it? If the banker made the decision based on the company that would have better cash flow associated with the inventory costing method choice, which company would have received the loan?

8. Describe some business and economic conditions that might make the lower of cost or net realizable value more likely to be used.

9. Under which of the inventory methods, periodic or perpetual, would a company be better equipped to detect inventory shrinkage? Why?

10. If a company is having a harder time selling its products, even at discounted prices compared to last year, would this year's inventory turnover rate be higher or lower than last year's rate? What about the gross profit rate?

SELF CHECK

1. During February, Peter's Hardware made sales of $38,600 and ended the month with inventories totaling $5,400. Cost of Goods Sold was $23,200. Total operating expenses were $8,700. How much net income did Peter's Hardware earn for the month?

   a. $1,300
   b. $15,400
   c. $6,700
   d. $10,000

2. Which inventory costing method assigns the newest, most recent, costs incurred during the period to ending inventory?

   a. Specific-unit cost
   b. First-in, first-out (FIFO)
   c. Moving average cost
   d. Weighted average cost

3. Which inventory costing method results in the lowest net income during a period of declining inventory costs?

   a. Weighted average cost
   b. Specific-unit cost
   c. First-in, first-out (FIFO)
   d. Moving average cost

4. Assume HPC, Inc. began December with 60 units of inventory that cost a total of $720. During December, HPC, Inc. purchased and sold goods as follows:

Dec 6	Purchased 120 units @ $13 each
15	Sold 145 units @ $28 each
22	Purchased 100 units @$15
30	Sold 85 units @ $29 each

   HPC, Inc. uses perpetual inventory. Under the FIFO inventory method, how much is HPC's cost of goods sold for the sale on December 15?

   a. $455
   b. $1,740
   c. $1,860
   d. $1,825

5. Assume HPC, Inc. began December with 60 units of inventory that cost a total of $720. During December, HPC, Inc. purchased and sold goods as follows:

Dec 6	Purchased 120 units @ $13 each
15	Sold 145 units @ $28 each
22	Purchased 100 units @ $15 each
30	Sold 85 units @ $29 each

HPC, Inc. uses perpetual inventory. Under the FIFO inventory method, how much is HPC's cost of inventory on hand after the sale on December 30?

a. $645
b. $750
c. $600
d. $650

6. Assume HPC, Inc. began December with 60 units of inventory that cost a total of $720. During December, HPC, Inc. purchased and sold goods as follows:

Dec 6	Purchased 120 units @ $13 each
15	Sold 145 units @ $28 each
22	Purchased 100 units @ $15 each
30	Sold 85 units @ $29 each

HPC, Inc. uses perpetual inventory. Under the average cost inventory method, how much is HPC's cost of goods sold for the sale on December 15? Round unit cost to the nearest cent.

a. $1,812.50
b. $1,836.67
c. $1,825.75
d. $1,934.30

7. Which of the following prevents a company from switching its inventory costing method to a different method each year?

a. Disclosure principle
b. Consistency principle
c. Lower of cost or net realizable value
d. Materiality concept

8. Which of the following is most closely linked to accounting conservatism?

a. Materiality concept
b. Consistency principle
c. Disclosure principle
d. Lower of cost or net realizable value

9. At December 31, 2015, Inland Equipment understated ending inventory by $2,800. How does this error affect cost of goods sold and net income for 2015?

a. Overstates cost of goods sold and understates net income
b. Understates costs of goods sold and overstates net income
c. Overstates both cost of goods sold and net income
d. Leaves both cost of goods sold and net income correct because the errors cancel each other

10. Suppose Ironman, Inc. lost all of its inventory in a flood. Beginning inventory was $43,000, net purchases totalled $524,000, and sales came to $875,000. Ironman's normal gross profit percentage is 44%. Use the gross profit method to estimate the cost of the inventory lost in the flood.

a. $308,000
b. $182,000
c. $77,000
d. $34,000

Answers are given after Written Communication.

SHORT EXERCISES

S6-1. Inventory methods (*Learning Objective 1*) 5 min.

Motion Auto would like to assign the newest costs of inventory items to its ending inventory. Which inventory costing method should Motion Auto choose?

S6-2. Inventory methods (*Learning Objective 1*) 5–10 min.

Hamilton Furniture doesn't expect prices to change dramatically and wants to use a method that averages price changes.

Which inventory method would best meet Hamilton Furniture's goal? What if Hamilton Furniture wanted to expense out the older purchases of goods instead? Which inventory method would best meet that need?

S6-3. FIFO (*Learning Objective 2*) 5–10 min.

Mike's Powersports uses the FIFO inventory method. Mike's Powersports started August with 10 helmets that cost $54 each. On August 19, Mike's Powersports bought 15 helmets at $56 each. On August 28, Mike's Powersports sold 12 helmets.

Prepare an inventory subsidiary ledger for Mike's Powersports.

S6-4. Specific-identification (*Learning Objective 2*) 5–10 min.

Mike's Powersports uses the specific-identification inventory method. Mike's Powersports started August with 10 helmets that cost $54 each. On August 19, Mike's Powersports bought 15 helmets at $56 each. On August 28, Mike's Powersports sold 12 helmets. Four units were taken from the batch of the beginning inventory and 8 units from the purchase on August 19.

Calculate the cost of goods sold and ending inventory for Mike's Powersports.

S6-5. Average cost (*Learning Objective 2*) 5–10 min.

Mike's Powersports uses the average cost inventory method. Mike's Powersports started August with 10 helmets that cost $54 each. On August 19, Mike's Powersports bought 15 helmets at $56 each. On August 28, Mike's Powersports sold 12 helmets.

Prepare an inventory subsidiary ledger for the average cost method. Round average cost per unit to the nearest cent and all other amounts to the nearest dollar.

S6-6. Recording inventory transactions (*Learning Objective 2*) 5–10 min.

Mike's Powersports uses the (perpetual) average cost inventory method. Mike's Powersports started August with 10 helmets that cost $54 each. On August 19, Mike's Powersports bought 15 helmets at $56 each. On August 28, Mike's Powersports sold 12 helmets.

1. The August 19 purchase of inventory was on account.
2. The August 28 sale of inventory was on account. Mike's Powersports sold each helmet for $95.

Prepare the required journal entries for the purchase and sale of inventory.

S6-7. FIFO versus average cost (*Learning Objective 2*) 5–10 min.

Consider the FIFO and average cost inventory costing methods. Answer the following questions assuming that inventory costs are increasing:

1. Which method of inventory costing will produce the lower cost of goods sold?
2. Which method of inventory costing will produce the higher cost of goods sold?
3. If prices had been declining instead of rising, which inventory method will produce the higher cost of goods sold?

S6-8. Terms (*Learning Objectives 4 & 5*) 5–10 min.

Match the terms with the definitions.

a. Full disclosure

b. Materiality

c. Consistency

d. Prudence

_____ 1. A company must perform strictly proper accounting only for items that are significant to the business's financial statements.

_____ 2. Reporting the realistic figures in the financial statements.

_____ 3. A business's financial statements must report enough information for users to make knowledgeable decisions about the company.

_____ 4. A business should use the same accounting methods and procedures from period to period.

S6-9. Lower of cost or net realizable value (*Learning Objective 4*) 5–10 min.

Assume that Bonsai Boards has the following FIFO inventory subsidiary ledger for snowboards for the month of November:

		Snowboards		
Date	Purchases	Cost of Goods Sold	Inventory on Hand
Nov 1			$1,320
8	$ 840		$2,160
19		$1,640	$ 520
30	$1,130		$1,650

At November 30, the accountant for Bonsai Boards determines that the current replacement cost of the ending inventory is $1,615. Make any adjusting entry needed to apply the lower of cost or net realizable value rule. Inventory would be reported on the statement of financial position at what value on November 30?

S6-10. Reporting inventory on the statement of financial position (*Learning Objective 5*) 5–10 min.

At the end of the current year, Cuppa Joes' Inventory account balance was $12,600. A physical count of the inventory revealed that inventory on hand totalled $12,200.

What amount should Cuppa Joes report on its statement of financial position?

S6-11. Inventory principles and terminology (*Learning Objectives 1, 4, & 5*) 5–10 min.

Match the accounting terms on the left with the corresponding definitions on the right.

_____ 1. Prudence

_____ 2. Full disclosure

_____ 3. Moving average cost

_____ 4. FIFO

_____ 5. Consistency

_____ 6. Materiality

_____ 7. Specific identification

a. Assigns the most recent inventory costs to ending inventory.

b. Inventory costing method where a new weighted average cost per unit is computed and is used to value ending inventory and cost of goods sold.

c. This is the basis for using lower of cost or net realizable value.

d. Principle that prevents a company from using a different inventory costing method each year.

e. Identifies exactly which inventory item was sold. Usually used for unique inventory items.

f. Requires that a company report enough information for outsiders to make decisions.

g. Principle that states significant items must conform to IFRS and ASPE.

S6-12. Inventory errors (*Learning Objective 6*) 5–10 min.

Bonsai Board's income statement data for the year ended December 31, 2015, follow.

Sales Revenue	$237,500
Cost of Goods Sold	142,800
Gross Profit	$ 94,700

Assume that the ending inventory was accidentally overstated by $3,300. What are the correct amounts for cost of goods sold and gross profit?

S6-13. Inventory errors (*Learning Objective 6*) 10–15 min.

Bonsai Board's income statement data for the year ended December 31, 2015, follow.

Sales Revenue	$237,500
Cost of Goods Sold	142,800
Gross Profit	$ 94,700

Assume that the ending inventory was accidentally overstated by $3,300. How would the inventory error affect Bonsai Boards' cost of goods sold and gross profit for the year ended December 31, 2016, if the error is not corrected in 2015?

S6-14. Estimating ending inventory (*Learning Objective 7*) 10–15 min.

Inland Lumber began the year with inventory of $52,200 and made purchases of $316,700 during the year. Sales for the year are $503,800, and Inland Lumber's gross profit percentage is 42% of sales.

Compute Inland Lumber's estimated cost of ending inventory using the gross profit method.

S6-15. Inventory turnover (*Learning Objective 8*) 5–10 min.

Mackay Industries' sales for the year ended December 31, 2015, were $1,287,000 and cost of goods sold amounted to $707,000. Beginning inventory was $58,000 and ending inventory was $77,000.

a. Compute Mackay Industries' rate of inventory turnover for the year ended December 31, 2015. Round answer to the nearest tenth.

b. Compute days held in inventory.

EXERCISES (GROUP A)

E6-1A. FIFO (*Learning Objective 2*) 10–15 min.

Jameson's Sports Shop carries a line of waterproof watches. Jameson's Sports Shop uses the FIFO method and a perpetual inventory system. The sales price of each watch is $188. Company records indicate the following activity for waterproof watches for the month of August:

Date	Item	Quantity	Unit Cost
Aug 1	Balance	10	$104
7	Purchase	12	$108
11	Sale	14	
19	Purchase	11	$116
28	Sale	10	

Requirements

1. Prepare an inventory subsidiary ledger for the waterproof watches to determine the amount Jameson's Sports Shop should report for ending inventory and cost of goods sold using the FIFO method.

2. Journalize Jameson's Sports Shop's inventory transactions using the FIFO method. Assume that all purchases and sales are on account.

E6-2A. Specific-identification (*Learning Objective 2*) 10–15 min.

Refer to the data for E6-1A. However, instead of the FIFO method, assume Jameson's Sports Shop uses the specific-identification method, assuming the following for each sale:

August 11 sale: Two units were from the beginning inventory, and the rest from the August 7 purchase.

August 28 sale: All units are from the August 19 purchase.

Requirements

1. Prepare an inventory subsidiary ledger for the watches on the specific identification basis to determine the cost of ending inventory and cost of goods sold for the month.

2. Journalize Jameson's Sports Shop's inventory transactions using the perpetual specific identification method. Assume that all purchases and sales are on account.

E6-3A. Average cost (*Learning Objective 2*) 10–15 min.

Refer to the data for E6-1A. However, instead of the FIFO method, assume Jameson's Sports Shop uses the average cost method.

Requirements

1. Prepare an inventory subsidiary ledger for the watches on the average cost basis to determine the cost of ending inventory and cost of goods sold for the month. Round average cost per unit to the nearest cent and all other amounts to the nearest dollar.

2. Journalize Jameson's Sports Shop's inventory transactions using the perpetual average cost method. Assume that all purchases and sales are on account.

E6-4A. FIFO versus average cost (*Learning Objective 2*) 10–15 min.

Assume that Midway Cycles bought and sold a line of mountain bikes during May as follows:

Date	Item	Quantity	Unit Cost
May 1	Balance	10	$243
5	Sale	5	
12	Purchase	12	$252
21	Sale	7	
30	Sale	6	

Midway Cycles uses the perpetual inventory system.

Requirements

1. Compute the cost of ending inventory under FIFO.

2. Compute the cost of ending inventory under average cost.

3. Which method results in higher cost of ending inventory?

E6-5A. FIFO versus average cost (*Learning Objective 2*) 10–15 min.

Refer to the data for Midway Cycles in E6-4A.

Requirements

1. Compute the cost of goods sold under FIFO.

2. Compute the cost of goods sold under average cost.

3. Which method results in the higher cost of goods sold?

Quick solution:
1. FIFO cost of goods sold = $4,446; 2. Weighted average cost of goods sold = $4,456

E6-6A. FIFO versus average cost (*Learning Objectives 2 & 3*) 15–20 min.

Assume that a Firestone Tire store completed the following perpetual inventory transactions for a line of tires.

Aug 5	Beginning Inventory	34 tires @ $ 82
Aug 14	Purchase	25 tires @ $ 88
Aug 20	Sale	40 tires @ $134

Requirements

1. Compute cost of goods sold and gross profit under FIFO.

2. Compute cost of goods sold and gross profit using average cost. Round average cost per unit to the nearest cent and all other amounts to the nearest dollar.

3. Which method results in the larger gross profit and why?

E6-7A. Lower of cost or net realizable value (*Learning Objective 4*) 10–15 min.

GDL Enterprises has the following account balances at December 31, 2015. The inventory balance was determined using FIFO.

Inventory		Cost of Goods Sold		Sales Revenue	
Beg Bal 26,500					
End Bal 31,800		Bal 106,000			Bal 176,000

GDL Enterprises has determined that the replacement cost (current market value) of the December 31, 2015, ending inventory is $32,400.

Requirements

1. What value would GDL Enterprises report on the statement of financial position at December 31, 2015, for inventory assuming the company uses the lower of cost or net realizable value rule?

2. Prepare any adjusting journal entry required from the information given.

E6-8A. Reporting inventory on the statement of financial position (*Learning Objective 5*) 5–10 min.

Eagle Eye Sunglasses had the following FIFO inventory subsidiary ledger at June 30, the end of the fiscal year.

Date	Purchases Quantity	Purchases Unit Cost	Purchases Total Cost	Cost of Goods Sold Quantity	Cost of Goods Sold Unit Cost	Cost of Goods Sold Total Cost	Inventory on Hand Quantity	Inventory on Hand Unit Cost	Inventory on Hand Total Cost
Jun 1							200	$9.00	$1,800.00
Jun 3	125	$9.25	$1,156.25				200	$9.00	$1,800.00
							125	$9.25	$1,156.25
Jun 7				180	$9.00	$ 1,620.00	20	$9.00	$ 180.00
							125	$9.25	$1,156.25
Jun 13	100	$9.40	$ 940.00				20	$9.00	$ 180.00
							125	$9.25	$1,156.25
							100	$9.40	$ 940.00
Jun 18				20	$9.00	$ 180.00	30	$9.25	$ 277.50
				95	$9.25	$ 878.75	100	$9.40	$ 940.00
Jun 25				30	$9.25	$ 277.50			
				35	$9.40	$ 329.00	65	$9.40	$ 611.00
Jun 30	225		$2,096.25	360		$3,285.25	65		$ 611.00

A physical count of the inventory performed at year end revealed $587.00 of inventory on hand.

Requirements

1. Journalize the adjusting entry for inventory, if any is required.
2. What could have caused the value of the ending inventory based on the physical count to be lower than the amount based on the inventory subsidiary ledger?

E6-9A. Adjusting inventory based on a physical count (*Learning Objective 5*) 5–10 min.

The Inventory account for McCormack Tire Company had a balance of $112,600 at the end of its fiscal year. A physical count taken at year end revealed that the value of inventory on hand amounted to $110,800.

Requirements

1. Journalize the adjustment for inventory shrinkage.
2. What could cause the inventory balance according to the physical count to be different from the ledger balance?

E6-10A. Inventory errors (*Learning Objective 6*) 10–15 min.

Motion Auto reported sales revenue of $138,000 and cost of goods sold of $76,000.

Requirements

1. Compute Motion Auto's correct gross profit assuming the company's ending inventory is overstated by $1,300. Show your work.
2. Compute Motion Auto's correct gross profit assuming the company's ending inventory is understated by $2,700. Show your work.

E6-11A. Inventory errors (*Learning Objective 6*) 10–15 min.

Hanson's Furniture Outlet reported the following comparative income statement for the years ended December 31, 2015 and 2014.

		2015		2014
Hanson's Furniture Outlet Comparative Income Statement For the Years Ended December 31, 2015 and 2014				
Sales Revenue		$187,600		$164,000
Cost of Goods Sold:				
Beginning Inventory	$ 12,300		$ 9,100	
Net Purchases	114,500		101,600	
Cost of Goods Available	126,800		110,700	
Ending Inventory	14,600		12,300	
Cost of Goods Sold		112,200		98,400
Gross Profit		75,400		65,600
Operating Expenses		32,900		26,700
Net Income		$ 42,500		$ 38,900

During 2015, Hanson's Furniture Outlet discovered that the 2014 ending inventory, as previously reported, was understated by $2,100.

Requirements

1. Prepare the corrected comparative income statement for the two-year period, complete with a heading for the statement.
2. What was the effect of the error on net income for the two years combined? Explain your answer.

E6-12A. Estimating ending inventory (*Learning Objective 7*) 5–10 min.

Totally Tunes sells and installs audio equipment. During a recent fire that occurred at its warehouse, Totally Tunes' entire inventory was destroyed. Totally Tunes' accounting records reflect the following information.

Beginning Inventory	$ 46,400
Net Purchases	243,900
Net Sales	404,000
Gross Profit Rate	35%

Requirement

1. Use the gross profit method to estimate the amount of Totally Tunes' inventory loss.

E6-13A. Inventory turnover (*Learning Objective 8*) 10–15 min.

Gibson's Nursery has the following information as of December 31, 2015:

Sales Revenue		$1,287,500
Cost of Goods Sold:		
Beginning Inventory	$ 44,300	
Net Purchases	750,600	
Cost of Goods Available	794,900	
Ending Inventory	48,700	
Cost of Goods Sold		746,200
Gross Profit		541,300
Operating Expenses		388,700
Net Income		$ 152,600

Requirements

1. Compute the rate of inventory turnover for Gibson's Nursery for the year ended December 31, 2015. Round the result to two decimal places.

2. The rate of inventory turnover for Gibson's Nursery was 17.36 in 2014. Has the rate improved or deteriorated?

E6-14A. FIFO versus average cost and inventory turnover (*Learning Objectives 2, 3, & 8*) 20–25 min.

Kimco's sales for the year 2015 were $575,000 ($230/unit). On January 1, 2015, Kimco's beginning inventory showed 450 units, costing $40,500. During 2015, Kimco purchased 2,650 units at $95 each. Kimco's income statement is as follows.

Income Statement
Inventory Costing Method

	Units	FIFO	Weighted Average
Sales			
Cost of Goods Sold:			
Beginning Inventory			
Purchases			
Goods Available for Sale			
Ending Inventory			
Cost of Goods Sold			
Gross Profit			
Operating Expenses		$265,000	$265,000
Operating Income			
Income Tax Expense (30%)			
Net Income			

Requirements

1. Complete the income statement for Kimco, using FIFO and weighted average cost methods.

2. Calculate the inventory turnover, using FIFO and weighted average cost methods.

3. Which method shows higher profit and inventory turnover? Explain.

EXERCISES (GROUP B)

E6-1B. FIFO (*Learning Objective 2*) 10–15 min.

Underwater World carries a line of waterproof watches. Underwater World uses the FIFO method and a perpetual inventory system. The sales price of each watch is $185.

Company records indicate the following activity for waterproof watches for the month of March:

Date	Item	Quantity	Unit Cost
Mar 1	Balance	6	$100
7	Purchase	8	$108
11	Sale	10	
19	Purchase	13	$112
28	Sale	9	

Requirements

1. Prepare an inventory subsidiary ledger for the waterproof watches to determine the amount Underwater World should report for ending inventory and cost of goods sold using the FIFO method.

2. Journalize Underwater World's inventory transactions using the FIFO method.

Assume that all purchases and sales are on account.

E6-2B. Specific-identification (*Learning Objective 2*) 10–15 min.

Refer to the data for E6-1B. However, instead of the FIFO method, assume Underwater World uses the specific-identification method, assuming the following for each sale:

March 11 sale: Two units were from the beginning inventory, and the rest from the March 7 purchase.
March 28 sale: All units are from the March 19 purchase.

Requirements

1. Prepare an inventory subsidiary ledger for the watches on the specific identification basis to determine the cost of ending inventory and cost of goods sold for the month.

2. Journalize Underwater World's inventory transactions using the perpetual specific-identification method. Assume that all purchases and sales are on account.

E6-3B. Average cost (*Learning Objective 2*) 10–15 min.

Refer to the data for E6-1B. However, instead of the FIFO method, assume that Underwater Way uses the average cost method.

Requirements

1. Prepare an inventory subsidiary ledger for the watches on the average cost basis to determine the cost of ending inventory and cost of goods sold for the month. Round average cost per unit to the nearest cent and all other amounts to the nearest dollar.

2. Journalize Underwater Way's inventory transactions using the perpetual average cost method. Assume that all purchases and sales are on account.

E6-4B. FIFO versus average cost (*Learning Objective 2*) 10–15 min.

Assume that Cycle Guys bought and sold a line of mountain bikes during December as follows:

Date	Item	Quantity	Unit Cost
Dec 1	Balance	12	$225
5	Sale	6	
12	Purchase	10	$220
21	Sale	8	
30	Sale	6	

Cycle Guys uses the perpetual inventory system.

Requirements

1. Compute the cost of ending inventory under FIFO.
2. Compute the cost of ending inventory under average cost.
3. Which method results in a higher cost of ending inventory?

E6-5B. FIFO versus average cost (*Learning Objective 2*) 10–15 min.

Refer to the data for Cycle Guys in E6-4B.

Requirements

1. Compute the cost of goods sold under FIFO.
2. Compute the cost of goods sold under average cost.
3. Which method results in a higher cost of goods sold?

E6-6B. FIFO versus average cost (*Learning Objectives 2 & 3*) 15–20 min.

Assume that RB Tire Store completed the following perpetual inventory transactions for a line of tires.

Sep 5	Beginning Inventory	32 tires @ $ 73
Sep 14	Purchase	37 tires @ $ 67
Sep 28	Sale	38 tires @ $154

Requirements

1. Compute cost of goods sold and gross profit under FIFO.
2. Compute cost of goods sold and gross profit using average cost. Round average cost per unit to the nearest cent and all other amounts to the nearest dollar.
3. Which method results in the larger gross profit and why?

E6-7B. Lower of cost or net realizable value (*Learning Objective 4*) 10–15 min.

Clarmont Resources has the following account balances at October 31, 2015. The inventory balance was determined using FIFO.

Inventory		Cost of Goods Sold		Sales Revenue	
Beg Bal 22,400					
End Bal 35,500		Bal 114,000			Bal 188,000

Clarmont Resources has determined that the replacement cost (current market value) of the October 31, 2015, ending inventory is $38,000.

Requirements

1. What value would Clarmont Resources report on the statement of financial position at October 31, 2015, for inventory assuming the company uses the lower of cost or net realizable value rule?

2. Prepare any adjusting journal entry required from the information given.

E6-8B. Reporting inventory on the statement of financial position (*Learning Objective 5*) 5–10 min.

Ray Blocker Sunglasses had the following FIFO inventory subsidiary ledger at April 30, the end of the fiscal year.

	Purchases			Cost of Goods Sold			Inventory on Hand		
Date	Quantity	Unit Cost	Total Cost	Quantity	Unit Cost	Total Cost	Quantity	Unit Cost	Total Cost
Apr 1							150	$9.00	$1,350.00
Apr 3	150	$9.50	$1,425.00				150	$9.00	$1,350.00
							150	$9.50	$1,425.00
Apr 7				110	$9.00	$ 990.00	40	$9.00	$ 360.00
							150	$9.50	$1,425.00
Apr 13	110	$9.70	$1,067.00				40	$9.00	$ 360.00
							150	$9.50	$1,425.00
							110	$9.70	$1,067.00
Apr 18				40	$9.00	$ 360.00	90	$9.50	$ 855.00
				60	$9.50	$ 570.00	110	$9.70	$1,067.00
Apr 25				90	$9.50	$ 855.00			
				35	$9.70	$ 339.50	75	$9.70	$ 727.50
Apr 30	260		$2,492.00	335		$3,114.50	75		$ 727.50

A physical count of the inventory performed at year-end revealed $672.50 of inventory on hand.

Requirements

1. Journalize the adjusting entry for inventory, if any is required.

2. What could have caused the value of the ending inventory based on the physical count to be lower than the amount based on the inventory subsidiary ledger?

E6-9B. Adjusting inventory based on a physical count (*Learning Objective 5*) 5–10 min.

The Inventory account for Brady Company had a balance of $137,900 at the end of its fiscal year. A physical count taken at year end revealed that the value of inventory on hand amounted to $136,400.

Requirements

1. Journalize the adjustment for inventory shrinkage.

2. What could cause the inventory balance according to the physical count to be different from the ledger balance?

E6-10B. Inventory errors (*Learning Objective 6*) 10–15 min.

Boston Auto reported sales revenue of $160,000 and cost of goods sold of $90,000.

Requirements

1. Compute Boston Auto's correct gross profit assuming the company's ending inventory is overstated by $1,400. Show your work.

2. Compute Boston Auto's correct gross profit assuming the company's ending inventory is understated by $2,400. Show your work.

E6-11B. Inventory errors (*Learning Objective 6*) 10–15 min.

Healthy Bite Mart reported the following comparative income statement for the years ended November 30, 2015 and 2014.

		2015		2014	
	Healthy Bite Mart **Comparative Income Statements** For the Years Ended November 30, 2015 and 2014				
Sales Revenue			$137,000		$120,000
Cost of Goods Sold:					
Beginning Inventory		$15,500		$11,000	
Net Purchases		70,000		69,000	
Cost of Goods Available		85,500		80,000	
Ending Inventory		18,500		15,500	
Cost of Goods Sold			67,000		64,500
Gross Profit			70,000		55,500
Operating Expenses			24,000		20,000
Net Income			$ 46,000		$ 35,500

During 2015, Healthy Bite Mart discovered that the 2014 ending inventory, as previously reported, was understated by $2,500.

Requirements

1. Prepare the corrected comparative income statement for the two-year period, complete with a heading for the statement.

2. What was the effect of the error on net income for the two years combined? Explain your answer.

E6-12B. Estimating ending inventory (*Learning Objective 7*) 5–10 min.

Speaker Shop sells and installs audio equipment. During a recent fire that occurred at its warehouse, Speaker Shop's entire inventory was destroyed. Speaker Shop's accounting records reflect the following information.

Beginning Inventory.........................	$ 47,500
Net Purchases.................................	288,500
Net Sales..	440,000
Gross Profit Rate	30%

Requirement

1. Use the gross profit method to estimate the amount of Speaker Shop's inventory loss.

E6-13B. Inventory turnover (*Learning Objective 8*) 10–15 min.

Pete's Plants has the following information as of October 31, 2015:

Sales Revenue...	$1,345,000
Cost of Goods Sold:	
Beginning Inventory .... $ 30,000	
Net Purchases.. 840,600	
Cost of Goods Available 870,600	
Ending Inventory.. 41,000	
Cost of Goods Sold	829,600
Gross Profit...	515,400
Operating Expenses	109,000
Net Income	$ 406,400

Requirements

1. Compute the rate of inventory turnover for Pete's Plants for the year ended October 31, 2015. Round the result to two decimal places.

2. The rate of inventory turnover for Pete's Plants was 21.96 in 2014. Has the rate improved or deteriorated?

E6-14B. FIFO versus average cost and inventory turnover (Learning Objectives 2, 3, & 8) 20–25 min.

Calco's sales for the year 2015 were $115,000 ($92/unit). On January 1, 2015, Calco's beginning inventory showed 120 units, costing $4,800. During 2015, Calco purchased 1,420 units at $38 each. Calco's income statement is as follows

	Units	Income Statement Inventory Costing Method FIFO	Weighted Average
Sales	_____	_____	_____
Cost of Goods Sold:			
Beginning Inventory	_____	_____	_____
Purchases	_____	_____	_____
Goods Available for Sale	_____	_____	_____
Ending Inventory	_____	_____	_____
Cost of Goods Sold	_____	_____	_____
Gross Profit		_____	_____
Operating Expenses		$25,000	$25,000
Operating Income		_____	_____
Income Tax Expense (30%)		_____	_____
Net Income		_____	_____

Requirements

1. Complete the income statement for Calco, using FIFO and weighted average cost methods.

2. Calculate the inventory turnover, using FIFO and weighted average cost methods.

3. Which method shows higher profit and inventory turnover? Explain.

EXERCISES (ALTERNATES 1, 2, AND 3)

These alternative exercise sets are available for your practice benefit on **MyAccountingLab**.

PROBLEMS (GROUP A)

P6-1A. Computing FIFO and journalizing inventory transactions (*Learning Objectives 1 & 2*) 15–20 min.

Inland Equipment sells hand-held engine analyzers to automotive service shops. Inland Equipment started April with an inventory of 85 units that cost a total of $12,750. During the month, Inland Equipment purchased and sold merchandise on account as follows:

Apr 6	Purchased 125 units @ $160
13	Sold 110 units @ $310
19	Purchased 130 units @ $168
25	Sold 80 units @ $310
29	Sold 75 units @ $310

Inland Equipment uses the FIFO method. Cash payments on account totalled $21,700. Operating expenses for the month were $12,000, with two-thirds paid in cash and the rest accrued as Accounts Payable.

Requirements

1. Which inventory method (excluding specific-unit) most likely mimics the physical flow of Inland Equipment's inventory?

2. Prepare an inventory subsidiary ledger, using FIFO cost, for this merchandise.

3. Journalize all transactions using FIFO. Record the payments on account and the operating expenses on the 30th.

P6-2A. Computing average cost and journalizing inventory transactions (*Learning Objectives 2 & 5*) 15–20 min.

Refer to the data for Inland Equipment in P6-1A. However, assume Inland Equipment uses the average cost method.

Requirements

1. Prepare an inventory subsidiary ledger using average cost. Round the average unit cost to the nearest cent and all other amounts to the nearest dollar.

2. Prepare a multi-step income statement for Inland Equipment for the month of April.

P6-3A. FIFO and average cost (*Learning Objectives 2 & 3*) 15–20 min.

MAC Industries completed the following inventory transactions during the month of August:

Date	Item	Quantity	Unit Cost
Aug 1	Balance	25	$80
4	Purchase	40	$78
12	Sale	52	
22	Purchase	30	$77
31	Sale	22	

Requirements

1. Without resorting to calculations, determine which inventory method will result in MAC Industries paying the lowest income taxes.

2. Prepare an inventory subsidiary ledger using FIFO.

3. Prepare an inventory subsidiary ledger using average cost.

P6-4A. Lower of cost or net realizable value (*Learning Objective 4*) 10–15 min.

Titan Offroad Equipment uses the FIFO inventory method and values its inventory using the lower of cost or net realizable value rule. Titan Offroad Equipment has the following account balances at December 31, 2015, prior to releasing the financial statements for the year:

Inventory		Cost of Goods Sold		Sales Revenue	
Beg Bal 54,300					
End Bal 61,100		Bal 258,600		Bal 419,500	

The accountant for Titan Offroad Equipment has determined that the replacement cost (current market value) of the ending inventory as of December 31, 2015, is $58,300.

Requirements

1. Which accounting principle or concept is most relevant to Titan Offroad Equipment's decision to utilize LCNRV?

2. What value would Titan Offroad Equipment report on the statement of financial position at December 31, 2015, for inventory?

3. Prepare any adjusting journal entry required from the information given.

P6-5A. Lower of cost or net realizable value (*Learning Objective 4*) 10–15 min.

Due to a nationwide recession, PC World's merchandise inventory is gathering dust. It is now December 31, 2015, and the $162,000 that PC World paid for its ending inventory is $14,000 higher than current replacement cost. Before any adjustments at the end of the period, PC World's Cost of Goods Sold account has a balance of $628,000. PC World uses lower of cost or net realizable value to value its ending inventory.

Requirements

1. What amount should PC World report for inventory on the statement of financial position?

2. What amount should PC World report for cost of goods sold?

3. Journalize any required entries.

P6-6A. Inventory errors (*Learning Objective 6*) 20–25 min.

A & R Industrial Supply shows the following financial statement data for 2013, 2014, and 2015. Prior to issuing the 2015 statements, auditors found that the ending inventory for 2013 was understated by $8,000 and that the ending inventory for 2015 was overstated by $9,000. The ending inventory at December 31, 2014, was correct.

(In thousands)	2015		2014		2013	
Sales Revenue		$210		$191		$186
Cost of Goods Sold:						
Beginning Inventory	$ 12		$ 18		$ 15	
Net Purchases	143		121		128	
Cost of Goods Available	155		139		143	
Ending Inventory	16		12		18	
Cost of Goods Sold		139		127		125
Gross Profit		71		64		61
Operating Expenses		46		43		42
Net Income		$ 25		$ 21		$ 19

Requirements

1. State whether each year's net income before corrections is understated or overstated and indicate the amount of the understatement or overstatement.

2. Prepare corrected income statements for the three years.

3. What is the impact on the 2015 income statement if the 2013 inventory error is left uncorrected?

P6-7A. Estimating ending inventory (*Learning Objective 7*) 15–20 min.

Amtran Enterprises lost its entire inventory in a hurricane that occurred on May 31, 2015. Over the past five years, gross profit has averaged 32% of net sales. The company's records reveal the following data for the month of May:

Beginning Inventory	$ 38,600
Net Purchases	341,900
Sales	530,400
Sales Returns and Allowances	12,300
Sales Discounts	6,500

Requirements

1. Estimate the May 31 inventory using the gross profit method.

2. Prepare the May income statement through gross profit for Amtran Enterprises.

Quick solution:

1. May 31 estimated inventory = $32,612;
2. Gross Profit = $163,712

P6-8A. Inventory turnover (*Learning Objective 8*) 10–15 min.

Motion Auto has the following information for the years ending December 31, 2015 and 2014:

(In thousands)	2015		2014	
Sales Revenue		$242		$239
Cost of Goods Sold:				
Beginning Inventory	$ 22		$ 38	
Net Purchases	152		144	
Cost of Goods Available	174		182	
Ending Inventory	13		22	
Cost of Goods Sold		161		160
Gross Profit		81		79
Operating Expenses		55		54
Net Income		$ 26		$ 25

Requirements

1. Compute the rate of inventory turnover for Motion Auto for the years ended December 31, 2015 and 2014. Round the result to two decimal places.

2. What is a likely cause for the change in the rate of inventory turnover from 2014 to 2015?

P6-9A. Inventory turnover (*Learning Objective 8*) 20–25 min.

Luson's manager is quite concerned about its inventory turnover and would like to improve the turnover. The following is the financial information for the past two years:

	2014	2015
Sales	$150,000	$165,000
Inventory	20,500	24,500

Luson's financial objective is to continue with the same growth rate in sales for 2016. Its cost of goods sold is 60% of the sales.

Requirements

1. What is the inventory turnover for 2015?

2. What are the projected sales in 2016?

3. With the projected growth in sales in 2016, if Luson wants to increase inventory turnover to 5.5 times, what should the inventory be?

P6-10A. Computing FIFO, specific-identification, average cost, and journalizing inventory transactions (*Learning Objectives 2, 3, & 9*) 40–45 min.

Silverin Gifts, Inc. had the following transactions related to purchases and sales of merchandise for the last month. The selling price of silver plates was $120 each, with a credit term of 2/10, n/30. All purchases were on credit, with a term of 2/10, n/30.

Mar 5	Purchased 25 silver plates at $55 each.
7	Sold 15 silver plates to Botan, Inc.
10	Purchased 20 silver plates at $58 each.
15	Sold 10 silver plates to Zenith Co.
17	Zenith returned 5 silver plates to Silverin.
21	Purchased 40 silver plates at $60 each.
25	Sold 12 silver plates to Raj Co.
30	Sold 15 silver plates to Kito Co.

On March 1, Silverin had five silver plates in inventory, with a total cost of $260.

Requirements

1. Calculate the ending inventory and cost of goods sold, using a perpetual inventory system:

   a. FIFO

   b. Average cost (round the average unit cost to the nearest cent and all other amounts to the nearest cent)

2. Calculate the ending inventory and cost of goods sold, using a periodic inventory system:

   a. FIFO

   b. Average cost (round the average unit cost to the nearest cent and all other amounts to the nearest cent)

3. Prepare the journal entries, using a perpetual inventory system:

   a. FIFO

   b. Average cost (round the average unit cost to the nearest cent and all other amounts to the nearest cent)

4. Calculate the ending inventory and cost of goods sold, assuming Silverin uses the specific-identification method. Silverin provided the following additional information:

   - Mar 7 sale: All units were taken from the March 5 purchase.
   - Mar 15 sale: Five units were taken from the beginning inventory, five units from the Mar 10 purchase.
   - Mar 17 sales return: Five units were returned to the March 10 purchase.
   - Mar 25 sale: All units were taken from the March 21 purchase.
   - Mar 30 sale: All units were taken from the March 21 purchase.

P6-11A. Correcting inventory errors (*Learning Objective 6*) 20–25 min.

Raj Trading reported the following amounts in its financial statements:

	Financial Statement for Year Ended Dec. 31		
	2015	2016	2017
(a) Cost of Goods Sold	$ 715,000	$ 847,000	$ 735,000
(b) Net Income	275,000	220,000	292,000
(c) Total Current Assets	865,000	764,000	847,000
(d) Shareholders' Equity	1,287,000	1,169,000	1,232,000

In making the physical count of inventory, the following errors were made:

1. Inventory on December 31, 2015, included $25,000 of goods that were on consignment from a friend of the owner.

2. Inventory on December 31, 2016, did not count a section of inventory, $42,000.

Requirements

For each of the preceding financial statement items—(a), (b), (c), and (d)—prepare a schedule and show the adjustments that would have been necessary to correct the reported amounts.

Cost of Goods Sold	2015	2016	2017
Reported			
Adjustments for (1)			
Adjustments for (2)			
Corrected			

Total Current Assets	2015	2016	2017
Reported			
Adjustments for (1)			
Adjustments for (2)			
Corrected			

Net Income	2015	2016	2017
Reported			
Adjustments for (1)			
Adjustments for (2)			
Corrected			

Shareholders' Equity	2015	2016	2017
Reported			
Adjustments for (1)			
Adjustments for (2)			
Corrected			

PROBLEMS (GROUP B)

P6-1B. Computing FIFO and journalizing inventory transactions (*Learning Objectives 1 & 2*) 15–20 min.

Builder Bee Equipment sells hand-held engine analyzers to automotive service shops. Builder Bee Equipment started April with an inventory of 45 units that cost a total of $5,760. During the month, Builder Bee Equipment purchased and sold merchandise on account as follows:

Apr 6	Purchased 115 units @ $142
13	Sold 100 units @ $300
19	Purchased 80 units @ $152
25	Sold 40 units @ $300
29	Sold 75 units @ $300

Builder Bee Equipment uses the FIFO method. Cash payments on account totalled $20,000. Operating expenses for the month were $15,000, with two-thirds paid in cash and the rest accrued as Accounts Payable.

Requirements

1. Which inventory method (excluding specific-unit) most likely mimics the physical flow of Builder Bee Equipment's inventory?

2. Prepare an inventory subsidiary ledger using FIFO cost for this merchandise.

3. Journalize all transactions using FIFO. Record the payments on account and the operating expenses on the 30th.

P6-2B. Computing average cost and journalizing inventory transactions (*Learning Objectives 2 & 5*) 15–20 min.

Refer to the data for Builder Bee Equipment in P6-1B. However, assume Builder Bee Equipment uses the average cost method.

Requirements

1. Prepare an inventory subsidiary ledger using average cost. Round the average unit cost to the nearest cent and all other amounts to the nearest dollar.

2. Prepare a multi-step income statement for Builder Bee Equipment for the month of April.

P6-3B. FIFO and average cost (*Learning Objectives 2 & 3*) 15–20 min.

Widget, Corp. completed the following inventory transactions during the month of January:

Date	Item	Quantity	Unit Cost
Jan 1	Balance	15	$50
4	Purchase	55	$55
12	Sale	66	
22	Purchase	35	$58
31	Sale	24	

Requirements

1. Without resorting to calculations, determine which inventory method will result in Widget, Corp. paying the lowest income taxes.

2. Prepare an inventory subsidiary ledger using FIFO.

3. Prepare an inventory subsidiary ledger using average cost.

P6-4B. Lower of cost or net realizable value (*Learning Objective 4*) 10–15 min.

Richmond Sporting Goods uses the FIFO inventory method and values its inventory using the lower of cost or net realizable value (LCNRV) rule. Richmond Sporting Goods has the following account balances at May 31, 2015, prior to releasing the financial statements for the year:

Inventory		Cost of Goods Sold		Sales Revenue	
Beg Bal 41,800					
End Bal 68,900		Bal 206,000			Bal 303,000

The accountant for Richmond Sporting Goods has determined that the replacement cost (current market value) of the ending inventory as of May 31, 2015, is $54,000.

Requirements

1. Which accounting principle or concept is most relevant to Richmond Sporting Goods' decision to utilize LCNRV?

2. What value would Richmond Sporting Goods report on the statement of financial position at May 31, 2015, for inventory?

3. Prepare any adjusting journal entry required from the information given.

P6-5B. Lower of cost or net realizable value (LCNRV) (*Learning Objective 4*) 10–15 min.

Due to a nationwide recession, Amesbury Systems' merchandise inventory is gathering dust. It is now October 31, 2015, and the $163,300 that Amesbury Systems paid for its ending inventory is $18,500 higher than current replacement cost. Before any adjustments at the end of the period, Amesbury Systems' Cost of Goods Sold account has a balance of $695,000. Amesbury Systems uses lower of cost or net realizable value to value its ending inventory.

Requirements

1. What amount should Amesbury Systems report for inventory on the statement of financial position?
2. What amount should Amesbury Systems report for cost of goods sold?
3. Journalize any required entries.

P6-6B. Inventory errors (*Learning Objective 6*) 20–25 min.

Lally Industries shows the following financial statement data for 2013, 2014, and 2015.

(In thousands)	2015		2014		2013	
Net Sales Revenue		$205		$170		$175
Cost of Goods Sold:						
Beginning Inventory	$ 12		$ 27		$ 24	
Net Purchases	138		103		126	
Cost of Goods Available	150		130		150	
Ending Inventory	21		12		27	
Cost of Goods Sold		129		118		123
Gross Profit		76		52		52
Operating Expenses		47		31		36
Net Income		$ 29		$ 21		$ 16

Prior to issuing the 2015 statements, auditors found that the ending inventory for 2013 was understated by $5,000 and that the ending inventory for 2015 was overstated by $12,000. The ending inventory at December 31, 2014, was correct.

Requirements

1. State whether each year's net income before corrections is understated or overstated and indicate the amount of the understatement or overstatement.
2. Prepare corrected income statements for the three years.
3. What is the impact on the 2015 income statement if the 2013 inventory error is left uncorrected?

P6-7B. Estimating ending inventory (*Learning Objective 7*) 15–20 min.

Olympic Village Enterprises lost its entire inventory in a hurricane that occurred on July 31, 2015. Over the past five years, gross profit has averaged 30% of net sales. The company's records reveal the following data for the month of July:

Beginning Inventory	$ 37,100
Net Purchases	294,600
Sales	540,100
Sales Returns and Allowances	72,200
Sales Discounts	8,300

Requirements

1. Estimate the July 31 inventory using the gross profit method.
2. Prepare the July income statement through gross profit for Olympic Village Enterprises.

P6-8B. Inventory turnover (*Learning Objective 8*) 10–15 min

Hulu's Hybrids has the following information for the years ending January 31, 2015 and 2014:

(In thousands)	2015		2014	
Sales Revenue		$235		$213
Cost of Goods Sold:				
Beginning Inventory	$ 23		$ 33	
Net Purchases	141		147	
Cost of Goods Available	164		180	
Ending Inventory	6		23	
Cost of Goods Sold		158		157
Gross Profit		77		56
Operating Expenses		59		42
Net Income		$ 18		$ 14

Requirements

1. Compute the rate of inventory turnover for Hulu's Hybrids for the years ended January 31, 2015 and 2014. Round the result to two decimal places.

2. What is a likely cause for the change in the rate of inventory turnover from 2014 to 2015?

P6-9B. Inventory turnover (*Learning Objective 8*) 20–25 min.

Taiping's owner thinks he manages his inventory quite well. However, his accountant advises him that the industry average of inventory turnover is nine times higher than his. The following is the financial information for the past two years:

	2014	2015
Sales	$360,000	$378,000
Inventory	42,500	33,100

Taiping's financial objective is to continue with the same growth rate in sales for 2016. Its cost of goods sold is 70% of the sales.

Requirements

1. What is the inventory turnover for 2015?

2. What are the projected sales in 2016?

3. With the projected growth in sales in 2016, if Taiping wants to increase inventory turnover by nine times, what should the inventory be?

P6-10B. Computing FIFO, specific-identification, average cost, and journalizing inventory transactions (*Learning Objectives 2, 3, & 9*) 40–45 min.

Hamada Hand Tools, Inc. (HHT) had the following transactions related to purchases and sales of merchandise for the last month. The selling price of hand tools was $80 each, with a credit term of 2/10, n/30. All purchases were on credit, with a term of 2/10, n/30.

May 2	Purchased 30 hand tools at $45 each.
6	Sold 15 hand tools to CAT Construction, Inc.
10	Purchased 25 hand tools at $42 each.
14	Sold 20 hand tools to Max Tools.
16	Max Tools returned 2 hand tools to HHT.
18	Sold 12 hand tools to Parker Co.
22	Purchased 40 hand tools at $44 each.
27	Sold 25 hand tools to Bibby Co.

On May 1, HHT had 10 hand tools in inventory, with a total cost of $480.

Requirements

1. Calculate the ending inventory and cost of goods sold using a perpetual inventory system:

   a. FIFO

   b. Average cost (round the average unit cost to the nearest cent and all other amounts to the nearest dollar)

2. Calculate the ending inventory and cost of goods sold using a periodic inventory system:

   a. FIFO

   b. Average cost (round the average unit cost to the nearest cent and all other amounts to the nearest dollar)

3. Prepare the journal entries using a perpetual inventory system:

   a. FIFO

   b. Average cost (round the average unit cost to the nearest cent and all other amounts to the nearest dollar)

4. Calculate the ending inventory and cost of goods sold, assuming HHT is using the specific-identification method. HHT provided the following additional information:

   - May 6 sale: All units were taken from the May 2 purchase.

   - May 14 sale: Ten units were taken from the beginning inventory and 10 units from the May 10 purchase.

   - May 16 sales return: Two units were returned to the beginning inventory cost.

   - May 18 sale: All units were taken from the May 10 purchase.

   - May 27 sale: All units were taken from the May 22 purchase.

P6-11B. Correcting inventory errors (*Learning Objective 6*) 20–25 min.

Suresh Import, Inc. reported the following amounts in its financial statements:

	Financial Statement for Year Ended Dec. 31		
	2015	2016	2017
(a) Cost of Goods Sold	$425,000	$369,000	$406,000
(b) Net Income	128,000	240,000	148,000
(c) Total Current Assets	465,000	547,000	527,000
(d) Shareholders' Equity	782,000	896,000	876,000

In making the physical count of inventory, the following errors were made:

1. Inventory on December 31, 2015: did not count a section of inventory, $45,000.

2. Inventory on December 31, 2016: included $32,000 of goods that were sold and set aside to be shipped the next day.

Requirements

For each of the preceding financial statement items—(a), (b), (c), and (d)—prepare a schedule and show the adjustments that would have been necessary to correct the reported amounts.

Cost of Goods Sold	2015	2016	2017
Reported			
Adjustments for (1)			
Adjustments for (2)			
Corrected			

Total Current Assets	2015	2016	2017
Reported			
Adjustments for (1)			
Adjustments for (2)			
Corrected			

Net Income	2015	2016	2017
Reported			
Adjustments for (1)			
Adjustments for (2)			
Corrected			

Shareholders' Equity	2015	2016	2017
Reported			
Adjustments for (1)			
Adjustments for (2)			
Corrected			

PROBLEMS (ALTERNATES 1, 2, AND 3)

These alternative problem sets are available for your practice benefit on
MyAccountingLab.

CONTINUING EXERCISE

This exercise continues the Graham's Yard Care, Inc. exercise begun in Chapter 1. Consider the July transactions for Graham's Yard Care that were presented in Chapter 5. (Cost data have been removed from the sale transactions.)

Jul 2	Completed lawn service and received cash of $500.
5	Purchased 100 plants on account for inventory, $250, plus freight in of $10.
15	Sold 40 plants on account, $400.
17	Consulted with a client on landscaping design for a fee of $150 on account.
20	Purchased 100 plants on account for inventory, $300.
21	Paid on account, $100.
25	Sold 100 plants for cash, $700.
31	Recorded the following adjusting entries:
	Accrued salaries for the month of July equal $225
	Depreciation on equipment $30
	Physical count of plant inventory, 50 plants

Refer to the T-accounts for Graham's Yard Care, Inc. from the continuing exercise in Chapter 3.

Requirements

1. Prepare inventory subsidiary ledgers for July for Graham's Yard Care, Inc. using the FIFO method.

2. Journalize and post the July transactions using the inventory subsidiary ledger created in Requirement 1. Omit explanations. Key all items by date. Compute each account balance, and denote the balance as *Bal*.

3. Journalize and post the adjusting entries. Denote each adjustment amount as *Adj*.

4. Journalize and post closing entries. After posting all closing entries, prove the equality of debits and credits in the ledger.

CONTINUING PROBLEM

This continues our accounting for Aqua Elite, Inc. As stated in the continuing problem in Chapter 5, Aqua Elite, Inc. began selling pools and spas in August. For this problem, we will focus on the purchase and sales of spas during the month of September. The purchases and sales of spa inventory for the month of September are as follows:

Spa Inventory		
	Unit @ Cost	Total Cost
August 31 balance	3 units @ $1,800/each	$ 5,400
September 5 purchase	5 units @ $2,000/each	$10,000
September 11 sale	4 units	
September 17 purchase	6 units @ $2,100/each	$12,600
September 21 sale	5 units	
September 25 purchase	5 units @ $2,200/each	$11,000
September 29 sale	4 units	

Requirements

1. Assuming that Aqua Elite, Inc. uses the FIFO inventory cost flow assumption, what is the September 30 ending spa inventory balance and September cost of goods sold for spas?

2. Assuming that Aqua Elite, Inc. uses the average cost inventory cost flow assumption, what is the September 30 ending spa inventory balance and September cost of goods sold for spas?

APPLY YOUR KNOWLEDGE

ETHICS IN ACTION

Case 1.   Julie Robertson recently went to work for K & K Enterprises as the accounting manager. At the end of the year, Jeffrey Baker, the CEO, called Julie into his office for a meeting. Mr. Baker explained to Julie that K & K Enterprises was in the midst of obtaining a substantial investment of cash by a major investor. Mr. Baker explained that he was concerned that the investor would decide not to invest in K & K Enterprises when it saw the current year's results of operations. Mr. Baker then asked Julie to revise the current year's financial statements by increasing the value of the ending inventory in order to decrease cost of goods sold and increase net income. Mr. Baker tried to reassure Julie by explaining that the company is undertaking a new advertising campaign that will result in a significant improvement in the company's income in the following year. Julie is concerned about the future of her job, as well as others within the company, if the company does not receive the investment of cash.

Requirements

1. What would you do if you were in Julie's position?

2. If Julie increases the value of the current year's ending inventory, what will be the effect on the following year's net income?

Case 2.   Inland Standard Equipment, which sells industrial handling equipment, values its inventory using FIFO. During the recent year, Inland Standard Equipment has experienced a significant decrease in the cost of its inventory items. Although the net income for the current year has been fairly good, Roberta Hill, the company president, wishes it was higher because the company has been considering borrowing money to purchase a new building. Mrs. Hill has heard that a company's choice of inventory valuation method can impact the net income of the company. Mrs. Hill has asked the controller, Vicki Simpson, to explore the possibility of changing the company's inventory valuation method.

Requirement

1. If you were in Vicki's position how would you respond to Mrs. Hill? Address potential ethical implications and applicable accounting principles in your answer.

KNOW YOUR BUSINESS

FINANCIAL ANALYSIS

Purpose: To help familiarize you with the financial reporting of a real company to further your understanding of the chapter material you are learning.

The Bombardier Annual Report, Year Ended January 31, 2012 is included in MyAccountingLab. Access the annual report and answer the following questions.

Requirements

1. Which note discusses the inventory costing method used by Bombardier Inc.? What types of costs are included in inventories?

2. Which note discloses the types of inventories held by Bombardier? Describe the types of inventory that Bombardier has and why? What are the Advances and Progress Billings and why are these deducted in determining inventories? What is included in "Finished Products"?

3. What is the amount of inventories recognized in cost of sales for 2012? What is the gross inventory balance (before taking the deduction for the Advances and Progress Billings) for 2012? Using these two numbers, calculate an inventory turnover ratio for 2012. Why might an inventory turnover ratio not be very relevant or useful in the case of Bombardier?

INDUSTRY ANALYSIS

Purpose: To help you understand and compare the performance of two companies in the same industry.

Now access The Boeing Company's 2012 Annual Report. To do this from the internet, go to their webpage for the Investor Relations at http://www.boeing.com/companyoffices/financial/quarterly.htm and, under Annual Report, go to the 2012 Annual Report.

Requirement

1. Calculate the inventory turnover for both companies (calculate the turnover for January 31, 2012 for Bombardier and for December 31, 2012 for Boeing). For both companies, use the inventory balances before the deduction for Advances and Progress Billings in calculating the turnover ratio. Who has the highest inventory turnover? Is that good or bad? Is it better to have a high inventory turnover or a low inventory turnover?

SMALL BUSINESS ANALYSIS

Purpose: To help you understand the importance of cash flows in the operation of a small business.

It's the end of the year and your warehouse manager just finished taking a physical count of the inventory on hand. Because you are utilizing the perpetual inventory method with a relatively sophisticated inventory software program, you expect that the ending inventory balance will be pretty close to the balance on your general ledger. In the past, you've had to make some pretty large adjustments for inventory shrinkage, but with the new security measures you've installed to safeguard your inventory, you're expecting that any shrinkage adjustment this year will be minimal. At least you hope that's the case, because your net income can't take many more adjustments. This year's financial statements are very important to your banker because of the loan renewal coming up early next year.

You look at the amount from the final inventory count and it reads $467,450. You go to the general ledger Merchandise Inventory account and it reads $498,500. You look at the preliminary income statement, which doesn't reflect any of these adjustments yet, and the net income is $128,400. You remember that the banker said that he really wanted to see a net income of at least $100,000 this year.

Requirements

1. Calculate the effect that the required inventory adjustments will have on the net income for the year. Would your banker be happy or not so happy when you presented the financial statements to him after these adjustments?

2. If the adjustment you made for inventory shrinkage last year was about $10,000, should that cause you any concern for the amount of adjustment you have to make this year?

3. In addition to the impact that the inventory adjustment might have on your loan renewal, what effect did it have on your cash flow during the year?

WRITTEN COMMUNICATION

You just got off the telephone with one of your clients who has decided to expand her business by beginning to offer some merchandise for sale. Previously the company had only been a consulting business, but now it has an opportunity to sell some product from a new line offered by one of its clients.

The client's question to you seems rather simple, at least in her eyes. Which inventory costing method should the client use that will give the highest amount of net income? Because the consulting part of the business has not been doing very well lately, the company wants to have a lot of net income from this new side of the business so that the income statement will look good at the end of the year. The company has heard that either average cost or FIFO will result in higher net income, but it is not certain which it is. Plus, the company definitely plans to always sell the oldest merchandise first, so will this have any impact on which method it chooses? The question does seem simple, but is the answer simple?

Requirement

1. Respond to your client either with a memo, a letter, or an email.

Self Check Answers
1. c 2. b 3. c 4. d 5. b 6. b 7. b 8. d 9. a 10. b

COMPREHENSIVE PROBLEM

THE ACCOUNTING CYCLE FOR A MERCHANDISER INCLUDING INVENTORY VALUATION

Wild Wheels, Inc. wholesales a line of custom mountain bikes. Wild Wheels' inventory as of November 30, 2015, consisted of 20 bikes costing $550 each. Wild Wheels' trial balance as of November 30 appears as follows:

	ACCOUNT	DEBIT	CREDIT
	Wild Wheels, Inc. **Trial Balance** **November 30, 2015**		
	Cash	$ 9,150	
	Accounts Receivable	12,300	
	Inventory	11,000	
	Supplies	900	
	Office Equipment	18,000	
	Accumulated Depreciation, Office Equipment		3,000
	Accounts Payable		1,325
	Note Payable, Long-Term		5,000
	Common Shares		8,500
	Retained Earnings		21,425
	Dividends	4,250	
	Sales Revenues		93,500
	Sales Returns and Allowances	1,700	
	Sales Discounts	1,275	
	Cost of Goods Sold	46,750	
	Sales Commissions	11,300	
	Office Salaries Expense	7,425	
	Office Rent Expense	5,500	
	Shipping Expense	3,200	
	Total	$132,750	$132,750

During the month of December 2015 Wild Wheels, Inc., had the following transactions:

Dec 4	Purchased 10 mountain bikes for $575 each from Slickrock Bicycle, Co. on account, terms 2/15, n/45, FOB destination.
6	Sold 14 mountain bikes for $1,100 each on account to Allsport, Inc., terms 3/10, n/30, FOB destination.
8	Paid $175 freight charges to deliver goods to Allsport, Inc.
10	Received $6,200 from Cyclemart as payment on a November 17 purchase. Terms were n/30.
12	Purchased $350 of supplies on account from Office Maxx, terms 2/10, n/30, FOB destination.
14	Received payment in full from Allsport, Inc. for the December 6 sale.
16	Purchased 15 mountain bikes for $600 each from Slickrock Bicycle, Co. on account, terms 2/15, n/45, FOB destination.
19	Sold 18 mountain bikes for $1,125 each on account to Bikeworld, Inc., terms 2/15, n/45, FOB shipping point.

20	Paid Slickrock Bicycle, Co. the amount due from the December 4 purchase in full.
20	Paid for the supplies purchased on December 12.
22	Paid sales commissions, $875.
30	Paid current month's rent, $500.

Requirements

1. Using the transactions listed above, prepare an inventory subsidiary ledger for Wild Wheels, Inc. for the month of December. Wild Wheels, Inc. uses the FIFO inventory costing method.

2. Open four-column general ledger accounts and enter the balances from the November 30 trial balance.

3. Record each transaction in the general journal. Explanations are not required. Post the journal entries to the general ledger, creating new ledger accounts as necessary. Omit posting references. Calculate the new account balances.

4. Prepare an unadjusted trial balance as of December 31, 2015.

5. Journalize and post the adjusting journal entries based on the following information, creating new ledger accounts as necessary:

   a. Depreciation expense on office equipment, $1,650.

   b. Supplies on hand, $125.

   c. Accrued salaries expense for the office receptionist, $675.

6. Prepare an adjusted trial balance as of December 31, 2015. Use the adjusted trial balance to prepare Wild Wheels, Inc.'s multi-step income statement, statement of retained earnings, and classified statement of financial position for the year ending December 31, 2015.

7. Journalize and post the closing entries.

8. Prepare a post-closing trial balance at December 31, 2015.

Appendix 6A

L.O. **9** (Appendix 6A) Compute inventory costs using different methods under a periodic inventory system

HOW DOES A COMPANY VALUE INVENTORY UNDER A PERIODIC INVENTORY SYSTEM?

When using the FIFO method in a periodic inventory system, the method of calculating the cost of goods sold and ending inventory is different from that used in a perpetual inventory system. However, the amounts of both the cost of goods sold and the ending inventory are the *same*.

When using the average cost method in a periodic inventory system, the method of calculating the cost of goods sold and ending inventory is different from that used in a perpetual inventory system, and the amounts of both the cost of goods sold and the ending inventory are *different* as well. This is because in the periodic inventory system there is only one average cost, which we call a **weighted average cost**, while in the perpetual inventory system we have a new average cost every time we sell or purchase new inventory, which we call a **moving average cost**.

In a periodic inventory system, the inventory level is not updated until the end of the accounting period. Let's use the data from Northwest Outfitters used in the chapter to illustrate. Northwest would add the beginning inventory to all the purchases incurred during the accounting period and conduct a physical count of inventory at the end of the accounting period. At this point, we need to assign the cost to the inventory. Using the FIFO costing method, the first costs incurred by the company are the first ones to get assigned to COGS; therefore, the ending inventory costs will come from the last inventory items purchased. Since nine parkas were purchased on different dates, we will need to get the purchase price from the most recent purchase and then go back to the previous purchase price, if needed.

		Unit	Cost $	Total $
Sep 1	Beginning Inventory	1	$40	$ 40
5	Purchase	6	$45	$270
26	Purchase	7	$50	$350
	Goods Available for Sale	14		$660

Northwest will first assign $50 to the two unsold parkas, since these items are from the most recent purchase price. The following shows the calculations for the ending inventory and the cost of goods sold:

FIFO Method:

Ending Inventory	2 × $50 =	$100
		$100
Goods Available for Sale		$660
− Ending Inventory		100
= Cost of Goods Sold		$560

or

Cost of Goods Sold:

1 × $40 =	$ 40
6 × $45 =	$270
5 × $50 =	$250
	$560

Cost Available for Sale	$660
− Cost of Goods Sold	$560
= Ending Inventory	$100

As you can see, even though Northwest used the periodic system instead of the perpetual system, the ending inventory and COGS amounts are the same as the results from the perpetual system. (Refer to the calculation of the FIFO method using a perpetual system in Exhibit 6-4 on page 340.)

Using the weighted average cost method in a periodic system, Northwest needs to find out the average cost per parka for the entire inventory. Since the goods available for sale is $660 for 14 parkas, the weighted average cost per parka is $47.14 ($660/14). This is the cost that Northwest will use to assign the cost of goods sold and ending inventory amounts.

Weighted Average Cost Method:

Ending Inventory	2 × $47.14 =	$ 94.28
Goods Available for Sale		$660.00
− Ending Inventory		94.28
= Cost of Goods Sold		$565.72

or

Cost of Goods Sold:	12 × 47.14 =	$565.78
Cost Available for Sale		$660
− Cost of Goods Sold		$565.78
= Ending Inventory		$ 94.22

Notice that there are 4 cents difference between the two methods due to rounding.

Journalizing Inventory Transactions

Assuming that all purchases and sales in September were made on account and that the sales price of a parka was $80, the following journal entries would be necessary to record the above transactions:

DATE	ACCOUNTS	Periodic FIFO DR.	CR.	Periodic Moving Average DR.	CR.
Sep 5	Purchases	270		270	
	Accounts Payable		270		270
	Purchase inventory on account (6 parkas @ $45 each)				
15	Accounts Receivable	320		320	
	Sales Revenue		320		320
26	Purchases	350		350	
	Accounts Payable		350		350
	Purchase inventory on account (7 parkas @ $50 each)				
30	Accounts Receivable	640		640	
	Sales Revenue		640		640
30	Cost of Goods Sold	560		565.72	
	Inventory (100 − 40), (94.28 − 40)	60		54.28	
	Purchases		620		620
	Adjusting entry to set up ending inventory, clear out purchases account, and record COGS.				

Assets = Liabilities + Shareholders' Equity
+270   −270

Assets = Liabilities + Shareholders' Equity
+320   +320

Assets = Liabilities + Shareholders' Equity
+350   −350

Assets = Liabilities + Shareholders' Equity
+640   +640

Assets = Liabilities + Shareholders' Equity
FIFO +60   −560 +620

Assets = Liabilities + Shareholders' Equity
Average +54.28   −565.72 +620

Notice that the journal entries to record the purchases of inventory on account are almost the same, regardless of the costing method chosen. *The differences occur in the second part of the sales entries, which removes the cost of the parkas sold from the Inventory account and transfers it to Cost of Goods Sold as previously illustrated in Chapter 5.*

LEARNING OBJECTIVES

1. Describe the different types of revenue and identify when revenue is recognized
2. Identify the different types of sales and receivables and discuss related internal controls for accounts receivable
3. Use the allowance method to account for uncollectible accounts
4. Report accounts receivable on the statement of financial position
5. Account for notes receivable
6. Calculate the quick ratio and accounts receivable turnover

CHAPTER OUTLINE

CHAPTER 7

Sales and Receivables

BUSINESS, ACCOUNTING, AND YOU

Walk into a Best Buy and observe the employees operating cash registers. What are they doing? Customers are buying and paying for products, but look closely at how they are paying for their purchases. They often pay with cash or credit cards. A credit card is a promise to pay cash in the future; it's a receivable to Best Buy. It's a good receivable, since banks or credit card companies guarantee that Best Buy will collect the entire amount when it is due. Best Buy can also sell goods to other businesses on credit, which is also a receivable to Best Buy, but some businesses might default and not pay their debts.

Now think about what Best Buy does with its cash. It takes the cash and deposits it in a bank account, which it then uses to pay its bills. Best Buy must pay for the inventory it purchased, the wages it owes its employees, and the other liabilities that it incurs to operate. If it cannot pay its bills, it cannot stay in business. Being in business is about taking risks, and managing cash is a very important part of managing risk.

Accountants use accrual accounting to recognize, measure, record, and report business transactions. But managing cash and the promise of future cash is important in operating a successful business. Business is about earning net income, but to earn net income you need to be able to pay the bills. As an accountant or manager, you need to understand how businesses account for cash transactions and receivables.

In earlier chapters we have seen that net income is the result of deducting all of a business's expenses from its revenues. Therefore, it makes sense that to increase net income a business must either reduce its expenses or increase its revenues. The choice of what methods of payment a business is willing to accept from its customers can have a significant effect on the amount of revenues it is able to generate. The method of payment a business accepts is determined by the type of sales it makes.

HOW DO YOU ACCOUNT FOR REVENUE?

L.O. ① Describe the different types of revenue and identify when revenue is recognized

SALES REVENUE

Accounting for the sale of goods is similar under IFRS and ASPE. The seller recognizes sales revenue when goods and ownership are transferred to the buyers and the seller has no control over the goods. The transfer of ownership or the title is usually specified in the sales contract or the invoice. In Chapter 5, we discussed FOB shipping point and FOB destination. The point of delivery specifies when the ownership passes on to the buyer. This also has an impact on the inventory count.

REVENUE RECOGNITION

IFRS

ASPE

Sometimes, it is clear when revenue should be recognized. However, there are also situations when companies can record revenues at other points in the process of selling a product or service. The guidelines according to IFRS and the ASPE are similar in that both guidelines stipulate that revenue is recognized when (1) the risks and rewards of ownership of the goods are passed to the buyer, (2) the revenues can be reasonably measured, and (3) collection from the customer is reasonably assured. The IFRS guidelines also add that the costs associated with the goods sold should be able to be measured reliably and the seller no longer has control or managerial influence over the item to a degree that would be normally associated with ownership. We can find the specific revenue recognition principles and policies that companies use in the notes to their financial statements.

SERVICE REVENUE

Service companies recognize revenue when they have performed services for a client. Some guidelines of recognizing revenue for goods applies to services too, such as the requirements that revenues can be reasonably measured and collection from customers is reasonably assured. However, additional conditions should be satisfied, such as the stage of completion of the service can be measured reliably and that costs incurred for providing the service and those that are necessary to complete it can be measured reliably. It can sometimes be difficult to determine when precisely a service is completed, which requires judgment to be used. For example, if a company provided maintenance service to a vehicle with a guarantee that it could repair any problem arising from such services within the next 30 days, the question would be whether the revenue should be recognized directly after completing the maintenance or if the company should wait until the 30 days elapse. This is a judgment call that depends on previous experience and industry practice; in some cases, it will also require creating an allowance in case additional costs arise.

ACCOUNTING FOR REVENUE IN LONG-TERM CONTRACTS

Long-term projects such as construction of a cruise ship or a building may take more than one year to complete. If the company waited to record revenue until the delivery of the cruise ship or passing the ownership of the building when the project was completed, then the company would show only expenses and no revenues during the years when the projects were being constructed and show a huge revenue during the year of delivery. This method is called the **completed contract method**; however, this method distorts the company's economic activities. Under IFRS, the completed contract method is prohibited. Instead, the revenue from long-term contracts must be recognized using the **percentage of completion method**, if percentage of completion can be measured reliably. ASPE provides an option to use the percentage of completion or completed contract method.

IFRS

ASPE

Under the percentage of completion method, the total revenues and expenses are estimated. Then, the revenue for the first year is recognized based on the percentage of expenses incurred during the year over the total expenses of the project. For example, Kidel Constructions, Inc. estimated total revenue for a new office building of $25 million and total expenses of $20 million. During the first year of the project, Kidel incurred $8 million of expenses, which is 40% of the contract expenses ($8 million ÷ $20 million). Kidel will recognize 40% of revenue, which is $10 million ($25 million × 40%). During the second year of the project, Kidel incurred $7 million in expenses, and the total expenses incurred to date were $15 million ($8 million + $7 million). If the total estimated expenses were not expected to change, then the total expenses incurred to date were 75% ($15 million ÷ $20 million) of the total estimated expenses. The revenue for the second year is $8.75 million ([$25 million × 75% – $10 million] or [75% – 40%] × $25 million), calculated by taking 75% of the total estimated revenue and subtracting the revenue that has been recognized in the previous year, as shown in **Exhibit 7-1**:

	Year 1	Year 2
Expenses Incurred to Date	$ 8,000,000	$15,000,000
Total Estimated Expenses	$20,000,000	$20,000,000
Percentage of Completion	40%	75%
Revenue Recognized to Date	$10,000,000	$18,750,000
Revenue Recognized for the Year	$10,000,000	$ 8,750,000

Exhibit 7-1 ▲

7.1 STILL DON'T GET IT?
Visit MyAccountingLab for an alternate explanation of this important accounting concept.

The revenue to be recognized in following years would work in the same way as the second year, until the long-term project was complete.

Based on such guidelines, it is obvious that revenue recognition requires a lot of judgment to fulfill the revenue recognition criteria. For example, Kidel needs to use judgment to determine what percentage of completion the building is at when each period comes to an end to calculate the realized revenue. Another example is the manufacture of a special order for a customer. After the order is prepared but is still in the warehouse of the manufacturer waiting for the customer to pick it up, is the sale complete? Accountants have to use a high degree of judgment to determine whether revenue should be realized in this case or not. They have to review the terms of the contract, the risk of having the goods at the warehouse, and so on to determine whether the title and risk of the goods has been transferred to the customer and hence if the revenue could be realized.

WHAT ARE THE DIFFERENT TYPES OF SALES?

CASH SALES

Cash sales are the most desirable form of sales because the business receives cash immediately upon delivering goods or services. Cash sales are also the easiest type to track because customers give currency or a cheque at the time of sale. The business

L.O. ❷ Identify the different types of sales and receivables and discuss related internal controls for accounts receivable does not need to keep records of the individual customers. As demonstrated in earlier chapters, a cash sale is recorded as follows (assume the sale amount is $500):

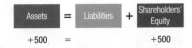

Assets	=	Liabilities	+	Shareholders' Equity
+500	=			+500

DATE	ACCOUNTS	POST REF.	DR.	CR.
	Cash		500	
	Sales			500

Although cash sales are easy to account for, businesses may limit their sales potential by not providing options for customers to buy now and pay later.

CREDIT CARD SALES

An alternative that helps businesses attract more customers is the acceptance of credit cards. There are two main types of credit cards:

- Credit cards issued by a financial institution such as a bank or a credit union, such as Scotiabank or Bank of Montreal. The most common types of these cards are Visa and MasterCard.

- Credit cards issued by a credit card company on behalf of a retail store or other corporation, such as MBNA or Hudson's Bay Company.

One of the primary benefits of credit cards is that they allow customers to buy now and pay later. Retailers who accept credit card payments do not have to worry about collecting from the customer or keeping accounts receivable records because the entity that issued the card bears the responsibility of collecting the amounts due from the customers. Instead of collecting cash from the customer, the retailer will receive payment from the issuer of the card. Another benefit of credit card sales is that they facilitate purchases made via telephone or online due to the fact that no cash has to change hands at the time of sale. One drawback to accepting credit card payments is that retailers typically pay a service fee to cover the cost of processing the transaction.

DEBIT CARD SALES

Businesses can also attract customers by accepting debit card payments in addition to cash and credit card payments. From the retailer's perspective, debit cards are nearly identical to credit cards and have the same benefits and drawbacks. The primary difference between a debit card and a credit card is how and when the cardholder must pay the card issuer.

CREDIT/DEBIT CARD PROCESSING

Most businesses hire a third-party processor to process credit and debit card transactions. Transactions are typically entered into an electronic terminal that is often rented from the processor. Businesses may also purchase a terminal if they would rather own the terminal than rent it. As previously discussed, there is a fee associated with credit and debit card transactions. The fees vary depending on the type of card processed and depending upon the specific agreement the business has with the card processor. The agreement also specifies when and how fees are paid. The most common methods of fee payment follow:

- The fees are deducted from the proceeds of each sale at the time the sale proceeds are deposited into the business's bank account.

- The fees for all transactions processed are deducted from the business's bank account on a monthly basis.

Proceeds from credit and debit card transactions are typically deposited into a business's bank account within a one- to three-day period. Therefore, credit and debit card sales are journalized in a manner similar to cash sales. Assume a business has a credit/debit card sale of $500, with a cost of the product being $350. The customer paid by credit card. The business pays $8 of processing fees, which are deducted from the proceeds. The journal entry to record the card sale is as follows:

DATE	ACCOUNTS	POST REF.	DR.	CR.
Mar 31	Cash		492	
	Credit Card Expense		8	
	Sales			500
	Cost of Goods Sold		350	
	Inventory			350

The expense associated with processing the transactions is recorded at the same time the sale proceeds are recorded. Now, assume that instead of having the processing fees deducted from the sales proceeds, the business has the fees deducted from its bank account at the end of each month. The journal entry to record the day's card sales would now look like this:

DATE	ACCOUNTS	POST REF.	DR.	CR.
Mar 31	Cash		500	
	Sales			500
	Cost of Goods Sold		350	
	Inventory			350

Notice that this entry is exactly the same as the entry required for cash sales. The expense associated with processing the transactions will be recorded at the time a statement is received from the processor or at the time the monthly bank reconciliation is prepared.

SALES ON ACCOUNT

In Chapter 5, we discussed sales of merchandise on account. When businesses agree to sell on credit, sales increase, but so does the risk of not being able to collect what is owed as a result of these sales. Accordingly, companies bear the risk of **bad debts**, or **uncollectible accounts**, which occur when a customer does not pay for the goods or services they received. Regardless of its size, a business must manage its customer relationships to avoid bad debts.

HOW DO YOU ACCOUNT FOR RECEIVABLES?

TYPES OF RECEIVABLES

Companies often make sales on account that create a receivable from the customer. The two major types of receivables are **accounts receivable** and **notes receivable**. Remember from Chapter 1 that a business's accounts receivable are current assets that reflect the amounts due from customers for credit sales of goods or services. Also recall from Chapter 2 that notes receivable are written promises by customers to pay an amount of cash to the business in the future. Notes receivable are more formal and usually longer in term than accounts receivable. Notes also usually include a charge for interest. A detailed discussion of notes receivable will follow later in the chapter.

A company may also have other receivables, such as loans to employees and interest receivable. These other receivables may be either current or long-term assets, depending on their due dates.

INTERNAL CONTROL OVER ACCOUNTS RECEIVABLE

Most companies have a credit department to evaluate customers' credit applications. The extension of credit requires a balancing act. The company wants to avoid receivables that will never be collected while at the same time granting credit to as many customers as possible. Also, companies that sell on credit often receive the related payment by mail, so internal control over collections is important. Remember, a critical element of internal control is the separation of cash-handling and cash-accounting duties.

Good internal control over accounts receivable dictates that the granting of credit, the receipt of cash, and the recording of accounts receivable transactions is done by different individuals preferably from different departments. For example, if the employee who handles the daily cash receipts also records the accounts receivable transactions, the company would have no separation of duties. The employee could pocket money received from a customer. He or she could then label the customer's account as uncollectible, and the company would **write off** the account receivable, as discussed in the next section. The company would stop billing that customer, and the employee would have covered his or her theft. For this reason, separation of duties is important.

ACCOUNTING FOR UNCOLLECTIBLE ACCOUNTS RECEIVABLE

Unfortunately, when a business chooses to sell goods or services on account, there will likely be customers who fail to pay the amount owed. When this happens, the customer's account is referred to as an uncollectible account. Uncollectible accounts reflect a cost associated with selling goods and services on account. Companies that make sales on account expect that the benefit of granting credit to customers outweighs the cost.

- **The benefit:** Increased revenues and profits from making sales to a wider range of customers.
- **The cost:** Some customers don't pay, and that creates an expense called **bad debt expense** (sometimes referred to as uncollectible accounts expense).

HOW DO YOU ACCOUNT FOR BAD DEBTS?

When businesses agree to sell on credit, sales increase, but so does the risk of not being able to collect what is owed as a result of these sales. The amount of bad debt is unknown when the sales are made. Therefore, the bad debt amount needs to be estimated. This amount is used to reduce the income and also to reduce the accounts receivable, and this amount needs to be recorded at the end of an accounting period.

THE DIRECT WRITE-OFF METHOD

The simplest way to account for uncollectible accounts is to use the **direct write-off method**. Under the direct write-off method, at the time it is determined the business will not collect from a specific customer, the business writes off that customer's account receivable. The account receivable is written off by debiting Bad Debt Expense and crediting the customer's Account Receivable. This method could be accepted if the business is doing most of its sales in cash and insignificant amounts of its sales are on account.

Otherwise, this method is not accepted for financial reporting purposes because it does not show the realizable value of accounts receivable. In addition it could violate the matching principle, because if the client defaults in the following accounting period(s), then expenses from previous periods (when the sale happened) are matched with revenues of the current period (when the client defaults), which violates the matching principle. **Exhibit 7-2** illustrates how such a situation affects the matching principle, where the expenses related to 2015 sales revenue are matched with 2016 sales revenue instead.

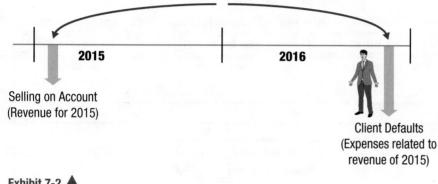

2015

Selling on Account
(Revenue for 2015)

2016

Client Defaults
(Expenses related to
revenue of 2015)

Exhibit 7-2 ▲

THE ALLOWANCE METHOD

The **allowance method** is a method of accounting for bad debts in which bad debt expense is recorded in the same period as sales revenue. Under the allowance method, a business will use an adjusting entry at the end of the period to record the bad debt expense for the period. Since the business does not know which customers will eventually not pay them, it must estimate the amount of bad debt expense based on past experience. This expense must be recognized during the same period when the credit sales are generated. The debit side of the adjusting entry will be to the Bad Debt Expense account. However, instead of crediting Accounts Receivable, a contra-account called **Allowance for Doubtful Accounts (AFDA)** will be credited. The Allowance for Doubtful Accounts is "tied" to the Accounts Receivable account and serves to reduce the **net realizable value** of the accounts receivable. The adjusting entry will look like this:

L.O. ③ Use the allowance method to account for uncollectible accounts

DATE	ACCOUNTS	POST REF.	DR.	CR.
Dec 31	Bad Debt Expense		XXX	
	Allowance for Doubtful Accounts			XXX
	To record estimated bad debts.			

The Allowance for Doubtful Accounts is utilized because the specific customers who will ultimately not pay are unknown at the time the adjusting entry is made. Companies usually create the Accounts Receivable **control account** in the general ledger. Each customer has an account in the accounts receivable subsidiary ledger under the Accounts Receivable control account. **Exhibit 7-3** illustrates the relationship between the accounts receivable subsidiary ledger and the Accounts Receivable control account on the general ledger. The subsidiary ledger shows the balances of individual customers. The beginning balance of all customers on the subsidiary ledger must comply with the total beginning balance on the Accounts Receivable control account in the general ledger (notice the beginning balances and follow the red line to find out how the balances add up to $10,000). On the other hand, customers pay during the period some or all of the amounts due. Such amounts are credited to the individual account of each customer in the subsidiary ledger and are reflected as a total in the Accounts Receivable control account. Notice the credited amount circled in green and follow the green lines to see how they add up to the $4,000 credit in balance in the Accounts Receivable general ledger account; for simplicity and to focus on the concept, it is assumed that no credit sales happened during the period. You could also now notice that the sum of the balance of all accounts receivables in the subsidiary ledger matches the balance of the Accounts Receivable control account within the general ledger.

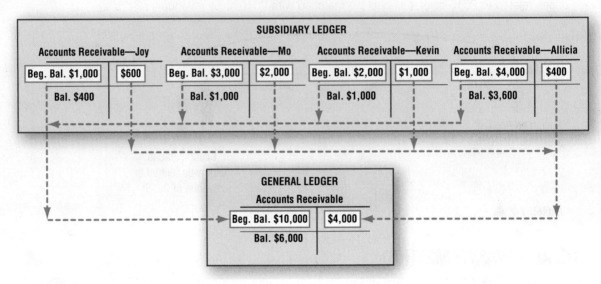

Exhibit 7-3 ▲

7.2 **STILL** DON'T GET IT **?**
Visit MyAccountingLab for an alternate explanation of this important accounting concept.

To reduce Accounts Receivable, the specific customer would have to be known so that his or her Account Receivable could be reduced in the subsidiary ledger. As we will demonstrate later in the chapter, once it is known that a specific customer's account is uncollectible, his or her Account Receivable will be written off. The offset to this entry will be to reduce the Allowance for Doubtful Accounts by an equal amount.

Estimating the Amount of Uncollectible Accounts

In order to estimate the amount of bad debt expense, a company will use its past bad debt experience to make an educated guess of how much will be uncollectible. The state of the economy, the industry the business operates in, and other variables are also used to arrive at the best estimate possible. There are two basic ways to estimate the amount of uncollectible accounts:

- Percentage of sales method or income statement approach
- Aging method or statement of financial position approach

Percentage of Sales Method The **percentage of sales method** computes the estimated amount of uncollectible accounts as a percentage of **net credit sales**. This amount is the bad debt amount. As both sales and bad debt expense are income statement accounts, this method of estimating the amount is also called the **income statement approach**. To demonstrate, let's assume that Allied Enterprises has the following selected account balances as of December 31, 2015, prior to adjusting for bad debts:

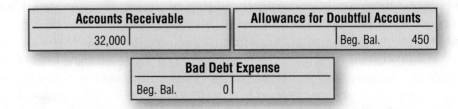

It is important to note that when using the allowance method, the Allowance for Doubtful Accounts will almost always have a balance at the end of the period. The balance in the account may have a debit or a credit balance depending on the amount of the adjusting entry from the prior period and the amount of uncollectible accounts that have been written off during the current period. Also note that the Bad Debt Expense account will always have a zero balance. This is because, as an expense account, it was closed at the end of the prior period.

Now, let's assume that Allied Enterprises estimates bad debt expense to be 1/2 of 1% of net credit sales, which totalled $300,000 during 2015. The estimated amount of bad debts is $1,500 ($300,000 × 0.005). Under the percentage of sales method, once the estimated amount of uncollectible accounts has been determined, the adjusting entry is made for that amount. The required journal entry at December 31, 2015, would be as follows:

DATE	ACCOUNTS	POST REF.	DR.	CR.
Dec 31	Bad Debt Expense		1,500	
	Allowance for Doubtful Accounts			1,500
	To record estimated bad debts.			

After posting the adjusting entry, Allied Enterprises' accounts would look like this:

Accounts Receivable	
32,000	

Allowance for Doubtful Accounts	
	Beg. Bal. 450
	1,500
	1,950

Bad Debt Expense	
Beg. Bal. 0	
1,500	
1,500	

The net realizable value of Allied Enterprises' Accounts Receivable is $30,050 at December 31, 2015 ($32,000 A/R less $1,950 Allowance for Doubtful Accounts). Notice that Bad Debt Expense reflects the calculated amount of uncollectible accounts ($1,500), whereas Allowance for Doubtful Accounts reflects a different amount ($1,950). This shows why this method is also called the income statement approach: It focuses more on the income statement than on the statement of financial position. After the adjusting entry has been posted, the income statement account (Bad Debt Expense) reflects the calculated amount of uncollectible accounts rather than the statement of financial position account (Allowance for Doubtful Accounts).

Aging Method The other method for estimating uncollectible accounts is the **aging method**. This method is more accurate because it takes into consideration the quality of the accounts receivables outstanding, allowing the business to get a better idea of which accounts are likely to default by analyzing the ages of the accounts receivables. Once again, let's assume Allied Enterprises had the following account balances at December 31, 2015, prior to adjusting for bad debts:

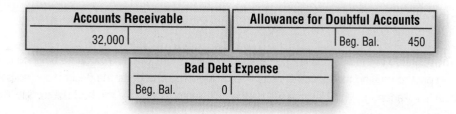

MEMORYTIPS
The result of multiplying net credit sales by the estimated bad debt expense percentage will be used in the entry regardless of the previous balance of Allowance for Doubtful Accounts.

When using the aging method, a schedule is created that reflects all of the company's individual credit customers with their account balances broken down based on how long they've been outstanding. This is known as an accounts receivable aging report. **Exhibit 7-4** reflects the accounts receivable aging report for Allied Enterprises at December 31, 2015.

| | Customer | Balance | Current | Days Past Due | | | | |
				1–30	31–60	61–90	91–180	> 181
1	B. Ashford	$ 450		150	300			
2	L. Clark	875	875					
32	M. Reynolds	575	575					
33	R. Turlock	225						225
34	K. Wilson	950				125	825	
	Total	$32,000	26,850	2,800	475	325	1,250	300

Exhibit 7-4 ▲

Once the aging report has been prepared, an estimated percentage of bad debts is determined for each age category. This percentage is then multiplied by the balance for each age category to determine the estimated bad debts for that category. These amounts are then added together to arrive at the total estimated amount of allowance for doubtful accounts for the period. The calculation for Allied Enterprises would look like this:

Account Age	Balance	Estimated Percent Uncollectible	Estimated Uncollectible Amount
Current	$26,850	2%	$ 537
1–30	2,800	5%	140
31–60	475	20%	95
61–90	325	40%	130
91–180	1,250	50%	625
> 181	300	80%	240
Total	$32,000		$1,767

Now that we know the total estimated amount of bad debts, $1,767, we are ready to make the adjusting entry. The most significant difference between the two methods is that, unlike when using the percentage of sales method, we do not simply take the calculated amount of Allowance for Doubtful Accounts and use this as the amount of the journal entry. Instead, we must look at the existing balance in Allowance for Doubtful Accounts and perform a calculation to determine the amount to use in the adjusting entry. When using the aging method, the goal is for Allowance for Doubtful Accounts to reflect the calculated amount of bad debts *after* the adjusting entry has been recorded and posted. The easiest way to determine the correct amount of the required adjusting entry is to do a T-account analysis of Allowance for Doubtful Accounts as follows:

Allowance for Doubtful Accounts	
	Beg. Bal. 450
	?
	1,767

The first step in the analysis is to enter the Allowance for Doubtful Accounts balance that existed prior to making the adjusting entry. Next, skip a line and enter the desired ending balance in the T-account. This balance will be the calculated amount of the bad debts, $1,767.

The question mark represents the adjusting entry amount that is required. This amount is determined by calculating the credit needed to bring the ending balance up to the desired amount. It is important to pay attention to whether the Allowance for Doubtful Accounts balance that existed prior to making the adjusting entry was a debit or a credit. Also, remember that the ending balance in the account will always be a credit balance. By looking at the T-account analysis, we can see that the required adjusting entry amount is $1,317 ($1,767 – $450). The required journal entry at December 31, 2015, would be as follows:

DATE	ACCOUNTS	POST REF.	DR.	CR.
Dec 31	Bad Debt Expense		1,317	
	Allowance for Doubtful Accounts			1,317
	To record estimated bad debts.			

After posting the adjusting entry, Allied Enterprises' accounts would look like this:

Accounts Receivable	
32,000	

Allowance for Doubtful Accounts		
	Beg. Bal.	450
		1,317
		1,767

Bad Debt Expense		
Beg. Bal.	0	
	1,317	
	1,317	

The net realizable value of Allied Enterprises' Accounts Receivable is $30,233 at December 31, 2015 ($32,000 A/R less $1,767 Allowance for Doubtful Accounts). Notice that Allowance for Doubtful Accounts reflects the calculated amount of estimated uncollectible accounts ($1,767) based on the aging schedule above whereas Bad Debt Expense reflects a different amount ($1,317). This shows why this method is also called the **statement of financial position approach**. This method focuses more on the statement of financial position than on the income statement. After the adjusting entry has been posted, the statement of financial position account (Allowance for Doubtful Accounts) reflects the estimated amount of uncollectible accounts rather than the income statement account (Bad Debt Expense), which represents the period's bad debt expense.

WRITING OFF BAD DEBTS UNDER THE ALLOWANCE METHOD

The entry to write off a customer's account under the allowance method begins with a credit to Accounts Receivable to remove it from the company's books with a debit made to Allowance for Doubtful Accounts. Assume that on March 5, 2016, Allied Enterprises determined that Bill Johnson's $400 account receivable was uncollectible. The entry to write off Bill Johnson's account under the allowance method would be as follows:

DATE	ACCOUNTS	POST REF.	DR.	CR.
Mar 5	Allowance for Doubtful Accounts		400	
	Accounts Receivable—Bill Johnson			400
	Wrote off Bill Johnson's account.			

Remember that the expense related to writing off Bill Johnson's account was recognized in 2015 when Allied Enterprises made the adjusting entry to record the estimated bad debts.

The Adequacy of the Allowance for Doubtful Accounts

The Allowance for Doubtful Accounts balance is built on an estimate, which is based on industry practice and previous experience. Sometimes estimates are wrong, though; for instance, the amount of actual bad debt during a period might exceed the estimated allowance, which would lead to the Allowance for Doubtful Accounts account having a debit balance. In this situation, it is preferable to revise the estimates and to accrue such unexpected expenses during the current period.

To illustrate, let's assume that Allied Enterprises had an Allowance for Doubtful Accounts balance of $2,000 on December 1, 2015. During the period, $2,500 of receivables defaulted. In this case, the Allowance for Doubtful Accounts balance ends up having a $500 debit balance—defaulted accounts receivables exceeded the original expectations of $2,000 by $500. The journal entry and the effect on the Allowance for Doubtful Accounts account would be as follows when the account is written off:

+2,500 =
−2,500

DATE	ACCOUNTS	POST REF.	DR.	CR.
Dec 15	Allowance For Doubtful Accounts		2,500	
	Accounts Recievable—Adam Tyler			2,500
	Wrote off Adam Tyler's account			

Note that a decrease in a contra-asset account would be a debit, which means an increase in assets:

Allowance for Doubtful Accounts			
Dec 15	2,500	Dec 1	2,000
Dec 31 Bal.	500		

Now, assume that Allied Enterprises reviewed their estimates and calculated the amount of bad debt based on the aging method to be $3,500. This means that the new balance in the Allowance for Doubtful Accounts after adjustments should show a credit balance of $3,500. Accordingly, the bad debt expenses for the period would be $500 + $3,500 = $4,000. The journal entry and the effect on the Allowance for Doubtful Accounts account would be as follows:

−4,000 = −4,000

DATE	ACCOUNTS	POST REF.	DR.	CR.
Dec 31	Bad Debt Expense		4,000	
	Allowance For Doubtful Accounts			4,000
	Wrote off Adam Tyler's account			

Allowance for Doubtful Accounts			
Dec 15	2,500	Dec 1	2,000
Dec 31 Bal.	500	adj.	4,000
		Bal.	3,500

MEMORY TIPS

For the aging method and to calculate bad debt expense for the period:
If the AFDA balance is a **debit, ADD** it to the estimated uncollectible accounts.
If the AFDA balance is a **credit, SUBTRACT** it from the estimated uncollectible accounts.

CONCEPT CHECK...

Will writing off Bill Johnson's $400 account reduce the net realizable value of Allied Enterprises' accounts receivable?

Answer: No, the write-off of uncollectible receivables has no impact on the net realizable value of accounts receivable. Remember that the net realizable value of accounts receivable equals the balance in the Accounts Receivable account less the balance in the related contra-account, Allowance for Doubtful Accounts. When Bill Johnson's account was written off, the asset account, Accounts Receivable, was reduced by $400. However, the Allowance for Doubtful Accounts was also reduced by $400, so the total change in the net realizable value of the accounts receivable is zero.

ALLOWANCE METHOD: RECOVERY OF ACCOUNTS PREVIOUSLY WRITTEN OFF

Entries are required to record the receipt of cash from a customer whose account was previously written off. First, the customer's Account Receivable is reinstated. Then, the payment on the account is recorded. Let's assume once again that on August 10, 2016, Bill Johnson unexpectedly sent Allied Enterprises a cheque for $250 as payment on his previously written-off account. Allied Enterprises would first reinstate the Account Receivable as follows:

DATE	ACCOUNTS	POST REF.	DR.	CR.
Aug 10	Accounts Receivable—Bill Johnson		250	
	Allowance for Doubtful Accounts			250
	Reinstated Bill Johnson's account.			

Notice again that the accounts debited and credited in this entry are exactly opposite of those used in the entry to write off the account. Allied Enterprises now records the receipt of cash as follows:

DATE	ACCOUNTS	POST REF.	DR.	CR.
Aug 10	Cash		250	
	Accounts Receivable—Bill Johnson			250
	Collected cash on account.			

Exhibit 7-5 summarizes the transactions that cause changes in Accounts Receivable and Allowance for Doubtful Accounts, and the entries required when using the allowance method.

Cash

Dr (+)	Cr (−)
(2) Collection of credit sales	
(6) Collection of written-off AR	

Accounts Receivable

Dr (+)	Cr (−)
(1) Sales on credit	(2) Collection of credit sales
	(4) Write-off of uncollectable AR
(5) Recovery of previously written-off AR	(6) Collection of written-off AR

Allowance for Doubtful Accounts

Dr (−)	Cr (+)
	(3) Adj. estimated uncollectable amount
(4) Write-off of uncollectable AR	
	(5) Recovery of previously written-off AR

Bad Debt Expense

Dr (+)	Cr (−)
(3) Adj. estimated uncollectable amount	

Sales

Dr (−)	Cr (+)
	(1) Sales on credit

Event	Journal Entries	DR.	CR.
(1) Sales	Accounts Receivable	XXXX	
	Sales		XXXX
(2) Collection of credit sales	Cash	XXXX	
	Accounts Receivable		XXXX
(3) Period-end adjusting entry	Bad Debt Expense	XXXX	
	Allowance for Doubtful Accounts		XXXX
(4) Entry to write off customer account	Allowance for Doubtful Accounts	XXXX	
	Accounts Receivable—Customer Name		XXXX
(5) and (6) Entries to record receipt of payment on an account previously written off	Accounts Receivable—Customer Name	XXXX	
	Allowance for Doubtful Accounts		XXXX
	Cash	XXXX	
	Accounts Receivable—Customer Name		XXXX

Exhibit 7-5 ▲

HOW ARE ACCOUNTS RECEIVABLE REPORTED ON THE STATEMENT OF FINANCIAL POSITION?

L.O. 4 Report accounts receivable on the statement of financial position

Accounts receivable are reported at "net realizable value" in the current assets section of the statement of financial position. There are two ways to show accounts receivable at net realizable value. For example, assume that at December 31, 2015, Allied Enterprises' Accounts Receivable balance is $32,000 and its Allowance for Doubtful Accounts balance is $1,767. Allied Enterprises could report its accounts receivable in either of the two ways shown here:

Allied Enterprises Statement of Financial Position (partial): December 31, 2015	
Accounts Receivable	$32,000
Less: Allowance for Doubtful Accounts	1,767
Accounts Receivable, Net	$30,233

Allied Enterprises Statement of Financial Position (partial): December 31. 2015	
Accounts Receivable, Net of Allowance for Doubtful Accounts of $1,767	$30,233

Most companies use the second method, but either is acceptable. The key is to show accounts receivable at net realizable value.

 CRITICAL THINKING

Take a minute to think about the impact of the following independent cases on the assets and net income, based on each of the scenarios.

1. When the company determined an uncollectible accounts receivable of $1,200, the journal entry was recorded as debit to Bad Debt Expense $1,200 and credit to Accounts Receivable $1,200.

2. When the company determined an uncollectible accounts receivable of $900, the journal entry was recorded as debit to Allowance for Doubtful Accounts $900 and credit to Accounts Receivable $900.

3. When the company determined an uncollectible accounts receivable of $2,500, the journal entry was recorded as debit to Allowance for Doubtful Accounts $2,500 and credit to Accounts Receivable $2,500. As the result, the balance of the Allowance for Doubtful Accounts has a debit balance of $2,000.

Solutions:

	Impact on Account		
	Assets	Net Income	Entry in Accounting Record
1.	−1,200	−1,200	Assets and net income would be understated. The correct entry should be: Allowance for Doubtful Accounts (Dr); Accounts Receivable (Cr).
2.	NE	NE	This is the correct entry. There is no impact on accounts for the subsequent accounting period when the allowance method is used.
3.	NE	NE	Assets and net income would not be impacted. However, the debit balance of Allowance for Doubtful Accounts indicates that the estimation for bad debts was too low for this period.

DECISION GUIDELINES

DECISION	GUIDELINE	ANALYZE
As an entrepreneur, I am in the process of setting up my first business. Should I use the direct write-off method or the allowance method to account for bad debts?	Both IFRS and ASPE dictate the use of the allowance method.	Because the allowance method matches bad debt expense with the credit sales that resulted in the bad debts, it is generally viewed as the preferred method. The allowance method also reports accounts receivable at its net realizable value, which is a better indicator of the amount of cash that will ultimately be collected from the receivables.

HOW DO YOU ACCOUNT FOR NOTES RECEIVABLE?

L.O. **5** Account for notes receivable

Notes receivable are more formal than accounts receivable. The debtor signs a promissory note as evidence of the transaction. Before launching into the accounting, let's define the terms related to notes receivable.

■ **Promissory note:** A written promise to pay a specified amount of money on a particular future date.

■ **Maker of a note (debtor):** The entity that signs the note and promises to pay the required amount; the maker of the note is the **debtor**.

■ **Payee of a note (creditor):** The entity to whom the maker promises future payment; the payee of the note is the **creditor**.

■ **Principal:** The amount loaned out by the payee and borrowed by the maker of the note.

■ **Interest:** The amount charged for loaning money. Interest is an expense to the debtor and income to the creditor.

■ **Interest rate:** The percentage rate of interest specified by the note. Interest rates are almost always stated for a period of one year. A 10% note usually means that the amount of interest for *one year* is 10% of the note's principal.

■ **Maturity date:** This is the date when final payment of the note is due. Also called the **due date**.

■ **Maturity value:** The sum of the principal plus interest due at maturity.

■ **Note term:** The period of time during which interest is earned. It extends from the original date of the note to the maturity date.

Exhibit 7-6 illustrates a promissory note. As you study the promissory note, look for the items mentioned previously.

IDENTIFYING THE MATURITY DATE

Some notes specify the maturity date. For example, March 31, 2016, is the maturity date of the note shown in Exhibit 7-6. Other notes state the period of the note in days or months. When the period is given in months, the note's maturity date falls on the same day of the month as the date the note was issued. For example, a three-month note dated March 1, 2015, would mature on June 1, 2015.

When the period is given in days, the maturity date is determined by counting the actual days from the date of issue. A 180-day note dated February 16, 2015, matures on August 15, 2015.

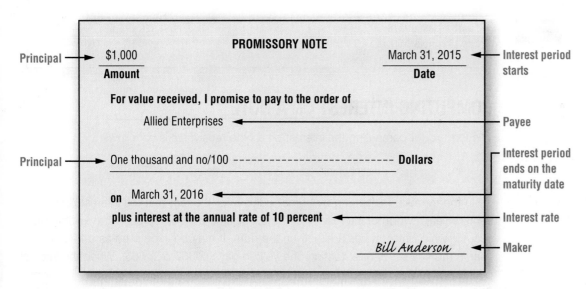

Exhibit 7-6 ▲

When counting the days for a note term remember to

- count the maturity date.
- omit the date the note was issued.

ORIGINATION OF NOTES RECEIVABLE

Notes receivable typically originate from a company doing one of the following:

- Lending money
- Providing goods or services in exchange for a promissory note
- Accepting a promissory note as payment on an account receivable

Assume that on August 1, 2015, Allied Enterprises lent $800 to Kim Simmons on a six-month, 8% promissory note. The journal entry to record the note would be as follows:

DATE	ACCOUNTS	POST REF.	DR.	CR.
Aug 1	Note Receivable—K. Simmons		800	
	Cash			800

Next, assume that on September 5, Allied Enterprises sells goods for $2,500 to Don Hammond. Hammond signs a nine-month promissory note at 10% annual interest. Allied Enterprises' entry to record the sale is as follows:

DATE	ACCOUNTS	POST REF.	DR.	CR.
Sep 5	Note Receivable—D. Hammond		2,500	
	Sales			2,500

A company may also accept a note receivable from a credit customer who is unable to pay his or her account receivable on time. The customer signs a promissory note and gives it to the creditor. Assume that on November 18, 2015, Sandra Fisher cannot pay her $1,200 account when it comes due and that Allied Enterprises accepts a 60-day, 12% note receivable in lieu of payment. Allied Enterprises would record this as follows:

DATE	ACCOUNTS	POST REF.	DR.	CR.
Nov 18	Note Receivable—S. Fisher		1,200	
	Accounts Receivable—S. Fisher			1,200

COMPUTING INTEREST ON A NOTE

The formula for computing the interest on a note receivable is as follows:

Amount of interest = Principal × Interest rate × Time

In the formula, multiplying by "Time" adjusts for the fact that the interest rate represents a year's worth of interest. The "Time," or time period, represents the portion of a year for which interest has accrued on the note. It may be expressed as a fraction of a year in months (x/12) or a fraction of a year in days (x/360 or x/365). When the interest period is stated in days, interest may be computed based on either a 360-day year or a 365-day year. Using the data in Exhibit 7-6, Allied Enterprises computes interest revenue for one year as follows:

The maturity value of the note is $1,100 ($1,000 principal + $100 interest). The time element is 12/12 or 1 because the note's term is 1 year.

Interest on a $2,000 note at 6% for nine months is computed as follows:

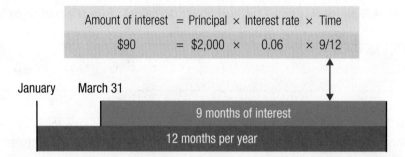

Interest on a $4,000 note at 8% for 90 days (assuming a 360-day year) is computed as follows:

ACCRUING INTEREST REVENUE

Notes receivable are often outstanding at the end of an accounting period. The interest revenue earned on the notes up to year-end should be recorded as part of that year's earnings. Recall that interest revenue is earned over time, not just when cash is received. We want to record the earnings from notes in the year in which they were earned.

Let's continue with the Allied Enterprises note receivable from Exhibit 7-5. Allied Enterprises' accounting period ends December 31.

- How much of the total interest revenue does Allied Enterprises earn in 2015 (from March 31 through December 31, 2015)?

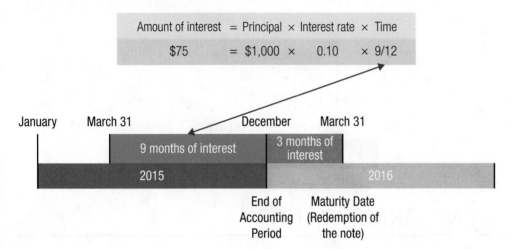

Allied Enterprises makes the following adjusting entry at December 31, 2015:

DATE	ACCOUNTS	POST REF.	DR.	CR.
Dec 31	Interest Receivable		75	
	Interest Revenue			75
	Accrue interest revenue.			

- How much interest revenue does Allied Enterprises earn in 2016 (from January 1 through March 31, 2016)?

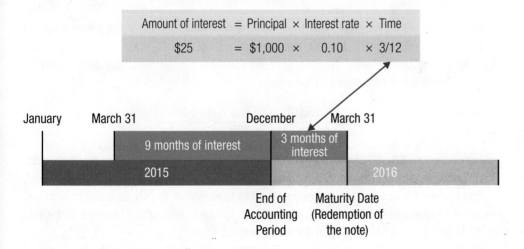

On the note's maturity date, Allied Enterprises makes the following entry:

DATE	ACCOUNTS	POST REF.	DR.	CR.
Mar 31	Cash (Maturity Value)		1,100	
	Note Receivable—B. Anderson			1,000
	Interest Receivable			75
	Interest Revenue			25
	Record repayment of note at maturity.			

Earlier we determined that total interest on the note was $100 ($1,000 × 0.10 × 12/12). These entries assign the correct amount of interest to each year.

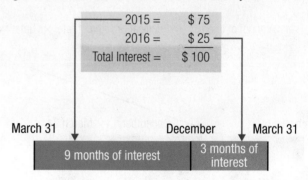

FOCUS ON DECISION MAKING: RATIOS

L.O. 6 Calculate the quick ratio and accounts receivable turnover

QUICK RATIO

In Chapter 5, we discussed the current ratio, which measures the ability to pay current liabilities with current assets. A more stringent measure of a company's ability to pay current liabilities is the **quick ratio**. The quick ratio, also called the **acid-test ratio**, compares a company's **quick assets** to its current liabilities. The quick ratio reveals whether the entity could pay all of its current liabilities if they were to become due immediately. The formula for the quick ratio is as follows:

$$\text{Quick ratio} = \frac{\text{Cash} + \text{Net current receivables} + \text{Short-term investments}}{\text{Total current liabilities}}$$

Let's assume that Mackay Industries has the following current asset information for December 31, 2015: cash, $3,100; net current receivables, $2,500; inventory, $6,300; and short-term investments, $1,600. Current liabilities are $4,300. The quick ratio for Mackay Industries is calculated as follows:

$$\text{Quick ratio} = \frac{\$3,100 + \$2,500 + \$1,600}{\$4,300} = 1.67$$

Notice that the $6,300 of inventory was not considered in the calculation of the quick ratio. This is because, although inventory is a current asset, it is not considered to be a "quick" asset.

The higher the quick ratio, the more able the business is to pay its current liabilities. Mackay Industries has a very strong quick ratio: Its quick ratio of 1.67 means that it has $1.67 of quick assets to pay each $1 of current liabilities.

What is an acceptable quick ratio? The answer depends on the industry. Walmart operates smoothly with a quick ratio of less than 0.20. Several things make this low ratio possible: Walmart collects cash rapidly and has almost no receivables. The quick ratios for most department stores cluster around 0.80, while travel agencies average 1.10. In general, a quick ratio of 1.00 is considered safe.

DECISION GUIDELINES

ACCOUNTS RECEIVABLE TURNOVER

Accounts receivable turnover measures the ability to collect cash from credit customers. The higher the ratio, the more successful the business is in collecting cash. However, an accounts receivable turnover that is too high may indicate that a company is not extending credit freely enough to make sales to all potentially good customers. Accounts receivable turnover is calculated as follows:

$$\text{Accounts receivable turnover} = \frac{\text{Net Credit Sales}}{\text{Average net Accounts Receivable}}$$

Assume that Mackay Industries has net credit sales for the year of $486,000, beginning net accounts receivable of $64,000, and ending net accounts receivable of $52,000. Mackay Industries would calculate the accounts receivable turnover for the year as follows:

$$\text{Accounts receivable turnover} = \frac{\$486,000}{\$58,000} = 8.38$$

The average net accounts receivable, $58,000, is figured by adding the beginning accounts receivable balance of $64,000 to the ending balance of $52,000 and dividing the result by 2. The determination of whether a company's accounts receivable turnover rate is good or bad depends on the company's credit terms. If Mackay Industries grants 30-day credit terms, its 8.38 accounts receivable turnover rate would be viewed as poor. With 30-day credit terms, you would expect a ratio of closer to 12 (360 days divided by 30 days). If Mackay Industries grants 45-day credit terms, its 8.38 accounts receivable turnover rate would be viewed as good. With 45-day credit terms, you would expect a ratio of closer to 8 (360 days divided by 45 days).

 DECISION GUIDELINES

FOCUS ON USERS

Concept	User	Why Is This Important to This User?
Revenue Recognition	**Bookkeepers** **Managers** **Shareholders** **Creditors** **Competitors** **Government and Regulatory Bodies** **Unions**	The point at which revenue is recognized is critically important to all users as this has a significant impact on the amount of revenues that are recognized by a company in any period. This will affect the company's net income and performance measures and impact decisions that revolve around income such as shareholders purchasing shares, creditors loaning funds, unions negotiating for additional benefits, competitors developing strategies, etc. The rules around revenue recognition are subjective, which means that different people would come up with different responses to how much should be recorded for revenues in the period. This can lead to the potential for unethical practices, so users of financial statements need to understand the principles that were used to create the statements.
Net Accounts Receivable	**Bookkeepers** **Managers** **Shareholders** **Creditors** **Competitors**	Competitors are interested in a company's accounts receivable for a number of reasons. A competitor would examine the accounts receivable and net accounts receivable to determine the amount recorded in the Allowance for Doubtful Accounts. This would provide a competitor with an idea of how much another company in the same industry is experiencing bad debts to know whether its own level of bad debts is similar, larger, or smaller. A competitor would also calculate the accounts receivable turnover to determine how long it takes to collect the accounts on average. Again this would provide a competitor with a comparison figure, particularly for how quickly its competitors pay their accounts in relation to the credit terms that the company offers.

📄 DEMO DOC

MyAccountingLab   Visit MyAccountingLab to watch animated versions of similar Demo Docs.

ACCOUNTS RECEIVABLE

LEARNING OBJECTIVE ③

Advantage Cycle accounts for its bad debts using the allowance method. Advantage Cycle had the following account balances as of September 1:

Accounts Receivable		Allowance for Doubtful Accounts	
Bal 32,000			Bal 1,700

During the month of September, Advantage Cycle had the following transactions:

    a. Made $57,000 of sales on account.

    b. Collected $49,000 on account from credit customers.

    c. Wrote off $2,300 of accounts receivable as uncollectible.

    d. Unexpectedly collected $250 of accounts receivable that had previously been written off.

REQUIREMENTS:

① Journalize Transactions a–d (because information about individual customers has not been given, record all entries as summary entries to the Accounts Receivable control account). Post the entries to the Accounts Receivable and Allowance for Doubtful Accounts T-accounts and calculate the account balances.

② Assume that on September 30, based on an aging of its accounts receivable, Advantage Cycle estimates that $2,100 of accounts receivable will be uncollectible. Journalize the entry to record bad debt expense for the month of September. What is the net realizable value of Accounts Receivable at September 30?

③ Ignoring Requirement 2, assume instead that Advantage Cycle estimates that accounts receivable equal to 3% of all credit sales will eventually be uncollectible. Journalize the entry to record bad debt expense for the month of September. What is the net realizable value of Accounts Receivable at September 30?

DEMO DOC SOLUTIONS

REQUIREMENT ①

Journalize Transactions a–d.

Part 1	Part 2	Part 3	Demo Doc Complete

a. Made $57,000 of sales on account.

Because the sales were on account, Accounts Receivable is increased (debited) by $57,000. Sales is also increased (credited) by $57,000.

DATE	ACCOUNTS	POST REF.	DR.	CR.
	Accounts Receivable		57,000	
	Sales			57,000
	Sold merchandise on account.			

b. Collected $49,000 on account from credit customers.

When cash is collected from customers, Cash is increased (debited) by $49,000 and Accounts Receivable is decreased (credited) by $49,000.

DATE	ACCOUNTS	POST REF.	DR.	CR.
	Cash		49,000	
	Accounts Receivable			49,000
	Received cash on account.			

c. Wrote off $2,300 of accounts receivable as uncollectible.

When receivables are uncollectible, they no longer have value. Therefore, they are no longer considered to be valid assets, so Accounts Receivable needs to be decreased (credited) by $2,300. Because Advantage Cycle uses the allowance method, the debit side of the entry is made to Allowance for Doubtful Accounts. Remember that under the allowance method, the Allowance for Doubtful Accounts account is created when the period-end adjusting entry is made to record the estimated bad debt expense.

DATE	ACCOUNTS	POST REF.	DR.	CR.
	Allowance for Doubtful Accounts		2,300	
	Accounts Receivable			2,300
	Wrote off uncollectible accounts.			

d. Unexpectedly collected $250 of accounts receivable that had previously been written off.

When an account is written off, it is removed from the accounting records. If it is subsequently collected, it must first be put back into the accounting records. To reinstate the receivable, we must reverse the entry that removed the account. In other words, we must debit the accounts that were originally credited and credit the accounts that were originally debited. The entry to write off accounts receivable debits the allowance and credits the accounts receivable (as in Transaction c). To reverse this entry, we must do the opposite: Debit the accounts receivable and credit the allowance by $250.

+250
−250

DATE	ACCOUNTS	POST REF.	DR.	CR.
	Accounts Receivable		250	
	Allowance for Doubtful Accounts			250
	Reinstated Accounts Receivable.			

Once this journal entry has been made, the cash collection is recorded as usual. Cash is increased (debited) by $250 and Accounts Receivable is decreased (credited) by $250.

+250
−250

DATE	ACCOUNTS	POST REF.	DR.	CR.
	Cash		250	
	Accounts Receivable			250
	Received cash on account.			

Post the entries to the Accounts Receivable and Allowance for Doubtful Accounts T-accounts and calculate the account balances.

The entries are posted to the T-accounts and the ending balances are calculated as follows:

Accounts Receivable			
Bal	32,000	b.	49,000
a.	57,000	c.	2,300
d.	250	d.	250
Bal	37,700		

Allowance for Doubtful Accounts			
c.	2,300	Bal	1,700
		d.	250
		Bal	350

REQUIREMENT ②

Assume that on September 30, based on an aging of its accounts receivable, Advantage Cycle estimates that $2,100 of accounts receivable will be uncollectible. Journalize the entry to record bad debt expense for the month of September. What is the net realizable value of Accounts Receivable at September 30?

Part 1	**Part 2**	Part 3	Demo Doc Complete

The phrase "based on an aging of its accounts receivable" tells us that Advantage Cycle is using the accounts receivable aging method to determine its allowance for doubtful accounts. Under the aging method, the ending balance in the allowance account should equal the estimated amount of bad debts that was determined based on the aging of accounts receivable ($2,100).

What do we need to do to bring the allowance account to a balance of $2,100? By inserting the desired ending balance into the allowance account's T-account, we can determine how much we must credit the account for in order to bring its balance to $2,100.

Allowance for Doubtful Accounts			
c.	2,300	Bal	1,700
		d.	250
Bal	350		?
		Bal	2,100

The question mark represents the required credit to the account. Notice that the account has a debit balance prior to making the adjusting entry. This is because the amount of accounts written off during the period exceeds the balance that was in the allowance account at the beginning of the period. Remember, it is possible for the allowance account to have either a debit or a credit balance prior to making the period-end adjusting entry. It is very important to pay attention to whether the account has a debit or a credit balance as this has an impact on the calculation of the required adjusting entry.

To bring the account from a debit balance of $350 to a credit balance of $2,100 we must credit the account for a total of $2,450 ($350 + $2,100). This represents a credit of $350, which brings the account to a zero balance, plus an additional credit of $2,100, which brings the account to the desired $2,100 balance. The debit side of the entry is to Bad Debt Expense.

DATE	ACCOUNTS	POST REF.	DR.	CR.
Sep 30	Bad Debt Expense		2,450	
	Allowance for Doubtful Accounts			2,450
	Record estimated uncollectible accounts.			

Assets	=	Liabilities	+	Shareholders' Equity
−2,450				−2,450

The net realizable value of accounts receivable is calculated by subtracting the ending Allowance for Doubtful Accounts balance from the ending balance of Accounts Receivable calculated in Requirement 1.

Accounts Receivable	$37,700
− Allowance for Doubtful Accounts	(2,100)
= Accounts Receivable, Net	$35,600

REQUIREMENT ③

Ignoring Requirement 2, assume instead that Advantage Cycle estimates that accounts receivable equal to 3% of all credit sales will eventually be uncollectible. Journalize the entry to record bad debt expense for the month of September. What is the net realizable value of Accounts Receivable at September 30?

Part 1	Part 2	**Part 3**	Demo Doc Complete

The phrase "that accounts receivable equal to 3% of all credit sales will eventually be uncollectible" tells us that Advantage Cycle is using the percentage of sales method to determine its allowance for doubtful accounts. From Requirement 1, Transaction a, we know that credit sales were $57,000 for the month. The amount of estimated bad debts is calculated as follows:

Estimated uncollectible accounts = 3% of credit sales

$1,710 = 3% × $57,000

Unlike with the aging method, it is not necessary to consider the Allowance for Doubtful Accounts balance to determine the amount of the required period-end adjusting entry. Once the estimated amount of bad debts has been calculated, that amount is used as the debit to Bad Debt Expense and the credit to Allowance for Doubtful Accounts as follows:

DATE	ACCOUNTS	POST REF.	DR.	CR.
Sep 30	Bad Debt Expense		1,710	
	Allowance for Doubtful Accounts			1,710
	Record estimated uncollectible accounts.			

Assets	=	Liabilities	+	Shareholders' Equity
−1,710				−1,710

Before we can calculate the net realizable value of Accounts Receivable we need to post the adjusting entry to the allowance account and calculate the ending balance.

Allowance for Doubtful Accounts			
c.	2,300	Bal	1,700
		d.	250
Bal	350	Adj	1,710
		Bal	1,360

The net realizable value of Accounts Receivable can now be calculated as in Requirement 2.

Accounts Receivable	$37,700
− Allowance for Doubtful Accounts	(1,360)
= Accounts Receivable, Net	$36,340

DEMO DOC COMPLETE

Part 1	Part 2	Part 3	**Demo Doc Complete**

DECISION GUIDELINES

What decisions might you encounter while accounting for cash and receivables within your business?

DECISION	GUIDELINE	ANALYZE
As an entrepreneur, I am in the process of setting up my first business. Should I use the direct write-off method or the allowance method to account for bad debts?	Both IFRS and ASPE dictate the use of the allowance method.	Because the allowance method matches bad debt expense with the credit sales that resulted in the bad debts, it is generally viewed as the preferred method. The allowance method also reports accounts receivable at its net realizable value, which is a better indicator of the amount of cash that will ultimately be collected from the receivables.
As a manager, I would like to know if I need to make changes to our credit terms for our customers. What can I examine to help with this decision?	Use the quick ratio.	The quick ratio provides an indicator of a business's ability to pay its obligations as they come due. Although the quick ratio takes into account a business's short-term investments, the primary components are cash and receivables. A quick ratio that is below 1.0 is generally an indicator that a business has an inadequate amount of cash and receivables on hand. If too many liabilities come due at once, the business is likely to encounter cash flow problems.
As a supplier, I need to determine whether or not to extend credit to customers. As part of this assessment, I need to look at how easily the company can pay its short-term debts. What is the best way to assess this?	Use the accounts receivable turnover ratio. Compare the ratio to other companies in the industry and to the ratio the company had last year.	A low accounts receivable turnover ratio is often an indicator that a business is not properly managing its credit accounts. A low ratio is usually the result of credit accounts becoming delinquent. This can adversely affect a company because it negatively impacts cash flows. However, an accounts receivable turnover that is too high may also be an indicator that accounts receivable is being poorly managed. This often occurs when credit is not granted freely enough, resulting in lost sales.

POINT OF COMPARISON	IFRS	ASPE
Revenue recognition in the case of selling of goods	Same as ASPE. In addition, it is probable that the selling entity will be able to collect the economic benefits of such transactions and that the costs of the transaction can be measured reliably.*	Revenue recognition occurs when two conditions have been met: (1) When the seller of the goods has transferred to the buyer the significant risks and rewards of ownership, and (2) there is a reasonable assurance regarding the measurement of the amount that will be derived from the sales of goods.**
Revenue recognition in the case of rendering services and long-term contracts	The percentage of completion method is the accepted method.	The percentage of completion method or the completed contract method can be used, provided that reasonable assurance exists regarding the measurement of the amount that will be derived from rendering the service or performing the long-term contract.**
Use of the allowance method (in calculating bad debts)	Both IFRS and ASPE require adopting the allowance method for accounting for bad debts.	

*CICA Handbook - Accounting, The Canadian Institute of Chartered Accountants, 2013 edition. Parts I and IV, pages 542–544
**CICA Handbook - Accounting, The Canadian Institute of Chartered Accountants, 2013 edition, Parts II and III, page 360

ACCOUNTING VOCABULARY

THE LANGUAGE OF BUSINESS

Accounts receivable (p. 399)

Accounts receivable turnover (p. 415)

Acid-test ratio (p. 414)

Aging method (p. 403)

Allowance for Doubtful Account (AFDA) (p. 401)

Allowance method (p. 401)

Bad debt (p. 399)

Bad debt expense (p. 400)

Completed contract method (p. 397)

Control account (p. 401)

Creditor (p. 410)

Debtor (p. 410)

Direct write-off method (p. 400)

Due date (p. 410)

Income statement approach (p. 402)

Interest (p. 410)

Interest rate (p. 410)

Maker of a note (p. 410)

Maturity date (p. 410)

Maturity value (p. 410)

Net credit sales (p. 402)

Net realizable value (p. 401)

Note term (p. 410)

Notes receivable (p. 399)

Payee of a note (p. 410)

Percentage of completion method (p. 397)

Percentage of sales method (p. 402)

Principal (p. 410)

Promissory note (p. 410)

Quick assets (p. 414)

Quick ratio (p. 414)

Statement of financial position approach (p. 405)

Uncollectible account (p. 399)

Write off (p. 400)

ACCOUNTING PRACTICE

DISCUSSION QUESTIONS

1. What are the different types of sales? Explain the difference between gross sales and net sales.

2. What is the benefit of using the percentage of net credit sales to estimate the bad debt expense? What is the benefit of using the aging method to estimate the bad debt expense?

3. What would be the surest way to eliminate the possibility of having any bad debts? Why don't companies operate this way if it could help them eliminate this costly expense?

4. Why does the allowance method of accounting for bad debts conform to IFRS and ASPE while the direct write-off method does not?

5. How is allowance for doubtful accounts reported on the financial statements? Why is it important for companies to report net realizable value of accounts receivable on the statement of financial position?

6. Why is the percentage of sales method called the "income statement approach" while the aging method is called the "statement of financial position approach"?

7. Under which method, percentage of sales or aging, would the balance in Allowance for Doubtful Accounts just before the adjusting entry affect the amount of the adjusting entry? Why?

8. How would the net realizable value of accounts receivable change when an account is written off under the allowance method?

9. If a company with a December 31 year-end lends money in the form of a six-month note on November 1, which accounts will be credited when the note is paid off on 4/30?

10. When in a deep recession, what would be the expected effect of the recession on accounts receivable turnover ratios?

SELF CHECK

MyAccountingLab

The exercises and problems in this chapter can be found on MyAccountingLab. You can practise them as often as you want, and they feature step-by-step guided solutions to help you find the right answer.

1. ADI Company's ledger shows the following balances on December 31: Sales $365,000, Accounts Receivable, $146,000, Allowance for Doubtful Accounts $7,300, Sales Returns and Allowances $3,650, Sales Discounts $5,475, and Credit Card Expense $4,380. Calculate the amount of net sales reported on the income statement.

   a. $355,875
   b. $351,495
   c. $348,575
   d. $211,700

2. Which type of sales will not increase the company's operating expenses?

   a. Cash sales
   b. Debit card sales
   c. Credit card sales
   d. Sales on account

3. Which of the following statements is true when a company has a debit balance for the Allowance for Doubtful Accounts?

   a. The company over-estimated the bad debt expense.
   b. The bad debt is smaller than the allocated amount for the Allowance for Doubtful Accounts.
   c. The company should not record bad expense for the current year.
   d. None of the above.

4. GIA Company's net credit sales for the year were $468,000, Accounts Receivable, $192,000, Allowance for Doubtful Accounts, $3,600 (Dr.). GIA uses 5% of net credit sales as the bad debt expense. The amount of the bad debt expense to be recorded is

   a. $13,200

   b. $19,800

   c. $23,400

   d. $27,000

5. What is the impact on the quick ratio of recording the bad debt expense adjusting entry?

   a. Increase

   b. Decrease

   c. Remain the same

   d. Cannot be determined

6. Uncollectible accounts are the same as

   a. bad debts.

   b. notes receivable.

   c. both a and b.

   d. none of the above.

7. Which method of estimating uncollectible receivables focuses on net credit sales?

   a. Aging approach

   b. Percentage of sales approach

   c. Net realizable value approach

   d. All of the above

8. Your business uses the allowance method to account for uncollectible receivables. At the beginning of the year, Allowance for Doubtful Accounts had a credit balance of $1,100. During the year you wrote off bad receivables of $2,100 and recorded bad debt expense of $2,000. What is your year-end balance in Allowance for Doubtful Accounts?

   a. $1,000

   b. $2,000

   c. $3,100

   d. $3,200

9. Niko Company's net credit sales for the year were $480,000 and the average accounts receivable was $96,000. To improve accounts receivable turnover to six times, what should the average accounts receivable be, if the net credit sales are expected to increase by 10%?

   a. $80,000

   b. $87,273

   c. $88,000

   d. $105,600

10. On December 31, you have a $10,000 note receivable from a customer. Interest of 8% has also accrued for six months on the note. What will your financial statements report for this situation?

   a. Nothing will be reported because you haven't received the cash yet.

   b. The statement of financial position will report the note receivable of $10,000.

   c. The statement of financial position will report the note receivable of $10,000 and interest receivable of $400.

   d. The income statement will report a note receivable of $10,000.

Answers are given after Written Communication.

S7-1. Reporting net sales with sales returns and allowances and sales discounts (*Learning Objective 2*) 10 min.

The total sales for April were $265,000, of which 60% was on credit. One percent of the total sales was defective and returned. Two percent of the net credit sales were sales discounts. What are the amounts of sales returns and allowance, sales discounts, and net sales?

S7-2. Missing information (*Learning Objective 3*) 15 min.

The following data were selected from Chow's ledger. Chow's accounting policy related to estimated bad debt expense is to keep the same relation between the Accounts Receivable and Allowance for Doubtful Accounts.

Accounts Receivable			
	42,000	(2)	?
(1)	252,000	(3)	226,800
	58,500		

Allowance for Doubtful Accounts			
(2)	?		3,360
		(4)	?
			4,680

Sales		
	(1)	252,000

Requirements

1. Calculate the missing information.
2. What is the percentage used to estimate the bad debts?
3. Explain the transactions (1) to (4).

S7-3. Comparing two methods of estimating bad debts (*Learning Objective 3*) 15 min.

Gupta Electronic recorded $425,000 of credit sales during its first year of operation. Gupta reported $102,000 (Dr.) in Accounts Receivable and $2,800 (Dr.) in Allowance for Doubtful Accounts before the adjustments at the end of the year. The Accounts Receivable account has $65,000 that is current and $37,000 that is 30 days or older. The accountant is wondering which method to use to estimate the bad debts. She has two options:

a. 3% of credit sales
b. aging of accounts receivable: 1% of current Accounts Receivable, 20% of 30+

Requirements

1. Calculate the bad debt expense using (1) the percentage of credit sales, and (2) the aging of accounts receivable.
2. Prepare the adjusting journal entry to record bad debt expense using the two different methods.
3. Explain the main differences between the two methods of estimating bad debts.

S7-4. Receivable terms (*Learning Objectives 1, 2, & 3*) 5–10 min.

Match the term with its definition by placing the corresponding letter in the space provided:

__c__	Example: Amounts owed to a business by another business or individual	a. Creditor
___ 1.	A contra-account, related to accounts receivable, that holds the estimated amount of uncollectible receivables	b. Debtor
		c. Receivables
		d. Bad debt expense
___ 2.	A method of accounting for uncollectible receivables in which the company waits until a specific customer's account receivable is uncollectible before recording bad debt expense	e. Allowance method

_____ 3. A method of recording receivable losses on the basis of estimates instead of waiting to see which customers the company will not collect from

_____ 4. The party to a credit transaction who sells goods or a service and obtains a receivable

_____ 5. A way to estimate bad debts by analyzing individual accounts receivable according to the length of time they have been receivable

_____ 6. The party to a credit transaction who makes a purchase and has a payable

_____ 7. Cost to the seller of credit sales; arises from the failure to collect from credit customers

_____ 8. A method of estimating uncollectible receivables that calculates bad debt expense based on net credit sales

f. Allowance for Doubtful Accounts

g. Percentage of sales method

h. Aging method

i. Direct write-off method

S7-5. Allowance method (_Learning Objective 3_) 5–10 min.

Antonio Galvan, an attorney, uses the allowance method to account for uncollectible receivables. On August 31, Galvan's accounts receivable were $8,000. During September, he earned service revenue of $20,000 on account and collected $22,000 from clients on account. He also wrote off uncollectible receivables of $2,000. What is Galvan's balance of Accounts Receivable on September 30? Does he expect to collect this entire amount? Why or why not?

S7-6. Percentage of sales allowance method (_Learning Objectives 3 & 4_) 5–10 min.

During its first year of operations, Atlas Travel earned revenue of $400,000 on account. Industry experience suggests that Atlas Travel's bad debts will amount to 2% of revenues. On December 31, 2015, accounts receivable total $90,000. The company uses the allowance method to account for uncollectibles.

Journalize Atlas Travel's bad debt expense using the percentage of sales method. Show how Atlas should report Accounts Receivable on its statement of financial position on December 31, 2015.

S7-7. Percentage of sales allowance method (_Learning Objective 2_) 5–10 min.

Atlas Travel ended 2014 with Accounts Receivable of $90,000 and an Allowance for Doubtful Accounts balance of $8,000. During 2015, Atlas Travel had the following activity:

a. Service revenue earned on account, $600,000.

b. Collections on account, $580,000.

c. Write-offs of uncollectibles, $15,000.

d. Bad debt expense, estimated as 2% of service revenue.

Journalize Atlas Travel's activity for 2015.

S7-8. Aging of accounts receivable allowance method (_Learning Objective 3_) 5–10 min.

Gorav Dental Group started 2015 with Accounts Receivable of $120,000 and an Allowance for Doubtful Accounts balance of $6,000. The following information relates to Gorav Dental's 2015 operations:

a. Credit sales, $400,000.

c. Collections on account, $320,000.

c. Write-offs of uncollectibles, $15,000.

d. At December 31, the aging of accounts receivable showed that Gorav will probably _not_ collect $5,000 of its accounts receivable.

Journalize Gorav's 2015 transactions based on the information provided. Prepare a T-account for the Allowance for Doubtful Accounts to show your computation of bad debt expense for the year.

S7-9. Aging of accounts receivable allowance method (*Learning Objective 3*) 5–10 min.

Limo.com had the following balances on December 31, 2015, before the year-end adjustments:

Accounts Receivable	Allowance for Doubtful Accounts
104,000	1,300

The aging of receivables yields these data:

	Age of Accounts				
	1–30 Days	31–60 Days	61–90 Days	Over 90 Days	Total Receivables
Accounts Receivable..............................	$70,000	$20,000	$10,000	$4,000	$104,000
Estimate Percentage Uncollectible	× 1%	× 2%	× 5%	× 50%	

Journalize Limo.com's entry to adjust the allowance account to its correct balance on December 31, 2015.

S7-10. Internal controls—credit sales (*Learning Objective 2*) 10–15 min.

Claire Billiot, the office manager of a local office supply company, is designing its internal control system. Billiot proposes the following procedures for credit checks on new customers, sales on account, cash collections, and write-offs of uncollectible receivables:

a. The credit department runs a credit check on all customers who apply for credit. When an account proves uncollectible, the credit department authorizes the write-off of the account receivable.

b. Cash receipts come into the credit department, which separates the cash received from the customer remittance slips. The credit department lists all cash receipts by customer name and amount of cash received.

c. The cash goes to the treasurer for deposit in the bank. The remittance slips go to the accounting department for recording of the collections.

d. The controller compares the daily deposit slip to the total amount of the collections recorded. Both amounts must agree.

For each of the four procedures, indicate whether the procedure includes an internal control weakness. Explain how employee fraud could occur because of the weakness. What can Claire do to strengthen the internal control system?

S7-11. Notes receivable terms (*Learning Objective 5*) 10–15 min.

Match the term with its definition by placing the corresponding letter in the space provided:

____ 1. A written promise to pay a specified amount of money at a particular future date

____ 2. The date when final payment of the note is due; also called the due date

____ 3. The percentage rate of interest specified by the note for one year

a. Interest
b. Note term
c. Interest rate
d. Maker of the note
e. Maturity date

_____ 4. The entity to whom the maker promises future payment

_____ 5. The period of time during which interest is earned

_____ 6. The amount loaned out by the payee and borrowed by the maker of the note

_____ 7. The sum of the principal plus interest due at maturity

_____ 8. The entity that signs the note and promises to pay the required amount

_____ 9. The revenue to the payee for loaning money; the expense to the debtor

f. Maturity value

g. Payee of the note

h. Principal

i. Promissory note

S7-12. Accounting for notes receivable (*Learning Objective 5*) 10–15 min.

For each of the following notes receivable, compute the amount of interest revenue earned during 2015. Use a 360-day year, and round to the nearest dollar.

	Principal	Interest Rate	Interest Period During 2015
Note 1	$100,000	8%	6 months
Note 2	30,000	12%	75 days
Note 3	20,000	9%	60 days
Note 4	50,000	10%	3 months

S7-13. Accounting for notes receivable (*Learning Objective 5*) 10–15 min.

Bank of Montreal lent $100,000 to Christine Kleuters on a 90-day, 8% note. Record the following transactions for Bank of Montreal (explanations are not required):

1. Lending the money on June 12.

2. Collecting the principal and interest at maturity. Specify the date. For the computation of interest, use a 360-day year.

S7-14. Quick ratio (*Learning Objective 6*) 5–10 min.

Calculate the quick assets and the quick ratio for each of the following companies:

	Jaxon	Kilborn
Cash	$10,000	$ 25,000
Short-term Investments	5,000	15,000
Net Receivables	45,000	52,000
Current Liabilities	45,000	100,000

S7-15. Accounts receivable turnover (*Learning Objective 6*) 5–10 min.

Calculate accounts receivable turnover for the following two companies.

	Moore	Noel
Net Credit Sales	$73,000	$45,625
Net Accounts Receivable, Beginning	12,000	23,000
Net Accounts Receivable, Ending	13,000	21,000

EXERCISES (GROUP A)

E7-1A. Accounting for revenue in long-term contracts (*Learning Objective 1*) 10 min.

On January 1, 2015, Niagara Constructions Inc. signed a contract for constructing a high-rise condominium complex with a client for $20 million over a period of three years. The costs of construction are estimated to be $14 million. On December 31, 2015, the company incurred $5 million of the costs. At the end of 2016, total expenses incurred amounted to $12 million.

Requirements

1. Determine the revenue to be recognized in both 2015 and 2016 using the percentage of completion method.

E7-2A. Reporting net sales with sales returns and allowances and sales discounts (*Learning Objective 2*) 10–15 min.

Cheng Enterprises completed the following transactions during May. Cheng uses the periodic inventory system in accounting for inventory.

May 4	Sold merchandise to a customer for $2,500. Customer paid with a credit card. The credit card company charged a 2% service fee.
6	Sold merchandise worth $6,200 to Wang on account, with terms of 2/10, n/30, FOB shipping point.
8	Wang returned $300 of merchandise.
12	Sold merchandise worth $4,800 to Jung on account, with terms of 2/10, n/30, FOB shipping point.
15	Received payment from Wang.
22	Received payment from Jung.

Requirements

1. Calculate the net sales for May.

2. Prepare the journal entries to record the transactions that occurred in May.

E7-3A. Bad debt write-offs and cash collections (*Learning Objective 3*) 10–15 min.

Sun's ledger shows the following account balances on December 31:

	2015	2014
Accounts Receivable	$ 530,000	$ 450,000
Allowance for Doubtful Accounts	26,500	18,000
Sales on Account	3,500,000	2,700,000

During 2015, Sun wrote off $12,500 of uncollectible accounts receivable, and reinstated $1,500 of previously written-off accounts receivable.

Requirements

1. Calculate the bad debt expense for 2015.

2. Calculate cash collections from accounts receivable, assuming that all sales were on credit.

E7-4A. Allowance method (*Learning Objective 2*) 5–10 min.

Blue Mountain, Inc., uses the allowance method to account for bad debts. Record the following transactions that occurred during the year:

May 3	Provided $4,450 of services to Ken Reeve on account.
Nov 8	Wrote off Ken Reeve's $4,450 account as uncollectible.
Dec 10	Unexpectedly collected $1,000 from Ken Reeve on the account that had been written off. Blue Mountain, Inc., does not expect to collect the remaining balance.

E7-5A. Percentage of sales allowance method (*Learning Objective 3*) 10–15 min.

Rice Automotive ended December 2014 with Accounts Receivable of $30,000 and Allowance for Doubtful Accounts of $1,500. During January 2015, Rice Automotive completed the following transactions:

- Sales of $180,000, which included $120,000 in credit sales and $60,000 of cash sales.
- Cash collections on account, $90,000.
- Write-offs of uncollectible receivables, $1,200.
- Bad debt expense, estimated as 2% of credit sales.

Requirements

1. Prepare journal entries to record sales, collections, write-offs of uncollectibles, and bad debt expense by the percentage of sales method.

2. Calculate the ending balances in Accounts Receivable, Allowance for Doubtful Accounts, and net Accounts Receivable at January 31. How much does Rice Automotive expect to collect?

E7-6A. Aging of accounts receivable allowance method (*Learning Objective 3*) 15–20 min.

On December 31, 2015, the Accounts Receivable balance of Alterations Express is $300,000. The Allowance for Doubtful Accounts has a $3,900 credit balance. Alterations prepares the following aging schedule for its accounts receivable:

	Age of Accounts			
	1–30 Days	31–60 Days	61–90 Days	Over 90 Days
Accounts Receivable..............................	$140,000	$80,000	$70,000	$10,000
Estimated Percentage Uncollectible	0.5%	1.0%	6.0%	50%

Requirements

1. Journalize the year-end adjusting entry for bad debts on the basis of the aging schedule. Calculate the resulting ending balance of the allowance account based on the account aging. Show the T-account for the allowance on December 31, 2015.

2. Assume that instead of a $3,900 credit balance, there is a $1,300 debit balance in the allowance account prior to adjustment. Journalize the year-end adjusting entry for bad debts on the basis of the aging schedule. Calculate the resulting ending balance of the allowance account based on the account aging. Show the T-account for the allowance on December 31, 2015.

E7-7A. Percentage of sales and aging of accounts receivable allowance methods (*Learning Objective 3*) 15–20 min.

Inland Equipment uses the allowance method to account for bad debts. On December 31, 2015, Allowance for Doubtful Accounts has a $600 credit balance. Journalize the year-end adjusting entry for bad debts assuming the following *independent* scenarios:

1. Inland Equipment estimates bad debts as 1/2 of 1% of net credit sales. Net credit sales for the year equal $550,000.

2. Based on an aging of accounts receivable, Inland Equipment estimates that bad debts will equal $2,575.

E7-8A. Sales, bad debt write-offs, and cash collections (*Learning Objectives 2 & 3*) 20–25 min.

Momo Industries began operations on January 1, 2015. During the next two years, the company completed a number of transactions involving credit sales, accounts receivable collections, and bad debts. Momo uses a perpetual inventory system, and the gross margin is 40% of the sales. These transactions are summarized as follows:

2015

a. Sold merchandise on credit for $1,500,000, terms n/30.

b. Wrote off uncollectible accounts receivable in the amount of $20,000.

c. Received cash of $720,000 in payment of outstanding accounts receivable.

d. December 31, Momo estimated that 3.5% of the outstanding accounts receivable would become uncollectible.

2016

e. Sold merchandise on credit for $1,750,000 terms n/30.

f. Wrote off uncollectible accounts receivable in the amount of $28,000.

g. Received cash of $1,250,000 in payment of outstanding accounts receivable.

h. Momo uses the same method as in 2015 to estimate and record the uncollectible accounts receivable.

Requirements

1. Prepare the journal entries to record the transactions that occurred in 2015 and 2016, and the adjusting entries to record bad debt expense at the end of each year.

2. Is the estimated amount for the bad debt expense sufficient?

E7-9A. Accounting for notes receivable (*Learning Objective 5*) 15–20 min.

On April 30, 2015, Scotiabank loaned $100,000 to Grant Hughes on a one-year, 6% note.

Requirements

1. Compute the interest for the years ended December 31, 2015 and 2016, on the Hughes note.

2. Which party has

    a. a note receivable?

    b. a note payable?

    c. interest revenue?

    d. interest expense?

3. How much in total would Hughes pay the bank if he pays off the note early—say, on November 30, 2015?

E7-10A. Accounting for notes receivable (*Learning Objective 5*) 15–20 min.

Journalize the following transactions of Cramer, Inc., which ends its accounting year on June 30:

Apr 1	Loaned $20,000 cash to R. Simpson on a one-year, 8% note.
Jun 6	Sold goods to Friday, Corp., receiving a 90-day, 10% note for $3,000.
30	Made a single compound entry to accrue interest revenue on both notes.

Use a 360-day year for interest computations.

E7-11A. Accounting for notes receivable (*Learning Objective 5*) 15–20 min.

Gorman Enterprises sells on account. When a customer account becomes four months old, Gorman converts the account to a note receivable. During 2015, Gorman completed these transactions:

Jun 29	Sold goods on account to I. Happy, $10,000.
Nov 1	Received a $10,000,60-day, 9% note from I. Happy in satisfaction of his past-due account receivable.
Dec 31	Collected the I. Happy note at maturity.

Requirement

1. Record the transactions in Gorman Enterprises' journal.

E7-12A. Quick ratio (Learning Objective 6) 15–20 min.

Consider the following data:

	A	B	C	D
Cash..	$ 92,000	$ 64,000	$23,000	$107,000
Short-term Investments.................	70,000	28,000	15,000	53,000
Net Receivables..............................	125,000	110,000	52,000	140,000
Current Liabilities...........................	205,000	101,000	60,000	350,000

Requirements

1. Calculate the quick assets and the quick ratio for each company.

2. Which of the companies should be concerned about its liquidity?

E7-13A. Quick ratio and accounts receivable turnover (Learning Objective 6) 15–20 min.

Vision Equipment reported the following items on February 28, 2015 (amounts in thousands, with last year's amounts also given as needed):

Accounts Payable........................	$ 449	Accounts Receivable, Net:	
Cash..	215	February 28, 2015..................	$ 220
Inventory:		February 28, 2014..................	150
February 28, 2015..................	190	Cost of Goods Sold.....................	1,200
February 28, 2014..................	160	Short-term Investments..............	165
Net Credit Sales..........................	1,930	Other Current Assets..................	90
Long-term Assets........................	410	Other Current Liabilities..............	145
Long-term Liabilities...................	10		

Requirements

1. Compute Vision Equipment's (a) quick ratio and (b) accounts receivable turnover for 2015.

2. Evaluate each ratio value as strong or weak. Assume Vision Equipment sells on terms of net 30.

EXERCISES (GROUP B)

E7-1B. Accounting for revenue in long-term contracts (Learning Objective 1) 10 min.

On January 1, 2015, Global Constructions Inc. signed a contract for constructing a mall with a client for $30 million over a period of three years. The costs of construction are estimated to be $24 million. On December 31, 2015, company incurred $10 million of the costs. At the end of 2016, total expenses incurred amounted to $18 million.

Requirement

1. Determine the revenue to be recognized in both 2015 and 2016 using the percentage of completion method.

E7-2B. Reporting net sales with sales returns and allowances and sales discounts (Learning Objective 2) 10–15 min.

Wu International completed the following transactions during July. Wu uses the periodic inventory system in accounting for inventory.

Jul 2	Sold merchandise worth $4,500 to Hung on account, with terms of 2/15, n/30, FOB shipping point.
7	Sold merchandise worth $7,800 to Lee on account, with terms of 2/15, n/30, FOB shipping point.
8	Lee returned $300 of merchandise.
14	Sold merchandise to a customer for $2,500. Customer paid with a credit card. The credit card company charged a 2% service fee.
17	Received payment from Hung.
21	Received payment from Lee.

Requirements

1. Calculate the net sales for July.

2. Prepare the journal entries to record the transactions that occurred in July.

E7-3B. Bad debt write-offs and cash collections (*Learning Objective 3*) 10–15 min.

Moto's ledger shows the following account balances on December 31:

	2015	2014
Accounts Receivable	$ 720,000	$ 540,000
Allowance for Doubtful Accounts	36,000	24,000
Sales on Account	3,600,000	2,970,000

During 2015, Moto reinstated $2,500 of previously written-off accounts receivable, and recorded $21,000 bad debt expense.

Requirements

1. Calculate the written-off accounts receivable for 2015.

2. Calculate cash collections from accounts receivable, assuming that all sales were on credit.

E7-4B. Allowance method (*Learning Objective 3*) 5–10 min.

Keene Industries uses the allowance method to account for bad debts. Record the following transactions that occurred during the year:

May 3	Provided $1,100 of services to Fred Whittaker on account.
Nov 8	Wrote off Fred Whittaker's $1,100 account as uncollectible.
Dec 10	Unexpectedly collected $900 from Fred Whittaker on the account that had been written off. Keene Industries does not expect to collect the remaining balance.

E7-5B. Percentage of sales allowance method (*Learning Objective 3*) 10–15 min.

Ortiz Automotive ended December 2014 with Accounts Receivable of $20,000 and Allowance for Doubtful Accounts of $5,900. During January 2015, Ortiz Automotive completed the following transactions:

- Sales of $260,000, which included $160,000 in credit sales and $100,000 of cash sales.
- Cash collections on account, $54,000.
- Write-offs of uncollectible receivables, $2,500.
- Bad debt expense estimated as 4% of credit sales.

Requirements

1. Prepare journal entries to record sales, collections, write-offs of uncollectibles, and bad debt expense by the percentage of sales method.

2. Calculate the ending balances in Accounts Receivable, Allowance for Doubtful Accounts, and Net Accounts Receivable at January 31. How much does Ortiz Automotive expect to collect?

E7-6B. Aging of accounts receivable allowance method (*Learning Objective 3*)
15–20 min.

On July 31, 2015, the Accounts Receivable balance of Questor Application, Inc. is
$320,000. The Allowance for Doubtful Accounts has a $6,400 credit balance. Questor
prepares the following aging schedule for its accounts receivable:

	Age of Accounts			
	1–30 Days	31–60 Days	61–90 Days	Over 90 Days
Accounts Receivable...............................	$175,000	$70,000	$60,000	$15,000
Estimated Percentage Uncollectible	0.8%	3.0%	5.0%	60%

Requirements

1. Journalize the year-end adjusting entry for uncollectible accounts on the basis of
the aging schedule. Calculate the resulting ending balance of the allowance
account based on the account aging. Show the T-account for the allowance on
July 31, 2015.

2. Assume that instead of a $6,400 credit balance, there is a $500 debit balance in
the allowance account prior to adjustment. Journalize the year-end adjusting
entry for uncollectible accounts on the basis of the aging schedule. Calculate the
resulting ending balance of the allowance account based on the account aging.
Show the T-account for the allowance on July 31, 2015.

E7-7B. Percentage of sales and aging of accounts receivable allowance methods
(*Learning Objective 3*) 15–20 min.

Cotton, Corp. uses the allowance method to account for uncollectible accounts.
On May 31, 2015, Allowance for Doubtful Accounts has a $1,300 credit balance.
Journalize the year-end adjusting entry for Allowance of Doubtful Accounts assuming
the following *independent* scenarios:

1. Cotton, Corp. estimates doubtful accounts as 3/4 of 1% of net credit sales. Net
credit sales for the year equal $750,000.

2. Based on an aging of accounts receivable, Cotton, Corp. estimates that
Allowance of Doubtful Accounts will equal $3,120.

E7-8B. Sales, bad debt write-offs, and cash collections (*Learning Objectives 2 & 3*)
20–25 min.

Vihn Luggage Manufacturing began operations on January 1, 2015. During the next
two years, the company completed a number of transactions involving credit sales,
accounts receivable collections, and bad debts. Vihn uses a perpetual inventory
system, and the gross margin is 30% of the sales. These transactions are summarized
as follows:

2015

a. Sold merchandise on credit for $850,000, terms n/30.
b. Wrote off uncollectible accounts receivable in the amount of $15,000.
c. Received cash of $320,000 in payment of outstanding accounts receivable.
d. December 31, Vihn estimated that 2% of the outstanding accounts receivable
would become uncollectible.

2016

e. Sold merchandise on credit for $920,000, terms n/30.
f. Wrote off uncollectible accounts receivable in the amount of $20,000.
g. Received cash of $480,000 in payment of outstanding accounts receivable.
h. Vihn uses the same method as in 2015 to estimate and record the uncollectible
accounts receivable.

Requirements

1. Prepare the journal entries to record the transactions that occurred in 2015 and 2016, and the adjusting entries to record bad debt expense at the end of each year.

2. Is the estimated amount for the bad debt expense sufficient?

E7-9B. Accounting for notes receivable (*Learning Objective 5*) 15–20 min.

On June 30, 2015, Nature Bank loaned $2,000,000 to Gary Simon on a one-year, 7% note.

Requirements

1. Compute the interest for the years ended December 31, 2015 and 2016, on the Simon note.

2. Which party has

   a. a note receivable?

   b. a note payable?

   c. interest revenue?

   d. interest expense?

3. How much in total would Simon pay the bank if he pays off the note early—say, on January 31, 2016?

E7-10B. Accounting for notes receivable (*Learning Objective 5*) 15–20 min.

Journalize the following transactions of Coral, Inc., which ends its accounting year on April 30:

Feb 1	Loaned $15,000 cash to Carroll Fadal on a one-year, 10% note.
Apr 6	Sold goods to Lawn Pro, receiving a 90-day, 4% note for $6,000.
30	Made a single compound entry to accrue interest revenue on both notes.

Use a 360-day year for interest computations.

E7-11B. Accounting for notes receivable (*Learning Objective 5*) 15–20 min.

Professional Enterprises sells on account. When a customer account becomes four months old, Professional converts the account to a note receivable. During 2015, Professional completed these transactions:

Mar 29	Sold goods on account to Montclair, Inc., $21,000.
Aug 1	Received a $21,000, 60-day, 5% note from Montclair, Inc., in satisfaction of its past-due account receivable.
Sep 30	Collected the Montclair, Inc. note at maturity.

Requirement

1. Record the transactions in Professional Enterprises' journal.

E7-12B. Quick ratio (*Learning Objective 6*) 15–20 min.

Consider the following data:

	A	B	C	D
Cash	$ 93,000	$ 67,000	$23,000	$111,000
Short-term Investments	75,000	27,000	18,000	49,000
Net Receivables	126,000	110,000	54,000	144,000
Current Liabilities	335,000	280,000	35,000	220,000

Requirements

1. Calculate the quick assets and the quick ratio for each company.

2. Which of the companies should be concerned about its liquidity?

E7-13B. Quick ratio and accounts receivable turnover (*Learning Objective 6*)
15–20 min.

Algonquin Equipment reported the following items on November 30, 2015 (amounts in thousands, with last year's amounts also given as needed):

Accounts Payable.........................	$ 434	Accounts Receivable, Net:	
Cash...	210	November 30, 2015	$200
Inventory:		November 30, 2014	110
November 30, 2015	170	Cost of Goods Sold.........................	800
November 30, 2014	130	Short-term Investments...................	170
Net Credit Sales	2,450	Other Current Assets.......................	30
Long-term Assets	410	Other Current Liabilities	170
Long-term Liabilities..................	60		

Requirements

1. Compute Algonquin Equipment's (a) quick ratio and (b) accounts receivable turnover for 2015.

2. Evaluate each ratio value as strong or weak. Assume Algonquin Equipment sells on terms of net 30.

EXERCISES (ALTERNATES 1, 2, AND 3)

These alternative exercise sets are available for your practice benefit on **MyAccountingLab**.

PROBLEMS (GROUP A)

P7-1A. Prepare journal entries for various types of sales (*Learning Objective 2*)
20–25 min.

Ace Party Supplies, Ltd. completed the following transactions during December. Ace uses the perpetual inventory system in accounting for inventory.

Dec 2	Sold party supplies for $1,800 to Goody Bags on account, with terms of 2/10, n/30, FOB shipping point. The cost of the sale was $1,125.
4	Sold party supplies to a customer for $500, with cost of $350. Customer paid with a credit card. The credit card company charged a 2% service fee.
6	Sold party supplies for $1,200 to Party Queen on account, with terms of 2/10, n/30, FOB shipping point. The cost of the sale was $750.
12	Party Queen returned $200 of the party supplies. The cost of the returned products was $125. These products were returned to the warehouse for resale.
15	Sold party supplies to customer for $320 cash. The cost of the sale was $200.
16	Received payment from Party Queen, less returns and discount.
23	Sold party supplies to a customer for $400, with cost of $280. Customer paid with a debit card. The bank charged a 2% of service fee.
31	Received payment from Goody Bags.

Requirements

1. Record the transactions in the journal.

2. What are the amounts for total sales, sales returns and allowances, and sales discounts to be reported in the income statement?

P7-2A. Allowance method and accounts receivable reporting (*Learning Objectives 3 & 4*) 20–25 min.

On August 31, Pro Tennis Equipment had a $150,000 debit balance in Accounts Receivable ($70,000 current, $55,000 30 to 60 days, $35,000 60+). During September, Pro Tennis Equipment had the following transactions:

- Sales of $500,000, all on credit.
- Collections on account, $550,000.
- Write-offs of uncollectible receivables, $7,000.

Requirements

1. Assume that Pro Tennis Equipment uses the allowance method to account for doubtful accounts and that there was a $9,000 credit balance in the allowance account on August 31. Prepare journal entries to record sales, collections on account, and write-offs of doubtful accounts for the month of September. Next, assuming that doubtful accounts expense is estimated at 2% of credit sales, prepare the adjusting journal entry to record bad debts expense. Enter the beginning balances and post all September activity in T-accounts for Accounts Receivable, Allowance for Doubtful Accounts, and Bad Debt Expense.

2. Suppose that instead of the percentage of sales method, Pro Tennis Equipment uses the aging of accounts receivable method. The estimated bad debt is as follows: 1% of current A/R, 5% of A/R 30–60 days, 20% of A/R 60+ days. Prepare journal entries to record sales, collections on account, and write-offs of doubtful accounts for the month of September. Enter the beginning balances and post all September activity in T-accounts for Accounts Receivable and Bad Debt Expense.

3. What amount of bad debt expense would Pro Tennis Equipment report on its September income statement under each of the two methods?

4. What amount of net accounts receivable would Pro Tennis Equipment report on its September 30 statement of financial position under each of the two methods?

P7-3A. Aging of accounts receivable allowance method (*Learning Objectives 3 & 4*) 15–20 min.

Regents Supply completed the following selected transactions during the year:

Jan 17	Sold inventory to Abe Gomez, $600, on account. Ignore cost of goods sold.
Jun 29	Wrote off the Abe Gomez account as uncollectible after repeated efforts to collect from him.
Aug 6	Received $200 from Abe Gomez, along with a letter stating his intention to pay within 30 days. Reinstated his account in full.
Sep 4	Received the balance due from Abe Gomez.
Dec 31	Made a compound entry to write off the following accounts as uncollectible: Bernard Clark, $700; Marie Montrose, $300; and Terry Forman, $600.
Dec 31	Based on an aging of accounts receivable, estimated uncollectible accounts as $2,300.

Requirements

1. Open T-accounts for Allowance for Doubtful Accounts and Bad Debt Expense. These accounts have beginning balances of $1,800 (Cr.) and 0, respectively.

2. Record the transactions in the journal, and post to the two T-accounts.

3. The December 31 balance of Accounts Receivable is $139,000. Show how Accounts Receivable would be reported on the statement of financial position at that date.

Quick solution:

2. Adjusting journal entry amount to record bad debts expense = $2,100; Allowance for Doubtful Accounts ending balance = $2,300; Bad Debt Expense ending balance = $2,100

P7-4A. Aging of accounts receivable allowance method (*Learning Objectives 3 & 4*)
30–35 min.

Goto Foods International, Inc. uses the aging of accounts receivable method to account for bad debts at the end of each year. All of its customers are on account with the credit terms 2/10, n/30. Accounts receivable are grouped into three aging periods: (1) current—within the current month, (2) 31 to 60 days, and (3) 61+ days. Goto's accounting policy for estimating the uncollectible accounts receivable is calculated based on (1) 5% on the current, (2) 10% on the second aging period, and (3) 30% on the third aging period.

At December 31, Goto Foods' Accounts Receivable was $92,800, and the unadjusted Allowance for Doubtful Accounts was $3,200 (Cr.). The following is a list of the accounts receivable subsidiary ledger for five customers:

Date	Document	Debit	Credit	Balance
		Bua Foods		
Oct 28	Invoice 337	$ 6,850		$ 6,850
Nov 28	Invoice 395	4,750		11,600
Dec 5	Receipt Inv 337		3,360	8,240
Dec 23	Invoice 456	7,240		15,480
		Nitesh Grocers		
Oct 08	Invoice 263	6,500		6,500
Oct 10	Credit Memo 105		700	5,800
Oct 17	Receipt Inv 263		5,800	0
Oct 30	Invoice 346	12,500		12,500
		Pusan Export, Inc.		
Nov 18	Invoice 279	30,200		30,200
		Vuong Company		
Oct 22	Invoice 302	8,520		8,520
Dec 10	Invoice 418	3,400		11,920
		Wang Enterprise		
Oct 26	Invoice 328	8,600		8,600
Nov 05	Receipt Inv 328		4,300	4,300
Dec 30	Invoice 468	18,400		22,700

Requirements

1. Prepare the customer aging schedule based on the three aging groups.
2. Calculate the estimated uncollectible accounts for the year.
3. Prepare the journal entry for the bad debt expense.
4. Which company has taken the sales discounts? What was the amount of the sales discounts taken?

P7-5A. Sales and bad debt write-offs (*Learning Objectives 2 & 3*) 20–25 min.

MinTech Computer Supplies, Inc.'s accounting data show the following balances for 2015 and 2016:

	2015	2016
Sales (40%—Cash, 60%—Credit)	$280,000	$322,000
Sales Returns and Allowances	5,600	6,400
Accounts Receivable written off during the year	2,700	11,000
Accounts Receivable, December 31	84,000	108,000
Allowance for Doubtful Accounts (credit balance), December 31	4,200	5,400

The accountant also provided the following additional information:

a. MinTech uses the perpetual inventory system and its gross margin is 40% of the sales.

b. During 2016, there was a large write-off of $11,000 due to an unexpected bankruptcy of a major customer.

c. During 2016, $500 of the previously written-off amount was collected in full.

Requirements

1. Calculate the bad debt expense for the year ended December 31, 2016.

2. Calculate the cash collections from accounts receivable for 2016.

3. Prepare journal entries to record all the transactions for MinTech in 2016.

4. What is the impact on each of assets, shareholders' equity, and net income when the uncollectible accounts are written off? Please identify as increase (I), decrease (D), or no effect (NE).

P7-6A. **Accounting for notes receivable (*Learning Objective 5*) 20–25 min.**

The Bailey Insurance Agency received the following notes during 2015:

Note	Date	Principal Amount	Interest Rate	Term
(1)	Dec 23	$13,000	9%	1 year
(2)	Nov 30	12,000	12%	6 months
(3)	Dec 7	9,000	10%	30 days

Requirements

1. Identifying each note by number, compute interest using a 360-day year, and determine the due date and maturity value of each note.

2. Journalize a single adjusting entry on December 31, 2015, to record accrued interest revenue on all three notes. Explanations are not required.

3. For note (1), journalize the collection of principal and interest at maturity. Explanations are not required.

P7-7A. **Accounting for notes receivable (*Learning Objective 5*) 20–25 min.**

Record the following transactions in the journal of Bingham Phone Accessories. Explanations are not required.

2014	
Dec 19	Received a $3,000, 60-day, 12% note on account from Arnold Collins.
31	Made an adjusting entry to accrue interest on the Collins note.
31	Made a closing entry for interest revenue.

2015	
Feb 17	Collected the maturity value of the Collins note.
Jun 1	Loaned $10,000 cash to Electra Mann, receiving a six-month, 11% note.
Oct 31	Received a $1,500, 60-day, 12% note from Mark Phillips on his past-due account receivable.
Dec 1	Collected the maturity value of the Electra Mann note.

P7-8A. **Quick ratio and accounts receivable turnover (*Learning Objective 6*) 20–25 min.**

The comparative financial statements of Bien Taco Restaurants for 2015, 2014, and 2013 include the following selected data:

	(In Thousands)		
	2015	**2014**	**2013**
Statement of Financial Position			
Current Assets:			
Cash	$ 82	$ 80	$ 60
Short-term Investments	140	174	122
Receivables, Net of Allowance for Doubtful Accounts of $6, $6, and $5 respectively	257	265	218
Inventory	429	341	302
Prepaid Expenses	21	27	46
Total Current Assets	929	887	748
Total Current Liabilities	$ 680	$ 700	$ 600
Income Statement			
Sales Revenue	$5,189	$4,995	$4,206
Cost of Goods Sold	2,734	2,636	2,418

Requirements

1. Compute these ratios for 2015 and 2014:

   a. Quick ratio.

   b. Accounts receivable turnover. Assume all sales are credit sales.

2. Write a memo explaining to the company owner which ratios improved from 2014 to 2015, which ratios deteriorated, and which items in the financial statements changed and caused changes in some ratios. Discuss whether this conveys a favourable or an unfavourable impression about the company.

PROBLEMS (GROUP B)

P7-1B. Prepare journal entries for various types of sales (*Learning Objective 2*)
20–25 min.

Bill Building Supplies, Ltd. completed the following transactions during June. Bill uses the perpetual inventory system in accounting for inventory.

Jun 2	Sold plumbing supplies to a customer for $1,100, with cost of $660. Customer paid with a credit card. The credit card company charged a 2% service fee.
6	Sold building supplies for $2,600 to Goh Development on account, with terms of 2/15, n/30, FOB shipping point. The cost of the sale was $1,560.
12	Goh Development returned $600 of the building supplies. The cost of the returned products was $360. These products were returned to the warehouse for resale.
15	Sold building supplies for $1,800 to Lum Contractors on account, with terms of 2/15, n/30, FOB shipping point. The cost of the sale was $1,080.
16	Sold building supplies to a customer for $820 cash. The cost of the sale was $500.
21	Received payment from Goh Development, less returns and discount.
23	Sold building supplies to a customer for $1,400, with cost of $840. Customer paid with a debit card. The bank charged a 2% service fee.
30	Received payment from Lum Contractors, less discount.

Requirements

1. Record the transactions in the journal.
2. What are the amounts for total sales, sales returns and allowances, and sales discounts to be reported in the income statement?

P7-2B. Allowance method and accounts receivable reporting (*Learning Objectives 3 & 4*) 20–25 min.

On March 31, Daisy Tennis Equipment had a $165,000 debit balance in Accounts Receivable ($80,000 current, $65,000 30 to 60 days, $20,000 60+). During April, Daisy Tennis Equipment had the following transactions:

- Sales of $490,000, all on credit.
- Collections on account, $425,000.
- Write-offs of uncollectible receivables, $6,000.

Requirements

1. Assume that Daisy Tennis Equipment uses the allowance method to account for doubtful accounts and that there was an $8,000 credit balance in the allowance account on March 31. Prepare journal entries to record sales, collections on account, and write-offs of doubtful accounts for the month of April. Next, assuming that bad debt expense is estimated at 2% of credit sales, prepare the adjusting journal entry to record bad debts expense. Enter the beginning balances and post all April activity in T-accounts for Accounts Receivable, Allowance for Doubtful Accounts, and Bad Debt Expense.

2. Suppose that instead of the allowance method, Daisy Tennis Equipment uses the aging of accounts receivable method. The estimated bad debt is as follows: 0.5% of current A/R, 5% of A/R 30–60 days, 30% of A/R 60+ days. Prepare journal entries to record sales, collections on account, and write-offs of doubtful accounts for the month of April. Enter the beginning balances and post all April activity in T-accounts for Accounts Receivable and Bad Debt Expense.

3. What amount of bad debt expense would Daisy Tennis Equipment report on its April income statement under each of the two methods?

4. What amount of net accounts receivable would Daisy Tennis Equipment report on its April 30 statement of financial position under each of the two methods?

P7-3B. Aging of accounts receivable allowance method (*Learning Objectives 3 & 4*) 15–20 min.

Beta Supply completed the following selected transactions during the year:

Jan 17	Sold inventory to Abe Gomez, $800 on account. Ignore cost of goods sold.
Jun 29	Wrote off Abe Gomez's account as uncollectible after repeated efforts to collect from him.
Aug 6	Received $250 from Abe Gomez, along with a letter stating his intention to pay within 30 days. Reinstated Gomez's account in full.
Sep 4	Received the balance due from Abe Gomez.
Dec 31	Made a compound entry to write off the following accounts as uncollectible: Brian Kemper, $1,000; Marie Montrose, $200; and Tanya Wayne, $900.
Dec 31	Based on an aging of accounts receivable, estimated uncollectible accounts as $2,600.

Requirements

1. Open T-accounts for Allowance for Doubtful Accounts and Bad Debt Expense. These accounts have beginning balances of $1,500 (Cr.) and 0, respectively.

2. Record the transactions in the journal, and post to the two T-accounts.

3. The December 31 balance of Accounts Receivable is $133,000. Show how Accounts Receivable would be reported on the statement of financial position at that date.

P7-4B. Aging of accounts receivable allowance method (Learning Objectives 3 & 4)
30–35 min.

Yangzi International, Inc. uses the aging of accounts receivable method to account for uncollectible accounts at the end of each year. All of its customers are on account with the credit terms 2/10, n/30. Accounts receivable are grouped in three aging periods: (1) current—within the current month, (2) 31 to 60 days, and (3) 61+ days. Yangzi's accounting policy for estimating the uncollectible accounts receivable is calculated based on (1) 5% on the current, (2) 10% on the second aging period, and (3) 40% on the third aging period.

On March 31, the end of this fiscal year, Yangzi's Accounts Receivable was $130,600, and the unadjusted Allowance for Doubtful Accounts was $5,800 (credit). The following is a list of the accounts receivable subsidiary ledger for five customers:

Date	Document	Debit	Credit	Balance
	Chen Enterprise			
Jan 8	Invoice 121	26,500		26,500
Jan 10	Credit Memo 52		1,200	25,300
Jan 21	Invoice 130	14,600		39,900
Feb 7	Receipt Inv 121		25,300	14,600
	Dong Gifts			
Jan 22	Invoice 132	25,800		25,800
Feb 21	Receipt Inv 132		15,480	10,320
Mar 10	Invoice 158	32,400		42,720
Mar 15	Receipt Inv 132		5,320	37,400
	Jeevan Export, Inc.			
Jan 28	Invoice 145	12,400		12,400
Feb 28	Invoice 159	8,600		21,000
Mar 5	Receipt Inv 145		6,400	14,600
Mar 25	Invoice 178	32,400		47,000
	Prasad Trades Company			
Jan 18	Invoice 128	13,200		13,200
	Zhou International			
Jan 26	Invoice 143	7,500		7,500
Feb 5	Receipt Inv 143		7,500	0
Mar 30	Invoice 168	18,400		18,400

Requirements

1. Prepare the customer aging schedule based on the three aging groups.

2. Calculate the estimated uncollectible accounts for the year.

3. Prepare the journal entry for the bad debt expense.

4. Which company has taken the sales discounts? What was the amount of the sales discounts taken?

P7-5B. Sales and bad debt write-offs (*Learning Objectives 2 & 3*) 20–25 min.

ATel Electronics, Inc.'s accounting data show the following balances for 2015 and 2016:

	2015	2016
Sales (40%—Cash, 60%—Credit)	$420,000	$546,000
Sales Returns and Allowances	12,600	13,650
Accounts Receivable written off during the year	5,200	15,800
Accounts Receivable, December 31	128,000	164,000
Allowance for Doubtful Accounts (credit balance), December 31	6,400	8,200

The accountant also provided the following additional information:

a. ATel Electronics uses the perpetual inventory system and its gross margin is 40% of the sales.

b. During 2016, there was a large write-off of $15,800 due to an unexpected bankruptcy of a major customer.

c. During 2016, $1,200 of the previously written-off amount was collected in full.

Requirements

1. Calculate the bad debt expense for the year ended December 31, 2016.

2. Calculate the cash collections from accounts receivable for 2016.

3. Prepare journal entries to record all the transactions for ATel in 2016.

4. What is the impact on each of assets, shareholders' equity, and net income, when the uncollectible accounts are written off? Please identify as increase (I), decrease (D), or no effect (NE).

P7-6B. Accounting for notes receivable (*Learning Objective 5*) 20–25 min.

The Buffalo Insurance Agency received the following notes during 2015:

Note	Date	Principal	Interest Rate	Term
(1)	Oct 23	$13,000	8%	1 year
(2)	Sep 30	8,000	11%	2 months
(3)	Oct 7	10,000	12%	45 days

Requirements

1. Identifying each note by number, compute interest using a 360-day year, and determine the due date and maturity value of each note.

2. Journalize a single adjusting entry on October 31, 2015, to record accrued interest revenue on all three notes. Explanations are not required.

3. For note (1), journalize the collection of principal and interest at maturity. Explanations are not required.

P7-7B. Accounting for notes receivable (*Learning Objective 5*) 20–25 min.

Record the following transactions in the journal of Birds Eye Music. Explanations are not required.

2014

Dec 19   Received a $6,000, 60-day, 12% note on account from AVC Company.
31   Made an adjusting entry to accrue interest on the AVC Company note.
31   Made a closing entry for interest revenue.

2015

Feb 17   Collected the maturity value of the AVC Company note.
Jun 1   Loaned $12,000 cash to Lincoln Music, receiving a six-month, 11% note.
Oct 31   Received a $5,500, 60-day, 13% note from Ying Yang Music on its past-due account receivable.
Dec 1   Collected the maturity value of the Lincoln Music note.

P7-8B. Quick ratio and accounts receivable turnover (*Learning Objective 6*)
20–25 min.

The comparative financial statements of Perfection Taco Restaurants for 2015, 2014, and 2013 include the following selected data:

	(In Thousands)		
	2015	2014	2013
Statement of Financial Position			
Current Assets:			
Cash	$ 82	$ 80	$ 55
Short-term Investments	130	178	125
Receivables, Net of Allowance for Doubtful Accounts of $7, $6, and $4, respectively	290	305	256
Inventory	434	335	315
Prepaid Expenses	24	30	55
Total Current Assets	960	928	806
Total Current Liabilities	$ 780	$ 800	$ 625
Income Statement			
Sales Revenue	$5,223	$5,039	$4,250
Cost of Goods Sold	2,768	2,650	2,490

Requirements

1. Compute these ratios for 2015 and 2014:

   a. Quick ratio.

   b. Accounts receivable turnover. Assume all sales are credit sales.

2. Write a memo explaining to the company owner which ratios improved from 2014 to 2015, which ratios deteriorated, and which items in the financial statements changed and caused changes in some ratios. Discuss whether this change conveys a favourable or an unfavourable impression about the company.

PROBLEMS (ALTERNATES 1, 2, AND 3)

These alternative problem sets are available for your practice benefit on **MyAccountingLab**.

CONTINUING EXERCISE

In this exercise, we continue our accounting for Graham's Yard Care, Inc. from Chapter 6. Refer to the Continuing Exercise from Chapter 6. On August 18, Graham's Yard Care, Inc. received $250 on account from Jim Henderson related to his July 15 purchase. On October 12, Jim notified Graham's Yard Care, Inc. that he was filing for bankruptcy and that he would not be able to pay the remaining amount owed.

Requirement

1. Journalize the entry to record the payment from Jim and to record the write-off of Jim's uncollectible account. Assume that Graham's Yard Care, Inc. uses the allowance method to account for Doubtful Accounts.

In this problem, we continue our accounting for Aqua Elite, Inc. from Chapter 6. Refer to the Continuing Problem in Chapters 5 and 6. Assume that all 13 of the spas Aqua Elite, Inc. sold in September were sold on account for $4,000 each. At September 30, Aqua Elite, Inc. estimates that 5% of the sales will not be collected.

Requirements

1. Calculate the ending balance in Accounts Receivable at September 30.
2. Journalize the entry to record Aqua Elite's Bad Debt Expense for September.
3. How will Accounts Receivable be reflected on Aqua Elite's statement of financial position at September 30?

APPLY YOUR KNOWLEDGE

ETHICS IN ACTION

Case 1. Ed Hanson is the controller of Casey's Collectibles. The business uses the accrual method of accounting and recognizes sales revenue in the period in which the sale is made. As a result, the Accounts Receivable balance at year-end was $92,480, which was net of the Allowance for Doubtful Accounts of $1,260. Ed was completing the year-end financial statements for the business to apply for a much needed business loan when he saw a letter from a district court. The letter was to inform him as controller of Casey's Collectibles that Charlie Smith had declared bankruptcy. As it turned out, Charlie was Casey's Collectibles' largest customer and his account receivable balance was $24,295, which the bankruptcy notification letter stated was never going to be paid. When Ed looked over the account receivable aging schedule he saw that Charlie's account was more than 90 days past due, and even though Ed had been suspicious, he still hoped that Charlie would pay his account balance. Ed looked at his statement of financial position and thought that if he wrote off Charlie's account, the bank would become concerned about all of the accounts receivable listed. He then thought that had he not been so quick to open the mail, he would have not known that Charlie was bankrupt, and the statement of financial position he was about to present to the bank would be fine. Knowing how potentially damaging this new information could be, Ed decided to just ignore it for the moment and simply go ahead with the statement of financial position he had originally planned to give to the bank.

Should Ed provide the bank with a new statement of financial position that reflects this new information? Would Ed have been fine with the original statement of financial position had he simply waited to open his mail? Are any ethical issues involved with updating financial statement information for subsequent events? Did Ed not properly use the allowance method as he only had a balance for doubtful accounts totalling $1,260? Would Ed need to inform the bank had the bankruptcy letter been from a customer with an account receivable balance of $120?

Case 2. Bob and Larry were finishing the financial statements for their business when they saw the net income for the year was not going to be as high as they had hoped. Concerned that the bank would question the lower reported net income, Bob suggested that they reduce the percentage used to estimate doubtful accounts for the current year from 5% of credit sales to 1% of credit sales. Larry quickly pointed out that for the last seven years, the bad debts always approximated 5% of the total credit sales. Bob then said that the key was simply that an "estimate" was used to compute the bad debt expense, so why not simply change the percentage from the "5% estimate" to a "1% estimate"? Larry was concerned because the change was not due to new business information; rather it was due to pressure to increase the current year profit by reducing the amount of bad debt expense currently included in the income statement. He told Bob that the current year credit sales were $6,587,000 and the bad debt expense should be 5% or $329,350, not 1% or $65,870, because they could expect that over the next fiscal year approximately $329,000 of accounts receivable would end up as uncollectible. Bob pointed out, however, that by only using a 1% estimate the current year net income would be much higher since the amount of bad debt expense would only be $65,870 instead of the larger $329,350. He also noted that the allowance account would also be reduced so the net Accounts Receivable on the statement of financial position would be larger as well. Besides, Bob told Larry that they could worry about it in the next fiscal year. Larry told Bob that the bank would find out what they had done, to which Bob said there would be no problem; they could just say they made a mistake in their estimate.

Would it be unethical to change the percentage used to compute the current year's bad debt expense? Would it be acceptable to change the percentage amount if the change was disclosed? Would it be acceptable if they compromised and used 3%? If they had used a new screening method to determine the credit-worthiness of customers and, as a result, they were certain that the bad debts would be drastically reduced, could they change the percentage amount used? What do you think would happen if they used the 1% of credit sales for the current year financial statements? What would you recommend?

KNOW YOUR BUSINESS

FINANCIAL ANALYSIS

Purpose: To help familiarize you with the financial reporting of a real company to further your understanding of the chapter material you are learning.

This case will address the accounts receivable reflected on Bombardier Inc.'s statement of financial position. We will once again refer to the annual report for Bombardier Inc. located in MyAccountingLab to answer some questions related to Bombardier Inc.'s receivables.

Requirements

1. What was the Accounts Receivable balance as of January 31, 2012? What was the Accounts Receivable balance as of January 31, 2011? Did the amount of accounts receivable increase or decrease during the year?

   How much of the trade accounts receivable is estimated not likely to be collected?

2. How much of the trade receivables are impaired and how does the company determine impairment?

INDUSTRY ANALYSIS

Purpose: To help you understand and compare the performance of two companies in the same industry.

Find the Bombardier Annual Report, Year Ended January 31, 2012 located in MyAccountingLab. Now access the Boeing Company's 2012 Annual Report. To do this from the internet, go to their webpage for the Investor Relations at http://www.boeing.com/companyoffices/financial/quarterly.htm and under Annual Report, go to the 2010 Annual Report.

Requirement

1. Calculate the accounts receivable turnover for Bombardier for 2012 and Boeing for 2012 using the gross trade receivable amounts for each company. Who has the highest accounts receivable turnover? Is that good or bad? Is it better to have a high accounts receivable turnover or a low accounts receivable turnover? Explain your answer.

SMALL BUSINESS ANALYSIS

Purpose: To help you understand the importance of managing accounts receivable of a small business.

Louise was horrified when she realized, too late, that it was only five days until the end of the month, and there was insufficient cash available to pay all her employees and the rent. What happened? The last four weeks had been a whirlwind of activity, as her small software training company had been immersed in the biggest, most profitable training initiative of the firm's existence, during which time she had ignored her usual weekly activity of calling clients whose accounts receivable were three days overdue, to remind them to process the invoice for payment.

Since the firm typically sent out dozens of invoices weekly for training completed, but customers often needed reminding to send the invoices to their accounts payable department for processing, Louise had found from past experience that it was necessary to follow up by phone on approximately thirty percent of invoices, or else they would not get processed.

Requirements

1. What happened? Why did Louise find she wouldn't have enough cash to pay all her employees and the rent at month end?

2. If the accounts receivable were not collected, what happens to the accounts receivable turnover?

WRITTEN COMMUNICATION

You're pretty excited about your cash balance at the end of the month because this was the month you were going to take the big bonus from the business and make a down payment on a new house. You were waiting on a big cheque to come in from a client who has owed you for several months. You had considered writing it off because you had heard through some business associates that the company had been experiencing some financial difficulties. However, after your telephone call to the company the first of the week, the cheque finally arrived. You rushed the cheque down to the bank and deposited it. A couple days later, you access your account online at the bank to figure out how much of a bonus cheque you can afford to write yourself. After depositing the $30,000 from your client, you expect to have a balance of at least $40,000 and since you always like to keep a balance of at least $10,000 in your account as a buffer, you figure you can easily write a bonus check for $25,000 for your down payment. After reviewing your account, you're really concerned when you see that your bank balance is only $9,500! What happened? You scroll down through the screen for an explanation and you see the following:

NSF cheque—Burns & Associates, Inc.—$30,000.00
Return cheque charge $200.00
Monthly service charge $300.00

Prepare an email to the owner of Burns & Associates, Inc., explaining the situation with the returned cheque and the charge that the bank applied to your account for processing the returned cheque. Also request payment for this entire amount, as it is now several months overdue. However, keep in mind that the tone of the email might have some bearing on whether or not Burns continues to utilize your services.

Self Check Answers
1. a 2. a 3. d 4. c 5. b 6. a 7. b 8. a 9. c 10. c

8
Long-Term Assets

BUSINESS, ACCOUNTING, AND YOU

Drive or walk up to a Best Buy store. What does it look like? It is a big building with a big blue and yellow Best Buy sign. There is also a lot of land around the store and a parking lot. Go inside and you will see many pieces of furniture and equipment needed to display the inventory and operate the store.

You go to Best Buy to buy products, but Best Buy needs more than just inventory to operate. It needs assets such as land, buildings, and equipment. These assets have a long life and can be used for more than one year; hence they are called long-term assets. They are necessary to attract customers and deliver the inventory customers want—without these assets, no sales will occur, and without sales, the business cannot survive.

Businesses like Best Buy need long-term assets such as land, buildings, and equipment, but these assets are often very expensive. As the business uses these assets, the assets depreciate. If the business needs to sell these assets, it is often difficult to find a buyer. As such, investing money in these assets is risky and must be done carefully.

So how do accountants recognize, measure, record, and report long-term asset transactions? As an accountant or manager, you need to understand how a business accounts for long-term assets because it impacts a business's net income and value.

WHAT ARE THE DIFFERENT TYPES OF LONG-TERM ASSETS?

L.O. ❶ Describe the difference between plant assets, intangible assets, and natural resources

Most businesses will own at least one of the following types of long-term assets:

- **Plant assets.** Plant assets, also called fixed assets, are "physical assets"—meaning they can be seen, touched, or held. This includes assets such as land, buildings, vehicles, desks, and equipment. In addition to assets that have a physical form, plant assets are also sometimes referred to as **tangible assets**.

- **Intangible assets.** Patents, trademarks, brands, and goodwill are examples of **intangible assets**. Unlike plant assets, intangible assets cannot be seen, touched, or held. For example, even though there may be a piece of paper that provides written evidence of a patent, the paper is not the patent. The patent (the intangible asset) is actually the specific rights that are conveyed to the owner of the patent. Similarly, a logo, such as the Tim Hortons logo below, identifies a brand and is an intangible element of creating the image of the company that is recognizable by customers and the public at large.

- **Natural resources.** Assets that come from the earth and can ultimately be used up are called **natural resources**. Timber, oil, minerals, and coal are all examples of natural resources.

As we learned in Chapter 3, the cost of a long-term asset must be allocated to an expense as the asset is used up. Although the process of cost allocation is similar for the different types of assets, the terminology used to describe the process is different for each type of asset. **Exhibit 8-1** summarizes the different asset types and the cost allocation terminology used with each. Note that IFRS uses the term *depreciation* when referring to allocating the cost of property, plant, and equipment, and *amortization* when referring to allocating the cost of intangible assets. ASPE uses *amortization* to refer to cost allocation of both tangible and intangible assets. The cost allocation methods for each type of asset will be covered later in the chapter.

Companies may also own long-term assets that are classified as *other long-term assets*. Other long-term assets typically consist of long-term investments made by a business. These will be discussed near the end of the chapter. Further, companies may use long-term assets that they don't own, such as assets that are leased for more than one accounting period. Accounting for leases will be discussed in Appendix 8A of this chapter.

Exhibit 8-1 ▲

HOW IS THE COST OF A PLANT ASSET CALCULATED?

Both IFRS and ASPE require that the *cost principle,* which we learned about in Chapter 1, be applied when determining the cost of a plant asset. Therefore, the actual amount paid for an asset is to be used as the asset's cost. The amount paid for an asset should include all amounts paid to acquire the asset and to prepare it for its intended purpose. These costs vary depending on the type of plant asset being purchased, so let's discuss each asset type individually.

**L.O. ② ** Calculate and record the acquisition of plant assets

LAND AND LAND IMPROVEMENTS

The cost of land includes, but is not limited to, the following amounts paid by the purchaser:

- Purchase price
- Realtor commissions
- Survey and legal fees
- Unpaid property taxes owed on the land
- Fees associated with transferring the ownership (title) on the land
- Cost of clearing the land and removing unwanted buildings

To summarize, any cost that is paid to acquire and make the land ready for use is included in the cost of the land. Any revenue derived from the land during the process of making it ready for use (such as selling material from demolished buildings) is deducted from the cost of the land.

The cost of land does *not* include the following costs:

- Fencing
- Paving
- Sprinkler systems
- Lighting
- Signs

These costs are recorded as separate plant assets called **land improvements**.

Suppose that Apex Industries purchases land for $75,000 by signing a note payable for the same amount. Apex Industries also pays cash as follows: $2,500 in realtor commission, $1,200 in transfer fees, a $1,700 survey fee, $4,500 to remove an old building, $2,200 to have the land graded and levelled, $6,300 to have the land fenced, $1,300 for a sprinkler system, and $2,700 for outdoor lighting. What amount would Apex Industries record as the cost of the land? How much would Apex record as land improvements? Apex Industries would assign the costs to land and land improvements as follows:

Cost Incurred	Land	Land Improvements
Purchase price	$75,000	
Realtor commission	2,500	
Transfer fees	1,200	
Survey fee	1,700	
Building removal	4,500	
Grading	2,200	
Fencing		$ 6,300
Sprinkler system		1,300
Lighting		2,700
Total cost	$87,100	$10,300

The purchase of the land and the subsequent cash payments are recorded as follows:

Assets	=	Liabilities	+	Shareholders' Equity
+75,000	=	+75,000		

Assets	=	Liabilities	+	Shareholders' Equity
+12,100	=			
+10,300				
−22,400				

DATE	ACCOUNTS	POST REF.	DR.	CR.
	Land		75,000	
	Note Payable			75,000
	Purchased land on a note payable.			
	Land		12,100	
	Land Improvements		10,300	
	Cash			22,400
	Paid cash for land and land improvements.			

MEMORY TIPS

Remember that costs attached to the land are usually one-time costs before the land can be used, while costs paid for land improvements could recur in the future.

We would say that Apex Industries *capitalized* the cost of the land at $87,100 ($75,000 + $12,100) and the land improvements at $10,300. **Capitalized** means that an asset account is debited (increased) for the cost of an asset. Notice that Land and Land Improvements are two entirely separate assets. Land is a special plant asset because it is never really used up. Therefore, land is not depreciated. However, the cost of land improvements *is* depreciated over the useful life of the improvements.

BUILDINGS

The cost of a building depends on whether the building is constructed or whether an existing building is purchased. If a building is constructed, the cost of the building includes the following:

- Architectural fees
- Building permit fees
- Contractor charges
- Payments for material, labour, and overhead

The time to complete a building can be months, even years. If a company constructs its own assets, the cost of a building may also include interest charged during the time of construction on any borrowed money.

If a company purchases an existing building, the cost of the building includes the following:

- Purchase price
- Realtor commissions
- Survey and legal fees
- Unpaid property taxes owed on the building
- Fees associated with transferring the ownership (title) on the building
- Costs of repairing and renovating the building for its intended use

MACHINERY AND EQUIPMENT

The cost of machinery and equipment includes the following:

- Purchase price (less any discounts)
- Transportation (delivery) charges
- Insurance while in transit

- Sales and other taxes
- Purchase commission
- Installation costs
- Cost of testing the asset before it is used

After the asset is up and running, the company no longer debits insurance, taxes, and maintenance costs to the Equipment account. From that point on, insurance, taxes, repairs, and maintenance costs are recorded as expenses.

FURNITURE AND FIXTURES

Furniture and fixtures include desks, chairs, file cabinets, display racks, shelving, and so forth. The cost of furniture and fixtures includes the basic cost of each asset (less any discounts), plus all other costs to ready the asset for its intended use. For example, for a desk, this may include the costs to ship the desk to the business and the cost paid to a handyman to assemble the desk.

Exhibit 8-2 summarizes the costs associated with the different types of plant assets.

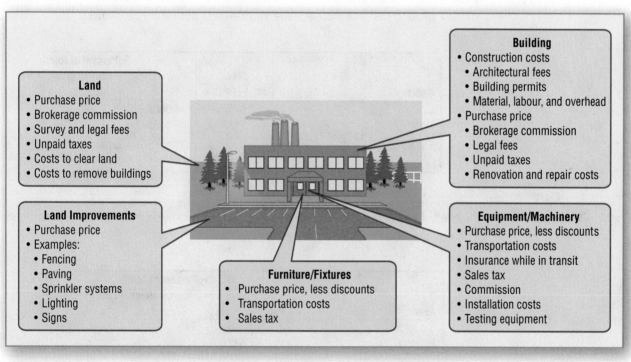

Land
- Purchase price
- Brokerage commission
- Survey and legal fees
- Unpaid taxes
- Costs to clear land
- Costs to remove buildings

Land Improvements
- Purchase price
- Examples:
  - Fencing
  - Paving
  - Sprinkler systems
  - Lighting
  - Signs

Furniture/Fixtures
- Purchase price, less discounts
- Transportation costs
- Sales tax

Building
- Construction costs
  - Architectural fees
  - Building permits
  - Material, labour, and overhead
- Purchase price
  - Brokerage commission
  - Legal fees
  - Unpaid taxes
  - Renovation and repair costs

Equipment/Machinery
- Purchase price, less discounts
- Transportation costs
- Insurance while in transit
- Sales tax
- Commission
- Installation costs
- Testing equipment

Exhibit 8-2 ▲

LUMP-SUM (BASKET) PURCHASE OF ASSETS

When a company pays a single price for several assets as a group it is referred to as a **lump-sum purchase**, or **"basket" purchase**. For example, Apex Industries may pay one price ($625,000) for land, a building, and equipment. For accounting purposes, the company must allocate a portion of the total cost to each individual asset, as shown in the following diagram:

Total Purchase Price
$625,000

Land
?

Building
?

Equipment
?

Shutterstock   Jelwolf/Fotolia   Terex/Fotolia

The total cost is allocated to the different assets based on their relative market values. Let's assume that an appraisal revealed that the land's market value is $75,000, the building's market value is $480,000, and the equipment's market value is $130,000. Apex Industries got a good deal, paying only $625,000 for assets with a combined market value of $685,000 ($75,000 + $480,000 + $130,000). To allocate the total purchase price to the different assets, Apex Industries must first determine the ratio of each asset's market value to the total market value for all assets combined as follows:

Asset	Market Value		Percent of Total Market Value (Rounded)
Land	$ 75,000	÷ $685,000	11%
Building	480,000	÷ $685,000	70%
Equipment	130,000	÷ $685,000	19%
Total	**$685,000**		**100%**

Next, the cost that is allocated to each asset is found by multiplying the total purchase price by the ratios determined previously.

Asset	Total Purchase Price	×	Percent of Total Market Value (Rounded)	Cost Allocated to Asset
Land	$625,000	×	11%	$ 68,750
Building	$625,000	×	70%	437,500
Equipment	$625,000	×	19%	118,750
Total			**100%**	**$625,000**

If we assume that Apex Industries purchased the combined assets on a note payable, the purchase is recorded as follows:

Assets	=	Liabilities	+	Shareholders' Equity
+68,750	=	+625,000		
+437,500				
+118,750				

DATE	ACCOUNTS	POST REF.	DR.	CR.
	Land		68,750	
	Building		437,500	
	Equipment		118,750	
	Note Payable			625,000
	Purchased land, building, and equipment on a note payable.			

HOW ARE COSTS MEASURED?

Asset values should be measured based on the amount of cash that is exchanged. However, in some situations, companies do not pay cash for their assets; instead, companies may issue shares in exchange for assets. In the case of a share-based payment, if the asset value can be reliably determined, then the fair value of the asset should be used; otherwise, the fair value of the shares given in exchange should be used. If a company's shares are publicly traded, then the fair value of the shares is easily obtainable and verifiable. Therefore, the share value given up should be used. If it is a private company whose shares are not traded, then it is more reliable to use the fair value of the asset acquired.

 DECISION GUIDELINES

DECISION	**GUIDELINE**	**ANALYZE**
How do I determine the cost of an asset?	All costs associated with acquiring an asset, and preparing it for its intended use, should be considered as part of the cost of the asset.	It is tempting to treat costs related to the purchase of an asset (delivery fees, taxes, set-up costs, etc.) as current period expenses. However, if these costs are expensed in the current period, then the cost of the asset does not reflect all of the costs that are necessary for the asset to be able to be used. This causes the current period's net income to be understated and future periods' net income to be overstated.

HOW ARE PLANT ASSETS DEPRECIATED?

As we saw in Exhibit 8-1, the process of allocating a plant asset's cost to expense over its useful life is referred to as depreciation. In accounting, the "using up" of a plant asset is also referred to as **depreciation**. For example, a delivery truck can only go so many kilometres before it is worn out, or used up. As the truck is driven, it depreciates, or is used up. Physical factors, like age and weather, will also contribute to the depreciation of assets. So, depreciation refers to the "using up" of a plant asset as well as to the process of allocating the asset's cost to expense over the asset's useful life.

L.O. ❸ Calculate and record the depreciation of plant assets

Both IFRS and ASPE require companies to develop a componentization policy. **Componentization** is to group assets into separate component parts, where the cost of each of these components is significant in relation to the total cost of the asset. Each of the component parts is recognized and depreciated separately. For example, an aircraft can be grouped into several components, such as engine, cabin interior modifications, and the aircraft itself, each of which could be depreciated on a different time scale.

ASPE

IFRS

For example, Air Canada's aircraft and flight equipment are componentized into aircraft frame, engine, and cabin interior equipment and modifications. Aircraft frame and engines are depreciated over 20 to 25 years, with 10% to 20% estimated residual values. Cabin interior equipment and modifications are depreciated over the lesser of 5 years or the remaining useful life of the aircraft.

Let's contrast this with what depreciation is *not*.

- **Depreciation is not a process of valuation.** Businesses do not record depreciation based on changes in the asset's market (sales) value.

- **Depreciation does not mean that the business sets aside cash to replace an asset when it is used up.** Depreciation is a non-cash expense.

ACCOUNTING IN YOUR WORLD

Have you ever bought a new car, or know someone who has? If so, then you have probably heard people comment on how much the car "depreciated" the minute it was driven off the car lot. These people were referring to the fact that the resale value of the car was most likely less than what had been paid for it. In everyday life, the term depreciation is commonly used to describe a decrease in the market value of an asset, such as a car. However, from an accounting point of view, the car had not depreciated merely because it was driven off the lot. In accounting, depreciation refers to the allocation of the cost of an asset to expense during the life of the asset rather than to a decline in the market value of the asset.

Thinkstock/Stockbyte/Getty Images

MEASURING DEPRECIATION

Depreciation of a plant asset is based on three factors:

1. Cost
2. Estimated useful life
3. Estimated residual value

Cost is known and, as mentioned earlier in this chapter, includes all amounts incurred to prepare the asset for its intended purpose. The other two factors are estimates.

Estimated **useful life** represents the expected life of an asset during which it is anticipated to generate revenues. Useful life may be measured in years, or in units of output. For example, a building's life is usually stated in years, a truck's in the number of kilometres it can be driven, and a photocopier's in the number of copies it can make. For each asset, the goal is to define the estimated useful life that best matches the "using up" of the asset.

Some assets, such as computers and software, may become **obsolete** before they wear out. An asset is obsolete when a newer asset can perform the job more efficiently. As a result of obsolescence, an asset's useful life may be determined to be shorter than its physical life. In all cases, an asset's cost is depreciated over its useful life.

Estimated **residual value**—also called salvage value or scrap value—is the asset's expected cash value at the end of its useful life. A delivery truck's useful life may be 150,000 kilometres. When the truck has driven that distance, the company will sell or scrap it. The expected cash value at the end of the truck's life is the truck's estimated residual value. Because the estimated residual value represents a portion of the asset's cost that will be recovered, it is not depreciated. The residual value is subtracted from the cost of the asset to arrive at the asset's **depreciable cost**.

> Cost
> − Residual Value
> = Depreciable Cost

A business will use past experience as well as information obtained from other sources to make the best estimates it can of useful life and residual value.

DEPRECIATION METHODS

The most commonly used depreciation methods are as follows:

- Straight-line
- Units-of-production
- Declining-balance

These methods work differently in *how* the yearly depreciation amount is calculated, but they all result in the same total depreciation over the useful life of the asset. To demonstrate the different depreciation methods, let's assume that Apex Industries purchased and placed in service a new delivery truck on January 1. The data related to Apex Industries' new delivery truck is presented next:

Purchase price (cost)...	$43,000
Estimated residual (salvage) value..	$ 4,000
Estimated useful life...	5 years

Straight-Line Method   The **straight-line (SL) depreciation method** allocates an equal amount of depreciation to each year. Apex Industries might want to use this method for the truck if it thinks time is the best indicator of the truck's depreciation. The equation to find yearly depreciation using straight-line depreciation is as follows:

$$\text{Straight-line depreciation} = \frac{\text{Cost} - \text{Residual value}}{\text{Estimated useful life in years}} = \text{Depreciation per year}$$

The yearly depreciation expense for Apex Industries' delivery truck is as follows:

$$\frac{\text{Cost} - \text{Residual value}}{\text{Estimated useful life}} = \frac{\$43,000 - \$4,000}{5} = \$7,800 \text{ per year}$$

or

$$SL = \frac{1}{\text{Estimated useful life in years}} \times (\text{Cost} - \text{Residual Value}) = \text{Depreciation per year}$$

$$SL = \frac{1}{5}(\$43,000 - \$4,000) = \$7,800$$

Because Apex Industries purchased the delivery truck on January 1, an entire year's worth of depreciation will be recorded for the first year as follows on December 31:

DATE	ACCOUNTS	POST REF.	DR.	CR.
Dec 31	Depreciation Expense, Vehicles		7,800	
	Accumulated Depreciation, Vehicles			7,800
	Record yearly depreciation.			

Assets	=	Liabilities	+	Shareholders' Equity
−7,800	=			−7,800

Exhibit 8-3 demonstrates a straight-line depreciation schedule that has been prepared for Apex Industries' delivery truck.

Year	Asset Cost	Yearly Depreciation	Accumulated Depreciation	Book Value
0	$43,000			$43,000
1		$7,800	$ 7,800	35,200
2		7,800	15,600	27,400
3		7,800	23,400	19,600
4		7,800	31,200	11,800
5		7,800	39,000	4,000

Exhibit 8-3 ▲

The final column shows the asset's *book value*, which is its cost less accumulated depreciation.

Notice that as an asset is depreciated, its accumulated depreciation increases and its book value decreases. Observe the Accumulated Depreciation and Book Value columns in Exhibit 8-3. At the end of its useful life, the asset is said to be **fully depreciated**. Once an asset has been fully depreciated its final book value should equal its residual value, $4,000 in this case.

Units-of-Production (UOP) Method   The **units-of-production (UOP) depreciation method** (also known as the unit-of-output method) allocates a fixed amount of depreciation to each unit of output as follows:

$$\text{Units-of-production depreciation} = \frac{\text{Cost} - \text{Residual value}}{\text{Estimated useful life in units}} = \text{Depreciation per unit}$$

Assume that instead of straight-line, Apex Industries depreciates its delivery truck using units-of-production depreciation. Apex Industries might want to use UOP depreciation for the truck if it thinks kilometres are the best measure of the truck's depreciation. The delivery truck is estimated to be driven 35,000 kilometres the first year, 30,000 the second, 30,000 the third, 20,000 the fourth, and 15,000 during the fifth (for a total of 130,000 kilometres). The UOP depreciation each period varies with the number of units (kilometres, in the case of the truck) the asset produces. The depreciation per unit for Apex Industries' delivery truck is calculated as follows:

$$\frac{\text{Cost} - \text{Residual value}}{\text{Estimated useful life in units}} = \frac{\$43,000 - \$4,000}{130,000 \text{ kilometres}} = \$0.30 \text{ per kilometre}$$

Apex Industries would record $10,500 (35,000 kilometres × $0.30) of depreciation at December 31 of the first year as follows:

DATE	ACCOUNTS	POST REF.	DR.	CR.
Dec 31	Depreciation Expense, Vehicles		10,500	
	Accumulated Depreciation, Vehicles			10,500
	Record yearly depreciation.			

A depreciation schedule similar to the one prepared for straight-line depreciation is presented in **Exhibit 8-4** for units-of-production depreciation.

Notice once again that the ending book value of the delivery truck, $4,000, equals its residual value as it did with straight-line depreciation.

Year	Asset Cost	Yearly Depreciation					
		Number of Units		Depreciation Per Unit		Depreciation Expense	Accumulated Depreciation	Book Value
0	$43,000							$43,000
1		35,000 km	×	$0.30	=	$10,500	$10,500	32,500
2		30,000 km	×	$0.30	=	9,000	19,500	23,500
3		30,000 km	×	$0.30	=	9,000	28,500	14,500
4		20,000 km	×	$0.30	=	6,000	34,500	8,500
5		15,000 km	×	$0.30	=	4,500	39,000	4,000

Exhibit 8-4 ▲

Double-Declining-Balance Method   The **double-declining-balance (DDB) method** is also known as an **accelerated depreciation method**. An accelerated depreciation method writes off more depreciation near the start of an asset's life and less at the end. The use of DDB by Apex Industries would be appropriate if Apex anticipates the delivery truck will be significantly more productive in its early years. The DDB method multiplies the asset's decreasing book value by a constant rate that is twice the straight-line depreciation rate. DDB amounts can be computed using the following formula:

$$SL = \frac{1}{\text{Estimated useful life in years}} \times 2 \times \text{Cost} = \text{Depreciation per year}$$

Straight-line rate   To double it   Notice that the residual value is not subtracted

Note that residual value is not included in the formula. Unlike with straight-line and units-of-production, with double-declining-balance depreciation, residual value is ignored until the end of an asset's life.

For the first year of the delivery truck, the calculation would be as shown here:

$$\frac{1}{5} \times 2 = \frac{2}{5}$$

$$\text{DDB depreciation for first year} = \frac{2}{5} \times \$43,000 = \$17,200$$

MEMORY TIPS
To calculate the DDB rate, divide 1 by the number of years of useful life then multiply by 2.

Exhibit 8-5 reflects a depreciation schedule for the delivery truck using double-declining-balance depreciation.

Year	Asset Cost	Yearly Depreciation					
		DDB Rate*		Book Value		Depreciation Expense	Accumulated Depreciation	Book Value
0	$43,000							$43,000
1		2/5	×	$43,000	=	$17,200	$17,200	25,800
2		2/5	×	25,800	=	10,320	27,520	15,480
3		2/5	×	15,480	=	6,192	33,712	9,288
4		2/5	×	9,288	=	3,715**	37,427	5,573
5						1,573***	39,000	4,000

*$\frac{1}{5} \times 2 = \frac{2}{5}$
**rounded
***5,573 − 4,000 = 1,573

Exhibit 8-5 ▲

8.1 **STILL** DON'T GET IT?
Visit MyAccountingLab for an alternate explanation of this important accounting concept.

Under double-declining-balance, the depreciation schedule is altered in the final years to prevent the asset from being depreciated below the residual value. In the case of Apex Industries' delivery truck, the residual value was given as $4,000. In the DDB schedule in Exhibit 8-5, notice that after year 4, the truck's book value is $5,573. Depreciation expense calculated using DDB would reduce the book value below the residual value. Therefore, in the final year, the depreciation expense is reduced to $1,573, which is the book value of $5,573 less the $4,000 residual value. If the residual value is high enough, it is possible that the second to last year's depreciation expense could be reduced and there would be no depreciation in the final year.

Some companies change to the straight-line method during the last years of an asset's life to "level-off" the yearly depreciation expense in the final years. The yearly depreciation when switching to straight-line is calculated as follows:

$$\frac{\text{Remaining book value} - \text{Residual value}}{\text{Remaining useful life}} = \text{Depreciation per year}$$

Exhibit 8-6 reflects a depreciation schedule for the delivery truck using double-declining-balance depreciation with a switch to straight-line after year 3.

8.2 **STILL** DON'T GET IT**?**
Visit MyAccountingLab for an alternate explanation of this important accounting concept.

Year	Asset Cost	DDB Rate*		Book Value		Depreciation Expense	Accumulated Depreciation	Book Value
0	$43,000							$43,000
1		2/5	×	$43,000	=	$17,200	$17,200	25,800
2		2/5	×	25,800	=	10,320	27,520	15,480
3		2/5	×	15,480	=	6,192	33,712	9,288
4						2,644*	36,356	6,644
5						2,644*	39,000	4,000

*(9,288 − 4,000) ÷ 2 = 2,644

Exhibit 8-6 ▲

COMPARING DEPRECIATION METHODS

Let's compare the depreciation methods. Annual amounts vary, but total accumulated depreciation equals $39,000 for all three methods.

Year	Straight-Line	Units-of-Production	Double-Declining-Balance
1	$ 7,800	$10,500	$17,200
2	7,800	9,000	10,320
3	7,800	9,000	6,192
4	7,800	6,000	3,715
5	7,800	4,500	1,573
Total Depreciation	$39,000	$39,000	$39,000

Exhibit 8-7 illustrates graphically the difference between the three depreciation methods. It is clear that the straight-line method distributes the costs evenly over the useful life. The double-declining-balance method adds more depreciation costs during the early years of the asset and decreases depreciation over time. Increasing the depreciation expense in

the early years would decrease profitability, but profitability would increase as the depreciation expense decreases over the years. As for the units-of-production method, its graph would change according to the plan of production during the asset's life. If the asset is not used intensively in its early years, the depreciation expense would be lower but would increase in the years that the asset is used more.

Exhibit 8-7 ▲

Which method is best? That depends on the asset. A business should match an asset's expense against the revenue that the asset produces. Following are some guidelines:

- **Straight-Line.** For an asset that generates revenue evenly over time, the straight-line method will demonstrate the even usage of the asset over time as well. For example, Cameco Corporation (mainly a mining company) depreciates its building over 15 to 25 years and plant equipment over 4 to 15 years by using the straight-line depreciation method.

- **Units-of-Production.** The UOP method works best for an asset whose use varies from year to year. More use causes greater depreciation. UOP might be good for depreciating assets such as copy machines, vehicles, and machinery. For example, Cameco Corporation amortizes its intellectual property on a unit-of-production basis.

- **Double-Declining-Balance.** The DDB method works best for assets that produce more revenue in their early years and less in their later years. Higher depreciation in the early years is matched against the greater revenue. DDB would be good for depreciating assets such as computers. For example, The Depository Trust Company depreciates its furniture and equipment over estimated useful lives ranging from five to seven years using an accelerated double-declining-balance method.

PARTIAL YEAR DEPRECIATION

In the examples for Apex Industries' delivery truck, it was assumed that the truck was purchased on January 1 and used for an entire year. However, most assets are not purchased on the first day of the year and used for the entire year. When an asset is not used for an entire year, the depreciation expense for that year must be prorated for the number of months the asset was actually used during the year. If an asset is in service for more than one half of the month, it is considered to be in service for the entire month. The formula for prorating the depreciation expense is as follows:

$$\text{Depreciation expense for the entire year} \times \frac{\text{\# of months asset was used}}{12} = \text{Prorated yearly depreciation expense}$$

Let's return to our example using Apex Industries' delivery truck. Assume that instead of purchasing the delivery truck on January 1, Apex Industries purchased the delivery truck on May 1. **Exhibits 8-8** and **8-9** reflect new depreciation schedules for Apex Industries' delivery truck using straight-line and double-declining-balance depreciation respectively.

Year	Asset Cost	Yearly Depreciation	Accumulated Depreciation	Book Value
0	$43,000			$43,000
1		$7,800 × 8/12* = $5,200	$ 5,200	37,800
2		7,800	13,000	30,000
3		7,800	20,800	22,200
4		7,800	28,600	14,400
5		7,800	36,400	6,600
6		$7,800 × 4/12** = 2,600	39,000	4,000

*Prorated for May through December
**Prorated for January through April

Exhibit 8-8 ▲

Year	Asset Cost	Yearly Depreciation			Accumulated Depreciation	Book Value
		DDB Rate	Book Value	Depreciation Expense*		
0	$43,000					$43,000
1		2/5 ×	$43,000 =	$17,200 × 8/12** = $11,467	$11,467	31,533
2		2/5 ×	31,533 =	12,613	24,080	18,920
3		2/5 ×	18,920 =	7,568	31,648	11,352
4		2/5 ×	11,352 =	4,541	36,189	6,811
5		2/5 ×	6,811 =	2,724	38,913	4,087
6				(4,087 − 4,000) = 87	39,000	4,000

*Rounded
**Prorated for May through December

Exhibit 8-9 ▲

Notice that both schedules now reflect six years even though the delivery truck has a five-year life. Because the truck was only depreciated for eight months in the first year instead of twelve, the sixth year is added to "pick up" the final four months of depreciation. With units-of-production depreciation, there is no need to prorate the depreciation for partial years. This is because UOP is based on the quantity of units produced by an asset, regardless of how many months the asset was in service during the year.

CHANGING THE USEFUL LIFE OF A DEPRECIABLE ASSET

Estimating the useful life and residual value of a plant asset can be difficult. Sometimes, as the asset is used, a business may determine that it needs to revise the useful life and/ or the residual value of the asset. For example, at the end of year 3, Apex Industries may find that its delivery truck is expected to last seven years instead of five. Accounting changes like this are not uncommon because the original estimates are not based on perfect foresight. The formula used to calculate the new yearly depreciation amount if the useful life or residual value is changed looks like this:

$$\frac{\text{(Remaining book value} - \text{New residual value)}}{\text{(New estimated useful life} - \text{Number of years already depreciated)}} = \text{Revised annual depreciation}$$

In effect, the asset's remaining depreciable book value is spread over the asset's remaining life.

Let's return to our Apex Industries' example. If we look back at Exhibit 8-3, we see that the remaining book value for Apex Industries' delivery truck after year 3 is $19,600. Now let's suppose that in addition to revising the estimated useful life from five to seven years, the residual value is also revised from $4,000 to $3,000. Apex Industries would calculate the new yearly depreciation as follows:

$$\frac{(\$19,600 - \$3,000)}{(7 \text{ years} - 3 \text{ years})} = \frac{\$16,600}{4} = \$4,150$$

A new straight-line depreciation schedule reflecting the changes in estimates appears in **Exhibit 8-10**.

Year	Yearly Depreciation	Accumulated Depreciation	Book Value
0			$43,000
1	$7,800	$ 7,800	35,200
2	7,800	15,600	27,400
3	7,800	23,400	19,600
4	4,150	27,550	15,450
5	4,150	31,700	11,300
6	4,150	35,850	7,150
7	4,150	40,000	3,000

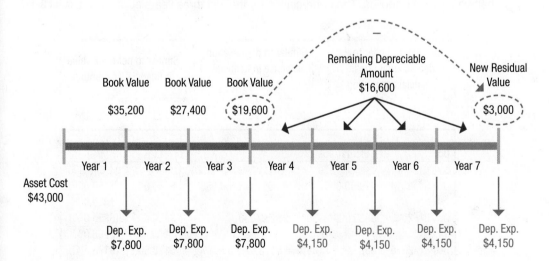

Exhibit 8-10 ▲

USING FULLY-DEPRECIATED ASSETS

As explained earlier in the chapter, a fully-depreciated asset is one that has reached the end of its *estimated* useful life. No more depreciation is recorded for the asset. If the asset is no longer useful, it is disposed of. If the asset is still useful, the company may continue using it. The asset account and its accumulated depreciation remain on the books, but no additional depreciation is recorded. In short, the asset never goes below its residual value.

DEPRECIATION FOR TAX PURPOSES (CAPITAL COST ALLOWANCE)

Companies are free to use different depreciation and amortization methods for financial reporting purposes. However, when reporting for income tax calculations purposes, they have to comply with Canada Revenue Agency (CRA) regulations. The CRA requires that companies calculate the depreciation and amortization of their assets based on a specific depreciation method called **capital cost allowance (CCA)** and according to specific depreciation rates (known as the capital cost allowance rate).

The CRA has categorized long-term assets into categories. Assets falling in a certain category are depreciated by the rate set by the CRA for this category. The CRA has set the rates based on several criteria, including the nature of the assets and the willingness of the government to encourage companies to invest in certain assets. For example, assets falling in class 1 (including lighting fixtures, sprinkler systems, heating equipment, etc.) are depreciated by a rate of 4%, while assets in class 52 (including electronic process control, data handling equipment, system software, etc.) are depreciated at a rate of 100%.

The depreciation method used is similar to the double-declining-balance method. However, there are some differences. For example, only 50% depreciation can be allocated for the first year the asset is used in (the half-year rule), after which full depreciation is applied. CCA is calculated for each class separately at year end by multiplying the balance of the undepreciated capital cost (UCC) of the assets for each category by its rate. The maximum amount that can be claimed cannot be greater than the UCC times the specific CCA rate.

To illustrate, assume that on January 1, 2015, Gold Oil Corp. bought an excavating machine (which falls into class 38) for $1,000,000. Assets in class 38 are depreciated with a CCA rate of 30%. The equipment has 10 years of life and a residual value of $100,000. Even though the equipment is acquired only one month before year end, the half-year rule still applies. The depreciation for the first three years appears in **Exhibit 8-11**.

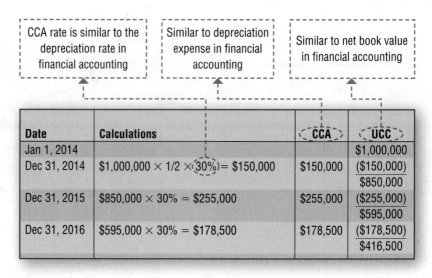

CCA rate is similar to the depreciation rate in financial accounting		Similar to depreciation expense in financial accounting		Similar to net book value in financial accounting

Date	Calculations	CCA	UCC
Jan 1, 2014			$1,000,000
Dec 31, 2014	$1,000,000 × 1/2 × 30% = $150,000	$150,000	($150,000)
			$850,000
Dec 31, 2015	$850,000 × 30% = $255,000	$255,000	($255,000)
			$595,000
Dec 31, 2016	$595,000 × 30% = $178,500	$178,500	($178,500)
			$416,500

Exhibit 8-11 ▲

It is worth mentioning that the CCA calculation is used *only* for income tax calculation purposes and it is not used for financial reporting purposes. The company would still use its financial accounting depreciation (amortization) method as illustrated in this chapter for the preparation of the financial statements. Later, the financial accounting income is adjusted to calculate the taxable income to file for taxation. This means that the above calculations for CCA will not be reflected in the company books.

Detailed coverage of capital cost allowance will be left to a more advanced financial accounting course.

 ## DECISION GUIDELINES

DECISION	GUIDELINE	ANALYZE
I'm a new business owner and have made numerous purchases of capital assets to begin my operations. Which depreciation method is the best for my assets?	The choice of depreciation method depends upon the specific asset being depreciated as well as what the intended use of that asset is. The best method is one that most closely matches the cost of an asset against the future revenues it helps generate.	Straight-line depreciation is best for assets that will be used evenly throughout their lives and that will incur repair and maintenance cost evenly.
		Units-of-production depreciation is best for assets that will be utilized on an irregular basis throughout their lives.
		Double-declining-balance depreciation is best for assets that will be utilized significantly more in the early years of their lives. It is also best for assets that will require significantly more repair and maintenance expenditures in the later years of the asset's life.

HOW ARE COSTS OF REPAIRING PLANT ASSETS RECORDED?

When a business has to repair an existing plant asset, the method of accounting for the expenditure is determined by the type of repair that occurred. Repairs are generally broken down into three types:

 L.O. ❹ Account for repairs to plant assets

- Ordinary repairs
- Extraordinary repairs
- Betterments

ORDINARY REPAIRS

Expenditures incurred to maintain an asset in proper working order are called **ordinary repairs**. For example, the cost of repairing the radiator, changing the oil and filter, or replacing the tires on a company vehicle would be considered ordinary repairs. Ordinary repairs do not extend the useful life of an asset beyond its original useful life nor do they increase the productivity of the asset. They simply keep the asset running. Ordinary repairs are recorded as an expense (usually by debiting Repairs and Maintenance Expense) in the period in which they are incurred. Ordinary repairs are also called **revenue expenditures** because the repair expense is matched against the revenues for the period.

EXTRAORDINARY REPAIRS

When an expenditure extends the useful life of an asset, it is called an **extraordinary repair**. Replacing the engine on a four-year-old company vehicle is an example of an extraordinary repair. This extraordinary repair would extend the vehicle's useful life past its original expected life. Extraordinary repairs are not expensed when they are incurred because they provide value beyond the current period. Instead, the expenditure is capitalized by debiting the cost of the repair to an asset account. The asset is then depreciated over its remaining useful life. For this reason, extraordinary repairs are also called **capital expenditures**.

BETTERMENTS

Expenditures that increase an asset's capacity or productivity are called **betterments**. An addition to an existing building is an example of a betterment. As with extraordinary repairs, betterments are capital expenditures that provide value that extends beyond the current period. The cost of a betterment is capitalized (debited to an asset account) and depreciated over the life of the betterment.

Treating a capital expenditure as an expense, or vice versa, creates an accounting error. Suppose Mackay Machine Works replaces the engine in a company vehicle. This would be an extraordinary repair because it increases the vehicle's life. If Mackay Machine Works expenses the cost by debiting Repair and Maintenance Expense, rather than capitalizing it (debiting an asset), Mackay Machine Works makes an accounting error. This error would

- overstate Repair and Maintenance Expense.
- understate net income and, therefore, retained earnings.
- understate assets on the statement of financial position.

Incorrectly capitalizing an expense creates the opposite error. Assume a minor repair, such as replacing the alternator on a vehicle, was incorrectly debited to an asset account. The error would result in expenses being understated and net income (and therefore retained earnings) being overstated. Furthermore, the statement of financial position would overstate assets by the amount of the repair bill. Knowingly capitalizing an ordinary repair or expensing a capital expenditure is a violation of proper ethical behaviour!

CHANGES IN COST AND ESTIMATES

As a result of repairing assets or changes of estimates of the useful life and/or residual value, calculations of depreciation will have to change accordingly. For example, Apex Industries' delivery truck was purchased for $43,000, on January 1, with an estimated residual value of $4,000 after five years of useful life. Apex uses the straight-line depreciation method. On July 1, year 3, Apex overhauled the engine with a cost of $5,000. As a result of the overhaul, Apex estimated its residual value would increase by $500 and its useful life would increase by 1.5 years.

Exhibit 8-12 illustrates how to calculate the new depreciation expense.

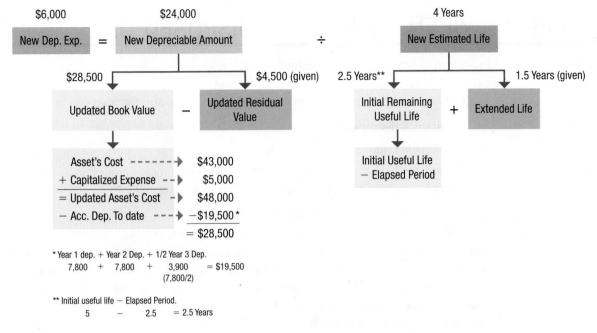

* Year 1 dep. + Year 2 Dep. + 1/2 Year 3 Dep.

7,800	+	7,800	+	3,900	= $19,500
				(7,800/2)	

** Initial useful life − Elapsed Period.

5	−	2.5	= 2.5 Years

Exhibit 8-12 ▲

Total depreciation expense for year 3 is $6,900 ($3,900 for the first half of the year + $6,000/2 for the second half).

Exhibit 8-13 shows the new straight-line depreciation schedule reflecting the changes in estimates.

Year	Cost	Yearly Depreciation	Accumulated Depreciation	Book Value
0	$43,000			$43,000
1	43,000	$7,800	$7,800	35,200
2	43,000	7,800	15,600	27,400
3	$48,000	6,900	22,500	25,500*
4	48,000	6,000	28,500	19,500
5	48,000	6,000	34,500	13,500
6	48,000	6,000	40,500	7,500
6.5	48,000	3,000	43,500	4,500

*Year 3 book value = ($43,000 + $5,000) − ($15,600 + $6,900)

Exhibit 8-13

8.3 **STILL** DON'T GET IT**?**
Visit MyAccountingLab for an alternate explanation of this important accounting concept.

 DECISION GUIDELINES

DECISION	**GUIDELINE**	**ANALYZE**
Should I expense the cost of repairing my assets?	The effect of the repair and whether or not it betters the asset will determine when the cost of the repair should be expensed.	Ordinary repairs are repairs that simply maintain an asset in a state of operation. The cost of ordinary repairs is expensed in the period incurred because no future benefit is expected to arise from the repair. If a repair extends the useful life of an asset or makes it more efficient, it is known as an extraordinary repair. The cost of the repair should be capitalized and depreciated over the remaining life of the asset because it will provide future benefits. If an extraordinary repair is incorrectly expensed in the current period, the net income for that period will be understated and the net income for future periods will be overstated.

WHAT HAPPENS WHEN AN ASSET IS DISPOSED OF?

L.O. 5 Account for the disposal of plant assets

In addition to acquiring and depreciating plant assets, businesses often dispose of plant assets. This may happen before, or after, the asset has reached the end of its useful life. The following are the most common ways that plant assets are disposed of:

1. The asset is discarded (thrown out).

2. The asset is sold.

3. The asset is exchanged for another asset. This occurs most often when an asset is used as a trade-in toward the purchase of another asset.

Regardless of the method of disposal, it is important to ensure that depreciation expense on the asset is up to date prior to recording the disposal. Therefore, for any asset that has not been fully depreciated, a business must record the current period's depreciation expense before recording the disposal of the asset. In many cases, the depreciation needs to be prorated because the asset is not in service for the entire year in which it is disposed of. Prorating depreciation was covered earlier in the chapter in the discussion of partial-year's depreciation.

Once depreciation is up to date, the disposal of an asset is recorded using the following steps:

Step 1 *Record "what you got."* In other words, if you received any cash as part of the disposal transaction, then you would debit Cash for the amount of cash received. If you received a piece of equipment, then you would debit the Equipment account for the cost of the equipment you received.

Step 2 *Record the disposition of the asset that you are giving up.* In other words, its balance together with its accumulated depreciation must be equal to zero. Hence, the asset's balance would be credited and the balance of its Accumulated Depreciation account would be debited to close them. In addition, if you are exchanging the asset with a new one, then the amount of cash paid should be also credited.

Step 3 *Record any gain or loss recognized on the transaction.* If total debits are greater than total credits ("what you got" is more than the value of "what you gave up"), then there is a gain in selling the asset by the difference, and it will be recognized by crediting Gains on Sale of the asset by such an amount. If total credits are greater than total debits ("what you got" in the transaction is less than "what you gave up"), then there is a loss on disposing the asset and it is recognized by debiting Loss on Disposal of the asset by the amount of difference.

Let's demonstrate asset disposals by once again using the Apex Industries' delivery truck as an example. At the end of its useful life, the delivery truck is represented in the books as follows:

Truck		Accumulated Depreciation, Truck	
43,000			39,000

Consider these three situations in which Apex Industries disposes of the delivery truck. All disposals are assumed to take place after the delivery truck has been fully depreciated.

Situation A: The truck is completely worthless and is scrapped for $0. Let's apply the three steps for disposal outlined previously to demonstrate this:

Step 1 Record "what you got." In this case Apex Industries received nothing for the truck so there will be nothing to record.

Step 2 Record the disposition of the asset that you are giving up. In this case, Apex Industries gave up the old delivery truck and should remove it from the books. To remove the asset, we must zero out both the Asset and Accumulated Depreciation accounts. To do this we will need to debit the Accumulated Depreciation account for $39,000 and credit the Truck account for $43,000.

Step 3 Record any gain or loss on the transaction. This is a loss on disposal because Apex Industries received nothing for a truck that had a net book value (cost minus accumulated depreciation) of $4,000. Apex Industries will debit Loss on Disposal for $4,000. Remember that when total credits are greater than total debits, there is a loss.

Apex Industries will record the disposal as follows:

DATE	ACCOUNTS	POST REF.	DR.	CR.
	Accumulated Depreciation, Truck		39,000	
	Loss on Disposal of Truck		4,000	
	Truck			43,000
	Record discarding of truck.			

Notice that the debit to the loss account equals the amount needed to bring the entire entry into balance.

Situation B: Apex Industries sells the truck for $5,000 cash. The three steps for disposal outlined previously can be applied to this situation as follows:

Step 1 Record "what you got." Apex Industries received $5,000 for the truck, so Cash will be debited for $5,000.

Step 2 Record the disposition of the asset that you are giving up. Once again, Apex Industries gave up the old delivery truck and should remove it from the books. Accumulated Depreciation is debited for $39,000 and the Truck account is credited for $43,000.

Step 3 Record any gain or loss on the transaction. This is a gain on sale because Apex Industries received $5,000 for a truck that had a net book value (cost – accumulated depreciation) of $4,000. Apex Industries will credit Gain on Sale for $1,000.

Apex Industries will record the disposal as follows:

DATE	ACCOUNTS	POST REF.	DR.	CR.
	Cash		5,000	
	Accumulated Depreciation, Truck		39,000	
	Truck			43,000
	Gain on Sale of Truck			1,000
	Record sale of truck.			

Observe that the credit to the gain account equals the amount needed to bring the entire entry into balance.

Situation C: Apex Industries trades the delivery truck in on a new truck that costs $48,000. Apex is granted a trade-in allowance of $5,500 and pays for the difference in cash. Here again we will apply the three-step process to record the disposal.

Step 1 Record "what you got." In this transaction, Apex Industries received a $48,000 new truck. So, Truck (new) will be debited for $48,000.

Step 2 Record the disposition of the asset that you are giving up. As in the previous situations, Apex Industries gave up the old delivery truck and should remove it from the books. Accumulated Depreciation is debited for $39,000 and the Truck (old) account is credited for $43,000. In addition to giving up the truck, Apex Industries paid cash in the amount of $42,500, so Cash is also credited for $42,500. With a trade-in, the amount of cash paid is determined by subtracting the trade-in allowance from the purchase price of the new asset. So, the $48,000 cost of the new truck less the $5,500 trade-in allowance equals the $42,500 cash paid. This same process is used to determine the amount of a note payable if a note is given instead of cash.

Step 3 Record any gain or loss on the transaction. A gain on the exchange occurs because Apex Industries received $48,000 of equipment for assets worth $46,500 (a truck that had a net book value of $4,000 plus cash of $42,500). Apex Industries will credit Gain on Exchange for $1,500.

Apex Industries will record the disposal as follows:

Assets	=	Liabilities	+	Shareholders' Equity
+48,000	=			+1,500
+39,000				
−43,000				
−42,500				

DATE	ACCOUNTS	POST REF.	DR.	CR.
	Truck (New)		48,000	
	Accumulated Depreciation, Truck		39,000	
	Truck (Old)			43,000
	Cash			42,500
	Gain on Exchange of Assets			1,500
	Record trade-in of old truck on a new truck.			

Once again, the gain equals the amount necessary to bring the entry into balance.

HOW DO YOU ACCOUNT FOR INTANGIBLE ASSETS?

L.O. 6 Account for intangible assets

As we saw earlier, *intangible assets* have no physical form. Instead, in most cases, these assets convey special rights to their owner. Intangible assets include patents, copyrights, trademarks, and other creative works. IFRS refers to the process of allocating the cost of an intangible asset to expense as **amortization**. However, ASPE uses the term *amortization* for both tangible and intangible assets. Amortization applies to intangible assets exactly as depreciation applies to plant assets and depletion to natural resources.

Amortization is computed over the intangible asset's estimated useful life—usually by the straight-line method. The residual value of most intangible assets is zero. Also, obsolescence can sometimes cause an intangible asset's useful life to be shortened from its original expected length. Amortization expense for an intangible asset is usually credited directly to the asset account instead of using an accumulated amortization account.

SPECIFIC INTANGIBLES

Patents A **patent** is an intangible asset that is a federal government grant conveying an exclusive 20-year right to produce and sell an invention. The patent may cover a product, process, or technology. The useful life of a patent is often much less than 20 years because newer, better products and processes are invented, rendering the patent obsolete. As an international example, from 1993 to 2007, IBM was granted over 38,000 U.S. patents, more than any other U.S. company. When an intangible asset is acquired, the acquisition cost is debited to an asset account.

Suppose Apex Industries pays $160,000 on January 1 to acquire a patent on a new manufacturing process. Apex Industries believes this patent's useful life is only five years, because it is likely that a new, more efficient process will be developed within that time. Amortization expense is $32,000 per year ($160,000/5 years). The acquisition and year-end amortization entries for this patent are as follows:

DATE	ACCOUNTS	POST REF.	DR.	CR.
Jan 1	Patents		160,000	
	Cash			160,000
	Purchase patent.			
Dec 31	Amortization Expense		32,000	
	Patents			32,000
	Record yearly amortization.			

At the end of the first year, Apex Industries will report this patent at $128,000 ($160,000 minus first-year amortization of $32,000), the next year at $96,000, and so forth. Each year for five years the value of the patent will be reduced by $32,000 until the end of its five-year life, at which point its net book value will be $0.

Copyrights   A **copyright** is the exclusive right to reproduce and sell a book, musical composition, film, or other work of art or intellectual property. Copyrights also protect computer software programs such as Microsoft Vista™. Copyrights are issued by the federal government and extend 50 years beyond the author's life, although the useful life of most copyrights is relatively short. A copyright is accounted for in the same manner as a patent.

Trademarks and Brand Names   **Trademarks** and **brand names** (also known as **trade names**) convey the exclusive right to utilize a symbol, slogan, or name that represents a distinctive product or service such as Sony's Blu-ray Disc™, Intel's Centrino®, and Apple's iPad. The cost of a trademark or trade name is amortized over its useful life.

Franchises and Licences   **Franchises** and **licences** are privileges granted by a private business or a government to sell goods or services under specified conditions. The Toronto Blue Jays baseball team is a franchise granted by Major League Baseball. Subway restaurants and Midas Muffler centres are well-known business franchises. The acquisition cost of a franchise or licence is amortized over its useful life.

Goodwill   *Goodwill* in accounting has a different meaning from the everyday phrase "goodwill among men." **Goodwill** is generated over time, and it reflects the trust, reputation, and confidence of clients in the business operation, which has a positive effect on its net income. A lot of factors contribute to generating goodwill internally, and of course there are costs associated with goodwill. However, a business cannot record internally generated goodwill on its books. Goodwill is only recognized on the buyer's books when one company acquires another and the purchase price of the acquired company exceeds the market value of its net assets (assets minus liabilities).

Suppose Apex Industries acquires Mackay Machine Works for $1,350,000. At the time of the purchase, the market value of Mackay Machine Works' assets is $1,750,000 and its liabilities total $500,000. In this case, Apex Industries pays $100,000 above the value of Mackay Machine Works' net assets of $1,250,000 ($1,750,000 − $500,000). The extra $100,000 is considered to be goodwill and is recorded as follows:

+1,750,000 = +500,000
+100,000
−1,350,000

DATE	ACCOUNTS	POST REF.	DR.	CR.
	Assets (Cash, Accounts Receivable, Equipment, etc.			
	recorded at market value)		1,750,000	
	Goodwill		100,000	
	Liabilities (Accounts Payable, Notes Payable, Accrued			
	Liabilities, etc.)			500,000
	Cash			1,350,000
	To record purchase of Mackay Machine Works.			

Goodwill has some unique features from other intangible assets:

1. Goodwill is recorded only by an acquiring company when it purchases another company. An outstanding reputation may create goodwill, but that company never records goodwill for its own business.

2. Intangible assets with indefinite lives are not subject to amortization. Goodwill is not amortized; however, companies are required to apply an impairment test. Under IFRS, the companies should test **impairment** on an annual basis, while under ASPE, companies need to test impairment when events or changes occur that indicate impairment. If the goodwill has increased in value, there is nothing to record. But if goodwill's value has decreased, or become impaired, then the company records a loss and writes the goodwill down. For example, suppose Apex Industries' goodwill—which it acquired in the purchase of Mackay Machine Works—is worth only $80,000 a year after the purchase. In this case, Apex Industries would make the following entry:

−20,000 = −20,000

DATE	ACCOUNTS	POST REF.	DR.	CR.
	Loss on Goodwill		20,000	
	Goodwill ($100,000 − $80,000)			20,000
	To record decrease in value of goodwill.			

Apex Industries would then report this goodwill at its reduced current value of $80,000.

ACCOUNTING FOR RESEARCH AND DEVELOPMENT COSTS

Research and Development   Research and development (R&D) costs are the lifeblood of companies such as BlackBerry, Bombardier, Apple, and Ford. Companies should charge all research costs to expense accounts. Development costs may be capitalized but only after a new product is commercially feasible for sale or use. If a company cannot separate the research phase from the development phase, the company should treat the expenditure as if it were incurred in the research phase only, and expense the cost.

HOW ARE NATURAL RESOURCES ACCOUNTED FOR?

L.O. 7 Account for natural resources

Natural resources are assets that come from the earth. Examples include minerals, oil, natural gas, precious metals, coal, and timber. As stated earlier in the chapter, the process of allocating the cost of a natural resource to an expense is called **depletion**. Depletion expense is that portion of the cost of a natural resource that is used up in a particular period. Depletion expense is computed in a manner almost identical to units-of-production depreciation. The formula used to calculate the depletion per unit of a natural resource is as follows:

$$\text{Depletion per unit of natural resource} = \frac{\text{Cost}}{\text{Estimated total units of natural resource}} = \text{Depletion expense per unit}$$

Notice that, unlike UOP depreciation, there is no residual value in the calculation of depletion expense. This is because when a natural resource is used up, there is nothing left to sell.

To illustrate, let's assume that Pegasus Gold owns gold reserves that cost $8,500,000. A geological study estimates that the reserves hold 20,000 (Troy) ounces of gold. Pegasus Gold would calculate the depletion per ounce of gold as follows:

$$\frac{\$8,500,000}{20,000 \text{ ounces}} = \$425 \text{ per ounce}$$

If 600 ounces of gold are removed during the month, depletion is $255,000 (600 ounces × $425 per ounce) and would be recorded as follows:

DATE	ACCOUNTS	POST REF.	DR.	CR.
	Inventory or Cost of Goods Sold		255,000	
	Accumulated Depletion—Gold Reserves			255,000
	Record monthly depletion.			

Accumulated Depletion is a contra-account similar to Accumulated Depreciation. It is deducted from the cost of the natural resource to determine the net book value of the natural resource.

The depletion of natural resources can be recorded as Cost of Goods Sold (if sold right away) or be recorded in the Inventory account (if kept at the end of the period). When the gold is sold, the inventory will be reduced and the cost of inventory will be transferred to cost of goods sold.

WHAT ARE THE OTHER TYPES OF LONG-TERM ASSETS?

Other long-term assets may consist of any assets a business owns that we have not already discussed. Two common long-term assets that a business might own are real estate (land or buildings) that are being held for resale rather than for use, and investments in marketable securities. Marketable securities are investments, such as shares, also known as equity securities, and bonds, also called debt securities. Bonds will be discussed more in Chapter 9, but basically buying bonds is a way of loaning money to an entity. Marketable securities are classified as current assets if management intends to sell them, or they mature within a year. However, if they are not intended to be sold, or they do not mature within a year, they are shown as other long-term assets.

L.O. 8 Account for other long-term assets

A company investing in marketable securities earns income when it receives dividends on shares or interest on bonds that it holds. Also, changes in the value of a security can impact a company's income in two ways:

- Realized gains and losses occur when a security is sold for an amount different from its cost.

- Unrealized gains and losses occur when a security's market value changes while the company still owns it. These are considered "unreal" because the company won't actually gain or lose money until it sells the investment.

Accounting for marketable securities depends on the type of investment and on management's intention for the investment. Marketable securities are classified as trading securities, held-to-maturity securities, or available-for-sale securities.

- Trading securities include equity or debt securities that are actively managed to maximize profit as a result of short-term changes in price. These are shown as current assets on the statement of financial position at their market value as of the statement date. Any increase or decrease in price during the period is shown as an unrealized gain or loss on the income statement. Any interest or dividends earned during the period are reported as income on the income statement.

- Held-to-maturity securities are debt securities that a company intends and is able to hold until they mature. These are valued at their cost on the statement of financial position as either current or long-term assets based on their maturity date. Any interest income earned on these securities is reported on the income statement.

- Available-for-sale securities include equity or debt securities that cannot be classified as trading or held-to-maturity securities. These are valued at their current market value on the statement of financial position date. Any interest or dividends earned during the period is included in net income on the income statement. However, increases or decreases in value during the period are not reported as part of net income on the income statement. Instead, they are shown as separate changes in shareholders' equity for the period.

IFRS

ASPE

If the assets are classified as an investment, such as real estate, then the initial cost of acquisition, under both IFRS and ASPE, is to be recorded based on the cost principle. However, after the acquisition, a company needs to make an accounting policy as to how to treat the investment property. A company has two choices—to record the investment property at cost or fair value. If a company chooses to record the investment at cost, it has to disclose the fair value information or describe why it cannot reliably obtain the fair value in the notes to the financial statements. On the other hand, if a company chooses to record the investment at fair value, it will need to adjust the value of the assets by recording the unrealized gains or losses in either net income or in other comprehensive income. The details of this topic will be covered in higher level accounting courses.

HOW ARE LONG-TERM ASSETS REPORTED ON THE STATEMENT OF FINANCIAL POSITION?

L.O. ⑨ Report long-term assets on the statement of financial position

In Chapter 5, we learned that current assets appear first on a classified statement of financial position. Following the current assets, a business will report its long-term assets. Fixed assets are usually the first long-term asset reported and are often shown as "Property, Plant, and Equipment." Property, plant, and equipment includes the original cost, accumulated depreciation, and book value of assets such as land, buildings, and equipment. Natural resources are typically shown after the fixed assets and include the original cost, accumulated depletion, and book value of any natural resources the business owns. A business may choose to show only the net book value of fixed assets and natural resources on the statement of financial position. In this case, the business will disclose the costs and accumulated depreciation or depletion for each asset group in the financial statement notes.

When a business has intangible assets, the statement of financial position will typically show the amount after the fixed assets and the natural resources. The notes to the financial statements will include a description of the intangible asset and its estimated useful life.

Other long-term assets are typically shown last in the long-term assets section of a statement of financial position. **Exhibit 8-14** illustrates a typical long-term assets section of a statement of financial position.

Total Current Assets		$ 165,000
Property, Plant, and Equipment:		
Land	$ 175,000	
Buildings	680,000	
Equipment	240,000	
	1,095,000	
Less: Accumulated Depreciation	385,000	
Net Property, Plant, and Equipment		710,000
Gold Reserves, Net of Accumulated Depletion of $260,000		620,000
Patents		80,000
Other Long-Term Assets		145,000
Total Assets		$1,720,000

Exhibit 8-14 ▲

IFRS
ASPE

Both IFRS and ASPE require the initial acquisition on property, plant, and equipment, as well as investment properties, to be recorded based on the cost principle. However, after the acquisition, when reporting the value of assets in the financial statements, a company, depending on whether it is publicly accountable (uses IFRS) or a private enterprise (uses ASPE), can choose among various cost methods. **Exhibit 8-15** summarizes the differences.

	IFRS	Canadian ASPE
Initial Acquisition		
Property, Plant, Equipment	Cost	Cost
Investment Property	Cost	Cost
After Acquisition		
Property, Plant, Equipment	Cost or Revaluation	Cost
Investment Property	Cost or Fair Value	Cost

Exhibit 8-15 ▲

As shown in Exhibit 8-15, under ASPE, companies do not re-measure property, plant, and equipment and investment property at fair value. Property, Plant, and Equipment is only measured at fair value if it is lower than the original cost of the asset, as a result of an impairment loss. Under IFRS, companies can choose to report their property, plant, and equipment either at cost and depreciation, or at fair value using the **revaluation model** and depreciation. The revaluation model can be used only if the asset's fair value can be measured reliably. In the revaluation model, any increase from fair value is recognized in revaluation surplus under other comprehensive income in the statement of changes in equity. Since this increase goes directly to equity, it does not impact the current year's income statement. If in a subsequent year the fair value decreases, then we will first reduce the revaluation surplus. If the amount of decrease goes below the revaluation surplus, then we will record the decrease in the income statement. In essence, revaluations often do not impact the income statement and are recognized in shareholders' equity; however, when the revaluation decreases an asset below its original cost, the loss from the revaluation will be recognized in the income statement.

ASSET IMPAIRMENT

When an asset's carrying value is greater than its recoverable amount, we say that the asset is impaired. The **recoverable amount** is the higher of the future discounted cash flow that the asset can provide (or **value in use**) and the amount it can be disposed for. Unlike inventory, we don't apply the lower of cost and net realizable value, because Property, Plant, and Equipment is expected to be used in operations for a long period of time. Instead, we will need to perform an impairment test. Some indications of asset impairment include market value declines; negative changes in technology, the economy, or laws; physical damage of the asset; or worse economic performance than expected. Similar to goodwill, IFRS requires that assets be tested for impairment at the end of each reporting period, while ASPE requires the test only when events and changes in circumstances indicate that an asset's carrying amount may not be recoverable.

For example, in the fifth year after the initial purchase by Apex Industries and the overhauling of the engine, the accountant obtains the following amounts: fair value of the truck $12,000, the value in use $14,000, and the carrying value $13,500.

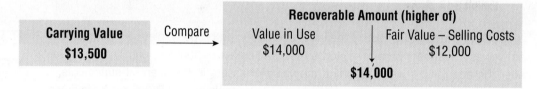

There is no impairment, because the carrying value is less than the recoverable amount. However, if the accountant obtains the following: fair value of the truck $12,000, value in use $12,500, and carrying value $13,500, then the impairment loss is $1,000 ($13,500 − $12,500).

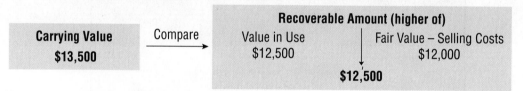

The journal entry to record the impairment is as follows:

DATE	ACCOUNTS	POST REF.	DR.	CR.
Dec 31	Loss on Impairment		1,000	
	Accumulated Impairment Losses			1,000

FOCUS ON DECISION MAKING: RATIOS

L.O. 10 Calculate the assets turnover ratio and return on assets

ASSET TURNOVER RATIO

The assets turnover ratio measures the efficiency of the company in using its assets. This ratio shows how many dollars of sales are generated by one dollar invested in assets. The ratio is calculated by relating net sales to average total assets as follows:

$$\text{Assets Turnover Ratio} = \frac{\text{Net Sales}}{\text{Average Total Assets}}$$

Let's assume that Mackay Industries has the following information for the year ended December 31, 2015: net sales $100,000; total assets at the beginning of 2015, $120,000; and total assets on December 31, 2015, $110,000. The assets turnover ratio for Mackay Industries is calculated as follows:

$$\text{Assets Turnover Ratio} = \frac{100,000}{\dfrac{120,000 + 110,000}{2}} = 0.87 \text{ times}$$

Notice that the average total assets is calculated by dividing the total assets at the beginning and at the end of the year by 2. The ratio indicates that each dollar Mackay invests in assets yields $0.87 of sales.

There is another version of this ratio, where only long-term assets are used. In this case, the ratio will show the company's efficiency in using its long-term assets and is calculated as follows:

$$\text{Long-Term Assets Turnover Ratio} = \frac{\text{Net Sales}}{\text{Average Long-Term Assets}}$$

If we assume that Mackay Industries' long-term assets at the beginning of 2015 are $90,000 and at the end of 2015 are $85,000, the ratio would be calculated as follows:

$$\text{Long-Term Assets Turnover Ratio} = \frac{100,000}{\dfrac{90,000 + 85,000}{2}} = 1.14 \text{ times}$$

The ratio of 1.14 means that each dollar Mackay invests in long-term assets yields $1.14 of net sales.

As a general rule, the higher the ratio of asset turnover, the more efficient the company is using its long-term assets. Ratio levels vary widely from one industry to another, though, so companies usually compare their ratio over a period of time to measure how efficiently they are using their assets.

RETURN ON ASSETS

The return on assets ratio shows another dimension of the efficiency of using assets: It shows how many dollars of net income are generated by each dollar invested in assets. The ratio is calculated by relating net income to average total assets as follows:

$$\text{Return on Assets} = \frac{\text{Net Income}}{\text{Average Total Assets}}$$

Let's assume that Mackay Industries has generated net income of $30,000 for the year ended December 31, 2015. The return on assets ratio for Mackay Industries is calculated as follows:

$$\text{Return on Assets} = \frac{30,000}{\dfrac{120,000 + 110,000}{2}} = 0.26 \text{ or } 26\%$$

The ratio indicates that each dollar Mackay invests in assets yields $0.26 of net income.

There is also another version of this ratio, where only long-term assets are used. In this case, the ratio will show the company's efficiency in using its long-term assets and is calculated as follows:

$$\text{Return on Long-Term Assets} = \frac{\text{Net Sales}}{\text{Average Long-Term Assets}}$$

If we assume that Mackay Industries' long-term assets at the beginning of 2015 are $90,000 and at the end of 2015 are $85,000, the ratio would be calculated as follows:

$$\text{Return on Long-Term Assets} = \frac{30,000}{\dfrac{90,000 + 85,000}{2}} = 0.34 \text{ or } 34\%$$

The ratio of 0.34 means that each dollar Mackay invests in long-term assets yields $0.34 of net income.

 DECISION GUIDELINES

DECISION	GUIDELINE	ANALYZE
As a financial analyst, I need to know if the company I'm analyzing is efficiently using its assets. How can I know that?	Use the assets turnover ratio and return on assets.	The assets turnover ratio will provide an indicator of how efficiently the company is using its assets. Another indicator would be the return on assets. You should compare your results with industry averages for equivalent indicators or for comparing your results with another company of a similar size working in the same industry.

FOCUS ON USERS

Concept	User	Why Is This Important to This User?
Depreciation	Bookkeepers Managers Shareholders and Potential Investors Creditors Competitors Government and Regulatory Bodies Unions	Since depreciation expense impacts the income statement and also the statement of financial position through both assets and retained earnings, depreciation and the choices that are made regarding the various depreciation methods and estimations are important to all users of financial statements. For a user of financial statements who is interested in the amount of net income (for example, a union representative would want to know the quality of the earnings on the statement and the impact on the cash holdings of the company, and a competitor would want to make comparisons of performance), a net loss may be able to be explained through the use of an accelerated depreciation schedule by the company. For a user of financial statements who is interested in the amount of assets that are shown on the statement of financial position (for example, shareholders would want to know what it is that they would have rights to should the company be liquidated, and creditors would want to know what might be used for collateral), the book value of the assets can be deceiving as this is not reflective of what the assets are actually worth. A good understanding of the recording of assets is essential for being able to make decisions that are based on the assets owned by the company.
Goodwill	Shareholders and Potential Investors	Shareholders will need to pay attention to goodwill and changes in goodwill. Goodwill cannot be created within a company, but can be recorded when another company is purchased. However, quite often the amount paid to acquire another company is too high and impairments of goodwill are recorded in the years following the purchase.
	Competitors	Acquisitions of companies can signal movements in new strategies (for example, a company may purchase one of its own suppliers to have more control over the quality of the materials going into the manufacture of a product, or a company may purchase a competitor in order to facilitate growth).

DEMO DOC

MyAccountingLab   Visit MyAccountingLab to watch animated versions of similar Demo Docs.

DEPRECIATION AND DISPOSAL OF DEPRECIABLE ASSETS

LEARNING OBJECTIVES &

Jensen, Inc. purchased a machine for $100,000 on January 1, 2015. The machine was expected to last for six years and to produce 180,000 units during that time. The machine has a residual value of $10,000.

Jensen, Inc. produced 50,000 units in 2015, 20,000 in 2016, and 40,000 in 2017.

REQUIREMENTS:

① Prepare a depreciation table showing depreciation calculations for the years 2015, 2016, and 2017 under the following depreciation methods: (a) straight-line, (b) units-of-production, and (c) double-declining-balance.

② On May 1, 2018, Jensen, Inc. sold the machine for $60,000 cash. Assume that Jensen, Inc. was using the straight-line method of depreciation. Journalize all transactions on this date.

DEMO DOC SOLUTIONS

REQUIREMENT ①

Prepare a depreciation table showing depreciation calculations for the years 2015, 2016, and 2017 under the following depreciation methods: (a) straight-line, (b) units-of-production, and (c) double-declining-balance.

Part 1	Part 2	Demo Doc Complete

STRAIGHT-LINE

Refer to the straight-line depreciation table as shown in Exhibit 8-3. On the machine's purchase date (January 1, 2015), the machine's cost of $100,000 must be input. Because no depreciation has been taken yet, the book value is the same as the original cost.

Date	Asset Cost	Yearly Depreciation	Accumulated Depreciation	Book Value
Jan 1, 2015	$100,000			$100,000
Dec 31, 2015				
Dec 31, 2016				
Dec 31, 2017				

Remember that

$$\text{Straight-line depreciation} = \frac{\text{Cost} - \text{Residual value}}{\text{Estimated useful life in years}} = \frac{\$100,000 - \$10,000}{6} = \$15,000 \text{ per year}$$

So for each year, the depreciation expense will be $15,000:

Date	Asset Cost	Yearly Depreciation	Accumulated Depreciation	Book Value
Jan 1, 2015	$100,000			$100,000
Dec 31, 2015		$15,000		
Dec 31, 2016		15,000		
Dec 31, 2017		15,000		

Accumulated depreciation is all of the depreciation expense that has *ever* been taken. So, to calculate accumulated depreciation, we take the previous year's accumulated depreciation and add on the current year's depreciation expense.

The first year of the machine's life is 2015, so in that year no prior depreciation has accumulated. Therefore, accumulated depreciation at December 31, 2015, is the same as the depreciation expense for 2015: $15,000.

For 2016, the accumulated depreciation is the December 31, 2015, accumulated depreciation plus the 2016 depreciation expense. Accumulated depreciation at December 31, 2016, is as follows:

$$\$15,000 + \$15,000 = \$30,000$$

For 2017, the accumulated depreciation is the December 31, 2016, accumulated depreciation plus the 2017 depreciation expense. So accumulated depreciation at December 31, 2017, is as follows:

$$\$30,000 + \$15,000 = \$45,000$$

Date	Asset Cost	Yearly Depreciation	Accumulated Depreciation	Book Value
Jan 1, 2015	$100,000			$100,000
Dec 31, 2015		$15,000	$15,000	
Dec 31, 2016		15,000	30,000	
Dec 31, 2017		15,000	45,000	

The book value of the machine is its cost minus its accumulated depreciation. So to calculate the book value for each year, subtract the accumulated depreciation from the total cost of $100,000.

Book Value at December 31, 2015 = $85,000 ($100,000 − $15,000)
Book Value at December 31, 2016 = $70,000 ($100,000 − $30,000)
Book Value at December 31, 2017 = $55,000 ($100,000 − $45,000)

Date	Asset Cost	Yearly Depreciation	Accumulated Depreciation	Book Value
Jan 1, 2015	$100,000			$100,000
Dec 31, 2015		$15,000	$15,000	85,000
Dec 31, 2016		15,000	30,000	70,000
Dec 31, 2017		15,000	45,000	55,000

UNITS-OF-PRODUCTION

Refer to the units-of-production depreciation table as shown in Exhibit 8-4. As with straight-line, the cost and starting book value of the machine are both $100,000.

Date	Asset Cost	Yearly Depreciation			Accumulated Depreciation	Book Value
		Number of Units	Depreciation Per Unit	Depreciation Expense		
Jan 1, 2015	$100,000					$100,000
Dec 31, 2015						
Dec 31, 2016						
Dec 31, 2017						

Remember that

$$\text{Units-of-production depreciation per unit} = \frac{\text{Cost} - \text{Residual value}}{\text{Estimated useful life in years}} = \frac{\$100,000 - \$10,000}{180,000 \text{ units}} = \$0.50 \text{ per page}$$

Each year, the depreciation expense is calculated as the depreciation cost per page multiplied by the number of units produced.

2015 Depreciation Expense = \$0.50 Depreciation expense per page × 50,000 Units produced
= \$25,000

2016 Depreciation Expense = \$0.50 Depreciation expense per page × 20,000 Units produced
= \$10,000

2017 Depreciation Expense = \$0.50 Depreciation expense per page × 40,000 Units produced
= \$20,000

Date	Asset Cost	Yearly Depreciation Number of Units		Depreciation Per Unit		Depreciation Expense	Accumulated Depreciation	Book Value
Jan 1, 2015	$100,000							$100,000
Dec 31, 2015		50,000	×	$0.50	=	$25,000		
Dec 31, 2016		20,000	×	$0.50	=	$10,000		
Dec 31, 2017		40,000	×	$0.50	=	$20,000		

Accumulated depreciation and book value are calculated in the same manner as was used for straight-line.

Accumulated Depreciation at December 31, 2015 = \$0 + \$25,000 = \$25,000
Book Value at December 31, 2015 = \$100,000 − \$25,000 = \$75,000

Accumulated Depreciation at December 31, 2016 = \$25,000 + \$10,000 = \$35,000
Book Value at December 31, 2016 = \$100,000 − \$35,000 = \$65,000

Accumulated Depreciation at December 31, 2017 = \$35,000 + \$20,000 = \$55,000
Book Value at December 31, 2017 = \$100,000 − \$55,000 = \$45,000

The completed table would look as follows:

Date	Asset Cost	Yearly Depreciation Number of Units		Depreciation Per Unit		Depreciation Expense	Accumulated Depreciation	Book Value
Jan 1, 2015	$100,000							$100,000
Dec 31, 2015		50,000	×	$0.50	=	$25,000	$25,000	75,000
Dec 31, 2016		20,000	×	$0.50	=	$10,000	35,000	65,000
Dec 31, 2017		40,000	×	$0.50	=	$20,000	55,000	45,000

DOUBLE-DECLINING-BALANCE

Refer to the double-declining-balance (DDB) depreciation table as shown in Exhibit 8-5. As with straight-line and units-of-production, the cost and starting book value of the machine are both \$100,000.

| Date | Asset Cost | Yearly Depreciation | | | | Accumulated Depreciation | Book Value |
		DDB Rate*		Book Value	Depreciation Expense*		
Jan 1, 2015	$100,000						$100,000
Dec 31, 2015							
Dec 31, 2016							
Dec 31, 2017							

*Rounded

The DDB depreciation rate is calculated as follows:

$$\text{Double-declining-balance depreciation} = \frac{1}{\text{Estimated useful life in years}} \times 2 = 1/6 \times 2 = 2/6 \text{ or } 1/3$$

Each year, the depreciation rate is multiplied by the book value of the machine *at the beginning of the year*. So for 2015, the depreciation expense is as follows:

$$\$100,000 \times 1/3 = \$33,333$$

Accumulated depreciation and book value at the end of the year are calculated as under straight-line and units-of-production.

Accumulated Depreciation at December 31, 2015 = $0 + $33,333 = $33,333
Book Value at December 31, 2015 = $100,000 − $33,333 = $66,667

| Date | Asset Cost | Yearly Depreciation | | | | Accumulated Depreciation | Book Value |
		DDB Rate*		Book Value	Depreciation Expense*		
Jan 1, 2015	$100,000						$100,000
Dec 31, 2015		1/3	×	$100,000 =	$33,333	$33,333	66,667
Dec 31, 2016							
Dec 31, 2017							

*Rounded

Depreciation expense for 2016 is the book value of the machine *at the beginning* of 2016 multiplied by the depreciation rate. So for 2016, the depreciation expense is as follows:

$$\$66,667 \times 1/3 = \$22,222$$

Accumulated Depreciation at December 31, 2016 = $33,333 + $22,222 = $55,555
Book Value at December 31, 2016 = $100,000 − $55,555 = $44,445

| Date | Asset Cost | Yearly Depreciation | | | | Accumulated Depreciation | Book Value |
		DDB Rate*		Book Value	Depreciation Expense*		
Jan 1, 2015	$100,000						$100,000
Dec 31, 2015		1/3	×	$100,000 =	$33,333	$33,333	66,667
Dec 31, 2016		1/3	×	66,667 =	22,222	$55,555	44,445
Dec 31, 2017							

*Rounded

Depreciation expense for 2017 is the book value of the machine *at the beginning* of 2017 multiplied by the depreciation rate. So for 2017, the depreciation expense is as follows:

$$\$44,445 \times 1/3 = \$14,815$$

Accumulated Depreciation at December 31, 2016 = $55,555 + $14,815 = $70,370
Book Value at December 31, 2016 = $100,000 − $70,370 = $29,630

The completed table would look like this:

Date	Asset Cost	Yearly Depreciation DDB Rate*		Book Value		Depreciation Expense*	Accumulated Depreciation	Book Value
Jan 1, 2015	$100,000							$100,000
Dec 31, 2015		1/3	×	$100,000	=	$33,333	$33,333	66,667
Dec 31, 2016		1/3	×	66,667	=	22,222	$55,555	44,445
Dec 31, 2017		1/3	×	44,445	=	14,815	$70,370	29,630

*Rounded

REQUIREMENT ②

On May 1, 2018, Jensen, Inc. sold the machine for $60,000 cash. Assume that Jensen, Inc. was using the straight-line method of depreciation. Journalize all transactions on this date.

Part 1	**Part 2**	Demo Doc Complete

Before Jensen, Inc. can record the disposal of the machine, it must update the depreciation on the machine. Depreciation represents use of an asset and because the asset was used for four months of 2018 (January, February, March, and April), four months of depreciation expense must be recorded.

From Requirement 1, we know that the annual depreciation expense on the machine under the straight-line method is $15,000 per year (12 months). To adjust for only four months we must multiply by the fraction of 4/12.

Depreciation Expense for 2018 is as follows:

$$\$15,000 \times 4/12 = \$5,000$$

This depreciation expense must now be recorded in a journal entry. Depreciation Expense is increased (debit) by $5,000, and Accumulated Depreciation is increased (credit) by $5,000.

DATE	ACCOUNTS	POST REF.	DR.	CR.
May 1	Depreciation Expense, Machine		5,000	
	Accumulated Depreciation, Machine			5,000
	To record four months' depreciation on machine.			

Assets	=	Liabilities	+	Shareholders' Equity
−5,000				−5,000

Now that this journal entry is made, we can calculate the balance in Accumulated Depreciation immediately before the disposal.

The transactions that have affected the Accumulated Depreciation account are the depreciation expense recorded in each year (2015, 2016, 2017, and 2018). We can add the 2018 depreciation expense to the Accumulated Depreciation balance from the prior year (2017).

Machine		Accumulated Depreciation, Machine	
Bal	100,000	Dec 31, 2017 Bal	45,000
		May 1, 2018	5,000
		May 1, 2018 Bal	50,000

Now we are ready to journalize the disposal of the machine.

Jensen, Inc. is receiving cash, so Cash increases (debit) by the $60,000 of cash received.

The machine is being sold, so the machine asset will be decreased (credit) by its original cost of $100,000 (the amount in the machine T-account).

If the machine is sold, it no longer makes sense to have the accumulated depreciation on the machine. This account must be removed as well. Remember that Accumulated Depreciation is a contra-account, and so it goes wherever its associated asset goes. If we remove the machine from the accounting records, then the accumulated depreciation on that machine goes with it and is removed as well. We will, therefore, decrease Accumulated Depreciation (debit) by its balance of $50,000.

So far for the journal entry we have the following:

DATE	ACCOUNTS	POST REF.	DR.	CR.
May 1	Cash		60,000	
	Accumulated Depreciation, Machine		50,000	
	Machine			100,000

Unbalanced

To complete the journal entry, we need to record the gain or loss on the sale of the machine. Remember that the amount of gain or loss can be calculated by comparing "what you got" to "what you gave up." In this case, Jensen got $60,000 for a machine with a book value of $50,000 ($100,000 − $50,000), so it had a $10,000 ($60,000 − $50,000) gain. The amount of the gain or loss can also equal the amount required to balance the journal entry. So far, the total debits in this entry are $110,000 ($60,000 + $50,000), and the total credits are $100,000. So a credit of $10,000 ($110,000 − $100,000) is needed to balance the entry.

Because the balancing amount is a credit, it is *similar* to revenue in that it will increase net income (be a positive number on the income statement). Therefore, it is a gain, so we will credit Gain on Sale of Machine for $10,000.

DATE	ACCOUNTS	POST REF.	DR.	CR.
May 1	Cash		60,000	
	Accumulated Depreciation, Machine		50,000	
	Machine			100,000
	Gain on Sale of Machine			10,000
	Record sale of machine.			

DEMO DOC COMPLETE

Part 1	Part 2	Demo Doc Complete

DECISION GUIDELINES

Long-Term Assets

If your company has long-term assets, you will likely encounter one or more of the following decisions with regard to those assets:

DECISION		GUIDELINE		ANALYZE

DECISION

How do I determine the cost of an asset?

GUIDELINE

 All costs associated with acquiring an asset, and preparing it for its intended use, should be considered as part of the cost of the asset.

ANALYZE

It is tempting to treat costs related to the purchase of an asset (delivery fees, taxes, set up costs, etc.) as current period expenses. However, if these costs are expensed in the current period, then the cost of the asset does not reflect all of the costs that are necessary for the asset to be able to be used. This causes the current period's net income to be understated and future periods' net income to be overstated.

I'm a new business owner and have made numerous purchases of capital assets to begin my operations. Which depreciation method is the best for my assets?

 The choice of depreciation method depends upon the specific asset being depreciated as well as what the intended use of that asset is. The best method is one that most closely matches the cost of an asset against the future revenues it helps generate.

Straight-line depreciation is best for assets that will be used evenly throughout their lives and that will incur repair and maintenance cost evenly.

Units-of-production depreciation is best for assets that will be utilized on an irregular basis throughout their lives.

Double-declining-balance depreciation is best for assets that will be utilized significantly more in the early years of their lives. It is also best for assets that will require significantly more repair and maintenance expenditures in the later years of the asset's life.

Should I expense the cost of repairing my assets?

 The effect of the repair and whether or not it betters the asset will determine when the cost of the repair should be expensed.

Ordinary repairs are repairs that simply maintain an asset in a state of operation. The cost of ordinary repairs is expensed in the period incurred because no future benefit is expected to arise from the repair.

If a repair extends the useful life of an asset or makes it more efficient, it is known as an extraordinary repair. The cost of the repair should be capitalized and depreciated over the remaining life of the asset because it will provide future benefits.

If an extraordinary repair is incorrectly expensed in the current period, the net income for that period will be understated and the net income for future periods will be overstated.

As a financial analyst, I need to know if the company I'm analyzing is efficiently using its assets. How can I know that?

Use the assets turnover ratio and return on assets.

The assets turnover ratio will provide an indicator of how efficiently the company is using its assets. Another indicator would be the return on assets. You should compare your results with industry averages for equivalent indicators or for comparing your results with another company of a similar size working in the same industry.

Main Differences between IFRS and ASPE

POINT OF COMPARISON	IFRS	ASPE
Asset cost allocation terminology	*Depreciation* for tangible assets. *Amortization* for intangible assets. *Depletion* for natural resources.	*Amortization* for both tangible and intangible assets. *Depreciation* and *depletion* "D&D" used for natural resources.*
Disclosure	The method of depreciation/amortization/depletion is disclosed. Accumulated depreciation/amortization at the end of the period should be disclosed.**	Amortization is disclosed for each major category of assets. Amortization method should be disclosed.
Componentization of assets	Required	Required
Assets impairment	Impairment should be tested on an annual basis.	Impairment needs to be tested when events or changes occur that indicate impairment.
Investments	Initial cost is recorded at cost; however, the company could later choose either to record the investment at fair value or cost.	Only the cost model is allowed.

*CICA Handbook-Accounting, The Canadian Institute of Chartered Accountants, 2013 edition, Parts II and III, page 718
**CICA Handbook-Accounting, The Canadian Institute of Chartered Accountants, 2013 edition, Parts I and IV, page 520

ACCOUNTING VOCABULARY

THE LANGUAGE OF BUSINESS

Accelerated depreciation method (p. 459)

Amortization (p. 470)

Basket purchase (p. 453)

Betterment (p. 466)

Brand names (p. 471)

Capital cost allowance (CCA) (p. 464)

Capital expenditure (p. 466)

Capitalized (p. 452)

Componentization (p. 455)

Copyright (p. 471)

Depletion (p. 472)

Depreciable cost (p. 456)

Depreciation (p. 455)

Double-declining-balance (DDB) method (p. 459)

Extraordinary repair (p. 466)

Franchises (p. 471)

Fully-depreciated asset (p. 458)

Goodwill (p. 471)

Impairment (p. 472)

Intangible assets (p. 450)

Lessee (p. 515)

Lessor (p. 515)

Land improvements (p. 451)

Licences (p. 471)

Lump-sum purchase (p. 453)

Natural resources (p. 450)

Obsolete (p. 456)

Ordinary repair (p. 465)

ACCOUNTING PRACTICE

DISCUSSION QUESTIONS

1. When a company makes an expenditure, it can either capitalize or expense the cost, depending on the nature of the expenditure. What does it mean to capitalize an expenditure? What determines whether an expenditure can be capitalized?

2. If a company were to purchase a piece of land with a building on it that it demolishes to make room for its new building, in which account would the cost of demolition be recorded (land, building, demolition expense, or something else)? Why?

3. What is a lump-sum purchase of assets? How does a company determine how much to allocate to each asset purchased in a lump-sum purchase?

4. What is depreciation and why is it used in accounting?

5. Are useful life and physical life the same thing relative to plant assets? Provide some examples that illustrate your answer.

6. Which depreciation method would be most appropriate for each of the following assets?

   a. This machine is used as a backup to the other machines in the production process. As a result there are some years where it sees a lot of action and others where it is seldom used. It is not a high-tech machine. It will not become obsolete in the fore-seeable future.

   b. Typically this machine will work very effectively and with few repairs for the first three years, but will be down for maintenance quite a bit during its final four years of use.

   c. This machine is expected to run constantly over the entire period it is used. It requires regular maintenance over its lifetime to maintain its expected steady level of production.

7. What makes a repair "extraordinary" (as opposed to ordinary)? Give an example of an extraordinary and an ordinary repair. What is the financial statement effect of recording a repair as an extraordinary repair instead of an ordinary repair?

8. What is the book value of an asset? How is gain or loss on disposal of assets calculated?

9. If a machine that cost $10,000 was estimated to have a salvage value of zero after a useful life of 10 years and was sold for $4,500 after it had been owned for 6 complete years, what would be the amount of gain or loss recognized on the sale?

10. Complete the following analogies. What are some similarities and differences between the two concepts involved in each?

   a. Depreciation is to plant assets as _____ is to intangible assets.

   b. Depreciation is to plant assets as _____ is to natural resources.

SELF CHECK

MyAccountingLab

The exercises and problems in this chapter can be found on MyAccountingLab. You can practise them as often as you want, and they feature step-by-step guided solutions to help you find the right answer.

1. Which cost is *not* recorded as part of the cost of a building?

   a. Construction materials, labour, and overhead
   b. Annual building maintenance
   c. Real estate commission paid to buy the building
   d. Earthmoving for the building's foundation

2. Orbit Airways bought two used Boeing 707 airplanes. Each plane was worth $35 million, but Orbit bought the combination for $60 million. How much is Orbit Airways' cost of each plane?

   a. $30 million
   b. $35 million
   c. $60 million
   d. $70 million

3. How should a capital expenditure be recorded?

   a. Debit capital
   b. Debit an expense
   c. Debit a liability
   d. Debit an asset

4. Which depreciation method usually produces the most depreciation in the first year?

   a. Straight-line
   b. Units-of-production
   c. Double-declining-balance
   d. All produce the same amount of depreciation for the first year.

5. A FedEx airplane costs $50 million and is expected to fly 500 million miles during its 10-year life. Residual value is expected to be zero. If the plane travels 20 million miles the first year, how much depreciation should FedEx record under the units-of-production method?

   a. $2 million
   b. $5 million
   c. $10 million
   d. Cannot be determined from the data given

6. Which depreciation method will result in lower net income in the first years of the asset's life? Why?

   a. Straight-line, because it is simplest
   b. Units-of-production, because it best tracks the asset's use
   c. Double-declining-balance, because it gives the most total depreciation over the asset's life
   d. Double-declining-balance, because it gives higher depreciation deductions in earlier years

7. A copy machine cost $40,000 when new and has accumulated depreciation of $37,000. Suppose Copies R Us junks this machine, receiving nothing in return. What is the result of the disposal transaction?

   a. Gain of $3,000
   b. Loss of $3,000
   c. Gain of $37,000
   d. Loss of $40,000

8. Using information from the preceding question, suppose Copies R Us sold the machine for $5,000. What is the result of this disposal transaction?

   a. Gain of $2,000
   b. Loss of $2,000
   c. Gain of $3,000
   d. Gain of $5,000

9. Depletion is calculated in a manner similar to which depreciation method?

  a. Accelerated method

  b. Straight-line method

  c. Units-of-production method

  d. Double-declining-balance method

10. Which intangible asset is recorded only as part of the acquisition of another company?

  a. Copyright

  b. Patent

  c. Franchise

  d. Goodwill

Answers are given after Written Communication.

SHORT EXERCISES

S8-1. Long-term asset terms (*Learning Objective 1*) 5–10 min.

Identify each of the following assets as a plant asset (P) or an intangible asset (I):

____ 1. Franchises

____ 2. Vehicles

____ 3. Buildings

____ 4. Furniture

____ 5. Patents

____ 6. Copyrights

____ 7. Trademarks

____ 8. Land improvements

S8-2. Long-term asset terms (*Learning Objective 1*) 5–10 min.

For each of the following long-term assets, identify the type of expense that will be incurred to allocate the asset's cost as depreciation expense (DR), depletion expense (DL), amortization expense (A), or none of these (NA).

____ 1. Franchises

____ 2. Land

____ 3. Buildings

____ 4. Furniture

____ 5. Patents

____ 6. Copyrights

____ 7. Trademarks

____ 8. Land improvements

____ 9. Gold ore deposits

S8-3. Land or land improvements (*Learning Objective 2*) 5–10 min.

Identify each of the following as land (L) or land improvements (LI):

____ 1. Survey fees

____ 2. Fencing

____ 3. Lighting

____ 4. Clearing land

____ 5. Parking lot

S8-4. Lump-sum purchase (*Learning Objective 2*) 5–10 min.

Johnson purchased land having a current market value of $80,000, a building with a market value of $64,000, and equipment with a market value of $16,000. Journalize the lump-sum purchase of the three assets purchased for a total cost of $120,000 in exchange for a note payable.

S8-5. Errors in accounting for long-term assets (*Learning Objective 2*) 5–10 min.

Orbit Airways repaired one of its Boeing 767 aircraft at a cost of $600,000, which Orbit Airways paid in cash. Orbit Airways erroneously capitalized this cost as part of the cost of the plane.

Journalize both the incorrect entry the accountant made to record this transaction and the correct entry that the accountant should have made. How will this accounting error affect Orbit Airways' net income? Ignore depreciation.

S8-6. Concept of depreciation (*Learning Objective 3*) 10–15 min.

Jessica Brooks just slept through the class in which Professor Dominguez explained the concept of depreciation. Because the next test is scheduled for Wednesday, Jessica Brooks telephones Hanna Svensen to get her notes from the lecture. Hanna Svensen's notes are concise: "Depreciation—Sounds like Greek to me." Jessica Brooks next tries Tim Lake, who says he thinks depreciation is what happens when an asset wears out. David Coe is confident that depreciation is the process of building up a cash fund to replace an asset at the end of its useful life. Explain the concept of depreciation for Jessica Brooks. Evaluate the explanations of Tim Lake and David Coe. Be specific.

S8-7. Depreciation methods (*Learning Objective 3*) 10–15 min.

At the beginning of the year, Orbit Airways purchased a used Boeing aircraft at a cost of $45 million. Orbit Airways expects the plane to remain useful for five years (3 million kilometres) and to have a residual value of $5 million. Orbit Airways expects the plane to be flown 750,000 kilometres the first year and 1.5 million kilometres the second year.

Compute Orbit Airways' first-year depreciation on the plane using the following methods:

_____ a. Straight-line

_____ b. Units-of-production

_____ c. Double-declining-balance

Show the airplane's book value at the end of the first year under the straight-line method.

S8-8. Depreciation methods (*Learning Objective 3*) 10–15 min.

Refer to the data for S8-7. Compute second-year depreciation on the plane using the following methods:

a. Straight-line

b. Units-of-production

c. Double-declining-balance

S8-9. Straight-line depreciation method (*Learning Objective 3*) 5–10 min.

On March 31, 2015, Orbit Airways purchased a used Boeing aircraft at a cost of $45 million. Orbit Airways expects to fly the plane for five years and to have a residual value of $5 million. Compute Orbit Airways' depreciation on the plane for the year ended December 31, 2015, using the straight-line method.

S8-10. Straight-line depreciation method (*Learning Objective 3*) 5–10 min.

Big Boy's Hot Dogs purchased a hotdog stand for $40,000 with an estimated useful life of eight years and no residual value. Suppose that after using the hotdog stand for four years, the company determines that the asset will remain useful for only two more years. Record Big Boy's Hot Dogs' depreciation on the hotdog stand for year five by the straight-line method.

S8-11. Capitalized versus expensed costs for long-term assets (*Learning Objectives 2 & 4*) 10–15 min.

Classify each of the following expenditures as a capital expenditure (CAP) or a revenue expenditure (REV):

   a. Purchase price

   b. Ordinary recurring repairs to keep the machinery in good working order

   c. Lubrication of the machinery before it is placed in service

   d. Periodic lubrication after the machinery is placed in service

   e. Major overhaul to extend useful life by three years

   f. Sales tax paid on the purchase price

   g. Transportation and insurance while machinery is in transit from seller to buyer

   h. Installation

   i. Training of personnel for initial operation of the machinery

S8-12. Disposition of long-term assets (*Learning Objective 5*) 5–10 min.

Orbit Airways purchased a baggage-handling truck for $41,000. Suppose Orbit Airways sold the truck on December 31, 2015, for $28,000 cash, after using the truck for two full years and accumulating depreciation of $16,000. Make the journal entry to record Orbit Airways' sale of the truck.

S8-13. Goodwill (*Learning Objective 6*) 15–20 min.

When one media company buys another, goodwill is often the most costly asset acquired. World Media paid $700,000 to acquire the *Dandy Dime*, a weekly advertising paper. At the time of the acquisition, the *Dandy Dime's* statement of financial position reported total assets of $1,200,000 and liabilities of $600,000. The fair market value of the *Dandy Dime's* assets was $800,000.

How much goodwill did World Media purchase as part of the acquisition of the *Dandy Dime*? Journalize World Media's acquisition of the *Dandy Dime*.

S8-14. Amortization (*Learning Objective 6*) 5–10 min.

On April 1, Keystone Applications paid $500,000 to acquire a patent on software. Keystone Application expects the patent to have a useful life of five years.

Journalize the entry to record the purchase of the patent on April 1. Journalize the entry to record amortization on December 31.

S8-15. Depletion (*Learning Objective 7*) 5–10 min.

Kent Oil, a small Texas oil company, holds huge reserves of oil and gas assets. Assume that at the end of 2015, Kent Oil's cost of mineral assets totalled approximately $18 million, representing 2.4 million barrels of oil and gas reserves in the ground.

Calculate Kent Oil's depletion expense per barrel of oil. Suppose Kent Oil removed 0.8 million barrels of oil during 2016 and sold all of these barrels during the year. Record Kent Oil's depletion expense for 2016.

S8-16. Other long-term assets (*Learning Objective 8*) 5–10 min.

Classify each of the following as:

Trading security (T)
Available-for-sale security (A)
Held-to-maturity security (H)
None of the above (N)

_____ 1. A bond that management plans on owning until it is repaid. Management does not believe it will need to sell the bond to generate cash before the bond's scheduled maturity date.

_____ 2. Land that management is holding as an investment.

_____ 3. Intel shares that company management plans on selling quickly, as soon as its price is 10% more than what the company paid at the time it purchased the shares.

_____ 4. Ford Motor Company shares. Management does not actively manage these shares and intends to sell them only if they need to generate cash.

_____ 5. A bond that management plans on owning until it is repaid. However, management believes it may have to sell the bond within the year to provide enough cash for operations.

_____ 6. Inventory that management intends to sell within the year.

S8-17. Other long-term assets (*Learning Objective 8*) 5–10 min.

Specify how each of the following items would be reported in the financial statements of Tanaka Enterprises for its current fiscal year. Also specify the amount that would appear on the statement. Some items may be reported on more than one financial statement. In these cases, specify the amount that would appear on each statement.

Income Statement (IS)
Statement of Financial Position (SFP)
Change in Shareholders' Equity (SE)

1. Tanaka Enterprises received $55 of dividends during the year on shares it owned in Jasper, Inc.

2. At year-end, Tanaka Enterprises owned a $1,000 Canada Savings Bond.

3. Tanaka Enterprises sold shares for $110 cash that had been held as an available-for-sale security. The shares had been purchased for $90 and hadn't changed in value until the time of their sale.

4. Shares that Tanaka Enterprises purchased for $90 during the year as an available-for-sale security have a market value of $110 at the year-end statement of financial position date.

5. Shares that Tanaka Enterprises purchased for $90 during the year as a trading security had a market value of $110 at the year-end statement of financial position date.

6. Earned $75 of interest on a bond that Tanaka Enterprises purchased from the province of Quebec.

EXERCISES (GROUP A)

E8-1A. Capitalized costs for long-term assets (*Learning Objective 2*) 10–15 min.

Bozeman Systems purchased land, paying $80,000 cash as a down payment and signing a $120,000 note payable for the balance. In addition, Bozeman Systems paid delinquent property tax of $2,100, title insurance costing $2,500, and a $10,400 charge for levelling the land and removing an unwanted building. The company constructed an office building on the land at a cost of $800,000. It also paid $51,000 for a fence around the property, $15,000 for the company sign near the entrance, and $6,000 for special lighting of the grounds.

Requirements

1. Determine the cost of the company's land, land improvements, and building.
2. Which of the assets will Bozeman depreciate?

E8-2A. Capitalized costs for long-term assets (*Learning Objective 2*) 10–15 min.

Lynch Brothers manufactures conveyor belts. Early in January 2015, Lynch Brothers constructed its own building at a materials, labour, and overhead cost of $900,000. Lynch Brothers also paid for architect fees and building permits of $72,000.

Requirements

1. How much should Lynch Brothers record as the cost of the building in 2015?
2. Record Lynch Brothers' transactions related to the construction of the building.

Quick solution:
Land = $215,000; Land Improvements = $72,000; Building = $800,000

E8-3A. Capitalized costs for long-term assets (*Learning Objective 2*) 10–15 min.

Tonya's Tanning Salon bought three tanning beds in a $10,000 lump-sum purchase. An independent appraiser valued the tanning beds as follows:

Tanning Bed	Appraised Value
1	$3,000
2	5,000
3	4,000

Tonya's Tanning Salon paid $5,000 in cash and signed a note payable for $5,000. Record the purchase in the journal, identifying each tanning bed's cost by number in a separate Tanning Bed account. Round decimals to three places.

E8-4A. Errors in accounting for long-term assets (*Learning Objective 2*) 15–20 min.

Assume that early in year 1, Mariposa Company purchased equipment at a cost of $500,000. Management expects the equipment to remain in service for five years, with zero residual value. Mariposa Company uses the straight-line depreciation method. Through an accounting error, Mariposa Company accidentally expensed the entire cost of the equipment at the time of purchase.

Requirement

1. Prepare a schedule to show the overstatement or understatement in the following items at the end of each year over the five-year life of the equipment.
   a. Equipment, net
   b. Net income

E8-5A. Depreciation methods (*Learning Objective 3*) 15–20 min.

Memorial Medical Centre bought equipment on January 2, 2015, for $30,000. The equipment was expected to remain in service for four years and to perform 1,000 operations. At the end of the equipment's useful life, Memorial estimates that its residual value will be $6,000. The equipment performed 100 operations the first year, 300 the second year, 400 the third year, and 200 the fourth year.

Requirements

1. Prepare a schedule of depreciation expense per year for the equipment under the three depreciation methods. After two years under double-declining-balance depreciation, the company switched to the straight-line method. Show your computations.
2. Which method tracks the wear and tear on the equipment most closely?
3. Which method would result in the lowest net income over the first few year's of the asset's life? Why?

E8-6A. Straight-line depreciation (*Learning Objective 3*) 10–15 min.

LHD Freight purchased a building for $700,000 and depreciated it on a straight-line basis over a 40-year period. The estimated residual value was $100,000. After using the building for 15 years, LHD realized that wear and tear on the building would force the company to replace it before 40 years. Starting with the sixteenth year, LHD began depreciating the building over a revised total life of 30 years and increased the estimated residual value to $175,000. Record depreciation expense on the building for years 15 and 16.

E8-7A. Straight-line depreciation and long-term asset disposal (*Learning Objectives 3 & 5*) 15–20 min.

On January 2, 2015, Bright Lights purchased showroom fixtures for $10,000 cash, expecting the fixtures to remain in service for five years. Bright Lights has depreciated the fixtures on a straight-line basis, with zero residual value. On September 30, 2016, Bright Lights sold the fixtures for $5,000 cash. Record both the depreciation expense on the fixtures for 2016 and the sale of the fixtures on September 30, 2016.

E8-8A. Disposition of long-term assets (*Learning Objective 5*) 10–15 min.

Assume that Henson Corporation's comparative statement of financial position reported these amounts:

	December 31	
	2014	2013
Plant and Equipment...	$ 600,000	$ 595,000
Less: Accumulated Depreciation...............................	145,000	135,000
Net Plant and Equipment...	$ 455,000	$ 460,000

Requirement

1. Assume that on January 2, 2015, Henson sold 1/10 of its plant and equipment for $75,500 in cash. Journalize this transaction for Henson.

E8-9A. Trade-in on purchase of new asset (*Learning Objectives 3 & 5*) 15–20 min.

Mesilla Valley Transport is a large trucking company. Mesilla Valley Transport uses the units-of-production (UOP) method to depreciate its trucks. In 2014, Mesilla Valley Transport acquired a Mack truck costing $350,000 with a useful life of 10 years or 1 million kilometres. Estimated residual value was $100,000. The truck was driven 80,000 kilometres in 2014, 120,000 kilometres in 2015, and 160,000 kilometres in 2016. After 40,000 kilometres in 2017, Mesilla Valley Transport traded in the Mack truck for a new Freightliner that cost $480,000. Mesilla Valley Transport received a $275,000 trade-in allowance for the old truck and paid the difference in cash. Journalize the entry to record the purchase of the new truck.

E8-10A. Patents (*Learning Objective 6*) 10–15 min.

Part 1. Millennium Printing manufactures high-speed printers. Millennium Printing recently paid $1 million for a patent on a new laser printer. Although it gives legal protection for 20 years, the patent is expected to provide a competitive advantage for only 8 years. Using the straight-line method of amortization, make journal entries to record (a) the purchase of the patent and (b) amortization for year 1.

Part 2. After using the patent for four years, Millennium Printing learns at an industry trade show that another company is designing a more efficient printer. On the basis of this new information, Millennium Printing decides, starting with year 5, to amortize the remaining cost of the patent over two remaining years, giving the patent a total useful life of six years. Record amortization for year 5.

E8-11A. Goodwill (*Learning Objective 6*) 10–15 min.

Rutherford, Corp. aggressively acquired other companies. Assume that Rutherford, Corp. purchased Lancer, Inc. for $11 million cash. The market value of Lancer's assets is $15 million, and it has liabilities of $10 million.

Requirements

1. Compute the cost of goodwill purchased by Rutherford, Corp.
2. Record the purchase of Lancer, Inc. by Rutherford, Corp.

E8-12A. Depletion (*Learning Objective 7*) 10–15 min.

Asarco Mining paid $398,500 for the right to extract mineral assets from a 200,000-tonne mineral deposit. In addition to the purchase price, Asarco Mining also paid a $500 filing fee, a $1,000 licence fee to the Yukon Territory, and $60,000 for a geological survey of the property. Because the company purchased the rights to the minerals only, the company expected the asset to have zero residual value when fully depleted. During the first year, Asarco Mining removed 40,000 tonnes of minerals. Using the Mineral Assets account, make journal entries to record the following:

a. Purchase of the mineral rights
b. Payment of fees and other costs
c. Depletion for the first year (none of the minerals were sold during the year)

E8-13A. Statement of financial position disclosure of long-term assets (*Learning Objective 9*) 10–15 min.

At the end of 2015, Zeman, Corp. had total assets of $25 million and total liabilities of $13 million. Included in the assets were property, plant, and equipment with a cost of $9 million and accumulated depreciation of $3 million. During 2015, Zeman, Corp. earned total revenues of $20 million and had total expenses of $17 million. Show how Zeman, Corp. reported property, plant, and equipment on its statement of financial position on December 31, 2015. What was the book value of property, plant, and equipment on that date?

E8-14A. Depreciation methods (*Learning Objective 3*) 10–15 min.

Oteda purchased a machine on January 1 for $11,500. Oteda expected the machine will be used for four years and will have a residual value of $2,500. Oteda expects the machine to be used for 25,000 hours: first year, 5,200 hours; second year, 7,500 hours; third year, 8,600 hours; and the fourth year, 3,700 hours.

Requirement

1. Compute the annual depreciation amount using three different depreciation methods by filling in the following table:

	Straight-Line	Units-of-Production	Double-Declining
Year 1			
Year 2			
Year 3			
Year 4			
Total			

E8-15A. Identify asset impairment (Learning Objective 8) 10–15 min.

Gupta Ltd. has four assets. You are an accounting assistant who is in charge of identifying the recoverable amount and determining whether each of the assets is impaired. If so, what is the amount that should be recorded?

	Carrying Value	Value in Use	Fair Value	Recoverable Amount	Is Asset Impaired?	Impairment Amount
1. Equipment	$ 21,000	$ 18,000	$ 18,500			
2. Goodwill	150,000	80,000	75,000			
3. Building	560,000	620,000	750,000			
4. Patent	25,000	16,000	16,500			

E8-16A. Amortization (Learning Objectives 2 & 6) 10–15 min.

Trinh Technologies Company (TTC) has two intangible assets at the end of the year.

a. Signed a five-year lease for an office on March 1. TTC immediately spent $35,000 for leasehold improvements. TTC estimated the leasehold improvements would last for seven years. TTC moved into the office on April 1, after the improvements were completed.

b. TTC purchased a patent for $6,000 on June 1. The patent was registered with the Canadian Intellectual Property Office eight years ago. TTC estimated that it would keep the patent for eight years.

Requirements

1. Record the acquisition of the two intangible assets.
2. Calculate the amortization of each intangible asset at December 31.
3. Record the year-end adjusting entries.
4. What is the carrying value of each asset reported in the statement of financial position?

E8-17A. Depreciation methods (Learning Objective 3) 15–20 min.

On October 1, 2015, Alexander Corp. bought furniture for its new office for $20,000. (Furniture falls within class 8—CCA rate 20%). The residual value of the furniture is $2,000, and it is expected to remain in use for five years. The company uses the straight-line depreciation method.

Requirements

1. Calculate the depreciation expense and net book value on December 31, 2015 and 2016.
2. Calculate the CCA and UCC for 2015 and 2016.

E8-18A. Calculating the assets turnover ratio and return on assets (Learning Objective 10) 10–15 min.

The following information is provided for Interlink Industries Inc. for the year 2015 along with industry averages:

	December 31	
	2015	2014
Current Assets...	$60,000	$50,000
Long-Term Assets...	$140,000	$146,000

Net sales for 2015 amounted to $150,000 and net income was $50,000.

Requirements

1. Calculate the assets turnover ratio and the long-term assets turnover ratio.
2. Calculate return on assets and return on long-term assets.

EXERCISES (GROUP B)

E8-1B. Capitalized costs for long-term assets (*Learning Objective 2*) 10–15 min.

Ogden Systems purchased land, paying $110,000 cash as a down payment and signing a $140,000 note payable for the balance. In addition, Ogden Systems paid delinquent property tax of $1,500, title insurance costing $3,500, and a $10,400 charge for levelling the land and removing an unwanted building. The company constructed an office building on the land at a cost of $600,000. It also paid $46,000 for a fence around the property, $7,000 for the company sign near the entrance, and $5,000 for special lighting of the grounds.

Requirements

1. Determine the cost of the company's land, land improvements, and building.
2. Which of the assets will Ogden depreciate?

E8-2B. Capitalized costs for long-term assets (*Learning Objective 2*) 10–15 min.

White Brothers manufactures conveyor belts. Early in May 2015, White Brothers constructed its own building at a materials, labour, and overhead cost of $970,000. White Brothers also paid for architect fees and building permits of $76,000.

Requirements

1. How much should White Brothers record as the cost of the building in 2015?
2. Record White Brothers' transactions related to the construction of the building.

E8-3B. Capitalized costs for long-term assets (*Learning Objective 2*) 10–15 min.

Amy's Tanning Salon bought three tanning beds in a $20,000 lump-sum purchase. An independent appraiser valued the tanning beds as follows:

Tanning Bed	Appraised Value
1	$ 7,000
2	8,000
3	11,000

Amy's Tanning Salon paid $10,000 in cash and signed a note payable for $10,000. Record the purchase in the journal, identifying each tanning bed's cost by number in a separate Tanning Bed account. Round decimals to three places.

E8-4B. Errors in accounting for long-term assets (*Learning Objective 2*) 15–20 min.

Assume that early in year 1, Marginal Company purchased equipment at a cost of $520,000. Management expects the equipment to remain in service for five years, with zero residual value. Marginal Company uses the straight-line depreciation method. Through an accounting error, Marginal Company accidentally expensed the entire cost of the equipment at the time of purchase.

Requirement

1. Prepare a schedule to show the overstatement or understatement in the following items at the end of each year over the five-year life of the equipment:
   a. Equipment, net
   b. Net income

E8-5B. Depreciation methods (*Learning Objective 3*) 15–20 min.

General Medical Centre bought equipment on January 2, 2015, for $18,000. The equipment was expected to remain in service for four years and to perform 400 operations. At the end of the equipment's useful life, General estimates that its residual value will be $4,000. The equipment performed 40 operations the first year, 120 the second year, 160 the third year, and 80 the fourth year.

Requirements

1. Prepare a schedule of depreciation expense per year for the equipment under the three depreciation methods. After two years under double-declining-balance depreciation, the company switched to the straight-line method. Show your computations.

2. Which method tracks the wear and tear on the equipment most closely?

3. Which method would result in the lowest net income over the first few year's of the asset's life? Why?

E8-6B. Straight-line depreciation (*Learning Objective 3*) 10–15 min.

Chapin Freight purchased a building for $800,000 and depreciated it on a straight-line basis over a 30-year period. The estimated residual value was $110,000. After using the building for 15 years, Chapin realized that wear and tear on the building would force the company to replace it before 30 years. Starting with the sixteenth year, Chapin began depreciating the building over a revised total life of 20 years and increased the estimated residual value to $170,000. Record depreciation expense on the building for years 15 and 16.

E8-7B. Straight-line depreciation and long-term asset disposal (*Learning Objectives 3 & 5*) 15–20 min.

On January 2, 2015, Shine Lights purchased showroom fixtures for $18,000 cash, expecting the fixtures to remain in service for five years. Shine Lights has depreciated the fixtures on a straight-line basis, with zero residual value. On March 31, 2016, Shine Lights sold the fixtures for $5,000 cash. Record both the depreciation expense on the fixtures for 2016 and the sale of the fixtures on March 31, 2016.

E8-8B. Disposition of long-term assets (*Learning Objective 5*) 10–15 min.

Assume that Hector Corporation's comparative statement of financial position reported these amounts:

	December 31	
	2014	**2013**
Plant and Equipment	$ 610,000	$ 583,000
Less: Accumulated Depreciation	160,000	120,000
Net Plant and Equipment	$ 450,000	$ 463,000

Requirement

1. Assume that on January 2, 2015, Hector sold 1/2 of its plant and equipment for $237,000 in cash. Journalize this transaction for Hector.

E8-9B. Trade-in on purchase of new asset (*Learning Objectives 3 & 5*) 15–20 min.

Regional Highway Transport is a large trucking company. Regional Highway Transport uses the units-of-production (UOP) method to depreciate its trucks. In 2014, Regional Highway Transport acquired a Mack truck costing $410,000 with a useful life of 10 years or 1,250,000 kilometres. Estimated residual value was $10,000. The truck was driven 85,000 kilometres in 2014, 110,000 kilometres in 2015, and 150,000 kilometres in 2016. After 10,000 kilometres in 2017, Regional Highway Transport traded in the Mack truck for a new Freightliner that costs $524,400. Regional Highway Transport received a $314,400 trade-in allowance for the old truck and paid the difference in cash. Journalize the entry to record the purchase of the new truck.

E8-10B. Patents (*Learning Objective 6*) 10–15 min.

Part 1. Mayflower Printing manufactures high-speed printers. Mayflower Printing recently paid $9 million for a patent on a new laser printer. Although it gives legal protection for 20 years, the patent is expected to provide a competitive advantage for only 15 years. Using the straight-line method of amortization, make journal entries to record (a) the purchase of the patent and (b) amortization for year 1.

Part 2. After using the patent for seven years, Mayflower Printing learns at an industry trade show that another company is designing a more efficient printer. On the basis of this new information, Mayflower Printing decides, starting with year 8, to amortize the remaining cost of the patent over two remaining years, giving the patent a total useful life of nine years. Record amortization for year 8.

E8-11B. Goodwill (*Learning Objective 6*) 10–15 min.

Richardson, Corp. aggressively acquired other companies. Assume that Richardson, Corp. purchased Lawrence, Inc. for $14 million cash. The market value of Lawrence's assets is $22 million, and it has liabilities of $14 million.

Requirements

1. Compute the cost of goodwill purchased by Richardson, Corp.
2. Record the purchase of Lawrence, Inc. by Richardson, Corp.

E8-12B. Depletion (*Learning Objective 7*) 10–15 min.

McKenzie Mining paid $831,600 for the right to extract mineral assets from a 600,000-tonne mineral deposit. In addition to the purchase price, McKenzie Mining also paid a $600 filing fee, a $2,800 licence fee to the province of Quebec, and $65,000 for a geological survey of the property. Because the company purchased the rights to the minerals only, the company expected the asset to have zero residual value when fully depleted. During the first year, McKenzie Mining removed 75,000 tonnes of minerals. Using the Mineral Assets account, make journal entries to record the following:

a. Purchase of the mineral rights
b. Payment of fees and other costs
c. Depletion for the first year (none of the minerals were sold during the year)

E8-13B. Statement of financial position disclosure of long-term assets (*Learning Objective 9*) 10–15 min.

At the end of 2015, Zaney, Corp. had total assets of $26 million and total liabilities of $15 million. Included in the assets were property, plant, and equipment with a cost of $14 million and accumulated depreciation of $5 million. During 2015, Zaney, Corp. earned total revenues of $24 million and had total expenses of $15 million. Show how Zaney, Corp. reported property, plant, and equipment on its statement of financial position on December 31, 2015. What was the book value of property, plant, and equipment on that date?

E8-14B. Depreciation methods (*Learning Objective 3*) 10–15 min.

Wilson Mining (WM) purchased a truck on April 1 for $98,500. WM expected the truck will be used for five years and to have a residual value of $3,500. WM expects the truck to be used for 125,000 kilometres: first year, 23,000 km; second year, 28,500 km; third year, 26,400 km; the fourth year, 24,500 km; and the fifth year, 22,600 km.

Requirement

1. Compute the annual depreciation amount using three different depreciation methods by filling in the following table:

	Straight-Line	Units-of-Production	Double-Declining
Year 1			
Year 2			
Year 3			
Year 4			
Year 5			
Total			

500 CHAPTER 8

E8-15B. Identify asset impairment (*Learning Objective 8*) 10–15 min.

TaoYuen Ltd. has four assets. You are an accounting assistant who is in charge of identifying the recoverable amount and determining whether each of the assets is impaired. If so, what is the amount that should be recorded?

	Carrying Value	Value in Use	Fair Value	Recoverable Amount	Is Asset Impaired?	Impairment Amount
1. Truck	$52,000	$48,000	$45,000			
2. Franchise	45,000	52,000	$55,000			
3. Machine	60,000	52,000	$50,000			
4. Patent	12,000	16,000	$16,500			

E8-16B. Amortization (*Learning Objectives 2 & 6*) 10–15 min.

Lakeshore Company has two intangible assets at the end of the year.

1. On July 1, Lakeshore joined a franchise business and paid $60,000 for a five-year franchise agreement.
2. On October 1, Lakeshore purchased a copyright for $26,000. The copyright had 25 years of legal life remaining; however, Lakeshore estimated that the copyright will have no value after 20 years.

Requirements

1. Record the acquisition of the two intangible assets.
2. Calculate the amortization of each intangible asset at December 31.
3. Record the year-end adjusting entries.
4. What is the carrying value of each asset reported in the statement of financial position?

E8-17B. Depreciation methods (*Learning Objective 3*) 15–20 min.

On November 1, 2015, Fresh Manufacturers Inc. bought a line of production machinery for its new office for $500,000. (Machines fall within class 38—CCA rate 30%.) The residual value of the machinery is expected to be $50,000, and it is expected to remain in use for 10 years. The company uses the straight-line depreciation method.

Requirements

1. Calculate the depreciation expense and net book value on December 31, 2015 and 2016.
2. Calculate the CCA and UCC for 2015 and 2016.

E8-18B. Calculating the assets turnover ratio and return on assets (*Learning Objective 10*) 10–15 min.

The following information is provided for Canadian Industries Inc. for the year 2015 along with industry averages:

	December 31	
	2015	2014
Current Assets	$30,000	$25,000
Long-Term Assets	$70,000	$73,000

Net sales for 2015 amounted to $75,000 and net income was $25,000.

Requirements

1. Calculate the assets turnover ratio and the long-term assets turnover ratio.
2. Calculate return on assets and return on long-term assets.

These alternative exercise sets are available for your practice benefit on
MyAccountingLab.

PROBLEMS (GROUP A)

P8-1A. Long-term asset costs and partial year depreciation (*Learning Objectives 2 & 3*)
20–25 min.

Provincial Manufacturing incurred the following costs in acquiring land, making land
improvements, and constructing and furnishing a new building:

a.	Purchase price of four hectares of land	$193,000
b.	Additional dirt and earthmoving	9,400
c.	Fence around the boundary of the property	17,500
d.	Attorney fee for title search on the land	1,100
e.	Unpaid property taxes on the land to be paid by Provincial	5,900
f.	Company signs at the front of the property	4,700
g.	Building permit for the building	2,100
h.	Architect's fee for the design of the building	20,900
i.	Labour to construct the building	498,000
j.	Materials used to construct the building	400,000
k.	Landscaping	6,700
l.	Parking lot and concrete walks	29,100
m.	Lights for the parking lot and walkways	11,000
n.	Salary of construction supervisor (85% to building; 15% to parking lot and concrete walks)	60,000
o.	Furniture for the building	106,000
p.	Transportation and installation of furniture	2,000

Provincial Manufacturing depreciates buildings over 30 years, land improvements over
20 years, and furniture over 8 years, all on a straight-line basis with zero residual value.

Requirements

1. Set up columns for Land, Land Improvements, Building, and Furniture. Show
   how to account for each cost by listing the cost under the correct account.
   Determine the total cost of each asset.

2. All construction was complete and assets were placed in service on September 1.
   Record partial-year depreciation for the year ended December 31.

P8-2A. Journalize long-term asset transactions (*Learning Objectives 2, 3, & 5*)
20–25 min.

Regal Freightway provides freight service. The company's statement of financial position includes Land, Buildings, and Motor-Carrier Equipment. Regal Freightway uses a
separate accumulated depreciation account for each depreciable asset. During 2015,
Regal Freightway completed the following transactions:

Jan 1	Traded in motor-carrier equipment with accumulated depreciation of $90,000 (cost of $130,000) for new equipment with a cash cost of $176,000. Regal Freightway received a trade-in allowance of $70,000 on the old equipment and paid the remainder in cash.
Jul 1	Sold a building that cost $550,000 and had accumulated depreciation of $250,000 through December 31 of the preceding year. Depreciation is computed on a straight-line basis. The building has a 40-year useful life and a residual value of $50,000. Regal Freightway received $100,000 cash and a $600,000 note receivable.

Oct 31   Purchased land and a building for a cash payment of $300,000. An independent appraisal valued the land at $115,000 and the building at $230,000.

Dec 31   Recorded depreciation as follows:

New motor-carrier equipment has an expected useful life of 1 million kilometres and an estimated residual value of $26,000. Depreciation method is the units-of-production method. During the year, Regal Freightway drove the truck 150,000 kilometres.

Depreciation on buildings is straight-line. The new building has a 40-year useful life and a residual value equal to $20,000.

Requirement

1. Record the transactions in Regal Freightway's journal.

P8-3A. Capitalize long-term asset costs and several depreciation methods (*Learning Objectives 2, 3, & 9*) 20–25 min.

On January 3, 2015, Jose Rojo, Inc. paid $224,000 for equipment used in manufacturing automotive supplies. In addition to the basic purchase price, the company paid $700 transportation charges, $100 insurance for the equipment while in transit, $12,100 sales tax, and $3,100 for a special platform on which to place the equipment in the plant. Jose Rojo, Inc. management estimates that the equipment will remain in service for five years and have a residual value of $20,000. The equipment will produce 50,000 units the first year, with annual production decreasing by 5,000 units during each of the next four years (i.e., 45,000 units in year 2; 40,000 units in year 3; and so on for a total of 200,000 units). In trying to decide which depreciation method to use, Jose Rojo, Inc. requested a depreciation schedule for each of the three depreciation methods (straight-line, units-of-production, and double-declining-balance).

Requirements

1. For each depreciation method, prepare a depreciation schedule showing asset cost, depreciation expense, accumulated depreciation, and asset book value. For the units-of-production method, round depreciation per unit to three decimal places.

2. Show how Jose Rojo, Inc. would report equipment on the December 31, 2015, statement of financial position for each depreciation method.

P8-4A. Disposing of an asset (*Learning Objective 5*) 15–20 min.

Atco Industries had a piece of equipment that cost $25,000 and had accumulated depreciation of $23,000.

Requirement

Quick solution:
a. $2,000 loss; b. $1,000 gain;
c. $3,000 gain; d. $1,000 loss

1. Record the disposition of the equipment assuming the following independent situations:

   a. Atco discarded the equipment, receiving $0.

   b. Atco sold the equipment for $3,000 cash.

   c. Atco traded the equipment in on a new piece of equipment costing $30,000. Atco was granted a $5,000 trade-in allowance for the old equipment and paid the difference in cash.

   d. Atco traded the equipment in on a new piece of equipment costing $20,000. Atco was granted a $1,000 trade-in allowance for the old equipment and signed a note payable for the difference.

P8-5A. Goodwill (*Learning Objective 6*) 15–20 min.

Benny's Restaurants acquired Hungry Boy Diners. The financial records of Hungry Boy Diners included the following:

Book Value of Assets	$2.4 million
Market Value of Assets	2.7 million
Liabilities	2.2 million

Requirements

1. Make the journal entry to record Benny's Restaurants' purchase of Hungry Boy Diners for $3 million cash, including any goodwill.

2. How should Benny's Restaurants account for this goodwill after acquiring Hungry Boy Diners? Explain in detail.

P8-6A. Depletion (*Learning Objective 7*) 20–25 min.

Wright Oil Company's statement of financial position includes three assets: natural gas, oil, and coal. Suppose Wright Oil Company paid $2.8 million in cash for the right to work a mine with an estimated 100,000 tonnes of coal. Assume the company paid $60,000 to remove unwanted buildings from the land and $45,000 to prepare the surface for mining. Further, assume that Wright Oil Company signed a $30,000 note payable to a company that will return the land surface to its original condition after the mining ends. During the first year, Wright Oil Company removed 40,000 tonnes of coal, which it sold on account for $39 per tonne. Operating expenses for the first year totalled $252,000, all paid in cash.

Requirements

1. Record all of Wright Oil Company's transactions, including depletion, for the year.

2. Prepare the company's income statement for its coal operations for the year.

P8-7A. Lump-sum basket purchase of long-term assets (*Learning Objective 2*) 20–25 min.

On March 1, Taikin Manufacturing Ltd. purchased a factory with a lot of land and a machine for $818,000. Taikin paid legal fees of $2,000 for this purchase, renovation costs on the building of $27,000, and the $8,000 cost of overhauling the machine. The appraisal value for the land was $225,000, for the building was $585,000, and for the machine was $90,000.

Taikin estimated that the building's useful life was 15 years with a residual value of $20,000 and the machine's production hours would be 43,000 machine hours, with a residual value of $4,000. Taikin uses the straight-line method to depreciate buildings and the units-of-production method to depreciate machines. Taikin's year-end is December 31. Taikin used the machine 3,600 hours for the first year and 4,500 hours for the second year.

Requirements

1. Apportion the cost of the factory on the basis of the appraised value. Show your calculations.

2. Record the journal entry for the purchase of the building, land, and machine.

3. Record the adjusting entry for the depreciation for the first year.

4. What would be the carrying value of each asset at the end of the first year and the second year?

P8-8A. Changes in estimates and disposal (*Learning Objectives 3 & 5*) 20–25 min.

On January 1, 2015, Nami Inc.'s ledger shows its capital asset of $79,000 (at cost) and accumulated depreciation of $28,125. When the capital asset was purchased, Nami estimated that its useful life would be 12 years. On July 1, 2015, Nami paid

$18,000 for property betterment and, as a result, it estimated its residual value had increased from $4,000 to $6,000; as well, the useful life had increased by 2.5 years. Nami uses straight-line amortization. On October 1, 2017, Nami sold the capital asset for $45,000.

Requirements

1. What was the age of the capital asset as of Janary 1, 2015? What was the annual depreciation amount?
2. Prepare the journal entry to record the betterment.
3. Prepare the adjusting entry for the depreciation expense at the end of the year.
4. What is the impact on the income statement after the betterment has been completed?
5. Prepare the journal entry to record the disposal of the capital asset.

P8-9A. Natural resources and depletion (*Learning Objective 7*) 20–25 min.

Golden Gate Mining (GGM) purchased a mineral deposit for $1,350,000 in May, 2015. In June, GGM spent $50,000 to prepare for the exploitation. The mineral deposit was ready for exploitation on July 1. GGM estimated 800,000 ounces of minerals could be economically extracted and sold. On January 2, 2017, GGM spent $80,000 for further development cost. As a result, GGM estimated an additional 110,000 ounces of mineral could be extracted and sold. The amount of mineral extracted for 2015, 2016, and 2017 is as follows:

Year	Ounces
2015	72,000
2016	88,000
2017	75,000

Requirements

1. Calculate the acquisition cost of the minerals and record the journal entry for the acquisition in 2015.
2. Record the journal entries for the depletion expense for 2015 and 2016.
3. What is the carrying value for the mineral deposit on December 31, 2016?
4. Record the journal entry for additional development cost in 2017.
5. Calculate the depletion expense for 2017 and record the journal entry for the depletion on December 31, 2017.

P8-10A. Disposal of assets (*Learning Objective 5*) 20–25 min.

Qasim Manufacturing Ltd. has three assets. Their costs, estimated residual value, useful life in years, and their carrying value on January 1, 2015, are listed in the following table:

	Cost	Residual Value	Useful Life	Carrying Value
Equipment A	$125,000	$5,000	8	$ 46,250
Equipment B	224,000	8,000	15	101,600
Equipment C	86,000	2,000	12	38,750

During 2015, Qasim completed the following transactions related to asset retirement:

Apr 1   Sold Equipment A for $42,500 cash.
Jul 31   Sold Equipment B for $112,500; received $12,500 cash and an interest-bearing (6%) note receivable for the remainder due on July 31, 2016.
Oct 2   Sold Equipment C for $30,000; received $20,000 and a note receivable due on December 31, 2015.

Requirements

1. What is the age of each asset on January 1, 2015?

2. Prepare all journal entries related to the disposal of each of the assets in 2015.

3. Record adjusting entries on December 31, 2015.

4. What is the total gain or loss from the disposal of these three assets?

P8-11A. Journalize long-term asset transactions (*Learning Objectives 2, 3, & 5*) 25–30 min.

On October 1, 2015, Lyndon, Inc. purchased a computer system for $86,000 from AIT Systems. The computer system had an estimated life of five years and residual value of $3,000. Lyndon paid $2,820 for shipping and insurance and hired an engineering company to install and set up the computer system for $7,500. AIT asked for $20,000 cash payment immediately; in addition, AIT accepted a one-year note payable of $50,000 plus 6% interest due on September 30, 2016. The remaining $16,000 is due in 30 days; however, AIT allowed a 2% discount on this $16,000 if Lyndon makes a payment by October 15. Lyndon paid the invoice on October 31. Lyndon uses the straight-line depreciation method.

On July 1, 2017, Lyndon replaced a hard drive costing $12,000 and, as a result, the useful life of the computer system increased by two years.

On January 10, 2018, the computer system experienced irreparable damage. Lyndon made a claim to the insurance company. Subsequently, Lyndon received $40,000 cash on January 31, 2018.

Requirements

1. Calculate the acquisition cost of the computer system.

2. Prepare all journal entries for 2015, 2016, 2017, and 2018.

P8-12A. Lump-sum basket purchase of long-term assets, depreciation, and disposal (*Learning Objectives 2, 3, 4, & 5*) 30–35 min.

On July 1, 2015, Park and Kim, Ltd. purchased a factory, including factory building, land, machine, and fixtures, for $825,000. Park and Kim hired an appraiser to provide the appraisal value for each asset: building $600,000, land $120,000, machine $420,000, and fixtures $60,000. To prepare the factory for use in production, Park and Kim spent $21,250 to renovate the factory building and $5,250 to overhaul the machine. The following table shows the estimates and the method of depreciation for each of the assets:

	Method	Life	Residual Value
Building	Straight-Line	15 years	$13,750
Machine	Unit-of-Production	20,000 hours	10,000
Fixtures	Double-Declining	5 years	6,250

The machine was used 2,000 hours in 2015 and 3,000 hours in 2016.

Park and Kim had several transactions related to maintaining and upgrading the assets. On April 15, 2016, Park and Kim spent $1,200 to repair the fixtures, and on January 5, 2017, Park and Kim spent $49,500 to overhaul the engine. As a result, the total remaining machine hours were estimated at 21,000 hours. The machine was used 2,400 hours in 2017.

On January 2, 2018, Park and Kim sold the factory for $785,000.

Requirements

1. Apportion the cost of the factory on the basis of the appraisal value. Show your calculations.

2. Calculate the depreciation expense for each asset for 2015, 2016, and 2017:

	Building	Machine	Fixtures
2015			
2016			
2017			
Total			

3. Record all journal entries for 2015, 2016, and 2017. Park and Kim's year-end is December 31.

4. Record the sale of the factory on January 2, 2018.

PROBLEMS (GROUP B)

P8-1B. Long-term asset costs and partial year depreciation (*Learning Objectives 2 & 3*) 20–25 min.

Marsellus Manufacturing incurred the following costs in acquiring land, making land improvements, and constructing and furnishing a new building.

a.	Purchase price of four hectares of land	$206,000
b.	Additional dirt and earthmoving	8,400
c.	Fence around the boundary of the property	16,000
d.	Attorney fee for title search on the land	1,000
e.	Unpaid property taxes on the land to be paid by Marsellus	5,800
f.	Company signs at the front of the property	4,200
g.	Building permit for the building	1,200
h.	Architect's fee for the design of the building	20,100
i.	Labour to construct the building	526,000
j.	Materials used to construct the building	352,000
k.	Landscaping	6,700
l.	Parking lot and concrete walks	29,200
m.	Lights for the parking lot and walkways	11,180
n.	Salary of construction supervisor (85% to building; 15% to parking lot and concrete walks)	40,000
o.	Furniture for the building	106,000
p.	Transportation and installation of furniture	2,300

Marsellus Manufacturing depreciates buildings over 30 years, land improvements over 20 years, and furniture over 10 years, all on a straight-line basis with zero residual value.

Requirements

1. Set up columns for Land, Land Improvements, Building, and Furniture. Show how to account for each cost by listing the cost under the correct account. Determine the total cost of each asset.

2. All construction was complete and the assets were placed in service on November 1. Record partial-year depreciation for the year ended December 31.

P8-2B. Journalize long-term asset transactions (*Learning Objectives 2, 3, & 5*) 20–25 min.

Russell Freightway provides freight service. The company's statement of financial position includes Land, Buildings, and Motor-Carrier Equipment. Russell uses a separate accumulated depreciation account for each depreciable asset. During 2015, Russell Freightway completed the following transactions:

Jan 1	Traded in motor-carrier equipment with accumulated depreciation of $83,000 (cost of $136,000) for new equipment with a cash cost of $136,000. Russell received a trade-in allowance of $63,000 on the old equipment and paid the remainder in cash.
Jul 1	Sold a building that cost $565,000 and had accumulated depreciation of $265,000 through December 31 of the preceding year. Depreciation is computed on a straight-line basis. The building has a 40-year useful life and a residual value of $45,000. Russell received $90,000 cash and a $620,000 note receivable.
Oct 31	Purchased land and a building for a cash payment of $400,000. An independent appraisal valued the land at $139,500 and the building at $310,500.
Dec 31	Recorded depreciation as follows: New motor-carrier equipment has an expected useful life of 1 million kilometres and an estimated residual value of $24,000. Depreciation method is the units-of-production method. During the year, Russell drove the truck 180,000 kilometres. Depreciation on buildings is straight-line. The new building has a 40-year useful life and a residual value equal to $20,000.

Requirement

1. Record the transactions in Russell Freightway's journal. (Round your depreciation expense to the nearest whole dollar.)

P8-3B. Capitalize long-term asset costs and several depreciation methods (*Learning Objectives 2, 3, & 9*) 20–25 min.

On January 7, Red Tucker, Inc. paid $254,700 for equipment used in manufacturing automotive supplies. In addition to the basic purchase price, the company paid $500 transportation charges, $300 insurance for the equipment while in transit, $12,000 sales tax, and $2,500 for a special platform on which to place the equipment in the plant. Red Tucker, Inc. management estimates that the equipment will remain in service for five years and have a residual value of $30,000. The equipment will produce 60,000 units the first year, with annual production decreasing by 5,000 units during each of the next four years (i.e., 55,000 units in year 2, 50,000 units in year 3, and so on for a total of 250,000 units). In trying to decide which depreciation method to use, Red Tucker, Inc. requested a depreciation schedule for each of the three depreciation methods (straight-line, units-of-production, and double-declining-balance).

Requirements

1. For each depreciation method, prepare a depreciation schedule showing asset cost, depreciation expense, accumulated depreciation, and asset book value. For the units-of-production method, round depreciation per unit to three decimal places.

2. Prepare the statement of financial position disclosure for Red Tucker's equipment at December 31 of the first year.

P8-4B. Disposing of an asset (*Learning Objective 5*) 15–20 min.

Mackay Industries had a piece of equipment that cost $32,000 and had accumulated depreciation of $28,000.

Requirement

1. Record the disposition of the equipment assuming the following independent situations:

   a. Mackay discarded the equipment receiving $0.

   b. Mackay sold the equipment for $6,000 cash.

c. Mackay traded the equipment in on a new piece of equipment costing $35,000. Mackay was granted a $5,000 trade-in allowance for the old equipment and paid the difference in cash.

d. Mackay traded the equipment in on a new piece of equipment costing $25,000. Mackay was granted a $3,000 trade-in allowance for the old equipment and signed a note payable for the difference.

P8-5B. Goodwill (*Learning Objective* 6) 15–20 min.

Tico's Restaurants acquired Tin Bus Diners. The financial records of Tin Bus Diners included the following:

Book Value of Assets	$2,300,000
Market Value of Assets	2,750,000
Liabilities	2,250,000

Requirements

1. Make the journal entry to record Tico's Restaurants' purchase of Tin Bus Diners for $3,200,000 cash, including any goodwill.

2. How should Tico's Restaurants account for this goodwill after acquiring Tin Bus Diners? Explain in detail.

P8-6B. Depletion (*Learning Objective* 7) 20–25 min.

Airheart Oil Company's statement of financial position includes three assets: natural gas, oil, and coal. Suppose Airheart Oil Company paid $1,900,000 cash for the right to work a mine with an estimated 200,000 tonnes of coal. Assume the company paid $68,000 to remove unwanted buildings from the land and $45,000 to prepare the surface for mining. Further, assume that Airheart Oil Company signed a $33,000 note payable to a company that will return the land surface to its original condition after the mining ends. During the first year, Airheart Oil Company removed 41,000 tonnes of coal, which it sold on account for $36 per tonne. Operating expenses for the first year totalled $248,000, all paid in cash.

Requirements

1. Record all of Airheart Oil Company's transactions, including depletion, for the year.

2. Prepare the company's income statement for its coal operations for the year.

P8-7B. Lump-sum basket purchase of long-term assets (*Learning Objective* 2) 20–25 min.

On May 1, Chippewa Brewery, Ltd. purchased a bottling factory including land and equipment for $920,000. Chippewa paid legal fees of $20,000, renovation costs on the building of $38,000, and the $18,000 cost of overhauling the equipment. The appraisal value for the land was $300,000, for the building was $780,000, and for the equipment was $120,000.

Chippewa estimated that the building's useful life was 20 years with a residual value of $16,000 and that the equipment would produce 2,000,000 bottles of beer, with a residual value of $2,000. Chippewa uses the straight-line method to depreciate buildings and the units-of-production method to depreciate equipment. Chippewa's year-end is December 31. The equipment produced 350,000 bottles for the first year and 420,000 bottles for the second year.

Requirements

1. Apportion the cost of the factory on the basis of the appraised value. Show your calculations.

2. Record the journal entry for the purchase of the factory, land, and machine.

3. Record the adjusting entry for the depreciation for the first year.

4. What would be the carrying value of the asset at the end of the first year and the second year?

P8-8B. Changes in estimates and disposal (*Learning Objectives 3 & 5*) **20–25 min.**

On July 1, 2015, Yama Inc.'s ledger shows its capital assets at $144,000 (at cost) and accumulated depreciation of $55,000. When the capital assets were purchased, Yama estimated that their useful life would be seven years. On October 1, 2015, Yama paid $26,000 for additional investment on the capital assets, and as a result, it estimated its residual value had increased from $4,000 to $8,000, and the useful life had increased by two years. Yama uses straight-line amortization. On April 1, 2017, Yama sold these capital assets for $60,000. Yama's year-end date is June 30.

Requirements

1. What was the age of the capital assets? What was the annual depreciation amount?
2. Prepare the journal entry to record the betterment.
3. Prepare the adjusting entry for the depreciation expense at the end of the year.
4. What is the impact on the income statement after the betterment has been completed?
5. Prepare the journal entry to record the disposal of the capital assets.

P8-9B. Natural resources and depletion (*Learning Objective 7*) **20–25 min.**

TinTin Mining (TTM) purchased a mineral deposit for $2,480,000 in June 2015. In July, TTM spent $120,000 to prepare for the exploitation. The mineral deposit was ready for exploitation on August 1. TTM estimated $1,300,000 ounces of minerals could be economically extracted and sold. On January 2, 2017, TTM spent $62,000 for further development. As a result, TTM estimated an additional 121,000 ounces of minerals could be extracted and sold. The amount of minerals extracted for 2015, 2016, and 2017 are as follows:

Year	Ounces
2015	65,000
2016	156,000
2017	180,000

Requirements

1. Calculate the acquisition cost of the mineral deposit and record the journal entry for the acquisition in 2015.
2. Record the journal entries for the depletion expense for 2015 and 2016.
3. What is the carrying value for the mineral deposit on December 31, 2016?
4. Record the journal entry for additional development costs in 2017.
5. Calculate the depletion expense for 2017 and record the journal entry for the depletion on December 31, 2017.

P8-10B. Disposal of assets (*Learning Objective 5*) **25–30 min.**

Aslam Manufacturing Ltd. has three assets. Aslam's year-end is June 30. The assets' costs, estimated residual value, useful life, and their carrying value on July 1, 2015, are listed in the following table:

	Cost	Residual Value	Useful Life	Carrying Value
Machine 1	$228,000	$ 4,000	7	$ 52,000
Machine 2	426,000	12,000	12	210,375
Machine 3	332,000	8,000	9	161,000

During 2015, Aslam completed the following transactions related to asset retirement:

Aug 1	Sold Machine 2 for $200,000; received $50,000 cash and an interest-bearing (6%) note receivable for the remainder, due on July 31, 2016.
Dec 31	Sold Machine 1 for $50,000 cash.
Feb 2, 2016	The engine of Machine 3 broke down and was determined irreparable. The insurance company agreed to compensation of $120,000 and sent a cheque for $20,000 and a note receivable for the remaining $100,000, due on February 28, 2016.

Requirements

1. What is the age of each asset on July 1, 2015?
2. Prepare all journal entries related to the disposal of each of the assets in 2015 and 2016.
3. What is the total gain or loss from the disposal of these three assets?

P8-11B. Journalize long-term asset transactions (*Learning Objectives 2, 3, & 5*) 25–30 min.

On July 1, 2015, Seto, Inc. purchased a fire extinguisher system for $130,000 from MTI Systems. The fire extinguisher system had an estimated life of 15 years and residual value of $2,800. Seto paid $4,500 for shipping and insurance, and hired an engineering company to install and set up the fire extinguisher system for $12,500. MTI asked for $80,000 cash payment upon purchase, $10,000 is due on July 31, 2015, with a 2% discount if Seto makes the payment by July 10, and a $40,000 one-year note payable plus 6% interest due on June 30, 2016. Seto paid the invoice on July 31. Seto uses the straight-line depreciation method.

On January 1, 2017, Seto replaced a valve component costing $38,700, and as a result, the useful life of the fire extinguisher system increased by three years.

On September 3, 2018, the fire extinguisher system was destroyed by a factory fire. Seto made a claim to the insurance company. Subsequently, Seto received $125,000 cash on September 30, 2018.

Requirements

1. Calculate the acquisition cost of the fire extinguisher system.
2. Prepare all journal entries for 2015, 2016, 2017, and 2018.

P8-12B. Lump-sum basket purchase of long-term assets, depreciation, and disposal (*Learning Objectives 2, 3, 4, & 5*) 30–35 min.

On April 1, 2015, KD Candies, Ltd. purchased a candy factory, including a building, computer system, and equipment for $550,000. KD Candies hired an appraiser to provide the appraisal value for each asset: building $350,000, computer system $150,000, and equipment $125,000. To prepare the factory for use in production, KD Candies spent $30,000 to renovate the factory facilities, $23,000 to upgrade the computer system, and $25,000 to upgrade the equipment. The following table shows the estimates and the method of depreciation for each of the assets:

	Method	Life	Residual Value
Building	Straight-Line	12 years	$14,000
Computer System	Double-Declining	5 years	5,000
Equipment	Units-of-Production	25,000 hours	15,000

The machine was used 3,800 hours in 2015 and 5,200 hours in 2016.

KD Candies had several transactions related to maintaining and upgrading the assets. On July 1, 2016, KD Candies spent $6,500 to upgrade the computer system, and on January 5, 2017, KD Candies spent $13,200 to upgrade the equipment. As a result, the total remaining machine hours were estimated at 20,000 hours. The machine was used 6,500 hours.

On January 2, 2018, KD Candies sold the factory for $350,000.

Requirements

1. Apportion the cost of the factory on the basis of the appraisal value. Show your calculations.

2. Calculate the depreciation expense for each asset for 2015, 2016, and 2017:

	Building	Computer System	Equipment
2015			
2016			
2017			
Total			

3. Record all journal entries for 2015, 2016, and 2017. KD Candies' year-end is December 31.

4. Record the sale of the factory on January 2, 2018.

PROBLEMS (ALTERNATES 1, 2, AND 3)

These alternative problem sets are available for your practice benefit on **MyAccountingLab**.

CONTINUING EXERCISE

This exercise continues our accounting for Graham's Yard Care, Inc. from previous chapters. In this exercise, we will account for the annual depreciation expense for Graham's Yard Care, Inc. In the Continuing Exercise in Chapter 2 we learned that Graham's Yard Care, Inc. had purchased a lawn mower and a weed whacker on June 3 and that they were expected to last four years.

Requirements

1. Calculate the annual depreciation expense amount for each asset assuming both assets are using straight-line depreciation for both assets.

2. Record the entry for the partial year's depreciation for 2015. Date it December 31, 2015. Assume that no depreciation has been recorded yet in 2015.

CONTINUING PROBLEM

This problem continues our accounting for Aqua Elite, Inc. from Chapter 7. During 2015, Aqua Elite made the following purchases:

- On May 3, Aqua Elite, Inc. purchased a copy machine for $4,700 cash. The copy machine has an estimated useful life of four years and no salvage value. Aqua Elite uses double-declining-balance depreciation for the copy machine.

- On May 18, Aqua Elite, Inc. purchased a $31,000 truck financed by a note payable bearing 8% annual interest. The truck has an estimated useful life of 200,000 kilometres and a residual value of $3,000. The truck was driven 28,000 kilometres in 2015 and is depreciated using the units-of-production method.

- On June 2, Aqua Elite, Inc. paid $15,000 for land.

- On June 22, $3,300 of furniture was purchased on account. The furniture has a five-year life and a residual value of $500. Furniture is depreciated using straight-line depreciation.

- On August 10, $1,200 of furniture was purchased. The furniture has a four-year life and no residual value, and is depreciated using straight-line depreciation.

- On September 1, Aqua Elite, Inc. purchased a building for $85,000 financed by a mortgage bearing 6% annual interest. The building has an estimated salvage value of $10,000 and is being depreciated over 25 years using the straight-line method.

Requirements

1. Calculate the depreciation expense as of December 31, 2015, for all assets purchased in 2015.

2. Assuming these are Aqua Elite's only assets, how will fixed assets be reflected on the statement of financial position at December 31, 2015?

APPLY YOUR KNOWLEDGE

ETHICS IN ACTION

Case 1. Larry Johnson owns Larry's Limousine, which operates a fleet of limousines and shuttle buses. Upon reviewing the most recent financial statements, he became confused over the recent decline in net income. He called his accountant and asked for an explanation. The accountant told Larry that the numerous repairs and maintenance expenses, such as oil changes, cleaning, and minor engine repairs, had totalled up to a large amount. Further, because several drivers were involved in accidents, the fleet insurance premiums had also risen sharply. Larry told his accountant to simply capitalize all the expenses related to the vehicles rather than expensing them. These capitalized repair costs could then be depreciated over the next 10 or 20 years. By capitalizing those expenses, the net income would be higher, as would property and equipment assets; therefore, both the income statement and statement of financial position would look better. His accountant, however, disagreed because the costs were clearly routine maintenance and because they did not extend the fleet's useful life. Larry then told his accountant that the estimated useful life of the vehicles needed to be changed from 5 years to 20 years to lower the amount of depreciation expense. His accountant responded that capitalizing costs that should be expensed and extending the estimated lives of assets just to increase the reported net income was unethical and wrong. Larry said that it was his business and, therefore, demanded that the financial statements be changed to show more net income. As a result, the accountant told Larry to pick up his files and find another accountant. What ethical concerns did the accountant have? If the total amount of repairs and maintenance were so large, couldn't a case be made that the amount should be capitalized? Is it unethical to change the estimated life of an asset? Was it unethical for the accountant to sever the business relationship? Do you have any suggestions?

Case 2. Table Corporation purchased Chairs Unlimited for $10 million. The fair market value of Chairs' net assets at the time was $8 million, so Table Corporation recorded $2 million of goodwill. Also included in the purchase was a patent valued at $1 million with an estimated remaining life of 10 years. To comply with accounting guidelines, the goodwill was not amortized, but the patent was amortized over the remaining 10-year life. However, the Chairs Unlimited business was not as profitable as anticipated and, as a result, the accountant for Table Corporation stated that the goodwill needed to be written off. Further, the accountant discovered that the remaining life of the patent was only 6 years and that it should be amortized over the remaining 6-year life rather than the 10-year life originally estimated. The CEO became concerned because these adjustments would cause net income to be extremely low for the year. As a result, he told the accountant to wait before writing off the goodwill because of the possibility that the purchase could be profitable in the future. Also, he argued, the life of the patent should be left alone because it was originally based upon what was thought to be a 10-year life. After much debate, the CEO then agreed with the accountant as long as the amount of goodwill was not completely written off in the current year. What ethical concerns are involved? Should the accountant change the amortizable life of an intangible asset? Should the accountant completely write off the goodwill account in the current year? Does the CEO's concern for higher net income create any ethical problems when the accountant agrees to not completely write off the goodwill? Do you have any other thoughts?

KNOW YOUR BUSINESS

Purpose: To help familiarize you with the financial reporting of a real company to further your understanding of the chapter material you are learning.

This case addresses the long-term assets of Bombardier Inc. The majority of these assets consist of tangible assets and intangible assets. In the text, you learned how most long-term tangible assets used in business are capitalized and depreciated over their estimated useful lives. Further, you learned that certain intangible assets are amortized over time while others are not. In this case, you will not only see and understand the classification and presentation of these assets, but also explore the methods used by Bombardier Inc. to depreciate and amortize them. Refer to Bombardier Inc.'s financial statements in MyAccountingLab. Also consider the information presented in Note 7, under the heading Property, Plant, and Equipment, and in Note 8 titled Intangible Assets.

Requirements

1. What were the balances of Property, Plant, and Equipment on December 31, 2012, and December 31, 2011? Did the amount of ending Property, Plant, and Equipment increase or decrease? Assume Bombardier Inc. removed fully depreciated equipment having a cost of $357 (million) in 2012. What effect would this have on the value of the Property, Plant, and Equipment balance? Explain your answer.

2. What kinds of tangible assets does Bombardier Inc. have? What kinds of intangible assets does Bombardier Inc. have? Which intangible assets are amortized by Bombardier Inc. and which are not? Why?

3. What was the percentage of tangible assets compared to the total assets on December 31, 2012? What was the percentage of tangible assets compared to the total assets on December 31, 2011? Did the percentage increase or decrease during the year?

4. What depreciation policies does Bombardier use for its Property, Plant, and Equipment? How much amortization was expensed during the year related to its property, plant, and equipment?

5. For the intangible assets, how much was internally generated and how much was the accumulated amortization during 2012?

Purpose: To help you understand and compare the performance of two companies in the same industry.

Find the Bombardier Annual Report, Year Ended December 31, 2012, located in MyAccountingLab and go to the Notes to Consolidated Financial Statements on page 145. Now access The Boeing Company's 2012 Annual Report. To do this from the internet, go to their webpage for the Investor Relations at http://www.boeing.com/companyoffices/financial/quarterly.htm and, under Annual Report, go to the 2012 Annual Report.

Requirement

1. Find the section in the notes for each company where the company discusses its Property, Plant, and Equipment, net. Also find the section where the company discusses Intangible Assets. Compare the two and note any major differences. Also examine the depreciation and amortization policies used by the two companies. What are some differences between these two companies related to these policies?

SMALL BUSINESS ANALYSIS

Purpose: To help you understand the importance of cash flows in the operation of a small business.

You've made an appointment to take your year-end financial statements down to the bank. You know that your banker is usually concerned about two things, your net income and the amount of cash you have. You are a little concerned because you know that your current year net income was down a little bit from the prior year. You figure that a significant cause for the decline was due to a large equipment purchase you made early in the year, which resulted in a lot of depreciation expense. However, as you look at your statement of financial position, it says that cash increased from last year to this year. That's a little puzzling, but you're hoping the banker can figure it out.

A couple of days later, you get a call from the banker. You're expecting him to tell you the bank won't be able to extend any more credit to you because your net income has declined. Imagine your surprise when he tells you how pleased he is with your financial performance this year, and that he doesn't anticipate any problems extending more credit to you. You want to know what he saw in your financial statements that you didn't see so you say to him, "Bob, thanks for the good news and the good report on my financial condition, even though our cash increased this year. I was afraid that the decline in our income might cause you some concern. How come it didn't?"

Requirement

1. What kind of response do you think that you might get from the banker regarding your net income as it relates to cash flow?

WRITTEN COMMUNICATION

A client of yours notified you that she just closed a deal to purchase an existing business. It's a pretty hefty purchase. As part of the purchase of the business, she received the land, the building, all the equipment, and the entire merchandise inventory of the company purchased. Your client emailed you a copy of the closing statement along with the breakdown of the purchase price shown below. In the email, your client expressed concern about how the $1,500,000 paid for the land and building should be accounted for. She also wanted to know the proper way to account for the merchandise inventory and the goodwill that was purchased.

Asset List	
Description	**Amount**
Land and Building	$1,500,000
Equipment	675,000
Inventory	425,000
Goodwill	1,400,000
Total Purchase Price	$4,000,000

Requirement

1. Prepare an email to your client explaining how the $1,500,000 should be allocated between the land and building as well as how the merchandise inventory and goodwill should be accounted for.

Self Check Answers
1. b 2. a 3. d 4. c 5. a 6. d 7. b 8. a 9. c 10. D

Appendix 8A

HOW ARE LEASED ASSETS ACCOUNTED FOR?

As mentioned earlier, some companies use assets that they don't own. This usually takes place through leasing. "A lease is an agreement whereby the **lessor** (the party who is providing the asset) conveys to the **lessee** (the party who is using the asset) in return for a payment or series of payments the right to use an asset for an agreed period of time."[1] There may or may not be an agreement to transfer the title to the lessee at the end of the lease agreement. Accounting for leases is a topic for intermediate accounting; in this appendix we just introduce the topic to get a sense of what it means and its effect on accounting.

L.O. ⑪ (Appendix 8A) Account for leases

Types of Leases

There are mainly two types of leases: a finance lease (sometime called a capital lease) or an operating lease. The main difference lies in who inherits the risks and rewards of using the asset. Determining whether a lease is an operating lease or a financial lease is critical since the accounting treatment of each differs substantially. However, this goes beyond the scope of this text.

Financial Leases

A financial lease is a lease that transfers substantially all of the risks and rewards of ownership of an asset to the lessee. Title may or may not eventually be transferred.[2] For example, a lot of airline companies lease their aircrafts or factories lease machines for a long period of time, almost covering the entire economic life of the asset. This situation is regarded as a financial lease because the lessee is using the asset as if it is its own property and for a period of time that covers almost the entire economic life of the asset. The lessee acquires the risks of using the asset and also the benefits from its returns. It is also liable to pay to the lessor a series of payments to cover the lease agreement. Such payments usually cover part of the lease liability in addition to an interest expense covering the financing costs (which are usually included in the payment amount).

From a lessee accounting perspective, such an asset would be recorded on the books of the lessee, and an equivalent liability (representing the future amounts to be paid to the lessor) would be added on the lessee statement of financial position. The lessee would also record depreciation expense for the asset. From a lessor accounting perspective, the lease would be recorded as a receivable at an amount equal to the net investment in the lease.

Exhibit 8A-1 illustrates the accounting effect of a financial lease agreement on both the lessee's and lessor's books at the commencement of the lease and then the payments in subsequent years.

---

[1]CICA Handbook, Part 1 International Financial Reporting Standards, The Canadian Institute of Chartered Accountants, 2013, page 524
[2]CICA Handbook, Part 1 International Financial Reporting Standards, The Canadian Institute of Chartered Accountants, 2013, page 524

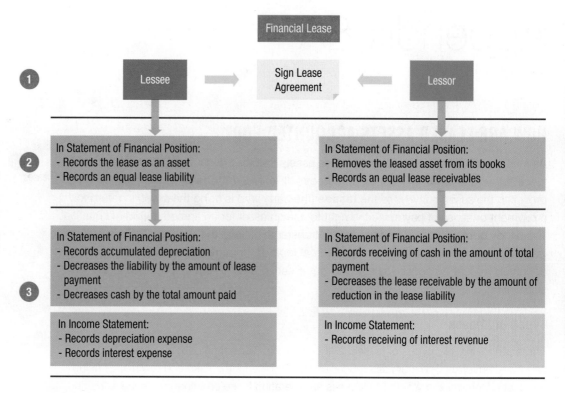

Exhibit 8A-1 ▲

The following illustrates how the periodic lease payment is divided between interest and the decrease in the amount of the lease from both a lessee and lessor perspective.

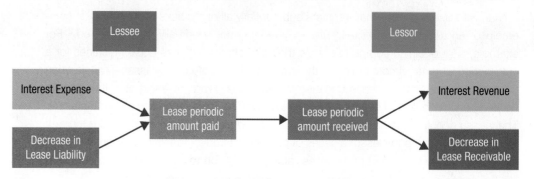

At the beginning of the lease, the lessee and lessor should sign a lease agreement that identifies the lease terms and the amount of each periodic payment. This agreement would determine whether this is a financial or an operating lease, the amount of annual deduction in the lease, and the amount of interest that would be recognized. (The method of determining such amounts is an issue that goes beyond the scope of this text.)

In a financial lease, the lessor would remove the asset from its books and replace it with a lease receivable. On the other hand, the lessee would record the lease as an asset and record an equivalent liability (lease liability). Usually, the amount of both the asset and its liability would be equivalent to the present value of the future periodic payments, which is based on the cost of the asset, the financing costs, and any other applicable charges.

In the following years, the lessee would pay the agreed-upon lease payment (thus reducing the lease liability) and interest expense (which appears on the income statement) to cover the cost of financing. It also records depreciation expense and shows the accumulated depreciation on the statement of financial position. On the other hand, the lessor would record the total cash amount received, decrease its Lease Receivables account by the amount of reduction in the lease on the statement of financial position, and add interest revenue to the income statement.

Operating Leases

An operating lease is any lease that is not considered a financial lease. Usually it covers a shorter period of time and the lessor still substantially shares the asset's risks and returns. An example would be leasing an aircraft to another airline company for three years.

From a lessee perspective, the lease payment will be recognized as an expense on a straight-line basis over the lease term unless another systematic basis is more representative of the time pattern of the user's benefit. The leased asset will not appear on the statement of financial position of the lessee.[3]

From a lessor perspective, the asset would appear in most cases on the statement of financial position as "assets held for operating leases" or according to the nature of the asset, while the lease income would be recognized on a straight-line basis over the lease term, unless another systematic basis is more representative of the time pattern in which the benefit derived from the leased asset is diminished.[4]

Exhibit 8A-2 illustrates the accounting effect of an operating lease on both the lessee's and lessor's books at the commencement of the lease and then the payments in subsequent years.

Exhibit 8A-2 ▲

In an operating lease situation, the lessor would keep the asset on its book and also record depreciation for the asset as it still retains the title of the asset. It will also record the periodic payments from the lessee as lease revenue. The lessee, on the other hand, will only record lease expense and will not record the asset on its books. This is sometimes called *off-balance sheet financing*, since the lessee will neither show the asset nor its liabilities on its statement of financial position.

It should be noted that most companies adopting IFRS will soon be required to treat most leases as financial leases.

---

[3]CICA Handbook, Part 1 International Financial Reporting Standards (International Accounting Standard 17.50), The Canadian Institute of Chartered Accountants, 2013, page 532

[4]CICA Handbook, Part 1 International Financial Reporting Standards (International Accounting Standard 17.50), The Canadian Institute of Chartered Accountants, 2013, page 535

CHAPTER 9

Current Liabilities and Long-Term Debt

▲ Photo Alto/Eric Audras/Getty Images

BUSINESS, ACCOUNTING, AND YOU

Best Buy has assets in the form of cash, accounts receivable, inventory, land, and buildings—it takes a lot of assets to operate Best Buy! But how does Best Buy purchase or fund these assets? It takes money to make money.

Remember your accounting equation. Assets equal liabilities plus shareholders' equity. The owners of Best Buy, the shareholders, provide money. But Best Buy also uses money obtained with debt, called liabilities. Liabilities are amounts owed to lenders (like a bank) or other creditors (like a supplier).

By agreement, some liabilities need to be paid quickly. Suppliers deliver inventory to Best Buy with the understanding that Best Buy will pay the supplier within 30 to 60 days. Employees provide labour to Best Buy believing that they will be paid within a few weeks. But by agreement, some liabilities are paid over long periods of time. Think about Best Buy spending millions of dollars to build a store. If Best Buy borrows this money from a bank or other lender, it would probably want to repay that money over many years. That long period of time also means Best Buy will pay interest to the lender.

Understanding liabilities is important. Remember that if a business cannot pay its liabilities, it has taken too much risk and will fail. You need to know how accountants recognize, measure, record, and report liabilities. As an accountant or manager, you need to understand how and when a business borrows money and repays money.

WHAT IS THE DIFFERENCE BETWEEN KNOWN, ESTIMATED, AND CONTINGENT LIABILITIES AND PROVISIONS?

L.O. **1** Distinguish among known, estimated, and contingent liabilities and provisions

IFRS

ASPE

Both IFRS and ASPE have similar definitions of liabilities. Liabilities are the present obligations of an entity that arise from past events and require future settlement using the entity's resources. Liabilities can generally be broken down into three categories as follows:

- **Known liabilities:** The majority of a company's liabilities fall into this category. **Known liabilities** can be defined as known obligations of known amounts. In other words, the business knows that it owes something and it knows how much it owes. Examples of known liabilities include accounts payable, notes payable, unearned revenues, and accrued liabilities such as interest or taxes payable.

- **Estimated liabilities:** An **estimated liability** is defined as a known obligation of an unknown amount. A business will sometimes encounter a situation where it knows that a liability exists but it does not know the exact amount of the liability. In these situations, the amount of the liability must be estimated. A typical example is estimated warranties payable, which is common for companies that manufacture or sell products; for example, General Motors presented on its statement of financial position dated December 31, 2012, an estimated warranty liability of $2.1 million.

- **Contingent liabilities and provisions: Contingent liabilities** and **provisions** are unique liabilities that differ from all other types of liabilities. These liabilities arise because of a *past* event, but they are dependent upon the outcome of a *future* event. In other words, whether or not a company has an obligation depends upon the result of an event that has not yet occurred. In addition, the amount of a contingent liability may be either known or unknown. Current or pending litigation is an example of a contingent liability; for example, British American Tobacco disclosed the possibility of paying contingencies representing possible damages and health care cost recovery in different provinces in the notes of its 2013 financial statements.

As we learned in Chapter 2, a liability is classified as a current liability if the related obligation will be settled within one year or an operating cycle, whichever is longer. All liabilities not classified as current liabilities are classified as long-term debt. It is possible for known, unknown, or contingent liabilities and provisions to be classified as either current or long term. We will begin our discussion of accounting for liabilities by looking at current liabilities of a known amount.

HOW DO YOU ACCOUNT FOR CURRENT LIABILITIES OF A KNOWN AMOUNT?

L.O. **2** Account for current liabilities of a known amount

A large portion of liabilities for most companies will be made up of known liabilities that are due within one fiscal year. In the following paragraphs, we will learn how to account for the majority of the types of current liabilities of a known amount that most companies are likely to encounter.

ACCOUNTS PAYABLE

As we have learned in previous chapters, amounts owed for purchases on account are known as accounts payable. Since accounts payable are typically due in 30 to 45 days, they are classified as current liabilities. The largest portion of accounts payable for most merchandising companies is related to the purchase of inventory on account. Merchandising and service businesses also incur accounts payable when they purchase items such as supplies, electricity, or telephone service on account. Accounts payable transactions are recorded by debiting the related asset or expense account and crediting Accounts Payable. For example, assume that Mackay Industries receives a utility bill for $680. The bill represents prior electricity usage and is not due for 30 days. Mackay Industries would record the receipt of the bill as follows:

DATE	ACCOUNTS	POST REF.	DR.	CR.
	Utilities Expense		680	
	Accounts Payable			680
	Record utility bill due in 30 days.			

When Mackay Industries pays the utility bill, it will record the payment on account as follows:

DATE	ACCOUNTS	POST REF.	DR.	CR.
	Accounts Payable		680	
	Cash			680
	Record payment on account.			

NOTES PAYABLE

When a business borrows money, usually from a financial institution, the signing of a promissory note is generally required. Businesses also often finance purchases of long-term assets through the use of notes payable. Any note payable that must be paid within one year from the statement of financial position date is classified as a current liability. All notes not classified as a current liability are classified as long-term debt (discussed later in the chapter).

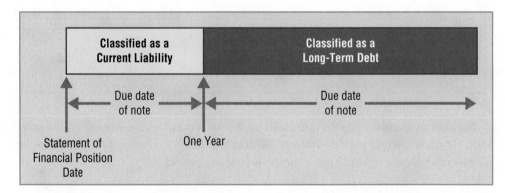

In Chapter 7 we learned about promissory notes when we studied notes receivable. The terms and concepts we learned about then will also apply to notes payable. However, we are now learning about the promissory note transaction from the opposite perspective. To illustrate a note payable, assume that on September 1, 2015, Mackay Industries borrows $8,000 from First National Bank on a nine-month, 6% note payable. Mackay Industries would record the transaction as follows on September 1:

DATE	ACCOUNTS	POST REF.	DR.	CR.
Sep 1, 2015	Cash		8,000	
	Notes Payable			8,000
	Record 6%, nine-month note.			

At December 31, 2015, it is necessary for Mackay Industries to accrue interest expense for the four months from September to December. The accrued interest is recorded as follows:

Assets	=	Liabilities	+	Shareholders' Equity
	=	+160		−160

DATE	ACCOUNTS	POST REF.	DR.	CR.
Dec 31, 2015	Interest Expense		160*	
	Interest Payable			160
	Accrue four months' interest expense.			

*$160 = ($8,000 × 0.06 × 4/12)

The interest accrual at December 31, 2015, allocated $160 of the interest on this note to 2015. The remaining $200 ($8,000 × 0.06 × 5/12) of interest expense on this note will be allocated to 2016 at the time the note is paid off as follows:

Assets	=	Liabilities	+	Shareholders' Equity
−8,360	=	−8,000		−200
		−160		

DATE	ACCOUNTS	POST REF.	DR.	CR.
Jun 1, 2016	Notes Payable		8,000	
	Interest Payable		160	
	Interest Expense		200	
	Cash			8,360
	Repay 6%, nine-month note.			

Notice that the $160 debit to Interest Payable zeros out the amount that was accrued in the liability account at December 31, 2015. The $8,000 debit to Notes Payable removes the note from Mackay Industries' books. The $200 debit to Interest Expense records the interest expense for 2016. In addition, the $8,360 credit to Cash reflects the payment of the entire maturity value of the note. If the term of the note had not spanned the end of the period, no adjusting entry to accrue interest would have been necessary. If this had been the case for Mackay Industries in the previous example, the final entry to repay the note would look like this:

Assets	=	Liabilities	+	Shareholders' Equity
−8,360	=	−8,000		−360

DATE	ACCOUNTS	POST REF.	DR.	CR.
	Notes Payable		8,000	
	Interest Expense		360	
	Cash			8,360
	Repay 6%, nine-month note.			

Notice that Interest Expense is debited for the full amount of the interest on the note, $360. There is also no debit to Interest Payable because no interest had been accrued on the note (since it did not span over the end of the period).

SALES TAX PAYABLE

Most provinces levy harmonized sales tax (HST) or provincial sales tax (PST), and goods and services tax (GST) on retail sales. Retailers collect the sales tax from their customers in addition to the price of the item sold. The sales tax collected must then be remitted, or paid, to the Canada Revenue Agency (CRA) on a periodic basis, usually monthly or quarterly. Sales Tax Payable is a current liability because the retailer must pay the CRA in less than a year. Let's apply this to Mackay Industries.

Suppose December's taxable sales for Mackay Industries totalled $22,000. Assume that Mackay Industries is required to collect an additional 13% of sales tax (HST), which would equal $2,860 ($22,000 × 0.13). Mackay Industries would record December sales as follows:

DATE	ACCOUNTS	POST REF.	DR.	CR.
	Accounts Receivable or Cash		24,860	
	Sales Revenue			22,000
	HST Payable			2,860
	Record December sales.			

+24,860 = +2,860 +22,000

To determine how much needs to be paid to the CRA for the HST collected, Mackay Industries also needs to incorporate the amount of HST that Mackay has paid out on purchases. The amount of HST paid on purchases (HST receivable) is deducted from the amount of HST collected from customers to determine the amount that needs to be remitted to the government. Assume that Mackay Industries paid $13,200 for merchandise in the same period as the sales recorded above, and also paid 13% HST. Mackay Industries would record the December purchase as follows:

9.1 STILL DON'T GET IT?
Visit MyAccountingLab for an alternate explanation of this important accounting concept.

DATE	ACCOUNTS	POST REF.	DR.	CR.
	Inventory		13,200	
	HST Receivable		1,716	
	Accounts Payable			14,916
	Record December inventory purchases.			

+13,200 = +14,916
+1,716

The entry recorded when Mackay Industries remits the HST to the government looks like this:

DATE	ACCOUNTS	POST REF.	DR.	CR.
	HST Payable		2,860	
	HST Receivable (Paid on Purchases)			1,716
	Cash			1,144
	Remit HST.			

−1,716 = −2,860
−1,144

ACCRUED EXPENSES (ACCRUED LIABILITIES)

In Chapter 3, we learned that an accrued expense is any expense that has been incurred but has not yet been paid. That's why accrued expenses are also called accrued liabilities. Most businesses will often have accrued liabilities for one or more of the following:

- Interest
- Salaries and wages
- Payroll
- Income taxes

Payroll liabilities are employee deductions withheld by employers, such as Canada Pension Plan (CPP), employment insurance (EI), and employee income tax. Employers must remit these deductions to the appropriate government agencies. In addition, if employees participate in any additional benefits, such as pension plans, union dues, or extended health plans, then the employers have to deduct these fees and remit them to the appropriate agencies.

So, in addition to salaries expense, employers also incur employee benefits expenses, which include employers' contributions to CPP, EI, private pension plans, extended health plans, etc. Employers have to pay CPP contributions in the same amount as the employees' deduction, but must pay 1.4 times the EI contribution of employees. For example, in December, Mackay Industries' gross pay, or salaries expense, was $10,000. Mackay Industries would make two transactions to record (1) salaries expense and payroll deductions, and (2) employee benefits expense and payroll payable:

DATE	ACCOUNTS	POST REF.	DR.	CR.
	Salaries Expense		10,000	
	CPP Payable – Employees			495
	EI Payable – Employees			175
	Income Taxes Payable			2,500
	Union Dues Payable			25
	Salaries Payable			6,805
	To record payroll and employee deductions for the month of December.			

DATE	ACCOUNTS	POST REF.	DR.	CR.
	Employee Benefits Expense		740	
	CPP Payable – Employer			495
	EI Payable – Employer			245*
	To record employer's payroll costs for the month of December.			

*175 × 1.4 = 245

Suppose Mackay Industries remits the payroll payable to the Canada Revenue Agency (CRA) on January 15. It would record the following entry:

DATE	ACCOUNTS	POST REF.	DR.	CR.
	CPP Payable – Employees		495	
	CPP Payable – Employer		495	
	EI Payable – Employees		175	
	EI Payable – Employer		245	
	Income Taxes Payable		2,500	
	Cash			3,910
	To record December payroll payable remittance to CRA.			

Notice that the union dues payable is not included in the payment to the CRA. The union dues payable will be paid to the employees' union organization, which is separate from the CRA. It is worth noting that CPP and EI deductions from the employees' paycheques are the employees' expense, while the employer portion of CPP and EI is the employer's payroll expense, in addition to the salaries expense.

Accrued liabilities are recorded by debiting the related expense account and crediting a liability account. For example, the entry to record $7,000 of accrued corporate income tax would be as follows:

DATE	ACCOUNTS	POST REF.	DR.	CR.
	Corporate Income Tax Expense		$7,000	
	Corporate Income Tax Payable			$7,000
	Record accrued income tax expense.			

UNEARNED REVENUES

As we saw in Chapter 3, unearned revenues, also called deferred revenues, arise when a business receives cash in advance of providing goods or services. As a result, the business has an obligation to provide goods or services to the customer in the future. Unearned revenues are typically classified as current liabilities because customers do not usually pay for more than one year's worth of goods or services in advance.

CURRENT PORTION OF LONG-TERM DEBT

Many long-term debt obligations (discussed later in the chapter) are paid in instalments. The principal amount of these obligations, due within one year from the statement of financial position date, is referred to as **current portion of long-term debt**. Because it is due within one year from the statement of financial position date, the current portion of long-term debt is classified as a current liability on the statement of financial position. Let's assume that Mackay Industries signs a $30,000, 6% note payable on June 1, 2015. The note requires that annual instalments of $6,000, plus interest, be paid on June 1 of each of the next five years. On Mackay Industries' December 31, 2015, statement of financial position, what amount will be reflected as the current portion of long-term debt? Because the $6,000 payment that is due on June 1, 2016, is due within one year from the statement of financial position date, it will be classified as the current portion of long-term debt. The remaining $24,000 ($30,000 − $6,000) will be classified as long term.

 CONCEPT CHECK...

Jill and Alan both work in the accounting department of a large retail business that has a significant amount of long-term debt. Jill was commenting to Alan how important it is to ensure that the current portion of the company's long-term debt be properly classified as such on the statement of financial position. Alan argued that it really didn't matter how the debt was classified as long as the correct total amount of debt was included somewhere on the statement of financial position. Is Alan's point of view correct?

Answer: No, Jill's point of view is correct. In Chapter 5 we learned that the current ratio is one of the most widely used tools investors, creditors, and suppliers use to evaluate a company's ability to pay its obligations as they come due. So, even though a company includes the correct amount of total liabilities on the statement of financial position, if the liabilities are not properly classified as current versus long term, the current ratio will not be correct. As a result, investors, creditors, and suppliers will be unable to correctly assess the ability of a business to pay its obligations as they come due. Therefore, it is important for a business to analyze all of its long-term debt at the end of each accounting period to ensure that it is being properly classified as current versus long-term.

HOW DO YOU ACCOUNT FOR CURRENT LIABILITIES OF AN UNCERTAIN AMOUNT?

A business may know that a liability exists but not know the exact amount of the liability. It cannot simply ignore the liability. The liability must be reported on the statement of financial position. Although there are other types of estimated liabilities, the most common example occurs when a company guarantees its products or services against

L.O. ❸   Account for liabilities of an uncertain amount

defects under a **warranty** agreement. Therefore, we will focus our attention on accounting for estimated warranties.

ESTIMATED WARRANTY LIABILITY

It is common for companies to provide either 90-day or 1-year warranties on the goods or services they provide. When a sale is made, it is reasonable to assume that there is a potential for a warranty claim to be made. Without recognizing this potential expense (and liability), the financial statements will not accurately reflect the true nature of the sale. The expense, therefore, is incurred when sales are made, not when warranty claims are settled. At the time of sale, the company does not know how many warranty claims will be filed. Therefore, the amount of warranty expense for a period is unknown and must be estimated.

Assume that Mackay Industries makes sales on account of $75,000 during the month of August and that Mackay Industries extends its customers a 90-day warranty on all products sold. Mackay Industries estimates that its products will require warranty repairs at a rate of 2% of the sales amounts. The company would record sales and warranty expense for the month of August as follows:

DATE	ACCOUNTS	POST REF.	DR.	CR.
	Accounts Receivable		75,000	
	Sales Revenue			75,000
	Record monthly sales.			
	Warranty Expense		1,500	
	Estimated Warranty Payable			1,500
	Record estimated warranty expense.			

Now assume that during September Mackay Industries paid $450 to settle warranty claims filed by customers. Mackay would make the following entry to record payment of the warranty claims:

DATE	ACCOUNTS	POST REF.	DR.	CR.
	Estimated Warranty Payable		450	
	Cash			450
	Settled warranty claims.			

If, instead of paying cash to settle the warranty claims, Mackay Industries had replaced the defective goods with new items, the entry would have been as follows:

DATE	ACCOUNTS	POST REF.	DR.	CR.
	Estimated Warranty Payable		450	
	Inventory			450
	Settled warranty claims.			

Estimated liabilities are generally current liabilities. However, if the estimated liability is expected to be settled more than one year from the statement of financial position date, it would be classified as long term.

DECISION GUIDELINES

DECISION		GUIDELINE		ANALYZE
What should I do if I do not know the exact amount of a liability?		Use professional judgment and estimate the amount.		To properly reflect the true financial position and the results of operations of a company, it is important that all obligations of the business be recorded. When the exact amount of a liability is unknown, an estimate of the amount owed should be made. It is important to use professional judgment to estimate a reasonable amount.
My company started a warranty program for its products last year. I started getting some products back for maintenance. What should I do to represent the real economic situation on the financial statements?		Consider forming an estimated warranty expense and liability.		To have an accurate matching between revenues and expenses, estimated future maintenance costs for products that have been sold in the current period must be expensed within the current period too. A liability is formed and it decreases when such products use the maintenance service in the future.

HOW DO YOU ACCOUNT FOR CONTINGENT LIABILITIES AND PROVISIONS?

L.O. **4** Account for contingent liabilities and provisions

IFRS

ASPE

As stated earlier, although contingent liabilities and provisions arise as the result of a past event, they are dependent upon the outcome of a future event. Therefore, contingent liabilities or provisions represent potential, rather than actual, obligations.

There are differences in terminology used between IFRS and ASPE. Under IFRS, a *provision* is a liability that has uncertain timing or an uncertain amount, while a *contingent liability* is a possible obligation that will be confirmed by uncertain future events. Under ASPE, there is no specific definition for provisions. A contingency is an uncertain situation that will involve a possible gain or loss to a company. The outcome of the future event will determine whether or not a company will incur an obligation. Examples of contingent liabilities are as follows:

- Pending, or actual, legal action
- Potential fines resulting from investigations conducted by regulatory agencies
- Loan guarantees that occur when one entity co-signs a note payable for another entity

One example of a provision is an asset retirement obligation. Companies may be required to clean up pollution, or remove or dismantle an asset at the end of its useful life. This is a present obligation and will require future outflow of resources to fulfil the obligation; however, the timing and the amount of resources required is uncertain.

Suppose Mackay Industries guarantees a note for Tucker Enterprises. If Tucker Enterprises fails to pay the note when it comes due, Mackay Industries would be obligated to pay the amount due. This represents a contingent liability to Mackay Industries. Although Mackay Industries cosigned the note (a past event), it will only incur an obligation if Tucker Enterprises fails to pay the note (the future event).

The accounting treatment of a contingent liability or a provision depends on the likelihood of an actual obligation occurring. **Exhibit 9-1** outlines the accounting treatment of contingent liabilities.

Likelihood of Obligation Occurring	Accounting Treatment
Remote (very unlikely)	No action is necessary.
Possible (it could occur)	Disclose the existence of the contingent liability in the financial statement notes. An explanation of the circumstances related to the contingent liability should be included in the note.
Probable (more likely than not)	If the amount of the potential obligation is known (or can be reasonably estimated), the contingent liability should be recorded. The circumstances related to the contingent liability should also be disclosed in the financial statement notes.
	If the amount of the obligation is not known and cannot be reasonably estimated, then only note disclosure is required.

Exhibit 9-1 ▲

Exhibit 9-2 shows the comparison of the measurement and accounting treatment of contingent liabilities and provisions under IFRS and ASPE.

Exhibit 9-2 ▲

Let's return to our earlier example of the loan guarantee. As long as Tucker Enterprises is in sound financial condition, the likelihood of Mackay Industries being required to pay the loan is remote and, therefore, no action is required. If Mackay Industries becomes aware of the fact that Tucker Enterprises is experiencing financial difficulties, it is now possible that Mackay Industries will be obligated to repay the loan. In this case, Mackay Industries would be required to disclose the contingent liability in the notes to its financial statements. If Tucker Enterprises files for bankruptcy or defaults on the loan, it is probable that Mackay Industries will be obligated to repay the loan. Now, in addition to disclosing the contingent liability in the financial statement notes, Mackay Industries will have to record the contingent liability in the financial statements. The contingent liability would be recorded by debiting a loss account and crediting a liability account. Contingent liabilities and provisions are classified as current versus long-term based upon when the liability is expected to be paid.

CRITICAL THINKING

Take a minute to think about each of the following cases. What is the appropriate accounting treatment for each case—report a liability on the financial statement, recognize a provision, or not report the situation? What is the impact on the company's financial statements?

Cases	Accounting Treatment	Impact on Financial Statements
1. Star Café sells hot beverages. The owner of Star Café is concerned about the hot temperature of the hot beverages that it sells. She is wondering whether to book a $500,000 provision in the liability.		
2. DIT is a chemical company that sells pesticides. The auditor of DIT recently found that DIT has leaked a small quantity of the chemical in the nearby river. The cleanup of the chemical is likely to cost $1 million to $2 million.		
3. Dia Mine, Inc. mines diamonds. Under provincial law, the company must clean up any pollution at the end of operations. Current estimates indicate that the cleanup will cost up to $3 million.		

Solutions:

Cases	Accounting Treatment	Impact on Financial Statements
1. Star Café sells hot beverages. The owner of Star Café is concerned about the hot temperature of the hot beverages that it sells. She is wondering whether to book a $500,000 provision in the liability.	No Disclosure Required • No past event and no current obligation • No potential future outflow of assets due to past events and current obligations	No impact on the financial statements
2. DIT is a chemical company that sells pesticides. The auditor of DIT recently found that DIT has leaked a small quantity of the chemical in the near-by river. The cleanup of the chemical is likely to cost $1 million to $2 million.	Recognize • Past event—chemical leak—caused the current obligation to clean up the river • The future outflow of $1 million or $2 million is required	Expense and Provision will reduce income and increase liabilities
3. Dia Mine, Inc. mines diamonds. Under provincial law, the company must clean up any pollution at the end of operations. Current estimates indicate that the cleanup will cost up to $3 million.	Disclose • Dia Mine has not polluted the environment in the past. However, under provincial law the company will possibly have a cash outflow of up to $3 million.	No impact on the financial statements

HOW DO YOU ACCOUNT FOR LONG-TERM DEBT?

L.O. ⑤ Account for long-term debt

The long-term debt of most companies is comprised of the following types of obligations:

- Notes payable
- Bonds payable

There are many similarities in the accounting for these different obligations. However, there are also some unique differences. Therefore, we will examine each of the three separately.

NOTES PAYABLE

As discussed previously, a note payable is a debt obligation that is supported by a promissory note. Notes payable that are due to be repaid more than one year from the statement of financial position date are classified as long-term debt. Most long-term notes payable represent loans taken out for the purchase of land, buildings, or both that are repaid over a long-term period. A note payable used to purchase land or buildings is a special type of note called a **mortgage**. A mortgage is an example of a secured note because it gives the lender the right to take specified assets, called **collateral**, if the borrower is unable to repay the loan.

A mortgage is typically paid off through instalment payments that include both principal and interest. The entries required to record mortgage note transactions are similar to those for note payable transactions. Let's assume that Mackay Industries signed a $155,000, 8%, 20-year mortgage note on January 1, 2015, to finance the purchase of a new building. Payments of $7,831 on the mortgage will be made semi-annually on June 30 and December 31 of each year. The purchase of the building is recorded as follows:

Assets	=	Liabilities	+	Shareholders' Equity
+155,000	=	+155,000		

DATE	ACCOUNTS	POST REF.	DR.	CR.
Jan 1	Buildings		155,000	
	Mortgage Payable			155,000
	Issued mortgage to purchase building.			

ACCOUNTING IN YOUR WORLD

If you have ever borrowed money to purchase a car, then you probably know that you do not get the title to the car until the loan has been paid off. The vehicle title represents legal ownership of the vehicle. Lenders often secure car loans by using the car as collateral for the loan and placing a lien on the title. This means that the lender gets the title to the car (and has legal ownership of the car) until the loan is repaid. If the borrower fails to repay the loan, the lender has the right to repossess, or take back, the car to compensate it for the unpaid loan. Once the loan has been repaid, the lender will release the lien on the title by "signing it over" to the borrower. This transfers legal ownership of the car to the borrower.

Echo/Cultura/Getty Images

In order to keep track of the portion of each payment that is allocated to principal and to interest, an amortization schedule is usually prepared. **Exhibit 9-3** illustrates an amortization schedule for the first four years of Mackay Industries' mortgage.

Date	A Payment	B Interest (D × .08 × 1/2)*	C Principal (A − B)	D Loan Balance (D − C)
1/01/2015				$155,000
6/30/2015	$7,831	$6,200	$1,631	153,369
12/31/2015	7,831	6,135	1,696	151,673
6/30/2016	7,831	6,067	1,764	149,909
12/31/2016	7,831	5,996	1,835	148,074
6/30/2017	7,831	5,923	1,908	146,166
12/31/2017	7,831	5,847	1,984	144,182
6/30/2018	7,831	5,767	2,064	142,118
12/31/2018	7,831	5,685	2,146	139,972

*Rounded

Column B is calculated by multiplying the loan balance from the prior period (column D) by the interest rate (8%) and then multiplying by 1/2 to account for the fact that the payment is made semiannually.

Column C is calculated by subtracting the interest (column B) from the payment (column A).

Column D is calculated by subtracting the principal portion of the payment (column C) from the loan balance from the prior period (column D).

Exhibit 9-3 ▲

Based on information found in Exhibit 9-3, Mackay Industries will record the June 30, 2015, loan payment as follows:

DATE	ACCOUNTS	POST REF.	DR.	CR.
Jun 30	Interest Expense		6,200	
	Mortgage Payable		1,631	
	Cash			7,831
	Record semiannual loan payment.			

Assets	=	Liabilities	+	Shareholders' Equity
−7,831	=	−1,631		−6,200

As discussed previously in the chapter, the principal portion of any mortgage payments due within one year from the statement of financial position date will be classified under the current portion of long-term debt on the statement of financial position.

BONDS PAYABLE

In addition to using notes payable to acquire needed cash, a business may obtain money by issuing **bonds payable**. Bonds payable are long-term, interest-bearing notes that are issued to multiple lenders, called bondholders. By issuing bonds, it is often possible for a business to borrow hundreds of thousands (or even millions) of dollars. Instead of depending on one large loan from a single bank or lender, with bonds, a large number of smaller amounts are borrowed from different investors. For example, Mackay Industries could raise $1,000,000 by borrowing $1,000 each from 1,000 different investors.

Before we move on, let's explore some of the terminology associated with bonds.

- **Term bonds** all mature at the same specified time. For example, $500,000 of term bonds may all mature 10 years from today. With term bonds, the company issuing the bonds will have to repay all $500,000 at the same time.

- **Serial bonds** are bonds from the same bond issuance that mature at different times. For example, a $1,500,000 serial bond issuance may specify that one-third of the bonds mature in 10 years, one-third mature in 15 years, and one-third mature in 20 years.
- **Secured bonds** are bonds that are backed with some form of collateral. Secured bonds give the bondholders the right to take specified assets of the issuer if the issuer fails to pay principal or interest.
- **Unsecured bonds** are bonds that are not backed by any assets. They are backed only by the general credit of the company issuing the bond. Unsecured bonds are also called **debentures**.
- **Convertible bonds** are bonds that give the bondholder the option of exchanging the bond for common shares in the company.
- **Callable bonds** are bonds that may be bought back and retired (called) by the bond issuer at a pre-arranged price.
- **Zero coupon bonds** are bonds issued at a price lower than the face value that do not pay interest during the bond's duration. However, the face value is paid in full at maturity. In other words, the amount of the discount represents the compounded interest of the bond that is paid at maturity.
- **Principal amount** is the amount the borrower must pay back to the bondholders on the maturity date. The principal amount is also called **maturity value**, or **par value**.
- **Maturity date** is the date on which the borrower must repay the principal amount to the bondholders.
- **Stated interest rate**, or coupon rate, determines the amount of cash interest the bond issuer pays each year. The stated interest rate is printed on the bond and *does not change* from year to year. For example, if a $1,000 bond has a stated interest rate of 9%, the bond issuer pays $90 of interest annually on the bond.
- **Market interest rate**, or yield, is the rate of interest a business is willing to pay for similar bonds of equal risk at the current time. Bonds are often issued with a stated interest rate that differs from the market interest rate. This is due to the time gap between when the stated rate is determined and when the bonds are actually issued.

Bond Prices

The price of a bond is determined mainly by the relationship between its interest rate and the market rate for an equal-risk investment at the time the bond is issued. Accordingly, a bond could be issued at its par (or face) value (which is the amount payable on the maturity date), at a **premium** (above par), or at a **discount** (below par). Regardless of the amount the company receives on the issuance date, on the maturity date, the company has to pay back the principal amount, or par value.

To illustrate, let's assume that Mackay Industries issues 6% bonds when the market rate for similar bonds of equal risk is higher, say 6.5%. Mackay Industries will have a hard time attracting investors to buy its bonds when investors can earn higher returns on bonds of other companies. Therefore, to attract investors, Mackay Industries will offer to sell its bonds at a price less than maturity value, or at a discount. So, for example, Mackay Industries may offer to sell its $1,000, 6% bonds for only $920 each. Mackay Industries will pay the investors annual interest payments equal to $60 ($1,000 par value $\times$ 6% stated interest) on each bond. However, because the investors only paid $920 for each bond, the $60 interest payment represents a return of approximately 6.5% ($60 interest/$920 invested).

On the other hand, if the market interest rate is 5.5%, for example, Mackay Industries' 6% bonds will be so attractive that investors will pay more than maturity value, or a premium, for them. So Mackay Industries may offer to sell its $1,000, 6% bonds for $1,085 each. Mackay Industries will still pay the investors yearly interest payments equal to $60 ($1,000 par value × 6% interest) on each bond. However, because the investors paid $1,085 for each bond, the $60 interest payment represents a return of approximately 5.5% ($60 interest/$1,085 invested). The actual price of a bond represents a price that makes the return on the bond effectively the same as the market rate of interest at the time the bond is sold. **Exhibit 9-4** illustrates the relationship between the stated interest rate and the market interest rate and how it affects the sales price of a bond.

Relationship of Stated Interest Rate to Current Market Interest Rate	Bond Is Sold At	Why?
Stated rate = Market rate	Par	Investors are willing to pay the full maturity value for the bond because it offers the same interest rate as similar bonds with equal risk.
Stated rate < Market rate	Discount	Investors are willing to pay a lower price for the bond because they will receive a lower rate of interest from this bond than from similar bonds with equal risk.
Stated rate > Market rate	Premium	Investors are willing to pay a higher price for the bond because they will receive a higher rate of interest from this bond than from similar bonds with equal risk.

Exhibit 9-4 ▲

The issue price of a bond determines the amount of cash the company receives when it issues the bond. However, the issue price of a bond does not affect the required payment at maturity. A company must always pay the maturity value (par value) of the bonds when they mature.

After bonds have been issued, investors may buy and sell them on the bond market just as they buy and sell shares on the stock market.

Bond prices are quoted as a percentage of maturity value. For example,

- a $1,000 bond quoted at 100 is bought or sold for 100% of maturity value, ($1,000 × 1.00).
- a $1,000 bond quoted at 96.4 has a price of $964 ($1,000 × 0.964).
- a $1,000 bond quoted at 102.8 has a price of $1,028 ($1,000 × 1.028).

Issuing Bonds Payable at Par

The journal entry to record the issuance of bonds payable depends on whether the bond is issued at par, at a discount, or at a premium. Let's assume that on April 1, 2015, Mackay Industries issues $500,000 of 8% bonds payable that mature in five years. The bonds will pay interest semi-annually on March 31 and September 30 of each year. First, let's assume that the market rate of interest on April 1, 2015, is 8%. Because the stated interest rate equals the market interest rate, Mackay Industries will issue these bonds at maturity (par) value. Let's look at how this amount is calculated. The cash receipt for the bond is the sum of the present value of the bond at maturity ($500,000) and the present value of the 10 interest payments ($20,000). The concept of present value is discussed in Appendix B. The present value of interest factors are in Table B-3 and Table B-4 of Appendix B. We will use the market rate, or yield, to discount the principal and interest payment amounts, and use the stated rate, or coupon rate, to calculate the interest payment. The cash receipt is calculated as follows:

Facts:
Principal: $500,000
Interest payments: $500,000 × 8% ÷ 2 = $20,000
Period: 5 years × 2 payments per year = 10 periods
Yield: 8% ÷ 2 = 4%
Cash receipt = $500,000

To know how the cash receipts are calculated:
Present value of Principal: $500,000 × PVIF$_{(4\%, 10)}$ = $500,000 × 0.6756 = $337,800
Present value of Interest Payments: $20,000 × PVIFA$_{(4\%, 10)}$ = $20,000 × 8.1100 = $162,200
                                                                                           Cash Receipt = $500,000

The journal entry to record the receipt of cash and issuance of bonds payable is as follows:

DATE	ACCOUNTS	POST REF.	DR.	CR.
Apr 1	Cash		500,000	
	Bonds Payable			500,000
	Issued bonds at par.			

Interest payments occur March 31 and September 30 each year. Mackay Industries' first semi-annual interest payment on September 30, 2015, is journalized as follows:

DATE	ACCOUNTS	POST REF.	DR.	CR.
Sep 30	Interest Expense		20,000*	
	Cash			20,000
	Paid semiannual interest.			

*$500,000 × 0.08 × 1/2

Each semi-annual interest payment made until the bonds mature will be the same as the September 30, 2015, entry.

At maturity on March 31, 2020, after making the journal entry to record the final interest payment, Mackay Industries will record the repayment of the bonds as follows:

DATE	ACCOUNTS	POST REF.	DR.	CR.
2025				
Mar 31	Bonds Payable		500,000	
	Cash			500,000
	Repaid bonds at maturity.			

Now let's look at how bonds issued at a discount are accounted for.

Issuing Bonds Payable at a Discount

Suppose the market rate of interest is higher than 8% on April 1, 2015, when Mackay Industries issues the $500,000 of bonds. Remember from our previous discussion, if the market rate of interest is higher than the stated rate of interest, bonds will sell at a discount. Suppose the market rate of interest is 10% on April 1, 2015. The cash receipt and discount on bonds payable are calculated as follows:

Facts:
Principal: $500,000
Interest payments: $500,000 × 8% ÷ 2 = $20,000
Periods: 5 years × 2 payments per year = 10 periods
Yield: 10% ÷ 2 = 5%
Cash Receipt = $461,384

To know how the cash receipts are calculated:

Present value of Principal: $500,000 × $PVIF_{(5\%,\ 10)}$ = $500,000 × 0.6139 = $306,950

Present value of Interest Payments: $20,000 × $PVIF_{(5\%,\ 10)}$ = $20,000 × 7.7217 = _154,434_

           Cash Receipt = $461,384

           Bonds Payable at Maturity = $500,000

           Discount on Bonds Payable = $(38,616)

Mackay Industries receives $461,384, instead of $500,000. The difference ($38,616) is the discount on bonds payable. Mackay Industries receives less money on the issuance date. However, at the maturity date, Mackay Industries will pay bondholders the whole $500,000. Mackay Industries makes the following journal entry to record the issuance of the bonds at a discount:

DATE	ACCOUNTS	POST REF.	DR.	CR.
Apr 1	Cash		461,384	
	Bonds Payable			461,384
	Issued bonds at discount.			

Assets	=	Liabilities	+	Shareholders' Equity
+461,384	=	+461,384		

After posting, the Bonds Payable account has the following balance:

Bonds Payable

	461,384

Bonds payable *minus* the discount gives the **carrying amount** of the bonds. The carrying amount of the bonds represents the "net" bond liability that is carried on the company's books. The carrying value of Mackay Industries' bonds immediately after issue would be as follows:

Bonds Par Value	$500,000
Less, Discount on Bonds Payable	38,616
Carrying Value of Bonds Payable	$461,384

Interest Expense on Bonds Payable with a Discount

When Mackay Industries issued the bonds, it received $461,384, but it still must repay $500,000 when the bonds mature. The $38,616 difference between what it received and what it must pay back (the discount) ultimately represents additional interest expense to Mackay Industries. This additional interest effectively raises Mackay Industries' true interest rate on the bonds to the market interest rate, 10%, which was higher than the stated interest rate of 8%. The discount is allocated to interest expense through the process of amortization.

Amortizing interest can be done by one of two methods: the **effective interest method** (which is required by IFRS and which is accepted by ASPE) or the straight-line method (which is not accepted by IFRS, but accepted by ASPE if it does not differ significantly than the effective interest method).

Effective interest amortization method: According to the effective interest method, interest expense is calculated by taking the bond carrying value (the borrowed amount) and multiplying by the market rate or yield. The interest payment is calculated by taking the par value and multiplying by the stated rate. The interest expense amount is not the same as the interest payment—the difference is the amortization amount. This is the preferred method because interest expense is calculated based on the amount owed. **Exhibit 9-5** illustrates the calculation of discount amortization for Mackay Industries based on the effective interest method.

	A	B	C	D	E
Semi-Annual Interest Period	Interest Paid ($500,000 × 8% × 1/2)	Interest Expense = Previous Period Carrying Amount × Market Rate (10% × 1/2)	Discount Amortization Amount (B − A)	Unamortized Amount (D − C)	Bond Carrying Value ($500,000 − D)
0				38,616	461,384
1	20,000	23,069	3,069	35,547	464,453
2	20,000	23,223	3,223	32,324	467,676
3	20,000	23,384	3,384	28,940	471,060
4	20,000	23,553	3,553	25,387	474,613
5	20,000	23,731	3,731	21,657	478,343
6	20,000	23,917	3,917	17,740	482,260
7	20,000	24,113	4,113	13,627	486,373
8	20,000	24,319	4,319	9,308	490,692
9	20,000	24,535	4,535	4,773	495,227
10	20,000	24,773	4,773	0	500,000

Exhibit 9-5 ▲

Using the effective interest method, Mackay Industries' first semi-annual interest payment is recorded as follows:

DATE	ACCOUNTS	POST REF.	DR.	CR.
Sep 30	Interest Expense		23,069	
	Bonds Payable			3,069
	Cash			20,000
	Paid semi-annual interest.			

The Bonds Payable account will be credited on each interest payment date by the amount calculated for discount amortization for that period until it reaches its par value of $500,000 at maturity, as illustrated in Exhibit 9-5.

Straight-line amortization method: Under ASPE, private enterprises may choose to use *straight-line amortization* if the amortization amount is not significantly different. The straight-line method is similar to the amortization of intangible assets, like patents, which we learned about in Chapter 8. Under straight-line amortization, the discount on bonds payable is divided by the number of periods; therefore, an equal amount of the discount is allocated to interest expense at the time of each semi-annual interest payment.

In our example, the discount on bonds payable is $38,616, and there are 10 semi-annual interest periods during the bonds' five-year life. Therefore, 1/10 of the $38,616 bond discount ($3,862) is amortized each interest period. As a result, the interest expense is the sum of the amortization amount and interest payment.

Using the straight-line method, Mackay Industries' first semi-annual interest payment is recorded as follows:

DATE	ACCOUNTS	POST REF.	DR.	CR.
Sep 30	Interest Expense		23,862	
	Bonds Payable			3,862
	Cash			20,000
	Paid semi-annual interest.			

Bonds Payable is credited each time by the amortization amount. By maturity (the end of the tenth period), the Bonds Payable amount will be equal to its par value of $500,000.

Exhibit 9-6 illustrates bonds amortization using the straight-line amortization method.

	A	B	C	D	E
Semi-Annual Interest Period	Interest Paid ($500,000 × 8% × 1/2)	Interest Expense = Previous Period Carrying Amount × Market Rate (10% × 1/2)	Discount Amortization Amount (B − A)	Unamortized Amount (D − C)	Bond Carrying Value ($500,000 − D)
0				38,616	461,384
1	20,000	23,862	3,862	34,754	465,246
2	20,000	23,862	3,862	30,893	469,107
3	20,000	23,862	3,862	27,031	472,969
4	20,000	23,862	3,862	23,170	476,830
5	20,000	23,862	3,862	19,308	480,692
6	20,000	23,862	3,862	15,446	484,554
7	20,000	23,862	3,862	11,585	488,415
8	20,000	23,862	3,862	7,723	492,277
9	20,000	23,862	3,862	3,862	496,138
10	20,000	23,862	3,862	0	500,000

Exhibit 9-6 ▲

At maturity, after making the journal entry to record the final interest payment, Mackay Industries, whether using the effective interest or the straight-line amortization method, will record the repayment of the bonds as follows:

DATE	ACCOUNTS	POST REF.	DR.	CR.
2020				
Mar 31	Bonds Payable		500,000	
	Cash			500,000
	Repaid bonds at maturity.			

Notice that the entry to record the repayment of the bonds is the same as it was for bonds that were issued at par. This is because, at maturity, the carrying value of the bonds is equal to the par value of the bonds.

Issuing Bonds Payable at a Premium

To illustrate a bond premium, let's change the Mackay Industries example. Suppose the market rate of interest is 6% on April 1, 2015, when Mackay Industries issues the $500,000 of bonds. Mackay Industries' 8% bonds are attractive when the market interest rate is less than 8% so investors will pay a premium to acquire them. In this case, Mackay Industries receives $542,654 cash upon issuance. The cash receipt and premium on bonds payable are calculated as follows:

Facts:
Principal: $500,000
Interest payments: $500,000 × 8% ÷ 2 = $20,000
Periods: 5 years × 2 payments per year = 10 periods
Yield: 6% ÷ 2 = 3%
Cash receipt = $542,654

To know how the cash receipts are calculated:

Present value of Principal: $500,000 × PVIF$_{(3\%, 10)}$ = $500,000 × 0.7441 = $372,050

Present value of Interest Payments: $20,000 × PVIF$_{(3\%, 10)}$ = $20,000 × 8.5302 = $\underline{170,604}$

Cash Receipt = $542,654

Bonds Payable at Maturity = $500,000

Premium on Bonds Payable = $\underline{\$ \ 42,654}$

Mackay Industries receives $542,654, instead of $500,000. The difference ($42,654) is the premium on bonds payable. Mackay Industries receives more money on the issuance date. However, at the maturity date, Mackay Industries will pay bondholders the whole $500,000. Mackay Industries makes the following journal entry to record the issuance of the bonds at a premium:

DATE	ACCOUNTS	POST REF.	DR.	CR.
Apr 1	Cash		542,654	
	Bonds Payable			542,654
	Issued bonds at premium.			

After posting, the Bonds Payable account has the following balance:

Bonds Payable	
	542,654

Therefore, we add the premium on bonds payable to Bonds Payable to determine the bond carrying value. The carrying value of the Mackay Industries' bonds immediately after issuance is as follows:

Bonds Payable	$500,000
Plus, Premium on Bonds Payable	42,654
Carrying Value of Bonds Payable	$542,654

Interest Expense on Bonds Payable with a Premium

When Mackay Industries issued the bonds, it received $542,654, but it must pay back only $500,000 at maturity. The $42,654 difference between what it received and what it must pay back (the premium) ultimately represents a reduction of interest expense to Mackay Industries. This reduced interest effectively lowers Mackay Industries' true interest rate on the bonds to the market interest rate that was lower than the stated interest rate of 8%. As with a discount, a premium is allocated to interest expense through the process of amortization. Only in the case of a premium, the amortization decreases interest expense over the life of the bonds.

As was the case with amortization of the discount, amortizing interest can be done by two methods: the effective interest method (which is required by IFRS and which is accepted by ASPE) or the straight-line method (which is not accepted by IFRS, but is accepted by ASPE only in cases where it does not differ significantly than the effective interest method).

IFRS

ASPE

Effective interest amortization method: The effective interest method is calculated exactly as it was illustrated for amortizing a bond's discount. However, the amortization amount is *deducted* from the bond's carrying value rather than added to it. **Exhibit 9-7** illustrates the calculation of premium amortization for Mackay Industries based on the effective interest method.

	A	B	C	D	E
Semi-Annual Interest Period	Interest Paid ($500,000 × 8% × 1/2)	Interest Expense = Previous Period Carrying Amount × Market Rate (6% × 1/2)	Premium Amortization Amount (A − B)	Unamortized Amount (D − C)	Bond Carrying Value ($500,000 + D)
0				42,654	542,654
1	20,000	16,280	3,720	38,934	538,934
2	20,000	16,168	3,832	35,102	535,102
3	20,000	16,053	3,947	31,155	531,155
4	20,000	15,935	4,065	27,089	527,089
5	20,000	15,813	4,187	22,902	522,902
6	20,000	15,687	4,313	18,589	518,589
7	20,000	15,558	4,442	14,147	514,147
8	20,000	15,424	4,576	9,571	509,571
9	20,000	15,287	4,713	4,858	504,858
10	20,000	15,142	4,858	0	500,000

Exhibit 9-7 ▲

Using the effective interest method, Mackay Industries' interest expense and Mackay Industries' first semi-annual interest payment is recorded as follows:

Assets	=	Liabilities	+	Shareholders' Equity
−20,000	=	−3,720		−16,280

DATE	ACCOUNTS	POST REF.	DR.	CR.
Sep 30	Interest Expense		16,280	
	Bonds Payable		3,720	
	Cash			20,000
	Paid semi-annual interest.			

MEMORY TIPS

When bonds are issued at a *premium*, **subtract** the amount of premium amortization from the cash paid to get the interest expense.

The Bonds Payable account will be debited on each interest payment date by the amount calculated for premium amortization for that period until it reaches its par value of $500,000 at maturity, as illustrated in Exhibit 9-7.

Straight-line amortization method: In our example, the premium on bonds payable is $42,654, and there are 10 semi-annual interest periods during the bonds' five-year life. Therefore, using the straight-line method, 1/10 of the $42,654 bond premium ($4,265) is amortized each interest period. As a result, the interest expense is the net of the interest paid and amortization amount.

Using the straight-line method, Mackay Industries' first semi-annual interest payment is recorded as follows:

DATE	ACCOUNTS	POST REF.	DR.	CR.
Sep 30	Interest Expense		15,735	
	Bonds Payable		4,265	
	Cash			20,000
	Paid semi-annual interest.			

Assets	=	Liabilities	+	Shareholders' Equity
−20,000	=	−4,265		−15,735

At the end of each period, the carrying value of the bonds decreases by debiting the Bonds Payable account by the amount of the amortization. At maturity on March 31, 2020, the bond premium will have been fully amortized (it will have a zero balance), and the bonds' carrying amount will be $500,000 (the amount in the Bonds Payable account). Therefore, the entry to record the repayment of the bonds will be the same as it was when the bonds were issued at par or at a discount.

Exhibit 9-8 illustrates amortization of the bond premium for Mackay Industries using the straight-line method.

	A	B	C	D	E
Semi-Annual Interest Period	Interest Paid ($500,000 × 8% × 1/2)	Interest Expense = Interest Paid + Premium Amortization (A − C)	Premium Amortization Amount	Unamortized Amount (D − C)	Bond Carrying Value ($500,000 + D)
0				42,654	542,654
1	20,000	15,735	4,265	38,389	538,389
2	20,000	15,735	4,265	34,123	534,123
3	20,000	15,735	4,265	29,858	529,858
4	20,000	15,735	4,265	25,592	525,592
5	20,000	15,735	4,265	21,327	521,327
6	20,000	15,735	4,265	17,062	517,062
7	20,000	15,735	4,265	12,796	512,796
8	20,000	15,735	4,265	8,531	508,531
9	20,000	15,735	4,265	4,265	504,265
10	20,000	15,735	4,265	(0)	500,000

Exhibit 9-8▲

9.3 STILL DON'T GET IT?

Visit MyAccountingLab for an alternate explanation of this important accounting concept.

Exhibit 9-9 illustrates how both the bond premium and discount amortization ends up with the bonds' carrying value equal to its par value.

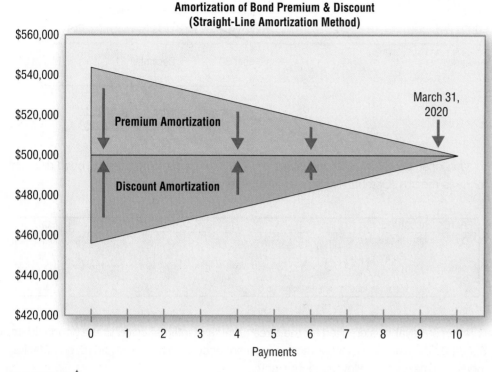

**Amortization of Bond Premium & Discount
(Straight-Line Amortization Method)**

Exhibit 9-9 ▲

Adjusting Entries for Bonds Payable

Interest payments on bonds seldom occur on a company's fiscal year-end date, so interest expense must be accrued at year end. The accrual entry should also amortize any related bond discount or premium. Let's return to our Mackay Industries example where Mackay Industries sold $500,000 of bonds at a discount for $461,384 on April 1, 2015. Mackay Industries made an interest payment on September 30, 2015. Using the effective interest method, Mackay Industries' interest expense and the amortization of the discount on bonds payable was calculated in Exhibit 9-5. Based on that data, the carrying value of the bonds after the September 30 payment is $464,453 as follows:

> Par value of bonds − Discount amount on issuance − Discount amortization on September 30
> $500,000 − $38,616 − $3,069 = $464,453

The second payment is due on March 31, including six months of interest and amortization. Since the financial statements are prepared on December 31, which is half the period (3/6 = 1/2), we would divide the interest payable, interest expense, and discount amortization of the second semi-annual interest period (in Exhibit 9-5) by 2:

> Interest Payable = $20,000/2 = $10,000
>
> Interest Expense = 23,223/2 = $11,612 (rounded)
>
> Discount Amortization Amount = $ 3,223/2 = 1,612 (rounded)

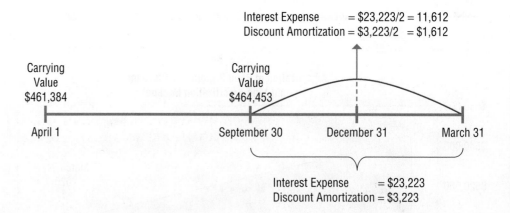

On December 31, Mackay Industries accrues interest and amortizes the bond discount for three months (October, November, and December) as follows:

DATE	ACCOUNTS	POST REF.	DR.	CR.
Dec 31	Interest Expense		11,612	
	Bonds Payable			1,612
	Interest Payable			10,000
	Accrued three months' interest expense.			

Interest Payable is credited for the three months of interest owed to the bondholders, $10,000. The next semi-annual interest payment occurs on March 31, 2016, and Mackay Industries makes the following journal entry:

DATE	ACCOUNTS	POST REF.	DR.	CR.
Mar 31	Interest Expense		11,612	
	Interest Payable		10,000	
	Bonds Payable			1,612
	Cash			20,000
	Paid semi-annual interest.			

The interest expense of $11,612 and the discount on bonds payable of $1,612 are half of the six-month amounts. Interest Payable is debited for $10,000 to reflect the fact that the amount accrued at December 31, 2015, is being paid. The $20,000 credit to Cash represents the stated interest that is paid to the bondholders.

EARLY RETIREMENT OF BONDS

As discussed earlier, the bond principal will be paid back by the maturity date. However, some bonds may come with special features, such as offering the bond issuer or bond-holders an option to retire all or part of the outstanding bonds before the bond maturity date. These are callable (redeemable) bonds. Companies might choose to retire their bonds early if the yield (the market interest rate of a similar-risk investment) is significantly lower than the coupon rate. They can issue new bonds at the new yield and pay a lower interest rate than they are currently paying, and thus save on the interest payment.

Suppose the yield drops to 6% on April 1, 2018, from a yield of 10% when the bonds were issued on April 1, 2015 (with a stated rate of 8%). If Mackay Industries decides to call the bonds and issue new ones at the current yield, the semi-annual interest payment on $500,000 would be reduced from $20,000 to $15,000 ($500,000 × 6% × 1/2). Mackay Industries would save $5,000 every six months for two years until the maturity date. This means that Mackay Industries would save $18,586 ($5,000 × PVIFA$_{(3\%, 4)}$) on April 1, 2018.

Another option is for Mackay Industries to retire its bonds in the open market. Once Mackay Industries owns the bonds it can retire them; however, Mackay must offer to pay a price for the bonds that is attractive to the bondholders. This price is stated as a percentage of the par value. In this case, Mackay Industries decides to retire its bonds in the open market at 98 (that is, 98% of par value). Mackay Industries needs to calculate whether there is a gain or loss as a result of the early retirement. The gain or loss on bond retirement is calculated as follows:

Carrying value of Bonds Payable on April 1, 2018:
Principal: $500,000
Interest payments: $500,000 × 8% ÷ 2 = $20,000
Periods remaining: 2 years × 2 payments per year = 4 periods
Yield on the issuing date (April 1, 2015): 10% ÷ 2 = 5%

Present value of Principal: $500,000 × PVIF$_{(5\%, 4)}$ = $500,000 × 0.8227 = $411,350
Present value of Interest Payments: $20,000 × PVIFA$_{(5\%, 4)}$ = $20,000 × 3.5455 = $\underline{70,910}$
Bonds Carrying Value on April 1, 2018 = $482,260
Bonds Payable at Maturity = $500,000
Discount on Bonds Payable on April 1, 2018 = $(17,740*)

Cash payment for bonds retirement: $500,000 × 98% = $490,000

Cash payment	$(490,000)
Carrying value of Bonds Payable	$\underline{482,260}$
Loss on Bonds Retirement	$ (7,740)

*You can calculate the same figure by deducting the bond's carrying value from its par value at period 6 in Exhibit 9-5 (500,000 − 482,260).

Mackay Industries makes the following journal entry to record the bonds retirement:

DATE	ACCOUNTS	POST REF.	DR.	CR.
Apr 1, 2018	Bonds Payable		482,260	
	Loss on Bonds Retirement		7,740	
	Cash			490,000
	Retired bonds at a loss.			

Assets	=	Liabilities	+	Shareholders' Equity
−490,000	=	−482,260		−7,740

 # DECISION GUIDELINES

DECISION		GUIDELINE		ANALYZE
What should I do if my business needs more cash than the bank will lend me?		Consider issuing bonds.		With notes payable, a business typically borrows a large sum of money from one lender, usually a bank. With bonds, a business borrows smaller amounts, often in $1,000 increments, from many different investors. By utilizing bonds payable, a business can often borrow very large sums of money because no single investor is exposed to a significant amount of risk.

HOW ARE LIABILITIES REPORTED ON THE STATEMENT OF FINANCIAL POSITION?

L.O. 6 Report liabilities on the statement of financial position

In Chapter 5, we learned how to prepare a classified statement of financial position. Throughout the chapter, we have seen how all of a company's liabilities are classified as either current liabilities or long-term liabilities. This classification determines where the liabilities are reported on the company's classified statement of financial position. An example of what the liabilities section of Mackay Industries' statement might look like is presented in **Exhibit 9-10**.

Mackay Industries Statement of Financial Position—Partial	
Current Liabilities:	
Accounts Payable	$ 2,200
Salaries Payable	8,700
Payroll Taxes Payable	2,610
Interest Payable	1,850
Sales Tax Payable	975
Estimated Warranty Payable	1,310
Unearned Revenue	1,400
Income Tax Payable	6,200
Current Portion of Long-Term Debt	11,700
Total Current Liabilities	36,945
Long-Term Debt	
Mortgage Payable	85,000
Bonds Payable, Net of $20,350 Discount	479,650
Lease Payable	36,650
Total Long-Term Debt	601,300
Total Liabilities	$638,245

Exhibit 9-10 ▲

Proper accounting for liabilities can also pose an ethical challenge. Classifying current liabilities as long-term, or vice versa, can have a big impact on a company's current ratio. Owners and managers may also be tempted to overlook expenses and their related liabilities at the end of the accounting period in an effort to make a business look more profitable. For example, a company might neglect to accrue warranty expense and the related warranty liability. This will cause reported liabilities and total expenses to be understated. Net income will also be overstated.

Provisions or contingent liabilities also pose an ethical challenge. Because contingencies are based on the outcome of a future event, they are easier to overlook. However, a contingency can turn into a real liability and can significantly change the company's financial position. Successful businesspeople refuse to play games with their accounting. Falsifying financial statements can result, and has resulted, in prison terms.

FOCUS ON DECISION MAKING: RATIOS

In Chapter 5 we learned how the current ratio is used to analyze a business's ability to pay its obligations as they come due. The **debt ratio** also uses liabilities to help examine a business; however, instead of focusing on current liabilities, the debt ratio focuses on the total liabilities of an organization. The debt ratio is found by dividing the total liabilities (debt) of an organization by the total assets:

L.O. 7 Compute the debt ratio

$$\text{Debt ratio} = \frac{\text{Total liabilities}}{\text{Total assets}}$$

The debt ratio reveals what percentage of a company's assets would be required to pay off all of its liabilities. The debt ratio is an indicator of a company's solvency. It is also a good indicator of a company's ability to incur, or take on, more debt. Let's assume that Mackay Industries has assets totalling $685,000, total liabilities of $425,000, and total shareholders' equity of $260,000. Mackay Industries' debt ratio is as follows:

$$\text{Debt ratio} = \frac{\text{Total liabilities}}{\text{Total assets}} = \frac{\$425,000}{\$685,000} = 62\% \text{ (rounded)}$$

Mackay Industries' debt ratio of 62% indicates that 62% of Mackay Industries' assets would be required to pay off all of its liabilities. Another way of looking at it is that after paying off all liabilities, 38% of Mackay Industries' assets would be left for the shareholders. The higher the debt, the higher the leverage, and thus the higher the business risk. The average debt ratio for most companies ranges from 57% to 67%, with relatively little variation from company to company. Mackay Industries' debt ratio falls right in the middle of the range of industry averages.

FOCUS ON USERS

Concept	User	Why Is This Important to This User?
Payroll Liabilities	**Unions**	The union will be very interested in the recording of payroll liabilities to ensure that the elements that are removed from employees' paycheques are ultimately forwarded to the correct agencies and that they are recorded at the correct amounts. It could create quite a problem if pension amounts were recorded and accounted for incorrectly and not noticed until the employees retire.
Debt Ratio	**Creditors**	The debt ratio will be watched by creditors as this ratio is a good indication of the long-term ability of the organization to pay its debt. A high ratio is not necessarily a bad thing because the debt ratio is very industry-dependent. Some industries will rely heavily on debt financing, while others may have very little debt financing, with each debt structure being a valid way of financing an organization. Competitor comparisons become quite important when examining the debt ratio and assessing whether or not the amount that was calculated is an indication of a strength or a weakness of the organization.

DEMO DOC

MyAccountingLab   Visit MyAccountingLab to watch animated versions of similar Demo Docs.

KNOWN AND ESTIMATED CURRENT LIABILITIES

Advantage Audio, Inc. began operations on January 1, 2015, selling personal music players. Each player comes with a one-year warranty included in the selling price. Advantage Audio, Inc. also sells digital songs that owners can download to their players. Customers prepay $100 for 100 songs and can download them whenever they wish.

 LEARNING OBJECTIVES ❶–❸

During 2015, Advantage Audio, Inc. had the following information:

Sales revenue from sale of music players sold to customers	$100,000
Purchase cost of music players sold to customers	$ 40,000
Sales tax rate (sales tax charged on player sales only)	7%
Music downloads purchased by customers...	20,000 songs
Songs downloaded by customers..	6,000 songs
Repairs made to players under warranty	$ 1,200

Advantage Audio, Inc. estimates that the repairs it will have to make to music players under the warranty provided will cost 2% of the selling price. Advantage Audio, Inc. has made an up-front cash payment to contract with a local repair shop to service any players as required.

At December 31, 2015, Advantage Audio, Inc. estimated that of the remaining prepaid music downloads, 10,000 songs would be downloaded in 2016, with the rest downloaded in 2017.

REQUIREMENTS:

① **Journalize the following transactions:**

    a. The sale of all music players in 2015 (assume cash sales)

    b. Payment of the year's sales taxes to the Canada Revenue Agency (CRA)

    c. The sale of music downloads in 2015 (assume cash sales)

    d. Song downloads in 2015

    e. Repairs made under warranty in 2015

② **Are the following liabilities current or long-term for Advantage Audio, Inc.?**

    a. Sales Tax Payable

    b. Unearned Music Downloads Revenue

    c. Estimated Warranty Payable

DEMO DOC SOLUTIONS
REQUIREMENT ①

Journalize the following transactions:

Part 1	Part 2	Demo Doc Complete

a. The sale of all music players in 2015 (assume cash sales)

When the players are sold, a number of accounts are affected. First, Advantage Audio, Inc. must record the sales revenue and cash collected. We are told in the problem that $100,000 of music players were sold, so "Sales Revenue—Players" increases (credit) by $100,000.

Cash also increases, but is $100,000 the *only* amount the customers paid? No, in addition to the selling price, customers must also pay sales tax when they buy a player. The total cash paid by customers was $107,000 [$100,000 + ($100,000 × 7%)]. So, Cash is increased (debit) by $107,000.

The extra $7,000 ($100,000 × 7%) collected by Advantage Audio, Inc. *does not belong* to it. It belongs to the government and must be paid to the CRA at a future date. A future payment (or *obligation*) is a liability. Therefore, Advantage Audio, Inc. must record (credit) a Sales Tax Payable of $7,000.

DATE	ACCOUNTS	POST REF.	DR.	CR.
	Cash ($100,000 × 1.07)		107,000	
	Sales Revenue—Players			100,000
	Sales Tax Payable ($100,000 × 7%)			7,000
	Record sales for cash.			

In addition to recording the sales revenue, Advantage Audio, Inc. must record the cost of the players sold. The players cost $40,000 to purchase, so we must record (debit) Cost of Goods Sold for $40,000. As the players are sold, Inventory is also decreased (credit) by $40,000.

DATE	ACCOUNTS	POST REF.	DR.	CR.
	Cost of Goods Sold		40,000	
	Inventory			40,000
	Record cost of sales.			

One other issue must be addressed when recording the sales of the players: the warranties included in the selling price. Warranty costs are recorded at the time of sale so that the liabilities and the expenses are accurately reflected in the financial statements.

Advantage Audio, Inc. estimates that the warranty costs will be 2% of selling price, so Advantage Audio, Inc. must record (debit) Warranty Expense for $2,000 ($100,000 × 2%). Advantage Audio, Inc. is now *obligated* to pay for these repairs when customer players break down. In accounting, *a future obligation is a liability*. So, Advantage Audio, Inc. must record an Estimated Warranty Payable liability (credit) of $2,000.

DATE	ACCOUNTS	POST REF.	DR.	CR.
	Warranty Expense ($100,000 × 0.02)		2,000	
	Estimated Warranty Payable			2,000
	Record estimated warranty expense.			

b. Payment of the year's sales taxes to the CRA

The sales taxes must be sent to the government. When this payment is made, Sales Tax Payable is decreased (debit) by $7,000 and Cash is decreased (credit) by $7,000.

DATE	ACCOUNTS	POST REF.	DR.	CR.
	Sales Tax Payable		7,000	
	Cash			7,000
	Record payment of sales tax collected.			

Notice that this entry is nearly identical to the entry to record payment of general accounts payable.

c. The sale of music downloads in 2015 (assume cash sales)

The customer pays for the music downloads before he or she receives them. In other words, Advantage Audio, Inc. has received the cash but has not provided the songs yet. So, Advantage Audio, Inc. has an *obligation* (a liability) to provide these songs to the customer.

Advantage Audio, Inc. *has not yet earned* the download revenue because it has not yet provided the songs to customers. Revenue will be earned as customers download their songs.

With 20,000 songs prepaid for $1 per song, we must record Unearned Music Download Revenue (credit) of $20,000 (20,000 × $1). We must also record an increase in Cash (debit) of $20,000.

DATE	ACCOUNTS	POST REF.	DR.	CR.
	Cash		20,000	
	Unearned Music Download Revenue			20,000
	Record cash received for music downloads in advance			
	of providing songs.			

d. Song downloads in 2015

Once songs are downloaded, Advantage Audio, Inc. earns the revenue from the sale of the songs. Then, it records "Sales Revenue—Music Downloads" of $6,000 (6,000 × $1). Because Advantage Audio, Inc. is now meeting its obligation to its customers by providing songs, the Unearned Music Download Revenue account is decreased (debit) by $6,000.

DATE	ACCOUNTS	POST REF.	DR.	CR.
	Unearned Music Download Revenue		6,000	
	Sales Revenue—Music Downloads (6,000 × $1)			6,000
	Record downloads revenue earned.			

After this transaction is recorded, the Unearned Revenue and related Sales Revenue accounts are as follows:

Unearned Music Download Revenue		
	(Downloads prepaid)	20,000
(Songs downloaded) 6,000		
	Dec 31 Bal	14,000

Sales Revenue—Music Downloads	
	6,000

e. Repairs made under warranty in 2015

When repairs are made under warranty, Advantage Audio's obligation to pay for these repairs is being met. This causes Estimated Warranty Payable to decrease (debit) by $1,200.

The repairs are being paid for in cash, so Cash is also decreased (credit) by $1,200.

DATE	ACCOUNTS	POST REF.	DR.	CR.
	Estimated Warranty Payable		1,200	
	Cash			1,200
	Record payment of warranty claims.			

Notice that warranty expense is *not* affected by this transaction! The expense was *already* recorded back when the players were sold (see Transaction a). To record warranty expense now would be double-counting the expense.

After this transaction is recorded, the warranty-related accounts are as follows:

Estimated Warranty Payable				Warranty Expense	
	(Players sold)	2,000		2,000	
(Repairs made) 1,200					
	Dec 31 Bal	800			

REQUIREMENT ②

Are the following liabilities current or long-term for Advantage Audio, Inc.?

Part 1	Part 2	Demo Doc Complete

a. Sales Tax Payable

Governments usually do not want to wait long for their money. Most sales taxes are remitted to the government within one month (or sooner) of being collected. In this example, Advantage Audio, Inc. already remitted the 2015 sales taxes before the end of the year. A real company could send sales tax collections to the CRA once a month. Because sales tax liabilities are paid well within one year, the Sales Tax Payable account is a current liability.

b. Unearned Music Downloads Revenue

The prepaid music downloads are unearned revenue. But when will that revenue be earned? In 2015, 6,000 songs were downloaded, and Advantage Audio, Inc. expects that another 10,000 will be downloaded in 2016, with the remaining 4,000 songs (20,000 − 6,000 − 10,000) being downloaded in 2017.

At December 31, 2015, Advantage Audio, Inc. has an Unearned Music Download Revenue liability of $14,000 for 14,000 songs (see Transaction d). Of this $14,000, $10,000 is a current liability (because it will be earned during the next year of 2016 as songs are downloaded) and $4,000 is a long-term liability (for songs downloaded after 2016).

c. Estimated Warranty Payable

Warranties can cover many years, so it is possible that an Estimated Warranty Payable liability could have both current and long-term portions (as Advantage Audio's Unearned Revenue does). However, the warranties Advantage Audio, Inc. provides are only one year long, so we know that all obligations under the warranty will be met within one year. Therefore, the entire Estimated Warranty Payable is a current liability.

DEMO DOC COMPLETE

Part 1	Part 2	Demo Doc Complete

DECISION GUIDELINES

Accounting for Current Liabilities and Long-Term Debt

Within your business, you will likely encounter some, or all, of these decisions related to liabilities:

DECISION		GUIDELINE		ANALYZE
What should I do if I do not know the exact amount of a liability?		Use professional judgment and estimate the amount.		In order to properly reflect the true financial position and results of operations of a company, it is important that all obligations of the business be recorded. When the exact amount of a liability is unknown, an estimate of the amount owed should be made. It is important to use professional judgment to estimate a reasonable amount.
My company started a warranty program for its products last year. I started getting some products back for maintenance. What should I do to represent the real economic situation on the financial statements?		Consider forming an estimated warranty expense and liability.		To have an accurate matching between revenues and expenses, estimated future maintenance costs for products that have been sold in the current period must be expensed within the current period too. A liability is formed and it decreases when such products use the maintenance service in the future.
What should I do if my business needs more cash than the bank will lend me?		Consider issuing bonds.		With notes payable, a business typically borrows a large sum of money from one lender, usually a bank. With bonds, a business borrows smaller amounts, often in $1,000 increments, from many different investors. By utilizing bonds payable, a business can often borrow very large sums of money because no single investor is exposed to a significant amount of risk.

Main Differences between IFRS and ASPE

POINT OF COMPARISON	IFRS	ASPE
Provision	A liability that has uncertain timing or an uncertain amount.	No specific definition given.
Contingent liability	A possible obligation that will be confirmed by uncertain future events.	An uncertain situation that will involve a possible gain or loss to a company.
Recognition of contingent liabilities	When it is virtually certain or probable.	When it is virtually certain.
Disclosing contingent liabilities	If it is possible.	If it is probable.
No disclosure required for contingent liabilities	If it is remote.	If it is possible or remote.
Bond premium/discount amortization	Effective interest method.	Effective interest method or straight-line method.

ACCOUNTING VOCABULARY

THE LANGUAGE OF BUSINESS

Bonds payable (p. 531)

Callable bonds (p. 532)

Carrying amount (p. 535)

Collateral (p. 530)

Contingent liability (p. 520)

Convertible bonds (p. 532)

ACCOUNTING PRACTICE

DISCUSSION QUESTIONS

1. Provide an example of a known liability, an estimated liability, and a contingent liability or provision.

2. If a company with a 12/31 year-end were to borrow money in the form of a four-month note on 11/1, what accounts would be debited on 3/1 when it pays the note off?

3. What journal entry is made when unearned revenue is earned?

4. What is the difference between a current liability for an uncertain amount and a contingent liability? Give an example of each and demonstrate how they differ with respect to the difference that you identified in the first part of this question.

5. What is the distinguishing feature of each of the following types of bonds:

   a. Convertible   **b.** Callable   **c.** Secured
   d. Unsecured   **e.** Serial   **f.** Term

6. What do we know about the relationship between the market rate of interest and the stated interest rate for a particular bond when the bond is sold at

   a. par?   **b.** a premium?   **c.** a discount?

7. Will interest expense be greater than, less than, or equal to the interest payment made on bonds when the bonds are sold at

   a. par?   **b.** a premium?   **c.** a discount?

8. What happens to the difference between the carrying amount of bonds and the principal amount of the bonds over time?

9. What are the differences between an operating lease and a capital lease?

10. What are some ways that companies might use improper recording of liabilities to manipulate financial statements?

SELF CHECK

1. Known liabilities of uncertain amounts should be

   a. estimated and accrued when they occur.
   b. ignored; record them when they are paid.
   c. reported on the income statement.
   d. described in the notes to the financial statements.

MyAccountingLab

The exercises and problems in this chapter can be found on MyAccountingLab. You can practise them as often as you want, and they feature step-by-step guided solutions to help you find the right answer.

2. On January 1, 2015, you borrowed $10,000 on a five-year, 8% note payable. At December 31, 2015, you should record a journal entry that includes which of the following?

a. Note Payable of $10,000
b. Nothing; the note has already been recorded
c. Interest Payable of $800
d. Cash receipt of $10,000

3. Your company sells $100,000 of goods and you collect sales tax of 3%. What current liability does the sale create?

a. Accounts Payable of $3,000
b. Unearned Revenue of $3,000
c. Sales Revenue of $103,000
d. Sales Tax Payable of $3,000

4. Sony owed Estimated Warranty Payable of $1,000 at the end of 2015. During 2016, Sony made sales of $100,000 and expects product warranties to cost the company 3% of the sales. During 2016, Sony paid $2,500 for warranties. What is Sony's Estimated Warranty Payable at the end of 2016?

a. $1,500
b. $2,500
c. $3,000
d. $3,500

5. What is the term used to describe an unsecured bond?

a. Debenture bond
b. Mortgage bond
c. Serial bond
d. Callable bond

6. Which interest rate on a bond determines the amount of the semi-annual interest payment?

a. Market rate
b. Effective rate
c. Stated rate
d. None of the above

7. Plavix Corporation's bonds payable carry a stated interest rate of 7%, and the market rate of interest at the time of issuance is 8%. Plavix Corporation's bonds will be sold at

a. a premium.
b. a discount.
c. par value.
d. maturity value.

8. Bonds issued at a premium always have

a. interest expense less than the interest payments.
b. interest expense greater than the interest payments.
c. interest expense equal to the interest payments.
d. none of the above.

9. Milton's bonds pay interest semi-annually on July 1 and January 1. If its fiscal year ends on September 30, which statement is *true* of Milton's year-end adjusting journal entry for bond interest?

a. Milton must record three month's accrued interest expense and amortize three month's discount or premium.
b. Milton will record nine month's accrued interest expense and amortize nine month's discount or premium.
c. Milton must record three month's accrued interest expense only.
d. Milton will record nine month's accrued interest expense and amortize three month's discount or premium.

10. Which of the following statements is correct?

a. The effective interest method will yield the same amortization amount as the straight-line method.
b. When amortizing a bond discount by using the effective interest method, the amortization amount decreases when the bond approaches maturity.
c. When amortizing a bond discount by using the effective interest method, the amortization amount increases when the bond approaches maturity.
d. The straight-line method is more accurate because it distributes the amortization amount evenly over the bond's duration.

Answers are given after Written Communication.

SHORT EXERCISES

S9-1. Accounting for notes payable (*Learning Objective 2*) 5–10 min.

On June 30, 2015, Harper, Co. purchased $9,000 of inventory for a one-year, 9% note payable. Journalize the following for the company:

1. Accrual of interest expense on December 31, 2015
2. Payment of the note plus interest on June 30, 2016

S9-2. Accounting for notes payable (*Learning Objective 2*) 5–10 min.

On September 30, 2015, Tucker, Co. borrowed $15,000 on a one-year, 7% note payable. What amounts would Tucker, Co. report for the note payable and the related interest payable on its statement of financial position at December 31, 2015, and on its income statement for the year ended December 31, 2015?

S9-3. Warranties (*Learning Objective 3*) 5–10 min.

Lake Country Boats guarantees its boats for three years or 1,500 hours, whichever comes first. Past experience of other boat makers indicates that Lake Country can expect warranty costs will equal 6% of sales. Assume in its first year Lake Country Boats had sales totalling $600,000, receiving cash for 30% of sales and notes receivable for the remainder. Warranty payments totalled $22,000 during the year.

1. Record the sales, warranty expense, and warranty payments for Lake Country Boats.
2. Post relevant portions of the journal entries to the Estimated Warranty Payable T-account. At the end of the first year, how much in estimated warranty payable does Lake Country owe its customers?
3. What amount of warranty expense will Lake Country report during its first year of operations? Does the warranty expense for the year equal the year's cash payments for warranties?

S9-4. Commitments and contingencies (*Learning Objective 4*) 5–10 min.

Phatboy Motorcycles, Inc., a motorcycle manufacturer, included the following note in its annual report:

Notes to Consolidated Financial Statements

9: Commitments and Contingencies

The Company self-insures its product liability losses in Canada up to $2.5 million.

Catastrophic coverage is maintained for individual claims in excess of $2.5 million up to $25 million.

1. Why are product liability losses considered contingent liabilities?
2. How can a contingent liability become a real liability for Phatboy Motorcycles?

S9-5. Accounting for mortgages (*Learning Objective 5*) 10–15 min.

Ling Company issued a $200,000, 8%, 30-year mortgage on January 1, 2015, to purchase a building. Payments of $8,840 are made semi-annually. Complete the following amortization schedule (partial) for Ling Company.

Date	Payment	Interest	Principal	Loan Balance
Jan 1, 2015				$200,000
Jun 30, 2015	$8,840			
Dec 31, 2015				
Jun 30, 2016				
Dec 31, 2016				

S9-6. Accounting for mortgages (*Learning Objective 5*) 5–10 min.

Apex, Co. issued a $225,000, 9% mortgage on January 1, 2015. Payments of $10,900 are made semi-annually on June 30 and December 31 each year. Calculate and record the journal entries for (a) issuance of the mortgage on January 1, 2015, and (b) the first semi-annual payment on June 30, 2015.

S9-7. Bond terms (*Learning Objective 5*) 5–10 min.

Match the following terms with the correct definition.

____ 1. Bonds that all mature at the same time.

____ 2. Interest rate investors are willing to pay for similar bonds of equal risk.

____ 3. Unsecured bonds backed only by the good faith of the borrower.

____ 4. Amount of a bond's issue price over its maturity value.

____ 5. Bonds that may be converted into the common shares of the issuing company at the option of the investor.

____ 6. Amount of a bond's maturity value over its issue price.

____ 7. Interest rate that determines the amount of cash interest the borrower pays and the investor receives.

____ 8. Bonds in the same bond issuance that mature at different times.

____ 9. Bonds that the issuer may call or pay off at a specified price whenever the issuer wants.

a. Convertible bonds
b. Premium on bond
c. Callable bonds
d. Debentures
e. Term bonds
f. · Serial bonds
g. Discount on bond
h. Stated interest rate
i. Market interest rate

S9-8. Determining the issue price for bonds (*Learning Objective 5*) 5–10 min.

Determine whether the following bonds payable will be issued at par, at a premium, or at a discount:

a. The market interest rate is 7%. Owens, Corp. issues bonds payable with a stated rate of 8 1/2%.

b. Bakers, Inc. issued 7% bonds payable when the market rate was 7 1/2%.

c. Saratoga Corporation issued 8% bonds when the market interest rate was 8%.

d. Tacoma Company issued bonds payable that pay cash interest at the stated rate of 7%. At the date of issuance, the market interest rate was 8 1/4%.

S9-9. Analyzing bond terms (*Learning Objective 5*)10–15 min.

All Star Amusements is planning to issue long-term bonds payable to borrow for a major expansion. For each of the following questions, identify whether the bond price involves a discount, a premium, or par value.

a. The stated interest rate on the bonds is 7%, and the market interest rate is 8%. What type of price can All Star Amusements expect for the bonds?

b. All Star Amusements could raise the stated interest rate on the bonds to 9% (market rate is 8%). In that case, what type of price can All Star Amusements expect for the bonds?

c. At what type of bond price will All Star Amusements have total interest expense equal to the cash interest payments?

d. At which type of price will All Star Amusements' total interest expense be less than the cash interest payments?

e. At which type of price will All Star Amusements' total interest expense be greater than the cash interest payments?

S9-10. Accounting for bonds (*Learning Objective 5*) 15–20 min.

Delta, Corp. issued 6%, five-year bonds payable with a maturity value of $5,000 on January 1, 2015. Journalize the following transactions and include an explanation for each entry. The market rate of interest equalled the stated rate at the date of issuance.

    a. Issuance of the bonds payable at par on January 1, 2015.

    b. Payment of semi-annual interest on July 1, 2015.

    c. Payment of semi-annual interest and the bonds payable at maturity. (Give the date.)

S9-11. Accounting for bonds (*Learning Objective 5*) 15–20 min.

Hastings, Corp. issued 6%, five-year bonds payable with a maturity value of $5,000 at a price of $4,550 when the market rate was 8% on January 1, 2015. Journalize the following transactions for Hastings, Corp. Include an explanation for each entry.

    a. Issuance of the bonds payable on January 1, 2015.

    b. Payment of semi-annual interest and amortization of bond discount on July 1, 2015. (Use the effective interest method to amortize the discount.)

S9-12. Accounting for bonds (*Learning Objective 5*) 15–20 min.

Hastings, Corp. issued 6%, five-year bonds payable with a maturity value of $5,000 at a price of $5,450 when the market rate was 4% on January 1, 2015. Journalize the following transactions for Hastings, Corp. Include an explanation for each entry.

    a. Issuance of the bonds payable on January 1, 2015.

    b. Payment of semi-annual interest and amortization of bond premium on July 1, 2015. (Use the effective interest method to amortize the premium.)

S9-13. Accounting for bonds (*Learning Objective 5*) 15–20 min.

Hastings, Corp. issued 6%, five-year bonds payable with a maturity value of $5,000 at par on May 1, 2015. Assume that the fiscal year ends on December 31. Journalize the following transactions and include an explanation for each entry.

    a. Issuance of the bonds payable on May 1, 2015.

    b. Payment of the first semi-annual interest amount on November 1, 2015.

    c. Accrual of semi-annual interest expense on December 31, 2015.

S9-14. Classification of liability accounts as current or long-term. (*Learning Objective 6*) 5–10 min.

Identify the section of the statement of financial position in which the following accounts would be located: Current Liabilities (CL) or Long-Term Liabilities (LTL).

    _____ 1. Bonds Payable

    _____ 2. Interest Payable

    _____ 3. Six Month Notes Payable

    _____ 4. Mortgage Notes Payable

S9-15. Statement of financial position of long-term liabilities (*Learning Objective 5*) 5–10 min.

FastTrack Magazine, Inc. includes the following selected accounts in its general ledger at December 31, 2015:

Mortgage Notes		Interest Payable	
Payable	$100,000	(due next year)....................	7,000
Bonds Payable	344,000	Accounts Payable	$19,000

Prepare the liabilities section of FastTrack Magazine's statement of financial position at December 31, 2015, to show how the company would report these items. Report a total for current liabilities.

EXERCISES (GROUP A)

E9-1A. HST payable (*Learning Objective 2*) 5–10 min.

Make journal entries to record the following transactions. Explanations are not required.

Mar 31	Recorded cash sales of $200,000 for the month, plus HST of 13% collected for the Province of Ontario.
Apr 6	Sent March HST to CRA.

E9-2A. Accounting for notes payable (*Learning Objective 2*) 5–10 min.

Record the following note payable transactions of Lisbon, Corp. in the company's journal. Explanations are not required.

2015	
May 1	Purchased equipment costing $15,000 by issuing a one-year, 6% note payable.
Dec 31	Accrued interest on the note payable.
2016	
May 1	Paid the note payable at maturity.

E9-3A. Subscriptions (*Learning Objective 2*) 5–10 min.

Ozark Publishing Company completed the following transactions during 2015:

Nov 1	Sold a six-month subscription, collecting cash of $180, plus sales tax of 5%.
Dec 15	Remitted the sales tax to the CRA.
31	Made the necessary adjustment at year-end to record the amount of subscription revenue earned during the year.

Requirements

1. Journalize these transactions. Explanations are not required.
2. What amounts would Ozark Publishing Company report on the statement of financial position at December 31, 2015?

Quick solution:

2. December 31, 2015, balance in Estimated Warranty Payable = $6,000

E9-4A. Warranties (*Learning Objective 3*) 5–10 min.

The accounting records of Osgood Carpets showed a balance of $3,000 in Estimated Warranty Payable at December 31, 2015. In the past, Osgood's warranty expense has been 5% of sales. During 2016, Osgood made sales of $300,000 on account and paid $12,000 to satisfy warranty claims.

Requirements

1. Journalize Osgood's sales, warranty expense, and cash payments made to satisfy warranty claims during 2016. Explanations are not required.
2. What balance of Estimated Warranty Payable will Osgood report on its statement of financial position at December 31, 2016?

E9-5A. Accounting for mortgages (*Learning Objective 5*) 10–15 min.

Orbit, Corp. issued a $400,000, 10%, 15-year mortgage on January 1, 2015, to purchase warehouses.

Date	Payment	Interest	Principal	Loan Balance
Jan 1, 2015				$400,000
Jun 30, 2015	$26,021			
Dec 31, 2015				
Jun 30, 2016				
Dec 31, 2016				
Jun 30, 2017				

Requirements

1. Complete the amortization schedule for Orbit, Corp. assuming payments are made semi-annually.

2. Record the journal entries for (a) issuance of mortgage on January 1, 2015, and (b) the first semi-annual payment on June 30, 2015.

E9-6A. Accounting for bonds (*Learning Objective 5*) 15–20 min.

Pluto Corporation issued 8%, 20-year bonds payable with a maturity value of $500,000 on March 31. The bonds were issued at par and pay interest on March 31 and September 30. Record (a) issuance of the bonds on March 31, (b) payment of interest on September 30, and (c) accrual of interest on December 31.

E9-7A. Accounting for bonds (*Learning Objective 5*) 15–20 min.

On January 1, Quizmo, Corp. issues 8%, 20-year bonds payable with a maturity value of $100,000. The bonds sell at 98 and pay interest on January 1 and July 1. Quizmo, Corp. amortizes any bond discount or premium by the straight-line method. Record (a) the issuance of the bonds on January 1, and (b) the semi-annual interest payment and amortization of any bond discount or premium on July 1.

E9-8A. Accounting for bonds (*Learning Objective 5*) 15–20 min.

Datil, Inc. issued $100,000 of 10-year, 6% bonds payable on January 1. Datil, Inc. pays interest each January 1 and July 1 and amortizes any discount or premium by the straight-line method. Datil, Inc. can issue its bonds payable under various conditions:

a. Issuance at par value

b. Issuance at a price of $90,000 when the market rate was 7%

c. Issuance at a price of $105,000 when the market rate was 5.5%

Requirements

1. Journalize Datil's issuance of the bonds and first semi-annual interest payment for each situation. Explanations are not required.

2. Which condition results in the most interest expense for Datil, Inc.? Explain in detail.

E9-9A. Classifying notes payable as current or long-term (*Learning Objectives 5 & 6*) 10–15 min.

Carruthers Medical Group borrowed $300,000 on July 1, 2015, by issuing a 9% long-term note payable that must be paid in three equal annual instalments plus interest each July 1 for the next three years.

Requirement

1. Insert the appropriate amounts to show how Carruthers would report its current and long-term liabilities.

	December 31		
	2015	**2016**	**2017**
Current Liabilities:			
Current Portion of Long-Term Note Payable	$	$	$
Interest Payable			
Long-Term Liabilities:			
Long-Term Note Payable			

E9-10A. Statement of financial position disclosure of liabilities (*Learning Objective 6*) 15–20 min.

At December 31, Deming Drapes owes $50,000 on accounts payable, plus salaries payable of $14,000 and income tax payable of $8,000. Deming Drapes also has $300,000 of bonds payable that require payment of a $30,000 instalment next year and the remainder in later years. The bonds payable also require an interest payment of $7,000 at the end of each year. Report Deming Drapes' liabilities on its year-end classified statement of financial position.

E9-11A. Debt ratio (*Learning Objective 7*) 5–10 min.

Appleway Company had the following balances as of December 31, 2015:

Total Current Assets	$ 87,000
Total Long-Term Assets	358,000
Total Current Liabilities	42,000
Total Long-Term Liabilities	217,000
Total Shareholders' Equity	186,000

Requirement

1. Calculate Appleway Company's debt ratio as of December 31, 2015. Does it appear that Appleway Company is in a position to take on more debt?

E9-12A. Accounting for bonds (*Learning Objective 5*) 20–25 min.

Jung Inc. issued $500,000 of 10-year, 7% bonds payable on April 1, when the market rate was 8%. Jung, Inc. pays interest each September 30 and March 31 and amortizes any discount or premium by the effective interest method. Jung's year-end is December 31.

Requirements

1. Calculate the cash receipt for the bond issuance.

2. Journalize Jung's issuance of the bonds.

3. Journalize Jung's first semi-annual interest payment, year-end adjustment, and the second semi-annual interest payment. Explanations are not required.

E9-13A. Accounting for bonds and bonds retirement (*Learning Objective 5*) 20–25 min.

Yamada Inc. issued $1,000,000 of 5-year, 5% bonds payable on January 1, 2015, when the market rate was 6%. Yamada Inc. pays interest each June 30 and December 31 and amortizes any discount or premium by the effective interest method. On July 1, 2018, Yamada retired 60% of its bonds at 99.5 in the open market.

Requirements

1. Calculate the cash receipt for the bond issuance.

2. Calculate the bond carrying value on July 1, 2018.

3. Calculate the gain or loss on bond retirement.

4. Journalize Yamada's issuance of the bonds on January 1, 2015 and bond retirement on July 1, 2018.

E9-14A. Accounting for payroll payable (*Learning Objective 2*) 15–20 min.

The following is Kiten's payroll information on employees' deductions for December:

Gross Pay	EI	CPP	Income Tax	Union Dues
52,000	910	2,574	10,400	520

Kiten pays its employees at the end of each month, and is required to remit employees' deductions and payroll payable to CRA by January 15.

Requirements

1. Record the journal entries for salaries expense and employee benefit expense on December 31.

2. Record the journal entry for the remittance to CRA on January 15.

E9-15A. Accounting treatment of provisions and contingent liabilities (*Learning Objective 3*) 10–15 min.

Wulai Company is facing the following situations, and the owner of the company needs your help in identify the accounting treatment:

1. A customer sued Wulai for selling a defective product. The time that the customer took to fix the defective product caused the customer's company productivity loss, which was estimated around $30,000. Wulai claimed that the product was not defective, but was misused by the customer. Wulai's lawyer is confident that the court will dismiss the case.

2. A competitor sued Wulai for infringing their patent for one of Wulai's best-selling smart phones. The court has awarded the plantiff $1 million. The owner of Wulai is appealing the case and believes that the company will win the lawsuit, but the lawyers believe that it could lose the appeal.

Requirements

Determine the appropriate accounting treatment. Based on your analysis, identify whether the company should (1) recognize a provision, (2) disclose a provision liability, or (3) determine no disclosure is required.

EXERCISES (GROUP B)

E9-1B. Sales tax payable (*Learning Objective 2*) 5–10 min.

Make journal entries to record the following transactions. Explanations are not required.

Aug 31	Recorded cash sales of $770,000 for the month, plus sales tax of 7% collected for the Province of Alberta.
Sep 6	Sent August sales tax to the CRA.

E9-2B. Accounting for notes payable (*Learning Objective 2*) 5–10 min.

Record the following note payable transactions of Concilio, Corp. in the company's journal. Explanations are not required.

2015

Oct 1	Purchased equipment costing $8,000 by issuing a one-year, 8% note payable.
Dec 31	Accrued interest on the note payable.

2016

Oct 1	Paid the note payable at maturity.

E9-3B. Subscriptions (*Learning Objective 2*) 5–10 min.

TransWorld Publishing Company completed the following transactions during 2015:

Aug 1	Sold a six-month subscription, collecting cash of $3,000, plus sales tax of 4%.
Dec 15	Remitted the sales tax to the provincial tax authority.
31	Made the necessary adjustment at year-end to record the amount of subscription revenue earned during the year.

Requirements

1. Journalize these transactions. Explanations are not required.
2. What amounts would TransWorld Publishing Company report on the statement of financial position at December 31, 2015?

E9-4B. Warranties (*Learning Objective 3*) 5–10 min.

The accounting records of Atkinson Books showed a balance of $2,000 in Estimated Warranty Payable at December 31, 2015. In the past, Atkinson's warranty expense has been 6% of sales. During 2016, Atkinson made sales of $329,000 on account and paid $6,000 to satisfy warranty claims.

Requirements

1. Journalize Atkinson's sales, warranty expense, and cash payments made to satisfy warranty claims during 2016. Explanations are not required.
2. What balance of Estimated Warranty Payable will Atkinson report on its statement of financial position at December 31, 2016?

E9-5B. Accounting for mortgages (*Learning Objective 5*) 10–15 min.

Jupiter, Corp. issued a $500,000, 8%, 15-year mortgage on January 1, 2015, to purchase warehouses.

Date	Payment	Interest	Principal	Loan Balance
Jan 1, 2015				$500,000
Jun 30, 2015	$28,915			
Dec 31, 2015				
Jun 30, 2016				
Dec 31, 2016				
Jun 30, 2017				

Requirements

1. Complete the amortization schedule for Jupiter, Corp. assuming payments are made semi-annually.
2. Record the journal entries for (a) issuance of the mortgage on the January 1, 2015, and (b) the first semi-annual payment on June 30, 2015.

E9-6B. Accounting for bonds (*Learning Objective 5*) 15–20 min.

Daffy Corporation issued 4%, 20-year bonds payable with a maturity value of $330,000 on January 31. The bonds were issued at par and pay interest on January 31 and July 31. Record (a) issuance of the bonds on January 31, (b) payment of interest on July 31, and (c) accrual of interest on December 31.

E9-7B. Accounting for bonds (*Learning Objective 5*) 15–20 min.

On January 1, Danvers, Corp. issues 5%, four-year bonds payable with a maturity value of $110,000. The bonds sell at 94 and pay interest on January 1 and July 1. Danvers, Corp. amortizes any bond discount or premium by the straight-line method. Record (a) the issuance of the bonds on January 1, and (b) the semi-annual interest payment and amortization of any bond discount or premium on July 1.

E9-8B. Accounting for bonds (*Learning Objective 5*) 15–20 min.

Jefferson, Inc. issued $200,000 of 10-year, 4% bonds payable on January 1. Jefferson, Inc. pays interest each January 1 and July 1 and amortizes any discount or premium by the straight-line method. Jefferson, Inc. can issue its bonds payable under various conditions:

a. Issuance at par value

b. Issuance at a price of $130,000 when the market rate is 6.2%

c. Issuance at a price of $250,000 when the market rate is 3.2%

Requirements

1. Journalize Jefferson's issuance of the bonds and first semi-annual interest payment for each situation. Explanations are not required.

2. Which condition results in the most interest expense for Jefferson, Inc.? Explain in detail.

E9-9B. Classifying notes payable as current or long-term (*Learning Objectives 5 & 6*) 10–15 min.

Bon Secour Medical Group borrowed $600,000 on July 1, 2015, by issuing a 14% long-term note payable that must be paid in three equal annual instalments plus interest each July 1 for the next three years.

Requirement

1. Insert the appropriate amounts to show how Bon Secour would report its current and long-term liabilities.

	December 31		
	2015	**2016**	**2017**
Current Liabilities:			
Current Portion of Long-Term Note Payable	$	$	$
Interest Payable			
Long-Term Liabilities:			
Long-Term Note Payable			

E9-10B. Statement of financial position disclosure of liabilities (*Learning Objective 6*) 15–20 min.

At December 31, Trumpette Drapes owes $59,000 on accounts payable, plus salaries payable of $15,000 and income tax payable of $13,000. Trumpette Drapes also has $270,000 of bonds payable that require payment of a $25,000 instalment next year and the remainder in later years. The bonds payable also require an interest payment of $5,500 at the end of each year. Report Trumpette Drapes' liabilities on its year-end classified statement of financial position.

E9-11B. Debt ratio (*Learning Objective 7*) 5–10 min.

Pine City Company had the following balances as of December 31, 2015:

Total Current Assets	$154,000
Total Long-Term Assets	501,000
Total Current Liabilities	95,000
Total Long-Term Liabilities	195,000
Total Shareholders' Equity	365,000

Requirement

1. Calculate Pine City Company's debt ratio as of December 31, 2015. Does it appear that Pine City Company is in a position to take on more debt?

E9-12B. Accounting for bonds (*Learning Objective 5*) 20–25 min.

Yip Inc. issued $800,000 of 8-year, 9% bonds payable on October 1, when the market rate was 8%. Yip Inc. pays interest each March 31 and September 30 and amortizes any discount or premium by the effective interest method. Yip's year-end is December 31.

Requirements

1. Calculate the cash receipt for the bond issuance.
2. Journalize Yip's issuance of the bonds.
3. Journalize Yip's first semi-annual interest payment, year-end adjustment, and the second semi-annual interest payment. Explanations are not required.

E9-13B. Accounting for bonds and bonds retirement (*Learning Objective 5*) 20–25 min.

Tran Inc. issued $500,000 of 8-year, 7% bonds payable on July 1, 2015 when the market rate was 6%. Tran Inc. pays interest each June 30 and December 31 and amortizes any discount or premium by the effective interest method. On January 1, 2020, Tran retired 50% of its bonds at 101.5 in the open market.

Requirements

1. Calculate the cash receipt for the bond issuance.
2. Calculate the bond carrying value on January 1, 2020.
3. Calculate the gain or loss on bond retirement.
4. Journalize Tran's issuance of the bonds on January 1, 2015, and bond retirement on January 1, 2020.

E9-14B. Accounting for payroll payable (*Learning Objective 2*) 15–20 min.

The following is Hoshi's payroll information on employees' deductions for March:

Gross Pay	EI	CPP	Income Tax	Extended Health Insurance
68,000	1,190	3,366	16,320	1,360

Hoshi pays its employees at the end of each month, and is required to remit employees' deductions and payroll payable to CRA by April 15.

Requirements

1. Record the journal entries for salaries expense and employee benefit expense on March 31.
2. Record the journal entry for the remittance to CRA on April 15.

E9-15B. Accounting treatment of provisions and contingent liabilities (*Learning Objective 3*) 10–15 min.

Chemco Company is facing the following situations, and the owner of the company needs your help in identify the accounting treatment:

1. In making one of Chemco's products, Chemco leaked out waste into a nearby lake. Under provincial law, Chemco has to clean the polluted lake and also pay a fine. The total estimates for the incident would likely be $3 million.

2. A customer purchased pesticides from Chemco. The customer was injured due to inappropriate handling of the pesticides. The customer is suing Chemco $100,000 for his damage.

Requirement

1. Determine the appropriate accounting treatment. Based on your analysis, identify whether the company should (1) recognize a provision, (2) disclose a provision liability, or (3) determine no disclosure is required.

EXERCISES (ALTERNATES 1, 2, AND 3)

These alternative exercise sets are available for your practice benefit at **MyAccountingLab**.

PROBLEMS (GROUP A)

P9-1A. Accounting for several current liabilities (*Learning Objectives 2 & 3*) 20–25 min.

The following transactions of Austin's Marine Supply occurred during 2015 and 2016:

2015	
Feb 3	Purchased equipment for $15,000, signing a six-month, 4% note payable.
28	Recorded the week's sales of $60,000, one-third for cash, and two-thirds on account. All sales amounts are subject to a 5% sales tax. Ignore cost of goods sold.
Mar 7	Sent last week's sales tax to the province.
Apr 30	Borrowed $210,000 on a four-year, 11% note payable that calls for annual payment of interest each April 30.
Aug 3	Paid the six-month, 4% note at maturity.
Nov 30	Purchased inventory at a cost of $3,000, signing a three-month, 8% note payable for that amount.
Dec 31	Accrued warranty expense, which is estimated at 1% of total sales of $790,000.
31	Accrued interest on all outstanding notes payable. Accrued interest for each note separately.
2016	
Feb 28	Paid off the 8% inventory note, plus interest, at maturity.
Apr 30	Paid the interest for one year on the long-term note payable.

Requirement

1. Record the transactions in the company's journal. Explanations are not required.

P9-2A. Accounting for several current and long-term liabilities (*Learning Objectives 2, 3, & 5*) 20–25 min.

Following are pertinent facts about events during the current year at Greely Snowboards.

a. December sales totalled $404,000, and Greely collected sales tax of 5%. The sales tax will be sent to Ontario early in January.

b. Greely owes $75,000 on a long-term note payable. At December 31, 6% interest for the year plus $25,000 of principal are payable within one year.

c. On August 31, Greely signed a six-month, 6% note payable to purchase a machine costing $80,000. The note requires payment of principal and interest at maturity.

d. Sales of $909,000 were covered by the Greely product warranty. At January 1, estimated warranty payable was $11,300. During the year, Greely recorded warranty expense of $27,900 and paid warranty claims of $30,100.

e. On October 31, Greely received cash of $2,400 in advance for the rent on a building. This rent will be earned evenly over six months.

Requirement

1. For each item, indicate the account and the related amount to be reported as a current liability on Greely's December 31 statement of financial position.

P9-3A. Accounting for mortgages (*Learning Objective 5*) 20–25 min.

Jordan, Corp. completed the following transactions in 2015:

Jan 1	Purchased a building costing $100,000 and signed a 10-year, 10% mortgage note payable for the same amount.
Jun 30	Made the first semi-annual payment on the mortgage note payable.
Dec 1	Signed a five-year lease to rent a warehouse for $7,000 per month due at the end of each month. The lease is considered an operating lease.
31	Paid for one month's rent on the warehouse.
31	Made the second semi-annual payment on the mortgage note payable.

Requirements

1. Complete the following amortization schedule for the first four mortgage payments on the $100,000 mortgage note, assuming semi-annual payments of $8,024.

Date	Payment	Interest	Principal	Loan Balance
Jan 1, 2015				$100,000
Jun 30, 2015	$8,024			
Dec 31, 2015				
Jun 30, 2016				
Dec 31, 2016				

2. Record the journal entries for the 2015 transactions.

3. Prepare the long-term liabilities section of the statement of financial position on December 31, 2015.

P9-4A. Analyzing bond terms and accounting for bonds (*Learning Objective 5*) 20–25 min.

Assume that on April 1, 2015, Roland, Corp. issues 8%, 10-year bonds payable with a maturity value of $400,000. The bonds pay interest on March 31 and September 30. Roland's fiscal year-end is December 31.

Requirements

1. If the market interest rate is 7 1/2% when Roland, Corp. issues its bonds, will the bonds be priced at par, at a premium, or at a discount? Explain.

2. If the market interest rate is 9% when Roland, Corp. issues its bonds, will the bonds be priced at par, at a premium, or at a discount? Explain.

3. Assume that the issue price of the bonds is $404,000. Journalize the following bonds payable transactions, first using the straight-line method and second using the effective interest method (Note: you will need a financial calculator to calculate the market rate for the effective interest method):

   a. Issuance of the bonds on April 1, 2015.

   b. Payment of interest and amortization of premium on September 30, 2015.

   c. Accrual of interest and amortization of premium on December 31, 2015.

   d. Payment of interest and amortization of premium on March 31, 2016.

P9-5A. Analyzing bond terms and accounting for bonds (*Learning Objective 5*) 20–25 min.

On January 1, 2015, Cave Creek Golf Club issued $600,000 of 20-year, 9% bonds payable. The bonds were sold for $600,000. The bonds pay interest each June 30 and December 31 and any discount or premium is amortized using effective interest amortization.

Requirements

1. Fill in the blanks to complete these statements:

   a. Cave Creek Golf Club's bonds are priced at (express the price as a percentage)___.

   b. When Cave Creek Golf Club issued its bonds, the market interest rate was (higher than, lower than, or equal to) ___ 9%.

   c. The amount of bond discount or premium is $___.

2. Record the following transactions:

   a. Issuance of the bonds payable on January 1, 2015.

   b. Payment of interest (and amortization of discount or premium, if any) on June 30, 2015.

   c. Payment of interest (and amortization of discount or premium, if any) on December 31, 2015. Explanations are not required.

3. At what amount will Cave Creek Golf Club report the bonds on its statement of financial position at December 31, 2015?

P9-6A. Statement of financial position disclosure of long-term liabilities (*Learning Objective 6*) 15–20 min.

The accounting records of Stokes, Corp. include the following items at December 31, 2015:

Salaries Payable	$32,000	Accounts Payable	$ 60,000
Bonds Payable,		Mortgage Note Payable,	
Current Portion	25,000	Long-Term	90,000
Discount on Bonds Payable	7,000	Interest Payable	20,000
Income Tax Payable	16,000	Bonds Payable	300,000

Requirement

1. Report these liabilities on Stokes' statement of financial position at December 31, 2015, including headings.

Quick solution:

Total current liabilities = $153,000; total long-term liabilities = $383,000

P9-7A. Calculation of debt ratio (*Learning Objective 7*) 10–15 min.

The classified statement of financial position for Tipke, Inc. as of December 31, 2015, is presented next.

Tipke, Inc. Statement of Financial Position December 31, 2015				
Current Assets:			**Current Liabilities:**	
Cash		$ 17,500	Accounts Payable	$ 1,100
Accounts Receivable		5,400	Salaries Payable	2,400
Supplies		400	Unearned Service Revenue	650
Prepaid Rent		3,600	Note Payable	10,000
Total Current Assets		26,900	Total Current Liabilities	14,150
Fixed Assets:			**Long-Term Debt:**	
Land		55,000	Mortgage Note Payable	10,000
Equipment	38,000		Bonds Payable	140,000
Less Accumulated			Total Long-Term Debt	150,000
Depreciation, Equipment	8,000	30,000		
			Shareholders' Equity:	
Building	225,000		Common Shares	20,000
Less Accumulated			Retained Earnings	122,750
Depreciation, Building	30,000	195,000	Total Shareholders' Equity	142,750
Total Fixed Assets		280,000	Total Liabilities and	
Total Assets		$306,900	Shareholders' Equity	$306,900

Requirements

1. Calculate Tipke's debt ratio as of December 31, 2015.
2. What percentage of Tipke's assets belong to the shareholders?
3. Would you be willing to extend credit to Tipke, Inc.? Why or why not?

P9-8A. Accounting for bonds (*Learning Objective 5*) 30–35 min.

Misan Inc. is planning to issue $2,000,000, 5-year, 6% bonds. Interest is payable semi-annually each June 30 and December 31. All of the bonds will be sold on July 1, 2015; they mature on June 30, 2020. Misan's year-end is December 31.

Requirements

1. Compute the issue (sale) price on July 1, 2015, if the yield is:
   a. 6%
   b. 8%
   c. 4%
2. Prepare all journal entries for the above three cases in 2015.
3. Prepare all journal entries for the above three cases in 2016, using the effective interest method.
4. Show how the bond interest expense and the bonds payable, for each case, should be reported on the annual financial statements for 2015 and 2016.

P9-9A. Accounting for bonds, year-end adjustment, and bond retirement (*Learning Objective 5*) 30–35 min.

Lamon Inc. issued $1,000,000, 5-year, 7% bonds on March 1, 2015, when the yield was 6%. Interest is payable semi-annually each August 31 and February 28. All of the bonds were sold on March 1, 2015; they mature on February 28, 2020. Lamon's year-end is December 31.

Requirements

1. Compute the issue (sale) price on March 1, 2015.

2. Record all journal entries for 2015. Lamon used the effective interest method.

3. Record the journal entry for the interest payment on February 28, 2016.

4. Assume on September 1, 2017, Lamon retired 70% of its bonds at 102.75. What is the carrying value of the bonds payable? Calculate the gain or loss on the bond retirement.

5. Record the journal entry for the bond retirement on September 1, 2017.

P9-10A. Accounting for various short-term and long-term liabilities and their impact on the debt ratio (Learning Objectives 2, 3, 6, & 7) 30–35 min.

Binco Inc. completed the following transactions during month of December. The company's fiscal year ends on December 31. The HST of 13% is included on all purchases and sales. Cost of goods sold is 60% of the sales.

December 1	Borrowed $50,000 from the PC Bank by signing a five-year note at 6% interest rate. The interest is paid monthly on the 1st of the month.
3	Purchased merchandise inventory on credit for $50,850, terms 2/10, n/30. Binco uses a perpetual inventory system.
8	Sold merchandise on credit for $14,125, including HST, terms 2/10, n/30.
17	Received a cheque from a customer who purchased merchandise on December 8.
20	Purchased merchandise inventory on credit for $40,680, (including HST) terms 2/10, n/30.
24	Received a $300 deposit for back-ordered merchandise to be shipped at the beginning of the new year.
31	Salaries Expense for the month were $10,000, of which employees deductions included CPP, $450; EI, $160; and income tax, $2,400. Binco also recorded the employee benefits expense.

Requirements

1. Record all journal entries, including adjusting entries, for the month of December.

2. Show the liability section of the statement of financial position on December 31.

PROBLEMS (GROUP B)

P9-1B. Accounting for several current liabilities (Learning Objectives 2 & 3) 20–25 min.

The following transactions of Handy Andy's stores occurred during 2015 and 2016:

2015	
Feb 3	Purchased equipment for $10,000, signing a six-month, 11% note payable.
28	Recorded the week's sales of $48,000, one-third for cash, and two-thirds on account. All sales amounts are subject to a 7% sales tax. Ignore cost of goods sold.
Mar 7	Sent last week's sales tax to the province.
Apr 30	Borrowed $120,000 on a four-year, 6% note payable that calls for annual payment of interest each April 30.
Aug 3	Paid the six-month, 11% note at maturity.
Nov 30	Purchased inventory at a cost of $6,000, signing a three-month, 5% note payable for that amount.

Dec 31	Accrued warranty expense, which is estimated at 6% of total sales of $580,000.
31	Accrued interest on all outstanding notes payable. Accrued interest for each note separately.
2016	
Feb 28	Paid off the 5% note, plus interest, at maturity.
Apr 30	Paid the interest for one year on the long-term note payable.

Requirement

1. Record the transactions in the company's journal. Explanations are not required.

P9-2B. Accounting for several current and long-term liabilities (*Learning Objectives 2, 3, & 5*) 20–25 min.

Following are pertinent facts about events during the current year at Laughton Snowboards.

a. December sales totalled $405,000, and Laughton collected sales tax of 5%. The sales tax will be sent to Alberta early in January.

b. Laughton owes $70,000 on a long-term note payable. At December 31, 6% interest for the year plus $45,000 of principal are payable within one year.

c. On August 31, Laughton signed a six-month, 6% note payable to purchase a machine costing $78,000. The note requires payment of principal and interest at maturity.

d. Sales of $101,000 were covered by a Laughton product warranty. At January 1, estimated warranty payable was $11,100. During the year, Laughton recorded warranty expense of $27,800 and paid warranty claims of $30,050.

e. On October 31, Laughton received cash of $3,990 in advance for the rent on a building. This rent will be earned evenly over six months.

Requirement

1. For each item, indicate the account and the related amount to be reported as a current liability on Laughton's December 31 statement of financial position.

P9-3B. Accounting for mortgages (*Learning Objective 5*) 20–25 min.

Franco, Corp. completed the following transactions in 2015:

Jan 1	Purchased a building costing $140,000 and signed a 10-year, 11% mortgage note payable for the same amount.
Jun 30	Made the first semi-annual payment on the mortgage note payable.
Dec 1	Signed a five-year lease to rent a warehouse for $9,000 per month due at the end of each month. The lease is considered an operating lease.
31	Paid for one month's rent on the warehouse.
31	Made the second semi-annual payment on the mortgage note payable.

Requirements

1. Complete the following amortization schedule for the first four mortgage payments on the $140,000 mortgage note, assuming semi-annual payments of $9,633.

Date	Payment	Interest	Principal	Loan Balance
Jan 1, 2015				$140,000
Jun 30, 2015	$9,633			
Dec 31, 2015				
Jun 30, 2016				
Dec 31, 2016				

2. Record the journal entries for the 2015 transactions.

3. Prepare the long-term liabilities section of the statement of financial position on December 31, 2015.

P9-4B. Analyzing bond terms and accounting for bonds (*Learning Objective 5*)
20–25 min.

Assume that on February 1, 2015, Atlantic, Corp. issued 9%, 10-year bonds payable with maturity value of $800,000. The bonds pay interest on January 31 and July 31. Atlantic's fiscal year-end is October 31.

Requirements

1. If the market interest rate is 8.5% when Atlantic, Corp. issues its bonds, will the bonds be priced at par, at a premium, or at a discount? Explain.

2. If the market interest rate is 10% when Atlantic, Corp. issues its bonds, will the bonds be priced at par, at a premium, or at a discount? Explain.

3. Assume that the issue price of the bonds is $832,000. Journalize the following bonds payable transactions, first using the straight-line method and second using the effective interest method (Note: you will need a financial calculator to calculate the market rate for the effective interest method):

   a. Issuance of the bonds on February 1, 2015.

   b. Payment of interest and amortization of premium on July 31, 2015.

   c. Accrual of interest and amortization of premium on October 31, 2015.

   d. Payment of interest and amortization of premium on January 31, 2016.

P9-5B. Analyzing bond terms and accounting for bonds (*Learning Objective 5*)
20–25 min.

On January 1, 2015, De La Terre Bistro issued $700,000 of 15-year, 7% bonds payable. The bonds were sold for $725,000. The bonds pay interest each June 30 and December 31.

Requirements

1. Fill in the blanks to complete these statements:

   a. De La Terre Bistro's bonds are priced at (express the price as a percentage)___.

   b. When De La Terre Bistro issued its bonds, the market interest rate was (higher than, lower than, or equal to)____7%.

   c. The amount of bond discount or premium is $___.

2. Record the following transactions, first using the straight-line method and second using the effective interest method (Note: you will need a financial calculator to calculate the market rate for the effective interest method):

   a. Issuance of the bonds payable on January 1, 2015. Explanations are not required.

   b. Payment of interest (and amortization of discount or premium, if any) on June 30, 2015. Explanations are not required.

   c. Payment of interest (and amortization of discount or premium, if any) on December 31, 2015. Explanations are not required.

3. At what amount will De La Terre Bistro report the bonds on its statement of financial position at December 31, 2015?

P9-6B. Statement of financial position disclosure of long-term liabilities (*Learning Objective 6*) 15–20 min.

The accounting records of Green, Corp. include the following items at December 31, 2015:

Salaries Payable......................	$10,000	Accounts Payable..................	$ 52,000
Bonds Payable,		Mortgage Note Payable,	
Current Portion	17,000	Long-Term	120,000
Discount on Bonds Payable	13,000	Interest Payable	16,000
Income Tax Payable.................	8,000	Bonds Payable	220,000

Requirement

1. Report these liabilities on Green's statement of financial position at December 31, 2015, including headings.

P9-7B. Calculation of debt ratio (*Learning Objective 7*) 10–15 min.

The classified statement of financial position for Thorn, Inc. as of December 31, 2015, is presented next.

Thorn, Inc.
Statement of Financial Position
December 31, 2015

ASSETS			LIABILITIES	
Current Assets:			Current Liabilities:	
Cash		$ 6,600	Accounts Payable	$ 10,200
Accounts Receivable		10,100	Salaries Payable	1,900
Supplies		1,300	Unearned Service Revenue	17,700
Prepaid Rent		2,800	Note Payable	10,000
Total Current Assets		$ 20,800	Total Current Liabilities	39,800
Fixed Assets:			Long-Term Debt:	
Land		55,000	Mortgage Note Payable	30,000
Equipment	$ 40,000		Bonds Payable	110,000
Less: Accumulated			Total Long-Term Debt	140,000
Depreciation, Equipment	14,000	26,000		
Building	225,000		**SHAREHOLDERS' EQUITY**	
Less: Accumulated			Common Shares	8,000
Depreciation, Building	90,000	135,000	Retained Earnings	49,000
Total Fixed Assets		216,000	Total Shareholders' Equity	57,000
			Total Liabilities and	
Total Assets		$236,800	Shareholders' Equity	$236,800

Requirements

1. Calculate Thorn's debt ratio as of December 31, 2015.
2. What percentage of Thorn's assets belong to the shareholders?
3. Would you be willing to extend credit to Thorn, Inc.? Why or why not?

P9-8B. Accounting for bonds (*Learning Objective 5*) 30–35 min.

Sansen Inc. is planning to issue $5,000,000, 8-year, 4% bonds. Interest is payable semi-annually each June 30 and December 31. All of the bonds will be sold on July 1, 2015; they mature on June 30, 2023. Sansen's year-end is December 31.

Requirements

1. Compute the issue (sale) price on July 1, 2015, if the yield is:

   a. 4%

   b. 6%

   c. 2%

2. Prepare all journal entries for the above three cases in 2015.

3. Prepare all journal entries for the above three cases in 2016 using the effective interest method.

4. Show how the bond interest expense and the bonds payable, for each case, should be reported on the annual financial statements for 2015 and 2016.

P9-9B. Accounting for bonds, year-end adjustment, and bond retirement (*Learning Objective 5*) 30–35 min.

Chura Inc. issued $5,000,000, 10-year, 5% bonds on February 1, 2015, when the yield was 6%. Interest is payable semi-annually each July 31 and January 31. All of the bonds were sold on February 1, 2015; they mature on January 31, 2025. Chura's year-end is December 31. The effective interest method is used.

Requirements

1. Compute the issue (sale) price on February 1, 2015.

2. Record all journal entries for 2015.

3. Record the journal entry for the interest payment on January 31, 2016.

4. Assume on February 1, 2022, Chura retired 60% of its bonds at 96.75. What is the carrying value of the bonds payable? Calculate the gain or loss on the bond retirement.

5. Record the journal entry for the bond retirement on February 1, 2022.

P9-10B. Accounting for various short-term and long-term liabilities and their impact on the debt ratio (*Learning Objectives 2, 3, 6, & 7*) 30–35 min.

Budai Inc. completed the following transactions during the month of December. The company's fiscal year ends on December 31. The HST of 13% is included in all purchases and sales. Cost of goods sold is 50% of the sales.

December 3	Purchased merchandise inventory on credit for $28,250, terms 2/10, n/30. Budai uses a perpetual inventory system.
10	Sold merchandise on credit for $18,080, terms 2/10, n/30.
12	Paid the invoice for the purchase on December 3.
16	Borrowed $30,000 from the CT Bank by signing a three-year note at 4% interest rate. The interest is paid monthly on the 15th of the month.
19	Received a cheque from a customer who purchased merchandise on December 10.
23	Purchased merchandise inventory on credit for $47,460, terms 2/10, n/30.
28	Received a $500 deposit for back-ordered merchandise to be shipped at the beginning of the new year.
31	Salaries Expense for the month were $25,000, of which employee deductions included CPP, $1,230; EI, $430; and income tax, $6,250. Budai also recorded the employee benefits expense.

Requirements

1. Record all journal entries, including adjusting entries, for the month of December.

2. Show the liability section of the statement of financial position on December 31.

PROBLEMS (ALTERNATES 1, 2, AND 3)

These alternative problem sets are available for your practice benefit on **MyAccountingLab**.

CONTINUING EXERCISE

In this exercise we will continue the accounting for Graham's Yard Care, Inc. Assume that on September 1, 2015, Graham's Yard Care, Inc. borrowed $5,000 from First National Bank, signing a nine-month, 10% note.

Requirement

1. Prepare the journal required on September 1, 2015, December 31, 2015, and May 31, 2016, to record the transactions related to the note.

CONTINUING PROBLEM

This continues the Aqua Elite, Inc. example from the Continuing Problem in Chapter 8. Aqua Elite, Inc. purchased some of its fixed assets during 2015 using long-term debt. The following table summarizes the nature of this long-term debt.

Date	Item	Annual Interest Rate	Amount	Payment Terms
May 18	Note payable	8%	$31,000	Five equal annual payments of principal plus accrued interest are due on May 18 of each year.
Sep 1	Mortgage payable	6%	$85,000	Semiannual payments of $3,677 due on March 1 and September 1 of each year.

Requirements

1. Calculate the interest expense that Aqua Elite, Inc. should accrue as of December 31, 2015.
2. Prepare the statement of financial position presentation for all long-term debt indicating the portion that should be classified as current and the portion that should be classified as long-term.

APPLY YOUR KNOWLEDGE

ETHICS IN ACTION

Case 1. The Transmission Shop was the largest company in Ontario specializing in rebuilding automobile transmissions. Every transmission rebuilt by the business was covered by a six-month warranty. The owner, Ron Wood, was meeting with his accountant to go over the yearly financial statements. In reviewing the statement of financial position, Ron became puzzled by the large amount of current liabilities being reported, so he asked his accountant to explain them. The accountant said that most of the current liabilities were the result of accruals, such as the estimated warranty payable, some additional wages payable, and interest accrued on the note owed to the bank. The employees were not actually paid until the first week of the new year, so some of their wages had to be recorded and properly matched against revenues in the current period. Also, several months of interest expense had to be accrued on a bank loan, but the largest amount of the accrued liabilities was due to the estimated warranty expense. Ron asked whether the wages payable and the interest payable could be removed because they would be paid off shortly after the year ended. The accountant stated that accrued liabilities had to be properly recognized in the current accounting period, and, thus, they could not be removed. Ron agreed but then asked about the large accrued liability based upon the estimated warranty amounts. Again, the accountant stated that in previous years actual warranty cost had been about 5% of the total sales and, therefore, in the current year the estimate was accrued at 5%. Ron then informed the accountant that a new conditioning lubricant had been added to each transmission rebuilt, which dramatically reduced the amount of rebuilt transmissions being returned under warranty. As a result, Ron strongly felt that the warranty estimate should be reduced to only 2% of total sales and, thereby, the accrued warranty liability and related expense would also be reduced. The accountant argued that the only reason Ron wanted to reduce the estimated percentage was to improve the financial statements, which would be unethical and inappropriate.

Requirements

1. What is the impact of accrued liabilities on the financial statements? Should the accrued liabilities for wages and interest payable be removed from the statement of financial position?

2. Does Ron have a valid reason for wanting to reduce the estimated warranty liability? Are the concerns expressed by the accountant valid?

3. What ethical issues are involved?

Case 2. On December 28, Sam Hanna, CEO of a pharmaceutical manufacturing company (which is adopting IFRS), was meeting with the company controller to discuss a major issue facing the company. The company has been testing a medicine on a group of volunteers. Two of the volunteers experienced critical side effects and have sued the company for damages. Sam told the controller that the company's lawyer just left and she informed him that the company's chances of having to pay a penalty are pretty high. She recommended an out-of-court settlement of $2,000,000 for each claimant. Sam told the controller that they have been experiencing a rough year. He suggested the company ignore this issue in the annual financial statements and let it be recognized when the liability is paid. The controller responded that this issue cannot be overlooked. He mentioned that having to pay the indemnification is more likely than not, and hence it should be recognized now. Sam mentioned that if the lawyer told them this information a week later they wouldn't have been having this conversation at all. He told the controller to simply assume that you heard about this liability next week.

Requirements

1. Why does Sam want to postpone recognizing the amount paid to the claimants until next year?

2. Does the controller have a legitimate argument? Does Sam have a legitimate argument?

3. What ethical issues are involved here?

KNOW YOUR BUSINESS

FINANCIAL ANALYSIS

Purpose: To help familiarize you with the financial reporting of a real company to further your understanding of the chapter material you are learning.

This case focuses on the liabilities of Bombardier Inc. Current liabilities are those obligations that will become due and payable within the next year or operating cycle (whichever is longer), while long-term liabilities are those that are due and payable more than one year from the statement of financial position date. It is important to properly classify and report these liabilities because they affect liquidity. We will now consider the current and long-term liabilities of Bombardier Inc. Refer to the Bombardier Inc. financial statements found in MyAccountingLab. Also, consider Note 12 and Note 13 in the footnotes included in the annual report.

Requirements

1. What was the balance of Accounts Payable and Accrued Liabilities at December 31, 2012 and December 31, 2011? Did the amount increase or decrease over the year?

2. What do the Advances on Aerospace Programs represent?

3. How much is owed for long-term debt at December 31, 2012? Look at the financing activities section of the Consolidated Statements of Cash Flows. What is the amount of proceeds from issuance of long-term debt over the last year? What is the amount of repayments of long-term debt over the last year? Does it appear that Bombardier Inc. is borrowing more than it repays or repaying more than it borrows? From Note 24, determine how much of the long-term debt must be repaid in the next twelve months, i.e., during the year ended December 31, 2013?

4. What are the total liabilities that Bombardier owes at December 31, 2012? What type of liabilities represents the highest percentage of total liabilities and what is this percentage for 2012 and 2011? Is the amount of total shareholders' equity more than or less than the total of all the liabilities at December 31, 2012? What does this result mean?

INDUSTRY ANALYSIS

Purpose: To help you understand and compare the performance of two companies in the same industry.

Find the Bombardier Annual Report, Year Ended December 31, 2012, located in MyAccountingLab and go to the Financial Statements. Now access The Boeing Company's 2012 Annual Report. To do this from the internet, go to their webpage for the Investor Relations at http://www.boeing.com/companyoffices/financial/quarterly.htm and under Annual Report, go to the 2012 Annual Report.

Requirement

1. Calculate the debt to total asset ratio (total liabilities to total assets) for both companies for the past two years. Generally speaking, what does this ratio tell you? Using these calculations, what comments can you make about these two companies?

SMALL BUSINESS ANALYSIS

Purpose: To help you understand the importance of cash flows in the operation of a small business.

Your business has been doing pretty well since you first opened the doors five years ago. You've been thinking for the last six months or so about expanding the business. There is some property right next door that would work well into your expansion plans. It would take some renovations to the building, but to continue to grow, you know you're going to need more room. But here's the problem. How are you going to pay for the building and the renovations? Your cash account is in pretty good shape, but you remember the sage advice of the business consultant who helped you when you were just getting started. That advice was to always have enough available cash to cover three months' worth of expenses just in case of some unexpected business interruption. Your available cash and short-term investments of $100,000 is right at that benchmark.

Some preliminary investigation into the property next door indicates that the existing owner would probably be willing to accept $200,000 for the property. You also have a discussion with a contractor associate who tells you that the renovations to your specifications would cost about $50,000. So your dilemma is how are you going to come up with $250,000? You figure the best place to start is with a visit to your banker.

At that meeting with the banker, he tells you something like this:

"Frank, we would be pleased to help you out with your expansion plans. We would require you to take out a mortgage on the building and we would need a 20% down payment of the total amount up front. So the balance that we would be lending you would be 80% of the total you need, or $200,000. Your down payment amount would be $50,000. At 8% for 20 years, your monthly payments would be $1,672.88."

You are somewhat pleased with the outcome of the meeting, but you tell the banker you will get back to him in a day or two. You know that this is a big step and a long-term investment for the business.

Requirements

1. After considering the details of the plan the banker gave you, what are your thoughts? Since the down payment is going to use up about half of your available cash, how does that concern you? What about the long-term commitment of 20 years?

2. Assuming you go ahead with the mortgage and the purchase and renovation of the property, journalize the transactions to acquire the property and make the renovations. Where will the building and the renovations show up on your financial statements? Where will the mortgage show up on your financial statements? If the interest portion of your first payment is going to be $1,333.33, journalize the transaction to make your first mortgage payment.

WRITTEN COMMUNICATION

Your boss has just asked you to write a short note to one of his clients that had expressed some concerns about the difference between liabilities that are of an unknown amount versus contingent liabilities. The client is in the midst of a lawsuit with a governmental agency that its attorney thinks has about a 50-50 chance of winning. However, if the company loses, it could cost a substantial amount of money. The client is wondering if it needs to account for the lawsuit, and if so, how?

Requirement

1. Write a note to the client explaining the difference between a liability of an unknown amount and a contingent liability. Also, make a suggestion as to how this particular situation might need to be accounted for.

Self Check Answers
1. a 2. c 3. d 4. a 5. a 6. c 7. b 8. a 9. a 10. c

LEARNING OBJECTIVES

1. Review the characteristics of a corporation
2. Describe the two sources of shareholders' equity and the classes of shares
3. Journalize the issuance of shares
4. Account for cash dividends
5. Account for stock dividends and stock splits
6. Account for treasury shares
7. Report shareholders' equity
8. Evaluate return on shareholders' equity and return on common shareholders' equity

CHAPTER OUTLINE

HOW Are Corporations Organized? p. 578

WHAT Makes Up the Shareholders' Equity of a Corporation? p. 579

HOW Is the Issuance of Shares Recorded? p. 580

HOW Are Cash Dividends Accounted For? p. 581

HOW Are Stock Dividends and Stock Splits Accounted For? p. 584

HOW Are Treasury Shares Accounted For? p. 589

HOW Is Shareholders' Equity Reported? p. 592

FOCUS On Decision Making: Ratios p. 593

CHAPTER 10
Corporations: Share Capital and Retained Earnings

BUSINESS, ACCOUNTING, AND YOU

Best Buy needs a lot of money to operate. It gets some of that money from lenders, such as banks, but it also gets money from owners, who are called shareholders in a corporation. But why would someone want to own part of a company like Best Buy? Why would someone invest money in a company? The answer is that owners seek value—they seek net income that compensates them for the use of their money over time and for taking risks.

How do Best Buy's shareholders provide Best Buy with money? There are two ways. First, the shareholders of Best Buy can buy shares from the company. The shareholders give Best Buy money, and Best Buy gives them a certificate of ownership called a share certificate. The share certificate permits the shareholders to vote for who will manage the company. Second, Best Buy's net income belongs to its shareholders. However, the business can decide to retain its net income or distribute it to shareholders through distributions called dividends. If the net income is retained in the business, it can be used to grow the business, to pay off liabilities, or for other actions management feels are needed.

It's important to understand how much money shareholders provide to a company. Every company tries to generate net income and, thus, create value for shareholders. The investor must decide if the net income generated was worth the time and risk assumed. Remember, the objective of a business is to create value for its owners. Whether an accountant or manager, you need to know how accountants recognize, measure, record, and report shareholders' equity.

HOW ARE CORPORATIONS ORGANIZED?

A **corporation** is a separate legal entity from its owners. Corporations in Canada are established as a result of an application to either the federal government or to a particular provincial government. The process of becoming a corporation is known as incorporating. To incorporate, an organization's founders file an application to the appropriate government authorities, specifying information including the name of the corporation, the type of business, the location of the business, the number and types of shares to be authorized, and so forth.

Once the organization has become a corporation, it is authorized to sell individuals an ownership interest, or shares, in the corporation. When you invest in a corporation, you may call yourself a **shareholder**, or stock holder. Different classes of shares may be issued, but it is the "common shareholders" who actually own the company.

It is important to distinguish between a private corporation and a public corporation. A public corporation has its shares listed for trading in a stock market such as the Toronto Stock Exchange (TSX). Many large Canadian corporations, including companies like BlackBerry, Loblaws, Shoppers Drug Mart, and Tim Hortons, have their shares listed on the TSX. Private corporations, on the other hand, are typically, though not always, smaller companies, and usually only have a small number of shareholders, and the shares are not "liquid"; that is, the shares are not easily traded, or transferred from one person to another.

While other forms of business activity such as proprietorships and partnerships are plentiful in Canada, it is the corporate form of ownership that dominates.

A corporation has a separate legal existence from its common shareholders, and may act independently of its owners. It may sue and be sued, must pay taxes as a separate entity, and, crucially, enables the limited liability of its shareholders. This means that creditors cannot generally make a claim against individual shareholders for liabilities associated with the corporation.

Exhibit 10-1 summarizes some of the advantages and disadvantages of the corporate form of business.

Advantages	Why?	Disadvantages	Why?
Shareholders have limited liability because the corporation is a separate legal entity.	The maximum shareholders can lose is their invested amount in shares.	Costly	Establishing a corporation is more costly than other forms of business.
A corporation can raise more money than a proprietorship or partnership.	A corporation can issue shares to numerous people, and on top of that it can also issue bonds.	Requires preparation of dual tax returns	As an owner of a corporation, you have to file a tax return for the corporation and another personal tax return.
A corporation has a continuous life.	Because the shares pass from one person to another, a corporation is not affected by the life of its shareholders.	Lots of government regulations	If the shares are going to be publicly traded, then the corporation needs to implement IFRS and follow strict government regulations.
The transfer of corporate ownership is easy.	Shares can be traded on the stock market.		

Exhibit 10-1 ▲

WHAT MAKES UP THE SHAREHOLDERS' EQUITY OF A CORPORATION?

Recall from Chapter 1 that the shareholders' equity of a corporation is divided into two categories:

L.O. ② Describe the two sources of shareholders' equity and the classes of shares

- **Share capital** (also called contributed capital) represents amounts received from the shareholders. **Common shares**, discussed in Chapter 1, are the main source of share capital. This is *externally* generated capital and results from transactions with outsiders.
- **Retained earnings** is capital earned by profitable operations. This is *internally* generated capital and results from internal corporate decisions and earnings. In other words, it is the re-investment of the undistributed net income back into the business.

SHAREHOLDERS' RIGHTS

There are four basic rights a shareholder may have:

1. **Vote.** Shareholders participate in management by voting on corporate matters. This is the only way in which a shareholder can help to manage the corporation. Normally, each common share carries one vote.
2. **Dividends.** Shareholders receive a proportionate part of any dividend. Each share receives an equal dividend so, for example, a shareholder who owns 1% of the total shares in the company receives 1% of any dividend.
3. **Liquidation.** Shareholders receive their proportionate share of any assets remaining after the corporation pays its debts and liquidates (goes out of business).
4. **Preemption.** Shareholders can maintain their proportionate ownership in the corporation. Suppose you own 5% of a corporation's shares. If the corporation issues 100,000 new shares, it must offer you the opportunity to buy 5% (5,000) of the new shares. However, if it is not stated explicitly in the shareholders' agreement, shareholders might not have such right.

CLASSES OF SHARES

Every corporation must issue common shares, which represent the basic ownership of the corporation. The real "owners" of the corporation are the common shareholders. Some companies issue Class A common shares, which carry the right to vote, and Class B common shares, which could have different voting rights or no voting rights at all. For example, Class A shares could have 10 voting rights, while Class B shares could have only 1 voting right. There must be at least one voting "class" of shares. However, there is no limit to the number or types of classes of shares that a corporation may issue. Each class of shares has a separate account. For example, Rogers Communication Inc. has Class A voting shares and Class B non-voting shares.

In addition to common shares, a corporation may also issue **preferred shares**. Preferred shares give their owners certain advantages over the owners of common shares. Most notably, preferred shareholders receive dividends before the common shareholders. They also receive assets before common shareholders if the corporation liquidates. Corporations pay a fixed dividend on preferred shares, which is printed on the face of the preferred share certificate. Investors usually buy preferred shares to earn those fixed dividends. With these advantages, preferred shareholders take less investment risk than common shareholders. For example, Canadian Banc Corporation is authorized to issue an unlimited number of preferred shares.

Owners of preferred shares may also have the four basic shareholder rights, unless a right is withheld. The right to vote, however, is usually withheld from preferred shares. Companies may issue different series of preferred shares (Series A and Series B, for example). Each series is recorded in a separate account.

PAR VALUE

Shares may carry a par value, a stated value, or they may be no-par shares. **Par value** is an arbitrary amount assigned by a company to a share.

Shares that had a face value printed on the share certificate were called "par value." Typically, this value represented the amount for which the shares had originally been issued by the corporation. However, immediately after the issue of the shares, the marketplace would set the new value of the shares, which made the par value meaningless. Therefore, under the Canada Business Corporations Act (CBCA), shares must be no par value.

HOW IS THE ISSUANCE OF SHARES RECORDED?

L.O. 3 Journalize the issuance of shares

Corporations such as Best Buy and Canadian Tire need huge quantities of money to operate. They cannot finance all their operations through borrowing, so they raise capital by issuing shares. A company can sell its shares directly to shareholders or it can use the services of an **underwriter**, such as the brokerage firms RBC Dominion and TD Waterhouse. An underwriter usually agrees to buy all the shares it cannot sell to its clients.

The price that the corporation receives from issuing shares is called the **issue price**. We use Mackay Industries to show how to account for the issuance of shares.

ISSUING COMMON SHARES

How does a company record the issuance of shares? Let's assume that the shares for Mackay Industries were trading at $15 per share on January 1. Remember that we do not need to refer to these shares as "no-par shares" because all Canadian shares are no-par value. The entry to record the issuance of 500,000 shares for $15 per share would be as follows:

+7,500,000 = +7,500,000

DATE	ACCOUNTS	POST REF.	DR.	CR.
Jan 1	Cash (500,000 × $15)		7,500,000	
	Common Shares			7,500,000
	Issued 500,000 common shares for $15 per share.			

Issuing Shares for Assets Other Than Cash

A corporation may issue shares for assets other than cash. It records the assets received at their current market value and credits the share accounts accordingly. The assets' prior book value is irrelevant. Now let's reconsider the January 1 entry for Mackay Industries. Assume that, instead of cash, Mackay Industries received a building worth $7,500,000 in exchange for the 500,000 shares of its $15 common shares on January 1. How would the entry change?

Under IFRS and ASPE, non-monetary exchanges, such as shares exchanged for an asset, should be measured at the more reliable measure of the fair value of the asset received. However, if the value of the shares can be more reliably measured, for instance when the share price can be easily obtained from the stock market, then the asset exchanged should be recorded at the fair value of the share price. If Mackay Industries is not a publicly traded company, the fair market value of the building is a more reliable measure, which would make the value of each share $15 ($7,500,000 / 500,000 shares = $15 per share). If Mackay Industries is a publicly traded company, the share value given up will also be valued at $15 per share (500,000 × $15 = $7,500,000).

DATE	ACCOUNTS	POST REF.	DR.	CR.
Jan 1	Building (fair market value)		7,500,000	
	Common Shares ($15 × 500,000)			7,500,000
	Issued 500,000 common shares in exchange for a building.			

+7,500,000 = +7,500,000

ISSUING PREFERRED SHARES

Accounting for preferred shares is similar to the process illustrated for issuing common shares. Let's assume that Mackay Industries decides to issue 10,000 of its 10% preferred shares on February 15 for $20 per share. The entry to record the issuance would be as follows:

DATE	ACCOUNTS	POST REF.	DR.	CR.
Feb 15	Cash (10,000 × $20)		200,000	
	Preferred Shares (10,000 × $20)			200,000
	Issued 10,000 preferred shares for $20 per share.			

+200,000 = +200,000

HOW ARE CASH DIVIDENDS ACCOUNTED FOR?

As discussed in Chapter 1, a profitable corporation may distribute cash to the shareholders in the form of **dividends**. Dividends cause a decrease in both assets and shareholders' equity (retained earnings). Companies are prohibited from using share capital for dividends. Accountants, therefore, use the term **legal capital** to refer to the portion of shareholders' equity that cannot be used for dividends. Corporations declare cash dividends from retained earnings and then pay them with cash.

L.O. 4 Account for cash dividends

DIVIDEND DATES

A corporation declares a dividend before paying it. There are three dates associated with the declaration and payment of a cash dividend.

1. **Declaration date.** On the declaration date—say, March 5—the board of directors announces the intention to pay the dividend. The declaration of a cash dividend creates an obligation (liability) for the corporation.

2. **Date of record.** Those shareholders holding the shares at the end of business on the date of record—usually several weeks after declaration, say, March 19—will receive the dividend cheque even if they sell the shares the next day.

3. **Payment date.** Payment of the dividend usually follows the record date by several weeks, say, March 31.

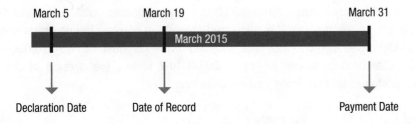

DECLARING AND PAYING DIVIDENDS

The annual dividend rate on *preferred shares* is usually expressed as a flat dollar amount per share, such as $2 per share. It could also be expressed as a percentage of its value. Let's look at how to compute preferred dividends, using Mackay Industries' 10,000 outstanding 10% preferred shares which are issued at $20.

Outstanding shares × flat dividend rate = preferred dividend
10,000 shares × $2 per share = $20,000
or
Value of outstanding shares × percentage = preferred dividends
10,000 × $20 × 10% = $20,000

Cash dividends on *common shares* are computed the same way.

Remember from Chapter 3 that the Dividends account is closed to Retained Earnings at the end of the year. So, instead of using the Dividends account, companies may record the declaration of a dividend by debiting the Retained Earnings account instead of Dividends. In this case, there will be no entry required at year-end to close the Dividends account. To account for Mackay Industries' declaration of a cash dividend, we debit Retained Earnings and credit Dividends Payable on the date of declaration, as follows:

DATE	ACCOUNTS	POST REF.	DR.	CR.
Mar 5	Retained Earnings		20,000	
	Dividends Payable			20,000
	Declared a cash dividend.			

On the date of record, no journal entry is required. On the payment date, Mackay Industries will record the payment of the dividend as follows:

DATE	ACCOUNTS	POST REF.	DR.	CR.
Mar 31	Dividends Payable		20,000	
	Cash			20,000
	Paid cash dividend.			

When a company has issued only common shares, the common shareholders will receive any dividend that is declared. However, if both preferred and common shares are issued, the preferred shareholders get their dividends first. The common shareholders receive dividends only if the total dividend declared is larger than the amount of the annual preferred dividend. In other words, the common shareholders get the leftovers. Let's see how dividends are divided between preferred and common shareholders.

DIVIDING DIVIDENDS BETWEEN PREFERRED AND COMMON SHAREHOLDERS

Assume that Mackay Industries has 500,000 common shares outstanding and 10,000 preferred shares outstanding. We calculated earlier that Mackay Industries' annual preferred dividend was $20,000. So, total declared dividends must exceed $20,000 for the common shareholders to get anything. **Exhibit 10-2** shows the division of dividends between preferred and common for two situations.

Situation A—Total Dividend of $15,000:		
Preferred dividend (the full $15,000 goes to the preferred		
shareholders because the annual preferred dividend is $20,000)	$15,000	
Common dividend (none because the total dividend did not cover		
the preferred annual dividend)	0	
Total dividend	$15,000	
Situation B—Total Dividend of $30,000:		
Preferred dividend (10,000 shares × $2 per share)	$20,000	
Common dividend ($30,000 − $20,000)	10,000	
Total dividend	$30,000	

Exhibit 10-2 ▲

If Mackay Industries' dividend is large enough to cover the preferred dividend (Situation B), the preferred shareholders get their regular dividend ($20,000), and the common shareholders get the remainder ($10,000). But if the year's dividend falls below the annual preferred amount (Situation A), the preferred shareholders will receive all of the dividend paid by the company, and the common shareholders get nothing that year.

DIVIDENDS ON CUMULATIVE AND NONCUMULATIVE PREFERRED SHARES

Preferred shares can be either

- cumulative, or
- noncumulative.

Preferred shares are assumed to be cumulative unless they are specifically designated as noncumulative. Most preferred shares are cumulative. Let's see what effect the cumulative versus noncumulative designation has on the payment of dividends.

As we saw with Mackay Industries in Situation A in Exhibit 10-2, a corporation may fail to pay the entire annual preferred dividend. This may happen if, for example, the company does not have enough cash to fund the entire dividend. This is called *passing the dividend*, and the dividends are said to be in **arrears**. **Cumulative preferred shares** shareholders must receive the current year's dividends and all dividends in arrears before the common shareholders get any dividend.

The preferred shares of Mackay Industries are cumulative. How do we know this? Because they are not labelled as noncumulative.

Suppose Mackay Industries passed the entire 2015 preferred dividend of $20,000. Before paying any common dividend in 2016, Mackay Industries must first pay preferred dividends of $20,000 for 2015 in addition to $20,000 for 2016, a total of $40,000. In 2016, Mackay Industries declares a $75,000 dividend. How much of this dividend goes to preferred? How much goes to common? The allocation of this $75,000 dividend is as follows:

MEMORYTIPS

Cumulative preferred shares receive dividends in arrears *plus* current year's dividends when dividends are declared.

Total dividend		$75,000
Preferred shareholders get:		
2015 dividend (10,000 × $2 per share)......................	$20,000	
2016 dividend (10,000 × $2 per share)......................	20,000	
Total to preferred...		40,000
Common shareholders get the remainder.............................		$35,000

If Mackay Industries declared the $75,000 dividend on November 10, 2016, it would make the following entry:

Assets	=	Liabilities	+ Shareholders' Equity
	=	+40,000	−75,000
		+35,000	

DATE	ACCOUNTS	POST REF.	DR.	CR.
Nov 10	Retained Earnings		75,000	
	Dividends Payable—Preferred			40,000
	Dividends Payable—Common			35,000
	Declared a cash dividend.			

MEMORY TIPS

Noncumulative preferred shares receive dividends only for the year in which dividends are declared.

10.1 STILL DON'T GET IT?

Visit MyAccountingLab for an alternate explanation of this important accounting concept.

If the preferred shares are *noncumulative*, the corporation is not required to pay any dividends in arrears. Suppose Mackay Industries' preferred shares were noncumulative and the company passed the 2015 dividend. The preferred shareholders would lose the 2015 dividend of $20,000 forever. Then, before paying any common dividends in 2016, Mackay Industries would only have to pay the 2016 preferred dividend of $20,000, which would leave $55,000 for the common shareholders.

Dividends in arrears are *not* a liability. A liability for dividends arises only after the board of directors declares a dividend. It is possible that the board may never declare another dividend in the future. However, a corporation does report cumulative preferred dividends in arrears in the notes to the financial statements. This shows the common shareholders how big the declared dividend will need to be for them to get any dividends in the future.

 DECISION GUIDELINES

DECISION	GUIDELINE	ANALYZE
As a member of the board of directors, I make decisions on when to declare dividends, how much to declare, and whether they will be cash dividends or something else. When making these decisions, when is a cash dividend appropriate?	Consider the amount of available cash as well as the balance in retained earnings.	A cash dividend is a distribution of earnings to the company's shareholders. So, a company cannot declare and distribute dividends unless the balance in retained earnings (counting the current year's earnings) exceeds the amount of the desired dividend. In addition, the company must have the cash available to pay the dividend if it is declared. A business should carefully analyze its future cash needs so that it does not deplete its cash with a dividend and end up with cash flow issues in the future.

HOW ARE STOCK DIVIDENDS AND STOCK SPLITS ACCOUNTED FOR?

L.O. 5 Account for stock dividends and stock splits

RECORDING STOCK DIVIDENDS

A **stock dividend** is a distribution of a corporation's own shares to its shareholders. Unlike cash dividends, stock dividends do not give any assets to the shareholders.

As with a cash dividend, there are three dates associated with a stock dividend:

- Declaration date
- Date of record
- Distribution date

The board of directors announces the stock dividend on the declaration date. The date of record determines who will receive the additional shares. The distribution date is the date the additional shares are distributed to the shareholders. Unlike with a cash dividend, the declaration of a stock dividend does *not* create a liability. This is because the corporation is not obligated to distribute any assets to the shareholders. (Recall that a liability is a claim on assets.) With a stock dividend, the corporation has simply declared its intention to distribute more of its shares. A stock dividend affects the following accounts:

- Retained Earnings is reduced (debited) by an amount equal to the number of shares being distributed times the current market price of the company's shares.

- Common Shares is increased (credited) by an amount equal to the number of shares being distributed times the value of the share. If the company declares a stock dividend of an amount that is less than 20%–25% of the total number of shares outstanding, then the market value of the shares will be used. If the company declares a stock dividend of more than 20%–25%, then the average issuing price (or par value) will be used.

The net effect of a stock dividend is to transfer an amount equal to the market value of the dividend from retained earnings into share capital.

Assume that Mackay Industries has the following shareholders' equity on June 1, prior to declaring a stock dividend:

Mackay Industries, Inc. Shareholders' Equity June 1	
Share Capital:	
Preferred Shares, 500,000 shares authorized,	
10,000 shares issued	$ 200,000
Common Shares, 2,000,000 shares authorized,	
500,000 shares issued	7,500,000
Total Share Capital	7,700,000
Retained Earnings	2,000,000
Total Shareholders' Equity	$9,700,000

Now, assume Mackay Industries declares a 5% stock dividend on June 15 when the market value of Mackay Industries common shares is $40 per share. Once Mackay declares the stock dividend, the Retained Earnings account is reduced or debited; however, this is not the date to distribute the additional shares. Mackay will need to credit an account called Stock Dividends Distributable. The Stock Dividends Distributable account is one of the shareholders' equity accounts and is increased when stock dividends are declared and decreased when stock dividends are distributed to shareholders. Mackay would record the declaration and distribution of the stock dividend as follows:

DATE	ACCOUNTS	POST REF.	DR.	CR.
Jun 15	Retained Earnings (500,000 × 5% × $40)		1,000,000	
	Stock Dividends Distributable			1,000,000
	Declared 5% common share dividend.			

DATE	ACCOUNTS	POST REF.	DR.	CR.
Jun 30	Stock Dividends Distributable		1,000,000	
	Common Shares			1,000,000
	Distributed 5% common share dividend.			

As we did with cash dividends, we debited Retained Earnings directly instead of using a dividend account. Remember that a stock dividend does not affect assets, liabilities, or total shareholders' equity. A stock dividend merely rearranges the balances in the equity accounts, leaving total equity unchanged. Immediately after the stock dividend, Mackay Industries' shareholders' equity looks like this:

Mackay Industries, Inc. **Shareholders' Equity** June 30		
Share Capital:		
Preferred Shares, 500,000 shares authorized,		
10,000 shares issued		$ 200,000
Common Shares, 2,000,000 shares authorized,		
525,000 shares issued		8,500,000
Total Share Capital		8,700,000
Retained Earnings		1,000,000
Total Shareholders' Equity		$9,700,000

Note that the number of outstanding shares is now 525,000 [500,000 + (500,000 × 0.05)]. Note also that total shareholders' equity is still $9,700,000. The effect of the stock dividend was simply to transfer $1,000,000 from retained earnings to share capital.

Based on the previous illustration it could be concluded that stock dividends:

- affect only shareholders' equity accounts (including Retained Earnings and Common Shares).

- have no effect on total shareholders' equity.

- have no effect on assets or liabilities.

A corporation distributes stock dividends to shareholders in proportion to the number of shares they already own. Suppose you own 5,000 shares of Mackay Industries' common shares. If Mackay Industries distributes a 5% stock dividend, you would receive 250 (5,000 × 0.05) additional shares. You would now own 5,250 shares. All other Mackay Industries' shareholders also receive additional shares equal to 5% of the amount of shares they currently have. Because the amount of shares every shareholder has increases by 5%, the shareholders would all own the same percentage share of Mackay Industries' shares as they did before the stock dividend.

Companies issue stock dividends for several reasons:

1. To continue a history of declaring dividends while conserving cash. A company may wish to continue dividends to keep shareholders happy but needs to keep its cash for operations. A stock dividend is a way to do so without using any cash.

2. To reduce the market price of its shares. A stock dividend will usually cause the company's share price to fall. This happens because after the stock dividend there will be more shares representing the same value of shareholders' equity. Suppose that Mackay Industries' shares traded at $40 recently. Increasing the shares outstanding by issuing a 10% stock dividend would likely drop Mackay Industries' shares market price to around $36 per share. The objective behind a stock dividend is to make the shares less expensive and, therefore, more available and attractive to investors.

3. To reward investors. Investors often feel like they've received something of value when they get a stock dividend.

STOCK SPLITS

When a company's share price is too high, the board of directors may consider reducing the share price in the market by splitting (dividing) the shares. The effect of a **stock split** is to increase the total number of shares and reduce the share price. The purpose of a stock split is to increase the liquidity of the shares in the market. Many shareholders do not like or have the ability to buy high-priced shares. The illiquidity of share trading in the stock market is not good for companies. Although a stock split does not change the total value of a company, many investors interpret a stock split as a positive sign. In general, shares perform well after a company announces a stock split.

On the other hand, when a company's share price is too low, the board of directors may consider increasing the share price in the market by a reverse stock split. For example, a 1-for-2 reverse stock split will result in a reduction of the number of shares outstanding by half. Since the total share capital does not change, the share price will double.

Both a stock dividend and a stock split will increase the number of shares outstanding. However, a stock split is fundamentally different from a stock dividend. A stock split increases not only the number of outstanding shares, but also the number of issued shares. For example, if Mackay Industries splits its common shares 2-for-1, the number of outstanding shares is doubled.

Assume the market price of a common share of Mackay Industries has been approximately $40. If Mackay Industries initiates a 2-for-1 split of its common shares on August 1, the market price per share will drop to around $20. A 2-for-1 stock split means that Mackay Industries will have twice as many shares outstanding after the split as before. **Exhibit 10-3** shows the before and after of how a 2-for-1 split affects Mackay Industries' shareholders' equity.

Mackay Industries, Inc. Shareholders' Equity—Before Split August 1		
Share Capital:		
Preferred Shares, 500,000 shares authorized, 10,000 shares issued and outstanding		$ 200,000
Common Shares, 525,000 shares issued authorized, 2,000,000 shares and outstanding		8,500,000
Total Share Capital		8,750,000
Retained Earnings		1,000,000
Total Shareholders' Equity		$9,750,000

Mackay Industries, Inc. Shareholders' Equity—After Split August 1		
Share Capital:		
Preferred Shares, 500,000 shares authorized, 10,000 shares issued and outstanding		$ 200,000
Common Shares, 1,050,000 shares issued authorized, 2,000,000 shares* and outstanding		8,500,000
Total Share Capital		8,750,000
Retained Earnings		1,000,000
Total Shareholders' Equity		$9,750,000

*Authorized shares are not affected by the split. If the company needs to increase the number of authorized shares, it would submit a petition to the authorities.

Exhibit 10-3 ▲

Study the exhibit and you'll see that a 2-for-1 stock split does the following:

- Doubles the shares issued and outstanding
- Leaves all account balances and total equity unchanged

Because the stock split does not affect any account balances, no formal journal entry is needed to record a stock split. Instead, the split is recorded in a **memorandum entry**, a journal entry that "notes" a significant event, but which has no debit or credit amount. Following is an example of a memorandum entry:

DATE	ACCOUNTS	POST REF.	DR.	CR.
Aug 1	Split the common stock 2-for-1.			
	OLD: 2,000,000 shares authorized; 525,000 shares issued			
	NEW: 2,000,000 shares authorized; 1,050,000 shares issued			

⊕ ACCOUNTING IN YOUR WORLD

Getty Images

Robert invited three friends over to watch a football game and share a "take-and-bake" pizza he had purchased. On game day, Robert pulled the pizza out of the oven and was just about to slice it into eight pieces (two slices for each of them) when he began to wonder if there was enough pizza. Robert had an idea. He figured that if he cut the pizza into twelve slices instead of eight slices, each person would get three slices of pizza instead of two. Robert knew that each person would still receive the same amount of pizza but he figured that his friends would feel more satisfied if they received three slices instead of only two slices. It worked; no one complained that they did not get enough to eat.

The logic behind a stock split is similar to the logic behind Robert slicing the pizza into more pieces. When a company splits its shares, each shareholder still owns the same amount of the company (think the whole pizza). However, the shareholders' ownership is now represented by more shares (think slices of pizza). For example, after a 3-for-2 stock split, each shareholder would own the same amount of the company. Each shareholder would just own three shares now for every two shares he or she used to own.

STOCK DIVIDENDS AND STOCK SPLITS COMPARED

Stock dividends and stock splits have some similarities and some differences. **Exhibit 10-4** summarizes the effects of each on shareholders' equity. Cash dividends have also been included in the exhibit for comparison purposes.

Event	Number of Common Shares	Share Capital	Retained Earnings	Total Shareholders' Equity
Cash dividend	—	—	⬇	⬇
Stock dividend	⬆	⬆	⬇	—
Stock split	⬆	—	—	—

Exhibit 10-4 ▲

DECISION GUIDELINES

DECISION	**GUIDELINE**	**ANALYZE**
I am a member of the board of directors and we are having difficulty selling our shares on the stock market. We've been told that our share price is too high because the company has been performing very well. To decrease the market price of a company's shares, is it better to use a stock dividend or a stock split?	The amount by which a company wishes to reduce the market price of the shares influences the decision to use a stock dividend or a stock split.	Because both a stock dividend and a stock split increase the number of outstanding shares (with no increase in the company's shareholders' equity), they both reduce the market value of a company's shares. A stock split usually increases the number of outstanding shares by a larger amount than a stock dividend. Therefore, it tends to have a bigger impact on the market price of the shares and should be used when a significant decrease in the market price is desired. For example, a 2-for-1 split will typically reduce the market price of a company's shares by 50%.

HOW ARE TREASURY SHARES ACCOUNTED FOR?

After a company has issued shares, it is possible for that company to reacquire, or buy back, some of its shares at a later date. In general, when a company buys back its own shares, it cancels these shares and the number of common shares and the balance of the Common Shares account are reduced. However, if a company buys back its own shares and holds these shares, then the reacquired shares are called **treasury shares** because they are, in effect, held in the company's treasury. A corporation such as Mackay Industries may purchase treasury shares for several reasons:

 L.O. ⑥ Account for treasury shares

1. Management wants to support the company's share price.
2. Management wants to avoid a takeover by an outside party. If the company purchases the available shares, the shares are not available for others to purchase.
3. Management wants to reward valued employees with shares. Treasury shares can be given to employees as a reward.

Treasury share transactions are common among larger corporations.

TREASURY SHARE BASICS

Before we see how treasury shares are accounted for, let's review some basic concepts related to treasury shares:

- The Treasury Shares account is a contra-equity account. Therefore, Treasury Shares has a debit balance, which is the opposite of the other equity accounts.
- Treasury shares are recorded at average cost.
- The Treasury Shares account is reported beneath retained earnings on the statement of financial position as a reduction to total shareholders' equity.

Although treasury shares are still considered to be issued shares, they decrease the company's shares that are outstanding. This is because the shares are no longer held by outsiders (the shareholders). We compute outstanding shares as follows:

Outstanding shares = Issued shares − Treasury shares

Outstanding shares are important because only outstanding shares have voting rights and receive cash dividends. Treasury shares don't have voting rights, and they get no dividends. Now let's illustrate how to account for treasury shares, continuing with Mackay Industries.

PURCHASE OF TREASURY SHARES

Assuming that there was no stock split or stock dividend, Mackay Industries' shareholders' equity on August 1, the same as on June 30, is shown in **Exhibit 10-5**.

Mackay Industries, Inc. **Shareholders' Equity** August 1		
Share Capital:		
Preferred Shares, 500,000 shares authorized,		
10,000 shares issued		$ 200,000
Common Shares, 2,000,000 shares authorized,		
500,000 shares issued		7,500,000
Total Share Capital		7,700,000
Retained Earnings		2,000,000
Total Shareholders' Equity		$9,700,000

Exhibit 10-5 ▲

Assume that on August 10, Mackay Industries purchased 5,000 treasury shares (common shares). If cash paid is less than the average cost of the shares (value of shares ÷ outstanding number of shares), then the Contributed Surplus account will be increased to record the difference. If cash paid is more than the average cost of the shares, then Retained Earnings should be reduced if there is no credit balance in the Contributed Surplus account. For example, Mackay Industries pays $12 per share to purchase back 5,000 of its shares. Mackay would record the purchase as follows:

DATE	ACCOUNTS	POST REF.	DR.	CR.
Aug 10	Treasury Shares ($7,500,000 ÷ 500,000) × 5,000		75,000	
	Contributed Surplus			15,000
	Cash			60,000
	Purchased 5,000 treasury shares.			

Suppose MacKay purchases another 10,000 shares at $17 per share on October 1. Since the purchase price per share is higher than the average price, MacKay needs to reduce the contributed surplus to zero. If the balance in the Contributed Surplus account is not enough, then MacKay needs to reduce Retained Earnings. The entry for the October 1 purchase follows:

DATE	ACCOUNTS	POST REF.	DR.	CR.
Oct 1	Treasury Shares ($7,500,000 ÷ 500,000) × 10,000		150,000	
	Contributed Surplus		15,000	
	Retained Earnings		5,000	
	Cash			170,000
	Purchased 10,000 treasury shares.			

After posting the entry, the Treasury Shares account would look like this:

Treasury Shares		
8/10	75,000	
10/1	150,000	
	225,000	

CRITICAL THINKING

Take a minute to think about each of the following cases. What would be the impact from the company's perspective and the shareholders' perspective?

Cases	Impact on Company	Impact on Shareholders
(1) Sida's shares are trading at $100. Sida's management thinks that the share price is too high and is considering three courses of action: (1) 4-for-1 stock split, (2) 20% stock dividend, or (3) $10 cash dividend. What is your recommendation?		
Recommendation:		
(2) Darcy's has 1,000,000 shares outstanding and the shares are trading at $10. Darcy's management thinks that the share price is too low and is considering two courses of action: (1) purchase back 500,000 shares, or (2) 1-for-2 reverse stock split. What is your recommendation?		
Recommendation:		

Solutions:

Cases	Impact on Company	Impact on Shareholders
(1) Sida's shares are trading at $100. Sida's management thinks that the share price is too high and is considering three courses of actions: (1) 4-for-1 stock split, (2) 20% stock dividend, or (3) $10 cash dividend. What is your recommendation?	(1) The number of shares will quadruple and the share price will drop to approximately $25. (2) The number of shares will increase by 20% and the share price will be approximately $83.33. (3) The number of shares is unchanged and the share price will drop to approximately $90.	(1) The number of shares increases but not the value of their investment. However, a 4-for-1 stock split sends a positive signal to investors that usually results in the shares performing well. (2) The number of shares increases but not the value of their investment. (3) The number of shares is unchanged but the investors receive cash in their account.
	Recommendation: All three actions will reduce the share price. However, the 4-for-1 stock split has the biggest impact on share price reduction and a potential benefit of better share performance.	

Cases	Impact on Company	Impact on Shareholders
(2) Darcy's has 1,000,000 shares outstanding and the shares are trading at $10. Darcy's management thinks that the share price is too low and is considering two courses of action: (1) purchase back 500,000 shares, or (2) 1-for-2 reverse stock split. What is your recommendation?	(1) The company's cash will be reduced by $5,000,000, and the number of shares outstanding will reduce to 500,000 shares. But the share price will remain approximately unchanged. (2) The company's shares will be reduced by 500,000 shares, but the total share capital remains unchanged. Therefore, the share price will approximately double to $20 per share.	(1) The share price does not change; however, those shareholders who keep their shares see their percentage ownership stake in the company double. (2) The number of shares owned by each shareholder is cut in half, but the share price approximately doubles. Therefore, the ownership stake in the company does not change.

Recommendation:

Since the goal is to increase the share price, the reverse stock split achieves that goal. However, a share buyback often sends a positive signal to investors, which may result in a small increase in share price.

HOW IS SHAREHOLDERS' EQUITY REPORTED?

L.O. 7 Report shareholders' equity

The components of shareholders' equity include two major categories:

1. **Contributed Capital:** the items included in this category are share capital, such as common and preferred shares, and contributed surplus.

2. **Earned Capital:** the items included in this category are retained earnings and accumulated other comprehensive income.

IFRS

Accumulated other comprehensive income (AOCI) is the cumulative change in equity related to other comprehensive income that bypasses net income. Under IFRS, companies need to present the following items as other comprehensive income (OCI):

1. Foreign currency translation adjustments

2. Changes in the fair value of available-for-sale financial assets

3. Revaluations of property, plant, and equipment

4. Changes in the fair value of a financial instrument in a cash flow hedge

Under IFRS, companies need to prepare a statement of comprehensive income and statement of changes in equity showing every account, including Accumulated Other Comprehensive Income. This statement is used to show investors the significant changes in all of the equity categories that occurred during the year. An example of a statement of shareholders' equity is presented in **Exhibit 10-6**.

ASPE

Under ASPE, companies usually need to prepare a statement of retained earnings only since disclosure of comprehensive income is not required.

	Example Company Statement of Shareholders' Equity Year Ended December 31, 2015					
	Preferred Shares	Common Shares	Contributed Surplus	Retained Earnings	Other Comprehensive Income	Total
Balance, December 31, 2014	$250,000	$5,000,000	$15,000	$450,000	$35,000	$5,750,000
Increase in OCI					5,000	5,000
Issue of Preferred Shares	100,000					100,000
Purchase of Common Shares		(75,000)	(15,000)			(90,000)
Stock Dividend		50,000		(50,000)		0
Cash Dividend:						0
Preferred				(25,000)		(25,000)
Common				(50,000)		(50,000)
Balance, December 31, 2015	$350,000	$4,975,000	$ 0	$325,000	$40,000	$5,690,000

Exhibit 10-6 ▲

FOCUS ON DECISION MAKING: RATIOS

Investors are constantly evaluating companies' profits to determine performance. Two important ratios to use for comparison are return on shareholders' equity and return on common shareholders' equity.

L.O. **8**   Evaluate return on shareholders' equity and return on common shareholders' equity

RATE OF RETURN ON SHAREHOLDERS' EQUITY

Rate of return on shareholders' equity, or **return on equity**, shows the relationship between net income and the average shareholders' equity. The numerator is net income and the denominator is average shareholders' equity. Let's assume Mackay Industries has the following data:

Net income for 2015..	$136,000
Total shareholders' equity, 12/31/2015..	$943,000
Total shareholders' equity, 12/31/2014..	$825,000

Mackay Industries' rate of return on common shareholders' equity for 2015 is computed as follows:

$$\text{Rate of return on shareholders' equity} = \frac{\text{Net income}}{\text{Average shareholders' equity}}$$

$$= \frac{\$136,000}{(\$943,000 + \$825,000)/2}$$

$$= \frac{\$136,000}{\$884,000}$$

$$= 15.4\% \text{ (rounded)}$$

RATE OF RETURN ON COMMON SHAREHOLDERS' EQUITY

Rate of return on common shareholders' equity, or **return on common equity**, shows the relationship between the net income available to the common shareholders and their average shareholders' equity. The numerator is net income minus preferred dividends. The preferred dividends are subtracted because they represent part of the net income that is unavailable to the common shareholders. The denominator is average common shareholders' equity (total shareholders' equity minus preferred share capital). Let's assume Mackay Industries has the following data:

Net income for 2015..	$136,000
Preferred dividends for 2015...	$ 18,000
Common shareholders' equity, 12/31/2015..	$847,000
Common shareholders' equity, 12/31/2014..	$723,000

Mackay Industries' rate of return on shareholders' equity for 2015 is computed as follows:

$$\text{Rate of return on common shareholders' equity} = \frac{\text{Net income} - \text{preferred dividends}}{\text{Average common shareholders' equity}}$$

$$= \frac{\$136,000 - 18,000}{(\$847,000 + \$723,000)/2}$$

$$= \frac{\$118,000}{\$785,000}$$

$$= 15.0\% \text{ (rounded)}$$

Return on equity can be compared to returns that can be earned from other investments, such as investments in other companies or even investments in money market accounts or certificates of deposit. Returns on equity above 12% are generally considered to be good returns. Mackay Industries' return on equity of 15.4% and return on common equity of 15.0% are both strong.

FOCUS ON USERS

Concept	User	Why Is This Important to This User?
Dividends	**Shareholders and Potential Investors**	Shareholders are able to receive a financial benefit from owning shares in two ways: the value of the share increasing and receiving dividends. As an investor, if you are preparing to purchase some shares, you may wish to examine the financial statements to determine the history of dividend payments. This will provide an indication of what you may expect in the way of dividends should you decide to purchase the shares.
Treasury Shares	**Shareholders and Potential Investors**	Shareholders will want to watch the Treasury Shares account. Since a company will purchase its own shares for specific reasons, such as to fend off a hostile takeover, the appearance of new treasury shares can signal some interesting developments with the company.
Stock Splits	**Competitors Shareholders and Potential Investors**	Competitors and potential investors will want to watch the market for actions such as stock splits. A stock split can be used when the share price for a company has become high and perhaps a little too expensive for the average investor to make the stock more affordable. A stock split could indicate that the company is expecting further good results for the company or that the company may be looking to raise funds by issuing more shares. Raising additional funds is usually a sign that the company will be expanding or going through a growth phase and requires funds to support this action. If a competitor can read these signs and have an idea of the competition's movements before they happen, then the competitor can plan its own strategy to deal with the changes in the market too.

DEMO DOC 📄

MyAccountingLab   Visit MyAccountingLab to watch animated versions of similar Demo Docs.

EQUITY TRANSACTIONS

At January 1, 2015, Sara, Corp. had 2,000 common shares outstanding, $20,000. During 2015, Sara had the following transactions:

LEARNING OBJECTIVES **3**–**6**

Jan 31	Issued 500 common shares for $10 cash per share.
Mar 31	Declared cash dividends of $0.40 per common share.
May 31	Paid the cash dividends declared in March.
Jul 31	Purchased 300 treasury shares for $11 cash per share.
Sep 30	Declared and distributed a 5% stock dividend when the market price was $12 per share.
Dec 31	Declared 2-for-1 stock split.

REQUIREMENT:

① **Journalize all of Sara's equity transactions for 2015. After each transaction determine how many common shares are outstanding.**

DEMO DOC SOLUTIONS

REQUIREMENT ①

Journalize all of Sara's equity transactions for 2015. After each transaction determine how many common shares are outstanding.

Part 1	Demo Doc Complete

Jan 31 Issued 500 common shares for $10 cash per share.

Issuing common shares means that brand new share certificates were printed by Sara and sold to outside investors. It means an increase (credit) to Common Shares.

Sara receives $10 cash per share, so Cash is increased (debited) by $5,000 (500 shares × $10 per share), and Common Shares increase (credited) by $5,000.

DATE	ACCOUNTS	POST REF.	DR.	CR.
Jan 31	Cash (500 shares × $10)		5,000	
	Common Shares (500 shares × $10)			5,000
	Issued shares.			

Assets	=	Liabilities	+	Shareholders' Equity
+5,000				+5,000

Selling common shares to outside investors increases the number of outstanding shares. So after this transaction, Sara has 2,500 (2,000 + 500) common shares outstanding.

Mar 31 Declared cash dividends of $0.40 per common share.

DATE	ACCOUNTS	POST REF.	DR.	CR.
Mar 31	Retained Earnings		1,000	
	Dividends Payable (2,500 shares × $0.40)			1,000
	Declared cash dividends.			

Assets	=	Liabilities	+	Shareholders' Equity
		+1,000		−1,000

Declaring cash dividends decreases (debits) Retained Earnings and increases (credits) Dividends Payable by the amount to be paid. Sara declares $1,000 (2,500 shares outstanding × $0.40 per share) in cash dividends.

Declaring cash dividends does not change the number of outstanding shares, so 2,500 common shares remain outstanding after this transaction.

May 31 Paid the cash dividends declared in March.

When the dividends are paid, the Dividends Payable account is decreased (debited), in this case by $1,000, and Cash is also decreased (credited) by $1,000.

DATE	ACCOUNTS	POST REF.	DR.	CR.
May 31	Dividends Payable		1,000	
	Cash			1,000
	Paid cash dividends.			

Paying cash dividends does not change the number of outstanding shares, so 2,500 common shares remain outstanding after this transaction.

Jul 31 Purchased 300 treasury shares for $11 cash per share.

When treasury shares are purchased, the Treasury Shares account is increased by the cost of the treasury shares. Treasury Shares is a *contra-equity* account, which means that it has a balance *opposite* to normal equity accounts. Most equity accounts have credit balances, so Treasury Shares has a debit balance. *Treasury shares decrease equity*. Cash is also decreased because Sara is *buying* (that is, paying for) the treasury shares.

In this case, the Treasury Shares account is increased (debit) by $3,000 (300 shares × $10 average cost per share), Retained Earnings is reduced (debit) by $300, and Cash is decreased (credit) by $3,300 (300 shares × $11 per share).

DATE	ACCOUNTS	POST REF.	DR.	CR.
Aug 10	Treasury Shares (300 shares × $10)		3,000	
	Retained Earnings		300	
	Cash			3,300
	Purchased 300 treasury shares.			

Treasury shares are *no longer outstanding*. Because they are held by the company, they no longer have votes at shareholder meetings, nor do they receive dividends. So the number of outstanding shares is now 2,200 (2,500 − 300).

Sep 30 Declared and distributed a 5% stock dividend when the market price was $12 per share.

Stock dividends are similar to cash dividends except that a stock dividend is distributed in shares instead of paid in cash. The stock dividend will issue brand new common shares to investors who already own shares of the corporation.

Dividends (both shares and cash) only apply to *outstanding* shares. The treasury shares are considered inactive and *do not* receive dividends of any kind.

Just as with cash dividends, stock dividends decrease Retained Earnings. Retained Earnings is decreased by the *market value* of the new shares issued. Retained Earnings is decreased (debit) by $1,320 (2,200 shares × 5% × $12 per share), and the Common Shares account is increased by $1,320.

The remainder of the entry is similar to the entry to issue common shares. The only difference between this transaction and the one on January 31 is that Retained Earnings is debited *instead of* Cash.

DATE	ACCOUNTS	POST REF.	DR.	CR.
Sep 30	Retained Earnings (2,200 × 5% × $12)		1,320	
	Common Shares (2,200 × 5% × $12)			1,320
	Declared and distributed a stock dividend.			

Because the stock dividend increases the number of common shares held by outside investors, it increases the number of outstanding common shares by 110 shares (2,200 shares × 5%). So after this transaction, Sara has 2,310 (2,200 + 110) common shares outstanding.

Dec 31 Declared 2-for-1 stock split.

A stock split does not affect any account balances, and no journal entry is required. However, a note disclosure is necessary. Sara, Corp. would state that on December 31, the board of directors declared a 2-for-1 common stock split. The total number of common shares outstanding after the split is 4,620 shares.

DEMO DOC COMPLETE

Part 1	Demo Doc Complete

 DECISION GUIDELINES

Corporations: Contributed Capital and Retained Earnings
The corporate form of business organization is very popular. You will possibly work for a corporation someday. Or, you may even have an opportunity to organize your own corporation. If you do, you will most likely encounter the following decisions.

DECISION	▶	**GUIDELINE**	▶	**ANALYZE**
As a member of the board of directors, I make decisions on when to declare dividends, how much to declare, and whether they will be cash dividends or something else. When making these decisions, when is a cash dividend appropriate?		Consider the amount of available cash as well as the balance in Retained Earnings.		A cash dividend is a distribution of earnings to the company's shareholders. So a company cannot declare and distribute dividends unless the balance in retained earnings (counting the current year's earnings) exceeds the amount of the desired dividend. In addition, the company must have the cash available to pay the dividend if it is declared. A business should carefully analyze its future cash needs so that it does not deplete its cash with a dividend and end up with cash flow issues in the future.

Main Differences between IFRS and ASPE

POINT OF COMPARISON	IFRS	ASPE
Issuing shares in a non-monetary exchange	Should be measured at the more reliable measure, either the fair value of the assets received or the fair value of the share price.	
Comprehensive income	Must present accumulated other comprehensive income in the statement of comprehensive income and statement of changes in equity.	Companies usually need to prepare a statement of retained earnings only as disclosure of comprehensive income is not required.

ACCOUNTING VOCABULARY

THE LANGUAGE OF BUSINESS

Accumulated other comprehensive income (p. 592)

Arrears (p. 583)

Common shares (p. 579)

Corporation (p. 578)

Cumulative preferred shares (p. 583)

Dividends (p. 581)

Issue price (p. 580)

Legal capital (p. 581)

Memorandum entry (p. 588)

Par value (of shares) (p. 580)

Preferred shares (p. 579)

Rate of return on common shareholders' equity (p. 593)

Rate of return on shareholders' equity (p. 593)

Retained earnings (p. 579)

Return on common equity (p. 593)

Return on equity (p. 593)

ACCOUNTING PRACTICE

DISCUSSION QUESTIONS

1. What are the four basic rights of shareholders?

2. Assume that you are a CFO of a company that is attempting to raise additional capital to finance an expansion of its production facility. You are considering either issuing bonds or additional shares. What are some of the differences in the two options?

3. What accounts, if any, are involved in the journal entries to record the events associated with each of the following dates associated with cash dividends?

   a. Declaration date
   b. Date of record
   c. Payment date

4. With which type of shares would dividends in arrears be associated? Why?

5. What accounts are affected by the declaration and distribution of a stock dividend? What is the effect of a stock dividend on

   a. Total shareholders' equity?
   b. Total assets?
   c. Total liabilities?
   d. Cash?

6. What are some of the reasons for issuing a stock dividend?

7. What kind of account is treasury shares? What is its normal balance? Where would it be reported on the financial statements?

8. What could you reasonably conclude if a company reports more shares issued than outstanding?

9. Why are preferred dividends subtracted from the numerator in calculating the return on common equity ratio?

SELF CHECK

MyAccountingLab

The exercises and problems in this chapter can be found on MyAccountingLab. You can practise them as often as you want, and they feature step-by-step guided solutions to help you find the right answer.

1. Which characteristic of a corporation is considered to be an advantage?

   a. Ease of transferring ownership
   b. Indefinite life
   c. Limited shareholder liability
   d. All of the above

2. Which of the following is a disadvantage of organizing as a corporation?

   a. Separate legal entity
   b. Limited ability to raise capital
   c. Double taxation
   d. Limited shareholder liability

3. What are the two basic sources of corporate capital?

   a. Share capital and retained earnings
   b. Shares and bonds
   c. Common shares and preferred shares
   d. Retained earnings and dividends

4. Which of the following statements is correct?

   a. A stock split results in a transfer of retained earnings while a stock dividend does not.
   b. A stock dividend changes the proportion of ownership while a stock split does not.

c. While a stock split does not require any journal entries, it does require disclosure in the notes to the financial statements.

d. None of the above

5. Chewning Corporation has 10,000 shares of 5%, $10, cumulative preferred shares and 50,000 common shares outstanding. Chewning Corporation declared no dividends in 2015. In 2016, Chewning Corporation declares a total dividend of $25,000. How much of the dividends goes to the common shareholders?

    a. $ 5,000

    b. $10,000

    c. $15,000

    d. None; it all goes to preferred.

6. Techster Company has 10,000 common shares outstanding, which Techster Company issued at $5 per share. Techster Company also has retained earnings of $80,000. How much is Techster Company's total shareholders' equity?

    a. $ 50,000

    b. $ 80,000

    c. $ 90,000

    d. $130,000

7. What is the term for a company's own shares that it has issued and repurchased?

    a. Issued shares

    b. Stock dividend

    c. Outstanding shares

    d. Treasury shares

8. What does a stock dividend do?

    a. Increases Common Shares

    b. Has no effect on total equity

    c. Decreases Retained Earnings

    d. All of the above

9. What happens with a stock split?

    a. Increases the number of shares issued

    b. Reduces Retained Earnings

    c. Both a and b

    d. None of the above

10. Assume that Pier 1 Imports pays $10 per share to purchase 1,000 of its common shares as treasury shares. What is the effect of purchasing the treasury shares?

    a. Decreases total shareholders' equity by $1,000

    b. Decreases total shareholders' equity by $10,000

    c. Increases total shareholders' equity by $1,000

    d. Increases total shareholders' equity by $10,000

Answers are given after Written Communication.

SHORT EXERCISES

S10-1. Shareholders' equity terminology (*Learning Objectives 1 & 2*) 10–15 min.

Match the following terms with the correct definition.

a. Common shares	____ 1. Share capital plus Retained Earnings
b. Share capital	____ 2. Capital from investments by the shareholders
c. Dividends	
d. Legal capital	____ 3. Capital earned through profitable operation of the business
e. Outstanding shares	
f. Preferred shares	____ 4. The basic form of capital shares

g. Retained earnings

h. Treasury shares

i. Shareholders' equity

____ 5. Shares in the hands of shareholders

____ 6. Distributions by a corporation to its shareholders

____ 7. Shares that give their owners certain advantages over common shareholders, such as the right to receive dividends before the common shareholders

____ 8. The portion of shareholders' equity maintained for the protection of creditors

____ 9. A corporation's own shares that it reacquires

S10-2. Shares issuance (*Learning Objectives 3, 4, & 7*) 15–20 min.

Tricor, Corp. was incorporated on January 20, 2015. During 2015, Tricor had the following transactions related to share capital:

1. Issued 300,000 common shares for $3 million.

2. Issued 20,000 cumulative preferred shares for $25 per share, distributing $1.50 dividend per share.

3. Tricor showed a $35,000 net loss.

Requirements

1. Prepare journal entries.

2. Prepare the shareholders' equity section of the statement of financial position at December 31, 2015.

3. Assuming that you are a preferred shareholder, would you expect to receive a dividend in 2015? Explain.

S10-3. Issuance of shares for cash and noncash assets (*Learning Objective 3*) 10–15 min.

This exercise shows the similarity and the difference between two ways to acquire plant assets.

Case A—Issue shares and buy the assets in separate transactions:

Atar, Inc. issued 10,000 common shares for cash of $700,000. In a separate transaction, Atar, Inc. purchased a building for $500,000 and equipment for $200,000. Journalize the two transactions.

Case B—Issue shares to acquire the assets:

Atar, Inc. issued 10,000 common shares to acquire a building valued at $500,000 and equipment worth $200,000. Journalize this single transaction.

Compare the balances in all accounts after making both sets of entries. Are the account balances similar or different?

S10-4. Share issuance (*Learning Objectives 2 & 3*) 5–10 min.

The Kingston Company reported the following on its statement of financial position at December 31, 2015:

Common Shares, 500,000 shares authorized, 350,000 shares issued and outstanding		$ 473,000
Retained Earnings		2,500,000

1. Assume Kingston Company issued all of its shares during 2015. Journalize the company's issuance of the shares for cash.

S10-5. Analyzing shareholders' equity (*Learning Objectives 2 & 3*) 5–10 min.

At December 31, 2015, Kingston Company reported the following on its comparative statement of financial position, which included 2014 amounts for comparison:

	December 31	
	2015	**2014**
Common Shares, 500,000 shares authorized, 350,000 shares issued and outstanding in 2015; 349,000 shares in 2014	$ 473,000	$ 439,250
Retained Earnings	2,500,000	2,250,000

1. How much did Kingston Company's total share capital increase during 2015? What caused total share capital to increase? How can you tell?

2. Did Kingston Company have a profit or a loss for 2015? How can you tell?

S10-6. Shares issuance (*Learning Objectives 2 & 3*) 5–10 min.

Bruner Corporation has two classes of shares, common shares and preferred shares. Journalize Bruner's issuance of the following:

a. 1,000 common shares for $50 per share

b. 1,000 preferred shares for a total of $32,000

Explanations are not required.

S10-7. Accounting for cash dividends (*Learning Objective 4*) 10–15 min.

Midas Company earned net income of $85,000 during the year ended December 31, 2015. On December 15, 2015, Midas Company declared the annual cash dividend on its 6% preferred shares ($100,000) and a $0.50 per share cash dividend on its common shares (50,000 shares outstanding). Midas Company then paid the dividends on January 4, 2016.

Journalize for Midas Company

a. declaring the cash dividends on December 15, 2015.

b. paying the cash dividends on January 4, 2016.

S10-8. Accounting for cash dividends (*Learning Objective 4*) 10–15 min.

Holiday.com prepared the following shareholders' equity section as of December 31, 2015:

Shareholders' Equity	
Share Capital:	
Preferred Shares, 5%, 5,000 shares authorized,	
400 shares issued and outstanding	$ 40,000
Common Shares, 20,000 shares authorized,	
5,000 shares issued and outstanding	120,000
Total Share Capital	$160,000
Retained Earnings	90,000
Total Shareholders' Equity	$250,000

Answer the following questions about Holiday.com's dividends:

1. How much in dividends must Holiday.com declare each year before the common shareholders get any cash dividends for the year?

2. Suppose Holiday.com declares cash dividends of $20,000 for 2015. How much of the dividends goes to preferred? How much goes to common?

3. Are Holiday.com's preferred shares cumulative or noncumulative? How can you tell?

4. Suppose Holiday.com passed the preferred dividend in 2016 and 2017. In 2018, the company declares cash dividends of $9,000. How much of the dividends goes to preferred? How much goes to common?

S10-9. Accounting for stock dividends (*Learning Objective 5*) 10–15 min.

Transtech, Inc. has 200,000 common shares outstanding. Transtech, Inc. declares and distributes a 5% stock dividend when the market value of its shares is $10 per share.

1. Journalize Transtech's declaration and distribution of the stock dividend on September 30. An explanation is not required.

2. What is the overall effect of the stock dividend on Transtech's total assets? On total shareholders' equity?

S10-10. Comparing cash and stock dividends (*Learning Objectives 4 & 5*) 10–15 min.

Compare and contrast the accounting for cash dividends and stock dividends. In the space provided, insert either "Cash dividends," "Stock dividends," or "Both" to complete each of the following statements:

1. _____ increase share capital by the same amount that they decrease retained earnings.

2. _____ decrease both total assets and total shareholders' equity.

3. _____ decrease retained earnings.

4. _____ have no effect on a liability.

S10-11. Accounting for stock splits (*Learning Objective 5*) 5–10 min.

Suppose Pier 1 Imports has common shares, 500,000 shares authorized, and 100,000 shares issued and outstanding. The book value of the common shares is $500,000. The company decided to split its common shares 2-for-1 to decrease the market price of its shares. The company's shares were trading at $20 immediately before the split.

1. Show how the common shareholders' equity would appear in the shareholders' equity section of Pier 1 Imports' statement of financial position after the stock split.

2. Which account balances changed after the stock split? Which account balances were unchanged?

S10-12. Accounting for treasury shares (*Learning Objective 6*) 10–15 min.

Classic Corporation began operations in 2015. After issuing its common shares to the public, Classic Corporation completed the following treasury shares transaction:

a. Purchased 2,000 shares of the company's $1 average price common shares as treasury shares, paying cash of $5 per share.

Journalize the transaction. Explanations are not required. Show how Classic Corporation will report treasury shares on its December 31, 2015 statement of financial position. In reporting the treasury shares, focus solely on the Treasury Shares account. You may ignore all other accounts.

S10-13. Statement of financial position disclosure of shareholders' equity (*Learning Objective 7*) 5–10 min.

The financial statements of Nason Corporation reported the following accounts (in thousands):

Contributed Surplus........................	$170	Net Sales......................................	$1,080
Cost of Goods Sold........................	588	Accounts Payable........................	60
Common Shares, 400 shares		Retained Earnings........................	166
issued and outstanding..............	400	Other Current Liabilities..............	52
Cash..	240	Operating Expenses....................	412
Long-Term Debt.............................	76	Total Assets.................................	?

Prepare the shareholders' equity section of Nason Corporation's statement of financial position. Net income has already been closed to Retained Earnings.

S10-14. Analyzing shareholders' equity (*Learning Objective 7*) 10–15 min.

Use the statement of shareholders' equity in Exhibit 10-6 to answer the following questions:

1. Make journal entries to record the declaration and payment of cash dividends during 2015.

2. How much cash did the issuance of preferred shares bring in during 2015?

3. What was the cost of the treasury shares that were purchased during 2015?

EXERCISES (GROUP A)

E10-1A. Shares issuance (*Learning Objective 3*) 10–15 min.

Stanley Systems completed the following shares issuance transactions:

Apr 19	Issued 1,000 common shares for cash of $10.50 per share.
May 3	Sold 300 shares of $4.50, preferred shares for $15,000 cash.
11	Received inventory valued at $23,000 and equipment with a market value of $11,000. Issued 3,000 common shares in exchange.

Requirement

1. Journalize the transactions. Explanations are not required.

E10-2A. Share issuance (*Learning Objectives 3 & 7*) 10–15 min.

The charter for Zycor, Inc. authorizes the company to issue 100,000 preferred shares and 500,000 common shares. During its start-up phase, Zycor, Inc. completed the following transactions:

2015	
Aug 6	Issued 500 common shares to the promoters who organized the corporation, receiving cash of $15,000.
12	Issued 300 preferred shares for cash of $20,000.
14	Issued 1,000 common shares in exchange for land valued at $26,000.

Requirements

1. Record the transactions in the journal.

2. Prepare the shareholders' equity section of Zycor's statement of financial position at December 31, 2015. Assume that the company earned net income of $25,000 during this period.

E10-3A. Share issuance and financial statement presentation (*Learning Objectives 3 & 7*) 15–20 min.

BiBa Manufacturing's charter authorized the company to issue an unlimited number of common shares and 750,000 preferred shares. The following transactions occurred during BiBa's first year of business:

Jan 10	Issued 5,000 common shares to the firm's promoters for the work done to set up the corporation. This work has an estimated value of $60,000.
May 21	40,000 shares were issued for cash of $15 per share.
July 25	15,000 preferred shares were issued for cash totalling $225,000.
Oct 1	50,000 common shares in total were issued for land, buildings, and equipment with appraised values of $250,000, $380,000, and $170,000 respectively.

Requirements

1. Prepare journal entries for all the transactions.
2. Prepare the shareholders' equity section of the statement of financial position at December 31, 2015.

E10-4A. Issuance of shares for cash and noncash assets (*Learning Objective 3*) 10–15 min.

Victor, Co. recently organized. The company issued common shares to an attorney in exchange for his patent with a market value of $40,000. In addition, Victor, Co. received cash for 2,000 of its $50 preferred shares, and 26,000 of its common shares sold at $10 per share. Retained Earnings at the end of the first year was $70,000.

Requirement

1. Without making journal entries, determine the total share capital created by these transactions.

E10-5A. Accounting for cash dividends (*Learning Objective 4*) 10–15 min.

Horizon Communications has the following shareholders' equity:

Horizon Communications Shareholders' Equity		
Share Capital:		
Preferred Shares, 8%, unlimited number of shares authorized,		
20,000 shares issued and outstanding		$ 200,000
Common Shares, 500,000 shares authorized,		
300,000 shares issued and outstanding		750,000
Total Share Capital		$ 950,000
Retained Earnings		150,000
Total Shareholders' Equity		$1,100,000

Quick solution:

2015 dividends = $15,000 preferred, $0 common; 2016 dividends = $17,000 preferred, $33,000 common

Requirement

1. Assume the preferred shares are cumulative. Compute the amount of dividends to preferred and common shareholders for 2015 and 2016 if total dividends are $15,000 in 2015 and $50,000 in 2016.

E10-6A. Accounting for cash dividends (*Learning Objective 4*) 10–15 min.

The following elements of shareholders' equity are adapted from the statement of financial position of Scribner Corporation:

Shareholders' Equity	$ Thousands
Preferred Shares, cumulative, $0.40, 50,000 shares issued and outstanding	$100
Common Shares, 9,000,000 shares issued and outstanding	900

Scribner Corporation paid no preferred dividends in 2015 but paid the designated amount of cash dividends per share to preferred shareholders in all prior years.

Requirement

  1. Compute the dividends to preferred and common shareholders for 2016 if total dividends are $150,000.

E10-7A. Accounting for stock dividends (*Learning Objectives 5 & 7*) 10–15 min.

The shareholders' equity for Blade, Inc. on December 31, 2014, follows:

Shareholders' Equity	
Share Capital:	
Common Shares, 100,000 shares authorized,	
50,000 shares issued and outstanding	$450,000
Total Share Capital	$450,000
Retained Earnings	120,000
Total Shareholders' Equity	$570,000

On April 30, 2015, the market price of Blade's common shares was $16 per share and the company distributed a 10% stock dividend.

Requirements

  1. Journalize the declaration and distribution of the stock dividend.

  2. Prepare the shareholders' equity section of the statement of financial position after the stock dividend.

E10-8A. Accounting for cash and stock dividends (*Learning Objectives 4 & 5*) 10–15 min.

Rolly Racing Motors is authorized to issue an unlimited number of common shares. The company issued 80,000 shares at $4 per share, and all 80,000 shares are outstanding. When the market price of common shares was $5 per share, Rolly Racing Motors declared and distributed a 10% stock dividend. Later, Rolly Racing Motors declared and paid a $0.50 per share cash dividend.

Requirements

  1. Journalize the declaration and distribution of the stock dividend.

  2. Journalize the declaration and the payment of the cash dividend.

E10-9A. Accounting for stock splits (*Learning Objectives 5 & 7*) 10–15 min.

Lipton Travel, Inc. had the following shareholders' equity at May 31:

Shareholders' Equity	
Share Capital:	
Common Shares, 200,000 shares authorized,	
50,000 shares issued and outstanding	$600,000
Total Share Capital	$600,000
Retained Earnings	200,000
Total Shareholders' Equity	$800,000

On June 30, Lipton Travel, Inc. split its common shares 2-for-1.

Requirement

  1. Make any necessary entries to record the stock split.

  2. Prepare the shareholders' equity section of the statement of financial position immediately after the split.

E10-10A. Accounting for shares issuance, splits, and treasury shares (*Learning Objectives 3, 5, & 6*) 20–25 min.

Consider each of the following transactions separately from every other transaction:

a. Issuance of 50,000 common shares at $15.

b. Purchase of 1,000 treasury shares (average price is $0.50) at $5 per share.

c. Issuance of a 10% stock dividend. Before the dividend, 500,000 common shares were outstanding; market value was $7 at the time of the dividend.

d. Split shares 3-for-1. Prior to the split, 60,000 common shares were outstanding.

Requirement

1. Identify whether each transaction increased, decreased, or did not change total shareholders' equity.

E10-11A. Accounting for treasury shares (*Learning Objectives 3 & 6*) 10–15 min.

Journalize the following transactions of Goddard Sports, Inc., a chain of sports stores:

Feb 4	Issued 20,000 common shares at $15 per share.
Apr 22	Purchased 1,000 treasury shares at $14 per share.
Jun 20	Purchased 2,000 treasury shares at $16 per share.

E10-12A. Accounting for treasury shares (*Learning Objectives 6 & 7*) 20–25 min.

Franklin, Inc. had the following shareholders' equity on November 30:

Shareholders' Equity	
Share Capital:	
Common Shares, unlimited number of shares authorized,	
50,000 shares issued and 45,000 shares outstanding	$400,000
Contributed Surplus (purchase of treasury shares, June 30)	10,000
Retained Earnings	520,000
Less: 5,000 Treasury Shares	(40,000)
Total Shareholders' Equity	$890,000

On December 30, Franklin, Inc. purchased another 8,000 treasury shares at $10 per share.

Requirement

1. What is the average price per common share? What is the amount paid to purchase treasury shares on June 30?

2. Journalize the purchases of the treasury shares on June 30 and December 30.

3. Prepare the shareholders' equity section of the statement of financial position at December 31.

E10-13A. Statement of financial position disclosure of shareholders' equity (*Learning Objective 7*) 10–15 min.

Casey Manufacturing, Co. has the following selected account balances at June 30, 2015:

Common Shares, unlimited number of shares authorized, 100,000 shares issued and outstanding..........................	$100,000	Inventory................................	$112,000
		Machinery and Equipment	109,000
		Preferred Shares, 5%, 20,000 shares authorized, 5,000 shares issued and	
Accumulated Depreciation, Machinery and Equipment...	62,000		
Retained Earnings	110,000	outstanding	190,000
		Cost of Goods Sold	81,000

Requirement

1. Prepare the shareholders' equity section of the company's statement of financial position.

E10-14A. Accounting for various shareholders' equity transactions (*Learning Objectives 3, 4, 5, 7, & 8*) 20–25 min.

Smart Tech Inc.'s shareholders' equity on December 31, 2014, was as follows:

Shareholders' Equity	
Share Capital:	
Preferred Shares, $1 accumulated deferred dividends,	
150,000 shares authorized, 50,000 issued and outstanding	$1,000,000
Common Shares, unlimited number of shares authorized,	
100,000 shares issued and outstanding	$2,000,000
Retained Earnings	450,000
Total Shareholders' Equity	$3,450,000

During 2015, the following transactions occurred:

Jan 2	10,000 preferred shares were issued at $22.00 per share.	
Feb 1	12,000 common shares were issued in exchange for a building with a fair value of $300,000.	
Nov 25	Declared preferred dividends to be paid on December 23.	
Dec 27	Declared 5% common stock dividend, when the market price was $25, to be distributed on January 30, 2016.	
Dec 31	Net income for the year was $520,000.	

Requirements

1. Journalize the above transactions.

2. Prepare the shareholders' equity section of the Smart Tech Inc. statement of financial position as of December 31, 2015.

E10-15A. Accounting for cash, stock dividends, and stock split (*Learning Objectives 4 & 5*) 20–25 min.

Try-Fly Corp. had the following shares outstanding and retained earnings as of December 31, 2015:

Preferred shares, 6%, 5,000 shares outstanding	$150,000
Common shares, with 50,000 shares outstanding	$550,000
Retained earnings	$160,000

No dividends have been paid since 2013. The board is considering a cash dividend to both the preferred and the common shareholders.

Requirements

1. Assume that the total amount of dividends is $27,000:

   a. What is the amount of dividends distributed to preferred shareholders and common shareholders if the preferred shares are noncumulative?

   b. What is the amount of dividends distributed to preferred shareholders and common shareholders if the preferred shares are cumulative?

2. Assuming that the total amount of dividends is $57,000, what is the amount of dividends distributed to preferred shareholders and common shareholders?

E10-16A. Calculating return on equity (*Learning Objective 8*) 10–15 min.

Assume that Apex, Inc. has the following data:

Net income for 2015	$ 127,000
Preferred dividends for 2015	23,000
Total shareholders' equity, 12/31/2015	1,627,000
Total shareholders' equity, 12/31/2014	1,589,000
Common shareholders' equity, 12/31/2015	1,484,000
Common shareholders' equity, 12/31/2014	1,392,000

Requirements

1. Calculate Apex's return on equity for 2015.
2. Calculate Apex's return on common equity for 2015.
3. Comment on Apex's performance during 2015.

EXERCISES (GROUP B)

E10-1B. Share issuance (*Learning Objective 3*) 10–15 min.

Sierra Systems completed the following share issuance transactions:

Sep 19 Issued 1,300 common shares for cash of $10.00 per share.
Oct 3 Sold 500 preferred shares for $25,000 cash.
    11 Received inventory valued at $21,000 and equipment with a market value of $16,000. Issued 12,000 common shares in exchange.

Requirement

1. Journalize the transactions. Explanations are not required.

E10-2B. Share issuance (*Learning Objectives 3 & 7*) 10–15 min.

The charter for Zerron, Inc. authorizes the company to issue 500,000 preferred shares and 700,000 common shares. During its start-up phase, Zerron, Inc. completed the following transactions:

2015
Jul 6 Issued 575 common shares to the promoters who organized the corporation, receiving cash of $17,250.
    12 Issued 650 preferred shares for cash of $23,000.
    14 Issued 1,200 common shares in exchange for land valued at $19,000.

Requirements

1. Record the transactions in the journal.
2. Prepare the shareholders' equity section of Zerron's statement of financial position at December 31, 2015. Assume that the company earned net income of $37,000 during this period.

E10-3B. Share issuance and financial statement presentation (*Learning Objectives 3 & 7*) 15–20 min.

HoShi Electronics' charter authorized the company to issue an unlimited number of common shares and 250,000 preferred shares. The following transactions occurred during Hoshi's first year of business:

Mar 10	Issued 3,000 common shares to the firm's promoters for the work done to set up the corporation. This work has an estimated value of $90,000.
Jul 21	20,000 shares were issued for cash of $32 per share.
Sep 1	12,000 preferred shares were issued for cash totalling $300,000.
Dec 11	27,000 common shares in total were issued for land, buildings, and equipment with appraised values of $225,000, $450,000, and $270,000 respectively.

Requirements

1. Prepare journal entries for all the transactions.
2. Prepare the shareholders' equity section of the statement of financial position at December 31, 2015.

E10-4B. Issuance of shares for cash and noncash assets (*Learning Objective 3*) 10–15 min.

Arilla, Co. recently organized. The company issued common shares to an attorney in exchange for his patent with a market value of $52,000. In addition, Arilla, Co. received cash for 1,000 shares of its $60 preferred shares and for 30,000 common shares sold at $15 per share. Retained Earnings at the end of the first year was $88,000.

Requirement

1. Without making journal entries, determine the total share capital created by these transactions.

E10-5B. Accounting for cash dividends (*Learning Objective 4*) 10–15 min.

Eastern Communications has the following shareholders' equity:

Eastern Communications Shareholders' Equity	
Share Capital:	
Preferred Shares, 15%, unlimited number of shares authorized	
28,000 shares issued and outstanding	$ 280,000
Common Shares, 500,000 shares authorized	
320,000 shares issued and outstanding	710,000
Total Share Capital	990,000
Retained Earnings	160,000
Total Shareholders' Equity	$1,150,000

Requirement

1. Assume the preferred shares are cumulative. Compute the amount of dividends to preferred and common shareholders for 2015 and 2016 if total dividends are $36,000 in 2015 and $51,000 in 2016.

E10-6B. Accounting for cash dividends (*Learning Objective 4*) 10–15 min.

The following elements of shareholders' equity are adapted from the statement of financial position of Sacchetti Corporation.

Shareholders' Equity	$ Thousands
Preferred Shares, cumulative, $0.75, 45,000 shares issued and outstanding	$225
Common Shares, 8,750,000 shares issued and outstanding	875

Sacchetti Corporation paid no preferred dividends in 2015 but paid the designated amount of cash dividends per share to preferred shareholders in all prior years.

Requirement

1. Compute the dividends to preferred and common shareholders for 2016 if total dividends are $185,000.

E10-7B. Accounting for stock dividends (*Learning Objectives 5 & 7*) 10–15 min.

The shareholders' equity for Pondwood, Inc. on December 31, 2014, follows:

Shareholders' Equity	
Share Capital:	
Common Shares, 350,000 shares authorized,	
40,000 issued and outstanding	$200,000
Total Share Capital	200,000
Retained Earnings	360,000
Total Shareholders' Equity	$560,000

On September 30, 2015, the market price of Pondwood's common shares was $11 per share and the company distributed a 30% stock dividend.

Requirements

1. Journalize the declaration and distribution of the stock dividend.
2. Prepare the shareholders' equity section of the Pondwood, Inc. statement of financial position after the stock dividend.

E10-8B. Accounting for cash and stock dividends (*Learning Objectives 4 & 5*) 10–15 min.

Artistic Expression is authorized to issue an unlimited number of common shares. The company issued 71,000 shares at $4 per share, and all 71,000 shares are outstanding. When the market price of common shares was $12 per share, Artistic Expression declared and distributed a 20% stock dividend. Later, Artistic Expression declared and paid a $0.45 per share cash dividend.

Requirements

1. Journalize the declaration and distribution of the stock dividend.
2. Journalize the declaration and the payment of the cash dividend.

E10-9B. Accounting for stock splits (*Learning Objectives 5 & 7*) 10–15 min.

Clubhouse Landing, Inc. had the following shareholders' equity at May 31:

Shareholders' Equity	
Share Capital:	
Common Shares, 30,000 shares authorized,	
10,000 issued and outstanding	$ 30,000
Total Share Capital	30,000
Retained Earnings	700,000
Total Shareholders' Equity	$730,000

On June 30, Clubhouse Landing, Inc. split its common shares 5-for-1.

Requirements

1. Make any necessary entries to record the stock split.
2. Prepare the shareholders' equity section of the statement of financial position immediately after the split.

E10-10B. Accounting for shares issuance, splits, and treasury shares (*Learning Objectives 3, 5, & 6*) 20–25 min.

Consider each of the following transactions separately from every other transaction:

a. Issuance of 57,000 common shares at $13.

b. Purchase of 1,800 treasury shares at $8 per share.

c. Issuance of a 10% stock dividend. Before the dividend, 500,000 common shares were outstanding; market value was $9 at the time of the dividend.

d. Split shares 3-for-1. Prior to the split, 120,000 common shares were outstanding.

Requirement

1. Identify whether each transaction increased, decreased, or did not change total shareholders' equity.

E10-11B. Accounting for treasury shares (*Learning Objectives 3 & 6*) 10–15 min.

Journalize the following transactions of Goddard Sports, Inc., a chain of sports stores:

Mar 4	Issued 30,000 common shares at $12 per share.
Jul 22	Purchased 3,000 treasury shares at $14 per share.
Oct 20	Purchased 2,000 treasury shares at $11 per share.

E10-12B. Accounting for treasury shares (*Learning Objectives 6 & 7*) 20–25 min.

Southern, Inc. had the following shareholders' equity on November 30:

Shareholders' Equity	
Share Capital:	
Common Shares, unlimited number of shares authorized,	
40,000 shares issued and 30,000 outstanding	$480,000
Contributed Surplus (purchase of treasury shares, May 30)	20,000
Retained Earnings	520,000
Less: 10,000 Treasury Shares	(120,000)
Total Shareholders' Equity	$900,000

On December 10, Southern purchased 5,000 treasury shares at $15 per share.

Requirement

1. What is the average price per common share? What is the amount paid to purchase treasury shares on May 30?

2. Journalize the purchases of the treasury shares on May 30 and December 10.

3. Prepare the shareholders' equity section of the statement of financial position at December 31.

E10-13B. Statement of financial position disclosure of shareholders' equity (*Learning Objective 7*) 10–15 min.

Bretton Manufacturing, Co. has the following selected account balances at April 30, 2015.

Common Shares, 140,000 shares authorized, issued, and outstanding.....	$560,000	Inventory..................................	$ 55,000
		Machinery and Equipment	77,000
Accumulated Depreciation, Machinery and Equipment...	14,000	Preferred Shares, 5%, 20,000 shares authorized, 6,000 shares issued and	
Retained Earnings	150,000	outstanding	102,000
		Cost of Goods Sold................	76,000

Requirement

1. Prepare the shareholders' equity section of the company's statement of financial position.

E10-14B. Accounting for various shareholders' equity transactions (*Learning Objectives 3, 4, 5, 7, & 8*) 20–25 min.

Shohei Inc.'s shareholders' equity on December 31, 2014, was as follows:

Shareholders' Equity	
Share Capital:	
Preferred Shares, $0.75 accumulated deferred dividends, 500,000 shares authorized, 100,000 issued and outstanding	$1,000,000
Common Shares, unlimited number of shares authorized, 250,000 shares issued and outstanding	$4,000,000
Retained Earnings	750,000
Total Shareholders' Equity	$5,750,000

During 2015, the following transactions occurred.

Jan 2	10,000 preferred shares were issued at $22.00 per share.
Feb 1	12,000 common shares were issued in exchange for a building with a fair value of $300,000.
Nov 25	Declared preferred dividends to be paid on December 23.
Dec 27	Declared 5% common stock dividend, when the market price was $25, to be distributed on January 30, 2016.
Dec 31	Net income for the year was $520,000.

Requirements

1. Journalize the above transactions.
2. Prepare the shareholders' equity section of the Shohei Inc. statement of financial position as of December 31, 2015.

E10-15B. Accounting for cash, stock dividends, and stock split (*Learning Objectives 4 & 5*) 20–25 min.

Dragonfly Corp. had the following shares outstanding and retained earnings as of December 31, 2015:

Preferred shares, 5%, 10,000 shares outstanding	$200,000
Common shares, with 80,000 shares outstanding	$720,000
Retained earnings	$150,000

No dividends have been paid since 2013. The board is considering a cash dividend to both the preferred and the common shareholders.

Requirements

1. Assume that the total amount of dividends is $30,000:

   a. What is the amount of dividends distributed to preferred shareholders and common shareholders if the preferred shares are noncumulative?

   b. What is the amount of dividends distributed to preferred shareholders and common shareholders if the preferred shares are cumulative?

2. Assume that instead of a cash dividend, the company gave the common shareholders a 15% stock dividend when the common shares were trading at $10 each. Prepare the shareholders' equity section of the statement of financial position before and after the dividend. Describe what has happened to the total and each account.

E10-16B. Calculating return on equity (*Learning Objective 8*) **10–15 min.**

Assume that Skippito, Inc. has the following data:

Net income for 2015	$ 223,000
Preferred dividends for 2015	23,000
Total shareholders' equity, 12/31/2015..	1,009,000
Total shareholders' equity, 12/31/2014..	1,384,000
Common shareholders' equity, 12/31/2015.................................	987,000
Common shareholders' equity, 12/31/2014.................................	1,207,000

Requirements

1. Calculate Skippito's return on equity for 2015.

2. Calculate Skippito's return on common equity for 2015.

3. Comment on Skippito's performance during 2015.

EXERCISES (ALTERNATES 1, 2, AND 3)

These alternative exercise sets are available for your practice benefit on **MyAccountingLab**.

PROBLEMS (GROUP A)

P10-1A. Shares issuance (*Learning Objectives 3 & 7*) **10–15 min.**

Partners Pat and Quincy wish to avoid the unlimited personal liability of the partnership form of business, so they are incorporating the company as P & Q Services, Inc., which is authorized to issue 25,000 shares of 5%, $100 par preferred shares and 300,000 shares of no-par common shares. In its first month, P & Q Services, Inc. completed the following transactions:

Jan 3	Issued 6,100 common shares to Pat and 3,600 shares to Quincy, both for cash of $5 per share.
12	Issued 900 preferred shares to acquire a patent with a market value of $90,000.
22	Issued 1,400 common shares to other investors for $5 cash per share.

Requirements

1. Record the transactions in the journal.

2. Prepare the shareholders' equity section of the P & Q Services, Inc. statement of financial position at December 31. The ending balance of Retained Earnings is $59,000.

P10-2A. Analyzing shareholders' equity (*Learning Objectives 2, 3, 4, & 7*) **20–25 min.**

Gamma Corporation was organized in 2014. At December 31, 2014, Gamma Corporation's statement of financial position reported the following shareholders' equity:

Shareholders' Equity	
Share Capital:	
Preferred Shares, $2, 50,000 shares authorized, none issued	$ 0
Common Shares, 100,000 shares authorized,	
10,000 shares issued and outstanding	50,000
Total Share Capital	50,000
Retained Earnings (deficit)	(5,000)
Total Shareholders' Equity	$45,000

Requirements

Answer the following questions and make journal entries as needed:

1. What does the $2 mean for the preferred shares? After Gamma Corporation issues preferred shares, how much in annual cash dividends would Gamma Corporation expect to pay on 1,000 shares?

2. At what price per share did Gamma Corporation issue the common shares during 2014?

3. Were first-year operations profitable? Give your reason.

4. During 2015, the company completed the following selected transactions. Journalize each transaction. Explanations are not required.

   a. Issued for cash 5,000 preferred shares at $10 per share.

   b. Issued for cash 1,000 common shares at a price of $7 per share.

5. Prepare the shareholders' equity section of the Gamma Corporation statement of financial position at December 31, 2015. Assume net income for the year is $50,000.

P10-3A. Analyzing shareholders' equity (*Learning Objectives 2, 3, & 4*) 20–25 min.

Radisson, Inc. included the following shareholders' equity on its year-end statement of financial position at December 31, 2015, with all dollar amounts adapted and in millions:

Shareholders' Equity	$ Millions
Share Capital:	
Preferred Shares, 6% cumulative	$ 65
Common Shares, 650,000,000 shares authorized,	
236,000,000 shares issued and outstanding	306
Total Share Capital	371
Retained Earnings	247
Total Shareholders' Equity	$618

Requirements

1. Identify the different issues of shares Radisson, Inc. has outstanding.

2. Give the two entries to record issuance of the Radisson, Inc. shares. Assume that all the shares were issued for cash. Explanations are not required.

3. Assume that preferred dividends are in arrears for 2014 and 2015. Record the declaration of a $50 million cash dividend on December 30, 2016. Use separate Dividends Payable accounts for preferred and common shares. Round to the nearest $1 million. An explanation is not required.

P10-4A. Accounting for cash dividends (*Learning Objective 4*) 15–20 min.

Klammer Consulting, Inc. has 10,000 shares of $4.50 preferred shares and 50,000 common shares outstanding. Klammer Consulting, Inc. declared and paid the following dividends during a three-year period: 2013, $20,000; 2014, $100,000; and 2015, $200,000.

Requirements

1. Compute the total dividends to preferred shareholders and to common shareholders for each of the three years if

   a. preferred is noncumulative.

   b. preferred is cumulative.

2. For case 1(b), journalize the declaration of the 2015 dividends on December 28, 2015, and the payment of the dividends on January 17, 2016. Use separate Dividends Payable accounts for preferred and common shares.

P10-5A. Accounting for various shareholders' equity transactions (*Learning Objectives 4, 5, & 6*) 20–25 min.

Ralston Sports Corporation completed the following selected transactions during 2015:

Jan 6	Declared a cash dividend on the 10,000 $2.25 preferred shares outstanding. Declared a $0.20 per share dividend on the 10,000 common shares outstanding. The date of record is January 17, and the payment date is January 20.
Jan 20	Paid the cash dividends.
Mar 21	Split the common shares 2-for-1 by calling in the 10,000 common shares and issuing new shares in their place.
Apr 18	Declared and distributed a 10% stock dividend on the common shares. The market value of the common shares was $27 per share.
Jun 18	Purchased 2,000 treasury common shares at $25 per share.

Requirement

1. Record the transactions in the journal.

P10-6A. Accounting for stock split, stock dividends, and reporting shareholders' equity on the statement of financial position (*Learning Objectives 5, 6, & 7*) 20–25 min.

Mingu Inc. had the following balances in its shareholders' equity accounts at December 31, 2014:

Share Capital

Common Shares, unlimited number of shares authorized, 30,000 shares issued and outstanding..	$4,500,000
Retained Earnings..	625,000
Total Shareholders' Equity...	$5,125,000

During 2015, Mingu completed the following selected transactions related to shareholders' equity:

Feb 15	Purchased and retired 2,500 common shares at $130 per share.
Jun 28	Purchased and retired 3,500 common shares at $160 per share.
Dec 18	Declared a 3-for-2 stock split effective on this date.
Dec 30	Mingu reported net income for the year of $150,000.

Requirements

1. Prepare journal entries to account for the transactions during 2015.

2. Assume that instead of a 3-for-2 split, the board of directors declared a 5% stock dividend when the market price was $165. The stock dividends were to be distributed on January 15, 2016. Prepare the journal entry to account for the stock dividend.

3. Prepare the company's shareholders' equity section at December 31, 2015 for (a) the stock split and (b) the stock dividend.

P10-7A. Accounting for various shareholders' equity transactions (Learning Objectives 3, 4, 5, & 7) 30–35 min.

At December 31, 2014, Eaton Corp. reported the following shareholders' equity:

Shareholders' Equity	
Share Capital:	
Common Shares, 400,000 shares authorized,	
120,000 shares issued and 100,000 outstanding	$1,440,000
Contributed Surplus (purchase of treasury shares)	20,000
Retained Earnings	730,000
Less: 20,000 Treasury Shares	(240,000)
Total Shareholders' Equity	$1,950,000

During 2015, Eaton Corp. completed these transactions and events:

Jan 15	Paid cash dividends of $0.50 per share, which were declared on December 15, 2014.
Apr 1	Issued 50,000 common shares at $15 per share.
Jun 30	Declared a 10% stock dividend to be distributed on July 31. The market price was $16.
July 31	Distributed stock dividend.
Dec 20	Declared a 2-for-1 stock split.
Dec 31	Net income for the year was $200,000.

Requirements

1. Prepare journal entries to record the above transactions.
2. Prepare Eaton's shareholders' equity section of the statement of financial position at December 31, 2015.
3. Prepare Eaton's statement of changes in equity for 2015.

P10-8A Analyzing shareholders' equity (Learning Objective 7) 15–20 min.

Market Analysts, Inc. reported the following statement of shareholders' equity for the year ended September 30, 2015:

Market Analysts, Inc.					
Statement of Shareholders' Equity					
Year Ended September 30, 2015					
(Dollar amounts in thousands)	Common Shares	Contributed Surplus	Retained Earnings	Treasury Shares	Total
Balance, September 30, 2014	$2,289		$1,704	$(20)	$3,973
Net Income			519		519
Cash Dividends			(117)		(117)
Issuance of Shares (4,000 shares)	66				66
Stock Dividend	117		(117)		0
Sale of Treasury Shares		7		9	16
Balance, September 30, 2015	$2,472	$7	$1,989	$(11)	$4,457

Requirements

1. At what price per share did the company issue its common shares during the year?
2. What was the cost of treasury shares sold during the year? What was the selling price of the treasury shares sold? What was the increase in total shareholders' equity from selling the treasury shares?
3. What overall effect did the stock dividend have on total shareholders' equity?

PROBLEMS (GROUP B)

P10-1B. Shares issuance (*Learning Objectives 3 & 7*) 10–15 min.

Partners Dahl and Sullivan wish to avoid the unlimited personal liability of the partnership form of business, so they are incorporating the company as D & S Services, Inc., which is authorized to issue 25,000 shares of 5%, $75 par preferred shares and 300,000 shares of no-par common shares. In its first month, D & S Services, Inc. completed the following transactions:

Jan 3	Issued 5,400 common shares to Dahl and 4,100 shares to Sullivan, both for cash of $8 per share.
12	Issued 1,000 preferred shares to acquire a patent with a market value of $75,000.
22	Issued 1,400 common shares to other investors for $8 cash per share.

Requirements

1. Record the transactions in the journal.
2. Prepare the shareholders' equity section of the D & S Services, Inc. statement of financial position at December 31. The ending balance of Retained Earnings is $73,000.

P10-2B. Analyzing shareholders' equity (*Learning Objectives 2, 3, 4, & 7*) 20–25 min.

Robert Corporation was organized in 2014. At December 31, 2014, Robert Corporation's statement of financial position reported the following shareholders' equity:

Shareholders' Equity	
Share Capital:	
Preferred Shares $10, 6%, 35,000 shares authorized, none issued	$ 0
Common Shares, 120,000 shares authorized,	
11,000 shares issued and outstanding	44,000
Total Share Capital	44,000
Retained Earnings (deficit)	(5,000)
Total Shareholders' Equity	$39,000

Requirements

Answer the following questions and make journal entries as needed:

1. What does the 6% mean for the preferred shares? After Robert Corporation issues preferred shares, how much in annual cash dividends would Robert Corporation expect to pay on 1,000 shares?
2. At what price per share did Robert Corporation issue the common shares during 2014?
3. Were the first-year operations profitable? Give your reasons.
4. During 2015, the company completed the following selected transactions. Journalize each transaction. Explanations are not required.

   a. Issued for cash 2,000 preferred shares at $10 per share.

   b. Issued for cash 1,500 common shares at a price of $5 per share.

5. Prepare the shareholders' equity section of the Robert Corporation statement of financial position at December 31, 2015. Assume net income for the year was $65,000.

P10-3B. Analyzing shareholders' equity (*Learning Objectives 2, 3, & 4*) 20–25 min.

Madison Hotel, Inc. included the following shareholders' equity on its year-end statement of financial position at December 31, 2015, with all dollar amounts in millions:

Shareholders' Equity	$ Millions
Share Capital:	
Preferred Shares, 6.5% cumulative	$ 45
Common Shares; 500,000,000 shares authorized,	
176,000,000 shares issued and outstanding	228
Total Share Capital	273
Retained Earnings	142
Total Shareholders' Equity	$415

Requirements

1. Identify the different issues of shares Madison Hotel, Inc. has outstanding.

2. Give the two entries to record issuance of the Madison Hotel, Inc. shares. Assume all the shares were issued for cash. Explanations are not required.

3. Assume that preferred dividends are in arrears for 2014 and 2015. Record the declaration of a $37 million cash dividend on December 30, 2016. Use separate Dividends Payable accounts for preferred and common shares. Round to the nearest $1 million. An explanation is not required.

P10-4B. Accounting for cash dividends (*Learning Objective 4*) 15–20 min.

Krystal Consulting, Inc. has 13,000 shares of $4.00 preferred shares and 90,000 common shares outstanding. Krystal declared and paid the following dividends during a three-year period: 2013, $24,000; 2014, $115,000; and 2015, $230,000.

Requirements

1. Compute the total dividends to preferred shareholders and to common shareholders for each of the three years if

   a. preferred is noncumulative.

   b. preferred is cumulative.

2. For case 1(b), journalize the declaration of the 2015 dividends on December 28, 2015, and the payment of dividends on January 17, 2016.

Use separate Dividends Payable accounts for preferred and common shares.

P10-5B. Accounting for various shareholders' equity transactions (*Learning Objectives 4, 5, & 6*) 20–25 min.

Triton Triathlete Corporation completed the following selected transactions during 2016:

Jan 6	Declared a cash dividend on the 7,000 shares of $3.00, preferred shares outstanding. Declared a $0.10 per share dividend on the 15,000 common shares outstanding. The date of record is January 17, and the payment date is January 20.
Jan 20	Paid the cash dividends.
Mar 21	Completed a 2-for-1 stock split on common shares by calling in the 15,000 common shares and issuing new shares in their place.
Apr 18	Declared and distributed a 15% stock dividend on the common shares. The market value of the common shares was $34 per share.
Jun 18	Purchased 2,000 treasury shares at $31 per share.

Requirement

1. Record the transactions in the journal.

P10-6B. **Accounting for stock split, stock dividends, and reporting shareholders' equity on the statement of financial position (*Learning Objectives 5, 6, & 7*) 20–25 min.**

Fuken Inc. had the following balances in its shareholders' equity accounts at December 31, 2014:

Share Capital	
Common Shares, unlimited number of shares authorized,	
50,000 shares issued and outstanding	$8,000,000
Retained Earnings	750,000
Total Shareholders' Equity	$8,750,000

During 2015, Fuken completed the following selected transactions related to shareholders' equity:

Mar 15	Purchased and retired 4,500 common shares at $150 per share.
Jul 21	Purchased and retired 3,500 common shares at $170 per share.
Dec 28	Declared a 2-for-1 stock split effective on this date.
Dec 30	Fuken reported net income for the year of $325,000.

Requirements

1. Prepare journal entries to account for the transactions during 2015.

2. Assume that instead of a 2-for-1 split, the board of directors declared a 5% stock dividend when the market price was $175. The stock dividends were to be distributed on January 31, 2016. Prepare the journal entry to account for the stock dividend.

3. Prepare the company's shareholders' equity section at December 31, 2015 for (a) the stock split and (b) the stock dividend.

P10-7B. **Accounting for various shareholders' equity transactions (*Learning Objectives 3, 4, 5, & 7*) 30–35 min.**

At December 31, 2014, Maloney, Corp. reported the following shareholders' equity.

Shareholders' Equity	
Share Capital:	
Common Shares, unlimited number of shares authorized,	
200,000 shares issued and 180,000 outstanding	$5,600,000
Stock Dividends Distributable	270,000
Retained Earnings	690,000
Less: 20,000 Treasury Shares	(560,000)
Total Shareholders' Equity	$6,000,000

During 2015, Maloney, Corp. completed these transactions and events:

Jan 20	Distributed stock dividends (5% of outstanding common shares), which were declared on December 1, 2014.
May 1	Issued 21,000 common shares at $31 per share.
Sep 30	Declared cash dividends of $1 per share.
Oct 31	Paid cash dividends declared on September 30.
Dec 20	Declared a 2-for-1 stock split.
Dec 31	Net income for the year was $240,000.

Requirements

1. What is the market price per share on December 1, 2014?
2. Prepare journal entries to record the above transactions.
3. Prepare Maloney's shareholders' equity section of the statement of financial position at December 31, 2015.
4. Prepare Maloney's statement of shareholders' equity for 2015.

P10-8B Analyzing shareholders' equity (*Learning Objective 7*) 15–20 min.

Commerce Analysts, Inc. reported the following statement of shareholders' equity for the year ended September 30, 2015.

		Commerce Analysts, Inc. Statement of Shareholders' Equity Year Ended September 30, 2015				
(Dollar amounts in thousands)	Common Shares	Contributed Surplus	Retained Earnings	Treasury Shares	Total
Balance, September 30, 2014	$2,292		$1,704	$(21)	$3,975
Net Income			519		519
Cash Dividends			(113)		(113)
Issuance of Shares (4,000 shares)	65				65
Stock Dividend	107		(107)		0
Sale of Treasury Shares		4		9	13
Balance, September 30, 2015	$2,464	$4	$2,003	$(12)	$4,459

Requirements

1. At what price per share did the company issue its common shares during the year?
2. What was the cost of treasury shares sold during the year? What was the selling price of the treasury shares sold? What was the increase in total shareholders' equity from selling the treasury shares?
3. What overall effect did the stock dividend have on total shareholders' equity?

PROBLEMS (ALTERNATES 1, 2, AND 3)

These alternative problem sets are available for your practice benefit on **MyAccountingLab**.

CONTINUING EXERCISE

This exercise continues our accounting for Graham's Yard Care, Inc. from Chapter 9. In this exercise, we will account for the declaration and issuance of a cash dividend by Graham's Yard Care, Inc. On October 15, 2015, Graham's Yard Care, Inc. declared a $5,000 dividend. The dividend was payable to all common shareholders of record on October 31 and was paid on November 15, 2015.

Requirements

1. Journalize the entries related to the dividends.
2. What was the effect of the dividend on the following?

   - Cash
   - Retained Earnings
   - Total Shareholders' Equity

CONTINUING PROBLEM

This problem continues our accounting for Aqua Elite, Inc. from Chapter 9. Aqua Elite, Inc. has been authorized to sell 500,000 common shares and 100,000 8% preferred shares. During the year, Aqua Elite had the following transactions related to shareholders' equity:

May 5	Issued 5,700 common shares to Mike Hanson in exchange for $15,000 cash and a truck valued at $13,500.
Jun 13	Issued an additional 2,000 shares to Mike Hanson for $10,000 cash.
Jul 18	Sold 4,000 common shares to investors for $45,000.
Aug 6	Sold 1,500 preferred shares to investors for $20,000.
Oct 22	Purchased 1,000 common shares for $12 per share to hold in the company's treasury.
Nov 14	Declared a $5,000 dividend payable on December 15 to shareholders on record on December 1. Used separate payable accounts for preferred and common dividends.
Dec 15	Paid the dividend.

Requirements

1. Record the transactions in the journal. Explanations are not required.

2. Prepare the shareholders' equity section of the statement of financial position at December 31, 2015, assuming Aqua Elite, Inc. earned $96,000 of net income during the year. In addition to the dividends paid on December 15, $3,400 of dividends were paid earlier in the year.

APPLY YOUR KNOWLEDGE

ETHICS IN ACTION

Case 1. Ted was a wealthy, 20% shareholder of TDS Corporation. He was looking over the financial statements of the corporation and saw that TDS Corporation was in need of a large loan. Furthermore, he knew that December sales were weaker than expected and that the yearly financial statements would show a lower net income than anticipated. He then decided to loan the company $3 million at 5% interest and also become a customer and purchase $250,000 of merchandise. By Ted becoming a customer, it would increase the business's December sales and net income, and give the company sufficient cash to meet expenses. When approached with the ideas, the CEO objected, stating that the "loan" would have to be recorded as additional capital because a shareholder could not loan money to a company. Ted stated that as long as the money was treated as a loan with interest and the expectation of repayment, it should be allowed. The CEO then stated that it would be unethical for the company to "borrow" money from a shareholder. Also, it would be unethical for the company to "sell" merchandise to a shareholder, because it would merely be done to improve the December sales. Ted stated that the loan agreement and 5% interest would make the arrangement reasonable. He stated that if the interest rate were 25%, then the CEO might have a valid ethical concern. Ted also argued that the sale of merchandise to him was completely ethical, because he was not going to return the merchandise. He further contended that it should not matter whether he was a shareholder because in these transactions he would be a lender and a customer, which would not involve any ethical issues.

Can a shareholder ethically lend money to the corporation? What potential ethical issues would be involved? Can a shareholder ethically become a customer to make purchases just to improve the sales and net income? Does the amount of the purchase matter? Why do you think the CEO was concerned?

Case 2. The board of directors for Atlantic Corporation met in January to address growing concerns about the declining share price of the firm. Because the price per share was so low, the board decided that the company would buy back 10 million outstanding shares. During the year, Atlantic Corporation repurchased the shares at a total cost of $62 million. With fewer shares in the hands of shareholders, the board of directors declared and paid a dividend on only those remaining shares outstanding. As a result of these activities, the price per share rose dramatically in only 10 months. The board of directors then felt it best to reissue the treasury shares at the highest per share price possible. Accordingly, Atlantic Corporation reissued the 10 million shares for $142 million. When the board of directors looked over the yearly financial statements, however, it could not find the $80 million "gain" from the treasury shares sale, equal to the reissue price of $142 million less the purchase cost of $62 million. The accountant had recorded the excess as "Additional Share Capital" rather than as a gain on sale. The board of directors met with the accountant and demanded that a gain be recorded; the board wanted more revenue to be included on the income statement. It argued that shares had been sold at a price higher than they were purchased for, and, therefore, it really did not matter whether the shares were Atlantic Corporation shares or any other company's shares, because all share sales result in either a gain or loss.

Why does the board of directors want to recognize the $80 million excess from the treasury share transactions as a gain? Why does the accountant want to recognize the $80 million as an increase in total equity? Who is right and are any ethical issues involved? Does the board of directors have a strong argument that it does not matter whether the shares were Atlantic Corporation shares or any other company since all shares are the same? Do you have any additional thoughts?

KNOW YOUR BUSINESS

FINANCIAL ANALYSIS

Purpose: To help familiarize you with the financial reporting of a real company in order to further your understanding of the chapter material you are learning.

This case continues our examination of Bombardier Inc. We will now study the shareholders' equity of Bombardier Inc. Refer to the Bombardier Inc. financial statements found in MyAccountingLab. Look for the Consolidated Balance Sheets as well as the Consolidated Statements of Changes in Equity and Note 27.

Requirements

1. What was the balance of total shareholders' equity at December 31, 2012 and December 31, 2011? Did the amount of ending total shareholders' equity increase or decrease? What seems to be the main reason for the change in total shareholders' equity? What is the largest component of total equity? (Hint: Look at the Consolidated Statements of Changes in Equity to help answer this last question.)

2. Does Bombardier Inc. have any preferred shares authorized? Issued? Describe the preferred shares: voting or non-voting; cumulative or noncumulative; redeemable (at what price) or not redeemable and their dividend rates.

3. Describe the classes of common shares that Bombardier has authorized and issued. How many common shares are issued and outstanding at the end of the 2012 fiscal year for each class? How many shares were issued and outstanding at the beginning of the year?

4. Look at the consolidated statements of shareholders' equity. Did Bombardier Inc. declare any dividends in 2012?

INDUSTRY ANALYSIS

Purpose: To help you understand and compare the performance of two companies in the same industry.

Find the Bombardier Annual Report, Year Ended December 31, 2012, located in MyAccountingLab and go to the Financial Statements. Now access the The Boeing Company's 2012 Annual Report. To do this from the internet, go to their webpage for the Investor Relations at http://www.boeing.com/companyoffices/financial/quarterly.htm and, under Annual Report, go to the 2012 Annual Report.

Requirement

1. On the Consolidated Balance Sheets and the statement of changes in equity for each company, look at the Shareholders' Equity section. What type or class of shares has each company issued? What is the book value per common share outstanding for each company? How might this compare to the market value per share?

SMALL BUSINESS ANALYSIS

Purpose: To help you understand the importance of cash flows in the operation of a small business.

You are the chief operating officer (COO) of a small public corporation. The company just completed its fiscal year, and the annual meeting is just a few weeks away. Your company has had a pretty good year despite the rough economic climate your industry has been weathering. In spite of that, the share price has maintained its high level. But here's the dilemma: The corporation has paid out a cash dividend every year since its inception, but this year you have some concerns about continuing that tradition. Cash flows during the latter part of the year have been slow because your customers are taking longer to pay than they normally do. There's also the concern about the lump sum payment on the mortgage that is due in a couple of months. You've got to have sufficient cash for that. You've already had some inquiries from shareholders about the amount of the dividend that the company will be paying out this year. You've answered all the inquiries with a very positive tone, but the whole while you're wondering if there will even be a dividend this year. You're certain that the important shareholders would understand if the corporation had to forego paying a dividend this year. Or would they? You decide to have a meeting with the controller to discuss the situation.

Requirement

1. What would be the most viable suggestion that your controller might make to you as an alternative to paying out a cash dividend this year? What are the implications of your recommendation?

WRITTEN COMMUNICATION

You just got off the telephone with one of your clients who is wanting to start a new business as a corporation. His question to you was concerning the different types of shares that can be issued to the potential shareholders of this new corporation. You had explained it to him during the telephone call, but you thought you should follow up your conversation with a letter.

Requirement

1. Prepare a letter to your client explaining the different types or classes of shares that can be issued, and the characteristics of each different type.

Self Check Answers
1. d 2. c 3. a 4. c 5. c 6. d 7. d 8. d 9. a 10. b

LEARNING OBJECTIVES

1. Understand the role of the statement of cash flows

2. Differentiate among cash flows from operating, investing, and financing activities

3. Prepare the statement of cash flows using the indirect method

4. Prepare the statement of cash flows using the direct method

5. Evaluate a company's performance with respect to cash

CHAPTER OUTLINE

CHAPTER

11

The Statement of Cash Flows

BUSINESS, ACCOUNTING, AND YOU

Close your eyes and imagine that you are the head accountant (who is often called the controller) at Best Buy. As Best Buy's controller, what is your role in the company? Your job is to provide understandable, relevant, and reliable information to decision makers. Many of those decisions deal with cash, which, as we've discussed throughout this text, is required for a lot of things, including running day-to-day operations, investing in assets, and paying debts.

Decisions about cash are very important. As noted in Chapter 7, a business must have enough cash to operate and pay its bills. But where does a business get cash, and how does it use cash? How does cash flow in and out of a business like Best Buy? You cannot tell by looking at the statement of financial position, because that financial statement only tells you how much cash a business has at a point in time. You cannot tell by looking at the income statement, since income statements are based on accrual accounting, where revenues and expenses are recognized when they occur and not when the cash is received or paid. Hence, net income shown is not necessarily reflected in the cash balance. So accountants need to provide information in addition to a statement of financial position and an income statement—they need to create a statement that reports where and when the business gets and uses cash during a period of time. So, they create the statement of cash flows.

WHAT IS THE STATEMENT OF CASH FLOWS?

L.O. ① Understand the role of the statement of cash flows.

Cash is often considered to be the "life blood" of a business. As we have seen throughout the text, the statement of financial position reports the amount of cash a business has at the end of the accounting period. When a comparative statement of financial position is presented, the balance of cash the business has at the end of two consecutive periods is reported. The comparative statement of financial position shows whether cash increased or decreased from one period to the next. However, the comparative statement of financial position does not show *why* cash increased or decreased.

Further, managers and owners are interested in the profitability of their companies. In an accrual accounting system, the income statement shows the profitability of a company, yet net income shown is not necessarily reflected in the cash balance. Managers cannot rely on the net income figure to build plans for new expansions and plan dates to pay invoices, simply because the net income (on an accrual basis) could be different from the cash surplus at the end of the period. There is an increasing need for management to know whether the net income appearing on the income statement is reflected in the business's cash flows. Neither the income statement nor the statement of financial position provides such information.

Therefore, a **statement of cash flows** is usually prepared to show why the cash amount changed during the year. It also helps managers to know the sources of these changes and enables them to make effective decisions regarding cash management. The statement of cash flows reports

- all sources of cash during the period. In other words, it shows where a company got its cash during the year.
- all uses of cash during the period. In other words, it shows where a company spent its cash during the year.

🌐 ACCOUNTING IN YOUR WORLD

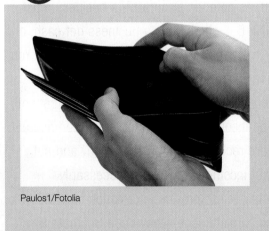

Paulos1/Fotolia

Have you ever taken a weekend road trip with some of your friends? If so, you probably went to the bank to get some cash before you took off. Then, at least once, you probably had to find an ATM to get a little more cash. When you got home, you probably looked in your wallet to see how much money you had left. Upon realizing that you had very little money left, you probably wondered "Where did all my money go?" At this point, you might have taken out a piece of paper and written down how much money you started with and how much additional cash you got along the way (your sources of cash). Then, you probably recorded all the things you spent money on, such as gas $120, food $73, movies $28, etc. (your uses of cash). Finally, you subtracted all of your uses of cash from your sources of cash and, sure enough, it equalled the amount of money left in your wallet. In essence, you prepared a statement of cash flows for the period of your road trip.

The statement of cash flows helps managers, investors, and creditors do the following:

1. **Predict future cash flows.** Past cash receipts and payments help predict future cash flows.

2. **Evaluate management decisions.** Wise investment decisions help the business prosper. Unwise decisions cause problems. Investors and creditors use cash-flow information to evaluate managers' decisions.

3. **Predict ability to pay debts and dividends.** Lenders want to know whether they'll collect on their loans. Shareholders want dividends on their investments. The statement of cash flows helps make these predictions.

PREPARING A STATEMENT OF CASH FLOWS

Individuals and businesses need to understand cash flow. The method businesses use to prepare a statement of cash flows is different than the method used by individuals. Unlike individuals, businesses do not go to their cash account and look at the beginning balance, deposits, withdrawals, and ending balance. Businesses use the statement of financial position and income statement to figure out where their cash came from and where it went. A business's statement of cash flows is designed to supplement the statement of financial position and income statement, and to show how transactions reported in the statement of financial position and income statement impact cash. As such, the statement of cash flows is a very important statement in giving the user a complete picture of a business's operations. The statement of financial position and income statement use accrual accounting to reflect the business's assets, liabilities, shareholders' equity, revenue, and expenses. The statement of financial position and income statement reflect transactions when they occur, even though it may take time before cash is affected. The statement of cash flows takes the information on the statement of financial position and income statement and shows how these transactions affect or do not affect cash. In essence, the statement of cash flows is the communicating link between the accrual-based statement of financial position and income statement and the cash reported on the statement of financial position.

Exhibit 11-1 illustrates that a statement of cash flows is prepared based on the information provided by two successive statements of financial position and an income statement. It also illustrates that the statement of cash flows explains the difference in the cash balance from one period to the next.

However, accountants must decide if they will include only cash in the statement of cash flows or other items that are very close to cash, such as treasury bonds, as well.

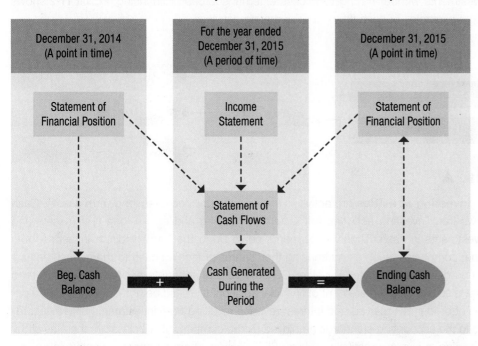

Exhibit 11-1 ▲

WHAT TO INCLUDE IN THE STATEMENT OF CASH FLOWS

Mainly cash and cash equivalents are included in the statement of cash flows. Cash equivalents are short-term, highly liquid investments that usually mature within three months and whose cash value is determined with a high degree of certainty. These investments are usually debt instruments; however, they could also represent a bank "overdraft" that is payable on demand. It should be noted that there are some noncash investing and financing activities that are not reported in the body of the statement of cash flows (because they are not in cash) but instead are disclosed in its notes. Such activities include, for example, issuing shares for assets other than cash (as mentioned in Chapter 10). The disclosure of such activities in the statement of cash flows is important to provide the user with an explanation of why cash is not affected by such activities.

So where does a business get and use cash? Every business, including Best Buy, gets cash and uses cash from one of three activities: operating, investing, and financing.

WHAT IS THE DIFFERENCE AMONG OPERATING, INVESTING, AND FINANCING ACTIVITIES?

L.O. 2 Differentiate among cash flows from operating, investing, and financing activities

CLASSIFICATION OF CASH FLOWS

To provide useful information for decision makers, the statement of cash flows is classified into three categories based on the activity that resulted in a source or use of cash. Those activities are broad categories of all the activities a business can carry out: operating, investing, and financing activities.

Operating activities are the day-to-day activities that create revenues or expenses related to the core business of the company. In other words, operating cash flows result from the main operations of the business. Most of those items are related to the income statement and current assets and current liabilities sections of the statement of financial position. The amount of cash flows arising from operating activities is a key indicator of the extent to which the operations of the entity have generated sufficient cash flows to repay loans, maintain the operating capability of the entity, pay dividends, and make new investments without having to access external sources of financing. **Exhibit 11-2** shows some examples of cash flows from operating activities.

Exhibit 11-2 ▲

Investing activities are activities that increase or decrease long-term assets. Cash flows from investing activities will result from buying and selling long-term assets and investments in cash. Those investments could be in the form of direct investments in other companies, such as purchasing their shares or lending cash to them, such as with bonds or long-term notes payable. Generally, these accounts appear in the long-term assets section of the statement of financial position. It should be noted that the classification of dividends received and interest revenue resulting from investments differs according to the accounting standards employed by the company. IFRS classifies them as either operating or investing activities, while ASPE classifies them as operating activities.

Exhibit 11-3 shows some examples of cash flows from investing activities.

Exhibit 11-3 ▲

Financing activities are activities related to the issuance and repayment of long-term debt, the issuance of shares, or the payment of dividends. Cash flows from financing activities occur when a company obtains financing in the form of equity or loans, as well as repayment of these loans to owners or lenders. These cash flows relate to the long-term liabilities and equity section of the statement of financial position. It is important to note that dividends distributed are considered financing activities and that the classification of interest expense resulting from paying interest on bonds or loans differs according to the accounting standards employed by the company. IFRS classifies interest on bonds as either operating or financing activities as long as it is consistently applied and relevant to the users, while ASPE classifies them as operating activities. In this text interest is regarded as operating activities.

Exhibit 11-4 shows some examples of cash flows from financing activities.

Exhibit 11-4 ▲

Exhibit 11-5 shows the relationship among operating, investing, and financing activities and the various parts of the statement of financial position they affect.

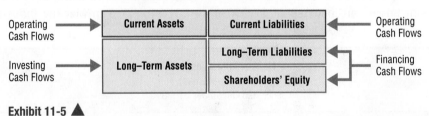

Exhibit 11-5 ▲

As you can see, operating cash flows affect the current accounts, investing cash flows affect the long-term assets, and financing cash flows affect long-term liabilities and equity.

TWO FORMATS FOR OPERATING ACTIVITIES

The *operating activities* section of the statement of cash flows may be prepared using either the **direct method** or **indirect method**. Both methods will result in the exact same cash flow amount, and the investing and financing activities are also prepared in the same way using each method.

Both methods are accepted by IFRS and ASPE. The direct method is preferred by both standards because it provides more transparency and information to the users of financial statements. However, most companies prefer to use the indirect method because its format makes it easier to reconcile net income to the change in cash for the period, and it does not reveal detailed information that could be used by competitors.

In this text, we will focus on the indirect method because it is most commonly used; however, the direct method will be also illustrated.

DECISION GUIDELINES

DECISION	GUIDELINE	ANALYZE
A bank is in the process of granting a loan to a business. Information is requested by the credit department to report on how the company is managing its cash and whether it is successful in doing so.	Review the statement of cash flows to determine the financial health of the company.	The statement of cash flows is divided into three categories: • Operating activities—shows the cash flow from business operations. • Investing activities—shows the cash flow from buying and selling long-term assets. • Financing activities—shows the cash flow from borrowing and repaying long-term debt, as well as from shareholders' equity transactions. For a business to remain successful, operating activities must be the main source of its cash over the long run.

HOW IS THE STATEMENT OF CASH FLOWS PREPARED USING THE INDIRECT METHOD?

L.O. ③ Prepare the statement of cash flows using the indirect method

In order to prepare the cash flows from operating activities using the indirect method, you will need the following information:

- Comparative statements of financial position (two statements)
- The current period's income statement
- Any additional disclosures that reveal how cash was used or generated during the period
- Information deduced from the statement of retained earnings (if necessary)

Let's illustrate the steps required to prepare the statement of cash flows using the indirect method through the following example.

Mackay Industries' financial statements are presented in **Exhibit 11-6**. The Cash account shows an increase of $7,000 from 2014 to 2015 in Mackay Industries'

Mackay Industries, Inc.
Income Statement
Year Ended December 31, 2015

		Revenue:		
		Sales Revenue	$268,000	
		Interest Revenue	13,000	
		Dividend Revenue	5,000	
		Total Revenues		$286,000
		Expenses:		
		Cost of Goods Sold	$137,000	
		Salaries Expense	48,000	
	B*	Depreciation Expense	18,000	
		Other Operating Expense	12,000	
		Interest Expense	11,000	
		Income Tax Expense	9,000	
	C	Loss on Sale of Fixed Assets	3,000	
		Total Expenses		238,000
	A	Net Income		$ 48,000

*These letters correspond to other illustrations and discussions in the text.

Exhibit 11-6 ▲

Mackay Industries, Inc.
Statement of Retained Earnings
Year Ended December 31, 2015

	Retained Earnings, December 31, 2014	$121,000
	Add: Net Income for the Year	48,000
	Subtotal	169,000
M	Less: Dividends	23,000
	Retained Earnings, December 31, 2015	$146,000

First step: Deduce the change in the balances of each account and categorize the activity.

Mackay Industries, Inc.
Statement of Financial Position
December 31, 2014 and 2015

		2015	2014	SOURCE (USE) OF CASH/CASH FLOWS CATEGORY	
	ASSETS				
	Current:				
	Cash	$ 18,000	$ 11,000	($ 7,000)	N/A
D	Accounts Receivable	76,000	93,000	17,000	O
E	Inventory	132,000	124,000	(8,000)	O
	Total Current Assets	226,000	228,000		
H/I	Plant Assets, Net	385,000	315,000	(70,000)	I
	Total Assets	$611,000	$543,000		
	LIABILITIES				
	Current:				
F	Accounts Payable	$ 84,000	$ 96,000	$(12,000)	O
G	Accrued Liabilities	12,000	8,000	4,000	O
	Total Current Liabilities	96,000	104,000		
J/K	Long-Term Notes Payable	147,000	98,000	49,000	F
	Total Liabilities	243,000	202,000		
	SHAREHOLDERS' EQUITY				
L	Common Shares	240,000	220,000	20,000	F
A/M	Retained Earnings	146,000	121,000	25,000	
N	Less Treasury Shares	(18,000)	(0)	(18,000)	F
	Total Shareholders' Equity	368,000	341,000		
	Total Liabilities and	$611,000	$543,000		
	Shareholders' Equity				
	Totals				

O = operating activities; I = investing activities; F = financing activities.

Additional Information:
- Purchased equipment in cash for $195,000.
- Sold equipment with net book value of $107,000 (cost of $134,000 and accumulated depreciation of $27,000) for $104,000 in cash.
- Borrowed $75,000 cash by issuing a note payable and paid back a note payable of $26,000.
- No shares were retired during the period, and new shares were issued in cash.
- Dividends were paid in cash.
- No treasury shares have been sold during the period.

Exhibit 11-6 ▲ (*continued*)

statement of financial position. The statement of cash flows is to show where this increase of $7,000 came from, through three business activities. Please note that the sum of the three business activities subtotals should equal the difference in the Cash account.

Now, let's prepare Mackay Industries' statement of cash flows one section at a time. To make things easier to follow, each item on the statement of cash flows has been cross referenced to the financial statements by a letter.

CASH FLOWS FROM OPERATING ACTIVITIES

The operating activities section of Mackay Industries' statement of cash flows would look like this:

		Cash flows from operating activities:		
A		Net Income		$48,000
		Adjustments to reconcile net income to net cash provided by operating activities:		
B		Depreciation Expense	$ 18,000	
C		Loss on sale of fixed assets	3,000	
D		Decrease in Accounts Receivable	17,000	
E		Increase in Inventory	(8,000)	
F		Decrease in Accounts Payable	(12,000)	
G		Increase in Accrued Liabilities	4,000	22,000
		Net cash provided by operating activities		70,000

Operating cash flows begin with net income, taken from the income statement.

A Net Income

The statement of cash flows—indirect method—begins with net income because revenues and expenses, which affect net income, produce cash receipts and cash payments. Revenues bring in cash receipts and expenses must be paid. But net income is accrual based and the accrual basis of revenues and expenses don't always equal the cash flows (cash basis net income). For example, sales *on account* are revenues that increase net income, but the company hasn't yet collected cash from those sales. Accrued expenses decrease your net income, but you haven't paid cash *if the expenses are accrued*.

To go from net income to cash flow from operations, we must make some adjustments to net income on the statement of cash flows. These additions and subtractions follow net income and are labelled "Adjustments to reconcile net income to net cash provided by operating activities." There are three items to be adjusted: (1) noncash items from the income statement, such as depreciation, (2) non-operating items from the income statement, such as a gain or loss from the sale of fixed assets, and (3) noncash working capital accounts from the statement of financial position.

B Depreciation, Depletion, and Amortization Expenses

These expenses are added back to net income to reconcile it to cash flows from operations. Let's see why. Depreciation is recorded as follows:

Assets	=	Liabilities	+	Shareholders' Equity
−18,000	=			−18,000

DATE	ACCOUNTS	POST REF.	DR.	CR.
	Depreciation Expense		18,000	
	Accumulated Depreciation			18,000

You can see that depreciation does not affect cash because there's no Cash account in the journal entry. However, depreciation, like all the other expenses, decreases net income. Therefore, to go from net income to cash flows, we must add the depreciation back to net income.

Example: Suppose you had only two transactions during the period:

- $50,000 cash sale
- Depreciation expense of $20,000

In this example, net income is $30,000 ($50,000 – $20,000). But cash flow from operations is $50,000 because depreciation is a noncash expense. To reconcile the net income of $30,000 to the cash flow from operations of $50,000, add back the $20,000 of depreciation expense. You would also add back depletion and amortization expenses because they are noncash expenses similar to depreciation.

It is worth mentioning that if no long-term assets are sold or retired during the period, and the accumulated depreciation is provided on the statement of financial position, the change in accumulated depreciation would be equal to the depreciation expense. This is simply because the increase in accumulated depreciation is a result of the increase in the depreciation expense.

C Gains and Losses on the Sale of Assets

Sales of long-term assets such as land and buildings are investing activities. The total cash proceeds from these sales are included in the investing section of the statement of cash flows. However, these sales usually result in a gain or a loss, which is included in net income. Gains and losses do not represent cash flows. They are simply a function of the difference between the cash proceeds and the book value of the asset. Therefore, gains and losses must be removed from net income on the statement of cash flows.

Mackay Industries' income statement includes a loss on the sale of plant assets. During 2015, Mackay Industries sold equipment resulting in a loss of $3,000 on the sale. Because the loss reduces net income, it is added back to net income to arrive at cash flows from operating activities. On the other hand, a gain on the sale of plant assets would increase net income. So, it would be subtracted from net income to arrive at cash flows from operating activities. The impact on cash from the sale of a capital asset will be properly calculated in the cash flow from the investing activities section.

D, E, F, & G Changes in the Current Assets and the Current Liabilities

Most current assets and current liabilities result from operating activities. For example,

- accounts receivable result from sales,
- inventory and accounts payable relate to cost of goods sold,
- prepaid assets and accrued liabilities relate to operating expenses, and so on.

Changes in the current asset and current liability accounts create adjustments to net income on the statement of cash flows, as follows:

1. **A decrease in a current asset other than cash causes an increase in cash.** Mackay Industries' Accounts Receivable decreased by $17,000 D. What caused the decrease? During the year, Mackay Industries must have collected more cash from credit customers than the current year's credit sales. This means that $17,000 more was collected from customers than what is represented by the revenues on the income statement. Therefore, the $17,000 decrease in Accounts Receivable is added to net income to arrive at cash flows from operating activities. A decrease in any current asset other than cash will be added to net income to arrive at cash flows from operating activities. The last column in the statement of financial position in Exhibit 11-6 also shows that this decrease in Accounts Receivable represents a "source" or inflow of cash.

11.1 **STILL** DON'T GET IT**?**
Visit MyAccountingLab for an alternate explanation of this important accounting concept.

MEMORY **TIPS**
Gain on sale of assets → Subtract
Loss on sale of assets → Add

11.2 **STILL** DON'T GET IT**?**

Visit MyAccountingLab for an alternate explanation of this important accounting concept.

MEMORY TIPS

Increase in assets → Subtract
Decrease in assets → Add

MEMORY TIPS

Increase in liabilities → Add
Decrease in liabilities → Subtract

11.3 **STILL** DON'T GET IT**?**

Visit MyAccountingLab for an alternate explanation of this important accounting concept.

2. **An increase in a current asset other than cash causes a decrease in cash.** It takes cash to acquire assets. If Accounts Receivable, Inventory, or Prepaid Expenses increase, then Cash decreases. Therefore, subtract the increase in the current asset from net income to get cash flow from operations. For example, Mackay Industries' Inventory went up by $8,000 **E** . The $8,000 increase in inventory is not reflected in Cost of Goods Sold on the income statement. However, this increase required the payment of cash so it is deducted from net income to arrive at cash flows from operating activities. An increase in any current asset other than cash will be subtracted from net income to arrive at cash flows from operating activities. The last column in the statement of financial position in Exhibit 11-6 also shows that this increase in Inventory represents a "use" or outflow of cash.

3. **A decrease in a current liability causes a decrease in cash.** Mackay Industries' Accounts Payable went down $12,000 **F** . This means that Mackay Industries paid $12,000 more on its payables than it charged during the current year. However, the amount that Mackay Industries charged on its payables is what is reflected in Cost of Goods Sold and Operating Expenses on the income statement. So, the $12,000 decrease in Accounts Payable is subtracted from net income to arrive at cash flows from operating activities. A decrease in any current liability will be subtracted from net income to arrive at cash flows from operating activities. The last column in the statement of financial position in Exhibit 11-6 also shows that this decrease in Accounts Payable represents a "use" or outflow of cash.

4. **An increase in a current liability causes an increase in cash.** Mackay Industries' Accrued Liabilities increased by $4,000 **G** . This means that $4,000 of the operating expenses on the income statement have not yet been paid for. Accordingly, even though net income was reduced by the $4,000, cash was not reduced. Therefore, the $4,000 increase in current liabilities is added to net income to arrive at cash flows from operations. An increase in any current liability will be added to net income to arrive at cash flows from operating activities. The last column in the statement of financial position in Exhibit 11-6 also shows that this increase in Accrued Liabilities payable represents a "source" or inflow of cash.

During 2015, Mackay Industries' operations provided net cash flow of $70,000. This amount exceeds net income (due to the various adjustments discussed previously). However, to fully evaluate a company's cash flows, we must also examine its investing and financing activities.

To summarize the adjustments, **Exhibit 11-7** shows a summary of the adjustments required to transfer net income into operating cash flows using the indirect method.

CASH FLOWS FROM INVESTING ACTIVITIES

As shown in Exhibit 11-5, investing activities affect long-term assets, such as plant assets and investments. The investing section of Mackay Industries' statement of cash flows, which is based on the additional information provided in Exhibit 11-6, is presented next:

		Cash flows from investing activities:		
	H	Acquisition of fixed assets	$(195,000)	
	I	Proceeds from sale of fixed assets	104,000	
		Net cash used in investing activities		(91,000)

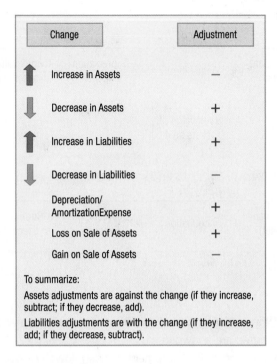

Change	Adjustment
Increase in Assets	–
Decrease in Assets	+
Increase in Liabilities	+
Decrease in Liabilities	–
Depreciation/ AmortizationExpense	+
Loss on Sale of Assets	+
Gain on Sale of Assets	–

To summarize:

Assets adjustments are against the change (if they increase, subtract; if they decrease, add).

Liabilities adjustments are with the change (if they increase, add; if they decrease, subtract).

Exhibit 11-7 ▲

Computing Acquisitions and Sales of Plant Assets

Companies usually keep a separate account for each type of plant asset. However, for computing investing cash flows, it is helpful to combine all the plant assets into a single Plant Assets account. We subtract accumulated depreciation from the assets' cost to work with a single net figure for plant assets, such as Plant Assets, Net $385,000. This simplifies the computations.

To illustrate, observe that Mackay Industries' financial statements presented in Exhibit 11-6 show the following:

- The statement of financial position reports plant assets, net of depreciation, of $385,000 at the end of 2015 and $315,000 at the end of 2014.

- The income statement shows depreciation expense of $18,000 and a $3,000 loss on sale of plant assets.

Mackay Industries' acquisitions of plant assets during 2015 consisted of $195,000 of cash purchases. The $195,000 of cash used to purchase the plant assets will be reported as a cash outflow (item **H**) in the investing section of the statement of cash flows. If any portion of the purchase of plant assets is financed with notes payable, the amount financed is not included in the cash outflow.

On the other hand, Mackay Industries also sold equipment with a cost of $134,000 and accumulated depreciation of $27,000 for a cash price of $104,000. Hence, there is a loss on sale of assets of $3,000. It would be journalized as follows:

DATE	ACCOUNTS	POST REF.	DR.	CR.
	Cash		104,000	
	Accumulated Depreciation		27,000	
	Loss on sale of assets		3,000	
	Plant Asset			134,000

As you can see, the loss amount does not represent cash flows. The only cash inflow from this transaction is the $104,000 cash receipts, which is shown as item **I** in the investing activities section of the statement of cash flows. **Exhibit 11-8** summarizes the

Cash Receipts

From sale of plant assets

$$\text{Beginning plant} \atop \text{assets (net)} + \text{Acquisition*} - \text{Depreciation} \atop \text{Expense} - \text{Book value of} \atop \text{assets sold} = \text{Ending plant} \atop \text{assets (net)}$$

$$\text{Cash receipt} = \text{Book value of} \atop \text{assets sold} \begin{cases} + & \text{Gain on sale} \\ \text{or} & \\ - & \text{Loss on sale} \end{cases}$$

Cash Payments

For acquisition of plant assets

$$\text{Beginning plant} \atop \text{assets (net)} + \text{Acquisition*} - \text{Depreciation} \atop \text{Expense} - \text{Book value of} \atop \text{assets sold} = \text{Ending plant} \atop \text{assets (net)}$$

*Any portion of the acquisition that is financed by a note payable must be deducted from the amount of cash paid.

Exhibit 11-8 ▲

computation of the investing cash flows from the acquisition and sale of plant assets. Items to be computed are shown in blue.

The investing section of the statement of cash flows will also include cash outflows for the purchase of investments and for any amounts lent to others under long-term notes receivable. Cash inflows reported in the investing section of the statement of cash flows will include proceeds from the sale of investments and any payments received on long-term notes receivable.

As we can see, Mackay Industries used $91,000 in investing activities. Now let's examine the financing section of the statement of cash flows.

CASH FLOWS FROM FINANCING ACTIVITIES

As shown in Exhibit 11-5, financing activities affect the liability and shareholders' equity accounts, such as Long-Term Notes Payable, Bonds Payable, Common Shares, and Retained Earnings. The financing section of Mackay Industries' statement of cash flows, which is based on the additional information provided in Exhibit 11-6, is presented next:

	Cash flows from financing activities:		
J	Proceeds from issuance of notes payable	$ 75,000	
L	Proceeds from issuance of common shares	20,000	
K	Payment of notes payable	(26,000)	
M	Payment of dividends	(23,000)	
N	Purchase of treasury shares	(18,000)	
	Net cash provided by financing activities		28,000

Computing Issuances and Payments of Long-Term Notes Payable

The beginning and ending balances of Notes Payable or Bonds Payable are found on the statement of financial position. If either the amount of new issuances or payments is known, the other amount can be computed. For Mackay Industries, it is given that during 2015, $75,000 was borrowed on a long-term note payable. We can use the amount of the note proceeds and the beginning and ending balances of Notes Payable from Mackay Industries' statement of financial position in Exhibit 11-6 to create the following incomplete T-account:

Notes Payable			
		12/31/14 Bal	98,000
Note payments	?	New notes	75,000
		12/31/15 Bal	147,000

Then, solve for the missing payments value:

12/31/14 Bal + New notes issued − Note payments? = 12/31/15 Bal

$98,000	+	$ 75,000	− Note payments? =	$147,000
		$173,000	− Note payments? =	$147,000
			Note payments =	$ 26,000

The completed T-account looks like this:

Notes Payable			
		12/31/14 Bal	98,000
Note payments	26,000	New notes	75,000
		12/31/15 Bal	147,000

The $75,000 cash received is reflected as a cash inflow (item **J**) in the financing section of the statement of cash flows. The payment of $26,000 is reflected as a cash outflow (item **K**) in the financing section of the statement of cash flows. The difference between $75,000 and $26,000 is the net cash inflow showing in Exhibit 11-6 as a "source" of $49,000.

Computing Issuances of Shares

Cash flows for these financing activities can be determined by analyzing the share accounts. We can see from looking at the data in Exhibit 11-6 that the balance in the Common Shares account increased by $20,000. Since it is given that there were no share retirements during 2015 and shares issued were in cash, the $20,000 will be reflected as a cash inflow (item **L**) in the financing section of the statement of cash flows.

Computing Dividend Payments

The amount of dividends that were declared during the year can be found on the statement of retained earnings. From the statement of retained earnings in Exhibit 11-6, we see that Mackay Industries declared $23,000 of dividends during 2015. Remember, a share dividend has *no* effect on cash and is, therefore, *not* reported on the statement of cash flows. However, it is given that all of Mackay Industries' dividends were cash dividends. Because there were no beginning or ending balances in Dividends Payable on the statement of financial position, we can conclude that the entire $23,000 (and no more) was paid during 2015. Therefore, the $23,000 will be reflected as a cash outflow (item **M**) in the financing section of the statement of cash flows.

If the statement of retained earnings is unavailable, the amount of dividends can be computed by analyzing the Retained Earnings account. Remember, Retained Earnings increases when companies earn net income. Retained Earnings also decreases when companies have a net loss and when they declare dividends. We can use the amount of the net income and the beginning and ending balances of Retained Earnings (from Mackay Industries' financial statements in Exhibit 11-6) to create the following incomplete T-account:

Retained Earnings		
	12/31/14 Bal	121,000
Dividends ?	Net income	48,000
	12/31/15 Bal	146,000

Then, solve for the missing amount of dividends declared:

$$12/31/14 \text{ Bal} + \text{Net income} - \text{Dividends?} = 12/31/15 \text{ Bal}$$
$$\$121,000 + \$48,000 - \text{Dividends?} = \$146,000$$
$$\$169,000 - \text{Dividends?} = \$146,000$$
$$\text{Dividends} = \$23,000$$

The completed T-account looks like this:

Retained Earnings		
	12/31/14 Bal	121,000
Dividends 23,000	Net income	48,000
	12/31/15 Bal	146,000

11.4 **STILL** DON'T GET IT?
Visit MyAccountingLab for an alternate explanation of this important accounting concept.

Another way to determine the amount of dividends declared is to compare the net income and the amount of increase in the Retained Earnings account. The statement of financial position in Exhibit 11-6 shows that there is a "source" or inflow of cash of $25,000. However, Mackay Industries reported a net income of $48,000. The difference of $23,000 was declared as dividends.

Purchases and Sales of Treasury Shares

The last item that changed on Mackay Industries' statement of financial position was Treasury Shares. Since there were no treasury shares sold during the period, $18,000 is shown as a cash outflow in the financing section of the statement of cash flows for purchase of treasury shares (item **N**).

NET CHANGE IN CASH AND CASH BALANCES

The cash provided by or used in operating, investing, and financing activities is totalled to arrive at the net increase of $7,000 in cash. Next, the beginning cash of $11,000 from December 31, 2014, is listed. The net increase of $7,000 is added to the beginning cash of $11,000 to get the ending cash balance on December 31, 2015, of $18,000. The completed statement of cash flows for Mackay Industries is presented in **Exhibit 11-9**.

You can see why the statement of cash flows is so valuable. It explains why the cash balance for Mackay Industries increased by only $7,000, even though the company reported net income for the year of $48,000.

NONCASH INVESTING AND FINANCING ACTIVITIES

The operating, investing, and financing sections of the statement of cash flows only reflect activity that results from the exchange of cash; however, companies may make investments that do not require cash. They may also obtain financing for other reasons than to acquire cash. These types of transactions are called noncash investing and financing activities. Although these transactions do not affect cash, they still affect the long-term assets, long-term liabilities, and equity of a business. To provide financial statement users with complete information, all noncash investing and financing activities are

Mackay Industries
Statement of Cash Flows
Year Ended December 31, 2015

Cash flows from operating activities:			
A	Net Income		$ 48,000
	Adjustments to reconcile net income to net cash provided by operating activities:		
B	Depreciation Expense	$ 18,000	
C	Loss on sale of fixed assets	3,000	
D	Decrease in Accounts Receivable	17,000	
E	Increase in Inventory	(8,000)	
F	Decrease in Accounts Payable	(12,000)	
G	Increase in Accrued Liabilities	4,000	22,000
	Net cash provided by operating activities		70,000
	Cash flows from investing activities:		
H	Acquisition of fixed assets	(195,000)	
I	Proceeds from sale of fixed assets	104,000	
	Net cash used in investing activities		(91,000)
	Cash flows from financing activities:		
J	Proceeds from issuance of notes payable	75,000	
L	Proceeds from issuance of common shares	20,000	
K	Payment of notes payable	(26,000)	
M	Payment of dividends	(23,000)	
N	Purchase of treasury shares	(18,000)	
	Net cash provided by financing activities		28,000
	Net increase in cash:		7,000
	Cash balance, December 31, 2014		11,000
	Cash balance, December 31, 2015		$ 18,000

Exhibit 11-9 ▲

reported. Noncash investing and financing activities can be reported in a separate schedule that accompanies the statement of cash flows, or they can be disclosed in a financial statement note.

Our Mackay Industries example did not include noncash transactions because the company did not have any transactions of this type during the year. So, to illustrate the reporting of noncash transactions, let's consider the following three noncash transactions for Tucker Enterprises.

1. Tucker Enterprises issues $450,000 of common shares in exchange for a building. The journal entry to record the purchase would be as follows:

DATE	ACCOUNTS	POST REF.	DR.	CR.
	Building		450,000	
	Common Shares			450,000
	Exchanged shares for a building.			

The purchase of the building is an investing activity. The issuance of common shares is a financing activity. However, this transaction is not reported in the investing and financing sections of the statement of cash flows because no cash is exchanged. Instead, this transaction is reported as a *noncash investing and financing activity.*

2. Tucker Enterprises acquired $120,000 of land by issuing a note. The journal entry to record the purchase would be as follows:

Assets = Liabilities + Shareholders' Equity

+120,000 = +120,000

DATE	ACCOUNTS	POST REF.	DR.	CR.
	Land		120,000	
	Notes Payable			120,000
	Purchased land.			

The purchase of the land is an investing activity. The issuance of the note is a financing activity. Once again, this transaction is not reported in the investing and financing sections of the statement of cash flows because no cash is exchanged. Instead, this transaction is reported as a *noncash investing and financing activity*.

3. Tucker Enterprises issued $100,000 of common shares to pay off a debt. The journal entry to record the payment would be as follows:

Assets = Liabilities + Shareholders' Equity

= −100,000 +100,000

DATE	ACCOUNTS	POST REF.	DR.	CR.
	Notes Payable		100,000	
	Common Shares			100,000
	Paid note with shares.			

The payment on the note and the issuance of the common shares are both financing activities. But, because no cash is involved, this transaction will not be reported in the financing section of the statement of cash flows. It is reported as a *noncash investing and financing activity*.

Exhibit 11-10 illustrates how the noncash investing and financing activities for Tucker Enterprises would be presented.

Tucker Enterprises
Statement of Cash Flows—Partial
Year Ended December 31, 2015

Noncash investing and financing activities:		
Issued 10,000 common shares in exchange for a building		$450,000
Issued a note in exchange for land		120,000
Issued 1,800 common shares as repayment of note		100,000

Exhibit 11-10 ▲

 CONCEPT CHECK...

Alpine Manufacturing purchased a new piece of equipment costing $45,000. Alpine paid $5,000 cash down and signed a note for the remainder. What types of activities (operating, financing, or investing) are represented by this transaction? How would this transaction be reported in Alpine Manufacturing's statement of cash flows?

Answer: Because this transaction involves both the purchase of new plant assets and the issuance of a note payable, it represents both an investing activity and a financing activity. However, on Alpine Manufacturing's statement of cash flows, only $5,000 will be reflected in the investing section as an outflow of cash for the purchase of plant assets. The remaining $40,000 will be reflected as a noncash investing and financing activity in a separate schedule.

HOW IS THE STATEMENT OF CASH FLOWS PREPARED USING THE DIRECT METHOD?

Although most companies utilize the indirect method of reporting cash flows from operating activities, both IFRS and ASPE prefer the direct method. This is one instance when companies choose to use an accounting method that is contrary to the general rules. But since most companies use the indirect method, the discrepancy is overlooked. The direct method provides clearer information about the sources and uses of cash than the indirect method. Investing and financing cash flows are presented exactly the same under both methods.

To illustrate how the operating section of the statement of cash flows differs for the direct method, we will be using the Mackay Industries data we used with the indirect method.

Mackay Industries' completed direct method statement of cash flows for 2015 is presented in **Exhibit 11-11**.

L.O. ④ Prepare the statement of cash flows using the direct method

		Mackay Industries **Statement of Cash Flows** Year Ended December 31, 2015		
		Cash flows from operating activities:		
		Receipts:		
A		Collections from customers	$ 285,000	
B		Interest received	13,000	
C		Dividends received	5,000	
		Total cash receipts		$ 303,000
		Payments:		
D		To suppliers	(165,000)	
E		To employees	(48,000)	
F		For interest	(11,000)	
G		For taxes	(9,000)	
		Total cash payments		(233,000)
		Net cash provided by operating activities		70,000
		Cash flows from investing activities:		
		Acquisition of plant assets	(195,000)	
		Proceeds from sale of plant assets	104,000	
		Net cash used in investing activities		(91,000)
		Cash flows from financing activities:		
		Proceeds from issuance of notes payable	75,000	
		Proceeds from issuance of common shares	20,000	
		Payment of notes payable	(26,000)	
		Payment of dividends	(23,000)	
		Purchase of treasury shares	(18,000)	
		Net cash provided by financing activities		28,000
		Net increase in cash:		7,000
		Cash balance, December 31, 2014		11,000
		Cash balance, December 31, 2015		$ 18,000

Exhibit 11-11 ▲

Now, we'll explain how we calculated each number.

CASH FLOWS FROM OPERATING ACTIVITIES

In the indirect method, we start with net income and then adjust it to "cash-basis" through a series of adjusting items. In the direct method, we convert each line item on the income statement from accrual to cash basis. So, in essence, the operating activities section of the direct method statement of cash flows is really just a cash-basis income statement.

Depreciation, Depletion, and Amortization Expense

Because these expenses do not require the payment of cash, they are *not* reported on the direct method statement of cash flows.

Gains and Losses on the Sale of Plant Assets

The last item on the income statement is a loss on sale of plant assets of $3,000. Remember that gains and losses do not represent cash flows. The cash flow related to the sale of a plant asset equals the proceeds from the sale of the asset. As with the indirect method, the proceeds from the sale of the asset are reported in the investing section, not the operating section.

A Cash Collections from Customers

The first item on the income statement is Sales Revenue of $268,000. Sales Revenue represents the total of all sales, whether for cash or on account. The statement of financial position accounts related to Sales Revenue are Accounts Receivable and Unearned Revenues. Accounts Receivable decreased $17,000 from $93,000 at 12/31/2014 to $76,000 at 12/31/2015. A decrease in Accounts Receivable means that Mackay Industries collected more cash than it made in sales during the current year, as shown in the statement of financial position in Exhibit 11-6 source of cash of $17,000. This means that the cash receipts during the year are $17,000 greater than sales revenues. The statement of financial position shows no unearned revenues, so no adjustment is needed for unearned revenues. We can calculate the cash received from customers as follows:

Sales Revenue	$268,000
Plus decrease in Accounts Receivable	17,000
Cash receipts from customers	$285,000

B Cash Receipts of Interest

The second item on the income statement is Interest Revenue of $13,000. The statement of financial position account related to Interest Revenue is Interest Receivable. Since there is no Interest Receivable account on the statement of financial position, the Interest Revenue must have all been received in cash. So, the statement of cash flows shows interest received of $13,000. Had there been interest receivable in either year, the accrual basis Interest Revenue would have been converted to cash basis in a manner similar to that used for Sales Revenue and Accounts Receivable.

C Cash Receipts of Dividends

Dividend Revenue of $5,000 is the third item reported on the income statement. The statement of financial position account related to Dividend Revenue is Dividends Receivable.

As with the interest, there is no Dividends Receivable on the statement of financial position. Therefore, the dividend revenue must have all been received in cash. So, the statement of cash flows shows cash received from dividends of $5,000.

◻ Payments to Suppliers

Payments to suppliers include all payments for

- inventory and
- operating expenses except employee compensation, interest, and income taxes.

Suppliers are those entities that provide the business with its inventory and essential services. The accounts related to payments to suppliers for inventory are Cost of Goods Sold, Inventory, and Accounts Payable. Cost of Goods Sold on the income statement was $137,000. Inventory increased from $124,000 at 12/31/2014 to $132,000 at 12/31/2015. The $8,000 ($132,000 − $124,000) increase in Inventory means that Mackay Industries purchased more inventory than it sold during the year. This means that the total amount of inventory purchased during the year would be $145,000.

Cost of Goods Sold	$137,000
Plus increase in Inventory	8,000
Total inventory purchased	$145,000

Next we need to consider the change in Accounts Payable to determine the total cash payments for inventory purchased during the year. Accounts Payable decreased from $96,000 at 12/31/2014 to $84,000 at 12/31/2015. The $12,000 decrease ($96,000 − $84,000) in Accounts Payable means that Mackay Industries paid $12,000 more during the year than the amount of inventory purchased. So, the cash payments for inventory purchased during the year can be calculated as follows:

Total inventory purchased	$145,000
Plus decrease in Accounts Payable	12,000
Cash payments for inventory	$157,000

The accounts related to payments to suppliers for operating expenses are Operating Expenses, Prepaid Expenses, and Accrued Liabilities. Operating Expenses on the income statement were $12,000. There are no Prepaid Expenses on the statement of financial position so no adjustment is needed for changes in prepaid expenses. Accrued Liabilities increased from $8,000 at 12/31/2014 to $12,000 at 12/31/2015. This means that Mackay Industries incurred more operating expenses than it paid for during the year. By subtracting the $4,000 ($12,000 − $8,000) from the operating expenses we get the amount of cash payments made to suppliers for operating expense:

Operating Expenses	$12,000
Less increase in Accrued Liabilities	4,000
Cash payments for operating expenses	$ 8,000

Finally, by adding the cash paid to suppliers for inventory to the cash paid to suppliers for operating expenses we get the total cash paid to suppliers of $165,000.

Cash payments for inventory	$157,000
Cash payments for operating expenses	8,000
Total cash payments to suppliers	$165,000

E Payments to Employees

This category includes payments for salaries, wages, and other forms of employee compensation. The accounts related to employee payments are Salaries Expense from the income statement and Salaries Payable from the statement of financial position. Since there aren't any Salaries Payable on the statement of financial position, the Salaries Expense account must represent all amounts paid in cash to employees. So, the statement of cash flows shows cash payments to employees of $48,000. Had there been any Salaries Payable, the Salaries Expense account would have been adjusted to arrive at the cash paid to employees in a manner similar to how operating expenses were adjusted for accrued liabilities above.

F Payments for Interest Expense

These cash payments are reported separately from the other expenses. The accounts related to interest payments are Interest Expense from the income statement and Interest Payable from the statement of financial position. Since there is no Interest Payable on the statement of financial position, the Interest Expense from the income statement must represent all amounts paid in cash for interest. So, the statement of cash flows shows cash payments for interest of $11,000.

G Payments for Income Tax Expense

Like interest expense, these cash payments are reported separately from the other expenses. The accounts related to income tax payments are Income Tax Expense from the income statement and Income Tax Payable from the statement of financial position. Again, since there is no Income Tax Payable on the statement of financial position, the Income Tax Expense from the income statement must represent all amounts paid in cash for income tax. Therefore, the statement of cash flows shows cash payments for income tax of $9,000.

Net Cash Provided by Operating Activities

To calculate net cash provided by operating activities using the direct method, we add all the cash receipts and cash payments described previously and find the difference. For Mackay Industries, Inc., total cash receipts were $303,000. Total cash payments were $233,000. So, net cash provided by operating activities is $70,000. If you refer back to the indirect method statement of cash flows shown in Exhibit 11-9, you will find that it showed the same $70,000 for net cash provided by operating activities—only the method by which it was calculated was different.

The remainder of Mackay Industries' statement of cash flows is exactly the same as what we calculated using the indirect method (see Exhibit 11-9).

Exhibit 11-12 summarizes the differences between the two methods of preparing the statement of cash flows.

Exhibit 11-12 ▲

 CRITICAL THINKING

Take a minute to think about the following items. How do companies record journal entries for each of these items? What do they do in preparing the statement of cash flows?

- Premium on bonds payable
- Discount on bonds payable
- Warranty expense
- Bad debt expense
- Contributed surplus

Solution:

		DR.	CR.	STATEMENT OF CASH FLOWS
1	Interest Expense	xxx		Need to subtract this amount from net income to get cash amount paid for interest.
	Premium on Bonds Payable	xx		
	Cash		xxx	
2	Interest Expense	xxx		Need to add this amount to net income to get cash amount paid for interest.
	Discount on Bonds Payable		xx	
	Cash		xxx	
3	Warranty Expense	xxx		This is a noncash item. This amount needs to be added back to net income.
	Estimated Warranty Liabilities		xxx	
4	Bad Debt Expense	xxx		This is a noncash item. This amount needs to be added back to net income.
	Allowance for Doubtful Accounts		xxx	
5	Common Shares	xxx		Need to subtract this amount from the changes in the Common Shares account to get total cash amount paid to buy back common shares.
	Contributed Surplus		xx	
	Cash		xxx	

 DECISION GUIDELINES

DECISION	GUIDELINE	ANALYZE
I just started my own business and I want to make sure that I report things properly. Should the direct or indirect method be used to prepare the statement of cash flows?	Although the direct method is preferred by IFRS and ASPE, most financial statement users find the indirect method more useful.	Because the indirect method reconciles net income as reported on the income statement to net cash provided by operating activities, it is more useful to most financial statements users. It helps answer the questions "How can the company have so much income when it has so little cash?" or "How can the company have so much cash when it made so little income?"

FOCUS ON DECISION MAKING: FREE CASH FLOW AND THE CASH CONVERSION CYCLE

L.O. ⑤ Evaluate a company's performance with respect to cash

A business needs cash. If it doesn't have enough cash, it will fail. However, it may also have too much cash. Managing and financing cash is expensive; the benefits of holding cash should exceed the costs. So how do businesses look at and manage cash flow? They often use two measures: free cash flow and the cash conversion cycle.

FREE CASH FLOW

The statement of cash flows is a useful tool for examining the sources and uses of cash during an accounting period. However, investors may want to know how much cash a company anticipates it can "free up" for new opportunities, to reduce debt, or to pay dividends. **Free cash flow** is the amount of cash available from operations after paying for investments in long-term assets. Fundamentally, free cash flow is net cash flow from operations minus cash payments for investments in long-term assets. Free cash flow can be computed as follows:

Free Cash Flow = Net Cash Flow from Operations − Cash Payments for Investments in Long-Term Assets

Many companies use free cash flow to manage their operations. Suppose Tucker Enterprises has net cash provided by operations of $160,000 during the year, and the company spent $85,000 to purchase new equipment. In this case, Tucker Enterprises' free cash flow would be $75,000 ($160,000 – $85,000). If a good investment opportunity comes along (or an unanticipated need for cash arises), Tucker Enterprises should have $75,000 of free cash available. It could also use the $75,000 to pay off debts or to pay dividends.

CASH CONVERSION CYCLE

The **cash conversion cycle** represents the time it takes a company to sell its inventory and collect its receivables, less the time it takes the company to pay its payables. In other words, the cash conversion cycle represents the number of days a company's cash is "tied up" in the operations of the business. The cash conversion cycle is calculated as follows:

Cash Conversion Cycle = (Days Sales in Inventory) + (Receivable Collection Period) − (Accounts Payable Payment Period)

Days sales in inventory tells you how many days it takes to convert inventory into a sale (the computation for this ratio is covered in Chapter 6). The receivable collection period tells you how many days it takes to convert the accounts receivable into cash (the computation for this ratio is covered in Chapter 7). The accounts payable payment period tells you how many days it takes to pay accounts payable. The accounts payable payment period is calculated as follows:

Accounts Payable Payment Period = Average Accounts Payable/(Cost of Goods Sold/365 Days)

Average accounts payable is computed by adding the beginning and ending accounts payable and dividing the total by 2. Remember that the statement of financial position accounts, such as accounts payable, carry their balances from one period to the next. The ending accounts payable for one year becomes the beginning accounts payable for the next year.

Let's assume that Tucker Enterprises has a days sales in inventory of 52 days, a receivable collection period of 34 days, and an accounts payable payment period of 39 days. Tucker Enterprises' cash conversion cycle would equal 47 days (52 + 34 − 39). This means that, on average, Tucker Enterprises' cash is tied up for 47 days. Generally, the shorter the cash conversion cycle is, the healthier the company is. This is because cash is the lifeblood of a business, and the less amount of time it is "tied up," the better. Over time, if the cash conversion cycle for a business grows longer, it can be a sign that the business may be facing a pending cash flow "crunch."

HOW THEY DO IT: A LOOK AT BUSINESS

Let's look at a real-world example, Procter & Gamble. Procter & Gamble (P&G) is the manufacturer of household products such as Cover Girl cosmetics, Gillette razors, Crest toothpaste, Duracell batteries, and Tide detergent. It buys ingredients and makes products. These ingredients and products are P&G's inventory. It then sells its inventory to retailers such as Loblaw. However, Loblaw does not immediately pay P&G, and P&G has a receivable from Loblaw. When Loblaw pays P&G, cash is received and the receivable goes away. P&G then has cash to pay its ingredients' suppliers.

This process creates operating cash flow that can then be used to make planned investments in long-term assets, such as new factories. What results is free cash flow. For the fiscal year ending June 30, 2012, P&G's days sales in inventory was 60.7 days, receivable collection period was 26.9 days, and accounts payable payment period was 68.7 days. Therefore, P&G's cash conversion cycle was 18.9 days (60.7 days + 26.9 days − 68.7 days = 18.9 days).

 DECISION GUIDELINES

DECISION	GUIDELINE	ANALYZE
As the manager of a department, I would like to have renovations done on my retail area. Does the company have sufficient cash available?	Calculate the company's free cash flow and its cash conversion cycle.	For a business to be able to take advantage of unforeseen opportunities, it is important that it has free cash available. A lack of free cash will probably not negatively impact a business's normal operations but it will most likely result in lost income due to forgone opportunities. The cash conversion cycle indicates how long a company's cash is being "tied up" in its operations. The longer cash is tied up, the more likely it is that the company will encounter cash flow problems in the future. A company with a long cash conversion cycle should consider obtaining a line of credit to provide some insurance against cash flow problems.

FOCUS ON USERS

Concept	User	Why Is This Important to This User?
Statement of Cash Flows	**Bookkeepers Managers Shareholders Creditors Competitors Government and Regulatory Bodies**	All users of financial statements will spend a great deal of time examining the statement of cash flows for the signals that it will send. For example, a new company may not have sufficient sales to generate positive cash flows from operations because the company will be purchasing inventory, selling to customers on credit, but paying for their purchases and expenses such as payroll; investing activities will also likely be a use of cash because the company needs to purchase the assets that will make the company productive; and, in order to support the operating and investing activities, a new company would need to have significant cash inflows from financing activities by selling shares, acquiring long-term debt, or both. A company that has been around long enough to be in its mature phase will likely have positive cash flows from operations that are significant enough to support any new purchases of capital assets in the investing activities (to replace older equipment), and uses of cash in the financing activities for paying down debt and paying dividends to shareholders. Each combination of sources and uses of cash in the three areas of activities will tell a story of how the company is performing. Since cash is the most important asset of an organization (because a company cannot exist without sufficient cash to satisfy its needs), understanding where a company is receiving cash and where a company uses its cash is critical for understanding its long-term potential. The cash flow needs to be understood in combination with the other financial statements and other information, though. For example, negative cash flow from a company's operating activities without understanding that this company is a start-up organization could lead to a misinterpretation of how the organization is performing. Overall, the statement of cash flows can provide users with important information for analyzing whether creditors want to extend credit, competitors want to adjust their own strategies, investors want to purchase shares, or management needs to adjust their priorities for cash.

DEMO DOC

PREPARING THE STATEMENT OF CASH FLOWS USING THE INDIRECT METHOD

Cassidy, Inc. has the following information for 2015:

LEARNING OBJECTIVE ❸

Cassidy, Inc.
Income Statement
Year Ended December 31, 2015

Sales Revenue		$550,000
Cost of Goods Sold		320,000
Gross Profit		230,000
Operating Expenses:		
Salaries Expense	$165,000	
Depreciation Expense	21,000	
Insurance Expense	19,000	
Total Operating Expenses		205,000
Income from Operations		25,000
Other Income:		
Gain on Sale of Fixed Assets		3,000
Net Income		$ 28,000

Cassidy, Inc.
Statement of Financial Position
December 31, 2015 and 2014

ASSETS	2015	2014	LIABILITIES	2015	2014
Current:			Current:		
Cash	$ 28,000	$ 33,000	Accounts Payable	$ 20,000	$ 23,000
Accounts Receivable	26,000	15,000	Salaries Payable	10,000	8,000
Prepaid Insurance	30,000	42,000	Total Current		
Total Current Assets	84,000	90,000	Liabilities	30,000	31,000
Furniture, net	90,000	74,500	Notes Payable	40,000	50,000
			SHAREHOLDERS' EQUITY		
			Common Shares	4,000	3,500
			Retained Earnings	100,000	80,000
			Total Liabilities and		
Total Assets	$174,000	$164,500	Shareholders' Equity	$174,000	$164,500

During 2015 Cassidy

- sold furniture with a book value of $15,000 for cash. New furniture was purchased for cash.
- repaid notes payable with a principal value of $22,000. Issued new notes for cash.

- issued new common shares for cash.
- paid cash dividends.

REQUIREMENT:

① **Prepare Cassidy's statement of cash flows using the indirect method.**

DEMO DOC SOLUTION
REQUIREMENT ①
Prepare Cassidy's statement of cash flows using the indirect method.

Part 1	Demo Doc Complete

OPERATING ACTIVITIES

As with income statements and statements of financial position, every statement of cash flows needs a proper title. The first line of the title is the company name, next is the name of the statement (statement of cash flows), and last is the date (year ended December 31, 2015). Put all together, the title is as follows:

> **Cassidy, Inc.**
> **Statement of Cash Flows**
> Year Ended December 31, 2015

The first section of the statement of cash flows is operating activities. This section begins with net income. We can find net income on the income statement. According to Cassidy's income statement, net income for the year is $28,000.

Items are added or subtracted on the statement of cash flows based on their impact to cash. In this case, net income increases cash, so it is added on the statement of cash flows.

Next, we must take a quick look through the income statement and look for any noncash items. Noncash items are *not* part of cash flows, so any noncash items in net income must be removed.

The most frequent noncash item on the income statement is depreciation expense. Depreciation expense is subtracted to arrive at net income (if you look at the income statement, you will see a subtraction for depreciation expense), so to *remove* its impact, the *opposite* must be done: Depreciation expense of $21,000 must be added back to net income.

The other noncash item that you will see on many income statements is gains/losses on sale of assets. In this example, Cassidy has a gain on sale of furniture of $3,000. As you can see on the income statement, this gain was added to arrive at net income. To *remove* its effect, we do the *opposite*: subtract it. So the gain of $3,000 is subtracted.

Now that we have gotten all necessary information from the income statement, we can turn to the statement of financial position.

Operating activities deal with everyday transactions of the business, the kind of things the company normally does to earn a profit. What kinds of accounts do businesses deal with on a daily basis? Some accounts are Accounts Receivable, Accounts Payable, Inventory, and so forth. In other words, they are the current assets and current liabilities of the company. Changes in the balances of these accounts impact income differently than they impact cash flows. So, adjustments must be made to reconcile net income to the cash flows for the period.

Other than Cash (which we are trying to analyze in preparing the statement of cash flows), what is the first current asset on the statement of financial position? It is Accounts Receivable. What happened to Accounts Receivable during the year? It increased from $15,000 to $26,000. This means that $11,000 ($26,000 – $15,000) of the revenues on the income statement have not yet been collected in cash. So the $11,000 increase to Accounts Receivable is subtracted from net income on the statement of cash flows.

The other current asset is Prepaid Insurance. This account decreased from $42,000 to $30,000. A decrease to Prepaid Insurance indicates that part of the expenses for the period were not paid for with cash. Instead, we used something we had prepaid—that is something we had already paid for in an earlier period. So, the decrease of $12,000 ($42,000 – $30,000) will be added to net income on the statement of cash flows.

So far, operating activities show the following information:

Cash flows from operating activities:		
Net Income		$28,000
Adjustments to reconcile net income to net cash		
provided by operating activities:		
Depreciation Expense	$ 21,000	
Gain on sale of plant assets	(3,000)	
Increase in Accounts Receivable	(11,000)	
Decrease in Prepaid Insurance	12,000	

Now that we have looked at the current assets, we can look at the current liabilities. The first current liability is Accounts Payable. During the year, Accounts Payable decreased from $23,000 to $20,000. This means that $3,000 ($23,000 – $20,000) more was paid for during the current year than was charged on account. So, the $3,000 will be subtracted from net income on the statement of cash flows.

The other current liability is Salaries Payable. During the year, Salaries Payable increased from $8,000 to $10,000. The increase in this payable account means that part of the current year's salaries expense was not paid for with cash. So $2,000 ($10,000 – $8,000) will be added to net income on the statement of cash flows.

Now that we have looked at all of the current assets and liabilities, we can total the operating activities section:

Cash flows from operating activities:		
Net Income		$28,000
Adjustments to reconcile net income to net cash		
provided by operating activities:		
Depreciation Expense	$ 21,000	
Gain on sale of plant assets	(3,000)	
Increase in Accounts Receivable	(11,000)	
Decrease in Prepaid Insurance	12,000	
Decrease in Accounts Payable	(3,000)	
Increase in Salaries Payable	2,000	18,000
Net cash provided by operating activities		46,000

INVESTING ACTIVITIES

Investing activities deal with long-term assets. The only long-term asset is Furniture. Unfortunately, we cannot just say "increase in Furniture" or "decrease in Furniture" and look at the overall change because Furniture is a major account. We must look at each significant transaction affecting the account.

From the additional information we were given with the question, we know that Cassidy purchased furniture and sold furniture during the year. Each of these transactions will be a separate line in investing activities.

Cash flows from investing activities:		
Acquisition of furniture	???	
Proceeds from sale of furniture	???	
Net cash used for investing activities		???

We do not know these totals, but we can calculate them with the information we already have.

First, we should analyze the Furniture, Net T-account. From the statement of financial position, we know that in 2015, Furniture, Net has a beginning balance of $74,500 and an ending balance of $90,000. During the year, Furniture, Net increased and decreased.

Furniture, Net			
Beginning balance	74,500		
Increases	???	Decreases	???
Ending balance	90,000		

Furniture, Net increases when new furniture is purchased (acquisitions). Furniture, Net decreases by the book value of furniture sold and when depreciation expense is recorded. Depreciation expense of $21,000 can be obtained from the income statement (or the operating activities section of the statement of cash flows). The book value of $15,000 for the assets sold was given in the problem. Putting these items into the T-account is shown next:

Furniture, Net			
Beginning balance	74,500	Depreciation	21,000
Acquisitions	X	Book value of assets sold	15,000
Ending balance	90,000		

We can use this information to calculate the cost of furniture purchased (acquisitions), X.

$$\$74{,}500 - \$21{,}000 - \$15{,}000 + X = \$90{,}000$$
$$X = \$90{,}000 - \$74{,}500 + \$21{,}000 + \$15{,}000$$
$$X = \$51{,}500$$

So acquisitions of furniture were $51,500. Purchasing furniture caused Cash to decrease, so the $51,500 will be subtracted on the statement of cash flows.

We still need to determine the cash received when furniture was sold (proceeds). We can use the gain/loss formula for this calculation:

$$\text{Proceeds} = \text{Book value of assets sold} \quad + \text{Gain, or} - \text{Loss}$$
$$\text{Proceeds} = \$15{,}000 \text{ Book value of assets sold} + \text{Gain of } \$3{,}000$$
$$\text{Proceeds} = \$18{,}000$$

So the proceeds from sale of furniture were $18,000. Selling furniture caused Cash to increase, so the $18,000 will be added on the statement of cash flows. Filling this information into the investing activities, we have the following:

Cash flows from investing activities:		
Acquisition of furniture	$(51,500)	
Proceeds from sale of furniture	18,000	
Net cash used for investing activities		$(33,500)

FINANCING ACTIVITIES

Financing activities deal with long-term liabilities (debt financing) and equity (equity financing).

Cassidy only has one long-term liability: Notes Payable. As with Furniture, we know that we must report the major transactions in this account separately.

From the additional information we were given with the question, we know that Cassidy paid off notes payable and issued new notes payable during the year. Each of these transactions will be a separate line in financing activities.

Cash flows from financing activities:		
Proceeds from issuance of long-term notes payable	???	
Payment of long-term notes payable	???	

We need to calculate the value of new notes issued. As we did with furniture, we can make this calculation by analyzing the T-account. In 2015, Notes Payable had a beginning balance of $50,000 and an ending balance of $40,000.

Notes Payable			
		Beginning balance	50,000
Decreases	???	Increases	???
		Ending balance	40,000

Notes Payable is increased when new notes are issued and is decreased when notes are paid off. From the additional information given in the problem, we know that $22,000 of notes were paid off. Putting this information into the T-account, we have the following:

Notes Payable			
		Beginning balance	50,000
Payments	22,000	Issuance of new notes payable	X
		Ending balance	40,000

We can use this information to calculate the value of new notes issued:

$$\$50,000 - \$22,000 + X = \$40,000$$
$$X = \$40,000 - \$50,000 + \$22,000$$
$$X = \$12,000$$

So, issuance of new notes payable was $12,000. Because issuing notes payable increased Cash, $12,000 will be added on the statement of cash flows.

Putting this information into the financing activities section, we have the following:

	Cash flows from financing activities:		
	Proceeds from issuance of long-term notes payable	$ 12,000	
	Payment of long-term notes payable	(22,000)	

Now that we have examined the long-term liabilities, we only have equity remaining. The first account in equity is Common Shares. From the additional information, we know that new common shares were issued during the year. Because this is the only transaction affecting Common Shares, we know that the change in the Common Shares account represents the issuance of these shares. Using the T-account we have the following:

Common Shares		
	Beginning balance	3,500
	Issuance of new shares	X
	Ending balance	4,000

We use this information to calculate the value of new common shares issued, X.

$$\$3,500 + X = \$4,000$$
$$X = \$4,000 - \$3,500$$
$$X = \$500$$

So issuance of common shares (proceeds) was $500. Because issuing common shares increases Cash, $500 will be added on the statement of cash flows.

The last account in equity is Retained Earnings. This account changed during 2015. Looking at the T-account we have the following:

Retained Earnings			
		Beginning balance	80,000
Decreases	???	Increases	???
		Ending balance	100,000

Retained Earnings is increased when the company earns net income and is decreased when the company declares dividends. If we put the net income from the income statement into the T-account, we have the following:

Retained Earnings			
		Beginning balance	80,000
Dividends	X	Net income	28,000
		Ending balance	100,000

We use this information to calculate the amount of cash dividends declared, X.

$$\$80,000 + \$28,000 - X = \$100,000$$
$$X = \$80,000 + \$28,000 - \$100,000$$
$$X = \$8,000$$

So, since there were no dividends payable, the cash dividends declared and paid were $8,000. Because the payment of dividends decreased Cash, $8,000 will be subtracted on the statement of cash flows.

Notice that we *do not record net income* in the financing activities (even though it affects Retained Earnings), because net income was already accounted for in the operating activities section.

Putting all of this information into the financing activities section, we have the following:

Cash flows from financing activities:		
Proceeds from issuance of long-term notes payable	$ 12,000	
Payment of long-term notes payable	(22,000)	
Proceeds from issuance of common shares	500	
Payment of dividends	(8,000)	
Net cash used for financing activities		$(17,500)

FINISHING THE STATEMENT OF CASH FLOWS

Now that we have completed the three main sections of the statement of cash flows, we can add the totals of the three sections together to determine cash flow (the net change in cash).

Net change in cash =	Cash provided by operating activities	−	Cash used for investing activities	−	Cash used for financing activities
Net change in cash =	$46,000	−	$33,500	−	$17,500
Net change in cash = $(5,000)					

Because the change in cash is negative, we know that it means a net *decrease* in cash.

The statement began with net income (from the income statement). Now we tie it to the statement of financial position to bring cash flows full circle. We add the decrease of $5,000 in cash to the $33,000 Cash balance at the beginning of the year (from Cassidy's statement of financial position). This gives us the cash balance at the end of the year of $(5,000) + $33,000 = $28,000.

Putting this information in statement of cash flows format, we have the following:

Net decrease in cash	$ (5,000)
Cash balance, December 31, 2014	33,000
Cash balance, December 31, 2015	$28,000

This section of the statement is also a nice check to ensure that our calculations are correct. The $28,000 calculated *is the number reported for cash* on the statement of financial position at December 31, 2015.

To finish the statement of cash flows, we just put all of these pieces together:

Cassidy, Inc.		
Statement of Cash Flows		
Year Ended December 31, 2015		
Cash flows from operating activities:		
Net Income		$ 28,000
Adjustments to reconcile net income to net cash		
provided by operating activities:		
Depreciation Expense	$ 21,000	
Gain on sale of plant assets	(3,000)	
Increase in Accounts Receivable	(11,000)	
Decrease in Prepaid Insurance	12,000	
Decrease in Accounts Payable	(3,000)	
Increase in Salaries Payable	2,000	18,000
Net cash provided by operating activities		$ 46,000
Cash flows from investing activities:		
Acquisition of furniture	(51,500)	
Proceeds from sale of furniture	18,000	
Net cash used for investing activities		(33,500)
Cash flows from financing activities:		
Proceeds from issuance of long-term notes payable	12,000	
Payment of long-term notes payable	(22,000)	
Proceeds from issuance of common shares	500	
Payment of dividends	(8,000)	
Net cash used for financing activities		(17,500)
Net decrease in cash		$ (5,000)
Cash balance, December 31, 2014		33,000
Cash balance, December 31, 2015		$ 28,000

DEMO DOC COMPLETE

Part 1   **Demo Doc Complete**

DECISION GUIDELINES

The Statement of Cash Flows

As you examine the performance of a company (perhaps someday even your own) you may encounter some of the following decisions related to cash:

DECISION	**GUIDELINE**	**ANALYZE**
A bank is in the process of granting a loan to a business. Information is requested by the credit department to report on how the company is managing its cash and whether it is successful in doing so.	Review the statement of cash flows to determine the financial health of the company.	The statement of cash flows is divided into three categories: • Operating activities—shows the cash flow from business operations. • Investing activities—shows the cash flow from buying and selling long-term assets. • Financing activities—shows the cash flow from borrowing and repaying long-term debt, as well as from shareholders' equity transactions. For a business to remain successful, operating activities must be the main source of its cash over the long run.
I just started my own business and I want to make sure that I report things properly. Should the direct or indirect method be used to prepare the statement of cash flows?	Although the direct method is preferred by IFRS and ASPE, most financial statement users find the indirect method more useful	Because the indirect method reconciles net income as reported on the income statement to net cash provided by operating activities, it is more useful to most financial statements users. It helps answer the questions "How can the company have so much income when it has so little cash?" or "How can the company have so much cash when it made so little income?"

DECISION		GUIDELINE		ANALYZE
As the manager of a department, I would like to have renovations done on my retail area. Does the company have sufficient cash available?		Calculate the company's free cash flow and its cash conversion cycle		For a business to be able to take advantage of unforeseen opportunities, it is important that it has "free cash" available. A lack of "free cash" will probably not negatively impact a business's normal operations but it will most likely result in lost income due to foregone opportunities. The cash conversion cycle indicates how long a company's cash is being "tied up" in its operations. The longer cash is tied up, the more likely it is that the company will encounter cash flow problems in the future. A company with a long cash conversion cycle should consider obtaining a line of credit to provide some insurance against cash flow problems.

Main Differences Between IFRS and ASPE

POINT OF COMPARISON	IFRS	ASPE
Statement title	Statement of Cash Flows	Cash Flow Statement
Dividends or interest received	Usually classified as operating activities, although it is acceptable to classify them as investing activities.	Classified as operating activities.
Interest paid	Usually classified as an operating activity, although it is acceptable to classify it as a financing activity.	Classified as operating activity.
Dividends paid	Usually classified as a financing activity, although it is acceptable to classify it as an operating activity.	Classified as financing activity.

ACCOUNTING VOCABULARY

THE LANGUAGE OF BUSINESS

Cash conversion cycle (p. 647)

Direct method (p. 629)

Financing activities (p. 629)

Free cash flow (p. 646)

Indirect method (p. 629)

Investing activities (p. 628)

Operating activities (p. 628)

Statement of cash flows (p. 626)

ACCOUNTING PRACTICE

DISCUSSION QUESTIONS

1. What are some of the reasons why a statement of cash flows may be important to users of financial statements?

2. A company used cash to build a new factory and received cash when it sold off the machines in the old factory. In which section of the statement of cash flows would the cash flows from these activities be reported?

3. A company used cash to pay employees and received cash from performing services. In which section of the statement of cash flows would the cash flows from these activities be reported?

4. A company issued bonds during the year. Would this be reported as a source or use of cash on the statement of cash flows? In which section would it be reported?

5. Why is net income a good place to start when attempting to determine the cash flows from operating activities using the indirect method? Why is it not the same as the cash flows from operating activities?

6. When using the indirect method, why are gains on the sale of plant assets subtracted from net income in the operating activities section of the statement of cash flows? Why are losses on the sale of plant assets added to net income?

7. How does an increase in accounts receivable during the year affect the statement of cash flows (if at all)? Why?

8. Why would a decrease in accounts payable be shown as a decrease in cash when using the indirect method of calculating the cash flows from operating activities?

9. How would the sale of treasury shares that were acquired three years ago appear in the statement of cash flows (if at all)?

10. A company's cash conversion cycle increased from 55 days in Year 1 to 68 days in Year 3. What are the implications of this increase? What do you think happens to the cash conversion cycles of companies during a recession?

SELF CHECK

MyAccountingLab

The exercises and problems in this chapter can be found on MyAccountingLab. You can practise them as often as you want, and they feature step-by-step guided solutions to help you find the right answer.

1. The three main categories of cash flows are
   a. direct, indirect, and hybrid.
   b. current, long-term, and fixed.
   c. operating, investing, and financing.
   d. short-term, long-term, and equity.

2. The purpose of the statement of cash flows is to
   a. predict future cash flows.
   b. evaluate management decisions.
   c. predict ability to make payments to lenders.
   d. All of the above

3. Financing activities are most closely related to
   a. current assets and current liabilities.
   b. long-term assets.
   c. long-term liabilities and shareholder's equity.
   d. net income and dividends.

4. Which item does not appear on a statement of cash flows prepared by the indirect method?
   a. Collections from customers
   b. Net income
   c. Depreciation
   d. Gain on sale of land

5. Advanced Robotics earned net income of $60,000 after deducting depreciation of $4,000 and all other expenses. Current assets increased by $3,000 and current liabilities decreased by $5,000. Using the indirect method, how much was Advanced Robotics' cash flows from operating activities?
   a. $48,000
   b. $50,000
   c. $52,000
   d. $56,000

6. The Plant Assets account of Betterbuilt, Inc. shows the following:

Plant Assets, Net			
Beginning balance	100,000	Depreciation	30,000
Purchase	400,000	Sale	?
Ending balance	420,000		

Betterbuilt, Inc. sold plant assets at a $10,000 gain. How much should Betterbuilt, Inc. report for the sale?

a. Cash flows from investing activities, $40,000
b. Cash flows from investing activities, $50,000
c. Cash flows from investing activities, $60,000
d. Cash flows from investing activities, $10,000

7. Widget Corporation borrowed $15,000, issued common shares of $10,000, and paid dividends of $25,000. What was Widget Corporation's net cash provided or used by financing activities?

a. $0
b. $25,000
c. $(25,000)
d. $50,000

8. Which item appears on a statement of cash flows prepared by the indirect method?

a. Net income
b. Payment to suppliers
c. Collections from customers
d. Payment of income tax

9. Structural Systems, Inc. had accounts receivable of $20,000 at the beginning of the year and $50,000 at year-end. Revenue for the year totalled $100,000. How much cash did Structural Systems collect from customers?

a. $170,000
b. $150,000
c. $120,000
d. $70,000

10. Allied Enterprises had operating expenses of $40,000. At the beginning of the year, Allied Enterprises owed $5,000 on accrued liabilities. At year-end, accrued liabilities were $8,000. How much cash did Allied Enterprises pay for operating expenses?

a. $35,000
b. $37,000
c. $43,000
d. $45,000

Answers are given after Written Communication.

SHORT EXERCISES

S11-1. Purpose of the statement of cash flows (*Learning Objective 1*) 5–10 min.

Describe how the statement of cash flows helps investors and creditors perform each of the following functions:

1. Predict future cash flows

2. Evaluate management decisions

3. Predict the ability to make debt payments to lenders and pay dividends to shareholders

S11-2. Basics of the statement of cash flows (*Learning Objectives 2 & 3*) 5–10 min.

Answer these questions about the statement of cash flows:

1. What is the "check figure" for the statement of cash flows? Where do you get this check figure?

2. List the categories of cash flows as they are presented on the Statement of Cash Flows.

3. What is the first dollar amount reported using the indirect method?

S11-3. Purpose of the statement of cash flows (*Learning Objective 1*) 5–10 min.

Intermountain, Inc. experienced an unbroken string of 10 years of growth in net income. Nevertheless, the business is facing bankruptcy. Creditors are calling all of Intermountain's outstanding loans for immediate payment, and Intermountain, Inc. has no cash available to make these payments because managers placed undue emphasis on net income and gave too little attention to cash flows.

Write a brief memo in your own words to explain to the managers of Intermountain, Inc. the purposes of the statement of cash flows.

S11-4. Classification of items as operating, investing, or financing (*Learning Objective 2*) 10–15 min.

Identify each of the following transactions as one of the following:

- Operating activity (O)
- Investing activity (I)
- Financing activity (F)
- Noncash investing and financing activity (NIF)

For each item, indicate whether it represents an increase (+) or a decrease (–) in cash. The indirect method is used to report cash flows from operating activities.

____ a. Cash sale of land

____ b. Issuance of long-term note payable in exchange for cash

____ c. Depreciation of equipment

____ d. Purchase of treasury shares

____ e. Issuance of common shares for cash

____ f. Increase in Accounts Payable

____ g. Net income

____ h. Payment of cash dividend

____ i. Decrease in Accrued Liabilities

____ j. Loss on sale of land

____ k. Acquisition of building by issuance of notes payable

____ l. Payment of long-term debt

____ m. Acquisition of building by issuance of common shares

____ n. Decrease in Accounts Receivable

____ o. Decrease in Inventory

____ p. Increase in prepaid expenses

S11-5. Classification of items as operating, investing, or financing (*Learning Objectives 2 & 3*) 10–15 min.

Indicate whether each of the following transactions would result in an operating activity, an investing activity, a financing activity, or a transaction that does not affect cash for a statement of cash flows prepared by the indirect method.

DATE	ACCOUNTS	POST REF.	DR.	CR.
a.	Equipment		18,000	
	Cash			18,000
b.	Cash		7,200	
	Long-Term Investment			7,200
c.	Bonds Payable		45,000	
	Cash			45,000
d.	Building		164,000	
	Notes Payable, Long-Term			164,000
e.	Loss on Disposal of Equipment		1,400	
	Equipment			1,400
f.	Dividend Payable		16,500	
	Cash			16,500
g.	Cash		81,000	
	Common Shares			81,000
h.	Treasury Shares		13,000	
	Cash			13,000
i.	Cash		60,000	
	Sales Revenue			60,000
j.	Land		87,700	
	Cash			87,700
k.	Depreciation		9,000	
	Accumulated Depreciation			9,000

S11-6. Operating activities—indirect method (*Learning Objective 3*) 10–15 min.

C. Kirk Corporation reported the following data for 2015:

Income statement:	Net Income	$50,000
	Depreciation...	8,000
Statement of Financial Position:	Increase in Accounts Receivable...	6,000
	Decrease in Accounts Payable	4,000

Compute C. Kirk Corporation's net cash provided by operating activities according to the indirect method.

S11-7. Operating activities—indirect method (*Learning Objective 3*) 10–15 min.

Inland Equipment's accountants assembled the following data for the year ended June 30, 2015.

Net Income	$60,000	Purchase of equipment	$40,000
Proceeds from issuance of		Decrease in	
common shares	20,000	current liabilities..................	5,000
Payment of dividends..............	6,000	Payment of note payable..........	30,000
Increase in current assets		Proceeds from	
other than cash	30,000	sale of land..........................	60,000
Purchase of treasury shares	5,000	Depreciation Expense..............	15,000

Prepare Inland Equipment's statement of cash flows for the year ended June 30, 2015 using the direct method. Inland Equipment's cash balance at June 30, 2014 was $12,000.

S11-8. Operating activities—direct method (*Learning Objective 4*) 5–10 min.

Uhura Health Spas began 2015 with cash of $104,000. During the year, Uhura earned service revenue of $600,000 and collected $590,000 from customers. Expenses for the year totalled $420,000, of which Uhura paid $410,000 in cash to suppliers and employees. Uhura also paid $140,000 to purchase equipment and paid a cash dividend of $50,000 to its shareholders during 2015. Prepare the company's statement of cash flows for the year ended December 31, 2015. Format cash flows from operating activities by the direct method.

S11-9. Operating activities—direct method (*Learning Objective 4*) 5–10 min.

Inland Equipment, Inc. assembled the following data related to its cash transactions for the year ended June 30, 2015:

Payment of dividends...	$ 6,000
Proceeds from issuance of shares...	20,000
Collections from customers...	200,000
Proceeds from sale of land	60,000
Payments to suppliers	80,000
Purchase of equipment...	40,000
Payments to employees..	70,000
Payment of note payable...	30,000

Prepare Inland Equipment's statement of cash flows for the year ended June 30, 2015 using the direct method. Inland Equipment's cash balance at June 30, 2014 was $12,000.

S11-10. Calculate certain operating information for direct method
(*Learning Objective 4*) 5–10 min.

McCoy Medical Company reported the following financial statements for 2015:

McCoy Medical Company Income Statement Year Ended December 31, 2015 (Amounts in Thousands)			
Revenue:			
Sales Revenue			$710
Expenses:			
Cost of Goods Sold		$340	
Depreciation Expense		60	
Other Expenses		200	
Total Expense			600
Net Income			$110

McCoy Medical Company Comparative Statement of Financial Position December 31, 2015 and 2014					
	(in thousands)			**(in thousands)**	
ASSETS	**2015**	**2014**	**LIABILITIES**	**2015**	**2014**
Current:			Current:		
Cash	$ 19	$ 16	Accounts Payable	$ 47	$ 42
Accounts Receivable	54	48	Salaries Payable	23	21
Inventory	80	84	Accrued Liabilities	8	11
Prepaid Expenses	3	2	Long-Term Notes Payable	66	68
Long-Term Investments	75	90			
Plant Assets, Net	225	185	**SHAREHOLDERS' EQUITY**		
			Common Shares	40	37
			Retained Earnings	272	246
			Total Liabilities and		
Total Assets	$456	$425	Shareholders' Equity	$456	$425

Use the information in McCoy Medical Company's financial statements to compute the following:

1. Collections from customers

2. Payments for inventory

S11-11. Calculate certain investing and financing information from financial statements (*Learning Objective 3*) 10–15 min.

Use the McCoy Medical Company data in S11-10 to compute the amount of plant assets acquired by McCoy Medical Company, assuming McCoy sold no plant assets in 2015.

S11-12. Calculate certain investing and financing information from financial statements (*Learning Objective 3*) 10–15 min.

Use the McCoy Medical Company data in S11-10 to compute the following amounts for 2015:

1. Borrowing or payment of long-term notes payable, assuming McCoy had only one long-term note payable transaction during the year

2. Issuance of common shares, assuming McCoy had only one common shares transaction during the year

3. Payment of cash dividends

EXERCISES (GROUP A)

E11-1A. Operating activities—indirect method (*Learning Objective 3*) 10–15 min.

The accounting records of Action Athletics, Inc. reveal the following:

Net Income	$22,000
Depreciation Expense...	9,000
Sales Revenue..	21,000
Decrease in current liabilities	28,000
Loss on sale of land	2,000
Increase in current assets other than Cash	10,000
Acquisition of land	39,000

Requirements

1. Compute cash flows from operating activities by the indirect method. Use the format of the operating activities section shown in Exhibit 11-9.

2. Evaluate the operating cash flow of Action Athletics, Inc. Give the reason for your evaluation.

E11-2A. Operating activities—indirect method (*Learning Objective 3*) 10–15 min.

The March accounting records of Jackson & Associates include these accounts:

Cash			
Mar 1	5,000	Payments	448,000
Receipts	447,000		
Mar 31	4,000		

Accounts Receivable			
Mar 1	18,000	Collections	447,000
Sales	443,000		
Mar 31	14,000		

Inventory			
Mar 1	19,000	Cost of goods sold	335,000
Purchases	337,000		
Mar 31	21,000		

Accounts Payable			
Payments	332,000	Mar 1	14,000
		Purchases	337,000
		Mar 31	19,000

Accumulated Depreciation			
		Mar 1	52,000
		Depreciation	3,000
		Mar 31	55,000

Retained Earnings			
Dividends	18,000	Mar 1	64,000
		Net income	69,000
		Mar 31	115,000

Requirement

1. Compute Jackson & Associates' net cash provided by operating activities during March. Use the indirect method.

E11-3A. Prepare statement of cash flows—indirect method (*Learning Objective 3*)
20–25 min.

The income statement and additional data of Specialized Services, Inc. follow:

Specialized Services, Inc.
Income Statement
Year Ended June 30, 2015

Revenues:		
Sales Revenue	$229,000	
Dividend Revenue	8,000	
Total Revenues		$237,000
Expenses:		
Cost of Goods Sold	$103,000	
Salaries Expense	45,000	
Depreciation Expense	28,000	
Advertising Expense	12,000	
Interest Expense	2,000	
Income Tax Expense	9,000	
Total Expenses		199,000
Net Income		$ 38,000

Additional data follow:

a. Acquisition of plant assets totalled $116,000. Of this amount, $101,000 was paid in cash and a $15,000 note payable was signed for the remainder.

b. Proceeds from sale of land totalled $24,000. No gain was recognized on the sale.

c. Proceeds from issuance of common shares totalled $30,000.

d. Payment of long-term note payable was $15,000.

e. Payment of dividends was $11,000.

f. Data from the comparative statement of financial position follow:

June 30	2015	2014
Current Assets:		
Cash	$26,000	$20,000
Accounts Receivable	43,000	58,000
Inventory	92,000	85,000
Current Liabilities:		
Accounts Payable	$35,000	$22,000
Accrued Liabilities	13,000	21,000

Requirements

1. Prepare Specialized Services' statement of cash flows for the year ended June 30, 2015, using the indirect method.

2. Evaluate Specialized Services' cash flows for the year. In your evaluation, mention all three categories of cash flows and give the reason for your evaluation.

Quick solution:

1. Cash dividends = $34,000;

2. Cash proceeds from sale = $6,000

E11-4A. Calculate certain investing and financing information from financial statements (*Learning Objective 3*) 10–15 min.

Compute the following items for the statement of cash flows:

1. The beginning and ending Retained Earnings balances are $45,000 and $73,000, respectively. Net income for the period is $62,000. How much are cash dividends?

2. The beginning and ending Plant Assets, Net, balances are $103,000 and $107,000, respectively. Depreciation for the period is $16,000, and acquisitions of new plant assets total $27,000. Plant assets were sold at a $1,000 loss. What were the cash proceeds of the sale?

E11-5A. Operating activities—direct method (*Learning Objective 4*) 10–15 min.

The accounting records of The Fenceman, Inc. reveal the following:

Net Income	$ 22,000	Payment of	
Payment of income tax	13,000	salaries and wages..............	$34,000
Collection of		Depreciation............................	12,000
dividend revenue...............	7,000	Payment of interest.................	16,000
Payment to suppliers	54,000	Payment of	
Collections from customers...	102,000	dividends............................	7,000

Requirements

1. Compute cash flows from operating activities by the direct method.

2. Evaluate the operating cash flow of The Fenceman, Inc. Give the reason for your evaluation.

E11-6A. Prepare statement of cash flows—direct method (*Learning Objective 4*) 20–25 min.

The income statement and additional data of Specialized Services, Inc. follow:

Specialized Services, Inc.
Income Statement
Year Ended June 30, 2015

Revenues:		
Sales Revenue	$229,000	
Dividend Revenue	8,000	
Total Revenues		$237,000
Expenses:		
Cost of Goods Sold	$103,000	
Salaries Expense	45,000	
Depreciation Expense	28,000	
Advertising Expense	12,000	
Interest Expense	2,000	
Income Tax Expense	9,000	
Total Expenses		199,000
Net Income		$ 38,000

Additional data follow:

a. Collections from customers are $15,000 more than sales.

b. Payments to suppliers are the sum of cost of goods sold plus advertising expense.

c. Payments to employees are $2,000 more than salaries expense.

d. Dividend revenue, interest expense, and income tax expense equal their cash amounts.

e. Acquisition of plant assets for cash is $101,000.

f. Proceeds from sale of land total $24,000.

g. Proceeds from issuance of common shares for cash total $30,000.

h. Payment of long-term note payable is $15,000.

i. Payment of dividends is $11,000.

j. Cash balance, June 30, 2014, was $20,000.

Requirement

1. Prepare Specialized Services' statement of cash flows for the year ended June 30, 2015. Use the direct method.

E11-7A. Calculate certain information for direct method (*Learning Objective 4*)
10–15 min.

Compute the following items for the statement of cash flows:

1. The beginning and ending Accounts Receivable balances are $22,000 and $18,000, respectively. Credit sales for the period total $81,000. How much are cash collections?

2. Cost of Goods Sold is $90,000. Beginning Inventory balance is $25,000, and ending Inventory balance is $21,000. Beginning and ending Accounts Payable are $11,000 and $8,000, respectively. How much are cash payments for inventory?

E11-8A. Calculate certain information for direct method (*Learning Objective 4*)
20–25 min.

Top Ten Corporation, a nationwide insurance chain, reported the following selected amounts in its financial statements for the year ended August 31, 2015 (adapted, in millions):

Income Statement

	2015	2014
Net Sales	$24,623	$21,207
Cost of Goods Sold	18,048	15,466
Depreciation Expense	269	230
Other Expenses	4,883	4,248
Income Tax Expense	537	486
Net Income	886	777

Statement of Financial Position

	2015	2014
Cash and Cash Equivalents	$ 17	$ 13
Accounts Receivable	798	615
Inventories	3,482	2,831
Property and Equipment, Net	4,345	3,428
Accounts Payable	1,547	1,364
Accrued Liabilities	938	848
Long-Term Liabilities	478	464
Common Shares	676	446
Retained Earnings	4,531	3,788

Requirement

1. Determine the following for Top Ten Corporation during 2015. (Enter all amounts in millions.)

   a. Collections from customers

   b. Payments for inventory

   c. Payments of operating expenses

   d. Acquisitions of property and equipment; no sales were made during 2015

   e. Long-term borrowing, assuming Top Ten made no payments on long-term liabilities

   f. Proceeds from issuance of common shares

   g. Payment of cash dividends

EXERCISES (GROUP B)

E11-1B. Operating activities—indirect method (*Learning Objective 3*) 10–15 min.

The accounting records of Elite Talent Agency reveal the following:

Net Income	$40,000
Depreciation Expense	3,000
Sales Revenue	13,000
Decrease in current liabilities	24,000
Loss on sale of land	2,000
Increase in current assets other than Cash	15,000
Acquisition of land	39,000

Requirements

1. Compute cash flows from operating activities by the indirect method. Use the format of the operating activities section shown in Exhibit 11-9.
2. Evaluate the operating cash flow of Elite Talent Agency. Give the reason for your evaluation.

E11-2B. Operating activities—indirect method (*Learning Objective 3*) 10–15 min.

The October accounting records of Morrison & Associates include these accounts:

Cash			
Oct 1	12,000	Payments	400,000
Receipts	394,000		
Oct 31	6,000		

Accounts Receivable			
Oct 1	16,000	Collections	394,000
Sales	391,000		
Oct 31	13,000		

Inventory			
Oct 1	20,000	Cost of goods sold	309,000
Purchases	321,000		
Oct 31	32,000		

Accounts Payable			
Payments	319,000	Oct 1	19,000
		Purchases	321,000
		Oct 31	21,000

Accumulated Depreciation			
		Oct 1	49,000
		Depreciation	10,000
		Oct 31	59,000

Retained Earnings			
Dividends	24,000	Oct 1	67,000
		Net income	50,000
		Oct 31	93,000

Requirement

1. Compute Morrison & Associates' net cash provided by operating activities during October. Use the indirect method.

**E11-3B. Prepare statement of cash flows—indirect method (*Learning Objective 3*)
20–25 min.**

The income statement and additional data of Rayborn Services, Inc. follow:

Rayborn Services, Inc.		
Income Statement		
Year Ended April 30, 2015		
Revenues:		
Sales Revenue	$262,000	
Dividend Revenue	11,000	
Total Revenues		$273,000
Expenses:		
Cost of Goods Sold	$107,000	
Salaries Expense	60,000	
Depreciation Expense	18,000	
Advertising Expense	14,000	
Interest Expense	9,000	
Income Tax Expense	8,000	
Total Expenses		216,000
Net Income		$ 57,000

Additional data follow:

a. Acquisition of plant assets totalled $116,000. Of this amount, $101,000 was paid in cash and a $15,000 note payable was signed for the remainder.

b. Proceeds from the sale of land totalled $22,000. No gain was recognized on the sale.

c. Proceeds from issuance of common shares total $34,000.

d. Payment of long-term note payable was $15,000.

e. Payment of dividends was $14,000.

f. Data from the comparative statement of financial position follow:

June 30	2015	2014
Current Assets:		
Cash	$30,000	$21,000
Accounts Receivable	42,000	57,000
Inventory	89,000	83,000
Current Liabilities:		
Accounts Payable	$38,000	$31,000
Accrued Liabilities	12,000	20,000

Requirements

1. Prepare Rayborn Services' statement of cash flows for the year ended April 30, 2015, using the indirect method.

2. Evaluate Rayborn Services' cash flows for the year. In your evaluation, mention all three categories of cash flows and give the reason for your evaluation.

E11-4B. Calculate certain investing and financing information from financial statements (*Learning Objective 3*) 10–15 min.

Compute the following items for the statement of cash flows:

1. The beginning and ending Retained Earnings balances are $47,000 and $71,000, respectively. Net income for the period is $93,000. How much are cash dividends?

2. The beginning and ending Plant Assets, Net balances are $104,000 and $113,000, respectively. Depreciation for the period is $13,000, and acquisitions of new plant assets total $30,000. Plant assets were sold at a $6,000 loss. What were the cash proceeds of the sale?

E11-5B. Operating activities—direct method (*Learning Objective 4*) 10–15 min.

The accounting records of Fence Up, Inc. reveal the following:

Net Income	$ 64,000	Payment of	
Payment of income tax	20,000	salaries and wages..............	$30,000
Collection of		Depreciation.............................	15,000
dividend revenue...............	7,000	Payment of interest..................	18,000
Payment to suppliers	36,000	Payment of	
Collections from customers...	113,000	dividends............................	7,000

Requirements

1. Compute cash flows from operating activities by the *direct* method.

2. Evaluate the operating cash flow of Fence Up, Inc. Give the reason for your evaluation.

E11-6B. Prepare statement of cash flows—direct method (*Learning Objective 4*) 20–25 min.

The income statement and additional data of Rayborn Services, Inc. follow:

Rayborn Services, Inc. Income Statement Year Ended April 30, 2015		
Revenues:		
Sales Revenue	$262,000	
Dividend Revenue	11,000	
Total Revenues		$273,000
Expenses:		
Cost of Goods Sold	$107,000	
Salaries Expense	60,000	
Depreciation Expense	18,000	
Advertising Expense	14,000	
Interest Expense	9,000	
Income Tax Expense	8,000	
Total Expenses		216,000
Net Income		$ 57,000

Additional data follow:

a. Collections from customers are $15,000 more than sales.

b. Payments to suppliers are the sum of cost of goods sold plus advertising expense.

c. Payments to employees are $7,000 more than salaries expense.

d. Dividend revenue, interest expense, and income tax expense equal their cash amounts.

e. Acquisition of plant assets for cash is $101,000.

f. Proceeds from sale of land total $22,000.

g. Proceeds from issuance of common shares for cash total $34,000.

h. Payment of long-term note payable is $15,000.

i. Payment of dividends is $14,000.

j. Cash balance, April 30, 2014, was $21,000.

Requirement

1. Prepare Rayborn Services' statement of cash flows for the year ended April 30, 2015. Use the direct method.

E11-7B. Calculate certain information for direct method (*Learning Objective 4*)
10–15 min.

Compute the following items for the statement of cash flows:

1. The beginning and ending Accounts Receivable balances are $18,000 and $22,000, respectively. Credit sales for the period total $115,000. How much are cash collections?

2. Cost of Goods Sold is $76,000. Beginning Inventory balance is $26,000, and ending Inventory balance is $28,000. Beginning and ending Accounts Payable are $15,000 and $12,000, respectively. How much are cash payments for inventory?

E11-8B. Calculate certain information for direct method (*Learning Objective 4*)
20–25 min.

A-One Corporation, a nationwide insurance chain, reported the following selected amounts in its financial statements for the year ended March 31, 2015 (adapted, in millions):

Income Statement

	2015	2014
Net Sales	$24,859	$21,099
Cost of Goods Sold	18,026	15,497
Depreciation Expense	270	230
Other Expenses	4,801	4,460
Income Tax Expense	539	488
Net Income	1,223	424

Statement of Financial Position

	2015	2014
Cash and Cash Equivalents	$ 30	$ 28
Accounts Receivable	804	626
Inventories	3,484	3,264
Property and Equipment, Net	4,225	3,825
Accounts Payable	1,543	1,373
Accrued Liabilities	939	848
Long-Term Liabilities	450	445
Common Shares	675	575
Retained Earnings	4,936	4,502

Requirement

1. Determine the following for A-One Corporation during 2015. (Enter all amounts in millions.)

   a. Collections from customers

   b. Payments for inventory

   c. Payments of operating expenses

   d. Acquisitions of property and equipment; no sales were made during 2015

   e. Long-term borrowing, assuming A-One made no payments on long-term liabilities

   f. Proceeds from issuance of common shares

   g. Payment of cash dividends

EXERCISES (ALTERNATES 1, 2, AND 3)

These alternative exercise sets are available for your practice benefit on
MyAccountingLab.

PROBLEMS (GROUP A)

P11-1A. Prepare statement of cash flows—indirect method (*Learning Objective 3*)
20–25 min.

O'Malley Corporation accountants assembled the following data for the year ended
December 31, 2015:

O'Malley Corporation		
December 31	**2015**	**2014**
Current Assets:		
Cash and Cash Equivalents	$85,000	$22,000
Accounts Receivable...	69,200	64,200
Inventory...	80,000	83,000
Current Liabilities:		
Accounts Payable..	$57,800	$55,800
Income Tax Payable..	14,700	16,700

Transaction Data for 2015:	
Net Income	$ 57,000
Purchase of treasury shares	14,000
Issuance of common shares for cash	41,000
Loss on sale of equipment..	11,000
Payment of cash dividends	18,000
Depreciation Expense..	21,000
Issuance of long-term note payable in exchange for cash	34,000
Purchase of building for cash	125,000
Retirement of bonds payable by issuing common shares....................	65,000
Sale of equipment for cash	58,000

Requirement

1. Prepare O'Malley Corporation's statement of cash flows using the indirect method
to report operating activities. List noncash investing and financing activities on an
accompanying schedule.

Quick solution:

*1. Cash provided by operating
activities = $87,000;
Cash used for investing
activities = ($67,000);
Cash provided by financing
activities = $43,000*

P11-2A. Prepare statement of cash flows—indirect method (*Learning Objective 3*)
20–25 min.

Data from the comparative statement of financial position of Izzie Company at March
31, 2015, follow:

March 31	2015	2014
Current Assets:		
Cash and Cash Equivalents	$ 6,200	$ 4,000
Accounts Receivable...	14,900	21,700
Inventory...	63,200	60,600
Current Liabilities:		
Accounts Payable..	$30,100	$27,600
Accrued Liabilities...	10,700	11,100
Income Tax Payable..	8,000	4,700

Izzie Company's transactions during the year ended March 31, 2015, included the following:

Payment of cash dividend........	$30,000	Depreciation Expense...............	$17,300
Purchase of		Purchase of	
equipment for cash	78,700	building for cash	47,000
Issuance of long-term		Net Income	70,000
note payable in exchange		Issuance of	
for cash	50,000	common shares	11,000

Requirements

1. Prepare Izzie Company's statement of cash flows for the year ended March 31, 2015, using the indirect method to report cash flows from operating activities.

2. Evaluate Izzie's cash flows for the year. Mention all three categories of cash flows and give the reason for your evaluation.

P11-3A. Prepare statement of cash flows—indirect method (*Learning Objective 3*) 20–25 min.

The 2015 comparative statement of financial position and income statement of A. Karev Medical Supplies follow:

A. Karev Medical Supplies Comparative Statement of Financial Position December 31, 2015 and 2014			
	2015	**2014**	**INCREASE (DECREASE)**
Current Assets:			
Cash and Cash Equivalents	$ 6,700	$ 5,300	$ 1,400
Accounts Receivable	25,300	26,900	(1,600)
Inventory	91,800	89,800	2,000
Plant Assets:			
Land	89,000	60,000	29,000
Equipment, Net	53,500	49,400	4,100
Total Assets	$266,300	$231,400	$ 34,900
Current Liabilities:			
Accounts Payable	$ 30,900	$ 35,400	$ (4,500)
Accrued Liabilities	30,600	28,600	2,000
Long-Term Liabilities:			
Notes Payable	75,000	100,000	(25,000)
Shareholders' Equity:			
Common Shares	88,300	64,700	23,600
Retained Earnings	41,500	2,700	38,800
Total Liabilities and Shareholders' Equity	$266,300	$231,400	$ 34,900

A. Karev Medical Supplies
Income Statement
Year Ended December 31, 2015

Revenues:		
Sales Revenue	$213,000	
Interest Revenue	8,600	
Total Revenues		$221,600
Expenses:		
Cost of Goods Sold	$ 70,600	
Salaries Expense	27,800	
Depreciation Expense	4,000	
Other Operating Expenses	10,500	
Interest Expense	11,600	
Income Tax Expense	29,100	
Total Expenses		153,600
Net Income		**$ 68,000**

A. Karev Medical Supplies had no noncash investing and financing transactions during 2015. During the year, A. Karev Medical Supplies made no sales of land or equipment, no issuance of notes payable, no retirement of shares, and no treasury share transactions.

Requirements

1. Prepare the 2015 statement of cash flows, formatting operating activities by the indirect method.

2. How will what you learned in this problem help you evaluate an investment in A. Karev Medical Supplies?

P11-4A. Prepare statement of cash flows—direct method (*Learning Objective 4*) 20–25 min.

The accounting records for R. Webber Associates, Inc. for the year ended April 30, 2015, contain the following information:

a. Purchase of plant assets for cash, $59,400

b. Proceeds from issuance of common shares, $8,000

c. Payment of dividends, $48,400

d. Collection of interest, $4,400

e. Payment of salaries, $93,600

f. Proceeds from sale of plant assets, $22,400

g. Collections from customers, $620,500

h. Cash receipt of dividend revenue, $4,100

i. Payments to suppliers, $368,500

j. Depreciation expense, $59,900

k. Proceeds from issuance of long-term notes, $19,600

l. Payments of long-term notes payable, $50,000

m. Interest expense and payments, $13,300

n. Income tax expense and payments, $37,900

o. Cash balances: April 30, 2014, $39,300; April 30, 2015, $47,200

Requirement

1. Prepare R. Webber Associates' statement of cash flows for the year ended April 30, 2015. Use the direct method for cash flows from operating activities.

P11-5A. Prepare statement of cash flows—direct method (*Learning Objective 4*)
20–25 min.

Use the A. Karev Medical Supplies data from P11-3A. The cash amounts for Interest Revenue, Salaries Expense, Interest Expense, and Income Tax Expense are the same as the accrual amounts for these items.

Requirements

1. Prepare the 2015 statement of cash flows by the direct method.
2. How will what you learned in this problem help you evaluate an investment in A. Karev Medical Supplies?

P11-6A. Prepare statement of cash flows—direct method (*Learning Objective 4*)
20–25 min.

To prepare the statement of cash flows, accountants for C. Yang, Inc. summarized 2015 activity in the Cash account as follows:

Cash			
Beginning balance	53,600	Payment on accounts payable	399,100
Receipts of interest	17,100	Payment of dividends	27,200
Collections from customers	673,700	Payment of salaries and wages	143,800
Issuance of common shares	47,300	Payment of interest	26,900
		Payment for equipment	10,200
		Payment of operating expenses	34,300
		Payment of notes payable	67,700
		Payment of income tax	18,900
Ending balance	63,600		

Requirement

1. Prepare the statement of cash flows of C. Yang, Inc. for the year ended December 31, 2015, using the direct method for operating activities.

P11-7A. Prepare statement of cash flows—indirect and direct methods (*Learning Objectives 3 & 4*) 25–30 min.

Comparative selected account balances and an unclassified income statement for THK Company follow:

THK Company Account Balances as at December 31		
	2015	**2014**
Cash	$28,400	$ 4,700
Accounts Receivable	35,200	18,600
Inventory	15,000	21,000
Accounts Payable	15,500	21,000
Wages Payable	3,500	1,200

THK Company Income Statement For the Year Ended December 31, 2015		
Sales		$241,800
Cost of Goods Sold	$180,000	
Wages	43,500	
Supplies	4,800	
Property Taxes	2,400	
Utilities	1,600	
Loss on Disposal of Equipment	5,000	
Depreciation of Capital Assets	3,200	240,500
Net Income		$ 1,300

In addition, the following information is available:

- Accounts Payable balances resulted from merchandise inventory purchases.
- The book value of the equipment was $13,000.
- Signed a 6%, 10-year note payable in exchange for a building with a market value of $80,000.
- Issued 2,000 new common shares at $10 per share.

Requirements

1. Prepare a statement of cash flows for THK, using the indirect method.
2. Prepare the cash flow from operating activities section by using the direct method.

P11-8A. Identify source or use of cash and prepare statement of cash flows—indirect and direct methods (*Learning Objectives 2, 3, & 4*) 30–35 min.

The following is the financial information for TinTing School Supplies, Ltd.:

TinTing School Supplies, Ltd.
Statement of Financial Position
As of December 31

	2015	2014	SOURCE/ (USES)
Current Assets:			
Cash	$ 3,600	$ 6,500	
Accounts Receivable	23,600	21,400	
Packaging Supplies	1,300	1,600	
Prepaid Insurance	1,400	2,340	
Inventory	12,100	10,400	
Total Current Assets	42,000	42,240	
Capital Assets			
Store Equipment	27,000	18,200	
Accumulated Depreciation, Store Equipment	(5,400)	(3,640)	
Delivery Trucks	168,000	116,500	
Accumulated Depreciation, Delivery Trucks	(33,600)	(23,300)	
Total Capital Assets	156,000	107,760	
Total Assets	$198,000	$150,000	
Current Liabilities			
Accounts Payable	$ 23,700	$ 14,200	
Income Tax Payable	4,030	3,500	
Total Current Liabilities	27,730	17,700	
Long-term Liabilities			
Long-Term Note Payable	36,250	31,000	
Bank Loan	71,300	45,300	
Total Long-Term Liabilities	107,550	76,300	
Shareholders' Equity			
Common Shares	35,000	35,000	
Retained Earnings	27,720	21,000	
Total Shareholders' Equity	62,720	56,000	
Total Liabilities & Shareholders' Equity	$198,000	$150,000	

TinTing School Supplies, Ltd.
Income Statement
For the Year Ended December 31, 2015

Revenues:			$125,000
Cost of Goods Sold			50,000
Gross Profit			75,000
Operating Expenses			
Depreciation Expense		$12,060	
Wages Expense		35,000	
Other Expenses		8,240	
Total Operating Expenses			55,300
Income Before Taxes			19,700
Income Taxes (40%)			7,880
Net Income			$ 11,820

Additional information:

1. Store equipment was purchased by signing a two-year long-term note payable.
2. Additional bank loan was borrowed as a partial payment for the purchase of delivery trucks.
3. TinTing declared and paid dividends on December 28, 2015.
4. TinTing's net income was $11,820.

Requirements

1. Identify source and use of cash for each account in the statement of financial position.
2. Prepare a statement of cash flows, using the indirect method.
3. Prepare the cash flow from operating activities section by using the direct method.

P11-9A. Identify source or use of cash and prepare statement of cash flows—indirect and direct methods (*Learning Objectives 2, 3, & 4*) 35–40 min.

ShinFu Electronic, Inc.'s income statement and comparative statement of financial position appear as follows:

ShinFu Electronic, Inc.
Income Statement
For the Year Ended December 31, 2015

Sales Revenue			$610,000
Cost of Goods Sold			(366,000)
			244,000
Depreciation Expense — Patent		$ 1,500	
Depreciation Expense — Equipment		15,200	
Salaries Expense		62,000	
Other Operating Expenses		83,300	
Interest Expense		14,500	
Loss on Sale of Equipment		12,500	189,000
Income Before Income Taxes			55,000
Income Tax Expense			16,500
Net Income			$ 38,500

ShinFu Electronic, Inc.
Statement of Financial Position
As of December 31

	2015	2014	SOURCE/ (USE)
Cash	$ 12,500	$ 15,200	
Accounts Receivable	32,500	43,500	
Inventory	72,700	68,400	
Prepaid Expenses	4,100	2,600	
Equipment	189,800	145,200	
Accumulated Depreciation	(45,000)	(67,200)	
Land	183,000	135,000	
Patents	11,000	12,500	
Total	$460,600	$355,200	
Accounts Payable	48,600	36,200	
Accrued Liabilities	26,200	58,900	
Salaries Payable	14,500	10,200	
Dividends Payable	8,600	7,200	
Interest Payable	12,200	18,000	
Income Tax Payable	32,000	24,200	
Mortgage	20,000	0	
Common Shares	240,000	170,000	
Retained Earnings	58,500	30,500	
Total	$460,600	$355,200	

Additional information related to business activities during 2015:

1. All accounts payable pertain to inventory purchases, and accrued liabilities pertain to other operating expenses.
2. The original cost of the equipment sold was $80,400. New equipment was purchased and 5,000 common shares at $14 per share were issued as a partial payment.
3. ShinFu purchased some land and borrowed $20,000 from a mortgage company as a partial payment.
4. ShinFu declared a dividend on December 15 to be paid on January 15, 2016.

Requirements

1. Identify source and use of cash for each account in the statement of financial position.
2. Calculate the cash receipt from the sale of equipment and the cost of the new equipment, using T-accounts to show your calculations.
3. Calculate the amount of cash dividend declared and cash dividend paid, using T-accounts to show your calculations.
4. Prepare a statement of cash flows, using the indirect method.
5. Prepare the cash flow from operating activities section by using the direct method.

P11-10A. Identify source or use of cash and prepare statement of cash flows—indirect and direct methods (_Learning Objectives 2, 3, & 4_) 35–40 min.

Sawada Trading Company's income statement and comparative statement of financial position appear as follows:

Sawada Trading Company
Income Statement
For the Year Ended December 31, 2015

Sales Revenue		$420,000
Cost of Goods Sold		(252,000)
		168,000
Depreciation Expense — Equipment	$25,500	
Salaries Expense	52,000	
Other Operating Expenses	65,000	
Interest Expense	12,000	
Loss on Sale of Equipment	9,500	164,000
Income Tax Expense		1,600
Net Income (Loss)		$ 2,400

Sawada Trading Company
Statement of Financial Position
As of December 31

	2015	2014	SOURCE/ (USE)
Cash	$ 7,600	$ 9,200	
Accounts Receivable	20,200	13,400	
Inventory	25,600	22,000	
Prepaid Expenses	3,600	4,400	
Equipment	170,000	148,000	
Accumulated Depreciation	(33,000)	(28,000)	
Total	$194,000	$169,000	
Accounts Payable	$ 21,600	$ 18,200	
Unearned Revenue	4,000	2,600	
Salaries Payable	15,500	12,000	
Interest Payable	7,700	6,200	
Income Tax Payable	12,000	23,200	
Common Shares	85,000	60,000	
Retained Earnings	48,200	46,800	
Total	$194,000	$169,000	

Additional information related to business activities during 2015:

1. All accounts payable pertain to inventory purchases, and accrued liabilities pertain to other operating expenses.

2. The original cost of the equipment sold was $43,000. New equipment was purchased and 5,000 common shares at $5 per share were issued as a partial payment.

3. Sawada declared and paid a dividend on December 30.

Requirements

1. Identify source and use of cash for each account in the statement of financial position.

2. Calculate the cash receipt from the sale of equipment and the cost of the new equipment, using T-accounts to show your calculations.

3. Prepare a statement of cash flows, using the indirect method.

4. Prepare the cash flow from operating activities section by using the direct method.

PROBLEMS (GROUP B)

P11-1B. Prepare statement of cash flows—indirect method (*Learning Objective 3*)
20–25 min.

Morgensen Corporation accountants assembled the following data for the year ended December 31, 2015:

Morgensen Corporation		
December 31	**2015**	**2014**
Current Assets:		
Cash and Cash Equivalents	$85,000	$23,000
Accounts Receivable	69,600	64,700
Inventory	80,900	83,500
Current Liabilities:		
Accounts Payable	$57,700	$55,600
Income Tax Payable	14,800	16,400

Transaction Data for 2015:	
Net Income	$ 57,800
Purchase of treasury shares	14,500
Issuance of common shares for cash	36,200
Loss on sale of equipment	11,000
Payment of cash dividends	18,100
Depreciation Expense	21,900
Issuance of long-term note payable in exchange for cash	34,500
Purchase of building for cash	122,000
Retirement of bonds payable by issuing common shares	62,000
Sale of equipment for cash	57,000

Requirement

1. Prepare Morgensen Corporation's statement of cash flows using the indirect method to report operating activities. List noncash investing and financing activities on an accompanying schedule.

P11-2B. Prepare statement of cash flows—indirect method (*Learning Objective 3*)
20–25 min.

Data from the comparative statement of financial position of Johnson Company at March 31, 2015, follow:

March 31	2015	2014
Current Assets:		
Cash and Cash Equivalents	$13,400	$ 4,600
Accounts Receivable	14,800	21,400
Inventory	54,300	53,600
Current Liabilities:		
Accounts Payable	$29,000	$28,400
Accrued Liabilities	14,600	16,200
Income Tax Payable	8,300	4,800

Johnson Company's transactions during the year ended March 31, 2015, included the following:

Payment of cash dividend........	$33,500	Depreciation Expense...............	$17,500
Purchase of		Purchase of	
equipment for cash	78,300	building for cash	47,800
Issuance of long-term		Net Income	73,500
note payable in exchange		Issuance of	
for cash.............................	56,000	common shares	13,000

Requirements

1. Prepare Johnson Company's statement of cash flows for the year ended March 31, 2015, using the indirect method to report cash flows from operating activities.

2. Evaluate Johnson Company's cash flows for the year. Mention all three categories of cash flows and give the reason for your evaluation.

P11-3B. Prepare statement of cash flows—indirect method (*Learning Objective 3*) 20–25 min.

The 2015 comparative statement of financial position and income statement of Goldman Medical Supplies follow:

Goldman Medical Supplies Comparative Statement of Financial Position December 31, 2015 and 2014			
	2015	**2014**	**INCREASE (DECREASE)**
Current Assets:			
Cash and Cash Equivalents	$ 6,700	$ 5,400	$ 1,300
Accounts Receivable	25,200	26,800	(1,600)
Inventory	91,500	89,600	1,900
Plant Assets:			
Land	89,200	60,300	28,900
Equipment, Net	53,200	49,200	4,000
Total Assets	$265,800	$231,300	$ 34,500
Current Liabilities:			
Accounts Payable	$ 30,200	$ 35,400	$ (5,200)
Accrued Liabilities	30,400	28,100	2,300
Long-Term Liabilities:			
Notes Payable	72,000	100,000	(28,000)
Shareholders' Equity:			
Common Shares	88,900	64,700	24,200
Retained Earnings	44,300	3,100	41,200
Total Liabilities and Shareholders' Equity	$265,800	$231,300	$ 34,500

Goldman Medical Supplies
Income Statement
Year Ended December 31, 2015

Revenues:			
Sales Revenue		$217,000	
Interest Revenue		8,500	
Total Revenues			225,500
Expenses:			
Cost of Goods Sold		$ 70,700	
Salaries Expense		27,400	
Depreciation Expense		4,400	
Other Operating Expenses		10,400	
Interest Expense		11,100	
Income Tax Expense		29,700	
Total Expenses			153,700
Net Income			$ 71,800

Goldman Medical Supplies had no noncash investing and financing transactions during 2015. During the year, Goldman Medical Supplies made no sales of land or equipment, no issuance of notes payable, no retirement of shares, and no treasury share transactions.

Requirements

1. Prepare the 2015 statement of cash flows, formatting operating activities by the indirect method.

2. How will what you learned in this problem help you evaluate an investment in Goldman Medical Supplies?

P11-4B. Prepare statement of cash flows—direct method (*Learning Objective 4*)
20–25 min.

The accounting records for L. Lee Associates, Inc. for the year ended April 30, 2015, contain the following information:

a. Purchase of plant assets, $55,400

b. Proceeds from issuance of common shares, $45,000

c. Payment of dividends, $44,400

d. Collection of interest, $8,500

e. Payments of salaries, $93,600

f. Proceeds from sale of plant assets, $27,000

g. Collections from customers, $630,000

h. Cash receipt of dividend revenue, $4,600

i. Payments to suppliers, $374,800

j. Depreciation expense, $58,500

k. Proceeds from issuance of long-term notes, $46,100

l. Payments of long-term notes payable, $39,000

m. Interest expense and payments, $14,000

n. Income tax expense and payments, $45,000

o. Cash balance: April 30, 2014, $39,400; April 30, 2015, $134,400

Requirement

1. Prepare L. Lee Associates' statement of cash flow for the year ended April 30, 2015. Use the direct method for cash flows from operating activities.

P11-5B. Prepare statement of cash flows—direct method (*Learning Objective 4*)
20–25 min.

Use the Goldman Medical Supplies data from P11-3B. The cash amounts for Interest Revenue, Salaries Expense, Interest Expense, and Income Tax Expense are the same as the accrual amounts for these items.

Requirements

1. Prepare the 2015 statement of cash flows by the direct method.

2. How will what you learned in this problem help you evaluate an investment in Goldman Medical Supplies?

P11-6B. Prepare statement of cash flows—direct method (*Learning Objective 4*) 20–25 min.

To prepare the statement of cash flows, accountants for H. Laurie, Inc. summarized 2015 activity in the Cash account as follows:

Cash			
Beginning balance	91,700	Payment on accounts payable	347,400
Receipts of interest	15,100	Payment of dividends	30,000
Collections from customers	492,300	Payment of salaries and wages	63,500
Issuance of common shares	90,000	Payment of interest	21,100
		Payment for equipment	11,000
		Payment of operating expenses	21,100
		Payment of notes payable	77,000
		Payment of income tax	18,900
Ending balance	99,100		

Requirement

1. Prepare the statement of cash flows of H. Laurie, Inc. for the year ended December 31, 2015, using the direct method for operating activities.

P11-7B. Prepare statement of cash flows—indirect and direct methods (*Learning Objectives 3 & 4*) 25–30 min.

Comparative selected account balances and an unclassified income statement for KTA Company follow:

KTA Company Account Balances As at December 31		
	2015	2014
Cash	$22,800	$30,100
Accounts Receivable	27,600	42,800
Inventory	15,000	21,000
Prepaid Insurance	3,600	1,400
Accounts Payable	26,000	18,000
Accrued Liabilities	14,200	16,800
Tax Payable	4,600	1,800

KTA Company Income Statement For the Year Ended Dec 31, 2015		
Sales		$338,000
Cost of Goods Sold	$219,700	
Salaries Expense	52,600	
Other Operating Expenses	22,800	
Gain on Disposal of Equipment	(6,000)	
Depreciation of Capital Assets	6,400	295,500
Income Taxes		2,400
Net Income		$ 40,100

In addition, the following information is available:

- Accounts Payable balances resulted from merchandise inventory purchases.
- The book value of the equipment was $24,000.
- Declared and paid $25,000 dividends.
- Purchased a truck costing $100,000 by issuing a long-term note payable of $20,000 as a partial payment.

Requirements

1. Prepare a statement of cash flows for KTA using the indirect method.
2. Prepare the cash flow from operating activities section by using the direct method.

P11-8B. Identify source or use of cash and prepare statement of cash flows—indirect and direct methods (*Learning Objectives 2, 3, & 4*) 30–35 min.

The following is the financial information for Shine Hair Supplies, Ltd.:

Shine Hair Supplies, Ltd. Statement of Financial Position As of December 31			
	2015	2014	SOURCE/ (USES)
Current Assets:			
Cash	$ 5,400	$ 2,700	
Accounts Receivable	8,600	10,300	
Store Supplies	1,800	1,200	
Prepaid Insurance	1,020	1,920	
Inventory	12,900	10,400	
Total Current Assets	29,720	26,520	
Capital Assets			
Store Equipment	16,500	12,000	
Accumulated Depreciation, Store Equipment	(3,300)	(2,400)	
Delivery Trucks	72,600	37,600	
Accumulated Depreciation, Delivery Trucks	(14,520)	(7,520)	
Total Capital Assets	71,280	39,680	
Total Assets	$101,000	$66,200	
Current Liabilities			
Accounts Payable	16,600	10,800	
Interest Payable	2,800	1,700	
Total Current Liabilities	19,400	12,500	
Long-Term Liabilities			
Long-Term Note Payable	21,500	17,000	
Bank Loan	27,500	7,500	
Total Long-Term Liabilities	49,000	24,500	
Shareholders' Equity			
Common Shares	15,000	15,000	
Retained Earnings	17,600	14,200	
Total Shareholders' Equity	32,600	29,200	
Total Liabilities & Shareholders' Equity	$101,000	$66,200	

Shine Hair Supplies, Ltd.
Income Statement
For the Year Ended December 31, 2015

Revenues:			$86,000
Cost of Goods Sold			34,400
Gross Profit			51,600
Operating Expenses:			
Depreciation Expense		$ 7,900	
Wages Expense		26,000	
Other Expenses		6,000	
Total Operating Expenses			39,900
Interest Expense			2,450
Income Before Taxes			9,250
Income Taxes (40%)			3,700
Net Income			$ 5,550

Additional information:

1. Store equipment was purchased by signing a two-year long-term note payable.
2. Additional bank loan of $35,000 was obtained for the purchase of delivery trucks.
3. Shine Hair declared and paid dividends on December 24, 2015.

Requirements

1. Identify source and use of cash for each account in the statement of financial position.
2. Prepare a statement of cash flows, using the indirect method.
3. Prepare the cash flow from operating activities section by using the direct method.

P11-9B. Identify source or use of cash and prepare statement of cash flows—indirect and direct methods (*Learning Objectives 2, 3, & 4*) 35–40 min.

DelTek, Inc.'s income statement and comparative statement of financial position appear as follows:

DelTek, Inc.
Income Statement
For the Year Ended December 31, 2015

Sales Revenue			$212,000
Cost of Goods Sold			(84,800)
			127,200
Depreciation Expense — Patent		$ 1,200	
Depreciation Expense — Equipment		12,600	
Salaries Expense		52,500	
Other Operating Expenses		37,500	
Interest Expense		9,000	
Gain on Sale of Equipment		(2,600)	110,200
Income Before Income Taxes			17,000
Income Tax Expense			5,100
Net Income			$ 11,900

DelTek, Inc.
Statement of Financial Position
As of December 31

	2015	2014	SOURCE/ (USE)
Cash	$ 8,000	$ 5,200	
Accounts Receivable	12,500	16,800	
Inventory	36,700	42,600	
Prepaid Expenses	2,500	4,300	
Equipment	143,500	86,700	
Accumulated Depreciation	(41,000)	(34,600)	
Land	83,000	35,000	
Patents	4,800	6,000	
Total	$250,000	$162,000	
Accounts Payable	24,300	16,200	
Accrued Liabilities	6,700	8,900	
Salaries Payable	14,500	10,200	
Dividends Payable	8,600	9,200	
Interest payable	12,200	18,000	
Income Tax Payable	3,600	4,800	
Mortgage	20,000	0	
Common Shares	130,000	70,000	
Retained Earnings	30,100	24,700	
Total	$250,000	$162,000	

Additional information related to business activities during 2015:

1. All accounts payable pertain to inventory purchases, and accrued liabilities pertain to other operating expenses.

2. The original cost of the equipment sold was $19,600. New equipment was purchased and 6,000 common shares at $10/share were issued as a partial payment.

3. DelTek purchased some land and borrowed $20,000 from a mortgage company as a partial payment.

4. DelTek declared a dividend on December 24 to be paid on January 24, 2016.

Requirements

1. Identify source and use of cash for each account in the statement of financial position.

2. Calculate the cash receipt from the sale of equipment and the cost of the new equipment, using T-accounts to show your calculations.

3. Calculate the amount of cash dividend declared and cash dividend paid, using T-accounts to show your calculations.

4. Prepare a statement of cash flows, using the indirect method.

5. Prepare the cash flow from operating activities section by using the direct method.

P11-10B. Identify source or use of cash and prepare statement of cash flows—indirect and direct methods (*Learning Objectives 2, 3, & 4*) 35–40 min.

Kenji International, Inc.'s income statement and comparative statement of financial position appear as follows:

Kenji International, Inc.
Income Statement
For the Year Ended December 31, 2015

Sales Revenue		$160,000
Cost of Goods Sold		(64,000)
		96,000
Depreciation Expense — Equipment	$14,500	
Salaries Expense	48,500	
Bad Debt Expense	2,400	
Other Operating Expenses	35,200	
Interest Expense	6,000	106,600
Operating Income (Loss)		(10,600)
Gain on Sale of Equipment		3,500
Net Loss		($ 7,100)

Kenji International, Inc.
Statement of Financial Position
As of December 31

	2015	2014	SOURCE/ (USE)
Cash	$ 2,800	$ 4,800	
Accounts Receivable	26,000	12,800	
Allowance for Doubtful Accounts	(3,600)	(1,200)	
Inventory	24,500	27,800	
Prepaid Expenses	4,800	2,100	
Equipment	167,000	85,000	
Accumulated Depreciation	(37,500)	(42,500)	
Total	$184,000	$88,800	
Accounts Payable	10,400	7,200	
Salaries Payable	4,000	6,400	
Interest Payable	3,500	2,000	
Long-Term Note Payable	100,000	0	
Common Shares	50,000	50,000	
Retained Earnings	16,100	23,200	
Total	$184,000	$88,800	

Additional information related to business activities during 2015:

1. All accounts payable pertain to inventory purchases, and accrued liabilities pertain to other operating expenses.

2. The original cost of the equipment sold was $38,000. New equipment was purchased by issuing a 6%, $100,000, five-year long-term note payable as a partial payment.

Requirements

1. Identify source and use of cash for each account in the statement of financial position.

2. Calculate the cash receipt from the sale of equipment and the cost of the new equipment, using T-accounts to show your calculations.

3. Prepare a statement of cash flows, using the indirect method.

4. Prepare the cash flow from operating activities section by using the direct method.

PROBLEMS (ALTERNATES 1, 2, AND 3)

These alternative problem sets are available for your practice benefit on MyAccountingLab.

CONTINUING EXERCISE

This exercise continues the accounting for Graham's Yard Care, Inc. from the Continuing Exercise in Chapter 10. Assume that Graham's Yard Care, Inc. had the following comparative statement of financial position at the end of 2016, its second year of operations.

Graham's Yard Care, Inc.
Comparative Statement of Financial Position
December 31, 2016 and 2015

	2016	2015
ASSETS		
Cash	$1,500	$6,480
Accounts Receivable	2,200	150
Lawn Supplies	150	70
Equipment	4,900	1,400
(Less Accumulated Depreciation)	(495)	(146)
Total Assets	$8,255	$7,954
LIABILITIES		
Accounts Payable	$ 350	$1,400
Notes Payable		5,000
SHAREHOLDERS' EQUITY		
Common Shares	2,000	1,000
Retained Earnings	5,905	554
Total Liabilities and Sharesholders' Equity	$8,255	$7,954

Requirement

1. Prepare the statement of cash flows for Graham's Yard Care, Inc. for 2016, using the indirect method. The following additional information applies to 2016:

- Common shares were issued.
- No dividends were declared or paid during the year.
- No equipment was sold during the year and all purchases of equipment were for cash.

CONTINUING PROBLEM

In this problem, we continue our accounting for Aqua Elite, Inc. from Chapter 10. We will assume that Aqua Elite, Inc. is now in its second year of operations.

Assume that the comparative statement of financial position for Aqua Elite, Inc. at July 31, 2015, and the income statement for the month ended July 31, 2015, are as follows.

Aqua Elite, Inc.
Comparative Statement of Financial Position
July 31 and June 30, 2015

	July 31	June 30
ASSETS		
Cash	$ 5,333	$3,270
Accounts Receivable, net	2,280	1,000
Inventory	4,175	180
Supplies	105	125
Total Current Assets	11,893	4,575
Fixed Assets	67,250	2,250
Less: Accumulated Depreciation	(352)	(47)
Net Fixed Assets	66,898	2,203
Total Assets	$78,791	$6,778
LIABILITIES		
Accounts Payable	$ 1,805	$ 450
Unearned Revenue	5,800	2,000
Salaries Payable	950	900
Interest Payable	375	17
Payroll Taxes Payable	188	—
Dividend Payable	500	—
Current Portion of Long-Term Debt	4,410	2,000
Total Current Liabilities	14,028	5,367
Notes Payable	20,000	—
Mortgage Payable	42,590	—
Total Liabilities	76,618	5,367
SHAREHOLDERS' EQUITY		
Common Shares	1,000	1,000
Retained Earnings	1,173	411
Total Shareholders' Equity	2,173	1,411
Total Liabilities & Shareholders' Equity	$78,791	$6,778

Aqua Elite, Inc.
Income Statement
Month Ended July 31, 2015

Revenue	$6,300
Expenses:	
Cost of Goods Sold	1,080
Depreciation Expense	305
Bad Debt Expense	220
Interest Expense	375
Insurance Expense	150
Supplies Expense	210
Salaries Expense	2,400
Payroll Taxes Expense	268
Bank Service Fees	30
Net Income*	$1,262

*Income taxes ignored

Additional information follows:

Aqua Elite, Inc. purchased a $20,000 truck financed with a note payable; it purchased a $45,000 building site financed with a mortgage payable; and it did not sell any fixed assets during the month.

Requirement

1. Prepare the statement of cash flows using the indirect method for the month of July.

APPLY YOUR KNOWLEDGE

ETHICS IN ACTION

Case 1. Design Incorporated experienced a downturn in December sales. To make matters worse, many of the recent sales were on account, and because many customers were not paying on their accounts, the ending balance of Accounts Receivable at December 31 was higher than the beginning balance. Because the business had a dramatic need for cash, a prime piece of land owned by the company was sold for cash in December at a substantial gain. Design had purchased the land 10 years earlier and properly classified it as a long-term investment. The CEO, Jim Shady, was looking over the financial statements and saw the company's weak operating cash flows. He approached the accountant to ask why the December cash flows provided from operations were so weak, given that the land had been sold. The accountant explained that because the indirect method was used in preparing the statement of cash flows, certain adjustments to net income were required. To begin with, the increase in accounts receivable was a decreasing adjustment made in arriving at the net cash provided from operating activities. Next, the large gain recognized on the sale of land had to be adjusted by subtracting it from the net income in arriving at the cash provided by operating activities. These large negative adjustments drastically reduced the reported cash provided from that category of cash flows. The accountant then explained that all the cash proceeds from the land sale were included as cash inflows in the investing activities section.

Jim became worried because he remembered the bank telling him about the importance of strong operating cash flows, so he told the accountant to redo the statement but not to reduce the net income by the accounts receivable increase or the gain on the land sale. The accountant refused because these adjustments were necessary to properly arrive at the net cash provided from operating activities. If these adjustments were not made, then the net change in cash could not be reconciled. Jim finally agreed but then told the accountant to just include the cash proceeds from the sale of land in the operating activities rather than in the investing activities. The accountant said that would be wrong. Besides, everyone would know that proceeds from the sale of land should be an investing activity. Jim then suggested listing it as "other" in the operating section so no one would ever know that it wasn't an operating cash flow.

Why didn't Jim want the accountant to decrease the net income by the increase in accounts receivable and the gain on the land sale? Why do you think Jim finally agreed with the accountant? Could the operating cash flows be increased by including the cash proceeds from the sale but listing them as "other" rather than as land sale proceeds? What ethical concerns are involved? Do you have any other thoughts?

Case 2. Kevin Sailors, the CEO of Candle Corporation, was discussing the financial statements with the company accountant. Weak cash flows had resulted in the company borrowing a lot of money. Kevin wanted to know why the money borrowed was included as cash inflows in the financing section of the statement of cash flows but the interest paid on the amounts borrowed was not. The accountant replied that the interest paid on loans was an expense included in the calculation of net income, which was in the operating activities section. Kevin then asked why the dividends Candle Corporation paid to shareholders were included as an outflow of cash in the financing section. The accountant then explained that dividends paid, unlike interest paid, were a return to shareholders and not an expense; therefore, it would not be included in net income, nor would it appear in the operating activities section. Kevin replied that he did not care, and instructed the accountant to include both the interest paid and the dividends paid in the financing section. The accountant said that such a move would not be proper. Kevin then said to not provide the statement of cash flows at all because too many people would see the weakening operating cash flows. He further stated that investors and creditors who really analyzed the income statements and statement of financial position would be able to understand the company without the need for a statement of cash flows spelling out the net changes in cash flows.

Why would Kevin want the interest paid to be included in the financing activities section? Why would the accountant state that interest paid should not be included in the financing activities section? Can the statement of cash flows be omitted? What ethical issues are involved? Do you have any additional thoughts?

KNOW YOUR BUSINESS

FINANCIAL ANALYSIS

Purpose: To help familiarize you with the financial reporting of a real company to further your understanding of the chapter material you are learning.

This case focuses on the cash flows of Bombardier Inc. Recall that inflows and outflows of cash are classified as operating activities, investing activities, or financing activities. The statement of cash flows presents cash flows from each of these three activities. It is, therefore, important to understand the information provided in this revealing financial statement. The statement of cash flows and additional related information for Bombardier Inc. are disclosed in its annual report found in MyAccountingLab.

Requirements

1. Look at the operating activities section of the Consolidated Statements of Cash Flows. Compare the net cash provided by operating activities to the net income for each of the two years presented. Are the net income amounts reported on the statement of cash flows the same as on the income statement? How does the total cash flows provided by operating activities compare to the net income? Why do they differ? Is this difference good or bad? Have the cash flows provided from operations been increasing or decreasing? On average, what is the largest noncash adjustment item in the operating cash flows section? Why is this amount added back each year?

2. Review Note 29. Explain what it means when receivables show a negative cash flow in 2012 and a positive cash flow in 2011. Explain what it means when the accounts payable and accrued liabilities have positive cash flows for both 2012 and 2011.

3. Look at the investing activities section of the Consolidated Statements of Cash Flows. What has created the largest outflow of cash related to investing activities? Did investing activities provide or use cash for the two years presented? Is this good or bad for the company?

4. Look at the financing activities section of the Consolidated Statements of Cash Flows. Did financing activities provide or require cash for the two fiscal years presented? What is the significance of this information? What was the largest item in the financing section for the 2012 year-end?

5. How do you feel about the overall sufficiency of cash flows? Does the cash provided from operations cover the cash required for investing activities?

6. What was the net change in cash and cash equivalents for the most recent fiscal year? Does the ending cash and cash equivalents amount agree with the cash and cash equivalents reported on the statement of financial position? Do you have any other observations about the statement of cash flows?

7. What was the amount of cash actually paid for interest in 2012? Why does the cash paid for interest not agree with the financing expense for the year?

INDUSTRY ANALYSIS

Purpose: To help you understand and compare the performance of two companies in the same industry.

Find the Bombardier Annual Report, Year Ended January 31, 2012, located in MyAccountingLab and go to the Consolidated Cash Flows. Now access The Boeing Company's 2011 Annual Report. To do this from the internet, go to their webpage for the Investor Relations at http://www.boeing.com/companyoffices/financial/quarterly.htm and under Annual Report, go to the 2011 Annual Report.

Requirement

1. Which method (direct or indirect) does each of these companies use to prepare its statement of cash flows? How can you tell? Which activities provided cash for each of the companies? Which activities used cash for each of these companies? What conclusions can you draw from these results?

SMALL BUSINESS ANALYSIS

Purpose: To help you understand the importance of cash flows in the operation of a small business.

You just received your year-end financial statements from your accountant. Although receiving the year-end financial package is important every year for your financing institutions and your investors, it is especially important this year because of the potential investment opportunity that just became available to you. Yesterday you got a telephone call from one of your competitors with whom you have been discussing the possibility of a merger. The gist of the conversation was that the board of directors wanted to sell outright to you instead of merging. You're pretty happy about that except for the fact that it could create some potential cash flow problems. The other company wants $1,000,000 cash and it wants to do it soon or the deal is off. You've got that amount of cash and cash equivalents available right now, but you know there are some cash commitments coming up soon for capital expenditures and dividend payments. You decide to call one of your financial investors. He or she suggests that you calculate free cash flow from the end of the year to determine if that amount of cash is available to complete the deal.

You look at your statement of cash flows from the financial statements and see that cash flows from operations was $1,725,000 and you expect that same amount for this year. From the capital budget, anticipated capital expenditures in the short term are $550,000. And from the board of director's minutes of the last meeting, the cash dividend approved for payout next month is $275,000.

Requirement

1. Define free cash flow and calculate it based on the information previously provided. With your understanding of free cash flow, is this new investment something that this company should pursue?

WRITTEN COMMUNICATION

You have been asked by your accounting professor to prepare a paper outlining the importance of the statement of cash flows, the details of what is included in each of the three sections of the statement, and how it provides a link between the income statement and the statement of financial position.

CANDEAL FIXED INCOME PRICES					CHANGE
			HIGH	LOW	-0.040
09:52:33		YIELD	99.640	99.571	-0.038
INSTRUMENT	BID	0.949	99.991	99.895	-0.037
	99.640	0.999	101.582	101.418	-0.032
2Y T-BOND	99.991	1.143	110.427	110.134	-0.023
3Y T-BOND	101.582	1.602	137.493	136.921	
5Y T-BOND	110.425	2.230			
10Y T-BOND	137.493				
30Y T-BOND					

Toronto Stock Excha

HUSKY ENERGY INC (HSE)
100 @ 25.64 ▲ 0.06

ROYAL BANK OF CANADA (RY)
100 @ 52.18 ▼ -0.30

SHERRITT INTERNA
100 @ 4.7

LEARNING OBJECTIVES

1. Understand items on corporate income statements
2. Perform a horizontal analysis of financial statements
3. Perform a vertical analysis of financial statements
4. Compare one company to another using common-size financial statements and benchmarking
5. Compute various financial ratios

CHAPTER OUTLINE

12
Financial Statement Analysis

BUSINESS, ACCOUNTING, AND YOU

In the previous chapters, you learned about the different types of transactions and how accountants classify those transactions. You learned how these transactions feed into the financial statements to show to interested parties, creditors, vendors, and investors how successful the business was or was not.

Now let's look at how these interested parties, or stakeholders, use this information in the financial statements. Let's look at how to analyze a business's financial statements to figure out what the business is doing and whether the business is successful or not.

Go back and look over Chapter 1. Remember that businesses exist to create value. Think about the businesses we've looked at in this text : Best Buy, Hudson's Bay, Google, Target, John Deere, Apple, and others. How can you tell if these businesses are doing a good or bad job of creating value? Are these businesses creating enough net income to compensate shareholders for the use of their money over time and for taking risks? Would you buy shares in these companies?

It's time to consider what accountants tell us in the financial statements and how you can use that information to evaluate the value of a business. Accounting information is designed to be used by decision makers either to invest, lend, or extend credit. In other words, it's time to learn how to analyze financial statements.

In Chapter 1, we learned that the study of accounting is important because it teaches us about the "language of business." In this chapter, we will learn that another important reason to study accounting is that it teaches us how to use financial information to make better decisions. Managers, investors, and creditors can all benefit from being able to make better decisions regarding the performance of a company. As we begin our discussion of financial statement analysis, there are several important points that should be considered:

1. Financial statement analysis usually does not indicate that a problem definitely exists within a company. Also, even if a problem does exist, financial statement analysis generally will not identify what the specific problem is. Instead, financial statement analysis indicates that a problem may exist and it gives clues as to what the problem might be.

2. A company's performance is best evaluated by examining more than one year's data. This is why most financial statements cover at least two periods. In fact, most financial analysis covers trends of up to five years.

3. A company's performance is best evaluated by comparing it against the following:

   ■ Its own past performance
   ■ The performance of competitors
   ■ Industry averages for the industry the company is in

There are three main ways to analyze financial statements:

■ Horizontal analysis
■ Vertical analysis
■ Ratio analysis

Before we begin our discussion of financial statement analysis, let's take a closer look at the income statements of a corporation.

⊕ ACCOUNTING IN YOUR WORLD

So just how badly did you do on that test?

Have you ever received a test or an assignment back and, after looking at your score, you were sure you failed? Then you found out your score wasn't so bad after all because there were only 80 points possible. Or perhaps you found out that your score, although low, was higher than the class average. Until you had a point of reference, your raw score did not tell the whole story about your performance. The results of financial statement analysis are similar: they have minimal value without a point of reference. This is why, when conducting financial statement analysis, a company's performance is compared to past performance and industry averages.

Creatas Images/Creatas/360/Getty Images

WHAT IS THE DIFFERENCE BETWEEN OPERATING INCOME AND NET INCOME ON THE INCOME STATEMENT?

In Chapter 5, we examined the multi-step income statement format. Recall that the multi-step format provides detailed information about the items comprising net income so that financial statement users can make more informed decisions about a company's results of operations. Corporate income statements often contain additional items that are reported to better inform users about a company's results of operations. The income items we will examine are as follows:

L.O. ❶ Understand items on corporate income statements

- Continuing operations

- Discontinued operations

- Effects of changes in accounting principles

For illustration purposes, refer to the income statement for Best Way, Inc. presented in **Exhibit 12-1**.

Best Way, Inc. Income Statement Year Ended December 31, 2015	
Net Sales Revenue	$1,877,000
Cost of Goods Sold	1,145,000
Gross Profit	732,000
Operating Expenses (detailed)	423,000
Operating Income	309,000
Other income (expense):	
Interest Expense	(32,000)
Loss on Sale of Fixed Assets	(14,000)
Income from continuing operations before income tax	263,000
Income tax expense	72,000
Income from continuing operations	191,000
Income from discontinued operations, net of income tax of $11,000	26,000
Net Income	$ 217,000
Earnings per common share (100,000 shares outstanding):	
Income from continuing operations	$ 1.91
Income from discontinued operations	0.26
Net Income	$ 2.17

Exhibit 12-1 ▲

INCOME FROM CONTINUING OPERATIONS

In Exhibit 12-1, the top-most section reports income from continuing operations. Continuing operations consist of business activities that will most likely continue from period to period. Reporting income from continuing operations, therefore, helps investors make predictions about a company's future earnings. The continuing operations of Best Way, Inc. include two items that need explanation:

- *Other income (expense)* includes items that, although a normal part of business operations, fall outside of a company's core business activities. Therefore, these items are not included in sales, cost of goods sold, or operating expenses but are instead reported separately. Gains and losses on the sale of fixed assets as well as interest income and interest expense are examples of items reported as part of other income (expense). Best Way, Inc. reported interest expense of $32,000 and a loss on the sale of fixed assets of $14,000.

- *Income tax expense* reflects the income tax expense that is assessed on the company's operating income. Best Way, Inc. was assessed $72,000 of income tax on its operating income.

After continuing operations, an income statement may include the following items:

- Discontinued operations
- Cumulative effects of changes in accounting principles

DISCONTINUED OPERATIONS

Corporations often consist of many different business segments. A business segment is a distinguishable part of a business that is subject to a different set of risks and returns than other parts of the business. Information on any of the company's segments that have been sold (or otherwise discontinued) is reported separately from the results of continuing operations. This is because the discontinued segment will not be part of the company's operations in the future. The results of discontinued operations are generally reported net of income tax expense (or income tax savings in the case of a loss). Best Way, Inc. reported net income from discontinued operations of $26,000. This amount represents income of $37,000 less income tax expense of $11,000.

EFFECTS OF CHANGES IN ACCOUNTING PRINCIPLES

Occasionally, a company will change from the application of one accounting principle to another. For example, a business may change from weighted average to FIFO inventory valuation. Both IFRS and ASPE require retrospective application to account for the effects of most changes in accounting principles. Retrospective application means that a change in accounting principle is accounted for by restating comparative financial statements to reflect the new method as though it had been applied all along.

EARNINGS PER SHARE

The final segment of a corporate income statement reports the company's earnings per share, abbreviated as EPS. Earnings per share reports the amount of net income for each share of the company's *outstanding common shares.* The computation of EPS is discussed later in the chapter. Corporations report a separate EPS figure for each element of income. Some corporations must report two sets of EPS figures, as follows:

- Basic EPS—EPS based on outstanding common shares.
- Diluted EPS—EPS based on outstanding common shares plus the additional common shares that would arise if convertible preferred shares (or other dilutive items) were exchanged for common shares. Diluted EPS is always lower than basic EPS.

Best Way, Inc. had no convertible (dilutive) items and therefore reported only one set of EPS figures for each element of income.

Now let's examine financial statement analysis. As previously discussed, the three most popular forms of financial statement analysis are horizontal analysis, vertical analysis, and ratio analysis. We will begin our discussion with horizontal analysis.

WHAT IS HORIZONTAL ANALYSIS?

The study of percentage changes in the line items on comparative financial statements is called **horizontal analysis**. Although it can be useful to know if individual financial statement amounts (such as sales, wages expense, or accounts receivable) have increased or decreased from the prior period, the *percentage change* is often more relevant and, therefore, more helpful to know. For example, sales may have increased by $80,000, but considered alone, this fact is not very helpful. For some companies, an $80,000 increase in sales would be significant while for others, it would be minor. It is better to know by what percentage sales have increased from the prior year. For instance, knowing that sales have increased by 15% is more meaningful than knowing sales increased by $80,000.

L.O. ② Perform a horizontal analysis of financial statements

To compute the percentage change in the line items on comparative financial statements,

1. compute the dollar amount of the change from the earlier period to the later period.

2. divide the dollar amount of change by the earlier period amount and multiply by 100. We call the earlier period the base period.

To illustrate horizontal analysis, let's consider the comparative income statement and statement of financial position for Tucker Enterprises presented in **Exhibits 12-2** and **12-3**.

Tucker Enterprises, Inc.
Income Statement
Years Ended December 31, 2015 and 2014

(in thousands)	2015	2014
Net Sales	$824	$596
Cost of Goods Sold	375	277
Gross Profit	449	319
Operating Expenses:		
Selling, General, and Administrative	213	167
Other	48	34
Income Before Income Tax	188	118
Income Tax Expense	33	21
Net Income	$155	$ 97

Exhibit 12-2 ▲

The increase in sales is computed as follows:

Step 1 Compute the dollar amount of change in sales from 2014 to 2015:

$$\frac{\text{2015 Amount}}{\$824} - \frac{\text{2014 Amount}}{\$596} = \frac{\text{Dollar Change}}{\$228}$$

Step 2 Compute the percentage change for the period by dividing the dollar amount of change by the base period (2014) amount and multiplying the result by 100:

$$\text{Percentage change} = \frac{\text{Dollar change}}{\text{Base period amount}} \times 100 = \frac{\$228}{\$596} \times 100 = 38.3\%\text{(rounded)}$$

Tucker Enterprises, Inc.
Statement of Financial Position
December 31, 2015 and 2014

(in thousands)	2015	2014
Assets		
Current Assets:		
Cash and Cash Equivalents	$ 36	$ 47
Accounts Receivable, Net	61	52
Inventory	144	116
Total Current Assets	241	215
Property, Plant, and Equipment, Net	319	179
Total Assets	$560	$394
Liabilities		
Current Liabilities:		
Accounts Payable	$121	$ 74
Accrued Liabilities	24	33
Total Current Liabilities	145	107
Long-Term Liabilities	173	104
Total Liabilities	318	211
Shareholders' Equity		
Common Shares	35	30
Retained Earnings	207	153
Total Shareholders' Equity	242	183
Total Liabilities and Shareholders' Equity	$560	$394

Exhibit 12-3 ▲

The percentage changes in the remaining items are computed in the same manner. The completed horizontal analyses for Tucker Enterprises' financial statements are shown in **Exhibit 12-4** and **Exhibit 12-5**.

Tucker Enterprises, Inc.
Income Statement
Years Ended December 31, 2015 and 2014

(in thousands)	2015	2014	INCREASE (DECREASE) AMOUNT	PERCENTAGE
Net Sales	$824	$596	$228	38.3%
Cost of Goods Sold	375	277	98	35.4
Gross Profit	449	319	130	40.8
Operating Expenses:				
Selling, General, and Administrative	213	167	46	27.5
Other	48	34	14	41.2
Income Before Income Tax	188	118	70	59.3
Income Tax Expense	33	21	12	57.1
Net Income	$155	$ 97	58	59.8%

Exhibit 12-4 ▲

HORIZONTAL ANALYSIS OF THE INCOME STATEMENT

Tucker Enterprises' comparative income statement reveals strong growth during 2015. The 38.3% increase in sales coupled with only a 35.4% increase in cost of goods sold resulted in an increase in gross profit of 40.8%. The item on Tucker Enterprises' income

		Tucker Enterprises, Inc. Statement of Financial Position December 31, 2015 and 2014		INCREASE (DECREASE)	
(in thousands)	**2015**	**2014**	**AMOUNT**	**PERCENTAGE**
Assets				
Current Assets:				
Cash and Cash Equivalents	$ 36	$ 47	$ (11)	(23.4)%
Accounts Receivable, Net	61	52	9	17.3
Inventory	144	116	28	24.1
Total Current Assets	241	215	26	12.1
Property, Plant, and Equipment, Net	319	179	140	78.2
Total Assets	$560	$394	$166	42.1 %
Liabilities				
Current Liabilities:				
Accounts Payable	$121	$ 74	$ 47	63.5
Accrued Liabilities	24	33	(9)	(27.3)
Total Current Liabilities	145	107	38	35.5
Long-Term Liabilities	173	104	69	66.3
Total Liabilities	318	211	107	50.7
Shareholders' Equity				
Common Shares	35	30	5	16.7
Retained Earnings	207	153	54	35.3
Total Shareholders' Equity	242	183	59	32.2
Total Liabilities and Shareholders' Equity	$560	$394	$166	42.1 %

Exhibit 12-5 ▲

statement with the lowest growth rate is selling, general, and administrative expense, with an increase of only 27.5%. Even though other operating expenses and income tax expense increased by 41.2% and 57.1% respectively, they were the smallest dollar amounts on the income statement. So, on the bottom line, net income grew by a very respectable 59.8%.

HORIZONTAL ANALYSIS OF THE STATEMENT OF FINANCIAL POSITION

Tucker Enterprises' comparative statement of financial position also shows significant growth with total assets increasing by 42.1%. Accounts receivable and inventory increased 17.3% and 24.1% respectively. These increases are likely related to the increase in sales during the year. Cash actually decreased by 23.4%, which could be a concern for Tucker Enterprises' management. If a decrease in cash becomes a trend, the company could face cash flow problems in the future. Tucker Enterprises' property, plant, and equipment also grew notably at a rate of 78.2%.

Total liabilities increased by 50.7%. Accounts payable increased notably at a rate of 63.5%; however, accrued liabilities actually decreased by 27.3%. The 66.3% increase in long-term liabilities is probably not a concern for management as it is most likely related to the increase in property, plant, and equipment. The strong growth in net income for the year helped Tucker Enterprises achieve a 32.2% increase in total shareholders' equity during 2015.

TREND PERCENTAGES

Trend percentages are a form of horizontal analysis. Trends indicate the direction a business is taking. How have sales changed over a five-year period? What trend does net income show? These questions can be answered by looking at trend percentages over a period of time, such as three to five years.

To calculate trend percentages, a base year must first be selected. The base-year amounts are then set equal to 100%. Next, the amounts for each subsequent year are expressed as a percentage of the base-year amount. To compute trend percentages, divide each item for the years following the base year by the base-year amount and multiply the result by 100:

$$\text{Trend percentage} = \frac{\text{Any year \$}}{\text{Base year \$}} \times 100$$

Let's assume Tucker Enterprises' net sales were $387,000 in 2011 and rose to $824,000 in 2015. To illustrate trend analysis, let's review the trend of net sales during 2011–2015, with dollars in thousands. The base year is 2011, so that year's percentage is set equal to 100. We compute the trend percentages by dividing each year's net sales amount by the 2011 net sales amount and multiplying the result by 100.

(in thousands)	2015	2014	2013	2012	2011
Net Sales..	$ 824	$ 596	$ 467	$ 411	$387
Trend Percentage (base year amount)............	212.9%	154.0%	120.7%	106.2%	100%
Trend Percentage (previous year's amount)....	38.2%	27.6%	13.6%	6.2%	—

The trend analysis shows that Tucker Enterprises' net sales increased moderately from 2011 to 2013 and then more significantly in 2014 and substantially in 2015.

Alternatively, you could calculate the trend from one year to another. This will help you monitor the annual fluctuations during a period. To do this you should use the amount of change in an item (net sales in this case) and divide it by the previous year's total. It would be calculated as follows for 2013 for example:

$$\frac{\text{Amount of change (recent year's amount} - \text{previous year's amount)}}{\text{Previous year's amount}}$$

$$\text{For 2013} = \frac{467 - 411}{411} \times 100 = 13.6\%$$

You can perform a trend analysis on any one item or multiple items you consider important. Trend analysis is widely used to predict future performance.

WHAT IS VERTICAL ANALYSIS?

L.O. ❸ Perform a vertical analysis of financial statements

In addition to a horizontal analysis, a **vertical analysis** can also be performed to help evaluate a company's performance. A vertical analysis of a financial statement reflects each item on the financial statement as a percentage of another item (the base amount) on the financial statement. The vertical analysis percentages are calculated as follows:

$$\text{Vertical analysis percentage} = \frac{\text{Financial statement item \$}}{\text{Base amount \$}} \times 100$$

On the income statement, net sales is used as the base amount and is shown as 100%. On the statement of financial position, total assets is used as the base amount and is shown as 100%. The completed vertical analysis of Tucker Enterprises' 2014 and 2015 income statement and statement of financial position is presented in **Exhibits 12-6** and **12-7**.

Tucker Enterprises, Inc. **Income Statement** **Years Ended December 31, 2015 and 2014**				
(in thousands)	**2015**	**PERCENT**	**2014**	**PERCENT**
Net Sales	$824	100.0%	$596	100.0%
Cost of Goods Sold	375	45.5	277	46.5
Gross Profit	449	54.5	319	53.5
Operating Expenses:				
Selling, General, and Administrative	213	25.8	167	28.0
Other	48	5.8	34	5.7
Income Before Income Tax	188	22.8	118	19.8
Income Tax Expense	33	4.0	21	3.5
Net Income	$155	18.8%	$ 97	16.3%

Exhibit 12-6 ▲

Tucker Enterprises, Inc. **Statement of Financial Position** **December 31, 2015 and 2014**				
(in thousands)	**2015**	**PERCENT**	**2014**	**PERCENT**
Assets				
Current Assets:				
Cash and Cash Equivalents	$ 36	6.4%	$ 47	11.9%
Accounts Receivable, Net	61	10.9	52	13.2
Inventory	144	25.7	116	29.4
Total Current Assets	241	43.0	215	54.6
Property, Plant, and Equipment, Net	319	57.0	179	45.4
Total Assets	$560	100.0%	$394	100.0%
Liabilities				
Current Liabilities:				
Accounts Payable	$121	21.6%	$ 74	18.8%
Accrued Liabilities	24	4.3	33	8.4
Total Current Liabilities	145	25.9	107	27.2
Long-Term Liabilities	173	30.9	104	26.4
Total Liabilities	318	56.8	211	53.6
Shareholders' Equity				
Common Shares	35	6.2	30	7.6
Retained Earnings	207	37.0	153	38.8
Total Shareholders' Equity	242	43.2	183	46.4
Total Liabilities and Shareholders' Equity	$560	100.0%	$394	100.0%

Exhibit 12-7 ▲

A Note About Rounding

An interesting issue often arises when preparing vertical analyses of financial statements. This issue occurs when the calculated percentage amounts are added or subtracted from each other in the same manner that was used to prepare the financial statements (i.e., the cost of goods sold percentage is subtracted from the net sales percentage to get the gross profit percentage, etc.). Some of the percentage amounts arrived at in this manner often differ slightly from the percentage amounts that were initially calculated when doing the vertical analysis. For example, in Exhibit 12-6 for 2015, if the calculated percentages for operating expenses are subtracted from the calculated percentage for gross profit, the result is 22.9 (54.5 – 25.8 – 5.8). This amount differs from the 22.8 which was calculated when preparing the vertical analysis of the income statement. These differences are the result of the rounding that took place when calculating the percentages for the vertical analysis. These differences are insignificant and will be ignored for purposes of our discussion of vertical analysis. All of the amounts in the vertical analyses that are performed in this text will be the result of the calculated percentages.

VERTICAL ANALYSIS OF THE INCOME STATEMENT

The vertical analysis reveals that Tucker Enterprises' 2015 cost of goods sold is 45.5% of net sales compared to 46.5% in 2014. The fact that Tucker Enterprises was able to decrease the cost of goods sold as a percent of net sales while increasing net sales by over $200,000 is a positive sign. The analysis also indicates that Tucker Enterprises was able to decrease selling, general, and administrative expenses from 28.0% of net sales in 2014 to only 25.8% in 2015. This indicates that Tucker Enterprises' management appears to be doing a good job of controlling these expenses. We also see that Tucker Enterprises' 2015 net income is 18.8% of net sales. In other words, Tucker Enterprises earned $188 for every thousand dollars of net sales it had.

VERTICAL ANALYSIS OF THE STATEMENT OF FINANCIAL POSITION

The vertical analysis of Tucker Enterprises' statement of financial position reveals several things that warrant discussion. First, cash and cash equivalents decreased from 11.9% of total assets to only 6.4% of total assets. This should concern management since it could indicate a potential cash flow problem in the future. In addition to cash and cash equivalents, accounts receivable and inventory also decreased as a percentage of total assets. As a result, total current assets decreased from 54.6% of total assets to 43.0% of total assets. However, as we saw in the horizontal analysis, the current assets actually increased in total from 2014 to 2015. So, the decrease of current assets as a percentage of total assets was not due to a decrease in total current assets. It was actually the result of the significant increase in property, plant, and equipment during the year. Also, total liabilities increased from 53.6% to 56.8% of total liabilities and shareholders' equity while total shareholders' equity decreased from 46.4% to 43.2%. This indicates that creditors have claims to a higher percentage of Tucker Enterprises' assets in 2015 than they did in 2014.

HOW DO WE COMPARE ONE COMPANY WITH ANOTHER?

L.O. ❹ Compare one company to another using common-size financial statements and benchmarking

Horizontal and vertical analyses are useful tools to assess a company's performance. However, they only evaluate a company's performance against itself. To better assess a company's performance, it is often useful to compare the company against other companies. To compare Tucker Enterprises to another company we can use common-size statements. A **common-size statement** reports only percentages—the same percentages that appear in a vertical analysis. Common-size statements make it easier to compare companies of different sizes. By only reporting percentages, it removes **dollar value bias** when comparing the companies. Dollar value bias is the bias one sees from comparing numbers in absolute (dollars) rather than relative (percentages) terms. For example, it may appear that one company performed better than another because it had higher net income. However, the company with the lower net income might actually have been the better performer of the two companies in relative (percentage) terms.

To illustrate, let's assume that Tucker Enterprises, Inc. and Mackay Industries, Inc. compete in the same industry. Which company achieves a higher gross margin? Which company earns a higher percentage of revenues as profits for its shareholders? We can use a common-size income statement to compare the two companies and answer these questions. **Exhibit 12-8** gives both companies' common-size income statements for 2015 so that we may compare them on a relative, not absolute, basis. The figures for Tucker Enterprises are taken from the vertical analysis in Exhibit 12-6 and the figures for Mackay Industries are assumed.

Tucker Enterprises, Inc. versus Mackay Industries, Inc.
Common-Size Income Statement
Year Ended December 31, 2015

(in thousands)	TUCKER ENTERPRISES	MACKAY INDUSTRIES
Net Sales	100.0%	100.0%
Cost of Goods Sold	45.5	47.2
Gross Profit	54.5	52.8
Operating Expenses:		
Selling, General, and Administrative	25.8	26.3
Other	5.8	4.9
Income Before Income Tax	22.8	21.6
Income Tax Expense	4.0	3.7
Net Income	18.8%	17.9%

Exhibit 12-8 ▲

Exhibit 12-8 shows that in 2015, Tucker Enterprises was more profitable than Mackay Industries. Tucker Enterprises' gross profit percentage is 54.5%, compared to 52.8% for Mackay Industries. This means that Tucker Enterprises is getting more profit from every dollar of net sales than Mackay Industries. And, more importantly, Tucker Enterprises' percentage of net income to net sales is 18.8%. That means that nearly one-fifth of Tucker Enterprises' net sales end up as profits for the company's shareholders. On the other hand, although close, Mackay Industries' percentage of net income to net sales is 17.9%. Both percentages are good; however, the common-size statement highlights Tucker Enterprises' advantage over Mackay Industries.

A common-size statement of financial position can also be prepared to compare the two companies' statements of financial position. **Exhibit 12-9** gives both companies' common-size statements of financial position for 2015 so that we may compare them. The figures for Tucker Enterprises are taken from the vertical analysis in Exhibit 12-7 and the figures for Mackay Industries are assumed.

Tucker Enterprises, Inc. versus Mackay Industries, Inc.
Common-Size Statement of Financial Position
December 31, 2015

(in thousands)	TUCKER ENTERPRISES	MACKAY INDUSTRIES
Assets		
Current Assets:		
Cash and Cash Equivalents	6.4%	11.1%
Accounts Receivable, Net	10.9	9.3
Inventory	25.7	26.5
Total Current Assets	43.0	46.9
Property, Plant, and Equipment, Net	57.0	53.1
Total Assets	100.0%	100.0%
Liabilities		
Current Liabilities:		
Accounts Payable	21.6%	20.7%
Accrued Liabilities	4.3	6.4
Total Current Liabilities	25.9	27.1
Long-Term Liabilities	30.9	32.2
Total Liabilities	56.8	59.3
Shareholders' Equity		
Common Shares	6.2	5.2
Retained Earnings	37.0	35.5
Total Shareholders' Equity	43.2	40.7
Total Liabilities and Shareholders' Equity	100.0%	100.0%

Exhibit 12-9 ▲

As we can see from the figures in Exhibit 12-9, Tucker Enterprises' cash represents only 6.4% of its total assets compared to 11.1% for Mackay Industries. This might concern Tucker Enterprises' managers since it could indicate cash flow issues for Tucker Enterprises in the future. We can also see that Tucker Enterprises' total liabilities represents 56.8% of the total liabilities and shareholders' equity compared to 59.3% for Mackay Industries. This means that a higher percentage of assets are financed by creditors rather than shareholders for Mackay Industries.

BENCHMARKING

The practice of comparing a company with other leading companies is known as **benchmarking**. The common-size financial statements presented in Exhibits 12-8 and 12-9 represent benchmarking against a key competitor. Mackay Industries, Inc. is a good company to use to benchmark Tucker Enterprises' performance because the two companies compete in the same industry. As we saw in the common-size income statement, Tucker Enterprises is slightly more profitable than Mackay Industries.

It is also possible to utilize industry averages as a benchmark for evaluating a company. An industry comparison would show how Tucker Enterprises is performing alongside the average for the industry it operates in. A popular source for industry averages is *Annual Statement Studies* published by The Risk Management Association. You can even find industry averages online at BizStats.com. To compare Tucker Enterprises, Inc. to the industry average, simply insert the industry average common-size financial statements in place of Mackay Industries in Exhibits 12-8 and 12-9.

DECISION GUIDELINES

WHAT IS RATIO ANALYSIS?

A ratio is a relation between two numbers. **Ratio analysis**, therefore, is a form of financial statement analysis in which items on the financial statements are compared to one another. These ratios are then compared to ratios from prior years, ratios of other companies, or industry average ratios to evaluate a company's performance. Remember, however, that no single ratio tells the whole picture of any company's performance. Different ratios explain different aspects of a company. It is important to note that in order to get reliable results from ratio analysis, great care should be considered regarding the classifications of assets and liabilities. If the assets and liabilities are not correctly categorized, all your results will be unreliable and even misleading. The ratios we discuss in this chapter may be classified as follows:

L.O. 5 Compute various financial ratios

- **Liquidity ratios** measure a company's ability to meet short-term obligations with current assets.
- **Asset management ratios** measure how efficiently a company utilizes its operating assets.
- **Solvency ratios** measure a company's ability to meet its long-term obligations or take on more debt.
- **Profitability ratios** measure a company's ability to generate profits.
- **Market analysis ratios** are used to evaluate a company's stock market performance.

In earlier chapters, we introduced many of these ratios. In this chapter, we will review previously introduced ratios and examine new ratios. To illustrate ratio analysis, we will return to the comparative income statement and statement of financial position for Tucker Enterprises, which were presented in Exhibits 12-2 and 12-3. Let's start by discussing liquidity ratios.

LIQUIDITY RATIOS

Working Capital

Working capital is defined as current assets less current liabilities. Working capital measures the amount of current assets that are left over after settling all current liabilities.

Tucker Enterprises' working capital is $96,000 in 2015 and $108,000 in 2014, calculated as follows:

Working capital = Current assets − Current liabilities =

2015	$241,000 − 145,000 = $ 96,000
2014	$215,000 − 107,000 = $108,000

The following is a visual illustration of the working capital calculation for 2015:

Current Ratio

The **current ratio** is the most widely used liquidity ratio. The current ratio is calculated by dividing current assets by current liabilities. Tucker Enterprises' current ratio for 2015 and 2014 is calculated as follows:

		2015	**2014**
Current ratio =	$\dfrac{\text{Current assets}}{\text{Current liabilities}}$ =	$\dfrac{\$241,000}{\$145,000} = 1.66$	$\dfrac{\$215,000}{\$107,000} = 2.01$

A high current ratio indicates that the business has sufficient current assets to pay its current liabilities as they come due. But, what is an acceptable current ratio? The answer depends on the industry. For companies in most industries, a current ratio around 1.50 is considered good, as reported by The Risk Management Association. Tucker Enterprises' current ratio of 1.66 in 2015 and 2.01 in 2014 are both strong. However, the decrease in the current ratio from 2014 to 2015 may be a cause for concern. Keep in mind that a current ratio that is too high would also be a cause for concern. This would indicate that the company is too liquid and, therefore, is not using its assets effectively.

Acid-Test Ratio

The **acid-test ratio** (or **quick ratio**) tells us whether the entity could pay all its current liabilities if they came due immediately. Inventory and prepaid expenses are *not* included in the acid-test ratio because they are not available to pay current liabilities. To compute the acid-test ratio, we add cash, short-term investments, and net current receivables (accounts and notes receivable, net of allowances) and divide this sum by current liabilities. Tucker Enterprises' acid-test ratios for 2015 and 2014 follow:

		2015	**2014**
Acid-test (Quick) ratio =	$\dfrac{\text{Cash + Short-term investments + Net current receivables}}{\text{Current liabilities}}$ =	$\dfrac{\$97,000}{\$145,000} = 0.67$	$\dfrac{\$99,000}{\$107,000} = 0.93$

The company's acid-test ratio declined from 0.93 in 2014 to 0.67 in 2015. An acid-test ratio of 0.90 to 1.00 is acceptable in most industries. Therefore, although it appears that Tucker Enterprises' acid-test ratio was acceptable in 2014, it is somewhat low in 2015.

DECISION GUIDELINES

DECISION	GUIDELINE	ANALYZE
As a supplier, how can I check a customer's ability to pay their obligations as they come due in order to know whether or not to extend them credit?	Use liquidity ratios: • Working capital • Current ratio • Acid-test ratio	Monitoring a business's liquidity ratios can often provide an indicator that the business may experience cash flow problems. Action should be taken so that the business does not encounter difficulty meeting its obligations as they come due. For most businesses, a current ratio that drops below 1.50 or an acid-test ratio that drops below 0.90 may be cause for concern.

It is not only important for a company to have good liquidity ratios. It is also important that a company manage its operations effectively. There are three ratios we will look at that measure how well a company manages its inventory and accounts receivable.

ASSET MANAGEMENT RATIOS

Inventory Turnover

The **inventory turnover** measures the number of times a company sells its average level of inventory during a year. A high rate of turnover indicates ease in selling inventory; a low rate indicates difficulty. A value of 6 means that the company sold its average level of inventory six times, or once every two months, during the year. To compute inventory turnover, we divide cost of goods sold by the average inventory for the period. We use the cost of goods sold—not sales—because both cost of goods sold and inventory are stated *at cost.* Tucker Enterprises' inventory turnover for 2015 and 2014 is calculated as follows:

$$\text{Inventory turnover ratio} = \frac{\text{Cost of goods sold}}{\text{Average inventory}} = \frac{\overset{\textbf{2015}}{\$375,000}}{(\$116,000 + \$144,000)/2} = 2.88$$

$$= \frac{\overset{\textbf{2014}}{\$277,000}}{(\$68,000^* + \$116,000)/2} = 3.01$$

*2013 inventory is $68,000.

Cost of goods sold comes directly from the income statement. Average inventory is calculated by adding the beginning inventory to the ending inventory and dividing by two.

When calculating any ratio, if one number is taken from the income statement and the other number is taken from the statement of financial position, then the statement of financial position number to be used has to be an average number. This is because the income statement number is accumulated for the whole year, while the statement of financial position number is on a specific date. The statement of financial position number may be skewed on the last day of the accounting period; therefore, we need to use the average number.

Inventory turnover varies widely with the nature of the business. For example, the inventory turnover ratio for a heavy equipment dealer will be significantly lower than that for a grocery store. Because of the high profit margin on heavy equipment, it is not necessary to turn the inventory over as many times and still be profitable. Let's assume the industry average inventory turnover ratio in Tucker Enterprises' industry is 2.5. In this case, Tucker Enterprises turnover ratio would be considered good in both 2014 and 2015. However, the decrease in the turnover from 2014 to 2015 should be investigated as it could be an indicator that Tucker Enterprises has some obsolete inventory.

Days' Sales in Inventory

The **days' sales in inventory** also measures how long it takes a company to turn its inventory into sales. To compute, we divide 365 by the preceding inventory turnover. It is more intuitive for users of financial statements to understand the number of days it takes to turn inventory to sales, rather than the number of times it turns over in a year. Tucker Enterprises' days' sales in inventory for 2015 and 2014 is calculated as follows:

$$\text{Days' sales in inventory} = \frac{365}{\text{Inventory turnover}}$$

2015
$$= \frac{365}{2.88} = 127 \text{ days}$$

2014
$$= \frac{365}{3.01} = 122 \text{ days}$$

Accounts Receivable Turnover

The **accounts receivable turnover** measures the ability to collect cash from credit customers. The higher the ratio, the faster the company collects cash. However, a receivable turnover ratio that is too high may indicate that credit is too tight, causing the loss of sales to good customers. To compute accounts receivable turnover, net credit sales is divided by average net accounts receivable. Average net accounts receivable is calculated by adding the beginning and ending balances in net accounts receivable together and dividing the result by two. We will assume that all of Tucker Enterprises' sales were on account. Tucker Enterprises' accounts receivable turnover for 2015 and 2014 is computed as follows:

$$\text{Accounts receivable turnover ratio} = \frac{\text{Net credit sales}}{\text{Average net accounts receivable}}$$

2015
$$= \frac{\$824,000}{(\$52,000 + \$61,000)/2} = 14.58$$

2014
$$= \frac{\$596,000}{(\$43,000^* + \$52,000)/2} = 12.55$$

*2013 Accounts Receivable is $43,000.

Tucker Enterprises' receivable turnover of 14.58 in 2015 is an improvement over the 12.55 turnover in 2014. Considering Tucker Enterprises' credit terms are 2/10, n/30, it appears that Tucker Enterprises is doing a good job of collecting its receivables.

Days' Sales in Receivables

The **days' sales in receivables** also measures the ability to collect receivables. Days' sales in receivables tell us how many days' sales remain in accounts receivable. To compute, we divide 365 by the preceding accounts receivable turnover. Tucker Enterprises' days' sales in receivables for 2015 and 2014 is calculated as follows:

$$\text{Days' sales in receivables} = \frac{365}{\text{Accounts receivable turnover}}$$

2015
$$= \frac{365}{14.58} = 25 \text{ days}$$

2014
$$= \frac{365}{12.55} = 29 \text{ days}$$

An alternate method of calculating the days' sales in receivables is to do the following:

1. Divide net sales by 365 to determine the average sales for one day.

2. Divide this average day's sales amount into the average net accounts receivable.

Tucker Enterprises' ratio tells us that on average, 25 days' sales remain in accounts receivable in 2015 compared to 29 days in 2014. As with the accounts receivable turnover, this is an indicator that Tucker Enterprises has improved its ability to collect its accounts.

Fixed Asset Turnover

In addition to measuring how efficient the company is in managing its working capital accounts, we can also measure the company's operating efficiency by evaluating the company's **fixed asset turnover ratio**. The fixed asset turnover measures a company's ability to generate sales from fixed asset investments, specifically property, plant, and equipment (PPE). A higher turnover ratio shows that the company is more effective in using the investment in fixed assets to generate sales. Tucker Enterprises' fixed asset turnover for 2015 and 2014 is calculated as follows:

$$\text{Fixed asset turnover} = \frac{\text{Net sales}}{\text{Average net fixed assets}}$$

2015
$$= \frac{\$824{,}000}{(\$179{,}000 + \$319{,}000)/2} = 3.31$$

2014
$$= \frac{\$596{,}000}{(\$165{,}000^* + \$179{,}000)/2} = 3.47$$

*2013 Fixed Assets is $165,000.

Total Asset Turnover

Another asset management ratio is total asset turnover. The **total asset turnover ratio** measures the ability of a company to utilize its assets to generate sales. The higher the ratio, the more efficient the company is in generating sales. Tucker Enterprises' total asset turnover for 2015 and 2014 is calculated as follows:

$$\text{Total asset turnover} = \frac{\text{Net sales}}{\text{Average total assets}}$$

2015
$$= \frac{\$824{,}000}{(\$394{,}000 + \$560{,}000)/2} = 1.73$$

2014
$$= \frac{\$596{,}000}{(\$318{,}000^* + \$394{,}000)/2} = 1.67$$

*2013 Fixed Assets is $318,000.

DECISION GUIDELINES

DECISION	GUIDELINE	ANALYZE
As the manager, how do I determine if the inventory and accounts receivable are being managed effectively?	Use assets management ratios: • Inventory turnover • Accounts receivable turnover • Days' sales in receivables	Monitoring the asset management ratios can provide an indicator that a business is not managing its inventory and accounts receivables effectively. A decrease in the inventory turnover may indicate that a business has obsolete inventory or that it is purchasing too much inventory. Carrying high levels of inventory results in decreased profits due to the increased costs associated with maintaining the increased inventory levels. A decrease in the accounts receivable turnover may be due to poor collection practices related to past due accounts. This can result in decreased profits for the business due to increased bad debts expense. The longer a receivable is past due, the less likely it is to be collected.

SOLVENCY RATIOS

The ratios discussed so far yield insight into a company's ability to pay current liabilities and manage its assets. Most businesses also have long-term debt. Solvency ratios help assess a business's ability to pay long-term liabilities and evaluate its capital structure. These ratios are good indicators of a business's financial risks.

Debt Ratio

The **debt ratio** shows the relationship between total liabilities and total assets. In other words, it shows the proportion of assets financed with debt. If the debt ratio is 1, then all the assets are financed with debt. A debt ratio of 0.50 means that half the assets are financed with debt and the other half are financed by the owners of the business. The higher the debt ratio, the higher the company's financial risk. The debt ratios for Tucker Enterprises at the end of 2015 and 2014 follow:

$$\text{Debt ratio} = \frac{\text{Total liabilities}}{\text{Total assets}} = \begin{array}{cc} \mathbf{2015} & \mathbf{2014} \\ \frac{\$318,000}{\$560,000} = 0.57 & \frac{\$211,000}{\$394,000} = 0.54 \end{array}$$

Tucker Enterprises' debt ratio in 2015 of 0.57 is slightly higher than the 2014 debt ratio of 0.54. However, neither ratio is considered to be very high. The Risk Management Association reports that the average debt ratio for most companies ranges from 0.57 to 0.67, with relatively little variation from company to company. Tucker Enterprises appears to be very solvent and in a position to take on more debt should the need arise.

Debt to Equity Ratio

The **debt to equity ratio** shows the relationship between total liabilities and total equity. A high debt to equity ratio means that a company has been aggressive in financing its growth with debt; in other words, the company is more leveraged. Generally, companies with higher ratios are thought to be more risky because they have more liabilities and less equity. Tucker Enterprises' debt to equity ratio for 2015 and 2014 is calculated as follows:

		2015
Debt to equity ratio $=$	$\dfrac{\text{Total liabilities}}{\text{Total shareholders' equity}}$	$\dfrac{\$318{,}000}{\$242{,}000} = 1.31$
		2014
		$\dfrac{\$211{,}000}{\$183{,}000} = 1.15$

Times-Interest-Earned Ratio

The **times-interest-earned ratio**, also known as **interest-coverage ratio**, indicates a company's ability to continue to service its debt. It measures the number of times operating income can cover (pay) interest expense. A high ratio means that a company is able to meet its interest obligations because earnings are significantly greater than annual interest obligations. A low ratio indicates that a company may encounter difficulty meeting its obligations. To compute this ratio, we divide operating income by interest expense. Before we can calculate the times-interest-earned ratio for Tucker Enterprises, we must calculate its operating income. If Tucker Enterprises' interest expense was $28,000 and $17,000 in 2015 and 2014 respectively, we can calculate operating income for the two years as follows:

$$\text{Operating income} = \text{Income before income tax} + \text{Interest expense}$$
$$2015 = \$188{,}000 + \$28{,}000 = \$216{,}000$$
$$2014 = \$118{,}000 + \$17{,}000 = \$135{,}000$$

Next, we can calculate the times-interest-earned ratios as follows:

		2015		**2014**	
Times-interest-earned ratio $=$	$\dfrac{\text{Operating income}}{\text{Interest expense}}$	$\dfrac{\$216{,}000}{\$28{,}000} =$	$\begin{array}{c}7.7 \\ \text{times}\end{array}$	$\dfrac{\$135{,}000}{\$17{,}000} =$	$\begin{array}{c}7.9 \\ \text{times}\end{array}$

Tucker Enterprises' times-interest-earned ratio has declined slightly from 7.9 in 2014 to 7.7 in 2015. However, the norm, as reported by The Risk Management Association, falls in the range of 2.0 to 3.0. So, it appears that Tucker Enterprises will have little difficulty servicing its debt in the future.

 DECISION GUIDELINES

DECISION	**GUIDELINE**	**ANALYZE**
As an entrepreneur, the long-term health of my company revolves around making my debt payments. Will my business be able to service (pay off) its long-term debt?	Use solvency ratios: • Debt ratio • Times-interest-earned	Monitoring a company's solvency ratios can provide an indicator that the company may have difficulty servicing its long-term debt. In addition to creditors, a company's shareholders should pay attention to the solvency ratios. If a company is unable to pay back its creditors, there will be no value left in the company for the shareholders.

Now let's look at how the profitability of a business can be evaluated. We will examine four profitability ratios.

PROFITABILITY RATIOS

Rate of Return on Net Sales

The **rate of return on net sales**, or simply **return on sales**, shows the portion of each dollar of net sales that a firm is able to turn into income. Tucker Enterprises' rate of return on sales is calculated as follows:

			2015	**2014**
Rate of return on sales $=$	$\dfrac{\text{Net income}}{\text{Net sales}}$	$=$	$\dfrac{\$155,000}{\$824,000} = 18.8\%$	$\dfrac{\$97,000}{\$596,000} = 16.3\%$

Companies strive for a high rate of return on sales. The higher the rate of return, the more sales dollars end up as profit. The increase in Tucker Enterprises' return on sales from 16.3% in 2014 to 18.8% in 2015 is a good sign.

Rate of Return on Total Assets

The **rate of return on total assets**, or simply **return on assets**, measures a company's effectiveness in using assets to generate earnings. In other words, it gives investors an idea of how well the company is converting its assets into income. The assets of a company are financed by both debt and equity. The creditors have loaned money to the company and they earn interest. The shareholders have invested in shares and their return is net income. Therefore, the sum of interest expense and net income is added together when calculating the return to the two groups. The sum of these amounts is then divided by the average total assets to determine the return on assets. Average total assets is calculated by adding the beginning and ending total assets for the year together and dividing by two. Tucker Enterprises' return on assets for 2015 and 2014 is calculated as follows:

			2015
Rate of return on total assets $=$	$\dfrac{\text{Net income} + \text{Interest expense}}{\text{Average total assets}}$	$=$	$\dfrac{\$155,000 + \$28,000}{(\$394,000 + \$560,000)/2} = 38.4\%$
			2014
		$=$	$\dfrac{\$97,000 + \$17,000}{(\$318,000^* + \$394,000)/2} = 32.0\%$

*2013 Total Assets is $318,000.

Remember from our discussion of the times-interest-earned ratio that Tucker Enterprises' interest expense was $28,000 and $17,000 in 2015 and 2014 respectively. Investors would like Tucker Enterprises' return on assets for both years as they generally look for a return on assets that is high and growing.

Rate of Return on Common Shareholders' Equity

The **rate of return on common shareholders' equity**, often shortened to **return on common equity**, is another popular measure of profitability. The return on common equity shows the amount of net income returned as a percentage of common shareholders' equity.

To compute this ratio, we first subtract preferred dividends from net income to get net income available to the common shareholders. Because Tucker Enterprises has no preferred shares issued, preferred dividends are zero. The net income available to common shareholders is then divided by average common equity during the year. Common equity is total shareholders' equity minus preferred shareholders' equity. Average equity is the average of the beginning and ending balances.

The 2015 and 2014 rate of return on common shareholders' equity for Tucker Enterprises follows:

$$
\begin{array}{l}
\text{Rate of return on common} \\
\text{shareholders' equity}
\end{array}
=
\frac{\text{Net income} - \text{Preferred dividends}}{\text{Average common shareholders' equity}}
=
\begin{array}{c}
\textbf{2015} \\
\dfrac{\$155{,}000 - \$0}{(\$183{,}000 + \$242{,}000)/2} = 72.9\% \\[4pt]
\textbf{2014} \\
\dfrac{\$97{,}000 - \$0}{(\$165{,}000^* + \$183{,}000)/2} = 55.7\%
\end{array}
$$

*2013 Total common shareholders' equity is $165,000.

As we can see, the return on equity was higher than 50% for both years, which is exceptional. The significant increase from 2014 to 2015 is sure to make the shareholders happy.

Earnings per Share of Common Shares

Perhaps the most widely quoted of all financial statistics is **earnings per share of common shares**, or simply *earnings per share* (EPS). EPS is the only ratio that is required to be shown on the income statement. EPS is the amount of net income earned for each of the company's outstanding common shares.

Earnings per share is computed by dividing net income available to common shareholders by the number of common shares outstanding during the year. As with return on equity, preferred dividends are subtracted from net income because the preferred shareholders have a prior claim to dividends. Tucker Enterprises has no preferred shares outstanding and, therefore, paid no preferred dividends. To calculate earnings per share, we must know the number of common shares outstanding. Tucker Enterprises had 15,000 common shares outstanding in 2014 and 17,000 shares outstanding in 2015. Tucker Enterprises' earnings per share is calculated as follows:

$$
\begin{array}{l}
\text{Earnings per} \\
\text{common share}
\end{array}
=
\frac{\text{Net income} - \text{Preferred dividends}}{\begin{array}{c}\text{Number of common} \\ \text{shares outstanding}\end{array}}
=
\begin{array}{c}
\textbf{2015} \\
\dfrac{\$155{,}000 - \$0}{17{,}000} = \$9.12 \\[4pt]
\textbf{2014} \\
\dfrac{\$97{,}000 - \$0}{15{,}000} = \$6.47
\end{array}
$$

Tucker Enterprises' EPS increased by $2.65 from 2014 to 2015. This represents a 41% increase in the EPS. This is a good sign for Tucker Enterprises' shareholders; however, they should not expect this much increase in EPS every year. Most companies strive to increase EPS by 10% to 15% annually, and leading companies do so. But even the most successful companies have an occasional bad year.

 DECISION GUIDELINES

DECISION	GUIDELINE	ANALYZE
As an investor, how do I assess the profitability of a company that I'm interested in?	Use profitability ratios: • Return on sales • Return on assets • Return on common equity • Earnings per share	The profitability of a business over the long run is critical to the survival of the business. By monitoring the profitability ratios, potential problems can be detected early and steps can be taken to prevent business failure. Many companies that have failed have shown warning signs well in advance of the company's collapse.

DUPONT ANALYSIS

The financial ratios show the company's performance; however, they may not pinpoint where the problems are. In certain cases, management might need to dig further to understand why the return on assets (ROA) is increasing or decreasing. For example, if the company shows a low rate of return on total assets, it would be difficult to know whether the problem lies with a low return, which is related to operations, or lies with the total assets, which is related to asset management. In the 1920s, DuPont Corporation started using the decomposed formula of the ROA ratio to help analyze performance so that management could improve results.

Exhibit 12-10 shows the decomposed formula:

Exhibit 12-10 ▲

Companies can achieve a higher ROA by increasing the net income through better management of costs, or decreasing the average total assets through eliminating non-productive assets.

 CRITICAL THINKING

Take a minute to think about the following case, using the DuPont analysis to help you analyze the case:

■ BJ Enterprises just finished its second year of operations. The CEO of the company is pleased with the profit margin, or return on sales, as it had a slightly better performance than its competitor. The asset management ratios, in particular related to the working capital accounts, also showed the company was doing a fair job in managing its current assets. However, the CEO was disappointed by the low return on assets. What would you recommend the company to investigate? What would you recommend the company do to improve the return on assets?

Solution:
Return on assets can be examined in two parts: (1) return on sales (or profit margin), and (2) total asset turnover. If the return on sales does not show a problem, then the problem must reside with the total asset turnover. However, BJ was able to manage its current assets well; therefore, the only possible problem is related to long-term assets. This may mean that BJ has a lot of non-productive fixed assets, and was not able to effectively utilize these fixed assets to generate a sales level that met the desired return on assets.

MARKET ANALYSIS RATIOS

Investors purchase shares with the hope of earning a return on their investments. There are two ways that investors earn returns on their shares. They have gains (or losses) from selling shares at prices above or below what they paid for them. They also may receive distributions of cash in the form of dividends from the company. The following tools are used to help people evaluate share investments.

Price/Earnings Ratio

The **price/earnings ratio** is the ratio of the market price of a common share to the company's earnings per share. This ratio, abbreviated P/E, shows how much investors are willing to pay per dollar of earnings. The market prices of common shares for publicly traded companies can be found in *The Globe and Mail*, or online from sources such as www.tmx.com. The market price of Tucker Enterprises' common shares was $67 at the end of 2015 and $44 at the end of 2014. Tucker Enterprises' P/E ratios for 2015 and 2014 are calculated as follows.

$$\text{Price/earnings ratio} = \frac{\text{Market price per share}}{\text{Earnings per share}}$$

	2015	2014
	$\dfrac{\$67.00}{\$9.12} = 7.35$	$\dfrac{\$44.00}{\$6.47} = 6.80$

Tucker Enterprises' P/E ratio increased slightly from 2014 to 2015. This indicates that investors are willing to pay more for $1 of earnings in 2015 than in 2014.

Dividend Yield

The ratio of dividends per share to a share's market price per share is called the **dividend yield**. This ratio measures the percentage of a share's market value that is returned annually as dividends. Dividend yield may be calculated on common shares, preferred shares, or both, depending on what type of shares a company issues. Because *preferred* shareholders invest primarily to receive dividends, they should pay special attention to dividend yield.

Tucker Enterprises paid annual cash dividends on common shares of $3.50 per share in 2015 and $2.25 in 2014. Remember, Tucker Enterprises has no preferred shares. As noted previously, market prices of the company's common shares were $67 in 2015 and $44 in 2014. Tucker's dividend yield on common shares for 2015 and 2014 is calculated next.

$$\text{Dividend yield} = \frac{\text{Dividend per share}}{\text{Market price per share}}$$

	2015	2014
	$\dfrac{\$3.50}{\$67.00} = 5.2\%$	$\dfrac{\$2.25}{\$44.00} = 5.1\%$

Based on the dividend yield, investors who buy Tucker Enterprises' common shares can expect to receive about 5% of their investment in the form of cash dividends.

RED FLAGS IN FINANCIAL STATEMENT ANALYSIS

As stated earlier in the chapter, financial statement analysis usually will not indicate that a problem definitely exists with a company. Also, even if a problem does exist, financial statement analysis generally will not identify what the specific problem is. Instead, financial statement analysis generates *red flags* that may signal financial trouble. Recent accounting scandals highlight the importance of these red flags. The following conditions may be cause for concern:

- **Decreased Cash Flow.** Cash flow validates net income. Is cash flow from operations consistently lower than net income? If so, the company is in trouble. Are the sales of plant assets a major source of cash? If so, the company may face a cash shortage.

- **Inability to Collect Receivables.** Are days' sales in receivables growing faster than for competitors? A cash shortage may be looming.

- **Buildup of Inventories.** Is inventory turnover too slow? If so, the company may have obsolete inventory, or it may be overstating inventory.

- **Movement of Sales, Inventory, and Receivables.** Sales, receivables, and inventory generally move together. Increased sales lead to higher receivables and require more inventory to meet demand. Unexpected or inconsistent movements among sales, inventory, and receivables make the financial statements look suspect.

- **Earnings Problems.** Has net income decreased significantly for several years in a row? Has income turned into a loss? Most companies cannot survive consecutive losses year after year.

- **Too Much Debt.** How does the company's debt ratio compare to that of major competitors? If the debt ratio is too high, the company may be unable to pay its debts.

Based on our financial statement analysis of Tucker Enterprises, the company appears to be in a strong financial condition. The only area of concern could be the company's cash position. Tucker Enterprises should monitor its cash position to ensure that it does not encounter any cash flow problems in the future.

Exhibit 12-11 summarizes the ratios we have learned in this chapter.

DEMO DOC

MyAccountingLab   Visit MyAccountingLab to watch animated versions of similar Demo Docs.

HORIZONTAL AND VERTICAL ANALYSIS

Cassidy, Inc. has the following information for 2015 and 2014:

Cassidy, Inc. Income Statement Years Ended December 31, 2015 and 2014		
	2015	**2014**
Sales Revenue	$550,000	$600,000
Cost of Goods Sold	320,000	350,000
Gross Profit	230,000	250,000
Salaries Expense	165,000	158,000
Depreciation Expense	21,000	16,000
Insurance Expense	19,000	23,000
Income from Operations	25,000	53,000
Gain on Sale of Furniture	3,000	0
Net Income	$ 28,000	$ 53,000

Liquidity Ratios	To measure a company's ability to meet short-term obligations with current assets.
Working Capital	Current assets − Current liabilities
Current Ratio	$\dfrac{\text{Current assets}}{\text{Current liabilities}}$
Acid-test (Quick) Ratio	$\dfrac{\text{Cash} + \text{Short-term investments} + \text{Net current receivables}}{\text{Current liabilities}}$
Asset Management Ratios	To measure how efficiently a company utilizes its operating assets.
Inventory Turnover	$\dfrac{\text{Cost of goods sold}}{\text{Average inventory}}$
Days' Sales in Inventory	$\dfrac{365}{\text{Inventory turnover ratio}}$
Accounts Receivable Turnover	$\dfrac{\text{Net credit sales}}{\text{Average net accounts receivable}}$
Days' Sales in Receivable	$\dfrac{365}{\text{Accounts receivable turnover ratio}}$
Fixed Asset Turnover	$\dfrac{\text{Net sales}}{\text{Average net fixed assets}}$
Total Asset Turnover	$\dfrac{\text{Net sales}}{\text{Average total assets}}$
Solvency Ratios	To measure a company's ability to meet its long-term obligations or take on more debt.
Debt Ratio	$\dfrac{\text{Total liabilities}}{\text{Total assets}}$
Debt to Equity Ratio	$\dfrac{\text{Total liabilities}}{\text{Total equity}}$
Times-interest-earned Ratio	$\dfrac{\text{Operating income}}{\text{Interest expense}}$
Profitability Ratios	To measure a company's ability to generate profits.
Return on Sales	$\dfrac{\text{Net income}}{\text{Net sales}}$
Return on Assets	$\dfrac{\text{Net income} + \text{Interest expense}}{\text{Average total assets}}$
Return on (Common Shareholder's) Equity	$\dfrac{\text{Net income} - \text{Preferred dividends}}{\text{Average common shareholders' equity}}$
Earnings per (Common) Share	$\dfrac{\text{Net income} - \text{Preferred dividends}}{\text{Number of common shares outstanding}}$
Market Analysis Ratio	To measure a company's stock market performance.
Price/Earnings Ratio	$\dfrac{\text{Market price per share}}{\text{Earnings per share}}$
Dividend Yield	$\dfrac{\text{Dividend per share}}{\text{Market price per share}}$

Exhibit 12-11 ▲

Cassidy, Inc.
Statement of Financial Position
December 31, 2015 and 2014

ASSETS	2015	2014	LIABILITIES	2015	2014
Current:			Current:		
Cash	$ 28,000	$ 33,000	Accounts Payable	$ 20,000	$ 23,000
Accounts Receivable	26,000	15,000	Salaries Payable	10,000	8,000
Prepaid Insurance	30,000	42,000	Total Current Liabilities	30,000	31,000
Total Current Assets	84,000	90,000	Notes Payable	40,000	50,000
Furniture, Net	90,000	74,500			
			SHAREHOLDERS' EQUITY		
			Common Shares	4,000	3,500
			Retained Earnings	100,000	80,000
			Total Liabilities and		
Total Assets	$174,000	$164,500	Shareholders' Equity	$174,000	$164,500

REQUIREMENTS:

① Prepare a horizontal analysis of Cassidy's income statement and statement of financial position for 2015.

② Prepare a vertical analysis of Cassidy's income statement and statement of financial position for 2015.

DEMO DOC SOLUTIONS
REQUIREMENT ①

Prepare a horizontal analysis of Cassidy's income statement and statement of financial position for 2015.

Part 1	Part 2	Demo Doc Complete

Horizontal analysis goes across the rows of each financial statement, looking at one account and how it has changed from the prior year.

To prepare a horizontal analysis, we need to calculate the dollar amount of change and the percentage change for every number on the income statement and statement of financial position.

Dollar amount of change = This year's amount (balance) − Last year's amount (balance)

For example, the dollar amount of change for sales revenue and accounts receivable would be as follows:

Sales Revenue = $550,000 − $600,000 = $(50,000) Change
Accounts Receivable = $26,000 − $15,000 = $11,000 Change

Notice that the parentheses around the change in sales revenue indicate that it decreased, whereas the positive value of the change in the amount of accounts receivable indicates that it increased.

Expenses are assumed to be negative numbers on the income statement, in that they are subtracted to calculate net income. However, we use the absolute value of the expenses (ignoring the fact that they are already negative numbers) to calculate the dollar amount of change. So the dollar amount of change of depreciation expense and insurance expense would be as follows:

$$\text{Depreciation Expense} = \$21,000 - \$16,000 = \$5,000 \text{ Change}$$
$$\text{Insurance Expense} = \$19,000 - \$23,000 = \$(4,000) \text{ Change}$$

The positive amount of change indicates that depreciation expense increased and the negative amount of change indicates that insurance expense decreased.

$$\text{Percentage change} = \frac{\text{Dollar amount of change}}{\text{Base-year amount}}$$

The base-year amount is last year's amount (balance).

Using this formula, the percentage changes in sales revenue and accounts receivable would be as follows:

$$\text{Percentage Change in Sales Revenue} = \frac{\$(50,000)}{\$600,000}$$
$$= (8.3)\% \text{ Change}$$

$$\text{Percentage Change in Accounts Receivable} = \frac{\$11,000}{\$15,000}$$
$$= 73.3\% \text{ Change}$$

Notice that the percentage change numbers are negative for sales revenue (which had a dollar amount decrease for 2015) and positive for accounts receivable (which had a dollar amount increase for 2015).

The percentage changes of depreciation expense and insurance expense would be as follows:

$$\text{Percentage Change in Depreciation Expense} = \frac{\$5,000}{\$16,000}$$
$$= 31.3\% \text{ Change}$$

$$\text{Percentage Change in Insurance Expense} = \frac{\$(4,000)}{\$23,000}$$
$$= (17.4)\% \text{ Change}$$

If an account did not exist in the prior year (such as the gain on sale of furniture in this example), then horizontal analysis is irrelevant and a percentage change cannot be calculated. Extending these calculations to all of the accounts on the income statement and statement of financial position would appear as follows:

			2015	2014	INCREASE (DECREASE) AMOUNT	PERCENTAGE
		Cassidy, Inc. **Income Statement** Years Ended December 31, 2015 and 2014				
		Sales Revenue	$550,000	$600,000	$(50,000)	(8.3)%
		Cost of Goods Sold	320,000	350,000	(30,000)	(8.6)%
		Gross Profit	230,000	250,000	(20,000)	(8.0)%
		Salaries Expense	165,000	158,000	7,000	4.4 %
		Depreciation Expense	21,000	16,000	5,000	31.3 %
		Insurance Expense	19,000	23,000	(4,000)	(17.4)%
		Income from Operations	25,000	53,000	(28,000)	(52.8)%
		Gain on Sale of Furniture	3,000	0	3,000	—
		Net Income	$ 28,000	$ 53,000	$(25,000)	(47.2)%

			2015	2014	INCREASE (DECREASE)	
					AMOUNT	PERCENTAGE
	ASSETS					
	Current:					
		Cash	$ 28,000	$ 33,000	$ (5,000)	(15.2)%
		Accounts Receivable	26,000	15,000	11,000	73.3 %
		Prepaid Insurance	30,000	42,000	(12,000)	(28.6)%
		Total Current Assets	84,000	90,000	(6,000)	(6.7)%
	Furniture, Net		90,000	74,500	15,500	20.8 %
	Total Assets		$174,000	$164,500	9,500	5.8 %
	LIABILITIES					
	Current:					
		Accounts Payable	$ 20,000	$ 23,000	$ (3,000)	(13.0)%
		Salaries Payable	10,000	8,000	2,000	25.0 %
		Total Current Liabilities	30,000	31,000	(1,000)	(3.2)%
	Notes Payable		40,000	50,000	(10,000)	(20.0)%
	Total Liabilities		70,000	81,000	(11,000)	(13.6)%
	SHAREHOLDERS' EQUITY					
	Common Shares		4,000	3,500	500	14.3 %
	Retained Earnings		100,000	80,000	20,000	25.0 %
	Total Shareholders' Equity		104,000	83,500	20,500	24.6 %
	Total Liabilities and					
	Shareholders' Equity		$174,000	$164,500	$ 9,500	5.8 %

Cassidy, Inc. Statement of Financial Position December 31, 2015 and 2014

REQUIREMENT ②

Prepare a vertical analysis of Cassidy's income statement and statement of financial position for 2015.

Part 1	**Part 2**	Demo Doc Complete

Vertical analysis compares every number on a financial statement to all others in the same year (that is, down the columns of the financial statements).

To prepare a vertical analysis, we need to calculate the vertical analysis percentage for each account.

INCOME STATEMENT

On the income statement, each number is calculated as a percentage of net sales revenues.

$$\text{Vertical analysis \% (Income statement)} = \frac{\text{Income statement amount}}{\text{Net sales revenue}}$$

So in the case of gross profit, it is as follows:

$$\text{Vertical analysis \% (2015 Gross Profit)} = \frac{\$230,000}{\$550,000}$$
$$= 41.8\%$$

This figure means that $0.418 of gross profit resulted from every dollar of sales revenue.

The calculation is the same for expenses. The vertical analysis percentages for depreciation expense and insurance expense would be as follows:

$$\text{Vertical analysis \% (2015 Depreciation Expense)} = \frac{\$21,000}{\$550,000}$$
$$= 3.8\%$$

$$\text{Vertical analysis \% (2015 Insurance Expense)} = \frac{\$19,000}{\$550,000}$$
$$= 3.5\%$$

STATEMENT OF FINANCIAL POSITION

On the statement of financial position, each number, whether it be for an asset, a liability, or an equity account, is calculated as a percentage of total assets.

$$\text{Vertical analysis \% (Statement of Financial Position)} = \frac{\text{Statement of financial position amount}}{\text{Total assets}}$$

So in the case of accounts receivable, we have the following:

$$\text{Vertical analysis \% (2015 Accounts Receivable)} = \frac{\$26,000}{\$174,000}$$
$$= 14.9\%$$

In other words, approximately 15% of all the assets are accounts receivable.

Extending these calculations to all of the accounts on the income statement and statement of financial position gives us the following:

		2015		2014	
Cassidy, Inc. **Income Statement** Years Ended December 31, 2015 and 2014		AMOUNT	PERCENTAGE	AMOUNT	PERCENTAGE
Sales Revenue		$550,000	100.0%	$600,000	100.0%
Cost of Goods Sold		320,000	58.2%	350,000	58.3%
Gross Profit		230,000	41.8%	250,000	41.7%
Salaries Expense		165,000	30.0%	158,000	26.3%
Depreciation Expense		21,000	3.8%	16,000	2.7%
Insurance Expense		19,000	3.5%	23,000	3.8%
Income from Operations		25,000	4.5%	53,000	8.8%
Gain on Sale of Furniture		3,000	0.5%	0	0.0%
Net Income		$ 28,000	5.1%	$ 53,000	8.8%

			2015		2014	
			AMOUNT	PERCENTAGE	AMOUNT	PERCENTAGE
	Assets					
	Current:					
	Cash		$ 28,000	16.1%	$ 33,000	20.1%
	Accounts Receivable		26,000	14.9%	15,000	9.1%
	Prepaid Insurance		30,000	17.2%	42,000	25.5%
	Total Current Assets		84,000	48.3%	90,000	54.7%
	Furniture, Net		90,000	51.7%	74,500	45.3%
	Total Assets		$174,000	100.0%	$164,500	100.0%
	Liabilities					
	Current:					
	Accounts Payable		$ 20,000	11.5%	$ 23,000	14.0%
	Salaries Payable		10,000	5.7%	8,000	4.9%
	Total Current Liabilities		30,000	17.2%	31,000	18.8%
	Notes Payable		40,000	23.0%	50,000	30.4%
	Total Liabilities		70,000	40.2%	81,000	49.2%
	Shareholders' Equity					
	Common Shares		4,000	2.3%	3,500	2.1%
	Retained Earnings		100,000	57.5%	80,000	48.6%
	Total Shareholders' Equity		104,000	59.8%	83,500	50.8%
	Total Liabilities and Shareholders' Equity		$174,000	100.0%	$164,500	100.0%

The table is titled:

Cassidy, Inc.
Statement of Financial Position
December 31, 2015 and 2014

DEMO DOC COMPLETE

Part 1   Part 2   **Demo Doc Complete**

 DECISION GUIDELINES

Financial Statement Analysis

The following guidelines can help you determine how best to analyze the financial statements of different companies.

DECISION	**GUIDELINE**	**ANALYZE**

DECISION

As the CEO, I need to present the performance of the organization to the board of directors. I know that we had a bad year, but I also know that we are in a good position compared to our competitors. How do I show this comparison to competitors that are all different sizes?

GUIDELINE

Use common-size financial statements.

ANALYZE

Common-size financial statements can be used to compare two different companies even if they are of dissimilar sizes. This is because common-size financial statements report financial statement items as percentages instead of as dollar amounts. The percentages for the two companies can be compared to see which company has the highest gross profit percentage and the lowest expense percentages.

Common-size financial statements can also be used to compare a company against the best companies in the industry. This is known as benchmarking. A business may not be able to achieve the same results as the industry leader, but benchmarking gives a company a goal to shoot for.

DECISION	GUIDELINE	ANALYZE
As a supplier, how can I check a customer's ability to pay their obligations as they come due in order to know whether or not to extend them credit?	Use liquidity ratios: • Working capital • Current ratio • Quick ratio	Monitoring a business's liquidity ratios can often provide an indicator that the business may experience cash flow problems. Action should be taken so that the business does not encounter difficulty meeting its obligations as they come due. For most businesses, a current ratio that drops below 1.50 or a quick ratio that drops below 0.90 may be cause for concern.
As the manager, how do I determine if the inventory and accounts receivable are being managed effectively?	Use asset management ratios: • Inventory turnover • Accounts receivable turnover • Days' sales in receivables	Monitoring the asset management ratios can provide an indicator that a business is not managing its inventory and accounts receivables effectively. A decrease in the inventory turnover may indicate that a business has obsolete inventory or that it is purchasing too much inventory. Carrying high levels of inventory results in decreased profits due to the increased costs associated with maintaining the increased inventory levels. A decrease in the accounts receivable turnover may be due to poor collection practices related to past due accounts. This can result in decreased profits for the business due to increased bad debts expense. The longer a receivable is past due, the less likely it is to be collected.
As an entrepreneur, the long-term health of my company revolves around making my debt payments. Will my business be able to service (pay off) its long-term debt?	Use solvency ratios: • Debt ratio • Times-interest-earned	Monitoring a company's solvency ratios can provide an indicator that the company may have difficulty servicing its long-term debt. In addition to creditors, a company's shareholders should pay attention to the solvency ratios. If a company is unable to pay back its creditors, there will be no value left in the company for the shareholders.
As an investor, how do I assess the profitability of a company that I'm interested in?	Use profitability ratios: • Return on sales • Return on assets • Return on common equity • Earnings per share	The profitability of a business over the long run is critical to the survival of the business. By monitoring the profitability ratios, potential problems can be detected early and steps can be taken to prevent business failure. Many companies that have failed have shown warning signs well in advance of the company's collapse.

Main Differences between IFRS and ASPE

POINT OF COMPARISON	IFRS	ASPE
Financial statement analysis	There are no significant differences between IFRS and ASPE regarding financial statement analysis. The only thing that would differ is in the presentation and classifications of financial statements, which have been covered in previous chapters.	

ACCOUNTING VOCABULARY

THE LANGUAGE OF BUSINESS

Accounts receivable turnover (p. 708)

Acid-test ratio (p. 706)

Asset management ratios (p. 705)

Benchmarking (p. 704)

Common-size statement (p. 702)

Current ratio (p. 706)

Days' sales in inventory (p. 708)

Days' sales in receivables (p. 708)

ACCOUNTING PRACTICE

DISCUSSION QUESTIONS

1. How is percentage change calculated?

2. Which amount is the base amount for vertical analysis on the income statement?

3. Which amount is the base amount for vertical analysis on the statement of financial position?

4. What is the purpose of common-size financial statements?

5. The Accounting Standards Board (AcSB) and the International Accounting Standards Board have identified the goal of comparability of financial statements as one toward which all companies should strive and consistency as the means toward achieving that goal. How are these characteristics important to horizontal and vertical analysis?

6. What is benchmarking? What should a company that wishes to use benchmarking look for in establishing benchmarks?

7. What are the major goals of each of the following types of ratios:
   a. Liquidity ratios
   b. Asset management ratios
   c. Solvency ratios
   d. Profitability ratios
   e. Market analysis ratios

8. How would you expect a recession to affect asset management ratios?

9. What is a "red flag" with respect to financial statement analysis?

10. A company has experienced increases in accounts receivable and inventory turnover ratios and has cash flows from operations that exceed net income. All other things constant, what could you conclude about the company's performance this year relative to last year?

SELF CHECK

1. Net income was $245,000 in 2013, $240,000 in 2014, and $276,000 in 2015. The change from 2014 to 2015 is an

   a. increase of 5%.
   b. increase of 10%.
   c. increase of 15%.
   d. increase of 20%.

2. Horizontal analysis of a financial statement shows

   a. the relationship of each statement item to a specified base.
   b. percentage changes in comparative statements of financial position.
   c. percentage changes in comparative income statements.
   d. both b and c.

3. A statement that reports only percentages is called

   a. a comparative statement.
   b. a common-size statement.
   c. a condensed statement.
   d. a cumulative statement.

4. Working capital is

   a. a measure of the ability to meet short-term obligations with current assets.
   b. defined as current assets minus current liabilities.
   c. defined as current assets divided by current liabilities.
   d. both a and b.

5. Cash is $15,000, net accounts receivable amount to $6,000, inventory is $10,000, prepaid expenses total $4,000, and current liabilities are $20,000. What is the quick ratio?

   a. 1.05
   b. 1.55
   c. 1.25
   d. 1.75

6. Days' sales in receivables is computed by

   a. dividing net sales by 365.
   b. dividing 365 by accounts receivable turnover.
   c. dividing sales by average net accounts receivable.
   d. dividing accounts receivable turnover ratio by 365.

7. Rubble Company is experiencing a severe cash shortage due to its inability to collect accounts receivable. Which of the following would most likely identify this problem?

   a. Current ratio
   b. Working capital
   c. Accounts receivable turnover
   d. Return on sales

8. Which of the following statements is *true* of financial statement analysis?

   a. Horizontal analysis expresses all items on a financial statement as percentages of a common base.
   b. Vertical analysis involves comparing amounts from one year's financial statements to another year's statements.
   c. Ratio analysis is more important than either horizontal or vertical analysis.
   d. None of the above.

9. Which statement is most likely to be *true*?

   a. An increase in inventory turnover indicates that inventory is not selling as quickly as it was.
   b. A decrease in inventory turnover indicates that inventory is not selling as quickly as it was.
   c. A change in inventory turnover cannot be accurately assessed without considering the change in profit margin.
   d. None of the above.

MyAccountingLab

The exercises and problems in this chapter can be found on MyAccountingLab. You can practise them as often as you want, and they feature step-by-step guided solutions to help you find the right answer.

10. How are financial ratios used in decision making?

a. They eliminate uncertainty regarding cash flows.

b. They can be used as a substitute for consulting financial statements.

c. They are only used in evaluating business liquidity.

d. They help to identify reasons for business success and failure.

Answers are given after Written Communication.

SHORT EXERCISES

S12-1. Corporate financial statements (*Learning Objective 1*) 5–10 min.

Identify whether each of the following items would be classified as:

- Income from continuing operations (C)
- Income from discontinued operations (D)
- A change in accounting principle (P)

_____ a. $2,500 gain on the sale of office furniture

_____ b. $18,000 increase in income as a result of changing from DDB depreciation to straight-line depreciation

_____ c. Income tax expense

_____ d. $85,000 loss incurred as a result of closing the Coeur d'Alene, Quebec store location

_____ e. $4,600 loss incurred as a result of a company vehicle being involved in an accident

S12-2. Horizontal analysis (*Learning Objective 2*) 10–15 min.

Aztec, Inc. had net sales of $250,000 and cost of goods sold of $150,000 in 2013, net sales of $275,000 and cost of goods sold of $165,000 in 2014, and net sales of $300,000 and cost of goods sold of $177,000 in 2015.

1. Find the percentage change in net sales from 2013 to 2014 and from 2014 to 2015.

2. Find the percentage change in gross profit from 2013 to 2014 and from 2014 to 2015.

S12-3. Vertical analysis (*Learning Objective 3*) 10–15 min.

The 2015 accounting records of Star Records showed the following: Cash, $15,000; Net Accounts Receivable, $8,000; Inventory, $5,000; Prepaid Expenses, $4,000; Net Plant and Equipment, $18,000.

Construct a vertical analysis of the asset section of Star Records' statement of financial position for 2015.

S12-4. Ratio definitions (*Learning Objective 5*) 10–15 min.

Match the following terms to their definitions:

_____1. Tells whether a company can pay all its current liabilities if they become due immediately

_____2. Measures a company's success in using assets to earn income

_____3. The practice of comparing a company with other companies that are leaders

_____4. Indicates how rapidly inventory is sold

_____5. Shows the proportion of a company's assets that is financed with debt

a. Inventory turnover

b. Return on sales

c. Quick ratio

d. Dividend yield

e. Return on assets

f. Accounts receivable turnover

g. Benchmarking

h. Debt ratio

_____6. Tells the percentage of a share's market value that the company returns to shareholders annually as dividends

_____7. A measure of profitability

_____8. Measures a company's ability to collect cash from credit customers

S12-5. Purpose of select ratios (*Learning Objective 5*) 10–15 min.

Identify each of the following financial ratios as follows:

- Profitability ratio (P)
- Asset management ratio (A)
- Liquidity ratio (L)
- Solvency ratio (S)

_____a. Inventory turnover

_____b. Debt ratio

_____c. Return on equity

_____d. Days' sales in receivables

_____e. Quick ratio

_____f. Return on assets

_____g. Return on sales

_____h. Receivables turnover

_____i. Current ratio

_____j. Earnings per share

_____k. Times-interest-earned ratio

S12-6. Accounts receivable turnover, days' sales in accounts receivable, and inventory turnover (*Learning Objective 5*) 10–15 min.

The 2014 and 2015 statements of financial position for Jackson and Sons showed net accounts receivable of $10,000 and $14,000, respectively, and inventory of $8,000 and $6,000, respectively. The company's 2015 income statement showed net sales of $109,500 and cost of goods sold of $70,000. Compute the following ratios for 2015:

1. Accounts receivable turnover
2. Days' sales in receivables
3. Inventory turnover

S12-7. Current ratio and quick ratio (*Learning Objective 5*) 10–15 min.

In addition to the information from S12-6, assume that cash on the 2015 statement of financial position was $20,000 and current liabilities totaled $24,000. Compute the following ratios for 2015:

1. Current ratio
2. Quick ratio

S12-8. Return on sales, return on assets, return on common equity, times-interest-earned ratio, and debt ratio (*Learning Objective 5*) 10–15 min.

The 2015 financial statements for Country Cousin Stores show total assets of $490,000, total liabilities of $290,000, net sales of $1,800,000, net income of $450,000, income from operations of $520,000, cost of goods sold of $1,080,000, preferred dividends of $225,000, and interest expense of $20,000. Total assets and total liabilities for 2014 were $430,000 and $270,000, respectively. Preferred equity for both years is $35,000. Compute the following ratios for 2015:

1. Return on sales

2. Return on assets

3. Return on common equity

4. Times-interest-earned ratio

5. Debt ratio

S12-9. EPS and price/earnings ratio (*Learning Objective 5*) 10–15 min.

Using the information from S12-8, a market price of $25 per common share, and 100,000 common shares outstanding, compute the following for 2015:

1. Earnings per share

2. Price/earnings ratio

S12-10. Dividend yield (*Learning Objective 5*) 10–15 min.

In 2015, common shareholders received $2 per share in annual dividends. The market price per share for common shares was $12. Compute the dividend yield for common shares.

EXERCISES (GROUP A)

E12-1A. Horizontal analysis (*Learning Objective 2*) 15–20 min.

What were the dollar and percentage changes in Axel's Pawn Shop's working capital during 2014 and 2015? Is this trend favourable or unfavourable?

	2015	2014	2013
Total Current Assets	$410,000	$380,000	$360,000
Total Current Liabilities	250,000	217,000	240,000

E12-2A. Horizontal analysis (*Learning Objective 2*) 15–20 min.

Prepare a horizontal analysis of the following comparative income statement of R. Hanson, Inc. Round percentage changes to the nearest tenth of a percent.

R. Hanson, Inc. Comparative Income Statement Years Ended December 31, 2015 and 2014		
	2015	**2014**
Revenue	$492,000	$447,600
Expenses:		
Cost of Goods Sold	242,000	226,000
Selling and General Expenses	117,600	111,600
Interest Expense	8,000	5,000
Income Tax Expense	50,500	44,600
Total Expenses	418,100	387,200
Net Income	$ 73,900	$ 60,400

Requirement

1. Why did net income increase by a higher percent than total revenues increased during 2015?

E12-3A. Horizontal analysis (*Learning Objective 2*) 15–20 min.

Compute trend percentages for net sales and net income for the following five-year period, using year 1 as the base year:

	Year 5	Year 4	Year 3	Year 2	Year 1
Net Sales.................	$2,405	$2,185	$2,125	$2,005	$2,045
Net Income	717	714	683	671	685

Requirement

1. Which grew faster during the period, net sales or net income?

E12-4A. Vertical analysis (*Learning Objective 3*) 15–20 min.

Lori's Boutique requested that you perform a vertical analysis of its statement of financial position to determine the component percentages of its assets, liabilities, and shareholders' equity. Round to the nearest tenth of a percent.

Lori's Boutique **Statement of Financial Position** **December 31, 2015**			
ASSETS		**LIABILITIES**	
Current Assets	$108,000	Current Liabilities	$ 87,000
Long-Term Investments	52,500	Long-Term Debt	177,000
Property, Plant, and		Total Liabilities	264,000
Equipment, Net	325,500		
		SHAREHOLDERS' EQUITY	
		Shareholders' Equity	222,000
		Liabilities and	
Total Assets	$486,000	Shareholders' Equity	$486,000

E12-5A. Common-size income statement (*Learning Objective 4*) 15–20 min.

Prepare a comparative common-size income statement for R. Hanson, Inc. using the 2015 and 2014 data of E12-2A. Round percentages to the nearest tenth of a percent.

E12-6A. Current ratio, quick ratio, inventory turnover, accounts receivable turnover, and days' sales in accounts receivable (*Learning Objective 5*) 15–20 min.

The financial statements of Hernandez & Sons, Inc. include the following items:

	Current Year	Previous Year
Statement of Financial Position		
Cash..	$ 27,000	$ 33,000
Short-Term Investments	22,000	28,000
Accounts Receivable, Net..	54,000	72,000
Inventory..	65,000	42,000
Prepaid Expenses..	7,000	9,000
Total Current Assets...	175,000	184,000
Total Current Liabilities	87,500	92,000
Income Statement		
Net Credit Sales...	$554,800	
Cost of Goods Sold	331,700	

Requirement

1. Compute the following ratios for the current year: (a) current ratio, (b) quick ratio, (c) inventory turnover, (d) accounts receivable turnover, and (e) days' sales in accounts receivable.

E12-7A. Current ratio, quick ratio, debt ratio, times-interest-earned ratio (*Learning Objective 5*) 15–20 min.

Brandy Pitts Winery requested that you determine whether the company's ability to pay its current liabilities and long-term debts improved or deteriorated during 2015. To answer this question, compute the following ratios for 2015 and 2014: (a) current ratio, (b) quick ratio, (c) debt ratio, and (d) times-interest-earned ratio. Summarize the results of your analysis.

	2015	2014
Cash	$ 32,000	$ 45,000
Short-Term Investments	35,000	–
Accounts Receivable, Net	130,000	142,000
Inventory	340,000	360,000
Prepaid Expenses	15,000	12,000
Total Assets	580,000	560,000
Total Current Liabilities	220,800	245,600
Long-Term Liabilities	24,200	29,400
Income From Operations	185,000	179,000
Interest Expense	42,000	44,000

E12-8A. Financial statement analysis (*Learning Objective 5*) 15–20 min.

For 2014 and 2015, compute the four ratios that measure the ability to earn profits for Fabulous Fashions, Inc., whose comparative income statement follows:

Fabulous Fashions, Inc.
Income Statement
Years Ended December 31, 2015 and 2014

	2015	2014
Net Sales	$261,000	$237,000
Cost of Goods Sold	140,000	132,000
Gross Profit	121,000	105,000
Selling and General Expenses	72,000	65,000
Income From Operations	49,000	40,000
Interest Expense	32,000	15,000
Income Before Income Tax	17,000	25,000
Income Tax Expense	5,000	8,000
Net Income	$ 12,000	$ 17,000

Additional data follow:

	2015	2014	2013
Total Assets	$320,000	$292,000	$282,000
Common Shareholders' Equity	$148,000	$140,000	$132,000
Preferred Dividends	$ 4,000	$ 4,000	
Number of Common Shares Outstanding	25,000	25,000	

Requirement

1. Did the company's operating performance improve or deteriorate during 2015?

E12-9A. Financial statement analysis (*Learning Objective 5*) 15–20 min.

Evaluate the common shares of TomCat Incorporated as an investment. Specifically, use the two market analysis ratios to determine whether the shares increased or decreased in attractiveness during the past year. Assume that TomCat Incorporated paid the full amount of preferred dividends.

Quick solution:

Price/earnings ratio = 22 in 2015 and 17.9 in 2014; Dividend yield = 2.0% in 2015 and 2.6% in 2014.

	2015	2014
Net Income	$ 87,000	$ 83,000
Total Dividends	48,000	48,000
Common Shareholders' Equity at Year-End (100,000 shares)	780,000	750,000
Preferred Shareholders' Equity, 6%, at Year-End (3,000 shares)	300,000	300,000
Market Price of Common Shares at Year-End	$ 15.18	$ 11.63

E12-10A. Complete financial statement given certain information (*Learning Objective 5*) 15–20 min.

The following data (dollar amounts in millions) are adapted from the financial statements of Valco, Inc.:

Total Current Assets	$12,201
Accumulated Depreciation	1,738
Total Liabilities	14,755
Preferred Shares	10
Debt Ratio	55.145%
Current Ratio	2.1

Requirement

1. Complete the following condensed statement of financial position. Report amounts rounded to the nearest $1 million:

Current Assets		$?
Property, Plant, and Equipment	$?	
Less: Accumulated Depreciation	(?)	?
Total Assets		$?
Current Liabilities		$?
Long-Term Liabilities		?
Shareholders' Equity		?
Total Liabilities and Shareholders' Equity		$?

EXERCISES (GROUP B)

E12-1B. Horizontal analysis (*Learning Objective 2*) 15–20 min.

What were the dollar and percentage changes in Hillary's Hair Salon's working capital during 2014 and 2015? Is this trend favourable or unfavourable?

	2015	2014	2013
Total Current Assets	$600,000	$320,000	$270,000
Total Current Liabilities	479,000	232,000	190,000

E12-2B. Horizontal analysis (*Learning Objective 2*) 15–20 min.

Prepare a horizontal analysis of the following comparative income statement of Zinkowski, Inc. Round percentage changes to the nearest tenth of a percent.

		2015	2014
Zinkowski, Inc.			
Comparative Income Statement			
Years Ended December 31, 2015 and 2014			
Revenue		$480,000	$411,100
Expenses:			
Cost of Goods Sold		$254,000	$226,000
Selling and General Expenses		110,000	105,500
Interest Expense		6,500	2,000
Income Tax Expense		46,600	45,000
Total Expenses		417,100	378,500
Net Income		$ 62,900	$ 32,600

Requirement

1. Why did net income increase by a higher percent than total revenues increased during 2015?

E12-3B. Horizontal analysis (*Learning Objective 2*) 15–20 min.

Compute trend percentages for net sales and net income for the following five-year period, using year 1 as the base year:

	Year 5	Year 4	Year 3	Year 2	Year 1
Net Sales.............	$2,332	$2,310	$2,266	$2,244	$2,200
Net Income	755	717	659	640	640

Requirement

1. Which grew faster during the period, net sales or net income?

E12-4B. Vertical analysis (*Learning Objective 3*) 15–20 min.

Mary's Gift Store requested that you perform a vertical analysis of its statement of financial position to determine the component percentages of its assets, liabilities, and shareholders' equity. Round to the nearest tenth of a percent.

Mary's Gift Store
Statement of Financial Position
December 31, 2015

ASSETS		LIABILITIES	
Total Current Assets	$192,000	Total Current Liabilities	$120,000
Long-Term Investments	38,500	Long-Term Debt	155,000
Property, Plant, and		Total Liabilities	275,000
Equipment, Net	330,500		
		SHAREHOLDERS' EQUITY	
		Total Shareholders' Equity	286,000
		Total Liabilities and	
Total Assets	$561,000	Shareholders' Equity	$561,000

E12-5B. Common-size income statement (*Learning Objective 4*) 15–20 min.

Prepare a comparative common-size income statement for Zinkowski, Inc. using the 2015 and 2014 data of E12-2B. Round percentages to the nearest tenth of a percent.

E12-6B. Current ratio, quick ratio, inventory turnover, accounts receivable turnover, and days' sales in accounts receivable (*Learning Objective 5*) 15–20 min.

The financial statements of Vacation, Inc. include the following items:

	Current Year	Previous Year
Statement of Financial Position		
Cash	$ 25,000	$ 37,000
Short-Term Investments	10,000	24,000
Accounts Receivable, Net	64,000	86,000
Inventory	80,000	47,000
Prepaid Expenses	4,000	16,000
Total Current Assets	183,000	210,000
Total Current Liabilities	95,000	90,000
Income Statement		
Net Credit Sales	$475,000	
Cost of Goods Sold	325,500	

Requirement

1. Compute the following ratios for the current year: (a) current ratio, (b) quick ratio, (c) inventory turnover, (d) accounts receivable turnover, and (e) days' sales in accounts receivable.

E12-7B. Current ratio, quick ratio, debt ratio, times-interest-earned ratio (*Learning Objective 5*) 15–20 min.

Hudson Crowe Winery requested that you determine whether the company's ability to pay its current liabilities and long-term debts improved or deteriorated during 2015. To answer this question, compute the following ratios for 2015 and 2014: (a) current ratio, (b) quick ratio, (c) debt ratio, and (d) times-interest-earned ratio. Summarize the results of your analysis.

	2015	2014
Cash	$ 41,000	$ 49,000
Short-Term Investments	50,000	—
Accounts Receivable, Net	90,000	156,000
Inventory	320,000	395,000
Total Assets	570,000	650,000
Total Current Liabilities	250,000	244,700
Long-Term Liabilities	30,200	32,000
Income From Operations	145,000	203,000
Interest Expense	46,000	40,000

E12-8B. Financial statement analysis (*Learning Objective 5*) 15–20 min.

For 2014 and 2015, compute the four ratios that measure the ability to earn profits for Waldorf Fashions, Inc., whose comparative income statement and additional data follow:

Waldorf Fashions, Inc.
Income Statement
Years Ended December 31, 2015 and 2014

	2015	2014
Net Sales	$320,000	$298,000
Cost of Goods Sold	134,000	139,000
Gross Profit	186,000	159,000
Selling and General Expenses	66,000	68,000
Income from Operations	120,000	91,000
Interest Expense	32,000	19,000
Income Before Income Tax	88,000	72,000
Income Tax Expense	10,000	7,000
Net Income	$ 78,000	$ 65,000

Additional data follow:

	2015	2014	2013
Total Assets	$330,000	$286,000	$290,000
Common Shareholders' Equity	$150,000	$142,000	$134,000
Preferred Dividends	$ 6,000	$ 6,000	
Number of Common Shares Outstanding	45,000	45,000	

Requirement

1. Did the company's operating performance improve or deteriorate during 2015?

E12-9B. Financial statement analysis (*Learning Objective 5*) 15–20 min.

Evaluate the common shares of Shamrock Incorporated as an investment. Specifically, use the two market analysis ratios to determine whether the shares increased or decreased in attractiveness during the past year. Assume that Shamrock Incorporated paid the full amount of preferred dividends.

	2015	2014
Net Income	$117,000	$113,000
Total Dividends	30,000	30,000
Common Shareholders' Equity at Year-End (130,000 shares)	887,000	800,000
Preferred Shareholders' Equity, 4%, at Year-End (3,700 shares)	370,000	370,000
Market Price of Common Shares at Year-End	$ 9.40	$ 11.63

E12-10B. Complete financial statement given certain information (*Learning Objective 5*) 15–20 min.

The following data (dollar amounts in millions) are adapted from the financial statements of Drawler, Inc.

Total Current Assets	$11,983
Accumulated Depreciation	1,429
Total Liabilities	15,200
Preferred Shares	8
Debt Ratio	77.79%
Current Ratio	1.4

Requirement

1. Complete the following condensed statement of financial position. Report amounts rounded to the nearest $1 million:

Current Assets		$?
Property, Plant, and Equipment	$?	
Less: Accumulated Depreciation..	(?)	?
Total Assets		$?
Current Liabilities..		$?
Long-Term Liabilities		?
Shareholders' Equity...		?
Total Liabilities and Shareholders' Equity..................................		$?

EXERCISES (ALTERNATES 1, 2, AND 3)

These alternative exercise sets are available for your practice benefit on **MyAccountingLab**.

PROBLEMS (GROUP A)

P12-1A. Horizontal and vertical analysis (*Learning Objectives 2 & 3*) 20–25 min.

Net sales, net income, and total assets for Majestic Clothing Emporium for a four-year period follow:

(in thousands)	2015	2014	2013	2012
Net Sales..	$480	$460	$420	$400
Net Income	31	30	22	20
Ending Total Assets	280	250	230	200

Requirements

1. Compute trend percentages for each item for the years 2012 through 2015. Use 2012 as the base year.

2. Compute the return on assets for the years 2013 through 2015, rounding to three decimal places.

3. Majestic's main competitor had a return on assets of just over 11% for the years 2013 through 2015. How does Majestic Clothing Emporium's return on assets compare with its main competitor?

P12-2A. Common-size financial statements and profitability ratios (*Learning Objectives 4 & 5*) 20–25 min.

Love Bug Used Auto Sales asked for your help in comparing the company's profit performance and financial position with the average for the auto sales industry. The proprietor has given you the company's income statement and statement of financial position as well as the industry average data for retailers of used autos.

Love Bug Used Auto Sales
Income Statement Compared with Industry Average
Year Ended December 31, 2015

		LOVE BUG	INDUSTRY AVERAGE
Net Sales		$521,000	100.0%
Cost of Goods Sold		331,000	62.1%
Gross Profit		190,000	37.9%
Operating Expenses		110,000	27.8%
Operating Income		80,000	10.1%
Other Expenses		3,000	0.4%
Net Income		$ 77,000	9.7%

Love Bug Used Auto Sales
Statement of Financial Position Compared with Industry Average
December 31, 2015

		LOVE BUG	INDUSTRY AVERAGE
Current Assets		$230,000	70.9%
Plant Assets, Net		49,000	23.6%
Intangible Assets, Net		3,000	0.8%
Other Assets		15,000	4.7%
Total Assets		$297,000	100.0%
Current Liabilities		$136,000	48.1%
Long-Term Liabilities		41,000	16.6%
Shareholders' Equity		120,000	35.3%
Total Liabilities and Shareholders' Equity		$297,000	100.0%

Requirements

1. Prepare a two-column, common-size income statement and a two-column, common-size statement of financial position for Love Bug Used Auto Sales. The first column of each statement should present Love Bug Used Auto Sales' common-size statement and the second column should show the industry averages.

2. For the profitability analysis, examine Love Bug Used Auto Sales' (a) ratio of gross profit to net sales, (b) ratio of operating income to net sales, and (c) ratio of net income to net sales. Compare these figures with the industry averages. Is Love Bug's profit performance better or worse than the industry average?

3. For the analysis of financial position, examine Love Bug Used Auto Sales' (a) ratio of current assets to total assets, and (b) ratio of shareholders' equity to total assets. Compare these ratios with the industry averages. Is Love Bug Used Auto Sales' financial position better or worse than the industry average?

P12-3A. Current ratio, debt ratio, EPS (*Learning Objective 5*) 20–25 min.

Financial statement data of Barb Wired Fencing, Inc. include the following items:

Cash...	$ 17,000
Short-Term Investments...	22,000
Accounts Receivable, Net..	103,000
Inventory...	119,000
Prepaid Expenses..	10,000
Total Assets	660,000
Short-Term Notes Payable...	45,000
Accounts Payable..	105,000
Accrued Liabilities...	40,000
Long-Term Notes Payable...	158,000
Other Long-Term Liabilities	33,000
Net Income	75,000
Number of Common Shares Outstanding	35,000 shares

Requirements

1. Compute Barb Wired Fencing's current ratio, debt ratio, and earnings per share. Assume that the company had no preferred shares outstanding. Round all ratios to two decimal places.

2. Compute each of the same three ratios after evaluating the effect of each transaction that follows.

    a. Purchased merchandise of $38,000 on account, debiting Inventory.

    b. Issued 2,000 common shares, receiving cash of $80,000.

    c. Borrowed $80,000 on a long-term note payable.

    d. Received cash on account, $22,000.

Quick solution:

1. Current ratio = 1.43;
debt ratio = 0.58;
earnings per share = $2.14

P12-4A. Calculate various ratios for analysis (*Learning Objective 5*) 20–25 min.

Comparative financial statement data of Lounge Around Furniture Company follow:

Lounge Around Furniture Company Income Statement Years Ended December 31, 2015 and 2014		
	2015	**2014**
Net Sales	$482,000	$457,000
Cost of Goods Sold	238,000	229,000
Gross Profit	244,000	228,000
Operating Expenses	140,000	138,000
Income from Operations	104,000	90,000
Interest Expense	12,000	14,000
Income Before Income Tax	92,000	76,000
Income Tax Expense	28,000	23,000
Net Income	$ 64,000	$ 53,000

Lounge Around Furniture Company
Statement of Financial Position
December 31, 2015 and 2014
(Selected 2013 amounts given for computation of ratios)

	2015	2014	2013
Current Assets:			
Cash	$ 98,000	$ 99,000	
Accounts Receivable, Net	108,000	112,000	$104,000
Inventory	164,000	154,000	185,000
Prepaid Expenses	28,000	20,000	
Total Current Assets	398,000	385,000	
Property, Plant, and Equipment, Net	191,000	180,000	
Total Assets	$589,000	$565,000	
Total Current Liabilities	$208,000	$228,000	
Long-Term Liabilities	121,000	117,000	
Total Liabilities	329,000	345,000	
Preferred Shareholders' Equity, 8%	100,000	100,000	
Common Shareholders' Equity	160,000	120,000	100,000
Total Liabilities and Shareholders' Equity	$589,000	$565,000	

Other information follows:

a. Market price of common shares was $48 at December 31, 2015, and $30.75 at December 31, 2014.

b. Common shares outstanding were 10,000 during 2015 and 9,000 during 2014.

c. All sales were made on credit.

d. The full amount of preferred dividends was paid.

Requirements

1. Compute the following ratios for 2015 and 2014:

    a. Current ratio

    b. Inventory turnover

    c. Accounts receivable turnover

    d. Times-interest-earned ratio

    e. Return on common shareholders' equity

    f. Earnings per share of common shares

    g. Price/earnings ratio

2. Decide (a) whether Lounge Around Furniture Company's financial position improved or deteriorated during 2015, and (b) whether the investment attractiveness of its common shares appears to have increased or decreased.

3. How will what you learned in this problem help you evaluate an investment?

P12-5A. Calculate various ratios for analysis (*Learning Objective 5*) 20–25 min.

Assume you are purchasing an investment and decide to invest in a company in the home remodelling business. You narrow the choice to Build It Right, Inc. or Structurally Sound, Corp. You assemble the following selected data.

Selected income statement data for the current year follow:

	Build It Right, Inc.	Structurally Sound, Corp.
Net Sales (all on credit)	$298,000	$223,000
Cost of Goods Sold	155,000	125,000
Income from Operations.............................	83,000	47,000
Interest Expense	13,000	—
Net Income	43,000	29,000

Selected statement of financial position and market price data at the end of the current year follow:

	Build It Right, Inc.	Structurally Sound, Corp.
Current Assets:		
Cash	$ 12,000	$ 13,000
Short-Term Investments	11,000	12,000
Accounts Receivable, Net	28,000	25,000
Inventory	60,000	52,000
Prepaid Expenses	2,000	1,000
Total Current Assets..............................	113,000	103,000
Total Assets	197,000	159,000
Total Current Liabilities	59,000	65,000
Total Liabilities	79,000	65,000
Preferred Shares, 5%	20,000	
Common Shares, 6,000 Shares		6,000
3,000 Shares	7,500	
Total Shareholders' Equity	118,000	94,000
Market price per share of common shares..	$ 67	$ 31

Selected statement of financial position data at the beginning of the current year follow:

	Build It Right, Inc.	Structurally Sound, Corp.
Accounts Receivable, Net	$ 29,000	$ 24,000
Inventory	53,000	56,000
Total Assets	162,000	155,000
Preferred Shares, 5%, 200 shares	20,000	
Common Shares, 6,000 Shares		6,000
3,000 Shares	7,500	
Total Shareholders' Equity	76,000	71,000

Your investment strategy is to purchase the shares of the company that has a low price/earnings ratio but appears to be in good shape financially. Assume that you analyzed all other factors and your decision depends on the results of the ratio analysis to be performed.

Requirement

1. Compute the following ratios for both companies for the current year and decide which company's shares better fits your investment strategy.

   a. Quick ratio

   b. Inventory turnover

   c. Days' sales in receivables

   d. Debt ratio

   e. Earnings per share of common shares

   f. Price/earnings ratio

P12-6A. Financial statement ratio analysis (*Learning Objective 5*) 20–25 min.

You have been hired as an investment analyst at McNeice Securities, Inc. It is your job to recommend investments for your client. The only information you have are the following ratio values for two companies in the video game industry:

Ratio	Tomb Crater, Co.	Resident Upheaval, Inc.
Days to collect receivables	46	52
Inventory turnover	8	10
Gross profit percentage	67%	59%
Net income as a percent of sales	15%	21%
Times-interest-earned ratio	16	12
Return on equity	35%	26%
Return on assets	13%	18%

Requirement

1. Write a memo to your client recommending the company you believe to be a more attractive investment. Explain the reasons for your recommendation.

PROBLEMS (GROUP B)

P12-1B. Horizontal and vertical analysis (*Learning Objectives 2 & 3*) 20–25 min.

Net sales, net income, and total assets for Regal Clothing Emporium for a four-year period follow:

(in thousands)	2015	2014	2013	2012
Net Sales...	$1,350	$1,200	$1,150	$1,025
Net Income	82	77	53	49
Ending Total Assets	650	620	550	500

Requirements

1. Compute trend percentages for each item for the years 2012 through 2015. Use 2012 as the base year.
2. Compute the return on assets for the years 2013 through 2015, rounding to three decimal places.
3. Regal's main competitor had a return on assets of just under 12% for the years 2013 through 2015. How does Regal Clothing Emporium's return on assets compare with its main competitor?

P12-2B. Common-size financial statements and profitability ratios (*Learning Objectives 3 & 4*) 20–25 min.

Verifine Used Auto Sales asked for your help in comparing the company's profit performance and financial position with the average for the auto sales industry. The proprietor has given you the company's income statement and statement of financial position as well as the industry average data for retailers of used autos.

Verifine Used Auto Sales
Income Statement Compared with Industry Average
Year Ended December 31, 2015

		VERIFINE	INDUSTRY AVERAGE
Net Sales		$548,000	100.0%
Cost of Goods Sold		348,528	62.1%
Gross Profit		199,472	37.9%
Operating Expenses		122,752	27.8%
Operating Income		76,720	10.1%
Other Expenses		1,096	0.4%
Net Income		$ 75,624	9.7%

Verifine Used Auto Sales
Statement of Financial Position Compared with Industry Average
December 31, 2015

		VERIFINE	INDUSTRY AVERAGE
Current Assets		$229,034	70.9%
Plant Assets, Net		50,830	23.6%
Intangible Assets, Net		8,970	0.8%
Other Assets		10,166	4.7%
Total Assets		$299,000	100.0%
Current Liabilities		$118,105	48.1%
Long-Term Liabilities		50,830	16.6%
Shareholders' Equity		130,065	35.3%
Total Liabilities and Shareholders' Equity		$299,000	100.0%

Requirements

1. Prepare a two-column, common-size income statement and a two-column, common-size statement of financial position for Verifine Used Auto Sales. The first column of each statement should present Verifine Used Auto Sales' common-size statement and the second column should show the industry averages.

2. For the profitability analysis, examine Verifine Used Auto Sales' (a) ratio of gross profit to net sales, (b) ratio of operating income to net sales, and (c) ratio of net income to net sales. Compare these figures with the industry averages. Is Verifine Used Auto Sales' profit performance better or worse than the industry average?

3. For the analysis of financial position, examine Verifine Used Auto Sales' (a) ratio of current assets to total assets, and (b) ratio of shareholders' equity to total assets. Compare these ratios with the industry averages. Is Verifine Used Auto Sales' financial position better or worse than the industry average?

P12-3B. Current ratio, debt ratio, EPS (*Learning Objective 5*) 20–25 min.

Financial statement data of ABC Fencing, Inc. include the following items:

Cash..	$ 21,000
Short-Term Investments...	25,000
Accounts Receivable, Net..	102,000
Inventory...	121,000
Prepaid Expenses..	15,000
Total Assets	660,500
Short-Term Notes Payable...	45,000
Accounts Payable...	106,000
Accrued Liabilities..	44,000
Long-Term Notes Payable..	160,000
Other Long-Term Liabilities	37,000
Net Income	77,000
Number of Common Shares Outstanding	37,000 shares

Requirements

1. Compute ABC Fencing's current ratio, debt ratio, and earnings per share. Assume that the company had no preferred shares outstanding. Round all ratios to two decimal places.

2. Compute each of the same three ratios after evaluating the effect of each transaction that follows:

   a. Purchased merchandise of $40,000 on account, debiting Inventory.

   b. Issued 2,000 common shares, receiving cash of $78,000.

   c. Borrowed $78,000 on a long-term note payable.

   d. Received cash on account, $18,000.

P12-4B. Calculate various ratios for analysis (*Learning Objective 5*) 20–25 min.

Comparative financial statement data of Danfield Furniture Company follow:

Danfield Furniture Company Income Statement Years Ended December 31, 2015 and 2014			
		2015	**2014**
	Net Sales	$483,000	$458,000
	Cost of Goods Sold	244,000	234,000
	Gross Profit	239,000	224,000
	Operating Expenses	145,000	137,000
	Income from Operations	94,000	87,000
	Interest Expense	14,000	24,000
	Income Before Income Tax	80,000	63,000
	Income Tax Expense	28,000	24,000
	Net Income	$ 52,000	$ 39,000

Danfield Furniture Company
Statement of Financial Position
December 31, 2015 and 2014
(Selected 2013 amounts given for computation of ratios)

	2015	2014	2013
Current Assets:			
Cash	$ 95,000	$ 98,000	
Accounts Receivable, Net	104,000	114,000	$107,000
Inventory	161,000	151,000	193,000
Prepaid Expenses	38,000	28,000	
Total Current Assets	398,000	391,000	
Property, Plant, and Equipment, Net	196,000	175,000	
Total Assets	$594,000	$566,000	
Total Current Liabilities	$212,000	$228,000	
Long-Term Liabilities	129,000	116,000	
Total Liabilities	341,000	344,000	
Preferred Shareholders' Equity, 8%	99,000	99,000	
Common Shareholders' Equity	154,000	123,000	97,000
Total Liabilities and Shareholders' Equity	$594,000	$566,000	

Other information follows:

1. Market price of common shares was $48.50 at December 31, 2015, and $31.75 at December 31, 2014.

2. Common shares outstanding were 17,000 during 2015 and 15,000 during 2014.

3. All sales were made on credit.

4. The full amount of preferred dividends was paid.

Requirements

1. Compute the following ratios for 2015 and 2014:

   a. Current ratio

   b. Inventory turnover

   c. Accounts receivable turnover

   d. Times-interest-earned ratio

   e. Return on common shareholders' equity

   f. Earnings per share of common shares

   g. Price/earnings ratio

2. Decide (a) whether Danfield Furniture Company's financial position improved or deteriorated during 2015, and (b) whether the investment attractiveness of its common shares appears to have increased or decreased.

3. How will what you learned in this problem help you evaluate an investment?

P12-5B. Calculate various ratios for analysis (*Learning Objective 5*) 20–25 min.

Assume you are purchasing an investment and decide to invest in a company in the home remodelling business. You narrow the choice to Bob's Home Repair, Inc. or Stellar Stability, Corp. You assemble the following selected data.

Selected income statement data for the current year follow:

	Bob's Home Repair, Inc.	Stellar Stability, Corp.
Net Sales (all on credit)	$282,000	$226,000
Cost of Goods Sold	158,000	129,000
Income from Operations	88,000	48,000
Interest Expense	15,000	—
Net Income	44,000	24,000

Selected statement of financial position and market price data at the end of the current year follow:

	Bob's Home Repair, Inc.	Stellar Stability, Corp.
Current Assets:		
Cash	$ 13,000	$ 14,000
Short-Term Investments	12,000	15,000
Accounts Receivable, Net	30,000	25,000
Inventory	69,000	50,000
Prepaid Expenses	5,000	4,000
Total Current Assets	129,000	108,000
Total Assets	201,000	166,000
Total Current Liabilities	54,000	68,000
Total Liabilities	80,000	71,000
Preferred Shares, 5%, 180 shares	18,000	
Common Shares, 7,000 Shares		7,000
4,000 Shares	10,000	
Total Shareholders' Equity	121,000	95,000
Market price per common share	$ 43.12	$ 30.87

Selected statement of financial position data at the beginning of the current year follow:

	Bob's Home Repair, Inc.	Stellar Stability, Corp.
Accounts Receivable, Net	$ 29,000	$ 26,000
Inventory	52,000	62,000
Total Assets	162,000	157,000
Preferred Shares, 5% (180 shares)	18,000	
Common Shares, 7,000 Shares		7,000
4,000 Shares	10,000	
Total Shareholders' Equity	77,000	72,000

Your investment strategy is to purchase the shares of the company that has a low price/earnings ratio but appears to be in good shape financially. Assume that you analyzed all other factors and your decision depends on the results of the ratio analysis to be performed.

Requirement

1. Compute the following ratios for both companies for the current year and decide which company's shares better fit your investment strategy.

   a. Quick ratio

   b. Inventory turnover

   c. Days' sales in receivables

d. Debt ratio

e. Earnings per share of common shares

f. Price/earnings ratio

P12-6B. Financial statement ratio analysis (*Learning Objective 5*) 20–25 min.

You have been hired as an investment analyst at Harriet Winston Company. It is your job to recommend investments for your client. The only information you have are the following ratio values for two companies in the video game industry.

Ratio	Mario and Luco, Co.	Witches and Warlocks, Inc.
Days to collect receivables	60	54
Inventory turnover	10	8
Gross profit percentage	69%	75%
Net income as a percent of sales	17%	11%
Times-interest-earned ratio	14	18
Return on equity	37%	45%
Return on assets	15%	13%

Requirement

1. Write a memo to your client recommending the company you believe to be a more attractive investment. Explain the reasons for your recommendation.

PROBLEMS (ALTERNATES 1, 2, AND 3)

These alternative problem sets are available for your practice benefit on **MyAccountingLab**.

CONTINUING EXERCISE

This concludes the accounting for Graham's Yard Care, Inc. that we began in Chapter 1. For this exercise, refer to the comparative statement of financial position that was presented in the Continuing Exercise in Chapter 11.

Requirements

1. Prepare a horizontal analysis of the statement of financial position for Graham's Yard Care, Inc.

2. Prepare a vertical analysis of the statement of financial position for Graham's Yard Care, Inc.

CONTINUING PROBLEM

In Chapter 11, we prepared a statement of cash flows for Aqua Elite, Inc. Now, we will analyze Aqua Elite's financial statements using the tools we learned in this chapter.

Following are the statements of financial position for the months ended July 31 and June 30, 2015, and the income statement for the month ended July 31, 2015, for Aqua Elite, Inc.

Aqua Elite, Inc.
Comparative Statement of Financial Position
July 31 and June 30, 2015

		JULY 31	JUNE 30
Assets			
Cash		$ 5,333	$3,270
Accounts Receivable, Net		2,280	1,000
Inventory		4,175	180
Supplies		105	125
Total Current Assets		11,893	4,575
Fixed Assets		67,250	2,250
Less: Accumulated Depreciation		(352)	(47)
Net Fixed Assets		66,898	2,203
Total Assets		$78,791	$6,778
Liabilities			
Accounts Payable		$ 1,805	$ 450
Unearned Revenue		5,800	2,000
Salaries Payable		950	900
Interest Payable		375	17
Payroll Taxes Payable		188	—
Dividend Payable		500	—
Current Portion of Long-Term Debt		4,410	2,000
Total Current Liabilities		14,028	5,367
Notes Payable		20,000	—
Mortgage Payable		42,590	—
Total Liabilities		76,618	5,367
Shareholders' Equity			
Common Shares		1,000	1,000
Retained Earnings		1,173	411
Total Shareholders' Equity		2,173	1,411
Total Liabilities & Shareholders' Equity		$78,791	$6,778

Aqua Elite, Inc.
Income Statement
Month Ended July 31, 2015

Revenue		$6,300
Expenses:		
Cost of Goods Sold		1,080
Depreciation Expense		305
Bad Debt Expense		220
Interest Expense		375
Insurance Expense		150
Supplies Expense		210
Salaries Expense		2,400
Payroll Taxes Expense		268
Bank Service Fees		30
Net Income*		$1,262

*Income taxes ignored

Requirements

1. Prepare a vertical analysis of the income statement using a multi-step income statement.

2. Calculate the current ratio for Aqua Elite, Inc. at July 31, 2015.

3. Calculate the quick ratio for Aqua Elite, Inc. at July 31, 2015.

4. Why do you think the current and quick ratios are unfavourable? Do you believe that this is a temporary problem or a long-term problem?

APPLY YOUR KNOWLEDGE

ETHICS IN ACTION

Case 1.   Robin Peterson, the CEO of Teldar Incorporated, was reviewing the financial statements for the first three months of the year. He saw that sales and net income were lower than expected. Because the reported net income and the related earnings per share were below expectations, the price of the shares declined. Robin held a meeting with top management and expressed his concerns over the declining trend in sales and income. He stated that the reduced profitability meant that he needed to formulate a plan to somehow increase the earnings per share. The vice president of marketing suggested that more advertising might help sales increase. Robin stated that spending more money on advertising would not guarantee an increase in sales. Then he announced that the excess company cash would instead be used to buy back outstanding common shares; this move would help increase the earnings per share because fewer shares would be outstanding. Robin reminded everyone that the yearly financial statements would be analyzed and the current year would be compared to previous years' results. He then stated that the treasury shares would lower the total shareholders' equity, which could then provide a stronger EPS so the current year would not look as bad. Finally, Robin reminded everyone that with fewer shares outstanding, the dividend per share could be increased and that would help make Teldar shares more attractive. The CFO argued that buying back shares merely to increase performance measures such as EPS was manipulative and unethical, and financial analysts would easily see what Teldar was trying to do.

Why did the CEO want to repurchase shares of Teldar common shares? Would the repurchase of common shares really have any impact on the financial ratios? Would an investor or financial analyst be able to see that financial performance measures were improved because of the share repurchase? Are any ethical issues involved? Were the concerns expressed by the CFO valid? Do you have any other thoughts?

Case 2.   Crane Corporation was in the process of completing the financial statements for the latest fiscal year. Susan Randal, Crane's CEO, was reviewing the comparative financial statements and expressed some concerns. In comparing the current year's income statement against those of the prior years, she noticed that total sales had decreased slightly. Further, salaries expense had increased while the advertising and research and development expenses had decreased. Although the total operating expenses were essentially the same, Susan was concerned that the increased salaries expense would be questioned by the investors and financial analysts in light of the decreases in advertising and research and development. She knew that the lower sales would be blamed on reduced advertising and less spending on research and development. As a result, Susan ordered the accountants to issue a condensed income statement that would present all operating expenses as a single amount. Also, during the year Crane Corporation had purchased another company for a price higher than the total fair market value of the purchased business. Crane properly recorded the excess cost as goodwill, but the total amount of goodwill had increased substantially because of this purchase. Susan was concerned that this rather large increase in goodwill would be seen as an unnecessary purchase and investors and analysts would become upset. Thus, Susan ordered that the goodwill be lumped in with the other assets rather than listed separately on the statement of financial position where it could easily be seen. The accountants argued that attempting to hide these items from investors and analysts would be unethical. They further argued that IFRS and ASPE required full disclosure, and that if Susan insisted on providing condensed statements, details would need to be provided in the footnotes anyway. Susan reluctantly agreed to the disclosure, knowing that often footnotes are not read.

Why would Susan want all the operating expenses lumped together? Why would Susan want the goodwill included as other assets? Were the ethical concerns raised by the accountants valid? Are any ethical issues involved in providing condensed information with the details included in the footnotes? Do you have any additional thoughts?

KNOW YOUR BUSINESS

FINANCIAL ANALYSIS

Purpose: To help familiarize you with the financial reporting of a real company to further your understanding of the chapter material you are learning.

This case focuses on the financial statement analysis of Bombardier Inc. Recall from the chapter that stakeholders use numerous ways to analyze and, thus, better understand the financial position and results of operations of a company. Tools such as vertical and horizontal analyses are available. In addition, financial ratios can be used to gain further insight into areas such as liquidity and profitability. Other measures include earnings per share and ratios that consider the share price of the company. Finally, nonfinancial information provides additional insights into the performance and financial position of the company. We will now apply some of the analytical tools contained in the chapter. Refer to the Bombardier Annual Report, Year Ended December 31, 2012, found in MyAccountingLab.

Requirements

1. Perform a vertical analysis on the income statements (Consolidated Statements of Operations). Discuss your results. What benefit do you see in performing this analysis? Perform a horizontal analysis of the statements of financial position (Consolidated Statements of Financial Position). Discuss your results. What benefit do you see in performing this analysis?

2. Look at the income statements (Consolidated Statements of Income). Can you find the Basic EPS for each fiscal year presented? Has the Basic Earnings per Share increased or decreased each year? Why do you think the Basic EPS has been changing?

3. Compute the return on assets and the return on equity ratios for 2012 and 2011. Use only the ending amount for total assets and shareholders' equity instead of the average to calculate ROA and ROE for both years. Has Bombardier Inc.'s profitability improved or deteriorated?

INDUSTRY ANALYSIS

Purpose: To help you understand and compare the performance of two companies in the same industry.

Find the Bombardier Annual Report, Year Ended December 31, 2012 located in MyAccountingLab. Now access The Boeing Company's 2012 Annual Report. To do this from the internet, go to their webpage for the Investor Relations at http://www.boeing.com/companyoffices/financial/quarterly.htm and under Annual Report, go to the 2012 Annual Report.

Requirement

1. In your opinion and based on what you have learned from this chapter, to which company would you offer a short-term loan? And based on these data, which company would you invest in?

SMALL BUSINESS ANALYSIS

Purpose: To help you understand the importance of financial statement analysis in the operation of a small business.

You just returned from a meeting with your bank loan officer and you were a little taken aback by his comments. You've been doing business with this bank for a number of years and he always seemed happy with your company's performance. This is why you can't understand the bank's hesitation to continue extending credit to your company. At this meeting, you had supplied him with the current year's financial information and even ran some of the financial ratios that you know the bank asks about. You thought the numbers looked decent for the current year, maybe not the best, but decent. Sure, sales had fallen a little bit since the previous year, but they were still pretty good. So when the discussion turned to a comparison of the last couple of year's financial information with this year's, you had to question what that has to do with anything. "Why shouldn't each and every year stand by itself?" you asked the banker. His comments to you were, "A company's performance is best evaluated by examining more than one year's data. This is why most financial statements cover at least two periods. In fact, most financial analysis covers trends of up to five years." He also said that a company's performance is best evaluated by comparing it against its own past performance, the performance of competitors, and the industry averages for the industry the company is in.

Requirement

1. Below are some selected financial data from the last four years. Calculate the trend percentages using 2012 as the base year and the return on sales for these four years and see if you can figure out what the concern is that the banker has for the financial health of your company.

	2015	2014	2013	2012
Total Sales	1,010,000	1,050,000	1,080,000	1,000,000
Total Expenses...	896,000	888,000	880,000	800,000
Net Income	114,000	162,000	200,000	200,000

WRITTEN COMMUNICATION

Below are selected financial data for your client for the current year and corresponding data for the client's industry.

	Company	Industry
Return on Sales	12.5%	10.0%
Return on Assets	23.0%	20.0%
Current Ratio..	1.6	1.5
Inventory Turnover	8.5	7.1
Accounts Receivable Turnover.......................................	8.5	11.0
Days Sales in Receivables..	42.9	33.2
Debt Ratio	0.6	0.5

Requirement

1. Write a memo to your client comparing his or her business to the industry averages and explain to the client the value of common-size financial statements.

COMPREHENSIVE PROBLEM FOR CHAPTERS 11–12

ANALYZING A COMPANY FOR ITS INVESTMENT POTENTIAL

In its annual report, BALLI Supply includes the following five-year financial summary:

BALLI Supply, Inc.
Five-Year Financial Summary (partial)

(Dollar Amounts in Thousands Except per Share Data)	2015	2014	2013	2012	2011
Net Sales	$244,524	$217,799	$191,329	$165,013	$137,634
Net Sales Increase	12%	14%	16%	20%	17%
% of Store Increase	5%	6%	5%	8%	9%
Other Income, Net	$ 2,001	$ 1,873	$ 1,787	$ 1,615	$ 1,391
Cost of Goods Sold	191,838	171,562	150,255	129,664	108,725
Selling, General, and					
Administrative Expenses	41,043	36,173	31,550	27,040	22,363
Interest Costs:					
Interest Expense	1,063	1,357	1,383	1,045	803
Interest Income	(138)	(171)	(188)	(204)	(189)
Net Income	8,039	6,671	6,295	5,377	4,430
Per Share of Common Shares:					
Net Income	1.81	1.49	1.41	1.21	0.99
Dividends	0.30	0.28	0.24	0.20	0.16
Financial Position					
Current Assets	$ 30,483	$ 27,878	$ 26,555	$ 24,356	$ 21,132
Inventories at FIFO Cost	24,891	22,614	21,442	19,793	17,076
Net Property, Plant, and Equipment	51,904	45,750	40,934	35,969	25,973
Total Assets	94,685	83,527	78,130	70,349	49,996
Current Liabilities	32,617	27,282	28,949	25,803	16,762
Long-Term Debt	19,608	18,732	15,655	16,674	9,607
Shareholders' Equity	39,337	35,102	31,343	25,834	21,112
Financial Ratios					
Current ratio	0.9	1.0	0.9	0.9	1.3
Return on assets	9.2%	8.5%	8.7%	9.5%	9.6%
Return on shareholders' equity	21.6%	20.1%	22.0%	22.9%	22.4%

Requirement

1. Analyze the company's financial summary for the fiscal years 2011 through 2015 to decide whether to invest in the common shares of BALLI. Include the following sections in your analysis, and fully explain your final decision.

   a. Trend analysis for net sales and net income (use 2011 as the base year)

   b. Profitability analysis

   c. Measuring ability to sell inventory

   d. Measuring ability to pay debts

   e. Measuring dividends

Appendix A

BOMBARDIER ANNUAL REPORT FOR THE FISCAL YEAR ENDED DECEMBER 31, 2012

MyAccountingLab

The Financial and Industry Analysis questions at the end of each chapter feature one company, Bombardier, allowing students to see how chapter concepts are connected. The financial statements for Bombardier can be found on MyAccountingLab.

Appendix B

TIME VALUE OF MONEY—FUTURE AND PRESENT VALUE CONCEPTS

Money earns interest over time, a fact called the **time value of money**. The time value of money idea is based on the thought that $1 today is worth more than $1 in the future. This is because $1 today can be invested and earn interest and therefore become worth more than $1 at a later date.

FUTURE VALUE

Future value refers to the amount that a given sum of money will be "worth" at a specified time in the future assuming a certain interest rate. The main application of future value is calculating the future value of an amount invested today (a present value) that earns a constant rate of interest over time. For example, assume that you invest $4,545 and it earns 10% interest per year. After one year, the $4,545 invested grows to a future value of $5,000, as shown next.

If the money were invested for two years, you would have to perform five such calculations. You would also have to consider the compound interest your investment is earning. **Compound interest** is the interest you earn not only on your principal amount, but also on the interest to date. Most business applications include compound interest. The following table shows the interest calculations for the first two years:

End of Year	Interest	Future Value
0	—	$4,545
1	$4,545 × 0.10 = $455	5,000
2	5,000 × 0.10 = 500	5,500

Earning 10%, a $4,545 investment grows to $5,000 at the end of one year, to $5,500 at the end of two years. (Throughout this discussion, we round dollar amounts to the nearest dollar.)

Future-Value Tables

Mathematical tables make computing a future value easy. **Table B-1** shows the table used to calculate the future value of $1 for various interest rates over various time periods. Future value depends on three factors:

❶ The amount of the investment

❷ The length of time the amount is invested

❸ The interest rate

The heading in Table B-1 states that the future value of $1 is being calculated. Future-value and present-value tables are based on $1 because $1 is so easy to work with.

									Future value of $1 per period at i% for n periods, FVIF$_{(i,n)}$											
n	1%	2%	3%	3.5%	4%	4.5%	5%	6%	7%	8%	9%	10%	11%	12%	13%	14%	15%	16%	18%	20%	25%
1	1.0100	1.0200	1.0300	1.0350	1.0400	1.0450	1.0500	1.0600	1.0700	1.0800	1.0900	1.1000	1.1100	1.1200	1.1300	1.1400	1.1500	1.1600	1.1800	1.2000	1.2500
2	1.0201	1.0404	1.0609	1.0712	1.0816	1.0920	1.1025	1.1236	1.1449	1.1664	1.1881	1.2100	1.2321	1.2544	1.2769	1.2996	1.3225	1.3456	1.3924	1.4400	1.5625
3	1.0303	1.0612	1.0927	1.1087	1.1249	1.1412	1.1576	1.1910	1.2250	1.2597	1.2950	1.3310	1.3676	1.4049	1.4429	1.4815	1.5209	1.5609	1.6430	1.7280	1.9531
4	1.0406	1.0824	1.1255	1.1475	1.1699	1.1925	1.2155	1.2625	1.3108	1.3605	1.4116	1.4641	1.5181	1.5735	1.6305	1.6890	1.7490	1.8106	1.9388	2.0736	2.4414
5	1.0510	1.1041	1.1593	1.1877	1.2167	1.2462	1.2763	1.3382	1.4026	1.4693	1.5386	1.6105	1.6851	1.7623	1.8424	1.9254	2.0114	2.1003	2.2878	2.4883	3.0518
6	1.0615	1.1262	1.1941	1.2293	1.2653	1.3023	1.3401	1.4185	1.5007	1.5869	1.6771	1.7716	1.8704	1.9738	2.0820	2.1950	2.3131	2.4364	2.6996	2.9860	3.8147
7	1.0721	1.1487	1.2299	1.2723	1.3159	1.3609	1.4071	1.5036	1.6058	1.7138	1.8280	1.9487	2.0762	2.2107	2.3526	2.5023	2.6600	2.8262	3.1855	3.5832	4.7684
8	1.0829	1.1717	1.2668	1.3168	1.3686	1.4221	1.4775	1.5938	1.7182	1.8509	1.9926	2.1436	2.3045	2.4760	2.6584	2.8526	3.0590	3.2784	3.7589	4.2998	5.9605
9	1.0937	1.1951	1.3048	1.3629	1.4233	1.4861	1.5513	1.6895	1.8385	1.9990	2.1719	2.3579	2.5580	2.7731	3.0040	3.2519	3.5179	3.8030	4.4355	5.1598	7.4506
10	1.1046	1.2190	1.3439	1.4106	1.4802	1.5530	1.6289	1.7908	1.9672	2.1589	2.3674	2.5937	2.8394	3.1058	3.3946	3.7072	4.0456	4.4114	5.2338	6.1917	9.3132
11	1.1157	1.2434	1.3842	1.4600	1.5395	1.6229	1.7103	1.8983	2.1049	2.3316	2.5804	2.8531	3.1518	3.4785	3.8359	4.2262	4.6524	5.1173	6.1759	7.4301	11.6415
12	1.1268	1.2682	1.4258	1.5111	1.6010	1.6959	1.7959	2.0122	2.2522	2.5182	2.8127	3.1384	3.4985	3.8960	4.3345	4.8179	5.3503	5.9360	7.2876	8.9161	14.5519
13	1.1381	1.2936	1.4685	1.5640	1.6651	1.7722	1.8856	2.1329	2.4098	2.7196	3.0658	3.4523	3.8833	4.3635	4.8980	5.4924	6.1528	6.8858	8.5994	10.6993	18.1899
14	1.1495	1.3195	1.5126	1.6187	1.7317	1.8519	1.9799	2.2609	2.5785	2.9372	3.3417	3.7975	4.3104	4.8871	5.5348	6.2613	7.0757	7.9875	10.1472	12.8392	22.7374
15	1.1610	1.3459	1.5580	1.6753	1.8009	1.9353	2.0789	2.3966	2.7590	3.1722	3.6425	4.1772	4.7846	5.4736	6.2543	7.1379	8.1371	9.2655	11.9737	15.4070	28.4217
16	1.1726	1.3728	1.6047	1.7340	1.8730	2.0224	2.1829	2.5404	2.9522	3.4259	3.9703	4.5950	5.3109	6.1304	7.0673	8.1372	9.3576	10.7480	14.1290	18.4884	35.5271
17	1.1843	1.4002	1.6528	1.7947	1.9479	2.1134	2.2920	2.6928	3.1588	3.7000	4.3276	5.0545	5.8951	6.8660	7.9861	9.2765	10.7613	12.4677	16.6722	22.1861	44.4089
18	1.1961	1.4282	1.7024	1.8575	2.0258	2.2085	2.4066	2.8543	3.3799	3.9960	4.7171	5.5599	6.5436	7.6900	9.0243	10.5752	12.3755	14.4625	19.6733	26.6233	55.5112
19	1.2081	1.4568	1.7535	1.9225	2.1068	2.3079	2.5270	3.0256	3.6165	4.3157	5.1417	6.1159	7.2633	8.6128	10.1974	12.0557	14.2318	16.7765	23.2144	31.9480	69.3889
20	1.2202	1.4859	1.8061	1.9898	2.1911	2.4117	2.6533	3.2071	3.8697	4.6610	5.6044	6.7275	8.0623	9.6463	11.5231	13.7435	16.3665	19.4608	27.3930	38.3376	86.7362
25	1.2824	1.6406	2.0938	2.3632	2.6658	3.0054	3.3864	4.2919	5.4274	6.8485	8.6231	10.8347	13.5855	17.0001	21.2305	26.4619	32.9190	40.8742	62.6686	95.3962	264.6978
30	1.3478	1.8114	2.4273	2.8068	3.2434	3.7453	4.3219	5.7435	7.6123	10.0627	13.2677	17.4494	22.8923	29.9599	39.1159	50.9502	66.2118	85.8499	143.3706	237.3763	807.7936
35	1.4166	1.9999	2.8139	3.3336	3.9461	4.6673	5.5160	7.6861	10.6766	14.7853	20.4140	28.1024	38.5749	52.7996	72.0685	98.1002	133.1755	180.3141	327.9973	590.6682	2,465.1903
40	1.4889	2.2080	3.2620	3.9593	4.8010	5.8164	7.0400	10.2857	14.9745	21.7245	31.4094	45.2593	65.0009	93.0510	132.7816	188.8835	267.8635	378.7212	750.3783	1,469.7716	7,523.1638
50	1.6446	2.6916	4.3839	5.5849	7.1067	9.0326	11.4674	18.4202	29.4570	46.9016	74.3575	117.3909	184.5648	289.0022	450.7359	700.2330	1,083.6574	1,670.7038	3,927.3569	9,100.4382	70,064.9232

Table B-1 ▲

In business applications, interest rates are usually stated for a one-year period unless specified otherwise. However, an interest rate can be stated for any period, such as 3% per quarter or 5% for a six-month period. For example, an investment may offer a return of 3% per quarter for two years. In that case, you would be working with 3% interest for eight periods (two years multiplied by four quarters per year). It would be incorrect to use 3% for two years because the interest in this case is 3% compounded quarterly, and different future values would result. Take care when calculating future-value and present-value problems to select the proper interest rate and the appropriate number of periods.

Let's demonstrate using Table B-1. The future value of $1.00 invested at 8% for one year is $1.08 ($1.00 × 1.0800, which appears at the intersection of the 8% column and the period 1 row). The factor 1.0800 includes both the principal (1.000) and the compound interest for one period (0.0800).

Suppose you deposit $5,000 in a savings account that pays annual interest of 8%. The account balance at the end of one year will be $5,400. To compute the future value of $5,000 at 8% for one year, multiply $5,000 by 1.0800 to get $5,400.

Now suppose you invest $5,000 in a 10-year, 8% certificate of deposit (CD). What will be the future value of the CD at maturity? To compute the future value of $5,000 at 8% for 10 periods, multiply $5,000 by 2.1589 (from Table B-1) to get $10,795. This future value of $10,795 indicates that $5,000 earning 8% interest compounded annually grows to $10,795 at the end of 10 years. You can find any present amount's future value at a particular future date. This is faster and easier than multiplying $5,000 times 1.08 ten times over.

Future Value of an Annuity

In the preceding example, we made an investment of a single amount. Other investments, called **annuities**, include multiple payments of an equal periodic amount at fixed intervals over the length of the investment. Consider the Gomez family members investing for their child's education. Let's assume the Gomez family can invest $4,000 annually to accumulate a college fund for 15-year-old Daniel. The investment can earn 7% annually until Daniel turns 18—a three-year investment. How much will be available for Daniel on the date of the last investment? The investment will have a future value of $12,860 as calculated next.

End of Year	Annual Investment +	Interest	= Increase for the Year	Future Value of Annuity
0	—	—	—	0
1	$4,000	—	$4,000	$ 4,000
2	4,000	+ ($4,000 × 0.07 = $280) =	4,280	8,280
3	4,000	+ ($8,280 × 0.07 = $580) =	4,580	12,860

As with the Future Value of $1 table, mathematical tables make calculating the future value of annuities much easier. **Table B-2**, Future Value of Annuity of $1, gives the future value of a series of investments, each of equal amount, made at regular intervals.

Future value of an ordinary annuity of $1 per period at *i*% for *n* periods, FVIFA$_{(i,n)}$

n	1%	2%	3%	3.5%	4%	4.5%	5%	6%	7%	8%	9%	10%	11%	12%	13%	14%	15%	16%	18%	20%	25%
1	1.0000	1.0000	1.0000	1.0000	1.0000	1.0000	1.0000	1.0000	1.0000	1.0000	1.0000	1.0000	1.0000	1.0000	1.0000	1.0000	1.0000	1.0000	1.0000	1.0000	1.0000
2	2.0100	2.0200	2.0300	2.0350	2.0400	2.0450	2.0500	2.0600	2.0700	2.0800	2.0900	2.1000	2.1100	2.1200	2.1300	2.1400	2.1500	2.1600	2.1800	2.2000	2.2500
3	3.0301	3.0604	3.0909	3.1062	3.1216	3.1370	3.1525	3.1836	3.2149	3.2464	3.2781	3.3100	3.3421	3.3744	3.4069	3.4396	3.4725	3.5056	3.5724	3.6400	3.8125
4	4.0604	4.1216	4.1836	4.2149	4.2465	4.2782	4.3101	4.3746	4.4399	4.5061	4.5731	4.6410	4.7097	4.7793	4.8498	4.9211	4.9934	5.0665	5.2154	5.3680	5.7656
5	5.1010	5.2040	5.3091	5.3625	5.4163	5.4707	5.5256	5.6371	5.7507	5.8666	5.9847	6.1051	6.2278	6.3528	6.4803	6.6101	6.7424	6.8771	7.1542	7.4416	8.2070
6	6.1520	6.3081	6.4684	6.5502	6.6330	6.7169	6.8019	6.9753	7.1533	7.3359	7.5233	7.7156	7.9129	8.1152	8.3227	8.5355	8.7537	8.9775	9.4420	9.9299	11.2588
7	7.2135	7.4343	7.6625	7.7794	7.8983	8.0192	8.1420	8.3938	8.6540	8.9228	9.2004	9.4872	9.7833	10.0890	10.4047	10.7305	11.0668	11.4139	12.1415	12.9159	15.0735
8	8.2857	8.5830	8.8923	9.0517	9.2142	9.3800	9.5491	9.8975	10.2598	10.6366	11.0285	11.4359	11.8594	12.2997	12.7573	13.2328	13.7268	14.2401	15.3270	16.4991	19.8419
9	9.3685	9.7546	10.1591	10.3685	10.5828	10.8021	11.0266	11.4913	11.9780	12.4876	13.0210	13.5795	14.1640	14.7757	15.4157	16.0853	16.7858	17.5185	19.0859	20.7989	25.8023
10	10.4622	10.9497	11.4639	11.7314	12.0061	12.2882	12.5779	13.1808	13.8164	14.4866	15.1929	15.9374	16.7220	17.5487	18.4197	19.3373	20.3037	21.3215	23.5213	25.9587	33.2529
11	11.5668	12.1687	12.8078	13.1420	13.4864	13.8412	14.2068	14.9716	15.7836	16.6455	17.5603	18.5312	19.5614	20.6546	21.8143	23.0445	24.3493	25.7329	28.7551	32.1504	42.5661
12	12.6825	13.4121	14.1920	14.6020	15.0258	15.4640	15.9171	16.8699	17.8885	18.9771	20.1407	21.3843	22.7132	24.1331	25.6502	27.2707	29.0017	30.8502	34.9311	39.5805	54.2077
13	13.8093	14.6803	15.6178	16.1130	16.6268	17.1599	17.7130	18.8821	20.1406	21.4953	22.9534	24.5227	26.2116	28.0291	29.9847	32.0887	34.3519	36.7862	42.2187	48.4966	68.7596
14	14.9474	15.9739	17.0863	17.6770	18.2919	18.9321	19.5986	21.0151	22.5505	24.2149	26.0192	27.9750	30.0949	32.3926	34.8827	37.5811	40.5047	43.6720	50.8180	59.1959	86.9495
15	16.0969	17.2934	18.5989	19.2957	20.0236	20.7841	21.5786	23.2760	25.1290	27.1521	29.3609	31.7725	34.4054	37.2797	40.4175	43.8424	47.5804	51.6595	60.9653	72.0351	109.6868
16	17.2579	18.6393	20.1569	20.9710	21.8245	22.7193	23.6575	25.6725	27.8881	30.3243	33.0034	35.9497	39.1899	42.7533	46.6717	50.9804	55.7175	60.9250	72.9390	87.4421	138.1085
17	18.4304	20.0121	21.7616	22.7050	23.6975	24.7417	25.8404	28.2129	30.8402	33.7502	36.9737	40.5447	44.5008	48.8837	53.7391	59.1176	65.0751	71.6730	87.0680	105.9306	173.6357
18	19.6147	21.4123	23.4144	24.4997	25.6454	26.8551	28.1324	30.9057	33.9990	37.4502	41.3013	45.5992	50.3959	55.7497	61.7251	68.3941	75.8364	84.1407	103.7403	128.1167	218.0446
19	20.8109	22.8406	25.1169	26.3572	27.6712	29.0636	30.5390	33.7600	37.3790	41.4463	46.0185	51.1591	56.9395	63.4397	70.7494	78.9692	88.2118	98.6032	123.4135	154.7400	273.5558
20	22.0190	24.2974	26.8704	28.2797	29.7781	31.3714	33.0660	36.7856	40.9955	45.7620	51.1601	57.2750	64.2028	72.0524	80.9468	91.0249	102.4436	115.3797	146.6280	186.6880	342.9447
25	28.2432	32.0303	36.4593	38.9499	41.6459	44.5652	47.7271	54.8645	63.2490	73.1059	84.7009	98.3471	114.4133	133.3339	155.6196	181.8708	212.7930	249.2140	342.6035	471.9811	1,054.7912
30	34.7849	40.5681	47.5754	51.6227	56.0849	61.0071	66.4388	79.0582	94.4608	113.2832	136.3075	164.4940	199.0209	241.3327	293.1992	356.7868	434.7451	530.3117	790.9480	1,181.8816	3,227.1743
35	41.6603	49.9945	60.4621	66.6740	73.6522	81.4966	90.3203	111.4348	138.2369	172.3168	215.7108	271.0244	341.5896	431.6635	546.6808	693.5727	881.1702	1,120.7130	1,816.6516	2,948.3411	9,856.7613
40	48.8864	60.4020	75.4013	84.5503	95.0255	107.0303	120.7998	154.7620	199.6351	259.0565	337.8824	442.5926	581.8261	767.0914	1,013.7042	1,342.0251	1,779.0903	2,360.7572	4,163.2130	7,343.8578	30,088.6554
50	64.4632	84.5794	112.7969	130.9979	152.6671	178.5030	209.3480	290.3359	406.5289	573.7702	815.0836	1,163.9085	1,668.7712	2,400.0182	3,459.5071	4,994.5213	7,217.7163	10,435.6488	21,813.0937	45,497.1908	280,255.6929

Table B-2 ▲

What is the future value of an annuity of three investments of $1 each that earn 7%? The answer, 3.2149, can be found in the 7% column and across from period 3 in Table B-2. This amount can be used to compute the future value of the investment for Daniel's education, as follows:

Amount of Each Periodic Investment ×	Future Value of Annuity of $1 (Table B-2)	= Future Value of Investment
$4,000	× 3.2149	= $12,860

You can compute the future value of any investment consisting of equal periodic amounts at regular intervals. Businesses make periodic investments to accumulate funds for plant expansion and other uses.

PRESENT VALUE

Often a person knows a future amount and needs to know the related **present value**. Present value is the value on a given date of a future amount, adjusted to reflect the time value of money. Suppose an investment promises to pay you $5,000 at the *end* of one year. How much would you pay *now* to acquire this investment? You would be willing to pay the present value of the $5,000 future amount.

Present value also depends on three factors:

❶ The amount of the future payment (or receipt)

❷ The time span between investment and future payment (or receipt)

❸ The interest rate

Bringing a future value back to the present is called **discounting** because the present value is *always less* than the future value.

In our example, the future receipt is $5,000. The investment period is one year. Assume that you demand an annual interest rate of 10% on your investment. With all three factors specified, you can compute the present value of $5,000 at 10% for one year as follows:

$$\frac{\text{Future Value}}{(1 + \text{Interest Rate})} = \frac{\$5,000}{1.10} = \$4,545$$

By turning the data around into a future-value problem, we verify the present-value computation:

Amount Invested (present value)	$4,545
Expected Earnings ($4,545 × 0.10)...	455
Amount to Be Received One Year from Now (future value)...................................	$5,000

This example illustrates that present value and future value are based on the same equation:

$$\text{Present Value} \times (1 + \text{Interest Rate}) = \text{Future Value}$$

$$\frac{\text{Future Value}}{(1 + \text{Interest Rate})} = \text{Present Value}$$

If the $5,000 is to be received two years from now, you will pay only $4,132 for the investment, as shown next:

By turning the data around, we verify that $4,132 accumulates to $5,000 at 10% for two years:

Amount Invested (present value)	$4,132
Expected Earnings for First Year ($4,132 × 0.10)	413
Amount of Investment after One Year	4,545
Expected Earnings for Second Year ($4,545 × 0.10)	455
Amount to Be Received Two Years from Now (future value)	$5,000

You would pay $4,132, the present value of $5,000, to receive the $5,000 future amount at the end of two years at 10% per year. The $868 difference between the amount invested, $4,132, and the amount to be received, $5,000, is the return on the investment; it is the sum of the two interest receipts: $413 + $455 = $868.

Present-Value Tables

We have shown the simple formula for computing present value. However, calculating present value this way for investments spanning many years is tedious. Present-value tables ease our work. Let's reexamine our examples of present value by using **Table B-3**, Present Value of $1.

Present value of $1 per period at i% for n periods, $PVIF_{(i,n)}$

n	1%	2%	3%	3.5%	4%	4.5%	5%	6%	7%	8%	9%	10%	11%	12%	13%	14%	15%	16%	18%	20%	25%
1	0.9901	0.9804	0.9709	0.9662	0.9615	0.9569	0.9524	0.9434	0.9346	0.9259	0.9174	0.9091	0.9009	0.8929	0.8850	0.8772	0.8696	0.8621	0.8475	0.8333	0.8000
2	0.9803	0.9612	0.9426	0.9335	0.9246	0.9157	0.9070	0.8900	0.8734	0.8573	0.8417	0.8264	0.8116	0.7972	0.7831	0.7695	0.7561	0.7432	0.7182	0.6944	0.6400
3	0.9706	0.9423	0.9151	0.9019	0.8890	0.8763	0.8638	0.8396	0.8163	0.7938	0.7722	0.7513	0.7312	0.7118	0.6931	0.6750	0.6575	0.6407	0.6086	0.5787	0.5120
4	0.9610	0.9238	0.8885	0.8714	0.8548	0.8386	0.8227	0.7921	0.7629	0.7350	0.7084	0.6830	0.6587	0.6355	0.6133	0.5921	0.5718	0.5523	0.5158	0.4823	0.4096
5	0.9515	0.9057	0.8626	0.8420	0.8219	0.8025	0.7835	0.7473	0.7130	0.6806	0.6499	0.6209	0.5935	0.5674	0.5428	0.5194	0.4972	0.4761	0.4371	0.4019	0.3277
6	0.9420	0.8880	0.8375	0.8135	0.7903	0.7679	0.7462	0.7050	0.6663	0.6302	0.5963	0.5645	0.5346	0.5066	0.4803	0.4556	0.4323	0.4104	0.3704	0.3349	0.2621
7	0.9327	0.8706	0.8131	0.7860	0.7599	0.7348	0.7107	0.6651	0.6227	0.5835	0.5470	0.5132	0.4817	0.4523	0.4251	0.3996	0.3759	0.3538	0.3139	0.2791	0.2097
8	0.9235	0.8535	0.7894	0.7594	0.7307	0.7032	0.6768	0.6274	0.5820	0.5403	0.5019	0.4665	0.4339	0.4039	0.3762	0.3506	0.3269	0.3050	0.2660	0.2326	0.1678
9	0.9143	0.8368	0.7664	0.7337	0.7026	0.6729	0.6446	0.5919	0.5439	0.5002	0.4604	0.4241	0.3909	0.3606	0.3329	0.3075	0.2843	0.2630	0.2255	0.1938	0.1342
10	0.9053	0.8203	0.7441	0.7089	0.6756	0.6439	0.6139	0.5584	0.5083	0.4632	0.4224	0.3855	0.3522	0.3220	0.2946	0.2697	0.2472	0.2267	0.1911	0.1615	0.1074
11	0.8963	0.8043	0.7224	0.6849	0.6496	0.6162	0.5847	0.5268	0.4751	0.4289	0.3875	0.3505	0.3173	0.2875	0.2607	0.2366	0.2149	0.1954	0.1619	0.1346	0.0859
12	0.8874	0.7885	0.7014	0.6618	0.6246	0.5897	0.5568	0.4970	0.4440	0.3971	0.3555	0.3186	0.2858	0.2567	0.2307	0.2076	0.1869	0.1685	0.1372	0.1122	0.0687
13	0.8787	0.7730	0.6810	0.6394	0.6006	0.5643	0.5303	0.4688	0.4150	0.3677	0.3262	0.2897	0.2575	0.2292	0.2042	0.1821	0.1625	0.1452	0.1163	0.0935	0.0550
14	0.8700	0.7579	0.6611	0.6178	0.5775	0.5400	0.5051	0.4423	0.3878	0.3405	0.2992	0.2633	0.2320	0.2046	0.1807	0.1597	0.1413	0.1252	0.0985	0.0779	0.0440
15	0.8613	0.7430	0.6419	0.5969	0.5553	0.5167	0.4810	0.4173	0.3624	0.3152	0.2745	0.2394	0.2090	0.1827	0.1599	0.1401	0.1229	0.1079	0.0835	0.0649	0.0352
16	0.8528	0.7284	0.6232	0.5767	0.5339	0.4945	0.4581	0.3936	0.3387	0.2919	0.2519	0.2176	0.1883	0.1631	0.1415	0.1229	0.1069	0.0930	0.0708	0.0541	0.0281
17	0.8444	0.7142	0.6050	0.5572	0.5134	0.4732	0.4363	0.3714	0.3166	0.2703	0.2311	0.1978	0.1696	0.1456	0.1252	0.1078	0.0929	0.0802	0.0600	0.0451	0.0225
18	0.8360	0.7002	0.5874	0.5384	0.4936	0.4528	0.4155	0.3503	0.2959	0.2502	0.2120	0.1799	0.1528	0.1300	0.1108	0.0946	0.0808	0.0691	0.0508	0.0376	0.0180
19	0.8277	0.6864	0.5703	0.5202	0.4746	0.4333	0.3957	0.3305	0.2765	0.2317	0.1945	0.1635	0.1377	0.1161	0.0981	0.0829	0.0703	0.0596	0.0431	0.0313	0.0144
20	0.8195	0.6730	0.5537	0.5026	0.4564	0.4146	0.3769	0.3118	0.2584	0.2145	0.1784	0.1486	0.1240	0.1037	0.0868	0.0728	0.0611	0.0514	0.0365	0.0261	0.0115
25	0.7798	0.6095	0.4776	0.4231	0.3751	0.3327	0.2953	0.2330	0.1842	0.1460	0.1160	0.0923	0.0736	0.0588	0.0471	0.0378	0.0304	0.0245	0.0160	0.0105	0.0038
30	0.7419	0.5521	0.4120	0.3563	0.3083	0.2670	0.2314	0.1741	0.1314	0.0994	0.0754	0.0573	0.0437	0.0334	0.0256	0.0196	0.0151	0.0116	0.0070	0.0042	0.0012
35	0.7059	0.5000	0.3554	0.3000	0.2534	0.2143	0.1813	0.1301	0.0937	0.0676	0.0490	0.0356	0.0259	0.0189	0.0139	0.0102	0.0075	0.0055	0.0030	0.0017	0.0004
40	0.6717	0.4529	0.3066	0.2526	0.2083	0.1719	0.1420	0.0972	0.0668	0.0460	0.0318	0.0221	0.0154	0.0107	0.0075	0.0053	0.0037	0.0026	0.0013	0.0007	0.0001
50	0.6080	0.3715	0.2281	0.1791	0.1407	0.1107	0.0872	0.0543	0.0339	0.0213	0.0134	0.0085	0.0054	0.0035	0.0022	0.0014	0.0009	0.0006	0.0003	0.0001	0.0000

Table B-3 ▲

For the 10% investment for one year, we find the intersection of the 10% column and the first row of the period column. The figure 0.9091 is computed as follows: 1 ÷ 1.10 = 0.9091. In preparing the table, this work has been done for us, so only the resulting present values are given in the table. The heading in Table B-3 states that the present value of $1 is being determined. To calculate present value for $5,000, we multiply $5,000 by 0.9091. The result is $4,545, which matches the result we obtained previously by hand.

For the two-year investment, we read down the 10% column and across the period 2 row. We multiply 0.8264 by $5,000 and get $4,132, which confirms our preceding computation of $4,132. Using the table, we can compute the present value of any single future amount.

Present Value of an Annuity

Let's return to the investment example that provided the investor with only a single future receipt of $5,000 at the end of two years. Annuity investments provide multiple receipts of an equal amount at fixed intervals over the investment's length.

Consider an investment that promises annual cash receipts of $10,000 to be received at the end of each of three years. Assume that you demand a 12% return on your investment. What is the investment's present value? What would you pay today to acquire the investment? The investment spans three periods, and you would pay the sum of three present values. The computation follows:

Year	Annual Cash Receipt	×	Present Value of $1 at 12% (Table B-3)	=	Present Value of Annual Cash Receipt
1	$10,000	×	0.8929	=	$ 8,929
2	10,000	×	0.7972	=	7,972
3	10,000	×	0.7118	=	7,118
			Total Present Value of Investment =		$24,019

The present value of this annuity is $24,019. By paying this amount today, you will receive $10,000 at the end of each of the three years while earning 12% on your investment.

The example illustrates repetitive computations of the three future amounts. One way to ease the computational burden is to add the three present values of a $1 from Table B-3, 0.8929 + 0.7972 + 0.7118, and multiply their sum of 2.4019 by the annual cash receipt of $10,000 to obtain the present value of the annuity, $24,019 ($10,000 × 2.4019).

An easier approach is to use a present value of an annuity table. **Table B-4** shows the present value of $1 to be received at the end of each period for a given number of periods. The present value of a three-period annuity at 12% is 2.4018, the junction of the period 3 row and the 12% column. Thus, the present value of $10,000 received annually at the end of each of three years, discounted at 12%, is $24,018 ($10,000 × 2.4018). The difference between 2.4019 and 2.4018 is due to rounding in the present value table.

									Present value of an annuity of $1 per period at i% for n periods, PVIFA$_{(i,n)}$											
n	1%	2%	3%	3.5%	4%	4.5%	5%	6%	7%	8%	9%	10%	11%	12%	13%	14%	15%	16%	18%	20%	25%
1	0.9901	0.9804	0.9709	0.9662	0.9615	0.9569	0.9524	0.9434	0.9346	0.9259	0.9174	0.9091	0.9009	0.8929	0.8850	0.8772	0.8696	0.8621	0.8475	0.8333	0.8000
2	1.9704	1.9416	1.9135	1.8997	1.8861	1.8727	1.8594	1.8334	1.8080	1.7833	1.7591	1.7355	1.7125	1.6901	1.6681	1.6467	1.6257	1.6052	1.5656	1.5278	1.4400
3	2.9410	2.8839	2.8286	2.8016	2.7751	2.7490	2.7232	2.6730	2.6243	2.5771	2.5313	2.4869	2.4437	2.4018	2.3612	2.3216	2.2832	2.2459	2.1743	2.1065	1.9520
4	3.9020	3.8077	3.7171	3.6731	3.6299	3.5875	3.5460	3.4651	3.3872	3.3121	3.2397	3.1699	3.1024	3.0373	2.9745	2.9137	2.8550	2.7982	2.6901	2.5887	2.3616
5	4.8534	4.7135	4.5797	4.5151	4.4518	4.3900	4.3295	4.2124	4.1002	3.9927	3.8897	3.7908	3.6959	3.6048	3.5172	3.4331	3.3522	3.2743	3.1272	2.9906	2.6893
6	5.7955	5.6014	5.4172	5.3286	5.2421	5.1579	5.0757	4.9173	4.7665	4.6229	4.4859	4.3553	4.2305	4.1114	3.9975	3.8887	3.7845	3.6847	3.4976	3.3255	2.9514
7	6.7282	6.4720	6.2303	6.1145	6.0021	5.8927	5.7864	5.5824	5.3893	5.2064	5.0330	4.8684	4.7122	4.5638	4.4226	4.2883	4.1604	4.0386	3.8115	3.6046	3.1611
8	7.6517	7.3255	7.0197	6.8740	6.7327	6.5959	6.4632	6.2098	5.9713	5.7466	5.5348	5.3349	5.1461	4.9676	4.7988	4.6389	4.4873	4.3436	4.0776	3.8372	3.3289
9	8.5660	8.1622	7.7861	7.6077	7.4353	7.2688	7.1078	6.8017	6.5152	6.2469	5.9952	5.7590	5.5370	5.3282	5.1317	4.9464	4.7716	4.6065	4.3030	4.0310	3.4631
10	9.4713	8.9826	8.5302	8.3166	8.1109	7.9127	7.7217	7.3601	7.0236	6.7101	6.4177	6.1446	5.8892	5.6502	5.4262	5.2161	5.0188	4.8332	4.4941	4.1925	3.5705
11	10.3676	9.7868	9.2526	9.0016	8.7605	8.5289	8.3064	7.8869	7.4987	7.1390	6.8052	6.4951	6.2065	5.9377	5.6869	5.4527	5.2337	5.0286	4.6560	4.3271	3.6564
12	11.2551	10.5753	9.9540	9.6633	9.3851	9.1186	8.8633	8.3838	7.9427	7.5361	7.1607	6.8137	6.4924	6.1944	5.9176	5.6603	5.4206	5.1971	4.7932	4.4392	3.7251
13	12.1337	11.3484	10.6350	10.3027	9.9856	9.6829	9.3936	8.8527	8.3577	7.9038	7.4869	7.1034	6.7499	6.4235	6.1218	5.8424	5.5831	5.3423	4.9095	4.5327	3.7801
14	13.0037	12.1062	11.2961	10.9205	10.5631	10.2228	9.8986	9.2950	8.7455	8.2442	7.7862	7.3667	6.9819	6.6282	6.3025	6.0021	5.7245	5.4675	5.0081	4.6106	3.8241
15	13.8651	12.8493	11.9379	11.5174	11.1184	10.7395	10.3797	9.7122	9.1079	8.5595	8.0607	7.6061	7.1909	6.8109	6.4624	6.1422	5.8474	5.5755	5.0916	4.6755	3.8593
16	14.7179	13.5777	12.5611	12.0941	11.6523	11.2340	10.8378	10.1059	9.4466	8.8514	8.3126	7.8237	7.3792	6.9740	6.6039	6.2651	5.9542	5.6685	5.1624	4.7296	3.8874
17	15.5623	14.2919	13.1661	12.6513	12.1657	11.7072	11.2741	10.4773	9.7632	9.1216	8.5436	8.0216	7.5488	7.1196	6.7291	6.3729	6.0472	5.7487	5.2223	4.7746	3.9099
18	16.3983	14.9920	13.7535	13.1897	12.6593	12.1600	11.6896	10.8276	10.0591	9.3719	8.7556	8.2014	7.7016	7.2497	6.8399	6.4674	6.1280	5.8178	5.2732	4.8122	3.9279
19	17.2260	15.6785	14.3238	13.7098	13.1339	12.5933	12.0853	11.1581	10.3356	9.6036	8.9501	8.3649	7.8393	7.3658	6.9380	6.5504	6.1982	5.8775	5.3162	4.8435	3.9424
20	18.0456	16.3514	14.8775	14.2124	13.5903	13.0079	12.4622	11.4699	10.5940	9.8181	9.1285	8.5136	7.9633	7.4694	7.0248	6.6231	6.2593	5.9288	5.3527	4.8696	3.9539
25	22.0232	19.5235	17.4131	16.4815	15.6221	14.8282	14.0939	12.7834	11.6536	10.6748	9.8226	9.0770	8.4217	7.8431	7.3300	6.8729	6.4641	6.0971	5.4669	4.9476	3.9849
30	25.8077	22.3965	19.6004	18.3920	17.2920	16.2889	15.3725	13.7648	12.4090	11.2578	10.2737	9.4269	8.6938	8.0552	7.4957	7.0027	6.5660	6.1772	5.5168	4.9789	3.9950
35	29.4086	24.9986	21.4872	20.0007	18.6646	17.4610	16.3742	14.4982	12.9477	11.6546	10.5668	9.6442	8.8552	8.1755	7.5856	7.0700	6.6166	6.2153	5.5386	4.9915	3.9984
40	32.8347	27.3555	23.1148	21.3551	19.7928	18.4016	17.1591	15.0463	13.3317	11.9246	10.7574	9.7791	8.9511	8.2438	7.6344	7.1050	6.6418	6.2335	5.5482	4.9966	3.9995
50	39.1961	31.4236	25.7298	23.4556	21.4822	19.7620	18.2559	15.7619	13.8007	12.2335	10.9617	9.9148	9.0417	8.3045	7.6752	7.1327	6.6605	6.2463	5.5541	4.9995	3.9999

Table B-4 ▲

ACCOUNTING VOCABULARY

THE LANGUAGE OF BUSINESS

Annuities (p. 753)

Compound interest (p. 752)

Discounting (p. 755)

Future value (p. 752)

Present value (p. 755)

Time value of money (p. 752)

ACCOUNTING PRACTICE

EXERCISES

MyAccountingLab

The exercises in this appendix can be found on MyAccountingLab. You can practise them as often as you want, and they feature step-by-step guided solutions to help you find the right answer.

EB-1A. Calculate present and future values. 10–15 min.

Presented next are four independent situations related to future and present values.

Requirement

1. Using the tables in this appendix, calculate the future or present value of each item as needed.

   a. $5,000 is deposited in the bank today for a period of eight years. Calculate the value of the $5,000 at the end of eight years assuming it earns 5% interest.

   b. How much must you invest today to receive $1,500 at the end of each year for the next four years, assuming you can earn 7% interest?

   c. $3,500 will be invested at the end of each year for a period of five years. Calculate the value of the investment at the end of five years, assuming it earns 9% interest.

   d. The company you work for wants to purchase a new piece of equipment that is estimated to cost $18,000 ten years from now. How much must it invest today to have the $18,000 necessary to purchase the equipment if it can earn 8% interest?

EB-2A. Future value concepts. 15–20 min.

Allen Hamilton is considering two plans for building an education fund for his children.

Plan A—Invest $2,000 each year for six years. This investment will earn 10% annual interest.

Plan B—Invest $10,000 now, earning 8% annual interest for six years.

Requirement

1. Before making any calculations, which plan would you expect to provide the larger future amount? Using the tables provided in this appendix, calculate the future value of each plan. Which plan provides the larger amount at the end of six years?

EB-3A. Present value concepts. 15–20 min.

Aztec Electronics, Inc. needs new manufacturing equipment. Two companies can provide similar equipment but under different payment plans:

   a. Fancher Manufacturing offers to let Aztec Electronics, Inc. pay $60,000 at the end of each year for five years. The payments include interest at 12% per year.

   b. Phoenix, Corp. will let Aztec Electronics, Inc. make a single payment of $400,000 at the end of five years. This payment includes both principal and interest at 12%.

Requirements

1. Calculate the present value cost of each payment plan.

2. In addition to the present value cost of the equipment, what other factors should Aztec Electronics consider when deciding which company to purchase the equipment from?

EB-4A. Present value concepts. 10–15 min.

Your tenant, Sandra, has just signed a one-year lease to rent the apartment from you at $850 per month, payable at the end of each month. However, you are short of cash and offer to accept a single payment now from Sandra of only $8,500. Sandra has been saving her money carefully for some time now, and has a large bank balance of more than $15,000, so has the money available to make the single payment now. If Sandra believes she can earn interest at a rate of 2% per month, should she take your offer, or not?

EB-5A. Future value concepts. 10–15 min.

Chan just won the grand prize at the city lottery, which consists of $100,000 at the end of one year, $200,000 at the end of two years, and $300,000 at the end of three years. The city lottery commission offers Chan the option of receiving a single payment of $700,000 at the end of five years, as an alternative to the three annual payments. If Chan believes that 8% is the right interest rate for borrowing or lending in the coming years, should Chan stick with the three payments or accept the single payment of $700,000? What if the annual interest rate is reduced to 5%? (Ignore taxes.)

EB-6A. Future value concepts. 10–15 min.

Hussain wants to buy a new car, which will cost him $23,000, tax included. Hussain has only $18,000 in his bank account, and does not like the idea of borrowing. He has decided to delay buying the car until he has enough money to do so. If Hussain is able to deposit $500 per month at the end of each month into his account, and if the money in his account earns interest at the rate of 2% per month, how long will Hussain have to wait until he can buy his new car?

EB-7A. Present value concepts. 10–15 min.

Rachel borrowed $10,000 and agreed to pay back the loan with five consecutive annual payments, with the first payment occurring in one year. If the annual interest rate is 5%, what is the amount of her annual payment?

EB-8A. Present value concepts. 10–15 min.

Hua Tran financed a new automobile by paying $7,500 cash and agreeing to make 40 monthly payments of $500 each, the first payment to be made one month after the purchase. The loan bears interest at an annual rate of 12%. What was the cost of the automobile?

Appendix C
Accounting for Investments

Let's say you got a job and you were able to save some money. What would you do with it? You could deposit it in a savings account or invest it in other forms of investments where you are investing your savings to get the highest possible return for a given level of risk to maximize your wealth. The same thing applies for companies. At a certain point almost all companies will have excess money. This could be as a result of the cyclical nature of their business, it could be that they are saving money to invest in a new project, or it could be that there is the absence of an investment opportunity related to their field of business. Keeping surplus funds idle in a bank account, earning low interest rates, will not contribute to maximizing the company's wealth. Accordingly, companies search for investment opportunities to maximize their rate of return on their capital. Such investments could be short term (which could be liquidated at any time), or they could be medium- or long-term investments that last for longer periods of time. In an investment situation, there are usually additional reasons behind the investment, such as influencing or controlling policies of other companies so that they can integrate, merge, expand, etc. For example, a car manufacturer would be interested in having influence on a tire manufacturing company to guarantee the supply of tires. When acquiring other companies, cost reductions from synergy effects could also be achieved. Companies could acquire other companies to expand their business line, to be present in new territories, or to seek more efficiency and stability.

WHAT ARE THE MAIN CLASSIFICATIONS OF INVESTMENTS?

L.O. 1 Identify the different types of investments

Investments can be classified in many ways:

- Time horizon of investment: Current or long-term investments
- Objective of holding investment: Strategic and non-strategic investments
- Type of investment: Investments in debt (bonds or treasury bills, for example) and investments in equity (shares)

Companies use different financial instruments to achieve their investment goals. They can invest in shares or bonds of other companies or in treasury bills. However, no matter what financial instrument a company chooses, it's the company's intention when acquiring the investment that determines the accounting method used to account for it. Accounting methods for investments differ substantially depending on what these investments are and how they are classified. There are also differences between IFRS and ASPE guidelines for accounting for investments. **Exhibit C-1** summarizes how investments are divided into non-strategic and strategic investments, how they are classified, and the accounting method used to account for each, according to IFRS.

IFRS

Exhibit C-1 ▲

L.O. ❷ Account for non-strategic investments

HOW DO YOU ACCOUNT FOR NON-STRATEGIC INVESTMENTS?

Non-strategic investments are generally short-term investments in financial instruments. According to IFRS, non-strategic investments fall into one of four categories:

- If a company invests in shares or bonds and its intention is to resell them in the short term (less than a year), this investment would be classified as a **held-for-trading investment**.
- If a company invests in bonds and its intention is to keep them until they mature, then this would be classified as a **held-to-maturity investment**.
- Any other investment would be classified as **available-for-sale securities**.
- If the company issues loans, these would be classified as loans and long-term receivables.

The accounting treatment of each classification of investment differs, which we will explore next.

HELD-FOR-TRADING INVESTMENTS

Held-for-trading securities are bonds or shares that are acquired with the intention of keeping them for a short period of time; these securities are traded in an open market. Held-for-trading securities are accounted for using the fair value model. According to the fair value model, bonds or shares are recorded at cost when they are acquired, and interest revenue or dividends received are recorded as revenue for the period. Bonds and shares are measured at their fair value at the end of the period and the bonds' and shares' value is adjusted by any gain or loss, as reflected in an Unrealized Holding Gains (Losses) account. The Unrealized Gains (Losses) account is included in Other Comprehensive Income. The term "unrealized" is used to note the fact that the gain or loss is not yet realized by selling the security. When the bonds are sold, any excess gains or losses are recognized within Other Income. The same method applies for shares, except that the dividends received would be recorded as part of the period's income.

To illustrate, let's assume the following simple example. Investco Inc. invests in Mackay Industries' bonds, which are issued for $100,000, and in 800 of Hay Corporation's shares at $100 each. Investco Inc.'s intention is to resell the bonds and shares within a short period of time when the need for cash arises. Investco Inc. would record the following entry:

Assets = Liabilities + Shareholders' Equity

100,000
80,000
−180,000

DATE	ACCOUNTS	POST REF.	DR.	CR.
Jun 30	Held-for-Trading Investments — Mackay Bonds		100,000	
	Held-for-Trading Investments — Hay Shares		80,000	
	Cash			180,000
	Investing in Mackay bonds and Hay shares.			

At year end, the price of the bonds went down to $99,000 and that of the shares went up to $84,000. The following table summarizes this information:

	Acquisition Price	Current Price	Gain/(Loss)
Mackay Bonds	$100,000	$ 99,000	$(1,000)
Hay Shares	$ 80,000	$ 84,000	$ 4,000
Total	$180,000	$183,000	$ 3,000

Since this is an investment that is accounted for according to the fair value model, the following entry would be recorded to recognize the change:

Assets = Liabilities + Shareholders' Equity

4,000
−1,000   3,000

DATE	ACCOUNTS	POST REF.	DR.	CR.
Dec 31	Held-for-Trading Investments — Hay Shares		4,000	
	Held-for-Trading Investments — Mackay Bonds			1,000
	Unrealized Gain (Loss) in Securities			3,000
	Recognizing the change in price in securities.			

Let's assume that on March 20 of the following year the bonds are sold for $101,000 and the shares are sold for $83,000. The following entry records this transaction:

Assets = Liabilities + Shareholders' Equity

184,000   1,000
−84,000
−99,000

DATE	ACCOUNTS	POST REF.	DR.	CR.
Mar 20	Cash		184,000	
	Held-for-Trading Investments — Hay Shares			84,000*
	Held-for-Trading Investments — Mackay Bonds			99,000**
	Gain (Loss) on Sale of Securities			1,000
	Recognizing the sale of securities.			

* This is the current book value for the shares after the latest adjustment on December 31.
** This is the current book value for the bonds after the latest adjustment on December 31.

In the fair value model, earnings are more volatile because the gains or losses are recognized at the time of preparing the financial statements rather than waiting until the investment is sold to recognize the overall gains or losses.

If ASPE is implemented, investments in equity instruments that are quoted in an active market are valued at fair value; otherwise, they would be valued at cost less any reduction for impairment. Investments in bonds are valued at amortized cost.

HELD-TO-MATURITY INVESTMENTS, LOANS, AND RECEIVABLES

The financial instruments that fall into this category are either bonds or loans that have a set maturity date and return interest. Shares don't fall into this category because they don't have a maturity date. If a company acquires these types of investments intending to keep them until maturity, it will classify them as held-to-maturity investments and will account for them using the amortized cost method, since the company is not intending to sell them in the near future. You have already been introduced to this method from an issuing company's perspective in Chapter 9. Now, we will deal with the same transactions from an investing company's perspective. We will use the Mackay Industries example from Chapter 9 (refer to the "Bonds Payable" section in Chapter 9, starting on page 531), but will explore the investor's perspective here.

Bonds Acquired at Face Value

Assume that on January 1, 2015, Investco Inc. acquired bonds issued by Mackay Industries for $500,000, which represents the face value of the bond. The bonds pay 8% semi-annual interest. Since the bonds are acquired and intended to be kept by Investco Inc. until maturity, they are going to be categorized as held-to-maturity investments and will be recorded as follows:

DATE	ACCOUNTS	POST REF.	DR.	CR.
Jan 1	Long-Term Investment in Bonds		500,000	
	Cash			500,000
	Acquiring bonds at face value.			

On June 30, the first semi-annual interest amount is paid:

DATE	ACCOUNTS	POST REF.	DR.	CR.
Jun 30	Cash		20,000	
	Interest Revenue			20,000
	Receiving semi-annual bond interest.			

The previous entry will recur every six months until the maturity date, when the bonds mature and Investco Inc. collects its money as follows:

DATE	ACCOUNTS	POST REF.	DR.	CR.
Jan 1	Cash		500,000	
	Long-Term Investment in Bonds			500,000
	Redeeming the value of bonds at maturity.			

Bonds Acquired at a Discount

As previously mentioned in Chapter 9, when a bond's interest rate is lower than the market rate, the bond will be issued at a discount and the difference between its face value and the issuing price will be amortized over its life by using the effective interest method (IFRS) or either the effective interest method or the straight-line method (ASPE) if the straight-line method does not differ significantly.

To illustrate using the effective interest method (which is acceptable by both IFRS and ASPE), let's return to the example from Chapter 9 (see page 535).

Assume that on January 1, 2015, Investco Inc. acquired $500,000 of face-value, five-year, 8% semi-annual bonds issued by Mackay Industries at $461,384. The market interest rate is 10%.

Exhibit C-2 illustrates how the effective interest method is used to calculate the interest revenue; for a detailed illustration of the calculations, please refer to Chapter 9.

Semi-annual interest period	A Interest collected ($500,000 × 8% × 1/2)	B Interest revenue = previous period carrying amount × market rate (10% × 1/2)	C Discount amortization amount (B − A)	D Unamortized amount (D − C)	E Bond carrying value ($500,000 − D)
0				38,616	461,384
1	20,000	23,069	3,069	35,547	464,453
2	20,000	23,223	3,223	32,324	467,676
3	20,000	23,384	3,384	28,940	471,060
4	20,000	23,553	3,553	25,387	474,613
5	20,000	23,731	3,731	21,657	478,343
6	20,000	23,917	3,917	17,740	482,260
7	20,000	24,113	4,113	13,627	486,373
8	20,000	24,319	4,319	9,308	490,692
9	20,000	24,535	4,535	4,773	495,227
10	20,000	24,773	4,773	0	500,000

Exhibit C-2 ▲

On the date of acquiring the bonds, the following entry is made:

DATE	ACCOUNTS	POST REF.	DR.	CR.
Jan 1	Long-Term Investment in Bonds		461,384	
	Cash			461,384
	Acquiring $500,000 worth of bonds at a discount price of $461,384.			

On the first interest date (June 30, 2015), the following entry is made to recognize the collection of interest and amortization of the discount:

DATE	ACCOUNTS	POST REF.	DR.	CR.
Jun 30	Cash		20,000	
	Long-Term Investment in Bonds		3,069	
	Interest Revenue			23,069
	Interest revenue for the period, including amortization of the discount.			

Long-Term Investment in Bonds will be debited on each payment date by the discount amortization amount calculated for that period until it reaches its par value of $500,000 at maturity, as illustrated in Exhibit C-2. On that date, Cash will be debited by $500,000 and the Long-Term Investment in Bonds account will be credited by $500,000 to close it. If ASPE is implemented, the straight-line amortization method for the discount could be used if the results do not differ significantly.

ASPE

Bonds Acquired at a Premium

As previously mentioned in Chapter 9, when a bond's interest rate is higher than the market rate, the bond will be issued at a premium and the difference between its face value and the issuing price will be amortized over its life by using the effective interest method (IFRS) or either the effective interest method or straight-line method (ASPE).

IFRS

ASPE

To illustrate using the effective interest method (which is acceptable by both IFRS and ASPE), let's return to the example from Chapter 9 (see page 538).

Assume that on January 1, 2015, Investco Inc. acquired $500,000 of face-value, five-year, 8% semi-annual bonds issued by Mackay Industries at $542,654. The market interest rate is 6%.

Exhibit C-3 illustrates how the effective interest method is used to calculate the interest revenue; for a detailed illustration of the calculations, please refer to Chapter 9.

Semi-annual interest period	A Interest collected ($500,000 × 8% × 1/2)	B Interest revenue = previous period carrying amount × market rate (6% × 1/2)	C Premium amortization amount (A − B)	D Unamortized amount (D − C)	E Bond carrying value ($500,000 + D)
0			0	42,654	542,654
1	20,000	16,280	3,720	38,934	538,934
2	20,000	16,168	3,832	35,102	535,102
3	20,000	16,053	3,947	31,155	531,155
4	20,000	15,935	4,065	27,089	527,089
5	20,000	15,813	4,187	22,902	522,902
6	20,000	15,687	4,313	18,589	518,589
7	20,000	15,558	4,442	14,147	514,147
8	20,000	15,424	4,576	9,571	509,571
9	20,000	15,287	4,713	4,858	504,858
10	20,000	15,142	4,858	0	500,000

Exhibit C-3 ▲

On the date of acquiring the bonds, the following entry is made:

DATE	ACCOUNTS	POST REF.	DR.	CR.
Jan 1	Long-Term Investment in Bonds		542,654	
	Cash			542,654
	Acquiring bonds at a premium for $542,654.			

On the first interest date (June 30, 2015), the following entry is recorded to recognize the collection of interest and amortization of the discount:

DATE	ACCOUNTS	POST REF.	DR.	CR.
Jun 30	Cash		20,000	
	Long-Term Investment in Bonds			3,720
	Interest Revenue			16,280
	Interest revenue for the period, including amortization			
	of the premium.			

ASPE Long-Term Investment in Bonds will be credited on each payment date by the amount calculated for the premium amortization for that period until it reaches its par value of $500,000 at maturity, as illustrated in Exhibit C-3. At that date, Cash will be debited by $500,000 and the Long-Term Investment in Bonds account will be credited by $500,000 to close it. If ASPE is used, the straight-line amortization method for the premium could be used.

AVAILABLE-FOR-SALE SECURITIES

Securities that are not classified as held for trading or held to maturity will be classified as available-for-sale securities. Available-for-sale securities are valued at fair value. However, the adjustments of gains or losses are included in Other Comprehensive Income on the income statement.

HOW DO YOU ACCOUNT FOR STRATEGIC INVESTMENTS?

L.O. 3 Account for strategic investments

Companies that are strategically investing in other companies are aiming to do more than just receive a return on their investment. They want to influence the strategies of the company to attain other goals, such as integrating with a supplier company, expanding to new territories, developing new product lines that appeal to a different customer segment, or reducing costs by merging with another company and thereby creating synergy effects, among others.

Strategic investments are long-term investments—the investing company is not intending to sell the investee's shares in the short run. The accounting method used to account for such investments differs depending on the degree of the investment.

INVESTING IN AN ASSOCIATED COMPANY (SIGNIFICANT INFLUENCE)

A company might decide to invest in another company to have **significant influence** over its policies. In this case, the investor company would not be intending to sell the investment in the short run. Significant influence usually can be attained by acquiring directly or indirectly a share between 20%–50% of the investee's voting right shares, by having a certain number of seats on the board of directors, or by any other means that allows the investor company to influence the strategies of the investee.

The equity method is used in this case to account for a significant influence investment. Under the equity method, the shares are recorded at cost when acquired. No upward adjustments are performed for the shares, but an impairment test is done at the end of each period, and the value is written off if there is impairment. At the end of each period, when the investee reports net income, the investor company will add a portion of such net income (in proportion to its investment in the investee) to its Investment in the Investee account. The rationale behind this is that the company's investment grew by the investee's increase in retained earnings represented by its undistributed net income. If dividends were distributed by the investee company, the amount of dividends received is deducted from the Investment in the Investee account. The rationale behind this deduction is that the company's investment in the investee will decrease by the amount of dividends distributed. The dividends in such a case are regarded as a reduction in the investor's investment in the investee.

To illustrate, let's assume the following example: On January 1, 2015, Investco Inc. invested in Mackay Industries by acquiring 300,000 shares at $100 per share, which represents 30% of Mackay's shares. The following entry is recorded to recognize this purchase:

DATE	ACCOUNTS	POST REF.	DR.	CR.
Jan 1	Investment in Associated Companies		30,000,000	
	Cash			30,000,000
	Acquiring shares in an associated company.			

30,000,000
−30,000,000

Let's assume that at the end of 2015, Mackay Industries reported $10,000,000 of net income and that their shares are trading for $105 per share. Since the equity method is used, no adjustments are made to reflect the increase in the share's price. However, Investco Inc.'s investment in Mackay Industries will increase by its share in net income (Investco Inc.'s percentage share in Mackay Industries × reported net income by Mackay Industries = 30% × $10,000,000 = $3,000,000). The following entry is prepared to reflect this change:

DATE	ACCOUNTS	POST REF.	DR.	CR.
Dec 31	Investment in Associated Companies		3,000,000	
	Equity Income in Associates			3,000,000
	Recognizing the increase in investment in associates.			

3,000,000   3,000,000

Equity Income in Associates is a revenue account that is included with other revenues on the income statement. Investco Inc.'s share in Mackay's net income is regarded as if it is reinvesting in Mackay Industries and, hence, its investment amount increases.

Let's assume that on January 15, 2016, Mackay Industries declares dividends that are distributed on January 28, 2016. Investco Inc.'s share of these dividends is $200,000. The entry to record the receipt of dividends follows:

DATE	ACCOUNTS	POST REF.	DR.	CR.
Jan 28	Cash		200,000	
	Investment in Associated Companies			200,000
	Received dividends.			

200,000
−200,000

Receiving dividends in this case is regarded as if Investco Inc. is getting back part of its investment.

If Investco Inc. decides that it no longer wants a significant influence over Mackay Industries, it can sell the Mackay shares. The difference between the cash collected from selling the shares and the balance in the Investment in Associated Companies account would be recorded as either a gain or loss depending on the balance in the Investment in Associated Companies account: If the cash collected is greater than the balance in the account, then it is a gain; otherwise it is a loss.

It should be noted that ASPE allows companies to also use the cost method to account for significant influence investments. However, if the securities are quoted on an active market, the investment should be recorded at its quoted amount, with changes recorded in net income.

ASPE

INVESTING IN SUBSIDIARIES (CONTROLLING THE INVESTEE COMPANY)

Before discussing an investment in subsidiaries, let's illustrate this type of investment with a simple example. Assume that you want to calculate the wealth of your family—meaning your family as a whole. The assets, liabilities, and income for the whole family would be added together. Accordingly, income that is gained from transactions between family members should be eliminated, as what is paid from one family member and what is received by the other family member does not add any value to the overall family's wealth. So only transactions with outsiders count. The same thing applies for companies.

If a company intends to control an investee company, it would invest in more than 50% of the investee's voting right shares, either directly or indirectly. The **controlling interest** indicates the investor's ability to direct the strategies of the investee. In such a case the investor company would be called the **parent company** and the investee would be called a **subsidiary**. A parent company can have more than one subsidiary, which is referred to as a "group" when they are all considered together. A set of financial statements are prepared for the whole group as if it is one company, which are called **consolidated financial statements**. In consolidation, the whole group of companies are dealt with as if they are one entity. Just as in our family example above, all inter-company transactions (if there are any) must be eliminated from these consolidated financial statements. Intercompany transactions are any transactions among the companies of the group, such as trading activities, lending money, etc. However, the method by which such consolidated financial statements are prepared is out of the scope of this text.

HOW ARE INVESTMENTS REPORTED ON THE FINANCIAL STATEMENTS?

L.O. 4 Report investments on the financial statements

Investment transactions affect three different financial statements. The results of investment activities (gains or losses) would affect the statement of comprehensive income, the investment itself would be presented on the statement of financial position, while all cash transactions related to such investments would appear on the statement of cash flows.

REPORTING INVESTMENT TRANSACTIONS ON THE INCOME STATEMENT

Investments could result in either gains or losses during a certain financial period. Because the investments dealt with in this chapter are mainly subordinate activities of the investor company (i.e., not related to their core business), the profit or loss of selling such investments would be presented on the income statement, usually under Other Income. If the investments are accounted for by the fair value method and there are unrealized gains or losses, they would be presented on the statement of comprehensive income under Other Comprehensive Income.

Exhibit C-4 illustrates how such transactions affect the income statement and statement of comprehensive income.

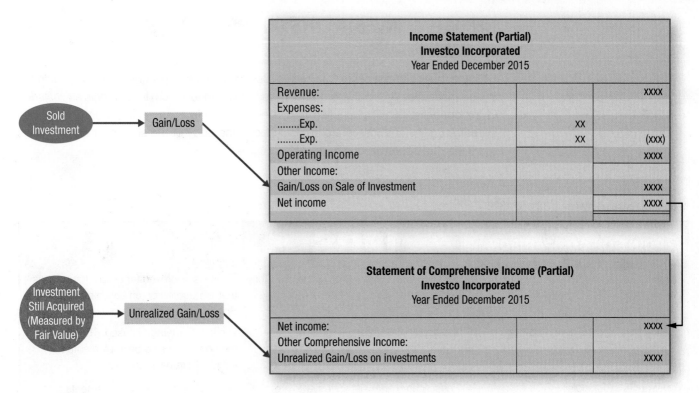

Income Statement (Partial) Investco Incorporated Year Ended December 2015		
Revenue:		XXXX
Expenses:		
........Exp.	XX	
........Exp.	XX	(XXX)
Operating Income		XXXX
Other Income:		
Gain/Loss on Sale of Investment		XXXX
Net income		XXXX

Statement of Comprehensive Income (Partial) Investco Incorporated Year Ended December 2015		
Net income:		XXXX
Other Comprehensive Income:		
Unrealized Gain/Loss on investments		XXXX

Exhibit C-4 ▲

REPORTING INVESTMENTS ON THE STATEMENT OF FINANCIAL POSITION

How investments are reported on the statement of financial position will depend on how the investment is classified. Trading or available-for-sale investments are reported within the current assets section because they are ready to be sold at any time. Investments in associate companies are included in the non-current assets section. If the company has investments in subsidiaries, a consolidated statement of financial position would need to be prepared.

Exhibit C-5 illustrates how the different investments are reported on the statement of financial position.

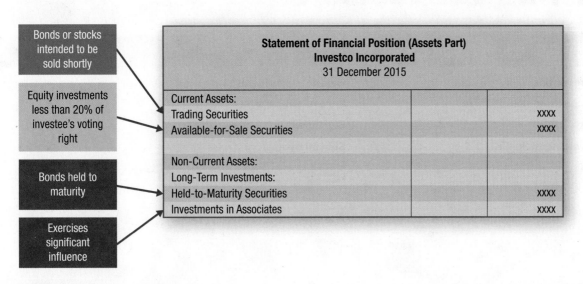

Statement of Financial Position (Assets Part) Investco Incorporated 31 December 2015		
Current Assets:		
Trading Securities		XXXX
Available-for-Sale Securities		XXXX
Non-Current Assets:		
Long-Term Investments:		
Held-to-Maturity Securities		XXXX
Investments in Associates		XXXX

Exhibit C-5 ▲

REPORTING INVESTMENTS ON THE STATEMENT OF CASH FLOWS

Selling or buying investments with cash appears on the statement of cash flows within the investing activities section, while gains, losses, and revenues from investments are included in the operating activities section to eliminate their effect, as explained in Chapter 12. Unrealized gains and losses are not included in the body of the statement of cash flows since they are not realized in cash yet.

Main Differences between IFRS and ASPE

POINT OF COMPARISON	IFRS	ASPE
Fair value model	Its use is approved and could be used for held-for-trading investments.	Its use is approved for equity instruments that are quoted on an active market. Bonds are valued at amortized cost.
Investments in associate companies	The equity method is used.	The equity method is used. The cost method could also be implemented, subject to impairment testing.
Investments in subsidiaries	Consolidated financial statements are prepared.	Consolidated financial statements are most likely prepared, but the equity or the cost methods could also be implemented.
Amortization of bond premiums and discounts	The effective interest method is used.	Either the effective interest method or straight-line amortization can be used as long as the difference is not significant.

ACCOUNTING VOCABULARY

THE LANGUAGE OF BUSINESS

Available-for-sale securities (p. 761)

Consolidated financial statements (p. 768)

Controlling interest (p. 768)

Held-for-trading investments (p. 761)

Held-to-maturity investments (p. 761)

Parent company (p. 768)

Significant influence (p. 766)

Subsidiary (p. 768)

ACCOUNTING PRACTICE

EXERCISES

EC-1A. Account for strategic investments (*Learning Objective 1*) 5 min.

State the accounting method used for each of the following investments according to IFRS:

1. Held-for-trading investment
2. Held-to-maturity investment
3. Having a significant influence over the investee company

EC-2A. Account for non-strategic investments (*Learning Objective 2*) 10 min.

On January 15, 2015, White Alberta Inc. invested in bonds issued for $200,000 by Wheat Grain Inc. and in 10,000 shares of Ontario Sun Inc. at $10 per share. White Alberta's intention is to resell the bonds and shares within a short period of time. At year-end the price of the bonds went down to $195,000 and the shares increased in value to $12 per share. The following table summarizes this information:

	Acquisition Price	Current Price	Gain/(Loss)
Wheat Grain Inc. Bonds	$200,000	$195,000	$(5,000)
Ontario Sun Inc. Shares	$100,000	$120,000	$20,000
Total	$300,000	$315,000	$15,000

On January 20, 2016, White Alberta Inc. sold the bonds and shares for $196,000 and $122,000, respectively.

Requirements

1. Prepare the necessary journal entry to record White Alberta's original investment in the bonds.
2. Prepare the required adjusting entries on December 31, 2015.
3. Prepare the necessary journal entries when White Alberta sold its investments.

EC-3A. Account for strategic investments (*Learning Objective 3*) 5 min.

On January 1, 2015, Super Magic Inc. acquired 600,000 shares representing 40% of Pure Water Inc.'s shares at $10 per share. Pure Water Inc.'s net income at year-end is $600,000 and Super Magic Inc. received dividends on January 15, 2016, in the amount of $80,000.

Requirement

1. Prepare the necessary journal entries to record Super Magic Inc.'s investment.
2. Prepare the journal entry to record Super Magic Inc.'s adjustments to recognize Pure Water Inc.'s net income.
3. Prepare the journal entry when Super Magic received dividends.

Glossary

Visit *MyAccountingLab* at **www.myaccountinglab.com** *to find Glossary Flashcards.*

A

Accelerated depreciation method. A depreciation method that writes off more of the asset's cost near the start of its useful life than the straight-line method does.

Account. The basic summary device of accounting; the detailed record of all the changes in a specific asset, liability, or shareholders' equity item as a result of transactions.

Account form. A statement of financial position format that lists assets on the left of the report and liabilities and shareholders' equity on the right, just as those accounts appear in the accounting equation.

Accounting. The information system that measures business activity, processes the results of activities into reports, and communicates the results to decision makers.

Accounting cycle. The sequence of steps used to record and report business transactions.

Accounting period. Generally, the time period reflected by a set of financial statements.

Accounting Standards for Private Enterprises (ASPE). A set of guidelines that have replaced the original Canadian Generally Accepted Accounting Principles (GAAP), but specifically used for private enterprises.

Accounts payable. A liability backed by the general reputation and credit standing of the debtor.

Accounts receivable. An asset representing amounts due from customers to whom the business has sold goods or for whom the business has performed services.

Accounts receivable turnover. Measures a company's ability to collect cash from credit customers. To compute accounts receivable turnover, divide net credit sales by average net accounts receivable.

Accrual basis accounting. An accounting system that records the business event based on when it occurs, not when cash is exchanged.

Accruals. Revenues earned or expenses incurred before cash has been exchanged.

Accrued expenses. Expenses that have been incurred prior to being paid for.

Accumulated Depreciation. A contra-asset account that reflects all of the depreciation recorded for an asset to date.

Accumulated other comprehensive income. The cumulative change in equity that is due to the revenues and expenses, and gains and losses derived from non-shareholder transactions.

Acid-test ratio. Ratio that reveals how well the entity can pay its current liabilities. The term is derived from how old gold miners tested a rock to see whether it was real gold. They used to submerge it in an acid. If it dissolves, then it is not gold, as gold does not dissolve in acid. It is calculated by dividing quick assets (cash, short-term investments, and net current receivables) by current liabilities. Also called the *quick ratio.*

Adjusted trial balance. A list of all the accounts of a business with their adjusted balances.

Adjusting entries. Journal entries made at the end of the accounting period to measure the period's income accurately and bring the related asset and liability accounts to correct balances before the financial statements are prepared.

Aging method. The method of estimating bad debts that focuses on accounts receivable; the accountant calculates the end-of-period allowance balance based on an aging of the Accounts Receivable; also called the *balance sheet method.*

Allowance for Doubtful Account (AFDA). A contra-asset account that holds the estimated amount of bad debts receivable.

Allowance method. The method of accounting for bad debts that estimates these amounts and uses an allowance account so that the statement of financial position shows the net amount of Accounts Receivable expected to be collected in the future.

Amortization. Systematic reduction of an intangible asset's carrying value on the books. An expense that applies to intangibles in the same way depreciation applies to plant assets and depletion to natural resources. ASPE uses this terminology to record the reduction in tangible assets, too.

Annuities. Multiple investments of an equal periodic amount at fixed intervals over the length of the investment.

Arrears. A cumulative dividend on preferred shares that has not been paid for the year.

Asset management ratios. Ratios that measure how efficiently a company utilizes its operating assets.

Assets. Items of value that a business possesses; also referred to as the economic resources or properties owned or controlled by the business that will provide future benefits to the business.

Audit. An examination of a company's financial statements performed to determine their fairness.

Audit trail. A trail of business documents and records that provides evidence of transactions.

Available-for-sale securities. Investments in financial instruments that are not categorized as held for trading or held to maturity. Such investments are usually non-strategic investments (i.e., the investor owns less than 20% of the investee's equity in the case of acquiring shares).

Average cost. Inventory costing method where a new average cost per unit is computed and is used to value ending inventory and cost of goods sold. There are two types of average cost: (1) moving average, and (2) weighted average. Moving average is applied in a perpetual inventory system. Weighted average is applied in a periodic inventory system.

B

Bad debt. An account receivable that is unable to be collected; also called an *uncollectible account.*

Bad debt expense. Selling expense caused by bad debts that reduce operating income.

Balance. The difference between an account's total debit and total credit amounts; the ending value of an account.

Balance sheet. Summary of an entity's assets, liabilities, and shareholders' equity as of a specific date; also called the *statement of financial position.*

Bank balance. The balance in the company's bank account according to the bank.

Bank collection. Collection of money by the bank on behalf of a depositor.

Bank reconciliation. A document that identifies and explains the differences between a depositor's record of a cash account and a bank's record of the same cash account.

Bank statement. A document the bank prepares to report the changes in the depositor's cash account for a period of time. It shows the beginning bank account balance, lists the month's cash transactions, and shows the ending bank account balance.

Basket purchase. Purchase of multiple assets for one price; also called a *lump-sum purchase*.

Benchmarking. The practice of comparing a company with other companies that are leaders.

Betterment. Expenditure that increases the capacity or efficiency of an asset.

Bonds payable. Long-term, interest-bearing notes payable issued to multiple lenders called bondholders.

Book balance. The balance in a company's bank account according to the company's accounting records, or books.

Book value. The asset's cost minus its accumulated depreciation; also called *carrying value*.

Brand names. Assets that represent distinctive identifications of a product or service; also called *trade names*.

Bribe. The payment of money to influence the conduct of a person.

Businesses. Organizations that sell products or services to customers.

C

Callable bonds. Bonds that the issuer may call or pay off at a specified price whenever the issuer wants.

Capital cost allowance (CCA). A method of calculating depreciation based on CRA tax regulations.

Capital expenditure. Expenditure that increases the capacity or efficiency of an asset or extends its useful life. Capital expenditures are debited to an asset account.

Capitalized. The process of debiting (increasing) an asset account for the cost of an asset.

Carrying amount. Bonds payable *minus* the discount or *plus* the premium.

Carrying value. The asset's cost minus its accumulated depreciation; also called *book value*.

Cash. Coin, currency, cheques, petty cash, chequing accounts, payroll accounts, money orders, traveller's cheques, and anything the bank will accept as a deposit.

Cash and Cash Equivalents. The statement of financial position item used to describe cash and items so closely resembling cash that they are presented as cash.

Cash-basis accounting. Accounting method that records revenues when cash is received and expenses when cash is paid.

Cash conversion cycle. A measurement of the amount of time a company's cash is tied up in its operations.

Cash equivalents. Highly liquid, highly safe investments that so closely resemble cash that they may be shown with cash on the statement of financial position.

Cash register scheme. A fraud scheme in which an employee steals cash by processing false refunds.

Chart of accounts. A list of all the accounts of a business and the numbers assigned to those accounts.

Cheque tampering. A fraud scheme in which an employee writes a fraudulent cheque and makes the cheque payable to him- or herself, or obtains a cheque intended for an outside party, endorses the cheque, and then cashes it.

Classified statement of financial position. A statement of financial position that separates assets and liabilities into current and long-term classes.

Closing entries. Journal entries that are prepared at the end of the accounting period. Closing entries zero out the revenue, expense, and dividends accounts so that accounting can begin for the next period.

Code of ethics. A formal written document that contains broad statements intended to guide proper ethical decision making.

Collateral. Assets pledged to secure repayment of a loan. In the case of nonpayment by the borrower, the lender has the right to take the collateral.

Collusion. Two or more individuals working together to commit fraud.

Common shares. Represents the investment of assets made by shareholders into a corporation.

Common-size statement. A financial statement that reports only percentages (no dollar amounts).

Comparability. One of the qualitative characteristics of accounting information that should enable users to compare one company's accounting information to another company's accounting information and to its own previous years' results.

Completed contract method. Under this method, revenues, costs, and gross profit are recognized only after the project is fully completed.

Componentization. To take the cost of an asset and divide it between its separate component parts, where the cost of each of these components is significant in relation to the total cost of the asset.

Compound interest. Interest earned not only on principal but also on the interest to date.

Compound journal entry. A journal entry affecting more than two accounts; an entry that has more than one debit and/or more than one credit.

Conceptual framework. A theoretical foundation that helps accounting standard setters develop consistent and coherent standards, and helps accountants determine the appropriate treatment of the events in the absence of specific guidance, so that financial information can be properly communicated to the users.

Consistency. Accounting principle that states that a business should use the same accounting methods and procedures from period to period.

Consolidated financial statements. Financial statements that are prepared by a parent company in which all of the parent company's subsidiaries are included and regarded as one economic unit.

Contingent liability. A potential liability that depends on the outcome of a future event.

Contra-account. An account that is linked to another account. A contra-account will have a normal balance opposite of the account it is linked to.

Control account. An account in the general ledger that summarizes the details of an account balance.

Control activities. The policies and procedures implemented in an internal control system.

Control environment. The overall attitude, awareness, and actions of management and staff regarding the internal control system and its importance to the business.

Controller. The individual in an organization responsible for the accounting system and financial statements.

Controlling interest. When an investor company owns enough of an investee company to direct the strategies of the investee company. Control exists even if the investor does not exercise it. A controlling interest usually results from the investor company acquiring more than 50% of the investee company's voting right shares, either directly or indirectly.

Convertible bonds. Bonds that may be converted into the common shares of the issuing company at the option of the investor.

Copyright. Exclusive right to reproduce and sell a book, musical composition, film, other work of art, or computer program. Issued by the federal government, copyrights extend 50 years beyond the author's life.

Corporation. A business owned by shareholders that is an entity legally separate from its owners.

Cost of goods available for sale. The cost of inventory on hand at the beginning of the period plus the net cost of inventory purchased during the period.

Cost of Goods Sold (COGS). The cost of the inventory that the business has sold to customers.

Cost vs. benefit. An analysis of what one option costs and what its benefits are to determine whether to implement the action or not.

Credit. The right side of any account; an entry made to the right side of an account.

Credit memorandum. A document that supports the return of goods from the customer and the adjustment to the customer's account balance.

Credit terms. The payment terms for customers who buy on account.

Creditor. The entity to whom the debtor promises future payment; also called the *payee of a note*.

Cumulative preferred shares. Preferred shares whose owners must receive all dividends in arrears before the corporation pays dividends to the common shareholders.

Current assets. Assets that are expected to be converted to cash, sold, or consumed within one year or the business's operating cycle if the cycle is longer than a year.

Current cost. The amount required to purchase the asset today.

Current liabilities. Debts due to be paid with cash or fulfilled with goods and services within one year or the entity's operating cycle if the cycle is longer than a year.

Current portion of long-term debt. The principal portion of a long-term liability that is payable within one year.

Current ratio. Current assets divided by current liabilities. Measures a business's ability to meet its short-term obligations with its current assets.

D

Days' sales in inventory. Measures a company's ability to turn inventory to sales. To compute the ratio, divide 365 by the inventory turnover.

Days' sales in receivables. Measures a company's ability to collect receivables. To compute the ratio, divide 365 by the accounts receivable turnover.

Debentures. Unsecured bonds backed only by the good faith of the borrower; also called *unsecured bonds*.

Debit. The left side of any account; an entry made to the left side of an account.

Debit memorandum. A document that supports the return of goods to the supplier and the adjustment to the balance owed to the supplier.

Debt ratio. The ratio of a company's total liabilities (debt) to its total assets. It measures a business's ability to pay long-term liabilities.

Debt to equity ratio. Total liabilities divided by total equity. It measures a business's financial leverage and indicates what proportion of equity and debt the company is using to finance its assets.

Debtor. The entity that promises future payment; also called the *maker of a note*.

Deferrals. Cash received or paid before revenues have been earned or expenses have been incurred.

Deferred expenses. Amounts that are assets of a business because they represent items that have been paid for but will be used later. Also called *prepaid expenses*.

Deferred revenue. A liability created when a business collects cash from customers in advance of providing goods or services; also called *unearned revenue*.

Depletion. Systematic reduction of a natural resource's carrying value on the books. Expense that applies to natural resource in the same way depreciation applies to plant assets and amortization to intangible assets. It is computed in the same way as units-of-production depreciation.

Deposits in transit. Deposits that have been recorded by a company but not yet by its bank.

Depreciable cost. The cost of a plant asset minus its estimated residual value.

Depreciation. Allocation of the cost of a long-term asset to expense over its useful life.

Direct method. Format of the operating activities section of the statement of cash flows; it lists the cash receipts and cash payments resulting from a company's day-to-day operations.

Direct write-off method. The method of accounting for bad debts in which a customer's account is written off as uncollectible when the business determines that the customer will not pay.

Disbursement scheme. A form of employee embezzlement in which an employee tricks a company into giving up cash for an invalid reason. Examples include cheque tampering, cash register schemes, and expense schemes.

Discount. Excess of a bond's maturity value over its issue price. Also called a *bond discount*.

Discount period. Period in which the buyer can make early payment for a purchase and receive a discount on that purchase.

Discounting. Computing a present value.

Dividend yield. Ratio of dividends per share to the share's market price. Tells the percentage of a share's market value that the company returns to shareholders annually as dividends.

Dividends. Distribution of earnings by a corporation to its shareholders.

Dollar value bias. The bias one sees from comparing numbers in absolute (dollars) rather than relative (percentages) terms.

Double-declining-balance (DDB) method. An accelerated depreciation method that computes annual depreciation by multiplying the asset's decreasing book value by a constant percent that is two times the straight-line rate.

Double-entry accounting. The rule of accounting that specifies that every transaction involves at least two accounts and is recorded with equal amounts of debits and credits.

Due date. The date when final payment of the note is due; also called the *maturity date*.

E

Earnings per share of common shares. Reflects the net income earned for each share of the company's outstanding common shares.

Economic entity assumption. The assumption that an organization or a section of an organization stands apart as a separate economic unit for accounting purposes.

Effective interest method. The calculation of interest on a bond based on the amount that is owed to bondholders.

Electronic data interchange (EDI). Direct electronic communication between suppliers and retailers.

Electronic funds transfer (EFT). System that transfers cash by electronic communication rather than by paper documents.

Employee embezzlement. Fraud where employees steal from employers by taking assets, bribes, or kickbacks, or engaging in disbursement schemes to steal cash.

Eom. Credit term specifying that payment for a purchase is due by the end of the month; also referred to as *n/eom*.

Estimated liabilities. A known obligation of an unknown amount.

Ethics. Principles of socially responsible behaviour.

Expense scheme. A fraud scheme in which an employee overcharges the company for travel and other business-related expenses, such as lunches, hotels, air travel, parking fees, and cab fares.

Expenses. Decreases to retained earnings caused by using resources to deliver goods or provide services to customers.

External audit. An audit of financial statements performed by public accountants.

Extraordinary repair. Repair work that extends the life of an asset.

F

Fair value. The anticipated market price to sell an asset or transfer a liability.

Financial accounting. A process used to track business transactions and to provide financial information about a business to external users.

Financial statements. Financial information prepared according to IFRS or Canadian Accounting Standards for Private Enterprises, that communicates an entity's performance or financial position.

Financing activities. Activities related to the issuance of, and repayment of, long-term debt or to the issuance of shares and the payment of dividends; it's a section of the statement of cash flows.

Finished goods. Inventory of goods ready to sell.

First-in, first-out (FIFO). Inventory costing method in which the first inventory costs incurred are the first costs to be assigned to cost of goods sold; FIFO leaves in ending inventory the last, the most recent, costs incurred.

Fiscal year. Any consecutive, 12-month period that a business adopts as its accounting year.

Fixed asset turnover ratio. Measures a company's ability to generate sales from fixed asset investments, specifically property, plant, and equipment (PPE).

Franchises. Privileges granted by a private business or a government to sell a product or service under specified conditions.

Fraud. Deceit or trickery involving intentional actions that cause harm to a business, its stakeholders, or both.

Fraud triangle. The combination of perceived pressure, rationalization, and perceived opportunity necessary to commit fraud.

Free cash flow. The anticipated amount of cash available from operations after paying for planned investments in long-term assets and paying dividends.

Free on board (FOB) destination. A shipping term specifying that title to goods passes to the buyer when the goods are received at the buyer's destination; thus, the seller pays the cost of shipping the goods to this destination.

Free on board (FOB) shipping point. A shipping term specifying that title to goods passes to the buyer when the goods are shipped at the seller's place of business; thus, the buyer pays the cost of shipping the goods to its location.

Freight charges. The cost of shipping merchandise from the seller to the buyer.

Full disclosure principle. An accounting principle that requires a company to provide all relevant information to the user of financial statements so that they can make an informed decision.

Fully depreciated asset. An asset that has reached the end of its estimated useful life. No more depreciation is recorded for the asset.

Fundamental accounting equation. The basic tool of accounting that measures the resources of a business and the claims to those resources: Assets = Liabilities + Shareholders' Equity.

Future value. The amount that a given sum of money will be "worth" at a specified time in the future assuming a certain interest rate.

G

General and administrative expenses. Office expenses, such as the salaries of the company president and office employees, depreciation of items used in administration, rent, utilities, and property taxes on the office building.

General journal. The chronological accounting record of the transactions of a business.

General ledger. The accounting record summarizing, in accounts, the transactions of a business and showing the resulting account balances.

Going-concern assumption. The assumption that the business entity will continue in operation for the foreseeable future.

Goodwill. Excess of the cost of an acquired company over the sum of the market values of its net assets (assets minus liabilities).

Gross margin. Net sales revenue minus cost of goods sold; also called *gross profit*.

Gross margin percentage. A measure of profitability equal to gross margin divided by net sales revenue; also called *gross profit percentage*.

Gross profit. Net sales revenue minus cost of goods sold; also called *gross margin*.

Gross profit method. A way of estimating inventory by estimating gross profit, using estimated gross profit to estimate cost of goods sold, and using estimated cost of goods sold to estimate ending inventory.

Gross profit percentage. A measure of profitability equal to gross profit divided by net sales revenue; also called *gross margin percentage*.

H

Held-for-trading investments. Shares and bonds quoted on an open market that a company acquires with the intention of reselling in the short term. The main goal of these investments is usually to get additional income in the short term.

Held-to-maturity investments. Bonds that a company acquires with the intention of holding until they mature.

Historical cost. The actual cost of goods and assets acquired.

Horizontal analysis. Study of dollar amount and percentage changes in comparative financial statements.

I

Impairment. An asset is impaired when its carrying amount exceeds its recoverable amount, which is the future undiscounted cash flow that the asset can provide and be disposed for.

Income from operations. Gross profit minus operating expenses; also called *operating income*.

Income statement. Summary of a business's revenues, expenses, and net income or net loss for a specific period. It is a component of the statement of comprehensive income.

Income statement approach. The method of estimating bad debts that focuses on net credit sales; also called the *percentage of sales method*.

Indirect method. Format of the operating activities section of the statement of cash flows; it starts with net income and reconciles to net cash provided by operating activities.

Intangible assets. Assets with no physical form. They are valuable because of the special rights they carry. Examples include patents and copyrights.

Interest. The fee for using money; revenue to the creditor for loaning money; expense to the debtor for borrowing money.

Interest-coverage ratio. Ratio of income from operations to interest expense. It measures the number of times that operating income can cover interest expense; also called the *times-interest-earned ratio.*

Interest rate. The percentage rate of interest specified by the note; almost always stated for a period of one year.

Interim financial statements. Financial statements that cover a period that is less than a year.

Internal audit. Assessment of a company's compliance with laws and regulations, operations, and policies and procedures performed by employees of the company.

Internal control. A system implemented within an organization to safeguard assets, operate efficiently and effectively, report financial information properly, and comply with applicable laws and regulations.

International Financial Reporting Standards (IFRS). A set of internationally accepted reporting standards that guide how business activities should be recognized, measured, and recorded, and how financial information should be reported. IFRS were developed by the International Accounting Standards Board.

Inventory. Goods purchased for resale to customers in the normal course of merchandising operations; also called *merchandise inventory.*

Inventory layer. A record of the quantity of and the cost of inventory items made in a single purchase.

Inventory shrinkage. The loss of inventory.

Inventory subsidiary ledger. A special type of subsidiary ledger where the quantity, cost, and value of each inventory item is tracked and recorded after each purchase, sale, or return. The quantity and value of inventory are recalculated after each transaction.

Inventory turnover. The ratio of cost of goods sold to average inventory. Measures the number of times a company sells its average level of inventory during a year.

Investing activities. Activities that increase or decrease long-term assets; it's a section of the statement of cash flows.

Issue price. The price the shares initially sell for the first time they are sold.

J

Journalize. Entering a transaction in a journal; also called *record.*

K

Kickback. The return of part of a sum received because of a confidential agreement.

Known liabilities. Known obligations of known amounts.

L

Land improvements. Depreciable improvements to land, such as fencing, sprinklers, paving, signs, and lighting.

Legal capital. The portion of shareholders' equity that cannot be used for dividends.

Lessee. The party who is using the lease.

Lessor. The party who is providing the asset for lease.

Liabilities. Third-party or creditor claims to the assets of a business; the debts owed by the business entity to third parties, which will reduce the future assets of a business or require future services or products.

Licences. Privileges granted by a private business or a government to sell a product or service under specified conditions.

Liquidity. The ability to convert an asset to cash quickly.

Liquidity ratios. Ratios that measure a company's ability to meet short-term obligations with current assets.

Lock-box system. A system in which customers send payments to a post office box of a business. The bank collects payments from the box and deposits them into the business's account.

Long-term asset. An asset that will be held for more than one year or longer than the operating cycle (also known as a fixed asset or non-current asset). A long-lived, tangible asset such as land, buildings, equipment, and furniture lasting for more than a year used in the operation of a business. Also called *plant assets* and commonly shown on the balance sheet as property, plant, and equipment.

Long-term liability. A liability that is expected to be paid after more than one year or after the period of one operating cycle (also known as a non-current liability).

Lower of cost or net realizable value (LCNRV) rule. The rule that a business must report inventory in the financial statements at whichever is lower, the historical cost or the net realizable value, of each inventory item.

Lump-sum purchase. Purchase of multiple assets for one price; also called a *basket purchase.*

M

Maker of a note. The entity that promises future payment; also called the *debtor.*

Management fraud. Management's intentional misstatement of the financial statements, driven by greed or the pressure to show that a business is more profitable than it really is.

Managerial accounting. A branch of accounting involved in the process of gathering cost information, budgeting, planning, performance evaluation, etc. for internal users.

Manufacturing business. A business that makes its own products that are sold to the final customer or to other companies.

Market analysis ratios. Ratios that are used to evaluate a company's stock market performance.

Market interest rate. Interest rate investors are willing to pay for similar bonds of equal risk at the current time. Also called *yield.*

Matching principle. The principle requiring revenues to be matched with their related expenses in a specified period to report net income.

Materiality. This is a measure of whether or not something is relevant to a decision. If an analysis leads to a response that something is significant or that it will change an opinion, then this is material, or of enough significance or size to matter.

Maturity date. The date when final payment of a note is due; also called the *due date.* Also, the date on which the bond issuer (the borrower) must repay the principal amount to the bondholders.

Maturity value. The sum of the principal of a note plus interest due at maturity. Also, the amount a borrower must pay back to the bondholders on the maturity date; also called *principal amount* or *par value.*

Memorandum entry. A journal entry that "notes" a significant event, but which has no debit or credit amount.

Merchandise inventory. Goods purchased for resale to customers in the normal course of merchandising operations; also called *inventory.*

Merchandising business. A business that sells products made by another company; also called *wholesale* and *retail business*.

Monetary unit assumption. The assumption that the purchasing power of the monetary unit (the dollar) is stable. In other words, a dollar from 50 years ago is worth a dollar today.

Mortgage. A long-term note payable that is secured by real estate.

Moving average cost. Inventory costing method where, after each purchase of inventory, a new average cost per unit is computed and is used to value ending inventory and cost of goods sold in the perpetual inventory system.

Multi-step income statement. Income statement format that calculates net income or net loss by listing important subtotals, such as gross profit and operating income.

N

N/30. Credit term specifying that payment for a purchase is due within 30 days after the date of the invoice.

Natural resources. Assets that come from the earth. Examples include minerals, gas, oil, and timber.

N/eom. Credit term specifying that payment for a purchase is due by the end of the month; also referred to as *eom*.

Net credit sales. The total credit sales less sales discounts and sales returns and allowances related to the credit sales.

Net income. The excess of total revenues over total expenses; also called *profit*.

Net loss. The excess of total expenses over total revenues.

Net realizable value. The net amount that the business expects to collect; the net realizable value of receivables is calculated by subtracting Allowance for Doubtful Accounts from Accounts Receivable.

Net sales revenue. Sales revenue less sales discounts and sales returns and allowances.

Net value. The amount found by subtracting the balance of a contra-account from the balance of the account it is linked to.

Nonsufficient funds (NSF) cheque. A cheque drawn against a bank account that has insufficient money to pay the cheque.

Normal balance. The balance that appears on the side of an account where increases are recorded; the expected balance of an account.

Note payable. A written promise of future payment made by the business.

Note term. The time span of the note during which interest is computed; it extends from the original date of the note to the maturity date.

Notes. Disclosures that accompany the financial statements.

Notes receivable. Written promises by customers to pay an amount of cash to the business in the future.

O

Obsolete. An asset that has lost part or all of its functionality or has become outdated.

On account. Buying or selling on credit.

Operating activities. Activities that create revenue or expense in the entity's major line of business; it's a section of the statement of cash flows. Operating activities affect the income statement.

Operating cycle. The time span during which the business obtains resources, uses them to sell goods and services to customers, and collects cash from these customers.

Operating expenses. Expenses of operating a business other than cost of goods sold. Examples include depreciation, rent, salaries, utilities, advertising, delivery expense, property taxes, and supplies expense.

Operating income. Gross profit minus operating expenses. Also called *income from operations*.

Ordinary repair. Repair work that is necessary to maintain an asset in normal operating condition.

Other revenues and expenses. Revenues and expenses that fall outside the main operations of a business, such as interest expense and a loss on the sale of long-term assets.

Outstanding cheques. Cheques that have been issued by a company and recorded in its books but have not yet been paid by its bank.

Owner(s) capital. The amount invested in a sole proprietorship or a partnership by an individual in exchange for ownership of the business.

P

Par value. The amount a borrower must pay back to the bondholders on the maturity date; also called *principal amount* or *maturity value*.

Par value (of shares). Arbitrary amount assigned to a share.

Parent company. A company that can exercise control over another company, such as by owning more than 50% of the capital of the other company.

Partnership. A business with two or more owners.

Patent. An intangible asset that is a federal government grant conveying an exclusive 20-year right to produce and sell a process or formula.

Payee of a note. The entity to whom the debtor promises future payment; also called the *creditor*.

Perceived opportunity. An element of the fraud triangle in which the employee believes a chance exists to commit fraud, conceal it, and avoid punishment.

Perceived pressure. An element of the fraud triangle in which the employee feels a need to obtain cash or other assets.

Percentage of completion method. Under this method, revenues and gross profit are recognized each period based on the percentage of expenses incurred, or the percentage of completion to date.

Percentage of sales method. The method of estimating bad debts that focuses on net credit sales; also called the *income statement approach*.

Periodic inventory system. An inventory system in which the business does not keep a continuous record of inventory on hand. At the end of the period, a physical count of inventory is taken and determines the inventory owned as well as the cost of the goods sold.

Permanent accounts. The asset, liability, and shareholders' equity accounts; these accounts are not closed at the end of the period.

Perpetual inventory system. An inventory system in which the business keeps a continuous record of inventory on hand and the cost of the goods sold.

Petty cash. Fund containing a small amount of cash that is used to pay for minor expenditures.

Post-closing trial balance. A list of the accounts and their balances at the end of the accounting period after closing entries have been journalized and posted.

Posting. Copying information from the general journal to accounts in the general ledger.

Posting reference. A notation in the journal and ledger that links these two accounting records together.

Preferred shares. Shares that give their owners certain advantages over common shareholders, such as the right to receive dividends before the common shareholders and the right to receive assets before the common shareholders if the corporation liquidates.

Premium. Excess of a bond's issue price over its maturity value. Also called *bond premium*.

Prepaid expenses. Amounts that are assets of a business because they represent items that have been paid for but will be used later.

Present value. The value on a given date of a future amount, adjusted to reflect the time value of a single amount or of an annuity.

Price/earnings ratio. Ratio of the market price of a common share to the company's earnings per share. It measures the value that the stock market places on $1 of a company's earnings.

Principal. The amount loaned out by the payee and borrowed by the maker of the note.

Principal amount. The amount a borrower must pay back to the bondholders on the maturity date; also called *par value* or *maturity value*.

Profit. The difference between the revenues (the sales price of the goods or services sold by the business) and expenses (the cost of the resources used to provide these goods and services); also called *net income*.

Profitability ratios. Ratios that measure a company's ability to generate profits.

Promissory note. A written pledge to pay a fixed amount of money at a later date.

Property, plant, and equipment. A heading often seen on the statement of financial position used to describe fixed, or plant, assets.

Provision. A liability that that has uncertain timing or uncertain amount.

Public accountant. A licensed accountant who serves the general public rather than one particular company.

Purchase discount. Discount received on purchases by paying early within a discount period.

Purchase order. A document showing details of merchandise being ordered from a supplier.

Purchase returns and allowances. A reduction in the amount owed for a purchase due to returning merchandise or accepting damaged goods.

Purchasing agent. The individual in an organization responsible for buying items for that organization.

Q

Quick assets. Highly liquid assets used to calculate the quick ratio, including cash and cash equivalents, short-term investments, and net accounts receivable.

Quick ratio. Items of assets that can be rapidly turned into cash (cash, short-term investments, and net current receivables) divided by current liabilities. Ratio that reveals how well the entity can pay its current liabilities; also called the *acid-test ratio*.

R

Rate of return on common shareholders' equity. Net income minus preferred dividends, divided by average common shareholders' equity. It is a measure of profitability; also called *return on common equity*.

Rate of return on net sales. Ratio of net income to net sales. It is a measure of profitability; also called *return on sales*.

Rate of return on shareholders' equity. Net income divided by average shareholders' equity. It is a measure of profitability; also called *return on equity*.

Rate of return on total assets. Ratio of net income plus interest expense to total assets. It measures a company's effectiveness in using assets to generate earnings; also called *return on assets*.

Ratio analysis. A form of financial statement analysis in which items on the financial statements are expressed as ratios of one number to another.

Rationalization. An element of the fraud triangle in which the employee justifies his or her actions and convinces him- or herself that fraud is not wrong.

Raw materials. Inventory items used in the production of goods.

Realizable value. The amount that is likely to be received in exchange for an asset, factoring in any cash or other benefit, less any costs or expenses to sell or distribute the asset.

Receiving report. A document evidencing the receipt of goods purchased.

Record. Entering a transaction in a journal; also called *journalize*.

Recoverable amount The higher of the future discounted cash flow that the asset can provide and the amount it can be disposed for.

Relevance. One of the qualitative characteristics of accounting information that makes a difference in a decision-making process. The information should be predictable and provide feedback in a timely manner.

Reliability. One of the qualitative characteristics of accounting information that it be verifiable, confirmable by any independent observer.

Remittance advice. A receipt of payment, usually sent by the customer informing the supplier that the payment is completed.

Report form. A statement of financial position format that reports assets at the top of the report, followed by liabilities, and ending with shareholders' equity at the end of the report.

Residual value. Expected cash value of an asset at the end of its useful life; also called *salvage (residual) value*.

Retail business. A business that sells products purchased from another company to the final consumer.

Retailers. Businesses that buy goods from manufacturers or wholesalers and resell them to the general public.

Retained earnings. Earnings of a business that are kept, or retained, in the business.

Return on assets. Ratio of net income plus interest expense to total assets. It measures a company's effectiveness in using assets to generate earnings; also called *rate of return on total assets*.

Return on common equity. Net income minus preferred dividends, divided by average common shareholders' equity. It is measure of profitability; also called *rate of return on common shareholders' equity*.

Return on equity. Net income divided by average shareholders' equity. It is a measure of profitability; also called *rate of return on shareholders' equity*.

Return on sales. Ratio of net income to net sales. It is a measure of profitability; also called *rate of return on net sales*.

Revaluation model. Under IFRS, property, plant and equipment can be revalued to the fair value if the value can be reliably measured.

Revenue. Increases to retained earnings created by delivering goods or providing services to customers.

Revenue expenditure. Expenditure that is debited to an expense account.

Revenue recognition principle. Recording revenues when they are earned by providing goods or services to customers.

Risk assessment. The process of identifying risks and gauging the probability that they will occur.

S

Sales Discount. Discount granted on sales for the customer's early payment within a discount period; a contra-account to Sales Revenue.

Sales invoice. A bill that documents the sale of goods to a business customer.

Sales Returns and Allowances. A reduction in the amount of sales due to customers returning merchandise or accepting damaged goods; a contra-account to Sales Revenue.

Sales Revenue. The amount that a retailer earns from selling its inventory.

Salvage (residual) value. The estimated value at the end of a long-term asset's useful life.

Sarbanes-Oxley Act (SOX). A law passed in 2002 by the U.S. Congress in response to large-scale fraud in publicly owned companies.

Secured bonds. Bonds that give bond-holders the right to take specified assets of the issuer if the issuer fails to pay principal or interest.

Selling expenses. Expenses related to advertising and selling products including sales salaries, sales commissions, advertising, depreciation on items used in sales, and delivery expense.

Serial bonds. Bonds from the same bond issuance that mature at different times.

Service business. A business that provides services to customers.

Share capital. Funds raised by the business entity in either cash or other consideration, and in exchange, the business entity issues ownership rights (preferred shares or common shares in a corporation) to the owner(s) who provided the funds.

Shareholder. A person who owns shares in a corporation.

Shareholders' equity. Represents the shareholders' ownership interest in the assets of a corporation.

Significant influence. When an investor company has the ability to direct or influence the strategies of the investee company, even if it has never exercised this ability in the past. Such ability is gained by having a significant amount of the voting power (usually obtained by acquiring between 20% and 50% of the voting right shares, either directly or indirectly) or by having a large enough number of seats on the board of directors to influence the board's decisions.

Single-step income statement. Income statement format that groups all revenues together and lists all expenses together, subtracting total expenses from total revenues and calculating net income or net loss without computing any subtotals.

Sole proprietorship. A business with a single owner.

Solvency ratios. Ratios that measure a company's ability to meet its long-term obligations or take on more debt.

Specific-identification. Inventory costing method in which a business uses the specific cost of each unit of inventory; also called the *specific-unit cost* method.

Specific-unit cost. Inventory costing method in which a business uses the specific cost of each unit of inventory; also called the *specific-identification* method.

Stated interest rate. Interest rate that determines the amount of cash interest the borrower pays and the investor receives each year. Also called the *coupon rate*.

Statement of cash flows. Summary of the changes in a business's cash balance for a specific period. A financial statement that shows all of the sources and all of the uses of cash for an accounting period.

Statement of changes in equity. Summary of the changes in shareholders' equity during a period by providing information on common shares, retained earnings, and other comprehensive income.

Statement of comprehensive income. Summary of a business's revenues, expenses, and net income or net loss for a specific period, as well as other comprehensive income, such as unrealized gains or losses from holding assets. The income statement is one of the components included in the statement of comprehensive income.

Statement of financial position. Summary of business's assets, liabilities, and shareholders' equity as of a specific date; also called the *balance sheet*.

Statement of financial position approach. The method of estimating bad debts that focuses on accounts receivable. The accountant calculates the end-of-period allowance balance based on an aging of the Accounts Receivable; also called the *aging method*.

Stock dividend. A distribution by a corporation of its own shares to shareholders.

Stock split. An increase in the number of outstanding shares coupled with a proportionate reduction in the value of the shares.

Straight-line (SL) depreciation method. Depreciation method in which an equal amount of depreciation expense is assigned to each year of asset use: (Cost of the Asset – Salvage Value)/Useful Life of the Asset.

Subsidiary. A company that is controlled by another company (called the parent company).

Subsidiary ledger. An accounting record that contains details of a main account called a controlling account, such as a list of customers and the accounts receivable due from each, a list of suppliers and the accounts payable due to each, etc.

T

T-account. An informal account form used to summarize transactions, where the top of the T holds the account title and the base divides the debit and credit sides of the account.

Tangible assets. Assets that are physical in form. They can be seen, touched, or held.

Temporary accounts. The revenue, expense, and dividend accounts; these accounts are closed at the end of the period.

Term bonds. Bonds that all mature at the same time.

Third party. Person or organization unrelated to the organization.

Time period assumption. The life of a business entity is divided into periods, which could be a month, a quarter, or a year.

Time value of money. The concept that states that a dollar today is worth more than a dollar received in the future.

Times-interest-earned ratio. Ratio of income from operations to interest expense. It measures the number of times that operating income can cover interest expense; also called the *interest-coverage ratio*.

Title. Ownership.

Total asset turnover ratio. Measures a company's ability to generate sales from its total assets, including current assets, investments, fixed assets, etc.

Trade names. Assets that represent distinctive identifications of a product or service; also called *brand names*.

Trademarks. Assets that represent distinctive identifications of a product or service.

Transaction. An event that has a financial impact on a business entity.

Treasurer. The individual in an organization responsible for the custody of assets, such as cash.

Treasury shares. A corporation's own shares that it has issued and later reacquired.

Trend percentages. A form of horizontal analysis in which percentages are computed by selecting a base year and then expressing amounts for following years as a percentage of the base-year amounts.

Trial balance. A list of all the accounts of a business and their balances in the order of the chart of accounts; its purpose is to verify that total debits equal total credits.

U

Unadjusted trial balance. A trial balance that is prepared prior to the adjusting entries being made.

Uncollectible account. An account receivable that is unable to be collected; also called a *bad debt*.

Understandability. One of the qualitative characteristics of accounting information, that it be understandable for users.

Underwriter. A firm, such as TD Waterhouse, that usually agrees to buy all the shares a company wants to issue if the firm cannot sell the shares to its clients.

Unearned revenue. A liability created when customers pay in advance for goods and services to be delivered in the future; also called *deferred revenue*. At the point when cash is received, the company has an obligation to fulfill and has not earned the revenue.

Units-of-production (UOP) depreciation method. Depreciation method by which a fixed amount of depreciation is assigned to each unit of output produced by an asset.

Unsecured bonds. Bonds that are backed only by the general credit of the company issuing the bond; also called *debentures*.

Useful life. The expected life of an asset during which it is anticipated to generate revenues. May be expressed in years or units of output.

V

Value in use. The discounted future cash flows expected to arise from the continuing use of an asset and from its disposal at the end of its useful life.

Vertical analysis. Analysis of a financial statement that reveals the relationship of each statement item to a specified base amount, which is the 100% figure.

W

Warranty. A guarantee that a product or service is free from defect.

Weighted average cost. Inventory costing method where the beginning inventory and all purchases of inventory are added and divided by the total number of units to get one average cost. This average cost is used to value ending inventory and cost of goods sold in the periodic system.

Whistleblower. A person who reports unethical behaviour.

Wholesale business. A business that purchases products from a manufacturer and sells them to a retail business.

Wholesaler. A business that buys goods from manufacturers and resells them to retailers.

Withdrawals. Income that is removed from the company and distributed to the owner(s).

Work in process. Inventory of partially completed goods.

Working capital. Current assets minus current liabilities. It measures a business's ability to meet its short-term obligations with its current assets.

Write off. Removing a customer's receivable from the accounting records because it is considered uncollectible.

Z

Zero coupon bond. A bond issued at a price lower than the face value and that does not pay interest during the bond's duration. The face value is paid in full at maturity.

Index

Company Index

Note: Company names in bold indicate real companies.